Theological Lexicon of the New Testament

Theological Lexicon of the New Testament

Volume 1

ἀγα–ἐλπ

CESLAS SPICQ, O.P.

Translated and Edited by JAMES D. ERNEST

Copyright © 1994 by Hendrickson Publishers, Inc.
P. O. Box 3473
Peabody, Massachusetts 01961-3473
All rights reserved
Printed in the United States of America on acid-free paper

ISBN 1-56563-035-1

Translated from: Ceslas Spicq, O.P., *Notes de lexicographie néo-testamentaire*, 3 volumes (Orbis Biblicus et Orientalis 22/1, 2, 3); © 1978, 1982, Editions Universitaires, Fribourg, Switzerland.

Library of Congress Cataloging-in-Publication Data

Spicq, Ceslas, 1901-1993
   [Notes de lexicographie néo-testamentaire.   English]
   Theological lexicon of the New Testament /   Ceslas Spicq; translated and edited by James D. Ernest.
   p. cm.
   Includes bibliographical references and index.
   ISBN 1-56563-035-1
   1. Greek language, Biblical—Semantics.   2. Greek language, Biblical—Glossaries, vocabularies, etc.   I. Ernest, James D.   II. Title.
PA875.S613   1994
487'.4—dc20   94-42932
                                                                                                          CIP

The article ἀπαρχή is a translation of "᾽ΑΠΑΡΧΗ. NOTE DE LEXICOGRAPHIE NÉO-TESTAMENTAIRE," by Ceslas Spicq, in *The New Testament Age. Essays in Honor of Bo Reicke* (Macon: Mercer University Press, 1984), volume 2, pages 493-502, and is used with permission by Mercer University Press, 1400 Coleman Avenue, Macon, GA 31207.

TABLE OF CONTENTS

VOLUME 1

PREFACE	vii
TRANSLATOR'S PREFACE	ix
TABLE OF GREEK WORDS IN VOLUME 1	xiii
ABBREVIATIONS: BIBLE, APOCRYPHA, PSEUDEPIGRAPHA, RABBINIC AND MISHNAIC WRITINGS, QUMRAN	xvii
ABBREVIATIONS: ANCIENT GREEK AND LATIN WRITERS	xx
ABBREVIATIONS: PAPYRI AND OSTRACA	xxxi
ABBREVIATIONS: INSCRIPTIONS	xliii
ABBREVIATIONS: GENERAL WORKS	il
ABBREVIATIONS: PERIODICALS	lxi
TRANSLITERATION TABLES	lxiv
ARTICLES IN VOLUME 1	1

VOLUME 2

TABLE OF GREEK WORDS IN VOLUME 2	v
ARTICLES IN VOLUME 2	1

VOLUME 3

TABLE OF GREEK WORDS IN VOLUME 3	v
ARTICLES IN VOLUME 3	1
LIST OF GREEK WORDS	519
LIST OF ENGLISH GLOSSES	528
INDEX OF ANCIENT SOURCES	547

PREFACE

I have often been asked to bring together in one volume the NT word studies scattered throughout my previous works, especially in the commentaries. I could not simply collect them as they were, even filling in the references and bringing the bibliographies up to date. Still less could I think of producing an exhaustive work, a project so perfectly completed by the dictionaries of W. Bauer or Moulton-Milligan,[1] not to mention the grammars,[2] some of the articles in the *Theologisches Wörterbuch* of G. Kittel and G. Friedrich,[3] and especially A. Deissmann's *Licht vom Osten* (Tübingen, 1923; ET *Light from the Ancient East*, New York, 1927), *Bibelstudien*, (Marburg, 1895) and *Neue Bibelstudien* (Marburg, 1897).

Not only do I study a restricted choice of words, but also *my intention is theological*. What interests me is not orthographic novelties, idioms, phonetics, or declensions, but the semantics and the religious and moral sense of the language of the NT.[4] This language has its own rules and its

---

[1] W. Bauer, *Griechisch-deutsches Wörterbuch zu den Schriften des Neuen Testaments und der übrigen urchristlichen Literatur*, 5th ed., Berlin, 1958 (English translation of the fourth edition by W. F. Arndt, F. W. Gingrich, *A Greek-English Lexicon of the New Testament and Other Early Christian Literature*, Chicago, 1957; second edition, revised and augmented by F. W. Gingrich and F. W. Danker from W. Bauer's fifth edition, Chicago, 1979); J. H. Moulton, G. Milligan, *The Vocabulary of the Greek Testament Illustrated from the Papyri and Other Non-Literary Sources*, 2d ed., London, 1949; reprinted Grand Rapids, 1982. Cf. T. Nägeli, *Der Wortschatz des Apostels Paulus*, Göttingen, 1905 (still indispensable, although it needs to be brought up to date).

[2] Always useful will be E. Mayser, *Grammatik der griechischen Papyri aus der Ptolemäerzeit*, multiple volumes; Leipzig, 1906–1934; cf. E. Pax, "Probleme des neutestamentlichen Griechisch," in *Bib*, 1972, pp. 557–564.

[3] Excellent translations are available: English by G. W. Bromiley, *Theological Dictionary of the New Testament*, Grand Rapids, 1964ff.; and Italian, by F. Mantagnini, G. Scarpatt, O. Soffritti, *Grande Lessico del Nuovo Testamento*, Brescia, 1965ff., and the articles published in French, in separate fascicles, under the title *Dictionnaire biblique Gerhard Kittel*, by Labor et Fides de Genève, under the signature of P. Reymond.

[4] Our model will be R. C. Trench, *Synonyms*, 12th ed., London, 1894. But, even though I group related words according to their root, I follow alphabetical order for the convenience of the reader, despite all of the criticism that has been directed against

own vocabulary. One cannot understand it except in light of the usages of the Greek language as it was spoken and written in the *oikoumenē* of the first century, which is called "standard Koine," the popular language understood by the hearers and readers of the NT authors.[5] That is why I have used many references—not only to the classical authors, but to the texts that are closest to the first century BC or AD. These references will undoubtedly be the most useful aspect of this work. Indeed, the many papyrological and epigraphical publications continually bring new findings.[6] It is my goal to serve students of the Bible by placing conveniently at their disposal the fruit of my studies. "The person who knows the papyri a little meets at every turn in the NT, parallels of subject matter and form that allow him to gain a more vivid grasp of the words of Scripture."[7]

---

this method from a scientific point of view. Cf. the observations of G. Friedrich, "Das bisher noch fehlende Begriffslexikon zum Neuen Testament," in *NTS*, vol. 19, 1973, pp. 127–152; idem, "Pre-History of the Theological Dictionary of the New Testament," in R. E. Pitkin, *Theological Dictionary of the New Testament*, vol. 10, Grand Rapids, 1976, pp. 650–661.

[5] Cf. F. M. Abel, *Grammaire du grec biblique*, Paris, 1927, pp. v, xl; G. Thieme, *Die Inschriften von Magnesia am Mäander und das Neue Testament; eine sprachgeschichtliche Studie*, Göttingen, 1906; J. Rouffiac, *Recherches sur les caractères du grec dans le Nouveau Testament d'après les Inscriptions de Priène*, Paris, 1911; H. G. Meechem, *Light from Ancient Letters*, London, 1923; G. Milligan, *Here and There Among the Papyri*, London, 1923; idem, *Selections from the Greek Papyri*, Cambridge, 1927; D. Brooke, *Private Letters Pagan and Christian*, 2d ed., London, 1929; J. G. Winter, *Life and Letters in the Papyri*, Ann Arbor, 1933; E. Gabba, *Iscrizioni greche e latine per lo studio della Bibbia*, Turin, 1958; H. Thierfelder, *Unbekannte antike Welt*, Gütersloh, 1963; G. D. Kilpatrick, "Atticism and the Text of the Greek New Testament," in *Festschrift für Prof. J. Schmid*, Regensburg, 1963, pp. 125–137; M. Guarducci, *Epigrafia greca*, Rome, vol. 2, 1969. R. Merkelbach, H. C. Youtie ("Der griechische Wortschatz und die Christen," dans *ZPE*, vol. 18, 1975, pp. 101–154) have underlined the evolution of the meaning of words according to epochs, cultural conditions, and above all religion; cf. O. Mentevecchi, "Dal Paganesimo al Cristianesimo: aspetti dell'evoluzione della lingua greca nei papiri dell'Egitto," in *Aeg*, 1957, pp. 41–59.

[6] Among the most important is a tomb inscription of Lower Egypt of the year 5 BC, which testifies that Arsinoë died in bringing forth her πρωτότοκος (cf. Luke 2:7. *CII*, n. 1510, 6; idem, "La signification du terme πρωτότοκος d'après une inscription juive," in *Bib*, 1930, pp. 373–390; *C.Pap.Jud.* III, 1510). Only in 1928 was there discovered in an inscription of Gerasa, dating from the time of Trajan, the verb θεατρίζω, "to play at the theater" (*SEG*, vol. 7, 825, 18), which was until then known only from Heb 10:33; cf. H. J. Cadbury, "θεατρίζω No Longer a NT Hapax Legomenon," in *ZNW*, 1930, pp. 60–63, etc.

[7] U. Wilcken, "Der heutige Stand der Papyrusforschung," in *Jahrbücher für das kl. Altertum*, 1901, p. 688; cf. M. J. Lagrange, "A travers les Papyrus grecs," in *Conférences de Saint Etienne 1909–1910*, Paris, 1910, pp. 55–88; N. Turner, "Philology in New Testament Studies," in *ExpT*, vol. 71, 1960, pp. 104–107.

Translator's Preface

In 1978 the original two volumes of Ceslas Spicq's *Notes de lexicographie néo-testamentaire* were published by Editions Universitaires of Fribourg, Switzerland (in the series Orbis Biblicus et Orientalis), and by Vandenhoeck & Ruprecht of Göttingen. These were followed four years later by a third volume, incorporating both newer material on some of the words covered in the original two volumes and also a large number of new entries. In 1991, Editions Universitaires collaborated with Cerf (Paris) in a single-volume reissue of the three-volume set. The reissue had a new title (*Lexique théologique du Nouveau Testament*) and merged the articles of the third volume into alphabetical order with the first two volumes but was otherwise unchanged. Meanwhile, an Italian translation had been published as a supplement to the Italian version of the Kittel-Friedrich *Theologisches Wörterbuch*.[1]

For reasons evident from the foregoing, in a certain number of instances the same word is treated in more than one article. We have followed the lead of the French one-volume edition in declining to omit or rearrange any of the material. Readers may find all the places a particular word is discussed by using the index of Greek words provided for this edition and the cross-references supplied at the beginnings of some articles.

English-language versions of Père Spicq's three-volume *Agapè dans le Nouveau Testament* (though without the notes) and of a couple of smaller works have been published. His solid reputation among North American scholars, however, rests largely on his biblical commentaries, especially those on Hebrews and the Pastoral Epistles, which have not been translated into English. As the preface to the first French edition notes, it is from the commentaries that Père Spicq culled the material that makes up the *Theological Lexicon*; he had been asked to bring together his painstaking word studies in a single collection. When informed that an English translation would be made, he expressed satisfaction that his work would thus be made

---

[1] *Note di lessicografia neotestamentaria*, edizione italiana a cura de Franco Luigi Viero (Brescia: Paideia Editrice, 1988).

available to the English-speaking world. We regret that Père Spicq did not live to see the publication of this translation.

The usefulness of Père Spicq's work for New Testament scholars should be evident. Nowadays graduate students are much more likely to have seminars in more recent methodological subdisciplines—various forms of sociological, literary, or ideological criticism—than in epigraphy, papyrology, or lexicography. Practitioners of most of the newer methodologies, however, note the continuing fundamental importance of basic historical-critical work; in most cases, their intention is not to obviate it but rather to note its limitations and build upon it. They will not be spending their own time sorting through the Fuad papyri or the Zeno archive, so they may be glad that Spicq and others have done it for them. This volume gives a summary of his findings plus references to hundreds of studies that today's biblical scholars might not easily find otherwise either because they were published in papyrological or epigraphical journals or *Festschriften* or else because they appeared too soon to be included in the computerized bibliographic databases upon which scholars increasingly rely.

Not only professional scholars in biblical studies and related fields, but also and especially pastors, teachers, and others interested in serious theological study of the Bible will profit from Spicq's work. In fact, Père Spicq's original preface points out that his primary interest was not in orthographical or grammatical details but in the religious or theological meaning of the words used in the biblical text. Obviously knowing some Greek is an advantage in using a work of this sort, but it is by no means an absolute requirement. For readers with little or no Greek, several conveniences have been supplied in the English version. In the main text, all of the Greek has been transliterated and where it seemed helpful translated as well. (The quotations in the footnotes, which are more likely to be helpful to scholars than to general readers, are printed in Greek characters.) Hebrew and Aramaic words are normally transliterated. The article titles are given in Greek characters, as in the original edition, but we have added transliterations; internal cross-references; cross-references to the Strong's word-numbering system used by Strong's *Concordance* and many other standard reference works; and English glosses.

It is important for readers to note that English glosses given with each article title are not original to Père Spicq; they have been added for the convenience of users of this work, especially those who do not know Greek. In a few odd cases a word or phrase has been lifted from Barclay Newman's *Concise Greek-English Dictionary of the New Testament*[2] or from LSJ, but in

---

[2] London: United Bible Societies, 1971.

general the glosses are extracted or otherwise derived from the articles themselves. (This procedure was necessary because sometimes Spicq disagrees with the commonly given definitions.) The glosses are intended to indicate concisely (not necessarily exhaustively) the range of meanings discussed within the article; thus they do not pretend to lexicographic rigor and should not be used as free-standing definitions. For words of special theological importance, no effort was made to represent in the gloss the semantic richness fully discussed in the article. The reader should consult the article to see which definitions Père Spicq applies to actual NT texts.

For the convenience of scholars, abbreviations for the papyri and inscriptions, as well as for classical works, have been standardized. The various bibliographies and tables of abbreviations are original to this edition. (The completed tables were compared with those in the Italian edition as a way of checking for omissions.)

Readers who know some Greek should be aware that many irregular spellings—especially itacisms, but also others—will be encountered in quotations from the papyri and inscriptions. At times it was not obvious to me whether an odd spelling was original (and should thus be retained) or arose as a typographical error in the French edition. (Naturally, in a work of this complexity, especially since it was prepared in the days before personal computers made possible the elimination of human intervention between author's original notes and final published product, there were many typos, especially in the Greek and Hebrew fonts.) In a relatively small number of egregious cases, I checked the published edition of the papyrus or inscription in question, but time was not available to verify a significant percentage of the large numbers of such citations. When in doubt, I retained the spelling printed in the French edition. There are also dialectal spelling variations (most commonly, alpha instead of eta and xi instead of sigma) that will look like misspellings to readers unfamiliar with the main Greek dialects.

Spicq's studies draw on the whole classical and Hellenistic Greek literary corpus. He appears to have paid special attention to Jewish writers (Philo, Josephus) and later pagan writers (Plutarch). The special value of his work, however, is the extent to which it draws upon the nonliterary papyri and the inscriptions. Many readers will be to some extent familiar with the discovery of many new such sources over the past century and some of the lexicographic and grammatical work that has been done upon them (Deissmann, Moulton-Milligan, etc.).[3] These papyri and inscriptions

---

[3] For titles and bibliographic information, see the general bibliography. Unfortunately Spicq did not have access to the formidable work of *New Documents Illustrating Early Christianity*, edited by G. H. R. Horsley (vols. 1–5) and Stephen Llewelyn

give us the language not as it was written by Plato five centuries before the birth of Christ but as it was used in everyday life by Greek and non-Greek peoples around the eastern Mediterranean during the early centuries of the spread of Christianity. Naturally, the language had changed. Readers of Spicq's articles will find many instances in which these nonliterary sources exemplify usages that make more sense of particular biblical passages than was possible before their discovery.

For readers who become interested in the social, economic, religious, and political institutions and circumstances constantly referred to in the papyri, various resources are available. Tarn and Griffith's *Hellenistic Civilization*[4] is a recognized classic. An up-to-date and authoritative study of the Egyptian papyri from the third through the fifth centuries of the common era is Roger S. Bagnall's *Egypt in Late Antiquity*.[5] Readers of Spicq may profitably consult Bagnall's appendices (on time, money and measures, and the nomes), brief glossary, and indexes for quick access to information on technical terms in the papyri. For the language of the papyri, readers may refer to the multivolume grammatical work of Francis Gignac.[6] A relatively recent work that demonstrates the way in which the nonliterary sources can illuminate and revise our understanding of the world in which ancient Christianity spread, especially with regard to popular religious life, is Robin Lane Fox's *Pagans and Christians*.[7] This latter work is mentioned by way of noting that although the papyri and inscriptions do not now generate the same excitement among students of the Bible that they did not so many decades ago, neither are they yet "old hat"; in some ways they are still a largely unmined treasure for the study of early Christianity. Spicq's work is one of the best available entrees to this material for readers interested in exploring the theological meaning of the words used in the New Testament.

(vol. 6) (The Ancient Documentary Research Centre: Macquarie University, 1981–). This work, which includes linguistic essays and reviews of recently published Greek papyri and inscriptions, is indispensable for advanced lexical studies.

[4]W. W. Tarn, *Hellenistic Civilization*, 3d ed. rev. by the author and G. T. Griffith (Cleveland: World, 1952); reprinted many times.

[5]Princeton: Princeton Univ. Press, 1993.

[6]*A Grammar of the Greek Papyri of the Roman and Byzantine Periods* (Milan: Istituto editoriale cisalpino-La goliardica, 1976–).

[7]San Franciso: Harper & Row, 1986.

Table of Greek Words in Volume 1

Greek Entry	English Gloss	Page
ἀγαθοποιέω, ἀγαθωσύνη	*agathopoieō*, to do good; *agathōsynē*, goodness	1
ἀγανακτέω, ἀγανάκτησις	*aganakteō*, to be indignant; *aganaktēsis*, indignation	5
ἀγάπη	*agapē*, love	8
ἀγγαρεύω	*angareuō*, to requisition	23
ἀγοράζω	*agorazō*, to buy	26
ἀγωγή	*agōgē*, conduct	29
ἀδιαλείπτως	*adialeiptōs*, unceasingly	32
ἀδύνατον	*adynaton*, impossible	35
ἀθετέω, ἀθέτησις	*atheteō*, to set aside, abrogate, reject; *athetēsis*, abrogation, rejection	39
αἰδώς, ἀναίδεια	*aidōs*, modesty; *anaideia*, shamelessness	41
αἰσχροκερδής, ἀφιλάργυρος	*aischrokerdēs*, eager for shameful gain; *aphilargyros*, free of the love of money	45
αἰφνίδιος, αἰφνιδίως, ἐξαίφνης	*aiphnidios*, sudden; *aiphnidiōs, exaiphnēs*, suddenly	49
ἄκακος	*akakos*, good, beneficent, innocent	53
ἄκαρπος	*akarpos*, fruitless, barren	56
ἀκατάγνωστος	*akatagnōstos*, unobjectionable, irreproachable	58
ἀκλινής	*aklinēs*, stable, unchanging, firm	59
ἀκρασία, ἐγκράτεια	*akrasia*, lack of self-control; *enkrateia*, self-control	60
ἀλαζονεία, ἀλαζών	*alazoneia*, boastful arrogance; *alazōn*, boaster	63
ἀλήθεια, ἀληθεύω, ἀληθής, ἀληθινός, ἀληθῶς	*alētheia*, truth; *alētheuō*, to speak the truth; *alēthēs*, true, truthful; *alēthinos*, authentic, genuine; *alēthōs*, truly	66
ἀμελέω, ἐπιμελέομαι	*ameleō*, to not matter; *epimeleomai*, to busy oneself with, see to	87
ἀμεταμέλητος	*ametamelētos*, leaving no room for regret, irrevocable	92
ἀμοιβή	*amoibē*, recompense, return	95
ἀναγκαῖος	*anankaios*, urgently necessary	97
ἀνάγνωσις	*anagnōsis*, reading (aloud, in public)	101
ἀνάδειξις	*anadeixis*, distinct demonstration, revelation, proclamation	103

Greek	Transliteration and meaning	Page
ἀναδέχομαι	anadechomai, to welcome, accept; to accept responsibility for	105
ἀναπέμπω	anapempō, to send, conduct, bring back, send up	107
ἀναστροφή	anastrophē, conduct	111
ἀνατρέφω	anatrephō, to nurture, raise	115
ἀναφέρω	anapherō, to cause to ascend, offer up, remove	117
ἀναψύχω	anapsychō, to refresh	120
ἀνθ' ὧν	anth' hōn, in place of, in exchange	122
ἀντιβάλλω	antiballō, to exchange	126
ἀντιδιατίθημι, ἀντικαθίστημι	antidiatithēmi, antikathistēmi, to oppose, resist	128
ἀντλέω, ἄντλημα	antleō, to draw (water), antlēma, bucket	131
ἀνυπόκριτος, γνήσιος	anypokritos, upright, unfeigned, authentic; gnēsios, authentic, dear, legitimate	134
ἅπαξ, ἐφάπαξ	hapax, ephapax, once	139
ἀπαράβατος	aparabatos, inviolable, nontransferable	143
ἀπαρχή	aparchē, firstfruit	145
ἀπάτη	apatē, deception, trickery, pleasure	153
ἀπελπίζω	apelpizō, to hope for something in return	156
ἀπέραντος	aperantos, endless, interminable, vain	159
ἀπερισπάστως	aperispastōs, without hindrance or distraction	160
ἀπέχω	apechō, to hold, collect, acknowledge receipt of payment in full; remain distant; abstain	162
ἁπλότης, ἁπλοῦς	haplotēs, simplicity, singleness, sincerity; haplous, morally whole, faithful	169
ἀποβλέπω	apoblepō, to look, observe, pay close attention	174
ἀποδοχή	apodochē, acceptance, enthusiastic reception, respect	176
ἀποκυέω	apokyeō, to deliver, give birth	178
ἀπόλαυσις	apolausis, enjoyment, happiness	181
ἀπολείπω	apoleipō, to leave behind	183
ἀπόστολος	apostolos, apostle	186
ἀργός	argos, inactive, inoperative	195
ἀρνέομαι, ἀπαρνέομαι	arneomai, aparneomai, to say no, deny, repudiate	199
ἀρχιποίμην	archipoimēn, chief shepherd	206
ἀρχιτέκτων	architektōn, master builder	209
ἀσφάλεια, ἀσφαλής, ἀσφαλίζομαι, ἀσφαλῶς	asphaleia, stability, safety, assurance, guarantee; asphalēs, safe, sure; asphalizomai, to secure, make sure, asphalōs, without slipping, securely, safely	212
ἀσωτία, ἀσώτως	asōtia, incurable dissoluteness; asōtōs, prodigally	220
ἀτακτέω, ἄτακτος, ἀτάκτως	atakteō, to be disorderly; ataktos, undisciplined, disorderly, rebellious; ataktōs, in disorder	223

TABLE OF GREEK WORDS

ἀτενίζω	atenizō, to look attentively, stare	227
αὐθάδης	authadēs, presumptuous, arrogant, ill-bred	229
αὐτόματος	automatos, spontaneous, self-moving	231
αὐτόπτης	autoptēs, eyewitness	235
ἄφεσις	aphesis, a sending out, point of departure, discharge, settlement, forgiveness, dispensation, acquittal, liberation	238
ἀφιλάργυρος	aphilargyros, free of the love of money	245
ἀφοράω	aphoraō, to look from a distance, gaze fixedly	247
βαθμός	bathmos, threshold, step, stage, rank	250
βαρύς	barys, important, serious, burdensome, grave, dangerous	252
βασιλεία, βασίλειος, βασιλεύς, βασιλεύω, βασιλικός, βασίλισσα	basileia, kingdom, reign; basileios, royal; basileus, king; basileuō, to be king, rule, reign; basilikos, royal; basilissa, queen	256
βασκαίνω	baskainō, to bewitch, cast a spell, regard enviously	272
βατταλογέω	battalogeō, to babble on	277
βέβαιος, βεβαιόω, βεβαίωσις	bebaios, solid, durable, sure, valid, guaranteed; bebaioō, to make sure, confirm, authenticate, guarantee, carry out; bebaiōsis, firmness, juridical definiteness	280
βέβηλος, βεβηλόω	bebēlos, accessible, profane, impure, impious; bebēloō, to profane, besmirch	284
βιάζομαι	biazomai, to use violence or force	287
βλαβερός	blaberos, harmful	292
γαστήρ	gastēr, belly, womb	293
γνήσιος	gnēsios, authentic, dear, legitimate	296
δειλία, δειλιάω, δειλός	deilia, faintheartedness, cowardice, fear; deiliaō, to be fearful; deilos, fearful	300
δειπνέω	deipneō, to dine	303
δεισιδαίμων, δεισιδαιμονία	deisidaimōn, superstitious, religious; deisidaimonia, superstition, religion, reverence	305
διαλάσσω	dialassō, to reconcile	309
διερμηνεύω, ἑρμηνεία, ἑρμηνεύω	diermēneuō, to translate, interpret, explain; hermēneia, interpretation; hermēneuō, to translate, interpret	312
δίκαιος, δικαιοσύνη, δικαιόω, δικαίωμα, δικαίωσις, δικαστής, δίκη	dikaios, conforming to law or custom, right, virtuous; dikaiosynē, justice, righteousness; dikaioō, to justify, pronounce just; dikaiōma, justification, righteousness, righteous decree, just requirement; dikaiōsis, justification; dikastēs, judge; dikē, custom, justice, punishment	318
δίστομος	distomos, having two mouths or two edges	348
διχοτομέω	dichotomeō, to cut in two	350

δοκιμάζω, δοκιμασία, δοκιμή, δοκίμιον, δόκιμος, ἀδόκιμος	*dokimazō*, to prove, test, verify, examine prior to approval, judge, evaluate, discern; *dokimasia*, verification, testing, authenticity; *dokimē*, proof, trial; *dokimion*, testing, proven worth; *dokimos*, proved, acceptable; *adokimos*, worthless	353
δόξα, δοξάζω, συνδοξάζω	*doxa*, expectation, opinion, reputation, honor, glory; *doxazō*, to think, hold an opinion, imagine, praise, glorify; *syndoxazō*, to sanction, agree to, glorify with	362
δοῦλος, οἰκέτης, οἰκεῖος, μίσθιος, μισθωτός	*doulos*, slave; *oiketēs*, slave or domestic servant; *oikeios*, family member; *misthios*, salaried domestic servant; *misthōtos*, day laborer	380
δύσκολος, σκολιός	*dyskolos*, difficult, causing frustration or unhappiness, disagreeable; *skolios*, crooked, difficult, perverse	387
ἔγγυος	*engyos*, guarantor	390
ἐγκαινίζω	*enkainizō*, to renew, inaugurate	396
ἐγκακέω	*enkakeō*, to conduct oneself badly, become weary, lose heart	398
ἐγκαταλείπω	*enkataleipō*, to leave, forsake, abandon	400
ἐγκομβόομαι	*enkomboomai*, to attach, fasten	404
ἔθος, εἰθισμένος (ἐθίζω)	*ethos*, custom; *eithismenos (ethizō)*, accustomed	405
εἰκών	*eikōn*, image, representation	412
εἰλικρίνεια, εἰλικρινής	*eilikrineia*, purity, unmixed quality; *eilikrinēs*, without mixture, sincere, candid	420
εἰρηνεύω, εἰρήνη, εἰρηνικός, εἰρηνοποιέω, εἰρηνοποιός	*eirēneuō*, to be at peace, live in peace; *eirēnē*, peace; *eirēnikos*, peaceful; *eirēnopoieō*, to make peace; *eirēnopoios*, making peace; a peacemaker	424
εἰσακούω, ἐπακούω, ὑπακούω, ὑπακοή	*eisakouō, epakouō*, to hear, listen to, heed; *hypakouō*, to heed, obey; *hypakoē*, obedience	439
ἐκδημέω	*ekdēmeō*, to leave, be in exile	453
ἐκλύομαι	*eklyomai*, to untie, dissolve, be physically or morally weak	455
ἐκτένεια, ἐκτενής, ἐκτενῶς	*ekteneia*, fervor, unfailing intensity; *ektenēs, ektenōs*, without ceasing, zealously, urgently	457
ἐκτρέπομαι	*ektrepomai*, to change direction, deviate, go astray	462
ἔκτρωμα	*ektrōma*, stillborn child, child born abnormally before term	464
ἐκψύχω	*ekpsychō*, to be short of breath, expire	467
ἔλαττον (ἐλάσσων), ἐλαττονέω, ἐλαττόω	*elatton (elassōn)*, smaller, lesser; *elattoneō*, to have less, have too little; *elattoō*, to diminish	468
ἐλεέω, ἔλεος	*eleeō*, to have compassion, show favor or mercy; *eleos*, compassion, mercy	471
ἐλπίζω, ἐλπίς	*elpizō*, to hope; *elpis*, hope	480

Abbreviations:
Bible, Apocrypha, Pseudepigrapha, Rabbinic and Mishnaic Writings, Qumran

A. Old Testament

Gen	Genesis	Cant	Canticles
Exod	Exodus	Isa	Isaiah
Lev	Leviticus	Jer	Jeremiah
Num	Numbers	Lam	Lamentations
Deut	Deuteronomy	Ezek	Ezekiel
Josh	Joshua	Dan	Daniel
Judg	Judges	Hos	Hosea
Ruth	Ruth	Joel	Joel
1-2 Sam	1-2 Samuel	Amos	Amos
1-2 Kgs	1-2 Kings	Obad	Obadiah
1-2 Chr	1-2 Chronicles	Jonah	Jonah
Ezra	Ezra	Mic	Micah
Neh	Nehemiah	Nah	Nahum
Esth	Esther	Hab	Habakkuk
Job	Job	Zeph	Zephaniah
Ps	Psalm(s)	Hag	Haggai
Prov	Proverbs	Zech	Zechariah
Eccl	Ecclesiastes	Mal	Malachi

B. Apocrypha

Tob	Tobit	Pr Azar	Prayer of Azariah
Jdt	Judith	Sus	Susanna
Add Esth	Additions to Esther	Bel	Bel and the Dragon
Wis	Wisdom (Ecclesiasticus)	1-2-3-4 Macc	1-2-3-4 Maccabees
Sir	Sirach	1-2 Esdr	1-2 Esdras
Bar	Baruch	Pr Man	Prayer of Manasseh
Ep Jer	Epistle of Jeremiah	4 Ezra	4 Ezra

C. New Testament

Matt	Matthew	Eph	Ephesians
Mark	Mark	Phil	Philippians
Luke	Luke	Col	Colossians
John	John	1-2 Thess	1-2 Thessalonians
Acts	Acts	1-2 Tim	1-2 Timothy
Rom	Romans	Titus	Titus
1-2 Cor	1-2 Corinthians	Phlm	Philemon
Gal	Galatians	Heb	Hebrews

THEOLOGICAL LEXICON OF THE NEW TESTAMENT

Jas	James
1-2 Pet	1-2 Peter
1-2-3 John	1-2-3 John

| Jude | Jude |
| Rev | Revelation |

D. Apocryphal and Pseudepigraphal Works and Early Christian Writings

Acts John	Acts of John
Acts Paul Thec.	Acts of Paul and Thecla
Acts Pet. Andr.	Acts of Peter and Andrew
Acts Phil.	Acts of Philip
Acts Thom.	Acts of Thomas
Adam and Eve	Life of Adam and Eve
2 Apoc. Bar.	Syriac Apocalypse of Baruch
3 Apoc. Bar.	Greek Apocalypse of Baruch
Apoc. Mos.	Apocalypse of Moses
Apoc. Paul	Apocalypse of Paul
Apoc. Pet.	Apocalypse of Peter
Asc. Isa.	Ascension of Isaiah
As. Mos.	Assumption of Moses
Barn.	Epistle of Barnabas
1 Clem.	First Clement
2 Clem.	Second Clement
Ep. Arist.	Letter of Aristeas
Did.	Didache
Gos. 12 App.	Gospel of the Twelve Apostles
Gos. Pet.	Gospel of Peter
Gos. Thom.	Gospel of Thomas
Herm. Man.	Hermas, Mandate(s)
Herm. Sim.	Hermas, Similitude(s)
Ign. Eph.	Ignatius, Letter to the Ephesians
Ign. Magn.	Ignatius, Letter to the Magnesians
Ign. Pol.	Ignatius, Letter to Polycarp
Ign. Rom.	Ignatius, Letter to the Romans
Ign. Smyrn.	Ignatius, Letter to the Smyrnaeans
Ign. Trall.	Ignatius, Letter to the Trallians

Jos. Asen.	Joseph and Aseneth
Jub.	Jubilees
Mart. Matt.	Martyrdom of Matthew
Mart. Paul	Martyrdom of Paul
Mart. Pol.	Martyrdom of Polycarp
Odes Sol.	Odes of Solomon
Par. Jer.	Paraleipomena of Jeremiah (= 4 Baruch)
Pol. Phil.	Polycarp, Letter to the Philippians
Prot. Jas.	Protevangelium of James
Ps.-Phocylides	Sentences of Pseudo-Phocylides
Pss. Sol.	Psalms of Solomon
Sent. Sextus	Sentences of Sextus
Sib. Or.	Sibylline Oracles
T. 12 Patr.	Testaments of the Twelve Patriarchs
T. Abr.	Testament of Abraham
T. Asher	Testament of Asher
T. Benj.	Testament of Benjamin
T. Dan	Testament of Dan
T. Gad	Testament of Gad
T. Issach.	Testament of Issachar
T. Job	Testament of Job
T. Jos.	Testament of Joseph
T. Jud.	Testament of Judah
T. Levi	Testament of Levi
T. Moses	Testament of Moses
T. Naph.	Testament of Naphtali
T. Reub.	Testament of Reuben
T. Sim.	Testament of Simeon
T. Sol.	Testament of Solomon
T. Zeb.	Testament of Zebulon

E. Rabbinic Writings

m. = Mishna, *t.* = Tosepta, *b.* = Babylonian Talmud, *y.* = Jerusalem Talmud

'Abod. Zar.	'Aboda Zara
'Arak.	'Arakin
B. Qam.	Baba Qamma
B. Bat.	Baba Batra
Bek.	Bekorot
Ber.	Berakot
Beṣa	Beṣa = Yom Ṭob

B. Meṣ.	Baba Meṣi'a
Dem.	Demai
'Ed.	'Eduyyot
'Erub.	'Erubin
Giṭ.	Giṭṭin
Ḥag.	Ḥagiga
Ḥul.	Ḥullin

ABBREVIATIONS

Qidd.	Qiddušin	Pesaḥ.	Pesahim
Ketub.	Ketubot	Roš Haš.	Roš Haššana
Kil.	Kil'ayim	Šabb.	Šabbat
Ma'aś.	Ma'aśerot	Sanh.	Sanhedrin
Mak.	Makkot	Šeqal.	Šeqalim
Meg.	Megilla	Soṭa	Soṭa
Menaḥ.	Menahot	Sukk.	Sukka
Nazir	Nazir	Ta'an.	Ta'anit
Nid.	Niddah	Tamid	Tamid
Pe'a	Pe'a	Yoma	Yoma = Kippurim

F. OTHER RABBINIC WORKS

'Abot R. Nat.	'Abot de Rabbi Nathan	Rab.	Rabbah
Mek.	Mekilta	Ṣem.	Ṣemahot
Midr.	Midraš	Sipre	Sipre
Pesiq. R.	Pesiqta Rabbati	Tanḥ.	Midraš Tanḥuma
Pirqe 'Abot	Pirqe 'Abot	Tg. Ps.-J.	Targum Pseudo-Jonathan
Pirqe R. El.	Pirqe Rabbi Eliezer		

G. QUMRAN[†]

1Q27	1QMyst = Book of Mysteries = "The Triumph of Righteousness" in G. Vermes, The Dead Sea Scrolls in English.	1QSb	= 1Q28b = Collection of Blessings Uttered Over the Faithful, the High Priest, the Priests, the Prince of the Congregation
1Q34	1QLitPr^a = Collection of Liturgical Prayers	4QFlor	= 4Q174 = "A Messianic Anthology" in G. Vermes, DSSE
1QH	Thanksgiving Psalms (Hôdāyôt) = "The Hymns" in G. Vermes, DSSE	4QM	War Scroll portions from Cave 4
1QM	War Scroll (Milḥāmāh) = "The War Rule" in G. Vermes, DSSE	4QMilMik	Words of Michael (Millê Mîkā'ēl) = Words of the book which Michael addressed to the angels
1QpHab	Pesher on Habakkuk = "Commentary on Habakkuk" in G. Vermes, DSSE	4QpHos	Pesher on Hosea = "Commentary on Hosea" in G. Vermes, DSSE
1QpMic	Pesher on Micah = 1Q14 = "Commentary on Micah" in G. Vermes, DSSE	4QpNah	Pesher on Nahum = "Commentary on Nahum" in G. Vermes, DSSE
1QS	Manual of Discipline = "Community Rule" in G. Vermes, DSSE	4QpPs	Pesher on Psalms = "Commentary on Psalm 37" in G. Vermes, DSSE
1QSa	= 1Q28a = Rule for all the Congregation of Israel in the End of Days = "The Messianic Rule" in G. Vermes, DSSE	11QPs^a	Psalms Scroll
		CD	Cairo geniza text of the Damascus Rule

[†]For fuller information, see Joseph A. Fitzmyer, *The Dead Sea Scrolls: Major Publications and Tools for Study* (rev. ed., Atlanta: Scholars Press, 1990).

ABBREVIATIONS:
ANCIENT GREEK AND LATIN WRITERS*

Achilles Tatius
   Leuc. et Clit. Τὰ κατὰ Λευκίππην καὶ Κλειτοφῶντα *(The Adventures of Leucippe and Cleitophon)*

Aelian
   NA   *De Natura Animalium*
   VH   *Varia Historia*
   Orat.   *Orationes*
   Orat. Rom.   *Oratio Romana*

Aeneas Tacticus
   Polior. Πολιορκητικά

Aeschines
   Fals. Leg.   *De Falsa Legatione*
   In Ctes.   Against Ctesiphon
   In Tim.   Against Timarchus

Aeschylus
   Ag.   *Agamemnon*
   Cho.   *Choephori*
   Eum.   *Eumenides*
   Pers.   *Persae*
   PV   *Prometheus Vinctus* (*Prometheus Bound*)
   Sept.   *Septem contra Thebas* (*Seven Against Thebes*)
   Suppl.   *Supplices*

Aesop
   Fab.   *Fabulae*

Albinus
   Didask. Διδασκαλικός

Alciphron
   Ep.   *Epistulae*

Alexander of Aphrodisias
   In Sens.   *In Librum de Sensu Commentarium*
   Mixt.   *De Mixtione*
   Pr.   *Problemata*

Ambrose
   In Luc.   Commentary on Luke
   Off.   *De Officiis Ministrorum*
   Sacr.   *De Sacramentis*

Anacreon
   Od.   *Odes*

Anaximenes
   Rhet. ad Alex.   *Rhetorica ad Alexandrum* (= *Ars rhetorica*)

Andocides
   [*C. Alcib.*]   *Against Alcibiades*
   Myst.   *De Mysteriis*

Andronicus
   [*Pass.*] Περὶ παθῶν (*De Passionibus*)

Anth. Pal.
   Palatine Anthology

Anth. Plan.
   Planudean Anthology

Antiphon (OCD 1)
   1 Tetr.   *First Tetralogy*
   2 Tetr.   *Second Tetralogy*
   3 Tetr.   *Third Tetralogy*
   Murd. Her.   *Murder of Herodes*

Antoninus Liberalis
   Met.   *Metamorphoses*

Apollodorus (OCD 6)
   Bibl.   *Bibliotheca*

Apollonius of Tyana
   Ep.   *Epistulae*

Apollonius Rhodius
   Argon.   *Argonautica*

Apollonius Sophista (OCD 13)
   Lex.   *Lexicon Homericum*

---

*Bracketed abbreviations indicate works that scholars now generally regard as pseudonymous. This list includes pagan, Jewish, and Christian authors.

ABBREVIATIONS

Appian
BCiv.   Bella Civilia
Hisp.   Ἰβηρική
Mith.   Μιθριδάτειος
Praef. Praefatio

Apuleius
Met.   Metamorphoses

Aratus
Phaen. Phaenomena

Archimedes
Aequil. Περὶ ἰσορροπιῶν (The Equilibriums of Planes)
Aren.   Ψαμμίτης (The Sand-reckoner)
Eratosth. Πρὸς Ἐρατοσθένην ἔφοδος (To Eratosthenes on the Method of Mechanical Theorems)
Sph. Cyl. Περὶ σφαίρας καὶ κυλίνδρου (On the Sphere and the Cylinder)
Spir.   Περὶ ἑλίκων (On Spirals)

Archytas of Tarentum
Antik. Περὶ ἀντικειμένων

Aretaeus
SA Περὶ αἰτιῶν καὶ σημείων ὀξέων παθῶν (Sign. Acut. Morb.)
SD Περὶ αἰτιῶν καὶ σημείων χρονίων παθῶν (Sign. Morb. Diuturn.)

Aristaenetus
Ep.   Epistulae

Aristophanes
Ach.   Acharnenses
Av.   Aves (Birds)
Eccl.   Ecclesiazusae
Eq.   Equites (Knights)
Lys.   Lysistrata
Nub.   Nubes (Clouds)
Plut.   Plutus
Ran.   Ranae (Frogs)
Thesm. Thesmophoriazusae
Vesp.   Vespae (Wasps)

Aristotle
An. Pr. Analytica Priora
Ath. Pol. Ἀθηναίων πολιτεία (Constitution of Athens)
Cael.   De Caelo
De An. De Anima
Eth. Eud. Ethica Eudemia
Eth. Nic. Ethica Nichomachea
Gen. An. De Generatione Anamalium
Gen. Cor. De Generatione et Corruptione
HA   Historia Animalium
MA   De Motu Animalium
[Mag. Mor.] Magna Moralia
Mem.   De Memoria
Metaph. Metaphysica
Mete.   Meteorologica
[Mir. Ausc.] De Mirabilibus Auscultationibus
[Mund.] De Mundo
[Oec.] Oeconomica
Part. An. De Partibus Animalium
Ph.   Physica
Poet.   Poetica
Pol.   Politica
[Pr.]   Problemata
Rh.   Rhetorica
[Rh. Al.] Rhetorica ad Alexandrum
Sens.   De Sensu
Top.   Topica

Arrian
Anab.   Anabasis

Artapanus
De Jud. De Judaeis (in Eusebius)

Artemidorus Daldianus
Onir.   Onirocriticus

Athanasius
Ep. Serap. Epistles to Serapion

Athenaeus
Deip.   Δειπνοσοφισταί

Athenagoras
Leg.   Legatio pro Christianis

Augustine
Civ.   De Civitate Dei
En. in Ps. Enarrationes in Psalmos
Op. Mon. De Opere Monachorum
Perf. Just. De Perfectione Justitiae Hominis
Serm.   Sermones
Tract. in Ev. Joh. Tractatus in Ioannis Evangelium

Aulus Gellius
NA   Noctes Atticae

Autolycus of Pitane
Risings Περὶ ἀνατολῶν καὶ δύσεων (Risings and Settings)

Babrius
Myth.   Μυθίαμβοι Αἰσώπειοι

Bell. Afr.
Bellum Africum

Bion Adon.
Ἀδώνιδος Ἐπιτάφιος (Lament for Adonis)
[Epith. Achil.] Epithalamium to Achilles and Deidamea

Caesar
BCiv.   Bellum Civile
BGall. Bellum Gallicum

Callimachus
Aet.   Aetia (in P.Oxy. 2079)
Epigr.   Epigrammata
Hec.   Hecale
Hymn.   Hymns
Hymn. Ap.   Hymn to Apollo
Hymn. Art.   Hymn to Artemis

Callixenus
Alex.   Peri Alexandreias

Can. App.
Apostolic Canons

Cato
Agr.   De Agricultura

Cebes of Thebes
[Tabula]   Κέβητος Θηβαίου Πίναξ

Cercidas
Mel.   Meliambi

Chariton
Chaer.   Chaereas and Callirhoe

Chio
Epist.   Epistulae

Cicero
Att.   Epistulae ad Atticum
Deiot.   Pro Rege Deiotaro
Fam.   Epistulae ad Familiares
Fat.   De Fato
Fin.   De Finibus
Flac.   Pro Flacco
Leg.   De Legibus
Leg. Man.   Pro Lege Manilia (De Imperio Cn. Pompeii)
Lig.   Pro Ligario
Marcell.   Pro Marcello
Nat. D.   De Natura Deorum
Off.   De Officiis
Part. Or.   Partitiones Oratoriae
Phil.   Orationes Philippicae
Rep.   De Republica
[Rhet. Her.]   Rhetorica ad Herennium
Sen.   De Senectute
Sull.   Pro Sulla
Tusc.   Tusculanae Disputationes
Verr.   In Verrem

Clement of Alexandria
Paed.   Paedagogus
Quis dives   Quis dives salvetur?
Strom.   Stromata

Codex Justin.
Codex Justinianus

Columella
Rust.   De re rustica

Const. App.
Apostolic Constitutions

Cornutus
Theol. Graec.   Ἐπιδρομὴ τῶν κατὰ τὴν Ἑλληνικὴν Θεολογίαν παραδεδομένων (=De Natura Deorum)

Corp. Herm.
Corpus Hermeticum

Cosmas Indicopleustes
Top.   Christian Topography

Crates of Thebes
Ep.   Epistulae

Cratinus
Dionysalex.   Dionysalexandros

Demetrius Phalereus
[Eloc.]   De Elocutione (Περὶ ἑρμηνείας)

Demosthenes
C. Andr.   Against Androtion
C. Apat.   Against Apaturius
1–3 C. Aphob.   Against Aphobus I–III
C. Aristocr.   Against Aristocrates
1–2 C. Aristog.   Against Aristogeiton I–II
C. Boeot.   Against Boeotos I
C. Call.   Against Callicles
C. Con.   Against Conon
C. Dionys.   Against Dionysodorus
C. Eub.   Against Eubulides
C. Euerg.   Against Evergus
C. Lacr.   Against Lacritus
C. Leoch.   Against Leochares
C. Lept.   Against Leptines
C. Macart.   Against Macartatus
C. Mid.   Against Meidias
C. Naus.   Against Nausimachus
[C. Neaer.]   Against Neaera
C. Nicostr.   Against Nicostratus
C. Olymp.   Against Olympiodorus
1–2 C. Onet.   Against Onetor I–II
C. Pant.   Against Pantaenetus
C. Poly.   Against Polycles
1–2 C. Steph.   Against Stephanus I–II
C. Theocr.   Against Theocrines
C. Tim.   Against Timothes
C. Timocr.   Against Timocrates
C. Zenoth.   Against Zenothemis
Chers.   On the Chersonese
Corona   On the Crown
Cor. Trier.   On the Trierarchic Crown
Embassy   On the False Embassy
Fun. Orat.   Funeral Oration
Halon.   On the Halonnesus
1–3 Olynth.   Olynthiac I–III

Org. Fin.   *On Organization*
Peace   *On the Peace*
P. Phorm.   *For Phormio*
1–4 Philip.   *Philippic I–IV*
Prooem.   *Prooemia (= Exordia)*
Treaty Alex.   *On the Treaty with Alexander*

Didymus
  Trin.   *On the Trinity*
  Zech.   *Commentary on Zechariah*

Dig.
  Digesta

Dinarchus
  C. Aristog.   *Against Aristogiton*
  C. Phil.   *Against Philocles*

Dio Chrysostom
  1 Mon.   *First Discourse, On Kingship*
  3 Mon.   *Third Discourse, On Kingship*
  Olymp.   *Olympic Discourse*
  Or.   *Discourse* (See LCL for discourse numbers)

Dionysius of Halicarnassus
  Amm. 1   *Epistula ad Ammaeum 1*
  Comp.   *De Compositione Verborum*
  Dem.   *De Demosthene*
  Din.   *De Dinarcho*
  Is.   *De Isaeo*
  Orat.   *De Oratoribus Veteribus*
  Pomp.   *Epistula ad Pompeium*
  Rh.   *Ars Rhetorica*
  Th.   *De Thucydide*

Dioscorides
  Alex.   *Alexipharmaca*
  Mat. Med.   *De Materia Medica* (also cited by author's name alone)

Duris of Samos
  Hist.   *Historiae* (in Athenaeus)

Epictetus
  Diatr.   *Diatribai*
  Ench.   *Enchiridion*

Epicurus
  Epist.   *Epistulae*
  Her.   *Letter to Herodotus*
  Men.   *Letter to Menoecus*
  Nat.   *De Rerum Natura*
  Pyth.   *Letter to Pythocles*
  Sent.   *Sententiae*

Epiphanius
  Pan.   *Panarion (Refutation of All Heresies)*

Etymol. Mag.
  Etymologicum Magnum

Euclid
  Elem.   *Elementa*

Euripides
  Alc.   *Alcestis*
  Andr.   *Andromache*
  Bacch.   *Bacchae*
  Cyc.   *Cyclops*
  Dict.   *Dictys*
  El.   *Electra*
  Hec.   *Hecuba*
  Hel.   *Helena*
  Heracl.   *Heraclidae*
  HF   *Hercules Furens*
  Hipp.   *Hippolytus*
  Hyps.   *Hypsipyle*
  IA   *Iphigenia Aulidensis*
  IT   *Iphigenia Taurica*
  Med.   *Medea*
  Or.   *Orestes*
  Phoen.   *Phoinissae*
  Rhes.   *Rhesus*
  Supp.   *Supplices*
  Tro.   *Troades*
  C. Marc.   *Against Marcellus*

Eusebius
  Dem. Evang.   *Demonstration of the Gospel*
  Hist. Eccl.   *Ecclesiastical History* (also cited by author's name alone)
  In Isa.   *Commentary on Isaiah*
  Mart. Palest.   *The Martyrs of Palestine*
  Praep. Evang.   *Preparation for the Gospel*

Firmicus Maternus
  Err. prof. rel.   *De errore profanarum religionum*
  Math.   *Mathesis*

Fronto
  Ep. ad M. Caes.   *Letter to Marcus Caesar*

Gaius
  Inst.   *Institutiones*

Galen
  Aliment. Comm.   *In Hippocratis De Alimento Commentarius*
  Anim. Pass.   Περὶ ψυχῆς παθῶν κτλ.
  Comm. Hipp.   *Galeni Comment. I in Hippocratis lib. I Epidemiorum*
  De Plac. Hipp. et Plat.   *De Placitis Hippocratis et Platonis*
  De simpl. medicam. temp.   *De Simplicium Medicamentorum Temperamentis*
  Def. Med.   *Definitiones Medicae*
  Med. Phil.   Ὅτι ὁ ἄριστος ἰατρὸς καὶ φιλόσοφος (= *That the Best Physician is Also a Philosopher*)
  Remed. Parab.   *De Remediis Parabilibus*

Geminus
  Intro. to Astronomy   Εἰσαγωγὴ εἰς τὰ
    φαινόμενα (Introduction to
    Astronomy)
Gorgias
  Hel.   Helena
Gregory of Nazianzus
  Ep.   Epistulae
  Or. Bas.   Oratio in Laudem Basilii
Gregory of Nyssa
  De Deitate   De Deitate Filii et Spiritus Sancti
Gregory the Great
  Moral.   Expositio in Librum Iob, sive
    Moralium Libri XXV
Heliodorus
  Aeth.   Aethiopica
Heraclitus
  All.   Allegoriae (Quaestiones Homericae)
Hero
  Spir.   Spiritalia (Pneumatica)
Herodian
  Hist.   Τῆς μετὰ Μάρκον βασιλείας
    ἱστορίαι
Hesiod
  Op.   Opera et Dies (Works and Days)
  [Sc.]   Scutum (Shield)
  Th.   Theogonia
Hierax
  Met.   Metamorphoses
Hippocrates
  Acut.   Περὶ διαίτης ὀξέων (De Ratione
    Victus in Morbis Acutis = Regimen
    in Acute Diseases)
  Aff.   Περὶ παθῶν (De Affectionibus =
    Affections)
  Alim.   Περὶ τροφῆς (De Alimento =
    Nutrition)
  Aph.   Ἀφορισμοί (Aphorismata =
    Aphorisms)
  Append.   Spurious appendix to Acut.
  Art.   Περὶ τέχνης (De Arte = The Art)
  Artic.   Περὶ ἄρθρων [ἐμβολῆς] (De
    Articulis Reponendis = Joints)
  Carn.   Περὶ σαρκῶν (De Carne = Fleshes
    or Tissues)
  Coac.   Κωακαὶ προγνώσεις (Praenotiones
    Coacae = Coan Prognoses)
  Decent.   Περὶ εὐσχημοσύνης (De Habitu
    Decenti = Decorum)
  Dent.   Περὶ ὀδοντοφυΐης (De Dentitione
    = Teething)
  Epid.   Ἐπιδημίαι (Epidemiae = Epidemics)
  Fist.   Περὶ συρίγγων (Fistulae)
  Fract.   Περὶ ἀγμῶν (De Fracturis =
    Fractures)
  Genit.   Περὶ γονῆς
  Int.   Περὶ τῶν ἐντὸς παθῶν (De
    Affectionibus Internis = Internal
    Affections)
  Jusj.   Ὅρκος (Jus Jurandum = The Oath)
  Lex   Νόμος (Lex = Decree)
  Liqu.   Περὶ ὑγρῶν χρήσιος (De
    Liquidorum Usu = Use of Fluids)
  Loc. Hom.   Περὶ τόπων τῶν κατὰ
    ἀνθρώπων (De Locis in Homine =
    Places in Man)
  Medic.   Περὶ ἰητροῦ (De Medico =
    Physician)
  Mochl.   Μοχλικόν (Instruments of
    Reduction or Nature of Bones)
  Morb.   Περὶ νούσων (De Morbis =
    Diseases)
  Morb. Sac.   Περὶ ἱερῆς νούσου (De
    Morbo Sacro = Sacred Disease)
  Mul.   Γυναικεῖα (De Morbis Mulierum =
    Diseases of Women)
  Nat. Hom.   Περὶ φύσιος ἀνθρώπου (De
    Natura Hominis)
  Nat. Mul.   Περὶ γυναικείης φύσιος (De
    Natura Muliebri)
  Nat. Puer.   Περὶ φύσιος παιδίου (De
    Nature Pueri)
  Oct.   Περὶ ὀκταμήνου (De Octimestri
    Partu = Eight Month's Child)
  Off.   Κατ' ἰητρεῖον (De Officina Medici =
    In the Surgery)
  Praec.   Παραγγελίαι (Praeceptiones =
    Precepts)
  Prog.   Προγνωστικόν (Prognostic)
  Prorrh.   Προρρητικόν (Prorhetic)
  Septim.   Περὶ ἑπταμήνου (De Septimestri
    Partu = Seven Month's Child)
  Steril.   Περὶ ἀφόρων (De Sterilitate =
    Sterile Women)
  Vict.   Περὶ διαίτης ὑγιεινῆς (De Ratione
    Victus Salubris = Regimen in
    Health); or Περὶ διαίτης (Regimen)
  VM   Περὶ ἀρχαίης ἰητρικῆς (De Vetere
    Medicina = Ancient Medicine)
Hippolytus
  Haer.   Refutation of All Heresies
  In Dan.   Commentary on Daniel
  Trad. ap.   The Apostolic Tradition
Homer
  [H. Aphr.]   Hymn to Aphrodite
  [H. Apol.]   Hymn to Apollo

ABBREVIATIONS

[H. Ares] Hymn to Ares
[H. Cast.] Hymn to Castor
[H. Demet.] Hymn to Demeter
[H. Diosc.] Hymn to the Dioscuri
[H. Hermes] Hymn to Hermes
[H. Pos.] Hymn to Poseidon
Il. Iliad
Od. Odyssey

Horace
Carm. Carmina
Epist. Epistulae
Epod. Epodi
Sat. Satirae

Hyginus
Poet. Astr. Poetica Astronomica

Hyperides
Ath. Adversus Athenogenem
Dem. Adversus Demosthenem
Eux. Pro Euxenippo
Lyc. Pro Lycophrone

Iamblichus
Agr. Letter to Agrippa (in Stobaeus)
Myst. De Mysteriis
Sophr. Letter concerning Prudence (in Stobaeus)
VP De Vita Pythagorica

Ignatius
[Ad Philip.] Letter to the Philippians

Irenaeus
Haer. Against Heresies

Isaeus
Philoct. On the Estate of Philoctemon

Isocrates
Ad Nic. To Nicocles
Aeginet. Aegineticus
Antid. Antidosis
Archid. Archidamus
Areop. Areopagiticus
Big. De Bigis (= On the Team of Horses)
Trapez. Trapeziticus (= On the Banker)
Bus. Busiris
C. Callim. Against Callimachus
De Pace On the Peace
[Demon.] To Demonicus
Ep. Epistulae
Evag. Evagoras
Hel. Helen
Nic. Nicocles
Panath. Panathenaicus
Paneg. Panegyricus
Phil. Philippus

Jerome
Epist. Epistulae
In Ep. ad Gal. In Epistolam Pauli ad Galatas
In Tit. In Epistolam Pauli ad Titum
Quaest. hebr. Quaestiones Hebraicae

John Chrysostom
Comp. reg. et mon. Comparatio regis et monachi
Ep. Theod. Letter to Theodore
Hom. Homilies
Sacerdot. De Sacerdotio

John Malalas
Chron. Chronography

John Philoponus
Comm. de An. In Aristotelis De Anima Libros Commentaria

Josephus
Ag. Apion Against Apion
Ant. Antiquities of the Jews
Life Life of Josephus
War The Jewish War

Justin
1 Apol. First Apology
2 Apol. Second Apology
Dial. Dialogue with Trypho

Justinian
Edict. Edicta
Nov. Novellae

Juvenal
Sat. Satirae

Lactantius
Mort. Pers. De Morte Persecutorum

Libanius
Autobiogr. Autobiography (Oration 1)

Longinus
[Subl.] Περὶ ὕψους (On the Sublime)

Longus
Daph. Daphnis and Chloe

Lucian
Alex. Alexander (Pseudomantis)
Am. Amores
Asin. Asinus (Lucius)
Bis Acc. Bis Accusatus
Cal. Calumniae Non Temere Credendum
Char. Charon
Demon. Demonax
Dial. D. Dialogi Deorum
Dial. Meret. Dialogi Meretricii
Dial. Mort. Diologi Mortuorum
Dom. De Domo

xxv

*Encom. Demosth.   Demosthenous
    Encomium (= In Praise of
    Demosthenes)*
Fug.   Fugitivi
Gall.   Gallus
Hermot.   Hermotimus (De Sectis)
Icar.   Icaromenippus
Im.   Imagines
Ind.   Adversus Indoctum
JConf.   Juppiter Confutatus
JTr.   Juppiter Tragoedus
Laps.   Pro Lapsu inter Salutandum
Luct.   De Luctu
Merc. Cond.   De Mercede Conductis
Nav.   Navigium
Nec.   Necyomantia
Par.   De Parasito
Peregr.   De Morte Peregrini
Phal.   Phalaris
[Philopatr.]   Philopatris
Philops.   Philopseudes
Pisc.   Piscator
Pseudol.   Pseudologista
Rh. Pr.   Rhetorum praeceptor
Sacr.   De Sacrificiis
Salt.   De Saltatione
Scyth.   Scytha
Somn.   Somnium (Vita Luciani)
Symp.   Symposium
Syr. D.   De Syria Dea
Tim.   Timon
Tox.   Toxaris
Tyr.   Tyrannicida
Ver. Hist.   Vera Historia
Vit. Auct.   Vitarum Auctio

Lycurgus
Leoc.   Against Leocrates

Lysias
[Amat.]   Amatorius
C. Agor.   Against Agoratus
C. Andoc.   Against Andocides
C. Leocr.   Against Leocrates
C. Nicom.   Against Nocomachus
C. Philo   Against Philo
C. Sim.   Against Simon
Def. Anon.   For an Anonymous Defendant
Inval.   For the Cripple
Mantith.   Defense of Mantitheus

Macrobius
Sat.   Saturnalia

Martial
Epigr.   Epigrammaton Libri

Menander
Dysk.   Dyskolos
Epit.   Epitrepontes
Georg.   Georgos
Mis.   Misoumenos
Mon.   Monostichoi
Phas.   Phasma
Pk.   Perikeiromene
Sam.   Samia
Sik.   Sikyonios
Thras.   Thrasonidis

Menander of Laodicea
Epidict.   Περὶ ἐπιδεικτικῶν

Methodius of Olympus
Symp.   Symposium

Minucius Felix
Oct.   Octavian

Mon. Anc.
Monumentum Ancyranum

Moschus
Eur.   Europa

Nicander
Alex.   Alexipharmaca
Ther.   Theriaca

Nichomachus of Gerasa
Ar.   Arithmetica Introductio

Nicolaus of Damascus
*Hist. Univ.   Universal History (in
    Athenaeus)*
Vit. Caes.   Vita Caesaris

Nonnus
Dion.   Dionysiaca

Ocellus of Lucania
Nat.   Περὶ τῆς τοῦ παντὸς φύσεως

Olympiodorus
*In Mete.   In Aristotelis Meteora
    Commentaria*

Orac. Chald.
Chaldaean Oracles

Origen
Cels.   Against Celsus
In Joh.   Commentary on John
Is.   Homilies on Isaiah
Prayer   On Prayer

Ovid
Am.   Amores
Ars am.   Ars amatoria
Fast.   Fasti
Her.   Heroides
Ib.   Ibis
Met.   Metamorphoses

ABBREVIATIONS

Pappus
   Coll.   Collectio (Συναγωγή)
Paulus
   Sent.   Sententiae
Peripl. M. Rubr.
   The Periplus of the Erythraean Sea
Persius
   Sat.   Satirae
Philo
   Abraham   On Abraham (De Abrahamo)
   Alleg. Interp.   Allegorical Interpretation (Legum Allegoriae)
   [Bib. Antiq.]   Biblical Antiquities
   Change of Names   On the Change of Names (Mut. nom.)
   Cherub.   On the Cherubim (De Cherubim)
   Conf. Tongues   On the Confusion of Tongues (De Confusione Linguarum)
   Contemp. Life   On the Contemplative Life (De Vita Contemplativa)
   Creation   On the Creation (De Opificio Mundi)
   Decalogue   On the Decalogue (De Decalogo)
   Dreams   On Dreams (De Somniis)
   Drunkenness   On Sobriety (De Ebrietate)
   Etern. World   On the Eternity of the World (De Aeternitate Mundi)
   Flacc.   Against Flaccus (In Flaccum)
   Flight   On Flight and Finding (De Fuga et Inventione)
   Giants   On the Giants (De Gigantibus)
   Good Man Free   Every Good Man Is Free (Quod Omnis Probus Liber Sit)
   Heir   Who Is the Heir (Quis Rerum Divinarum Heres)
   Husbandry   On Husbandry (De Agricultura)
   Hypoth.   Hypothetica (Apologia pro Iudaeis)
   Joseph   On Joseph (De Iosepho)
   Migr. Abr.   On the Migration of Abraham (De Migratione Abrahami)
   Moses   On the Life of Moses (De Vita Mosis)
   Plant.   On Noah's Work as a Planter (De Plantatione)
   Post. Cain   On the Posterity and Exile of Cain (De Posteritate Caini)
   Prelim. Stud.   On the Preliminary Studies (De Congressu Quaerendae Eruditionis Gratia)
   Prov.   On Providence (De Providentia)
   Quest. Exod.   Questions and Answers on Exodus (Quaestiones et Solutiones in Exodum)
   Quest. Gen.   Questions and Answers on Genesis (Quaestiones et Solutiones in Genesis)
   Rewards   On Rewards and Punishments (De Praemiis et Poenis)
   Sacr. Abel and Cain   On the Sacrifice of Abel and Cain (De Sacrificiis Abelis et Caini)
   Sobr.   On Sobriety (De Sobrietate)
   Spec. Laws   On the Special Laws (De Specialibus Legibus)
   To Gaius   On the Embassy to Gaius (De Legatione ad Gaium)
   Unchang. God   On the Unchangeableness of God (Quod Deus Immutabilis Sit)
   Virtues   On the Virtues (De Virtutibus)
   Worse Attacks Better   The Worse Attacks the Better (Quod Deterius Potiori Insidiari Solet)

Philodemus of Gadara
   Adv. Soph.   Adversus Sophistas
   D.   De Diis
   Hom.   De Bono Rege Secundum Homerum
   Ir.   De Ira
   Lib.   De Libertate Dicendi
   Mort.   De Morte
   Mus.   De Musica
   Piet.   De Pietate
   Rh.   Volumina Rhetorica
   Sign.   De Signis
   Vit.   De Vitiis X

Philostratus
   Ep.   Epistulae
   Gym.   De Gymnastica
   Imag.   Imagines
   VA   Vita Apollonii
   VS   Vitae Sophistarum

Photius
   Lex.   Lexicon

Pindar
   Isthm.   Isthmian Odes
   Nem.   Nemean Odes
   Ol.   Olympian Odes
   Paean.   Paeanes
   Pyth.   Pythian Odes
   Thren.   Threnoi

Plato
   [Alc. Maj.]   Alcibiades Major
   Ap.   Apologia
   [Ax.]   Axiochus
   Chrm.   Charmides
   Cra.   Cratylus
   [Def.]   Definitiones

Ep.   Epistulae (some authentic, some spurious)
[Epin.]   Epinomis
Euthd.   Euthydemus
Euthphr.   Euthyphro
Grg.   Gorgias
Hipparch.   Hipparchus
Hp. Ma.   Hippias Major
Hp. Mi.   Hippias Minor
Lach.   Laches
Leg.   Leges
Menex.   Menexenus
[Min.]   Minos
Phd.   Phaedo
Phdr.   Phaedrus
Phlb.   Philebus
Plt.   Politicus (Statesman)
Prm.   Parmenides
Prt.   Protagoras
Resp.   Respublica
Soph.   Sophista
Symp.   Symposium
Tht.   Theaetetus
Tim.   Timaeus

Plautus
Aul.   Aulularia
Bacch.   Bacchides
Mil. Glor.   Miles Gloriosus
Mostell.   Mostellaria
Poen.   Poenulus
Pseud.   Pseudolus
Trin.   Trinummus
Truc.   Truculentus

Pliny the Elder
HN   Natural History

Pliny the Younger
Ep.   Epistulae
Pan.   Panegyricus

Plotinus
Enn.   Enneades

Plutarch
Ad princ. iner.   Ad Principem Ineruditum
Adv. Col.   Adversus Colotem
Aem.   Aemilius Paulus
Ages.   Agesilaus
Agric.   Agricola
Alc.   Alcibiades
Alex.   Alexander
Amat.   Amatorius
[Amat. nar.]   Amatoriae Narrationes
An ignis   Aqua an Ignis Utilior
An seni   An Seni Respublica Gerenda Sit
Ant.   Antonius
An virt. doc.   An Virtus Doceri Possit
An vitiositas   An Vitiositas ad Infelicitatem Sufficiat
Apoph. lac.   Apophthegmata Laconica
Arat.   Aratus
Arist.   Aristides
Art.   Artaxerxes
Brut.   Brutus
Caes.   Caesar
Cam.   Camillus
Cat. Mai.   Cato the Elder
Cat. Min.   Cato the Younger
C. Gracch.   C. Gracchus
Cic.   Cicero
Cim.   Cimon
Cleom.   Cleomenes
Con. praec.   Coniugalia Praecepta
[Cons. ad Apoll.]   Consolatio ad Apollonium
Cons. ux.   Consolatio ad Uxorem
Conv. sept. sap.   Septem Sapientium Convivium
Cor.   Coriolanus
Crass.   Crassus
De adul. et am.   De Adulatore et Amico
De Alex. fort.   De Alexandri Fortuna
De amic. mult.   De Amicorum Multitudine
De am. prol.   De Amore Prolis
De audiendo   De Audiendo (= De Recta Ratione Audiendi)
De aud. poet.   De Audiendis Poetis
De cohib. ira   De Cohibenda Ira
De comm. not.   De Communibus Notitiis Contra Stoicos
De cupid. divit.   De Cupiditate Divitiarum
De curios.   De Curiositate
De def. or.   De Defectu Oraculorum
De E ap. Delph.   De E apud Delphos
De esu carn.   De Esu Carnium
De exil.   De Exilio
De fac.   De Facie in Orbe Lunae
De fort.   De Fortuna
De fort. Rom.   De Fortuna Romanorum
De frat. amor.   De Fraterno Amore
De garr.   De Garrulitate
De gen.   De Genio Socratis
De glor. Ath.   De Gloria Atheniensium
De inv. et ot.   De Invidia et Otio
De Is. et Os.   De Iside et Osiride
De laude   De Laude Ipsius
[De lib. ed.]   De Liberis Educandis
Dem.   Demosthenes
Demetr.   Demetrius
[De mus.]   De Musica
[De plac. philos.]   De Placita Philosophorum

De prim. frig.   *De Primo Frigido*
De prof. in virt.   *De Profectibus in Virtute*
De Pyth. or.   *De Pythiae Oraculis*
De sera   *De Sera Numinis Vindicta*
De sol. an.   *De Sollertia Animalium*
De Stoic. rep.   *De Stoicorum Repugnantiis*
De superst.   *De Superstitione*
De tranq. anim.   *De Tranquillitate Animi*
De trib. r. p. gen.   *De Tribus Rei Publicae Generibus*
De tu. san.   *De Tuenda Sanitate Praecepta*
De unius in rep. dom.   *De Unius in Republica Dominatione*
De virt. et vit.   *De Virtute et Vitio*
De virt. mor.   *De Virtute Morali*
De vit. aere al.   *De Vitando Aere Alieno*
De vit. et poes. Hom.   *De Vita et Poesi Homeri*
De vit. pud.   *De Vitioso Pudore*
Eum.   *Eumenes*
Fab.   *Fabius*
Flam.   *Flamininus*
Luc.   *Lucullus*
Lyc.   *Lycurgus*
Lys.   *Lysander*
Mar.   *Marius*
Marc.   *Marcellus*
Mor.   *Moralia*
Mulier. virt.   *Mulierum Virtutes*
Nic.   *Nicias*
Num.   *Numa*
Oth.   *Otho*
Pel.   *Pelopidas*
Per.   *Pericles*
Phil.   *Philopoemen*
Phoc.   *Phocion*
Pomp.   *Pompey*
Praec. ger. rei publ.   *Praecepta Gerendae Rei Publicae*
Publ.   *Publicola*
Pyrrh.   *Pyrrhus*
Quaest. conv.   *Quaestionum Convivialum Libri IX*
Quaest. nat.   *Quaestiones Naturales*
Quaest. Plat.   *Quaestiones Platonicae*
Quaest. Rom.   *Quaestiones Romanae*
[Reg. et imp. apoph.]   *Regum et Imperatorum Apophthegmata*
Rom.   *Romulus*
Sert.   *Sertorius*
Sol.   *Solon*
Suav. viv.   *Non Posse Suaviter Vivi Secundum Epicurum*
Sull.   *Sulla*

Them.   *Themistocles*
Thes.   *Theseus*
Ti. Gracch.   *Tiberius Gracchus*
Tim.   *Timoleon*
[X orat.]   *Vitae decem oratorum*

Polemo
Declam.   *Declamationes*

Pollux
Onom.   *Onomasticon*

Polyaenus
Strat.   *Strategemata*

Porphyry
Abst.   *De Abstinentia*
De antr. nymph.   *De Antro Nympharum*
VP   *Vita Pythagorae*

Proclus
Art. sacr.   *De Arte Sacra*

Procopius
Aed.   *De Aedificiis*
Goth.   *De Bello Gothico*

Ps.-Clem. Hom.
Clementine Homilies

Ptolemy (the Gnostic)
Flor.   *Letter to Flora*
Opt.   *Optica*
Tetr.   *Tetrabiblos (Ἀποτελεσματικά)*

Quintilian
Inst.   *Instituto oratoria*

Res gest. divi Aug.
Res gestae divi Augusti

Rufus of Ephesus   *Anat.*
Ἀνατομή

Rufus of Ephesus
Onom.   Περὶ ὀνομασίας
Ren. Ves.   *De Renum et Vesicae Affectionibus*

Sallust
Cat.   *Bellum Catalinae*
Iug.   *Bellum Iugurthinum*

Seneca
Ben.   *De Beneficiis*
Clem.   *De Clementia*
Dial.   *Dialogi*
Ep.   *Epistulae Morales*
Helv.   *Ad Helviam*
Herc.   *Hercules [Furens]*
Ira   *De Ira*
Lucil.   *Ad Lucilium*
Marc.   *Ad Marciam de Consolatione*
Phdr.   *Phaedra*
Polyb.   *Ad Polybium de Consolatione*

QNat.   Quaestiones Naturales
Tranq. De Tranquillitate Animi
Vit. Beat. De Vita Beata

Sextus Empiricus
Math.   Adversus Mathematicos
Pyr.   Πυρρώνειοι ὑποτυπώσεις (Outlines of Pyrrhonism)

Silius Italicus
Pun.   Punica

Sophocles
Aj.   Ajax
Ant.   Antigone
El.   Elektra
Ichn.   Ichneutae
OC   Oedipus Coloneus
OT   Oedipus Tyrannus
Phil.   Philoctetes
Trach. Trachiniae

Soranus
Gyn.   Γυναικεῖα

Statius
Silv.   Silvae

Stobaeus
Ecl.   Ἐκλογαί
Flor.   Ἀνθολόγιον

Strattis
Lemn.   Λημνομέδα

Suetonius
Aug.   Divus Augustus
Calig. Gaius Caligula
Claud. Divus Claudius
Iul.   Divus Iulius
Rhet.   De Grammaticis et Rhetoribus
Tib.   Tiberius
Tit.   Divus Titus
Vit.   Vitellius

Synesius
Epist. ad Paeonium   Epistula ad Paeonium
Hymn.   Hymni

Tacitus
Ann.   Annales
Dial.   Dialogus de Oratoribus
Germ.   Germania
Hist.   Historiae

Terence
Ad.   Adelphoe
Eun.   Eunuchus
Haut.   Hautontimorumenos
Phorm. Phormio

Tertullian
Apol.   Apology
Bapt.   On Baptism
Coron. De Corona (On the Crown)
Marc.   Against Marcion
Praescrip. Prescription of Heretics
Scap.   To Scapula

Themistius
Or.   Orations

Theocritus
Id.   Idylls

Theodoret
Car.   De Caritate
Hist. Eccl. Ecclesiastical History
Hist. Syr. Mon. History of the Monks of Syria

Theon of Alexandria
In Alm. Commentary on the Almagest

Theophilus
Ad Autol. Ad Autolycum

Theophrastus
Caus. Pl. De Causis Plantarum
Char.   Characteres (sometimes cited by author alone)
Hist. Pl. Historia Plantarum
Sens.   De Sensu

Varro
Rust.   De Re Rustica

Virgil
Aen.   Aeneid
G.   Georgics

Vitruvius
Arch.   De Architectura

Xenophon of Ephesus
Ephes. Ephesiaca

Xenophon
Ages.   Agesilaus
An.   Anab.
Ap.   Apologia Socratis
[Ath.] Respublica Atheniensium
Cyn.   Cynegeticus
Cyr.   Cyropaedia
Eq.   De Equitande Ratione
Eq. Mag. De Equitum Magistro
Hell.   Hellenica
Hier.   Hiero
Lac.   Respublica Lacedaemoniorum
Mem.   Memorabilia
Oec.   Oeconomicus
Symp.   Symposium

Zeno
Sign.   Περὶ σημείων

Abbreviations:
Papyri and Ostraca

A. Works Cited by an Abbreviation*

Apokrimata	*Apokrimata: Decisions of Septimius Severus on Legal Matters.* Ed. W. L. Westermann and A. A. Schiller. New York, 1954. (= *P.Col.* VI)
Berichtigungsliste	*Berichtigungsliste der griechischen Papyrusurkunden aus Ägypten.* Ed. F. Preisigke et al. Berlin, 1922–.
BGU	*Aegyptische Urkunden aus den Königlichen* (later *Staatlichen*) *Museen zu Berlin, Griechische Urkunden.* 15 vols. Berlin, 1895–1983.
Chrest.Mitt.	L. Mitteis and U. Wilcken, *Grundzüge und Chrestomathie der Papyruskunde* I. Band, Historischer Teil, II. Hälfte, Chrestomathie. Leipzig-Berlin, 1912.
Chrest.Wilck.	L. Mitteis and U. Wilcken, *Grundzüge und Chrestomathie der Papyruskunde* II. Band, Juristischer Teil, II. Hälfte, Chrestomathie. Leipzig-Berlin, 1912.
CPR	*Corpus Papyrorum Raineri.* 8 vols. Vienna, 1895–1983.
C.Ord.Ptol.	*Corpus des ordonnances des ptolémées.* Ed. M.-Th. Lenger. Brussels, 1964; 2d ed., 1980.

---

*Abbreviations generally follow the standard in *Checklist of Editions of Greek and Latin Papyri, Ostraca, and Tablets* (4th ed.; *BASP* Supplements 7; Atlanta, 1992), ed. John F. Oates, Roger S. Bagnall, William H. Willis, and Klaas A. Worp. In some instances the abbreviations derive from the 3d edition (1985), which occasionally differs slightly. The *Checklist* is an invaluable resource for anyone interested in additional information. (For example, the *Checklist* gives the distribution of inventory numbers through multivolumed works, such as *P.Hamb.* and *P.Oxy.*; it also gives references in the papyrological journals for publications from corpora partially published in the volumes cited here; and it tells where some of these have been reprinted.)

C.Pap.Jud.	*Corpus Papyrorum Judaicarum.* 3 vols. Ed. V. A. Tcherikover. Cambridge, Mass., 1957–1964.
C.P.Herm.	*Corpus Papyrorum Hermopolitanorum.* Ed. C. Wessely. Leipzig, 1905. (= *Stud.Pal.* V)
Jur.Pap.	*Juristische Papyri.* Ed. P. M. Meyer. Berlin, 1920.
MPER	*Mitteilungen aus der Sammlung der Papyrus Erzheurzog Rainer.* Ed. J. Karabacek. 6 vols. Vienna, 1887–1897.
MPER N.S.	*Mitteilungen aus der Papyrussammlung der Nationalbibliothek in Wien,* Neue Serie. 14 vols. Vienna, 1932–1982.
O.Aberd.	See *P.Aberd.*
O.Amst.	*Ostraka in Amsterdam Collections.* Ed. R. S. Bagnall, P. J. Sijpesteijn, and K. A. Worp. Zutphen, 1976.
O.Bodl.	*Greek Ostraca in the Bodleian Library at Oxford and Various Other Collections.* 3 vols. London, 1930–1964.
O.Brüss.Berl.	*Ostraka aus Brüssel und Berlin.* Ed. P. Viereck. Berlin-Leipzig, 1922.
O.Florida	*The Florida Ostraka: Documents from the Roman Army in Upper Egypt.* Ed. R. S. Bagnall. Durham, N.C., 1976.
O.Joach.	*Die Prinz-Joachim-Ostraka.* Ed. F. Preisigke and W. Spiegelberg. Strassburg, 1914.
O.Mich.	*Greek Ostraca in the University of Michigan Collection.* I = Ed. L. Amundsen. Ann Arbor, 1935. II and III = see *P.Mich.* VI and VIII.
O.Ont.Mus.	I = *Death and Taxes: Ostraka in the Royal Ontario Museum* I. Ed. A. E. Samuel et al. Toronto, 1971. II = *Ostraka in the Royal Ontario Museum* II. Ed. R. S. Bagnall and A. E. Samuel. Toronto, 1976.
O.Oslo	*Ostraca Osloënsia: Greek Ostraca in Norwegian Collections.* Ed. L. Amundsen. Oslo, 1933.
O.Wilb.	*Les Ostraca grecs de la collection Charles-Edwin Wilbour au Musée de Brooklyn.* Ed. C. Préaux. New York, 1935.
O.Wilck.	*Griechische Ostraka aus Aegypten und Nubien.* 2 vols. Ed. U. Wilcken. Leipzig-Berlin, 1899. Reprint Amsterdam, 1970, with addenda.
Pap.Brux.	*Papyrologica Bruxellensia.* 19 vols. Brussels, 1962–1980.

ABBREVIATIONS

Pap.Colon.	*Papyrologica Coloniensia.* 9 vols. Cologne/Opladen, 1964–1980.
Pap.Graec.Mag.	*Papyri Graecae Magicae.* Ed. K. Preisendanz. 2 vols. Leipzig-Berlin, 1928–1931.
Pap.Lugd.Bat.	*Papyrologica Lugduno-Batava.* 24 vols. Leiden, 1941–1983.
PSI	*Papiri greci e latine.* 15 vols. Florence, 1912–1979.
P.Aberd.	*Catalogue of Greek and Latin Papyri and Ostraca in the Possession of the University of Aberdeen.* Ed. E. G. Turner. Aberdeen, 1939.
P.Abinn.	*The Abinnaeus Archive: Papers of a Roman Officer in the Reign of Constantius II.* Ed. H. I. Bell et al. Oxford, 1962.
P.Achm.	*Les Papyrus grecs d'Achmîm à la Bibliothèque Nationale de Paris.* Ed. P. Collart. Cairo, 1930.
P.Adl.	*The Adler Papyri.* Greeks texts ed. E. N. Adler et al. Oxford, 1939.
P.Alex.	*Papyrus grecs du Musée Gréco-Romain d'Alexandrie.* Ed. A. Sawiderek and M. Vandoni. Warsaw, 1964.
P.Amh.	*The Amherst Papyri: Being an Account of the Greek Papyri in the Collection of the Right Hon. Lord Amherst of Hackney, F.S.A. at Didlington Hall, Norfolk.* Ed. B. P. Grenfell and A. S. Hunt. 2 vols. London, 1900–1901.
P.Amst.	*Die Amsterdamer Papyri* I. Ed. R. P. Salomons et al. Zutphen, 1980.
P.Ant.	*The Antinoopolis Papyri.* 3 vols. London, 1950–1967.
P.Apoll.	*Papyrus grecs d'Apollônos Anô.* Ed. R. Rémondon. Cairo, 1953.
P.Athen.	*Papyri Societatis Archaeologicae Atheniensis.* Ed. G. A. Petropoulos. Athens, 1939.
P.Bad.	*Veröffentlichungen aus den badischen Papyrus-Sammlungen.* 6 vols. Heidelberg, 1923–.
P.Berl.Möller	*Griechische Papyri aus dem Berliner Museum.* Ed. S. Möller. Göteborg, 1929.
P.Berl.Zill.	*Vierzehn Berliner griechische Papyri.* Ed. H. Zilliacus. Helsingfors, 1941.
P.Bodm.	*Papyrus Bodmer.* 26 vols. Cologny-Geneva, 1954–1969. XIV–XV = *Evangile de Luc chap. 3–24,*

	Evangile de Jean chap. 1–15. Ed. V. Martin and R. Kasser. 1961.
P.Bon.	*Papyri Bononienses.* Ed. O. Montevecchi. Milan, 1953.
P.Bour.	*Les Papyrus Bouriant.* Ed. P. Collart. Paris, 1926.
P.Brem.	*Die Bremer Papyri.* Ed. U. Wilcken. Berlin, 1936.
P.Brux.	*Papyri Bruxellenses Graecae.* Ed. G. Nachtergael. Brussels, 1974.
P.Cair.Goodsp.	*Greek Papyri from the Cairo Museum.* Ed. E. J. Goodspeed. Chicago, 1902.
P.Cair.Isid.	*The Archive of Aurelius Isidorus in the Egyptian Museum Cairo, and the University of Michigan.* Ed. A. E. R. Boak and H. C. Youtie. Ann Arbor, 1960.
P.Cair.Masp.	*Papyrus grecs d'époque byzantine, Catalogue général des antiquitiés égyptiennes du Musée du Caire.* Ed. J. Maspero. 3 vols. Cairo, 1911–1916.
P.Cair.Mich.	*A Tax List from Karanis.* Ed. H. Riad and J. C. Shelton. 2 parts. Bonn, 1976–1977.
P.Cair.Preis.	*Griechische Urkunden des Aegyptischen Museums zu Kairo.* Ed. F. Preisigke. Strassburg, 1911.
P.Cair.Zen.	*Zenon Papyri: Catalogue général des antiquités égyptiennes du Musée du Caire.* Ed. C. C. Edgar. 5 vols. Cairo, 1925–1940.
P.Catt.	See *Chrest.Mitt.* 88 and 372 and *SB* I, 4284.
P.Charite	*Das Aurelia Charite Archiv.* Ed. K. A. Worp. Zutphen, 1981.
P.Coll.Youtie	*Collectanea Papyrologica: Texts Published in Honor of H. C. Youtie.* Ed. A. E. Hanson. 2 vols. Bonn, 1976.
P.Col.	*Columbia Papyri,* Greek Series. 7 vols. New York, 1929–1954; Missoula, 1979.
P.Col.Zen.	*Zenon Papyri: Business Papers of the Third Century B.C. dealing with Palestine and Egypt.* 2 vols. New York, 1934–1940. (= *P.Col.* III-IV)
P.Copenhagen	See *P.Haun.*
P.Corn.	*Greek Papyri in the Library of Cornell University.* Ed. W. L. Westermann and C. J. Kraemer, Jr. New York, 1926.

ABBREVIATIONS

P.Dura   The Excavations at Dura-Europus Conducted by Yale University and the French Academy of Inscriptions and Leytters. Ed. C. B. Welles, R. O. Fink, and J. F. Gilliam. New Haven, 1959.

P.Edfou   Fouilles Franco-Polonaises. 3 vols. Cairo, 1937–1950.

P.Egerton   Fragments of an Unknown Gospel and Other Early Christian Papyri. Ed. H. I. Bell, and T. C. Skeat. London, 1935.

P.Eleph.   Elephantine-Papyri. Ed. O. Rubensohn. Berlin, 1907.

P.Enteux.   Ἐντεύξεις: Requêtes et plaintes addressées au Roi d'Égypte au IIIe siècle avant J.-C. Ed. O. Guéraud. Cairo, 1931.

P.Erl.   Die Papyri der Universitätsbibliothek Erlangen. Ed. W. Schubart. Leipzig, 1942.

P.Fam.Tebt.   A Family Archive from Tebtunis. Ed. B. A. van Groningen. Leiden, 1950. (= Pap.Lugd.Bat. VI).

P.Fay.   Fayûm Towns and Their Papyri. Ed. B. P. Grenfell, A. S. Hunt, and D. G. Hogarth. London, 1900.

P.Flor.   Papiri greco-egizii, Papiri Fiorentini. 3 vols. Milan, 1906–1915.

P.Fouad   Les Papyrus Fouad I. Ed. A. Bataille et al. Cairo, 1939.

P.Freib.   Mitteilungen aus der Freiburger Papyrussammlung. 3 vols. Heidelberg, 1914–1927.

P.Fuad I Univ.   Fuad I University Papyri. Ed. D. S. Crawford. Alexandria, 1949.

P.Genova   I = Papiri dell'Università di Genova I. Ed. M. Amelotti and L. Zingale Migliardi. Milan, 1974.
II = Ed. L. Migliardi Zingale. Florence, 1980.

P.Gen.   Les Papyrus de Genève. Ed. J. Nicole. Geneva, 1896–1906.

P.Giss.   Griechische Papyri im Museum des oberhessischen Geschichtsvereins zu Giessen. Ed. O. Eger, E. Kornemann, and P. M. Meyer. 3 parts. Leipzig/Berlin, 1910–1922.

P.Giss.Univ.   Mitteilungen aus der Papyrussammlung der Giessener Universitätsbibliothek. 6 vols. Giessen, 1924–1938.

P.Goodsp.	"A Group of Greek Papyrus Texts." Ed. E. J. Goodspeed. *Classical Philology*, vol. 1, 1906, pp. 167–173.
P.Got.	*Papyrus grecs de la Bibliothèque municipale de Gothembourg*. Ed. H. Frisk. Gothenburg, 1929.
P.Grad.	*Griechische Papyri der Sammlung Gradenwitz*. Ed. G. Plaumann. Heidelberg, 1914.
P.Grenf.	I = *An Alexandrian Erotic Fragment and Other Greek Papyri Chiefly Ptolemaic*. Ed. B. P. Grenfell. Oxford, 1896. II = *New Classical Fragments and Other Greek and Latin Papyri*. Ed. B. P. Grenfell and A. S. Hunt. Oxford, 1897.
P.Gron.	*Papyri Groninganae: Griechische Papyri der Universitätsbibliothek zu Groningen nebst zwei Papyri der Universitätsbibliothek zu Amsterdam*. Ed. A. G. Roos. Amsterdam, 1933.
P.Gron.Amst.	= the two Amsterdam paypri in *P.Gron*.
P.Gur.	*Greek Papyri from Gurob*. Ed. J. G. Smylky. Dublin, 1921.
P.Hal.	*Dikaiomata: Auszüge aus alexandrinischen Gesetzen und Verordnungen in einem Papyrus des Philologischen Seminars der Universität Halle mit einem Anhang weiterer Papyri derselben Sammlung*. Ed. by the Graeca Halensis. Berlin, 1913.
P.Hamb.	I = *Griechische Papyrusurkunden der Hamburger Staats- und Universitätsbibliothek* I. 3 parts. Ed. P. M. Meyer. Leipzig-Berlin, 1911–1924. II = *Griechische Papyri der Hamburger Staats- und Universitätsbibliothek mit einigen Stücken aus der Sammlung Hugo Ibscher*. Ed. B. Snell et al. Hamburg, 1954. III = *Griechische Papyri der Staats- und Universitätsbibliothek Hamburg*. Ed. B. Kramer and D. Hagedorn. Bonn, 1984.
P.Harr.	*The Rendel Harris Papyri of Woodbrooke College, Birmingham*. Ed. J. E. Powell. Cambridge, 1936.
P.Haun.	*Papyri Graecae Haunienses*. I. *Literarische Texte und ptolemäische Urkunden*. Ed. T. Larsen. Copenhagen, 1942. II. Ed. A. Bülow-Jacobsen and S. Ebbesen. Bonn, 1981.
P.Haw.	*Hawara, Biahmu and Arsinoe*. Ed. W. M. Flinders Petri. London, 1889.

P.Heid.	Veröffentlichungen aus der Heidelberger Papyrussammlung. 8 vols. in 2 series. Heidelberg, 1905-1964.
P.Hercul.	Herculanensium voluminum quae supersunt I-VI, VIII-XI. Naples, 1793-1855. Herculanensium voluminum quae supersunt collectio altera I-XI. Naples, 1862-1876. Fragmenta Herculanensia. Ed. W. Scott. Oxford, 1885. See Catalogo dei Papiri Ercolanesi. Ed. M. Gigante. Naples, 1979.
P.Herm.	Papyri from Hermopolis and Other Documents of the Byzantine Period. Ed. B. R. Rees. London, 1964.
P.Hib.	The Hibeh Papyri. 2 vols. London, 1906-1955.
P.Holm.	Papyrus graecus Holmiensis: Recepte für Silber, Steine und Purpur. Ed. O. Lagercrantz. Uppsala-Leipzig, 1913.
P.Iand.	Papyri Iandanae. Ed. C. Kalbfleisch and students. 8 vols. Leipzig, 1912-1938.
P.IFAO	Papyrus grecs de l'Institut Français d'Archéologie Orientale. Cairo. I = Ed. J. Schwartz. 1971. II = Ed. G. Wagner. 1971. III = Ed. J. Schwartz and G. Wagner. 1975.
P.Jena	Jenaer Papyrus-Urkunden. Ed. F. Zucker and F. Schneider. Jena, 1926.
P.Kar.Goodsp.	Papyri from Karanis. Ed. E. J. Goodspeed. Chicago, 1902.
P.Köln	Kölner Papyri. Ed. B. Kramer et al. 4 vols. Cologne/Opladen, 1976-1982.
P.Kroll	Eine ptolemäische Königsurkunde. Ed. L. Koenen. Wiesbaden, 1957.
P.Laur.	Dai Papiri della Biblioteca Medicea Laurenziana. Ed. R. Pintaudi and G. M. Browne. 5 vols. Florence, 1976-1984.
P.Leid.	Papyri Graeci Musei Antiquarii Lugduni-Batavi. Ed. C. Leemans. 2 vols. Leiden, 1843-1885.
P.Leit.	Leitourgia Papyri. Ed. N. Lewis. Philadelphia, 1963.
P.Lille	Papyrus grecs. 2 vols. I = Lille, 1907-1928. II = Papyrus de Magdôla. Ed. J. Lesquier. Lille, 1912.
P.Lips.	Griechische Urkunden der Papyrussammlung zu Leipzig. Ed. L. Mitteis. Leipzig, 1906.

P.Lond.	*Greek Papyri in the British Museum.* 7 vols. London, 1893–1974.
P.Lund	*Aus der Papyrussammlung der Universitätsbibliothek in Lund.* 6 parts. Lund, 1934–1952.
P.Magd.	*Papyrus de Magdôla.* Ed. J. Lesquier. Lille, 1912. (= P.Lille II)
P.Mert.	*A Descriptive Catalogue of the Greek Papyri in the Collection of Wilfred Merton.* 3 vols. 1948–1967.
P.Meyer	*Griechische Texte aus Aegypten.* Ed. P. M. Meyer. 2 vols. Berlin, 1916.
P.Michael.	*Papyri Michaelidae, Being a Catalogue of Greek and Latin Papyri, Tablets and Ostraca in the Library of Mr G. A. Michaïlidis of Cairo.* Ed. D. S. Crawford. Aberdeen, 1955.
P.Mich.	*Michigan Papyri.* 15 vols. 1931–1982.
P.Mich.Zen.	= P.Mich. I
P.Mil.	*Papiri Milanesi.* Ed. A. Calderini. Milan, 1928. 2d ed., ed. S. Daris, 1967.
P.Mil.Vogl.	7 vols. Milan, 1937–1981. I = *Papiri della R. Università di Milano.* Ed. A. Vogliano. 1937.
P.Monac.	*Byzantinische Papyri in der Königlichen Hof- und Staatsbibliothek zu München.* Ed. A. Heisenberg and L. Wenger.
P.Mur.	*Discoveries in the Judean Desert of Jordan.* 6 vols. Oxford, 1955–1977. All citations in Spicq are from vol. II, *Les Grottes de Murabba'ât.* Ed. P. Benoit, J. T. Milik, R. de Vaux. 1961.
P.Ness.	*Excavations at Nessana.* Vols. II–III. Princeton, 1950–1958. All citations in Spicq are from vol. III, *Non-Literary Papyri.* Ed. C. J. Kraemer, Jr.
P.NYU	*Greek Papyri in the Collection of New York University.* Ed. N. Lewis. Leiden, 1967.
P.Oslo	*Papyri Osloenses.* Ed. S. Eitrem and L. Amundsen. 3 vols. Oslo, 1925–1936.
P.Oxf.	*Some Oxford Papyri.* Ed. E. P. Wegener. Leiden, 1942–1948. (= Pap.Lugd.Bat. III A and III B)
P.Oxy.	*The Oxyrhynchus Papyri.* 51 vols. London, 1898–1984.
P.Oxy.Hels.	*Fifty Oxyrhynchus Papyri.* Ed. H. Zilliacus et al. Helsinki, 1979.

P.Panop.	Urkunden aus Panopolis. Ed. L. C. Youtie, D. Hagedorn, and H. C. Youtie. Bonn, 1980.
P.Panop.Beatty	Papyri from Panopolis in the Chester Beatty Library Dublin. Ed. T. C. Skeat. Dublin, 1964.
P.Paris	Notices et textes des papyrus du Musée du Louvre et de la Bibliothèque Impériale. Ed. J. A. Letronne, W. Brunet de Presle, and E. Egger. Paris, 1865.
P.Petaus	Das Archiv des Petaus. Ed. U. Hagedorn et al. Cologne/Opladen, 1969. (= Pap.Colon. IV)
P.Petr.	The Flinders Petrie Papyri. Ed. J. P. Mahaffy and J. G. Smyly. 3 vols. Dublin, 1891–1905.
P.Phil.	Papyrus de Philadelphie. Ed. J. Scherer. Cairo, 1947.
P.Princ.	Papyri in the Princeton University Collections. 3 vols. 1931–1942.
P.Rein.	2 vols. I = Papyrus grecs et démotiques recueillis en Egypte. Ed. T. Reinach, W. Spiegelberg, and S. de Ricci. Paris, 1905. II = Les Papyrus Théodore Reinach. Ed. P. Collart. Cairo, 1940.
P.Rev.	Revenue Laws of Ptolemy Philadelphus. B. P. Grenfell. Oxford, 1896. Reedited by J. Bingen, in Sammelbuch, Beiheft 1, Göttingen, 1952.
P.Ross.Georg.	Papyri russischer und georgischer Sammlungen. 5 vols. Tiflis, 1925–1935.
P.Ryl.	Catalogue of the Greek Papyri in the John Rylands Library. 4 vols. Manchester, 1911–1952.
P.Sakaon	The Archive of Aurelius Sakaon: Papers of an Egyptian Farmer in the Last Century of Theadelphia. Ed. G. M. Parássoglou. Bonn, 1978.
P.Sarap.	Les Archives de Sarapion et de ses fils: une exploitation agricole aux environs d'Hermoupolis Magna (de 90 à 133 p.C). Ed. J. Schwartz. Cairo, 1961.
P.Sorb.	Papyrus de la Sorbonne I. Ed. H. Cadell. Paris, 1966.
P.Soterichos	Das Archiv von Soterichos. Ed. S. Omar. Cologne/Opladen, 1979. (= Pap.Colon. VIII)
P.Stras.	Griechische Papyrus der kaiserlichen Universitäts- und Landesbibliothek zu Strassburg. 8 vols. 1912–1980. (Beginning with III 1948, title is Papyrus grecs de la Bibliothèque Nationale et Universitaire de Strasbourg.)

P. Tebt.	*The Tebtunis Papyri.* 4 vols. London, 1902–1976.
P. Tebt. Tait	*Papyri from Tebtunis in Egyptian and Greek.* Ed. W. J. Tait. London, 1977.
P. Thead.	*Papyrus de Théadelphie.* Ed. P. Jouguet. Paris, 1911.
P. Tor.	"Papiri graeci Regii Taurinensis Musei Aegyptii," in Reale Accademia de Torino, Classe di Scienze Morali, Storiche e Filologiche, *Memorie,* vol. 31, 1827, pp. 9–188 and vol. 33, 1829, pp. 1–80. Ed. A. Peyron.
P. Turner	*Papyri Greek and Egyptian edited by various hands in honour of Eric Gardner Turner on the occasion of his seventieth birthday.* Ed. P. J. Parsons et al. London, 1981.
P. Vars.	*Papyri Varsovienses.* Ed. G. Manteuffel, L. Zawadowski, and C. Rozenberg. Warsaw, 1935.
P. Vindob. Bosw.	*Einige Wiener Papyri.* Ed. E. Boswinkel. Leiden, 1942. (= Pap. Lugd. Bat. II)
P. Vindob. Sal.	*Einige Wiener Papyri.* Ed. R. P. Salomons. Amsterdam, 1976.
P. Vindob. Tandem	*Fünfunddreißig Wiener Papyri.* Ed. P. J. Sijpesteijn and K. A. Worp. Zutphen, 1976.
P. Vindob. Worp	*Einige Wiener Papyri.* Ed. K. A. Worp. Amsterdam, 1972.
P. Warr.	*The Warren Papyri.* Ed. M. David, B. A. van Groningen, and J. C. van Oven. Leiden, 1941. (= Pap. Lugd. Bat. I)
P. Wash. Univ.	*Washington University Papyri* I. Ed. V. B. Schuman. Missoula, 1980.
P. Wisc.	*The Wisconsin Papyri.* Ed. P. J. Sijpesteijn. I = Leiden, 1967. II = Zutphen, 1977.
P. Würzb.	*Mitteilungen aus der Würzburger Papyrussammlung.* Ed. U. Wilcken. Berlin, 1934.
P. Yale	*Yale Papyri in the Beinecke Rare Book and Manuscript Library.* 2 vols. 1967–1985.
SB	*Sammelbuch griechischer Urkunden aus Aegypten.* 14 vols. 1915–1983.
Sel. Pap.	*Select Papyri* (Loeb Classical Library). Ed. A. S. Hunt and C. C. Edgar. 3 vols. London and Cambridge, Mass., 1932–1942.

Stud.Pal.	Studien zur Palaeographie und Papyruskunde. Ed. C. Wessely. 23 vols. Leipzig, 1901–1924.
UPZ	Urkunden der Ptolemäerzeit (ältere Funde). Ed. U. Wilcken. 2 vols. Berlin-Leipzig, 1927–1957.

B. WORKS CITED BY AUTHOR AND TITLE (OR SHORTENED TITLE)

Austin, Comicorum Graecorum Fragmenta	C. Austin. Comicorum Graecorum Fragmenta in Papyris Reperta. Berlin, 1973.
Bell, Jews and Christians in Egypt	H. I. Bell. Jews and Christians in Egypt: The Jewish Troubles in Alexandria and the Athanasian Controversy. London, 1924. (= P.Lond. VI)
Hohlwein, Stratège du nome	N. Hohlwein. Le Stratège du nome. Brussels, 1969. (= Pap.Brux. IX)
Mason, Greek Terms	H. J. Mason. Greek Terms for Roman Institutions: A Lexicon and Analysis. American Studies in Papyrology XIII. Toronto, 1974.
Naldini, Cristianesimo in Egitto	M. Naldini. Il Cristianesimo in Egitto: Lettere private nei papiri dei secoli II-IV. Florence, 1968.
Vanderlip, Four Greek Hymns	V. F. Vanderlip. The Four Greek Hymns of Isidorus and the Cult of Isis. American Studies in Papyrology XII. Toronto, 1972.
Witkowski, Epistulae Privatae Graecae	S. Witkowski. Epistulae privatae graecae quae in papyris aetatis Lagidarum servantur. 2d ed. Leipzig, 1911.
Youtie, Scriptiunculae	H. C. Youtie. Scriptiunculae. 3 vols. Amsterdam, 1973–1975.

C. PUBLISHED PROCEEDINGS OF PAPYROLOGICAL CONGRESSES

Proceedings IV	Atti del IV Congresso Internazionale de Papirologia, Firenze, 28 aprile–2 maggio 1935 (Aegyptus, Serie scientifica 5). Milan, 1936.
Proceedings VIII	Akten des VIII. Internationalen Kongresses für Papyrologie, Wien 1955 (29 August–3 September). Vienna, 1956. (= MPER N.S. V)
Proceedings IX	Proceedings of the IX International Congress of Papyrology, Oslo, 19–22 August 1958. Hertford, England, 1961.
Proceedings X	Actes du Xe Congrès International de Papyrologie, Varsovie-Cracovie, 3–9 septembre 1961. Warsaw, 1964.

Proceedings XI	*Atti dell'XI Congresso Internazionale di Papirologia, Milano, 2–8 settembre 1965.* Milan, 1966.
Proceedings XII	*Proceedings of the Twelfth International Congress of Papyrology, Ann Arbor, 13–17 August 1968.* Toronto, 1970.
Proceedings XIII	*Akten des XIII. Internationalen Papyrologenkongresses, Marburg/Lahn, 2–6 August 1971.* Munich, 1974.
Proceedings XV	*Actes du XVe Congrès International de Papyrologie,* Brussels, 19 August–3 September 1977. Brussels, 1978. (= *Pap. Brux.* XVI–XIX)

ABBREVIATIONS: INSCRIPTIONS

A. WORKS CITED BY AN ABBREVIATION

CIG	*Corpus Inscriptionum Graecarum.* Ed A. Boeckh. 4 vols. Berlin, 1828–1877.
CII	*Corpus Inscriptionum Iudaicarum.* Ed. J. B. Frey. 2 vols. Rome, 1936–1952. Vol. 1 reprinted as *Corpus of Jewish Inscriptions: Jewish Inscriptions from the Third Century B.C. to the Seventh Century A.D.* New York, 1975.
CIL	*Corpus Inscriptionum Latinarum.* Berlin, 1862–.
CIRB	*Corpus Inscriptionum Regni Bosporani (Korpus bosporskikh nadpisei).* Moscow-Leningrad, 1965.
CIS	*Corpus Inscriptionum Semiticarum.* Paris, 1881–.
Dittenberger, *Or.*	*Orientis Graeci Inscriptiones Selectae.* Ed. W. Dittenberger. 2 vols. Leipzig, 1903–1905. Reprint Hildesheim-New York, 1970.
Dittenberger, *Syl.*	*Sylloge Inscriptionum Graecarum.* Ed. W. Dittenberger. 4 vols. 3d ed. Leipzig, 1915. Reprint Hildesheim-New York, 1982.
Fouilles de Delphes	*Fouilles de Delphes.* Vol. 3, *Epigraphie.* Paris, 1902–.
GDI	*Sammlung der griechischen Dialektinschriften.* Ed. F. Bechtel, H. Collitz, et al. 4 vols. in 7. Göttingen, 1884–1915. Reprint Nendeln-Liechtenstein, 1973–1975.
GIBM	*The Collection of Ancient Greek Inscriptions in the British Museum.* Ed. C. T. Newton. 4 vols. Oxford, 1874–1916. Reprint Milan, 1977–1979.
GVI	*Griechische Vers-Inschriften.* Vol. 1, *Grab-Epigramme.* Ed. W. Peek. Berlin, 1955.
IG	*Inscriptiones Graecae.* 14 vols. Berlin, 1873–.
IGLAM	*Inscriptions grecques et latines recueillies en Asie Mineure.* Ed. P. Le Bas and W. H. Waddington.

3 vols. Hildesheim-New York, 1968–1972. Originally published in Paris in 1870 as vol. 3, parts 5 and 6 of *Voyage archéologique en Grèce et en Asie Mineure*

IGLS   *Inscriptions grecques et latines de la Syrie*. Ed. L. Jalabert and R. Mouterde. Multiple volumes. Paris, 1929–.

IGRom.   *Inscriptiones Graecae ad Res Romanas Pertinentes*. Ed. R. Cagnat et al. 4 vols. Paris, 1911–1927. Reprint Rome, 1964.

IGUR   *Inscriptiones Graecae Urbis Romae*. Ed. L. Moretti. 4 vols. Rome, 1968–1990.

ILS   *Inscriptiones Latinae Selectae*. Ed. H. Dessau. 3d ed. 3 vols. in 5. Berlin, 1962.

ISE   *Iscrizioni storiche ellenistiche*. Ed. L. Moretti. 2 vols. Florence, 1967–1976.

I.Asok.   *Les Inscriptions d'Asoka*. Ed. J. Bloch. Paris, 1950.

I.Assos   *Die Inschriften von Assos*. Ed. R. Merkelbach. Bonn, 1976.

I.Bulg.   *Inscriptiones Graecae in Bulgaria Repertae*. Ed. G. Mihailov. Many vols. Sofia, 1956–. Revised ed. Sofia, 1970–.

I.Car.   *La Carie: histoire et géographie historique avec le recuel des inscriptions antiques*. Vol. 2, *Le Plateau de Tabai et ses environs*. Ed. L. and J. Robert. Paris, 1954–.

I.Chalced.   *Die Inschriften von Kalchedon*. Ed. R. Merlkelbach. Bonn, 1980.

I.Cor.   *Corinth: The Inscriptions*. Ed. J. H. Kent. Princeton, 1966.

I.Cos   *The Inscriptions of Cos*. Ed. W. R. Paton and E. L. Hicks. Oxford, 1891. Reprint Hildesheim-New York, 1990.

I.Cret.   *Inscriptiones Creticae*. Ed. M. Guarducci. 4 vols. Rome, 1935–1950.

I.Cumae   *Die Inschriften von Kyme*. Ed. H. Engelmann. Bonn, 1976.

I.Delos   *Inscriptions de Délos*. Ed. F. Durrbach et al. 4 vols. Paris, 1926–.

I.Did.   *Didyma*. Vol. 2, *Die Inschriften*. Ed. A. Rehm and R. Harder. Berlin, 1958.

I.Ephes.	*Die Inschriften von Ephesos.* 8 vols. Bonn, 1979–1984.
I.Erythr.Klaz.	*Die Inschriften von Erythrai und Klazomenai.* Ed. H. Engelmann and R. Merkelbach. 2 vols. Bonn, 1972–1973.
I.Gonn.	*Gonnoi.* Vol. 2, *Les Inscriptions.* Ed. B. Helly. 2 vols in 1. Amsterdam, 1973.
I.Ilium	*Die Inschriften von Ilion.* Ed. P. Frisch. Bonn, 1975.
I.Kour.	*The Inscriptions of Kourion.* Ed. T. B. Mitford. Philadelphia, 1971.
I.Lamps.	*Die Inschriften von Lampsakos.* Ed. P. Frisch. Bonn, 1978.
I.Lind.	*Lindos: Fouilles et recherches, 1902–1914.* Vol. 2, *Inscriptions.* Ed. C. Blinkenberg and K. Kinch. Copenhagen, 1941.
I.Magn.	*Die Inschriften von Magnesia am Mäander.* Ed. O. Kern. Berlin, 1900.
I.Olymp.	*Olympia: Die Ergebnisse der . . . Ausgrabung: Textband V, Die Inschriften.* Ed. W. Dittenberger and K. Purgold. Berlin, 1896.
I.Perg.	*Die Inschriften von Pergamon.* Ed. M. Fraenkel. Berlin, 1890–1895.
I.Priene	*Die Inschriften von Priene.* Ed. F. Hiller von Gärtringen. Berlin, 1906.
I.Rhamn.	*La Forteresse de Rhamnonte.* Ed. J. Pouilloux. Paris, 1954.
I.Salam.	*The Greek and Latin Inscriptions from Salamis.* Ed. T. B. Mitford and I. K. Nicolaou. Nicosia, 1974.
I.Sard.	*Sardis.* Vol. 7, *Greek and Latin Inscriptions.* Ed. W. H. Buckler and D. M. Robinson. Leiden, 1932.
I.Sard.Rob.	*Nouvelles Inscriptions de Sardes.* Ed. L. Robert. Paris, 1964–.
I.Side	"Inscriptions grecques de Sidé," *Rev. Phil.*, vol. 84, 1958, pp. 15–53. Cf. *The Inscriptions of Side.* Ed. G. E. Bean. Ankara, 1965.
I.Sinur.	*Le Sanctuaire de Sinuri près de Mylasa.* Vol. 1, *Les Inscriptions grecques.* Ed. L. Robert. Paris, 1945.
I.Thas.	*Recherches sur l'histoire et les cultes de Thasos.* Ed. J. Pouilloux and C. Dunant. 2 vols. Paris, 1954–1958.

LSAM	F. Sokolowski. *Lois sacrées de l'Asie Mineure*. Paris, 1955.
LSCG, LSCGSup	F. Sokolowski, *Lois sacrées des cités grecques*. Paris, 1969. *Supplément*. Paris, 1962.
Leg.Gort.	*Leges Gortynensium* (= *GDI* 4991).
MAMA	*Monumenta Asiae Minoris Antiqua*. 9 vols. Manchester-London, 1928–1988.
NCIG	*Nouveau choix d'inscriptions grecques*. Ed. Institut Fernand-Courby. Paris, 1971.
RIJG	*Recueil des inscriptions juridiques grecques*, Ed. R. Dareste, B. Haussoullier, and T. Reinach. 2 vols. Paris, 1891–1904. Reprint Rome, 1965.
SEG	*Supplementum Epigraphicum Graecum*. Alphen, 1923–.
TAM	*Tituli Asiae Minoris*. Vienna, 1901–.

B. Works Cited by Author and Title (or Shortened Title)

Bean & Mitford, *Cilicia*	G. E. Bean and T. B. Mitford, *Journeys in Rough Cilicia, 1964–1968*. Vienna, 1970.
A. & E. Bernand, *Memnon*	A. and E. Bernand. *Les Inscriptions grecques et latines du Colosse de Memnon*. Cairo, 1960.
A. Bernand, *Koptos*	A. Bernand. *De Koptos à Kosseir*. Leiden, 1972.
A. Bernand, *El-Kanaïs*	A. Bernand. *Le Paneion d'El-Kanaïs: Les Inscriptions grecques*. Leiden, 1972.
A. and E. Bernand, *Philae*	*Les Inscriptions grecques de Philae*. Vol. 1, *Epoque ptolémaïque*. Ed. A. Bernand. Vol. 2 (titled *Les Inscriptions grecques et latines de Philae*), *Haut et Bas Empire*. Ed. E. Bernand. Paris, 1969.
A. Bernand, *Fayoum*	A. Bernand. *Les Inscriptions grecques du Fayoum*. Cairo, 1981.
A. Bernand, *Pan*	A. Bernand. *Pan du Désert*. Leiden, 1977.
E. Bernand, *Inscriptions métriques*	E. Bernand. *Inscriptions métriques de l'Egypte gréco-romaine: Recherches sur la poésie épigrammatique des grecs en Egypte*. Paris, 1969.
E. Bernand, *Fayoum*	E. Bernand. *Recueil des inscriptions grecques du Fayoum*. 3 vols. Leiden, 1975–.
Breccia, *Iscrizioni*	E. Breccia. *Iscrizioni greche e latine. Catalogue générale des antiquités égyptiennes du musée d'Alexandrie*, 57. 1911. Reprinted as *Inscriptiones*

ABBREVIATIONS　　　　　　　　　　　　　　　　xlvii

	nunc Alexandriae in Museo = *Greek and Latin Inscriptions* = *Iscrizioni greche e latine*, Chicago, 1978.
Chalon, *T. Julius Alexander*	G. Chalon. *L'Edit de Tiberius Julius Alexander: Etude historique et exégetique*. Olten, 1964.
Cumont, *Fouilles de Doura-Europus*	F. Cumont. *Fouilles de Doura-Europus (1922-1923)*. Paris, 1926.
Cumont, *L'Egypte des astrologues*	F. Cumont. *L'Egypte des astrologues*. Brussels, 1937.
Cumont, *Lux Perpetua*	F. Cumont. *Lux Perpetua*. Paris, 1949.
Cumont, *Symbolisme funéraire*	F. Cumont. *Recherches sur le symbolisme funéraire des Romains*. Paris, 1942. Reprint New York, 1975.
Cumont, *Studia Pontica*	F. Cumont. *Studia Pontica*. Brussels, n.d.
des Gagniers, *Laodicée*	J. des Gagniers. *Laodicée du Lycos: Le Nymphée*. Quebec-Paris, 1969.
Drew-Bear, *Phrygie*	T. Drew-Bear. *Nouvelles inscriptions de Phrygie*. Zutphen, 1978.
Durrbach, *Choix*	F. Durrbach. *Choix d'inscriptions de Délos*. Paris, 1921. Vol. 1 reprinted Hildesheim, New York, 1976.
Ebert, *Griechische Epigramme*	J. Ebert. *Griechische Epigramme auf Sieger an gymnischen und hippischen Agonen*. Berlin, 1972.
Firatli & Robert, *Stèles funéraires*	N. Firatli and L. Robert. *Les Stèles funéraires de Byzance gréco-romaine*. Paris, 1964.
Grandjean, *Arétalogie d'Isis*	Y. Grandjean. *Une nouvelle arétalogie d'Isis à Maronée*. Leiden, 1975.
Grégoire, *Asie Mineure*	H. Grégoire. *Recueil des inscriptions grecques-chrétiennes d'Asie Mineure*. Amsterdam, 1968.
Guarducci, *Epigrafia greca*	M. Guarducci. *Epigrafia greca*. 4 vols. Rome, 1967-1978.
Hermann, *Ergebnisse*	P. Hermann. *Ergebnisse einer Reiser in Nordostlydien*. Vienna, 1962.
Holleaux, *Etudes d'épigraphie*	M. Holleaux. *Etudes d'épigraphie et d'histoire grecques*. 6 vols. Paris, 1952-1968.
Hutmacher, *Ehrendekret*	R. Hutmacher. *Das Ehrendekret für den Strategen Kallimachos*. Meisenheim am Glan, 1965.
Kaibel, *Epigrammata*	G. Kaibel. *Epigrammata Graeca ex Lapidibus Conlecta*. Berlin, 1878. Reprint Hildesheim, 1965.
Latyschev, *Inscriptiones Antiquae*	B. Latyschev. *Inscriptiones Antiquae Orae Septentrionalis Ponti Euxini Graecae et Latinae*. 2d ed. 2 vols. Hildesheim, 1965.

Letronne, *Egypte*	J. A. Letronne. *Recueil des inscriptions grecques et latines de l'Egypte*. 2 vols. Paris, 1842–1848. Reprint Aalen, 1974.
Lifshitz, *Synagogues juives*	B. Lifshitz. *Donateurs et fondateurs dans les synagogues juives*. Paris, 1967.
Michel, *Recueil*	C. Michel. *Recueil d'inscriptions grecques*. Paris, 1900. Reprint Hildesheim-New York, 1976. *Supplement*. 2 vols. Paris, 1912–1927. Reprint Hildesheim-New York, 1976.
Pfohl, *Grabinschriften*	G. Pfohl. *Untersuchungen über die attischen Grabinschriften*. Eisenstein, 1953.
Pleket, *Rijksmuseum*	H. W. Pleket. *The Greek Inscriptions in the Rijksmuseum van Oudheden at Leiden*. Leiden, 1958.
Pouilloux, *Choix*	J. Pouilloux. *Choix d'inscriptions grecques*. Paris, 1960.
L. Robert, *Documents*	L. Robert. *Documents de l'Asie mineure méridionale: inscriptions, monnaies et géographie*. Geneva-Paris, 1966.
L. Robert, *Etudes anatoliennes*	L. Robert. *Etudes anatoliennes: inscriptions, monnaies et géographie*. Paris, 1937. Reprint Amsterdam, 1970.
L. Robert, *Etudes épigraphiques*	L. Robert. *Etudes épigraphiques et philologiques*. Paris, 1938.
L. Robert, *Gladiateurs*	L. Robert. *Les Gladiateurs dans l'Orient grec*. Paris, 1940. Reprint Amsterdam, 1971.
L. Robert, *Noms indigènes*	L. Robert. *Noms indigènes dans l'Asie Mineure gréco-romaine*. Paris, 1963
L. Robert, *Opera Minora Selecta*	L. Robert. *Opera Minora Selecta: Epigraphie et antiquités grecques*. 7 vols. Amsterdam, 1969–1990.
L. Robert, *Villes d'Asie Mineure*	L. Robert. *Villes d'Asie Mineure: Etudes de géographie ancienne*. 2d ed. Paris, 1962.
Rougement, *Delphes*	*Corpus des inscriptions de Delphes*. Vol. 1, *Lois sacrées et règlements religieux*. Ed. G. Rougement. Paris, 1977.
Schwabe, *Beth She'arim*	*Beth She'arim: Report on the Excavations during 1936-1940*. Vol. 2, *The Greek inscriptions*. Ed. M. Schwabe and B. Lifshitz. New Brunswick, N.J., 1973–.
Welles, *Royal Correspondence*	C. B. Welles. *Royal Correspondence in the Hellenistic Period: A Study in Greek Epigraphy*. London, 1934. Reprint Chicago, 1974.

ABBREVIATIONS: GENERAL WORKS*

A. WORKS CITED BY AN ABBREVIATION

ANRW	H. Temporini and W. Haase. *Aufstieg und Niedergang der römischen Welt: Geschichte und Kultur Roms im Spiegel der neueren Forschung.* Many vols. Berlin–New York, 1972–.
Anth. Lyr. Graec.	*Anthologia Lyrica Graeca.* Ed. E. Diehl. Leipzig, 1954–.
BAGD	W. Bauer. *A Greek-English Lexicon of the New Testament and Other Early Christian Literature.* 2d ed. Trans. W. F. Arndt and F. W. Gingrich. Revised and edited F. W. Danker. Chicago, 1979.
BDF	F. Blass and A. Debrunner. *A Greek Grammar of the New Testament and Other Early Christian Literature.* Trans. and rev. of the 9th–10th German edition incorporating supplementary notes of A. Debrunner by R. W. Funk. Chicago, 1961.
CCAG	*Catalogus Codicum Astrologorum Graecorum.* 9 vols. Brussels, 1898–1953.
DACL	*Dictionnaire d'archéologie chrétienne et de liturgie.* 29 vols. Paris, 1903–1952.
DAGR	*Dictionnaire des antiquités grecques et romaines.* Ed. C. Daremberg and E. Saglio. 6 vols. in 10. Graz, 1962–63.
DBSup	*Dictionnaire de la Bible. Supplément.* Ed. L. Pirot and A. Robert. Paris, 1926–.
Dict.spir.	*Dictionnaire de spiritualité, ascétique et mystique, doctrine et histoire.* Ed. M. Viller et al. Paris, 1932–.

---

*Modern editions, aids, and studies. Cited here also are the resources referred to in the apparatus.

DTC	*Dictionnaire de théologie catholique.* Ed. A. Vacant, E. Mangenot, E. Amann, et al. 16 vols. Paris, 1903–1972.
DKP	*Der kleine Pauly: Lexikon der Antike auf der Grundlage von Pauly's Realencyclopädie der classischen Altertumswissenschaft.* Ed. K. Ziegler and W. Sontheimer. 5 vols. Stuttgart, 1964–1975.
EDNT	H. Balz and G. Schneider, eds. *Exegetical Dictionary of the New Testament.* Grand Rapids, 1990–1993.
F.Gr.H.	F. Jacoby. *Die Fragmente der griechischen Historiker.* 3 vols. in 15. Leiden, 1954–1964.
L&N	J. P. Louw and E. A. Nida, eds. *Greek-English Lexicon of the New Testament: Based on Semantic Domains.* 2d ed. New York, 1989.
LTGR	I. C. T. Ernesti. *Lexicon Technologiae Graecorum Rhetoricae.* 1795–1797. Reprint Hildesheim, 1962.
LSJ	H. G. Liddell and R. Scott. *A Greek-English Lexicon.* 9th ed. Ed. H. S. Jones and R. McKenzie. Oxford, 1940.
LSJSup	E. A. Barber et al. *H. G. Liddell, Robert Scott, H. Stuart Jones, Greek-English Lexicon: A Supplement.* Oxford, 1968.
LXX	Septuagint (Greek Old Testament)
Moulton-Milligan [MM in apparatus]	J. H. Moulton and G. Milligan. *The Vocabulary of the Greek Testament Illustrated from the Papyri and Other Non-literary Sources.* 2 vols. London, 1914–30. Reprint. Grand Rapids, 1985.
MT	Masoretic Text
ND	G. H. R. Horsley and Stephen Llewelyn, eds. *New Documents Illustrating Early Christianity.* North Ryde, N.S.W. 6 vols. 1981–.
NIDNTT	Colin Brown, ed. *The New International Dictionary of New Testament Theology.* Grand Rapids, 1986.
NJB	*New Jerusalem Bible*
NT	New Testament
OCD	*Oxford Classical Dictionary.* Ed. N. G. L. Hammond and H. H. Scullard. 2d ed. Oxford, 1970.

ODCC	*Oxford Dictionary of the Christian Church.* Ed. F. L. Cross and E. A. Livingstone. 2d ed., corrected. Oxford, 1983.
OT	Old Testament
PG	*Patrologiae Cursus Completus, Series Graeca.* Ed. J.-P. Migne. 161 vols in 166. Paris, 1857–87.
PL	*Patrologiae Cursus Completus, Series Latina.* Ed. J.-P. Migne. 221 vols. Paris, 1844–1864.
PO	*Patrologia Orientalis.* Ed. R. Fraffin and F. Nau. Paris, 1903–1922.
Prosop.Ptol.	*Prosopographia Ptolemaica.* Ed. W. Peremans and E. van't Dack. 9 vols. Louvain, 1950–1981.
PW	*Paulys Realencyclopädie der classischen Altertumswissenschaft.* New edition by G. Wissowa et al. 49 vols. in 50. Stuttgart, 1894–1980.
PWSup	*Paulys Real-Encyclopadie der classischen Altertumswissenschaft: Supplement.* 15 vols. Stuttgart, 1903–1980.
S	J. Strong. *Strong's Exhaustive Concordance of the Bible.* Reprint. Peabody, n.d.
Str-B	[H. L. Strack and] P. Billerbeck. *Kommentar zum Neuen Testament aus Talmud und Midrasch.* 6 vols. in 7. Munich, 1922–1961.
SVF	H. von Arnim. *Stoicorum Veterum Fragmenta.* 4 vols. Leipzig, 1903–1924. Reprint Stuttgart, 1978–1979.
TDNT	G. Kittel and G. Friedrich, eds. *Theological Dictionary of the New Testament.* Trans. G. W. Bromiley. 10 vols. Grand Rapids, 1964–1976.
TDOT	G. J. Botterweck and H. Ringgren. *Theological Dictionary of the Old Testament.* Grand Rapids, 1974–1990.
TWNT	G. Kittel and G. Friedrich. *Theologisches Wörterbuch zum Neuen Testament.* 10 vols. Stuttgart, 1932–1979. (References to *TWNT* have been retained only in a few instances in which bibliographies from *TWNT* were not included in *TDNT*. All others have been changed to the corresponding references in *TDNT*.)

B. Works Cited by Author and Title (or Shortened Title)

Abel, *Grammaire*	F. M. Abel. *Grammaire du grec biblique, suivie d'un Choix de papyrus*. Paris, 1927.
Abel, *Maccabées*	F. M. Abel. *Les Livres des Maccabées*. Paris, 1949.
Allo, *Première Epître aux Corinthiens*	E. B. Allo. *Saint Paul: Première Epître aux Corinthiens*. Paris, 1934.
Allo, *Seconde Epître aux Corinthiens*	E. B. Allo. *Saint Paul: Seconde Epître aux Corinthiens*. Paris, 1937. 2d ed., 1956.
Aujac, *Géminos*	G. Aujac. *Géminos: Introduction aux phénomènes*. Paris, 1975
Barclay, *NT Wordbook*	W. Barclay. *A New Testament Wordbook*. London, 1955.
Barr, *Semantics*	J. Barr. *The Semantics of Biblical Language*. London, 1961.
Barrett, *St. John*	C. K. Barrett. *The Gospel According to St. John*. London, 1955.
Barth, *Ephesians*	M. Barth. *Ephesians: Introduction, translation, and commentary*. 2 vols. New York, 1974.
Bengel	J. A. Bengel. *Gnomon Novi Testamenti*. 6th ed. Tübingen, 1858. ET *New Testament Word Studies*. Trans. C. T. Lewis and M. R. Vincent. 2 vols. Grand Rapids, 1971.
Benoit, *Exégèse et théologie*	P. Benoit. *Exégèse et théologie*. 4 vols. Paris, 1961–1983. Selections ET *Jesus and the Gospel*. Trans. B. Weatherhead. 2 vols. New York, 1973–1974.
Bergk, *Poetae Lyrici Graeci*	T. Bergk. *Poetae Lyrici Graeci*. 5th ed. 3 vols. Leipzig, 1900–1914.
Betz, *Lukian von Samosata*	H. D. Betz. *Lukian von Samosata und das Neue Testament: Religionsgeschichtliche und paranetische Parallelen*. Berlin, 1961.
Bickerman, *Institutions des Séleucides*	E. Bickerman. *Institutions des Séleucides*. Paris, 1938.
Black, *Aramaic Approach*	M. Black. *An Aramaic Approach to the Gospels and Acts*. 3d ed. Oxford, 1967.
Blinzler, *Trial of Jesus*	J. Blinzler. *The Trial of Jesus: The Jewish and Roman Proceedings against Jesus Christ Described and Assessed from the Oldest Accounts*. Translated by I. and F. McHugh from the 2d German ed. Westminster, 1959.

ABBREVIATIONS

Bogaert, *Banques et banquiers*	R. Bogaert. *Banques et banquiers dans les cités grecques.* Leiden, 1968.
Boisacq, *Dictionnaire étymologique*	E. Boisacq. *Dictionnaire étymologique de la langue grecque, étudiée dans ses rapports avec les autres langues indo-européennes.* 4th ed. Heidelberg, 1950.
Bompaire, *Lucien écrivain*	J. Bompaire. *Lucien écrivain: Imitation et création.* Paris, 1958.
Bonhöffer, *Epiktek*	A. Bonhöffer. *Epiktet und das Neue Testament.* Giessen, 1911.
Bonner, *Magical Amulets*	C. Bonner. *Studies in Magical Amulets, Chiefly Graeco-Egyptian.* Ann Arbor, 1950.
Bonsirven, *Judaïsme palestinien*	J. Bonsirven. *Le Judaïsme palestinien aux temps de Jésus-Christ: Sa théologie.* 2 vols. 2d ed. Paris, 1934–1935. ET *Palestinian Judaism in the time of Jesus Christ.* Abridged. Trans. W. Wolf. New York, 1964.
van Brock, *Vocabulaire médical*	N. van Brock. *Recherches sur le vocabulaire médical du grec ancien: Soins et guérison.* Paris, 1961.
Brown, *John*	R. E. Brown. *The Gospel According to John.* 2 vols. New York, 1970.
Cerfaux, *Recueil L. Cerfaux*	L. Cerfaux. *Recueil Lucien Cerfaux: Etudes d'exégèse et d'histoire religieuse.* 3 vols. Gembloux, 1954–1962.
Cerfaux & Tondriau, *Culte des souverains*	L. Cerfaux and J. Tondriau. *Le Culte des souverains dans la civilisation gréco-romaine.* Paris-Tournai, 1957.
Chantraine, *Dictionnaire étymologique*	P. Chantraine. *Dictionnaire étymologique de la langue grecque: Histoire des mots.* 4 vols. Paris, 1968–1980.
Conzelmann, *First Corinthians*	H. Conzelmann. *First Corinthians.* Trans. J. W. Leitch. Philadelphia, 1975. (ET of *Der erste Brief an die Korinther,* Göttingen, 1969.)
Le Déaut, *Nuit Pascale*	R. Le Déaut. *La Nuit Pascale: Essai sur la signification de la Paque juive à partir du Targum d'Exode XII 42.* AnBib 22. Rome, 1963.
Deissmann, *Bible Studies*	A. Deissmann. *Bible Studies.* Trans. A. Grieve. Edinburgh, 1901. Reprint Peabody, Mass., 1988.
Deissmann, *Light*	A. Deissmann. *Light from the Ancient East.* Trans. L. R. M. Strachan. New York, 1927. (ET of *Licht vom Osten,* Tübingen, 1923.)
Deissmann, *Neue Bibelstudien*	A. Deissmann. *Neue Bibelstudien.* Marburg, 1897.

Delebecque, *Etudes grecques*	E. Delebecque. *Etudes grecques sur l'Evangile de Luc.* Paris, 1976.
Delebecque, *Evangile de Luc*	E. Delebecque. *Evangile de Luc: texte traduit et annoté.* Paris, 1976. New edition, Paris, 1992.
Derrett, *Law in the NT*	J. D. M. Derrett. *Law in the New Testament.* London, 1970.
Dhorme, *Emploi métaphorique*	P. Dhorme. *L'Emploi métaphorique des noms de parties du corps en hébreu et en akkadien.* Paris, 1923. Reprint Paris, 1963.
Diels, *Fragmente der Vorsokratiker*	H. Diels and W. Kranz. *Die Fragmente der Vorsokratiker.* 10th ed., Berlin, 1960. ET (fragments only) in *Ancilla to the pre-Socratic philosophers: A complete translation of the fragments in Diels Fragmente der Vorsokratiker.* Trans. Kathleen Freeman. Oxford, 1962.
Dupont, *Béatitudes*	J. Dupont. *Les Béatitudes.* 2d ed. 3 vols. Bruges, 1958–1973.
Dupont, *Discours de Milet*	J. Dupont. *Le Discours de Milet.* Paris, 1962.
Dupont, *Union avec le Christ*	J. Dupont. *L'Union avec le Christ suivant saint Paul.* Bruges-Louvain, 1952.
Durham, *Vocabulary of Menander*	D. B. Durham. *The Vocabulary of Menander.* Amsterdam, 1969.
Edmonds, *Attic Comedy*	J. M. Edmonds. *The Fragments of Attic Comedy after Meineke, Bergk, and Kock.* 3 vols. in 4. Leiden, 1957–1961.
Festugière, *Dieu cosmique*	A. J. Festugière. *Le Dieu cosmique.* Vol. 2 of *Hermès Trismégiste.* Paris, 1949.
Festugière, *Dieu inconnu*	A. J. Festugière. *Le Dieu inconnu et la Gnose.* Vol. 4 of *Hermès Trismégiste.* Paris, 1954.
Festugière, *Etudes de religion*	A. J. Festugière. *Etudes de religion grecque et hellénistique.* Paris, 1972.
Festugière, *Etudes d'histoire*	A. J. Festugière. *Etudes d'histoire et de philologie.* Paris, 1975.
Festugière, *Hermès Trismégiste*	A. J. Festugière. *La Révélation d'Hermès Trismégiste.* 4 vols. Paris, 1949–1954.
Festugière, *Idéal religieux*	A. J. Festugière. *L'Idéal religieux des Grecs et l'Evangile.* Paris, 1932.
Festugière, *Monde gréco-romain*	A. J. Festugière and P. Fabre. *Le monde gréco-romain au temps de Notre-Seigneur.* 2 vols. Paris, 1935.

Festugière, *Personal Religion*	A. J. Festugière. *Personal Religion among the Greeks.* Berkeley, 1954.
Festugière, *Vie spirituelle*	A. J. Festugière. *La Vie spirituelle en Grèce à l'époque hellénistique: ou, Les Besoins de l'esprit dans un monde raffiné.* Paris, 1977.
Field, *Notes on the Translation*	F. Field. *Notes on the Translation of the New Testament.* Oxford, 1864–1881. Reprint Peabody, 1994.
Fitzmyer, *Semitic Background*	J. A. Fitzmyer. *Essays on the Semitic Background of the New Testament.* London, 1971. Reprint Missoula, Mont., 1974.
Fournier, *Les Verbes "dire"*	H. Fournier. *Les Verbes "dire" en grec ancien: Exemple de conjugaison supplétive.* Paris, 1946.
Gauthier, *Magnanimité*	R. A. Gauthier. *Magnanimité: L'Idéal de la grandeur dans la philosophie païenne et dans la théologie chrétienne.* Paris, 1951.
Gauthier, *Symbola*	P. Gauthier. *Symbola: Les Etrangers et la justice dans le cités grecques.* Nancy, 1972.
Gutierrez, *Paternité spirituelle*	P. Gutierrez. *La Paternité spirituelle selon saint Paul.* Paris, 1968.
Haenchen, *Acts*	E. Haenchen. *The Acts of the Apostles: A Commentary.* Trans. B. Noble et al. Philadelphia, 1971. (ET of *Die Apostelgeschichte*, 13th ed., Göttingen, 1961.)
Hengel, *Zealots*	M. Hengel. *The Zealots.* Trans. David Smith. Edinburgh, 1989. (ET of *Die Zeloten*, Leiden-Cologne, 1961.)
Héring, *Hébreux*	J. Héring. *L'Epître aux Hébreux.* Neuchâtel-Paris, 1954. ET *The Epistle to the Hebrews.* Trans A. W. Heathcote and P. J. Allcock. London, 1970.
Higgins, *New Testament Essays*	A. J. B. Higgins. *New Testament Essays: Studies in Memory of Thomas Walter Manson, 1893–1958.* Manchester, 1959.
Hill, *Greek Words and Hebrew Meanings*	D. Hill. *Greek Words and Hebrew Meanings: Studies in the Semantics of Soteriological Terms.* London, 1967.
Hobart, *Medical Language*	W. K. Hobart. *The Medical Language of St. Luke: A Proof from Internal Evidence that "The Gospel According to St. Luke" and "The Acts of the Apostles" Were Written by the Same Person, and that the Writer Was a Medical Man.* London-Dublin, 1882. Reprint Grand Rapids, 1954.

Hohlwein, *Termes techniques*	N. Hohlwein. *Recueil des termes techniques relatifs aux institutions politiques et administratives de l'Egypte romaine*. Brussels, 1912.
Hugedé, *Colossiens*	N. Hugedé. *Commentaire de l'Epître aux Colossiens*. Geneva, 1968.
Hugedé, *Ephésiens*	N. Hugedé. *L'Epître aux Ephésiens*. Geneva, 1974.
Hughes, *Hebrews*	P. E. Hughes. *A Commentary on the Epistle to the Hebrews*. Grand Rapids, 1977.
Jacquier, *Actes*	E. Jacquier. *Les Actes des Apôtres*. 2d ed. Paris, 1926.
Jeremias, *Abba*	J. Jeremias. *Abba: Studien zur neutestamentlichen Theologie und Zeitgeschichte*. Göttingen, 1966. ET *The Prayers of Jesus*. Naperville, 1967.
Jeremias, *Eucharistic Words*	J. Jeremias. *The Eucharistic Words of Jesus*. Trans. N. Perrin from 3d German ed. New York, 1966.
Jeremias, *Jerusalem*	J. Jeremias. *Jerusalem in the Time of Jesus: An Investigation into Economic and Social Conditions during the New Testament Period*. Philadelphia, 1969. (ET of *Jérusalem au temps de Jésus*, Paris, 1967.)
Jeremias, *Parables*	J. Jeremias. *The Parables of Jesus*. Trans. S. H. Hooke. 2d ed. New York, 1972.
Joly, *Genres de vie*	R. Joly. *Le Thème philosophique des genres de vie dans l'antiquité classique*. Brussels, 1956.
Jouguet, *Vie municipale*	P. Jouguet. *La Vie municipale dans l'Egypt romaine*. Paris, 1911. Reprint 1968.
Kaibel, *Comicorum Graecorum Fragmenta*	G. Kaibel. *Comicorum Graecorum Fragmenta*. Berlin, 1899. Reprint Berlin, 1958–.
Kakride, *Notion de l'amitié*	H. I. Kakride. *La Notion de l'amitié et de l'hospitalité chez Homère*. Thessaloníki, 1963.
Lagrange, *Galates*	M. J. Lagrange. *Saint Paul: Epître aux Galates*. 2d ed. Paris, 1926.
Lagrange, *Jean*	M. J. Lagrange. *Evangile selon saint Jean*. Paris, 1925.
Lagrange, *Luc*	M. J. Lagrange. *Evangile selon saint Luc*. 3d ed. Paris, 1927.
Lagrange, *Marc*	M. J. Lagrange. *Evangile selon saint Marc*. 4th ed. Paris, 1929.
Lagrange, *Matthieu*	M. J. Lagrange. *Evangile selon saint Matthieu*. 7th ed. Paris, 1948.

Lagrange, *Romains*	M. J. Lagrange. *St. Paul: Epître aux Romains*. Paris, 1931.
Landfester, *"Philos"*	M. Landfester. *Das griechische Nomen "philos" und seine Ableitungen*. Hildesheim, 1966.
Lattimore, *Epitaphs*	R. Lattimore. *Themes in Greek and Latin Epitaphs*. Urbana, 1942.
Launey, *Armées hellénistiques*	M. Launey. *Recherches sur les armées hellénistiques*. 2 vols. Paris, 1949–1950. Reprint with addenda 1987.
Leenhardt, *Romans*	F. J. Leenhardt. *The Epistle to the Romans: A Commentary*. Trans. H. Knight. Cleveland-New York, 1961. (ET of *L'Epître de saint Paul aux Romains*, Neuchâtel-Paris, 1957; 2d ed., Geneva, 1981.)
Mandilaras, *Verb*	B. G. Mandilaras [V. G. Mandelaras]. *The Verb in the Greek Non-Literary Papyri*. Athens, 1973.
Marrou, *History of Education*	H. I. Marrou. *A History of Education in Antiquity*. Trans. G. Lamb. New York, 1956. Reprint Madison, Wis., 1982. (ET of *Histoire de l'éducation dans l'antiquité*, Paris, 1948.)
Martin, *Architecture grecque*	R. Martin. *Manuel d'architecture grecque*. Paris, 1965–.
Martin, *Carmen Christi*	R. P. Martin. *Carmen Christi: Philippians ii. 5-11 in Recent Interpretation and in the Setting of Early Christian Worship*. London, 1967.
Mayser, *Grammatik*	E. Mayser. *Grammatik der griechischen Papyri aus der Ptolemäerzeit*. Leipzig, 1906. 2d ed., Berlin, 1970–. [Now see F. T. Gignac, *A Grammar of the Greek Papyri of the Roman and Byzantine Periods*. Milan, 1976–.]
Mélanges Rigaux	*Mélanges bibliques en hommage au R. P. Béda Rigaux*. Ed. A. Descamps and A. de Halleux. Gembloux, 1970.
Mélanges Tisserant	*Mélanges Eugène Tisserant*. 7 vols. Vatican City, 1964.
Moule, *Birth of the NT*	C. F. D. Moule. *The Birth of the New Testament*. 3d ed. New York, 1982.
Moule, *Idiom Book*	C. F. D. Moule. *An Idiom Book of New Testament Greek*. Cambridge, 1953.
Moulton & Howard, *Grammar*	J. H. Moulton and W. F. Howard. *A Grammar of New Testament Greek*. 4 vols. Edinburgh, 1908–1976.

Mugler, *Terminologie géométrique*	C. Mugler. *Dictionnaire historique de la terminologie géométrique des Grecs*. 2 vols in 1. Paris, 1958–1959.
Mugler, *Terminologie optique*	C. Mugler. *Dictionnaire historique de la terminologie optique des Grecs: Douze siècles de dialogues avec la lumière*. Paris, 1964.
Murphy O'Connor, *Paul on Preaching*	J. Murphy O'Connor. *Paul on Preaching*. New York, 1963.
Mussies, *Dio Chrysostom*	G. Mussies. *Dio Chrysostom and the New Testament: Parallels collected by G. Mussies*. Leiden, 1972.
Musurillo, *Acta Alexandrinorum*	H. Musurillo. *Acta Alexandrinorum: De Mortibus Alexandriae Nobilium Fragmenta Papyracea Graeca*. Leipzig, 1961.
Musurillo, *Christian Martyrs*	H. Musurillo. *The Acts of the Christian Martyrs*. Oxford, 1972.
Musurillo, *Pagan Martyrs*	H. Musurillo. *The Acts of the Pagan Martyrs* [tranlation of *Acta Alexandrinorum* with notes and commentary]. Oxford, 1954.
Nägeli, *Wortschatz*	T. Nägeli. *Der Wortschatz des Apostels Paulus: Beitrag zur sprachgeschichtlichen Erforschung des Neuen Testaments*. Göttingen, 1905.
Orlandos, *Technique architecturale*	A. Orlandos. *Les Matériaux de construction et la technique architecturale des anciens Grecs*. Paris, 1966.
Panagopoulos, *Vocabulaire*	C. Panagopoulos. "Vocabulaire et mentalité dans le *Moralia* de Plutarque," in *Dialogues d'histoire ancienne*, vol. 3, Besancon-Paris, 1977.
Pelekidis, *Ephébie attique*	C. Pelekidis. *Histoire de l'éphébie attique des origines à 31 avant Jésus-Christ*. Paris, 1962.
Pelletier, *Josèphe adaptateur*	A. Pelletier. *Flavius Josèphe, adaptateur de la Lettre d'Aristée*. Paris, 1962.
Plummer, *Second Corinthians*	A. Plummer. *A Critical and Exegetical Commentary on the Second Epistle of St. Paul to the Corinthians*. Edinburgh-New York, 1915. Reprint 1948.
Préaux, *Economie royale*	C. Préaux. *L'Economie royale des Lagides*. Brussels, 1939.
Preisigke, *Wörterbuch*	F. Preisigke. *Wörterbuch der griechischen Papyrusurkunden, mit Einschluss der griechischen Inschriften, Aufschriften, Ostraka, Mumienschilder usw., aus Ägypten*. 5 vols. Berlin, 1925–1971. Supplement. Ed. E. Kiessling. and W. Rübsam. Amsterdam, 1969–.

von Rad, *Genesis*	G. von Rad. *Genesis*. Trans. J. H. Marks. Philadelphia, 1971.
von Rad, *OT Theology*	G. von Rad. *Old Testament Theology*. Trans. D. M. G. Stalker. 2 vols. New York, 1962–1965.
Redard, *Noms grecs en -ΤΗΣ, -ΤΙΣ*	G. Redard. *Les Noms grecs en -ΤΗΣ, -ΤΙΣ et principalement en -ΙΤΗΣ, -ΙΤΙΣ: Etude philologique et linguistique*. Paris, 1949.
Rigaux, *Thessaloniciens*	B. Rigaux. *Saint Paul: Les Epîtres aux Thessaloniciens*. Paris-Gembloux, 1956.
Rouffiac, *Caractères du grec*	J. Rouffiac. *Recherches sur les caractères du grec dans le Nouveau Testament d'après les Inscriptions de Priène*. Paris, 1911.
Schnackenburg, *God's Rule*	R. Schnackenburg. *God's Rule and Kingdom*. New York, 1963.
Schnackenburg, *John*	R. Schnackenburg. *The Gospel according to St. John*. Trans. C. Hastings et al. 3 vols. New York, 1990. (ET of *Das Johannes-Evangelium*, Freiburg-Basel, 1971.)
Schürmann, *Lukasevangelium*	H. Schürmann. *Das Lukasevangelium*. Freiburg-Basel-Vienna, 1969–.
Sherwin-White, *Roman Society*	A. N. Sherwin-White. *Roman Society and Roman Law in the New Testament*. Oxford, 1963. Reprint Grand Rapids, 1978.
Snell, *Lexikon*	B. Snell et al. *Lexikon des frühgriechischen Epos*. Göttingen, 1955–.
Spicq, *Agapè*	C. Spicq. *Agapè dans le Nouveau Testament: Analyse des textes*. 3 vols. Paris, 1958–1959. ET (but without the notes) *Agape in the New Testament*. St. Louis, 1965.
Spicq, *Agapè: Prolégomènes*	Spicq, C. *Agapè: Prolégomènes à une étude de théologie néo-testamentaire*. Louvain-Leiden, 1955.
Spicq, *Charité et liberté*	C. Spicq. *Charité et liberté dans le Nouveau Testament*. Paris, 1964. ET *Charity and Liberty in the New Testament*. Trans. F. V. Manning. Staten Island, N.Y., 1965.
Spicq, *Dieu et l'homme*	C. Spicq. *Dieu et l'homme selon le Nouveau Testament*. Paris, 1961.
Spicq, *Epîtres aux Corinthiens*	C. Spicq. *Epîtres aux Corinthiens*. Paris, 1947.
Spicq, *Epîtres de saint Pierre*	C. Spicq. *Les Epîtres de saint Pierre*. Paris, 1966.

Spicq, *Epîtres Pastorales*	C. Spicq. *Saint Paul: Les Epîtres Pastorales*. 4th ed. 2 vols. Paris, 1969.
Spicq, *Hébreux*	C. Spicq. *L'Epître aux Hébreux*. Paris, 1953.
Spicq, *Justice*	C. Spicq. *La Justice*. Paris, 1935.
Spicq, *Péchés d'injustice*	C. Spicq. *Saint Thomas d'Aquin: Les Péchés d'injustice*. Paris-Tournai-Rome, 1934
Spicq, *Théologie morale*	C. Spicq. *Théologie morale du Nouveau Testament*. Paris, 1965.
Spicq, *Vie chrétienne*	C. Spicq. *Vie chrétienne et pérégrination selon le Nouveau Testament*. Paris, 1972.
Spicq, *Vie morale*	C. Spicq. *Vie morale et Trinité sainte selon Saint Paul*. Paris, 1957. ET *The Trinity and Our Moral Life according to St. Paul*. Trans. Sister Marie Aquinas. Westminster, Md., 1963 = *Saint Paul and Christian Living*. Dublin, 1964.
Swiderek, *Propriété foncière*	A. Swiderek. *La Propriété foncière dans l'Egypte de Vespasien*. Warsaw, 1960.
Taillardat, *Images d'Aristophane*	J. Taillardat. *Les Images d'Aristophane: Etudes de langue et de style*. Paris, 1962.
Taubenschlag, *Opera Minora*	R. Taubenschlag. *Opera Minora*. 2 vols. Warsaw-Paris, 1959.
Taubenschlag, *Law of Greco-Roman Egypt*	R. Taubenschlag. *The Law of Greco-Roman Egypt in the Light of the Papyri, 332 B.C.–640 A.D.* 2d ed., rev. and enlarged. Warsaw, 1955.
Trench, *Synonyms*	R. C. Trench. *Synonyms of the New Testament*. 12th ed. 2 vols. London, 1894.
de Vaux, *Ancient Israel*	R. de Vaux. *Ancient Israel: Its Life and Institutions*. Trans. J. McHugh. New York, 1961. (ET of *Les Institutions de l'Ancien Testament*, Paris, 1958.)
Vögtle, *Tugend- und Lasterkataloge*	A. Vögtle. *Die Tugend- und Lasterkataloge im Neuen Testament: Exegetisch, religions- und formgeschichtlich Untersucht*. Münster, 1936.
Wettstein	J. J. Wettstein. *Novum Testamentum. Post priores Steph. Curcellaei. . . .* Amsterdam, 1735.
Ysebaert, *Greek Baptismal Terminology*	J. Ysebaert. *Greek Baptismal Terminology: Its Origins and Early Development*. Nijmegen, 1962.
Zerwick, *Biblical Greek*	M. Zerwick. *Biblical Greek: Illustrated by Examples*. Adapted from the 4th Latin ed. of *Graecitas Biblica* by Joseph Smith. Rome, 1963. Reprint 1983.

Abbreviations: Periodicals

Aeg	Aegyptus
AJP	American Journal of Philology
AnBib	Analecta Biblica
Ang	Angelicum
Anton	Antonianum
APF	Archiv für Papyrusforschung
ASTI	Annual of the Swedish Theological Institute
ATR	Anglican Theological Review
BAGB	Bulletin de l'association G. Budé
BASOR	Bulletin of the American Schools of Oriental Research
BASP	Bulletin of the American Society of Papyrologists
BCH	Bulletin de correspondance hellénique
BerlSitzb	Sitzungsberichte der Preussischen Akademie der Wissenschaften
Bib	Biblica
BIFAO	Bulletin de l'institute français d'archéologie orientale
BJRL	Bulletin of the John Rylands University Library of Manchester
BSac	Bibliotheca Sacra
BSOAS	Bulletin of the School of Oriental and African Studies
BZ	Biblische Zeitschrift
CBQ	Catholic Biblical Quarterly
ChrEg	Chronique d'Egypte
ConNT	Coniectanea neotestamentica
CP	Classical Philology
CTM	Concordia Theological Monthly
DHA	Dialogues d'histoire ancienne
DivThom	Divus Thomas
EPap	Etudes de papyrologie
EstBib	Estudios bíblicos
ETL	Ephemerides theologicae lovanienses
ETR	Etudes théologiques et religieuses
EvQ	Evangelical Quarterly
ExpT	Expository Times
GRBS	Greek, Roman, and Byzantine Studies
Hellenica	Hellenica: Recueil d'épigraphie, de numismatique et d'antiquités grecques
HibJ	Hibbert Journal
HTR	Harvard Theological Review
HUCA	Hebrew Union College Annual

ITQ	*Irish Theological Quarterly*
JAC	*Jahrbuch für Antike und Christentum*
JBL	*Journal of Biblical Literature*
JEA	*Journal of Egyptian Archeology*
JHS	*Journal of Hellenic Studies*
JJP	*Journal of Juristic Papyrology*
JQR	*Jewish Quarterly Review*
JRS	*Journal of Roman Studies*
JSJ	*Journal for the Study of Judaism in the Persian, Hellenistic and Roman Period*
JSS	*Journal of Semitic Studies*
JTS	*Journal of Theological Studies*
LTP	*Laval théologique et philosophique*
MTZ	*Münchener theologische Zeitschrift*
MusHelv	*Museum Helveticum*
NJahrb	*Neue Jahrbücher für das klassische Altertum (1898–1925); Neue Jahrbücher für Wissenschaft und Jugendbildung (1925–1936)*
NKZ	*Neue kirkliche Zeitschrift*
NovT	*Novum Testamentum*
NRT	*La nouvelle revue théologique*
NTS	*New Testament Studies*
OTS	*Oudtestamentische Studiën*
RArch	*Revue archéologique*
RB	*Revue biblique*
REA	*Revue des études anciennes*
RechPap	*Recherches de papyrologie*
REG	*Revue des études grecques*
REJ	*Revue des études juives*
RevistB	*Revista bíblica*
RevPhil	*Revue de philologie*
RevQ	*Revue de Qumran*
RevThom	*Revue thomiste*
RHDFE	*Revue historique du droit français et étranger*
RhMus	*Rheinisches Museum*
RHPR	*Revue d'histoire et de philosophie religieuses*
RHR	*Revue de l'histoire des religions*
RIDA	*Revue internationale des droits de l'antiquité*
RQ	*Römische Quartalschrift für christliche Altertumskunde und Kirchengeschichte*
RSPT	*Revue des sciences philosophiques et théologiques*
RSR	*Recherches des science religieuses*
RTL	*Revue théologique de Louvain*
RTP	*Revue de théologie et de philosophie*
RTQR	*Revue de théologie et des questions religieuses*
ScEccl	*Sciences ecclésiastiques*
ScEs	*Science et esprit*
Scr	*Scripture*
SE	*Studia Evangelica* (in *Texte und Untersuchungen*)
SEÅ	*Svensk exegetisk Årsbok*

Sem	*Semitica*
SJT	*Scottish Journal of Theology*
SP	*Studia Patristica*
SPap	*Studia Papyrologica*
ST	*Studia Theologica*
TAPA	*Transactions of the American Philological Association*
TLZ	*Theologische Literaturzeitung*
TQ	*Theologische Quartalschrift*
TS	*Theological Studies*
TSK	*Theologische Studien und Kritiken*
TTZ	*Trierer theologische Zeitschrift*
TZ	*Theologische Zeitschrift*
VC	*Vigiliae Christianae*
VD	*Verbum Domini*
VSpir	*Vie spirituelle*
VT	*Vetus Testamentum*
VTSup	Vetus Testamentum Supplements
YCS	Yale Classical Studies
ZAW	*Zeitschrift für die alttestamentliche Wissenschaft*
ZKT	*Zeitschrift für katholische Theologie*
ZNW	*Zeitschrift für die neutestamentliche Wissenschaft*
ZPE	*Zeitschrift für Papyrologie und Epigraphik*
ZST	*Zeitschrift für systematische Theologie*
ZTK	*Zeitschrift für Theologie und Kirche*
ZWKL	*Zeitschrift für Wissenschaft und kirchliches Leben*

Transliterations

HEBREW

Consonants†

א	=	ʼ
ב	=	b
ג	=	g
ד	=	d
ה	=	h
ו	=	w
ז	=	z
ח	=	ḥ
ט	=	ṭ
י	=	y
ך כ	=	k
ל	=	l
ם מ	=	m
ן נ	=	n
ס	=	s
ע	=	ʻ
ף פ	=	p
ץ צ	=	ṣ
ק	=	q
ר	=	r
שׂ	=	ś
שׁ	=	š
ת	=	t

Vowels

ַ	=	a
ָ	=	ā
ָה	=	â (h)
ֲ	=	a
ֶ	=	e
ֵי	=	ē
ֵ	=	e
ֱ	=	e
ִ	=	i
ִי	=	î
וֹ	=	ô
ָ	=	o
ֹ	=	ō
ֻ	=	u
וּ	=	û

GREEK*

α	=	a
β	=	b
γ	=	g
δ	=	d
ε	=	e
ζ	=	z
η	=	ē
θ	=	th
ι	=	i
κ	=	k
λ	=	l
μ	=	m
ν	=	n
ξ	=	x
ο	=	o
π	=	p
ρ	=	r
σ ς	=	s
τ	=	t
υ	=	y‡
φ	=	ph
χ	=	ch
ψ	=	ps
ω	=	ō
ῥ	=	rh
γγ	=	ng
γκ	=	nk
γξ	=	nx

---

* Iota subscripts and accents are not represented; *h* = rough breathing.

† Spirant b, g, d, k, p, and t are underlined. Daghesh forte is represented by doubling of the transliterated consonant.

‡ υ = *u* in diphthongs: *au, eu, ou, ui*

ἀγαθοποιέω, ἀγαθωσύνη

agathopoieō, to do good; *agathōsynē*, goodness

Classical Greek and Koine had different formulas for saying "do something good,"[1] but it was the LXX—translating the hiphil of *yāṭab*—then the *Letter of Aristeas*[2] and the NT that were the first to use the combined form *agathopoieō*, unknown in the papyri.

In the OT, it refers to the performance of a good deed toward another,[3] either by God or by a human.[4] Thus Wis 1:12 juxtaposes "do good" and "do evil," just as the Lord asks whether it is permitted on the Sabbath to do good or to do evil—*agathopoiēsai* or *kakopoiēsai*—to save a life or to take a life (Luke 6:9). In its first occurrence in the Sermon on the Mount, the verb, used with an object in the accusative, has the same sense: to render good in return for good.[5] In Luke 6:35, however, it has a theological significance:

---

[1] Ἀγαθὸν ποιεῖν (Matt 19:16), καλὸν ποιεῖν (Jas 4:17), καλῶς ποιεῖν (Luke 6:27), εὖ ποιεῖν (Mark 14:7), ἔργον ἀγαθόν (2 Cor 9:8); cf. C. Spicq, *Epîtres Pastorales*, vol. 2, pp. 676ff.

[2] *Ep. Arist.* 242: He must pray God to shower them with all good things, πάντα ἀγαθοποιεῖν.

[3] Num 10:32; Judg 17:13; Tob 12:13; Wis 1:12; 1 Macc 11:33; 2 Macc 1:2; cf. *T. Benj.* 5.2—ἐὰν ἀγαθοποιοῦντες καὶ τὰ ἀκάθαρτα πνεύματα φεύξονται ἀφ' ὑμῶν.

[4] At Lystra, St. Paul refers to divine Providence as ἀγαθουργῶν (Acts 14:17), and in writing to Timothy he asks him to exhort the rich to do good (ἀγαθοεργεῖν; 1 Tim 6:18). Unlike Attic, Koine, heedless of euphony, does not avoid hiatus in compound words (BDF §124.)

[5] Luke 6:33—"If you do good to those who do good to you, what credit do you earn for that?"; cf. C. Spicq, *Agapè*, vol. 1, p. 108; W. Grundmann, "Die Bergpredigt nach der Lukasfassung," in K. Aland, F. L. Cross, *SE*, 1959, pp. 180–189; H. W. Bartsch, "Feldrede und Bergpredigt: Redaktionsarbeit in Luk. VI," in *TZ*, 1960, pp. 5–18; H. Kahlefeld, *Der Jünger. Eine Auslegung der Rede Lk VI, 20–49*, Frankfurt, 1962; B. Rigaux, *Témoignage de l'Evangile de Luc*, Desclée De Brouwer, 1970, pp. 168ff.

---

agathopoieō, S 15; *TDNT* 1.17–18; *EDNT* 1.4–5; *NIDNTT* 2.98, 100, 102; *L&N* 88.3; BAGD 2 ‖ **agathōsynē**, S 19; *TDNT* 1.18; *EDNT* 1.7; *NIDNTT* 2.98, 100–101; MM 1; *L&N* 57.109, 88.1; BAGD 3

"Love your enemies, do good," because *agathopoieite* explicates *agapate* and shows that *agapē* love, when seen clearly and in action, manifests itself in doing good; the context proves that this type of love is proper to the sons of God.[6]

On the other hand, if the four usages of *agathopoieō* in 1 Peter all have a religious meaning, since they refer the doing of good to the will of God and to God's grace,[7] the accent is not so much on the charity that gives and forgives, but on the virtue (cf. Gal 6:9–10), which is the virtue of servants who do well that which they ought to do[8] or of wives who are faithful to the obligations attaching to their position (1 Pet 3:6). Doing good is opposed to doing evil (2:14; 3:17), transgressing (2:20).

In the same way, the noun *agathopoiïa* refers to an upright moral life: "Let those who suffer according to the will of God entrust their souls to the faithful Creator in their doing of good."[9] Far from losing heart, or being paralyzed by panic, in these last days, Christians will occupy themselves with doing their best (cf. Eccl 9:10), seeking to fulfill the requirements of order and of justice: staying in their place, carrying out the responsibilities appropriate to their gender, their social status, and their function within the community (1 Pet 4:10; 5:2), having good morals, doing nothing blameworthy or mean. In short, their manner of life, their conduct (*anastrophē*; 1:15, 18; 2:12; 3:1, 2, 16), should be commendable and appealing to pagans.[10]

---

[6] 3 John 11 restates this concept, contrasting ὁ ἀγαθοποιῶν and ὁ κακοποιῶν: "Beloved one, do not imitate the evil, but the good. The one who does good is of God. The one who does evil has not seen God."

[7] 1 Pet 2:15, 20; 3:6, 17; cf. 4:19; this is a key word of the epistle, cf. W. C. van Unnik, "The Teaching of Good Works," in *NTS*, vol. 1, 1954, pp. 92–110; idem, "A Classical Parallel to I Petr. II, 14 and 20," ibid., vol. 2, 1956, pp. 198–202 (making reference to Diodorus Siculus, 15.1.1; cf. 11.46.1; for 1 Pet 2:15, G. Mussies, *Dio Chrysostom*, p. 236 gives as parallels Dio Chrysostom 4.58; 13.13; 69.7); C. Crowther, "Works, Work and Good Works," in *ExpT*, vol. 81, 1970, pp. 166–172.

[8] 1 Pet 2:20; cf. S. Daris, *Un Nuovo Frammento della Prima Lettera di Pietro* (1 Pet 2:20–3:12), Barcelona, 1967.

[9] 1 Pet 4:19. Because verse 18 has touched on the perfection of the judgment of God, one may include in ἀγαθοποιία the works of mercy, according to Matt 25:31–46; Acts 9:36; Heb 13:16. Cf. *T. Jos.* 18.2—καὶ ἐάν τις θέλει κακοποιῆσαι ὑμᾶς ἡμεῖς τῇ ἀγαθοεργείᾳ εὔχεσθε ὑπὲρ αὐτοῦ; Epictetus 4.1.122: "It is human nature to do good, to be useful to others."

[10] Cf. C. Spicq, *Epîtres de saint Pierre*, pp. 11, 27f. In Clement of Rome, *agathopoiïa* sums up morality, *1 Clem.* 2.2; 2.7; 33.1: "What shall we do? Become idle in doing good and forsake *agapē*?"; 34.2: "We must be eager to do good." *Agathopoiïa* in 1 Pet could be cited as a NT acknowledgement of natural law ethics.

If Christians are marked by their good conduct, they will be known as an honest persons, *agathopoioi:* governors are appointed "to punish evildoers (*kakopoiōn*) and to praise doers of good" (1 Pet 2:14). This adjective, which places the beneficent or charming woman in contrast to the *ponēria* of the man in Sir 42:14, is attested only in three late papyri.[11]

Closely related to *agathopoiïa* is *agathōsynē*, a strictly biblical term, unknown in secular Greek and in the papyri.[12] Its meaning is doubtful. Used more than a dozen times in the LXX (*tôb-tobah*), it refers to the beneficence that someone has shown (Judg 8:35; 2 Chr 24:16), to kind generosity (Neh 9:25, 35), to moral goodness,[13] to well-being and happiness.[14] It is used in the New Testament only by St. Paul, who sees it as a gift of God (2 Thess 1:11), a fruit of the Spirit (Gal 5:22) and of the light.[15] This would be first of all goodwill or the intention to do that which is good, linked with the power of faith to accomplish it (2 Thess 1:11); then a right disposition of the soul, which we would call "kind feelings,"[16] and which characterizes the person who is *agathos*, morally correct. This person's excellence is seen in all areas: "in all goodness, justice, and truth" (Eph 5:9). But in the list of virtues in Gal 5:22, *agathōsynē* comes between *chrēstotēs* and faithfulness; it no longer means moral goodness so much as goodness of heart. St. Jerome made this excellent comment: "Kindness or mellowness—the two senses of the Greek *chrēstotēs*—is a sweet, caressing, quiet virtue, disposed to sharing all of its goods; it invites familiarity; it is sweet in its words, steady in its ways. The Stoics briefly define it as a virtue naturally given to doing good. Goodness per se (*agathōsynē*) is not far removed from kindness, because it also is given to doing good. The difference is that goodness can be a bit somber and have knitted brows and an

---

[11] Two magical papyri of the fourth century AD, where ἀγαθοποιός is an astrological term meaning "auguring good, favorable"; *P.Lond.* 46, 48: μετὰ ἀγαθοποιῶν (referring to stars whose influence is favorable); 122, 16 qualifying Hermes: ἀγαθοποιὲ τῆς οἰκομένης. *Stud.Pal.* XX, 293, II, 8, which opposes ἀγαθ. to κακοποιός, is from the Byzantine era. According to Plutarch, Osiris is εὐεργέτης and ἀγαθοποιός (*Isis and Osiris* 12 and 42; commented on by H. Preisker, *Die urchristliche Botschaft von der Liebe Gottes*, Gießen, 1930, pp. 11ff.). Proclus describes Jupiter and Venus similarly.

[12] It is a derivative of ἀγαθός, like ἀγαθότης, which is unknown in the New Testament, cf. *P.Ryl.* 619, 6; Philo, *Sacr. Abel and Cain* 27.

[13] Ps 52:3—"You prefer the evil to the good"; cf. Neh 13:31.

[14] Eccl 4:8; 5:10, 17; 6:3, 6; 7:14; 9:18.

[15] Eph 5:9, where some manuscripts, including $\mathfrak{P}^{46}$, read πνεύματος instead of φωτός.

[16] Rom 15:14. The variant of F, G, and the Latin manuscripts, ἀγαπῆς, does not deserve to be considered.

austere moral tone, doubtless doing good and giving what is asked of it, but without being mellow in its dealings or drawing everyone in with its sweetness."[17] Thus *agathōsynē* will always take care to obtain for others that which is useful or beneficial, but it can have a stern side and apply itself to correcting and punishing; kindness adds to this basic and active goodness a shading of cordiality and sweetness (cf. Eph 4:32; Col 3:12).

---

[17]Jerome, *In Ep. ad Gal.* 5.22; *PL* 26, 420. The distinction that J. B. Lightfoot wanted to establish between these terms, corresponding to that between *benevolentia* and *beneficentia* (with ἀγαθωσύνη connoting more realization) doesn't account for actual usage (*Saint Paul's Epistle to the Galatians*, 8th ed., London, 1884, p. 213). The only possible NT translation in English is "goodness" (cf. E. De Witt Burton, *The Epistle to the Galatians*, 2d ed., Edinburgh, 1948, p. 316).

> ἀγανακτέω, ἀγανάκτησις
> ―――――――――――――――――――――――
> *aganakteō*, to be indignant; *aganaktēsis*, indignation

The etymology of these "emotional" terms has not been established.[1] Common in the Hellenistic period, especially in literary Greek, they are rare in the classics, where they express the idea of bubbling and fermenting, first in the physical sense,[2] then with respect to the soul that "is seething and irritated" like the gums of a person who is cutting teeth (Plato, *Phdr.* 251 *c*); "wailing with grief and roaring with anger";[3] "I am outraged at this encounter; my intestines are seething because I have to reply to this man" (Aristophanes, *Ran.* 1006; cf. *Vesp.* 287). Sometimes it is a case of mere discontent (Xenophon, *Hell.* 5.3.11), usually of indignation (Plato, *Ep.* 7.349 *d*; Plutarch, *Cam.* 28.5; Diodorus Siculus 4.63.3), and especially anger.[4]

The three occurrences of the verb in the LXX have a stronger meaning. Expressing God's punishment of his enemies: "the waves of the sea rage (or boil) against them" (Wis 5:22); "in their suffering they became incensed at those whom they had taken for gods."[5] The connotations are quite varied

---

[1] P. Chantraine, *Dictionnaire étymologique*, p. 7; cf. B. G. Mandilaras, *Verb*, n. 892; J. Holt, *Les Noms d'action en* -ΣΙΣ (-ΤΙΣ), Aarhus, 1940.

[2] Hippocrates, *Liqu.* 2.5: "the chest and the stomach, when penetrated by cold, become irritated and cause fatal accidents"; with respect to wine, Plutarch, *Quaest. conv.* 8.10.734 *e*.

[3] Plato, *Phd.* 117 *d*; 63 *b–c*: irritated at death; 64; Plato, *Euthd.* 283 *d*.

[4] Plato, *Lach.* 194 *a*: "I am angry" (ἀγανακτῶ); Thucydides 8.43.4; "Tissaphernes was indignant and left them in anger"; *P.Lond.* 1367, 3 (eighth century).

[5] Wis 12:27; Bel 28 (Theodotion): "the Babylonians were terribly indignant." In the papyri, where the verb is sometimes used with ὅτι (*P.Bon.* 15, 11, edict of Caracalla; *P.Ryl.* 625, 3), περί (*P.Berl.Zill.* 8, 11), κατά (*P.Fouad* 87, 17), and especially ἐπί (*P.Alex.* 2, 14; *P.Lond.* 44, 20; vol. 1, p. 34; *SB* 6711, 21; 7464, 14), the meaning is sometimes weakened: "do not be troubled" (*P.Mich.* 107, 7: Zeno's correspondence; *BGU* 1881, 6); sometimes it becomes rather official: in a rescript of Augustus in 6 BC, Asinius Gallus, governor of the province of Asia, seems to detest crime in an unnatural way,

---

aganakteō, S 23; *EDNT* 1.8; MM 1; L&N 88.187; BDF §229(2); BAGD 4 ‖ *aganaktēsis*, S 24; *EDNT* 1.8; MM 1; L&N 88.186; BAGD 4

in Philo and Josephus, first of all with respect to the subjects of the indignation: everyone, the people, even servants and slaves.[6] But this emotion is often personalized: Laban is irritated (Philo, *Alleg. Interp.* 3.20), as are a seer (Josephus, *Ag. Apion* 1.204), the leading people of Daphne (*War* 1.245), members of the Sanhedrin (*Ant.* 14.179) and of the senate (*P.Oxy.* 1119, 8), the king (Philo, *Moses* 1.236, 292, 328; cf. *Rewards* 77; Josephus, *Ant.* 2.284; *War* 1.564), Tiberias (2.180), Titus (5.554; 6.352), Vespasian (4.189), etc. God himself is angry at the outrages committed by the Sodomites (*Ant.* 1.202) and "when people scorn the gifts that he gives them."[7] There is, after all, such a thing as legitimate indignation (Philo, *Decalogue* 112; *Moses* 1.244; *Spec. Laws* 3.42), as against an inhumane proceeding (Josephus, *War* 2.415), "violation of the holy places, pillage, and murder" (4.162), indignation "on behalf of the temple at Jerusalem" (*Ant.* 13.77), assaults (Philo, *Husbandry* 117) and murders (*Moses* 1.45), curses (*Decalogue* 75), defamation (*Flacc.* 35), and insulting behavior (*To Gaius* 361).

As the subject of and reason for the emotion varies, *aganakteō* and *aganaktēsis* take on varying connotations. An individual can be merely

---

"becoming angry, as you did, not against these men who deserved it all . . . but against people who may have been unfortunate in their defense, but who had done no wrong" (Dittenberger, *Syl.* 780, 35; cf. *P.Thead.* 15, 10; *P.Oxy.* 1119, 8). It is pretty much a stock expression among lawyers: Antiphon, *3 Tetr.* 2.1: "I have the right, it seems to me, to be angry"; Andocides, *C. Alcib.* 4.18: "I am incensed when I think that . . ."; Lysias, *C. Sim.* 3.3: "Most of all, I resent Simon's forcing me to speak on so delicate a topic"; Isocrates, *Big.* 16.49: "I am especially incensed if I am to be punished by the very one whom I myself should be punishing." On the other hand, when an Egyptian woman poured water into the street where Heracleides was walking, he was "irritated" and reproached her (*P.Magd.* 24, 5; second century BC). The count John, hearing the complaints of three brothers of the monastery of Stratonikis against their superior Jeremias "flew into a rage against the same Jeremias" (*P.Fouad* 87, 17). For the substantive ἀγανάκτησις, an erroneous variant in A and B at Esth 8:12 *i* and a NT hapax (2 Cor 7:11), the only parallel cited by Moulton-Milligan is *P.Grenf.* II, 81, 17 (fifth century; cf. *P.Cair.Masp.* 202, 2); hardly anything else can be added apart from *P.Michael.* 32, 5 (Byzantine period).

[6] Philo, *Husbandry* 117; *Spec. Laws* 2.80; 3.119: "We must be angry against those who take the lives of newborns"; Philo, *Flacc.* 141: "everyone was unhappy"; *To Gaius* 361; Josephus, *War* 2.20: "the people, incensed at this conduct"; 2.42, 170, 175, 225, 293; 4.342: "everyone was irritated at the judges"; *Ant.* 13.368; 20.120; in *Gos. Pet.* 14, when Jesus' executioners heard the repentant thief confess Jesus as Savior, they "were irritated at him."

[7] Josephus, *War* 3.371; *Ant.* 8.360; *Ag. Apion* 1.306: the god Ammon was angry at impure and impious people; Philo, *Spec. Laws* 2.11: "God himself would be irritated to hear such things uttered"; 4 Macc 4:21—"divine justice, irritated at these crimes." Andocides, *Myst.* 1.139: "I think that the gods would be quite irritated and indignant to see humans trying to lose those whom they had saved."

displeased[8] or peeved (Josephus, *War* 1.564), but usually anger and rage are meant;[9] indignation "that a person would claim for himself the honor due to God" (Philo, *Dreams* 2.99, 197), fury.[10] Once a person's emotions are stirred up (Josephus, *War* 1.471) and he is seething with indignation (1.438) or upset (6.203), he is unable to master his irritation (1.449), explodes (2.604), and—like Tiron "in his excessive fury" (1.544)—goes mad.

In the Gospels, *aganakteō* never means indignation or displeasure[11] but anger. When the mother of Zebedee's two sons asks that they be seated at Jesus' left and right, "the ten, when they heard, were angry at the two brothers" (Matt 20:24, *ēganaktēsan peri;* Mark 10:41). The leading priests and scribes, seeing the wonders worked by Jesus and the way in which the children were praising him, "became irritated" (Matt 21:15), as the ruler of the synagogue was angry at Jesus' violation of the law of Sabbath rest (Luke 13:14, *aganaktōn hoti*) and as Jesus himself "became angry" when his disciples forbade parents to bring their children to him.[12]

The substantive *aganaktēsis* appears only once in the NT, regarding the repentance of the Corinthians who had rebelled against the apostle's authority but whose regret was reported by Titus. *Alla aganaktēsin* is usually translated "what indignation" (2 Cor 7:11), referring to their feeling about their offense; but we are to understand that they felt horror at what they had done. Today we would say "they were distraught" at their blindness.

---

[8] Josephus, *War* 1.471, 508, 546; 2.526, 598; *Ant.* 7.212; 16.386; 20.126.

[9] Philo, *Unchang. God* 68; *Worse Attacks Better* 69; *Decalogue* 75; *Moses* 1.45; Marcus Aurelius 7.66: without becoming angry. When they become irritated, princes prepare to make war (Josephus, *War* 1.133, 137), to kill (2.631), to imprison (2.180). Private individuals exchange insults and come to blows (3.439; 6.108, 203, 302; *Ag. Apion* 1.204). Cf. Thucydides 2.41.3: "Only our city never provoked the irritation of the enemies that attacked it."

[10] Josephus, *Ant.* 4.126: Balak was furious at not being blessed by the Israelites; 6.97: the Philistines were furious at the affront; 6.177: David was furious at the Philistines and wanted to do battle; 7.120, 206; 10.173; 13.292; 14.182; *Ant.* 20.193; *War* 4.541: "in his excessive fury, it would not have taken much for him to taste the flesh of his victims"; Numenius, frag. 26.62: the owner, fooled by his slaves, "became furious."

[11] The only exception is Matt 26:8—when Mary of Bethany anointed Jesus, the disciples expressed their displeasure ("Why this waste?" cf. Mark 14:4).

[12] Mark 10:14. Cf. S. Légasse, *Jésus et l'enfant*, Paris, 1969, pp. 187ff.

ἀγάπη
agapē, **love**

The etymology of *agapaō* is obscure. E. Boisacq and E. Stauffer offer no verdict,[1] Blass and Debrunner say not a word,[2] E. Risch and H. J. Mette admit their ignorance, as does P. Chantraine.[3] A. Ceresa-Gastaldo suggests a link to the Sanskrit *pā* with the sense of shelter or protect, and an analogy with the Greek *posis*.[4] A. Carnoy posits the primitive meaning "greet in a friendly manner" and goes back to the Indo-European *ghabh*, in Sanskrit *gabhasti*, "hand," with reference to the Homeric Greeks, who took each other's hand as a sign of friendship.[5] I myself would be tempted to trace this verb to the root *aga*, "very"; we know that the Greek *agē* means "admiration, astonishment."[6] Hence, no doubt, the first usages of this term in the sense of welcome: the surprise of the host who receives a stranger. At any rate, the only adequate translation is "love in the sense of charity"; in Latin, *caritas* or *dilectio*.[7]

---

[1] E. Boisacq, *Dictionnaire étymologique de la lange grecque*, 2d ed., Heidelberg, 1923, p. 6; E. Stauffer, ἀγαπάω, in *TDNT*, vol. 1, p. 36.

[2] BDF.

[3] E. Risch, H. J. Mette, ἀγαπάω, in B. Snell, *Lexikon;* P. Chantraine, *Dictionnaire étymologique*.

[4] Cf. the root *pô*, keep; A. Ceresa-Gastaldo, "ΑΓΑΠΗ nei documenti anteriori al Nuovo Testamento," in *Aeg*, 1951, pp. 302–303.

[5] A. Carnoy, *Dictionnaire étymologique du Proto-Indo-Européen*, Louvain, 1955, p. 3. He cites Homer, *Il.* 23.384: ἐν τ' ἄρα οἱ φῦ χειρί.

[6] Ἄγαμαι: to admire, to be astonished (cf. H. Cremer, J. Kögel, *Biblisch-theologisches Wörterbuch*, 10th ed., p. 9). J. Pollux associates ἀγαπῶ and ἄγαμαι (*Onom.* 5.20.113).

[7] H. Pétré, *Caritas. Etude sur le vocabulaire latin de la charité chrétienne*, Louvain, 1948; W. Thiele, *Wortschatzuntersuchungen zu den lateinischen Texten der Johannesbriefe*, Freiburg, 1958; P. Agaesse, *Saint Augustin: Commentaire de la première Epître de S. Jean*, Paris, 1961, pp. 31ff.; R. Völkl, *Frühchristliche Zeugnisse zu Wesen und Gestalt der christlichen Liebe*, Freiburg, 1963, pp. 91–95; R. T. Otten, "Amor, Caritas and Dilectio:

---

agapē, S 26; *TDNT* 1.21–55; *EDNT* 1.8–12; *NIDNTT* 2.538–551; MM 2; L&N 23.28, 25.43; BDF §163; BAGD 5–6; ND 4.258–259

The Greeks had four terms for expressing the major senses of love.[8] First, *storgē* (*stergō*) refers either to the tender feelings that parents naturally feel toward their children[9] or children toward their siblings and parents, or to the bond that unites husband and wife,[10] and also takes in sympathy for friends and compatriots.[11] *Erōs* (*eraō*), no doubt derived from an ancient neuter **eras*,[12] is not found in the New Testament; it expresses above all unreasoning passion and desire (an *alogos orexis*), the desire of the wolf for the sheep.[13] Although it is often used with no negative conno-

---

Some Observations on the Vocabulary of Love in the Exegetical Works of St. Ambrose," in *Mélanges Chr. Mohrmann*, Utrecht-Anvers, 1963, pp. 73–83.

[8] C. Spicq, *Agapè: Prolégomènes*, pp. 2ff. S. K. Wuest, "Four Greek Works for Love," in *BSac*, 1959, pp. 241–248; and the modern transposition by C. S. Lewis, *The Four Loves*, London, 1960.

[9] Cf. M. Raoss, "Iscrizione cristiana-greca di Roma anteriore al Terzo secolo?" in *Aevum*, 1963, pp. 11–30. Because of the propensity of the Koine to use compound words, *philostorgia* came to be used more and more for *storgē* (cf. Rom 12:10; C. Spicq, ΦΙΛΟΣΤΟΡΓΟΣ, in *RB* 1955, pp. 497–510); cf. Plutarch: "Does tenderness for one's children come naturally for humans?—Εἰ φυσικὴ πρὸς τὰ ἔκγονα φιλοστοργία;" (Plutarch, *Quaest. conv.* 3); *P.Oxy.* 1381, 104: ἡ μήτηρ ὡς ἐπὶ παιδί, καὶ φύσει φιλόστοργος; Ps.-Aristotle: "It is φιλοστοργία toward their children that inspires parents to draw up a will in their favor. . . . Children are so loved (ἀγαπωμένων) as being lovable objects per se" (cited by Stobaeus, II, 7, 13 = vol. 2, p. 120); a decree of Chersonesus for Thrasymedes of Heraclea: πατέρων ἀγαθῶν πρὸς υἱοὺς φιλοστόργους (cited by L. Robert, *Opera Minora Selecta*, vol. 1, p. 311, n. 2).

[10] Cf. *MAMA*, vol. 8, 367, 373, 374, 391, 392, 394; Menander: "I am ready to accept her without dowry and add an oath to cherish her always—διατελεῖν στέργων" (*Dysk.* 309, cf. P. Flury, *Liebe und Liebessprache bei Meinander, Plautus und Terenz*, Heidelberg, 1968). Alphaeus of Mitylene would take στέργω-ἐράω as synonyms (*Anth. Pal.* 9, 110).

[11] Cf. the letter of Panechotes in the second century: φθάνω μέν σοι δεδηλωκὼς ἦν ἔχω πρὸς σὲ στοργήν = I have already shown the affection that I have for you (*P.Oxy.* 2726, 5–8). This instinctive attraction was attibuted also to animals (Aristotle, *HA* 9.4.611ª12). The absence of this innate feeling (ἄστοργος, Rom 1:31; 2 Tim 3:3) is as noteworthy in humans as in cruel beasts (ἀστόργου θηρός; *GVI*, vol. 1, n. 1078, 4).

[12] A. Ernout, "Venus, Venia, Cupido," in *RevPhil*, 1956, p. 7.

[13] Epicurus defines *eros* thus: "a strong appetite for sexual pleasures, accompanied by furor and agony" (H. Usener, *Epicurea*, Frag. 483, Leipzig, 1887); cf. Alexis, in Stobaeus 63.13 (=4.20ª13H); Archilochus, *Epodes* 8.245: "So violent was the desire for love that welled up in my heart, pouring out an opaque fog upon by eyes"; D. M. Robinson, E. J. Fluck, *A Study of the Greek Love-names, including a Discussion of Paederasty and a Prosopographia*, Baltimore, 1937; F. Lasserre, *La Figure d'Eros dans la poésie grecque*, Lausanne, 1946; H. Licht, *Sexual Life in Ancient Greece*, 8th ed., London, 1956; M. F. Galizno, J. S. Lasso de la Vega, F. R. Adrados, *El descubrimiento del amor en Grecia*, Madrid, 1959; M. M. Laurent, *Réalisme et richesse de l'amour chrétien: Essai sur eros et agapè*, Issy-les-Moulineaux, 1962; J. Fürstauer, *Eros im alten Orient*, Stuttgart, 1965.

tation, this word for a type of covetousness can hardly express a love that is specifically divine, if only because it does not inspire respect.[14]

Friendship or amity (*philia, phileō*) moves on an entirely different plane,[15] even though it often refers to affection pure and simple, attachment, sympathy, always marked by a kindly attitude, and good will. But the Greek philosophers, especially Aristotle, turned it into a very elaborate concept. Strictly speaking, friendship wants reciprocity, does not take root except within a defined group of persons—thus we refer to "a pair of friends"—and above all between persons of the same standing: *amicitia pares aut invenit aut facit*.[16] If, then, in certain usages *phileō* is very close to *agapaō*,[17] the former verb was hardly appropriate for expressing a love

---

[14] Musaeus, *Hero and Leander* 98. On Eros as a warrior and fighter, cf. A. Spies, *Militat omnis amans. Ein Beitrag zur Bildersprache der antiken Erotik*, Tübingen, 1930; on Erōs as a mythic power, cf. G. Bornkamm, *Studien zu Antike und Urchristentum*, Munich, 1959, vol. 2, p. 31. The stoics give *erōs* a noble sense, cf. A. J. Festugière, *Le Dieu cosmique*, Paris, 1949, pp. 271ff.

[15] The first meaning of φίλος would have been possessive, "my," and by a semantic evolution it would have come to mean "dear," so that its opposite would have been ξένος, "stranger," meaning "one who does not belong to us" (H. I. Kakride, *Notion de l'amitié*. "Φίλος, regardless of the etymological details, literally expresses not an emotional attachment, but belonging to a social group, and this usage is linked to the use of the word as a possessive in Homer," P. Chantraine, *Etudes sur le vocabulaire grec*, Paris, 1956, p. 15). Cf. F. Dirlmeier, ΦΙΛΟΣ und ΦΙΛΙΑ *im vorhellenistischen Griechentum*, Munich, 1931; M. Landfester, *"Philos"*; Stählin, φιλέω-φίλος, in *TDNT*, vol. 9, pp. 115–116. On φιλέω in the inscriptions, cf. G. Pfohl, *Grabinschriften*, pp. 41, 44, 46, 101, etc.

[16] [Friendship either finds or makes equals.—Tr.] It is often said that charity is friendship, but St. Thomas Aquinas wrote *quasi-amicitia*, and he was making reference to the Aristotelian terminology concerning "friendships of superabundance," like those that link parents to their children.

[17] Cf. Menander, *Mis.* 307–308: Πρῶτος ἠγάπησά σε, ἀγαπῶ, φιλῶ, Κράτεια φιλτάτη (in *P.Oxy.* 2656, 20–21); Plutarch, *De virt. mor.* 8: in marriage, reasoning leads to a strengthening of affection and love, τὸ φιλεῖν καὶ τὸ ἀγαπᾶν; *Conv. sept. sap.* 2: one guest engages the others in friendship and mutual affection, πρὸς φιλίαν καὶ ἀγάπησιν ἀλλήλων; Dio Cassius 60.18: Messalina loved and favored (ἐφίλει καὶ ἠγάπα) indulgent husbands. Cf. John 3:35 and 5:20; 14:21b and 16:27; 11:3 and 5, 36; above all 21:15–17 (where P. S. Minear, *Images of the Church in the New Testament*, Philadelphia, 1960, p. 159, translates well, "Simon, are you my friend?"); Cf. C. Spicq, *Agapè*, vol. 3, pp. 219–245. The Pauline salutation "Greet those who love us in the faith" (Titus 3:15) and the Johannine salutation "The friends greet you. Greet the friends, each one individually" (3 John 15; cf. T. Y. Mullins, "Greeting as a New Testament Form," in *JBL*, 1968, pp. 418–426) use φιλέω in exactly the same sense as the contemporary protocol for letters (*P.Mert.* 83, 13–14): ἄσπασαι τοὺς φιλοῦντάς σε πάντας; 82, 16–19; *P.Abinn.* 6, 23–24: ἀσπάζομαι πάντες τὰ ἐν τῇ οἰκίᾳ κατ' ὄνομα; 25, 9–18; *P.Ross.Georg.* III, 4, 25–28; A. Bernand, *Philae*, n. 65; *P.IFAO* II, n. 40, 11; other papyrological citations in C. Spicq, *Agapè*, pp. 87ff., idem, "Le Lexique de l'amour

that unites God and humans and extends even to enemies,[18] especially since the noun *agapē* did not enter literary usage, except in the LXX, before the first century.

So what does *agapē* mean in the NT?[19] It is the most rational kind of love, inasmuch as it involves recognition and judgment of value, whence

---

dans les papyrus," in *Mnemosyné*, 1955, pp. 27–28). Συγγενής (literally "congener" or "fellow," used as an aulic title, cf. L. Mooren, "Über die ptol. Hofrangtitel," in *Antidorum W. Peremans*, Louvain, 1968, pp. 161ff.), is associated with ἀναγκαῖος φίλος in Acts 10:24, in accord with contemporary usage (on these terms, cf. C. Spicq, *Agapè*, pp. 92ff.; *I.Magn.*, 38, 52; *IG*, vol. 9, 2, n. 583, 58; *SB* 9415, 17; *SEG*, vol. 19, 468, 32; vol. 23, 547, 2; *P.Herm.* 1; *P.Mil.Vogl.* 59, 13; *IGLS*, vol. 6, 2859, 7; A. Bernand, *Philae*, n. 30; E. Bernand, *Inscriptions métriques*, p. 56; Plutarch, *Agric.* 3.1 and 3.5; L. Robert, *Hellenica*, vols. 11–12, Paris, 1960, p. 205; idem, *Opera minora selecta*, Amsterdam, 1960, p. 220; Michaelis, συγγενής, in *TDNT*, vol. 7, pp. 736–742. On the *necessarii regis*, cf. *Prosop.Ptol.*, vol. 2, p. xix). As for the formula φίλος τοῦ Καίσαρος (John 19:12; cf. *Agapè* vol. 3, pp. 239ff.), it should be considered together with the title "friend of the king," which seems to be of Egyptian origin (C. De Witt, "Enquête sur le titre de *śmr pr*," in *ChrEg*, 1956, pp. 89–104; H. Doner, "Der 'Freund des Königs,' " in *ZAW*, 1961, pp. 269–277; J. Gaudemet, *Institutions de l'antiquité*, Paris, 1967, pp. 227ff.), but used among the Persians, the Seleucids, and the Romans, referring to courtiers, courtesans, and royal favorites, the staff officers at headquarters, the ministers in charge, the councillors, and the personal couriers of the sovereign (*Ep. Arist.* 41, 45, 228, 268, 318). These dignitaries ranked after the "relatives of the king, συγγενεῖς" and there was a hierarchy among them, such that some were distinguished as "friends of the first order" (Dittenberger, *Or.*, vol. 1, 119; vol. 2, 754; *Syl.* 685, 121; *Pap.Lugd.Bat.* 14, 4th col.; *P.Dura*, 18, 10; 19, 18; 20, 3; *SEG*, vol. 8, 573; vol. 13, 552–557, 568–591; vol. 20, 208; *SB* 1078, 8876, 9963, 9986, 10122; Strabo 13.2.3; E. Bickerman, *Institutions des Séleucides*, pp. 40–50, 66, 188–189; M. Hollaux, *Etudes d'épigraphie*, vol. 3, pp. 220–225; E. Bammel, "Φίλος τοῦ Καίσαρος," in *TLZ*, 1952, col. 205–210; A. Pelletier, *Josèphe adaptateur*, p. 107; B. Lifshitz, "Sur le culte dynastique des Séleucides," in *RB*, 1963, pp. 76–81; G. Lumbroso, *Recherches sur l'économie politique de l'Egypte*, 2d ed., Amsterdam, 1967, pp. 191ff.; *Prosop.Ptol.*, vol. 6., pp. 21ff., 85; A. Bernand, *Philae*, n. 13, 2; C. Spicq, *Prolégomènes*, p. 165, *Agapè*, vol. 3, p. 167, 240).

[18] Matt 5:44. R. Joly (*Le Vocabulaire chrétien de l'amour est-il original?* Φιλεῖν et Ἀγαπᾶν, Brussels, 1968) challenges my semantics and quite often my exegesis. I will merely observe that from Plato to St. John Chrysostom and Basil of Ancyra, and in Philo along the way, it is ἐράω, much more than φιλέω, that is used in preference to the classical ἀγαπάω, "to be content with, be satisfied." Moreover, it is the vocabulary of the LXX—in which this verb occurs much more often (268 times, as opposed to around 30 for φιλέω) and with an affective sense—that determined that of the NT. Cf. B. Botte, in *Recherches de théologie ancienne et médiévale*, 1969, p. 235; J. Giblet, "Le Lexique chrétien de l'amour," in *RTL*, 1970, pp. 333–337.

[19] Cf. C. Spicq, *Prolégomènes*, pp. 65ff.; idem, "Les Composantes de la notion d'agapè dans le Nouveau Testament," in *Sacra Pagina*, Paris-Gembloux, 1959, pp. 440–455 (reprinted in *Charité et liberté*; developed in *Théologie morale*, vol. 2, pp. 481ff.); cf. N. Lazure, *Les valeurs morales de la théologie johannique*, Paris, 1965, pp. 207–250.

its frequent nuance of "preference."[20] The verb *agapaō* most often means "value, set great store by, hold in high esteem";[21] it is a love with deep respect (1 Pet 2:17), which often goes along with admiration and can become adoration.[22] This esteem and goodwill tend to be expressed in appropriate words and deeds.[23] Unlike other loves, which can remain hidden in the heart, it is essential to charity to manifest itself, to demonstrate itself, to provide proofs, to put itself on display;[24] so much so that in the NT it would almost always be necessary to translate *agapē* as "demonstration of love."[25] This affection—unlike *erōs*, which in the literature

---

[20] Rev 12:11; cf. Menander, *Dysk.* 824; *Sam.* 272; *P.Herc.* 1018, col. XII, 5; Plutarch, *Sol.* 6, 1; *Conv. sept. sap.* 2; Apollodorus, *Bibl.* 2.7.7; Dio Cassius 60.18; 61.7.

[21] 1 Thess 5:13; cf. Plato, *Resp.* 10.600c; Plutarch, *Rom.* 17.3; *Phoc.* 6.4; *Sert.* 14.1; *Conv. sept. sap.* 6; Dio Cassius 44.39; 59.20; 54.31; 71.31. Hence its opposition to καταφρονεῖν, "despise, scorn" (Matt 6:24; cf. C. Spicq, *Agapè*, vol. 1, Paris, 1958, pp. 31, 101); cf. Isocrates, *Antid.* 15.151.

[22] Cf. Phil 1:9–11; the precept "You shall love the Lord your God" can also be translated "You shall adore" (Matt 22:37); cf. Plutarch, *Arist.* 6.3: the people should love and venerate the gods. Cyrus, wishing to express his enthusiasm for the beauty of Milto, changed her name to Aspasia, the most "adorable" woman imaginable (*Per.* 24.12).

[23] 1 John 3:18—ἐν ἔργῳ καὶ ἀληθείᾳ (2 John 3; *Ep. Arist.* 260; *Pss. Sol.* 6.9; 10.4; 14.1; 15.3; *T. Jud.* 24.3; *T. Levi* 18.8; cf. I. de la Potterie, "La verità in S. Giovanni," in *RivistB*, 1963, pp. 3–24; N. Lazure, *Valeurs morales*, p. 87); ἔργῳ is opposed to λόγῳ as reality is opposed to appearances (Philo, *Cherub.* 41; Thucydides 2.65: "The democracy was such in name [λόγῳ], but in reality [ἔργῳ δέ] it was government by the first citizen"; cf. 8.78, nothing but words, without reality). In a personal letter of the first century, the writer complains about a certain Keramos who talks much and does nothing (*P.Alex.* 25, 19–20: πολλὰ λέγειν. . . οὐδὲν ἐποίει; *P.Alex.*, pp. 68ff.); *P.NYU* 1 *a* 8: ἔργῳ δὲ ἀληθεῖ καὶ δυνάμει; *I.Olymp.*, 356, 7: C. Asinius Quadratus τειμήσαντα τὴν Ὀλυμπίαν καὶ λόγῳ καὶ ἔργῳ; other references in *Agapè*, vol. 3, p. 263.

[24] Rom 5:8 (συνίστημι, cf. *Agapè*, vol. 2, p. 180); 1 John 4:9 (φανερόω; cf. 2 Tim 1:10); 2 Cor 8:24 (ἐνδείκνυμαι; cf. Heb 6:10); Titus 3:4 (ἐπιφαίνεν).

[25] It is clear, for example, that the authenticity of the followers of Jesus will be discernible only to the extent that they give proof of their mutual love (John 13:35; cf. likewise 15:13; 1 John 3:16, etc.; cf. C. Spicq, "Notes d'exégèse johannique: la charité est amour manifeste," in *RB*, 1958, pp. 358–370). Under the New Covenant, the keeping of commandments has no value except as a proof of love (John 14: 21). In an analogous use of the word, Ptolemy asks his very dear Apollonius to write him regularly so that he may know how much he loves him: Δι' ὅπερ παρακληθεὶς γράφε μοι συνεχῶς ἵνα διαγνῶ σε οὕτως με ἠγαπηκότα (*P.Mert.* 22, 8); cf. *SB* 7804, 5: μνησθεὶς τῆς ἀ[γάπη]ς, ἥν εἰς συνόμαιμον ἔδειξα (second century AD); *P.Oxy.* 11, 6: "You shall prove your love . . ."; *P.Berl.Zill.* 14, 12, 14; *P.Fouad* 86, 5: "Show me your love by saying . . ." etc.

brings endless suffering and disaster[26]—is accompanied by contentment, since the ordinary meaning of *agapaō* is to be happy, satisfied.[27] But in Christian usage, since it is a divine love, coming from heaven (Rom 5:5), it will be joyful and already a foretaste of blessedness.[28]

Finally, and perhaps above all, while friendship is properly used only of a relationship between equals, *agapē* links persons of different conditions: with rulers, benefactors, and fathers; it is a disinterested and generous love, full of thoughtfulness and concern. It is in this sense that God is *agapē* and loves the world.[29] With those who are indebted, for inferiors, for subjects, this *agapē*, which is first of all consent, welcome, acceptance,[30] is expressed in gratitude:[31] it is the love inspired in turn by generous love—

---

[26] Ps.-Lysias, *Amat.* 233 b: "Those who love deserve more pity than envy"; *Anth. Pal.* 9.157: "Who said that Eros is a god? We never see a god do evil, and Eros smilingly spills human blood."

[27] Plato, *Lysis* 218c: "I was joyful like a hunter, entirely happy (ἀγαπητῶς) to have at last that which I was pursuing"; Isocrates, *Ep.* 6.6: "I would be quite happy if . . . ἀγαπῴην ἂν εἰ"; Menander, *Dysk.* 745; "Each one would be content with his modest part"; *Sam.* 557; Synesius: "Ptolemy and his successors would be content to use only . . ." (*Epist. ad Paeonium* 311 B; edited by Terazghi, vol. 2, p. 138, 18); Plutarch, *Thes.* 17.2: The Athenians "were enchanted by the devotion that Theseus demonstrated toward the people"; *Crass.* 19.3: "Crassus rejoiced greatly"; *De gen.* 4 = 577d: "all too happy that their lives had been spared"; Dio Cassius 1.185, 307; 42.7; 61.4; Philo, *Post. Cain* 171; *Sacr. Abel and Cain* 37; *P.Panop.Beatty* 2, 6, 148: ἀγαπητῶς ἔχειν = to hold oneself to be satisfied, to account oneself happy.

[28] 1 Pet 1:8; cf. 1 Cor 2:9 (cf. *Agapè*, vol. 1, pp. 219ff.); P. Prigent, "Ce que l'œil n'a point vu," in *TZ*, 1958, pp. 416–429; M. Philonenko, "Quod oculus non vidit," ibid., 1959, pp. 51–56; J. B. Bauer, "ΤΟΙΣ ΑΓΑΠΩΣΙΝ ΤΟΝ ΘΕΟΝ," in *ZNW*, 1959, pp. 108–112; A. Feuillet, *Le Christ sagesse de Dieu*, Paris, 1966, pp. 37ff.); 1 Cor 13:6 (συγχαίρει); Gal 5:22; Rom 12:12, 15; Phil 2:2; John 14:28; 15:10–11. In the secular language, ἀγαπάω and χαίρω are already often synomyms (Epictetus 4.4.45; Plutarch, *Thes.* 17.2).

[29] John 3:16; 1 John 4:16; 5:1; Eph 2:4 (cf. *Agapè*, vol. 3, pp. 127ff., 288ff.; A. Feuillet, *Le Mystère de l'amour divin dans la théologie johannique*, Paris, 1972, pp. 179ff.). Caesar declared to his troops, "I love you as a father loves his children, ἀγαπῶ . . . ὡς πατὴρ παῖδας" (Dio Cassius 12.27; cf. 57; 53.18: the title of "father" given to emperors is "an invitation for them to love their subjects as their children"; 56.9; Stobaeus 2.7.13 = vol. 2, p. 120).

[30] Plutarch, *Num.* 4.3; 14.9; *Cor.* 39.13; *De frat. amor.* 6; Onasander 1.21.

[31] Cf. the exhortation of Antony to the Roman people at Caesar's funeral: ἐφιλήσατε αὐτὸν ὡς πατέρα, καὶ ἠγαπήσατε ὡς εὐεργέτην (Dio Cassius 44.48, 1; cf. 43.18: Caesar's soldiers were grateful to those who gave to them; 49.20: "Pacorus, because of his justice and mildness, was surrounded in Syria by more love [ὑπερηγάπων] than any king ever was." Compare Polybius 9.29.12; 5.11.6: διὰ τὴν εὐεργεσίαν καὶ φιλανθρωπίαν ἀγαπώμενον); Plutarch, *Alc.* 4.4; *Arist.* 23.6: "They bade him give thanks to Fortuna"; *Luc.* 20.6: "Lucullus was loved [with gratitude] by the peoples whom he had treated well"; 29.5: ". . . as a benefactor and a founder";

which is the meaning in 1 John 4:10—and it is translated into acclaim, applause, tokens of respect, congratulations, praises,[32] and even veneration,[33] so that Christian *agapē* is expressed in liturgy and worship: "To the one who loves us . . . to him be the glory and the power for ever and ever" (*Tō agapōnti hēmas . . . autō hē doxa kai to kratos eis tous aiōnas tōn aiōnōn*, Rev 1:5–6).

The verb *agapaō* makes its first appearance in Homer, and *agapēsis* is used in the classical period, but the noun *agapē* is unknown before its usage in the LXX. When it is attested before the Christian era,[34] it is almost

---

Cant 1:3; John 16:27; Eusebius, *Praep. Evang.* 9.3.3: διὰ ταῦτα ἀγαπηθῆναι; Theopompus of Chios: διὰ ταῦτα καὶ μᾶλλον αὐτὸν ἠγάπα τῶν πολιτῶν (in *FGr.H.*, II B, p. 580, 30). On this return of affection, cf. the Athenian poet Cantharus, frag. 6: καὶ πρότερον οὖσα παρθένος ἀμφηγάπαζες αὐτόν (in J. M. Edmonds, *Attic Comedy*, vol. 1, p. 450).

[32] Heraclitus, *All.* 6; Ps.-Lysias, *Amat.* 233e: "When one gives a dinner at one's own home, one should invite not one's friends, but beggars and starving folk. These are the people who will salute (ἀγαπήσουσιν) you, who will escort you, who will sit at your gate, who will be the most joyful, who will be the most grateful, who will wish you the greatest happiness"; Plutarch, *Publ.* 10.5; 19.3; Dio Cassius 45.4; the Pythagorean Diotogenes: the majesty of the king can draw the admiration and fear of the crowds, while his kindness provokes their love and applause, ἁ δὲ χρηστότας φιλεύμενον καὶ ἀγαπαζόμενον (*On Kingship*, in Stobaeus, 7.62 = vol. 4, p. 267, 14).

[33] Dio Cassius 44.48; 52.32: "It is natural for all people to rejoice when a superior deems them worthy to be addressed as if they were his equals; it is natural for them to approve all his decrees as if they were their own doing, to applaud them as if they themselves had thought of them first, καὶ ἀγαπᾶν ὡς αὐθαίρετα"; Polybius 9.29.12; 5.11.6. Cf. Theophilus: "Shall I depart, and betray my venerated master—τὸν ἀγαπητὸν δεσπότην?" (in J. M. Edmonds, *Attic Comedy*, vol. 2, p. 568).

[34] It is often difficult to date our documents with precision. For example, a tomb inscription preserved in the museum at Alexandria—μνησθεὶς τῆς ἀ[γάπη]ς εἰς συνόμαιμον ἔδειξα, μὴ παρίδῃς πέτρην οἶκον ὁμοφροσύνης—dated to 27 BC by A. Ceresa-Gastaldo (ΑΓΑΠΗ nei documenti estranei all' influsso biblico, in *Rivista di filologia e di istruzione classica*, 1953, pp. 347–356, taken up in like manner by *SB* 7804; *SEG*, vol. 8, 374; C. Spicq, "Le Lexique de l'amour dans les papyrus," in *Mnemosyne*, 1955, p. 32) is republished by W. Peek (*GVI*, vol. 1, n. 1143, 5), who not only dates it to the second century AD but also reads τῆς φιλίης instead of ἀγάπης (cf. *SEG*, vol. 14, 852). The truth is that "with the exception of the two first words, the line is totally effaced" (E. Bernand, *Inscriptions métriques*, n. 69 = p. 279). The inscription praising Amandos for his love of his country, τίς ὑπὸ πάτρης τόσσην ἔσχ' ἀγάπην (*SEG*, vol. 8, 11, 6) is from the third century (A. Ceresa-Gastaldo, "'Αγάπη nei documenti anteriori al Nuovo Testamento," in *Aeg*, 1951, p. 289). The inscription of Rhosos—ὑπὲρ μνήμης καὶ εὐχαριστίας καὶ ἀγάπης (*IGLS*, 727, 1–2)—is Christian and Byzantine (as *SB* 5314, 15) etc. In the third and fourth centuries, the formula of Ignatius of Antioch—ἀγάπην ποιεῖν, meaning "celebrate the *agapē*" (Ign. *Smyrn.* 8.2; cf. *SB* 1029, 6: εἰς τὴν ἀγάπην τοῦ ἁγίου Ἀπ' Ἀπολλῶ πάντως ἔρχομε, "I shall certainly come for the feast of Saint Abbot Apollos," republished and commented on by H. C. Youtie, in *ZPE*,

exclusively in Hellenic Judaism, and in each case it has a religious meaning.[35] One is inclined to think that it is not a biblical neologism but was borrowed by the inspired writers from the popular language of Egypt. In any case, contrary to what is often written, no certain attestation is available in any papyrus from the pre-Christian era.

P.Berlin 9869, an unintelligible fragment,[36] has often been cited: *en tois malista agapēs.* But not only do the editors point the final sigma as doubtful, but they also put a question mark both after their restoration[37] and after the word *agapē* in the index. Actually, the papyrus is mutilated; several letters have to be restored, and one could just as easily read the noun *agapēseōs,* the participle *agapēsas,* or the future *agapēseis.*[38] These verbal

---

vol. 16, 1975, pp. 259–264)—came to be used commonly to mean "give alms" (*P.Lond.* 1914, 28; cf. 1916, 28; C. Spicq, *Mnemosyne,* 1955, pp. 30ff.).

[35] *Ep. Arist.* 229 (with the note of the editor, A. Pelletier, Paris, 1962, p. 204); *Pss. Sol.* 18.4; Philo, *Unchang. God* 69; *Quest. Exod.* 23.27*a,* frag. 21 (edited by R. Marcus, pp. 60, 247; the *T. 12 Patr.* contains too many Christian glosses to be used here.) The absence of the noun in the secular literature (Josephus, Epictetus, Musonius, Julius Pollux, etc.) is notable (its first use would be a late scholium on Thucydides 1.51.5, glossing ἀρετῆς: φιλανθρωπίας καὶ ἀγάπης; cf. A. Deissmann, *Bible Studies,* 2d ed., Edinburgh, 1909, p. 200), as is its abundant usage in Christian language (cf. the papyri cited by N. Naldini, *Cristianesimo in Egitto,* pp. 16ff., 128, 130, 133, 140, 151, 154, 162, 174, 182, 189, 192, 196, 199, 210, 213, 220, 223, 226, 238, 278, 324, 331, 340, 362, 365). The magical papyrus from the end of the third century AD (Codex Paris 2316, fol. 436 r), edited by R. Reitzenstein (*Poimandrès,* 1904, pp. 297ff.) is probably of Christian origin: Γαβριὲλ ἐπὶ τῆς χαρᾶς . . . Ἀφαμαὴλ ἐπὶ τῆς ἀγάπης . . . οὗτοι εἰσιν οἱ ἄγγελοι οἱ προηγούμενοι ἐνώπιον τοῦ Θεοῦ (cf. A. Ceresa-Gastaldo, in *Aeg,* 1951, pp. 291–292). But the scholium on the *Tetrabiblos* of Ptolemaeus, where ἀγάπη expresses the mutual love of a man and a woman, and which I cited in my *Prolégomènes,* p. 32, n. 5, is by the Arab astrologer Abou Mas' aschar Apomasar (d. 885) whose work was translated into Greek in the eleventh century (cf. Charles E. Ruelle, "Deux identifications," in *Comptes rendus de l'Académie des Inscriptions et Belles Lettres,* Paris, 1910, pp. 32–39).

[36] Edited by H. Diels, W. Schubart, *Berliner Klassikertexte,* 2, Berlin, 1905, p. 55. It is no longer possible to refer to the document itself, because Professor P. Moraux tells us that *P.Berlin* 9869 disappeared in the turmoil of 1945, and officially no one knows where it is. Both he and M. Vogliano, having examined it several times, cast no doubt on Schubart's reading, but they cannot specify whether ΑΓΑΠΗΣ is the genitive singular of the noun or something like the first part of a verbal form whose end was obliterated (letter from Berlin dated 13 January 1952).

[37] Because of the -γμα that begins the following line, the editors restore "ἀγάπης [πρᾶ]γμα?"; cf. the analogy with *P.Erl.* 88, 13–14: μάλιστα . . . ἄμα, whose composition on the *Logos* seems close to this one.

[38] Professor Hombert of the Queen Elizabeth Egyptological Foundation of Brussels writes to me: "The Berlin papyrus is an extremely doubtful witness to the use of ἀγάπη in the second century BC, and ἀγάπησις seems to me to be just as possible" (letter dated 19 November 1951). This is also the opinion of A. Ceresa-Gastaldo in *Aeg,*

forms seem all the more likely since this is a philosophical dialogue, and Aristotle frequently uses *mallon* or *malista agapaō*.[39] Moreover, the date of this papyrus is unknown, and no positive data concerning its date are given.[40]

To this text, which is doubtful, to say the least, E. Stauffer[41] adds *P.Paris* 49, 3, dated by its editor W. Brunet de Presle to 164–58 BC.[42] But this citation should be challenged, because after F. Blass aired his doubts on this reading,[43] A. Deissmann consulted M. Pierret, conservator of Egyptian antiquities at the Louvre. The latter, after examining the papyrus, concluded, "One finds in papyrus no. 49 not a trace of the word *agapē*, but only on line 6 something that looks like it reads *tarachēn*."[44] On the authority of U. Wilcken, I shall adopt this reading: *dia te t[on] Sarapin kai tēn sēn eleuthe[ria]n kai pepeiramai*.[45]

The other texts brought forward are either suspect or of unverifiable date, and E. Peterson has shown that none of then are admissible.[46] An inscription from Tefeny in Pisidia, from the time of the empire, though the

---

1951, p. 293, who points out the oddity of the insertion from the popular Koine in a text of philosophical character.

[39] Cf. *GVI*, n. 1436: ἔπινον πίστεος, εὐνοίης, ἀρετῆς; ἀγάπης τε μάλιστα (funerary inscription of Padua from the second or third century); cf. 2090; Drimachos: ἐγώ σε πάντων ἀνθρώπων ἠγάπησα μάλιστα (*F.Gr.H.*, pp. 671, 10).

[40] The editors say that it is from the ptolemaic era, around the second century BC. It should be noted that F. Preisigke (*Wörterbuch*) and the supplement of E. Kiessling (1944) do not cite any usage of ἀγάπη in the papyri before the third century AD. Finally, cf. *P.Oxy.* 3004, 4: δίκαιον εὐθύς ἐστιν ἀγαπᾶν μητέρα (first century).

[41] E. Stauffer, ἀγάπη, in *TDNT*, vol. 1, p. 38, n. 87. The citation is probably borrowed from A. Deissmann (*Bible Studies*, p. 198 or from T. Nägeli (*Wortschatz*, pp. 38, 60).

[42] Letter from a certain Dionysius (commander at Memphis?) to Ptolemy, son of Slaucias; cf. W. Brunet de Presle (*Notices et extraits des manuscrits grecs de la bibliothèque impériale*, Paris, 1865, vol. 18, 2, p. 319) who read the text as follows: διά τε τὴν ἀγά[π]ην καὶ τὴν σὴν ἐλευθερίαν καταπεπείραμαι.

[43] A. Deissmann's summary of the work in *TLZ*, 1895, p. 488.

[44] Cited by A. Deissmann in his *Neue Bibelstudien* (pp. 26ff.) and the English translation *Bible Studies* by A. Grieve (Edinburgh, 1901, pp. 198–199). It is only more surprising to see the initial error taken up again (cf. again J. S. Banks, in *ExpT*, vol. 9, 1898, p. 501), because it was denounced by W. M. Ramsay (ibid., pp. 567–568) as by E. Buonaiuti, "I vocaboli d'amore nel N. T.," in *Rivista Storico-critica delle scienze teologische*, 1909, pp. 261–262; E. Jacquier, in *RB* 1915, p. 262; F. Prat, *La Théologie de saint Paul*, 2d ed., Paris, 1923, vol. 2, p. 562; E. B. Allo, *Première Epître aux Corinthiens*, p. 206.

[45] U. Wilcken edited *P.Paris* 49, which he believes to be earlier than 160, as number 62 in his *UPZ* I, p. 308.

[46] Article Ἀγάπη, in *BZ*, 1932, pp. 378–382. E. Peterson analyzes all the references supplied by W. Crönert, in F. Passow, *Wörterbuch der griechischen Sprache*, 2d ed., 1912, p. 25, and H. Lietzmann, *An die Korinther*, 3d ed., Tübingen, 1931, p. 68.

date can be narrowed down no further, reads: *penpsei d' eis aga[pē]n se philommeidēs Apphodeitē*,[47] but A. Deissmann has proved that the word must be restored *aga[tho]n*, not *agapēn*.[48] In *Lib.* 13a.3, Philodemus of Gadara (first century BC) wrote *philēsei kai di' a[g]apēs*;[49] but W. Crönert, who had not cited the text without caution in his new edition of F. Passow's *Wörterbuch der griechischen Sprache* (2d ed., 1912), finally rejects it[50] in adopting the reading *di' agapēseōs*.[51]

P.Oxy. XI, 1380, from the beginning of the second century AD, preserves a list of cultic names attributed in different places to the goddess Isis Polyōnymos. In the Egyptian villae of Thonis, she was invoked: *e]n Thōni agap[ēn . . .]ō*.[52] E. Peterson finds the conjecture unconvincing and reads *agap]ētēn*. At line 109, the first editors, Grenfell-Hunt (1915) read A[...]THN AΘ-OΛON = *en Italia agapēn theōn*.[53] But G. de Manteuffel, in making a more attentive collation of this papyrus, which is conserved at the Bod-

---

[47] *Papers of the American School of Classical Studies at Athens*, Boston, 1888, vol. 2, pp. 88, 87–88; again read in the same fashion by W.H.P. Hatch ("Some Illustrations of New Testament Usage from Greek Inscriptions of Asia Minor," in *JBL*, 1980, pp. 134–136), who underlines its pagan origin—Aphrodite is given her Homeric epithet.

[48] A. Deissmann, *Light*, p. 75, n. 3. He relies on the dissertation of F. Heinevetter, *Würfel- und Buchstabenorakel in Griechenland und Kleinasien*, Breslau, 1912, pp. 10 and 25.

[49] *P.Herc.* 1471, edited by A. Oliviere, Leipzig, 1914. Reading accepted by C. Jan Vooys, *Lexicon Philodemeum*, Purmerend, 1934, p. 2. Compare God's words to Abraham: τὸν ἠγαπημένον μου φίλον (*T. Abr.* A 1).

[50] Recension of the *Stoicorum Veterum Fragmenta*, vol. 4, of J. von Arnim, in *Gnomon*, 1930, p. 148. W. C. concludes his note 2: "Thus for the present ἀγάπη remains a Judeo-Christian word, commonly used in the language of the Byzantine epoch, as Preisigke has shown"; cf. *SB* 8705, 3.

[51] The reading that A. Ceresa-Gastaldo also reckons as the most probably, in *Aeg*, 1951, p. 297.

[52] Lines 27–28 (cf. G. Lafaye, "Litanie grecque d'Isis," in *RevPhil*, 1916, pp. 55ff.; F. Cumont, *Isis latina*, ibid., pp. 133–134; A. Ceresa-Gastaldo, loc. cit., pp. 293–294). At line 94 one sees ἐν Δώροις φιλίαν and at line 137 the appellation μισεχθής. Cf. the proscenium from the imperial period: ὃν ἀγαπᾷ ἡ Φαρία ᾿Ισις (*SB* 8542, 7). Reitzenstein (*Nachr. Götting. Gesell. d. Wiss.*, 1917, pp. 130ff.) compares *CIG*, vol. 12, 5, 217: ἐγὼ (Isis) γυναῖκα καὶ ἄνδρα συνήγαγα. . . ἐγὼ στέργεσθαι γυναῖκας ὑπ' ἀνδρῶν ἠνάγκασα. One might compare the hymns to Mandoulis: "the holy Talmis whom Mandoulis the sun loves, ὁ ἥλιος Μανδοῦλις ἀγαπᾷ" (E. Bernand, *Inscriptions métriques*, n. 166, 20; cf. 167, 1: "Mandoulis beloved of Athena, ᾿Αθηνᾶς ἀγάπημα"); cf. the invocation to the divinity: ῎Αδων ἀγαπατέ (Theocritus 15.149), ὦ Πὰν φίλε (ibid. 7.106), φίλα Σελάνα (ibid. 2.142); A. Bernand, *El-Kanaïs*, Leiden, 1972, n. viii, 9, 11.

[53] C. H. Roberts (in *JEA*, 1953, pp. 114) and R. E. Witt ("The Use of ΑΓΑΠΗ in *P.Oxy.* 1380: A Reply," in *JTS*, 1968, pp. 209–211) hold out for the originality of this reading.

leian, observed: "The epithet *agapē theōn* is very curious. The word *theōn* does not exist in the manuscript. τ instead of θ is a frequent enough mistake in the papyri. The greatest difficulty is in the division of the word *atholos*, but perhaps it can be explained in terms of the continuous script."[54] So the proper restoration is: *en Italia a[ga]thēn atholon.*[55]

We must therefore conclude that the term *agapē*, derived from *agapaō* (and not from *agapēsis*) is proper to the Koine. If the LXX gave the word its theological density, it also existed in the pagan language, but it is not attested before the first century AD.[56] It is nevertheless worth noting the names formed on this root, such as in the second century BC *Agapēnōr,* a name similar to that of the founder of the city of Paphos,[57] *Agapōmenos* at Lindos,[58] A*gapis* son of Annianos Neuthēnos, near the city

---

[54] G. de Manteuffel, "Quelques notes sur le Pap. Oxy. XI, 1380," in *RevPhil*, 1928, p. 163, n. 10.

[55] E. Peterson holds that this reading is convincing. It is retained with good reason by Miss St. West ("An Alleged Pagan Use of ΑΓΑΠΗ in *P.Oxy.* 1380," in *JTS*, 1967, pp. 142–143; idem, "A Further Note on ΑΓΑΠΗ in *P.Oxy.* 1380," *JTS*, 1969, pp. 228–230). Line 95, after all, has ἐν Στράτωνος Πύργῳ Ἑλλάδα ἀγαθήν (which corresponds to the *Bona Dea* of the Latins, cf. Plutarch, *Caes.* 9.2; *Cic.* 19.2). In an analogous fashion, in Titus 2:10 the miniscule 33 reads ἀγάπην for ἀγαθήν; in a Latin-Greek glossary, ἀπάτη is mistaken for ἀγάπη (cf. L. Robert, *Hellenica*, vol. 11, Paris, 1960, pp. 5–14) etc.

[56] Cf. D. J. Georgacas, "A Contribution to Greek Word History, Derivation and Etymology," in *Glotta*, 1957, pp. 105–106. The formula ἀγαπητὸς ἀδελφός (*P.Herm.* 4, 1; *SB* 9746, 1; *P.Abinn.* 6, 1 = *P.Lond.* 413) did not appear as a specifically Christian salutation formula (*P.Oxy.* 1870, 1; cf. B. R. Ress, in *Classical Review*, vol. 14, 1964, p. 102; but cf. *ChrEg*, 1969, p. 161), just as ἠγαπημένος ὑπὸ Φθᾶ (Dittenberger, *Or.* 90, 4 and 15) and the proper name Ἀγαπητός (*MAMA*, vol. 6, 339); σοφία Ἀγαπητοῦ (*IG*, vol. 3, 2199, cited by L. Vidmann, *Sylloge Inscriptionum Religionis Isiacae et Sarapiacae*, Berlin, 1969, n. 13 = first century AD, at Athens), but it was used by Christians: Ἐγὼ εἰμι ἁμαρτωλὸς Ἀγαπητός (*SB* 7496, 2; *P.Flor.* 300, 6; *P.Oxy.* 1919, 12: τῷ λαμπροτάτῳ Ἀγαπητῷ; cf. 2785, 1, 14: ἀγαπητὲ ἐν Κυρίῳ; cf. J. O'Callaghan, "Epitetos de trato en la correspondencia cristiana del siglo VI," in *SPap*, 1964, pp. 80ff.). It is known that this was one of the designations of the ascetics, tracing back by way of the LXX to the Hebrew *yaḥid* (cf. A. Guillaumont, "Le Nom des Agapètes," in *VC*, 1969, pp. 30–37), and that *Agapē* became a title of ecclesiastical dignity (L. Dineen, *Titles of Address in Christian Greek Epistolography*, Washington, 1929, pp. 15–20). In the first century AD neither ἀγαπητός nor ἠγαπημένοι has the intensive nuance that they acquire in the fourth century (*Vulg. dilectissimus, carissimus*). An expression like τὸ ἠγαπημένον τῶν τέκνων (Eusebius, *Praep. Evang.* 4.16.11) can only be late.

[57] *Suppl. IG*, vol. 9, 732, 3. Cf. Ἀγαπάνουρ (*SEG*, vol. 25, 664, 56; Thessaly, third century AD) and Φιλάνωρ (M. Landfester, "*Philos*," pp. 132, 136).

[58] S. Charitôniadou, ΑΙ ΕΠΙΓΡΑΦΑΙ ΤΗΣ ΛΕΣΒΟΥ, Athens, 1968, n. 102; cf. N. A. Bees, *Corpus der griech. Inschriften von Hellas*, Athens, 1941, n. 15.

ἀγάπη, *agapē* 19

of Carthage,[59] and *Agapios*.[60] Among women, we note *Agapēma*[61] and of course *Agapē*, which is common but which seems to have been used especially among the higher social classes, as in the second century AD in Phrygia: *hē kratistē Domna Agapē*.[62]

It is important to bring up to date H. Riesenfeld's excellent bibliography on *agapē*[63] and to complete the one that I myself began almost twenty years ago:[64]

A. H. Armstrong, "Platonic 'Eros' and Christian Agape," in *The Downside Review*, 1961, pp. 105–121; T. Barrosse, "The Relationship of Love to Faith in St. John," in *TS*, 1957, pp. 538–559; idem, "Christianity: Mystery of Love," in *CBQ*, 1958, pp. 137–172; idem, *Christianity: Mystery of Love*, Notre Dame, Indiana, 1964; D. Barsotti, *La Révélation de l'amour*, Paris, 1957; J. B. Bauer, " '. . . ΤΟΙΣ ΑΓΑΠΩΣΙΝ ΤΟΝ ΘΕΟΝ,' Röm. VIII, 28 (I Cor. II, 9; I Cor. VIII, 3)," in *ZNW*, 1959, pp. 106–112; K. Berger, *Die Gesetzesauslegung Jesu*, Neukirchen, 1972, pp. 56–257; M. Black, "The Interpretation of Romans VIII, 28," in *Freundesgabe O. Cullmann*, Leiden, 1962, pp. 166–172; G. Bornkamm, "Das Doppelgebot der Liebe," in *Gesammelte Aufsätze*, vol. 3, Munich, 1968, pp. 37–45; J. W. Bowman, "The Three Imperishables," in *Int*, 1959, pp. 433–443; P. I. Bratsiôtis, "Τὸ νόημα τῆς χριστιανικῆς ἀγάπης," in *Epistemonikè Epeteris t. Theol. Scholès*, Athens, 1955, pp. 1–3; C. Burchard,

---

[59] *SEG*, vol. 18, 775, 10.

[60] *P.Ross.Georg.* V, 59, 1 (fourth century AD). Of the same date, a tomb inscription of Tarsus, cf. H. Goldman, *Excavations at Gözlü Kule, Tarsus*, Princeton, 1950, vol. 1, p. 385, n. ix, 4. Eusebius tells of the martyrdom of "Agapios and Thecla, our contemporary" (*Mart. Palest.* 3.1 and 4; 6.3).

[61] N. Firatle, L. Robert, *Stèles funéraires*, p. 150. *CIRB*, Moscow-Leningrad, 1965, n. 337, 2–3: Ἀγάπημα γυνὴ Θεοφιλίσκου; F. Bechtel, *Die attischen Frauennamen*, Göttingen, 1902.

[62] *SEG*, vol. 6, 91 (B. Lavagnini, in *Aeg*, 1925, p. 339 reads otherwise). On a first-century stele of Alyzia in Acarnania this was added in the fourth century: καὶ ὑπὲρ μνήμης τῆς γυναικὸς αὐτοῦ Ἀγάπης (*IG*, vol. 9, 2, n. 446 b). According to Sulpicius Severus (*Chronicles* 2.46), the origin of the Priscillian heresy was the preaching of an Egyptian of Memphis named Marcus, who had as a student a certain Agape: *non ignobilis mulier* (likewise St. Jerome, *Epist.* 133). But *Caritas* is rare as a proper name (cf. the references given by H. I. Marrou, "Dame Sagesse et ses trois filles," in *Mélanges . . . Christ. Morhmann*, Utrecht-Anvers, 1963, pp. 181–183).

[63] "Etude bibliographique sur la notion biblique d'ΑΓΑΠΗ, surtout dans I Cor. 13," in *ConNT*, vol. 5, Leipzig-Uppsala, 1941, pp. 1–27; idem, "Note bibliographique sur I Cor. XIII," in *Nuntius*, vol. 6, Uppsala, 1952, col. 47–48; cf. BAGD, pp. 5–6. This translation of the fourth edition of the *Wörterbuch zum Neuen Testament* (Berlin, 1952) of W. Bauer could not take into account the clarification accomplished by G. Zuntz in his report in *Gnomon*, 1958, p. 23.

[64] C. Spicq, *Agapè*, vol. 1, pp. 317–324; as in that work, I shall here alphabetize according to the names of the authors.

"Das doppelte Leibesgebot in der frühen Überlieferung," in *Festschrift J. Jeremias*, Göttingen, 1970, pp. 39–62; J. Chmiel, *Lumière et charité d'après la première Epître de saint Jean*, Rome, 1971; S. Cipriani, "Dio è amore. La dottrina della carità in san Giovanni," in *La Scuola cattolica*, 1966, pp. 214–231; A. Colunga, "El amor y la misericordia hacia el prójimo," in *Teologia Espiritual*, 1959, pp. 445–462; J. Coppens, "La Doctrine biblique sur l'amour de Dieu et du prochain," in *ETL*, 1964, pp. 252–299; idem, "*Agapè et Agapan* dans les lettres johanniques," *ETL*, 1969, pp. 125–127; K.R.J. Cripps, "'Love Your Neighbor as Yourself' (Mt. XXII, 39)," in *ExpT*, vol. 76, 1964, p. 26; J. Deák, *Die Gottesliebe in den alten semitischen Religionen*, Eperjes, 1914; A. Dihle, *Die goldene Regal*, Göttingen, 1962; J. Egermann, *La charité dans la Bible*, Mulhouse, 1963 (popularization); F. Dreyfus, "'Maintenant, la foi, l'espérance et la charité demeurent toutes les trois' (I Cor. XIII, 13)," in *Studiorum Paulinorum Congressus*, Rome, 1963, pp. 403–412; E. Evans, "The Verb ΑΓΑΠΑΝ in the Fourth Gospel," in F. L. Cross, *Studies in the Fourth Gospel*, London, 1957, pp. 64–71; A. Feuillet, *Le Mystère de l'amour divin dans la théologie johannique*, Paris, 1972; E. Fischer, *Amor und Eros. Eine Untersuchung des Wortfeldes "Liebe" im Lateinischen und Griechischen*, Hildesheim, 1973; A. Fitzgerald, "Hebrew *yd* = 'Love' and 'Beloved,'" in *CBQ*, 1967, pp. 368–374; P. Foresi, *L'agape in S. Paolo e la carità in S. Tommaso d'Aquino*, Rome, 1965; G. Friedrich, *Was heißt das: Liebe?*, Stuttgart, 1972; R. H. Fuller, "Das Doppelgebot der Liebe," in G. Strecker, *Jesus Christus in Historie und Theologie* (Festschrift H. Conzelmann), Tübingen, 1975, pp. 317–329; V. P. Furnish, *The Love Command in the New Testament*, London, 1973; B. Gerhardsson, "I. Cor. 13. Om Paulus och hans rabbinska bakgrund," in *SEÅ*, vol. 39, 1974, pp. 121–144; G. Gilleman, "Charité théologale et vie morale," in *Lumen Vitae*, vol. 16, 1961, pp. 9–27; W. Grundmann, "Das Doppelgebot der Liebe," in *Die Zeichen der Zeit*, vol. 11, 1957, pp. 449–455; A. Guillaumont, "Le Nom des agapètes," in *VC*, 1969, pp. 30–37; A. J. Hultgren, "The Double Commandment of Love in Mt. XXII, 34–40: The Sources of Compositions," in *CBQ*, 1974, pp. 373–378; J.-P. Hyatt, "The God of Love in the O.T.," in *To Do and To Teach: Essays in Honor of C. L. Pyatt*, Lexington, 1953, pp. 15–26; J. Jeffrey, "The Love of God in Christ—Romans VIII, 38–39," in *ExpT*, vol. 69, 1958, pp. 359–361; R. Joly, *Le vocabulaire chrétien de l'amour est-il original?* Φιλεῖν et Ἀγαπᾶν, Brussels, 1968; J. Kahmann, *Die Offenbarung der Liebe Gottes im Alten Testament*, Witten, 1959; R. E. Ker, "Fear or Love?," in *ExpT*, vol. 72, 1961, pp. 195–196; R. Kieffer, *Le primat de l'amour: Commentaire épistémologique de I Corinthiens 13*, Paris, 1975; W. Klassen, "Love Your Enemy: A Study of N.T. Teaching on Coping with an Enemy," in *Mennonite Quarterly Review*, 1963, pp. 147–171; M. J. Lagrange, *La Morale de l'Evangile*, Paris, 1931 (the last chapter); idem, "L'Amour de Dieu, loi suprême de la morale de l'Evangile," in *VSpir, Supplé-*

ment, vol. 26, 1931, pp. 1–16; M. Landfester, *"Philos"*; M. Lattke, *Einheit im Wort: Die spezifische Bedeutung von "agapē," "agapan" und "filein" im Johannes-Evangelium*, Munich, 1975; M. M. Laurent, *Réalisme et richesse de l'amour chrétien: Essai sur Eros et Agapè*, Issy-les-Moulineaux, 1962; N. Lazure, *Les Valeurs morales de la théologie johannique*, Paris, 1965, pp. 207–250; E. H. van Leeuwen, "Ἀγαπητοί," in *Theologische Studien*, 1903, pp. 139–151; S. Légasse, "L'étendue de l'amour interhumain d'après le Nouveau Testament: Limites et promesses," in *RTL*, 1977, pp. 137–159; O. Linton, "S. Matthew V, 43," in *ST*, 1964, pp. 66–79; D. Muñoz Lion, "La Nouveauté du commandement de l'amour dans les écrits de S. Jean," in *La etica biblica* (vol. 29, Semana biblica española), Madrid, 1969, pp. 193–231; N. M. Loss, "Amore d'amicizia nel Nuovo Testamento," in *Salesianum*, 1977, pp. 3–55; J. B. Lotz, *Die Stufen der Liebe: Eros, Philia, Agapè*, Frankfurt, 1971; D. Lührmann, "Liebet eure Feinde (Lk. VI, 27–36; Mt. V, 39–48)," in *ZTK*, 1972, pp. 412–438; S. Lyonnet, *La carità pienezza della lege, secondo san Paulo*, 2d ed., Rome, 1971; F. Maas, "Die Selbstliebe nach Leviticus XIX, 18," in *Festschrift F. Baumgärtel*, Erlangen, 1959, pp. 109–113; D. J. McCarthy, "Notes on the Love of God in Deuteronomy," in *CBQ*, 1965, pp. 144–147; T. W. Manson, *On Paul and John*, London, 1963, pp. 104–127; H. Montefiore, "Thou Shalt Love Thy Neighbour as Thyself," in *NovT*, 1962, pp. 157–170; W. L. Moran, "The Ancient Near Eastern Background of the Love of God in Deuteronomy," in *CBQ*, 1963, pp. 77–87; J. Moss, "I Cor. XIII, 13," in *ExpT*, vol. 73, 1962, p. 253; D. Müller, "Das frühchristliche Verständnis der Liebe," in *Festschrift A. Alt*, Leipzig, 1953–1954, vol. 3, pp. 131–137; P. L. Naumann, "The Presence of Love in John's Gospel," in *Worship*, 1965, pp. 363–371; K. Niederwimmer, "Erkennen und Lieben: Gedanken zum Verhältnis von Gnosis und Agape im ersten Korintherbrief," in *KD*, 1965, pp. 75–102; A. Nissen, *Gott und der Nächste im antiken Judentum*, Tübingen, 1974; M. Oesterreicher, *The Bridge: A Yearbook of Judaeo-Christian Studies IV*, New York, 1962; C. Oggioni, *La dottrina della carità nel IV Vangelo e nella I^a Lettera di Giovanni*, Milan, 1953; G. Outha, *Agapè: An Ethical Analysis*, New Haven–London, 1972; A. Penna, *Amore nella Biblia*, Brescia, 1972; C. Perini, "Amicizia e carità fraterna nella vita della Chiesa," in *DivThom*, 1970, pp. 369–407; G. Quispel, "Love Thy Brother," in *Ancient Society*, Louvain, vol. 1, pp. 83–93; L. Ramlot, "Le Nouveau Commandement de la nouvelle alliance ou Alliance et commandement," in *Lumière et vie*, vol. 44, 1959, pp. 9–36; J. W. Rausch, *Agape and Amicitia: A Comparison Between St. Paul and St. Thomas*, Rome, 1958; C. C. Richardson, "Love: Greek and Christian," in *JR*, 1943, pp. 173–185; K. Romaniuk, *L'Amour du Père et du Fils dans la sotériologie de saint Paul*, Rome, 1961; G. Rotureau, *Amour de Dieu: Amour des hommes*, Tournai, 1958 (popularization); G. Schille, "Die Liebe Gottes in Christus: Beobachtungen zu Rm. VIII, 31–39," in *ZNW*, 1968, pp. 230–244; H. Schlier, *Die Zeit der Kirche*, Freiburg, 1956, pp. 186–193; idem, "Die Bruderliebe nach dem Evangelium und den Briefen des Johannes," in *Mélanges Rigaux*, pp. 235–245; G. Schneider, "Die Neuheit der christlichen Nächstenliebe," in *TTZ*, 1973, pp. 257–275; O.J.F. Seitz, "Love Your Enemies," in *NTS*, vol. 16, 1969, pp. 39–54; W. W. Sikes, "A Note on Agapē in Johannine Literature," in *Shane Quart.*, vol. 16, 1955, pp. 139–143; B. Snell, H. J. Mette, *Lexikon*, col. 45–46 (with the report of B. Marzullo, in *Philologus*, 1957, p. 205); M. Spanneut, "L'Amour, de l'hellénisme au christianisme," in *Mélanges de science religieuse*, 1964, pp. 5–19; C. Spicq, "Le Verbe ἀγαπάω et ses dérivés dans le grec classique," in *RB*, 1953, pp. 372–397; idem, "Die Liebe als Gestaltungsprinzip der Moral in den synoptischen Evangelien," in *Freiburger Zeitschrift für Philosophie und Theologie*, 1954, pp. 394–410; idem, "Le Lexique de l'amour dans les papyrus et dans quelques inscriptions de l'époque hellénistique," in *Mnemosyne*, 1955, pp. 25–33; idem, "Notes d'exégèse johannique: la charité est amour manifeste," in *RB*, 1958, pp. 358–370; idem, *Agapè*; idem, "La Justification du charitable (I Jo. III, 19–21)," in *Studia Biblica et Orientalia*, Rome, 1959, vol. 2, pp. 347–359; idem, "Les Composantes de la notion d'agapè dans le Nouveau Testament," in *Sacra Pagina*, Paris-Gembloux, 1959, vol. 2, pp. 440–455; idem, *Charité et liberté*; idem, *Théologie morale*, vol. 2, pp. 481–566; D. M. Stanley, " 'God So Loved the World,' " in *Worship*, 1957, pp. 16–23; K. Stendahl, "Hate, Non-retaliation, and Love," in *HTR*, 1962, pp. 343–355; J. B. Stern, "Jesus' Citation of Dt. VI, 5 and Lv. XIX, 18 in the Light of Jewish Tradition," in *CBQ*, 1966, pp. 312–316; T. Stramare, "La carità secondo S. Giovanni," in *Tabor*, 1965, pp. 47–58; D. W. Thomas, "The Root אהב 'Love' in Hebrew," in *ZAW*, 1939, pp. 57–64; G. Torralba, "La Caridad en S. Pablo," in *EstBib*, 1965, pp. 295–318; J. G. Trapiello, "El amor de Dios en los escritos de S. Juan," in *Verdad y vida*, 1963, pp. 257–279; W. C. van Unnik, "Die Motivierung der Feindesliebe in Lukas, VI, 32–35," in *Sparsa Collecta*, Leiden, 1973, vol. 1, pp. 111–128; F. Urtiz de Urtaran, "Esperanza y caridad en el N. T.," in *Scriptorium Victorense* (Vitoria), 1954, vol. 1, pp. 1–50; A. G. Vella, "Agapē in I Corinthians XIII," in *Melita Theologica*, vol. 18, 1966, pp. 22–31, 57–66; vol. 19, 1967, pp. 44–54; R. Völkl, *Die Selbstliebe in der heiligen Schrift und bei Thomas von Aquin*, Munich, 1956; idem, *Botschaft und Gebot der Liebe nach der Bibel*, Freiburg, 1964; V. Warnach, "Liebe," in J. B. Bauer, *Bibeltheologisches Wörterbuch*, Grass-Vienna, 1959, pp. 502–542; C. Wiéner, *Recherches sur l'amour pour Dieu dans l'Ancien Testament: Etude d'une racine*, Paris, 1957; S. K. Wuest, "Four Greek Words for Love," in *BibSac*, 1959, pp. 241–248.

ἀγγαρεύω

angareuō, **to requisition**

This verb of oriental, probably Iranian, origin[1] comes from *angaros*, which in Persian refers to the post riders who carried royal dispatches from relay post to relay post.[2] As this official delivery service involved requiring people to provide services and enlisting people as well as provisions, draft animals, or lodging, it came to mean "to requisition" and in general to make someone do something against his will. This explains its pejorative flavor from Menander[3] to modern times,[4] and well attested in the NT: the soldiers requisition Simon of Cyrene to carry the cross of Jesus.[5]

---

[1] A. Deissmann, *Bible Studies*, 2d ed., Edinburgh, 1909, pp. 86, 182; W. Barclay, *NT Wordbook*, pp. 15ff.; P. Chantraine, *Dictionnaire étymologique*, p. 8. F. Tailliez is inclined toward Akkadian ("Βασιλικὴ ὁδός," in *Miscellanea G. de Jarphanion*, Rome, 1947, pp. 346–348). It is also written ἐγγαρεύω, cf. BDF §42, 2.

[2] Hence ἀγγαρήιον, the royal postal service; cf. Herodotus 8.98 [here presented in the English of Aubrey de Selincourt—Tr.]: "Xerxes dispatched a courier to Persia with the news of his defeat. There is nothing in the world which travels faster than these Persian couriers. The whole idea is a Persian invention, and works like this: riders are stationed along the road, equal in number to the number of days the journey takes—a man and a horse for each day. Nothing stops these couriers from covering their allotted stage in the quickest possible time—neither snow, rain, heat, nor darkness. The first, at the end of his stage, passes the dispatch to the second, the second to the third, and so on along the line, as in the Greek torch-race which is held in honour of Hephaestus. The Persian word for this form of post is angarium." Cf. Xenophon, *Cyr.* 8.6–7; Aeschylus, *Ag.* 282; "like couriers of fire—ἀπ' ἀγγάρου πυρός—each light in turn hurried its signal toward us." At the beginning of the third century AD, this term again designated the *cursus publicus* (Dittenberger, *Syl.* 880, 54); cf. U. Wilcken, *Grundzüge*, Leipzig-Berlin, 1912, vol. 1, pp. 372–376; H. J. Mason, *Greek Terms*, p. 19; D. B. Durham, *Vocabulary of Menander*, p. 37; the note of A. J. Festugière on Artemidorus Daldianus, *La Clef des Songes* 5.16 (Paris, 1975, p. 268).

[3] Menander, *Sik.*, frag. 440 (J. M. Edmonds, *Attic Comedy*, vol. 3 B, p. 726); cf. A. Blanchard, A. Bataille, "Fragments sur papyrus du ΣΙΚΥΩΝΙΟΣ de Ménandre," in *RechPap*, vol. 3, Paris, 1964, p. 155.

[4] In modern Greek, ἐγγαρεία means "drudgery" (A. Mirambel, *Dictionnaire français-grec moderne*, Paris, 1960, p. 102).

[5] Matt 28:32 (M. J. Lagrange, *Matthieu*, pp. 113–114); Mark 15:21 (M. J. Lagrange, *Marc*, p. 425).

---

angareuō, S 29; *EDNT* 1.12; MM 2–3; L&N 37.34; BDF §§6, 42(2), 392(1e); BAGD 6; ND 2.77

The Egyptian papyri give examples of the many requisitions that were made for pack animals and drivers, farm animals, wheat and the barges that carried it, work, and provisions.[6] Normally, it was by public authority that individuals were coerced,[7] but many requisitions were arbitrary or illegitimate. This accounts for the numerous claims of individuals who complained that they had been wronged,[8] and hence the numerous interventions of sovereigns and prefects from the second century BC onward forbidding royal officers and soldiers to make requisitions for their personal interests. In 118, a decree (*prostagma*) of King Euergetes II and Queens Cleopatra II and Cleopatra III ordered: "Generals and other functionaries do not have the right to require the inhabitants of the country to work for their private interests, nor to use their beasts for their own purposes . . . nor to make them supply geese, fowl, wine, or grain, whether for money as a bribe for the renewal of their appointment, nor in short to make them work for free on any pretext."[9]

---

[6] *P.Tebt.* 5, 248–251; 703–704; 750 etc. (cf. Cl Préaux, *Economie royale*, pp. 139–144, 344–347, 529). *P.Stras.* 93 is a requisition order.

[7] Cf. in 252 BC the requisition of a boat for the postal service: τοῦ ὑπάρχοντος λέμβου ἀγγαρευθέντος ὑπό σου . . . ἀγγαρεύσας τὸν Ἀντικλέους λάμβον (*P.Paris* 2, 20).

[8] *P.Cair.Zen.* 59467; 59509, 5: Somoelis, warden at Philadelphia, ἀγγαρεύων διὰ παντός, asks Zeno to intervene; *P.Mich.Zen.* 29; *P.Enteux.* 88; *P.Cair.Isid.* 72, 32; 123, 5 (editor's note); *BGU* 21, col. III, 16; *PSI* 1333, 15: μὴ ἀγγαρευθῶσι = *SB* 7993, 15.

[9] *P.Tebt.* 5, 178–187; cf. line 252 (with the correction of U. Wilcken, in *APF,* vol. 3, p. 325, adopted by M. T. Lenger, *C.Ord.Ptol.* 53; cf. 55 = *PSI* 1401, 9: προστετάχασι δὲ μηθένα ἀγγαρεύειν πλοῖα κατὰ μηδεμίαν παρεύρεσιν εἰς τὰς ἰδίας χρείας). On 17 August 163, in a series of amnesty proclamations, Ptolemy VI Philometor condemned private and unpaid requisitions of boats: "He decreed that no one should requisition boats for a personal move, προστέταχεν δὲ μηδένα ἀγγαρεύειν πλοῖα" (M. T. Lenger, *C.Ord.Ptol.*, n. 34, 5; *SB* 9316, col. II, 5; cf. L. Koenen, *Eine ptolemäische Königsurkunde* [*P.Kroll*], Wiesbaden, 1957). Before 150, Demetrius I Soter forbade anyone to requisition for his service animals belonging to Jews: κελεύω δὲ μηδὲ ἀγγαρεύεσθαι τὰ Ἰουδαίων ὑποζύγια (Josephus, *Ant.* 13.52). On 1 February AD 49, an edict of the prefect C. Vergilius Capito forbade his soldiers to make requisitions, at least without written authorization from him: μηδὲν λαμβάνειν μηδὲ ἀνγαρεύειν εἰ μή τινες ἐμὰ διπλώματα ἔχουσιν (Dittenberger, *Or.*, 665, 24–25; *SEG*, vol. 8, 794; *SB* 8248, 24). In the year 19, Germanicus ordered that for his παρουσία no boat or beast of transport should be requisitioned without an order, and then only upon delivery of a receipt (*SB* 3924; A. S. Hunt, C. C. Edgar, *Select Papyri*, London, 1934, n. 211; W. Ehrenberg, A. H. M. Jones, *Documents Illustrating the Reigns of Augustus and Tiberius*, Oxford, 1955, n. 320). The edict of L. Aemilius Rectus of 29 April 42, prohibits the exactions on pain of very severe sanctions and orders the soldiers to make no requisition without making payment: μηδενὶ ἐξέστω ἐνγαρεύειν τοὺς ἐπὶ τῆς χώρας . . . ἄτερ ἐμοῦ διπλώματος (*P.Lond.* III, 1171; *Chrest.Wilck.*, n. 439). An

These facts and the number of documents that exhibit them show how frequent and burdensome these *angareiai* were. They show precisely the significance of the precept of the Sermon of the Mount: "If anyone requisitions you for a mile, go with him two miles."[10]

The case is so classic that it had perhaps become a topic of popular philosophy and of diatribe. At any rate, Epictetus also takes it up; but he advises only to comply for fear of suffering greater evils: "If an unforeseen requisition arises and a soldier takes your young ass, let it go. Do not resist, do not murmur, lest you receive blows as well as lose the ass" (4.1.79). For the sake of love, our Lord says to acquiesce[11] just as he said to bless persecutors. This attitude of acceptance toward impudent and vexatious people becomes a major theme of New Testament ethics: one must overcome evil with good.[12] The paradox of going two miles when only one was demanded puts the emphasis on interior good will, on its promptness and sincerity—or rather on the authentic *agapē* that is manifested in deed and in truth (1 John 3:18), in the most costly fashion (John 15:13). According to the principle of John 3:21, "The one who does the truth comes to the light," it was because Simon of Cyrene freely accepted his *angareia* that he and his children received the grace of faith.

---

identical prohibition from about 133–137 by the prefect Petronius Mamertinus (*PSI* 446; *Sel.Pap.* 221).

[10] Matt. 5:41. "In our case, one may imagine a soldier or a police officer arrogating to himself, without official mandate, the right of requiring someone to transport or carry something, for example" (M. J. Lagrange, on this verse, p. 113). For references to the Talmudic literature, cf. P. Fiebig, "ἀγγαρεύω," in ZNW, 1918, pp. 64–72.

[11] "It goes without saying that the lesson still applies when the first person who happens along lays claim to our services on some more or less plausible pretext. Give way, like good, defenseless folk. St. Thomas Aquinas let himself be led off to the marketplace by a lay brother" (M. J. Lagrange, *Matthieu*, p. 114).

[12] Rom 12:21. Cf. 15:1–7; 1 Cor 6:7—"Why not rather suffer wrong? Why not rather let yourself be defrauded?"; 13:7—"love bears all things"; Gal 5:14–15; 6:2; 1 Pet 2:13, 19: "It is meritorious to endure pains inflicted unjustly in order to please God"; 3:9, 17; 4:14; 1 John 3:16, etc.

ἀγοράζω

agorazō, **to buy**

This utterly commonplace verb originally meant "to go to market," then "to buy, make purchases,"[1] the counterpart of "to sell."[2] The NT uses it to designate redemption, emphasizing that there has been a transfer of property (Rev 14:3–4) and noting that the price has been paid: "You are no longer your own, because you have been bought and paid for" (*ēgorasthēte gar timēs*, 1 Cor 6:20). This mention of payment is significant; for, in the Hellenistic era, the contract of sale is not completed by the mere exchange of agreements; the seller must have received the *timē*, at least the partial down payment that guarantees good faith and excludes the possibility of retraction.[3] Only the payment of the price accomplishes the

---

[1] Luke 14:18; John 13:29. This is one of the ways of coming into possession (1 Cor 7:30) and of getting rich (Rev 3:18).

[2] Πωλέω; Matt 21:12; Luke 17:28; Rev 13:17. Cf. M.-J. Bry, *Essai sur la vente dans les papyrus gréco-égyptiens*, Paris, 1909.

[3] *I.Cor.*, vol. 8, 3, n. 530 (= *SEG*, vol. 9, 154): Euplous has bought the tomb at Anastasios (ἀγοράσας παρά) for one and a half pieces of gold: I gave him the price (καὶ δοὺς τὰς τιμάς) and I received from him the property (καὶ λαβὼν ἐξουσίαν παρ' αὐτοῦ); *P.Oxy.* 2951, 25 and 31; Theophrastus: "The purchase has no obligatory force (κυρία), and likewise the sale, in the matter of acquisition, until the price has been given and the parties have observed the legal procedures" (in Stobaeus 4.2.20; ed. Wachsmuth, vol. 4, p. 129, 19ff.). "When the seller has given the *amphourion* (the tax) and received the price, he will no longer be permitted to bring an action against the purchaser" (*P.Hal.* 1, 253, p. 140). One must pay the price to become the owner; cf. C. Appleton, "A l'époque classique, le transfert de propriété de la chose vendue et livrée était-il subordonné, en règle, au paiement du prix?" in *RHDFE*, 1928, pp. 11–12; P. Meylan, "Le paiement du prix et transfert de propriété de la chose vendue en droit romain classique," in *Studi in onore di P. Bonfante*, Milan, 1930, pp. 441–491; idem, "L'Origine de la vente consensuelle," in *RHDFE*, 1931, pp. 787–788; idem, "Le rôle de la 'bona fides' dans le passage de la vente au comptant à la vente consensuelle à Rome," in *Festgabe A. Simonius*, Basel, 1955, pp. 247–257.

---

agorazō, S 59; *TDNT* 1.124–128; *EDNT* 1.23; *NIDNTT* 1.267–268; MM 6; L&N 37.131, 57.188; BDF §179(1); BAGD 12–13

ἀγοράζω, *agorazō* 27

purchase of the property; so much so that the seller maintains his right to the item until he has received payment for it. This is why so many contracts mention that the payment has in fact been made.[4] In accord with these usages, Rev 5:9 specifies that the purchase has been accomplished by the blood of Christ; 1 Pet 1:19 that the price of the ransom was the precious blood, and this—according to Eph 1:7—was the means of redemption (*apolytrōsis*).

2 Pet 2:1 stigmatizes the false prophets who deny the Master (*despotēs* is the normal term for the owner of a slave, cf. 1 Tim 6:1–2) who purchased them, and 1 Cor 7:23 comments: "You have been bought and paid for! Do not become slaves of humans." As a result, the purchase-redemption by Christ is a metaphor that evokes the freeing of slaves[5] who gained their liberty through a fictive sale to the divinity, notably to the Pythian Apollo of Delphi; the owner, accompanied by his slave, whom he is leading to the god, presents himself at the sanctuary; the priest remits to the master the agreed price, which has been paid to him beforehand either by the slave himself or by his friends. The act of emancipation was inscribed on the walls of the temple: the master has sold his slave (*apedoto*) so that he is free;

---

[4] Cf. R. Taubenschlag, *Opera Minora*, vol. 1, pp. 527ff. L. Mitteis, *Reichsrecht und Volksrecht*, Leipzig, 1891, pp. 71ff. C. Préaux, "La Preuve," in *Recueils de la Société J. Bodin*, Brussels, 1965, pp. 197, 200. P.Dura 26, 13–14, moreover, associates the receiving of the *timē* and the transfer of possession (*paradosis*; cf. *Jur.Pap.*, n. 37, 13–16). On this mode of the structuring of consensual sale, cf. J. Demeyere, "La Formation de la vente et le transfer de la propriété in droit grec classique," in *RIDA*, 1952, pp. 215–266; idem, "Le Contrat de vente en droit classique: Les Obligations des parties," ibid., 1953, pp. 216–228; L. Gernet, "Sur l'obligation contractuelle dans la vente hellénique," ibid., p. 229–247; idem, *Droit et société dans la Grèce ancienne*, Paris, 1955, pp. 201–236.

[5] For Epictetus, the person who is in servitude to his passions is a "great slave" (μεγαλοδούλος), much more in subjection that the slave of any owner (4.1.55; cf. A. Pelletier, "Les Passions à l'assaut de l'âme d'après Philon," in *REG*, 1965, pp. 52–60). St. Paul declares himself "sold to the service of sin" (Rom 7:14; cf. Dio Cassius 62.3: "How much better it would be to be sold once—ἅπαξ πεπρᾶσθαι—than to be free in name only and have to buy ourselves back every year"). The verb πιπράσκω has here the pejorative sense which it has in the LXX and which is its first meaning in the secular language: to transport prisoners and slaves for sale (Deut 28:68; Lev 25:39, 42; Jer 34:14; 2 Macc 5:14; Matt 18:25), like Joseph (Ps 105:17) or the elect people (Esth 7:4; cf. S. Lyonnet, "Péché dans le Nouveau Testament," in *DBSup*, vol. 7, 506, 524, 551). But ἀγοράζειν is the most specific verb for the purchase-sale of slaves as merchandise that one buys like clothing, grain, wine, or fish (*P.Mich.* 657, 5; cf. M. P. Hervagault, M. M. Mactoux, "Esclaves et société d'après Démosthène," in *Actes du Colloque 1972 sur l'esclavage*, Paris, 1974, p. 62). On the slave markets and their sales, *C.Ord.Ptol.* 22 and 25; *IGLS* 4028, 37–39; Josephus, *War* 3.541; Plutarch, *Cat.* 21.1: "Cato used to buy especially prisoners of war who were still small so that he could raise them, train them like puppies or colts"; *Pap.Lugd.Bat.* XIII, 23; C. Spicq, *Théologie morale*, vol. 2, pp. 834ff.

the god accepts the abandoned one, purchases him, and guarantees his protection.[6] Henceforth the emancipated one is known as "sacred, slave of the goddess, being the god's" (*hieros, doulētheas, tou theou ōn*)[7] considering himself as consecrated to the service of the deity. That which was only a legal fiction in paganism is precisely the truth in Christianity. "Those who are in Christ"[8] cannot revert to their former servitude. The one who has paid the price of their emancipation requires that they be faithful to his worship and his service.[9]

---

[6] Delphi, 165/4 BC, in J. Pouilloux, *Choix*, n. 42; cf. P. Foucart, *Mémoire sur l'affranchissement des esclaves*, Paris, 1867; *RIJG*, vol. 2, pp. 251ff.; G. Daux, *Delphes au IIe et au Ier siècle*, Paris, 1936, p. 46–69, 615ff. Idem, "Note sur l'intérêt historique des affranchissements de Delphes," in *Proceedings* IX, pp. 286–292; A. Kränzlein, "Zu den Freilassungsinschriften aus Delphi," dans *Mélanges V. Arangio-Ruiz*, Naples, 1964, vol. 2, pp. 820–827. —At Butrini in Epirus, twenty-nine acts of emancipation by consecration to Asclepius have been recovered (J. and L. Robert, "Bulletin épigraphique," in *REG*, 1967, p. 503, n. 336; cf. 1969, p. 425, n. 1). Two slaves were emancipated at the sanctuary of Phisto (second century BC; cf. *IG*, vol. 9, 1^2, 99; L. Robert, *Noms indigènes*, p. 32). An analogous consecration to Sarapis (C. Michel, *Recueil*, n. 1393; P. M. Fraser, "Two Studies on the Cult of Sarapis," in *Opuscula Atheniensia*, Lund, 1960, pp. 43ff.), to Artemis Gazoria (*SEG*, vol. 2, 396). The Jews emancipated their slaves in the synagogue (*CII*, Vatican City, 1936, vol. 1, n. 690; sometimes to pagan gods, n. 711–712), just as Christians carried out this manumission in the church (St. Augustine, *Serm.* 21.6; cf. F. Fabrini, *La manumission in ecclesia*, Milan, 1965), etc.

[7] *SEG*, vol. 14, 529, 4: ἐλεύτερον ἱερὸν τᾶς θεοῦ; cf. H. W. Pleket, *Rijksmuseum*, pp. 19ff.; L. Robert, *Hellenica*, vol. 6, Paris, 1948, pp. 9, 46, 49.

[8] Οἱ τοῦ Χριστοῦ (possessive genitive), 1 Cor 15:23; Gal 5:24; cf. "Ce que signifie le nom de Chrétien" in C. Spicq, *Théologie morale*, vol. 1, pp. 407ff.

[9] St. Paul twice uses the compound form ἐξαγοράζω for "redeem the time" (Eph 5:16; Col 4:5; cited in a Christian letter of the fourth century, *P.Lond.* 1927, 45; cf. H. I. Bell, *Jews and Christians in Egypt*, pp. 110ff.; the only occurrence in the papyri. On the meaning of this expression, cf. C. Spicq, *Théologie morale*, vol. 2, p. 511; B. Häring, "La Théologie morale et la sociologie pastorale dans la perspective de l'histoire du salut: La Notion biblique de 'kairos,' " in *ScEccl*, 1964, pp. 209–224) and twice in Gal 3:13—"Christ has redeemed us from the curse of the law" (cf. W. Elert, "Redemptio ab Hostibus," in *TLZ*, 1947, pp. 265–270; E. Pax, "Der Loskauf: Zur Geschichte eines neutestamentlichen Begriffes," in *Anton*, 1962, pp. 239–278; S. Lyonnet, L. Sabourin, *Sin, Redemption and Sacrifice*, Rome, 1970, pp. 104ff.). It is clear that the compound form ἐξαγ. has the same meaning as the simple verb ἀγ. and that it is understood to involve redemption ἐπ' ἐλευθερίᾳ (cf. Gal 5:1). S. Lyonnet, "L'Emploi paulinien de ἐξαγοράζειν au sens de 'redimere' est-il attesté dans la littérature grecque?" in *Bib*, 1961, pp. 85–89, shows that the references often made to Diodorus Siculus 36.2.2; Polybius 3.43.2; Plutarch, *Crass.* 2.5; Dicaearchus 1.22 have the sense of purchasing and not of redeeming. But he cites Diodorus Siculus 15.7, where Plato, who has been sold on the slave market, is "redeemed" by his friends who thus restore his liberty. Of course, there is no question of a prisoner, or of the paying of ransom, but it is indeed a matter of emancipation from servitude ἐπὶ λύσει.

ἀγωγή

agōgē, conduct

St. Paul praises Timothy for having followed him "in teaching, *conduct*, purpose, faith, patience . . ." (2 Tim 3:10). Clearly, the NT hapax *agōgē*, here used in a figurative sense, should be translated "conduct, manner of life."[1] It is sometimes used in a derogatory sense, for foul schemes,[2] but for the most part it expresses either the culture[3] or the conduct or manner of life peculiar to a given race or a given individual (Diodorus Siculus 5.26), such as Esther, who changed nothing of her ways (Esth 2:20), or the Jews who preferred their particular way of life,[4] or Herod entreating, "Let everyone

---

[1] BGU 1247, 14 (second century BC); letter of Antiochus II Soter to the Erythraeans, after 261 BC, φαίνεσθε γὰρ καθόλου ἀγωγῇ ταύτῃ χρῆσθαι (C. B. Welles, *Royal Correspondence*, n. 15, 15). The word can be transitive or intransitive, designating education per se or its result (Polybius 6.2.13: ἡ ἐκ παίδων ἀγωγή). The philosophical schools distinguished themselves by their *agōgē* (Diogenes Laertius 1.19); cf. "the disciplines that belong to Hellenic education" (Marcus Aurelius 1.6); the "organization" of the Roman army (Josephus, *War* 3.109). The one who leads—the instructor—is ὁ παιδαγωγός; the instruction, ἡ παιδαγωγία; see K. L. Schmidt on this word in *TDNT*, vol. 1, p. 128, where he cites the Περὶ παίδων ἀγωγῆς of Plutarch. Plutarch uses *agōgē* in the sense of "reasoning" (*Cons. ad Apoll.* 9 [but this is a spurious work—Tr.]) as does Chrysippus (cf. *SVF*, vol. 2, 84; cf. "method" in Aristotle, *Rh.* 1.15.1375ᵇ12), but also with respect to "education" or the spartiate "discipline," a "hard and painful regimen, but one that teaches the young obedience" (*Ages.* 1.2; 3.5; *Lyc.* 16–23; *Cleom.* 11.3; 37.14) and also with respect to simplicity and philanthropy (*Ages.* 1.5).

[2] P.Tebt. 24, 57 (117 BC); cf. A. Pelletier, *Josèphe adaptateur*, pp. 301ff.

[3] *Ep. Arist.* 8: ἡ παιδείας ἀγωγή, the training that the culture gives; 124, 125: the culture and the eloquence of the philosophers (in the plural).

[4] 2 Macc 11:24; Josephus, *Ant.* 14.195: every question about the Jews' way of life; P.Paris 61, 12 (156 BC): πάντα ἐστὶν ἀλλότρια τῆς τε ἡμῶν ἀγωγῆς; cf. Polybius 1.32.1:

---

agōgē, S 72; *TDNT* 1.128–129; *EDNT* 1.25; *NIDNTT* 3.935; MM 8; L&N 41.3; BAGD 14–15

consider my age, the life that I lead (*tēn agōgēn tou biou*) and my piety" (Josephus, *War* 1.462).

Frequently—and this nuance is discernible in 2 Tim 3:10—this conduct is adopted in imitation of a master, of a model, of ancestors.[5] This is what St. Paul called "my ways in Christ" (*tas hodous mou tas en Christō*).[6] The subject for imitation, then, is not the conduct of the person but the manner of life of the apostle. It has to do with conforming to the requirements of the faith that are transmitted in the *didaskalia* and bear upon customs and specific mores:[7] practical, observable applications.[8] In the Pastorals, which develop a theology of beauty, this *agōgē* of the apostle seems to involve a sense of the brilliance or splendor (cf. Phil 3:17; 4:9) that this term can

---

"a Lacedaemonian who had received the Spartiate education." This education has as its goal "the training of the hoplites, the heavy infantry who had been responsible for Sparta's military superiority. . . . To have received the ἀγωγή, to have been educated in the proper fashion, was a necessary, if not a sufficient condition for the exercise of civic rights" (H. I. Marrou, *History of Education*, p. 42).

[5] 2 Macc 4:16—"In the very same people whose manner of life they wished to imitate and whom they wanted to be like in every respect they met their enemies and their executioners"; *Ep. Arist.* 43: Aristaeus a worthy representative of your own culture; 280: τὴν ἀγωγὴν μιμούμενοι; Josephus, *Ant.* 12.10: "determined to preserve their fathers' type of life"; 14.247: the Romans continuing their ancestors' way of life. In mathematics, *agōgē* would be the carrying out of a proof, the direction of an argument; hence: to follow out a line that one is drawing from a point (C. Mugler, *Terminologie géométrique*, p. 41). In law, *agōgē* is the "proceedings" (cf. R. Taubenschlag, *Law of Greco-Roman Egypt*, pp. 225, 331, 340, 381); in music, it isn't the tempo (*P.Oxy.* 2687, 5, 15) but a succession of elements following in a certain order (cf. Ps.-Plutarch, *De mus.* 29), "a rhythmic series" (W. J. W. Koster, "Quelques remarques sur l'étude de rythmique, P. Oxy. 2687," in *REG*, 1972, pp. 551–556).

[6] 1 Cor 4:17. Cf. *1 Clem.* 47.6: "It is shameful and unworthy of Christian conduct"; 48.1: "the noble and holy conduct of brotherly love." Cf., in the first century BC, the Περὶ θεῶν ἀγωγή of Philodemus of Gadara (ed. H. Diels, 1916).

[7] *I.Magn.* 164, 3: ἄνδρα φιλότειμον καὶ ἐνάρετον καὶ ἀπὸ προγόνων εὐσχήμονα καὶ ἔθει καὶ κόσμιον (edited anew by Dittenberger, *Or.* 485); *I.Car.* 70, A 9, an honorific decree in favor of Euneikos, a physician of Heraclea, whose good behavior is praised: διά τε τὴν ἰδίαν αὐτοῦ σωφροσύνην καὶ εὐταξίαν καὶ κοσμίαν ἀγωγήν; *MAMA*, vol. 8, 408, 6: ἀπὸ πρώτης ἡλικίας νεικήσας πάντας ἠθῶν τε σεμνότητι καὶ ἐναρέτου ἀγωγῆς; *P.Princ.* 75, 5: τὸν περὶ ἤθους καὶ ἀγωγῆς τρόπον (horoscope from the second century AD); *P.Ant.* 153, fr. 2, 17; whence the equivalence made by Hesychius: ἀγωγή = τρόπος, ἀναστροφή.

[8] 2 Macc 6:8; *Ep. Arist.* 246; 3 Macc 4:10; *SB* 9763, 35; *P.Oxy.* 2420, 7; 2478, 7; *P.Stras.* 229, 6. In the inscriptions and in numerous papyri, *agōgē* refers to the carrying capacity of the freight of a ship. Cf. *I.Did.*, 39 *a* 39–40; 40, 26; 41, 28, 483, 7; *BGU* 1925, 21 (before 131 BC); *P.Stras.* 519, 3; *P.Panop.Beatty* 1, 121; a load (*C.P.Herm.* 24, 7).

ἀγωγή, agōgē

connote in the first century,[9] and which is at the same time a characteristic of virtue and a grace of the apostle (2 Cor 4:6).

---

[9] Dittenberger, *Or.* 474, 9: διὰ τὴν κοσμιωτάτην αὐτῆς ἀγωγήν; cf. 223, 15. An honorific decree of AD 58 praises Ermadorus and his son Ermocrates, athletes who have distinguished themselves at the Pythian Games: πεποίηνται τὰν ἀναστροφὰν καλὰν καὶ εὐσχήμονα καὶ ἀξίαν τᾶς ἰδίας πατρίδος ... ἀπόδειξιν διδόντες καὶ τὰς περὶ τὸν βίον ἀγωγᾶς (*Syl.* 740, 2–6). An honorific decree of Plutarch son of Hermogenes in the first century BC, διὰ ... τὴν παρ' ὅλον τὸν βίον ἀγωγὴν καὶ σωφροσύνην καὶ τὴν πρὸς πάντας τοὺς πολίτας ἐκτένειαν καὶ φιλανθρωπίαν (P. Hermann, *Ergebnisse*, n. 3).

ἀδιαλείπτως

adialeiptōs, **unceasingly**

This adverb, which means "without interruption, incessantly," presents no difficulties. It is peculiar to the Koine and is not used in the Old Testament except in the books of the Maccabees.[1] But twice it qualifies continual prayer,[2] just as according to the *Letter of Aristeas* the priests maintain religious services without interruption.[3] This is the only sense in which the word is used by St. Paul, who is the only NT writer to use it;[4] hence it has a theological value, but one that is hard to pin down precisely.

The expression "make mention" of someone in prayer is traditional.[5] In general, people did one *proskynēma* each day;[6] but it was not extraordi-

---

[1] 2 Macc 3:26—two young men "whipped Heliodorus without respite"; 9:4—Antiochus Epiphanes "ordered the driver to drive his chariot without stopping"; 13:12—Maccabaeus maintained an unchangeable and unshakeable confidence.

[2] Onias declares: "We, then, at no time cease to make mention of you . . . in our prayers" (1 Macc 12:11); the Jews implore the Lord "prostrated for three days straight" (2 Macc 13:12); cf. 3 Macc 6:33—the king gave thanks to heaven without ceasing.

[3] *Ep. Arist.* 92; cf. *SB* 5156, 11: τυγχάνομεν ἀδιαλείπτως τάς τε θυσίας καὶ σπονδάς (inscription of Theadelphia, 57 BC); 7746, 14.

[4] 1 Thess 1:2; 2:13; 5:16; Rom 1:9; we might add the adjective ἀδιάλειπτος in 2 Tim 1:3—"I am full of gratitude toward God . . . when I ceaselessly make mention of you in my prayers, night and day."

[5] Μνείαν ποιοῦμαι (Plato, *Phaedrus* 254 *a*); 1 Thess 1:2; Rom 1:9; Eph 1:16; Phlm 4; cf. Phil 1:3; 2 Tim 1:3; *P.Cair.Zen.* 59076, 3; 59093, 3; *P.Lond.* 42, 6: "all members of the household remember you continually, οἱ ἐν οἴκῳ πάντες σου διαπαντὸς μνείαν ποιούμενοι" (24 July 172 BC); 1658, 6; *BGU* 632, 5: μνίαν σου ποιούμενος παρὰ τοῖς ἐνθάδε θεοῖς ἐκομισάμεν ἐν ἐπιστόλιον (second century BC); *I.Priene*, 50, 10: in the second century BC, the inhabitants of Erythrae decide to reward a judge, "so that it will be seen that the people remember good men, ὅπως οὖν καὶ ὁ δῆμος φαίνηται μνείαν ποιούμενος τῶν καλῶν καὶ ἀγαθῶν ἀνδρων."

[6] *P.Alex.* 28, 2–3: τὸ προσκύνημά σου ποιῶ καθ᾽ ἑκάστην ἡμέραν; 30, 3; *P.Hamb.* 89, 3; *PSI* 206, 4; cf. *P.Stras.* 268: "Each day, I prostrate myself on your behalf before all the gods of the place I am in" (published by F. Dunand, "Les noms théophores en -ammon," in *ChrEg*, 1963, p. 135).

---

adialeiptōs, S 88; *EDNT* 1.31; *NIDNTT* 3.229–230; L&N 68.55; BAGD 179

nary for this remembering before the deity to be referred to as perpetual.[7] Not only did St. Paul give thanks always (*pantote*) and on every occasion (*en panti kairō*), day and night,[8] but he agreed to register in the order of widows only women who had persevered night and day in prayer (1 Tim 5:5), and he instructed all Christians to "pray continually."[9] How is this to be understood? This precept should be linked to that of the Master when he bade his disciples to "pray under all circumstances and never give up,"[10] and understood in light of the tireless diligence of the primitive church in supplication.[11]

But does the choice of the adverb *adialeiptōs* have some special significance? The papyri shed hardly any light, except that they corroborate the sense "continual, uninterrupted"[12] and several times the nuance "without giving in to weakness."[13] A single pagan inscription mentions perseverance in prayer in this way: "I, Isio, son of Kallimachos, kinsman of the king, came and passed my time adoring our lady Isis."[14] Indeed, only the Christian religion gives this term for prayer its correct meaning. Certainly the point is not the counting of verbal invocations, which would run afoul of

---

[7] *P.Mich.* VIII, 502, 4: εὔχομαι καὶ τὸ προσκύνημά σου ἀδιαλείπτως ποιούμενος (second century BC); cf. a "perpetual institution" of lamps in the temple of Heracleopolis (*BGU* 1854, 4ff.). "Not only did they mention names in prayer, but they also inscribed them in the sanctuaries . . . as a perpetual prayer" (M. J. Lagrange, *Romains*, p. 14).

[8] 1 Thess 3:10, cf. C. Spicq, *Théologie morale*, vol. 1, pp. 358ff.

[9] 1 Thess 5:17—ἀδιαλείπτως προσεύχεσθε (present imperative).

[10] Luke 18:1 (C. Spicq, "La parabole de la veuve obstinée et du juge inerte aux décisions impromptues," in *RB* 1961, pp. 68ff.), cf. the intense prayer (ἐκτενῶς, Luke 22:44) that requires sustained effort.

[11] Acts 1:14; 2:42; 6:4; Col 4:2; cf. C. Spicq, *Théologie Morale*, p. 359.

[12] *Ep. Arist.* 86: the material of the veil was animated with a continual motion; *BGU* 180, 10: ἐν λειτουργίᾳ εἰμὶ ἀδιαλείπτως; *P.Mert.* 98, 3 and *P.Oxy.* 2420, 13: a stipulation that has perpetual validity; *P.Lond.* 122, 32: a continuous gift of food (magical papyrus of the fourth century; cf. *Pap.Graec.Mag.* VIII, 32). Cf. Marcus Aurelius 6.15: the incessant flight of time.

[13] Notably in oaths (cf. *P.Oxy.* 2764, 20; 2765, 11; 2767, 12). One takes watchful care of a tree so that it will live and prosper (*P.Oxy.* 2969, 10; 2994, 5). Diogenes of the village of Psoaphrē pledges to see that a boat is guarded night and day, without absence and without negligence, παραφυλάξειν νυκτός καὶ ἡμέρας . . . ἀδιαλείπτως καὶ ἀμέμπτως (*P.Oxy.* 2876, 18–20; third century); ἀμένπτως καὶ ἀδιαλείπτως (*PSI* 1229, 14); *T. Levi* 13.2—ἀναγινώσκοντες ἀδιαλείπτως τὸν νόμον τοῦ θεοῦ. There is then a psychological or mental note; cf. the joy of the king who has not let himself down (*Ep. Arist.* 294); *P.Tebt.* 27, 45: τὴν ἀδιαλίπτως προσφερομένην σπουδήν (AD 113); Dittenberger, *Syl.* 1104, 35.

[14] The duration of the act of adoration is expressed by the perfect διαγέωχα (A. Bernand, *Philae*, Paris, 1969, n. 61), 10 March 44.

the prohibition against *battalogia*;[15] and at any rate, even prayer day and night assumes some breaks.[16] Taken therefore in a qualitative sense, *adialeiptōs* is hyperbolic. It expresses the positive aspect of the attitude of watchfulness that characterizes the servant of God in the end times, when it is necessary to go without sleep (Luke 21:36; Eph 6:18). It would not be adequate to make an equation with what we call today "the spirit of prayer," a readiness to place oneself in the presence of God. It would be better to see it as "a spiritual life dominated by the presence of God"[17] and as a perpetual communion with God, after the fashion of a shoot vitally connected to the vine stock. If it is true that, according to the NT, the Christian life consists in the living out of the theological virtues,[18] then the believer's connection with the three divine Persons is continual, first of all as a creature who is radically and permanently dependent on the Almighty and then as a child of God in a dynamic relationship of love with the One who has predestined him to "exist in love."[19] We may speak of prayer without ceasing when the heart does not cease to be oriented toward God, just as love never stops or slackens when one's attention is temporarily diverted away from the beloved: everything is seen with reference to the beloved.[20]

---

[15] Matt 6:7–8; cf. C. Spicq, *Dieu et l'homme*, p. 64; F. Bussby, "A Note on . . . βατταλογέω in the Light of Qumran," in *ExpT*, vol. 74, 1964, p. 26; P. Gaechter, *Das Matthäus-Evangelium*, Innsbruck, 1963, pp. 205–209.

[16] Josephus uses the adjective ἀδ. with respect to continuous slaughter, renewed attacks (*War* 1.252; 2.489; 3.157; 5.31), which in every instance suppose some reprieves or lulls in even the most instense and constant action. By the same token, the "unceasing sorrow" felt by St. Paul (Rom 9:2) need not be actually experienced at every moment. Cf. ἀδιαλείπτως παραμεῖναι (*SB* 10944, 12).

[17] E. Delay, "ΑΔΙΑΛΕΙΠΤΟΣ," in *RTP*, 1950, p. 73.

[18] 1 Thess 1:3; cf. C. Spicq, *Agapè*, vol. 2, pp. 10ff.

[19] Eph 1:4; cf. C. Spicq, ibid., pp. 208ff.; K. Romaniuk, *L'Amour du Père et du Fils dans la sotériologie de saint Paul*, Rome, 1961, pp. 203ff.; J. Cambier, "La bénédiction d'Eph. I, 3–14," in *ZNW*, 1963, pp. 58–103; J. Winandy, "Le Cantique des cantiques et le N.T.," in *RB*, 1964, p. 163. I. Hausheer, *Prière de vie: Vie de prière*, Paris, 1964, pp. 16ff., 67ff., 307ff.

[20] Cf. Eph 6:24—"All those who love our Lord Jesus Christ with an imperishable love"; ἀφθαρσία means not just immortality, but indestructibility; cf. Philo, *Dreams* 1.181; Plutarch, *Aristides* 6.3; C. Spicq, *Agapè*, vol. 1, pp. 294ff.

ἀδύνατον

adynaton, **impossible**

The impossibility of the conversion of the apostate (Heb 6:4) is a difficult theological problem.[1] What kind of *adynaton* is this? In the OT, the term sometimes points to an absolute impossibility, like that of escaping the hand of God (Wis 16:15), but usually it denotes a relative or conditional impossibility, like the possibility that Onias could achieve a peaceful settlement without the intervention of the king.[2] In Jer 13:3, it is a rhetorical figure for expressing an absurd supposition, an event considered impossible because it is contrary to the laws of nature.[3]

---

[1] Cf. C. Spicq, *Hébreux*, vol. 2, pp. 167ff.; J. Héring, *Hébreux*, pp. 59ff. = ET pp. 45ff. It has been taken in the softened sense of a great difficulty (Nicolas of Lyra, Erasmus); in the Middle Ages, theologians set aside the possibility of pardon after death (Peter Lombard, Hugh of Saint Victor, Robert of Melun). Almost all the Fathers, and recently A. Richardson (*An Introduction to the Theology of the New Testament*, London, 1958, pp. 33, 348ff.) take this verse as a reference to the impossibility of receiving baptism again.

[2] 2 Macc 4:5 (cf. Thucydides 6.86.3: "We cannot remain in Sicily without your concurrence"). Josephus, *War* 5.57: "It was impossible for him to continue his advance, because the land was crisscrossed with trenches"; 3.172; cf. Alcimus declaring to Demetrius that as long as Judas is alive it will be impossible to restore peace to the state (2 Macc 14:10). The examples from Prov 30:18—to understand the course of the eagle in the sky or of the serpent on the rock—prove that *adynaton* is to be taken in its strict sense, even though it corresponds to the niphal of *pāla'*, "to be arduous, difficult."

[3] "Can a Cushite change his skin or a leopard its spots? And can you, who are addicted to doing evil, do good?" (cf. Dio Cassius 41.33: "Without obeying the laws of nature, nothing can last, not even for an instant"). To represent an impossible or implausible fact or action, one juxtaposes it with one or several natural impossibilities;

---

adynaton, S 102; *TDNT* 2.284–317; *EDNT* 1.33–34; *NIDNTT* 2.601, 606; MM 10; L&N 71.3, 74.22; BDF §127(2); BAGD 19

Clearly context is everything.[4] In the NT, almost all the occurrences are religious, and we should compare our text closely with the response of Jesus to the problem of the salvation of the rich and of everyone: "with humans this is impossible, but with God all things are possible" (*para anthrōpois touto adynaton estin, para de theō panta dynata*).[5] Or again: "It is impossible that the blood of bulls and goats should obliterate sins" (Heb 10:4) or that one could be pleasing to God without faith (11.6), because such is the providential disposition of the economy of salvation.[6] In the case of apostates, it is not stated that they will not be pardoned, but they are denied the possibility of reforming themselves and repenting, given their spiritual bearing and the nature of their sin: having rejected God, after having seen the light of the faith, they are psychologically incapable of making anotherabout-face; that would be contradictory to their apostate

---

this is comparison ἐκ or ἀπὸ τοῦ ἀδυνάτου (E. Dutoit, *Le Thème de l'adynaton dans la poésie antique*, Paris, 1936, pp. ix, 50, 167ff.), which lived on in the examples cited by Roman jurists of materially impossible conditions with respect to wills and stipulations, cf. J. Michel, "Quelques formules primitives de serment promissoire et l'origine de la comparaison par adynaton," in *RIDA*, 1957, pp. 139–150.

[4] St. Gregory of Nazianzus (*Orations* 30; *PG* 36.113–116) distinguishes six kinds of impossibility, based on (1) *powerlessness:* a child cannot fight (cf. *P.Lond.* 971, 4: ἀδύνατος γάρ ἐστιν ἡ γυνὴ διὰ ἀσθένιαν τῆς φύσεως, third-fourth century); (2) a condition *ut in pluribus:* a city locate on a mountain cannot be invisible; (3) *reason and propriety:* the friends of the groom cannot fast while the groom is with them (Josephus, *Ant.* 13.423: he saw the incapacity of his brother, who was supposed to succeed to the throne; *War* 7.144); (4) *the disposition of the will:* at Nazareth, Jesus could not perform many miracles because of the unbelief of the people; he did not want to perform miracles; (5) *nature*—but God can change nature: a camel entering through the eye of a needle (cf. Herodotus 1.32.39: "It isn't possible, so long as one is a human, to bring together all of the advantages of which I have spoken"; Josephus, *Ant.* 10.196); (6) *that which absolutely cannot be:* that God should be evil, that two times two plus four should equal ten. We have to add *scientific impossibility*, as with a method that would not cover actual results (Hippocrates, *De Vetere Medicina* 2.6; cf. Archimedes, *On Spirals* 16.9; 17.27; *The Equilibriums of Planes* 6; *The Sand-reckoner* 1, etc.; numerous examples in C. Mugler, *Terminologie géométrique*, pp. 41ff.).

[5] Matt 19:26; cf. Mark 10:27; Luke 18:27. Salvation is beyond the power of humans; the inability of the creature is radical; God must intervene; cf. Rom 8:3—that which was impossible for the law, because it was without power, God has accomplished. Josephus, *War* 2.390: without God's help, it is impossible that such a vast empire could have been established.

[6] On the other hand, "it is impossible for God to lie" (Heb 6:18) is an absolute impossibility which allows of no exception; cf. Philo, *Etern. World* 46: "It is impossible that the gods should lose their incorruptibility"; cf. 104: "In pairs of opposites, it is impossible for one term to exist without the other"; Herodotus 1.91.3: "it is impossible, even for a god, to escape destiny."

condition.[7] The best parallel is perhaps Philo: "It is not easy, and perhaps even impossible, for a defiant spirit to be educated."[8]

Certainly, that which is impossible for humans is possible for God,[9] and the whole gospel bears witness that divine initiative can change the spiritual condition of apostates, bring to them to a light and a power that will destroy the aforementioned impossibility.[10] But on the one hand the context emphasizes the seriousness of the crime—"crucifying for themselves the Son of God and holding him up for public ridicule"—in order to conclude that such a soul is "rejected and close to destruction; its end is to be burned" (verse 8); on the other hand, it seems that this sin of

---

[7] Ἀδύνατον in the sense of "not powerful," "unable," "there is no means," is common in secular Greek, cf. Thucydides 1.32.5; 1.73.4.; 1.141.6.; 6.85.1; 6.102.2; 7.44; 7.64.1. Dio Cassius 1.114: "It is [psychologically] impossible for those who have not been raised with the same mores and who do not have the same ideas concerning evil and good to be united in friendship"; 45.26: "It is morally impossible that a person raised in such disorder and in such shamelessness should not ruin his life altogether"; 5.27; 55.14: "It is impossible to satisy the passions of the wicked"; 61.2, Domitius, father of Nero, talking about his wife Agrippina: "It is impossible for an honest man to be born to me and her." Philo, *Alleg. Interp.* 3.4: without allegory, the exegete cannot discover a valid meaning in the letter of a text; 3.10: humans are incapable of praising and thanking God adequately; *Spec. Laws* 1.32: of understanding God; *Alleg. Interp.* 1.34: "for some people doing good is impossible"; *Change of Names* 49: "It is not possible to wash and completely clean away the stains that soil the soul" (cf. *Spec. Laws* 1.103); Josephus, *Ant.*3.230: those who are incapable of offering perfect sacrifices; *Ag. Apion* 5.442; *P.Oxy.* 2479, 19: "I cannot pay on that which I have not sown." J. Ebert, *Griechische Epigramme*, p. 69.

[8] *Rewards* 49: δύσκολον γάρ, μᾶλλον δ' ἀδύνατον ἀπιστοῦντα παιδεύεσθαι. Cf. the rigor of the Qumranians, who definitively excluded from the community those who transgressed the law in a plainly culpable manner (1QS 8.21–23, 1QM 1.6), and particularly their horror of apostasy (CD 2.17–18; 7.13; 8.1–13), which was especially accursed (cf. R. E. Brown, "The Qumran Scrolls and the Johannine Gospel and Epistles," in K. Stendahl, *The Scrolls and the New Testament*, New York, 1957, pp. 200ff.; A. M. Denis, *Les Thèmes de connaissance dans le Document de Damas*, Louvain, 1967, pp. 23, 140, 146). These "transgressors of the law" are opposed to "those who hold firm."

[9] Philo, *Moses* 1.174: τὰ ἀδύνατα παντὶ γενητῷ μόνῳ δυνατὰ καὶ κατὰ χειρός; cf. Gen 18:14; Matt 19:28; Luke 1:37. Even the pagans confess that the gods are capable of carrying out that which is ἀδύνατον for humans, cf. A. Cameron, "An Epigram of the Fifth Century B.C.," in *HTR*, 1940, pp. 118ff.

[10] A. J. Festugière has shown that the power of the soul in the order of salvation has to do with the will, with a basic disposition. If God saves only those who want to be saved, how will the apostate have this fundamental desire? (*Hermès Trismégiste*, Paris, 1953, vol. 3, pp. 110–115).

apostasy can be assimilated to the sin against the light and the blasphemy against the Holy Spirit, which is forgiven neither in this world nor in the one to come.[11]

---

[11] Matt 12:31–32; Mark 3:28–20; Luke 12:10; cf. 2 Pet 2:20–22; 1 John 5:16; cf. B. B. Warfield, "Misconception of Jesus and Blasphemy of the Son of Man," in *Biblical and Theological Studies*, Philadelphia, 1952, pp. 196–237; A. Michel, "Péché contre le Saint-Esprit?" in *Ami du clergé*, 1955, pp. 123–124; O. E. Evans, "The Unforgiveable Sin," in *ExpT*, vol. 58, 1957, pp. 240–244; G. Fitzer, "Die Sünde wider den Heiligen Geist," in *TZ*, 1957, pp. 161–182; R. Scroggs, "The Exaltation of the Spirit," in *JBL*, 1965, pp. 360ff.; C. Colpe, "Die Spruch von der Lästerung des Geistes," in *Festschrift J. Jeremias*, Göttingen, 1970, pp. 63–79.

ἀθετέω, ἀθέτησις

atheteō, to set aside, abrogate, reject; *athetēsis*, abrogation, rejection

The etymology of this verb (*tithēmi* with alpha-privative), literally "set aside," hardly provides a precise statement of its meaning in the language of the New Testament, but its use is varied as well as precise. First, there is the legal sense, "to abrogate, abolish, declare invalid"; thus the institution of the Aaronic priesthood has been abolished (Heb 7:18) and Christ has been manifested to destroy the reign of sin by his own sacrifice (9:26). In both cases, *athetēsis* is chosen to express a judicial and official annulment;[1] the hereditary priesthood is radically abolished; sin can never regain its power, since it has been conquered by the blood of Christ. *Athetēsis* is synonymous with *akyrōsis*, "annulment."[2]

In common usage, this "destruction" is only a repudiation, a refusal, or a withdrawal;[3] one challenges an authority: "The one who rejects you rejects me, and the one who rejects me rejects the one who sent me";[4] one

---

[1] Ἀθετέω is used for the rejection of a law (Isa 24:16; Ezek 22:26; Heb 10:28—τὸν νόμον), of a commandment (Mark 6:9—τὴν ἐντολήν), of a covenant (Gal 3:15—διαθήκην; 2 Macc 14:28—τὰ διεσταλμένα), of an agreement (2 Macc 13:25—περὶ τῶν συνθηκῶν). Cf. 1 Macc 15:27—"He revoked all that he had agreed with Simon."

[2] Cf. BGU 44, 16: διδόντα ἡμῖν ἀποχὴν καὶ ἀνδιδοῦντα τὴν διαγραφὴν εἰς ἀθέτησιν καὶ ἀκύρωσιν (14 July AD 102; cf. 196, 21; 281, 18; 394, 14); PSI 1131, 43 (28 August 44); P.Warr. 9, 22 (23 August 109); P.Fam.Tebt. 9, 15 (22 November 107); P.Mil.Vogl. 225, 15; P.Lips. 27, 20; P.Ryl. 174, 14: εἰς ἀθέτησιν καὶ ἀκύρωσιν (AD 112); P.Tebt. 397, 13; SB 7465, 8; 9839, 16. The invalidation of a document is the opposite of its confirmation, εἰς βεβαίωσιν (Heb 6:16; cf. Lev 25:23).

[3] Cf. the withdrawal of a lawsuit: οὕτως ἐξείσχυσεν τὰ βιβλείδια ἀθετηθῆναι (P.Oxy. 1120, 8), the liquidation of an account that is to be erased from a list (P.Tebt. 74, 59; 75, 77), the refusal of grain not fit for consumption (P.Lond. 237, 23). Cf. the rejection of the wisdom of the wise (1 Cor 1:19), the Pharisees and doctors of the law annulling the purpose of God (Luke 7:30; cf. Ps 33:10—ἀθετεῖ βουλὰς ἀρχόντων; Jdt 16:5). Esther rejects none of Hegai's instructions (Esth 2:15, LXX). Cf. 1 Macc 11:36—"Not one of these favors shall be cancelled, from this time forth for ever"; 14:44—"No one will be permitted . . . to reject one of these points"; Heb 10:28—"Does someone reject the law of Moses?"

[4] Luke 10:16; cf. John 12:48; 1 Thess 4:8.

---

atheteō, S 114; TDNT 8.158–159; EDNT 1.35; NIDNTT 1.74; MM 12; L&N 31.100, 76.24; BAGD 21 ‖ *athetēsis*, S 115; TDNT 8.158–159; EDNT 1.35; MM 12; L&N 13.36, 76.24; BAGD 21; ND 2.77

goes back on one's word or perjures oneself.⁵ Hence, *athetēsis* smacks of perfidy.⁶ This sense is the one that attaches to *atheteō*, used sixty times in the LXX, where it translates seventeen Hebrew words, but most frequently *bāgaḏ*," deceive, be unfaithful, betray," and *pāša'*, "defect, revolt," with the result that in biblical usage this verb almost always means "be unfaithful,"⁷ to revolt,⁸ or to betray,⁹ with the sense of "deceive" or "scorn."¹⁰ Hence the comparison in Jer 3:20—"As a woman betrays her lover, so have you betrayed me, house of Israel." It is not just a matter of violating an agreement, or even of breaking with a person (cf. Polybius 11.36.10), but of going back on one's decision and lying to most holy God.

It is in light of these texts that we must read 1 Tim 5:12, where the young widows, when their desires are stirred up against Christ, want to remarry, "having [their] condemnation, because they have rejected their former faith."¹¹ This *pistis* is not theological faith but the commitment of the widow to serve Christ and the poor, and doubtless also not to remarry. To revoke an agreement is to be unfaithful and to perjure oneself, to act toward God like a woman who betrays her lover.

---

⁵ Mark 6:26 (cf. Ps 15:4; Polybius 8.2.5; Dittenberger, *Or.* 444, 18: ἐὰν δέ τινες τῶν πόλεων ἀθετῶσι τὸ σύμφωνον). God never fails, doesn't change that which he has spoken (Ps 89:35; 132:11), he doesn't revoke his words (Isa 31:2); even though men break their oaths (1 Macc 6:62; cf. *BGU* 1123, 11: μηδενὶ ἡμῶν ἐξόντος ἀθετεῖν τῶν ὡμολογημένων—from the Augustan era).

⁶ Jdt 14:18; Isa 48:8; 1 Sam 24:12—"I bear no malice, no perfidy."

⁷ Judg 9:23; 1 Chr 2:7; 5:25; 2 Chr 10:19 (= 1 Kgs 12:19); 36:14 (the leaders of Judah, the priests, and the people have multiplied their acts of faithlessness, ἀθετῆσαι ἀθετήματα); Isa 1:2; Ezek 39:23; Dan 9:7 (Theod.).

⁸ 2 Kgs 1:1; 18:7, 20; 24:1, 20 = 2 Chr 36:13. Cf. Jude 8: the false teachers, "rejecting the sovereignty (κυριότητα δὲ ἀθετοῦσιν)." This revolt is not so much against the leaders of the community of the civil magistrates, nor against the elders or angels, but against the divine authority (verse 4), not taking into account the ordinances of God or the law of Christ.

⁹ 1 Kgs 8:50; Isa 21:2—the traitor betrays (ὁ ἀθετῶν ἀθετεῖ); 24:16; 33:1; Jer 5:11—"The house of Israel and the house of Judah have betrayed me"; 12:1—the instigators of treachery (οἱ ἀθετοῦντες ἀθετήματα).

¹⁰ 1 Sam 2:17—men who scorned the offering to Yahweh; Isa 63:8; Wis 5:1. Ἀθετεῖν = act faithlessly, cf. Exod 21:8; Deut 21:14. Compare the apostates who trample on the Son of God and treat as common the blood that he shed (Heb 10:28–29), as opposed to Paul who does not treat the grace of God as nothing (Gal 2:21).

¹¹ Τὴν πρώτην πίστιν ἠθέτησαν = *fidem irritam faciens* (cf. Polybius 8.36.5; 22.16.1; 22.17.5; 23.8.7). Cf. Rev 2:4—"You have relaxed your first love," which could also be translated, "You have deserted your first love" (on the sense of ἀφιέναι, cf. C. Spicq, *Agapè*, vol. 3, pp. 114ff.). Cf. 2:5—τὰ πρῶτα ἔργα ποίησον; 2:19; Jer 2:2). Cf. *I.Bulg.* 13, 25–26: ἐν τῇ πρώτῃ καὶ μεγίστῃ φιλίᾳ; Philodemus of Gadara, *Adv. Soph.*, frag. Y, col. XV, 8: τὴν πρώτην ὑπομονήν.

αἰδώς, ἀναίδεια

aidōs, **modesty;** *anaideia*, **shamelessness**

After the manner of the pagan cults, which often regulated the grooming of their participants—clothing, jewelry, hair[1]—St. Paul instructs the Ephesian women, when they pray at church, to adorn themselves with decency and sobriety (*meta aidous kai sōphrosynēs kosmein heautas*, 1 Tim 2:9), because the right way for a woman to arrange or accouter herself is to observe the rules of modesty and decency.[2]

Aidōs (from *aidomai*, to fear, respect) is a very old Greek concept[3] expressing the respectful and secret fear that one feels toward oneself (Democritus, frag. 264, Diels). With the Stoics it became a leading virtue.[4]

---

[1] Cf. *LSAM*, n. 14 (Pergamum), 16 (Gambreion), 69 (Stratonicea), 77, 79; idem, *LSCG*, n. 56 (Delos), 106 (Camiros); idem, *LSCG*, vol. 2, n. 68 (Lykosoura); C. Spicq, *Epîtres Pastorales*, vol. 1, pp. 419ff.

[2] The αἰδώς σωφροσύνη association is constant from Xenophon on (*Cyr.* 8.1.31; *Symp.* 1.8; Thucydides, 1.84.3; Diotogenes: "When, in his appearance, his thoughts, his sentences, his character, his deeds, his walk, and his carriage, the king enfolds himself in such decorum and pomp that he has a psychological effect on those who behold him, affected as they are by his dignity and his moderation" in Stobaeus 48.7.62; p. 268, 11); *GVI*, n. 1575 (first-second century); *MAMA*, vol. 7, 258, 5; Philo, *Who Is the Heir* 128: "the special task of human science is to give birth in the soul to restraint and moderation, virtues whose clearest manifestation is that one blushes when the occasion arises"; *Prelim. Stud.* 124: virtue manifests "a beauty remarkable for its modesty and propriety, beauty . . . truly virginal"; *Flight* 5; *Sacr. Abel and Cain* 27; notably in connection with κοσμεῖν-κοσμιότης (*Change of Names* 217: "If with an older companion at his side a young man adorns himself with modesty and restraint"; *Spec. Laws* 3.51).

[3] Cf. B. Snell, *Lexikon*, on this word; C. E. von Erffa, "Αἰδώς und verwandete Begriffe in ihrer Entwicklund von Homer bis Demokrit," in *Philologus*, Suppl. 30, 1937.

[4] Musonius Rufus: "*Aidōs* is the greatest good" (*That Women Too Should Study Philosophy*, frag. 3, p. 42, l. 24; ed. C. E. Lutz); "a feeling of shame toward all that is

---

aidōs, S 127; *TDNT* 1.169–171; *EDNT* 1.37; *NIDNTT* 3.826–827, 829; MM 13; L&N 88.49; BDF §47(4), 126(1*b*); BAGD 22 ‖ *anaideia*, S 335; *EDNT* 1.81; MM 33; L&N 66.12; BDF §23; BAGD 54

Plutarch distinguishes *aidōs*, "which often allows itself to be led by reason and places itself under the same laws," from an unhealthy shame whose hesitations and delays are contrary to reason.[5] In the first century AD, this sentiment is sometimes that of shame, notably the shame of soldiers who are in flight and know that they are defeated,[6] hence awareness of guilt;[7] it is sometimes that of respect for others,[8] the consideration owed others. It is then a restraint, a dignity,[9] a modesty, or a discretion that keeps one from excess;[10] thus a self-respect[11] and a sense of honor that is often identified with modesty.[12]

This virtue finds its highest expression in women. Philo explains why there was a wall of separation between Therapeutai and Therapeutrides, "to respect the modesty appropriate to the feminine nature,"[13] and he personifies the virtue as a woman who has "colors which are those of modesty . . . simple clothing, but more precious than gold, wisdom and

---

base" (*Should Daughters Receive the Same Education as Sons?*, frag. 4, p. 48, l. 3); the study of philosophy leads the king to have a sense of shame (frag. 8, p. 62, l. 18); a man who has many children has the respect of his neighbors (frag. 15, p. 98, l. 3); cf. Philo, *Sacr. Abel and Cain* 27: virtue is accompanied by modesty.

[5] Plutarch, *On Ethical Virtue* 8; cf. Epictetus, *Against Epicurus*, in Stobaeus 6.57 (vol. 3, p. 300).

[6] Josephus, *War* 3.19, 156; 4.285; 5.118; 6.20; Plutarch, *Tim.* 7.1: "Timoleon was ashamed before his mother."

[7] Josephus, *Ant.* 2.52; cf. *War* 2.351.

[8] Toward guests (Josephus, *Ant.* 1.201), parents (2.23), ancestral laws (5.108), age (6.262), dignity (19.102); old men (*War* 2.496), suppliants (2.317), the temple (4.311), neighbors (5.33), the prince (5.87; 6.263; *Ant.* 19.97); Plutarch, *Cleom.* 32.4; *Ti. Gracch.* 5.2; 11.3; *C. Gracch.* 16.1.

[9] Cf. the association with σεμνότης in Plutarch (*Con. praec.* 26) and Philo: the educators of Moses showed only restraint and seriousness, αἰδῶ καὶ σεμνότητα (Philo, *Moses* 1.20).

[10] Flaccus sojourning at Alexandria, μετὰ τοσθύτης αἰδοῦς (Philo, *Flacc.* 28).

[11] Epictetus 1.3.4; 3.14.13; 4.4.7: "It is no small thing that you are guarding; it is respect for yourself and good faith."

[12] Cf. Marcus Aurelius 3.7.1; 5.33.3; 10.13.2. Josephus, *Ant.* 1.44: Adam and Eve cover themselves out of modesty; *PSI* 1178, 6 (second century).

[13] Philo, *Contemp. Life* 33; cf. *Flacc.* 89: "Young girls who stay in their rooms out of modesty to avoid being seen by men"; *Flight* 5; *Spec. Laws* 3.51: "The republic of Moses has no room for the prostitute, to whom decency, chastity, modesty, and the other virtues are foreign"; *Moses* 2.234: The daughters of Salpaad "go to find the governor with the reserve appropriate to young girls"; Josephus, *War* 2.465: women from whom even the last veil of modesty has been taken away; cf. the "unspeakable shame" of Helen (Quintus of Smyrna, *Posthomerica* 9.144) and modesty in conjugal relations (Plutarch, *Quaest. Rom.* 65); ζήσαντα κοσμίως καὶ αἰδημόνως (*MAMA*, vol. 8, 490; cf. 414, 9: βίος αἰδήμων καὶ κόσμιος); "I hesitate to speak an indecent word in the presence of a matron" (Terence, *Haut.* 1042; cf. Propertius 2.6.18).

virtue for her finery" (*Sacr. Abel and Cain* 26). This is the closest parallel to 1 Tim 2:9.

If *aidōs* is sometimes associated with the agreeable equilibrium that is *epieikeia*,[14] it much more frequently connotes fear[15] and even *eulabeia*, the feeling of reverence that one experiences in the presence of majesty, whether of the emperor[16] or of God himself. It is in this sense that Christians offer worship to God (*latreuein meta aidous kai eulabeias*, cf. Heb 12:28).

If *aidōs* (Latin *verecundia*) keeps one from committing an act unworthy of oneself, makes one avoid that which is base, *anaideia* (NT hapax) is effrontery or impudence that shrinks from no means of achieving its goals.[17] It is the *anaideia* of the importunate friend who gets the three loaves that he asks for in the middle of the night.[18] This noun is rare in the papyri: it is found in a list of words (*P.Cair.Zen.* 59534, 21); in the complaint of Kronion, priest of Tebtunis in the second century, victim of the extreme insolence of Kronios;[19] in the complaint of Aurelius, attacked in the third century by a basely impudent woman;[20] and finally in an elegiac poem on Meleager.[21] If the Lord praises this boldness, it is because he has just

---

[14] Josephus, *Ant.* 13.319: Τιμαγένης, φύσει δ' ἐπιεικεῖ ἐκέχρητο καὶ σφόδρα ἦν αἰδοῦς ἥττων; Plutarch, *De vit. pud.* 2.529 c: "In shaking up false shame, one must fear taking along also its neighbors modesty, moderation, and mildness, τῆς αἰδοῦς καὶ τῆς ἐπιεικείας καὶ τῆς ἡμερότητος"; 3.530ᵃ; Dittenberger, *Or.* 507, 8 (second century AD).

[15] Philo, *Rewards* 97 (φόβος).

[16] When the Jews are brought into the presence of Caesar, they regard him with modesty and timidity, stretching out their hands toward him (Philo, *To Gaius* 352), cf. Diogenes Laertius 7.116.

[17] Josephus, *War* 1.224: "Malichos succeeded by effrontery in getting the better of Antipater's sons"; 1.504: "Pheroras, despairing of saving himself by honest means, sought deliverance through effrontery"; 1.616; Plutarch, *De vit. pud.* 11.533ᵈ: "feeling disgust and revulsion at the impudence (τὴν ἀναίδειαν) that upsets and assaults our reasoning"; 13.534ᵇ: "disagreeable folk lacking in modesty and without shame, ἀναιδῶς καὶ ἀδυσωπήτως"; Apollonius Rhodius, *Argon.* 2.407: "insolent eyes." Theognis associates it with hubris (291).

[18] Luke 11:8—διὰ τὴν ἀναιδείαν. The beggar breaks all the rules of politeness and discretion; his audacity knows no modesty (cf. Sir 25:22—shame and insolence, when it is the woman who supports her husband; 60:30—the lazy person, laying aside all pride, would rather live by begging than work).

[19] In *EPap*, vol. 8, 1957, p. 104, 11.

[20] Γυνὴ ἀναιδείᾳ μεγίστῃ καὶ θράσει κεχορηγημένη, *P.Oslo* inv. 1482, published by S. Eitrem and L. Amundsen, in *JEA*, 1954, p. 30; also in *SB* 9421, 12. In the first century, in the *Ninopedia* (ed. Wilcken, in *Hermes*, 1895, pp. 161ff.), lines 111, 113, 118, ἀναιδής means something close to rude in speech, crude and impudent in deed.

[21] Edited by M. Papathomopoulos, in *RechPap*, vol. 2, Paris, 1962, p. 101. There are two good parallels in Archilochus: "Drinking large amounts of pure wine and neglect-

instructed his disciples to pray to the heavenly Father and ask that his name be sanctified. But in accordance with *aidōs*—the religious fear that one experiences in the presence of the sacred—believers would be careful about being too free with their demands, would be hesitant to hail the holy God in an impetuous fashion, with too little concern for propriety. In truth, a child knows nothing of this timidity, but "pours out her heart" (1 Sam 1:15) before her Father, and the tradition of Israel validates this importunity.[22] It is a form of *parrhēsia*.

---

ing to pay your share of the tab . . . , without even being invited you came looking for us like someone finding himself among friends. In truth, your belly, taking away your reason, made you lose all modesty (εἰς ἀναιδείην)" (Frag. 94; ed. Laserre) and P.Cair.Isid. 55, 16: six villagers, drunk and emboldened by their luck to think that they would get away with it, forcibly entered and pillaged the house of Isidorus, and furthermore they impudently pretend that the law is on their side—ὅθεν τῆς τηλικαύτης αὐτῶν ἀναιδίας δεομένης κτλ. Cf. the impudence of a drunk (Josephus, *Ag. Apion* 1.46), P.Ryl. 141; refusing impudently to pay (AD 37) and the *incipit* of the edict of Cn. V. Capito, prefect of Emperor Claudius in Egypt, 7 December 48: "I have long since been informed of unjust charges caused by the exactions of persons abusing their powers with greed and impudence, πλεονεκτικῶς καὶ ἀναιδῶς" (SB 8248, 15–17; cf. the commentary of P. Jouguet, *Observations sur les inscriptions grecques de Khargeh*, in *Proceedings* IV, p. 8). Heraclitus, *All.* 70.11 includes among the "thousand faces of impudence" gluttony, brashness, and covetousness.

[22] Isa 62:7—"Give him no rest"; Ps 10:12 —"Arise, Yahweh"; 44:27 ; 74:22 ; 44:24—"Wake up! Why are you sleeping, Lord? Arise from your slumbers"; cf. the fight between Jacob and the angel (Gen 32:24ff.; S. H. Blank, "Men against God," in *JBL*, 1953, pp. 1–14; J. L. McKenzie, "Jacob at Peniel," in *CBQ*, 1963, pp. 71–76).

αἰσχροκερδής, ἀφιλάργυρος

aischrokerdēs, **eager for shameful gain;** *aphilargyros*, **free of the love of money**

→*see also* ἀφιλάργυρος; φιλαργυρία, φιλάργυρος

The Pharisees are stigmatized as "loving money,"[1] and according to 2 Tim 3:2 people in the last days will be *philargyroi*;[2] which can mean miserliness—often associated with meanness[3]—as well as covetousness. This is a vice of priests (*T. Levi* 17.1), above all of sophists, "vendors of words"[4] who shamefully hawk wisdom, and of false teachers (Titus 1:11). This *philargyria* is the "root of all evils."[5]

---

[1] Luke 16:14—φιλάργυροι. Ordinarily poor, Pharisees readily became spongers, soliciting gifts, asking for payment in kind for their services, abusing hospitality. Herod becomes irritated at the wife of Pheroras, who subsidized the Pharisees (Josephus, *War* 1.571), Alexander Jannaeus warns his wife against religious frauds, who on the outside resemble Pharisees (idem, *Ant.* 13.400–402) and who are eager for gain (*b. Soṭa* 22b; J. Jeremias, *Jerusalem*, pp. 114ff.). The scribes "devour the resources of widows" (Mark 12:40), concerning which M. J. Lagrange (on this verse) comments thus: "taking advantage of their knowledge of the law to despoil them. In societies where the rights of women depend in large measure on the protection of male relatives, widows are natural targets of greed."

[2] In the imperial era, Philargyrus is frequently used as a proper name, both among the slaves and freed slaves and also among the higher classes of society; cf. the citations brought forward by L. Robert, *Hellenica*, vol. 13, Paris, 1965, p. 260.

[3] Epictetus 2.9.12; 2.16.45; cf. Choricius of Gaza, *Apol. Min.* 73: Σμικρίνης δὲ φιλαργύρους ὁ δεδιώς, μή τι τῶν ἔνδον ὁ καπνὸς οἴχοιτο φέρων (Förster-Richsteig, pp. 360–361).

[4] Λογοπῶλοι; Philo, *Prelim. Stud.* 53 (*Quest. Gen.* 3.31), 127; cf. *Giants* 37, 39; *Moses* 2.212: "the sophists who sell, like any other commodity on the market, their principles and reasonings."

[5] 1 Tim 6:10. This might be a citation from a comic author (S. T. Byington, "I Tim. VI, 10," in *ExpT*, 1944, p. 54), but the sentence is traditional from the time of Plato:

---

aischrokerdēs, S 146; *EDNT* 1.41; *NIDNTT* 3.564; *L&N* 25.26; *BAGD* 25 ‖ *aphilargyros*, S 866; *EDNT* 1.183; *MM* 98; *L&N* 25.109; *BAGD* 126

Thus we can see the message of Heb 13:5 to its readers as being "Let your ways, or conduct, be free of all greed (*aphilargyros ho tropos*); be content with what you have."[6] The Greek Fathers supposed that the Hebrews had suffered or been threatened with the loss of their goods (10:34) and must have been trying too eagerly to rebuild their resources or guarantee their material security.[7] At any rate, trusting in Providence excludes any preoccupation with tomorrow, and one must be self-sufficient (*arkeō*, Matt 25:9; Luke 3:14; John 6:7; 1 Tim 6:8) with that which one currently has at one's disposal. In moral theology, *aphilargyria* and *tharreō theō* are linked.

St. Paul requires that the candidate for overseer at Ephesus be *aphilargyros* (1 Tim 3:3), that the Cretan overseer not be eager for shameful gain, *mē aischrokerdē* (Titus 1:7), and similarly the deacons (1 Tim 3:8). St. Peter

---

"The power that money has to give beget a thousand and one furies of insatiable greed, infinite . . . , this adoration of riches is the first and greatest source of the greatest cases of willful murder" (*Leg.* 9.870ᵃ). Preserved in the Jewish tradition (Sir 27:1–3; *T. Jud.* 19.1; Philo, *Post. Cain* 116; *Spec. Laws* 4.65: "the love of riches, a goad [or spur—ὁρμητήριον] of the greatest iniquities." *Sib. Or.* 2.115: χρυσέ, κακῶν ἀρχηγέ, βιοφθόρε, πάντα χαλέπτων; cf. 3.235) and attested in the secular literature: to love money is a supreme vice (Plutarch, *Aem.* 8.10); "The cause of all these evils was the desire for power arising from greed and ambition" (Thucydides 3.82.8; cf. Sir 10:8). Stobaeus attributes to Democrites the saying: πλοῦτος ἀπὸ κακῆς ἐργασίης περιγινόμενος ἐπιφανέστερον τὸ ὄνειδος κέκτηται, and to Bion: τὴν φιλαργυρίαν μητρόπολιν ἔλεγε πάσης κακίας εἶναι (10.36–37; vol. 3, p. 417; cf. Diogenes Laertius 6.50; Diodorus Siculus, *Exc.* 21.1); "inde fere scelerum causae" (Juvenal, *Sat.* 14.173); "Pecunia . . . semina curarum de capite orta tuo" (Propertius 3.7.4; 3.13.48ff.); τὸ κεφάλαιον τῶν κακῶν: ἐν φιλαργυρίᾳ γὰρ πάντ' ἔνι (Apollodorus of Gela, in Stobaeus, *Flor.* 16.12; vol. 3, p. 482). The image of the root implies the ideas of cause, principle, source, equally permanent and invisible. A. Plummer notes that all the other vices have their times of satiety, but cupidity has none; even its sleep is uneasy!

[6] The compound form ἀφιλάργυρος is well attested between the second century BC and the second century AD (*I.Priene* 137, 5; cf. the adverb ἀφιλαργύρως, Dittenberger, *Syl.* 708, 17; 1104, 26), notably *P.Oxy.* 33, col. II, 11: The emperor Antoninus Pius was "first of all the friend of wisdom, secondly he was no friend of money, thirdly he was the friend of the good" (cf. R. MacMullen, "The Roman Concept Robber-Pretender," in *RIDA*, 1963, pp. 224ff.). Cf. A. Deissmann, *Light*, pp. 85–86. Onasander declares that *aphilargyria* should receive the highest ranking as a chief virtue, because it makes him incorruptible and objective in the handling of business (1.8).

[7] We know the extent to which political troubles breed uncertainty and worry about tomorrow, and thus foster an awareness of provisions. Christians are exhorted to confide in Providence, which never fails (Heb 13:5–6). This Scripture citation, identical to that of Philo, *Conf. Tongues* 166, is not from Josh 1:5 but from Gen 28:15, supplemented with Deut 31:6, 8 (cf. P. Katz, "Hebr. 13, 5. The Biblical Source of the Quotation," in *Bib*, 1952, pp. 523–525).

urges the presbyters to shepherd the flock of God "not for sordid gain (*aischrokerdōs*), but out of devotion." The office of the presbyter is above all pastoral[8] and is not a sinecure: watchfulness and continual care for the sheep, providing food, guiding the movements of the flock (Num 27:17; Ps 80:2), leading them to pasture (2 Sam 5:2; Isa 40:11; Ezek 34:15; Ps 23; 95:7), keeping the sheep from dispersing and bringing back the strays (1 Kgs 22:17; Isa 53:6; Zech 11:16; 13:7; Ps 119:176), defending them against savage beasts (Exod 22:13; 1 Sam 17:34; Amos 3:12; Isa 31:4) and thieves (Gen 31:39; Job 1:17). Much courage and self-denial is therefore necessary in a "good shepherd" who seeks only the good of the flock and does not exploit them to his own profit.[9] All shepherds are susceptible to the degeneration of the hireling who is transformed by the spirit of lucre into a shameless profiteer.[10]

This probably explains why, in discussing ministers of the church, St. Paul and St. Peter substitute for the simple *aphilargyros* the highly pejorative *aischrokerdēs*.[11] A "steward" in the household of God has a subordinate

---

[8] Acts 20:28; cf. J. Dupont, *Discours de Milet*.

[9] Isa 56:11; Jer 12:10; 23:1; Ezek 34:1–10. Cf. J. Jeremias, ποιμήν, in *TDNT*, vol. 6, pp. 485–502.

[10] Notably the deacons who distribute the church's welfare provisions (Acts 6:3), manage funds, receive gifts, and are exposed to the corrupting power of "unrighteous mammon" (Luke 16: 9, 11). After defining αἰσχροκέρδεια as "the pursuit of sordid gain," Theophrastus gives this example: "He serves to his guests skimpy morsels of bread. . . . Charged with distributing meats, he pretends that the one who distributes has a right to a double portion and pays himself off immediately" (*Char.* 30.1–2). Certainly the worker is worthy of his food (Matt 10:10; Luke 10:7) and the cultivator of crops deserves part of the harvest (2 Tim 2:5). The first ministers of the gospel lived at the expense of the communities (1 Cor 9:4–14; 2 Cor 12:13–17) and received "honoraria" (1 Tim 5:17–18). But they had to remain disinterested (Acts 20:33). St. Jerome specifies: "Qui altario servierint, de altario vivant [1 Cor 4:13–14]. Vivant, inquit, non divites fiant" ("Let those who serve at the altar live by the altar. Let them live, it says, not let them become rich,"*In Tit.* 1.7). Nothing is as shameful as the spirit of lucre in the service of souls, which demands total devotion of oneself (2 Cor 12:14–15).

[11] This sordid greed is associated with villainy in Demosthenes (*3 C. Aphob.* 4). Aristotle makes it a vice against honor and moral beauty (*Eth. Nic.* 4.33.1121^{b}7ff.). The emphasis is less on grasping greed (Josephus, *Life* 75) than on the baseness of this covetousness and its consequences: an attack on human and religious dignity (cf. 1 Tim 3:8—σεμνούς); thus it is a literally "ignoble" passion (cf. Simon the Sorcerer, Acts 8:18ff.). Plautus designates in the same way the basely greedy man (*turpilucricupidus*) or "Mr. Vulture" (*Trin.* 100); cf. P. Monteil, *Beau et laid*, Paris, 1964, pp. 262ff. D. B. Durham, *Vocabulary of Menander*, p. 39. The adjective αἰσχροκερδής is not attested in the papyri before the fourth century (*P.Vindob.Tandem*, n. 4, 18), and similarly the noun (*P.Oxy.* 2267, 7).

function. He will have to turn over his accounts to his *Kyrios* (Luke 12:42–48); his uprightness, which must be beyond suspicion, is an essential element of the "ethic of the *oikonomos*" prescribed by the Lord to his servants.[12] This ethic opposes the service of mammon to the service of God (Luke 16:10–13). Xenophon had already defined it: "a good manager must not touch the goods of his master or steal them."[13] The Christian steward will be disinterested, no doubt in accord with *agapē* (1 Cor 13:5), but first of all in the name of honesty. His freedom from lust for money will guarantee not only his uprightness in the management of material goods but also his compassion toward all the miseries of his neighbors, because it is avarice that hardens the heart.[14]

---

[12] Cf. C. Spicq, "L'Origine évangélique des vertus épiscopales," in *RB*, 1946, pp. 36–46; D. Webster, "The Primary Stewardship," in *ExpT*, vol. 62, 1961, p. 274.

[13] *Oec.* 14.2; cf. P. Landvogt, *Epigraphische Untersuchungen über den* ΟΙΚΟΝΟΜΟΣ, Strasbourg, 1908.

[14] "Obduratio contra misericordiam" (St. Gregory the Great, *Moral.* 31.45).

αἰφνίδιος, αἰφνιδίως, ἐξαίφνης

aiphnidios, **sudden;** *aiphnidiōs, exaiphnēs,* **suddenly**

Derived from *aiphnēs-aipsa,* the adjective *aiphnidios* ("sudden, unforeseeable") is used for an unexpected arrival (Thucydides 8.14.1), but usually for a development that causes fear.[1] The courage of the optimist is seen in his remaining "unruffled and imperturbable when some cause for fear unexpectedly appears" (Aristotle, *Eth. Nic.* 3.11.1117ᵃ18), such as an epidemic ("pride is overcome by the sudden and unexpected [*to aiphnidion kai aprosdokēton*], that which does not conform to expectations," Thucydides 2.61.3) or especially death: "an unexpected death suddenly took his life" (Aeschylus, *PV* 680); "God who is responsible for sudden deaths";[2] especially in decrees of consolation, as at Cyzicus,[3] at Sebaste in Phrygia (*SEG* VI, 189, 4), etc.

---

[1] Plutarch, *Crass.* 9.3: "The Romans, dismayed by the suddenness of the attack, took flight." The adjective is unknown in the papyri, but the adverb αἰφνιδίως means "immediately, at once": "Before there was time to asked him when he wanted to leave, he told me at once, 'Today' " (*P.Fay.* 123, 21); a condemned man immediately asks that his remaining property be sold (*P.Stras.* 334 b 3). Numa had had a very simple meal served, but announcing that the goddess had arrived, he suddenly (αἰφνίδιον) had a magnificent table prepared for his guests (Plutarch, *Num.* 15.2); on the tombstone of a young woman who died at the age of twenty: "suddenly I was ravished by Hades" (E. Bernand, *Inscriptions métriques,* n. 84, 8 = *SB* 6178; *SEG* 8.484; *CII* 1508); on the tombstone of Politta, dead at age five: "I rest in Hades, to which I was suddenly carried off" (E. Bernand, *Inscriptions métriques* 96, 7).

[2] Heraclitus, *All.* 8.4: τοῖς αἰφνιδίοις θανάτοις; Thucydides 2.53.1: "prosperous men died suddenly."

[3] Κτανθεὶς αἰφνιδίως λαθρίου ἀνδρὸς ἄρε, W. Peek, in *Athenische Mitteilungen,* 1931, p. 129, n. 14. L. Robert ("Enterrements et épitaphes," in *L'Antiquité classique,* 1968, pp. 418ff.) cites an honorific decree from Olbia: When Nikratos was killed in an ambush, the people were suddenly thrown into distress (αἰφνίδιος συμφορὰν θεασάμενος, Dittenberger, *Syl.* 730, 20; cf. 709, 9; *Or.* 339, 18), the epitaph of Arkesine,

---

aiphnidios, S 160; *EDNT* 1.44; MM 16; L&N 67.113; BAGD 26 ‖ *exaiphnēs,* S 1810; *EDNT* 2.1; MM 221; L&N 67.113; BDF §25; BAGD 272

The LXX uses the adjective only twice: for a sudden and unexpected fear (*aiphnidios kai aprosdokētos phobos*, Wis 17:14), and for the sudden and terrifying arrival of enemies.[4] Philo uses it a few times in a positive sense (the sudden light of wisdom, *Sacr. Abel and Cain* 78; *Migr. Abr.* 156, 184; *Dreams* 2.137) or in the neutral sense of a sudden change (*Alleg. Interp.* 1.17; *Flacc.* 154), but the other occurrences are all pejorative: the wind and the storm that capsize ships (*Cherub.* 38; *Husbandry* 174–176; *Spec. Laws* 4.201), sudden floods (*Dreams* 2.125), the rising tide and waves that cause disasters (*Moses* 1.179; 2.254), a cloud of dust that causes a cruelly painful ulceration (ibid. 1.127), lightning that annihilates with one strike (ibid. 2.154, 283), the sudden collapse of a wall (*Etern. World* 129), the sudden attacks of criminals (*Spec. Laws* 1.75), the sudden death of animals as the prelude to pestilential epidemics (*Moses* 1.133). This suddenness is also a characteristic of evil: the sudden inability to grasp the idea of the good and keep it in oneself (*Giants* 20); errors attack the soul all at once and besmirch it (*Flight* 115); the sudden loss of moral precepts (*Unchang. God* 89; cf. 26); a sudden dissoluteness (*Spec. Laws* 3.126; *Rewards* 146); "a sudden and unexpected trouble seized them" (*aiphnidios kai aprosdokētos tarachē*, *Joseph* 211); "a blind and sudden onset of folly and rage" (*Flacc.* 140).

In Josephus, reference is also made to disasters that strike terror (*War* 5.472), to shakings of the earth (*Ant.* 4.51), to sudden death and sickness (7.325; 12.413; *Life* 48), to sudden reversals of fortune (18.197), and thus sudden fear (9.199). Suddenness is often neutral, however: the wind changes suddenly (*War* 7.318), a cloud descends suddenly (*Ant.* 4.326), flame suddenly bursts out (3.207; *War* 4.180), someone shows up unexpectedly (*Life* 253), guards wake up suddenly (*War* 6.69), defenders suddenly open the gates (4.553; *Ant.* 7.139); but especially attacks by soldiers are so described.[5]

In his warnings concerning the last days, the Lord urges vigilance, as at the prospect of a cataclysm. This is not the time for spiritual lethargy: "Watch yourselves, lest your hearts be weighed down with excessive eating and drinking and the preoccupation of life, lest that day come upon you unawares (*epistē eph' hymas aiphnidios hē hēmera ekeinē*) like a snare" (Luke 21:34). The unexpectedness of the coming of the divine Judge is supposed

---

or of Philostorgus, dead at age twenty, ἁρπασμ' ἐγενήθην αἰφνιδίου Μοίρης (*GVI*, n. 1097, 4), that of Amorgus or the young Bryto, who died suddenly at the peak of her youth and beauty (*IG* XII, 7, 239; cf. 52, 394, 395, 397, 399, 401).

[4] 2 Macc 14.17; cf. 3 Macc 3:24. αἰφνιδίως: a surprise attack on Jerusalem (2 Macc 5:5); fear of sudden treachery on the part of enemies (14:22).

[5] *War* 5.75; *Ant.* 6.79, 362; 7.73; 8.377; 9.82, 113; cf. the meaning "right away, immediately afterward" (*War* 4.420). Dionysius of Halicarnassus: "Caesar frightened Ariovistus by the suddenness of his attack" (τῷ αἰφνιδίῳ τῆς ἐφόδου, 38.47).

to inspire fear and thus wakefulness—a meaning of *aiphnidios* that conforms completely with classical Greek, the LXX, and Philo and is comparable to *en tachei* in the parable of the Widow and the Judge.[6] Thus the word here has a technical sense, almost equivalent to "formidable." St. Paul retains it: "When they say, 'Peace and security,' then ruin will suddenly befall them (*tote aiphnidios autois ephistatai olethros*), like the pains of a woman in labor" (1 Thess 5:3); the unforeseen character of the distress makes it all the harder to bear.

With the same meaning: "Watch, for you do not know when the master of the house is coming . . . lest coming suddenly (*mē elthōn exaiphnēs*) he find you sleeping" (Mark 13:36). The compound form *exaiphnēs*, referring to an unforeseen arrival, one that is not announced, for which there was no warning, is almost synonymous with the simple *aiphnidios* and could be translated "instantaneously, all at once."[7] In the LXX, with a single exception,[8] it is used only in the context of disaster (Prov 24:22; Isa 47:11—

---

[6] Luke 18:7–8 contrasts the slowness or patience of God—who delays (μακροθυμεῖ), takes a long time to do justice for his people—with his sudden and rapid (ἐν τάχει = speedily) intervention. The emphasis is on prompt execution (cf. Rev 22:12; Plutarch, *Tim.* 21.7). We may interpret "suddenly, all at once, at one stroke" or better "like lightning"; swiftness is a sign of diligence, of a resolute and sovereign will, cf. C. Spicq, "La Parabole de la Veuve obstinée et du Juge inique aux décisions impromptues," in *RB*, 1961, pp. 68–90; H. Riesenfeld, "Zu μακροθυμεῖν (Lk XVIII, 7)," in J. Blinzler, *Neutestamentliche Aufsätze: Festschrift J. Schmid*, Regensburg, 1963, pp. 214–217.

[7] Homer, *Il.* 17.738: "the fire that instantly flared up"; 21.14; Pindar, *Ol.* 9.52: "suddenly this tide went down"; Aeschylus, *PV* 1077: "it is not suddenly, unexpectedly, that you will find yourself caught in the inescapable net of woe"; Hierocles: διὰ τὰς ἐξαιφνιδίους καὶ ἀπροσδοκήτους ἐπιδρομὰς τῆς τύχης (in Stobaeus, *Flor.* 84.27.20; vol. 4, p. 664, 2; cf. Plato, *Cra.* 414 a). Plato defines the instantaneous (τὸ ἐξαίφνης) as "the point of departure for two inverse changes" (*Prm.* 156 d); likewise Aristotle: "the instantaneous is a change that happens in a time that is so quick that it cannot be noticed" (*Ph.* 4.13.222b15); Iamblichus: "The one (superior, perfect) can do everything at once and uniformly; the other (deficient, less perfect) cannot act all at once or suddenly (οὔτε ἐξαίφνης) or indivisibly" (*Myst.* 1.7 = 21.4); "the gods in an instant (ἐξαίφνης), so to speak, made a clean cut" (5.4 = 203.12). Suddenness is characteristic of miraculous manifestations (Plutarch, *De def. or.* 17) and dream images: "Suddenly I opened my eyes and saw the Twins" (*UPZ* 78, 7). In the papyri, ἐξαίφνης refers to the instantaneousness of a departure (*P.Giss.* 86; *P.Flor.* 175, 7; *SB* 9558, 10; cf. 8858, 48), to hearing news quickly (*P.Lond.* 1914, 3), "I warned you that very soon we would have no more hay for the horses" (*P.Mich.* 21, 2). Zoilus wanted to prepare for the feast of Arsinoë, καὶ μὴ ἐξαίφνης ἀπαράσκευοι καταληφθῶμεν (*P.Cair.Zen.* 59096, 4); a Libyan marauder broke in "suddenly at dawn" (ἐξαίφνης ὑπὸ τὸν ὄρθον, *P.Oxy.* 3292, 15; cf. Acts 5:21).

[8] Mal 3:1—"Suddenly the Lord whom you seek will arrive in his temple, the king of the covenant." Ἐξαίφνης translates the Hebrew *pit'ōm* or *peta'*, which may

apōleia); the desert wind striking the house, which collapses, burying the children (Job 1:19); suddenly falling prey to creditors (Hab 2:7); "in an instant, in a single day, the loss of children and widowhood" (Isa 47:9); "suddenly devastation comes to us" (Jer 6:26); "on the mother I have made sudden sleeplessness and terror to fall" (Jer 15:8). Philo, who gives this adverb the meaning "rapidly," uses it sometimes in a positive, even a religious sense,[9] or in a neutral context: to appear suddenly (*Sacr. Abel and Cain* 26), to burst in suddenly (*Flacc.* 113; *To Gaius* 217), a statue set up unexpectedly (*To Gaius* 337). By far the commonest use, however, is with woes: lightning that destroys everything (*Alleg. Interp.* 3.227), a torrent that overflows (*Post. Cain* 113), a ship that suddenly wrecks at port after a safe voyage (*Dreams* 2.143; cf. *Virtues* 49), bad weather and disasters (*Abraham* 138; *Moses* 1.118; *Etern. World* 141), human misery.[10]

Like *aiphnidios*, the adverb *exaiphnēs* means "suddenly, all at once," like the light that shone around Paul on the Damascus road (Acts 9:3; 22:6), as well as "immediately, immediately afterward, forthwith." When the angel had announced the birth of a Savior to the shepherds of Bethlehem, "suddenly" there was with the angel "a large number of the host of heaven praising God" (Luke 2:13); "a spirit seizes him (the epileptic), and suddenly he screams" (Luke 9:39); this meaning is entirely classical: "as soon as he heard their sudden bitter cry, . . . he said" (Sophocles, *OC* 1610); the judge sees each soul "immediately after death" (Plato, *Grg.* 523 *e*; cf. *Cra.* 396 *b*). The LXX has this usage: "these woes, from which you will not quickly extricate yourselves" (Mic 2:3), as do Philo (*Creation* 113) and Josephus (*Ant.* 7.225).

---

well come from the Akkadian *pitta, pittimma, ina pitta* = instantaneous; cf. D. Daube, *The Sudden in the Scripture,* Leiden, 1964, p. 3.

[9]*Unchang. God* 37: "the young plants quickly spring up"; 92: "all at once we find the treasury of faithfulness complete"; 97; *Migr. Abr.* 35; *Change of Names* 165; *Moses* 1.65, 283: "suddenly seized with a divine rapture"; *Rewards* 15: "suddenly seized by ardor and love for the better"; *Cherub.* 100.

[10]*Moses* 2.271: "the people were suddenly blinded"; *Spec. Laws* 1.57: the burning of rage; 3.96: of implacable torments; 107; *Joseph* 23, 238: of tears; 214: "Sorrow and fear, the bitterest of evils, fell suddenly upon them"; *Husbandry* 176: "involuntary offenses swoop down suddenly, thoughtlessly"; *To Gaius* 123: "suddenly to find oneself without shelter or hearth, expelled and banished." In Josephus, ἐξαίφνης is used for an unexpected arrival (*War* 1.87; 2.13; *Ant.* 7.218, 299, 333; 13.391), an abrupt about-face (*War* 1.101), a fire (2.49), a tower that collapses (2.436; 4.65), the shaking of the earth (*Ant.* 10.269), a sudden attack or violence (13.337; *War* 5.71).

ἄκακος

akakos, good, beneficent, innocent

This adjective is used only twice in the NT (Rom 16:18; Heb 7:26) and is rather rare in classical Greek, where *kakos* ("bad, of bad quality") is quite plentiful.[1] The alpha privative ("non-bad") should not throw us off the track. The first meaning of *akakos* is "positively good"; Aeschylus, *Pers.* 662: "Come, beneficent father Darius"; but there is also Demosthenes, *C. Euerg.* 47.46: "his pretended innocence made an impression on the judges"; Plato, *Tim.* 91 d: "these men who are devoid of evil but light-minded, with their thoughts turned toward the heavens"; Polybius 3.98.5: the Carthaginian general Bostar "was a man without malice (*akakon onta ton andra*) and by nature mild,"[2] like the Lacedaemonian general Callicratides, "of a mild character and a simple soul" (*akakos kai tēn psychēn haplous*, Diodorus Siculus 13.76); Menander, *Dysk.* 222: "you who leave an innocent young woman (*akakon korēn*) all alone, with no more precaution than if the house were empty."[3] Childlike innocence, meaning ignorance of error, of moral

---

[1] Cf. W. Grundmann, "κακός, ἄκακος," in *TDNT*, vol. 3, pp. 469–487. Having no known etymology, κακός expresses a lack, an incapacity, a weakness; the substantive κακόν, κακά: woe, suffering, ruin; κάκωσις: mistreatment (Acts 7:34); the denominative verb κακόω = mistreat, do evil, destroy (Acts 7:6, 19; 12:1; 14:2; 18:10; 1 Pet 3:13). The philosophers reflected on evil, its origin, nature, and consequences. On the moral level, κακός is the opposite of ἀγαθός and ἀρετή (Rom 7:19–21; 12:21; 13:3–4; 16:19; Philo, *Post. Cain* 32; *Good Man Free* 84; *Spec. Laws* 2.53; *Flight* 62, 79; Epictetus 2.4.4; 4.1.42; Stobaeus, *Ecl.* 2.7.5; [Zeno, vol. 2, p. 57, 19; p. 70, 14: κατὰ τὰ περὶ ψυχήν, 1.1.12; Cleanthes, vol. 1, p. 26, 6]; Plutarch, *De comm. not.* 17, 34; *De Stoic. rep.* 35), especially in the LXX, where the term is found ninety-five times in Proverbs alone. In the NT, (Mark 7:21, 23; 1 Tim 6:10; Jas 1:13; 3:8; 1 Pet 3:10, quoting Ps 31:13–17), κακός is replaced especially by ἁμαρτία and πονηρός; cf. Col 3:5—ἐπιθυμίαν κακήν (like Philo, *Spec. Laws* 4.84) and Luke 16:25—τὰ κακά, ruin, woe.

[2] Cf. Plutarch, *De aud. poet.* 7, contrasting θαυμαστικοὶ καὶ ἄκακοι with καταφρονητικοὶ καὶ θρασεῖς.

[3] Cf. Anaxilas, regarding flatterers: εἰς ἄκακον τὸν ἀνθρώπου τρόπον (Athenaeus 6.254 c; cf. J. M. Edmonds, *Attic Comedy*, vol. 2, p. 344, 9 A).

---

akakos, S 172; *TDNT* 3.482; *EDNT* 1.48; *NIDNTT* 1.561, 563; MM 17; L&N 31.34, 88.2; BAGD 29

evil, of vice, is often mentioned in the funerary epigrams,[4] as at Olympus: "Here lies Pisidis Hermaios, son of Hermas, an innocent child."[5]

This double meaning "perfect, whole," and "innocent, without malice" is also found in the fifteen occurrences in the LXX. It means the former when it translates the Hebrew *tām, tāmîm*, "whole, without defect": "Job was a perfect and upright man" (*anthrōpos akakos alēthinos amemptos*, Job 2:3, cf. 8:20; 36:5; Prov 2:21; 13:6). On the other hand, the meaning "simple, without malice" is clear in Jer 11:19—"I, like an innocent lamb (*hōs arnion akakon*) that is led to the slaughter." The Hebrew *'alûp*, "tame," was understood to mean "without malice, naive," not suspecting that it was being led to its death. *Akakos* is linked with uprightness (Ps 25:21). But the LXX created a new type of "simple" (Hebrew *p^e tî*), something like "ingenuous," almost foolishly simple,[6] as opposed to the crafty, the clever, the astute, the sly, the deceitful. The Book of Proverbs is addressed to those who are inexperienced and simple (*akakois*) to teach them discernment (Prov 1:4; 8:5); they need to be educated (15:10, *paideia akakou*) because they are ignorant and will only learn prudence little by little (21:11, *panourgoteros ginetai ho akakos*); they are considered simpletons and derided (1:22). They believe everything that they are told (14:15), and their ignorance of all malice leaves them incapable of resisting the temptations of concupiscence, so they let themselves be perverted (Wis 4:12). They are a bit dim.

This candor is a function of age ("the perfect innocence of newborns")[7] and of virtue (Diodorus Siculus 5.66). The high priests must not keep company with any but "totally innocent and upright folk" (Philo, *Spec. Laws* 1.105), but this naiveté or simplemindedness is dangerous, because it makes a person credulous, and astute and hypocritical people take advan-

---

[4] Cf. H. Herter, "Das unschuldige Kind," in *JAC*, 1961, pp. 146–162; L. Robert, "Enterrements et épitaphes," in *L'Antiquité classique*, Brussels, 1968, pp. 430–433.

[5] Πισίδις Ἑρμαῖος, υἱὸς Ἑρμοῦ, ἄκακον παιδείν (= παιδίον) ἐνθάδε κεῖται, *TAM* II, 3, n. 1147. The papyri provide only two occurrences of ἄκακος, which are cited by Moulton-Milligan: a rental contract on a house, λ[άχαν]ον νέον νέον καθαρὸν ἄδολ(ον) . . . ἄκακον, i.e., not damaged, intact (*BGU* IV, 1015, 1; third century AD); a receipt for the payment for a shipment of 1,485 1/4 *artabai* of grain: σίτου . . . καθαροῦ ἀκάκου (*P.Oxy.* 142, 5; sixth century).

[6] Ps.-Plato, *II Alc.* 140 c: "People share unreason (ἀφροσύνην). Those who have the most of it we call madmen (μαινομένους); those who have somewhat less we call fools and nuts . . . some are fanatics, some are simple; others are people without malice (ἀκάκους), without experience (ἀπείρους), simpletons (ἐνεούς)."

[7] Philo, *Spec. Laws* 3.119; *Virtues* 43: "They spared the young women out of pity for their innocent youth" (ἄκακον ἡλικίαν); *Flacc.* 68: these men burned people without pity for innocent youth (ἄκακον ἡλικίαν); *To Gaius* 234: τὴν ἄκακον ἡλικίαν; Plutarch, *Mulier. virt.* 23: παιδίσκη νέα καὶ ἄκακος; cf. Aristotle, *Rh.* 2.12.1389b9. Josephus does not use this adjective.

tage. Charlatans link up with "simple and ingenuous souls (*aplastous kai akakōtatois ēthesi*) whom they lure and deceive."[8]

These are the credulous simpletons who are in view in Rom 16:18, which warns against "those people," Judaizers or Gnostics who instigate dissension and scandal through their teaching (verse 17); "they seduce the hearts of the simple,"[9] i.e., of naive people who are easily duped. In contrast, when Heb 7:26 writes of Christ the heavenly high priest, "Such is the high priest that we needed, holy, innocent, undefiled" (*hosios, akakos, amiantos*),[10] this means absolute perfection in the sense of the Book of Job, with an extreme insistence on the absence of any stain, for in heaven he is even "separated from sinners." Hence the redundancy of these adjectives, which amounts to a superlative. *Hosios* implies (1) consecrated to God as a priest; (2) holy in the cultic sense, possessing the qualities necessary for the accomplishment of the sacred functions;[11] (3) holy in the moral sense, possessing a perfection that is lacking in nothing, carrying God's will completely. *Akakos* means that like an innocent lamb (Jer 11:19), Christ is the spotless victim, acceptable to God (Job 8:20). *Amiantos* means without stain, pure, is the adjective used for the chaste (Heb 13:4), for a consecrated temple (2 Macc 14:36; 15:34), for authentically religious acts (Jas 1:27). The perfection of the Christ-Priest is thus consummate, absolute, religious, and moral.

---

[8] Philo, *Spec. Laws* 3.101; *Husbandry* 96: "a serpent who speaks with a human voice, who insinuates himself into the most innocent ways of life (ἀκακωτάτοις ἤθεσιν), who deceives a woman through the false splendor of his seduction"; *Joseph* 6: "in his innocence (ἀκάκοις τοῖς ἤθεσιν), Joseph did not perceive his brothers' secret enmity"; *Pss. Sol.* 4.6—the judge who lives in iniquity "is ready to enter any house with a smile, like an innocent person" (ὡς ἄκακον); 4.25—"They deceived innocent souls (ψυχὰς ἀκακῶν) through their sophistry"; 12.4—"May God save the innocent from the tongue of the godless."

[9] Ἐξαπατῶσι τὰς καρδίας τῶν ἀκάκων. O. Michel, *Der Brief an die Römer*, Göttingen, 1955) translates "die Arglosen"; E. Käsemann (*An die Römer*, Tübingen, 1973), "die Arglosen" = "the simple" (ET *Commentary on Romans*, trans. G. W. Bromiley, Grand Rapids, 1980). Cf. W. Schmithals, "Die Irrlehrer von Rm XVI, 17–20," in *ST*, vol. 13, 1959, pp. 51–69 (mentions the νήπιοι ἐν Χριστῷ of 1 Cor 2:6ff.; 3:1ff); R. Devreesse, "La deuxième aux Corinthiens et la seconde finale aux Romains," in *Mélanges Tisserant*, vol. 1, pp. 146–161; R. Trvijano, "Εὐλογία in St. Paul and the Text of Rom. XVI, 18," in *SE*, vol. 6, Berlin, 1973, pp. 537–540.

[10] Cf. C. Spicq, *Hébreux*, vol. 2, pp. 199ff. R. A. Stewart, "The Sinless High-Priest," in *NTS*, vol. 14, 1967, pp. 126–135.

[11] S. Meinke, "Der Platonische und neutestamentliche Begriff der ὁσιότης," in *TSK*, 1884, pp. 743–768; H. van der Walk, "Zum Worte ὅσιος," in *Mnemosyne*, 1942, p. 118; H. Jeanmaire, "Le Substantif Hosia et sa signification comme terme technique dans le vocabulaire religieux," in *REG*, 1945, pp. 66–89; L. Moulinier, *Le Pur et l'impur dans la pensée des Grecs*, Paris, 1952.

ἄκαρπος

akarpos, fruitless, barren

Sterility or barrenness—the incapacity for generation, the condition of that which does not produce anything—is a term that applies literally to unproductive land,[1] of trees that bear no fruit,[2] and of unmarried persons with no children.[3] It is also used figuratively for a fruitless labor (Wis 15:4), a profitless work,[4] such as the *erga akarpa* of darkness which produce nothing good or valuable (Eph 5:11), as opposed to the fruit of the light (verse 9); and above all it is used of the word of God smothered in the hearts of some by the cares of the world.[5]

It is more difficult to say exactly what the meaning is in Titus 3:14— "Our people[6] must also learn to be first in good works . . . so that they will

---

[1] Jer 2:6 (the desert without water); Polybius 12.3.2; Josephus, *Ant.* 15.300 (cf. *War* 4.452: a bare and arid mountain); *P.Iand.* 142, col. II, 24–25, second century AD (unproductive soil).

[2] Jude 12; Dittenberger, *Syl.* 900, 30 (first century AD). In AD 316, Aurelius Irenaeus, president of the carpenters' guild, relates his evaluation of a tree that has been sterile for years and is still incapable of producing any fruit (*P.Oxy.* 53, 9). In the papyri, this phrase constantly recurs with respect to the transfer of fields: "with the trees [or plants] that bear fruit and those that do not bear fruit" (*P.Dura* 26, 11; *P.Michael.* 42 A 18; *P.Hamb.* 23, 19; 68, 7; *P.Avroman* 1; ed. E. H. Minns, in *JHS,* vol. 35, 1915, pp. 22–65); cf. Epictetus 1.17.9–10: "The bushel is made of wood, it is sterile. . . . Logic is also sterile."

[3] Dedicated epigram at Philoxenos: ὀρφανὸς ἐκ προγόνων, ἄγονος, 'θανεν, ᾧ τὸν ἄκαρπον βλαστόν (*I.Thas.*, 332, 10); cf. the adverbial usage from the fourth century BC in this epitaph of Elpis: "I have twice endured the pains of childbirth, not without fruit, οὐδ' ἐς ἄκαρπον" (*I.Sard.*, 104, 3). Cf. 4 Macc 16:7—"Futile these seven fattenings! Useless these seven gestations . . . barren (ἄκαρποι) the first care that I gave them." According to Josephus, Abraham returned thanks to God that Sarah, at first sterile (ἀκάρπως) was then made fecund (*Ant.* 2.213).

[4] 1 Cor 14:14 (cf. P. Bonnard, "L'Intelligence chez saint Paul," in *Mélanges F. J. Leenhardt,* Geneva, 1968, pp. 13–14); cf. the irascible athletes with dry and passionate dispositions who bring no returns for their trainers—ἄκαρποι τοῖς γυμνάζουσι—like the hot sand for the seedings of farmers (Philostratus, *Gym.* 42).

[5] Matt 13:22—ἄκαρπος γίνεται; cf. Luke 8:14—οὐ τελεσφοροῦσιν; Mark 4:7— καρπὸν οὐκ ἔδωκεν.

[6] Οἱ ἡμέτεροι designates a definite plurality (the suffix *-tero* added to ἡμεῖς has a differentiating function, cf. E. Benveniste, *Noms d'agent,* Paris, 1948, p. 119): members

---

akarpos, S 175; *TDNT* 3.616; *EDNT* 2.251–252; *NIDNTT* 1.721, 723; MM 17; L&N

ἄκαρπος, akarpos 57

not be without fruit" (hina mē ōsin akarpoi).⁷ It could refer to growth in virtue⁸ or to the gaining of a reward.⁹ Most likely, however, this is a reference to a law of fruitbearing, which is a major urgency of New Testament ethics.¹⁰ It appears in the Synoptics, from the Sermon on the Mount, where the plant is judged by its fruit (Matt 7:16–20), and the parable of the Sower (13:3–8) to the incident involving the barren fig tree (Luke 13:6–9); in St. Paul (Rom 7:4; Eph 2:10), who prescribes the bearing of fruit;¹¹ and in St. John, where the branch is judged by its productivity (John 15:2, 4–8; cf. 12:24). Hence akarpos gains a theological significance in the language of the New Testament: if every Christian is supposed to engage in fruitful activity,¹² the false teachers are without fruit (Jude 12), and the bad Christian is one who produces no fine and noble works. His barrenness is the proof that he is a counterfeit; he is not vitally connected to Christ.

---

of the same family (Plato, Menex. 248ᵇ; Strabo 6.3.3), clients (P.Oxy. 37, col. I, 16; from AD 49 P.Fam.Tebt. 24, 99, P.Oslo 80, 5), "our people" as belonging to a restricted group (P.Oxy. 787, a letter of recommendation from the year 16: ὡς ἔστιν ἡμέτερος = as he is one of ours; cf. in 116, at the time of the Jewish insurrection in Egypt: οἱ ἡμέτεροι ἡττήθησαν, C.Pap.Jud. 438, 7; P.Ryl. 696, 4; P.Oslo 127, 14). Here the group is Christians on Crete, as opposed to "those outside" (1 Thess 4:12; 1 Cor 5:12; Col 4:5; 1 Tim 3:7), Jews or pagans (cf. Titus 1:10).
⁷ Several commentators see here a proleptic response to the accusations of the Romans that the Christians are useless citizens, "infructuosi in negociis" ("unproductive in business"), as Tertullian puts it; he responds: "Navigamus nos vobiscum et militamus et rusticamur et mercamur: proinde miscemus artes nostras, operas nostras publicamus usui vestro" (Apol. 42: "We sail, fight, farm, and trade with you; so also we will share our arts; we publish our works for your use").
⁸ Cf. 2 Pet 1:8—These virtues "when you possess them and they abound keep you from being either inactive or without fruit—οὐκ ἀργοὺς οὐδὲ ἀκάρπους—in the knowledge of our Lord Jesus Christ." Ἀργός is used for a worker who is doing nothing (Matt 20:3, 6), for goods or properties that bring no return (P.Flor. 1, 4, 13), deeds or works that do not succeed (1 Tim 5:13; Jas 2:20).
⁹ Titus proclaims, "noble deeds should not go unrewarded" (Josephus, War 6.36).
¹⁰ J. Bommer, Die Idee der Fruchtbarkeit in den Evangelien, Pfullingen, 1950 (dissertation); C. Spicq, "Le Chrétien doit porter du fruit," in VSpir, 363, 1951, pp. 605–615; F. Böckle, Die Idee der Fruchtbarkeit in den Paulusbriefen, Fribourg, 1953; A. Lozeron, La Notion de fruit dans le N.T., Lausanne, 1957. Cf. H. Riesenfeld, "Le Langage parabolique dans les épîtres de saint Paul," in Recherches bibliques, vol. 5, Bruges, 1960, pp. 53ff.
¹¹ Cf. Col 1:6, 10, καρποφορεῖν; cf. Heb 6:7–8; 12:11. Origen, commenting on the parable of the talents (Luke 19:11–27) in terms of Gen 1:28 and Wis 14:4, explains that God does not want his gifts to humankind to remain unproductive: θέλει δὲ μὴ ἀργὰ εἶναι μηδὲ ἄκαρπα μήτε ἀτελεσφόρητα τὰ δοθέντα τῷ ἀνθρώπῳ (P.Giss. 17, 22).
¹² Ἔργα = καρπός; cf. Phil 1:22—καρπὸς ἔργου; Rom 6:22—ἔχετε τὸν καρπὸν ὑμῶν (subjective genitive: your personal fruit).

ἀκατάγνωστος

akatagnōstos, **unobjectionable, irreproachable**

In his preaching, Titus is to speak only "unattackable" words, so that the adversaries[1] will be disarmed, finding nothing blameworthy or unseemly to denounce (Titus 2:8). That is to say, in the church, which is a column or buttress of the truth (1 Tim 3:15), one proclaims only the truth, that to which no one can raise any objection (cf. 2 Cor 13:8).

The NT hapax *akatagnōstos*, literally "nothing known against," is a juridical term expressing the innocence of one acquitted in a trial.[2] It does not appear in the papyri except in the Byzantine period, with respect to an unimpeachable contract or an irreproachable person. Thus it has a moral value, often associated with *amemptōs*,[3] *deontōs*,[4] and *spoudeōs*:[5] the contractor agrees to work or to render his services, promising that he will be "without reproach" or irreproachable. Titus 2:8 is thus one of many cases where St. Paul seems to be ahead of his time with respect to linguistic usages.

---

[1] Ὁ ἐξ ἐναντίας is the one facing (Mark 15:39), hence opposing; the one who is against (Acts 28:17; *P.Ryl.* 144, 15). Here, it is pagan criticism in general (cf. Titus 2:5, 10; 1 Pet 2:12; ὁ ἀντικείμενος, 1 Tim 5:14), but above all the false teachers, the opposition by definition (Titus 1:9; 2 Tim 2:25), lying in wait for any possible grounds for dispute.

[2] 2 Macc 4:47—Antiochus IV "sent back Menelaus, the author of all this evil, absolved of the accusations brought against him and condemned to death some unfortunates who, if they had been able to defend their cause even before the Scythians [the cruelest of barbarians], would have been acquitted (ἀκατάγνωστοι)." The word, unknown in the literary language before the third century, is attested in the inscriptions, cf. A. Deissmann, *Bible Studies*, p. 200; Θεοδώρα δούλη θεοῦ ἀκατάγνωστος (A. C. Bandy, *The Greek Christian Inscriptions of Crete*, Athens, 1970, n. 8).

[3] *P.Michael.* 41, 41; *PSI* 932, 10; *Pap.Lugd.Bat.* XI, 7, 15; *P.Oxy.* 2478, 19. Cf. *P.Grenf.* 1.58, 11: τρεφομένων παρ' ἐμοῦ ἀναμφιβόλως καὶ ἀκαταφρονήτως καὶ ἀκαταγνώστως.

[4] *P.Ross.Georg.* III, 51, 19; *SB* 9293, 16: ἐνδέξασθαι ἐν αὐταῖς δεόντως καὶ ἀκαταφρονήτως; *P.Lond.* 113 (4), 15. Cf. *Stud.Pal.*, vol. 20, 219, 17.

[5] *Pap.Lugd.Bat.* XI, 10, 4; cf. *P.Oxy.* 140, 15: ἀμέμπτως καὶ ἀόκνως καὶ ἀκαταγνώστως μετὰ πάσης σπουδῆς; *P.Giss.* 56, 14; cf. *P.Mil.* 48, 6; *SB* 9011, 6; 9152, 10.

---

akatagnōstos, S 176; *TDNT* 1.714–715; *EDNT* 1.48; MM 17; L&N 33.415; BAGD 29

ἀκλινής

aklinēs, stable, unchanging, firm

Unknown in Josephus, attested by one late occurrence in the papyri,[1] *aklinēs*, literally "which does not bend, is straight," signifies "stable, set," then "unmoving, at rest"; it is a synonym of *bebaios*.[2] It is used of an enduring friendship (*Anth. Pal.* 12.158.4) and above all to unshakable reason or judgment.[3] The emphasis is on immutability.[4] It is Philo who gave this adjective its religious and moral sense by attributing stability on the one hand to God, as opposed to creatures,[5] and on the other hand to the perfectly regenerated human.[6] From that point one can see how the term made it into the vocabulary of the Epistle to the Hebrews, which exhorts us to hold fast the *homologia* of our hope (Heb 10:23). This hope, which is "firmly founded" on the promise of God,[7] must be guarded without wavering. Note that the content of faith is identical to its hope (cf. Heb 11:1), just as in 1 Pet 3:15.

---

[1] A fifth-century petition, εὐχαριστήσω ταῖς ἀκλεινεῖς ἀκοαῖς τῆς ὑμετέρας ἐξουσίας: I will give thanks to the impartial ears of your Authority (*P.Oxy.* 904, 9).

[2] Philo, *Spec. Laws* 2.2, of an oath: ὅρκος ἔστω βέβαιος, ἀκλινής; cf. Heb 6:19.

[3] 4 Macc 6:7 contrasts the body of Eleazer, which has become feeble, to his reason, which remains sound and unshakable; cf. Philo, *Giants* 54: "Moses establishes his judgment immutably"; Plotinus, *Enn.* 2.9.2: "There exists only one intelligence, which is unique, identical, always the same, unshakable (νοῦς ἀκλινής), and imitates her father as much as possible." Cf. Lucian, *Encom. Demosth.* 33, ἀ. τῆς ψυχῆς.

[4] 4 Macc 17:3—"You stood up to the upheaval of the tortures without giving ground"; Philo, *Moses* 1.30: "as if one had arranged for oneself an immutable and perfectly sealed success, when perhaps the following day will no longer find us in the same situation"; *Virtues* 158: "the trunk [of the tree] based on a firm foundation."

[5] Philo, *Alleg. Interp.* 2.83: "God explains the difference between himself and the creature; he himself remains always unmoving (ἀκλινής ἔστηκεν ἀεί) and the creature wavers and vacillates between opposite directions"; 2.89: "How can one believe in God? By learning that all else changes and he alone remains immutable (ἄτρεπτος)"; *Giants* 49: "Stability and immutable repose, these are what one finds with God, who always stands unmoving."

[6] Cf. A. J. Festugière, *Hermès Trismégiste*, vol. 2, p. 214, who cites *Quest. Exod.* 2.96 (*immutabilitas*).

[7] Cf. C. Spicq, *Théologie morale*, pp. 330ff.

---

aklinēs, S 186; EDNT 1.49; MM 18; L&N 31.80; BAGD 30

ἀκρασία, ἐγκράτεια

akrasia, lack of self-control; *enkrateia*, self-control

Both of these terms derive from *kratos*, "force"; the *enkratēs* is the person who is master of himself; the *a-kratēs* is the one who cannot contain himself, who is lacking in power. From the time of Socrates, who made *enkrateia* the basis and foundation of all the virtues,[1] and Aristotle, who distinguished between the perfectly chaste person who knows no impure desires (*sōphrōn*) and the continent person (*enkratēs*) who feels their power but resists them (*Eth. Nic.* 7.1–11; pp. 1145^a–1152^a), this control over impulses and this tempering of the passions are considered among the Greeks as an element of prudence-temperance (*sōphrosynē*), and consequently an essential virtue for the honest person.

In the OT, it appears only in the books influenced by Hellenism and has no distinctive meaning,[2] as opposed to the *Letter of Aristeas*.[3] In the NT, it is associated with righteousness,[4] with gentleness (Gal 5:23), or

---

[1] According to Xenophon, *Mem.* 1.5.4 (cf. T. Camelot, "Egkratéia," in *Dictionnaire de Spiritualité*, vol. 4, col. 358; O. Gogon, *Kommentar zum zweiten Buch von Xenophons Memorabilien*, Basel, 1959, p. 9), implicitly followed by Philo: "On the basis of self-control, the *Therapeutai* build up the other virtues of the soul" (*Contemp. Life* 34). This became a commonplace since Panetius defined *temperamentia* in similar terms (Cicero, *Part. Or.* 76–78).

[2] Notably in Sir 18:15, 30, evoking the soul that is master of itself: ἐγκράτεια ψυχῆς; cf. 26:15.

[3] "By nature, all men are *akrateis* and have a natural inclination to seek pleasure. . . . The state of virtue, on the other hand, restrains those who are being pulled away by the love of pleasure and invites them to give priority to *enkrateia* and justice" (*Ep. Arist.* 277–278).

[4] Acts 24:25; same association in *Acts John* 84. This theme of Paul's preaching is taken up in *Acts Paul Thec.* 5: λόγος θεοῦ περὶ ἐγκρατείας καὶ ἀναστάσεως. . . .

---

akrasia, S 192; *TDNT* 2.339–342; *EDNT* 1.54; *NIDNTT* 1.494–496; *L&N* 88.91; *BAGD* 33 ‖ *enkrateia*, S 1466; *TDNT* 2.339–342; *EDNT* 1.377–378; *NIDNTT* 1.494–496; *MM* 180; *L&N* 88.83; *BAGD* 216

ἀκρασία, akrasia, etc.   61

inserted between *gnōsis* and *hypomonē* (2 Pet 1:6), receiving no particular emphasis in these "catalogs of virtues." It seems that it is mentioned only because of the influence of Stoic ethics, which gave it its greatest prominence.[5] The fact is that Philo considers conversion to be a passing "from incontinence to self-control" (*ex akrasias eis enkrateian, Rewards* 116), the latter being the most useful of virtues,[6] allowing the courageous to triumph over the obstacles along the way and arrive at last in heaven (*Spec. Laws* 4.112); it is opposed to impure desire (1.149: *epithymia*), to the love of pleasure (*Abraham* 24: *philēdonia*), to gastronomic and sexual delights, and even to intemperance in language.[7] It is in this sense that 1 Cor 9:25 compares the Christian to an athlete, observing: "Whoever contends—*ho agōnizomenos*—submits to every kind of abstinence."[8] We know how rigorous the training of Greek athletes was,[9] and the self-mastery cited

---

Μακάριοι οἱ ἐγκρατεῖς; cf. Eleazer: "I will never abandon you, beloved temperance" (4 Macc 5:34).

[5] Cf. Musonius Rufus, frag. 5 (ed. C. E. Lutz, p. 50, 22), frag. 12 (p. 88, 3–4), frag. 16 (p. 104, 20). Cleanthes (in Plutarch, *De Stoic. rep.* 7); Galen, *De Plac. Hipp. et Plat.*, pp. 467, 5–468, 4, etc.

[6] *Spec. Laws* 1.173: ὠφηλιμωτάτη τῶν ἀρετῶν, guaranteeing the victory of healthy reason over the attacks of incontinence and cupidity (cf. 149–150; Josephus, *Ag. Apion* 1.319; 2.244, where ἀκρασία is a sort of drunkenness which bogs down one's reasoning ability). When the Scribes and the Pharisees, in their carefulness about external purity, wash the outsides of vessels, they do not dream that "the contents of the cup and the plate are the products of theft and intemperance, ἐξ ἁρπαγῆς καὶ ἀκρασίας" (Matt 23:25); cf. *Pss. Sol.* 4.3—ἔνοχος ἐν ποικιλίᾳ ἁμαρτιῶν, ἐν ἀκρασίαις.

[7] *Prelim. Stud.* 80: "Philosophy teaches mastery of the stomach (ἐγκράτειαν γαστρός), mastery of the guts (ἐγκράτειαν τῶν μετὰ γαστέρα), mastery also of the tongue (ἐγκράτειαν καὶ γλώττης)"; cf. *Worse Attacks Better* 102–103; *Good Man Free* 84; *Spec. Laws* 2.195. Cf. a votive epigram of the third century BC, found in Afghanistan: "As a child, be on your good behavior; as a young man, be master of yourself (ἐγκρατής); in midlife, be just; as an old man, be wise; at your death, do not be grieved" (in *NCIG*, n. 37).

[8] The scholia on Demosthenes in Codex Bavaricus mention an Orphic work, the *Steliteutica*, of which the only known fragment furnishes a parallel to 1 Cor 9:25; cf. A. Erhardt, "An Unknown Orphic Writing in the Demosthenes Scholia and St. Paul," *ZNW*, 1957, pp. 101–110.

[9] Philostratus, *Gym.* 25: The trainer must know whether or not the young athlete is self-controlled or not, εἰ ἐγκρατὴς ἢ ἀκρατής, if he is a drinker or a glutton; 52: "If athletes have just yielded to the pleasures of Venus, it is better not to exercise them. Are they perhaps men who will take shameful pleasure rather than wreaths and the proclamations of heralds?"; C. Spicq, *Epîtres aux Corinthiens*, p. 235. The only occurrence of ἐγκρατεύεσθαι in the NT is 1 Cor 7:9—"If they cannot remain continent, then let them marry"; cf. the ἀκρασία of spouses separated from one another, 1 Cor 7:5.

here as an example applies to all arenas. The people of the end-times will not have it (2 Tim 3:3, *akrateis*); it is not so much that they lead a dissolute life, but rather that they cannot control themselves, and so they no longer act as human beings—they are amoral beings.[10] In the first century AD, self-control is especially a virtue of the religious, who master their passions,[11] and of the leader, who cannot direct others unless he is *sui compos*. According to Onasander 1.2–3, the first quality of a good general is to be *sōphrōn* (so as not to be distracted from duty by sensual pleasures) and *enkratēs*, because slavery to the passions would cause him to lose all authority. For Ecphantus, the king who would govern in accord with virtue will be *enkratēs*.[12] The tradition lived on with Emperor Julian, who presented himself as an example to all his governors in that he administered the affairs of the empire "with such decorum and prudence and self-control" (*meta tosautēs kosmiotētos kai sōphrosynēs kai enkrateias*).[13] It is clear that we must interpret against this literary background the virtue demanded of candidates for overseer: that they be *enkratēs*, that is to say, self-controlled.[14] But with Christians, this virtue is a gift of the Holy Spirit (Gal 5:23).

---

[10] Cf. *Ep. Arist.* 222–223; 227–278; Epictetus 2.21.3, 7; 3.1.8.

[11] Among the Essenes, the candidate had to supply evidence of his temperance during a trial period (Josephus, *War* 2.138; cf. 120: "These men hold temperance and restraint of the passions to be virtues"). It is through temperance that the worshipers of Isis reached God (Plutarch, *De Is. et Os.* 2), as also the magi and Brahmins (Dio Chrysostom, *Or.* 49.7; cf. Hippolytus, *Haer.* 1.24.1–4) or the Egyptian priests after the model of Cheremon (Porphyry, *Abst.* 4.6–8; cf. A. J. Festugière, *Hermès Trismégiste*, vol. 1, pp. 30ff.).

[12] Cf. Stobaeus 7.66; vol. 4, p. 279, 6–19; likewise Diotogenes, in Stobaeus 7.62, vol. 4, p. 266, 11 (cf. L. Delatte, *Les Traités de la royauté d'Ecphante, Diotogène et Sthénidas*, Liège-Paris, 1942, p. 258); Musonius Rufus, frag. 8 (ed. C. E. Lutz, p. 62, 10ff.).

[13] *P.Fay.* 20.21. By way of contrast, Antiochus was carried away by the violence of his passions (ὑπὸ δὲ ἀκρασίας παθῶν, Josephus, *War* 1.34), and the sons of Herod did not control their tongues (ἀκρατεῖς λέγειν, idem, *Ant.* 16.399).

[14] Titus 1:8; cf. the tomb inscription of a martyr, around AD 300, Βερέκων ἐγκρατὸς μαρτυρήσας ἐκοιμή (*SB* 7315, 9).

ἀλαζονεία, ἀλαζών

alazoneia, **boastful arrogance;** *alazōn,* **boaster**

It is not easy to define precisely the nature of this vice. It is denounced in the pagan literature[1] as well as in the Bible; but each author has his own conception of what it is. Sometimes it has to do with bombastic braggarts of the sort so thoroughly caricatured in Greco-Roman comedy,[2] especially for the extravagance of their talk; sometimes it has to do with the boastful and presumptuous, whose chatter is tinged with insolence.[3] *Alazoneia* is a vice of the rich and of those in the public eye (Wis 5:8; Philo, Virtues 162),

---

[1] For Aristotle, the boaster sins against truthfulness, "he loves to seem to possess claims to glory that are not really his, or to exaggerate those that he does have. . . . His entire being is vile (because if it wasn't, he would derive no pleasure from lies), but he is apparently more vain than wicked. . . . Those who boast out of a desire for glory pretend to possess all that inspires praise and congratulations" (*Eth. Nic.* 4.13, pp. 1127ᵃ21ff.); cf. Cyrus: "ὁ ἀλαζών seems to me to apply to people who are richer or braver than they are and who promise to do things that are beyond their capabilities" (Xenophon, *Cyr.* 2.2.12; cf. 1.6.22). "Boasting, it seems to me, is pretending to have advantages that one does not have" (Theophrastus, *Char.* 23.1). Numerous texts in O. Ribbeck, *Alazon,* Leipzig, 1882, which outlines a portrait of the *alazon* and gives synonyms (cf. J. Pollux, *Onom.,* vol. 1, 195; vol. 9, 146). Cf. the commentary of H. Lloyd-Jones on Menander, *Perikeromenē,* 268, in *ZPE,* vol. 15, 1974, p. 209.

[2] Cf. the "empty-talking boasters" (Athenaeus 1.52 = 29ᶜ), bullies vaunting their exploits (the *miles gloriosus* of Plautus, or of Lucian in *Dial. Meret.* 1, 9, 13, 15; the soldier Thrason in Terence, *Eun.,* or Polēmon in Menander, *Pk.;* cf. J. P. Cèbe, *La caricature et la parodie,* Paris, 1966, pp. 50ff.); boastfulness, associated with exaggeration (περιττολογία; Josephus, *Ant.* 14.111) is synonymous with tall tales (Xenophon of Ephesus, *Hell.* 7.1.38); but is always severely judged, as is Isokos ἀλαζὼν ἀνὴρ καὶ ἀνόητος (Josephus, *Ant.* 8.264), "because *alazoneia* and haughtiness are characteristic of the limited soul," *Spec. Laws* 4.165). At banquets one should at least place "near the boaster, the modest," Plutarch, *Quaest. conv.* 1.2.6). "The prattle of those who get puffed up about themselves and their accomplishments" (Polybius 5.33.8).

[3] Prov 21:24—αὐθάδης καὶ ἀλαζών. *Moses* 2.240: "Step forward, now, you boasters, you who puff up your chests . . . who staighten your necks and raise your eyebrows, . . . you for whom the lot of widows is a joke and the condition of orphans

---

alazoneia, S 212; TDNT 1.226–227; EDNT 1.56; NIDNTT 3.28–32; MM 20; L&N 88.219; BAGD 34 ‖ *alazōn,* S 213; TDNT 1.226–227; EDNT 1.56; NIDNTT 2.435; L&N 88.219; BAGD 34

of the man of politics (*T. Job* 21.3) and of the ruler (2 Macc 15:6; Philo, *Virtues* 161; *Spec. Laws* 4.170), of the orator, the philosopher, the poet, the magician, the doctor,[4] that is, of all those who lay claim to intelligence (Wis 17:7), but also of superiors who abuse their authority vis-à-vis their inferiors.[5] *Alazōn* is thus a term of the wisdom vocabulary that associates arrogance, presumption,[6] and above all pride.[7] The *alazōn* takes himself for a god or boasts that God is his father (Wis 2:16). Thus he is an impostor and an ungodly person, after the fashion of Antiochus who "in his superhuman conceit thought that he could give orders to the waves of the sea" (2 Macc 9:8).

All of these nuances are found in the NT, especially the most ridiculous form of *alazoneia:* "Now you glory in your boastings; all vainglory of this sort is iniquitous" (Jas 4:16). At issue are presumptuous merchants and those "business travelers" who are puffed up in their imagination and in their speech,[8] considering themselves rich in intelligence, ease, and savoir-

---

a subject for mocking"; Josephus, *Ant.* 6.179; 4 Macc 1:26; 2:15; 8:19; *Jos. Asen.* 4.16: "his daughter had answered him with insolence and anger." Cf. Cicero, *Tusc.* 4.9.20: "Jactatio est voluptas gestiens et se offerens insolentius."

[4] Lucian, *Rh. Pr., Dial. Mort.* 1; 10.8; *Tim.* 54; *Merc. Cond.* 35–36; *Ind.* 29 (cf. J. Bompaire, *Lucien écrivain,* p. 205; H. D. Betz, *Lukian von Samosata,* p. 198). *Alazōn* is thus a term of insult, defined by Suetonius: παρὰ τὸ ἀλώμενος ζῆν (J. Taillardat, *Suétone, Des Termes injurieux,* Paris, 1967, pp. 56, 86). According to Strabo (4.4.5) and Arrian (*Anab.* 1.4), *alazoneia* is a flaw of the Celts and Gauls.

[5] *Spec. Laws* 3.137: "Masters should not prove their arrogance, pride, and frightful cruelty by abusing their power over servants." In Job 28:18, υἱοὶ ἀλαζόνων (Theodotion) are savage beasts. But Philo observes that "*alazoneia* exists also among unimportant people . . . like each of the other passions and moral disorders and weaknesses" *Virtues* 162; cf. 172); such is the one who vaunts himself before the king (Prov 25:6; this could be the flatterer, κόλαξ).

[6] *Virtues* 161, 165; *Flight* 33–34; *Spec. Laws* 4.88; 2.18–19.

[7] Hab 2:5—"ἀνὴρ ἀλαζών (*yāhîr*): the proud man . . . is never satisfied."*Prelim. Stud.* 41; *Virtues* 171–172, citing Pindar (Frag. 280): "every *alazōn* considers himself neither a human nor a demigod but an entirely divine being." *T. Jos.* 17.8: καὶ ὕψωσα ἐμαυτὸν ἐν αὐτοῖς ἐν ἀλαζονείᾳ διὰ τὴν κοσμικήν μου δόξαν, ἀλλ᾽ ἤμην ἐν αὐτοῖς ὡς εἷς τῶν ἐλαχίστων; *T. Dan* 1.6. The Pythagorean Callicratidas: ἀνάγκα γὰρ τὼς πολλὰ ἔχοντας τετυφῶσθαι πρᾶτον, τετυφωμένως δὲ ἀλαζόνας γίνεσθαι, ἀλαζόνας δὲ γενομένως ὑπερηφάνως ἦμεν (in Stobaeus, *Flor.* 85.16; vol. 4, p. 684, 3–5). This is why Philo declares that to repress and destroy *alazoneia* it is necessary to remember God in one's heart (*Virtues* 165). He opposes these boasters to the humble (*Moses* 2.240–241), as Clement of Rome also does constantly, *1 Clem.* 2.1: "You were all humble, free of conceit, more ready to obey than to command"; 13.1: "Let us be humble in heart, let us set aside all feelings of conceit, of vanity, of foolish pride"; 16.2: "The Lord Jesus Christ did not follow after conceit and pride . . . but with a humble heart"; cf. 35.5.

[8] Cf. *1 Clem.* 21.5: "Greeks all proud of their arrogant talk."

faire, proud of the importance of their enterprise and their profits, multiplying fine projects for the future. All of this is inane, vain presumption, ignorance of creaturely limitations. To pride oneself on one's own abilities is, religiously speaking, a sin.

This vice will be much more serious among the people of the end times, "impostors and arrogant," who are simultaneously proud and blasphemers: *alazones, hyperēphanoi, blasphēmoi*,[9] thus creatures in rebellion against divine authority who confine themselves to their own sufficiency, setting themselves up as their own standard for life. Henceforth, according to Rom 1:30, it is the province of the pagans to be "proud, blustery, inventors of evil." These are not vain people who exalt themselves thoughtlessly, but people who go to the extreme excess of abolishing their Creator in their thoughts and in their lives. God abhors this conceit (Philo, *Spec. Laws* 1.265).

This nuance seems necessary in interpreting 1 John 2:16—"All that is in the world—the lust of the flesh, the lust of the eyes, *hē alazonia tou biou*—is not of the Father."[10] If St. John did not mention as a third *epithymia* "the lust for riches or money," it is precisely because he had his sights set on a more serious vice than the ostentation of the wealthy or their arrogance toward the poor. He contrasts with God the creaturely pride, the mastery of one's own existence, of the person who decides and directs the course of his life without taking God into account.[11] This "sufficiency" is the exact opposite of the absolute duty of worshiping God and serving God devoutly; it follows that this is something altogether different from the classical and profane *alazoneia*.

---

[9] 2 Tim 3:2. In a sin list, comparable with that of Philo, *Sacr. Abel and Cain* 32, which juxtaposes ἀλαζὼν δοκησίσοφος αὐθάδης.

[10] On the basis of Polybius 6.57.6—ἡ περὶ τοὺς βίους ἀλαζονεία—and especially Wis 5:8—πλοῦτος μετὰ ἀλαζονείας—βίος is often understood as referring to riches (cf. 1 John 3:17; Mark 12:44; Luke 15:12, 30). The point would have to do with audacious confidence placed in worldly goods (P. Joüon, "I Jo. II, 16, la présomption des richesses," in *RSR*, 1938, pp. 479–481). Cf. J. Bonsirven: "The splendor of fortune, following the meaning of the two Greek words, ostentation, the display of all of one's possessions (St. Cyprian translates: *ambitio saeculi, jactantia hujus vitae*), splendid luxury, in short, all the pursuits of vanity, one of the grossest forms of pride" (*Epîtres de saint Jean*, 2d ed., Paris, 1954, p. 118). C. H. Lensky, *The Epistles of St. Peter, St. John*, Columbus, 1945, p. 426, F. M. Braun, *Jean le théologien*, vol. 3, 2, p. 208: "ἀλαζονεία τοῦ βίου, which we have rendered by 'pride of riches,' would be the appeal of the power conferred by the possession of material goods."

[11] This is the interpretation of J. Chaine, *Les Epîtres catholiques*, Paris, 1939, p. 164; R. Schnackenburg, *Die Johannesbriefe*, Freiburg, 1953, p. 114. Ἀλαζών does not occur in the papyri, but cf. *P.Lond.* 1927, 32 (Christian, mid-fourth century, H. I. Bell, *Jews and Christians in Egypt*, p. 111): τὴν τοῦ κόσμου ἀλαζονίαν ἀπεκήρυξας καὶ τὴν τῶν κενοδόξων μεγαλαυχίαν ἐβδέλυξας.

> ἀλήθεια, ἀληθεύω, ἀληθής, ἀληθινός, ἀληθῶς
>
> alētheia, truth; alētheuō, to speak the truth; alēthēs, true, truthful; alēthinos, authentic, genuine; alēthōs, truly

All of these terms derive from *lanthanō*, "go unnoticed, be unknown," and in the middle and passive, "forget." These compound forms with the alpha prefix mean "not hidden." *Alētheia* is that which is not concealed, a fact or a condition that can be seen or expressed as it really is. To speak the whole truth[1] is to conceal nothing, and *alētheia* is the opposite of lying or forgetfulness.[2] An event is true (*alēthēs*) when it is unveiled; a hidden reality becomes explicit. A person who is true or sincere is one who conceals nothing and does not try to deceive.

Greek philosophy and religious strivings were dominated by the search for truth (*hē zētēsis tēs alētheias*, Thucydides 1.20.3), as Plato explicates it: "By searching for truth I strive to make myself as perfect as possible in life and, when the time comes to die, in death."[3] The truth not only gives life;

---

[1] Cf. Homer, *Il.* 24.407: "Tell me all the truth; is my son still near the boats?" Herodotus 6.69: "Then do not accept any other story concerning your birth: the final word of the truth is what you have heard me speak with my own mouth"; Thucydides 4.120: "He had to consider them in truth as the Lacedaemonians' most faithful friends." R. Bultmann, "Untersuchungen zum Johannes-Evangelium: A. II. Aletheia in der griechischen und hellenistischen Literatur," in *ZNW*, 1928, pp. 134–163.

[2] Λήθη. Cf. W. Luther, *"Wahrheit" und "Lüge" im ältesten Griechentum*, Borna-Leipzig, 1935; H. Frisk, *"Wahrheit" und "Lüge" in den indogermanischen Sprachen*, Göteborg, 1936.

[3] Plato, *Grg.* 526 *d*; cf. Plutarch, *De Is. et Os.* 2: "To aspire to the truth is to incline toward divinity—especially the truth concerning the gods. This type of study and

---

alētheia, S 225; TDNT 1.232–247; EDNT 1.57–60; NIDNTT 3.874–878, 882–893; MM 21; L&N 70.4, 72.2; BDF §§234(7), 397(3); BAGD 35–36 ‖ *alētheuō*, S 226; TDNT 1.251; EDNT 1.57–60; NIDNTT 3.874, 877, 886–888; MM 21; L&N 33.251; BDF §101; BAGD 36 ‖ *alēthēs*, S 227; TDNT 1.247–249; EDNT 1.57–60; NIDNTT 3.874–877, 882–884, 888–891, 893; MM 21; L&N 70.3, 72.1, 88.39; BAGD 36 ‖ *alēthinos*, S 228; TDNT 1.249–250; EDNT 1.57–60; NIDNTT 3.874, 877, 883–884, 888–889, 891–893; MM 21–22; L&N 70.3, 72.1, 73.2; BDF §263(a); BAGD 37 ‖ *alēthōs*, S 230; EDNT 1.57–60; NIDNTT 3.874, 877, 883, 888, 893; L&N 70.3; BDF §243; BAGD 37

it gives the good life (Epictetus 1.4.31; 3.24.40), because it orients action: "If you knew the truth, you would necessarily act rightly."[4] It is a question of an ascent of the soul toward the "plane of truth" where it is possible to contemplate the Ideas, the veritable, authentic realities.[5] Finally *alētheia* as a metaphysical concept refers to the nature or essence of things—Being insofar as it is intelligible—and is contrasted to the terrestrial world of sensible phenomena. Not only is the true identical to being, the real;[6] but it is the divine reality as revealed to humans. Truth is God (especially in Gnosticism, cf. *Corp. Herm.*, chapters 7 and 13).

In the LXX, *alētheia* never expresses a metaphysical concept. It almost always translates *'emet*, from the root *'āman*, "be firm," and thus refers to that which is solid, firm, valid, durable. A "true" path is one that ends where it is supposed to go (Gen 24:48; cf. Ps 25:10). The true is that which is real;[7] "truly" relying on Yahweh means "actually" doing so (Isa 10:20). In a moral sense, truth is synonymous with sincerity and loyalty[8] and the

---

research is like an ascent toward the holy things, a more religious task than any ritual or priestly function"; Diogenes Laertius 9.10: ἀπὸ τοῦ πάντοτε ζητεῖν τὴν ἀλήθειαν; Marcus Aurelius 6.21.2: ζητῶ γὰρ τὴν ἀλήθειαν; Philo, *Moses* 1.24: the search for truth should be the great human preoccupation (τὴν ἀλήθειαν ζητεῖν); *Spec. Laws* 3.181; 4.5; *Good Man Free* 12; *Etern. World* 1: πόθος ἀληθείας; *Joseph* 90; *Contemp. Life* 63; *Ps.-Clem. Hom.* 19.6.6.

[4] Epictetus 1.17.14: σὺ δὲ κατεμεμάθηκας τὴν ἀλήθειαν, ἀνάγκη σε ἤδη κατορθοῦν; 1.24.4; 2.26.1–5. Cf. Plato, *Soph.* 228 c–d; *Prt.* 345 d–e; *Resp.* 3.413 a.

[5] *Phdr.* 248 b, τὸ ἀληθείας πεδίον. Cf. P. Courcelle, "La Plaine de la vérité: Platon, Phèdre 248 b," in *MusHelv,* 1969, pp. 199–203.

[6] Plato, *Tht.* 186 c: "Can that attain to the truth which does not even attain to being? —Impossible"; *Symp.* 211 b; 212 a; *Resp.* 6.508 d; 9.585 d; 10.596 d–605 c; Aristotle, *Ph.* 1.8.191ᵃ25: ζητοῦντες . . . τὴν ἀλήθειαν καὶ τὴν φύσιν τὴν τῶν ὄντων. Cf. R. Herbertz, *Das Wahrheitsproblem in der griechischen Philosophie*, Berlin, 1913; P. Wilpert, "Zum aristotelischen Wahrheitsbegriff," in *Philosophisches Jahrbuch,* 1940, p. 3–16; M. Heidegger, *Platos Lehre von der Wahrheit,* Bern, 1947; M. Detienne, "La Notion mythique d' Ἀλήθεια," in *REG,* 1960, pp. 27–36; E. Heitsch, "Die nicht-philosophische ἀλήθεια," in *Hermes,* 1962, pp. 24–33; H. D. Rankin, " Ἀ-λήθεια in Plato," in *Glotta,* 1963, pp. 51–54; G. Stammler, "Die Bedeutung des Wortes Wahrheit," in *Kerygma und Dogma,* vol. 2, 1965, pp. 234–243; E. des Places, *Platon: Lexique,* Paris, 1964, vol. 1, pp. 27ff.

[7] Deut 22:20—"if the matter is true, if (the signs of) her virginity are not found in the young woman" (ἐὰν δὲ ἐπ' ἀληθείας γένηται); Judg 9:15—"If you truly want to anoint me as king"; 2 Kgs 19:17—"It is true, Yahweh, that the kings of Assyria have laid waste the nations"; Job 9:2—"In truth [ἐπ' ἀληθείας], I know that it is so"; 19.4; 36:4; Dan 2:8 (Theodotion).

[8] Judg 9:16—"Have you acted in truth and in sincerity?" 2 Chr 32:1—"After these acts of loyalty by Hezekiah, Sennacherib came to invade Judah"; Tob 8:7—"It is not in lust that I take this my sister, but in truth" (ἐπ' ἀληθείας); Hos 4:1; Dan 9:13 (Theodotion); Wis 5:6; 1 Macc 7:18; Eccl 12:10—"The Preacher set himself to . . .

opposite of lying, falsehood, and counterfeiting (Prov 8:7; 22:21; 26:28). The Wisdom writings warn against hiding secrets (Wis 6:22) or speaking against the truth (Sir 4:25). Intentions are revealed (2 Macc 3:9—*epynthaneto de ei tais alētheiais*); the exhortation is given to fight to the death for truth (Sir 4:28). This is in conformity with secular Greek,[9] but, in accord with the underlying Hebrew, *alētheia* in the LXX suggests consistency and solidity and therefore fidelity. Hence Yahweh is called "God of truth"[10] on the basis of his unchangeableness, the solidity or stability of his works, the certainty that his promises will be fulfilled: what he says always comes to pass. His utterances and actual events coincide.[11] God does not lie and never fails (Ps 132:11); the principle of his speech is truth (119:160). All his gifts are characterized by stability, fixity, perseverance, continuity;[12] to say that he does the truth (*alētheian epoiēsas*, Neh 9:33; cf. Tob 4:6) is to say not only that his conduct is coherent but also that it corresponds to his

---

writing words of truth in uprightness." To make an oath "in truth" (μετὰ ἀληθείας) is to make it sincerely (Jer 4:2), hence honestly (Sir 7:20). One "speaks the truth according to one's heart" (Ps 15:3; cf. 5:9; 119:43—λόγον ἀληθείας). Cf. *Ep. Arist.* 205.

[9] Notably the revelation of the truth, ὑποδείξω σοι τὴν ἀλήθειαν (Tob 7:10); Jdt 5:5; 10:13; Ps 30:9; 88:11; Dan 11:2 (Theodotion). Ahab to Micaiah: "How many times do I have to adjure you to tell me only the truth" (2 Chr 18:15). Cf. C. H. Dodd, *The Bible and the Greeks*, London, 1935, pp. 65–75; J. Guillet, *Thèmes bibliques*, Paris, 1954, pp. 38–46; E. T. Ramsdall, "The Old Testament Understanding of Truth," in *Journal of Religion*, 1951, pp. 264–273; Y. Alanen, "Das Wahrheitsproblem in der Bibel und in der griechischen Philosophie," in *Kerygma und Dogma*, 1957, pp. 230–239; K. Koch, "Der hebräische Wahrheitsbegriff im griechischen Sprachraum," in H. R. Müller-Schwefe, *Was ist Wahrheit?*, Göttingen, 1965, pp. 47–65; P. Benoit "La Vérité dans la Sainte Ecriture," in *Exégèse et théologie*, pp. 143–156; J. Barr, *Semantics*, pp. 187–200.

[10] Ps 31:5; cf. 89:8—"your faithfulness envelops you"; 146:6—"Yahweh keeps faith forever"; 36:6—"Yahweh, your grace is in the heavens, your truth rises to the clouds"; 57:10; 89:2; 108:4.

[11] Isa 45:19—"I am Yahweh; I utter truth"; Jer 23:28; Zech 8:8—"I will be their God in truth and in justice"; Sir 41:19—"before the truth of God and the covenant"; Ps 25:5; 40:11—"I told of your faithfulness and your help; I did not hide your grace and your truth"; 57:4—"May Elohim send his grace and his truth"; 43:3; 66:8; 89:14, 25; 100:5; 69:13—"In your great grace, answer me, through the truth of your salvation"; 71:22—"I will give you thanks for your faithfulness, my God"; 89:1, 5; 92:2; 115:1; 117:2; 138:2; 89:50—"Where, O Adonai, are your former mercies which, in your faithfulness, you swore to David?" 98:3—"He remembered his grace and his faithfulness." Note the frequent link between faithfulness and benevolence, Gen 24:27; 32:10; 47:29; Josh 2:14; 2 Sam 2:6; 15:20; Tob 3:2; Ps 45:4; Mic 7:20. Cf. F. Asensio, "Misericoridia et Veritas: El ḥesed y 'ĕmet divinos: Su influjo religio-social en la historia de Israel," in *Analecta Gregoriana*, Rome, 1949.

[12] God's laws and commands are immutable truth (Neh 9:13; Ps 111:7; 119:86, 142, 151; Mal 2:6; *Midr. Ps.* 25 11: the Torah is *'emet*) as are his judgments (Isa 42:3; Ps 96:13; cf. *Pirqe 'Abot* 3.26; *Mek.* on Exod 14:18; *Exod. Rab.* on 6:2; 29:1; *b. Ber.* 46*b*).

prior declarations. Likewise, what is asked of the just is steadfast loyalty to the Lord: "If your sons watch their way, walking before me in truth with all their heart and all their soul."[13] Faithfulness and piety go together (Prov 14:22; 20:22). Not only is God near to all those who love truth-sincerity (Ps 145:18; Zech 8:19), he also showers blessings upon them.[14]

The usages of *alētheia* in Philo derive more from the word's etymology and the Greek tradition than from the Greek Bible, although a religious meaning is retained. The Alexandrian philosopher constantly contrasts authentic divine revelation (the truth) with philosophers and lawmakers who, "wrapping their thought in superfluous bombast, have deceived the masses with the smoke of illusion, masking the truth under mythic fictions."[15] He means the pure, naked, unadorned truth (*Creation* 45; *Drunkenness* 6, 34), unchanged, with nothing added and nothing taken away (*Creation* 170); thus a revealing, the light shed by revelation. "There is no light for actions more brilliant than the truth" (*Alleg. Interp.* 3.45; cf. *Unchang. God* 96), and "it is God's will to reveal the secrets of things to those who wish to know the truth" (*Joseph* 90). "Truth" is associated with clarity (*saphēneia, Alleg. Interp.* 3.124, 128, 140), with revealing[16] and light;[17] it is "the knowledge of the true God" (*Rewards* 58; cf. *Contemp. Life* 89).

But Philo Platonizes by contrasting truth and appearance (*Migr. Abr.* 158; *Moses* 1.48); the study of intelligible essences, which yields truth, with the study of sensible objects, which yields opinion (*Rewards* 28). God is "Being, the one who is in truth,"[18] "the one who is truth" (*Dreams* 1.60;

---

[13] 1 Kgs 2:4; 3:6; 2 Kgs 20:3; Tob 1:3—"I, Tobit, have walked in the ways of truth and of justice" (ὁδοῖς ἀληθείας); 13:6—"If you practice truth before him with all your soul" (ποιῆσαι ἐνώπιον αὐτοῦ ἀλήθειαν); Ps 26:3; 86:11; 119:30—"I have chosen the way of truth"; Sir 37:15; Isa 38:3.

[14] Sir 27:9—"Truth returns to those who practice it." It is a shield (Ps 91:40) and a belt (Isa 11:5). "All those who love the Lord with faithfulness and justice will have joy" (Tob 14:7).

[15] *Creation* 1. This contrast between the truth and myths, inventions and falsifications recurs at *Alleg. Interp.* 3.36, 232; *Cherub.* 94; *Sacr. Abel and Cain* 12; *Worse Attacks Better* 125; *Post. Cain* 52, 101; *Giants* 58; *Prelim. Stud.* 61; *Joseph* 106; *Spec. Laws* 1.28, 51, 319; 4.50; *Virtues* 102, 178; *Rewards* 8, 162; *Contemp. Life* 63; *Etern. World* 56, 68; *To Gaius* 77.

[16] Δήλωσις, *Alleg. Interp.* 3.24, 143; *Spec. Laws* 1.88; 4.69; *Moses* 2.113, 128–129. Cf. *Ep. Arist.* 77: τὴν τῆς ἀληθείας ἔμφασιν.

[17] *Dreams* 1.218: "the unclouded light and brilliance of the truth"; 2.106, 133; *Joseph* 68; *Migr. Abr.* 76; *Spec. Laws* 1.63; 4.52, 178; *Flight* 139; *Moses* 2.271; *Rewards* 25: "smoke is the enemy of truth"; 27, 58.

[18] *Change of Names* 7: ὅ ἐστι πρὸς ἀλήθειαν ὄν; he cannot be perceived by a human: "It is impossible for anyone to grasp true Being" (πρὸς ἀλήθειαν ὄν, *Abraham* 80; cf. *Moses* 2.67, 100); *Post. Cain* 167: "Being, which exists in reality" (τὸ δὲ πρὸς

Abraham 121), "truly existing" (*tou pros alētheian ontos theou, Decalogue* 81; *Spec. Laws* 1.313, 344). Truth basically means "reality"; "in truth" means "according to being" or "in reality";[19] true goods are real goods (*Creation* 21; *Sacr. Abel and Cain* 99; *Giants* 15; *Virtues* 17: *tou pros alētheian biou;* cf. *Ep. Arist.* 260, 306); "Do you believe that among mortal realities there is found one that has true being, true substance?" (*Unchang. God* 172). It is God alone who is "the sole Artisan of the true human being, that is, the spirit in all its purity" (*Flight* 71); "God placed the true human, that is, the Spirit, in us, among the most sacred shoots and plants of moral worth" (*Plant.* 42; *Dreams* 1.215; *Virtues* 20). Consequently, "true life is to walk according to the orders and commandments of God" (*Prelim. Stud.* 87), "to grasp the truth" (*Sacr. Abel and Cain* 13), to be "well in tune with it" (*Post. Cain* 88), to revere it (*Spec. Laws* 4.33, 43). That is what is most honorable (ibid. 69, 71) and most profitable.[20] In any event, Philo is far removed from the cult of truth in the Psalms and at Qumran.[21]

ἀλήθειαν ὄν); *Giants* 45: "I am the truly good being" (ἐγὼ τὸ πρὸς ἀλήθειαν ἀγαθόν); *Spec. Laws* 4.178: "going to dwell with the truth and with the veneration of the only venerable Being"; *Virtues* 65, 219, 221; *Rewards* 46; *Moses* 2.270: "the God of truth"; 2.177: "truth is God's handmaid"; *Unchang. God* 61: "truth initiates into the authentic mysteries of Being"; cf. *Conf. Tongues* 190: the meanings of the words of the oracles "are subsistent realities." Cf. Arius Didymus: "God has a vision of the truth" (θεὸς οἶδε τὴν ἀλήθειαν, in Stobaeus, *Ecl.* 2.1.17, vol. 2, n. 6). In *Pap.Graec.Mag.*, ἀλήθεια represents a divine entity (II, 156; IV, 1014; vol. 1, pp. 38 and 106); "I am the truth, the one who hates the injustices of the world" (V, 148; vol. 1, p. 186). The supreme God "possesses the truth unmixed with falsehood" (ὁ ἔχων τὴν ἄψευστον ἀλήθειαν, XII, 257; vol. 2, p. 75). A magical papyrus of the third century: "Great God, you who alone keep the truth on your head" (μόνος ὁ τὴν ἀλήθειαν ἔχων ἐπὶ τῆς κεφαλῆς, *P.Warr.* 21, 25). Cf. *Ep. Arist.* 140: σέβεται τὸν κατὰ ἀλήθειαν θεόν.

[19] *Worse Attacks Better* 162; *Creation* 136; *Alleg. Interp.* 2.10, 20; 3.63, 174, 178, 191; *Cherub.* 50; *Post. Cain* 12, 42, 119, 147; *Plant.* 164; *Sobr.* 11; *Heir* 20; *Change of Names* 94; *Abraham* 179; *Moses* 2.48; *Spec. Laws* 1.287, 3.155, 186; *Virtues* 56; *Rewards* 123; *Good Man Free* 41; cf. *Post. Cain* 136: "those who are the judges of reality"; 164: "the beautiful in its reality"; *Flacc.* 164: "it was a hallucination; it was not reality" (οὐκ ἀλήθεια); *To Gaius* 20, 60, 248, 279, 359; *Decalogue* 128: when a woman commits adultery, the identity (authenticity) of the child's father in unknown; *Joseph* 38: "in deed and in truth" (ἔργῳ δὲ καὶ ταῖς ἀληθείαις).

[20] *Drunkenness* 39, 70; *Dreams* 1.179. "Enamored of this most sacred good that is truth" (*Good Man Free* 158), following "the paths of truth" (*Contemp. Life* 27, cf. 39), seeking "undoctored truth" (*Spec. Laws* 3.53, 141; *Virtues* 6); just the opposite of the wicked person, the "enemy of truth, defender of lies" (*Conf. Tongues* 48; cf. *Migr. Abr.* 110; *Flacc.* 156; *Dreams* 2.97; *Moses* 1.235; 2.167; *Decalogue* 138; *Spec. Laws* 1.89; *Etern. World* 69).

[21] The sect's goal was "to carry out faithfulness ['*emet*], justice, and uprightness" (1QS 1.5) in contrast with impiety and perversity (1.19; 3.7, 19; 4.2, 17, 19, 23–25; 5.3; 6.15; 8.2–6; 1QH 16.7), "with regard to an eternal faithfulness" (1QS 9.3). Its members

On the grammatical level, note that apart from the plural,[22] most of the occurrences of *alētheia* with the preposition *pros* (cf. *epi, ek, en*) conform to the language of the papyri.[23] These provide no new data. They give this noun the meaning "sincerity, objectivity." In his edict in AD 68, Tiberius Julius Alexander writes, "As for the most important questions, I will make them known to him in all truth" (*autō dēlōsō meta pasēs alētheias*, BGU 1563, 24 = SB 8444). One tells the truth, especially in judicial settings;[24] it is

---

are "volunteers for his faithfulness" (1.11–12; 5.10), "the party of faithfulness" (4QM 13.12, 15), the sons of faithfulness (= the faithful, 1QS 4.5–6; 4QM 17.8; 1QH 6.69; 7.30; 9.35; 11.1), "men of faithfulness who practice the law . . . in the service of faithfulness" (1QpHab 7.10–12; cf. 8.9: the first name of the impious priest was "Faithfulness"); in fact, the congregation was called the "faithful house" (1QS 5.6; 8.9; CD A, 3.19). All the elect are faithful (1QH 14.15) and rely on God's faithfulness (6.25–26; 7.20; 9.32; 10.17; frag 2.15). God is faithful (1QS 4.20–21; 1QH 1.30; 3.34; 4.40; 6.9–12; 7.28; 9.10; 11.27, 29; 15.25; 16.40); "Faithfulness of God" is the inscription on the banners (4QM 4.6; cf. 11.14; 13.1–2, 9–10). The angel of faithfulness is the one who is in submission to God's will (1QS 3.24). *'Emet* also signifies the divine knowledge that the Teacher of Righteousness inculcates in the disciples (1QS 9.17; cf. CD 2.13: the seers of truth; 1QH 1.27; 10.4; 11.4, 9: the secret of truth). Cf. O. Betz, "Gottes 'Wahrheit' ('emet)," in *Offenbarung und Schriftforschung in der Qumransekte*, Tübingen, 1960, pp. 53–60; F. Nötscher, " 'Wahrheit' als theologischer Terminus in den Qumran-Texten," in *Vom Alten zum Neuen Testament*, bonn, 1962, pp. 112–125; P. Benoit, "Qumrân et le Nouveau Testament," in *NTS*, vol. 7, 1961, pp. 276–296; J. Murphy-O'Connor, "La 'Vérité' chez saint Paul et à Qumrân," in *RB*, 1965, pp. 29–76.

[22] Ταῖς ἀληθείαις (Philo, *Joseph* 38), as at 2 Macc 3:9; 7:6; Josephus, *Ant.* 6.59; 14.291; 16.235; *Life* 401; frequent in the papyri: *P.Oxy.* 2562, 13: the sums will actually be paid; *P.Petr.* 6, 14: "if the above-named is actually dead"; 7, 18; 8, 21; 9, 20; *P.Ryl.* 105, 26; *P.Mil.Vogl.* 98, 26; *PSI* 1064, 22; 1433, 3; *SB* 1114, 14; *Proceedings* XV, p. 81, line 76 (in AD 80).

[23] With (a) ἐπί, especially in traditional oath formulas: "we swear that we have soundly and faithfully presented the preceding account" (ἐξ ὑγιοῦς καὶ ἐπ' ἀληθείας ἐπιδεδωκέναι, *P.Amh.* 68, 33; *P.Bon.* 17, 8; *P.Brem.* 32, 25; *P.Oslo* 98, 29; *P.Stras.* 207, 5; *P.Brux.* 20, 22; *P.Oxy.* 480, 9; 2277, 4, 8, 12 [AD 13]; 2472, 18; *SB* 7365, 159; 9360, 22; 10633; 10638, 11; *P.Cair.Zen.* 59384, 7; 59484, 4); *P.Flor.* 112, 67: τὸν γέροντα ἐπ' ἀληθείας τύπτουσιν (Aristophanes); (b) ἐκ; cf. *P.Flor.* 32, 14: ἐξόμνυμι . . . ἐξ ἀληθείας καὶ πίστεως; *P.Oxy.* 1032, 33; *P.Stras.* 152, 14 (= *SB* 8942, 14); *P.Yale* 80, 11: ἀσπασάντας τοὺς φιλοῦντας ἡμᾶς ἐξ ἀληθείας; *P.Mich.* 477, 41: οἱ φιλοῦντές σε ἐξ ἀληθείας παντελῶς; (c) κατά, cf. *P.Cair.Zen.* 59202, 7: ἐὰν φαίνηται κατ' ἀλήθειαν (= *SB* 6739); *P.Oxy.* 2429, frag 1 (b), col. II, 41; frag. 7, 133: κατ' ἀλήθειαν (Epicharmus); (d) περί, cf. *P.Oxy.* 1860, 8: φιλογνωρίσαι αὐτὴν τὸ περὶ τῆς ἀληθείας; (e) πρός, cf. *Ep. Arist.* 161; the letters of Gemellus, *P.Fay.* 118, 26: ἀσπάζου τοὺς φιλοῦντές πάντες πρὸς ἀλήθιαν; 119, 26 (cf. 2 John 1; 3 John 1). On the very common use of πρός with the accusative case in the papyri, cf. the index of E. Mayser, *Grammatik*, II, 2, p. 620; with other prepositions, II, 1, pp. 13ff.

[24] *P.Ant.* 87, 13 (transcript of a trial): "tell the truth" (λέγε τὴν ἀλήθειαν); *UPZ* 70, verso 2; *P.Oxy.* 2419, 5: εἰπὲ μετὰ ἀληθείας; *P.Giss.* 84, 14. Cf. ἡ τῶν νόμων ἀλήθεια

revealed: "since the whole truth concerning the matters previously written about will hardly be made known" (*ex hou deēsei gnōsthēnai pasan tēn peri tōn progegrammenōn alētheian, P.Oxy.* 283, 13); one is faithful to the facts (*C.P.Herm.* 18, 16). "That by all means the actual sum disbursed may be known" (*P.Panop.Beatty* 1, 17). *Alētheia* is the real ("Let them not address us as people who have really been wronged"—*entynchanousin kat' alētheian plēmmeloumenoi, C.Ord.Ptol.* 35, 9; second century BC) and is the opposite of falsehood and lying ("hating deviousness but honoring truth").[25]

This same meaning, truth-reality, appears in the Synoptic Gospels and in Acts, where *alētheia* never has a theological meaning.[26] Sometimes it has to do with questions of noting or identifying facts,[27] but usually *en* or *ep' alētheias* is used with the verbs *didaskō, eipon, legō*[28] to point to an utterance that is true, exactly correct, trustworthy—the opposite of false or ambiguous.

St. Paul uses the term *alētheia* in a way that agrees with its Greek etymology (that which may be seen in the open, as it is) but also takes account of OT usage; in various texts, one or the other element predominates. If people are lost, it is because "they did not accept the love of truth

---

(*P.Lond.* 412, 5; vol. 2, p. 280; 897, 3, vol. 3, p. 206). *UPZ* 162, col. VI, 12: εἴπερ γε δὴ ἐνόμιζεν ἐκ τῆς ἀληθείας τῇ κατὰ νόμους ὁδῷ πορευόμενος, the *epistatēs* will attempt to bring out the truth by following the legal procedure; *SB* 8248, 54 = Dittenberger, *Or.* 665.

[25] Τὰ πανοῦργα μισῶν, τὴν δ' ἀλήθειαν σέβων, C. Austin, *Comicorum Graecorum Fragmenta*, n. 307, 5. Cf. *P.Apoll.* 31, 4: τῇ ἀληθείᾳ θέλω = "to tell the truth, I want the boat to be repaired."

[26] Mark 5:33—the woman with the hemorrhage "fell down before Jesus and told him the whole truth" (εἶπεν αὐτῷ πᾶσαν τὴν ἀλήθειαν); Acts 26:25, Paul to Festus: "I am not mad . . . I am speaking words of truth and good sense" (ἀληθείας ῥήματα).

[27] Luke 22:59—"In truth (ἐπ' ἀληθείας) he (Peter) was with him (Jesus)" (the parallels, Matt 26:73; Mark 14:70, use the adverb ἀληθῶς, "assuredly"); Acts 4:27—"Truly they joined together against your holy servant Jesus . . ."; 10:34—"In truth, I understand that God is no respecter of persons."

[28] Matt 22:16—"You teach the way of God in truth" (τὴν ὁδὸν τοῦ θεοῦ ἐν ἀληθείᾳ διδάσκεις = Mark 12:14; Luke 20:21); Mark 12:32—"you have spoken truly" (ἐπ' ἀληθείας εἶπες, which Lagrange translates "vraiment très bien"); Luke 4:25—"I tell you truly" (ἐπ' ἀληθείας λέγω ὑμῖν). This expression corresponds to Ἀμὴν λέγω ὑμῖν (Mark 9:1, 41; Luke 18:29; cf. Rev 5:14; 7:12; 19:4). The Hebrew *'āmēn* means "yes" (cf. Rev 1:7—ναί, ἀμήν; 22:20; 2 Cor 1:20). In this context, it is intended to support or emphasize a statement, make it stand out—especially when it is repeated, as in John (1:51, etc.) where Jesus wants to focus attention and inspire certainty: "this is absolutely true"; cf. G. Stählin, "Zum Gebrauch von Beteuerungsformeln im Neuen Testament," in *NovT*, 1926, pp. 122–130. Likewise Rom 9:1—ἀλήθειαν λέγω ἐν Χριστῷ, οὐ ψεύδομαι; 1 Tim 2:7.

in order to be saved. . . . they did not believe the truth."²⁹ Salvation depends first of all on the adherence and submission of the heart to the objective truth; these responses make it possible to recognize and accept it when it is revealed in the preaching of the gospel (verse 13, *pistis alētheias*). By being resistant toward God's commands (Rom 2:8), humans "held the truth captive through their unrighteousness" (Rom 1:18). In other words, when salvation and righteousness were revealed (1:16-17), humans refused to accept them; they shackled or gagged the revelation, as it were, through their impiety and their sins.³⁰ This opposing force is next identified as the lie.³¹

This "truth" of revelation is the correct knowledge of reality (Hebrew *'emet*). The Jews possess in the Torah the *morphōsis*, the form or expression of knowledge and truth (Rom 2:20); they are sure of the divine will respecting them. It has to be obeyed, after the fashion of submitting to a rule (Gal 5:7), with nothing added and nothing taken away (Gal 2:5); we must walk straight or firmly, according to the solidity of the gospel.³²

---

²⁹ 2 Thess 2:10-12, τὴν ἀγάπην τῆς ἀληθείας; cf. Ps 50:8; 83:12; Zech 8:9; Josephus, *Ag. Apion* 2.296: "To you, Epaphroditus, who love the truth above all things . . . I dedicate this book" (μάλιστα τὴν ἀλήθειαν ἀγαπῶντι); *War* 1.30: τοῖς γε τὴν ἀλήθειαν ἀγαπῶσιν. C. Spicq, *Agapè*, vol. 2, pp. 32-39.

³⁰ G. R. Castellino, "Il paganesimo de Romani I, Sapienza 13-14 e la storia delle religioni," in AnBib, vol. 18, Rome, 1963, pp. 255-263.

³¹ Rom 1:25—"They exchanged the truth of God for the lie," i.e., they exchanged the only true, real, existing God for false conceptions, "gods who are not" (C. H. Dodd, *The Bible and the Greeks*, London, 1935, p. 74); Rom 3:7—"If my lying enhances God's truthfulness and so redounds to his greater glory . . ."; the ψεῦσμα is the unbelief and faithlessness of the Jew; 15:8—"Christ was minister of the circumcision (in the service of the circumcised, i.e., Israel) to show God's truthfulness in carrying out his promises to the Fathers"; the realization of these promises proves God's veracity (*'emet*, that which can be relied on). Cf. the judgment of God κατὰ ἀλήθειαν, in accord with real facts (2:2).

³² Gal 2:14—οὐκ ὀρθοποδοῦσιν πρὸς τὴν ἀλήθειαν τοῦ εὐαγγελίου. The truth is the certain reality, the objective rule of conduct (cf. verse 5). Ὀρθοποδέω, unknown in secular and biblical Greek before the Christian era, was understood by the church fathers to mean "walk straight" (G. D. Kilpatrick, "Gal. II, 14," in *Neutestamentliche Studien für R. Bultmann*, Berlin, 1954, pp. 269-274), but it seems rather to mean "to have clean conduct, a steady stride" according to *P.Mil.* XXIV, 8: νὴ τὴν σήν μοι σωτηρίαν καὶ τὴν τοῦ τεκνίου μου καὶ ὀρθοποδίαν (AD 117; cf. C. H. Roberts, "A Note on Galatians II, 14," in *JTS*, 1939, pp. 55-56); a University of Michigan papyrus (inv. 337): τὸ πεδείον ὀρθοποδεῖ ἐν ἐμοὶ εἶνα (published by J. G. Winter, "Another Instance of ὀρθοποδεῖν," in *HTR*, 1941, pp. 161-162); Nicander, *Alex.* 419: ὀρθόποδες βαίνοντες ἄνις σμυγεροῖον τιθήνης. In these three instances (*P.Phil.* XXXV, 4-6 is not clear), the topic is children who are beginning to walk on their own, without having to hold a nurse's hand to keep from falling. Cf. Cyril of Alexandria, *In Matt.* 17.17, ὁ ἄπιστος ἔσται που καὶ διεστραμμένος καὶ κατ' οὐδένα τρόπον ὀρθοποδεῖν εἰδώς (in J. Reuss, *Matthäus-Kommentare*, Berlin, 1957, p. 220).

Preaching and teaching in the church are "conformable to the truth that is in Jesus" (Eph 4:21), and every baptized Christian puts on "the new humanity, created according to God in the righteousness and holiness of truth."[33] The Passover is to be celebrated "not with the old leaven, nor with the leaven of vice and perversity, but with the unleavened loaves of purity and truth" (*en azymois eilikrineias kai alētheias*, 1 Cor 1:8); here "truth" is sincerity, honesty,[34] with a nuance of firmness as well (cf. Gal 5:7–9). This meaning, "truth-honesty," is constant in the apostle.[35]

The most numerous occurrences are those that give *alētheia* its Greek sense of true teaching, the expression or manifestation of the truth (and in a religious sense). "We have put aside the deceits of [false] shame (*ta krypta tēs aischynēs*), we who do not walk in shrewdness (*en panourgia*) or falsify the word of God (*mē dolountes ton logon tou theou*) but who, through the manifesting of the truth (*tē phanerōsei tēs alētheias*), commend ourselves to every human conscience" (2 Cor 4:2). This is the preaching-proclaiming of the unabridged kerygma, out in the light, under God's watchful eye. Second Corinthians 6:4, 7: "recommending ourselves as ministers of God . . . in the word of truth" (*en logō tēs alētheias*), which is the gospel (Col 1:5), the good news of salvation (Eph 1:30), the divine revelation[36] that admits

---

[33] Eph 4:24; this *alētheia* is almost "authenticity," as opposed to the "deceitful desires" of the old self (verse 22); cf. 1 Tim 2:7.

[34] The Targum calls Abraham "the totally unleavened one," i.e., "pure, sincere" (R. Le Déaut, *Nuit Pascale*, p. 173, n. 110); a connotation confirmed by the link with εἰλικρινία. Ἐιλικρινῆ, from εἴλη (the sun's heat or light) means "purified in the sunlight"; the soul is purified when it is open to the light. The *a-zymoi* are freed from the old lying fermentation, i.e., the community's lack of straightforwardness and firmness toward those guilty of incest.

[35] 2 Cor 7:14—"We spoke truthfully to you in everything"; 12:6—"I would be speaking the truth" (J. Cambier, "Le Critère paulinien de l'apostolat en II Cor. XII, 6," in *Bib*, 1962, pp. 481–518; idem, "Une lecture de II Cor. XII, 6–7 a: Essai d'interprétation nouvelle," in AnBib, vol. 17, Rome, 1963, pp. 475–485); 11:10—"the truth of Christ is in me" (guaranteeing what I say); Phil 1:18—"In one way or another, whether hypocritically or honestly (εἴτε προφάσει εἴτε ἀληθείᾳ), Christ is proclaimed" (C. Spicq, *Agapè*, vol. 2, pp. 244–252); Eph 4:25—"No more lying; let each one speak the truth to his neighbor" (cf. Zech 8:16); 5:9—"the fruit of the light in all goodness, righteousness, and truth" (cf. 1QS 1.5; 2.24–25; 4.5; 5.3–4, 25; 8.2); Eph 6:14—"Stand fast, with truth as your belt, righteousness as your breastplate" (Isa 11:5; 59:17; M. Barth, *Ephesians*, vol. 2, pp. 767ff.); cf. Jas 3:14—"Do not lie against the truth" (μὴ ψεύδεσθε κατὰ τῆς ἀληθείας). A characteristic of love is that is applauds the truth (1 Cor 13:6), i.e., the good, with virtue, righteousness, moral rectitude; it rejoices in it and pours out praise upon it; cf. the proselytes who are ἀληθείας ἐρασταί (Philo, *Virtues* 182; cf. *T. Dan* 5.2; *T. Reub.* 6.9).

[36] Cf. Jas 1:18—"The father of lights . . . has brought us forth by a word of truth"; cf. C. Spicq, *Théologie morale*, vol. 1, pp. 89ff.

ἀλήθεια, alētheia, etc. 75

of no distortion or falsification.³⁷ Ultimately, Christianity is "the truth";³⁸ a person accepts it and submits to it through the profession of faith³⁹ and sets out to follow "the way of truth" (2 Pet 2:2). The church is a "pillar and supporting structure of the truth," which is unchanging.⁴⁰ The heterodox who deviate from the faith (1 Tim 2:4; 2 Tim 2:25; 3:7) are "without the truth" (1 Tim 6:5); heretics "turn their ears away from the truth" (2 Tim 4:4), turn their back on it (Titus 1:14, *apostrephomenōn tēn alētheian*), deviate or walk away from the truth (2 Tim 2:18, *ēstochēsan*), wander away from it and get lost (Jas 5:19) and end up opposing it.⁴¹ In a word, the Christian religion is a cult of the truth; to be converted is to "come to the knowledge of the truth" (*eis epignōsin alētheias elthein*, 1 Tim 2:4). This stereotyped formula, which appears in the later writings of the NT,⁴²

---

³⁷ Timothy must rightly dispense the word of truth (ὀρθοτομοῦντα τὸν λόγον τῆς ἀληθείας, 2 Tim 2:15). The rare verb ὀρθοτομέω corresponds to the vocabulary of rhetoric: ὀρθὸν λέγειν means to express oneself correctly (Aristotle, *Gen. Cor.* 1.314ᵇ13; Iamblichus, *Myst.* 1.3 = 7.13). The rule of Greek dialectic was ὀρθοέπεια, expressing oneself correctly and precisely, without error or flaw (Plato, *Phdr.* 267 c), the opposite of the work of bad exegetes who twist texts (2 Pet 3:16). Cf. the apology of Quadratus, who showed ἀποστολικὴ ὀρθοτομία, "apostolic correctness," i.e., orthodoxy, according to Eusebius, *Hist. Eccl.* 4.3.1.

³⁸ 2 Pet 1:12; cf. A. Vögtle, "Die Schriftwerdung der apostolischen Paradosis nach II Petr. I, 12–15," in *Neues Testament und Geschichte* (Festschrift O. Cullmann), Zurich, 1972, pp. 297–306.

³⁹ 1 Pet 1:22—"Having perfectly sanctified your souls by obeying the truth." In this ancient allusion to baptism, *alētheia* is the unveiling of what was hidden or unknown, the opposite of the times of ignorance or error in verses 14 and 18.

⁴⁰ 1 Tim 3:15; ἑδραίωμα (biblical hapax, unknown in secular Greek literature) is sometimes translated "rampart, buttress, flying buttress, support, post." It corresponds to the Latin *firmamentum* (Vulgate) and derives from the adjective ἑδραῖος, "firmly seated, solid." It suggests robustness, stability, and unshakeable permanence of the building-church, built on rock and capable of resisting the gates of hell (Matt 16:18). Cf. J. Murphy-O'Connor, "La 'Vérité' chez saint Paul et à Qumrân," in 67ff.

⁴¹ Cf. 2 Tim 3:8; cf. K. Berger, "Die königlichen Messiastraditionen des Neuen Testaments," in *NTS*, vol. 20, 1, 1973, p. 10, n. 38; cf. p. 12, n. 40.

⁴² 1 Tim 4:3—"believers and those who know the truth"; Titus 1:1—"the faith of God's elect and the knowledge of the truth that accords with piety"; 2 Tim 2:25—God may grant to opponents "conversion to the knowledge of the truth"; 3:7—women who are "always learning but never attaining to knowledge of the truth"; Heb 10:26—at baptism, the Christian receives from God a knowledge of the truth, which is correct and unchanging; 2 John 1 addresses "all who have known the truth" and remain in it (verb in the perfect, οἱ ἐγνωκότες; cf. R. Schnackenburg, "Zum Begriff der 'Wahrheit' in den beiden kleinen Johannesbriefen," in *BZ*, 1967, pp. 253–258). —Cf. M. Dibelius, " Ἐπίγνωσις ἀληθείας," in *Neutestamentliche Studien für G. Heinrici*, Leipzig, 1014, pp. 178–189 (reprinted in *Botschaft und Geschichte*, Tübingen,

refers to the correct knowledge of the true religion; the truth is the object of faith. The Christian profession is to adhere to it, to come to this knowledge, to receive it from God, and to keep it; this is salvation.[43] *Epignōsis* is not a deepened knowledge, but a precise, determinate knowledge, built on revelation, the gospel discerned as being real and not a myth; hence it is an orthodox knowledge, received from God, opposed to heretical deviations.[44]

In St. John, *alētheia* (twenty-five occurrences in the Fourth Gospel, twenty in the epistles) becomes a distinctively Christian term, belonging to the vocabulary of the revelation of *epigeia* and *epourania* (earthly things and heavenly things).[45] In the prologue, which summarizes the theology of his Gospel, John sets out to provide an unshakeable basis for the doctrine of the Revealer par excellence and presents him as "full of grace and

---

1953, vol. 2, pp. 1–13); C. Spicq, *Epîtres Pastorales*, 3d ed., Excursus XVI, pp. 362–365; H. von Lips, *Glaube, Gemeinde, Amt*, Göttingen, 1979, pp. 33–40.

[43] The few pagan parallels are thus merely verbal: "The magi search the works of nature to learn the truth (πρὸς ἐπίγνωσιν τῆς ἀληθείας) . . . and they receive and transmit the revelation of the divine virtues" (Philo, *Good Man Free* 74; cf. *Spec. Laws* 4.178, μεταναστὰς εἰς ἀλήθειαν, going to dwell with truth); Josephus, *Ant.* 8.33: recognize the truth of someone's sentiments; 20.128: know the truth more exactly; Epictetus 2.20.21: "Is there a faculty that permits discernment of the truth?" On ἐπίγνωσις—discernment and identification—cf. Matt 11:27; Josephus, *Ant.* 8.48; Plutarch, *Cor.* 34.3; *Ages.* 21. —K. Sullivan, "Epignosis in the Epistles of St. Paul," in AnBib, vol. 18, Rome, 1963, II, pp. 405–416; H. Clavier, "Recherche exégétique et théologique sur la notion paulinienne d'épignosis," in E. A. Livingstone, *SE*, vol. 6, Berlin, 1973, pp. 37–52.

[44] There was probably some influence from Qumran: the "volunteers of the truth of God" (1QS 1.11–12; 5.10) were converted to *'emet* (6.15), which is what distinguished them from those perverted in heart (4.24–25). They drew upon the "knowledge of the truth" (9.17–18; 1QH 7.26–27; 10.20–29). The "knowers" were God's faithful, those who held firm (CD 2.13). Cf. H. Kosmala, *Hebräer—Essener—Christen*, Leiden, 1959, pp. 155ff. J. Murphy-O'Connor, *RB*, 1965, pp. 61ff. A. M. Denis, *Les Thèmes de la connaissance dans le Document de Damas*, Louvain, 1967, pp. 51ff., 78ff., 200ff.

[45] John 3:12. F. Büchsel, *Der Begriff der Wahrheit in dem Evangelium und in den Briefen des Johannes*, Gütersloh, 1911; A. Augustinović, "ΑΛΗΘΕΙΑ nel IV Vangelo," in *Studii biblici Franciscani liber annuus I*, 1950–51, pp. 161–190; H. von Soden, "Was ist Wahrheit?" in *Urchristentum und Geschichte*, Tübingen, 1951, pp. 1–29; O. Betz, "Die 'Wahrheit' in den johanneischen Schriften," in *Offenbarung und Schriftforschung in der Qumransekte*, Tübingen, 1960, pp. 60–61; S. Aalen, " 'Truth' a Key Word in St John's Gospel," in *SE*, vol. 2, Berlin, 1964, pp. 3–24; N. Lazure, *Les Valeurs morales de la théologie johannique*, Paris, 1965, pp. 70–92; R. Schnackenburg, "The Johannine Concept of Truth" (Excursus 10), in *John*, vol. 2, pp. 225–237. The major books are Yu Ibuki, *Die Wahrheit im Johannesevangelium*, Bonn, 1972, and I. de la Potterie, *La Vérité dans saint Jean*, 2 vols., Rome, 1977. Cf. idem, "Storia e verità," in R. Latourelle, G. O'Collins, *Problemi e prospettive de teologia fondamentale*, Brescia, 1980, pp. 115–139.

truth."[46] This is the Word that was made flesh and dwelt among us. In this human condition, and on the level of history, *alētheia* is not the essential truth of the Logos but a divine gift: the knowledge of the truth communicated to human nature. Hence it is in the first place the beatific vision, then that quality which permits "bearing witness to the truth" (John 18:37), and finally the truth of the teachings of Jesus both regarding God (the Father) and regarding his own sonship and the salvation of humans. It is a truthful and sure teaching, worthy of trust. Jesus possesses this truth in its fullness and reveals, transmits, and explicates it.[47] He is the supreme Revealer, unveiling and manifesting to the fullest the divine secrets.

He specifies that he alone gives access to God: "I am the way and the truth and the life."[48] The emphasis is on the way,[49] an image explicated by the two ideas of truth and life. Jesus is the only way because he communicates the fullness of revelation and even the very life of God. He is the instrument of the truth that comes from God; it is inherent in him, and he affirms it unfailingly: "I, a man who spoke to you the truth that I heard from God."[50] After all, one testifies concerning that which one has seen and heard (3:11). The legal idea of testimony takes on a theological meaning (cf. Jer 42:5; Prov 14:25) when John the Baptist identifies Jesus as God's Chosen One and reveals him as such (5:33; cf. 1:7, 15, 19, 31, 34) and when

---

[46] Πλήρης χάριτος καὶ ἀληθείας, John 1:14; cf. verse 17: "From his fullness we have all received. . . . Grace and truth came through Jesus Christ." The pairing χάρις-ἀλήθεια recalls "mercy and truth" in the OT (Gen 24:27, 49; 32:11; 47:29; Exod 34:6; Josh 2:14; 2 Sam 2:6; 15:20; Hos 4:1; Mic 7:20; Ps 40:11; 85:11; 89:15; Tob 3:2); cf. I. de la Potterie, *La Vérité dans saint Jean*, vol. 1, pp. 76-78, 158-176.

[47] John 1:18—ἐξηγήσατο; the object of exegesis is τὰ θεῖα (Dionysius of Halicarnassus 2.23.6), the exegete interprets περὶ ἱερείων (Hesychius); cf. Sir 18:5; 43:31.

[48] Ἐγώ εἰμι ἡ ὁδὸς καὶ ἡ ἀλήθεια καὶ ἡ ζωή, John 14:6 (I. de la Potterie, *La Vérité dans saint Jean*, vol. 1, pp. 241-278). As the incarnate Son of God, Jesus is identical with the truth, is the living revelation of the Father (14:9-11). Cf. M. Comeau, "Le Christ, chemin et terme de l'ascension spirituelle d'après saint Augustin," in *Mélanges J. Lebreton* (RSR, 1952, pp. 80-89); T. Camelot, "Le Christ, sacrement de Dieu," in *Mélanges H. de Lubac*, Paris, 1963, vol. 1, pp. 355-363.

[49] The OT links way and truth (Ps 25:10; 26:3; 86:11; 119:30; Wis 5:6; Tob 1:3; Sir 24:18), but in the sense of moral rectitude (cf. *Odes Sol.* 41.11-12; 4 Ezra 5:1; 1QS 4.16-20). Cf. B. Couroyer, "Le Chemin et la vie en Egypte et en Israël," in *RB*, 1949, pp. 412-432; P. Courcelle, " 'Trames veritatis': La Fortune patristique d'une métaphore platonicienne (Phédon 66 b)," in *Mélanges E. Gilson*, Toronto-Paris, 1959, pp. 203-210.

[50] John 8:40, 45, 46 (or taught by God, verses 26, 28); cf. I. de la Potterie, *La Vérité dans saint Jean*, vol. 1, pp. 39-75. If Jesus makes a strange or paradoxical statement ("it is good for you that I go away"), he appeals to his perfect knowledge of things and of the future, as well as to his own veracity (16:7). If the Jews do not believe him, it is because their heart is dominated by the lie, because their father is the devil, a liar who has no truth in him (8:44; 1 John 1:8; 2:4).

the incarnate Christ makes known what he has heard in heaven, whence he has come "to bear witness to the truth,"[51] to manifest it. His life's work is to make this revelation so as to inspire faith (1:7; 19:35; 1 John 5:6).

To accept this testimony means not only being teachable and sincere, but also being in spiritual relationship with the truth and the words of Jesus, like sheep that recognize the voice of their true shepherd (John 10:16, 27). Better yet, it is to be "of the truth" (*ho ōn ek tēs alētheias*): "Whoever is of the truth hears my voice."[52] The concrete meaning of the expression is to be originally from a certain place, to have been born there; but it is synonymous with "son of" and means "depend on, abide in." Consequently, being "of the truth" means being permanently under God's influence, being obedient to revelation. This is what explains the way of life and the bearing of the believer who abides in the radiance of the truth of Christ. Hence the biblicism "do the truth";[53] "the one who does the truth (*ho poiōn tēn alētheian*) comes from the light, so that his works are clearly seen (*hina phanerōthē*) as being done in God."[54] In the genesis of faith, orthopraxy makes it possible to attain to the knowledge of revealed truth; it presupposes an interior choice—a right action and a true thought realized—that orients a person toward Christ. Thus a person becomes obedient to the Father's drawing, unconsciously submits to his will, and thus proves to be in communion with him.

"If you abide in my word, you will truly be my disciples, and you will know the truth, and the truth will deliver you" (John 8:32). *Alētheia* is the

---

[51] John 18:37 (I. de la Potterie, *La Vérité dans saint Jean*, pp. 79–116; cf. the "good confession before Pontius Pilate," 1 Tim 6:13). The members of the Qumran sect were "witnesses of truth," i.e., truthful witnesses (cf. F. M. Braun, "L'Arrière-fond judaïque du quatrième Evangile et la communauté de l'Alliance," in *RB*, 1955, pp. 5–44). 3 John 3: "Many brothers have given testimony of your truth" (your doctrinal fidelity and your Christian conduct).

[52] John 18:37; cf. 1 John 2:21; 3:19 (I. de la Potterie, *La Vérité dans saint Jean*, vol. 2, pp. 593–635). Compare being of God (John 8:47), of the devil (John 8:44; 1 John 3:8), of the world (John 7:14; 1 John 4:6), of our own (1 John 2:19). Knowing the truth (1 John 2:21; NT hapax; cf. Plato, *Phdr.* 262 c; *Resp.* 9.581 b; Lycurgus, *Leoc.* 22; Polybius 15.26.6; Josephus, *Ant.* 2.60) is a firm knowledge, a conviction (of the faith). Cf. loving in truth (1 John 3:18; 2 John 1; 3 John 1) = loving sincerely, really, but also according to the gospel, i.e., loving from the heart and showing it. Likewise "walking in the truth" (2 John 4; 3 John 3–4). Cf. R. Schnackenburg, "The Johannine Concept of Truth" (Excursus 10), in *John*, vol. 2, pp. 225–237.

[53] Gen 32:10; 47:29; Neh 9:33; Isa 26:10, referring to firm and persevering conduct (1QS 1.5; 5.3; *T. Benj.* 10.3).

[54] John 3:21; 1 John 1:6; M. Zerwick, "Veritatem facere, Joh. III, 21; I Joh. II, 6," in *VD*, 1938, pp. 338–341, 373–377; I. de la Potterie, *La Vérité dans saint Jean*, vol. 2, pp. 479ff.

content of Jesus' utterance, the full revelation concerning God and humanity, concerning their relationship (verses 40, 44, 45). To know this truth, a person must abide faithfully in this word and adhere to it (10:38; 2 Tim 3:14) firmly (2 Pet 1:12; *T. Jos.* 1.3). Then come (*a*) progress in becoming a true disciple through a more intimate attachment to Christ; (*b*) deeper penetration into the truth that is revelation and the Christian mystery;[55] (*c*) and finally liberation, because every sinner is considered a slave of error or vice;[56] but here it is a question of enslavement to the devil and of the sin of unbelief (1 John 3:4). There is thus a change of masters; for the former tyranny is substituted by the Lord's sovereignty (1 John 2:13–14; 5:18), then virtuous conduct characterized as service to God, and then finally and above all filiation takes the place of servitude. True liberty belongs to the one who lives in the household. It is a stable condition, characterized especially by a loving relationship with God; one is freed in order to be able to love. This is the noblest fruit of truth.[57]

As of Christ's advent, there are "true" worshipers (i.e., "real," or better, "perfect" worshipers) who worship the Father *en pneumati kai alētheia* ("in spirit and in truth").[58] In spirit (the highest faculty of the human person),

---

[55] Cf. 2 John 1: "to all those who have known the (unveiled) truth" (cf. Tob 5:14; recension S); one learns it better and better, discovers it more clearly (*Enoch* 106.7, 12; 1QS 9.17–19; 1QH 11.9–10), assimilates it more completely (1 Tim 2:4). This is the progress in faith (1 John 4:16; Wis 3:9) that is built on God but also and especially on Christ, his divine Sonship and his teaching.

[56] This was a Stoic doctrine (Epictetus 2.1.23; 4.1.113; Plutarch, *Cat. Min.* 67; Seneca, *Ep.* 88.2; etc. Cf. O. Schmitz, *Der Freiheitsgedanke bei Epiktet und das Freiheitszeugnis des Paulus*, Gütersloh, 1923; M. Pohlenz, *La Liberté grecque*, Paris, 1956; C. Spicq, *Théologie morale*, vol. 2, pp. 623–664, 828–849). Philo wrote a book to prove that the wise person is free, *Quod Omnis Probus Liber Sit* (*Every Good Man is Free*). Only submission to God secures freedom for those in servitude: "They have an invincible love of liberty, because they judge that God is the only leader and master" (Josephus, *Ant.* 18.23, cf. *War* 7.410; 2 Macc 1:27). "You will not find a free man other than the one who devotes himself to the study of Torah" (*Pirqe 'Abot* 6.2). The Messiah brings liberation to the people (*Tg.* Lam 2:22; 4:22; Shemoneh Esreh [the "Eighteen Benedictions"], number 10). Cf. D. Daube, *The New Testament and Rabbinic Judaism*, London, 1956, pp. 272–278.

[57] Cf. C. Spicq, *Charité et liberté*; L. Goppelt, "Wahrheit als Befreiung: Das neutestamentliche Zeugnis von der Wahrheit nach dem Jahannesevangelium," in H. R. Müller-Schwefe, *Was ist Wahrheit?*, Göttingen, 1965, pp. 80–93; D. Atal, "Die Wahrheit wird euch freimachen (Jo. VII, 32)," in H. Merklein, *Biblische Randbemerkungen: Schülerfestschrift für R. Schnackenburg*, Würzburg, 1974, pp. 283–299; I. de la Potterie, *La Vérité dans saint Jean*, vol. 2, pp. 551ff., 789–866.

[58] John 4:23–24. Cf. F. M. Braun, "In Spiritu et Veritate," in *RevThom*, 1952, pp. 245–274; 485–507; R. Schnackenburg, "Die 'Anbetung in Geist und Wahrheit' (Joh. IV, 23) im Lichte von Qumrân-Texten," in *BZ*, 1959, pp. 88–94 (reworked and developed

which allows being united with God, who is Spirit (John 4:24; no longer by material deeds or achievements). In truth means not as at Samaria and Jerusalem, but through the worship of the true God as revealed by Jesus, as children revering their heavenly Father. When Jesus prays to his father asking him to sanctify-consecrate the apostles *en tē alētheia*, as he himself is sanctified-consecrated *en alētheia*,[59] we may understand him to mean "really, actually" (Theodore of Mopsuestia), but since through this consecration the subject is not only set apart for a sacred office but prepared and adapted for it, *en* can have an instrumental meaning. Thus truth would be the instrument of sanctification (cf. 2 Thess 2:13; John 16:13). The disciples are invaded by it and transformed within. Finally, this consecration is conformable to that of Jesus and derives from it; they are devoted and reserved for the exclusive service of God.[60]

The Holy Spirit is described as the "Spirit of Truth." He continues the presence and action of Jesus on earth. He indwells the apostles, to whom he reveals the work of the Father and the Son, provided that their love is authentic (John 14:17). This divine being proceeds from the Father;[61] given to the disciples, he "will guide them into the entire truth . . . he will repeat all that he hears and will make future things known to you . . . he takes what is mine and makes it known to you" (John 16:13–15). An infallible teacher and guide,[62] worthy of trust, the Holy Spirit leads believers to

---

in *Christliche Existenz nach dem Neuen Testament*, Munich, 1968, vol. 2, pp. 75–96); D. Muñoz Leon, "Adoración en espíritu y verdad: Aportación targúmica a la inteligencia de Jn. IV, 23–24," in L. A. Verdes, E. J. A. Hernandez, *Homenaje a Juan Prado*, Madrid, 1075, pp. 387–403; I. de la Potterie, *La Vérité dans saint Jean*, vol. 2, pp. 673–705.

[59] John 17:17, 19. Cf. J. Giblet, "La sainteté de la vérité," in A. Dondeyne, J. Giblet, *Christianisme et vérité*, Brussels, 1959, pp. 7–42; I. de la Potterie, *La Vérité dans saint Jean*, vol. 2, pp. 706–787.

[60] God is most holy and is the only one who sanctifies (Exod 31:13; Lev 20:8; 21:8, 15; Ezek 20:12; 37:28; 1 Thess 5:23), sets people apart for himself alone (Num 3:13; Sir 33:12). This is an exclusive setting apart for a religious function (Exod 40:13; Lev 22:2–3; Matt 23:17).

[61] John 15:26—ἐκπορεύεται (present indicative): "flows from," as a river flows from its source (Rev 22:1). Historically, at a given moment, the Holy Spirit—who emanates (essentially, eternally) from the Father (eternal procession from deep within the Trinity)—is sent and given to the disciples. In other words, the historic acts of salvation rest on the eternal relationships of both the Son and the Spirit. The latter, "that one" (ἐκεῖνος), "bears witness regarding me" (περὶ ἐμοῦ). He has the authority of a divine witness. Knowing Jesus from all eternity, he alone, with the Father, knows perfectly who he is.

[62] Ὁδηγέω: show the way, lead someone in an unknown region (Rev 7:17). Cf. I. de la Potterie, *La Vérité dans saint Jean*, vol. 1, pp. 329–466. 1 John 4:6—"This is how we know the spirit of truth and the spirit of error" (τῆς πλάνης). In the trial between Jesus (who is innocent) and the world (which condemned him as guilty), the Holy

understand better the truth that is Christ so that they may better fathom; he does not complete it, but on the one hand he makes an exhaustive inventory of the data of the gospel, and on the other hand he illuminates to provide better understanding (cf. the Fourth Gospel vis-à-vis the Synoptics). He unveils its riches, progressively explicates its content, and in this way proclaims (*anangelei*); in this sense he is a teacher. But like Jesus (John 12:49; 14:10), he invents nothing, does not speak on his own; he only repeats what he has heard from God (cf. 8:26) and, through prophetic charisms, also unveils future things (1 Cor 12:29–30; Rev 19:10) and thus strengthens faith. Thus the Spirit is indeed a revealer.

Alētheuō. — Incontestably, this verb has only one meaning in secular Greek, "speak the truth,"[63] and that is its meaning in Gal 4:16—"Have I become your enemy because I told you the truth?" Nevertheless, there are shades of meaning. In Plato, *Resp.* 3.413 *a* and *Tht.* 202 *c, alētheuein* means "being right." Philo (*Etern. World* 48) contrasts the lover of truth (*alētheuontos*) to the concocter of paradoxes. The LXX puts these words in the mouth of Abimelech, addressing Sarah: "speak the truth in all things" (*panta alētheuson,* Gen 20:16; but the corresponding Hebrew verb is the

---

Spirit appears as a lawyer in the court of appeals and "will convict the world" (John 16:8). Every human being is called upon to take sides regarding this "sign spoken against" (Luke 2:34). Cf. T. Preiss, "La Justification dans la pensée johannique," in *Hommage et reconnaissance* (Mélanges K. Barth), Neuchâtel, 1946, pp. 100–118.

[63] Plato, *Cra.* 431 *b*: ἀληθεύειν . . . ψεύδεσθαι, "speak truthfully . . . speak falsehoods"; Xenophon, *An.* 4.4.15: "having spoken the truth . . . giving out as true that which was true and as false that which was not true"; Philo, *Alleg. Interp.* 3.124: hardly anyone who is angry speaks the truth, being dominated by a drunkenness of the soul; *Cherub.* 15: a physician does not tell the truth to (hides it from) his patient, and the wise person fears speaking it (unveiling it) to his adversaries; but "good faith speaks the truth" (*Drunkenness* 40; *Abraham* 107) and "interpreters of dreams have the obligation to speak the truth" (*Joseph* 95; *Moses* 2.177; *Spec. Laws* 4.60). Josephus, *Life* 132: "even the inhabitants of Tarichaeae came to believe that the young men were speaking the truth"; 338: the historian Justus "has said nothing true (correct) concerning his native city"; 339: "When writing history, one must tell the truth"; *War* 3.322: "was this man speaking the truth?"; *Ant.* 10.105: "Sacchias accepted as true what the prophet was saying"; *Ag. Apion* 1.223: "Certain authors do not tell the truth about how our ancestors came out of Egypt." Moulton-Milligan could only produce one weak attestation of this verb in the papyri: α]ληθευοντ (followed by a lacuna), *P.Amh.* II, 142, 1; but it has since been attested in the second century in a petition to the prefect: a mother, influenced by her depraved sons, did not tell the truth (*P.Oxy.* 232, 12); *P.Oxf.* 6, 15: "The villagers of Ogou did not tell the truth"; *P.Oxy.* 3129, 7: "if you find that he spoke the truth" (εἰ ἀληθεύοντα εὕροις). In *P.Hercul.* 1065, VIII, 12 (= Philodemus of Gadara, *Sign.*) this restoration has been made correctly: τὸ δόγμα [ἀληθεύεσθαι ν]ομίζομεν, "if we consider our philosophical doctrine to express the truth . . ."; cf. XI, 17.

niphal of *yākaḥ*, meaning that Sarah will be entirely justified in the sight of everyone). The LXX also contrasts telling the truth with lying (Sir 34:4); but when Joseph explains to his brothers that he is putting them in prison "to find out whether the truth is with you" (*ei alētheuete ē ou*, Gen 42:16, Hebrew *'emet*), that is, whether they are spies or not, the verb has the sense "be sincere."[64] The meaning is "realize, carry out" in Prov 21:3 (the one who pleases God) and Isa 44:26—"I carry out the words of my messengers" (Hebrew hiphil of *šālam*). These usages allow a somewhat original interpretation of Eph 4:15, *alētheuontes de en agapē*, which could be translated either "live by the truth and in love" (*NJB*) or, in line with the context, which denounces error and deceitfulness, "remaining in the truth, in love."[65] In any event, the emphasis is on remaining attached to the truth (of the gospel), holding fast to it, with the Johannine connotations of being of the truth, loving it, professing it, carrying it out; in other words, conforming one's conduct to it.[66]

Alēthēs. — This adjective, attested late, appears in the third century BC from the pen of Zeno: "if that is true (or correct)";[67] and it recurs in one form or another to modify something that has been said or written. It is the opposite of "false, lying";[68] this is in agreement with Wis 2:17 ("let us see if his words are true")[69] and with a goodly number of NT occurrences. In stating that she had no husband, the Samaritan woman spoke the truth, was correct and straightforward (John 4:18); John the Baptist and the evangelist spoke the truth (10:41; 19:35; cf. 2 Pet 2:22). This formula is used when security is posted or an obligation is taken on: "The note concerning

---

[64] This would seem to the nuance of *alētheuō* in Josephus, *War* 7.220: Caesennius Paetus "wrote to Caesar, either sincerely or out or hatred"; cf. *Ant.* 14.267: "make a sincere statement."

[65] N. Hugedé, *L'Epître aux Ephesiens*, Geneva, 1973, on this word. Cf. "being sincere in love" (M. Dibelius, *An die Kolosser, Epheser*, 3d ed., 1953, pp. 82ff.).

[66] Cf. C. Spicq, *Théologie morale*, vol. 2, p. 540, n. 1; J. D. Dubois, "Ephésiens IV, 15: ἀληθεύοντες δὲ or ἀλήθειαν δὲ ποιοῦντες," in *NovT*, 1974, pp. 30–34.

[67] *SB* 6744, 4: κἂν ᾖ ταῦτα ἀληθῆ; 6764, 4; *P.Yale* 46, col. I, 17; cf. *P.Tebt.* 782, 23; *SB* 7446, 7: ἃ ᾖ ἀληθῆ; 7520, 6; 9801, 19; 10044, 19.

[68] *P.Stras.* 41, 18: δεῖ γὰρ τὰ ἀληθῆ λέγειν; *P.Oxy.* 2419, 5: τὸ ἀληθὲς λέγω; *SB* 6097, 13: ἀληθές ἐστιν τὸν λόγον; *PSI* 816, 8: ἐὰν ᾖ ἃ γράφω ἀληθῆ; *P.Tebt.* 775, 14; *P.Magd.* I, 16; XI, 13; XII, 11; XIII, 10, etc. *P.Tebt.* 782, 23; *SB* 9605, 9: γράφω ὑμῖν, ἵν' ἰδῇ ἀληθές; 7258, 6.

[69] Cf. Job 42:7–8: speak the truth (niphal of *kûn*); *I.Thas.* XVIII, 1: "Anyone who informs on an insurrectionist movement . . . whose words prove to be correct"; *CII* 86: the praises of the deceased are true; Josephus, *War* 4.154.

ἀλήθεια, alētheia, etc. 83

this is true."[70] This adjective constantly occurs in oaths[71] and with testimony (John 5:31-32; 8:13, 14, 17; 21:24; Titus 1:13; 3 John 12; Josephus, Ant. 4.219). The nuance is then "authentic"[72] or "sincere, truthful";[73] it is used to describe reliable men (Neh 7:2; Hebrew 'emet), for Jesus and his candor (Matt 22:16 = Mark 12:14; John 7:18), especially for the true God and his word.[74] Finally, alēthēs often means "real" as opposed to imaginary or metaphorical,[75] as in Acts 12:9 where Peter, once freed from prison, "did not know that this was real but thought that he was having a vision," or in John 6:55—Jesus' flesh is truly (really) food and his blood is truly drink (the Textus Receptus substitutes the adverb alēthōs).

---

[70] Χειρογραφίαν περὶ τοῦ ἀληθῆ εἶναι, BGU 1573, 22; 1583, 23; 1756, 5; Pap.Lugd. Bat. VI, 29, 18; PSI 1064, 18; 1141, 13; 1225, 14; 1237, 20; 1328, 20; P.Oslo 99, 19; 111, 299; SB 7333, 32; 7599, 33; 7602, 12; 7817, 20; P.Oxy. 2186, 11: ἀληθῆ εἶναι τὰ προγεγραμμένα; 2564, 15; 2837, 22 (AD 50); 3034, 6; cf. P.Oslo 17, 14; τὸ ἀληθὲς ἐξομολογήσασθε.
[71] Ὅρκον ἀληθῆ, P.Corn. 19, 12 and 17; 20, 18; Pap.Lugd.Bat. VI, 33, 16; P.Cair.Isid. 2, 20; 3, 24; 4, 12; etc; P.Mich. 176, 22; PSI 1328, 69; P.Oxy. 2345, 8; SB 7602, 16; 7623, 20; 7672, 5; 7673, 13; 9317, a 35; 10726, 12, 17; P.Hal., p. 227; Philo, Cherub. 108, 124; Spec. Laws 2.10; Josephus, Ant. 4.219.
[72] Wis 6:17; 1 Pet 5:12. With respect to legitimate children (Philo, Migr. Abr. 69: τὸν ἀληθῆ πατέρα; Spec. Laws 1.326, 332; P.Tebt. 285, 3), civic rights (Prelim. Stud. 6), a circumcised child who is truly of a priestly family, ἀληθῆ εἶναι ἱερατικοῦ γένου (P.Tebt. 293, 17). Philo several times links ἀληθὲς καὶ γνήσιον (Conf. Tongues 72; Post. Cain 102; Joseph 258), several times uses the comparative ἀληθέστερον (Sacr. Abel and Cain 65; Moses 1.274; Etern. World 15), and nine times uses the superlative ἀληθέστατος (Creation 72; Alleg. Interp. 3.51; Sacr. Abel and Cain 26; Unchang. God 107, 123; Migr. Abr. 171; Heir 243; Abraham 60, 261). True is contrasted with false (Alleg. Interp. 3.229; Cherub. 127; Dreams 2.47, 64, 162; Virtues 205; Contemp. Life 10; etc.).
[73] P.Ant. 188, 16: τὸ δὲ ἀληθέστερον εἰπεῖν: "I urge you to express yourself quite frankly"; 2 Cor 6:8—ὡς πλάνοι καὶ ἀληθεῖς; taken as imposters, but nevertheless truthful. 1 John 2:27; cf. I. de la Potterie, S. Lyonnet, La Vie selon l'Esprit, Paris, 1965, pp. 126-143.
[74] Gen 41:32; Dan 2:47; 10:1; Wis 1:6; 12:27; 15:1; John 3:33; 8:26; Rom 3:34; Philo, Post. Cain 115; Drunkenness 45; Dreams 1.238; Abraham 50, 68; Joseph 254; Moses 2.171; Decalogue 8; Spec. Laws 1.36; To Gaius 290, 347; Josephus, Ant. 8.337, 343; 10.268; War 7.323.
[75] P.Panop.Beatty 2, 89: so that the true facts may be elucidated; P.Phil. I, 23: the estimation will be made "not according to a declaration with no official character, but according to their true circumstances" (ἐκ ἀληθοῦς αὐτῶν ὑποστάσεως); SB 8444, 57: "the tax charges will be made according to the true [state] of the grape crop and of the unflooded land"; P.Tebt. 739, 29. Cf. Job 5:12—"their hands do not the truth"—i.e., do not accomplish their plans. Alēthēs also has the psychological or moral connotation "honest, reasonable"; cf. Isa 41:26—"so that we may say that it was right" (ὅτι ἀληθῆ ἐστιν, Hebrew ṣadîq); 43:9 (Hebrew 'emet); Phil 4:8—"whatever is true (honest), whatever is worthy . . . let this be what counts for you."

Alēthinos.[76] — Less common than *alēthēs*, but having pretty nearly the same meaning, this adjective is used relatively little in the papyri, where it is contrasted with lying;[77] but its precise meaning is "authentic," with respect to either things[78] or persons: "true Egyptians (*hoi alēthinoi Aigyptioi*), easily recognizable by their speech" (*P.Giss.* 40, col. II, 27; edict of Caracalla). The LXX uses it with the nuance "perfect," sometimes with respect to people,[79] but with religious connotations. Usually it is applied to God (2 Chr 15:3; Isa 65:16; cf. *P.Oxy.* 925, 2; *BGU* 954, 28), his benevolence (Exod 34:6; Num 14:18; Ps 86:15; 103:8), his perfect works (Deut 32:4, Hebrew *tām;* Dan 3:27 [Theodotion]; 4:34), his words (2 Sam 7:28, Hebrew *'emet;* 1 Kgs 17:24), his commands and judgments (Ps 119:9; Tob 3:2, 5). Philo retained this meaning—"the one true God" (*Spec. Laws* 1.332; *To Gaius* 366)—but kept especially the nuance "authentic," referring to the essence, the deep truth. For example, false money is contrasted with "true value, that which exists really" (*ontōs ontos*).[80]

The NT is faithful to this semantic tradition. The true good (*to alēthinon*) is the authentic good, that of the soul (Luke 16:11). This adjective is applied almost exclusively to God and Christ,[81] but the Fourth Gospel and the

---

[76] This is the right spelling (Herodian 2.473.7), as opposed to *alētheinos* (ἀληθεινός) in certain papyri, cf. E. Mayser, *Grammatik,* p. 92, n. 7; I, 3, p. 100, 38.

[77] Moulton-Milligan (on this word) cite *P.Petr.* II, 19 (l. *a*) 6; (2) 3 (third century BC); cf. a death certificate: ἀληθινὰ εἶναι τὰ γεγραμμένα (*P.Phil.* 6, 24; from the second century AD); *P.Apoll.* 61, 10: "I made him swear that these were not lies but the truth"; 68, 2. A letter from the third century is addressed Σαραπίωνι τῷ ἀληθινῷ μωρῷ (*SB* 10557, 1); *BGU* 1141, 12: δέδωκα ἀποδείξεις ἀληθινάς (seventeenth year of Augustus; cf. Dittenberger, *Syl.* 684, 17).

[78] Autolycus of Pitane, *Risings,* intro. 4: "There are two types of sunrises and sunsets: true (ἀληθιναί = real) and apparent"; cf. 1.1 et passim. —Xenophon, *Oec.* 10.3: "If I passed off badly died fabric on you as authentic purple (πορφυρίδας ἀληθινάς)"; ἀληθινῆς μικτῆς πορφύρας (*SB* 11075, 8); the compound form ἀληθινοπόρφυρος (*P.Oxy.* 114, 7; *SB* 11075, 11). The verb ἀληθίζω means "die with purple," in *P.Holm.,* p. 28 = n. 18, 6; third-fourth century); ἀληθινός = purple, in John Malalas, *Chron.* 2.33.12; 17.413.14 (*PG,* vol. 97, 101 and 612).

[79] Job 1:1; 2:3; 4:7, 23; straightforward speech, 6:25; Prov 12:19; cf. the queen of Sheba: "Then what I heard about you is true" (1 Kgs 10:6; 2 Chr 9:5).

[80] *Prelim. Stud.* 159, 101: "true and just measure"; *Heir* 162: "let your weights be correct and just" (Deut 25:15) = *Dreams* 2.193. True wealth does not deceive (*Flight* 17) but is found in the heavens (*Rewards* 104). True goods are the object of divine benediction (*Virtues* 78). The "true man" is the one who corresponds to his spiritual nature (*Worse Attacks Better* 10; *Giants* 33; *Flight* 131; cf. *Moses* 1.289). "True life" is that of the religious soul (*Alleg. Interp.* 1.32, 35; 3.52); cf. authentic wisdom and virtue (*Flight* 82).

[81] John 17:3—"You, the only true God" (σε τὸν μόνον ἀληθινὸν θεόν); 1 Thess 1:9—"to serve the living and true God" (as opposed to idols); 1 John 5:20; Rev 3:7,

Epistle to the Hebrews give it a special meaning: "The Word was the true light" (*to phōs to alēthinon,* John 1:9; 1 John 2:8), meaning spiritual and divine, authentic or genuine. The opposite is not imperfect, veiled; *alēthinos* implies the idea of an ideal or a perfect model,[82] so that "the true" can properly mean only divine or heavenly realities; the earthly world is only a degraded participation in those realities. Hence Christ is not so much the "only and true" light as the "perfect" light, the source and model for all other light, the Revealer, the Illuminator par excellence. Likewise John 6:32—"The Father gives you true bread from heaven" (*ton arton ton alēthinon*). This is not only "real" bread, bread of heavenly origin, but divine bread in its very essence. John 7:28—"The One who sent me is true"; *alēthinos* means neither "authentic" nor "real" but the only Sender worthy of the name, having the power to send. The relations between the Father and Jesus are the ideal type for every human mission. John 15:1—"I am the true vine" (*egō eimi hē ampelos hē alēthinē*), not only by comparison with the degenerate vine that is Israel,[83] but the vine absolutely worthy of the name, the vine par excellence, doing in the highest degree "that which is proper to vines, bearing fruit that is very sweet and very wholesome" (M. J. Lagrange); the article before the adjective makes for a strong emphasis, a kind of superlative in apposition. Thus "true worshipers" (John 4:23) are authentic and perfect worshipers who actualize the precise concept of worship directed toward the true God. The tabernacle or sanctuary in which the high priest of the new covenant officiates in heaven (Heb 8:2; 9:24) is not "fabricated, an antitype of the true tabernacle," imperfect and transitory, but is authentic and divine.

Alēthōs. — In secular Greek this adverb means sometimes "truly, sincerely" as opposed to "falsely,"[84] sometimes "really" (Philo, *Alleg. Interp.* 1.17; *Post. Cain* 27; *Proceedings* XV, p. 94, line 16). Often the two meanings cannot be distinguished. The latter meaning surfaces in the LXX in ques-

---

14; 6:10; 19:11; his words (Rev 19:9; 21:5; 22:6), his judgments (16:7; 19:2), his ways are true (15:3). In a secular sense: the proverb spoke truly (John 4:37); in a moral sense: "let us draw near with a true heart," meaning upright and firm (Heb 10:22); in the OT sense: Christ's judgment (John 8:16) and the testimony of the evangelist (19:35) are true or perfect because well-founded.

[82] This suggests the Platonic theory of the Ideas, cf. R. C. Trench, *Synonyms,* pp. 27ff. J. H. Bernard, *Gospel According to St. John,* Edinburgh, 1928, vol. 1, p. 11.

[83] R. Borig, *Der wahre Weinstock, Untersuchungen zu Jo XV, 1–10,* Munich, 1967.

[84] Menander, *Dysk.* 915, 929; Dittenberger, *Or.* 223, 17; *C.P.Herm.* 6, 2, 32; 8, 18; SB 7635, 1: τῷ δεσπότῃ μου ὡς ἀληθῶς τιμιοτάτῳ; 8262, 1; 9444, 3; 9683, 1 (*P.Vindob.Sal.,* n. XXII, 1 and p. 195); Philo, *Alleg. Interp.* 2.81: πάνυ ἀληθῶς = quite true; 3.58; Philo uses the formula ὡς ἀληθῶς (= in truth) almost sixty times (*Cherub.* 76, 93; *Unchang. God* 125; *Rewards* 30, 43; *Etern. World* 10, 69; *Flacc.* 72; etc.).

tions: "Will I really give birth, now that I am old?" (Gen 18:13); "Will God really dwell on earth?" (1 Kgs 8:27 = 2 Chr 6:18; cf. Ps 58:1). But the adverb is used especially to give weight to an affirmation: "Truly, it is I who have sinned" (Josh 7:20; cf. 2 Macc 3:38). Hence its use in confessions of faith in the NT.[85] It expresses certitude in knowledge (John 17:8; Acts 12:11; cf. Exod 33:16), the reality of a fact (Matt 26:73 = Mark 14:70; John 7:46; cf. Dan 3:24) or of a condition, its authenticity—"You are really my disciples"[86]— and can be translated "actually."

---

[85] Christ is truly (the) son of God (Matt 14:33; 27:54; Mark 15:39), Savior of the world (John 4:42), the prophet who was to come (John 6:14; 7:40).

[86] John 8:31; cf. 1:47. 1 Thess 2:13—The Thessalonians received Paul's preaching "not as a human message, but as it really is, a message from God"; 1 John 2:5—"The one who keeps his word, the love of God is truly (actually) perfected in him."

ἀμελέω, ἐπιμελέομαι

ameleō, to not matter; *epimeleomai*, to busy oneself with, see to

The verb *melei* (construed with *moi tinos, peri tinos, hoti*) means: to care for someone with respect to something, to take an interest in or busy oneself with a matter;[1] hence *meletaō* is not only "think about, meditate on" but also "to be busy about, to exert oneself" and even "to practice."[2] More frequent is *ameleō*, "to be careless, negligent, not put oneself out." This indifference is that of the ones first invited to the marriage feast of the kingdom of God (Matt 22:5); it is cursed by Jer 48:10 and receives almost the same treatment in Heb 2:3—"How shall we escape if we neglect so great a salvation?"[3]—and Heb 8:9—"Since they have not remained in my covenant, I myself have also lost interest in them, says the Lord."[4] After asking Timothy to apply himself (*proseche*) to reading, to exhortation, and the like,

---

[1] In the Gospels, the construction is always negative: οὐ μέλει = the Lord doesn't care (Matt 22:16; Mark 4:38; Luke 10:40); the hireling thinks only of his own interests and does not bother himself about the sheep (John 10:13), nor Judas about the poor (John 12:6); nor does Gallio care that Sosthenes is being beaten before his tribunal (Acts 18:17). The nuance "busy oneself with, take care" is present in 1 Cor 7:21; 9:9; above all 1 Pet 5:7—"Unload all your cares upon God (Ps 55:23), for he is engaged on your behalf." Cf. Ps.-Plutarch, *De mus.* 26: "The ancient Greeks were right to devote the greatest care to musical education"; *P.Tebt.* 703, 174.

[2] Cf. Acts 4:25—the peoples have planned vain things (cf. Luke 21:14—προμελετᾶν); 1 Tim 4:15—Timothy is to meditate on the Paul's exhortations to virtue and on preaching—exert himself on, go to the trouble of putting into practice.

[3] Τηλικαῦτος (for τοσοῦτος), literally, of this age (2 Cor 1:10; Jas 3:4; Rev 16:18; *P.Oxy.* 900, 12; *P.Flor.* 58, 14), highlights the incomparable value of Christian salvation; cf. Diodorus Siculus 2.4.1: "Semiramis, a woman of modest estate, was exalted to just great renown, εἰς τηλικαύτην ... δόξαν"; Heraclitus, *All.* 25.11: "How can one heal such (τηλικαῦτα) sicknesses?"; Polybius 3.1.10: "such momentous developments"; cf. P. Chantraine, *Etudes sur le vocabulaire grec*, Paris, 1956, p. 153.

[4] Citing Jer 31:32 (a text exploited by the Qumran community, cf. J. T. Milik, *Dix ans de découvertes dans le désert de Judah*, Paris, 1957, p. 75). On this reciprocity, cf. the letter of Aurelius Sarapion to Aurelius Patas (third to fourth century): "Do not be negligent, knowing that I for my part do not neglect your affairs, μὴ ἀμαλήσῃς εἰδὼς

---

ameleō, S 272; *EDNT* 1.69; MM 26; L&N 30.50; BDF §176(2); BAGD 44–45 ‖ *epimeleomai*, S 1959; *EDNT* 2.31; MM 242; L&N 30.40, 35.44; BDF §§101, 176(2); BAGD 296

St. Paul instructs him: "Do not neglect the spiritual gift that is in you."[5] The litotes *mē amelei* occurs frequently in the papyrological literature to express a psychological orientation of zeal and urgency[6] or application to a task;[7] *mē ameleseis*, synonymous with *mē oknēseis* (P.Harr. 107, 15; P.Mich. III, 221, 12, 13); and opposed to *spoudason* (SB 9754, 3–4 = P.Mil. Vogl. 255), to *prothymōs* (cf. PSI 621, 7), and to *epimeleō* (cf. P.Eleph. 13, 7; P.Hib. 253, 3 and 8).

Ameleō is used in medicine for neglected patients, who are lost for lack of care,[8] but especially for functionaries in the public administration who

---

ὅτι κἀγὼ οὐκ ἀμελῶ εἰς σε" (B. Boyaval, "Le prologue du Misouménos de Ménandre et quelques autres papyrus grecs inédits," in ZPE, vol. 6, 1, 1970, p. 30; n. 14, 9–11), cf. P.Rein. 117, 11: "Do not neglect to write me a letter, taking into account that if you do something, you will receive it back quadruple." P.Phil. 32, 16: "If through negligence you send nothing, it is yourself that you will wrong" (end of the first century?).

[5] 1 Tim 4:14; ἀμελεῖν is the opposite of προσέχειν, "fix one's attention, attach oneself" (as in Heb 2:1, 3); cf. Hippocrates, *Acut*. 4.1; Demosthenes, *C. Poly*. 50.1; *C. Call*. 55.9). The verb plays a role in the vocabulary of Stoic ethics (Prelim. Stud. 65; Epictetus 4.12.7) and of the Christian pastoral writings (1 Tim 1:4; 3:8; 4:1, 3; 2 Pet 1:19; cf. J. Dupont, *Discours de Milet*, pp. 136ff.), where the sense of applying oneself and devoting oneself has a moral value. In a Christian papyrus of the third century, μὴ οὖν ἀμελήσητε, ἀδελφοί, διὰ ταχέων τοῦτο ποιῆσαι (SB 9557, 53) corresponds to καλῶς οὖν ποιήσαντες (line 37); one even specifies: νῦν οὖν μὴ ἀμελήσῃς, δέσποτα, διὰ τὸν θεόν (P.Herm. 7, 15).

[6] P.Mert. 85, 6: "Do not neglect to write, brother, concerning your health"; 112, 11; P.Princ. 186, 16 (AD 28); SB 10724, 18; Pap.Lugd.Bat. I, 19, 8; XI, 26, 19; P.Oxy. 113, 16: μὴ δόξῃς με ἠμεληκότα τῆς κλειδός; 1929, 4: μὴ ἀμελήσῃς τοῦ ζητῆσαι τουτό; 2982, 12; 2985, 9; P.Sorb. 62, 5: "Don't fail to see to that, because I absolutely need it"; P.Cair.Isid. 134, 8; P.Mich. VIII, 464, 15ff.: "Don't worry about us, take care of yourself" (first century AD).

[7] P.Yale 77, 8 (AD 100): "I ask you not to be negligent about the gold bracelet"; P.Mil. 74, 8; P.Oxy. 2149, 11: "Do it, do not neglect it"; 2781, 6 and 10; P.Harr. 107, 18: "Do not neglect to send me the coat"; Pap.Lugd.Bat. XIII, 18, 36; C.Pap.Jud. 424, 14: letter from Joanna to Epagathos, 15 December 87: "Do not neglect to take us"; P.Tebt. 315, 32: "Do not neglect yourself or that which I wrote you to buy for me"; 417, 31: "You shall not neglect any of these tasks"; P.Abinn. 43, 8: "Do not neglect to pay what you owe"; SB 10567, 53: τοῦτο μὴ ἀμελήσῃς ἀλλὰ ποίσον γυμνασθῆναι (third century, Antinoe); P.Vars. 26, 33: τοίνυν μὴ ἀμελήσῃς συντελεῖν τοῦτο. The exhortation is repeated at the beginning and the end of the letter (P.Oxy. 3199, 3, 10). Often the formula is ὅρα μὴ ἀμελήσῃς = See to it that you do not neglect (ibid. 42, 16; P.Ant. 192, 14; PSI 318, 7–8; P.IFAO II, n. 18, 8–9), and this exhortation concludes the letter, before the salutation: Μὴ οὖν ἀμελήσις. Ἔρρωσο (ibid. 19, 17–18, first century AD; cf. SB 9535, 12; P.Fay. 125, 3–4). Ἀμελῶς is used of a negligent sentinel (Thucydides 1.100).

[8] Hippocrates, *Epid*. 3.72.3; Thucydides 2.51.2: people were dying for lack of care (ἀμέλεια). The use of μελέτη for "treatment" is known (Hippocrates, *Artic*. 50;

default on their obligations as *epimelētes* (*P.Panop.Beatty* 1, 215; 2, 6, 74; Plutarch, *Tim.* 18.3: *argōs* and *amelōs*). *Ameleia* is typical offense of a proxy or of one responsible for carrying out a function, but who shirks his obligations.[9] It is obvious that we should understand 1 Tim 4:14 in this sense—Timothy should not lose sight of the fact that he was supernaturally equipped to carry out his duty, and he should take his stand on this divine gift in facing up to his responsibilities as model pastor and teacher.

In this pastoral context, it is natural that St. Paul uses *epimeleomai* with respect to the Ephesian overseers: "If anyone does not know how to rule his own household, how will he look after a church of God?" (*pōs ekklēsias theou epimelēsetai*, 1 Tim 3:5). This compound verb, meaning "busy oneself, take care, direct," suggestive of the public function carried out by the community minister and of the devotion that this function requires, is copiously attested in secular Greek, especially in epigraphy (see the index in Dittenberger, *Syl.* 4.345ff.), with respect to every occupation,[10] and it could be used here of any job or position of oversight in the *ekklēsia*. But the emphasis is on morality, because the term is used of a task that requires personal devotion, of effective leadership, of diligent application.[11] In this

---

Fract. 31, 35; *Int.* 44, 52). Hence the honorific inscription on behalf of Archelaos, doctor at Heraclea: διὰ τῆς ἰατρικῆς τέχνης εἰς τὴν τῶν ἀπόρων ὄνησιν πλείστην μελέτην ποιούμενον (*MAMA*, vol. 6, 114, 12–13 = *I.Car.*, n. 70, p. 177).

[9] *P.Hamb.* 192, 5: οὐκ ἠμέλησά σου τοῦ ἐντολίου; *PSI* 425, 13; *P.Oxy.* 62, 9; 1775, 15; *P.Princ.* 163, 7; 167, 9: μὴ ἀμελήσῃς περὶ ὧν σοι ἐνετειλάμην; *Pap.Lugd.Bat.* XVI, 34, 9 and 14; *P.Cair.Isid.* 77, 20; *P.Mil.Vogl.* 167, 13 "because of the carelessness of Mario, the inspector of seeds" (17 March 110); *P.Mich.* 591, 3 (ed. G. M. Browne).

[10] On the Sabbath, the Jews do not take care of any business, don't do any chores, μήτε ἄλλης ἐπιμελεῖσθαι λειτουργίας (Josephus, *Ag. Apion* 1.209). Simon made an inspection round, "taking care of matters related to the administration of the cities" (1 Macc 16:14). Used for the labor of architects (*CIRB*, Moscow-Leningrad, 1965, n. 1122; 1242, 1243, 1245, 1246). In its legal sense, ἐπιμελέομαι means "to be in charge of managing, to administrate, to watch over the interest of" (L. Gernet, *Démosthène: Plaidoyers civils*, vol. 4, Paris, 1960, p. 156; V. Arangio-Ruiz, *Lineamenti del sistema contrattuale nel diritto dei papyri*, Milan, 1928, pp. 22ff.).

[11] Cf. *P.Tebt.* 703, 183: ἐπιμέλου δὲ ἐπισκοπεῖν (third century BC); line 191: ἐπιμελές τέ σοι ἔστω (cf. line 70, 80, 149, 191, 215, 224, 241). A decree awarding public hospitality to Chairias, an adjunct official, mentions that "he demonstrates great care and devotion in his work and in all that he does for Antipatros" (P. Cabanes, "Les inscriptions de théâtre de Bouthôtos," in *Actes de Colloque 1972 sur l'esclavage*, Paris, 1974, p. 165, n. 32). Menander, *Dysk.* 213: "Look after your father"; 240: "take care of my sister"; 618: "See to his needs." *C.Pap.Jud.* 424, 27: "above all take good care of yourself, so that you may be well"; *P.Ross.Georg.* 2, 4; 18, 321; *UPZ* 1, 61, 29ff.; 59, 39; *PSI* 1312, 10; *P.Oxy.* 1479, 13: "take good care of yourself, so that you may be well," end of the first century BC; *P.Mert.* 62, 13, from AD 6). Cf. the funerary inscription of New Caesarea: "All the other gods who watch over good souls and take

sense it has a role in the medical vocabulary from the classical period,[12] where *epimelesthai/epimeleian poieisthai* means "care for medically." It is in this sense that, according to Doctor Luke, the good Samaritan, having taken the injured traveler to the inn "took care of him" (Luke 10:34) and instructed the innkeeper, *epimelētheti autou*.[13]

From Aristotle on, this verb has a political sense: to busy oneself with public affairs.[14] *Epimelētēs* designated especially the high magistrates who governed the city and whose dedicatory inscriptions praise their merit and their justice,[15] so much so that the holder of such a title was addressed in a letter as "Your Diligence"—*Epimeleia* (*P.Panop.Beatty* 1, 76, 85–86, 103). Clearly this political-moral sense applies well to the overseer called to guide

---

care of them" (in J. Pouilloux, *Choix*, n. 52, 13). Ζητεῖ ἐπιμελῶς (Luke 15:8) = search diligently, carefully. This adverb is used for education (Prov 13:24) and worship (Menander, *Dysk*. 37: the young girl "honors the nymphs diligently").

[12] Numerous examples not given in LSJ, mentioned by W. K. Hobart, *Medical Language*, pp. 269ff., and N. van Brock, *Vocabulaire médical*, pp. 237ff. "The lesions get worse if left alone, but if cared for (ἐπιμεληθέντα) they get better" Hippocrates, *Mochl*. 21; cf. *Art*. 8); "In the eyes of the common people, those who are not themselves in good bodily condition would not be able to take care of others either, οὐδ' ἂν ἑτέρων ἐπιμεληθῆναι καλῶς" Hippocrates, *Medic*. 1); Soranus, *Gyn*. 3.48.1. Honorific decree for a doctor of Cos (Dittenberger, *Syl*. 943, 30ff.), for the doctor Hermias at Gortyn (*I.Cret.*, vol. 4, p. 230, n. 168, 8ff.).

[13] Luke 10:35. At Sidon, the centurion Julius to be cared for by his friends, ἐπιμελείας τυχεῖν (Acts 27:3). Ἐπιμελεία, treatment, care provided for a sick person, cf. Prov 3:8; Sir 30:25.

[14] *Ath. Pol*. 16.3: ἐπιμελεῖσθαι τῶν κοινῶν; cf. *Pol*. 3.5.10: "the man of state is master of the administration of common affairs, κύριος τῶν κοινῶν ἐπιμελείας;" 7(6).8.1321ᵇ. In the technical usage, the Epimeletes at Athens were the twenty officials of the twenty *symmoriae*, with responsibility for overseeing the apportionment of charges, the enrolling of the members of the *symmoriae*, and the defense of the state; they could be compared to magistrates (cf. Glotz, *Epimélètes*, in *DAGR* p. 666). At Rome, the *epimelētēs* was the *curator* (cf. H. G. Mason, *Greek Terms*, p. 46).

[15] Cf. P. Roussel, *Délos colonie athénienne*, Paris, 1916, pp. 97–125; F. Durrbach, *Choix*, n. 77, 83, 95; P. Graindor, *Athènes de Tibère à Trajan*, Cairo, 1931, pp. 80ff. *I.Rhamn.*, pp. 84ff., 115ff., 118–120, 124ff. 129ff., 139. In an inscription of the port of Ostia, Valerius Serenus is ὁ ἐπιμελητὴς παντὸς τοῦ Ἀλεξανδρεινοῦ στόλου (*IG* vol. 14, 917). Aeneas Tacticus requires the leader and official (ἡγεμὼν καὶ ἐπιμελητής) to be prudent and dynamic (*Polior*. 1.7). Demetrius of Phalerum, who showed much benevolence and humaneness toward his fellow citizens, is ἐπιμελητὴς τῆς πόλεως (Diodorus Siculus 18.74.3; 20.45; cf. the ἐπιμελητὴς Καύδου in an inscription of Sparta, L. Robert, *Hellenica*, vol. 1, Limoges, 1940, pp. 109ff.). In Israel, two sorts of overseers and magistrates (ἐπιμελητὰς καὶ ἄρχοντα) maintained public security and good order (*Spec. Laws* 4.21); Moses was ὁ τοῦ ἔθνους ἐπιμελητὴς καὶ προστάτης (*Rewards* 77; cf. *Virtues* 57). On the *epimelētēs* of the city and the governor, cf. J. and L. Robert, "Bulletin épigraphique," in *REG*, 1974, pp. 202, n. 108; 291, n. 553.

ἀμελέω, ameleō, etc.   91

a Christian community,[16] but it works even better in light of the cultic usages of *epimeleia, epimeleomai* in the first century. In Israel, the *epimeleia tou hierou* or *tōn hiereōn* is entrusted to the priests and to the king:[17] they oversee the cultic celebrations, the organization of processions, the offering of sacrifices, and are responsible for the liturgy. In pagan cultic rules, the phrase *epimeleisthai tēs thysias* recurs frequently,[18] and the inscriptions provide *epimelētai tōn mysteriōn*.[19] In other words, the Christian minister does not necessarily have a financial role to play, as some have claimed, but is a leader who carries out a religious function and must apply himself to it with the greatest diligence.

---

[16] 1 Tim 3:15. We should note the analogous political meaning of the Greek Ἐπίσκοποι, especially at Ephesus; cf. the references in *DKP*, vol. 2, col. 323.

[17] Josephus, *Ag. Apion* 2.188; *Ant.* 20.222; *Ep. Arist.* 93; cf. *Husbandry* 51: the Logos, firstborn son of God, will receive the responsibility for caring for the sacred flock. At Delos, there were officials in charge of the sacrifices: ἐπιμελητὰς τῆς θυσίας (F. Durrbach, *Choix*, n. 21); at Ostia, Claudius Papirius is ἐπιμελητὴς τοῦ ἱεροῦ (*IG*, vol. 14, 926); at Oxyrhynchus, Sarapion is *epimelētēs* of the tribes of priests of the Serapeion and of other temples (*P.Oxy.* 2563, 5), like Demetrius at the temple of Artemis (*P.Thead.* 34, 14), Ἐπιμελητὴς, ναοῦ θεᾶς Ἀρτέμιδος (P. Hermann, *Ergebnisse*, n. 23, 2–3).

[18] *LSCG*, n. 93, 35 (Eretria, fourth–third century); 96, 19 (Mykonos, 200 BC); 103, 11 (Minoa of Amorgos, first century BC); 136, 5 (Ialysos, 300 BC); 171, 6, 9, 12 (Isthmos, second century BC); 177, 6, etc.

[19] Dittenberger, *Syl.* 384, 9 (Athens); 540, 11, 43 (Athens); 1029, 10; *SEG*, vol. 16, 92, 7 (Eleusis); 162, 10, 24 (Athens); vol. 21, 494, 19 (Eleusis, first century BC), etc.

> ἀμεταμέλητος
>
> *ametamelētos*, **leaving no room for regret, irrevocable**

Unknown in the OT, this adjective is used only twice in the NT,[1] notably in Rom 11:29, where it has a theological significance; with respect to the final salvation of Israel,[2] the apostle affirms: "The gifts and the calling of God are irrevocable." If we insist on an etymological definition (*a-metamelomai*), we will see this as meaning that God does not change his mind;[3] once God has chosen his people, he will not go back on the decision; God never breaks his word after making a promise (Ps 110:4 = Heb 8:21). Hence our adjective, a synonym of *ametanoētos*,[4] will express simply the absence of variation in the divine will. God is *am atablētos* (Aristotle, *Cael.* 1.9.279ᵃ).

---

[1] 2 Cor 7:10—"The sorrow that is according to God works a repentance unto salvation that leaves no room for regret." Most commentators connect ἀμεταμέλητον to μετάνοιαν and not to σωτηρίαν. A conversion that will not change is without turning back, definitive (Vulg. *stabilem*); cf. μεταμέλει, regret (Menander, *Dysk*. 12; E. G. Thomson, Μετανοέω and μεταμέλει *in Greek Literature until 100 A.D.*, Historical and Linguistic Studies in Literature Related to the N.T., second series, vol. 1, Chicago, 1909, p. 366).

[2] D. Judant, *Les deux Israël*, Paris, 1960 (with the review of P. Benoit, in *RB*, 1961, pp. 458–462); idem, *Judaïsme et Christianisme*, Paris, 1969, pp. 261ff. L. Goppelt, *Les Origines de l'Eglise*, Paris, 1961, pp. 116ff. The great majority of commentators have seen the Jewish people as the subject of this verse, but about half have not understood it to mean that this people as a whole would necessarily be converted (F. J. Caubet Iturbe, " 'Et sic omnis Israel salvus fieret' [Rom. XI, 26]," in *EstBib*, 1963, pp. 127–150); cf. S. Légasse, "Jésus a-t-il annoncé la conversion finale d'Israël (à propos de Mc. X, 23–27)?" in *NTS*, vol. 10, 1964, pp. 480–487; B. Noack, "Current and Backwater in the Epistle to the Romans," in *ST*, vol. 19, 1965, pp. 155–166.

[3] As opposed to men, Matt 21:30, 32; 27:3; *1 Clem.* 2.7: "You never regretted having done good"; 54.4: "they will not regret their conduct"; 58.2: "Accept our recommendations and you will not be sorry."

[4] This adjective occurs frequently in the papyri (wills, deeds of sale, of endowment, of gift) to express the irrevocable character of the decision, *P.Grenf.* 2.68, 4–5; *P.Cair.Preis.* 42, 3; *P.Flor.* 47, 4, 25; R. Taubenschlag, "Das babylonische Recht in den griechischen Papyri," in *JJP*, 1954, p. 179, n. 5; A. Bonhöffer, *Epiktet*, pp. 106ff. Cf. the *Inscription de Nazareth*, line 5: τούτους μένειν ἀμετακεινήτους τὸν αἰῶνα.

---

ametamelētos, S 278; *TDNT* 4.626–629; *EDNT* 1.69; *NIDNTT* 1.356–357; L&N 25.271; BAGD 45

But we must look at usage, which shows two partially overlapping semantics, one literary, the other legal.[5] Following Socrates' definition of happiness as "a pleasure that leaves no regret,"[6] Plato (*Tim.* 59^d), Crates of Thebes,[7] Plutarch (*De tu. san.* 26), Porphyry (*VP* 39; ed. A. Nauck, *Porphyrii opuscula*, Leipzig, 1886, p. 37), and the Neoplatonist Hierocles of Alexandria (ed. F. Jullach, *Fragmenta Philosophorum Graecorum*, Paris, 1875, vol. 1, p. 453) frequently modify *hēdonē* with the epithet *ametamelētos*. It is a scholastic tradition. But these same authors add that these pleasures are not vain but profitable (*ōpheleiai*), are not diluted with any sorrow (*alypon*), that nothing disturbs or diminishes their charm (*hēdeia*), and finally that they are characterized by permanence or fixity (*monimos*). This ensemble of subsidiary qualifiers tends to give to *ametamelētos* the sense "absolute, whole, unobscured."

Meanwhile, another series of texts gives this adjective the meaning "total" or "definitive," whether with respect to feelings, decisions, or personal resolutions.[8] Here and there appears a psychological or moral nuance of simplicity, good faith, or candor, which is the sense of the adverb *ameletētōs*. This meaning is predominant around the time of Christ, being used precisely with respect to benefits, to devotion, and—for the first time—to gifts. An honorific decree of Priene expresses the recognition of the city for the good grace and indefectible devotion of Zosimus toward it (*I.Priene*, 114, 8; end of the first century BC). According to Diodorus Siculus, "every benevolent act, done without afterthought, bears the good fruit of praise from those who are its beneficiaries" (10.15.3). The sure and definitive character of a donation in the first century AD is seen in the *Tabula* of Ps.-Cebes of Thebes: When an old man exhorts his interlocutor not to trust goods given by Fortune, who takes back what she gives, the stranger asks what characterizes gifts given by *alēthinē Paideia*. The rejoinder: "True knowledge of useful things, a sure and stable gift."[9]

This sense of *ametamelētos*—"irrevocable"—is exactly its meaning in the few papyri that use the adjective. On 10 November 41, Emperor Claudius

---

[5] Cf. the references supplied by H. Windisch, *Der zweite Korintherbrief*, 9th ed., Göttingen, 1924, p. 232.

[6] Ἡδονὴ ἀμεταμέλητος, in Stobaeus 103, 39, 18; ed. Wachsmuth, vol. 5, p. 906.

[7] *Ep.* 10, ed. R. Hercher, *Epistolographi*, Paris, 1873, p. 210.

[8] For example, there are those irrepressible fits of anger so blinding that one kills without hesitation and without a twinge of regret (Plato, *Leg.* 9.866^c); but there are also those serious characters who embark on an undertaking and never look back (Aristotle, *Eth. Nic.* 9.4.1166^{a}29). If they make promises or offer a treaty, they can be taken at their word; those who trust them will not be sorry (Polybius 23.16; 21.11.11; Dionysius of Halicarnassus 11.13).

[9] 32.12: ἀσφαλὴς δόσις καὶ βεβαία καὶ ἀμεταμέλητως (ed. C. Praechter, Leipzig, 1893, p. 26).

wrote to the Alexandrians: "I shall now address the disturbances and the anti-Jewish riots . . . reserving the right to bring an inflexible anger to bear against any who would start up again (reading *arxomenōn* for *arxamenōn*). I flatly declare to you that if you do not put an end to this murderous reciprocal furor, I shall be forced to give you a harsh demonstration of what the righteous anger of a philanthropic prince is."[10] Three other attestations are of juridical actions: writers of wills or parties to contracts declaring their decisions unchangeable and irrevocable,[11] such as Abraham, bishop of Hermonthis, at the end of the fourth century: *hothen eis tautēn hormēsa tēn engraphon ametamelēton eschatēn diathēkēmian asphaleian.*[12] The sense "immutable, unalterable" is confirmed by P.Lond. V, 1660, 37 (c. 353), if the restitution of C. Wessely is accepted:[13] *asaleuton kai ametamelēton kai ametanatrepton einai;*[14] and by P.Cair.Masp. 314, 3, 11, from the sixth century. These are late documents, but they provide good parallels to Rom 11:29, which has the value of a legal axiom.

The revelation will thus be this: The conduct of the beneficiaries of the covenant will have led God to abrogate it. Now God's faithfulness is not made false by the unfaithfulness of men (2 Tim 2:13); not only does God not repent of his generous gifts and his promises,[15] but they are irremissible by their very nature (1 Thess 5:24; 1 Cor 1:9; 2 Cor 1:19–22, etc.). Consequently, God will never go back on his choice and his gifts of grace.[16]

---

[10] P.Lond. 1912, 78 = H. I. Bell, *Jews and Christians in Egypt*, p. 25.

[11] R. Taubenschlag, *Law of Greco-Roman Egypt*, pp. 236ff. In the contract for the sale of some real estate in the Fayum on 8 September 512, "the said seller declares that it is his firm, freely arrived at, and irrevocable decision to sell from this time forth and forever" (A. Sayce, "Deux contrats grecs du Fayoum," in *Rev. des études grecques*, 1890, p. 131, A 3).

[12] P.Lond. I, 77, republished by *Chrest.Mitt.*, Leipzig-Berlin; 1912, vol. 2, n. 319; cf. P.Harr. 74, 25, from AD 99: διαθήκη, ἐφ᾽ ᾗ ἀμεταθέτῳ ἐτελεύτησεν.

[13] Cf. *Berichtigungsliste*, vol. 3, Leiden, 1958, p. 97.

[14] Cf. P.Michael. 45, 11; P.Berl.Zill., n. 4, 14.

[15] Cf. the texts cited by A. Vaccari, "Irrevocabilità dei favori divini: Nota a commento di Rom. XI, 29," in *Mélanges Tisserant*, vol. 1, pp. 437–442; cf. nevertheless the times that God had regrets under the Old Covenant, A. W. Argyle, "God's Repentance and the LXX," in *ExpT*, vol. 75, 1964, p. 367.

[16] The reason is not only that God is immutable (Mal 3:6), but that his election and his gifts are inspired by an *agapē* that is by definition an eternal love (cf. Phocylides 17.4: "Those who I respect, I love from the beginning to the end, τούτους ἐξ ἀρχῆς μέχρι τέλους ἀγαπῶ"; ed. E. Diehl, *Anth. Lyr. Graec.*, 3d ed., Leipzig, 1949, p. 60). A. Vaccari (loc. cit., p. 437) prefers to attach this immutability to the *ḥesed* that would be characterized by its durability and permanence. Obviously these are not mutually exclusive options.

ἀμοιβή
amoibē, **recompense, return**

The church takes charge only of those widows who have no family to support them. The children and grandchildren of a widow should learn to "give back [that which they owe] to their parents" (*amoibas apodidonai tois progonois*).[1] Solon imposed this obligation on sons on pain of dishonor.[2] In Egypt, it was the daughters who were bound to provide for their parents, sons being dispensed, at least unless they had agreed by contract to do so.[3] But in year 26 of Euergetes I and in the year 1 of Philopator, Pappos and Ctesicles, aged and infirm, complain that their son and daughter, respectively, have refused or ceased to pay a food pension (*P.Enteux.* 25 and 26); while the children and grandchildren of the general Diazelmis surround his old age with honor and care, in the second to third century BC.[4]

---

[1] 1 Tim 5:4. It is not certain that ἀμοιβάς is an accusative plural of intensity, because it is found often enough as an equivalent to the singular. Cf. Dittenberger, *Syl.* 798, 5: εὑρεῖν ἴσας ἀμοιβὰς οἷς εὐηργέτηνται νὴ δυναμένων (AD 37); Cagnat-Lafaye, *Inscriptions graecae*, vol. 4, col. II, 39: κομιζόμενος τῶν εὐεργεσιῶν ἀξίας τὰς ἀμοιβάς.

[2] Ἐάν τις μὴ τρέφῃ τοὺς γονέας ἄτιμος ἔστω (Diogenes Laertius 1.55); Plutarch, *Sol.* 22.1, 22.4.

[3] According to Herodotus 2.35; cf. E. Seidl, "Die Unterhaltspflicht der Töchter," in *Proceedings* XI, pp. 149–155. According to *P.Cair.Masp.* 67314, the sons, upon inheriting from their fathers, owe to their widowed mothers to γηροβοσκεῖσθαι and νοσοκομεῖσθαι (on γηροβοσκία, γηροτροφία, γηροκομία, the feeding, care, and lodging of aged and sick persons, cf. *P.Oxy.* 889, 19; 1210, 9; *BGU* 1578, 17; *P.Flor.* 382, 39; R. Taubenschlag, *Opera Minora*, vol. 2, pp. 339–345, 539–555).

[4] *SEG* vol. 8, 497, 11ff. In the sixth century, a son cares for his sick, aged father, *P.Lond.* 1708, 51ff.

---

amoibē, S 287; MM 27; L&N 57.168; BAGD 46

ἀμοιβή, amoibē

It is a question of natural law[5] and of filial devotion,[6] because it is a repayment or a just compensation of the part of children who after a fashion return to their parents from all that they have received from them.[7] To be precise, *amoibē* (a biblical hapax) expresses exchange[8] or substitution (*P.Oxy.* 1930, 2 and 4), a return gift, a recompense;[9] hence its constant usage as a sign of acknowledgement in expressions of gratitude.[10] In 84 BC, Zosimus, having received the title of citizen, felt no sterile gratitude (*ouk akarpon tēn tēs timēs dedeichen amoibēn*), for he loved the city as his homeland and poured benefits upon it.[11] Pagans and Christians often ask God to return benefit for benefit, like this black slave of the centurion Pallas at Antinoe: "In return, my God give my master a long life to live, and with it glory."[12]

---

[5] *P.Ryl.* 624, 16. Cf. Hierocles of Alexandria: "Children ought to regard themselves in the household of their parents as being in a temple where nature has placed them and made them priests and ministers, so that they should constantly look after the worship of these divinities who gave them life. . . . Children should supply to their fathers all necessary things, and, lest they should forget anything, should anticipate their desires and often go so far as to guess things that they cannot explain for themselves; for they have often guessed for us, when we could express our needs only through our cries, stammerings, and complaints" (in Stobaeus, *Flor.* 79.53, vol. 4, p. 640); cf. line 13: προθυμία πρὸς τὸ ἀμείβεσθαι τὰς εὐεργεσίας αὐτῶν). Cf. the parallels cited by C. Mussies, *Dio Chrysostom,* pp. 208–209.

[6] Cf. Antiochus I of Commagene, giving as a τύπος εὐσεβείας the respect of ἔκγονα toard their προγόνοι (*IGLS,* Paris, 1929, n. 1, 212ff.). One puts one's "religion" into practice (1 Tim 2:2) when one honors one's mother (Exod 20:12) and sustains her in her old age, cf. Sir 3:2, 14; 7:27–28; Prov 19:26; 28:24; 30:17.

[7] Cf. *P.Enteux.* 43, 5: "Let him restore [the sum] to me that I may have what I need for my old age: ἀποδῶι μοι καὶ ἔχω [εἰς τὸ] γῆρας τὰ ἀνάγκαια." On this value of iteration, cf. μέλλουσιν ὑπάτοις δευτέρᾳ ἀμοιβῇ (L. C. Youtie, D. Hagedorn, H. C. Youtie, "Urkunden aus Panopolis III," n. 26, 19, in *ZPE,* vol. 10, 1973, p. 125; reprinted in *P.Panop.*).

[8] *Etern. World* 108; Josephus, *War* 1.520: "He came to give him life as the price of his good deeds, the light of day in exchange for his hospitality"; cf. *I.Olymp.* 57, 56.

[9] *P.Oxy.* 705, 61 (AD 200–2); *P.Ryl.* 624, 3; Josephus, *Ant.* 5.13; *War* 3.445; 7.365: "their throats slit . . . that's the recompense the Jews received for their alliance"; *MAMA,* vol. 8, 418, 36; G. E. Bean, T. B. Mitford, *Cilicia,* n. 31, B, 7: τὴν ἐκ τούτων ἐλογίζοντο φιλοτιμίαν εἰς ἀμοιβήν.

[10] Cf. Josephus, *War* 1.293: certain ones attached themselves to Herod in return for the benefits that they had received from him and his father; *P.Brem.* 8, 3; *P.Oxy.* 2474, 37; *SB* 8026, 3.

[11] *I.Priene* 112, 17; cf. 113, 32; 119, 27; *I.Car.* 185, 9; the dedication by Menandros of an architectural work, in recognition: ἀμοιβῆς καὶ εὐνοίας ἕνεκεν.

[12] *SB* 8071, 19 (= E. Bernand, *Inscriptions métriques,* n. 26): τούτων δ'ἀμοιβὴν δεσπότην δοίη θεὸς βίου τε μακρεὶν οἶμον; *MAMA* vol. 7, 566, 11 (cf. N. Firatli, L. Robert, *Stèles funéraires,* p. 177); *P.Lond.* 1729, 22: only the Lord will be able to recompense you; Josephus, *Ant.* 4.266.

ἀναγκαῖος

anankaios, **urgently necessary**

The Epistle to Titus concludes with an exhortation to brotherly love: "Let our people[1] also learn to be first in good works, in the face of the urgent needs" (*eis tas anankaias chreias*, 3:14); which is parallel to Rom 12:13 on authentic *agapē:* "Take your part in the needs of the saints, practicing hospitality zealously." In the NT, the necessities of daily life—food, drink, clothing, shelter—are expressed by *chreia*,[2] which in the classical language often has the nuance of destitution, indigence, privation, distress.[3]

But here these "needs" are accentuated with the adjective *anankaios* —"pressing need"—in conformity with the usage of literature,[4] epigraphy,[5]

---

[1] Οἱ ἡμέτεροι designates a definite plurality (the suffix *-tero* added to ἡμεῖς has a differentiating function, cf. E. Benveniste, *Noms d'agent*, Paris, 1948, p. 119): members of the same family (Plato, *Menex.* 248ᵇ; Strabo 6.3.3), clients (*P.Oxy.* 37, col. I, 16; *P.Fam.Tebt.* 24, 99), "our people" as constituting a distinct group (*P.Oxy.* 787, 1, a letter of recommendation from the year AD 16: ὡς ἐστὶν ἡμέτερος = as he is one of ours; cf. *P.Brem.* 1.7). Here, it is a matter of Cretan Christians, as opposed to "those outside" (1 Tim 3:7; 1 Thess 4:12), pagan or Jewish (cf. Titus 1:10), οἱ λοιποί (1 Thess 4:13).

[2] Reference is sometimes to that which is indispensable (Acts 20:34; Eph 4:28; 1 John 3:17), sometimes to supplies and services (Acts 28:10), even generous charitable giving (Phil 4:16). Cf. *SB* 9844, 3: πρὸς χρείαν τῶν ἀδελφῶν ἡμῶν (Palestinian letter from the second century AD).

[3] Cf. G. Redard, *Recherches sur* ΧΡΗ, ΧΡΗΣΘΑΙ, Paris, 1953, p. 82.

[4] It probably comes from Homer, *Il.* 8, 57: "Necessity forces them, χρειοῖ ἀναγκαίη"; cf. Wettstein; Diodorus Siculus 1.34; Philo, *Good Man Free* 76; *Decalogue* 99: "Man, inasmuch as he depends upon a thousand things that the necessities of life require—πρὸς τὰς ἀναγκαίας τοῦ βίου χρείας—has the obligation of taking care of acquiring the necessities as long as he lives."

[5] In 129 BC, Moschion is the object of gratitude because he has provided for some urgent expenses, εἰς χρείας ἀναγκαίας (*I.Priene* 108, 80). We may compare ἀνάγκη, "distress, calamity" (Luke 21:23; 1 Thess 3:17; 1 Cor 7:26; 2 Cor 6:4; 12:10) and ἐγ καιροῖς ἀναγκαίοις (*I.Assos*, n. 11, 6; from the first century BC), ἐν τοῖς ἀναγκαιοτάτοις καιροῖς (*P.Paris* 46, 7; second century BC).

---

anankaios, S 316; *TDNT* 1.344–347; *EDNT* 1.77–79; *NIDNTT* 2.663; MM 31; L&N 34.14, 71.39; BAGD 52

and above all the papyri of the Hellenistic period.[6] Reference is sometimes made to repayment of cash advances (*P.Oxy.* 1891, 6; 1970, 20; *PSI* 964, 6), sometimes to services (*UPZ* 106, 11; 107, 13; 108, 11; *chrias pleious kai anankaias parechomenos*; October 99; cf. the "indispensable secretary" of Palmyra, in *IGLS*, 1859, 7), sometimes to necessary food supplies (*UPZ* 110, 104; 144, 33; *SB* 7758, 15; cf. 7205, 18; *P.Mert.* 91, 17). Thus St. Paul has in mind the several forms of aid that Christians should supply to those whom we still call "the needy."[7]

Curiously, *anankaios*, "constraining, necessary, indispensable,"[8] is used for blood relatives, literally the son or the daughter who cannot refuse the obligations of an inheritance;[9] for friends (*P.Oxy.* 2407, 36): *anankaioi philoi* are the most intimate friends.[10] In this sense, Cornelius, while await-

---

[6] *P.Grenf.* 2, 14 (c) 1: χρείαν ἔχομεν ἀναγκαίαν; *P.Oxy.* 56, 6; 1068, 16; *P.Stras.* 264, 10. Sometimes there is a simple formula: ἑτοίμως ἔχωμεν τῇ σῇ ἀρετῇ εἰς τὰς ἀναγκαίας σοῦ χραίας (*Pap.Lugd.Bat.* XI, 11, 20): "You will do well to pay me for my pressing necessities four talents of silver" (*P.Oxy.* 2600, 11; cf. *P.Michael.* 35 B 1; *PSI* 1122, 8). More often, the formula is developed: "I acknowledge having received for my personal and pressing necessity—εἰς ἰδίαν μου καὶ ἀναγκαίαν χρείαν—six pieces of imperial gold" (*P.Oxy.* 2237, cf. *PSI* 1340, 7; 1427, 9; *P.Harr.* 86, 2; *Pap.Lugd.Bat.* I, 10, 12; *P.Ant.* 102, 6; 103, 15; *P.Fouad* 53, 2; *SB* 9191, 4–5; 9270, 4–5; *American Studies in Papyrology*, vol. 9, 607, 14).

[7] [French *nécessiteux*. —Tr.] Cf. ἀναγκαῖος = that which is essential (*P.Fay.* 111, 19, from 95–96; *P.Oxy.* 2838, 7), the needs of orphans (*P.Mich.* IX, 532, 2).

[8] Cf. H. Schreckenberg, *Anankè*, Munich, 1964.

[9] Οἱ ἀναγκαῖοι, used absolutely, refers to parents and close relatives (Xenophon, *An.* 2.4.1: "At the home of Ariaeus arrived his brothers with other relatives, οἱ ἀδελφοὶ καὶ ἄλλοι ἀναγκαῖοι"; Demosthenes, *Embassy* 19.290: ὑπὲρ συγγενῶν καὶ ἀναγκαίων). These blood relationships are distinguished from relationships established with strangers (Lysias, *C. Philo* 31.23: τοὺς ἀναγκαίους is contrasted with τοὺς ἀλλοτρίους; Lysias, *Property of Aristophanes* 19.38: "Is this any reason for wanting his parents—τοὺς ἀναγκαίους—to be stripped of all their belongings?" Josephus, *Ant.* 7.121: the close relatives—οἵ τε ἀναγκαῖοι—and the chiefs of the Ammonite king realize that they have broken the treaty); the closest relatives are designated by the superlative οἱ ἀναγκαιότατοι (Josephus, *Ant.* 14.362); Epicharmus, frag. 186: ἐπιηρέστερον καὶ ἀναγκαιέστατον καὶ ὡραιέστατον; ed. G. Kaibel, *Comicorum Graecorum Fragmenta*, p. 125). G. D. Kypke offered the following definition: "*Necessarii* vocantur (1) consanguini, (2) adfinitate juncti, (3) familiaritatis et amicitiae connexe vinculis. Interdum vocabulum haec tria simul complectitur" (*Observationes Sacrae in Novi Foederis Libros*, Wratislavia, 1755, vol. 2, p. 49).

[10] "The notion that could justify this dual semantic development is that of linkage: it must be sought in ἀνάγκη. Nevertheless Schwyzer's idea (*Griechische Grammatik*) that ἀν-άγκη (with ἀν- from ἀνα-) expresses the idea 'take in one's arms' (cf. ἀγκών, perhaps ἀγκή in Hesychius), where 'grip, constraint' finds some support; cf. Sophocles, *Trach.* 831–832. The impossible Semitic etymology of Schreckenberg, *Anankè*, pp. 165–176" (P. Chantraine, *Dictionnaire étymologique*, vol. 1, p. 83 b).

ing the arrival of Peter from Caesarea, "had gathered his relatives and close friends."[11]

From Euripides on, the expression *philos anankaios* is commonly used.[12] In *Resp.* 9.574[bc], Plato contrasts the mother (*philē anankaia*) with the courtesan that someone wants to marry (*philē ouk anankaia*); then the father, the closest relative and relative of longest standing (*philos anankaios*) with the adolescent born yesterday (*philos ouk anankaios*). Josephus mentions "intimate friends" about ten times, but he is almost always talking about confidants of the king.[13] The son of Nebuchadnezzar, for example,

---

[11] Acts 10:24 συγκαλεσάμενος τοὺς συγγενεῖς αὐτοῦ καὶ τοὺς ἀναγκαίους φίλους. Συγγενής is literally "of common origin" (cf. Michaelis, συγγενής, in *TDNT*, vol. 7, pp. 736–742.). Συγγένεια is the name for a subdivision of a tribe (φυλή) or of a city (πόλις), so the members of these units are called συγγενεῖς (*I.Sinur.*, pp. 26–28, 96). Συγγενεῖς can mean the relatives of an individual when a modifier is used (αὐτοῦ, τοῦ δεῖνος); it can mean relations (Plutarch, *Publ.* 3.5: συγγενεῖς ὄντα ἅμα καὶ συνήθεις) and literal friends: φίλον ὄντα καὶ συγγενῆ καὶ σύμμαχον (*SEG*, vol. 19, 468, 32); φίλους καὶ συγγενεῖς τῆς πόλεως (Decree of Lebedos, in L. Robert, *Hellenica*, vol. 11–12, Paris, 1960, p. 205; cf. *SEG*, vol. 23, 547, 2); τοῖς συγγενέσι καὶ φίλοις καὶ εὐνοίοις (*I.Magn.*, 38, 52; other texts in L. Robert, *Opera Minora Selecta*, vol. 1, Amsterdam, 1969, p. 220). —It is also an aulic title; at the court of the Ptolemies, the rank of "king's relative—*syngeneis*" is the highest (Dittenberger, *Or.* 104, 2; 135, 5; A. Bernand, *Philae*, vol. 1, n. 30; E. Bernand, *Inscriptions métriquex*, n. 5, 5); cf. W. Peremans, "Sur la titulature aulique en Egypte," in *Symbolae... J. C. Van Oven*, Leiden, 1946, p. 157; Stählin, φίλος, in *TDNT*, vol. 9, pp. 148, 154–155; L. Mooren, "Über die ptolemäischen Hofrangtitel," in *Antidorum W. Peremans*, Louvain, 1968, pp. 161–180. The general is also qualified by this honorific title, N. Hohlwein, *Stratège du nome*, p. 135. —In Latin, the *necessarii* are friends. Legal *necessitudo*, equivalent to *cognatio*, is a designation of *adfinitas* (*Digesta*, vol. 42, 4, 5; Ulpien, 59 *ad ed*: the burden of defending a minor reverts to the *cognati*, the *adfines*, the *libertus*; the following reason is provided: Quod verisimile est defensionem pupilli pupillaeve non omissuros vel *propter necessitatem vel propter caritatem* vel qua aliter ratione). Festus borrows from Aelius Gallus his definition of necessarii as those *qui aut cognati aut adfines sunt, in quos necessaria officia conferuntur praeter ceteros* (cited by Klebs, in *RE*, vol. 1, 2 col. 492–493, under the word *necessitas*). Aulus Gellius defines: "Necessitas autem dicatur jus quoddam et vinculum religiosae conjunctionis . . . Necessitas sane pro jure officioque observantiae adfinitatisque infrequens est: Quamquam, *qui ob hoc ipsum jus adfinitatis familiaritatisque conjuncti sunt, necessariee dicuntur*" (*NA* 13.3). Necessitudo = affection in St. Jerome, *Ep.* 53.1; 68.11; etc.

[12] Euripides, *Andr.* 671: "You cry against your natural friends, τοὺς ἀναγκαίους φίλους," who are natural relatives; cf. Athenaeus 4.154[c].

[13] Φίλος is a court title (cf. *P.Dura* 18.10; *Pap.Lugd.Bat.* XVI, pp. 13ff. *I.Cret.*, vol. 3, p. 100; Dittenberger, *Or.* 119; E. Bammel, "Φίλος τοῦ Καίσαρος," in *TLZ*, 1952, col. 205–210; C. Spicq, *Agapē: Prolégomènes*, p. 165; R. Hutmacher, *Ehrendekret*, p. 32; *Prosop.Ptol.*, vol. 4, p. XIX; Stählin, "φίλος," in *TDNT*, vol. 9, p. 160, n. 114). In 167–166, for example, the Ionian cities greet the king of Pergamum, Eumenes II, congratulating him both on his good health and on the friends who accompanied him on his journey:

releases Jechonias and retains him as one of his closest friends.[14] In the letters among the papyri, the emphasis is always on confidence and affection, notably in letters of recommendation: "Ptolemaeus, the bearer of this letter, is my friend and an intimate" (*P.Col.Zen.* 7, 3; from March 257 BC); "Dioscoros, bearer of the letter, is my very close friend" (*estin mou leian anankaios philos*).[15] Sometimes a writer amplifies the effect by using the superlative: *philos anankaiotatos*.[16]

These examples, to which many more could be added, allow us to place the Lucan vocabulary against its background in the contemporary language. The "intimate friends" shared Cornelius's frame of mind and probably awaited with the same fervor as he the joyful message that St. Peter would bring them. In pointing out their presence, St. Luke intends to express more fully the social importance of the centurion of Caesarea; not only does he worship God "with all his house" (Acts 10:2), have devout soldiers in his service (verse 7), and enjoy a perfect reputation among "the whole nation of the Jews" (verse 22) but also he has numerous associates of quality (verse 27), including first of all some very dear friends. This pagan is a grand personage whose conversion should receive as much fanfare as possible in the church.

συνησθῆναι ἐπι τῷ ἐμέ καὶ τοὺς ἀναγκαίους ἐρρῶσθαι (Dittenberger, *Or.* 763, 31; cf. M. Holleaux, *Etudes d'épigraphie*, vol. 2, pp. 153–178). Attalus II traveled in similar company: συναγαγόντος μου οὐ νόνον Ἀθήναιον καὶ Σώσανδρον καὶ Μηνογένην, ἀλλὰ καὶ ἑτέρους πλείονας τῶν ἀναγκαίων (Dittenberger, *Or.* 315, 47 = C. B. Welles, *Royal Correspondence*, n. 61, 5).

[14] Josephus, *Ant.* 10.229: ἐν τοῖς ἀναγκαιοτάτοις τῶν φίλων εἶχε; cf. 10.5, 10.59; 11.208, 11.254; 13.224; 15.252.

[15] *P.Herm.* 1, 6–7 (first century AD); cf. *P.Oslo* 60, 5 (second century); *P.Mil.Vogl.* 59, 13 (second century); *BGU* 625, 26: ἔχω ἐν Ἀλεξανδρείᾳ ἀναγκαῖον φίλον; *P.Flor.* 142, 2: ἐποιδήπερ ἐντολικὸν ἔχω ἀναγκαίου φίλου (AD 264); *SB* 9415, 17, 11.

[16] *P.Brem.* 50, 4; *Stud.Pal.* XX, 233, 2. Cf. the ἀληθινοὶ φίλοι of Musonius, frags. 7 and 9 (ed. C. E. Lutz, pp. 56, 68), and the ἀεὶ φίλοι of Delos (J. and L. Robert, "Bulletin épigraphique," in *REG*, 1970, p. 418, n. 410).

ἀνάγνωσις

anagnōsis, reading (aloud, in public)

On the Sabbath day, the Jews congregate at the synagogue (*bêṯ sēper*) to hear the reading of and a commentary on a text from the Law and the Prophets.[1] The Christian church took up this tradition and turned "readers" into liturgical ministers.[2] But the reading of papyri and parchments was difficult, and it was necessary for the reader to know the text before reading it publicly.[3] "When you say, 'Come listen to a reading that I am

---

[1] Neh 8:7-8 (with the commentary of R. Le Déaut, *Introduction à la littérature targumique*, Rome, 1966, vol. 1, pp. 23ff.); Philo, *Dreams* 2.127; *Heir* 253; Josephus, *Ant.* 10.93-94; Luke 4:16; Acts 13:15 (cf. J. W. Bowker, "Speeches in Acts: A Study in Proem and Yelammedenu Form," in *NTS*, vol. 14, pp. 96-111); cf. 2 Cor 3:14. In the first third of the first century, Theodotus had a synagogue built at Jerusalem, εἰς ἀνάγνωσιν νόμου καὶ εἰς διδαχὴν ἐντολῶν (*CII* 1404). At Qumran, where a priest had the job of explaining clearly all the words of the prophets (1QpHab 2.6-9; cf. 1QS 8.11-12; 9.12-14), the monks met "to read in the Book," to examine the law, and pray together (1QS 6.6-8). Cf. A. Guilding, *The Fourth Gospel and Jewish Worship*, Oxford, 1960; J. R. Porter, "The Pentateuch and the Triennial Lectionary Cycle," in F. F. Bruce, *Promise and Fulfillment* (S. H. Hooke Festschrift), Edinburgh, 1963, pp. 163-174; R. Le Déaut, *Nuit pascale*, p. 219.

[2] St. Justin, *1 Apol.* 67; Tertullian, *Praescrip.* 41.8; *P.Apoll.* 99, 5; *P.Cair.Masp.* 67088. *IG*, vol. 10, 2, n. 1030, a tomb inscription of Aristea, ἀναγνώστης καὶ πακτωτὴς (administrator) γενάμενος τῆς Θεσσαλονικέων ἁγιωτάτης ἐκκλησίας; *I.Cor.*, 548; H. Grégoire, *Asie Mineure*, n. 131 *bis* (Lindos); 148 (Samos); 226 *quater* (Didyma); G. Lefebvre, *Recueil des inscriptions grecques-chrétiennes d'Egypte*, Cairo, 1907, n. 112 (Fayum), 350 (Akhmin), 581 (Aswan); *IGLS*, 1394 (region of Apamea). Cf. H. Leclercq, "Lecteur," in *DACL*, vol. 8, 2, col. 2242ff. J. M. Nielen, *Gebet und Gottesdienst im Neuen Testament*, Freiburg, 1937, pp. 182ff.

[3] Cf. H. I. Marrou, *Histoire de l'éducation*, pp. 230ff., 365ff. = ET, pp. 230ff., 375ff. Apprenticeship began in the school (Plato, *Leg.* 810^b; O. Guéraud, P. Jouguet, *Un livre d'écolier du IIIe siècle avant Jésus-Christ*, Cairo, 1938), and if the pupil stumbled over a syllable, his skin became more colorful than a nurse's apron (Plautus, *Bacch.* 423ff.; cf. Herondas, *Schoolmaster* 89-90); it then became an essential element in rhetorical education, exercising the intelligence and the memory, because in the recitation-declamation that was part of the official examination, commentary on and

---

anagnōsis, S 320; *TDNT* 1.343-344; *EDNT* 1.79; *NIDNTT* 1.245; MM 32; L&N 33.68; BAGD 52-53

going to do,' make sure that you do not grope your way through."⁴ This is the *anagnōsis* that St. Paul enjoins upon Timothy: "Apply yourself to *reading*, to exhorting, to teaching" (1 Tim 4:13).

Thus the letter to the Colossians would be read in the Laodicean community (*anaginōskō*, Col 4:16); public reading, which assured the maximum disclosure of the word of God,⁵ was used from the first days of the apostolic writings and the prophetic revelations (Rev 1:3). In the second century, the duty of the "lector" is entrusted to a competent minister,⁶ meaning on the one hand one who can produce an intelligible reading: *anagnōstēs kathistasthō euēkoos* (*Can. App.* 19; *Const. App.* 2.5: *polys en anagnōsmasin, hina tas graphas epimelōs hermēneuē* ["much given to reading, so that he may interpret the Scriptures carefully"]; cf. Ambrose, *Off.* 1.44.215); and on the other one who is intelligent: *ho anaginōskōn noeitō* (Mark 13:14; cf. Eph 3:4); since he must not only make an informed choice of the passages to read, but also comment on them. He does not have the right to be boring or esoteric (Ambrose, *Off.* 1.22.100–101; Eusebius, *Hist. Eccl.* 4.23.8).

---

criticism of the text that was sight-read were included (Plutarch, *De aud. poet.*; cf. I. Bruns, *De Schola Epicteti*, Kiel, 1897, pp. 3ff. J. Bompaire, *Lucien écrivain*, Paris, 1958, pp. 37ff. *P.Lips.* 32, 12: μετὰ τὴν ἀνάγνωσιν Ὠριγένης νεώτερος ῥήτωρ; A. C. Bandy, *The Greek Christian Inscriptions of Crete*, Athens, 1970, n. 6, 5: μνήμην Ἰωάννης ἀναγνώστης καὶ χαρτουλάριος; 37, 4; 104, 1). If the *anagnōstēs* is somtimes a specialist (Demosthenes, *C. Poly.* 1.65: the law will be read to you; *C. Tim.* 49.43: read me the testimony; cf. 1 Macc 14:19; *Ep. Arist.* 310; *P.Oxy.* 237, 5, 13; 7.33, 35; 2562, 4; 2963, 14; *BGU* 2244: the opening and public reading of a will, ἠνοίγη καὶ ἀνεγνώσθη; Dittenberger, *Syl.* 785, 1. T. C. Skeat, *The Use of Dictation in Ancient Book-Production*, London, 1956, pp. 179ff.; R. A. Coles, *Reports of Proceedings in Papyri*, Brussels, 1966, p. 47), it is also "someone who is studying a book" (Cicero, *Att.* 1.12; *Fam.* 5.9). Cf. *I.Magn.*, 100, 81.

⁴Epictetus 3.23.6; Pliny, *Ep.* 2.19; 5.12; 7.17; Plutarch, *Alex.* 1.1; 23.3; *P.Lond.* 1973, 1: "As soon as you read this letter—ὡς ἂν ἀναγνῷς τὴν ἐπιστολήν—send it to Ptolemais. . . ."

⁵ 1 Thess 5:27 (with the commentary of B. Rigaux, *Thessaloniciens*, on this verse); cf. 2 Cor 1:13; Eph 3:4. Justin, *1 Apol.* 67. On a literary level, cf. *P.Ant.* 93, 5: ἐδήλωσα . . . διὰ Σερήνου ἀναγνώστου (fourth century).

⁶Hippolytus, *Trad. ap.* 12; cf. *Const. App.* 8.22.2. The qualities of a lector had to do not only with voice quality and elocution, but also with intelligence for understanding the text of a papyrus or a codex in *scriptio continua*. The reader had to divide the words and make out the different elements of the sentence, which were not marked by any punctuation. (Cf. Plutarch, *An virt. doc.* 1: ἀναγινώσκειν γράμματα = decipher letters.) Even by the time of St. Augustine, there was no punctuated text of the Scriptures. Cassiodorus and Isidorus of Seville rightly insisted on the technical education of lectors. Cf. in the *Actes de la Conférence de Carthage in 411*, vol. 3, 255 (ed. S. Lancel), the criticisms aimed at the clerk: "He can't read, he doesn't separate the sentences (or: he doesn't distinguish the meaning of the words). . . . It is not the good faith of the clerk that is being criticized, but his pronunciation."

ἀνάδειξις

anadeixis, distinct demonstration, revelation, proclamation

This substantive makes a late appearance in the Koine and remains rather rare, unknown in the papyri, Philo, Josephus, etc. It retains the basic meaning of the verb *deiknymi*—"show something distinctly"[1]—and especially the meaning of the compound *anadeiknymi*: "make something visible by lifting it up,"[2] for example on the point of a spear (Plutarch, *Crass.* 26.4; cf. *De def. or.* 14), and is used for a shield (Herodotus 7.128; cf. 6.121, 124; Dio Cassius 77.13.5) and for the door of a house or of a sanctuary that is opened.[3] Hence the meaning "be revealed," "be uncovered" (Plutarch, *Them.* 25.2), "make oneself known" (idem, *Caes.* 38.5), "appear" (*Conf. Tongues* 103; *Sacr. Abel and Cain* 30). On the religious level, *anadeiknymi* often has God as its subject and means "reveal": "I have revealed initiations to men."[4] It is in this sense that the substantive *anadeixis* is used by Diodorus Siculus 1.85.4 regarding the cult of the Apis-bull: "When Osiris died, his soul passed into an animal of this species and . . . every time this god makes an *appearance* on earth, this soul passes successively . . . into the body of a bull."

The verb *anadeiknymi* also means "proclaim" (Xenophon, *Cyr.* 8.7.23), "declare" (2 Macc 9:14); "the God of victories proclaimed Abraham master of trophies" (Philo, *Prelim. Stud.* 93). It is used especially for the designation

---

[1] J. Gonda, ΔΕΙΚΝΥΜΙ, Amsterdam, 1929, pp. 58–67; H. Schlier, "δείκνυμι," in *TDNT*, vol. 2, p. 25.

[2] E. Bickerman, "ΑΝΑΔΕΙΞΙΣ," in *Mélanges E. Boisacq*, Brussels, 1937, vol. 1, pp. 117–124; cf. the index in C. B. Welles, *Royal Correspondence*, p. 311.

[3] Sophocles, *El.* 1458: "Let your doors open so that the inhabitants may see well"; Aristophanes, *Nub.* 304: opening a sanctuary; Dittenberger, *Syl.* 663, 15; *Or.* 234, 84.

[4] Aretalogy of Isis (Dittenberger, *Syl.* 1267, 28); *I.Magn.* 98, 21 (= *Syl.* 589); Acts 1:24—"Lord, show which of these two you have chosen"; Philo, *Sacr. Abel and Cain* 35; *Worse Attacks Better* 39, 44; *Conf. Tongues* 179; 3 Macc 2:14; *Sib. Or.* 3.15: "God has revealed himself as an eternal being."

---

anadeixis, S 323; *TDNT* 2.31; *EDNT* 1.80; *NIDNTT* 3.569; L&N 28.54; BAGD 53

of a sovereign through investiture ("I have designated my son to be king")[5] or of a high official in his office. It is in this sense that the substantive *anadeixis* is used for the first time by Polybius for "the coronations of the Lagids" (*kai tas anadeixeis tōn basileōn*, 15.25.11), then by Plutarch: the colleagues of Caius proclaim the results of his election to a third tribunate (Plutarch, *C. Gracch.* 12.7); "the day of the election" (of candidates to the magistracies, *hē kyria tēs anadeixeōs, Cat. Min.* 44.10); Metellus "did not let Marius leave until twelve days before the election of consuls" (*tēn tōn hypatōn anadeixin*).[6]

Curiously, the two biblical occurrences of *anadeixis* suggest both nuances, "show" and "institute." According to Sir 43:6, the moon is *anadeixin chronōn*,[7] that is, it indicates feasts and determines months; hence in the calendar it has the double function of announcing and ruling. According to Luke 1:80, John the Baptist was in the desert until the day of his manifesting to Israel (*heōs hēmeras anadeixeōs autou*). The solemnity of this "appearing" of the precursor, inaugurating his ministry, is noteworthy. The evangelist contrasts John's long, solitary, silent sojourn in the Judean desert east of Hebron to his official manifesting by God; it is like a revelation. The Vulgate translates well, "usque ad diem ostensionis." We may interpret, "He appeared publicly." But this is also the coming of a hero who heralds the king and prepares his way, his presentation before the whole nation. It was at this point that John, then about thirty years old, received his investiture as announcer of the messianic era.

---

[5] 2 Macc 9:25; 10:11—"the prince promoted Lysias governor general"; 14:26; Josephus, *Ant.* 13.113; 14.280; 20.227: designation of a high priest; Polybius 15.25.5; *I.Magn.* 100 *a* 24 and 37; C. Michel, *Recueil*, n. 55, 20; 57, 27. Cf. Luke 10:1—"The Lord designated seventy-two" disciples.

[6] Plutarch, *Mar.* 8.7. E. Bickerman, defines *anadeixis* as "the act of the solemn presentation of a prince to the people" ("ΑΝΑΔΕΙΞΙΣ," p. 123), which was part of the ceremonial investiture of Hellenistic sovereigns; but it is also used for the dedication of a temple. Lucullus's intention in asking Mummius to loan him statues was "to decorate the temple until its dedication" (μέχρι ἀναδείξεως, Strabo 8.6.23). Likewise the verb: a sanctuary is "dedicated" by the Gauls to Caesar Augustus (Strabo 4.3.2); cf. a declaration of war (Dittenberger, *Syl.* 742, 12; *Or.* 441, 49).

[7] The Greek would suggest nothing more than "indication" (cf. Philo, *Rewards* 153), but the Hebrew manuscript discovered at Cairo has *memšālāh* (in the construct), which means "dominion, rule" (the Hebrew manuscript from Masada has only the initial *mem*, followed by a lacuna; cf. Y. Yadin, *The Ben Sira Scroll from Masada*, Jerusalem, 1965; J. Le Moyne, *Les Sadducéens*, Paris, 1972, p. 68). Cf. the astrological meaning of *anadeiknymi* in Vettius Valens, p. 119, 25; *CPR* VII, 4, n. 24, 2: ἀναδεχομένου τὴν ἡμέραν.

ἀναδέχομαι

anadechomai, to welcome, accept; to accept responsibility for

The four biblical occurrences of this verb[1] are all of the first aorist middle participle *anadexamenos*. If the Bible gives it the well-attested sense of hospitality, "to welcome someone as a guest,"[2] it shows no trace of the common sense of accepting or receiving an object or a sum of money or of being subjected to an action.[3] At least in the case of Eleazer's "accepting" a glorious death in preference to an infamous existence (2 Macc 6:19), a voluntary and fervent consent is involved.

This verb is therefore not synonymous with *lambanō*. It very often means "take upon oneself, take on a burden or obligation"; one answers to someone for something. This was the case with Nicanor, who undertook to gain tribute money for the Romans by taking hostages from Jerusalem;[4]

---

[1] Cf. the doctoral thesis of S. Vitalini, *La notion d'accueil dans le Nouveau Testament*, Fribourg, 1961 (published in part as *La nozione d'accoglienza nel Nuovo Testamento*, Fribourg, 1963).

[2] "Publius received us and showed us hospitality" (Acts 28:7); cf. Dittenberger, *Or.* 339, 20: τάς τε πρεσβείας ἀνεδέχετο προθύμως (second century BC); 441, 9; *SB* 8029, 7.

[3] Josephus, *War* 1.338: "Those who escaped were received at sword-point"; 3.14: "Antonius received the first assaults with firmness"; 3.173: cattle hides to receive the stone projectiles; Dittenberger, *Syl.* 962, 65 (333 BC); *P.Tebt.* 329, 19 (AD 139); *P.Eleph.* 29, 13; Diodorus Siculus 4.29. A senatus consultum of Sulla: "undergo numerous dangers" (*I.Thas.*, 174 C 8).

[4] 2 Macc 8:36—ὁ τοῖς Ῥωμαίοις ἀναδεξάμενος φόρον; cf. Epictetus 3.24.64: "Diogenes joyfully took on so much bodily fatigue and misery"; Josephus, *War* 3.4: Vespasian able to assume the burden of so heavy a war; *Ant.* 14.315; Dittenberger, *Syl.* 685, 30: πᾶσαν ἀναδεχόμενοι κακοπαθίαν (139 BC); *SB* 7473, 6, 7738, 13: ἀναδεξάμενος πόνον ἐκ νυκτὸς καὶ μεθ' ἡμέραν, ἄχρι συνετέλεσεν (honorific decree for a general, from AD 22–23); 7996, 24: ἀναδεχομένου τὸν κίνδυνον τῆς πράσεως (18 September AD 430). *P.Oxy.* 71, 16; 1418, 18: ἀναδέξομαι τῷ παιδὶ τετραμήνιον γυμνασιαρχίαν; *P.Ryl.* 77, 38; *PSI* 1239 24; *BGU* 1762, 11. An honorific decree is voted

and it is said in Egypt concerning the son of Jason, who only lived five years, that he "accomplished all that he agreed to" (*SEG*, vol. 8, 799, 2). When one takes on a task, one agrees to carry it through to completion (*P.Cair.Isid.* 82, 5 and 8). Finally, *anadechomai* expresses someone's standing surety,[5] as attests the constant, albeit late, association *engyasthai kai anadechesthai*.[6]

This verb consequently has a legal meaning—to take on a responsibility[7]—which is almost certainly the sense in Heb 11:17—"By faith Abraham, when put to the test, offered Isaac—truly it was his only son that he was offering—he who had received the responsibility for the promises."[8] The "temptation" of Abraham was a trial of his faith, his love, and his obedience. All the commentators mention the nuance of the tense: the perfect *prosenēnochen* points to the sacrifice as completely accepted and, as it were, already accomplished in the heart of Abraham,[9] even as the imperfect *prosepheren* evokes the progressive realization of this offering without weakening throughout the preparations to the immolation on Moriah: "Having offered . . . he was in the process of offering"; while—as the recipient and agent of the promises of a posterity—he appeared to be nullifying this promise forever.

---

for Eirenias who "has taken responsibility for the costs entailed by the realization of these honors, τὰς δαπάνας τὰς εἰς τὴν συντέλειαν τῶν τιμῶν ἀναδέξασθαι παρ᾽ αὐτοῦ" (*NCIG*, n. 7, 12).

[5] Thucydides 8.81.3: "Tisaphernes would not entrust himself to the Athenians unless Alcibiades personally stood surety to him"; Polybius 5.16.8.

[6] *P.Oxy.* 1972, 6; 2238, 9; 2420, 10; 2478, 12; *P.Ross.Georg.* V, 34, 5; *Stud.Pal.* XX, 127, 9; 128, 8; *SB* 9146, 8–9; 9152, 7; 9592, 11–12; *PSI* 932, 5; *P.Stras.* 40, 18; *P.Lips.* 55, .8

[7] Josephus, *Ant.* 14.247; 17.304; *P.Oxy.* 513, 59: ἐγὼ αὐτὸς τοῦτο ἀναδέξομαι = I myself will take the responsibility (AD 184).

[8] Ὁ τὰς ἐπαγγελίας ἀναδεξάμενος. On Abraham and the sacrifice of Isaac, cf. R. Le Déaut, *La Nuit pascale*, Rome, 1963, pp. 131ff. 163, 206–207, 259ff. Idem, *La Présentation targumique du sacrifice d'Isaac et la sotériologie paulinienne*, in AnBib 18; Rome, 1963, vol. 2, pp. 563–574; M. McNamara, *The New Testament and the Palestinian Targum to the Pentateuch*, Rome, 1966, pp. 164ff. R. de Vaux, *Les Sacrifices de l'Ancien Testament*, Paris, 1964, p. 61; H. Cazelles, *DBSup*, vol. 7, 128ff. D. Lerch, *Isaaks Opferung christlich gedeutet*, Tübingen, 1950; F. M. Braun, *Jean le Théologien*, Paris, 1966, vol. 3, 1, p. 159. J. L. Vesco, "Abraham," in *RSPT*, 1971, pp. 33–80.

[9] "In certain cases, the perfect tense has considerable psychological significance; this aspect of 'dramatic past time' appears in passages where the perfect stands out from a background of aorists (2 Cor 11:25—πεποίηκα; Heb 11:17—προσενήνοχεν; Heb 11:28—πεποίηκεν)" (E. Osty, "Pour une traduction plus fidèle du Nouveau Testament," in *Ecole des Langues orientales . . . Mémorial de Cinquantenaire*, Paris, 1964, p. 88).

ἀναπέμπω

anapempō, **to send, conduct, bring back, send up**

During the Hellenistic period, this compound verb, unknown in the LXX, often has the same meaning as the simple form *pempō*, "send, conduct." "Herod sent subsidies to Antony's partisans" (Josephus, *War* 1.358, cf. 2.605; *Ant.* 18.313); "She sent us our provisions at the city of Antinous" (*Pap.Lugd.Bat.* VI, 37, 8); "Accept all that I send you."[1] It is used constantly in shipping orders: "Order from Ischyrion to Heroninos to load four camels with vetch (*orobos*) and send them into the city."[2] Documents are sent,[3] as are people.[4] Prayers are sent up to heaven.[5] Although there is this variety

---

[1] *P.Oxy.* 2273, 19 (H. C. Youtie, *Scriptiunculae*, vol. 1, p. 262), κομίσου πάντα ὅσα ἐὰν ἀναπέμπω σοι; *P.Yale* 84, 7: "As soon as you have received my letter, send the cakes"; *P.Hib.* 57, 1; *P.Warr.* 13, 5, 9; 14, 32: "send me the signed note immediately"; *P.Mich.* 500, 10: ἂν ἐθέλῃς ἀναπέμψασθαι; *P.Stras.* 171, 6; Philostratus, *Gym.* 31, "send the javelin"; Philo, *Unchang. God* 84: "the wind exhaled (ἀναπεμπόμενον) by the trachea"; Philo, *Dreams* 1.29; Philo, *Sacr. Abel and Cain* 74.

[2] *SB* 9058, 4: ἀνάπεμψον εἰς τὸν πόλιν; 9076, 7; 9077, 8; 9081, 5; 9408 [2], 67, 69, 73; 9409 [3], 98; 9415 [9], 5; 11129, 3: Βαυθλᾶν μοι ἀνάπεμψον μετὰ τῶν ὄνων; *P.Oxy.* 2153, 24: "I am sending the small boat with Isidorus"; 2784, 5: "For this reason, until today, have have not sent the cattle"; 2985, 13: "Send me six *keramia* of wine"; *P.Brem.* 20, 10.

[3] The summary of taxes sent by the *eklogistēs* of the nome (*P.Princ.* 126, 4); *P.Harr.* 75, 21: "I am sending the certificate for the act" (addressed to the keeper of archives). After a concluded agreement is registered, it is sent to the local authorities (*P.Oxy.* 2349, 3); a petition is addressed to the *stratēgos* with "a copy of the συγχώρησις, which has been sent to the keepers of the property registers" (τὸν ἀναπεμφέντα πρὸς τοὺς . . . βιβλιοφύλακας, 2473, 27); ὥστε ἀνάπεμψαι τὰ βιβλίδια (1653, 11).

[4] *P.Oxy.* 2182, 27; *SB* 9468, 6: ἀναπέμψαι τοὺς ἀνθρώπους εἰς τὸν ἀέρα.

[5] Josephus, commenting on 1 Kgs 8:23, 27: σοι τὰς εὐχὰς ἀναπέμπωμεν εἰς τὸν ἀέρα (*Ant.* 8.108); *C.P.Herm.* 8, 12: ἐν αἷς ἀναπέμπεις καὶ μεθ' ἡμέραν εὐχαῖς τῷ Κυρίῳ σωτῆρει ἡμῶν = prayers that you send up each day to our Lord Savior; *P.Oxy.* 2479, 17; *PSI* 1425, 6; *P.Alex.* 216 (p. 44): οὐ παύομε εὐχὰς ἀναπεμπόμενος ὑπὲρ σωτηρίας τῆς ὑμετέρας μεγαλοπρεποῦς (sixth century); *SB* 8728, 23: τὴν δόξαν ἰαναπέμπομεν τῷ πατρὶ καὶ τῷ υἱῷ καὶ τῷ ἁγίῳ πνεύματι (seventh century); 8334,

---

anapempō, S 375; *EDNT* 1.87; MM 37; L&N 15.70, 15.71; BAGD 59

of connotations, the basic meaning is moving a person or thing from the place where it is to another place, as is clear from the numerous "summonses" preserved among the papyri: "Immediately send Emes . . . who is accused by Aurelius Nilus. . . ."[6] The meaning "bring back, cause to return," is very common in literary Greek[7] and in the papyri: "I sent you a bag of sesame . . . send it back with Achilles" (*P.Oxy.* 3066, 4); a deceased woman's dowry was not restored to the heirs (*UPZ* 123, 22); "If there is some rupture between us, I agree to return the estate to Heracleia."[8] It is in this sense that we should understand Phlm 12, where St. Paul sent the slave Onesimus back to his legal owner: "I am sending him back to you" (*hon anepempsa* [epistolary aorist] *soi*).[9]

Anapempō often has a legal meaning: to send up an accused person or to refer a matter to the competent authorities.[10] This is the case in Luke 23:7, 11, 15: Pilate "sent Jesus up to Herod (*anepempsen pros*) . . . Herod sent

23: τῶν εἰς τὸν θεῖον ἀναπεμπομένων πάντων (cf. R. Hutmacher, *Ehrendekret*). We conclude that the verbal prefix ἀνα- specifies sending *up*, hence raising someone to a higher position, like the prophetess Martha, who was sent to the consul Marius by his wife and stirred his admiration (Plutarch, *Mar.* 17.3); cf. Dittenberger, *Or.* 329, 51: ἀναπέμψαι δὲ τὸ ψήφισμα τοὺς στρατηγοὺς πρὸς τὸν βασιλέα; *SB* 8728, 23.

[6] *P.Fay.* 37, 1: ἀνάπεμψον Ἔμην ἐνκαλούμενον ὑπὸ Αὐρηλίου Νείλου βουλευτοῦ ἐξαυτῆς (with the correction by H. C. Youtie, "P. Fay. 37," in *ZPE* 33, 1979, pp. 211–212); cf. *BGU* 1569, 2082–2083; *P.Tebt.* 594; *P.Oslo* 20; *P.Oxy.* 3035; *P.Grenf.* II, 66; *P.Aberd.* 60, 1; *SB* 9352, 11034; *P.Ryl.* 681 (with the corrections of H. C. Youtie, *Scriptiunculae*, vol. 1, p. 25); *P.Mich.* 589 (the editor, G. M. Browne, lists the fifty-five known arrest warrants). *P.Oxy.* 169 (published by S. Daris, in *SPap*, 1980, pp. 5–7). Often the verb ἀναπέμπω is replaced by ἐκπέμπω (B. Boyaval, in *ZPE*, vol. 6, 1970, p. 11; cf. Ursula Hagedorn, "Das Formular der Überstellungsbefehle im römischen Ägypten," in *BASP,* 1970, pp. 61–74).

[7] Josephus, *War* 1.666: "The king ordered that all these men be sent back home"; 5.84; *Ant.* 3.72; Plutarch, *Sol.* 4.6: "The tripod came back to Thebes."

[8] *P.Mich.* 341, 4 (from AD 47); cf. a grain shipment in 49/48 BC, ἀναπεπέμφθαι ἐκ τῆς πόλεως (*SB* 8754, 7 and 24); ἀναπέμπω τὸ πρᾶγμα ἐπὶ τὴν δι' αὐτοῦ διάγνωσιν (7601, 12; cf. 7338, 8). In 131 BC, τὸν αὐτόγραφον σὺν τῇ ἐπιστολῇ ταύτῃ ἀναπέμψας: "returning the original (of the bank account to me) with this letter" (*UPZ* 199, 14); in 127/126: ἀναπέμψαι ἡμῶν τὴν ἔντευξιν ἐπὶ τοὺς χρηματιστάς (ibid. 170 A 34; cf. B 33); *P.Oxy.* 1032, 50.

[9] This restoration of a runaway slave to his master is contrary to Deut 23:16— "You shall not hand over to his master a slave who takes refuge with you from his master" (cf. Str-B, vol. 3, pp. 668ff.), an arrangement without parallel in ancient laws (R. de Vaux, *Ancient Israel*, vol. 1, p. 87; cf. M. Robert, *La Lettera de S. Paolo a Filemone e la condizione giuridica dello schiavo fuggitivo*, Milan, 1933, pp. 39–49), but here neither the Mosaic law nor Greek or Roman law governs the case: Onesimus is a brother in the faith; cf. P. J. Verdam, "St. Paul et un serf fugitif," in *Symbolae van Oven*, Leiden, 1946, pp. 211–230.

[10] *P.Oxy.* 2712, 15: ὁ κύριος μου ἡγεμὼν ἀνέπεμψεν ἐπὶ σὲ τὸ πρᾶγμα.

him back to Pilate (*anepempsen tō*) . . . Herod sent him up to us (*anepempsen auton pros hēmas*)."[11] These variations of venue and jurisdiction are mentioned constantly.[12] Sometimes plaintiffs who are up against a scheming adversary and are unable to obtain a judgment before an easily influenced jury, appeal to a higher authority;[13] sometimes the highest authority decides on jurisdiction. Thus a *prostagma* of Cleopatra III and Ptolemy Soter II rules that only the *dioikētēs* Eirenaios will have jurisdiction to judge state agents: "they shall refer (*anapempein*) complaints against agents and their trials to Eirenaios the kinsman (of the king) and *dioikētēs*" (*P.Tebt*. 7, 7 = *C.Ord.Ptol*. 61; from 144 BC). According to an inscription from Metropolis, the legate P. Ranius Castus received from the governor the assignment of taking on a case that his predecessors could not bring to a conclusion: "Having read Sosthenes' petition . . . which was sent (*anapemphthēnai*) to me by the proconsul Stertinius Quartus, I am quite amazed that after so many letters from governors . . ."[14]

---

[11] Pilate expected the tetrarch to acquit Jesus, since Jesus was his subject (*forum domicilii*); cf. J. Blinzler, *Trial of Jesus*, pp. 196ff.; 200, n. 17; A. N. Sherwin-White, *Roman Society*, p. 65; H. W. Hoehner, "Why did Pilate hand Jesus over to Antipas?" in E. Bammel, *The Trial of Jesus: Cambridge Studies in Honour of C. F. D. Moule*, London, 1970, pp. 84–90 (supplies the variants on verse 15, pp. 89–90).

[12] Philo, *Spec. Laws* 4.190: "The pretender, since he found that his perceptions were blurred by the obscurity . . . had to stand down and send the matter back before more perspicacious judges (the priests)" (ἀναπεμπέτω πρὸς ἀκριβεστέρους δικαστάς); Josephus, *War* 2.571: in each city, Joseph designated seven elders to judge small cases; "As for important matters and capital trials, he ordered them transferred to himself and to the Seventy" (τὰ γὰρ μείζω πράγματα καὶ τὰς φονικὰς δίκας, ἐφ' ἑαυτὸν ἀναπέμπειν ἐκέλευσεν καὶ τοὺς ἑβδομήκοντα); *Ant*. 4.218: If the judges do not see how they should rule in the matter that is before them, let them send the case up to Jerusalem (ἀναπεμπέτωσαν τὴν δίκην εἰς τὴν ἱερὰν πόλιν); 15.351, Marcus Agrippa sends the Gadarene prisoners back without even hearing them (ἀναπέμπει τῷ βασιλεῖ δεσμίους); *BGU* 5, col. II, 19: ἑαυτὸν δὲ ἐν νόσῳ γενόμενον ἀναπεπόμφθαι ἀναφόριον τῷ δικαιοδότῃ; idem 15, col. I, 17; 168, 25: ἀναπέμπω οὖν τὸ πρᾶγμα ἐπὶ τὸν κράτιστον ἐπιστράτηγον.

[13] *P.Fouad* 26, 7. Hermias, having been unable to get anything from the magistrate, appealed to the highest official in the Thebaid, the *epistratēgos* Demetrius; this new suit also gets nowhere. He then appeals to the *stratēgos*, who reserves judgment for himself (ἀναπεμφθὲν δὲ ἐφ' ἡμᾶς, οὗ ἐστιν ἀντίγραφον, *UPZ* 162, col. I, 13). This referral conforms to the law of the land (ἐκ τῶν τῆς χώρας νόμων; col. VII, 1ff.). Cf. an accused official who falls under the prefect's jurisdiction (*P.Mil.Vogl*. 98, 3).

[14] Th. Drew-Bear, *Phrygie*, p. 20. It is apparent from this text that ἀναπέμπω does not always imply referral to a higher-up; cf. likewise the edict of the proconsul of Asia, Gaius Gabinius Barbarus Pompeianus: "Whereas the city of Euhippe, having had recourse to the great Fortune of our master Emperor Antoninus with regard to the wrongs that they have suffered at the hands of those soldiers and officials who have left the royal routes and great highways and come into their cities (requisitions,

Thus Festus's language is perfectly adequate when he presents to Agrippa the case of the prisoner Paul: "I asked him if he wished to go to Jerusalem to be judged there, but when Paul appealed for his case to be reserved for the judgment of Augustus (the emperor Nero), I ordered that he be kept until I could send him up to Caesar" (*anapempsō pros Kaisara*, aorist subjunctive, Acts 25:21). This referral to the highest jurisdiction has numerous parallels. Herod had three Arabs arrested who "were yet examined by Saturninus, governor of Syria, and sent to Rome" (*anakrithentes . . . anepemphthēsan eis Rhōmēn*, Josephus, *War* 1.577; cf. *Ant.* 14.97). Quadratus promises to examine in detail matters submitted to him (*diereunēsein hekasta*), hears the complaints of the Samaritans, and sends to Caesar (*anepempsen epi Kaisara*) two high priests, various eminent persons, and others (*War* 2.243; cf. 246, 253; 3.398; *Ant.* 20.131, 134). Felix rids Judea of brigands, arrests Eleazar, who pillaged the region for twenty years, and sends him to Rome in chains (*dēsas anepempsen eis Rhōmēn, Ant.* 20.161). According to an inscription from Priene, the *stratēgos* writes and defers to the Senate: "concerning whom the *stratēgos* Lucius Lucilius wrote and sent to the Senate" (*peri hōn ho stratēgos Leukios Leukilios egrapsen kai anepempsen pros tēn synklēton, I.Priene,* 111, 147; first century BC; cf. Josephus, *War* 2.207).

---

exactions, violence), was referred to the governor of the province" (ἀνεπέμφθησαν ἐπὶ τὸν ἡγούμενον τοῦ ἔθνους, published and translated by L. Robert, *Opera Minora Selecta*, vol. 1, p. 592). The inspector Maximus, having been accused of embezzlement, was referred by the prefect to the *epistratēgos* (ἀνέπεμψεν αὐτοὺς ἐπὶ Κράσσον τὸν κράτιστον ἐπιστράτηγον, *P.Tebt.* 287, 6); cf. *P.Stras.* 188, 1.

ἀναστροφή

anastrophē, **conduct**

The most banal sense of *anastrephō*—"return, come back from one place to another,"[1] hence "retrace one's steps" (1 Sam 25:12; 2 Sam 3:16; Jdt 1:13)—sometimes retains the etymological nuance "to return upside down,"[2] like runaways thrown back on top of each other (1 Macc 7:46; cf. Jdt 1:11); sometimes it has the sense of coming and going, "living."[3] Hence its metaphorical usage: "walk in virtue."[4]

Only this moral nuance is retained in the noun *anastrophē*, designating a mode of existence, a way of behaving.[5] This became a technical term in NT spirituality. Just as the way of life of the pagans is stigmatized,[6] so also

---

[1] Gen 8:9 (*šûḇ*); 18:14; 22:5; Judg 18:26; 1 Sam 3:5–6; Acts 5:22; 15:16.

[2] [The French phrase *sens dessus dessous*, literally upside down, can mean "in utter disorder, in a state of distress"—Tr.] But in a favorable sense, one "sets the situation aright" (Josephus, *Life* 273), one "reverts" (*P.Mich.* 24, 55, 7). In optical jargon, ἀναστρέφειν means "the reversing of images in mirrors with respect to the actual objects" (C. Mugler, *Terminologie optique*, p. 33). In geometry, ἀναστροφή expresses the conversion of a ratio (idem, *Terminologie géométrique*, p. 61).

[3] Ezek 3:15; 19:6. Ἀναστρέφειν is then synonymous with περιπατεῖν, cf. Epictetus 1.2.26: "pass his life"; 3.15.5: "You are behaving like a child" (cf. A. Bonhöffer, *Epiktet*, pp. 52, 201). Hence "busy oneself" (*P.Sarap.* 80, 11; *SB* 9779, 4), dedicate oneself to one's duty (*Ep. Arist.* 252). C. Spicq, *Théologie morale*, vol. 1, pp. 382ff.

[4] 1 Kgs 6:12 (*hālak*); Prov 8:20; 20:7; Zech 3:7. Hence the favored meaning of conversion: return to God (Jer 3:7; 8:4; 15:19; 22:10–11; Sir 8:8; 39:3; 50:28). Cf. *Ep. Arist.* 216: during sleep, one's thoughts *return* to the same matters that one was busy about when awake.

[5] Tob 4:14; Gal 1:13—"You have heard about my conduct when I was in Judaism"; cf. Eph 2:3; *1 Clem.* 63.3: ἀπὸ μεότητος ἀναστρέφοντας ἕως γήρους ἀμέμπτως ἐν ἡμῖν.

[6] 2 Macc 5:8 (κακῆς ἀναστροφῆς); Eph 4:22—"You were instructed to have done with your former way of life, that of the old man corrupted by lusts"; 1 Pet 1:18—"You have been freed from the senseless (μάταιος) way of life that you inherited from your fathers" (cf. W. C. van Unnik, "The Critique of Paganism in I Petr. I, 18," in *Neotestamentica et Semitica: Studies in Honour of M. Black*, Edinburgh, 1969, pp. 129–142); 2 Pet 2:7—just Lot is "distraught at the behavior of these people who are crazy in their debauchery"; 2:18—neophytes, fragile and unstable, "barely distanced

---

anastrophē, S 391; *TDNT* 7.715–717; *EDNT* 1.93; *NIDNTT* 3.933, 935; MM 38; L&N 41.3; BAGD 61

is "perfect conduct from childhood" praised (2 Macc 6:23, *kallistē*). When St. Paul testifies concerning his conscience ("It is with simplicity and the purity of God—not in fleshly wisdom, but in the grace of God—that we have conducted ourselves in the world, particularly in our dealings with you," 2 Cor 1:12), he contrasts two modes of existence and already gives *anastrophē* the exemplary sense that will be required especially of ministers of the church;[7] the model, who is particularly visible, ought to be inspiring. Life lived in the faith is a persuasive testimony.

It is above all St. Peter who demands of all Christians an unassailable comportment. Whether with respect to bearing, dress, or behavior in family and social relations, every action and reaction in the context of the community, that is, the concrete life of the believer, should be noble and radiant:[8] "Let your behavior among the nations be noble" (1 Pet 2:12; *kalē*), apt as a result to disarm criticisms (3:16), notably those of husbands won over by the chaste and quiet deportment of their wives (3:1–2).

It used to be claimed that these moral and religious meanings derived from the OT, but they are attested in the secular literature,[9] in the papyri,[10]

---

from those who live aberrant lives—τοὺς ἐν πλάνῃ ἀναστρεφομένους" barely resist such distractions. Cf. Heb 10:33, where Christians are in solidarity with those who are maltreated, "in a similar situation" (cf. *P.Tebt.* 703, 271: τῆς καθ' ἡμᾶς ἀναστροφῆς καὶ ἀγωνίας; third century BC).

[7] 1 Tim 3:15—"I write to you . . . that you may know how one must conduct onself in a house of God"; 4:12—"Become a model for the believers in speech, in conduct, in love . . ."; Heb 13:7—"Remember your leaders. . . and meditate carefully on the outcome of their manner of life, imitate their faith"; the *didaskalos* who wrote this letter certifies that he himself wishes to conduct himself well in all things: καλῶς θέλοντες ἀναστρέφεσθαι (Heb 13:18). Jas 3:13—"Who is wise and experienced among you? Let him manifest his works by a noble comportment—ἐκ τῆς καλῆς ἀναστροφῆς—with an amiable wisdom." Cf. *Ep. Arist.* 130: "You see the influence of conduct and company."

[8] 1 Pet 1:15—αὐτοὶ ἅγιοι ἐν πάσῃ ἀναστροφῇ γενήθητε; 1:17—"Conduct yourselves with a devout fear during the time of your sojourn"; 2 Pet 3:11—"Since all these things are thus to be dissolved, how ought you not to live with a devout comportment and with piety, ἐν ἁγίαις ἀναστροφαῖς καὶ εὐσεβείαις" (cf. W. Brandt, "Wandel als Zeugnis nach dem I. Petrusbrief," in *Verbum Dei Manet in Aeternum,* Witten, 1953, pp. 10–25; C. Spicq, *Epîtres de saint Pierre,* on this verse). Philodemus of Gadara, *Mus.* 4, p. 76 (ed. J. Kemke): Certain melodies incline the soul "to conversation and good relations—πρὸς τὴν ὁμειλίαν καὶ τὴν ἁρμόττουσαν ἀναστροφήν"; Epictetus 1.22.13; *1 Clem.* 21.8: ὁσίως ἀναστρεφομένους ἐν καθαρᾷ διανοίᾳ.

[9] Polybius 4.81.1: "Philip attracted admiration beyond his years for his conduct in general"; Epictetus 1.9.24: "God has established for us a line of conduct"; Josephus, *Ant.* 15.190.

[10] In the second-third century BC, the formula "if your conduct is not better—οὐκ ἀπὸ τοῦ βελτίστου ἀναστρεφομένου" is often used (*BGU* 1756, 12; 1769, 4; *P.Tebt.*

ἀναστροφή, anastrophē 113

and especially by epigraphy, notably in the honorific decrees that give particular honor to magistrates and functionaries whose conduct has been irreproachable: "Menander, in the magistracies to which he has elected, has shown himself irreproachable by his noble and splendid conduct."[11] "I respect this man, who conducts himself so generously in all things."[12] This *en hapasin anastrephomenon* is already attested in the first century AD in *I.Priene*,[13] in *I.Car.*: "In all his embassies, he has conducted himself properly and managed affairs justly,"[14] and in inscriptions from Pergamum.[15] There is a wealth of parallels to the formula in Heb 13:18 (*en pasin kalōs telontes anastrephesthai*) and to 1 Pet 1:15 (*en pasē anastrophē*).

786, 15; 904, 10; cf. *P.Michael.* 20, 5: εἰ ἐνδεῶς περὶ τοῦτο ἀναστραφείης). In 5 BC, ἔν τε τοῖς καιρὸν δείπνοις μεγαλοπόρως καὶ μεγαλοψύχως ἀναστραφείς (*SB* 8267, 31). In AD 276, a husband establishes his will in favor of his wife, who has conducted herself appropriately in his home: πρεπόντως περὶ τὴν συμβίωσιν ἀναστραφείσῃ, καταλείπω (*P.Oxy.* 907, 17); but a widow complains in 303 to the prefect that his assistant and his business agent have acted dishonestly toward her: οἵ τινες μὴ ὀρθῶς ἀναστραφέντες (*P.Oxy.* 71, col. II, 12), after the fashion of Diocles and others in 103: ἀναστρεφομένων ἀδικήματα εἴς με (*P.Fay.* 12, 7).

[11] *I.Delos*, 1498, 7 (between 159 and 151); cf. *SEG*, vol. 23, 447, 15: "the generosity and diligence that they showed toward those who conducted themselves well in their magistracies" (second century BC). The judges "in the course of their term put on a comportment worthy of themselves, of the city that sent them, and of ourselves" (second century BC, *NCIG*, n. 12, 17); in the second century BC, the judges of Scotoussa "acted in their bearing and in their judicial functions in a manner worthy of themselves, of the city that sent them, and of those who had cases before them" (*I.Gonn.*, 91, 12); Dittenberger, *Syl.* 738 B 4: "Lykinos conducted himself during his term in a manner worthy of his people and of our city" (Delphi, 86 BC); *I.Olymp.* 52, 24. In an honorific decree of Cheronea, the chiliarch Amatokos, leader of a Thracian troop, is praised: τὴν ἀναστροφὴν ἐποιήσατο εὐσχήμονα, and we learn that his good conduct consisted of his taking care of the interests of the Cheroneans, in enforcing equity between them and his soldiers, and in the soldiers' causing no harm to the territory (published by M. Holleaux, *Etudes d'épigraphie*, vol. 1, p. 144, lines 5, 13, 26).

[12] *I.Cor.*, vol. 8, n. 306, 8 (second century AD); cf. L. Robert, *Hellenica*, Limoges, 1940, vol. 1, pp. 43–53).

[13] *I.Priene*, 115, 5: ἀναστρεφόμενος ἐν πάσιν φιλανθρώπως; cf. 108, 284: πεποίηται δὲ καὶ διὰ τὴν πρέπουσιν ἀναστροφήν. Cf. Josephus, *Ant.* 19.72: εὐπρεπῶς ἀναστραφησομένου.

[14] *I.Car.*, 167, 16: ἐμ πάσαις δεόντως ἀναστραφεὶς καὶ ὀρθῶς χρησάμενος τοῖς πράγμασιν; cf. 70, 10: τῇ παρ' ὅλον τὸν βίον ἀναστροφῇ διαφέροντα (= *MAMA*, vol. 6, 114).

[15] *I.Perg.*, 470, 4: ἐν πᾶσιν ἀνεστραμμένον ἀξίως τῆς πόλεως; cf. 224 A 5; *I.Priene*, 108, 223: τῇ πόλει συμπερόντως ἀνεστράφη; cf. *P.Brem.* 53, 35–36. *MAMA*, vol. 8, 412 b, 4: Καλλίαν ... νεανίαν καλὸν καὶ ἀγαθὸν τὴν ἀναστροφὴν πεποιημένον ἐνάρετον; cf. line 12; 414, 13: τὰς ἐπὶ τῇ κοσμίῳ ἀναστροφῇ μαρτυρίας καὶ τειμὰς ἀποδιδόναι.

If the extension of "good conduct" to all areas is emphasized, its quality or distinguishing marks become even clearer. Just as the NT writers qualify conduct with noble, good, pure, holy, devout, the inscriptions praise it for its nobility, glory, and piety.[16]

---

[16] *I.Perg.*, 459, 5: καλῶς καὶ ἐνδόξως ἀναστραφῆναι; 496, 5: ἀναστρεφομένην καλῶς καὶ εὐσεβῶς; Dittenberger, *Syl.* 598^{c}7; 717, 95; *I.Magn.* 85, 11: τὴν ἀναστροφὴν ποιησάμενοι μετὰ πάσης εὐκοσμίας. 179, 5: κόσμιον ἀναστροφὴν φιλοτειμησάμενον; 165, 6; *I.Bulg.* 43, 15: τὴν ἀναστροφὴν εὐσχήνομα καὶ ἀξίαν τοῦ τε βασιλέως κτλ. At Patara ἐπὶ τῇ τοῦ βίου αἰδήμονι καὶ κοσμίῳ ἀναστροφῇ (cited by L. Robert, *Etudes anatoliennes*, 2d ed., Amsterdam, 1970, p. 89, n. 1); Dittenberger, *Syl.* 800, 21 (ὁσίως), *Or.* 323, 5 (ἀμέμπτως). In case of indecent conduct, the rules of the mysteries of Andania provide for punishments, in 92 BC, τὸν δὲ ἀπειθοῦντα ἢ ἀπρεπῶς ἀναστρεφόμενον εἰς τὸ θεῖον μαστιγούντω οἱ ἱεροί (*LSCG*, n. 65, 40 and 43); cf. *SB* 8852, 9: μὴ ὀρθῶς ἀναστρεφομένους.

ἀνατρέφω

anatrephō, to nurture, raise

→*see also* τρέφω, ἀνατρέφω

This verb, which means "nurture" a child so that it will grow, then "raise" it, is only used once in the OT, with respect to Solomon: "I was nurtured, surrounded with swaddling clothes and with care" (Wis 7:4). In the NT, it is perhaps used concerning Jesus, who "came to Nazareth, where he had been raised";[1] it is clearly used concerning Moses, "nurtured for three months in the house of his father,"[2] and St. Paul, who received his rabbinic education at Jerusalem.[3] Because of this range of uses, *anatrephō* encompasses the entire life of the child until his maturity, including feeding and physical care,[4] the formation of the mind and character;[5] in which case it is synonymous with *paideuō*.[6]

[1] Luke 4:16—οὗ ἦν ἀνατεθραμμένος (S, W, Θ, several miniscules); but the other authorities (including B, A) have τεθραμμένος, which has been adopted by all editors. H. Schürmann (*Das Lukasevangelium*, Freiburg-Basel, 1969, vol. 1, p. 226) translates well: *wo er aufgewachsen war*.

[2] Acts 7:20. Cf. *Moses* 1.11: "We nursed him for three full months" (ἀνεθρέψαμεν), but the verb τρέφειν in used for his nurture and education (1.5, 17; cf. τροφή, 8, 15, 20). Josephus, *Ant.* 2.232: Thermuthis carried the baby Moses to his father to raise him, ἀναθρεψαμένη παῖδα; education (ἀνατροφή) was regarded with suspicion by the Egyptians (2.237); cf. in the sense of "nurture" (7.149) and educate (4.261).

[3] Acts 22:3—"I was raised (ἀνατεθραμμένος) in this city." For the discussion of this verse and this verb, cf. W. C. van Unnik, *Tarsus or Jerusalem*, London, 1962, pp. 9ff.

[4] *P.Lips.* 28, 12: πρὸς τὸ δύνασθαι ἀνατρέφεσθαι εὐγενῶς καὶ γνησίως (an act of adoption, AD 381); *P.Cair.Zen.* 59379, 1–2; *P.Oxy.* 1873, 9: θυγάτριον νήπιον εὐγενῶς ἀνατεθραμμένον; 2479, 47: "That I might return to the same farm and raise my unhappy children." Hence the medical definition, cf. the numerous references to Hippocrates and Galen given by W. K. Hobart, *Medical Language*, p. 207.

[5] 4 Macc 10:2—"In the same doctrines that we were raised in"; 11:15.

[6] According to Porphyry, Ammonius was "raised by his parents in the Christian doctrines" (ἀνατραφείς), while "Origen, on the other hand, was raised in Greek studies" (παιδευθείς) cited by Eusebius, *Hist. Eccl.* 6.19.7.

anatrephō, S 397; *EDNT* 1.94; MM 39; L&N 33.232, 35.51; BAGD 62

We must note, however, that *anatrephō* designates by preference the education received at home, almost always in relation with family members—natural or adoptive—that is, with brothers and sisters.[7] Specifically, L. Robert, in his epigraphical studies, has noted that "the verb *anatrephesthai* denotes education by the foster father, and is an important term for anyone interested in studying family relations and, for example, the status of the *threptoi*."[8] He cites the tomb of Kladaios at Aphrodisias where *Aurēlia Glyptē hē anathrepsamenē auton* ("who raised him") is also buried (*MAMA*, vol. 8, 560, 4), or in Caria the tomb of a certain Zeno, buried together with *M. Aur. Eutychos ho anathrepsamenos auton*.[9] Soterichos gives some vines, etc., to a certain Lucius, his pupil (*Loukiō hō anethrepsamēn*).[10]

---

[7] Epictetus, 2.22.26: "Do not investigate . . . whether these people have the same parents, whether they were raised together (καὶ ὁμοῦ ἀνατεθραμμένοι) and by the same tutor"; 3.1.35: "That is the type of young people that we should hope to see born and raised in our homes" (ἡμῖν φύεσθαι καὶ ἀνατρέφεσθαι); 3.22.68: "his children shall be raised in the same manner." Heliodorus, *Aeth*. 10.14.1: "I am the one who took in the exposed infant and secretly raised him."

[8] L. Robert, *Hellenica*, vol. 13, Paris, 1965, p. 222; cf. *Hellenica*, vol. 3, p. 11: ἀνεθρέψατο υἱοὺς δύο (inscription at Heraclea).

[9] *IGLAM*, n. 1641 a.

[10] L. Robert, *Villes d'Asie Mineure*, p. 345. Other inscriptions in "Bulletin épigraphique" in *REG*, 1948, p. 202, n. 229; 1959, p. 254, n. 447: ὕπατον τὰ οἰκετικὰ παιδία [= θρεπτοί] τὰ ὑπ' αὐτοῦ ἀνατρεφόμενα.

ἀναφέρω

anapherō, to cause to ascend, offer up, remove

In the classical language, this verb means "to carry up" or "back" (*Ep. Arist.* 268; Josephus, *War* 4.404; *Ant.* 1.16; *Ag. Apion* 2.162). In biblical Greek, it is used for everything that ascends, physically or metaphorically, from the flower of the vine (Gen 40:10), incense (Exod 30:9), or smoke (Judg 20:38), to anger (1 Macc 2:24) and hymns (2 Macc 10:7). Hence: to ascend or to carry from one place to another.[1] Thus before the transfiguration Jesus made Peter, James, and John ascend a high mountain (Matt 17:1; Mark 9:2); and after the resurrection he himself "ascended into the sky."[2]

A good many OT meanings are unknown in the NT: "raise a levy" (1 Kgs 5:27), "to dress up a garment with jewelry" (2 Sam 1:24), "to bring something,"[3] "present" a matter to Moses (Deut 1:17) or to God.[4] But in

---

[1] Deut 14:24; Judg 15:13; 16:3; 20:26; 1 Sam 2:19; 1 Kgs 8:1; 10:22; 17:19; 2 Kgs 4:21; 1 Chr 15:3, 12; 2 Chr 1:4; 4:2, 5; Neh 12:31; Tob 6:3; 2 Macc 6:10. *P.Lille* 7, 17: "Now he has transferred me to the prison of Crocodilopolis"; *BGU* 1500, 15: 1511, 5; *SB* 9080, 6; Philo, *Etern. World* 64: "The fragrant breezes carried their perfumes to the flowers." Josephus, *War* 5.432: the starved "snatched the morsels of food almost from their throats."

[2] Luke 24:51. Cf. V. Larrañaga, *L'Ascension de Notre-Seigneur*, Rome-Paris, 1938, pp. 145ff., 368ff., 417ff.; P. Benoit, *Exégèse et théologie*, pp. 363–411 = ET, vol. 1, pp. 209–253; cf. *Gos. Pet.* 56: "He has left for the place from which he was sent"; Plutarch, *Num.* 2.4: "Proclus . . . swore that he had seen Romulus ascend to heaven, εἰς οὐρανὸν ἀναφερόμενον."

[3] 1 Sam 18:27; 2 Sam 21:13; Neh 10:38; Isa 18:7; Sir 8:19. *P.Ant.* 93, 41: "That I might bring it with me when I come"; *P.Mich.* VIII, 511, 19; *SB* 7376, 28 (11 October AD 3); 9188; *P.Sorb.* 18, 7.

[4] Exod 18:19, 22; 19, 8. Ἀναφέρω in the sense of "bring to the attention of, inform, communicate" is very frequent in Josephus, whether concerning a desire (*Ag. Apion* 1.232), an utterance (*Ant.* 16.10, 218, 223, 225, 306–307; 17.40; 20.40; cf. *LSCG*, n. 85, 10), or a decree (*dogma, Ant.* 14.198, 221; *LSCG*, n. 73 A 24); and in the papyri: the

---

anapherō, S 399; *TDNT* 9.60–61; *EDNT* 1.94; MM 39; L&N 15.176, 15.206, 53.17; BAGD 63

both testaments,[5] *ascend* or *cause to ascend* has above all a sacrificial usage and figures in the cultic vocabulary. The priests carry and transport the victim, raise it to place it on the altar, and offer it as a sacrifice (1 Macc 4:53). In this sense, the high priest of the new covenant offered himself once to take away the sins of the many (Heb 9:28) and has no need to offer himself anew (Heb 7:27). Abraham offered his son Isaac on the altar (Jas 2:21), and Christians, "a holy company of priests," offer spiritual sacrifices (1 Pet 2:5), their continual praise, to God (Heb 13:15); *anapherō* is in this sense synonymous with *prospherō*,[6] meaning "to offer."

There remains 1 Pet 2:24—"He bore our sins in his body on the cross,"[7] where most commentators see a reference to the LXX of Isa 53:12 and

---

production of a contract *P.Rein.* 8, 8; 26, 15; 31, 9); "communicate this writing to our lord the duke, for it is for him to pass judgment on such attacks" (*P.Thead.* 22, 16; 23, 15; *P.Abinn.* 3, 17; 18, 14; 44, 15); "the copy of the petition that I presented to my lord the prefect" (*P.Mert.* 91, 2; cf. 5, 17); hence: make a report, a notification (*P.Ryl.* 163, 13; *P.Sorb.* 63, 3; *C.Ord.Ptol.* 37, 1; *P.Princ.* 119, 24; *P.Oslo* 126, 15; *P.Oxy.* 1380, 17; 2407, 5, 8, 42; *P.Mil.Vogl.* 229, 28; *BGU* 1669; *PSI* 823, 2; 1433, 9), an agreement (*BGU* 2097, 13 from AD 83; *SB* 7404, 46; 7438, 4); to register (a death) on an official list (*P.Lond.* 281, 15; from AD 66); cf. C. Préaux, *Economie royale*, p. 320); and hence to affect (*P.Thead.* 4, 1; Josephus, *Ant.* 12.31), attribute (*P.Mich.* 620, 271, 307, 314; *P.Brem.* 68, 23, 32; 69, 7; *P.Oxy.* 2119, 8; Josephus, *Ant.* 2.285; 6.9; 14.312; 15.6; 16.167; *War* 4.179, 391). Note further: recover one's health (Philostratus, *Gym.* 42), come to, come around (Josephus, *War* 1.234, 658), recover serenity (1.662); recall a memory (5.182; *Ant.* 18.188; Dittenberger, *Syl.* 736, 112).

[5] Ἀναφέρειν most often translates the hiphil of *'ālâh* from its first occurrence in Gen 8:20, where Noah offers up holocausts on the altar, and means offer a sacrifice or an oblation; cf. Gen 22:2, 13; Exod 24:5; Lev 14:20; Num 23:30; Deut 12:13; 27:6; Judg 13:16, 19; 21:4; 1 Sam 6:14; 7:9–10;2 Sam 24:25; 1 Kgs 10:5; 2 Chr 1:6; 14:14; Isa 57:6; 60:7; 56:3; Ps 66:15; Bar 1:10 (S. Daniel, *Recherches sur le vocabulaire du culte dans la Septante*, Paris, 1966, pp. 240–255). This sense retained by Josephus, *Ant.* 7.86; 8.104; 11.76, 124; likewise in the second century AD, in a ruling relative to the cult of Sarapis in Magnesia (*LSAM*, n. 34, 26).

[6] Cf. John 16:2; Heb 11:17; C. Spicq, *Hébreux*, vol. 1, p. 303; *LSAM*, p. 100. On the "offering of the lips" (unknown in the OT, but cf. "the fruit of the lips," Hos 14:3), cf. 1QS 9.3–5; A. Jaubert, *La notion d'alliance dans le Judaïsme*, Paris, 1963, pp. 168ff. B. Gärtner, *The Temple and the Community in Qumran and the New Testament*, Cambridge, 1965, pp. 86ff.; H. J. Hermisson, *Sprache und Ritus im altisraelitischen Kult: Zur "Spiritualisierung" der Kultbegriffe im A.T.*, Neukirchen, 1965; I. Lévy, *Recherches esséniennes et pythagoriciennes*, Geneva-Paris, 1965, pp. 19ff.; R. Deichgräber, *Gotteshymnus und Christus-Hymnus in der frühen Christenheit*, Göttingen, 1967, pp. 117ff.; G. Klinzing, *Die Umdeutung des Kultus in der Qumrangemeinde und im N.T.*, Göttingen, 1971, pp. 93ff., 158, 218ff.

[7] H. Patsch, "Zum alttestamentlichen Hintergrund von Römer IV, 25 und I Petrus II, 24," in *ZNW*, 1969, pp. 273–278; C.F.D. Moule "Death 'to Sin,' 'to Law,' and 'to the World': A Note on Certain Datives," in *Mélanges Rigaux*, pp. 367–375.

understand 1 Pet in the same sense: bear sins = undergo punishment for sins. But A. Deissmann objects that quotations do not often have the same sense in their new context as in the original,[8] and that to undergo punishment on the cross would have been expressed by *epi tō xylō* (the dative case), while the accusative in 1 Pet, *epi to xylon*, evokes the idea of removal. He cites P.Petr. I, 16, 2 (vol. 1, p. 47) from 230 BC, in which the litigant protests against the debts that have been transferred upon him[9] and submits his case to Asclepiades. It is true that, in the papyri and the inscriptions, *anapherō* often signifies "transfer, pay money"[10] and that one can here get some idea of substitution. But Moulton-Milligan (on this word) rightly observe that nothing turns our thoughts in this direction in 1 Pet 2:24, where the accusative that follows *epi* is a person, which weakens considerably the parallel cited by A. Deissmann.

---

[8]A. Deissmann, *Bible Studies*, pp. 88ff.

[9]Ὀφειλήματα ἀναφερόμενα (cf. P.Hib. 212, 2). It would be better to cite the complaint of a vintner of the third century BC: The agents of the bank "enter to my credit the payment of the tax by writing it in for the thirty-seventh year; while I owe nothing, but I paid everything in full" (ἀναφέρουσίν μοι τὴν καταβολὴν τοῦ τέλους, *PSI* 383, 9–10). To transfer the debts of a debtor to a third party is to free the original debtor from paying off the debt (cf. 1 Sam 20:13; Aeschines 3.215; Isocrates 5.32). Hence the forensic meaning: the sins are no longer imputed to the person. A. Deissmann cites Col 2:14, where the "handwriting" (= bond) is annulled on the cross (*Light*, pp. 332f.).

[10] P.Kar.Goodsp. 554, 43; P.Yale 49, 14; P.Mich. 601, 21; P.Petr. II, 38 (b) 5: ὅπως ἀνενέγκωμεν ἐπὶ Θεογένην = that we may transfer this to Theogenes; *SB* 10444, 1, 3, 4, 9; Josephus, *Ant.* 4.71: the owners must pay to the priests a shekel and a half; *War* 1.605; pay off a tax (*SEG*, vol. 3, 378 C 1; Dittenberger, *Syl.* 204, 42; 736, 94). The legal equivalent of ἀναφέρειν is *referre*, cf. H. J. Mason, *Greek Terms*, p. 21.

ἀναψύχω

anapsychō, **to refresh**

St. Peter exhorts the Jerusalemites to be converted "so that the times of refreshing [or relief] may come."[1] These times are linked with the Parousia and coincide with the *apokatastasis:* the perfect restoring, the complete restoration of the creation. St. Paul for his part, while a prisoner at Rome, declares that Onesiphorus has often comforted him or relieved him by his visits (2 Tim 1:16).

The verb *anapsychō*, which suggests the idea of refreshing[2] and thus of invigorating, is used first for physical health,[3] then for spiritual fortifi-

---

[1] Acts 3:20—καιροὶ ἀναψύξεως (cf. O. Bauernfeind, "Tradition und Komposition in dem Apokatastasisspruch Apostelgeschichte," in *Abraham unser Vater: Festschrift O. Michel*, Leiden, 1963, pp. 13–23). Ψύχειν, in the compound form ἀναψύχειν, is more closely related to the idea of wind (ψυχή) than that of cold (ψῦχος); thus in Homer (exposing a wound to the air by taking off a bandage, *Il.* 5.795; hence ἀναψύχεσθαι, get one's breath back, 10.575; 13.84) and in the medical writers: leave a wound open to the air (Hippocrates, *Fract.* chapters 25 and 27); then "get one's wind back (between two painful operations)," "catch one's breath" (Hippocrates, *Steril.* chapter 222; cf. J. Jounna, *Hippocrate: La Nature de l'homme*, Berlin, 1975, pp. 304ff.). Ἀνάψυξις (OT hapax; Exod 8:15 [= 8:11 MT]—Pharaoh saw that there was a respite, r^ewāḥâh) suggests recreation and relaxation (Philo, *Abraham* 152), frequently used by physicians (cf. the numerous references to Hippocrates and Galen in W. K. Hobart, *Medical Language*, p. 166), is not attested in the papyri (*P.Ness.* 96, 5) and the tomb inscriptions except in a very late period and in Christian prayers asking God to place the deceased in repose (*anapausis*) and ἐν τόπῳ ἀναψύξεως = a place of refreshing; cf. *SB* 6035, 10; 7428, 11; 7429, 7; 7430, 8; 8235, 9; 8723, 10; 8728, 10; 8765, 10.

[2] Josephus, *Ant.* 15.54: ἀνέψυχον τὸ θερμότατον τῆς μεσημβρίας; *War* 2.155: a gentle west wind, blowing from the ocean, continually refreshes the place to which just souls have traveled; 2 Macc 4:46: Ptolemy leads King Antiochus IV under the peristyle "as if to take a breath of cool air, ὡς ἀναψύξοντα"; *Jos. Asen.* 3.3: "It is noon . . . great is the heat of the sun, and I shall take a breath of cool air beneath your roof"; cf. Luke 16:24—Let Lazarus "dip the end of his finger in the water and refresh my tongue (καταψύξῃ)."

[3] The sabbath rest allows the son of the servant and the guest to catch their breath (Exod 23:12, niphal of *nāpaš*). When Samson has taken a drink of water, "his spirit returned, and he revived" (Judg 15:18, *ḥāyâh*). When they arrived at the stopping place, the king and the people caught their breath (2 Sam 16:14; niphal of *nāpaš*).

---

anapsychō, S 404; *TDNT* 9.663–664; *EDNT* 1.95; *NIDNTT* 3.686; MM 40; L&N 25.149; BAGD 63

ἀναψύχω, anapsychō 121

cation, the relieving of anxiety,[4] then of well-being experienced after pain or exertion. This is the meaning of this verb that is found among the papyri only in private letters. In the second century AD, a child writes to his parents: "when I found out, I was delivered from my uneasiness" (*P.Osl.* 153, 10). Another, in the third century, assures his parents of his academic progress: "I worked very hard and am relaxing."[5] But the best parallel to 2 Tim 1:16, cited in a Christian letter from the time of Constantine (*SB* 7872, 12), is in the double appeal made to Hephaistios, who is cloistered in the Serapeum of Memphis (*en katochē en tō Sarapoeiō*) on the one hand from his wife Isias, presently very distressed and incapable of being comforted except by the return of her husband to the house,[6] and on the other hand from Dionysius, brother of Hephaistios, who writes to him along the same lines.[7] This calming or relieving can blossom into joy.[8] It is in any case rest,[9] relaxation,[10] in which the soul expands (cf. *platynō*; 2 Cor 6:11; 4QPs 8.14), is not constrained;[11] it is like an enlarging,[12] which—thanks to the brotherly love shown by Onesiphorus—presents a fine contrast with the apostle's incarceration.

---

[4] When David plays the harp, Saul finds relief and gets better (1 Sam 16:23, *rāwaḥ*; cf. Ps 39:14). A respite in the war allows the people to catch their breath (2 Macc 13:11). Cf. the episode that "revived the courage of the allies of the Lacedaemonians" (Xenophon, *Hell.* 1.19).

[5] *P.Oxy.* 1296, 7: φιλιπονοῦμεν καὶ ἀναψύχομεν (republished by A. S. Hunt, C. C. Edgar, *Sel.Pap.*, vol. 1, n. 137).

[6] *P.Lond.* 42, 18: δοκοῦσα νῦγ γε σοῦ παραγενομένου τεύξεσθαί τινος ἀναψυχῆς (second century), republished in *UPZ* 59 and by A. S. Hunt, C. C. Edgar, *Sel.Pap.*, n. 97.

[7] S. Witkowski, *Epistulae Privatae Graecae* 36, 14–15: ἔτι δὲ καὶ τοιούτους καιροὺς ἀνηντληκυῖα νῦγ γε τύχη τινὸς ἀναψυχῆς; republished in *UPZ* 60.

[8] *P.Yale* 80, 3: ὥστε τότε ἱλαροὺς εἶναι κἀγὼ ἀναψύχω (second century). Ἀνάψυξις brought to Paul by Mark and Jesus Justus during his first captivity (Col 4:11) is thus more "reinvigorating" than the "calming" (*parēgoria*) brought to Paul by Mark and Jesus Justus during his first captivity (Col 4:11).

[9] Cf. κατάπαυσις, Acts 7:49; Heb 3:11, 18; 4:1, 3, 5, 10, 11 (O. Hofius, *Katapausis: Die Vorstellung vom endzeitlichen Ruheort im Hebräerbrief,* Tübingen, 1970).

[10] Cf. ἄνεσις, Acts 24:23; 2 Cor 2:13; 7:5; 8:13; 2 Thess 1:7; Philo *Plant.* 170; *To Gaius* 12 (with the note of the editor, A. Pelletier, Paris, 1972, p. 323); Strabo, 5.4.7; C. Spicq, *Théologie morale,* vol. 1, pp. 301, n. 1; 338, n. 1.

[11] The Hebrew *rāwaḥ* means "to have room, be unconstrained." In the NT, ease, the feeling of well-being and of breathing easily, as it were, is characteristic of the "pneumatic," cf. C. Spicq, *Théologie morale,* vol. 2, p. 772; J.F.A. Sawyer, "Spaciousness," in *ASTI,* vol. 6, Leiden, 1968, pp. 20–34; R. R. Niebuhr, "The Widened Heart," in *HTR,* 1969, pp. 127–154; M. Philonenko, "L'Ame à l'étroit," in *Hommages A. Dupont-Sommer,* Paris, 1971, pp. 421–428.

[12] [French: to enlarge (*dilater*) the heart or the soul means to fill it with joy. —Tr.]

> ἀνθ' ὧν
>
> *anth' hōn (anti + hōn)*, **in place of, in exchange**

In the papyri, this expression,[1] used very often in business documents, means above all "in place of,"[2] "in return, in exchange, in compensation." For example, the farmer Idomeneus complains to King Ptolemy that his field, already sown, was flooded by Petobastis and Horos. He asks that he be indemnified, that the guilty parties "be forced to buy back my land at their own expense and pay the fees arising from the transaction, and that I be given in place of the one that they flooded (*anth' hōn*) a spread equal to the land that they themselves cultivate."[3] The substitute (*BGU* 2128, 4) is the equivalent; in contracts for work[4] and in transfers of land, the boss or the seller certifies that he has received such and such a sum of money from the buyer, or that he has undertaken certain obligations "in return" for the labor of the worker.[5] There is an exact correspondence between the work and the salary (cf. *SB* 10526, 8).

---

[1] Cf. F. M. Abel, *Grammaire*, 35e, 46j, k. E. Mayser, *Grammatik*, vol. 2, pp. 374ff.; vol. 2, 3, pp. 101ff.

[2] Cf. the successor to an obligation (*P.Cair.Isid.* 125, 18); the substitute (*P.Lond.* 1913, 8; *P.Petaus* 14, 10; *P.Oxy.* 3095, 12); the representative (*P.Mur.* 116, 11; *P.Brux.* 21, 34). But Ἑρμίας ἀνθ' οὗ Ἑρμῆς (*BGU* 1062, 1; cf. *P.Lond.* 1170, 727) is only the statement of a surname.

[3] *P.Enteux.* 60, 10; cf. *P.Oslo* 40, 37, *P.Ant.* 89, 12; *Pap.Lugd.Bat.* XIII, 11, 18; *P.Mich.* 605, 5. In records of disbursements, cf. *P.Oxy.* 1914, 2; 2029, 15; *P.Tebt.* 120, 43.

[4] *P.Mich.* 355, 4 (first century AD; the hiring of a weaver); *P.Lond.* 1994, 222 (third century BC); 2002, 39; *BGU* 2175, 4: δέξασθαι τὸ ἄλλο ἥμισο. μέρος ἀνθ' ὧν ποιούμεθα καμάτων; *P.Stras.* 286, 10.

[5] *P.Mich.* 427, 15 (second century AD): sale of land and of part of a house by a veteran who acknowledges having received two hundred drachmas in exchange; 564, 11; 609, 17; *PSI* 1050, 2, (third century); *BGU* 1731, 8 (first century BC); 1732, 8; 1733.

---

anth' hōn, S 475, 3739; *TDNT* 1.372; BDF §§17, 208(1), 294(4); MM 46, 47; *EDNT* 108, 109; BAGD 73, 74

Making compensation is the very basis of exchange, as Philo observes: "Those who give (*hoi didontes*) wish to receive honor in exchange, seeking a recompense in return for their favor (*antidosin*), and under the guise of flattering with a gift (*dōreas*), they in fact execute a sale; those who are in the habit of accepting something in exchange for (*anth' hōn*) that which they supply are in fact sellers."[6] From this developed a logical sense for *anth' hōn*—"because, consequently"[7]—and a moral sense, emphasizing exact repayment.[8] This double nuance is preponderant in the biblical texts.

Often enough, the expression *anth' hōn* is used in a legal sense, "in compensation." A young girl who has been violated must become the wife of her seducer, "since he has violated her, and he cannot repudiate her as long as he lives" (Deut 22:29); "Joab and his brother Abishai killed Abner,

---

10; 1734, 8; 1739, 13; 2346, 4; *P.Ryl.* 159, 19 (AD 31): ἀνθ' ὧν ἔλαβε παρὰ τῆς Ταχόιτος. *P.Coll.Youtie* II, n. 80, 15 (= *P.Oxy.* 3255); 89, 17: "in recompense for the pains that I took"; 90, 19. Cf. Atticus, frag. 6.2: "if the corps do not receive any compensation for their losses."

[6] Philo, *Cherub.* 122, cf. *Spec. Laws* 3.82; *Migr. Abr.* 173. E. Benveniste ("Don et échange dans le vocabulaire indo-européen," in *L'Année sociologique*, 3d series, 1948–49; 1951, pp. 7–20) noticed this functional relationship between gift and exchange: the spontaneity and unwarranted nature of the gift (δῶρον, present) oblige the beneficiary to make a compensatory counter-gift (*antidōron;* δώρων χάριν), a gift in exchange (δωτίνη; Homer, *Il.* 9.155, 297; *Od.* 9.267; 11. 351; Herodotus 6.62; cf. 1.61.69). 1 Macc 10:27, Demetrius to the Jews: "Continue even now to preserve your fidelity toward us, and we will provide you with benefits in exchange for what you do for us, καὶ ἀνταποδώσομεν ὑμῖν ἀγαθὰ ἀνθ' ὧν ποιεῖτε μεθ' ἡμῶν." *P.Lond.* 1941, 9, letter of Hierocles to Zeno: "Ptolemy hopes to gain you the crown in return for the benefits that you have voluntarily provided for him" (third century BC).

[7] Cf. Luke 12:3—"There is nothing hidden that ought not to be revealed . . . consequently (ἀνθ' ὧν) everything that you hear spoken in darkness will be heard in the light." The gospel must be proclaimed with the maximum degree of publicity *since* all must be revealed on the great day. E. Delebecque (*Evangile de Luc*) translates "Moyennant quoi tout ce que l'on a dit dans les ténèbres sera entendu dans la lumière" ("In return [or consideration] for which all that has been spoken in the darkness will be heard in the light").

[8] The collections that need to cover the expenses of worship (*UPZ* 175ᵃ42; *PSI* 1159, 6; *Pap.Lugd.Bat.* II, 1, 6); a decree in honor of Samos (405 BC): the decree praises the Samian delegates "taking into account their benefits (ἀντὶ ὧν εὖ πεποιήκασιν) with regard to the Athenians" (J. Pouilloux, *Choix*, n. 23, 11); a foundation for distributions of oil (AD 210): "Flaviana Philokrateia, in honor of her husband Julianus Alexandros and herself, in return for numerous honors (ἀνθ' ὧν) issued by the most powerful Council . . . makes a gift (ἐπέδωκεν) of 10,000 Attic drachmas . . ." (*NCIG*, n. 34, 6); 4 Macc 12:12—"Sacrilegious tyrant . . . you were not ashamed to torture those who practice piety. *Because of this*, Divine Justice reserves you for an intense, eternal fire"; 18:3—the seven brothers know that pious reason is master of sufferings; "*that is why* they offer their bodies to suffer for piety."

because he had put their brother to death" (2 Sam 3:30); "He shall pay back the sheep fourfold, since he has committed this deed and has not shown pity."[9] There is a strict reciprocity: "I will do you no more evil, since my life has been precious in your eyes on this day" (1 Sam 26:21). Most frequently, this correspondence occurs in relations between God and humans. Sometimes, when people are faithful God rewards them and blesses them: "In your race (Abraham's) will all the nations of the earth be blessed, because you have obeyed my voice" (Gen 22:18; cf. 26:5); "My covenant will be for Phineas and his descendants after him a covenant of eternal priesthood, because he has shown himself jealous for his God" (Num 25:13); "Since you have asked for yourself discernment for understanding justice, behold, I shall act according to your word; I give you a wise and intelligent heart" (1 Kgs 3:11; 2 Chr 1:11; 2 Kgs 10:30; 22:19; Jdt 13:20; Ezek 36:13; Zech 1:15).

Most of the biblical usages of *anth' hōn* underline the justice of punishments, the exact repayment by God for people's sins; the penalties are at the same time the necessary consequence of and the just payment for the fault: "The land will become desolate . . . they will pay for their sin, since and because (double conjunction in Hebrew) they have despised by judgment" (Lev 26:43); "Because you have not served Yahweh your God with joy and gladness of heart when you had everything in abundance, you will serve in hunger, thirst, nudity, and privation the enemy that God will send against you."[10] It is worth noting that of the five occurrences of *anth' hōn* in the NT, four express a punishment, the sanction for a trespass; the archangel Gabriel punished the unbelief of Zacharias: "You will remain silent . . . since you have not believed my words" (Luke 1:20). Jerusalem will be destroyed, "because you have not known the time or your visitation" (Luke 19:44); Herod Agrippa is struck dead "because he did not give the glory to God" (Acts 12:23). If certain people are given over to perdition, it is "because they have not accepted the love of the truth in order to be saved."[11]

---

[9] 2 Sam 12:6; cf. Amos 5:11; Joel 4:19; Isa 53:12; Ps 109:16—"Since he loved cursing, let it fall upon him!"

[10] Deut 33:47; cf. 62; Judg 2:20; 2 Sam 12:10; 1 Kgs 9:9—"Because they have forsaken Yahweh their God . . . that is why Yahweh has brought upon them all this evil"; 11:20; 20:36; 2 Kgs 21:11, 15; 22:17; 2 Chr 34:25; Hos 8:1; Amos 1:3, 9, 13; 2:1, 6; Mic 3:4; Mal 2:9; Jer 5:14, 19; 7:13; 16:11; 19:4; 22:9; 23:38; Ezek 5:7, 11; 13:8, 10; 15:8; 16:36, 43; 20:16, 24; 21:29; 22:19; 23:35; 25:3, 6; 29:7; 31:10; 39:23. Cf. *Pss. Sol.* 2.3—"Because the sons of Jerusalem have defiled the worship of the Lord . . . for this reason God has said, 'Cast them out from my presence.' "

[11] 2 Thess 2:10 (cf. C. Spicq, *Agapè*, vol. 2, pp. 32–39); cf. Philo, *Spec. Laws* 3.197: "The master shall suffer double punishment for his actions"; 4.227; Josephus, *War*

In contrast, Philo and Josephus use *anth' hōn* most often in a favorable context. Not only do they evoke the equity of the recompense,[12] but they emphasize that gratitude is a gift in return for benefits received.[13] There is an exact correspondence between the action of thanksgiving and the divine favor,[14] for example the celebration of the Passover in grateful tribute for deliverance from servitude in Egypt (Josephus, *Ant.* 11.110).

In Hellenistic piety, as expressed notably in dedications, the Greek is seen giving gifts to his god, whom he knows to be close and powerful and whose protection and benefits he expects in exchange (*anth' hōn*). The *dōron* is a "tribute of friendship" (*Anth. Pal.* 6.325), which counts on winning the favors of the divinity (6.340), because the person who needs protection thinks on the one hand of pleasing the god and on the other hand of receiving a benevolent reciprocity. It is an exchange of friendly services.[15] For example, three brothers dedicate their nets to Pan, and ask "Send to them in return (*anth' hōn*) a good hunt" (Leonidas of Tarentum, in *Anth. Pal.* 6.13; cf. 154). Selene asks Cybele for her daughter that she may grow in beauty and find a husband, a just favor "in return (*anth' hōn*) for the child's having often let her hair hang down in your *pronaos* and before your altar" (ibid., 281); some sailors call upon Phoebus, "Be favorable to us and send us a good wind."[16]

4.264: "As a result (of the crimes of the enemy), the best course of action is to destroy these criminals and punish them."

[12] Philo, *Joseph* 46: "Does he deserve the reward that you advise me to give him? A fine gift (δωρεάς) I would give him, a suitable return for favors received!"; *Moses* 2.242; Josephus, *War* 5.530: "Matthias asked this favor in exchange for his having opened the gates of the city to Simon." Peter of Rosetta: King Ptolemy V has the zeal of a benevolent god, he has built sanctuaries for him and restored their temples, "in recompense for which the gods have given him health, victory, might, and all other good things" (Dittenberger, *Or.* 110.35 = *SB* 8232, 3). "May this come to pass for you in recompense for your holy deeds for the divinity" (*UPZ* 34, 12; second century BC, 35, 25; 36, 21; 46, 13).

[13] Philo, *Virtues* 72: "Give thanks to God for benefits received (εὐχαριστίαν ἀποδιδούς ἀνθ' ὧν) from birth to old age," like Moses, (*Moses* 1.33; Josephus, *Ant.* 4.318).

[14] Josephus, *Ant.* 1.229; 6.338; 17.48, 201.

[15] Δώρων χάριν, *Anth. Pal.* 6.188; cf. ἀντιδιδούς δός, 42, 91, 280; χάριν ἀντιδίδου, 138, 184, 185. A. J. Festugière, "'ΑΝΘ' ὩΝ: La Formule 'En échange de quoi' dans la prière grecque hellénistique," in *RSPT*, 1976, pp. 389–418.

[16] From Philip, *Anth. Pal.* 6.251; cf. 17: in exchange for an offering, Cypris is asked to send profits; 63; 68; 99: may Pan grant that the goatherd's goats will give birth twice; 105: may the fisherman's net always be full; 154; 187; 278; 332; 346.

> ἀντιβάλλω
>
> *antiballō*, **to exchange**

The primitive sense of this verb is "to retaliate, return fire."[1] It is used figuratively in 2 Macc 11:13, in the sense of "reflect upon";[2] this English expression translates well the nuance of the Greek, "a return of the mind upon itself so as to examine and deepen a spontaneous deliverance of consciousness";[3] the subject returns upon itself and after a fashion is refracted. Hence the sense "dispute" or simply "converse with each other," like the pilgrims of Emmaus: "What then are these matters that you were discussing among yourselves along the way?"[4]

Literary and papyrological attestations are rare;[5] not one corroborates the meaning of the two biblical texts.[6] The clearest meaning is the com-

---

[1] The Syracusans, "crushed under stones . . . returned the volley with javelins and arrows" (Plutarch, *Nic.* 25.4); cf. Thucydides 7.25.6: "The Syracusans took aim at them, but they retaliated from their large ship"; Polybius 6.22.4.

[2] "Lysias, who was not lacking in intelligence, reflected on the reverse that he had just suffered" at Beth-zur (cf. 1 Macc 4:35). "Ἀντιβάλλειν is a metaphor drawn from tax-collecting. Lysias confronts the reality that he has just experienced with the advantages that he had been counting on. With these evaporated, he imagines an acceptable outcome, namely peace. The use of this verb with πρὸς ἑαυτόν, *secum reputare* from the old Latin for 'reflect on' is very rare if not unique in literature" (F. M. Abel, *Maccabées*, p. 425).

[3] P. Robert, *Dictionnaire . . . de la langue française*, Paris, 1964, vol. 6, p. 21a.

[4] Luke 24:17. M. J. Lagrange comments: ἀντιβάλλειν is the word used for the collation of manuscripts. Field concludes that this is a latinism, *conferre sermones*. But ἀντιβάλλειν used in the sense of exchanging blows could have come to mean "exchange views" (*Luc*, p. 603).

[5] Moulton-Milligan cite only the substantive ἀντιβλήματα, meaning the small stones inserted to fill in chinks (*P.Oxy.* 498, 16, from the second century; a contract with a stone-cutter). The meaning of the verb in *P.Oxy.* 2177, 27 (third century) can not be precisely determined because the papyrus is badly mutilated.

[6] *P.Mert.* 24, 15 (business letter, around AD 200): καλῶς ποιήσεις ἀντιβαλὼν Σεμπρωνίῳ τὸ λογαρίδιον (verify and settle the account?).

---

antiballō, S 474; EDNT 1.109; MM 47; L&N 33.160; BAGD 74

parison of two exemplars, for example of a copy and its original (Strabo 13.609; 17. 790), as in the annotation to the will of Antonius Silvanus in AD 142: *Antōnis Silbanos ho progegrammenos antebalon tēn prokimenēn mou diathēkēn.*[7]

---

[7] R. Cavenaille, *Corpus Papyrorum Latinorum*, Wiesbaden, 1958, n. 221, 9. "This is probably the only well-preserved original of a will *per aes et libram*" (O. Guéraud, P. Jouguet, "Un Testament latin per aes et libram," in *EPap*, vol. 6, 1940, p. 8). These two authors, after mentioning the glossing of ἀντιβάλλει as διορθοῖ by Hesychius and as "dictate" by Harpocration (ἀντιβλητέντος, ἀντὶ τοῦ ὑπαγαρευθέντος, Δείναρχος ἐν τῇ κατὰ Πυθέου εἰσαγγελίᾳ p. 19), but having difficulty seeing how ἀντιβάλλειν could have taken on this meaning, and the discourse of Deinarchos being lost, they conclude: "Thus we do not dare take a stand on the the exact meaning that should be given this verb here" (loc. cit., p. 20). In addition, *PSI* 1443, 8 (third century); *P.Oxy.* 1479, 4: "I did not receive the documents, but there is a collation—τὰ βυβλία . . . κεῖται ἀντιβεβλημένα"; cf. *BGU* 970, 4. —Cf. Josephus asking, in order to identify the author of the best laws and most just rulings on religion, to compare the laws themselves: τῶν νόμων ἀντιπαραβάλλοντας (*Ag. Apion* 2.163).

> ἀντιδιατίθημι, ἀντικαθίστημι
>
> *antidiatithēmi, antikathistēmi*, **to oppose, resist**

The first of these verbs appears only in the Koine; but, unknown in the papyri, it is attested in good literature.[1] Occurring in the Bible only in 2 Tim 2:25, the present middle participle *tous antidiatithemenous* refers to "those who oppose or resist" the preaching of the gospel.[2]

Antikathistēmi can have the sense of "put in place of, exchange" (Josh 5:7; cf. *P.Cair.Zen.* 59278, 4: *antikatastēsome eis ta nea*), "establish, position

---

[1] Ps.-Longinus, *Subl.* 17.1: to rebel against persuasive speech; Philo, *Spec. Laws* 4.103: it is not appropriate for victims to "repay [their persecutors] in like coinage"; cf. T. Nägeli, *Wortschatz*, pp. 30, 41, 87.

[2] It is synonymous with ἀντιλέγοντες in Titus 1:9, literally the contra-speakers, the protesters, those who "hold out against others" (Luke 10:27, probable reading), like the Jews who oppose what Paul says (Acts 13:34; cf. 28.19, 22). But to declare oneself against Caesar is to set up an opposition (John 19:12), and ἀντιλέγω has a nuance of insubordination (Rom 10:21; Titus 2:9). In its frequent usages in the papyri (*P.Hib.* 205, 32; *P.Tebt.* 734, 8, 13; *C.Ord.Ptol.* 14, 24; *SB* 6263, 23; 6720, 15; etc.), this contesting is often tantamount to refusal: "If he opposes, after having supplied guarantees, let him be doubly condemned" (*P.Sorb.* 10, 3); "if he contests, let him be judged with me after a hearing of all parties" (*P.Enteux.* 14, 8; cf. 25, 15, *P.Abinn.* 42, 10); "If anyone raised an objection on this topic, he should advise me of it" (letter of a governor of Achaea, *I.Cor.* vol. 8, 3, n. 306, 15); "I do not contest the [part that reverts to you]" *P.Phil.* 11, 42, = *Pap.Lugd.Bat.* XIV, p. 116; *P.Mich.Zen.* 66, 10, 32). On this sort of legal challenge, cf. A. Würstle, "Untersuchungen zu Cair. Zén. III, 59355," in *JJP*, vol. 5, 1951, p. 54; cf. C. B. Welles, *Royal Correspondence*, New Haven, 1934, n. 3, 28, 50, 107. Cf. also the ἀντικείμενοι (1 Cor 16:9; Phil 1:28; see below), and the "oppositions (ἀντιθέσεις) of a self-proclaimed gnostic" (1 Tim 6:20), evoking the dialectical methodology of the controversialists (C. Spicq, *Epîtres Pastorales*, p. 113, n. 1). But these have a spirit of contradiction (Titus 3:9—ἔριν καὶ μάχας; C. T. Ernesti, *LTGR*, 2d ed., Hildesheim, 1962, p. 67 gives as quasi-synonymns ἀντίθεσις and ἀντικειμένη), having an appetite for objections and for polemic (λογομαχεῖν, 2 Tim 2:14; λογομαχίας, 1 Tim 6:4; μάχεσθαι, 2 Tim 2:24) and oppose the teaching of the apostles (1 Tim 1:10, ἀντίκειται), the truth (ἀνθίστανται τῇ ἀληθείᾳ, 2 Tim 3:8). Their couterpropositions are contrary to the orthodoxy of the church (2 Tim 2:25; 3:8).

---

antidiatithēmi, S 475; *EDNT* 1.109; MM 47; L&N 39.1; BAGD 74 ‖ *antikathistēmi*, S 478; *EDNT* 1.109; MM 47; L&N 39.18; BAGD 74

opposite" with a nuance of hostility (Mic 2:8) and usually against an adversary in justice (Deut 31:21) or in a plea to higher authorities. This is the constant and frequent meaning in the papyri.[3] In observing that the Christians have not yet "resisted to the point of shedding blood," Heb 12:4 uses a sports metaphor,[4] that of two boxers or pancratists facing each other; their blows were often lethal.[5] There is also a judicial nuance, because the persecuted Christians have not given the supreme testimony, shed blood.[6] This usage of *antikathistēmi*, which agrees well with the language of the period, confirms the culture of the author of Heb as well as his familiarity with the language of the LXX.

Antikeimai, "to be situated facing, confronted" (Josephus, *War* 4.454; 5.70; Strabo 2.5.15), usually[7]—and always in the Bible—has the sense of "be against": the flesh and the spirit are opposed to each other as two irreducible principles (Gal 5:17), as the sinful life on the one hand and the rectitude and integrity of the gospel on the other (1 Tim 1:10). It occurs mostly in the form of the present participle: *ho antikeimenos*, "the opponent, the enemy, the adversary,"[8] sometimes without a complement (1 Cor 16:9;

---

[3] *P.Oxy.* 260, 8 (from AD 59); cf. 97, 9; in the division of a father's estate between two brothers, Lysias and Heliodorus: if anyone contests the will, the first brother will take the opposition and clearly establish the title of the second (*P.Dura* 25, 10 and 31); *BGU* 168, 11, 21; *P.Mil.Vogl.* 98, 26; *P.Ross.Georg.* II, 21, 10; *SB* 7472, 18 (taken up *P.Warr.* 1, 18; cf. P. R. Swarney, *The Ptolemaic and Roman Idios Logos*, Toronto, 1970, p. 99). Boulagoras "having opposed during his embassy the most illustrious friends of Antiochus" (*SEG*, vol. 1, 366, 12).

[4] Μέχρις αἵματος = μέχρι θανάτου (2 Macc 13:14; Phil 2:8; cf. Rev 12:11).

[5] The blood flowed (Homer, *Il.* 23.651ff.; Artemidorus of Daldis 12.11; Theocritus, *Id.* 22.119-133; Apollonius Rhodius, *Argon.* 2.1-98; Pausanias 8.40; Virgil, *Aen.* 5.360ff.). Cf. the epigram of Dorokleidas of Thera: Ἀ νίκα πύκταισι δι' αἵματος. ἀλλ' ἔτι θερμὸν ‖ πνεῦμα φέρων σκληρᾶς παῖς ἀπὸ πυγμαχίας ‖ ἔστα παγκρατίου βαρὺν ἐς πόνον. ἀ μία δ' ἀώς ‖ δὶς Δωροκλείδαν εἶδεν ἀεθλοφόρον (*IG*, vol. 12, 3, 390; cited by L. Robert, *Gladiateurs*, p. 20); cf. R. Lattimore, *Epitaphs*, p. 145.

[6] Cf. Eusebius, *Hist. Eccl.* 8.4.4: In undertaking the purification of the pagan army, Veturius, "the one who was carrying out the operation, did it with moderation and did not go so far as to shed blood—μέχρις αἵματος—except in a few cases."

[7] Dio Cassius 39.8: "Claudius combatted (ἀντέλεγε) them, but Milo stood up to him (ἀντέκειτο)"; *Ep. Arist.* 266: "The goal of eloquence ... is to succeed in persuading the adversary (τὸν ἀντιλέγοντα) . . . without seeming to contradict him (οὐκ ἀντικείμενος)"; 1 Macc 14:7—"No one was found to resist him." This verb is used in astronomy for the opposition of planets (Vettius Valens, cited by O. Neugebauer, H. B. van Hoesen, *Greek Horoscopes*, Philadelphia, 1959, p. 191, under this word). In the vocabulary of geometry, the participle ἀντικείμενος, "opposed," is used notably for the two branches of a hyperbola (C. Mugler, *Terminologie géométrique*, pp. 65–66).

[8] Exod 23:22—"I will be the enemy of your enemies and the adversary of your adversaries" = 2 Macc 10:26; cf. Esth 9:2—οἱ ἀντικείμενοι τοῖς Ἰουδαίοις; 8:11; Isa

Phil 1:28), sometimes with the dative.⁹ The term is common and characteristic in Christian language, applied sometimes to the antichrist, the adversary par excellence, "the one who is opposed and set himself up against all that bears the name of God" (2 Thess 2:4), sometimes to the devil, *ho antidikos*,¹⁰ the one who attacks *kat' exochēn* against the church (Matt 16:18), its ministers (1 Tim 3:6–7), and its faithful.¹¹ His aggression is directed against the most vulnerable, for example young widows (1 Tim 5:14), who go astray by following him.¹²

41:11; 45:16; 66:6. In Job 13:24, the adversary is ὑπεναντίον σου; in 1 Kgs 11:14, Satan. The participle is a traditional term in rhetoric, cf. Archytas of Tarentum, *Antik.* (in H. Thesleff, *The Pythagorean Texts*, Abo, 1965, pp. 14ff.); Aristotle, *Rh.* 1409ᵇ35; 1401ᵃ5; 1410ᵇ29.

⁹ Luke 13:17—"All his adversaries were confounded, οἱ ἀντικείμενοι αὐτῷ"; 21:15. In the only text from the papyri, the complement is in the accusative: Μενέδημον ἀντικείμενον ἡμῖν (3 August 152; S. Witkowski, *Epistulae Privatae Graecae* n. 46, 6; republished in *UPZ* 69, 6).

¹⁰ 1 Pet 5:8; cf. S. V. McCasland, " 'The Black One,' " in *Studies in Honor of H. R. Willoughby*, Chicago, 1961, p. 77.

¹¹ Matt 13:38–39; 1 John 3:8; cf. *1 Clem.* 51.1: "All the sins that we have committed as a result of the snares of the adversary, τοῦ ἀντικειμένου."

¹² 1 Tim 5:15. In *TDNT*, vol. 3, p. 655, n. 3, Büchsel concludes that ὁ ἀντικείμενος (verse 14) is generic and does not refer to Satan, who is not mentioned until verse 15. But it is precisely this latter verse that identifies "the adversary" who has just been referred to in the singular and with the article, and who is in fact the "devil," the author of λοιδορία. Neither does this formulation support the identification of the ἀντικείμενος with some anonymous pagan or Jew of the future.

ἀντλέω, ἄντλημα

antleō, to draw (water), *antlēma*, bucket

The verb *antleō* is derived from the noun *antlos*, "ship's hold,"[1] and literally refers to bilge water that is bailed out.[2] Hence it means "to empty water from the hull" and, by extension, "to draw." Cf. "empty the water that the sea casts on board" (Theognis 673); "you draw straight from the cask" (Theocritus 10.13); "to draw water with a sieve, or what is proverbially called a pierced cask" (Ps.-Aristotle, *Oec.* 1.6.1); "they draw the liquid off with a bascule to which is attached a half of a wineskin instead of a bucket."[3] Hence the figurative sense "to drain, exhaust": a life of woe (Euripides, *Hipp.* 898), destiny (Aeschylus, *PV* 375).

In the papyri, the verb is used sometimes in accounts for the pay of workers who pump water (usually in a vineyard): *antlousan eis ampelon* (*Pap.Lugd.Bat.* XII, 20, 7); "for the pay of two water-drawers";[4] sometimes

---

[1] Homer, *Od.* 12.411: "the storm collapsed all the running gear into the hold"; 15.479: the Sidonian woman "fell into the hull's bilge." Cf. P. Chantraine, *Dictionnaire étymologique*, p. 93.

[2] Cf. ἀντλία, "bilge, water from the hull"; Aristophanes, *Eq.* 434: "watch over the bilge." The bilge is the part of the hull where water collects and is thus a symbol of corruption.

[3] Herodotus 6.119; Euripides, *Hyps.*: ἀνηλώματος Φαύστῳ ἀντλοῦντι μηχανὴν (in *P.Oxy.* 985; cf. 147, 1); Plato, *Tim.* 79 a: in the watered body, food and drink are "drawn as from a fountain to be poured out in the channels of the veins"; Xenophon, *Oec.* 7.40: "people who pour into a bottomless jar" (futile toil); Diogenes Laertius 7.5.168–169: Cleanthes "by night drew water in the gardens"; Josephus, *War* 4.472: "water drawn before sunrise."

[4] Ὑπὲρ μισθοῦ ἐργατῶν β ἀντλούντων, *P.Oxy.* 1732, 12; *P.Mil.Vogl.* 69, 45: ἀντλοῦντες εἰς τὸ νεόφυτον; 64: ἀντλοῦντες ἐργάται; 97; B 6, 45, 64, 74, 88, 93; *P.Lond.* 131, 40; 1177, 66 (vol. 2, p. 183); *P.Tebt.* 120, 142; *BGU* 1732, 6 = *SB* 7420; cf.

---

antleō, S 501; *EDNT* 1.112; MM 49; BAGD 76 ‖ *antlēma*, S 502; *EDNT* 1.112; MM 49; BAGD 76 it is used for the hydraulic irrigation machine: "so that the machine may draw" (hopōs antlēsē hē mēchanē, SB 9654, b 9); a machine for drawing water for a vineyard.[5]

In the LXX, water is drawn from a well (Gen 24:13, 20, 43; Hebrew šā'ab; Exod 2:16, 19: Hebrew dālâh), and Abraham's servant asks Rebekah, "Please give me a little water from your jar";[6] but in a figurative sense: "You shall draw water with joy from the springs of salvation" (Isa 12:3).

The substantive antlēma, which is much rarer,[7] is still represented by only three attestations in the papyri. In a petition (from the first century AD) to a police chief regarding the "irrigating machine" (epantlion, line 21) of a vineyard at Theogonis, irrigation became impossible "with the water-drawing machine."[8] In the second century AD, in an account of workers and pay, each worker receives a drachma a day: "two workers building the waterwheel, two drachmas."[9] In the fifth century, in a contract for a bath

---

9379, col. II, 15; 9699, 25 (accounts from AD 78/79). Cf. the scribal error ἀτλητός for ἀντλητός in a papyrus from Medinet Madi (W. Clarysse, "ΑΤΛΗΤΟΣ, Athlete or Irrigation?" in ZPE, vol. 27, 1977, p. 192).

[5] Μηχανὴν τοῦ καινοῦ καλουμένην ἀντλοῦσαν εἰς ἄμπελον, P.Mil. 64, 6 (= SB 9503); P.Mil.Vogl. 308, 99: ἀντληθείσης τῆς μηχανῆς (cf. 5, 30, 35, 61, 94); P.Oxy. 2244, 82 and 85; 2779, 11; SB 11231, 5.

[6] Ὕδωρ ἐκ τῆς ὑδρίας σου (Gen 24:17). Philo only uses the verb twice commenting on Scripture; both uses are figurative. On Gen 24:20, Rebekah empties the contents of her jar (τὴν ὑδρίαν) in the trough, which means that "all that she knew had been poured out by virtue in the container that is the mind of the disciple" (Post. Cain 151). On Exod 2:16, the perceptions of the intellect "in a way draw sensible external data until they fill the soul's reservoirs" (Change of Names 111).

[7] Plutarch, De sol. an. 974 e: a kind of bucket for drawing water; this is in connection with the cattle of Susa, which could count: εἰσὶ γὰρ αὐτόθι τὸν βασιλικὸν παράδεισον ἄρδουσαι περιάκτοις ἀντλήμασιν, ὧν ὥρισται τὸ πλῆθος. ἕκαστον γὰρ ἑκάστη βοῦς ἀναφέρει καθ' ἡμέραν ἑκάστην ἀντλήματα; Dioscorides 4.64, water poured on a wound.

[8] Διακωλύων ἐπαντλεῖν εἰς τὸν ἀμπελῶνα δι' οὗ συνεχώρει ἀντλήματος, line 10; J. R. Rea, "Petition to a Chief of Police," in Scritti in onore di O. Montevecchi, Bologna, 1981, pp. 317–321. J. R. Rea cites a scholium on Aristophanes, Ran. 1332, which seems to refer to a container of constant size, all the more so since a version of the story in Aelian, NA 7.1 speaks of a hundred jars. The scholiast on Aristophanes mentions the ropes (σχοινίον) of the ἀντλήματα. Finally, J. R. Rea concludes that antlēma is a generic term for "the machine for drawing water," especially the simplest machines such as a beam on a pivot or the winch from which a bucket is dropped into a well. Finally, the word is used for the container itself.

[9] Οἰκοδομῆς ἀντλήματος ἐργάται β δρ., BGU 2354, 2; cf. line 4: ἀντλοῦντες; line 10: for pumping: ἀντλήσεως καινοῦ μὲν τόπου; cf. workers on the spillways, ἀνοικοδομοῦντες ἀντλητήρια ἐργάται (P.Mil.Vogl. 305, 14).

house, the text is less certain: *to on en [tō] [ant]lēmati tou autou loutrou mēchanostasion.*

This group of texts, in addition to the immediate context, leaves no room for doubt regarding the meaning of the biblical hapax *antlēma* in John 4:11, where the Samaritan woman says to Jesus, *oute antlēma echeis*, which has to mean, "Lord, you do not have a container for drawing water"; but since *antlēma* "actually serves as a name for an instrument" (P. Chantraine, *Dictionnaire étymologique*), the correct English would be "You have nothing to draw water with," no vessel of any sort, no rope, etc., and the well is deep.

ἀνυπόκριτος, γνήσιος

anypokritos, **upright, unfeigned, authentic;** *gnēsios*, **authentic, dear, legitimate**

→*see also* ὑποκρίνομαι, ὑπόκρισις, ὑποκριτής, ἀνυπόκριτος

Because it is unknown in the papyri and in the secular language prior to its NT occurrences,[1] *anypokritos* can be said to be a specifically biblical word. If it is used only twice in the OT, in the sense of "upright, straightforward" (Wis 5:18; 18:16), it is found six times in the epistolary corpus of the NT, qualifying wisdom (Jas 3:17), faith (1 Tim 1:5; 2 Tim 1:5), and brotherly love (Rom 12:9; 2 Cor 6:6; 1 Pet 1:22).

In accord with its etymology[2] and with the synonyms offered by Hesychius—*adolos, aprosōpolēptos*—it is usually translated "without hypocrisy," that is, without sham or dissimulation. It is indeed true that this sense of sincerity or rectitude is implied in all these occurrences, especially in Jas 3:17, where wisdom is first of all qualified by pure (*hagnē*) and finally by *adiakritos* (without partiality) and *anypokritos*, which forms an *inclusio* and expresses a purity without mixture, an absolute sincerity. But this text contrasts the wisdom that comes from above with wisdom that is terrestrial, animal, diabolical (verse 15), and the eight characteristics listed are intended to define the true *sophia* in terms of its essential components so that it can

---

[1] Cf. T. Nägeli, *Wortschatz*, pp. 43, 70, 79, 85.

[2] Ὑποκριτής refers to the Greek actor, the comic player (A. Lesky, "Hypokrites," in *Studi in onore U. E. Paoli*, Florence, 1956, pp. 469–476; H. Koller, "Hypokrisis und Hypokrites," in *MusHelv*, 1957, pp. 100–107; cf. P. Joüon, "ὙΠΟΚΡΙΤΗΣ dans l'Evangile et l'hébreu hanéf," in *RSR*, 1930, pp. 312–316); hence Hippocrates: "Comedians and deceivers—ὑποκριταὶ καὶ ἐξαπάται—say, in front of people who know them, certain things and have other things in mind; they go out the same and come back not the same" (*Acut.* 1.24). The first meaning of ἀνυπόκριτος is thus "not good at acting on stage" (cf. Ps.-Demetrius Phalereus, *Eloc.* 194), then "without dissimulation" (Iamblichus, *VP* 31.188). Cf. the adverb ἀνυποκρίτως: "One must be an honest person . . . without pretense" (Marcus Aurelius 8.5).

---

anypokritos, S 505; *TDNT* 8.570–571; *EDNT* 1.112; MM 50; L&N 73.8; BAGD 76 ‖
gnēsios, S 1103; *TDNT* 1.727; *EDNT* 1.255; MM 128–129; L&N 73.1; BAGD 162–163

be distinguished from counterfeits. Similarly the "unfeigned faith" of 1 Tim 1:5 and 2 Tim 1:5 evokes the *pistis* whose exterior profession in words and deeds translates the allegiance of the heart and the convictions of the spirit;[3] a "sincere" faith is faith that includes intellectual orthodoxy, pious conduct, faithfulness, and loyalty in keeping obligations. But this "truth" then amounts to conformity with the very nature of the virtue, and *anypokritos* must be translated "authentic."

This emerges more clearly with the expression *agapē* (*philadelphia*) *anypokritos*, which is probably a "love without hypocrisy," such that the manifestations of affection match the sincerity of the attachment: one does not play-act in brotherly relationships.[4] But this meaning does not account for Rom 12:9, where this independent noun phrase governs the whole section on charity (verses 9–21) and serves as a kind of chapter title.[5] St. Paul lists the specific characteristics of *agapē*, which is neither *erōs*, nor *philia*, nor *philostorgia*, although it takes on their values; it is a completely original, godly love, revealed by Jesus Christ, poured out in the heart by the Holy Spirit, a love of nobility and beauty whose first mark is a horror of evil. In other words, *agapē anypokritos* is specifically Christian love, characteristic of the baptized.[6] It is also the mark of the true apostle; St. Paul recommends himself as a minister of God *en agapēi anypokritōi* (2 Cor 6:6), not by a show of affection but by the authentic charity which is divine in origin and has all of the traits that can be pondered in the example in Jesus Christ. It is like a certificate of origin that proves that Paul is truly

---

[3] Cf. Rom 10:10. Pelagius commented, "Fides enim ficta est quae solo ore promittitur et actu negatur" ("For that faith is a fiction that is only promised with the mouth and denied in practice.")

[4] Cf. 1 John 3:18—ἀγαπᾶν ἐν ἀληθείᾳ; Heliodorus, *Aeth.* 1.2.9: a sincere love (ἔρως ἀκραιφής); Marcus Aurelius 6.39: τούτους (ἀνθρώπους) φίλει, ἀλλ' ἀληθινῶς"; Dio Cassius 53.17: "as we begin to love one another, without mental reservation (ἀνυπόπτως)." C. Spicq, *Théologie morale*, vol. 1, p. 291.

[5] P. F. Regard, *La Phrase nominale dans la langue du Nouveau Testament*, Paris, 1919, pp. 61–62, 210–211. C. Spicq, *Agapè*, pp. 141ff. C.E.B. Cranfield, *A Commentary on Romans 12–13*, Edinburgh, 1965, pp. 38ff.; C. H. Talbert, "Tradition and Redaction in Romans XII, 9–21," in *NTS*, vol. 16, 1969, pp. 83–93.

[6] 1 Pet 1:22—"Having perfectly sanctified your souls by obedience to the truth, in order to have an authentic brotherly love, love one another from the bottom of your heart." This latter expression insists that love be true, but the former makes it the peculiar possession of the baptized (a primitive baptismal formula), who alone are capable of loving one another like children of the same heavenly Father (cf. C. Spicq, *Epîtres de saint Pierre*, p. 73). The pagans can recognize its originality (cf. John 13:35). Compare with 1 Pet 1:22 the decree of Tenos in the first century BC, γνησίαν ἔχοντι πρὸς πάντας φιλοστοργίαν (C. Michel, *Recueil d'Inscriptions grecques*, Paris, 1900, n. 394, 49).

sent by God and is thus a qualified apostle whose authority cannot be contested, in contrast to the *pseudapostoloi* (2 Cor 11:13). This meaning is confirmed by 2 Cor 8:8, where the Corinthians are in a position to prove that their love is authentic (*to tēs hymeteras agapēs gnēsion dokimazōn*), in that their urgency to participate in the collection authenticates their invisible love for God.[7] Similarly Marcus Aurelius writes that "goodwill is invincible, if it is candid, without a mocking smile, without hypocrisy" (*to eumenes anikēton ean gnēsion ē kai mē sesēros mēde hypokrisis*, 11.18.15).

The adjective *gnēsios*, distinctively Pauline in the NT, is applied to three persons: *Timotheō gnēsiō teknō en pistei* (1 Tim 1:2), which must be translated "dear and authentic child in the faith"; to Titus (Titus 1:4); and to Syzygos, on whose name Paul makes a pun, "dear and authentic companion."[8] In secular usage, it is used for a son,[9] a wife,[10] a brother and sister,[11] a friend,

---

[7] Cf. "who loves authentic worship, ὅ γνησίους μέν θεραπείας ἀσπάζεται" (Philo, *Worse Attacks Better* 21; cf. *Unchang. God* 116). For the organizing of a collection, *P.Mert.* 63: on 18 January 57, Herennia writes to her father Pompeius to tell him about a collection to benefit the sanctuary of Souchos and to say that a contribution from him is desired, and furthermore that contributions are expected from everyone, even Romans, Alexandrians, and the colonists at Arsinoë. —On the theology of the collection, cf. E. B. Allo, *Seconde Epître aux Corinthiens*, pp. 204–210; C. H. Buck, "The Collection for the Saints," in *HTR*, 1950, pp. 1–19; *Recueil L. Cerfaux*, vol. 2, pp. 390–413; K. Prümm, *Theologie des zweiten Korintherbriefes*, Rome-Fribourg, 1962, vol. 2, pp. 17ff. A. Ambrosiano, "La 'Colletta paolina' in una recente interpretazione," in AnBib 18, Rome, 1963, pp. 591–600; D. Georgi, *Die Geschichte der Kollekte des Paulus für Jerusalem*, Hamburg, 1965; K. F. Nickle, *The Collection: A Study in Paul's Strategy*, London, 1966. It was a gesture of gratitude to the mother church, the center of catholicity, just as Jerusalem was the center of Israel (J. Jeremias, *Jerusalem*, p. 51) and . . . the center of poverty (ibid., p. 169). For J. Jervell, St. Paul wrote Romans to justify his theology and his conduct before the mother church ("Der Brief nach Jerusalem," in *ST,* 1971, pp. 61–73).

[8] Phil 4:3. Σύζυγος means "bearing the same yoke." On this verse, cf. C. Spicq, *Théologie morale*, vol. 2, p. 587, n. 5; 786, n. 2. According to J. Fleury, σύζυγε-συνεργός is Lydia, who is charged with reestablishing peace between Euodia and Syntyche ("Une Société de fait dans l'Eglise apostolique," in *Mélanges Ph. Maylan*, Lausanne, 1963, vol. 2, pp. 58–59). Cf. Delling, art. σύζυγος, in *TDNT*, vol. 7, pp. 748–750.

[9] Menander, *Dysk.* 842: "I send back my daughter to you to beget legitimate children"; Philo, *Spec. Laws* 4.184; *Good Man Free* 87; *Contemp. Life* 72; *P.Oxy.* 1267, 15 (cf. Boswinkel's note on *P.Vindob.Bosw.* 5, 11), *MAMA*, vol. 6, 358, 10: μόνοις γνησίοις ἡνῶν τέκνοις; 7.427, 565; 8.595: τὰ γνήσιά μου παιδία; of the father: τὸν γλυκύτατον καὶ γνήσιον πατέρα (*BCH*, 1883, p. 274, n. 15; cf. *MAMA*, vol. 1, 365, 4); Philo, *To Gaius* 62, 71.

[10] *MAMA*, vol. 4, 305: τῇ γλυκυτάτῃ τεκούσῃ Μελτίνῃ καὶ γνησίᾳ γυναικὶ Ἀμμίᾳ; *SEG*, vol. 6, 232: Ἀγελαΐδι γυναικὶ μνείας ἕνεκεν.

[11] Sir 7:18; *P.Gronig.* 10, 9: ἡ ἐμὴ γνησιοτάτη ἀδελφὴ Σενεπώνυχος; *Pap.Lugd.Bat.* XIII, 24, 4; *P.Oslo* 132, 8; *P.Michael.* 45, 3: Κολλοῦθος γνήσιος αὐτοῦ ἀδελφὸς ἐκ τῶν

and a citizen.[12] These usages show that in the Hellenistic period *gnēsios* goes beyond the legal definition whereby it describes the legitimate son, as opposed to the bastard.[13]

(a) It is an emotionally freighted term. Like Isaac, whom Abraham sired by his wife, *huios . . . gnēsios, atapētos kai monos* (Philo, *Abraham* 168), or the decree of Cersonesos for a certain Heracleotes: "he shows authentic love" (*agapan gnasian endeiknytai*).[14]

(b) It is used in the first century in a religious sense for those who pass on a revelation.[15]

(c) In an even broader sense, for the authorized interpreters of a teaching, like Aristotle, "the most authentic disciple of Plato."[16] "Legiti-

αὐτῶν γονέων; *SEG*, vol. 8, 621, 19; *P.Oxy.* 2584, 30; 2761, 5; ὁ ὁμογνήσιος ἀδελφός = my legitimate brother.

[12] "Eleazer . . . to King Ptolemy, his true friend, φίλῳ γνησίῳ" (*Ep. Arist.* 41; with the commentary of A. Pelletier, *Josèphe adaptateur,* p. 112). Callisthenus to Onesimus: τῷ ἰδίῳ γνησίῳ φίλῳ (B. Latyschev, *Inscriptiones Antiquae*, vol. 3, p. 425); *P.Fouad* 54, 34: "Let them not forget their true friends"; *P.Apoll.* 24, 1: ἔγραψα τῇ περιβλέπτῳ σου γνησίᾳ φιλίᾳ (= *PSI* 1267, 1). In a letter of the eighth century, the vocative Γνήσιε = my true friend (ibid. 37, 12); cf. 70, 9; γνήσιος ἐραστής in a Roman inscription from the imperial period (L. Robert, *Hellenica*, vol. 4, Paris, 1948, p. 33); *BGU* 547, 7.

[13] Cf. Heb 12:8 (νόθος). Demosthenes defines γνήσιος: "the title of legitimate child belongs to the one that is son by blood" (Demosthenes, *C. Leoch.* 44.49). Cf. Philo, *Dreams* 2.47: "Vainglory always adds the illegitimate to the authentic, προστίθησιν ἀεὶ γνησίῳ μὲν τὸ νόθον." With respect to things, γνήσιος is equivalent to "in line with the rule, regular, usual" (*P.Amh.* 86, 10 and 15; *P.Stras.* 2, 13; *P.Ryl.* 341, 2; *P.Oslo* 154, 12; *BGU* 747, 14; *SB* 7337, 19), hence "proper." Cf. the adverb—τὰ ἔργα τῶν ἀμπέλων ἰδίων γνησίως γενέσθω (second century)—adapted or appropriate to its end.

[14] B. Latyschev, *Inscriptiones Antiquae*, vol. 1, n. 359, 6 (cited by L. Robert, *Opera Selecta Minora*, vol. 1, p. 311, n. 2); cf. *MAMA*, vol. 8, 220: λούκιος Ἰωάνῃ ἀναγνώστῃ φιλτάτῳ καὶ γνησίῳ υἱῷ. *P.Lond.* 1917, 5, 14: ἀταπηταὶ, γνησιώταται καὶ ἀξιώταται παρὰ κυρίῳ θεῷ; *SB* 7655, 9 and 34; 7871, 19: "the good Philhermes was for me an affectionate and true brother—ἀδελφὸν ὄντα μοι καὶ γνήσιον—not according to nature, but according to his tenderness (στοργῇ)." L. Robert (*Hellenica*, vol. 13, Paris, 1965, pp. 218ff.) cites many examples of this emotional meaning of γνήσιος, "a sentimental epithet on the same order as γλυκύτατος, φίλτατος." This is obviously the sense of the term in the Pastorals. St. John Chrysostom recognized this, since he commented on 1 Tim 1:2—ἀπὸ πολλῆς φιλοστρογίας.

[15] Isis to Horus: "He made me swear not to pass on the revelation, εἰ μὴ μόνον τέκνῳ καὶ φίλῳ γνησίῳ" (in M. Berthelot, *Collection des anciens alchimistes grecs*, 2d ed., London, 1963, p. 34, 6); cf. A. J. Festugière, "L'Expérience religieuse du médecin Thessalos," in *RB*, 1939, p. 51; J. Bidez, F. Cumont, *Les Mages hellénisés*, Paris, 1938, vol. 2, pp. 119, 127.

[16] Dionysius of Halicarnassus, *Pomp.* 1. Letter of Claudius to the Alexandrians: "My brother Germanicus addressed himself to you γνησιωτέραις ὑμᾶς φωναῖς"

mate sons," natural heirs of their father, are especially qualified to pass on his commandments (Philo, *Virtues* 59) and to be named sole governors of his empire (*To Gaius* 24). The additional observation that the adverb *gnēsiōs*, "sincerely," is used in the sense of "efficaciously"[17] will enhance by this density of usages the meaning of *gnēsios* as applied to Timothy and Titus in order to boost their credibility with the Ephesians and Cretans: true children of the apostle, they are his most authentic representatives, interpreters of his teachings, faithful echoes of his own voice. Furthermore, they should be treated with reverence, because they are not simple "brothers" (1 Thess 3:2) or collaborators (Rom 16:21), but men who have lived with Paul in a profound intimacy like that between sons and their father; thus they are very dear to him (2 Tim 2:1). These are credentials that will inspire Christians to obedience and filial piety toward them.

(*P.Lond.* 1912, 27; with the note of H. I. Bell, *Jews and Christians in Egypt*, p. 31). Cf. Philodemus of Gadara, *Adv. Soph.* frag. Y.3.15: γνήσιος ἀναγηώστης = a faithful interpreter; Atticus, frag. 44: οἱ γνήσιοι φιλόσοφοι, authentic philosophers.

[17] 2 Macc 14:8; Phil 2:20{"I really have no one who like Timothy effectively involves himself (γνησίως μεριμνᾶν) on your behalf"; M. Naldini, *Il Cristianesimo in Egitto*, n. 58, 5: μετὰ τὸν θεὸν ἄλλον ἀδελφὸν οὐκ ἔχω οὔτε φίλος γνήσιον οὔτε εὐπροαίρετον ἄνθρωπον εἰ μὴ σὺ μόνος; *P.Tebt.* 326, 11: "He will protect the child effectively—προστήσεσθαι γνησίως τοῦ παιδίου"; *SEG*, vol. 15, 849, 2: "Soades . . . having efficaciously and generously—γνησίως καὶ φιλοτείμνως—assisted the merchants, the caravans, and citizens established at Vologesias in a number of critical situations"; *P.Berl.Zill.* 14, 18; *P.Lond.* 130, 3: γνησίως φιλοπονήσαντες; *P.Apoll.* 46, 10: "So that my master may be up to date, I announce it to him faithfully"; Dittenberger, *Or.* 308, 9: μετὰ πάσης ὁμονοίας γνησίως.

ἅπαξ, ἐφάπαξ

hapax, ephapax, **once**

In a listing, the adverb *hapax* has an arithmetic significance—*epirrhēma arithmētikon* (Hesychius)—the opposite of "several times." Thus 2 Cor 11:25—"once I was stoned, three times I was shipwrecked"; a constant usage in the literature.[1] The literature often uses the formula *hapax kai dis*, "a first and a second time," which can be translated "various times."[2] The same usage appears in St. Paul: "We have wanted to come to you a first time and a second time, but Satan has hindered us" (1 Thess 2:18); "When I was at Thessalonica you sent what I needed a first time and a second time" (Phil 4:16). Needless to say, uniqueness is the opposite of multiplicity,

---

[1] Philo, *Unchang. God* 82 (citation of Ps 62:11; cf. Job 33:14—"God speaks once and does not repeat twice"); *Dreams* 1.62: "The word *place* can have three meanings: first of all (ἅπαξ) . . . , according to a second meaning (κατὰ δεύτερον τρόπον) . . . , thirdly (κατὰ τρίτον)"; *Alleg. Interp.* 2.54; 3.51; *To Gaius* 58: "not once but three times"; 356; *Moses* 1.183; 2.258; Josephus, *Life* 82: "Four times I took Tiberias by force, once Gabara."

[2] David, burdened with armor, "tried to walk once and twice, because he had never tried it" (1 Sam 17:39); Neh 13:20; 1 Macc 3:30; Philo, *Prelim. Stud.* 4: "animals and plants bear fruit only once or twice a year, ἅπαξ ἢ δίς" (cf. *P.Oxy.* XI, 37: ἅπαξ ποτ' ἢ δίς, republished by C. Austin, *Comicorum Graecorum Fragmenta*, n. 254; inscription of Silko: ἅπαξ δύο = δίς, in Dittenberger, *Or.* 201, 2 = *SB* 8536); Diogenes Laertius 7.13: "Zeno rarely used boys, once or twice a girl"; *P.Oxy.* 2731, 9: ἅπαξ καὶ δὶς καὶ τρὶς ἐδήλωσά σου; 2596, 12. The papyri nevertheless prefer the expression ἅπαξ καὶ δεύτερον, cf. *P.Panop.Beatty* 1, 54, 112: to order or to give instructions a first and a second time; *P.Lund* II, 4, 6: "I wrote you a first time, a second time, and often" (republished *SB* 8091); *P.Cair.Isid.* 63, 17 (republished *SB* 9185); *P.Mil.* 83, 4 (republished ibid. 9013); *P.Oslo* 64, 4; *P.Oxy.* 2996, 7.

---

hapax, S 530; *TDNT* 1.381–383; *EDNT* 1.115–116; *NIDNTT* 2.716–719, 725; MM 53; L&N 60.67, 60.68, 60.70; BAGD 80 ‖ **ephapax**, S 2178; *TDNT* 1.383–384; *EDNT* 2.91–92; *NIDNTT* 2.716–718; MM 269; L&N 60.67, 60.68, 67.34; BDF §§12(3), 203; BAGD 330 "one time" of "often"[3] and "another time,"[4] but not of "once again," which is a repetition, even with significant changes, and with the nuance of a first time which contrasts with the last time (Heb 12:26-27 = Hag 2:5; cf. Judg 16:20, 28; 20:30-31; 1 Sam 3:10; 20:25; 2 Macc 3:37; *T. Abr.* A 8, 9, 15).

Often *hapax* has the meaning "one single time, unique."[5] "Only (and without exception) man gives orders to all other living beings that are mortal" (Philo, *Husbandry* 8; *Moses* 2.65), "a single bite inevitably brings death" (*Dreams* 2.88; cf. *Spec. Laws* 1.59). This uniqueness can be periodic: "Once a year, propitiation is made";[6] thus the high priest only enters the holy of holies once a year.[7] But many other texts emphasize that what is done is not repeatable, and these give *hapax* its definitive meaning: "Once for all Christ was manifested at the consummation of the ages" (Heb 9:26); "humans are destined to die only once" (Heb 9:27). "The faith is passed down to the saints once for all."[8]

This meaning occurs frequently in Philo and the papyri: "The parricide would not die at one stroke (*mē hapax*); he finished dying only with con-

---

[3] Πολλάκις; Philo, *Spec. Laws* 4.85: "*erōs* is not content with a single catastrophe (ἅπαξ) but has frequently (πολλάκις) inundated the civilized world with innumerable evils" (cf. *Sacr. Abel and Cain* 127: μὴ ἅπαξ ἀλλὰ διὰ παντός); Josephus, *Ant.* 4.314, οὐχ ἅπαξ ἀλλὰ πολλάκις; *P.Panop.Beatty* 1, 175; *P.Mich.* 213, 5: "I wrote you often, but you did not write even once . . ."; *P.Giss.* 48, 10.

[4] Ἄλλο ἅπαξ, *P.Ryl.* 435; *P.Mich.* 482, 5; *O.Bodl.* 2471, 9.

[5] Gen 18:32; Judg 6:39; 2 Sam 17:7—Ahithophel erred only once; *P.Cair.Zen.* 59028: περὶ τοῦ ὀψωνίου ὅλως οὐκ εἰλήφαμεν ἀλλ' ἢ ἅπαξ; 59218, 27; *P.Oxy.* 2151, 5: ὑμεῖς δέ μοι οὐδὲ ἅπαξ ἐδηλώσατε περὶ τῆς σωτηρίας ὑμῶν; *P.Tebt.* 760, 8. Eupolis, frag. 128 D, 2: "οὐκ ἀνεβίων οὐδ' ἥπαξ; once dead, I shall not live again, even once" (republished by J. M. Edmonds, *Attic Comedy*, vol. 1, p. 364; C. Austin, *Comicorum Graecorum Fragmenta*, n. 94, 4; cf. 92, 8). On the occasion of a soldier's desertion, the priest of the village of Hermopolis pleads: "συνχώρησε αὐτοῦ τούτω τὸ ἅπαξ, forgive him for this one time" (*P.Lond.* 416, 8; vol. 2, p. 299 = *P.Abinn.* 32 = *P.Berl.Zill.* 8, 15).

[6] Exod 30:10; Lev 16:34; 2 Chr 9:21—"Once every three years the ships of Tarshish would arrive"; Philo *Spec. Laws* 2.146.

[7] Heb 9:7, ἅπαξ τοῦ ἐνιαυτοῦ; similarly Philo, *Spec. Laws* 1.72; *Drunkenness* 136; *To Gaius* 306; *Giants* 306 (opposed to πάντα καιρόν, on every occasion); Josephus, *War* 5.236; cf. m. *Yoma* 5.

[8] Jude 3: τῇ ἅπαξ παραδοθείσῃ τοῖς ἁγίοις πίστει; verse 5: "You who know all things once for all"; Heb 6:4—"Those who were illuminated once for all and tasted the heavenly gift"; cf. Philo, *Drunkenness* 198: πιστεύει τοῖς ἅπαξ παραδοθεῖσι; Josephus, *War* 2.158: "Those who have once tasted the wisdom of the Essenes"; *Ant.* 4.140: the young man who has only once tasted foreign customs is intoxicated and insatiable; cf. *P.Oxy.* 471, 77: once accustomed to his shame, ἅπαξ γὰρ ἐν ἔθει τῆς αἰσχύνης γενόμενον; 1102, 8: "ἐπεὶ ἅπαξ προσῆλθε τῇ κληρονομίᾳ, having once entered into definitive possession of the inheritance"; *T. Abr.* A 20: "Stop questioning me once and for all."

tinual suffering, sorrow, and distress" (*Rewards* 72); "It would be better to take nothing away, to add nothing . . . and to leave alone that which was done once for all (*hapax* = definitively) at the beginning" (*Etern. World* 42); "Leave all the rest aside once for all."[9] The expression *pros hapax* at the end of a receipt (*P.Oxy.* 1138, 13; *BGU* 1020, 15; *PSI* 1040, 26; *P.Erl.* 79, 4) or a dossier (*P.Bour.* 20, 14) seems to mean that the item in question is complete and thus valid and definitive (cf. *P.Lips.* 34, 20; 35, 19; 39, 6). This would correspond to the Hebrew *pa'am*, often translated by *hapax* in the LXX, which means "anvil, step or pace, time or occurrence"; cf. Abishai to David: "let me pin him to the ground with a single throw of the spear" (1 Sam 26:8; cf. 1 Chr 1:11; Judg 16:18); "May sinners perish far from the face of the Lord, all together."[10]

Hapax usually is given the sense of "once for all" in Heb 9:28; 1 Pet 3:18—Christ offered himself and died one single time for sins, and it is indeed true that this oblation was perfect and unique, so that there is no need for it to be renewed. But if this translation suggests the definitive quality of Christ's sacrifice, it does not sufficiently emphasize that it is absolute,[11] complete; it takes *hapax* too exclusively as an adverb of quantity and inadequately reflects the word's etymology. *Hapax* may be an old nominative[12] whose root is found in *pēg-ny-mi*, "to fasten by driving well in, to drive into the ground, fasten by assembling, fix by compacting, solidifying, crystallizing, jelling, being congealed."[13] This quality of "compactness" seems to be retained in Josephus, *Ant.* 12.109: *hapax . . . eis aei diamenē*; 18.172; and the papyri where an initial act includes its effects. In AD 54, when the prefect of Egypt, L. Lucius Geta, wrote that his orders and decisions had been formulated "once," he means that they always remain binding and must be applied by everyone everywhere just as on the first

---

[9] Philo, *Migr. Abr.* 137; 40: "the words that concern God are all at once put to rout"; *Husbandry* 104: "once for all indifferent to all the rest"; 105; *Change of Names* 247: "Once something has been said it cannot come back"; Xenophon, *An.* 1.9.10: "He never betrayed them since he had once granted them his friendship"; *Jos. Asen.* 25.6: "Have you not sold Joseph once for all, οὐχ ἅπαξ πεπράκατε?"

[10] *Pss. Sol.* 12.8; Philo, *Moses* 1.46: "At one stroke, the people in their places seized the opportunity"; *Flight* 101: "The divine Word, the most venerable of the whole lot of intelligences, τῶν νοητῶν ἅπαξ ἁπάντων"; Josephus, *Ant.* 11.192: "she had not once obeyed"; Xenophon, *Oec.* 10.1: "I have only to say one word for her to obey me immediately."

[11] *P.Phil.* 35, 26: "ἀλλὰ ἅπαξ οὐ μέλι ἡμῖν περὶ ἐμοῦ, you care absolutely nothing for me" (second century); *P.Oxy.* 3006, 9: ἅπαξ ἀκοῦσαι.

[12] Cf. P. Chantraine, *Morphologie historique du grec*, 2d ed., Paris, 1964, 132. Only the prefix ἅ corresponds to *sem-el*, *sim-plex*.

[13] P. Chantraine, *Dictionnaire étymologique*, under πήγνυμι.

day.[14] In a contract for a nurse, dating to 21 May 26: "When the year is up Paapis will pay her once for all 60 silver drachmas for the second year" (*P.Rein*. 103, 14; republished *SB* 7619). Here *eis hapax* means not just "one time only" but "entirely, completely"; the sum will be paid in full. On the theological plane, to say that the sacrifice of Christ is "compact" would mean that it includes all of its effects (and its commemorations?), like the spring which contains potentially the whole river.

As for *ephapax* = *ha-pax epi* [*pasin*], unknown in the LXX, in Philo, in Josephus, and in the papyri before the sixth century,[15] it is used five times in the epistolary corpus. Four of these occurrences[16] have the same meaning as *hapax* in the last sense discussed above. In Rom 6:10, the death of Christ was a unique event that objectively included the death of all. In Heb 7:27, *ephapax* is opposed to *kath' hēmeran:* Christ does not have to renew his sacrifice daily; its value is absolute and definitive, complete; thus he enters the heavenly sanctuary and does not come out again; his one and only entrance is made in order to remain there forever (9:12). To say that we are sanctified by the sacrifice of the body of Jesus (*hēgiasmenoi esmen . . . ephapax*) means that this sanctification is not only definitive (note the perfect participle) but collective, thanks to this unique offering which contains his body.

---

[14] Τὰ ὑπ' ἐμοῦ ἅπαξ κεκριμένα ἢ προσταχθέντα (Dittenberger, *Or.* 664, 14 = *SB* 8900); cf. Ps 89:35—"I have sworn once = for all time." Philo, *To Gaius* 218: "He intends that what he has once decided shall be carried out"; Menander, *Dysk.* 392: "since once I have set myself to the task, that isn't the moment to weaken"; Josephus, *Life* 314: "Tiberias had ἅπαξ gone over to them," i.e. validly and definitively; the attribution remains forever effective.

[15] *P.Lond.* 1708, 242 (sixth century); 483, 88 (seventh century). In *P.Flor.* 158, 10 (third century), ἀφάπαξ should be read ἐφ' ἅπαξ (Vitelli, in *Berichtigungsliste*, vol. 1, p. 150).

[16] In 1 Cor 15:6, Christ resurrected "was seen by more than five hundred brothers at one time, all at once, ὤφθη ἐφάπαξ"; but "compact" is also a possible meaning (cf. *Enoch* [Greek] 16.1—"the great time will come to an end all at once"); the vision is collective; cf. C. Mugler, *Terminologie optique*, p. 43: "ἅπαξ = *semel, at one time*. Adverb expressing the synthetic character of the act of vision which the school of Aristotle defied the atomists to explain. Alexander (of Aphrodisias): δοκεῖ . . . ὡς ἅπαξ . . . καὶ ὡς ἓν ὁρᾶν (sc. ἡ ὄψις) τὸ ὁρώμενον; vision seems to take in the object in a single act and perceive it as a unity, *In Sens.* 60.5."

ἀπαράβατος

aparabatos, inviolable, nontransferable

How should we translate this biblical hapax in Heb 7:24—"Jesus, inasmuch as he remains for eternity, *aparabaton echei tēn hierōsynēn*"?[1] This rather rare verb is only found in late Greek; it is used only once in Philo and twice in Josephus. Etymologically speaking, (*parabainō*: pass along or pass beyond, violate) a *parabatēs* is a transgressor, a violator, or a denigrator,[2] so *aparabatos* should be that which ought not be transgressed, "inviolable," and that is the meaning—usually in a legal context—that is well attested in the papyri and even in literary writings, notably with the verb *menō*.[3] But this meaning does not fit in Heb 7:24.

---

[1] There are almost as many translations as translators: "priesthood which is not transmitted" (A. Loisy, *Les Livres du Nouveau Testament*, Paris, 1912; A. Tricot, in *La Sainte Bible* of C. Crampon, Paris-Tournai, 1952); "intransmissible" (M. Goguel, H. Monnier, *Le Nouveau Testament*, Paris, 1929); "inalienable" (Médebielle, in L. Pirot's *La Sainte Bible*, Paris, 1938; C.F.D. Moule, *Idiom Book*, 109); "the absolute priesthood" (J.-S. Javet, *Dieu nous parla*, Neuchâtel-Paris, 1945); "priesthood is . . . not transferable" (J. Héring, *Hébreux* = ET, p. 62); "perpetual" (*NJB*); "unsurpassable priesthood" (A. Vanhoye, *Traduction structurelle de l'Epître aux Hébreux*, Rome, 1963); etc.

[2] Cf. Hos 6:7; Ps 17:4; Rom 2:25, 27; Gal 2:18; Jas 2:11.

[3] The conclusion of a legal sentence of AD 67: μένειν κύρια καὶ ἀπαράβατα (*P.Ryl.* 65, 18); *SB* 9152, 10: παραμένοντα ἀπαραβάρως καὶ ἀκαταγνώστως; *P.Grenf.* 1.60, 7: βεβαίᾳ καὶ ἀπαραβάτῳ . . . πράσει. The Jews placed their confidence in God, protesting εἰς νῦν ἀπαράβατοι μεμενηκότες, i.e., that up to the present they have remained pure of any transgression, or better, that they have not changed, they have remained unalterable (Josephus, *Ant.* 18.266). "This sovereign equality keeps itself constantly, unceasingly sheltered from any transgression" (Philo, *Etern. World* 112); "I shall make a mysterious machine, linked to an infallible and inviolable doctrine, ἀπλανοῦς καὶ ἀπαραβάτου" (Stobaeus 1.49.44; vol. 1, p. 401, 20; [French] translation by A. J. Festugière, *Corpus Hermeticum*, Paris, 1954, vol. 4, p. 16, n. 18, 20); "In the Whole there are four places, which are under an inviolable law and authority, ἀπαραβάτῳ νόμῳ" (Stobaeus 1.49.45; vol. 1, p. 407, 21; [French] translation by A. J. Festugière, *Corpus Hermeticum*, p. 52); cf. Epictetus, *Ench.* 51.2: νόμος ἀπαράβατος.

---

aparabatos, S 531; *TDNT* 5.742–743; *EDNT* 1.116; *NIDNTT* 3.583–585; MM 53; L&N 13.61; BAGD 80

One might be tempted to give our adjective the otherwise well-attested meaning of "permanent, perpetual,"[4] "unchangeable"[5] as the word was understood by the Vulgate (*sempiternum*) and the Peshitta, and as it is most often used in literature.[6] But this would produce a tautology with the first part of the verse, even a banality; and in any case this notion of a priesthood unchangeable in character or quality is not in evidence elsewhere in the epistle.[7]

Alternatively, we can posit a derivative meaning, one for which no attestation has yet been found: "not passing from one to another" (= *mē parabainousan eis allon*). This was the interpretation of St. John Chrysostom (*adiadochon*) and Theodoret, followed by Bengel—"that cannot pass to successors"—and it is the meaning that flows out of the context. As opposed to the levitical priesthood, whose mortal ministers had to transmit their power to their descendants, an eternal priest remains unique and will never have to pass his priesthood on to any other minister (cf. the *hoi men . . . ho de* antithesis in verses 23–24). The term was apparently chosen because of its legal connotations and to justify the priestly "institution" of the new covenant—which was identified with a single person! So we translate: "He possesses the priesthood which is nontransferable."[8]

---

[4] *P.Lond.* 1015, 12: ἄτροπα καὶ ἀσάλευτα καὶ ἀπαράγατα; *Chrest.Mitt.*, n. 372, col. V, 19: ἔνια ἀπαραβατά ἐστιν = There are some things for which nothing has changed. Josephus, *Ag. Apion* 2.293: "What finer thing than undeviating piety."

[5] The meaning retained by J. Schneider (in his excellent article on this word in *TDNT*, vol. 5, pp. 742–743), O. Michel (*Der Brief an die Hebräer*, 10th ed., Göttingen, 1957, p. 175), G. W. Buchanan (*To the Hebrews*, New York, 1972).

[6] Epictetus 2.15.1: "They imagine that they must always remain unshakeable"; Plutarch, *De def. or.* 3: "The sun maintains its accustomed course unchangeably, according to the received tradition." It is worth noting that it is used for the course of the stars, which cannot be changed (F. Cumont, *L'Egypte des astrologues*, p. 17, n. 2) and for destiny or unyielding fate (Plutarch, *De fato* 1; Marcus Aurelius 12.14.1–2).

[7] W. L. Lorimer, "Hebrews VII, 23 f," in *NTS*, vol. 13, 1967, pp. 386–387, taking note of these problems, suggests that the author of the epistle wrote (or meant to write) ἀμετάβατον, "not passing to another"; the mistake resulted from the παραμένειν of verse 23.

[8] Obviously ἔχειν retains its strong sense "possess, hold, keep."

ἀπαρχή

aparchē, **firstfruit**

Most of the peoples of antiquity had the custom of offering to the deity, the master of nature and source of fertility, the firstfruits of their fields and the firstborn of their domestic animals.[1] This usage is well attested in Greece, not only by the first literary text to employ the term *aparchē*,[2] but by many inscriptions in which it can be seen that the *aparchai* are not only levies but personal gifts, and more precisely offerings to the deity:[3] "Firstfruits to the goddess Artemis."[4] An Athenian decree pertaining to the

---

[1] Aristotle, *Eth. Nic.* 8.9 (1160ᵃ): "Still today we see sacrifices and assemblies of ancient origin after the harvest as a feast of firstfruits"; cf. Stengel, s.v. "Ἀπαρχαί," PW, vol. 1/2, 2666–68. On the ἀπαχαὶ ἀνθρώπων, cf. Aristotle, *Constitution of the Boeotians* (cited by Plutarch, *Thes.* 16.2): "The Cretans, in discharge of an ancient vow, the firstfruits of their offspring"; Plutarch, *De Pyth. or.* 16: "I approve of the people of Eretria and Magnesia who offered the firstfruits of their population to the god as the dispenser of all fruit, to the father, author, and friend of humankind"; *Quaest. Graec.* 35; cf. Solon 6.1.6.

[2] Herodotus 1.92: "The offerings that Croesus made at Delphi and at the sanctuary of Amphiaraus came from his own property; they were levied on the wealth inherited from his father" (τῶν πατρωίων χρημάτων ἀπαρχήν); cf. Euripides, *Or.* 96; Euripides, *Phoen.* 1525; Plato, *Leg.* 7.806 D. In his speech in praise of agriculture, Xenophon (*Oec.* 5.10) cries, "What art supplies to the gods better firstfruits" (ἀπαρχάς); and Theophrastus justifies the offering made to the gods on the grounds of the importance of cereals for civilization (cited by Porphyry, *Abst.* 2.6). Thucydides 3.58.4: "All the ritual offerings with all the fruits of our land, the firstfruits of which we bring (to the tombs of your fathers), levied by friends on a friendly land."

[3] Cf. ἀπάρχεσθαι: one offers to the god the firstfruits of one's art (Dittenberger, *Syl.* 711.12; 795 A; Dittenberger, *Or.* 352.42), or the firstfruits of wisdom (Plato, *Prt.* 343 B; Dio Chrysostom 72.12), of a discourse (Euripides, *Ion* 402). *Pss. Sol.* 15.5—"a new psalm . . . firstfruits of the lips, from a holy and righteous heart." Cf. L. Robert, *Etudes épigraphiques*, 40–45.

[4] Ἀπαρχὴν τῇ θεᾷ Ἀρτέμιδι (*I.Magn.* 83.12-13); Νέαρχος ἀνέθεκεν ὁ κεραμεὺς ἔργον ἀπαρχὲν τἀθεναίᾳ, Dittenberger, *Syl.* 1139 (vol. 3, 294–95, fifth century BC); cf. *Syl.* 731.23 (vol. 2, 395): δοθῆναι δὲ αὐτοῖς ὑπὸ τοῦ δήμου καὶ εἰς ἀπαρχὴν καὶ

---

aparchē, S 536; *TDNT* 1.484–486; *EDNT* 1.116; *NIDNTT* 3.415–417; *MM* 54; *L&N* 53.23, 57.171, 61.8; *BAGD* 81

offering of the firstfruits of grain and to the Eleusinian feasts celebrated on this occasion modifies the payment of a certain otherwise unknown Chairemonid: *kata ton Chairēmonido nomon ton peri tēs aparchēs*.[5] Similarly, a decree probably found on the two steles at Eleusis and at Athens calls upon the Athenians to pay the *aparchē* used for the sacrifices.[6] This religious act takes quite different forms; it may be carried out at the beginning of a meal[7] or before the departure of an army (Xenophon, *Cyr.* 7.1.1; *Hier.* 4.2); but it is always an opening ritual.[8]

We know how insistent Moses was about making this custom obligatory, how one had to present the firstfruits at the sanctuary with a word of dedication and a prayer (Deut 26:1-4) and the portion reserved for the priests (Num 5:9; 18:11; 31:29).[9] The firstfruits are the levy (Hebrew $t^e r \hat u m \bar a h$)

σύνοδον χρυσοῦς τέσσαρας (first century); Dittenberger, *Or.* 179, 12 (vol. 1, 261): Aniketo, οἰκονόμος σιτικῶν of the merits of Herakleides, decides in 96 BC "to give in his own name and the name of those who work under his orders to the office of circumscription each year as firstfruits, to the sanctuary of the very great god Soknopaios, 182½ *artabai* of wheat" (= *SB* 8888, 12; E. Bernand, *Fayoum*, n. 71, 12). Dedication to a goddess in the fifth century BC: ἀπαρχὴν θεᾷ (*I.Rhamn.* 150, n. 36). Cf. Hans Beer, Ἀπαρχή und verwandte Ausdrücke in griechischen Weilinschriften, Würzburg, 1914.

[5] F. Sokolowski, *LSCGSup*, n. 13, 10. Cf. *LSAM*, n. 10, 39 = decree of the Ilian confederation regarding the *panēgyris* of Athena in 77 BC, τὰς δὲ ἀπαρχὰς διοικεῖσθαι καθότι καὶ πρότερον = *I.Ilium*, 10, 39, which cites the response of Attalis I to the Magnesians: ἀπαρχὴν ἐγώ τε ἔταξα δοῦναι; Dittenberger, *Or.* 282, 17 (vol. 1, 458) = C. B. Welles, *Royal Correspondence*, n. 34, 18; *I.Thas.*, n. 379, 2-3. Ἀπαρχαί for the Delian Pythiads, J. and L. Robert, "Bulletin épigraphique," in *REG*, 1946-47, 322, n. 96.

[6] *LSCG*, n. 43, 47 = Dittenberger, *Syl.* 83, 43, 37; around 422-23 BC; *LSCG*, n. 155 B 5: ἀπαρχαὶ ἐμβάλλωνται τῷ θεῷ.

[7] Cf. T. Homolie, s.v., "Damarium," *DAGR*, vol. 2/1, 363-82.

[8] A nuance strongly emphasized by Jean Rudhardt, *Notions fondamentales de la pensée religieuse et actes constitutifs du culte dans la Grèce classique: Etude préliminaire pour aider à la compréhension de la piété athénienne au IVme siècle*, Geneva, 1958, 219-22: "It was not after the victory, after the harvest, that this rite was carried out, but before the start of the harvest or the plundering. These two moments coincide. . . . The firstfruits, whether saved or destroyed, were levied on a collection of goods in consideration of which their consecration derived all its value"; and he cites Philochorus, *Tresp.* 35: πάσας τε τὰς ἀρχὰς προσῆθαν αὐτοῖς (τοῖς θεοῖς), ὀρθῶς ποιοῦντες. τοὺς γὰρ ἁπάντων ἄρχοντας τοῖς ὁμοίοις χρὴ γεραίρειν.

[9] Cf. tractate *Ma'aserot*; Ezek 44:30—"The choice firstfruits of everything and all levies whatsoever among your levies shall be for the priests"; Sir 45:20—"God allotted to Aaron the first of the firstfruits." Cf. J de Fraine, s.v. "Premices," *DBSup* 8, 446-61; R. de Vaux, *Ancient Israel*, vol. 2, pp. 379, 404; O. Eissfeldt, *Ein Beitrag zur Geschichte des israelitisch-jüdischen Kultus* (Beiträge zur Wissenschaft von Alten Testament 22; Leipzig, 1917).

ἀπαρχή, aparchē   147

assessed[10] on the firstfruits of the soil, considered as the best.[11] The consecration to God of the firstfruits that sanctifies the whole harvest is a "sacred levy" (Lev 22:12; Ezek 48:10; Sir 7:31). At the return from captivity, this levy, which is reserved either for the priests or for the prince as part of their emolument (Ezek 45:16; 48:12, 18, 20, 21; cf. Philo, *Spec. Laws* 1.151: *semnoteron phoron kai hagiōteron;* 2.120, 222), strongly resembles a tax; this meaning of *aparchē* becomes common in the papyri and the equivalent is found in Josephus.[12] Dio Cassius tells of when Emperor Commodius "ordered for his birthday that he be paid two gold denarii as firstfruits"; the term is also used in the inscriptions.[13]

Philo commented copiously on the texts of Scripture relative to the *aparchai.*[14] He most often gives these latter the meaning "offering" (*Joseph* 194; *Spec. Laws* 2.167, 184, 186) and emphasizes their value as the first portion, an initial offering (*Heir* 253; *Abraham* 196; cf. *Prelim. Stud.* 89: *archas, tas aparchas* [that which is original, first]), but above all he insists on their religious meaning as an expression of gratitude toward God, a

---

[10] Exod 25:2–5; 35:5; 36:6; 2 Sam 1:21; mountains of Gilboah, "mountains of firstfruits," i.e., fertile; 2 Chr 31:10; Mal 3:8; Ezek 20:40; 45:1, 6, 7, 13. Cf. the Mishnah tractate *Terumot.*

[11] Exod 23:19 (Hebrew *rēšît;* commented on by the tractate *Bikkurim*); Lev 2:12; 23:10; Num 15:20 (applications in tractate *Ḥallah*); 18:12; Deut 18:4; 26:2, 10; 33:21 (Gad "appropriated the firstfruits; he saw that a ruler's portion was reserved for himself"); 1 Sam 2:29, "making yourselves fat with the best (the firstfruits) of all the offerings of my people"); 2 Chr 31:5; Ezek 44:30. Cf. Hebrew *ḥēleb,* "the fat," meaning "the best" (Num 18:12, 29–32). In Ps 78:51; 105:36, the firstborn is "the firstfruits of vigor."

[12] Josephus, *War* 5.21: the party of Eleazar kept the sacred firstfruits (τὰς ἱερὰς ἀπαρχάς); *Ant.* 7.378: out of his own purse (τῆς ἰδίας ἀπαρχῆς) Solomon gives 3,000 talents of gold to the Temple; so also Ptolemy sends offerings as ἀπαρχάς for the Temple (*Ant.* 12.50), and Caesar Augustus and Agrippa allow the Jews to carry their ἀπαρχάς to Jerusalem as an act of piety toward God (εὐσεβείας ἕνεκα, *Ant.* 16.172). Otherwise, if the firstfruits are given in homage to God, the source of plenty (*Ant.* 3.250), they provide a living for the priests and assure their office (*Ant.* 9.273); and the firstfruits of plunder are reserved for God (*Ant.* 5.26). According to a rabbinic prescription that is not found in Scripture, the firstborn are redeemed for five shekels (*Ant.* 4.71; cf. the tractate *Šeqalîm*).

[13] The treasures kept in the temples were made up of money "coming from gifts, fines, ἀπαρχαί, property revenues, tithes of booty, confiscated goods" (R. Bogaert, *Banques et banquiers,* p. 91). The state bank, at Delos, paid an annual contribution—ἀπαρχή—of 200 drachmas to the god Apollo (*IG* 2² 2336, lines 179 and 267; cf. Bogaert, *Banques,* 185, 187, 191, 213, 238). Cf. *IG* 2.985 (first century BC).

[14] Philo considered that Abel offered firstfruits not only of the firstborn, but also of their fat (*Sacr. Abel and Cain* 136), while Cain kept for himself the firstfruits of his farming labors and did not present his produce to God until much later (*Sacr. Abel and Cain* 72; *Conf. Tongues* 124).

basic way of honoring him: "The *aparchai* are offerings of thanks (*charistērious*) to God" (*Spec. Laws* 1.152; cf. 1.138). The sacred obligation to offer the firstfruits (*Spec. Laws* 2.168; 4.99) is an act of religious virtue that honors the deity (*Virtues* 95; *Sacr. Abel and Cain* 74, 117); virtue "returns in thank offerings the firstfruits of goods received" (*Prelim. Stud.* 7).[15] If it is necessary to consecrate to God the firstfruits of all plunder (*Moses* 1.316),[16] it is because of the knowledge that the victory was given by God. These levies are so plentiful that they constitute a treasure in almost all the cities (*Spec. Laws* 1.77–78, 133, 153), as a benefice for the priests, for the priests' servants, or for a priest's daughter who has been widowed or divorced and is childless (*Spec. Laws* 1.117, 126, 128, 129); so much so that it is evaluated as a sum of money (*timatai tēn aparchēn argyriō rhētō, Spec. Laws* 1.139; cf. *m. Bek.* 8.7–8), and thus the Jews "gathered together the sacred funds (*chrēmata hiera;* cf. *Syl.* 416, 9), those of the firstfruits, which they sent to Jerusalem" (*To Gaius* 156, 157, 216, 291, 311, 312, 316).

In the usage of the papyri, *aparchē* hardly ever has the religious meaning,[17] but it retains its basic meaning of "beginning, first, initial" and most often designates the birth certificate, the identification document for free men,[18] corresponding to the *hypomnēma epigennēseōs;* and for Roman citizens it refers to the *professio liberorum natorum.*[19] According to the *Gnomon of the Idios Logos:* "A female citizen (of Alexandria) who by mistake married an Egyptian man, thinking that he was of the same estate as herself, is not held responsible. If the two spouses together present the birth certificates of their children (*hypo amphoterōn aparchē teknōn tethē*), these latter will retain the right of (Alexandrian) citizenship" (*tēreitai hē politeia*) from their mother (47, line 131). In a list of inscriptions of minors as new citizens in AD 133, the document itself is called the *aparchē*. It proves that the child of

---

[15] Cf. *Prelim. Stud.* 98: "It is right to offer the firstfruits (of all the faculties related to reason) to God, the giver of fertile intelligence"; *Dreams* 2.272. Collaborating in the making of the bronze basin, the women "offered their mirrors as most worthy firstfruits of their wisdom, of their chastity in marriage, and, in sum, of the beauty of their souls" (*Moses* 2.137); "firstfruits always keep the remembrance of God present" (*Spec. Laws* 1.133), "thanksgiving memorial" (*Moses* 1.317); *Virtues* 159. The feast of the sacred sheaf, the firstfruits of the grain, is an act of gratitude (*Spec. Laws* 2.167, 171, 175), because the levy is made on an abundant harvest that is a gift and favor from God (*Spec. Laws* 2.216, 219).

[16] Cf. *Moses* 1.252, 254; cf. Sophocles, *Trach.* 183, 761; Euripides, *Phoen.* 857; Ps.-Plato, *Alc.* 2.151 B.

[17] Cf. *BGU* 30, 1, P. 6815, n. 30 (second-third century): ἡ ἀπαρχὴ Μάκρου Ἀντωνίου Διασκόρου.

[18] *Jur.Pap.*, 54.

[19] Cf. T. Reinach, "Un code fiscal de l'Egypte romaine: Le Gnomon de l'Idiologue," *Nouvelle revue historique de droit française et étranger,* 3d series, 44 (1920), 31.

ἀπαρχή, aparchē   149

a citizen was inscribed for the first time on an official list of citizens, with sponsors (*gnōstēres*, line 8) guaranteeing not that the child was born but that he has the right to be called a citizen of Antinoöpolis (*Pap.Lugd.Bat.* VI, 30, 18).[20] At the beginning of the third century, Ermias and his wife Helen address a petition to the senate of Antinoe that their five-year-old son Castor be inscribed as a citizen (βουλόμενοι θέσθαι ἀπαρχὴν υἱοῦ Κάστορος ἐτῶν ε΄ . . . ἀξιοῦμεν συντάξαι τῷ γραμματεῖ θέσθαι τὴν τοῦ Καστορος ἀπαρχὴν ὡς καθήκει, *P.Stras.* 634, 9 and 14). The editor, J. Schwartz, explains the procedure followed: "The father first addresses a petition to the *boulē*; then he presents his child, probably accompanied by two sponsors (*gnōstēres*) and pays perhaps . . . a tax (*aparchē*); then the child is inscribed in the register; and finally a certificate (likewise called an *aparchē*) is delivered to the father by the *prytaneis*."[21] Under Hadrian's reign, the tutor of a certain child born to a soldier had to prove that this child was a citizen by producing his birth certificate, but he seems to have been unable to do so: "that which is sought concerning the child's *aparchē* . . . to seek out the birth *aparchē*."[22] In the third century, *PSI* 1067, 11 contains the request for a child's birth certificate: "desiring the *aparchē* that we had from our mutual daughter Eudaimonis."[23]

Requests for enrollment as an ephebe are rather common,[24] and as with the birth certificate *aparchai*,[25] the payment of a monetary tax is

---

[20] = Preisigke, *SB* 7603.

[21] *P.IFAO* I, pp. 50–51.

[22] *P.Oxy.* 2199, 19 and 21: τὸ ζητούμενον περὶ τῆς τοῦ παιδίου ἀπαρχῆς. This has to do with an inheritance; cf. the inheritance tax: τὴν ἀπαρχῆς κληρονομίαν ἀπογράψασθαι, *UPZ* I, p. 162, col. VII, 10; *O.Wilck.* I, p. 345). *P.Catt.*: ἠμελήθη ἀπαρχὴν αὐτοῦ ἀποτεθῆναι (*Chrest.Mitt.*, p. 421, n. 372, col. IV, 7); perhaps *P.Flor.* 57, 81: τοῦ παιδὸς ἀπαρχή: but the meaning is obscure (cf. the γραφὴ παίδων in *Chrest.Wilck.*, p. 168, n. 143, 81). The heir, who had to make known his right and the value of his inheritance within a set period of time, did not actually inherit until paying the tax (*P.Amh.* 2, 72). Cf. S. L. Wallace, *Taxation in Egypt from Augustine to Diocletian* (Princeton Univ. Studies in Papyrology 2, 1938), p. 234.

[23] G. Vitelli, et al., eds., *Pubblicazioni della Società italiana: Papiri greci et latini* (= *PSI*) 1067, 11.

[24] *P.Tebt.* 316, 10 (AD 99); *PSI* 1225, 16: χρηματίζειν ἡμῖν τελοῦσι τὰ πρὸς τὴν ἀπαρχὴν καὶ ἐφηβείαν τοῦ προγεγραμμένου μου υἱοῦ Μηνοδώρου (second century AD); *P.Ant.* 37, 4: τάσσεσθαι ἀπαρχήν (cf. τάξασθαι, *Berichtigungsliste* 4, 2). Cf. Wallace, *Taxation in Egypt*, 277.

[25] Cf. the *oikogeneia* of *PSI* 690, 14 (first-second century): Flavius Longus paid the ἀπαρχή of the slave Juliana Philotera: ἐτάξατο τῆς ὑπερθέσμου ἐβδομαίας ἡμέρας θεᾶς Βερνίκης Εὐεργέτιδος τὴν καθήκουσαν ἀπαρχήν (= *SB* 6995–96); *Pap.Lugd.Bat.* VI, 33, 8: "the tax whereby I paid my son's ἀπαρχή" (= *SB* 7602, 8).

mentioned (*omnyō tassesthai aparchēn*),[26] and the *aparchē* can mean a sum of money,[27] notably that put up as a guarantee[28] or the tax on Jews.[29]

These usages, which despite their diversity retain the same fundamental meaning, help us better understand the NT usages of *aparchē*, which are almost all metaphorical. Most of these point to some beginning, a newness or even a birth. First of all, Jas 1:18—"He begot us by the word of truth so that we might be as it were the firstfruits of his creatures."[30] Christians are the new Israel, constituting the "assembly of the firstborn" (*ekklēsia prōtotokōn*, Heb 12:23). Newly born, they are like the firstfruits of the harvest and belong to God, and are described in terms of their precedence in regard to generations to follow. The best parallel is Philo: Israel, an orphan-people that stirs God's compassion, is "like a sort of firstfruits of the whole human race" (*Spec. Laws* 4.180). In the same sense, Christ resurrects the dead, "the firstfruits of those who sleep" (1 Cor 15:20); this is put in necessary relation with the mass of the other dead, who cannot *not* be "awakened" in their turn by God. Jesus is "at the avant-garde of those who have passed on,"[31] part of the same company; his own resurrection cannot be an isolated event but precedes and guarantees the resurrection of the other deceased.

If Epenetus is greeted as "firstfruits of Asia [offered] to Christ" (Rom 16:5) and "the household of Stephanas, firstfruits of Achaea" (1 Cor 16:15), this is a title of honor or dignity attributed to an elite, to the "firstfruits" of those who consecrated themselves to Christ in a certain region,[32] the "firstborn" begotten to the divine life, but constituting a unity with those who will be converted in the future and stirred up by their example. The "firstfruits," in accord with the usage of the LXX, are always the best. If the virgins "follow the Lamb wherever he goes, they have been redeemed (and separated) from humankind as a firstfruits for God and for the Lamb"

---

[26] *PSI* 464, 7.

[27] *P.Mert.* 5, 28: "He paid to the god Soter the ἀπαρχή according to the custom in violation of my contract of sale, which is in the public archives" (second century BC).

[28] *BGU* 1150, 11 (from 19 BC), with the observations of O. Gradenwitz, *Berliner philologische Wochenschrift* 34 (1914), col. 134–135.

[29] Ostraca from the year AD 85, *C.Pap.Jud.* 183a. On the Ἰουδαίων τέλεσμα, cf. Wallace, *Taxation in Egypt*, 170–176.

[30] Εἰς τὸ εἶναι ἡμᾶς ἀπαρχήν τινα τῶν αὐτοῦ κτισμάτων. Cf. Carl-Martin Edsman, "Schöpferwille und Geburt Jac 1, 18: Eine Studie zur altchristlichen Kosmologie," *ZNW* 38 (1939), 11–44; L. Elliott-Binns, "James 1.18: Creation or Redemption?" *NTS* 3 (1956–1957), 148–161. C. Spicq, *Théologie morale*, vol. 1, pp. 89–91.

[31] "A l'avant-garde de trépassés," the translation of J. Héring, *La Première Epître de saint Paul aux Corinthiens*, 2d ed., p. 138.

[32] Cf. *1 Clem.* 42.4—"The apostles preached in the countryside and in the cities and established their firstfruits" (καθίστανον τὰς ἀπαρχὰς αὐτῶν).

(Rev 14:4); there has been a transfer of ownership.[33] The reference is to the redemption of slaves (*agorazō*), who have a new standing and become the property of the deity. In the case at hand, it is the best part of redeemed humanity, that which is specially consecrated to God and to God's service, but they are "firstfruits" with regard to the universal harvest of the elect.[34] If all Christians have the firstfruits of the Spirit (*tēn aparchēn tou pneumatos echontes*), groaning inwardly and longing for adoption, the deliverance of the body (Rom 8:23), this *aparchē* is not a first participation as compared to a second that would be more abundant; it is an anticipation. The Holy Spirit is the pledge of the gift of glory. By his very presence he guarantees that the condition of the sons of God in this world will not remain precarious, imperfect, and threatened, or merely inchoative. They aspire intensely, for their standing as adoptive children should not only be recognized, but should also bring along all its rights and results, notable among which is the transformation of the physical body into a body that is spiritual and glorious. The Holy Spirit in the heart of the believer gives much greater certitude than any *prytaneis* of their birthright in the heavenly world.[35] This integral fullness of adoption is a marvelous *novum*.

More delicate is the interpretation of Rom 11:16, where St. Paul wishes to prove by a reference to Num 15:20–21 that the Jews are a people consecrated to God: "If the firstfruits are holy, the rest of the dough is also, and if the root is holy, the branches are as well." It matters little here whether the *aparchai* are the first Jewish converts or rather the patriarchs, notably Abraham (11:25), who constitutes "the holy root." On first reading, one understands that the consecration of the firstfruits profits the ensemble, that it has the effect of consecrating the rest. But Fr. Lagrange observes that this theology is not found in the Bible, nor in Philo, nor in Josephus; the goal of the firstfruits is "rather to give the people free usage of the whole after a small part has been set aside for Yahweh (Lev 23:14). . . . This

---

[33] C. Spicq, *Théologie morale*, vol. 2, p. 557, n. 2; p. 835, n. 4, 5; R. Devine, "The Virgin Followers of the Lamb (Apoc. 14, 4)," *Scr* 16, 1964, pp. 1–5; C. H. Lindijer, "Die Jungfrauen in der Offenbarung des Johannes XIV 4," *Studies in John, Presented to Professor Dr. J. N. Sevenster on the Occasion of His Seventieth Birthday*, NovTSup 24, Leiden, 1970, pp. 124–142.

[34] E. B. Allo, *L'Apocalypse*, 3d ed., Paris, 1933, p. 217. Cf. Philo, *Spec. Laws* 2.134: "The firstfruits of those who were of the first rank among our children were offered to God the Savior"; *Good Man Free* 15: "It is good that all young people of all lands dedicate the firstfruits of the springtime of their age to the sole pursuit with which it is good to pass both youth and old age."

[35] H. S. Jones (" Ἀπαρχὴ πνεύματος," *JTS* 23, 1922, 282–283) precisely situated this expression in the language of the papyri, giving ἀπαρχή its technical sense of a birth certificate of a free person; as the οἰκογένεια was the birth certificate of a slave.

offering thus has as its result that it confers [on plants and fruits] a sort of legal purity,"[36] making the loaf edible for the people of God; its initial "impurity" is removed. In the case at hand, the descendants of Israel, though unbelievers at present, still benefit from the blessing granted their ancestors; they remain called to salvation by virtue of the very firstfruits: "the root is holy." Now, the first NT meaning of the word is "non-impure" and it is thus in a marriage between a Christian husband and a pagan wife, or conversely "the unbelieving husband is found sanctified in the wife, and the unbelieving wife is sanctified in the brother; since otherwise we would have to conclude that your children are impure, whereas in fact they are holy" (1 Cor 7:14). This latter case is explained by the "incorporating personality" of the Christian parent, who passes on qualities and privileges to his descendant.[37] But for the firstfruits, it seems that rabbinic theology granted it a value analogous to "sanctification" with regard to the whole harvest: the best part served for the whole (cf. 1 Cor 15:20, 23). The first includes the aggregate, and that is why the offering of the former is beneficial for the latter. This is the teaching of R. Josue ben Kabsai: "All my life I read this verse (Num 19:19), 'The pure man sprinkles the impure' and I believed that an individual could only annul the impurity of one person, until I learned that a sprinkling suffices for many" (*b. Dem.* 3.4); "The Mishna (*m. Šabb.* 21.2) permits the transporting of a pure oblation together with a part that is profane. If it is allowed to take away what is impure, it is thanks to the pure part which is the majority" (*b. Dem.* 7.2).[38]

Thus all the NT usages of *aparchē*, while referring to OT texts and theology, apply only to humans. Under the influence of Philo, and, it would seem, the rabbis, they emphasize less the offering to God than the link between the firstfruits and the whole of the harvest; the former represent the latter and in some way contain it. Conformably to contemporary papyrological usage, the sense of newness, beginning, and birth is strongly emphasized; but according to the Pauline parallels, the nuance of "pledge, guarantee" comes to the surface. If the OT insists on the setting apart of the firstfruits, the NT makes the most of their unity with the rest of the harvest: "the branches are also holy."

---

[36] M.-J. Lagrange, *Saint Paul: Epître aux Romains*, p. 279.

[37] Cf. J. de Fraine, *Adam et son lignage: Etudes sur la notion de "personnalité corporative" dans la Bible*, Museum Lessianum, Section Biblique 2, Bruges, 1959.

[38] Cf. *b. Ter.* 2.1: "A levy is not placed on pure produce to liberate the impure; but if it has been done, it is valid. . . . According to R. Eliezer, one can levy the pure for the impure." Cf. 1QS 3.4—"He shall not be cleansed by purifying waters," with the commentary of J. Schmitt, "La Pureté sacerdotale d'après 1QS 3, 4–9," *RSR* 33, 1970, 214–224.

ἀπάτη

apatē, deception, trickery, pleasure

The classical meaning "deception, seduction, trickery" is the meaning in the LXX, which has only four occurrences, all in Jdt.[1] It is the only meaning in St. Paul,[2] and in the papyri, from the law of Cyrene in the second-third century BC[3] and an imperial rescript of the second century[4] to the quasi-stereotyped formula reproduced in various forms in the sixth and seventh centuries: "I confess without any guile or fear or force or deceit or compulsion" (*homologō dicha dolou kai phobou kai bias kai apatēs kai anankēs pasēs*).[5]

---

[1] Jdt 9:10, 13; 16:8. In 9:3, the text is difficult because of a play on words and corruption of the manuscripts; it could mean that the bed of the rulers, "stained with their deception" or "their sensual pleasure," was soaked with blood. In Eccl 9:6, ἀγάπη should be read in place of ἀπάτη; in 4 Macc 18:8—ἀπάτης ὄφις (the devil). The verb ἀπατᾶν occurs very often in the OT: in Gen 3:13, Eve is duped by the serpent (cf. 1 Tim 2:14), and Hezekiah misleads the people (2 Kgs 18:32; cf. 2 Chr 32:11, 15; Isa 36:14, 18; 37:10). But in both occurrences in Sir (14:16; 30:23; in the latter text, ἀπάτα must be read in place of ἀγαπᾷ), the verb surely has the sense of "rejoice"—"delight your soul." In the NT, cf. Eph 5:6; Jas 1:26.

[2] 2 Thess 2:10—the Antichrist is known for all sorts of evil deceptions = numerous seductions; Col 2:8; philosophy is an illusion, a hollow deceit; Eph 4:22—the old man is corrupted by deceitful lusts. According to Heb 3:13, sin is a seducer that does not keep its promises, that deceives, and it is sensible to speak of the ἀπάτη τῆς ἁμαρτίας (on this verse, cf. W. L. Lorimar, in *NTS*, vol. 12, 1966, pp. 390-391). In 2 Pet 2:13, ἀγάπαις must be read rather than ἀπάταις (cf. E. M. Paperrousaz, "Le Testament de Moïse," in *Sem*, vol. 19, p. 65).

[3] *SB* 9949, 11: μηθενὶ δόλῳ τινὶ ἢ ἀπάτῃ. The word is attested in *P.Tebt.* 801, 29 (142-141 BC), which is mutilated.

[4] *P.Oxy.* 1020, 8: τὸν ἀγῶνα τῆς ἀπάτης ὁ ἡγούμενος τοῦ ἔθνους ἐκδικήσει; cf. *P.Princ.* 119, 40: τὴν ἐξ ἀπάτης εὑρήκασιν (a petition of the fourth century AD).

[5] *C.P.Herm.* 31, 7; 32, 23; *P.Michael.* 40, 50; 41, 67; 45, 60; 52, 28; 55, 10; *Stud.Pal.* XX, 269, 5; *SB* 8987, 10; 8988, 51; 9463, 3; cf. *P.Ross.Georg.* III, 37, 15: χωρὶς ἀπάτης.

---

apatē, S 539; *TDNT* 1.385; *EDNT* 1.117; *NIDNTT* 2.457-459; MM 54; L&N 31.12; BAGD 82

But in 1903, A. Deissmann announced another meaning of the term: "pleasure, delight."⁶ In 1911, J. Rouffiac mentioned that several Italia manuscripts (codd. Corbeiensis, Bobbiensis) translate *apatē* with *delectationes, voluptas, delectamentum*, and he located this sense in *I.Priene* 113, 64 (84 BC): Euergetes Zosimus gave a banquet for the city, hired artists, "did not only that which was pleasant, but desiring moreover to delight the spectators, (he hired [a flute-player?] and a pantomime)."⁷ Finally, with immense epigraphical erudition, L. Robert showed that in the popular Hellenistic language *apatē* was often synonymous with *hēdonē, tryphē, terpsis* (a species of sensual pleasure, pleasure in spectacles). Apart from the Latin-Greek glossaries of the third century, he cites the *Lexeis Attikōn kai Hellēnōn kata stoicheion* of the lexicographer Moeris in the second century: "*apatē*: deceit among the Attics; pleasure among the Greeks."⁸ The examples are numerous, from Polybius 2.56.12: tragedy is modeled on reality "for the pleasure of the spectators"; to 4.20.5: music was not brought to humans as a charlatan's pleasure (or illusion?); to Dio Chrysostom, *Or.* 32.4–5: spectacles are a delight for the city (cf. 4.114). According to Artemidorus of Ephesus, dreaming about peaches, apricots, plums, and cherries "signifies pleasures and sensual delights if these are seasonable."⁹

These attestations provide a framework for translating *hē apatē tou ploutou* in the explanation of the parable of the sower (Matt 13:22; Mark 4:19). Commentators usually say "the seductions of wealth stifle the word." But we should probably follow M. J. Lagrange, who in his commentary on

---

⁶ A. Deissmann, "Hellenisierung des semitischen Monotheismus," in *NJahrb*, 1903, p. 165. If we confined ourselves to biblical semantics, we could explain the evolution beginning with certain uses of ἀπάτη-ἀπατᾶν: "seduce a woman" (Exod 22:16; Judg 14:15; 16:5; Sus 56; Jdt 12:16). In Philo, *Joseph* 56, the γυναικῶν ἀπάτας could just as well be the deceptions as the pleasures of women (cf. *Creation* 165; *Sacr. Abel and Cain* 26; *Good Man Free* 151: ἔρωτος ἀπάτης). In any event, *Alleg. Interp.* 3.64 sets forward the principle: πᾶσα οὖν ἀπάτη οἰκειοτάτη ἡδονῇ! According to *Drunkenness* 217, the method of preparation and the form of pastries "are made not only for the pleasure of taste, but also for that of the eyes."

⁷ [French] translation of J. Rouffiac, *Caractères du grec*, p. 38.

⁸ Ἀπάτη· ἡ πλάνη παρ' Ἀττικοῖς ... ἡ τέρψις παρ' Ἕλλησιν. The edition of J. Pierson, 1759, p. 65; cf. L. Robert, *Hellenica*, vol. 11, Paris, 1960, pp. 5–15; Oepke, in *TDNT*, vol. 1, p. 385.

⁹ Artemidorus Daldianus, *Onir.* 1.73: προσκαίρους ἡδονὰς καὶ ἀπάτας σημαίνει. Cf. Plutarch, *Sol.* 21.4: Solon put on the same level "deception (ἀπάτην), constraint, sensual pleasure (ἡδονήν), suffering." —Ἀπάτη is attested several times as a proper name of a woman (*P.Petr.* III, 11, 21) or a place (*BGU* 1665, 6); does it suggest deception or delight?

St. Mark relies on A. Deissmann and translates "the pleasures of wealth." The parallel in Luke 8:14 is almost conclusive: *hēdonai tou biou*.[10]

The two meanings are brought together in Strabo 11.2.10, which explains the epithet *Apatouros* given to the Aphrodite of Phanagoria: Attacked by giants, "she called on Heracles for help and hid him in a cave, then, receiving each of the giants in turn in her home, she turned them over one at a time to Heracles to be killed, thanks to this ruse whereby she served as bait, *ex apatēs*."[11]

---

[10] J. Dupont, "La Parabole du Semeur dans la version de Luc," in *Apophoreta: Festschrift für E. Haenchen*, Berlin, 1964, pp. 97–108; cf. H. J. Cadbury, *The Making of Luke-Acts*, London, 1958, p. 179.

[11] Cf. W. Kastner, "ἀπάτη," in *MusHelv*, 1977, pp. 199–202.

ἀπελπίζω

apelpizō, to hope for something in return

In the Sermon on the Mount, the Lord, wishing to emphasize the disinterested quality of *agapē*, commanded "Love your enemies, do good, and lend *mēden apelpizontes.*"[1] If this were a matter of making interest-free loans, it would be an illustration of the gratuitousness of benevolence (*agathopoieō*), not as a profitable financial operation for the lender, even at the lowest rates, but as a brotherly service.[2] But if the righteous person

---

[1] Luke 6:35. Hebrew has several terms for lending. The verb *lāwâh*, "borrow" (in the qal), "lend" (in the hiphil; LXX δανείζειν, κιχρᾶν); the verb *nāšâ'*, "lend, charge interest," and in the hiphil "oppress" (*foenerari, foenum imponere*); or the noun *maššeh*, "usury, interest." The verb *nāšak*, "bite, oppress, exact interest," which yielded *nešek*, one of the proper names for usury (in the versions: τόκος and *usura*). From the verb *rābâh*, "increase, multiply," are derived two other kinds of interest, *marbit* and *tarbit* (πλεονασμός, *superabundantia*).

[2] Exod 22:25; Lev 25:46–47; Deut 23:19–20 require lending to a fellow-countryman without charging interest (cf. C. van Leeuwen, *Le développement du sens social en Israël avant l'ère chrétienne*, Assen, 1955, pp. 42–58). "The one who practices mercy lends to his neighbor" (Sir 29:1); "Happy is the man who is compassionate and lends" (Ps 112:5). The ungodly "lends today and insists on collecting tomorrow" (Sir 20:15). On loans in the OT, cf. J. Hejcl, "Das alttestamantliche Zinsverbot im Lichte der ethnologischen Jurisprudenz," in *BZ*, vol. 12, 4, Fribourg, 1907; C. Spicq, *Les Péchés d'injustice*, Paris, 1935, vol. 2, pp. 444–450 (bibliography, pp. 488ff.); S. Stein, "The Laws on Interest in the Old Testament," in *JTS*, 1953, pp. 161–170; R. North, *Sociology of the Biblical Jubilee*, Rome 1954, pp. 176–190; E. Neufeld, "The Rate of Interest and the Text of Nehemiah V, 11," in *JQR*, 1954, pp. 194–204; idem, "The Prohibitions against Loans at Interest in Ancient Hebrew Laws," in *HUCA*, 26, 1955, pp. 355–412; E. Szlechter, "Le Prêt dans l'Ancien Testament et dans les codes mésopotamiens d'avant Hammourabi," in *La Bible et l'orient*, Paris, 1953, pp. 16–25; R. de Vaux, *Ancient Israel*, vol. 1, p. 170; H. A. Rupprecht, *Untersuchungen zum Darlehen im Recht der graeco-aegyptischen Papyri der Ptoläerzeit*, Munich, 1967; R. P. Maloney, "Usury in Greek, Roman and Rabbinic Thought," in *Traditio*, 1971, pp. 79–109; P. W. Pestman,

---

apelpizō, S 560; *TDNT* 2.533–534; *EDNT* 1.437–441; *NIDNTT* 2.238, 241; MM 56–57; L&N 30.54; BAGD 83–84

ἀπελπίζω, apelpizō 157

lent money to his countrymen without charging interest,[3] debtors often abused his generosity (cf. Sir 29:1-7), so that the lender, defrauded of his capital, was tempted to refuse to make new advances. Hence the exhortation in Matt 5:42—"Do not turn away from one who wants to borrow"; note the continued action implied by the present imperative *danizete*—"lend habitually" (Luke 6:35)—and the clear instruction *mēden apelpizontes*— "without expecting anything in return." Lend with the willingness never to be repaid.

But this translation, which is an interpretation—the difficulty is well known[4]—does not match the unique and well-attested meaning of *apelpizō*: not to hope that something will happen, to despair.[5] Furthermore, it seems to contradict the motive given later in the verse for heeding the exhortation: "and your recompense will be great." Some have suggested a mistake in the text,[6] or else exploited the reading of certain manuscripts (א, Ξ, Π* 489) supported by the Syriac versions (*mēdena apelpizontes*) taking the neuter

---

"Loans Bearing No Interest?" in *JJP*, 1971, pp. 7-29; B. Menu, "Le Prêt en droit égyptien," in *Etudes sur l'Egypte et le Soudan anciens*, Lille-Paris, 1973, pp. 59-141.

[3] Ps 15:5; Ezek 18:17; cf. ἄτοκος: *P.Fouad* 44, 19, "Lucius will repay the loan to Didymus without interest" (28 August 44); *P.Rein.* 31, 10: "Dionysos will return this grain without interest to Hermias" (109 BC); *P.Amh.* 50, 10; *P.Ross.Georg.* II, 6, 21; *P.Tebt.* 342, 30; *C.Pap.Jud.* 143, 25.

[4] The best discussion is that of M. Lagrange, *Luc*, cf. C. Spicq, *Agapè*, vol. 1, p. 111.

[5] God "the Savior of those who despair" (Jdt 9:11); "those who are without hope among humans" (Isa 29:19); "If you have drawn the sword against a friend, do not despair; a return is possible" (Sir 22:21); "The one who has revealed the secrets (of his friend) can hope no more" (Sir 27:21); Lucillius "Diaphantus who took away all hope from others" (*Anth. Pal.* 11.114). In Josephus, it is always a matter of giving up hope of surviving (*War* 1.462), of receiving pardon (4.193; 5.354), the pity of the Romans (6.368), security (4.397); thus it means renouncing any future good, given present circumstances. Likewise Polybius, "Hannibal despaired of his situation" (1.19.12) and Diodorus Siculus: "These monsters had made them despair of saving their lives" (17.106.7; cf. 19.50). Unknown in Philo, this verb, attested for the first time by Hyperides 5.35, is also found in a number of inscriptions (cf. R. Bultmann, in *TDNT*, vol. 2, pp. 533-544), is used in Galen for illnesses without hope of cure, desperate cases, and—with negation—for not doubting, having confidence (cf. W. K. Hobart, *Medical Language*, pp. 118-119); finally, in two papyri (*P.Cair.Zen.* 59642, 4, mutilated; *BGU* 1844, 13, from AD 130) and an ostracon from 260 BC (*SB* 8266, 10b and 20). On the Theban stele on which is inscribed the honorific decree for the general Callimachus in 42 BC, τοῖς ἀπελπίζουσιν refers to the Egyptians reduced to a critical state by the insufficient rise in the Nile (Dittenberger, *Or.* 194, 19 = *SB* 8334), but this restored verb was not retained by R. Hutmacher, *Ehrendekret*, p. 22.

[6] Ἀντελπίζοντες. T. Reinach, "Mutuum date, nihil inde sperantes," in *REG*, 1894, p. 52; the restoration refused by M. J. Lagrange, in *RB*, 1895, p. 116. The variant ἀπηλπικότες (D, G, Lat., Peshitta, read ἀπηλγηκότες) at Eph 4:19 is too poorly attested to be retained.

plural *mēdena* as referring to rebuffed would-be borrowers, "not forcing anyone to despair."[7] But this reading is clearly a dittography (*mēden a-apelpizontes*). Finally, one could follow the Old Latin, *nihil desperantes*, not despairing of someday recovering your capital or of being repaid a hundredfold by God (cf. the thought in Eccl 11:1—the sea returns that which is given it). But M. J. Lagrange rightly rebels against the meaning, which he says is "absolutely repugnant in this heroic context" (*RB*, 1895, p. 196).

So we must follow the Clementine Vulgate (*nihil inde sperantes*), which takes the verb in the sense clearly demanded by the context,[8] specifying the practical consequences of *agapē* in the abrupt manner of Semitic formulations. Jesus is not entering the spheres of business or of the virtues of prudence or justice. He is pointing out the nature of Christian love: complete forgetfulness of oneself and absolute gratuitousness. "Lend without expecting anything in return."[9]

---

[7] F. Field, *Notes on the Translation*, p. 59.

[8] Opposition to παρ' ὧν ἐλπίζετε λαβεῖν (verse 34); cf. E. Klostermann, *Das Lukas-Evangelium*, 2d ed., Tübingen, 1929, p. 82, who cites the parallel text of *Exod. Rab.* 31 (91c): "The one who lends money without demanding interest, God esteems this so highly in him that it is as if he had kept all the commandments." "The Gentiles lend in hope of a return; lend without hoping for a return, without hoping to receive. Ἀπελπίζω never has this meaning, it is true, but it could have been invented by Luke as a parallel to ἀπολανβάνειν, which also has both senses, receiving and giving up. In the Middle Ages this verse was understood to refer to lending for interest, but there is no exegetical tradition for that meaning. . . . Merely to forego interest would be hardly be to live up to the ideal of total renunciation that is set forth in this passage. This is not an order, it is a counsel. The objection that lending is then tantamount to giving misses a fine distinction. Often a person who borrows would be embarrassed to accept a gift. So one lends to him, being open to receiving repayment if it is offered, but also with a willingness sometimes to sacrifice the whole amount, *nihil sperantes*, μηδὲν ἐλπίζοντες ἀπολαβεῖν (Field)" (M. J. Lagrange, *RB*, 1895, pp. 196–197).

[9] What follows in the verse—καὶ ἔσται ὁ μισθὸς ὑμῶν πολύς—agrees with the supernatural lex talionis operative everywhere in the Synoptics: whatever is sacrificed on earth is compensated a hundredfold in supernatural value. Is it permissible to cite the discourse of Nero to the Corinthians in 67: "From my greatness of heart one may have all hope, παρὰ τῆς ἐμῆς μεγαλοφροσύνης ἀνέλπιστον" (Dittenberger, *Syl.* 814, 11)?

ἀπέραντος

aperantos, endless, interminable, vain

The heterodox Ephesians are fond of "fables and endless genealogies," i.e., never completed and inconsequential (1 Tim 1:4). The adjective *aperantos* (NT hapax), unknown in the papyri (cf. *P.Tebt.* 847, 21, *apēramenou*) has these two connotations.[1] But in the first century it took on a technical rhetorical significance in the Stoic vocabulary, qualifying "reasonings that do not result in proof, arguments that do not conclude,"[2] sterile conversations (Josephus, *Ant.* 17.131). Cicero complains to the son of Amyntas, an intolerable babbler (*aperantologias aēdous, Att.* 12.9; cf. Strabo 13.1.41). One of the best parallels is in the satirical poet Timon of Phlius: the philosophers "dispute endlessly [and vainly] (*apeirita dērioōntes*) in the aviary of the muses [meaning the Museum of Alexandria] . . . until these table speakers are unburdened of their flow of words [literally, logodiarrhea]" (Athenaeus 1.22*d*). The other is in Philo: the happiness of the skeptics rides entirely upon the endless and fruitless (*aperantō kai anēnytō*) criticism of names and words (*Prelim. Stud.* 53). Minds of this sort know neither measure nor limit in their discourse, they speak indiscriminately, bringing chaos and confusion in all matters, mixing the true and the false, the sacred and the profane. Prattlers of this type, already exposed at Alexandria,[3] have taken up exegesis and theology at Ephesus and pose a threat to the faith (cf. Titus 3:9).

---

[1] Without limit, infinite. *Ep. Arist.* 156: an infinity of appitudes; Polybius 1.57.3: the historian cannot enumerate an infinity of events; Philo (*Prelim. Stud.* 53) expressing his disdain for tricks of logic: "the endless and pointless minute examination of nouns and verbs"; *Corp. Herm.* 1.11.4: εἰς ἀπέραντον τέλος; without issue, inextricable, without effect, without result (Job 36:26—the number of God's years is endless and unfathomable); Josephus, *Ant.* 17.131: Varus realizing that the affair was endless and without effect; *1 Clem.* 20.8—the ocean impassable by men; *Corp. Herm.* 9.8: "The Good is unsurpassable, limitless, and endless, ἀδιάβατον γὰρ τὸ ἀγαθὸν καὶ ἀπέραντον καὶ ἀτελές."

[2] Λόγοι ἀπέραντοι (Philodemus of Gadara, *Ir.*, p. 97; cf. Diogenes Laertius 7.78; Strabo 2.4.8).

[3] Philo, *Abraham* 20: πρὸς ἄμετρον καὶ ἀπέραντον καὶ ἄκριτον διήγησιν.

ἀπερισπάστως

aperispastōs, **without hindrance or distraction**

The Corinthians are exhorted to virginity, which would firmly position them near the Lord, without distraction (*euparedron tō Kyriō aperispastōs*, 1 Cor 7:35). This adverb is a biblical hapax and is relatively rare in the Hellenistic period.[1] Apart from errors, it is found only twice in the papyri,[2] but its meaning is clear. Derived from *perispaō*, "pull from another direction, pull against," *aperispastōs* means "without hindrance, without distraction"; which agrees with the meaning of the adjective *aperispastos*, "not drawn hither and thither," known in the OT[3] and very common in our papyri. The oldest attestation is from the third century BC,[4] and it is multiplied in

---

[1] Polybius 2.20.10: When the Romans had conquered the Gauls, nothing remained to distract them from the war against Pyrrhus; 4.18.6: They could not run without hindrance against those who were rushing through the gate; Epictetus 1.29.59: in contemplation (θεωρεῖν), "one must settle in well, not letting oneself be distracted . . . be very attentive" (cf. 3.22.69: The Cynic who remains free of all that could distract him, ἀπερίσπαστον εἶναι); cf. J. Weiss, *Der erste Korintherbrief*, 10th ed., Göttingen, 1925, p. 205.

[2] *P.Tebt.* 895, 57 (from 175 BC): ἀπερισπάστως γενέσθαι; D. Foraboschi, *L'Archivio de Kronion*, Milan, 1971, n. 38, 16: παρέξομεν δὲ τὸν Σασῶπιν ἀπαρανοχλήτως καὶ ἀνισπράκτως καὶ ἀπερισπάστως κατὰ πάντα τρόπον; cf. the decree of Euergetes II in 124 BC, ἀπερισπάστους γενηθέντας (*P.Tebt.* 700, 36; taken up again in *C.Ord.Ptol.* 50, 15); *P.Grenf.* 1, n. 11, col. II, 4: τούτου δὲ γενομένου καὶ ἀπερίσπαστος ὤν (discussion concerning a field, from 157 BC); Polybius 2.67.7: "Freed by this maneuver (ἀπερίσπαστον γενόμενον), the division of the Illyrians . . . threw themselves valiantly against the enemy."

[3] Sir 41:1—"O death, how bitter is the memory of you . . . to the man who has no cares—ἀνδρὶ ἀπερισπάστῳ—and is successful at everything"; Wis 16:11—"For fear lest they become careless of your benefits."

[4] *BGU* 1243, 13. In the second and third centuries BC, cf. 1057, 22; 1756, 5: παρασχοῦαὐτοὺς ἀπερισπάστους; *UPZ* 145, 23. Cf. Diodorus Siculus 17.9.4: "Alexander would like to have a free hand (ἀπερίσπαστον ἔχειν) in the war against the Persians."

---

aperispastōs, S 563; *EDNT* 1.120; MM 57; L&N 30.33; BAGD 84

the first and second centuries AD, so that it could be said that the word becomes common coinage.[5] Now a general orders, "see to it that he is left in peace until he has finished his sowing" (*P.Rein.* 18, 40; 12 October 108 BC); now the weavers of Philadelphia remark that they "have until now been left in peace to practice our trade" and ask not to be disturbed and to remain exempt from other public services (*P.Phil.* 10, 16; from AD 139); or someone requires "that the carrier not be bothered" (*ho diagōn aperispastos estai, UPZ* 226, 6). In AD 46, 48, and 52 the *homologia aperispastou* is a guarantee of immunity to any constraint, penalty, or disagreement that a contracting party might incur.[6]

In all these occurrences, the adjective emphasized the absence of troubles, bothers, inconveniences, freedom from worries; in other literary texts, the focus is on steadiness, attention, and refusal of any digression.[7] All of these nuances converge perfectly in the *aperispastōs* of the virgins in 1 Cor 7:15, who are spared the *perispasmoi* of the married life.[8] With good reason, the exegetes bring in Luke 10:38–42, where Mary of Bethany is seated, at rest, at the feet of the Lord,[9] all her attention focused on him; while Martha busies herself here and there (*periespato*), pulled between divergent concerns. Thus virginity allows exclusive concentration on God.[10]

---

[5] So much so that T. Nägeli (*Wortschatz*, p. 30) mentions this word as one of those which identify St. Paul as an authentic Hellenist.

[6] *P.Mich.* V, 238, 35 and 177; 353, 4; 354, 19; cf. *P.Oxy.* 286, 17 (from AD 82): ὅπως περέχωνται ἡμᾶς ἀπερισπάστους καὶ ἀπαρενοχλήτους ὑπὲρ προκειμένης ὀφειλῆς καὶ ἀποδώσειν ταῦτα = so that he can be free from any responsibility or trouble in connection with the aforementioned debt and may repay it; 898, 15 (AD 123), which the editors translate [into English]: "to mortgage all my property in the Oasis in return for a deed of release received from Dioscorus." The editors further explain γράμματα ἀπερισπάστου as "a deed of indemnification." Cf. A. Berger, *Die Strafklauseln in den Papyrusurkunden*, 2d ed., Aalen, 1965, pp. 203ff.

[7] Polybius 4.32.6: "The Lacedaemonians, without allowing themselves to be distracted, set out to harm them"; Dionysius of Halicarnassus, *Th.* 9: "In historical writing, everything should be connected and contribute to unity, ἀπερίστατον εἶναι." This nuance of uninterruptedness is that of Plutarch, *Arist.* 5.3: "The authority of Miltiades was reinforced by the continuity of his command."

[8] Cf. Hierocles the Stoic, *Marriage*, in Stobaeus, *Flor.* 67.22.24 (vol. 4, p. 504).

[9] Παρακαθεσθεῖσα, cf. εὐπάρεδρον—perhaps a neologism coined by St. Paul—to be well situated near someone; the meaning is someone "with an attentive demeanor toward a venerable or sacred object" (E. B. Allo, *Première Epître aux Corinthiens*, p. 184).

[10] Cf. C. Spicq, *Théologie morale*, vol. 2, pp. 564–565; L. Legrand, *La Virginité dans la Bible*, Paris, 1964, pp. 83ff.

ἀπέχω

apechō, to hold, collect, acknowledge receipt of payment in full; remain distant; abstain

This verb, which has several very different meanings, is a compound of *echō*, "to have," which expresses a relationship of possession: "to hold, keep," hence "collect." Thus after Asclepius has healed Demodike, Akeson's wife, Akeson writes on a tablet, "You have received the debt of Akeson."[1] According to Marcus Aurelius 9.42.12–13, when a person does something good, it is enough to have acted in accord with nature; no reward is to be sought (*misthon zēteis*) any more than that the eye should receive a reward (*apechei to idion*) for seeing. In fulfilling its role, it possesses that which belongs to it (*echei to heautou*).

Hence the commercial meaning of *apechō*, "acknowledge receipt of payment in full,"[2] which is copiously attested in the papyri and is highlighted by A. Deissmann:[3] to have something from someone's hand is to receive one's due. There are two types of receipts: some note the act of a person who has paid, with the verb in the perfect (for the abiding result of the action); others express the acknowledgment of the one who receives, with the verb in the present (*echō*, "I have"; *apechō*, "I have my due").[4] The

---

[1] Callimachus, *Epigr.* 54.1; cf. 50.4: "The old woman, in exchange for the milk of her breasts, received thanks" (ἀπέχει χάριτας); Plutarch, *Them.* 17.4: "Themistocles reaped the fruit of the labors (τὸν καρπὸν ἀπέχειν) that he had expended for Greece"; *Sol.* 22.4: τόν τε μισθὸν ἀπέχει; *Mor.* 2.124 c; Josephus, *War* 1.179: "Pompey had not touched the temple gold"; 596: "I receive the price of my impiety" (ἀπέχω τὸ ἐπιτίμιον). A Jewish epitaph, for Horaia and her family: "Stranger, you have all the information about us" (ἀπέχεις, ὦ ξεῖνε, σαφῶς τὰ ἅπαντα παρ' ἡμῶν).

[2] A contract to hire a nurse, in AD 26: "The declarer and her husband and guarantor Petseiris hereby acknowledge receipt (ἀπέχειν) from Paapis of sixty drachmas of silver" (*P.Rein.* 103, 12); 104, 5; *P.Ryl.* 588, 9 (78 BC). Ἀποχή is the "receipt" (*P.Oxy.* 91, 25; 296, col. II, 8; *P.Princ.* 181, 16; *P.Mich.* 596, 9, etc.); "Draw up the model and the receipt" (τὸν τύπον καὶ τὴν ἀποχήν, *P.IFAO* II, n. 9, 4); ἡ ἀποχὴ κυρία καὶ ἐπερωτηθεὶς ὡμολόγησα (*P.Charite*, n. 13, 7; cf. 8, 8 and 18).

[3] A. Deissmann, *Light*, pp. 110–112. Idem, *Bible Studies*, p. 229.

[4] *O.Bodl.* 690–693. C. Préaux, "Aspect verbal et préverbe: L'Usage de ἀπέχω dans les ostraca," in *ChrEg*, 1954, pp. 139–146. Presents, according to the place and time,

---

apechō, S 568; *TDNT* 2.828; *EDNT* 1.120–121; MM 57–58; L&N 57.137, 59.47, 85.16, 90.67; BDF §§ 129, 180(3), 180(5), 308, 322; BAGD 84–85; ND 6.3

ἀπέχω, apechō   163

oldest papyrological attestation of the verb is from 276 BC: *homologein apechein K* ... (*P.Hib.* 97, 5; republished as *P.Yale* 27; cf. *P.Alex.* 9, 10). Usually it is specified that the "price" (*tēn timēn*) of some land, a house, an ass, etc., has been received: "C. Anthistius Valens has received the price of these lands (*to autōn teimas apeschēkenai*) as stipulated in the papers" (*P.Phil.* 11, 13); "Sarapion acknowledges having received from the buyer the full price agreed upon, amounting to fifty-four thousand drachmas."[5] Also quite often, however, only the sum of money is mentioned: "I have received the prescribed drachmas of silver";[6] "I acknowledge (having from you) twelve staters and two denarii which I received (*apeschon*) and which were charged to my account, and which I will repay" (*P.Mur.* 114, 12); sometimes obols (*P.Genova* 88, 2), as with this new officer (*principalis*) who has drawn some money (*chalkon apeschon*) and would have liked to send a gift to his mother (*P.Mich.* 465, 7). Sometimes a dowry is in question (*phernē, P.Fam.Tebt.* 13, 38; *P.Mil.Vogl.* 185, 21, 36), sometimes expenditures (*da-*

---

alternate with the aorists ἔσχον, ἔλαβον (*O.Bodl.* 670-737; *O.Wilck.* I, pp. 86, 109; II, n. 1081-1090, 1616). This nuance of the aorist has been described as "Aorist-präsens" (A. Thumb, "Prinzipienfragen der Koine-Forschung," in *NJahrb,* 1906, pp. 246-263); the added prefix reinforces the aorist (referring to an outcome) to express the perfect idea. With good reason, this aoristic role of the verbal prefix was rejected by E. Mayser (*Grammatik,* II, 1, pp. 132-133), who places ἀπέχω among the presents with perfect meaning, and by H. Erman ("Die Habe-Quittung bei den Griechen," in *APF,* 1901, pp. 77-84) who translates "have in return." C. Préaux (*ChrEg,* 1954, p. 146) concludes "thus we cannot call upon the ostraca as testimony to the function of the prefix in expressing aspect with regard to the verb ἀπέχω." Cf. the index prepared for the Bodleian ostraca by J. Bingen and M. Wittek, *O.Bodl.* III, p. 245.

[5] *P.Thead.* 2, 8; 3, 10: "I have sold a white adult ass for the agreed price of ... talents of silver, and I have received the aforesaid money"; 12, 24, *P.Tebt.* 109, 17: this sum "has been received by the above-names parties from Petesuchos, hand to hand, apart from the house" (93 BC); *PSI* 39, 8; *P.Princ.* 19, 7 (second century BC), 149, 9; *P.Köln* 146, 2 (10 BC); 54, 5 (4 BC); 155, 17 (AD 6); *P.Mich.* 241, 15 (AD 16); 251, 33 (AD 19); 254, 4 (AD 30/31); 428, 6, 14, 17; 583, 12; 621, 6; *P.Fouad* 40, 19 (AD 35); *P.Athen.* 25, 10 (AD 61); *P.Alex.* 15, col. II, 3: Heracles acknowledges having received the agreed price (first century); *BGU* 1643, 20; 2036, 21; 2049, 12, 18; 2335, 8 (AD 42/43); *Pap.Lugd.Bat.* II, 6, 20: ἀπέσχον τὴν τιμήν; *P.Corn.* 13, 29; *P.Dura* 26, 13; *P.Erl.* 106, 25; *P.Harr.* 146, 5; *P.Cair.Isid.* 83, 16; *P.Mert.* 19, 7; *P.Mil.Vogl.* 78, 27; 161, col. I, 23; 239, 13; *P.Oslo* 45, 2; *P.Oxy.* 2138, 5; 2270, 16; 2951, 25; 3143, 27; *P.Wisc.* 59, 21; *P.Soterichos* 5, 40; *SB* 6001, 6; 6016, 28.

[6] *BGU* 2119, 8 (first century); 2338, 15; 2342, 10; *P.Fouad* 56, 8; *P.Athen.* 29, 16; *P.Fam.Tebt.* VI, 3, 17; 7, 6; 9, 10; 10, 7; XIII, 17, 21; *P.Cair.Isid.* 80, 8; 81, 17; *P.Mil.* 7, 11, 37 (AD 38); *P.Mich.* 189, 23; 194, 8 (AD 61); 252, 5 (AD 25/26); 256, 4 (AD 29/30); *P.Mil.Vogl.* 159, 8; 186, 8, 18; 225, 11; *P.Princ.* 141, 2 (AD 23); *P.Yale* 63, 19 (AD 64); *P.Soterichos* 22, 15; 25, 12; *P.Oxy.* 3254, 24; *SB* 7533, 23, 53; 7664, 12; 8053, 4; *O.Mich.* 138, 4: ἀπέχω παρά σου δραχμὰς ζ'; 146, 2. In AD 43: ἀπέχω τὰς τριάκοντα δύο δραχμὰς Ἁρμύσιος (*P.IFAO* I, n. 17, 2); cf. pieces of meat, 56, 2: ἀ. τὰ δύο κρεάδια.

panēmata, P.Fouad 64, 5; P.Hamb. 69, 6), *artabai* of grain,[7] of straw (SB 9782, 3), a cargo or load,[8] food[9] and fruit (*karpōn*, BGU 1587, 7); on occasion, "what is due to me."[10] A rental or lease that is paid in kind (*to ekphorion*)[11] and a lease paid in cash (*phoros*)[12] are mentioned either together or separately; but for the latter it is often specified that it is a loan or rent (*misthōsis*).[13] In contracts for service, receipt of the agreed-upon wage is acknowledged (*apeschēkenai . . . to symphōnēthen salarion*, P.Harr. 64, 25; SB 10205, 16). In AD 24, "He acknowledges . . . receiving from him the price and the wages" (*homologei . . . apeschēkenai par' autou tēn timēn kai tous misthous*, P.Mich. 337, 7); in the second century, "I have received the wage from Phaophi" (*apechō de ton tou Phaōphi misthon*, BGU 1647, 13; cf. 1663, 1, 16; P.Oxy. 1992, 19).

These usages shed light on Matt 6:2, 5, 16, where—with respect of almsgiving, prayer, and fasting—the Lord denounces the ostentation of the hypocrites who seek to be seen and praised by other people. He repeats three times, "Truly, I tell you, they have received their reward" (*apechousin ton misthon autōn*). The verb in the present indicative means that these apparently pious people have nothing more to expect in the beyond. They already have now that which is due them. They have in hand the receipt for what they have supplied . . . so much wind! The irony is plain. In the same sense, the rich are told in Luke 6:24, *apechete tēn paraklēsin hymōn*; they have had their portion of joy on earth and must not expect "consolation" in heaven!

---

[7] P.Mich. 195, 6, 19; P.Oslo 38, 17; P.Princ. 181, 10; P.Mil.Vogl. 158, 11, 27; 226, 9; that which has been sent: ἀπέχομεν παρ' ὑμῶν τὰς ἐπισταλείσας (BGU 2269, 5; 2270, 3; 2271, *a* 5; *b* 6; *c* 3; SB 7515, 33, 112, 133; 10889, 4); cf. P.Mich. 531, 2: ἐπεῖχον τὴν ἐπιστολήν; P.Oxy. 2964, 5; 2965, 5; 2968, 7.

[8] Γόμον; O.Brüss.Berl. 67.

[9] P.Fam.Tebt. 53, A 5: ἀπέσχον παρά σοῦ τὰ τροφῖα; B 5: τὰ ὠψώνια; P.Wisc. 68, 12; P.Amst. 41, 53 and 77.

[10] Ἀπέχω παρά σου ἃς ὤφιλές μοι, P.Mil.Vogl. 146, 2; P.Oxy. 2587, 5: ὁμολογῶ ἀπεσχηκέναι παρά σου ἀφ' ὧν μου ὀφείλεις ἀργυρίου; 2834, 2; P.Princ. 34, 14; 35, 3; P.Soterichos 23, 5; BGU 1656, 3; 1657, 4; 2047, 5; Pap.Lugd.Bat. II, 11, 4; P.IFAO III, 22, 4; SB 9201, 8; 9406 *b* 6; 9485, 2; 10723, 12; cf. 8307, 8, a tomb inscription from Doris: "The one who is good also receives at last an easy death."

[11] BGU 2038, 3: ἀπέχω παρά σού τὸ ἐκφόριον; 2039, 2; P.Corn. 41, 13; P.Aberd. 63, 3; 64, 3; P.Cair.Isid. 108, 6; 109, 4, 10; 122, 3; P.Mich. 196, 7, 20; 197, 7; 198, 6; 199, 7; P.Mil.Vogl. 54, 4: ἀπέχομεν παρά σου τὰ ἐκφόρια καὶ τοὺς φόρους; 105, 23; 161, col. II, 15; 168, 4; 169, 3; P.Princ. 37, 5, 18; P.Oxy. 2836, 4; P.Wisc. 57, 5; P.Col. VIII, 185, 6; P.Soterichos 8, 2; 10, 2; 11, 4; 12, 4; SB 7624, 5; 7677, 6; 9175, 3; 9650, 4; 10332, 2.

[12] P.Soterichos 6, 10; 7, 11; P.Warr. 12, 4; P.Yale 67, 15; SB 8014, 5; 9357, 6; 9833, 8; 10423, 2; cf. τὸ γενόμενον τέλος, 7580, 4, 8; 9552, 2, 4; O.Brüss.Berl. 25, 27. On the βαλανευτικόν tax paid to the collectors of the treasury, cf. O.Wilb. 44–48.

[13] BGU 612, 2; 1647, 13; 1663, 1, 16; 2344, 5; P.Athen. 20, 29; P.Mich. 337, 7; P.Oxy. 1992, 19; P.Corn. 45, 7, 20; P.Gron. 9, 15, 23; P.Princ. 146, 18; SB 6766, 39; 7607, 30.

In contrast, Philemon, whose runaway slave was temporarily separated from him (*echōristhē*), will recover him (*apechēs*) for good in heaven as a brother for eternity (Phlm 15). The same bookkeeping nuance appears in Phil 4:18, in a section where the apostle uses several expressions borrowed from the language of business.[14] He acknowledges receiving the help sent by the Philippians: "I have received everything and more than enough" (*apechō de panta kai perisseuō*); "through Epaphroditus, I received what you sent" (*dexamenos . . . ta par' hymōn*). We could translate, "I give a receipt for everything, and I have plenty."[15]

The verbal prefix *ap-* retains its full force when *apechō* means "be distant," first of all in a geographical sense: "Jesus was not far from the house" (Luke 7:6); the prodigal son was still far from his father (15:20); Emmaus is "a town about sixty stadia away from Jerusalem" (*apechousan stadious hexēkonta*, 24:13). The usage is classical[16] and is particularly common in the LXX: Joseph's brothers, having left the city, "had not gone far" (Hebrew hiphil of *rāḥaq*, Gen 44:4); "They were far from the Sidonians."[17] It is common even in the papyri.[18] From this spatial meaning comes the

---

[14] Phil 4:15—λόγος δόσεως καὶ λήμψεως, "account of giving and receiving"; ἐκοινώνησεν, was associated, having a common account in community property.

[15] J. Fleury, "Une société de fait dans l'Eglise apostolique," in *Mélanges P. Meylan*, Lausanne, 1963, vol. 2, pp. 41–59. Cf. Gen 43:23—"your money came to me" (Hebrew *bô'*); Num 32:19—"our inheritance has come to us across the Jordan."

[16] Herodotus 1.179: "There is another city, about an eight days' journey away from (ἀπέχουσα) Babylon, called Is"; Thucydides 6.97.1: "Leon is six or seven stadia away from Epipolae"; Xenophon, *Cyr.* 1.1.3: "Cyrus thought that he was obeyed by peoples who were several days' journey away"; 3.3.28: "the armies were no longer more than about a parasang away"; Aristotle, *Gen. An.* 5.1.781ª: the more distant objects are, the more distinct they appear; cf. *Part. An.* 2.9.655ª; τὰ ἀπέχοντα; Xenophon, *An.* 4.3.5; Euphron, frag. 11.3: ἀπὸ θαλάττης Νικομήδει δεσποτῇ ὁδὸν ἀπέχοντι δώδεκ' ἡμερῶν (third century BC; cf. J. M. Edmonds, *Attic Comedy*, vol. 3 A, p. 278); Diodorus Siculus 5.42; 12.33; Philostratus, *Gym.* 5: "the runners were placed at a distance of one *stadion*."

[17] Judg 18:7; Deut 12:21; Ezek 8:6; 22:5; Ps 103:12—"as the east is far from the west"; Isa 55:9—the heavens above the earth; 1 Macc 8:4—"the place (ὁ τόπος) was very far from them"; 2 Macc 11:5—"Beth-zur was about five leagues from Jerusalem"; 12:29; cf. Philo, *Joseph* 256: his father was not far from the border; *Dreams* 2.257; Josephus, *War* 2.516, 636; 3.10; 4.474; 5.70, 133, 7.217; *Ant.* 7.34, 243; 10.169; *Life* 64, 115, 214.

[18] Ἀπέχον εἰς τὴν πόλιν, *P.Princ.* 116, 15; *P.Lille* 1, 5: "nine transverse levees running from west to east, each separated from the next by a distance of ten *schoinoi*"; 2, 2: "distance from this land to the town: fifteen stadia"; *P.Stras.* 57, 6: "the two towns are not more than a mile apart"; cf. the decree at Iasos relative to the divisions of the *ekklēsiastikon*: ἀπέχον ἀπὸ τῆς γῆς ἐφ' ὅσον ποδῶν ἑπτά (C. Michel, *Recueil*, n. 466, 9).

definition "remain apart, stay distant,"[19] especially in a figurative and psychological sense: "You are much farther than we from saying things worthy to be believed."[20] This meaning is common in the LXX, where Job begs God to remove his hand (Job 13:21) and Yahweh is far from the wicked (Prov 15:29); as a reproach, "He has removed his heart far from me" (*apechei ap' emou*, Isa 29:13; the opposite of *engizei*, draw near). It is commanded to "stay away from a man who has the power to put to death" (Sir 9:13), from quarreling (28:8), from violence (Isa 54:14), from the snares that lie in the path of the perverse (Prov 22:5; cf. Wis 2:16). Matt 15:8 quotes Isa 29:13—"This people honors me with their lips, but their heart is far from me" (*apechei ap' emou*, cf. Mark 7:6).

To keep one's distance can be a sign of respect: "When the Lacedaemonians ravaged the rest of Attica, they respected Decelea" (Herodotus 9.13; cf. Thucydides 4.97.3); "certain people do not even respect corpses."[21] To be far from means to be unable to touch,[22] a negative connotation that can be translated either "hinder" ("In all of these parts [thorax, the head, the back], with their numerous clefts, nothing hinders [*ouden apechei*] the vessels from carrying various materials")[23] or "spare." Aristobulus gives the order to "spare Antigonus if he is unarmed."[24]

In the language of NT ethics, *apechō* (in the middle voice), as in classical Greek,[25] always has the nuance of prohibition: "to abstain." At the Jeru-

---

[19] Homer, *Il.* 6.96: "Remove the son of Tydeus from Ilium"; *Od.* 15.33: separate a ship from the isles; 20.263, Telemachus: "It is my task to keep you away from the abuse and blows of those claiming the lordship"; Xenophon, *Cyr.* 1.1.2: "the flocks stray far from (ἀπέχονται) places from which they are pushed away." Ps.-Homer, *H. Aphr.* 230: "Venerable Dawn leaves her bed behind."

[20] Isocrates, *Bus.* 11.32; cf. *Archid.* 6.70: "I am so far from carrying out any of these obligations" (ἀπέχω τοῦ ποιῆσαι).

[21] Philo, *To Gaius* ; *Spec. Laws* 2.94; 4.202; 3.12: "The law requires respect not only for married women but for single women as well"; 21; *Abraham* 253: Abraham "stayed away (ἀποσχέσθαι) from Sarah out of a continent nature and the respect he had for his spouse"; *Alleg. Interp.* 2.88: "the serpent of pleasure does not even respect the one much beloved of God, Moses"; Josephus, *Ag. Apion* 1.98: Ramesses ordered his brother to "respect the royal concubines."

[22] Aeschylus, *Eum.* 350: "the immortals must not lay a hand upon us." Cf. Deut 18:22—when the prophet speaks presumptuously, he is not to be respected (οὐκ ἀπείχοντο αὐτοῦ, be feared (Hebrew *gûr*).

[23] Hippocrates, *Art.* 10; cf. Plato, *Cra.* 407 b; *Resp.* 1.354 b: "I was not able to keep myself from leaving the previous subject for this one"; Plutarch, *De def. or.* 41.433 a.

[24] Josephus, *War* 1.75, 637; 2.307; 4.262; 7.265; *Ant.* 6.318; 16.404. The temple is spared (1.400); the wealth of Hyrcanus (1.268); a city (2.69; *Ant.* 17.289); carnage (*Ant.* 3.54); cf. *P.Mich.* 43, 7: μηθενὸς ἀπόσχῃ, "Do not spare any efforts!"

[25] Homer, *Il.* 8.35: "we will keep ourselves far from battle"; 12.248; 14.206: "They both abstain from bed and love"; Herodotus 1.66: "They refrained from attacking";

salem Council, St. James proposes, "Let us write to the Gentiles to abstain from the pollution of idols and fornication."[26] St. Paul gives this definition: "This is the will of God, namely, your sanctification, abstaining (*apechesthai hymas*) from sexual immorality" (1 Thess 4:3), from every kind of evil.[27] St. Peter writes, "I exhort you to abstain from fleshly desires that make war on the soul."[28] This means not just keeping one's distance, but refusing to have even the slightest contact; at least this is the ethical nuance given this verb by the LXX[29] and especially by Philo: "It is commanded to abstain from wickedness" (Philo, *Alleg. Interp.* 1.102; cf. 3.104), from injustice (*Husbandry* 113), offenses (*tōn hamartēmatōn apechou, Change of Names* 47; *Virtues* 163), from doing evil (*Spec. Laws* 2.15), "from returning to each other the wrongs that are done us" (*Virtues* 140; cf. *Moses* 1.308). Likewise, in Josephus God commands Adam and Eve to abstain from the tree of knowledge (*Ant.* 1.40), and commands Noah to abstain from shedding blood.[30]

There remains the difficult task of translating Mark 14:41—"Sleep now and rest. It's all up (*apechei*)! The hour has come; the Son of Man will be handed over."[31] The Vulgate translates "sufficit," but what does "it is

---

Plato charges the citizens not to abstain from geometry (*Resp.* 7.527 c), and Xenophon urges the most influential people not to abstain from agriculture (*Oec.* 5.1); cf. *Cyr.* 1.6.32: they did not refrain from exploiting even their own friends. Thucydides 1.20.2: refrain from attacking; 5.25.3; Plutarch, *De Is. et Os.* 4 and 7; *De sera* 22; *Ep. Arist.* 115, 143; Josephus, *War* 2.142: abstain from brigandage; 581; 3.461; from wine (2.313), from all scandalmongering (*Ag. Apion* 1.164). *P.Panop.Beatty* 2, 235 orders tax collectors to refrain entirely from such actions (τῶν τοιούτων παντελῶς ἀπέχεσθαι).

[26] Acts 15:20—ἀπέχεσθαι (middle infinitive); cf. D. R. Catchpole, "Paul, James and the Apostolic Decree," in *NTS*, vol. 23, 1977, pp. 428–444. In the first century, this is a technical meaning; cf. the six occurrences in Ps.-Phocylides 6, 31, 35, 76, 145, 149; Plutarch, *De gen.* 15: abstaining from shameful pleasures, etc.

[27] 1 Thess 5:22; cf. 1 Tim 4:3—impostors commanded abstinence from foods that God created to be taken with thanksgiving by believers.

[28] 1 Pet 2:11; cf. N. Lazure, "La Convoitise de la chair en I Jo. II, 16," in *RB*, 1969, pp. 161–205.

[29] 1 Sam 21:6—David's soldiers do not approach (Hebrew *'āṣar*, hold back) a woman during the campaign and are in a state of holiness; Job (1:1, 8) refrains from every evil action (Hebrew *sûr*, 2:3; 28:28; cf. Mal 3:6); like the wise person (Prov 3:7; 14:6; 14:16), who turns away from riches (23:4; Hebrew *ḥādal*) but does not abstain from doing good (*māna'*) to whom good is due (3:27) or from receiving instruction (23:13); Joel 1:13; 4 Macc 1:34.

[30] *Ant.* 1.102, 334; 2.237; 3.92; 6.117; the sons of Eli: οὐδενὸς ἀπείχοντο παρανομήματος (5.339; cf. 19.150); abstinence from certain animals (3.259–260; 7.155; 10.190; 11.228; *Ag. Apion* 1.239, 261; 2.141, 174), from things consecrated to God (*Ant.* 5.32; 12.250; cf. 11.101).

[31] The translation of M. J. Lagrange ("C'en est fait!"); R. Schnackenburg (*L'Evangile selon saint Marc*, Paris, 1973): "continuez à dormir et reposez-vous! C'est passé"

enough" mean?[32] F. Field noted[33] that apart from the [pseudo-] attestation in Hesychius, the translation "sufficit" can be supported only with a text of Ps.-Anacreon (*Od.* 28.23): the poet, having given his instructions to the painter for a portrait of his mistress, concludes, "Enough! For now I see the young woman herself" (*apechei. blepō gar autēn*). This would perhaps be a sufficient attestation, but it can be corroborated by *P.Stras.* 4, 19, from the sixth century, [34] and by the chorus in Aeschylus, *PV* 687—"Oh! Oh! Far from me! Enough!" (*ea, ea, apeche, pheu*)—and probably by other equivalent usages.[35] We have to remember that a word may commonly have a meaning in the spoken language that is not attested in written documents. In any event, this meaning is in harmony with "abstain" and "be distant." We may imagine that the apostles, already asleep, have risen, and that after a few minutes Jesus, referring to all that has happened at Gethsemane, utters the word *apechei* either meaning "You've had it"[36] or pointing out that the time has come: "The hour is now." They would have to leave the garden and prepare to go.

(the agony, the conflict in prayer, the anguish has been overcome); manuscripts ψ and *k* omit ἀπέχει; D, W, Θ, Φ add τὸ τέλος, "the end has arrived; the hour has come"; this is also the interpretation of the Sahidic version ("the work has been finished") and the Syriac version ("the end has come"). M. Black (*Aramaic Approach*, pp. 225–226) postulates an error in the Aramaic original, reading דחיק instead of דחק, "urge, press."

[32] Sometimes Hesychius is cited: ἀπέχει· ἀπόχρη, ἐξάρκει (not found in the edition by K. Latte, 1953). Taking up the hypothesis formulated by J. de Zwaan ("The Text and Exegesis of Mark XIV, 41 and the papyri," in *The Expositor*, 1905, pp. 459–472), H. Boobyer ("ἀπέχει in Mark XIV, 41," in *NTS*, vol. 2, 1955, pp. 44–48) and W. Barclay ("The New Testament and the Papyri," in H. Anderson, W. Barclay, *The New Testament in Historical and Contemporary Perspective: Essays in Memory of G. H. C. Macgregor*, Oxford, 1965, pp. 75ff.) suggest that this is a reference to Judas (cf. verse 43), who has received the money that was the price of his betrayal—he has been paid and can now arrest Jesus. This, however, is to make a great deal of a simple verb without an object.

[33] F. Field, *Notes on the Translation*, p. 39.

[34] Καὶ μεθ' ὃν ᾧ ἀπέσχε χρόνον ἔχειν; the editor, F. Preisigke, writes "ἀπέσχε steht hier unpersönlich im Sinne von 'satis est': καὶ μετὰ τὸν χρόνον, ᾧ ἀπέσχε ἔχειν"; cf. *P.Lond.* 1343, 38 (eighth century).

[35] Aeschylus, *Ag.* 1125: "Careful! Away from the cow"; Homer, *Il.* 12.321: "Let us leave the flocks"; Philo, *Husbandry* 91: to halt in an undertaking; Josephus, *Life* 80: give in to the passions.

[36] Cf. the conclusion of *Ep. Arist.* (322): ἀπέχεις τὴν διήγησιν—"There you have the whole story, Philostratus, just as I promised."

ἁπλότης, ἁπλοῦς

haplotēs, simplicity, singleness, sincerity; *haplous*, morally whole, faithful

These are two terms that cannot be well understood in the NT except in light of the LXX. In classical Greek, "*haplous* is the opposite of *diplous*, meaning simple or single rather than double . . . sometimes in the moral sense of straight, without turning aside."[1] But in the OT, this adjective translates the Hebrew *tām*, signifying all that is whole (hence upright [French *intègre*—Tr.], perfect); then well made; and finally peaceful, and hence innocent. *Tāmîm* refers to all that is complete, finished, done; hence intact or undefiled, without fault; and finally irreproachable, exemplary, impeccable.[2] This perfection, which the Vulgate calls *simplicitas*, is frequently associated with *yāšār*, expressing rectitude: that which corresponds to an objective norm; thus, in a physical sense, that which is straight, direct, unified; and in a moral sense that which is loyal, just, right.[3] This union (Ps 25:21; 37:37) points out that the perfection-integrity of the just is characterized by an absolute rectitude of conscience and life. Furthermore, the models of the pious person, like Noah and Job (Gen 5:9; Job 1:1, 8) are presented as "perfect and upright," they are seasoned, lacking in nothing, innocent and irreproachable.

This is not just a dictionary entry but an entire spirituality. This faultless innocence, this uncompromising rectitude, is blessed by God (Prov 2:7; 10:29; 11:20; 28:10) and is the way of salvation (Prov 28:18). It is the

---

[1] P. Chantraine, *Dictionnaire étymologique*, p. 97; cf. Bauernfeind on this word in *TDNT*, vol. 1, pp. 386–387.

[2] Whence the corresponding terms ἀληθινός, ἄμωμος, ὅσιος, εἰρηνικός, καθαρὰ καρδία, τέλειος. J. Lévêque, *Job et son Dieu*, Paris, 1970, vol. 1, pp. 137ff. Cf. C. Spicq, "La vertu de simplicité dans l'Ancien et le Nouveau Testament," in *RSPT*, 1933, pp. 5–26.

[3] Cf. "simplicity of heart," Gen 20:5; Josh 24:14; 1 Kgs 9:4; 1 Chr 29:17; Wis 1:1.

---

haplotēs, S 572; *TDNT* 1.386–387; *EDNT* 1.123–124; *NIDNTT* 3.571–572; MM 58; L&N 57.106, 88.44; BAGD 85–86 ‖ **haplous**, S 573; *TDNT* 1.386; *EDNT* 1.123–124; *NIDNTT* 3.571; MM 58; L&N 23.132, 57.107; BDF §§45, 60(1), 61(2); BAGD 86

virtue of the servants of God (Deut 18:13; Ps 19:24; 25:21; Prov 13:6), or better, a deep-seated purpose, a condition of the soul. As opposed to duplicitous people, those with divided hearts, those who are simple have no other concern than to do the will of God, to observe his precepts; their whole existence is an expression of this disposition of heart, this rectitude: "Let us all die in our simplicity" (1 Macc 2:37). In the first century BC, *haplotēs*, so exalted in the Wisdom writings, is considered the supreme virtue of the patriarchs.[4]

It is not easy to define precisely the meaning of *haplous* in the outline of the logion of the two lights,[5] which calls for checking the condition of this "lamp of the body," the eye,[6] because if it is "evil" (dark) it is unable to make out the exterior light of Christ; this would be blindness indeed, like that of a blind person facing the sun.[7] If we take *haplous* and *ponēros*

---

[4] In *T. 12 Patr.* the exhortation recurs endlessly to "walk in *haplotēs* according to the law" (*T. Levi* 13.1; cf. *T. Reub.* 4.1; *T. Sim.* 4.5) or "in simplicity of heart" (*T. Issach.* 4.1; cf. 3.8; 7.7) or "of soul" (*T. Issach.* 4.6), "before God" (*T. Issach.* 3.2; cf. 5.8). *Haplotēs*, the subject of joy (*T. Issach.* 3.6), is parallel to *akakia* (*T. Issach.* 5.1). In the last days, your sons will abandon *haplotēs*. (*T. Issach.* 6.1; cf. 7.7; *T. Benj.* 6.7) and will have "double vision" (*T. Asher* 4.1, διπρόσωπον). A. Jaubert (*La notion d'alliance dans le Judaïsme*, Paris, 1963, p. 274) sees an anti-Pharisee point in these texts.

[5] "The light of the body is the eye. If then your eye is simple, your whole body will be full of light; but if your eye is evil, your whole body will be darkened." Recorded similarly by Matt 6:22 and Luke 11:34, but in totally different contexts; inserted by Matt in the Sermon on the Mount (devotion to wealth produces blindness of heart); by Luke among other fragments without any definite connection, after the passage about Martha at home, where it serves as a warning that purity of outlook is necessary for recognizing the teaching of Jesus, or better the light on Jesus (H. J. Cadbury, "The Single Eye," in *HTR*, 1954, pp. 69–74. L. Vaganay, "L'Etude d'un doublet dans la Parabole de la Lampe," in *Le Problème synoptique*, Paris-Tournai, 1954, pp. 426–442). Cf. C. Edlund, *Das Auge der Einfalt*, Copenhagen-Lund, 1952 (cf. the summary by P. Benoit, in *RB*, 1953, pp. 603–605); E. Sjöberg, "Das Licht in dir: Zur Deutung von Matth. VI, 22 f Par.," in *ST*, vol. 5, 1952, pp. 89–105; J. Amstutz, ΑΠΛΟΤΗΣ, Bonn, 1968.

[6] For the Greeks, the eye emits visual rays which travel outward in a straight line (Plato, *Tim.* 45c; Archimedes, fragments edited by C. Mugler, vol. 4, p. 207; cf. J. Itard, "Optique et perspective," in *La Science antique et médiévale*, Paris, 1957, vol. 1, pp. 341ff.) Empedocles, frag. 84.3 (Diels, 7th ed.) compares it to a lantern with a flaxen veil (cf. *REG*, 1959, pp. xi, 58). There is a movement (flow) from the eye toward its object (Philo, *Conf. Tongues* 99; *Unchang. God* 78). Cf. the texts in C. Mugler, *Terminologie géométrique*, pp. 293ff. A. Lejeune, *Recherches sur la catoptrique grecque*, Brussels, 1957.

[7] To put it another way, seeing requires both the objective light (the sun) and the subjective light (the eye). It is the same in the spiritual order: the subjective light of the body or soul is necessary, and the whole practical issue is making sure that it is in good order for receiving the objective light of the revelation of Jesus Christ. The union of both lights is required. Only the "simple eye" sees things exactly as they are.

in a physical sense, they would mean respectively "healthy or normal" and "sick." Thus Socrates called myopia a "defect of the eyes, *ponēria ophthalmōn*" (Plato, *Hp. Mi.* 374d), but this meaning is not biblical, and in secular Greek a healthy eye is normally called *ophthalmos agathos;* consequently, what we are dealing with is a Septuagintism. It is best to take the logion as a whole in a moral sense—the "darkened eye" in the sense of *T. Issach.* 4.6 (cf. *T. Benj.* 4.2), a clouded eye or depraved will. The eye is the organ for recognizing divinity: *ho ophthalmos sou = to phōs to en soi* (cf. Prov 20:27) = *tous ophthalmous tēs kardias* (Eph 1:18). The point here is probably unclouded loyalty,[8] in the sense in which pure hearts will see God (Matt 5:8), but the deepest meaning is that of a simple soul, not parceled out, like that of a small child,[9] oriented exclusively toward God. This integrity, this rigorousness of basic purpose, introduces one to the light, the world of God.[10] The light is total and perfect; but if one's outlook is evil, deficient because the heart is pulled in different directions (cf. Matt 6:21), the whole person abides in darkness (the world of Satan?). Simplicity is thus total involvement and the unreserved giving of the self.

These same connotations of generosity or liberality are to be understood in the verses about the gifts of the Macedonians and the Corinthians to the community at Jerusalem (2 Cor 8:2; 11:11, 13), and about gifts given by the charismatic, who gives not grudgingly but generously (*ho metadidous en haplotēti,* Rom 12:8). On the other hand, the nuance of integrity and uprightness come to the fore in 2 Cor 11:3—"I fear that just as the serpent lured Eve through his wiliness (*en tē panourgia;* cf. Gen 3:1) your thoughts might be corrupted (and abased) from the simplicity and purity that are fitting with respect to Christ."[11] But if slaves must obey their masters "in

---

We must remember that in the Hellenistic period, φῶς-φωτίζειν refer to the light from the beyond, and that it was in this period that the religious use of candles developed; cf. S. Aalen, *Die Begriffe Licht und Finsternis im A. T., im Spätjudentum und im Rabbinismus,* Oslo, 1952; F. N. Klein, *Die Lichtterminologie bei Philon von Alexandrien und in den Hermetischen Schriften,* Leiden, 1962; J. Duncan M. Derrett, *Law in the NT,* pp. 188–207.

[8] C. Edlund, *Das Auge der Einfalt,* Copenhagen-Lund, 1952, p. 67, is right in understanding this logion as aimed against the legalists and scribes. The most intelligent rabbis cannot see (understand) anything of the Savior's manifestation so long as they claim to be φῶς τῶν ἐν σκότει (Rom 2:19).

[9] Mark 10:15; cf. S. Légasse, *Jésus et l'enfant,* Paris, 1969.

[10] In biblical anthropology, *body* is not opposed to *soul* but designates the whole person.

[11] 2 Cor 11:3, ἀπὸ τῆς ἁπλότητος καὶ τῆς ἁγνότητος; cf. Philo, *Creation* 156: the eating of the fruit "suddenly conveyed them from innocence and simplicity in their way of life to deceitfulness—ἐξ ἀκακίας καὶ ἁπλότητος ἠθῶν εἰς πανουργίαν μετέβαλεν."

simplicity of heart" (Col 3:22; Eph 6:5), purity of intention and wholehearted devotion cannot be separated in their service. The Christian slave will want to obey orders faithfully and not balk at his duties. He works as a person in a position of trust and with real nobility.[12]

The meaning of the adverb *haplōs* (NT hapax) in Jas 1:5 cannot be determined with certainty: "God gives to all *haplōs* and does not reproach."[13] Given the last part of the sentence, it is tempting to translate *haplōs* "sincerely, without reservation or restriction."[14] But the meaning of the Vulgate, supported by the Peshitta, agrees better with the language of the LXX: God gives perfectly, i.e., with abandon. The papyri shed hardly any light,[15] or rather they most often use *haplōs*, especially in the first century, to affirm a statement: "absolutely, quite plainly."[16] Contracting parties agree not to file any complaints whatsoever concerning debts, payments, stipulations, or "anything else at all."[17] Thus, in an act establishing ownership, "the declarer and his successors will not initiate any legal proceedings concerning the above-mentioned goods, nor for anything else, *absolutely*,

---

[12] In Philo (*Moses* 1.172) goodwill (ἁπλότης) is opposed to recrimination, hardness, and a spiteful personality (τὴν πικρίαν καὶ τὸ βαρύμηνι); cf. "the natural uprightness of Titus" (Josephus, *War* 5.319; cf. 529).

[13] Cf. H. Riesenfeld, "ΑΠΛΩΣ: Zu Jak. I, 5," in *ConNT,* vol. 9, 1941, pp. 33–41, where several occurrences of this adverb with δίδωμι are cited (Plutarch, *Sol.* 21.4; *Demetr.* 19.10); *P.Panop.Beatty* 2, 95. W. C. van Unnik (*De ἀφθονία van God in de oudchristelijke Literatuur*, Amsterdam-London, 1973, pp. 12ff.) juxtaposes Jas 1:5 and *Odes Sol.* 7.3.

[14] Cf. Dio Chrysostom 51.1: οὐχ ἁπλῶς ἀλλὰ μετὰ φροντίδος; Marcus Aurelius 5.7.2: "One must either not pray at all or pray naively, candidly"; Philo, *Drunkenness* 76: "serving loyally and candidly, ἀψευδῶς καὶ ἁπλῶς θεραπεύων." In Prov 10:9, "the one who walks in uprightness" is in antithetical parallel with "devious." Hence my earlier translation, "without mental reservation or ulterior motive" (C. Spicq, "ΑΜΕΤΑΜΕΛΗΤΟΣ in Rom. XI, 29," in *RB*, 1960, pp. 217).

[15] With respect to coins, ἁπλῶς means "genuine" (Dittenberger, *Syl.* 901, 9; *P.Ryl.* 709, 6; *P.Fouad* 53, 3; *P.Oxy.* 2237, 8; *Pap.Lugd.Bat.* XIII, 1, 7; cf. J. and L. Robert, "Bulletin épigraphique," in *REG,* 1960, p. 142, n. 59). In legal language: "the written contract in a single exemplar (without duplicates) is valid" (*P.Rein.* 105, 10; 108, 14; *P.Warr.* 10, 30; *Pap.Lugd.Bat.* XIII, 4, 8; 20, 22; *PSI* 1427, 23; cf. *P.Fouad* 20, 11; *P.Mert.* 36, 17; 98, 19; *P.Harr.* 66, 4 and 13; 81, 7; 83, 14; 141, 6; 145, 4; *BGU* 2117, 10; *C.P.Herm.* 32, 22; *P.Oxy.* 2237, 19; 2270, 14; 2350, col. III, 19; 2587, 9; etc.).

[16] Cf. Menander, *Dysk.* 507: "I said plainly to everyone around. . . ."

[17] The forumla περὶ ἄλλου οὐδενὸς ἁπλῶς (*P.Yale* 63, 15, from 7 July 64; cf. 65, 31; *UPZ* 218, col., 1, 24; 223, col, 1, 18) or περὶ ἑτέρου ἁπλῶς πράγματος (*P.Fouad* 56, 19, from 11 February 79; *P.Ryl.* 588, 23; 20 September 78 BC) recurs constantly: *P.Mich.* 337, 15 (AD 24); 345, 15 (AD 7); 351, 14 (AD 44); 352, 10 (AD 46); *P.Mert.* 111, 15; *P.Fam.Tebt.* 9, 18; 13, 23, 44, 58; 20, 30; 21, 15, 27; *P.Oxy.* 2185, 27 (AD 95); *P.Tebt.* 45, 25; 395, 10, 18; in two acts of divorce, *P.Dura* 31, 15; 32, 11; cf. Philo, *Drunkenness* 78; *Post. Cain* 114; Epictetus 3.13.10; 3.22.96; 4.1.172.

in any manner. . . . For his part, Anthistia Cronous will not start legal proceedings against the declarer concerning any of the above stipulations (*peri mēdenos haplōs pragmatos*) . . . in any fashion (*tropō mēdeni*)" (*P.Phil.* 11.16, 21). In AD 38, *emou mēthen haplōs lambanontos* means "without receiving absolutely anything."[18] Consequently, the best translation of Jas 1:5 would appear to be "purely and simply,"[19] without emphasizing one nuance or another, except that of pure gift.

---

[18] *P.Mich.* 266, 15; 276, 10, 24, 25, 32, 40 (AD 47); cf. 603, 18 "with nothing more"; *P.Mert.* 115, 16; *P.Tebt.* 392, 26, 35; *P.Sarap.* 36, 10.

[19] Cf. 2 Macc 6:6—"It wasn't even allowed to celebrate the Sabbath, nor to keep the festivals of our ancestors, nor *simply* to admit that one was Jewish"; Wis 16:27— "That which was not destroyed by the fire melted, simply heated by a brief ray of sunlight." Epictetus 2.2.13: "Do not let yourself be pulled in all directions, sometimes ready to serve, sometimes refusing, but serve simply and with all your heart, ἀλλ' ἁπλῶς καὶ ἐξ ὅλης τῆς διανοίας."

> ἀποβλέπω
>
> *apoblepō*, **to look, observe, pay close attention**
>
> →*see also* ἀφοράω

To describe the character of the faith whereby Moses, in the midst of his trials, took the promised reward into account, Heb 11:26 uses the verb *apoblepō*, "look, observe, pay attention." Faith "looks from a distance," or better, "considers steadfastly" and as it were exclusively. In the OT, *apoblepō* sometimes connotes lying in wait or scrutinizing (Ps 10:8; 11:5), or making a profitable observation (Prov 24:32); but when it translates the verb *pânâh* (Hos 3:1; Cant 6:1), which means turn to look (Exod 2:12) or to leave (Isa 13:14), it takes on the sense of turning away, of detaching oneself from other concerns to devote one's attention to one thing only. This meaning, which is the one that applies in Heb 11:26, is confirmed by Philo, *Spec. Laws* 1.293; Moses keeps his eyes fixed on the greatness of God. Cf. *P.Stras.* 305, 6: *apoblepōn kai eis ta mellonta; PSI* 414, 9, a letter from the vine-grower Meno claiming his pay from Zeno: *eis to opsōnion apoblepō*.

In secular Greek, *apoblepō* expresses the activity of the astronomer who "observes the heavenly motions,"[1] or that of a painter who fixes his gaze on a model, constantly checking in order to take in every detail.[2] The use of the word is extended from simple eyesight[3] to a "become aware of" (Epictetus 1.6.37) and especially to "take into consideration, take into

---

[1] Plato, *Resp.* 7.530a; cf. C. Mugler, *Terminologie optique,* p. 44: "ἀπ. Verbal expression designating the contemplation, out of curiosity or scientific interest, of an optical phenomenon."

[2] Plato, *Resp.* 6.484c. Cf. Philo, *Virtues* 70: Moses is contemplated as a model and example; cf. B. Snell, H. Ersbe, *Lexikon,* vol. 1, col. 1090ff.

[3] Josephus, *War* 7.200: "the place where he was best seen by the spectators"; 7.338: "they looked at each other"; *Ant.* 8.344; 9.14.

---

apoblepō, S 578; EDNT 1.125; MM 59; L&N 30.31; BAGD 89

account"[4] in order to pattern one's conduct accordingly.[5] This is exactly what Moses did in reckoning that there was no comparison between the treasures of Egypt and the divine "recompense."

---

[4] Josephus, *Life* 135: "take your ancestral laws into consideration"; *Ag. Apion* 1.31: "without taking into consideration fortune or other distinctions"; *War* 2.311: "Florus, considering neither the number of the dead nor the high birth of the suppliant"; *Ant.* 20.61: "Izates took into consideration . . . the fact that changes of fortune are the dowry of all people (ἀποβλέπων is parallel to λογισμῷ διδούς)." In a Christian letter of consolation to a friend who has lost his son: ἀπόβλεψον ὅτι οὐδεὶς ἐν ἀνθρώποις ἀθάνατος (*P.Princ.* 102, 13–14; from the fourth century).

[5] Josephus, *Ant.* 4.39: the companions of Dathan come with their wives and their children "to see what Moses would decide to do, τί καὶ μέλλοι ποιεῖν." Moulton-Milligan cite the edict of Ephesus, around AD 160, ἀποβλέπων εἴς τε τὴν εὐσέβιαν τῆς θεοῦ καὶ εἰς τὴν τῆς λαμπροτάτης Ἐφεσίων πόλεως τειμήν.

ἀποδοχή

apodochē, **acceptance, enthusiastic reception, respect**

"This saying is sure and worthy of all approbation" (*pasēs apodochēs axios*, 1 Tim 1:15; 4:9). This kerygma formula, influenced by Hellenism, and abundantly commented upon by exegetes,[1] can be clarified when *apodochē* is given its proper value. This noun, which only appears in late Koine (except for Thucydides 4.81.2), normally means "a good welcome, favorable reception,"[2] and it is thus that it is attested in *Ep. Arist.* 257: "How can one find a good welcome among strangers?" and in Josephus, *Ant.* 18.274: "their insuperable objection to receiving the statue" of the emperor.

But already in the last century F. Field pointed out that the connotation of approval and admiration stood out in numerous texts,[3] and in 1911 J. Rouffiac tracked it down in two inscriptions of Priene.[4] We could add *Ep. Arist.* 308—when Demetrius undertook a reading and a translation in the presence of the translators, "these were received with enthusiasm by the crowd"[5]—and Diodorus Siculus 1.69; 9.40; 15.35.

---

[1] H. B. Swete, "The Faithful Sayings," in *JTS*, 1917, pp. 1–7; J. M. Bover, " 'Fidelis sermo,' " in *Bib*, 1938, pp. 74–79; G. W. Knight, *The Faithful Sayings in the Pastoral Letters*, Kampen, 1968, pp. 22ff. C. Spicq, *Epîtres Pastorales*, vol. 1, p. 277; C.F.D. Moule, *Birth of the NT*, pp. 283–284; Grundmann, on this word in *TDNT*, vol. 2, pp. 55–56.

[2] Cf. ἀποδέχομαι (Acts 2:41). A. Calderini (ΘΗΣΑΥΡΟΙ, 2d ed., Milan, 1972, p. 97) relates it to ἀποδοχία, "the reserve, the place where one keeps things."

[3] F. Field, *Notes on the Translation*, p. 203. Cf. Josephus, *Ant.* 6.347: "It is right that they should receive approval."

[4] J. Rouffiac, *Caractères du grec*, p. 39. After 129 BC, ἐν ἀποδοχῇ τῇ μεγίστῃ γινομένους = enjoying the highest esteem (*I.Priene* 108, 312; likewise 109, 234; around 120 BC). Cf. *I.Magn.* 113, 21: εἶναι ἐν ἀποδοχῇ τῷ δήμῳ; *CIRB* 432 B: ἐπαίνου καὶ πλείστης ἀποδοχῆς ὑποστῆναι; J. Pouilloux, *Choix*, n. 8, 7: ἀποδοχαί = favors. Polybius associates ἀποδοχή and πίστις several times: "Alexo enjoyed their favor and confidence" (1.43.4; cf. 1.5.5).

[5] Οἵτινες μεγάλης ἀποδοχῆς καὶ παρὰ τοῦ πλήθους ἔτυχον.

---

apodochē, S 594; *TDNT* 2.55–56; *EDNT* 1.129; *NIDNTT* 3.744, 746; MM 62; L&N 31.52; BAGD 91

What is more, the expression *axios apodochēs*, already used by Philo ("He alone is worthy of approval who has placed his hope in God," Philo, *Rewards* 13; likewise *Flight* 129), is current in the literature: "Strato himself was a man worthy of much acceptance" (*autos de ho Stratōn anēr gegone pollēs tēs apodochēs axios*, Diogenes Laertius 5.64); "If the starting point is unknown . . . all that follows can in no way deserve assent and confidence" (Polybius 1.5.5); with respect to the tomb of the king Osymandyas, "not only was this work praiseworthy on account of its immense size (*to megethos apodochēs axios*), but it was also admirable from an artistic point of view" (Diodorus Siculus 1.47.4; cf. 5.31: *apodochēs megalēs axiountes autous*; 12.15: this law is "perfectly just and worthy of the greatest praise"); *andros ergon kai pollēs axion apodochēs* (Hierocles, in Stobaeus, *Flor.* 4.27.20; vol. 4, p. 662, 2). It is especially with respect to people that the meaning "consideration, high esteem" predominates in the inscriptions;[6] for example in honorific decrees. One of these from the village of Odessa, around 45 BC, in honor of Menogenes, a *kaloskagathos* who had bestowed many benefits on the city and its region: "with the king he was reckoned worthy of great esteem" (*para tō basilei megalēs apodochēs axioutai*, I.Bulg., 43, 13); another honors Menas of Sestos: "being considered worthy of the noblest esteem" (*tēs kallistēs apodochēs axioumenos par' autō*, Dittenberger, *Or.* 339, 13–14). Similarly, a second-century inscription from Ephesus honoring the *agōnothētēs* Priscus: "a most respected man and worthy of all honor and esteem" (*andros dokimōtatou kai pasēs teimēs kai apodochēs axiou*, Dittenberger, *Syl.* 867, 20).

Consequently, the apostolic preaching not only deserves to be accepted by all but also deserves the highest credit (*pas* is intensive; cf. 1 Tim 6:1). It is worthy of devout respect, the respect that everyone owes to the Truth.[7]

---

[6] Ἀποδοχή, unknown in the papyri, belongs to cultivated language. In Greek rhetoric, one uses ἄξιος ἀποδοχῆς to qualify an utterance, a discourse based on argumentation and in which one may place confidence, cf. I.C.T. Ernesti, *LTGR*, 2d ed. Hildesheim, 1982, p. 226.

[7] W. A. Oldfather, L. W. Daly ("A Quotation from Menander in the Pastoral Epistles?" in *CP*, 1943, pp. 202–204) mention this saying in Terence: "It is a universal defect that in old age we are too attached to things," followed by the sentence, "the saying is true and must be put into practice—*et dictum est vere et re ipsa fieri oportet*" (Terence, *Ad.* 954); and since Terence is transposing Menander, these writers suppose that the latter wrote πιστὸς ὁ λόγος καὶ πάσης ἀποδοχῆς ἄξιος, which the Pastorals preserved more precisely.

> ἀποκυέω
>
> *apokyeō*, to deliver, give birth

"Desire, when it has conceived (*syllambanō*), gives birth to sin (*tiktō*), and sin, when it has come to term, gives birth to death (*apokyō*)."[1] The Father of lights "by his own will gave birth to us (*apekyēsen*) by a word of truth, so that we should be something of a firstfruits of his creatures."[2]

---

[1] Jas 1:15. The metaphor is attested several times in the OT: "The one who carries sin in the womb, who conceives a misdeed and gives birth to a lie" (Ps 7:15; cf. G. J. Thierry, "Remarks on Various Passages of the Psalms," in *OTS*, vol. 13, 1963, pp. 77ff.); "They conceive mischief and bring forth iniquity" (Isa 59:4); Job 15:35. It is loved by Philo: "We speak of corruption and of the birthing of the virtues . . ." (Philo, *Cherub.* 42–46; cf. 57); "The proper name of imprudence is She Who Gives Birth, because the intelligence of the insane . . . is always suffering the pangs of child-bearing, when it desires riches, glory, pleasure, of some other object" (*Alleg. Interp.* 1.75); the soul, which conceives thoughts, vices, and passions, has a reproductive capacity comparable to that of a woman who conceives and gives birth to a child (*Sacr. Abel and Cain* 103); all the virtues are fertile and can be compared to a productive field or to a mother who gives birth (*Worse Attacks Better* 114), especially justice, "which brings into the world a male offspring (ἀποκεκύηκε), right reasoning" (121); and "prudence, which, like a mother, brings into the world (ἀποκυήσασα) the race capable of receiving her instruction" (*Change of Names* 137). "The one who beholds God . . . brought into the world (ἀποκυηθέν) by virtue" (*Post. Cain* 63). Cf. *T. Benj.* 7.2—"The *dianoia* is pregnant with the works of Beliar."

[2] Jas 1:18. Cf. Deut 32:18—"You despise the Rock that gave birth to you and you forget the God who brought you into the world"; Isa 66:7–11; the metaphorical and collective birthing of the people Israel. O. Michel, O. Betz ("Von Gott gezeugt," in *Festschrift J. Jeremias*, Berlin, 1960, p. 22, and in *NTS*, vol. 9, 1963, pp. 129–130) point out parallels at Qumran. C. M. Edsman ("Schöpferwille und Geburt, Jk. I, 18: Eine Studie zur altchristlichen Kosmologie," in *ZNW*, 1939, pp. 11–44; idem, "Schöpfung und Wiedergeburt: Nochmals Jac. I, 18," in *Spiritus et Veritas: Mélanges Kundzinu,* Auseklis, 1953, pp. 43–55) provides references to ecclesiastical writers who use this term to designate the begetting of the Word by the Father or of Jesus by the Virgin Mary (Justin, *1 Apol.* 32.14; *2 Apol.* 6.5; Irenaeus, *Haer.* 1.1.1; Origen, *Cels.* 5.52; 5.58;

---

apokyeō, S 616; *EDNT* 1.134; MM 65; L&N 13.12, 13.87; BDF §101; BAGD 94

ἀποκυέω, apokyeō 179

The verb *apokyeō* (biblical hapax), unknown even in Josephus, belongs to cultivated Hellenistic Greek.[3] It is much used by Philo, who gives it its precise, objective meaning as the last stage of begetting—"deliver" or "give birth"—even when the usage is metaphorical.[4] After the conception (*syllambanō*) and the gestation (*en gastri echō, kyō*), the woman brings her child into the world; the prefix *apo-* precisely emphasizes the "delivery." Although the compound verb under discussion sometimes includes the two preceding phases, it must normally be distinguished from the simple *kyō* ("carry in the womb, be or become pregnant,"[5] the opposite of *tiktō*, Isa 61:4) and even more from the very general *gennaō*,[6] because it refers to the moment when the mother, at the end of the period of gestation, brings forth into the world a fully formed child now capable of an

---

Eusebius, *Dem. Evang.* 3.2; 3.50; etc.). A. v. Harnack knows only two authors (Clement of Alexandria, *Paed.* 1.45.1, and Methodius of Olympus, *Symp.* 3.8) who use this verb to speak of baptismal generation (*Die Terminologie der Wiedergeburt und verwandter Erlebnisse in der ältesten Kirche: Texte und Untersuchungen*, vol. 42, 3; Leipzig, 1918, p. 109, n. 2; p. 120, n. 2). Cf. L. E. Elliott-Binns, "James I, 18: Creation or Redemption?" in *NTS*, vol. 3, 1957, pp. 148-161; above all J. Ysebaert, *Greek Baptismal Terminology*, pp. 108, 126, 139ff., 150.

[3] It is very rare in the papyri: *BGU* 665, col. II, 19 (first century AD); *SB* 6611, 15, 20 (a notarial act of divorce, AD 120), always meaning specifically "bring into the world"; cf. 4 Macc 15:7—"O woman, the only one who has brought into the world perfect piety."

[4] Philo, *Flight* 208: "Through an easy birthing (πραϋτόκοις ὠδῖσιν), you will bring forth a male child (ἄρρενα γενεὰν ἀποκυήσεις)"; Philo, *Post. Cain* 114: "This shadow, these ambiguous hallucinations, give birth to (ἀποκυεῖται) a son."

[5] Κυέω, *concipio*, is said of the mother: "be great with child"; cf. an inscription of Delphi: οὔτε κύουσα γυνή (*SEG*, vol. 16, 341, 7; R. Ferwerda, *La signification des images et des métaphores dans la pensée de Plotin*, Groningen, 1965, pp. 82ff.); "all the pregnant women (πᾶσαι αἱ κυοῦσαι γυναῖκες) brought malformed children into the world" (Plutarch, *Publ.* 21.2); "They saw that his brother's wife was pregnant (κύουσαν)" (Plutarch, *Lyc.* 3.1; cf. *Alex.* 2.5; 77.6); "The seventh day . . . was brought into the world without gestation, γεννηθεῖσαν ἄνευ κύσεως" (Philo, *Moses* 2.210); Abraham had relations with Hagar "until she conceived a child (ἄχρι τοῦ παιδοποιήσασθαι) and—as the most trustworthy narrators tell us—only until she was pregnant (ἄχρι τοῦ μόνον ἐγκύμονα γενέσθαι)" *Abraham* 253. "The essence of God is to inseminate (τὸ κύειν) and produce all things" *Corp. Herm.* 5.9. Obviously the term is sometimes used more broadly (cf. Philo, *Moses* 1.16: "A Jewish woman who had recently given birth, κυήσαντι"); according to Lucian, *Ver. Hist.* 22, the inhabitants of the moon carry their children (κύουσι) in the paunchy part of the leg. Otherwise, κύος = fetus; κυΐσκω = inseminate (E. Boisacq, *Dictionnaire étymologique*, under this word). Among the Gnostics, κύημα referred to spiritual or pneumatic generation.

[6] Cf. C. Spicq, *Théologie morale*, vol. 1, pp. 100ff.; A. Schlatter, *Der Brief des Jakobus*, Stuttgart, 1956, p. 136.

independent existence.[7] The *genuit* of the Vulgate must therefore be eliminated in favor of the *peperit* of the Old Latin (ed. Beuron, vol. 26, p. 17). In choosing this verb, St. James wanted to point out the efficaciousness of the divine action and the reality of baptismal generation. Christians had taken on a spiritual mode of existence by virtue of which they were capable of leading a really new life.

---

[7] Cf. Philo: "With women, and with all females, when the time of parturition (ἀποκυΐσκω) draws near, their sources of milk can be seen to begin to form so that their bodies may supply the newborn offspring with needed and appropriate food" (*Plant.*); "The Pythagoreans compare the number seven to a woman of perpetual virginity and without a mother, because it was not born and does not beget, ὅτι οὔτε ἀπεκυήθη οὔτε ἀποτέξεται" (*Alleg. Interp.* 1.15); God is the father of this world, and one could call its mother the knowledge with which he begot it, "this knowledge, having received the divine seed, after conceiving and bringing to term her only and well-beloved son, she then gave birth to our sensible universe (ἀπεκύησε)" (*Drunkenness* 30); "It is one and the same soul that carries both of these conceptions. Once they are brought forth into the world (ὅταν ἀποκυηθῶσι), they must necessarily be separated" (*Sacr. Abel and Cain* 3). Plutarch: "Valeria gave birth to a daughter (ἀπεκύησεν)" (*Sull.* 37.7); "In the middle of her dinner . . . she brought a boy into the world (ἀποκυηθὲν ἄρρεν)" (idem, *Lyc.* 3.5); *Corp. Herm.:* Mind-God, being male-and-female . . . gave birth by a word (ἀπεκύησε λόγῳ) to a second Mind demiurge" (1.9); "He gave virth to a Man like himself, whom he loved as his own child" (1.12).

ἀπόλαυσις

apolausis, enjoyment, happiness

This noun, unknown in the papyri before the sixth century (cf. *P.Flor.* 296, 11), is only used twice in the NT, and in accord with the double meaning that it has in the secular language. God provides us with "all things richly for our enjoyment, *eis apolausin*" (1 Tim 6:17). As opposed to the ascetic Manichaeism of the heterodox teachers, St. Paul affirms the optimism of revelation with respect to the earthly goods that divine providence obtains for us.[1] The end purpose *eis apolausin* had already been expressed by Philo and Josephus in reference to food, subsistence, and everyday necessities of life.[2] In 68, the prefect of Egypt, Tiberius Julius Alexander, promulgated an edict to the effect that his subjects should wait upon the "safety and material happiness" of the benevolent emperor Galba.[3] The meaning is "to derive benefit, to enjoy personally, to make the most of a possession."[4]

---

[1] Acts 14:17. A Stoic theme, cf. C. Spicq, *Théologie morale*, vol. 1, p. 236.

[2] Philo, *Moses* 2.70: Moses remained on the mountain, "having brought no privisions for necessary food, εἰς ἀναγκαίας ἀπόλαυσιν τροφῆς"; *Rewards* 135: prosperous people find life desirable for the enjoyment of good things, εἰς ἀπόλαυσιν ἀγαθῶν"; cf. God's words to Adam: thanks to Providence, all things contribute to "well-being and pleasure, πρὸς ἀπόλαυσιν καὶ ἡδονήν" (Josephus, *Ant.* 1.46); *Ant.* 8.153: "those goods conveniently arranged for pleasure and joy, εἰς ἀπόλαυσιν καὶ τρυφήν"; 16.13: Herod entertains Marcus Agrippa and his friends with all sorts of pleasures and food. *1 Clem.* 20.10: "inexhaustible springs, created for pleasure and health, πρὸς ἀπόλαυσιν καὶ ὑγείαν."

[3] Τά τε πρὸς σωτηρίαν καὶ τὰ πρὸς ἀπόλαυσιν (*SB* 8444, 8; cf. G. Chalon, *T. Julius Alexander*).

[4] Cf. enjoyment of succession to the throne or the benefits of royalty (Josephus, *War* 1.111, 1.587), and the verb ἀπολαύω, which occurs frequently in the papyri (*P.Herm.* 5, 10: ἀπολαύειν τῆς ἐπὶ σοὶ μεγίστης εὐφροσύνης) and the inscriptions, cf. the discourse of Nero at Corinth in 67: "a larger number of people enjoyed my favors, ἵνα μου πλείονες ἀπολαύωσι τῆς χάριτος"; (Dittenberger, *Syl.* 814, 18; cf. *Or.* 666, 10); an inscription on a ring from Homs: " Ἀπόλαυε χέρων—Enjoy with pleasure" *IGLS* 2482).

---

apolausis, S 619; *EDNT* 1.135; MM 65–66; L&N 25.115; BAGD 94

This enjoyment, well-being, and pleasure is extended to happiness in all its forms, whether culinary delights (Josephus, *Ant.* 12.98), marital *koinōnia* (2.52), the love of a woman,[5] the joys of youth (*I.Thas.* 334, 18), the diversion of activities,[6] the satisfaction of ownership,[7] or the present and lasting enjoyment of good things.[8] It is in light of these usages that we must understand Heb 11:25—Moses chose to be "mistreated with the people of God rather than to enjoy for a time the pleasure of sin."[9]

---

[5] Ἀπόλαυσις represented in the form of an elegant young woman (*IGLS* 871). The Hebrews did not try to flee the enchantment of the beauty of the daughters of the Midianites and the intimacy of relations with them (Josephus, *Ant.* 4.131).

[6] *Inscription of Antiochus I of Commagene* (*IGLS* 1.150; cf. 12 = Dittenberger, *Or.* 383, 12). Cf. the technical meaning of *voluptas*: ἐπίτροπος ἀπὸ τῶν ἀ. (*ILS* 8849; Suetonius, *Tib.* 42).

[7] Josephus, *Ant.* 5.95: τὴν ἀπόλαυσιν τῶν ὑπαρχόντων ὑμῖν ἀγαθῶν; cf. 14.160.

[8] Josephus, *Ant.* 2.48; 2.161; 4.178; every sort of satisfaction (*War* 7.388). Diodorus Siculus 17.67.3; 17.75.1; 17.75.6; 17.110.5: the pleasures of existence.

[9] Josephus, *Ant.* 4.42: ἀφεὶς τὴν ἐκείνων ἀπόλαυσιν τῶν ἀγαθῶν ἐμαυτὸν ἐπέδωκα ταῖς ὑπὲρ τούτων ταλαιπωρίαις; cf. 2.174: God's words to Jacob—"This son whom you believe to be lost (Joseph) has been preserved by my Providence, and I have led him into a greater happiness, hardly different from that of a king." Demetrius and Antonius gave themselves up to debauchery (ἀπολαύσεις), Plutarch, *Ant.* 90(3).1; cf. 91(4), 5.

ἀπολείπω

apoleipō, **to leave behind**

After a quick visit to Crete, St. Paul left Titus there, and when he reached Rome as a prisoner, he had left Trophimus behind sick at Miletus (2 Tim 4:20). As parallels to this meaning of *apoleipō* ("leave behind") one could cite 1 Macc 9:65, "Jonathan left his brother Simon in the city"; 2 Macc 4:29, "Menelaus left his own brother Lysimachus to replace him as high priest."[1] Not only people are left behind but also objects, just as the apostle left behind his cloak at the home of Carpos at Troas.[2]

This nuance of losing and missing, an extremely frequent usage, is pejorative;[3] it refers to any sort of failure or deficiency,[4] from lateness or

---

[1] Cf. 2 Macc 10:19; 1 Macc 10:79; Judg 9:5—"Only Jotham was left"; 2 Kgs 10:21; Josephus, *War* 2.108: "Aristobulus was intentionally left behind on Cyprus so that he would not be ambushed"; 4.107: "women and children were left behind"; *Ant.* 7.218; *P.Athen.* 1, 4 (letter of Amyntas to Zeno, from 16 March 257 BC): ἀξιοῖ δὲ ἐν Μέμφει ἀπολειφθεὶς ἐργάζεσθαι; Lucian, *Nav.* 32: "We easily took possession of the open cities, where we left governors behind."

[2] 2 Tim 4:13 (on the *paenula*, a long, heavy, and thick cloak, cf. C. Spicq, "Pèlerine et vêtements," in *Mélanges Tisserant*, pp. 389–417); Josephus, *War* 1.667: "Ptolemy read a letter left by Herod for the benefit of his soldiers"; 3.452: "they left their mounts"; *Ant.* 18.38: the city; 14.354: the country; *SB* 6775, 2 (list of objects, from 257 BC): ἐν Ἑρμουπόλει ἀπολελοίπαμεν; hence, in an abstract and figurative sense: leave behind an opinion (Philo, *Etern. World* 7), a subject for criticism (vision of Maximus, in E. Bernand, *Inscriptions métriques*, n. 168, 21), a souvenir (Wis 8:13; 10:8; Josephus, *Ant.* 15.298: Herod left for posterity a monument to his philanthropy), a job to finish (Josephus, *War* 7.303).

[3] Sir 3:13—"If he has lost his understanding, be patient"; Josephus, *Ant.* 16.13: "Herod left out nothing that might please Marcus Agrippa"; 1.115; 1.215; 3.102; 9.236: "the king did not lack any virtue"; 1.75; 12.96; *War* 3.91: "no one should be missing from the ranks"; 3.250: "nothing that could terrify the eyes or ears was missing"; 4.382: "they left the bodies to rot in the sun"; 5.200; 5.222; 7.169; 7.186: "springs of water not lacking in sweetness." Hence the connotation of inferiority (*Ant.* 14.129; *Ag. Apion* 2.39: a period of a little less than three thousand years). In some post-Euclidean mathematicians, ἀπολείπω, as a synonym of καταλείπω and ὑπολείπω refers to "the effect of a subtraction carried out on geometrical figures" (C. Mugler, *Terminologie géométrique*, p. 77).

[4] *P.Tebt.* 10, 5; 72, 110; *P.Rein.* 109, 1: ἐὰν ἀπολίπῃ = in case of default (second century BC); *P.Oslo* 85, 17; *P.Mert.* 70, 32: if it is still due (28 August AD 159).

---

apoleipō, S 620; *EDNT* 1.135; MM 66; L&N 13.140, 15.59, 85.65; BDF §393(6); BAGD 94 absence[5] to renunciation and abandonment, with connotations of disorder and betrayal.[6] It is certainly with this connotation of "desertion" that the angels, whose natural habitation is heaven, are said to have "left their proper abode."[7]

The idea of leaving[8] and perhaps the use of *apoleipō* to communicate that a deceased person leaves surviving progeny or leaves possessions behind[9] coincide with the technical usage of this verb in wills, as is attested in the papyri and the inscriptions:[10] the testator "leaves" his goods to his heirs. Thus, around 200 BC, Epicteta: "I leave as follows (*apoleipō kata tan gegenēmenan*) in accord with the recommendation of my husband Phoenix";[11] in the second century AD, the will of Taptollion (P.Wisc. 13, 6, 7, 11, 13) or P.Oxy. 105, 3–4: "If I die with this will unchanged, I leave as heir my daughter Ammonous . . . objects, furnishings, buildings, and all other property that I leave."[12]

---

[5] Menander, *Dysk.* 402: "Getas, my boy, you are quite late"; Josephus, *Ant.* 9.135: "He would punish with death any absent priest"; 6.236: "the son of Jesse had been absent from the meal."

[6] Prov 2:17 ('*āzab*); 19:27 (*ḥādal*); Sir 17:25; Isa 55:7; UPZ 19, 6: "our father deserted the community" (164 BC); P.Oxy. 1881, 19: not abandoning a lawsuit just because it has come to a conclusion; 2711, 6; Josephus, *Ant.* 7.136: they left him to fight alone; *War* 4.393: "many dissidents abandoned him"; *Ant.* 14.346: Phasael did not think it right to abandon Hyrcanus; 8.335: they abandoned the true God; 8.296 (his worship); 6.231—Jonathan's words to David: "God will not abandon you"; *1 Clem.* 3.4: "each one has abandoned the fear of God"; 7.2: "then let us leave behind vain and useless preoccupations."

[7] Jude 6: ἀπολιπόντας τὸ ἴδιον οἰκητήριον. In the Greek fragments of the book of *Enoch* found at Akhmim, Enoch receives this command: "Go say to the Watchers of heaven that, having left high heaven . . . they are unclean" (12.4); "why have you left high heaven?" (15.3). In *2 Enoch* 11, "the devil became Satan when he fled heaven" (ed. A. Vaillant, p. 103).

[8] Polybius 2.1.6; Josephus, *War* 2.13.

[9] Josephus, *Ant.* 8.285: Abias left twenty-two daughters behind; 8.272; 12.282; *War* 1.572; 588: Herod would take care not to leave any of his children alive. In AD 36: "My husband died, leaving me with three children" (P.Mich. 236, 5 = SB 7568, 5); BGU 1833, 5 (50 BC), τὰ ἀπολελειμμένα = things left by the deceased, inheritance (P.Mert. 26, 9; P.Harr. 68, 8; SB 9790, 7; 10500, 13, 16, 24, 27; 10756, 13); cf. P.Oxy. 2111, 22–24; 2583, 4.

[10] It is set forth especially by J. H. Moulton, G. Milligan, *The Vocabulary of the Greek Testament*, 2d ed., London, 1949, under this word.

[11] C. Michel, *Recueil*, n. 1001, col. I, 7; col. II, 3: "I leave (ἀπολείπω) the museum with the enclosure" (*RIJG*, vol. 2, p. 78); P.Rein. 96, 5; P.Mil.Vogl. 79, 14; 161, col. II, 7.

[12] *Chrest.Mitt.*, n. 371, col. IV, 9 (the time of Nero): κληρονόμον γὰρ αὐτὸν τῶν ἰδίων ἀπολελοιπέναι; cf. n. 100, 17; BGU 1098, 49; 1148, 22; 1164, 18; Josephus, *War* 1.71: "John had left everything to Aristobulus."

ἀπολείπω, *apoleipō* 185

This meaning of "survival" or of "things left," of definitive acquisition, is the meaning in Heb 4:6, 9, where participation in God's rest is still bestowed upon or granted to believers,[13] because God's promise is as unalterable as a *diathēkē*; it does not expire. But, on the other hand, "there remains no further sacrifice for the sins" of the apostates (10:26), because the divine economy has made no provision for their pardon.

---

[13] Cf. Polybius 6.58.9: ἐλπὶς ἀπολείπεται σωτηρίας.

ἀπόστολος

apostolos, **apostle**

This adjective (Plato, *Ep.* 7.346 *a*) and noun derives from the verb *apostellō*, "send, dispatch,"[1] and like this verb it has a large variety of nuances that flow from the context.[2]

---

[1] Herodotus 5.32: "Artaphernes sent the army to Aristagoras"; 4.150: Grinnus "did not dare to send out colonists to an uncertain destination"; 1.123: Harpagus "sent (a message)" to Persia; Aristotle, *Pol.* 5.7.2.1306ᵇ: "They were sent to colonize Tarentum"; Xenophon, *An.* 2.1.5: "Clearchus sent messengers" (ἀποστέλλει τοὺς ἀγγέλους); Thucydides 3.89.5: "with the tidal waves, the earth shook and the sea retreated"; 3.28.1 (an embassy); Sophocles, *Phil.* 125: "I am going to send him back to the ship" (πρὸς ναῦν ἀποστελῶ πάλιν); 1297; *El.* 71; Euripides, *Phoen.* 485: "send the army away" from the land. In the sense of "banish" (idem, *Med.* 281; Plato, *Resp.* 10.607 *b*). In the Hellenistic period, Vespasian "had dispatched (ἀπεσταλμένος) his son Titus to Syria" (Josephus, *War* 4.32); "Diogenes was sent as a scout and brought us other news" (Epictetus 1.24.6); with a religious meaning: "the cynic must know that he has been sent to humans by Zeus as a messenger" (ἄγγελος, idem 3.22.23), "as an example sent by God" (4.8.31); Joseph "was not sent (ἀπεστάλθαι) by humans but was chosen by God to govern the body and the outside world legitimately" (Philo, *Migr. Abr.* 22). We may recall Hecataeus of Abdera, in the third century AD, according to whom the Jews considered the high priest "the messenger of God's commands" (ἄγγελον γίνεσθαι τῶν τοῦ θεοῦ προσταγμάτων, cited by Diodorus Siculus 40.3; cf. T. Reinach, *Textes d'auteurs grecs et romains relatifs au Judaïsme*, 2d ed., Hildesheim, 1963, p. 17; F. R. Walton, "The Messenger of God in Hecataeus of Abdera," in *HTR*, 1955, pp. 25–257). Ἀποστέλλειν, "emit," express the shining out of light (C. Mugler, *Terminologie optique*, p. 53). — The bibliography, which is considerable, is given in *TWNT*, vol. 10, pp. 986–989. In *P.Grenf.* I, 43, 5 (letter from the second century BC), where all that remains is the ending of the perfect active infinitive -κέναι, we must read not ἠγορακέναι—"you wrote me that you had bought a mare" (*Chrest.Wilck.*, n. 57; S. Witkowski, *Epistulae Privatae Graecae* 58)—but ἀπεσταλκέναι "had sent" (*C.Pap.Jud.*, n. 135). The writer of the letter is letting his brother know that he has "received neither the mare nor the wagon"; the agent has not yet had time to carry our his mission (cf. J. M. Modrzejewski, "Sur l'antisémitisme païen," in *Pour Léon Poliakov: Le Racisme, mythes et sciences*, Brussels, 1981, p. 415).

[2] It is difficult to say exactly what the difference is between ἀποστέλλω and πέμπω, since each author has his own vocabulary and is not even always consistent

---

apostolos, S 652; *TDNT* 1.407–445; *EDNT* 1.142; *NIDNTT* 1.126–130, 133–134, 136; MM 70; L&N 33.194, 53.74; BAGD 99–100

From Herodotus on, *apostolos* refers to the bearer of a message, such as the herald sent by Alyattes to Miletus (1.21). Varus authorizes a "delegation" (*ton apostolon*) of Jews to Rome (Josephus, *Ant*. 17.300, the only occurrence; 1.146 is very poorly attested). The word means someone sent on a mission out of the country, or an "expedition,"[3] or a group of colonists (Dionysius of Halicarnassus 9.5). Beginning in the fourth century, however, *apostolos* almost always refers to a naval expedition, a fleet,[4] a transport ship (*P.Oxy*. 522, 1; *P.Tebt*. 486: *logos apostolou Triadelphou; PSI* 1229, 13). In the papyri, it is a technical term[5] for the *naulōtikai syngraphai*, the official

---

with himself. (Cf. J. Rademakers, "Mission et apostolat dans l'Evangile johannique," in F. L. Cross, *SE*, II, Berlin, 1964, pp. 100–121; J. Seynaeve, "Les Verbes ἀποστέλλω et πέμπω dans le vocabulaire théologique de saint Jean," in M. de Jonge, *L'Evangile de Jean*, Gembloux-Louvain, 1977, pp. 385–389). In principle, this latter verb means simply to pass something on (Herodotus 1.123: send gifts) or send a person (a herald, idem 1.21), an intermediary. In the third century AD, *P.Hal*. I, 124, 147, 154 (cf. *P.Hal*., p. 84) disallows lawsuits against the king's envoys (ἀπεσταλμένων ὑπὸ τοῦ βασιλέως); this perfect passive participle indicates that the mission with which they are entrusted is linked to the persons of these officers, these "representatives" who act with the monarch's authority; cf. K. H. Rengstorf, "ἀπόστολος," in *TDNT*, vol. 1, pp. 407–445.
[3] Demosthenes, *3 Olynth*. 3.5: "You have given up the expedition" (τὸν ἀπόστολον; cf. the inscription from Cyprus in J. and L. Robert, "Bulletin épigraphique," in *REG*, 1961, p. 257, n. 824). This is often the meaning of ἀποστολή: the mission of the sacred ambassadors to Alexandria (*SEG* I, 366, 25); "How shall we justify our mission?" (*Ep. Arist*. 15); the sending or departure of people (*P.Tebt*. 703, 22; Josephus, *Ant*. 20.50; *Life* 268); "an expedition of angels of woe" (Ps 78:49; cited by Philo, *Giants* 17); "Your shoots (ἀποστολαί σου) are a garden of pomegranates" (Cant 4:13); Philo translates Methuselah ἀποστολὴ θανάτου, expedition of death (*Post. Cain* 73). In 256 BC, Panakestor is superintendent of expeditions or shipments: ὁ πρὸς ταῖς ἀποστολαῖς (*P.Lond*. 1964, 6 and 18; cf. Pelops as ἀποστελεύς, ibid. 1940, 3). Frequently enough, ἀποστολή means "gift, present" (1 Macc 2:18; 2 Macc 3:12; 1 Esdr 9:51, 54; *P.Hamb*. 191, 8); it translates the Hebrew *šiluḥîm* (from the verb *šālaḥ* in the piel, "dismiss") in 1 Kgs 9:16—the dowry given by Pharaoh to his daughter, who took leave of him to marry.
[4] Dittenberger, *Syl*. 305, 50; Demosthenes, *Corona* 80: "I dispatched all the expeditions (τοὺς ἀποστόλους) that saved the Chersonese, Byzantium, and all the allies"; Lysias, *Property of Aristophanes* 19.21: "the envoys (πρέσβεις) from Cyprus ... lacked money for the departure of the fleet" (εἰς τὸν ἀπόστολον). Hesychius, taking up Demosthenes 18.107, defines the *apostolos* as an admiral: στρατηγὸς κατὰ πλοῦν πεμπόμενος. The *apostoleis* in Aeschines are maritime quartermasters (*Fals. Leg*. 2.177). T. Nägeli, *Wortschatz*, p. 23, quotes a lexicon: ὁ ἐκπεμπόμενος μετὰ στρατιᾶς καὶ παρασκευῆς ἀπόστολος καλεῖται.
[5] With the exception of late and Christian texts: the living expenses of a messenger during his sojourn and his voyage (*P.Apoll*. 89, 7; *P.Ross.Georg*. IV, 1, 7 and 31; 11, 3); Μααμετ ἀπόστολος θεοῦ (*SB* 7240, 5; seventh-eighth century); the apostle Paul (*P.Lond*. 1915, 14; 1927, 35; *SB* 8176; an inscription at Cappadocia, in J. and L. Robert, "Bulletin épigraphique," in *REG*, 1939, p. 518, n. 451), Peter (*SB* 6087, 18),

papers ordering the shipment of grain by boat on the Nile from the public granaries to Alexandria.[6] The *apostolos* is a passport, a safe-conduct, or, if the bearer wished to leave, an exit authorization (*prostagma*, *P.Oxy.* 1271; cf. Strabo 2.3.5), an export license. *Gnomon of the Idios Logos* 162 prescribes: "Legal proceeding against persons who have embarked (at Alexandria) without a passport (*chōris apostolou*) now fall under the jurisdiction of the prefects."[7]

None of these meanings from everyday or legal parlance, except for the basic meaning "envoy, emissary,"[8] can explain the extreme theological density of this term in the NT, especially in St. Paul. Paul's usage presupposes a Semitic substrate, namely that of the *šaliaḥ*,[9] an institution appar-

---

James (6206), Andrew (8179), the intercession of the apostles (*IGLS* 1587). The Latin epitaph of Faustina, a Jew who died at age fourteen, in the fifth-sixth century at Venosa in Apulia, states that "her funeral oration was done by two apostles and two rabbis" (*CII*, n. 611; gives the bibliography on *apostoli*, who date to the fourth century in Judaism; cf. Epiphanius, *Pan.* 30.11; Eusebius, *In Isa.* 18.11); cf. J. Jeremias, "Paarweise Sendung im Neuen Testament," in A. J. B. Higgins, *New Testament Essays*, pp. 136–143.

[6] The *nauklēros*, commanding eight transport ships, receives and measures his shipment "conformably to the message" of the *epitropos* (*P.Oxy.* 1259, 10). The formula ἐξ ἀποστόλου is constant (*P.Stras.* 205, 4–5; 202, 6; *P.Princ.* 26, 14; *SB* 9088, 8). In 64/63 BC, ναυκλήρων Ἱπποδροματῶν ἀποστόλου ἀντίγραφον (*BGU* 1741, 6); in AD 15, *P.Lond.* 256 recto *a* 10 (*Chrest.Mitt.*, n. 443). Cf. A. J. M. Meyer-Termeer, *Die Haftung der Schiffer im griechischen und römischen Recht*, Zutphen, 1978, pp. 6, 24; U. Wilcken, *Grundzüge*, pp. 379ff. *Chrest.Wilck.* (p. 21) compares *Dig.* 49.6.1: "litteras dimissorias sive apostolos."

[7] Cf. *P.Amh.* 138, 10 (cf. *Chrest.Mitt.*, n. 342); *P.Oxy.* 1197, 13; 1259, 10; *P.Princ.* 26, 14; *P.Stras.* 202, 6; 205, 4–5; 206, 4; *SB* 7405, 6; 8754, 9; 9088, 8.

[8] In the first century, *apostolos* is rare in literary Greek; unknown in Philo, used only once in Josephus, it is a LXX hapax: The prophet Ahijah was warned by God concerning the visit of Jereboam's wife, who was coming to consult him concerning her son's illness. When she arrived, he said, "I have been sent (ἐγώ εἰμι ἀπόστολος; Hebrew *šālaḥ*) to you with bad news" (1 Kgs 14:6). But ἀποστέλλω is used for a prophet's mission, cf. D. Müller, "Apostle," in *NIDNTT*, Grand Rapids, 1975.

[9] Cf. Rengstorf, "ἀπόστολος," in *TDNT*, vol. 1, pp. 407–445; H. Mosbech, "Apostolos in the New Testament," in *ST*, 1950, pp. 166–200; G. Dix, *Jurisdiction in the Early Church: Episcopal and Papal*, London, 1938; J. C. Margot, "L'Apostolat dans le Nouveau Testament et la succession apostolique," in *Verbum Caro*, 1957, pp. 213–225; J. Colson, *Les Fonctions ecclésiales aux deux premier siècles*, Paris, 1956, pp. 11ff.; J. Dauvillier, *Les Temps apostoliques: Ier siècle*, Paris, 1970, pp. 139ff., 151–156, 175ff., 225ff. M. Delcor, E. Jenni, article שלח, in *Theol. Handwörterbuch zum A. T.*, vol. 2, 909–916. The most nuanced studies are C. K. Barrett, "Shaliaḥ and Apostle" (in *Donum Gentilicium . . . in honour D. Daube*, Oxford, 1978, pp. 88–102) and A. L. Descamps, "Paul, apôtre de Jésus-Christ," in Lorenzo de Lorenzi, *Paul de Tarse apôtre de notre temps*, Rome, 1979, pp. 25–60. The *šaliaḥ* was not a missionary but a member of the Jewish community; the title was not applied to prophets; whereas the title of the Christian apostle

ently going back to Jehoshaphat.[10] This person is not a mere envoy but a chargé d'affaires, a person's authorized representative; his acts are binding upon the "sender."[11] At this point the principal and the proxy are equivalent: "A person's *šaliaḥ* is as the person himself."[12] This rule carries over into the religious sphere: when the *šaliaḥ* acts on God's orders, it is God himself who acts (*b. B. Meṣ.* 86*b*), as in the case of Abraham, Elijah, or Elisha (*Midr. Ps.* 78 5; 173*b*). The rabbis considered the priest who offered the sacrifice to be God's *šaliaḥ*, "doing more than we can do" (*b. Qidd.* 23*b*; cf. Rengstorf, "ἀπόστολος," in *TDNT*, vol. 1, pp. 407, 419, 424), and on the Day of Atonement they called the high priest "the people's representative before God" (*m. Yoma* 1.5; *m. Giṭ.* 3.6). On the other hand, in the Mishnah and the Talmud, the *šaliaḥ* represents the community (*m. Roš Haš.* 4.9), invested with the power given him by his constituents. These data were little by little transposed into the Christian tradition.

"Jesus spent the night praying to God. When it was day he called his disciples, and having chosen twelve from among them, he named them apostles" (*kai apostolous ōnomasen*).[13] Among the *mathētai* who followed him, shared his life, and belonged to him (cf. *talmîdîm*, students of a master), Christ marked out twelve who would represent him in a special way, would be more closely associated with him,[14] and would therefore

---

emphasizes the official status and especially the divine origin and authority of the envoy; the apostle has a religious character. Cf. E. M. Kredel, "Der Apostelbegriff in der neueren Exegese," in *ZKT*, 1959, pp. 169–193; 257–305.

[10] 2 Chr 17:7-9: "In the third year of his reign, he sent his officials Ben-Hail, Obadiah, Zechariah, Nethanel, and Micaiah to teach in the towns of Judah. He sent with them the Levites. . . ."

[11] We may recall Eliezer, Abraham's *šaliaḥ*, sent to Laban and Bethuel to arrange Isaac's marriage with Rebekah (Gen 24). According to *m. Qidd.* 2.1 (41*b*), a man or a woman can marry through the agency of a *šaliaḥ*.

[12] *M. Ber.* 5.5. The *šaliaḥ* is an agent (*b. Giṭ.* 14*b*; *t. Giṭ.* 1.4); a minor cannot appoint a proxy (*m. Giṭ.* 6.3). A mission to take someone something that belongs to him cannot be withdrawn (*t. Giṭ.* 1.8–9). Cf. Str-B, vol. 3, pp. 2ff., citing *Mek.* on Exod 12:4 (5*a*); 12:6 (7*a*); *b. Ḥag.* 10*b*; *b. Nazir* 12*b*.

[13] Luke 6:13. J. Dupont (*Le Nom d'Apôtres a-t-il été donné aux Douze par Jésus?*, Louvain, 1956), L. Cerfaux ("Pour l'histoire du titre Apostolos dans le Nouveau Testament," in *Recueil L. Cerfaux*, vol. 3, Gembloux, 1962, pp. 186–200) and others consider this title to be redactional and not given by Jesus, but (with Rengstorf, Descamps, A. Médebielle, "Apostolat," in *DBSup*, vol. 1, pp. 533–588) we must insist that Jesus could very well have used the word *šaliaḥ* to designate disciples given a special charge to represent him and participate in his ministry.

[14] Mark 3:14 specifies: "He appointed twelve *to be with him*," so as to train them better. In fact, we see them join together as *apostoloi* around Jesus (Mark 6:30), returning to him after their mission to report to him all that they had done (Luke 9:10). They ask him to increase their faith (Luke 17:5). It is to them alone that the

have special authority. For the moment nothing is said concerning their function, except that the word *šaliaḥ* in itself indicates that they would be envoys and proxies with appropriate powers.[15] This is what Mark 6:7 says on the occasion of the temporary mission in Galilee: "He called the Twelve to himself and began to send them (*apostellein*) two by two, giving them power over unclean spirits" (cf. Matt 10:1–2). With Jesus' *exousia* at their disposal, the apostles are prepared to carry out their mission. Here we already see the essential character of Christian apostleship.

1. — The apostle is a religious person, one set apart,[16] chosen from among others and *called* by Christ; which implies that the apostle will share Christ's condition, abandon his property, his trade, his family, will drink his cup (Matt 20:23), receiving the baptism with which the Master was baptized (Mark 10:39). St. Luke insists, "Jesus, having through the Holy Spirit given his orders to the apostles whom he had chosen (*hous exelexato*), he was taken away" (Acts 1:2; cf. John 15:16, 19). St. Paul always justifies his authority as a proxy: *klētos apostolos*, apostle by (God's) call (Rom 1:1), i.e., by virtue of a vocation. The recurrent formula is "apostle of Christ Jesus by God's will" (1 Cor 1:1; 2 Cor 1:1; Col 1:1; Eph 1:1). The genitive *Christou Iēsou* (1 Pet 1:1) is a genitive of possession and of origin (cf. Rom 1:5), as clarified by the reference to the appearance of the resurrected Christ (1 Cor 9:1; 15:3–9) and reinforced by the divine will (*thelēma*).[17] No surer basis can be given for the legitimacy of the apostolic mission: the mandate comes from God. "An apostle not in the name of humans, nor [appointed] by a human, but by Jesus Christ and God the Father" (Gal 1:1). This investiture is official and stable.[18]

Lord speaks confidentially at the Last Supper (Luke 22:14); he places his testament in their hands; they are his heirs (John 13:17); he will remain with them always (Matt 28:20), cf. Phil 3:12.

[15] Cf. L. Cerfaux, "La mission apostolique de Douze et sa portée eschatologique," in *Mélanges Tisserant*, vol. 1, pp. 4–66; A. L. Descamps, "Aux origines du ministère: La Pensée de Jésus," in *RTL*, 1971, pp. 3–45; 1972, pp. 121–159; F. Agnew, "On the Origin of the Term Apostolos," in *CBQ*, 1976, pp. 49–53.

[16] Rom 1:1, ἀφωρισμένος; cf. A. M. Denis, "Investiture de la fonction apostolique par 'apocalypse': Etude thématique de Gal. I, 16," in *RB*, 1957, pp. 335–362; 492–515; A. Satake, "Apostolat und Gnade bei Paulus," in *NTS*, vol. 15, 1968–1969, pp. 96–107.

[17] Cf. 2 Tim 1:1; θέλημα is replaced by ἐπιταγή (in 1 Tim 1:1; Titus 1:3), which expresses a particularly imperative command, notwithstanding any custom or order to the contrary, an irrevocable decree that is carried out.

[18] Cf. τίθημι, "install in a function" (1 Tim 2:7; cf. Acts 20:28; 1 Cor 12:28), and πιστευθῆναι (1 Tim 1:11–13; Titus 1:3). A. M. Denis, "L'Apôtre Paul prophète 'messianique' des Gentils," in *ETL*, 1957, pp. 300ff. G. Klein, *Die Zwölf Apostel: Ursprung und Gehalt einer Idee*, Göttingen, 1961.

2. — The apostle is essentially a person *sent* by someone to someone else. The purpose can be more or less secular;[19] as a delegate or representative, this "*apostolos* is not greater than the one who sent him" (John 13:16); nevertheless, "whoever receives the one whom I have sent receives me, and whoever receives me receives the one who sent me."[20] The attitude that a person takes toward the šaliaḥ is in reality directed toward the person of the sender. The apostle's mission is first of all that of preaching,[21] but also founding churches (1 Cor 9:2), forgiving sins (John 20:23), passing on the Holy Spirit (Acts 8:18), ordaining deacons (Acts 6:6), instituting presbyters (Titus 1:5). If need be, different audiences are specified: Peter is sent to the circumcised (Gal 2:7), Paul to the pagans (Rom 11:13; cf. 2 Cor 10:13–16).

3. — Such a role in God's plan of salvation requires that the apostle be invested with *power* and authority (Luke 24:49; 1 Thess 1:5). The Lord gave them the Holy Spirit and *exousia* over the demons. As heirs or proxies of Christ, the apostles live not only as itinerant missionaries but as heads of communities, repositories of Jesus' authority: "many wonders and signs were done by the apostles,"[22] or more precisely, "by the power of God"

---

[19] Paul left for Damascus as the šaliaḥ of the Sanhedrin, armed with letters of requisition (Acts 9:2; 22:5; 26:10, 12). The Jews of Rome had not received any šaliaḥ speaking ill of Paul (Acts 28:21); the church at Antioch sends Barnabas and Saul to Jerusalem (Acts 11:30; 13:3–4; 15:2); the church at Jerusalem sends Barsabbas and Silas to Antioch (Acts 15:23). The Philippians send Epaphroditus to help Paul (Phil 2:5). Titus and other brothers who receive gifts for the collection are ἀπόστολοι ἐκκλησιῶν (2 Cor 8:23), sent and authorized by the churches.

[20] John 13:20, the only occurrence of ἀπόστολος in John, who uses the verbs ἀποστέλλω and πέμπω. The mission of Jesus in the world (John 3:17, 34; 5:36–38; 6:29; 7:29; 8:42; 10:36; 11:42; 17:3, 8, 23) will be carried on by his own apostles (Matt 10:5; Luke 9:2; 11:49; John 4:38). "Just as you sent me into the world, so also have I sent them into the world" (John 17:18; cf. 20:21). Cf. J. Seynaeve, "Les Verbes ἀποστέλλω et πέμπω," pp. 385–389; F. Klostermann, *Das christliche Apostolat*, Innsbruck, 1962; Y. Congar, "Définition de l'apostolat par son contenu," in *VSpir*, n. 535, 1967, pp. 130–160; cf. L. M. Dewailly, "Note sur l'histoire de l'adjectif 'apostolique,'" in *Envoyés du Père*, 2d ed., Paris, 1960, pp. 114–140.

[21] Mark 3:14; Matt 28:20; 1 Cor 1:17, cf. proclaiming the gospel or Christ as Savior (1 Thess 2:2, 4; Rom 11:13–14; 1 Cor 1:17; Gal 1:16; Eph 3:8), bearing witness to him (Acts 1:22; 4:33; 1 Cor 1:6; 1 Tim 2:6), etc. The responsibility of Judas, which was a ministry (διακονία), is defined by St. Peter: an ἀποστολή (Acts 1:25), as Paul had "received χάριν καὶ ἀποστολήν" (Rom 1:5; cf. 1 Cor 9:2) and Peter, the apostle to the Jews (Gal 2:8); but its content is never specified. Cf. A. M. Denis, "La fonction apostolique et la liturgie nouvelle en esprit," in *RSPT*, 1958, pp. 401–436; 617–656; A. Ródenas, "El apostolado, ministerio de salvación en el Nuevo Testamento," in *Analecta Calasanctiana*, 1966, pp. 5–29.

[22] Acts 2:43; 4:33, 37; 5:12; Christians come to lay the proceeds from the sale of their property at the apostles' feet, as the holy women returning from the sepulcher

(2 Cor 6:7). This is what gives so much credibility to the teaching and the promises of the apostles (2 Pet 3:2; Jude 17), since in reality they only pass on the word that they have received from their Master (1 Thess 2:13—"The word that you heard from us is not the word of men but the word of God"). They are aware of this (Paul's message was with "a demonstration of the Spirit's power")[23] and conduct themselves as befits leaders,[24] even if they are considered the *peripsēma* ("offscouring") of the universe (1 Cor 4:13). They do not claim special privileges; they are servants (John 13:12–17; Luke 22:25–27), but they are at the top of the hierarchy of the kingdom of God. *Apostolos* is a title of honor ("I do not deserve to be called an apostle, because I persecuted the church of God" [1 Cor 15:9]; "As apostles of Christ, we could have looked down on you" [1 Thess 2:7]), because the "holy apostles" (Eph 3:5; Rev 18:20) are entirely consecrated to God (John 17:19).

4. — Since the Bible is neither a law code nor a theological handbook, words gain richer theological meaning from day to day and do not have a definite meaning that is fixed once and for all. In the NT, there are the high apostles, and there are second-order apostles. St. Luke knows only the Twelve as apostles: *hoi dōdeka*. Matt 10:2 specifies *hoi dōdeka apostoloi*. The Semitism *epoiēsen tous dōdeka* (literally, "he made the twelve") in Mark 3:13–19 confirms that Jesus did indeed himself establish the college of the Twelve to govern the new Israel.[25] These *šᵉlûḥîm* are proxies, repre-

---

announced what they had seen to the apostles (Luke 24:10); but Peter tries and convicts Ananias and Sapphira (Acts 5:2, 9). Miracles are signs that accredit the *apostolos* (2 Cor 12:12).

[23] 1 Cor 2:4–5; cf. Acts 4:7–33. St. Paul insisted more than anyone else on the *dynamis* of God as underlying the apostle's effectiveness, cf. 2 Cor 4:7; 6:7; 10:6; 13:9; Eph 3:7; Col 1:29.

[24] Cf. F. Giblet, "Les Douze: Histoire et théologie," in *Recherches bibliques*, vol. 7, Desclée De Brouwer, 1965, pp. 51–64A; reprinted in L. Descamps, *Le Prêtre, Foi et Contestation*, Gembloux-Paris, 1970, pp. 44–76.

[25] B. Rigaux, "Die 'Zwölf' in Geschichte und Kerygma," in H. Ristow, K. Matthiae, *Der historische Jesus und der kerygmatische Christus*, Berlin, 1961, pp. 468–486; cf. J. Giblet, "Les Douze: Histoire et théologie." "The Twelve" is a closed group. Judas is still referred to as εἷς τῶν δώδεκα (Mark 14:10, 20; Matt 26:14, 17; Luke 22:47; John 6:71). Since the Scripture required that the number of the Twelve be reconstituted in its totality (Ps 69:26; 109:8), Matthias was elected to replace the traitor (Acts 1:15–26), although he does not appear again and plays no role in the book of Acts. If the integrity of the college of the Twelve is so important, it is because it has a specific mission in the history of salvation and will be the guarantor of the Christian tradition (P. H. Menoud, "Les Additions au groupe des Douze Apôtres dans le Livre des Actes," in idem, *Jésus-Christ et la foi*, Neuchâtel-Paris, 1975, pp. 91–100). If Paul of Tarsus can claim the title of *apostolos* in its full meaning (Acts 22:15; 26:16) it is because on the one hand he has seen the resurrected Christ and been given this charge by him, and on the other hand because he is the missionary par excellence (cf. 2 Cor 5:20—"We

ἀπόστολος, *apostolos* 193

sentatives, plenipotentiaries, granted his own powers: "The one who listens to you listens to me, and the one who rejects you rejects me; but the one who rejects me rejects the One who sent me" (Luke 10:16; cf. Matt 10:14). In governing the church (cf. Matt 19:28; Luke 22:28–30), better than the "twelve men and three priests" who presided over the Qumran community, these apostles are "pillars" (Gal 2:9), "VIPs" (Gal 2:2, 6), judges and guarantors of orthodoxy, established to abide forever, forever united with Christ. They are the "twelve apostles of the Lamb" (Rev 21:14).

In a text whose importance cannot be overestimated, the resurrected Lord is said to have appeared first of all to Cephas, then to the Twelve, and then to "all the apostles, and after all them to me (Paul)" (1 Cor 15:5–8). These *apostoloi* named after the twelve could be divinely appointed missionary preachers, charismatics who are listed first among the official ministers of the church (1 Cor 12:28–31; Eph 4:11), which shows that there is no conflict between institutions and charisms. Their anonymity is like that of the "apostles and presbyters" who are associated in an indeterminate group in Acts 15:4, 6, 22, 23; 16:4. Nevertheless, we know of Barnabas, Paul's collaborator (Acts 14:4, 14; 2 Cor 12:7) and of particularly zealous missionaries like Andronicus and Junias, "outstanding among the apostles."[26] Just as there are always unfaithful stewards, there were Jewish-Christian missionaries, hardened in their prejudices, who took pride in the title of apostle and played up their prestige, *hoi hyperlian apostoloi* (2 Cor 12:11); these "super-apostles" (2 Cor 11:5) are "false apostles."[27] The church at Ephesus

---

are ambassadors for Christ, seeing that it is God who urges you through us"). He is the only one to go "to the ends of the earth" (Acts 1:8), traveling as far as Spain (cf. C. Spicq, "Saint Paul est venu en Espagne," in *Helmantica*, 1964, pp. 45–70; idem, *Les Epîtres Pastorales*, pp. 129–138). "Paul in himself is another circle, outside of and parallel to the circle of the Twelve. They are envoys to Israel and its proselytes; he goes to the pagans" (P. H. Menoud, *Jésus-Christ et la foi*, p. 100); cf. J. Munck, "La Vocation de l'Apôtre Paul," in *ST*, 1947, pp. 131–145; idem, "Paul, the Apostle, and the Twelve," *ST*, 1950, pp. 96–110; J. Cambier, "Paul, apôtre du Christ et prédicateur de l'Evangile," in *NRT*, 1959, pp. 1,009–1,028; idem, "Le Critère paulinien de l'apostolat en II Cor. XII, 6ff.," in *Bib*, 1962, pp. 481–518; F. Bovon, *Luc le théologien*, Neuchâtel-Paris, 1978, pp. 370–389.

[26] Rom 16:7. Cf. E. Lohse, *Ursprung und Prägung des christlichen Apostolates*, in *TZ*, 1953, pp. 259–257; J. Dauvillier, *Les Temps apostoliques: Ier siècle*, pp. 322ff. On the different meanings of the word *apostle* in the Pauline churches, cf. P. Grelot, "Les Epîtres de Paul, la mission apostolique," in J. Delorme, *Le Ministère et les ministères selon le Nouveau Testament*, Paris, 1973, pp. 48ff.

[27] 2 Cor 11:13. It is not easy to identify these enemies of Paul's ministry; were they Jewish Christians? false teachers (cf. ψευδοπροφῆται, Matt 7:15; Luke 6:26; Acts 13:6; 2 Pet 1:1)? uncommissioned missionaries? Cf. C. K. Barrett, "ψευδαπόστολοι (II Cor. XI, 13)," in *Mélanges Rigaux*, pp. 377–396. J. Dupont, "L'Apôtre comme

is congratulated for having identified them: "You have tested those who call themselves apostles but are not, and you have found them to be liars" (Rev 2:2).

5. — "Consider the apostle (Peshitta: šliho) and high priest of our faith, Jesus" (Heb 3:1). This is the only time that Christ is described as *apostolos* (before Justin, *1 Apol.* 1.12). Perhaps there is a reference to the angel of Yahweh (Hebrew *mal'āk*), messenger and guide who led Israel during their wanderings in the wilderness (Exod 14:19; 23:20, 23; 32:34; 33:2; Num 20:16), God's help personified for his people.[28] We might also think of a contrast with Moses, chosen from among the Israelites to lead them, but not coming from heaven like the Son;[29] more likely, however, the author of Hebrews is showing the influence of the Johannine tradition,[30] in which Christ is first and foremost the one "sent" from God.[31] Note John 9:7— "Siloam, which is translated Sent" (*Silōam, ho hermēneuetai Apestalmenos*). The Evangelist treats the substantive *Silōaḥ*, referring to a canal leading or "sending" water, as a passive participle and considers it a proper name (cf. Isa 8:6ff.; Gen 49:10, Hebrew *šîlōh*; given a messianic interpretation at *Gen. Rab.* 98.13; 99.10; *Tg. Onq.*), which he applies to Jesus, "the Sent One," by antonomasia (John 3:17, 34; 5:36; 7:29). Moreover, in Heb 3:1 the connection of "apostle" and "high priest" indicates that Jesus' divine mission is to "represent" humankind before God, to be the *šaliaḥ*, the one delegated by believers to plead their cause, a paraclete (1 John 2:1), interceding unceasingly on their behalf in the heavenly sanctuary (John 14:13–14). His "apostolate" is his permanent priestly office.

---

intermédiaire du salut dans les Actes des Apôtres," in *RTP,* 1980, pp. 342–358; J. Zumstein, "L'Apôtre comme martyr dans les Actes de Luc," *RTP,* 1980, pp. 371–390.

[28] "A sort of mediator of the covenant" and even of God's own appearance in human form (cf. Judg 6:17ff.); cf. G. von Rad, *OT Theology,* vol. 1, pp. 287ff.

[29] Cf. P. Borgen, "God's Agent in the Fourth Gospel," in J. Neusner, *Religions in Antiquity,* Leiden, 1970, pp. 137–148.

[30] Cf. C. Spicq, *Hébreux,* vol. 1, pp. 109–131. Moderns consider this Johannine tradition very old, cf. ibid., p. 132, n. 2; A. Gyllenberg, "Die Anfänge der johanneischen Tradition," in *Neutestamentliche Studien für R. Bultmann,* Berlin, 1954, pp. 144–147; B. P. W. Stather Hunt, *Some Johannine Problems,* London, 1958, pp. 105–123.

[31] Cf. John 17:3, 18; 20:21; 1 John 4:10—ἀπέστειλεν ... ἱλασμόν. In the discourse after the Last Supper, "the Teacher becomes the Intercessor; the Prophet, the High Priest" (H. B. Swete, *The Last Discourse and Prayer of Our Lord,* London, 1914, p. 159).

ἀργός

argos, inactive, inoperative

A contracted form of *aergos*, the adjective *argos* is the opposite of *energos*, "active, effective" (cf. *synergos:* one who helps; *euergetēs*, benefactor), and means "inactive, idle, not working" when it is used to describe people (cf. Diodorus Siculus 17.79.3) and "ineffectual, incapable of doing something, sterile, inoperative, ineffective, unfruitful" when it is used to describe things. These meanings occur constantly throughout classical Greek[1] and in the Koine. Menander: "He will call you a pest, a loafer" (*Dysk.* 366); "they reduce me to inaction";[2] Plutarch: "Marius did not spend this period in idleness" (*Cor.* 31.4); "a lazy and idle crowd" (*argon de kai scholastēn ochlon*, *Sol.* 22.3; cf. 31.5, Pisistratus promulgates the law on idleness, *ton tēs argias nomon;* cf. *Ti. Gracch.* 1.3). In Philo, the dozen occurrences of *argos* refer to a lazy and indolent life (Philo, *Conf. Tongues* 43; Philo, *Spec. Laws* 2.101), "the idlest (*argotatē*) and least formed soul has been allotted to the fish" (*Creation* 65; *Alleg. Interp.* 1.32), brute, unformed matter (*Flacc.* 148; *Moses* 2.136; *Spec. Laws* 1.21), idle land, meaning land lying fallow (*Spec. Laws* 2.86, 2.88). Likewise in Josephus: at the time for sowing "the people spent fifty days doing nothing" (*War* 2.200); David decided to march against the Philistines "being neither idle nor slack in his conduct of affairs" (*mēden argon mēde rhathymon en tois pragmasin*).[3]

---

[1] Aristophanes, *Ran.* 1498: διατριβὴν ἀργόν; numerous references in LSJ under this word.

[2] *Dysk.* 443: ποιοῦσιν γέ με ἀργόν; "he isn't a person to walk around all day doing nothing, ἀργὸς περιπατεῖν" (ibid. 755); Philostratus, *Gym.* 44: "instead of being active, they are lazy, ἀργοὶ δὲ ἐξ ἐνεργῶν"; 58: "older athletes should be exposed to the sun, for they lie resting (ἀργοὶ κείμενοι)" while others are full of vigor (ἐνεργοί); cf. 34, 35.

[3] *Ant.* 7.96; *War* 6.44: "if you remain idle with such powerful arms"; 4.309, a vain clamor opposed to an effective rescue; *Ant.* 12.378, land that hasn't been sown is *argēn*. The Sabbath and the sabbatical year are times of rest, of the cessation of all activity, *War* 1.60; 2.517; 4.100; 7.53; cf. 2 Macc 5:25.

---

argos, S 692; *TDNT* 1.452; *EDNT* 1.150; MM 74; L&N 30.44, 42.46, 65.36, 72.21, 88.248; BDF §59(1); BAGD 104

In the vocabulary of the papyri, *argos* almost always means "not busy, unused," whether describing persons[4] or things: a house or a place (*P.Mil.* 67, col. 1.7: *oikos prōtos argos; P.Mich.* 620, 58, 60, 73, 83, 90, 107, 108, *argē kella*), a chest that is empty or out of service (*P.Oxy.* 1269, 22), land that has not been sown (*P.Stras.* 144, 5; cf. *PSI* 837, 7; Dittenberger, *Syl.* 884, 23), an oil press that is not in working order,[5] unproductive money: "they say that their gold is sitting idle and that they are greatly wronged" (*P.Cair.Zen.* 59021, 25: *SB* 6711; cf. 10257, 18). Finally, the *onos argos* is a beast that is good for nothing, as opposed to others that carry loads (*P.Lond.* 1170 verso, 474, 483; *SB* 9150, 38).

The three occurrences of *argos* in the OT are rather in the sense of "inert, unproductive." God does not want for the works of wisdom to be ineffectual, *erga arga*, i.e., created in vain, remaining sterile, unexploited, unproductive (Wis 14:5); the feet of the idols are useless for walking (Wis 15:15); the idle or lazy servant is not consulted concerning a great labor (Sir 37:11), he must be put to work lest he remain idle (Sir 33:28, *hina mē argē*).

At least seven of the eight NT occurrences retain the meaning "not busy, idle, inactive." In the parable of the workers sent to the vineyard, certain ones have not yet been hired and wait around "not doing anything" (Matt 20:3, 6). Young widows who no longer have a household to manage, have no child to raise, and do not devote their time to prayer become idle (*argai manthanousin*), and not only idle but gossips and busybodies (1 Tim 5:13). Epimenides of Cnossos, in calling the Cretans "do-nothing bellies," means that they are gluttons who get fat doing nothing.[6] According to Jas 2:20 "faith without works is sterile,"[7] i.e., useless for salvation; but 2 Pet 1:8 recognizes "you are not inactive and without fruit (*ouk argous oude akarpous*) toward the exact knowledge of our Lord Jesus Christ."

On Matt 12:36 all the commentators take different tacks:[8] "For every idle word that one speaks one will give account on the day of judgment."

---

[4] *P.Lond.* 915, 8 (vol. 3, p. 27); *BGU* 833, 5; *Pap.Lugd.Bat.* XI, 24, 19; *SB* 9604, 24, 7: Ἄμμωνος ἄργου. —*P.Brem.* 13, 5: "καθήμεθα ἀργοί, we are here without work"; *BGU* 1078, 6: οὐ γὰρ ἀργὸν δεῖ με καθῆσθαι (letter of AD 39); *SB* 8247, 22: πορόεσθε ἕκαστος εἰς τὰ εἴδια καὶ μὴ γείνεσθε ἀργοί (around AD 63).

[5] Ἐλαιουργίου ἀργοῦ (*P.Amh.* 97, 9; *P.Flor.* 1, 4; cf. *SB* 10278, 10–12). In the third century, a *dioikētēs* writes to a subordinate: "if you are unable to find the available material" (*P.Tebt.* 703, 159).

[6] Titus 1:12; cf. Theopompus (in Athenaeus 12.527*a*): the laziest inhabitants of Pharsalus and the most luxurious of all people, ἀργότατοι καὶ πολυτελέστατοι.

[7] The reading of B, whereas ℵ, A, Peshitta have νεκρά.

[8] Cf. J. Viteau, "La 'Parole oiseuse': Sur saint Matthieu XII, 36," in *VSpir,* Supplément, 1931, pp. 16–28; E. Stauffer, "Von jedem unnützen Wort?" in *Gott und die Götter* (Festgabe E. Fascher), Berlin, 1958, pp. 94–102; L.-M. Dewailly, "La Parole sans

How should we take *pan rhēma argon*? As E. Stauffer has pointed out, it seems to be true that this warning must be assessed alongside the *paideai stomatos* of Sir 23 and the *disciplina oris* of Qumran, where there was a cult of silence.[9] In fact, the expression *logon argon* is found in Josephus, *Ant.* 15.224, where it refers to an inconsequential utterance or bit of advice, one that is not taken into account, that has no effect. In Philo, *Dreams* 1.29, sound issues from thought, and "it is in the mouth that it is articulated"; the tongue serves as the herald and interpreter of the intelligence and "does not produce a sound that is not just that, that is ineffectual (*argēn*)"; cf. the ban on hasty speech (*Spec. Laws* 1.53); *Sent. Sextus* 154: "words without thought are mere noise" (*rhēmata aneu nou psophos*). Pythagoras had instructed "It is better to throw a stone with no goal than to utter an idle word" (*ē logon argon*, in Stobaeus, *Ecl.* 3.34.11; vol. 3, p. 684); cf. Pindar, frag. 58: "Take care not to utter useless words (*ton achreion logon*) in front of everyone."[10] Finally, this expression was used for the fatalistic argument posed by Chrysippus, the conclusion of which was the rejection of any initiative at all,[11] which is the *argos logos* theorem taken up by Plutarch (*De fato* 11) and Cicero.[12] Thus, not only is *argos* commonly linked with *logos*

œuvre (Mt. XII, 36)," in *Mélanges M.-D. Chenu*, Paris, 1967, pp. 203–219. —It isn't certain that this logion is in its true location and fits in with the polemical pericope against the Pharisees.

[9] Cf. 1QS 6.11: "In the Assembly of the Congregation no one should speak a word without the permission of the Congregation"; 7.9, a penalty "for the one who utters with his mouth a profane word (*nbl*) and for interrupting his neighbor's speech"; 10.21–24: "no profanity will be heard in my mouth"; CD 10.17: "on the Sabbath day, no one must use any profane (*nbl*) or scornful language." —A number of the church fathers understood Matt 12:36 to refer to foul, blameworthy, shameful, or slanderous language (cf. J. Viteau, L.-M. Desailly); but the rabbis understood *debarîm betalîm* as referring to language that was superfluous, lacking in substance, trivial, vain (cf. Str-B, vol. 1, p. 640). It would be necessary to give an accounting even for the negative, for that which did not exist.

[10] *SVF*, vol. 2, 278, 19.

[11] Cf. the ἀχρεῖος slave (Matt 25:30; Luke 18:10), i.e., the one who does not work. "The adjective ἀχρεῖος . . . is hard to translate. It is used of men who are no good, or no longer good, for service; for soldiers not fit for duty because of their age or their injuries; and figuratively of persons from whom nothing can be had, or from whom one no longer has anything to get" (E. Delebecque, *Etudes grecques*, p. 106).

[12] Cicero, *Fat.* 12.28–29: "We do not burden ourselves with what is called the 'idle argument;' philosophers apply the label *argos logos* to an argument that would lead us to lead lives of total inactivity. This is how the question is posed: If it is your fate to recover from this illness, then whether you go to the doctor or not you will recover. Likewise, if it is your fate not to be cured of this disease, then whether you go to the doctor or not you will not recover. And one of the two is your fate. Thus it is useless to go to the doctor."

in the first century, but it always has the meaning "ineffective, inactive." Therefore this meaning must be applied in Matt 12:36, where it fits the meaning of the context (bearing good or bad fruit, verse 33) and of all the other biblical occurrences, especially since it accords with the theology of the word in the Old and New Testaments: the word of God is never ineffectual (Isa 55:11), because it is by definition *energēs* (Heb 4:12). Similarly the word of the Christian must issue in *ergon* (1 John 3:18; cf. Phlm 6); it would be out of line with its dynamism for it to be inoperative, without effect. Thus it seems to have been understood by *Did.* 2.5: "Your word shall not be empty (*ou kenos logos*), but fulfilled in action."[13]

---

[13] Cf. Plutarch, *De garr.* 2: "the speech of prattlers is infertile and leads to nothing"; Lyc. 19.3: "an intemperate tongue makes discourse empty and senseless."

> ἀρνέομαι, ἀπαρνέομαι
>
> arneomai, aparneomai, to say no, deny, repudiate

The grammarians point out that the Koine prefers the aorist middle of *arneomai* to the aorist passive form of the classical period;[1] furthermore, verbs expressing will, desire, or hindrance are rather commonly construed with the infinitive (without an article) or with the conjunctions *hina, hōste, hoti.* In the NT, however, only the infinitive follows *arneomai.*[2] Moreover, after "negative" verbs like *arneomai* ("deny"), *antilegō* ("object"), and *amphisbēteō* ("question"), the complementary clause takes the negative *ou* with *hoti* (1 John 2:22) and the negative *mē* with infinitive (Luke 22:34; cf. F. M. Abel, *Grammaire,* 75 *i*). Finally, of the *arneomai* compounds with the verbal prefixes *ap-, ex-, kat-,* the NT has only *aparneomai* and uses it with exactly the same meaning as the simple form, as is proved by the use of these two verbs in strictly parallel texts in the Synoptic Gospels.[3]

The simplest meaning of *arneomai* is "say no," in an oral context: "Sara denied it, saying, 'I did not laugh'" (Gen 18:15; cf. Philo, *Abraham* 112, 206; *Spec. Laws* 2.54); Leah is "the one refused by every madman and sent back with a denial."[4] Petronius vacillates between two options: "to the crowd he

---

[1] F. M. Abel, *Grammaire,* 18 *m;* B. G. Mandilaras, *Verb,* n. 315.
[2] F. M. Abel, *Grammaire,* 69 *m* R.
[3] Cf. C. K. Barrett, "Is There a Theological Tendency in Codex Bezae?" in *Text and Interpretation: Studies in the N. T. Presented to M. Black,* Cambridge, 1979, p. 23, n. 3; H. Riesenfeld, "The Meaning of the Verb ἀρνεῖσθαι," in *ConNT,* vol. 11, 1947, pp. 207-219; H. Schlier, "ἀρνέομαι," in *TDNT,* vol. 1, pp. 469-471.
[4] Philo, *Cherub.* 41. Ἀρνέομαι is used constantly from Homer on for the refusal of a marriage proposal: "refuse a marriage (ἀρ. γάμον) abhorrent to her" (Homer, *Od.* 1.249); Amasius "was afraid and could bring himself neither to give his daughter

---

arneomai, S 720; *TDNT* 1.469-471; *EDNT* 1.153-155; *NIDNTT* 1.454-56; MM 78; L&N 30.52, 31.25, 33.277, 34.48, 36.43, 88.231; BDF §§78, 311(2), 392(1a), 397(3), 420(2), 429; BAGD 107-108 ‖ *aparneomai,* S 533; *TDNT* 1.471; *EDNT* 1.153-155; *NIDNTT* 1.454-455; MM 53; L&N 30.52, 33.277, 34.49; BAGD 81

said neither yes nor no."[5] Thus when Jesus asked who had touched him "they all denied it" (*arnoumenōn de pantōn*, Luke 8:45); Moses "refused to be called (*ērnēsato legesthai*) son of Pharaoh's daughter."[6] This meaning—spoken denial—is the commonest meaning in the papyri. Just as today we say, "The accused denied that he was guilty" or "The accused denied everything," *arneomai* is in a way a legal or judicial verb. It shows up in petitions and in transcripts of trials, where it often has connotations of lying,[7] as it does also at 1 John 2:22. For example, on July 18, 142, the prefect of Egypt, Valerius Eudaemon, reacting against blackmail by debtors and denouncing their fraudulent maneuvering (*panourgia*), sets forth the legal means whereby they can resist: "If someone is being pursued for a debt and does not immediately state that he does not owe it (*mē parautika arnēsamenos opheilein*), that is, if he does not try to prove—by saying that the documents are falsified and filing charges—the falsification of the documents or fraud or inveigling, then either such a maneuver will be pointless for him . . . or he will not be shielded from punishment but will be liable for the statutory fines."[8] In 6 BC, Asinius Gallus, governor of the province of Asia, questioned some slaves who had been implicated in a murder during the course of a nocturnal row. Here is what happened: Philinus came three nights in a row, hurling insults, to besiege, as it were, the house of Eubulus and Tryphera. The third time he brought with him his brother Eubulus. So the masters of the house "ordered a slave not to kill him . . . but to chase him off by throwing their waste on him. But in pouring it out, the slave,

---

nor to refuse her" (Herodotus 3.1); Abraham does not refuse the marriage with Rebekah (Josephus, *Ant.* 1.245); Samson's parents refuse his marriage with Thamna (5.286). "King Ptolemy asked for Cornelia's hand in marriage; she said no" (Plutarch, *Ti. Gracch.* 1.7).

[5] Philo, *To Gaius* 247; cf. Malichos, who appeases the people by his denials (Josephus, *War* 1.227; *Ant.* 14.278, 282); Ladice protested (Herodotus 2.181).

[6] Heb 11:24. The formula used concerning John the Baptist's response when asked about his identity ("He acknowledged and did not deny . . . 'I am not the Christ,' " John 1:20) has analogies in Greek (Euripides, *El.* 1057: "I say it and do not deny"; Josephus, *Ant.* 6.151) and in Hebrew; cf. A. Schlatter, *Der Evangelist Johannes*, Stuttgart, 1948, p. 38.

[7] This usage is found already in Ps.-Homer: "this rascal of a child denies so artfully and with such sophistication in this bogus tale" (*H. Hermes* 3.390); Herodotus 1.24: "they were convicted of their crimes and could deny them no longer"; 3.74; 4.68; 6.69; Plutarch, *Amat.* 5 (752 a): "the love of boys denies sensual pleasure" because it is ashamed and afraid.

[8] *P.Oxy.* 237, col. VIII, 14—P. Collinet, "L'Edit du préfet d'Egypte Valerius Eudaemon (P. Oxy. II, 237, 7–8) (138 ap. J.-C.): Une hypothèse sur la 'Querela non numeratae pecuniae,' " in *Proceedings* IV, pp. 89–100).

ἀρνέομαι, *arneomai* 201

whether intentionally or not—for he persists in denying it (*autos men gar enemeinen arnoumenos*)—let the vase fall on Eubulus, who was killed."[9]

To say no is to deny consent, to refuse, to protest, sometimes to revolt. The nuances are numerous. One can simply refuse to take a meal (Homer, *Il.* 19.304) or to sing (Polybius 4.20.11), decline an invitation to dinner (Josephus, *Life* 222), or a favor, or honors.[10] Or one can refuse to admit something: the healing of the lame man at Jerusalem was so obvious that "we can not deny it."[11] There are friendly refusals,[12] sometimes mere omissions (Wis 18:9), or the results of ignorance (Philo, *Sacr. Abel and Cain* 23: *mē agnoun arnē*; cf. 79); usually, however, a resolute refusal is meant. According to St. Stephen, the Israelites rebuffed Moses, "saying, 'Who set you up as a leader and judge?' " (Acts 7:35). Pilate refused to remove the standards from Jerusalem (Josephus, *War* 2.171); when Vespasian declines

---

[9] Dittenberger, *Syl.* 780, 25 (rescript of Augustus to the city of Cnidos); cf. J. Colin, *Les Villes libres de l'Orient gréco-romain*, Brussels, 1965, p. 88; cf. *P.Flor.* 61, 49: ἠρνήσατο οὗτος τὴν κληρονομίαν τοῦ πατρὸς καὶ ἐγὼ τὴν τοῦ ἰδίου πατρός (first century AD); *BGU* 195, 22–23; *SB* 8945, 26; *P.Mil.Vogl.* 229, 12: ἠρνήσατο ἃ παρεθέμην αὐτῇ (cf. N. Lewis, "On Paternal Authority in Roman Egypt," in *RIDA*, 1970, pp. 251–258); Thucydides 6.60.3: "He will be safer if he confesses his crimes under a guaranty of impunity than if he is handed over for judgment while denying them" (ἀρνηθέντι); Philo, *Spec. Laws* 4.32: to contest the reality of a deposit that has been entrusted to us is to renege on a twofold deposit (διττὰς ἀρνεῖσθαι παρακαταθήκας); 4.40: "the thief denies and lies (ἀρνεῖται καὶ ψεύδεται) out of fear of the punishment that will follow his confession. The person who denies (ὅ τε ἀρνούμενος) does his best to shift the blame to someone else through slander"; 1.235: "He blames himself for his denials and perjury"; 1.278: refuse to restore; *Plant.* 107; Josephus, *War* 1.548: Tiron and his son, when put to the question, denied everything; 2.303, 603; *Ant.* 7.226: the woman did not deny having seen him; 11.341: the Samaritans, when they are in a difficult spot, deny the truth; 15.173: Hyrcanus denied having given his consent; 15.288; 17.135.

[10] Plato, *Soph.* 217 c. *Anth. Pal.* 6.47. Οὐκ ἀρνήσομαι = I do not deny it (Euripides, *Hec.* 303; cf. Aeschylus, *PV* 266). In AD 41, the emperor Claudius refuses two gold statues that his very good friend Barbillus, ambassador of the Alexandrians, wished to dedicate to *Pax Augusta Claudiana* and declines to introduce a Claudian tribe (*P.Lond.* 1912, 36 and 41; cf. A. Kasher, "Les Circonstances de la promulgation de l'édit de l'empereur Claude et de sa lettre aux Alexandrins," in *Sem*, vol. 26, 1976, pp. 99–108).

[11] Οὐ δυνάμεθα ἀρνεῖσθαι. Acts 4:16; cf. Plato, *Symp.* 192 *e*: "No one on earth would refuse such an offer"; *Grg.* 461 *c*: "who then would deny being . . . able to teach"; Epictetus 3.24.81: "you will not deny knowing"; Philo, *Dreams* 1.49; Josephus, *Ant.* 16.150: it is impossible to deny Herod's very generous nature; *Life* 255: "I produced the letter, so that no one could deny anything, since the text refuted their objections"; 385: "It was impossible to deny that the Tiberians had written to the king."

[12] The refusal to loan a bow (Homer, *Il.* 21.345) or to give tools (Hesiod, *Op.* 408). Longinus was quite willing to carry a letter, but he refused to deliver objects, "saying (ἠρνήσατο λέγων) that he was unable to take anything" (*P.Mich.* 466, 14); but to refuse to serve the city is a kind of treason (Demosthenes, *Corona* 18.282).

imperial honors, his officers become more insistent.[13] *Arneomai* can also mean "renounce," that is, to desist, detach oneself, and voluntarily forsake a person to whom one has been attached. Aseneth states, "My father and my mother have forsaken me, because I destroyed and shattered their gods."[14]

These usages are secular. It is the Wisdom of Solomon that gives this verb a religious meaning, with respect to the impious: refusing to know God.[15] Philo uses it to mean "repudiate, apostasize": "Whoever renounces the truly real God (*ho ton ontōs onta theon arnoumenos*)—what punishment does such a person deserve!" (*Spec. Laws* 2.255). These texts are few and late. Perhaps it could be suggested that is was the Lord who coined the idea of "repudiation" that would be preserved and exploited in the NT. The most important statement is, "Whoever confesses (*homologēsei*) me before men, him will I also confess (*homologēsō*) before my Father who is in heaven; but whoever denies me (*arnēsetai me*) before men, him will I also deny (*arnēsomai*) before my Father who is in heaven."[16] A strong contrast is made between confessing the faith and repudiating it;[17] the content, the object, and the publicness are the same. The reference is to a disciple who publicly professes that he knows Jesus as Savior and God, adheres to his teaching,

---

[13] Josephus, *War* 4.603; cf. 5.425: the refusal of the occupants of a house to hand over foodstuffs; *Ant.* 1.275: Isaac's refusal to bless Esau; 4.86: the king of the Ammonites refuses to allow Israel to pass through; 18.159: refusal of a loan; 20.222, or a request.

[14] *Jos. Asen.* 12.11 (cf. Ps 27:10); 4 Macc 8:7—speaking to the Maccabee brothers, the tyrant states, "You will get prominent posts in my administration if you renounce the ancestral law that governs you"; the fourth brother rejects this proposition: "I will not renounce our noble brotherhood"; cf. Josephus, *Ag. Apion* 1.191: to renounce ancestral customs. *P.Phil.* 2, 6, in a transcript of an audience: after as agreement has been concluded for the restoration of an inheritance to some children, a woman interrupts; contradicting her earlier commitments (ὁμολογήσασα), she reneges (ἠρνήσατο) and causes problems.

[15] Wis 12:27; 16:16. "To know" is to be understood in its Semitic sense as an existential relationship.

[16] Matt 10:32–33 (cf. Luke 12:9—ἀπαρνεῖσθαι); Epictetus 4.1.146: "Slaves, do not run away from your masters, do not repudiate them (μηδ' ἀπαρνοῦ), and do not have the audacity to produce your emancipator, when the proofs of your slavery are so numerous." Jesus' prophecy found its way into a liturgical hymn at Jerusalem, quoted at 2 Tim 2:12—"If we deny [him], he will also deny us."

[17] The ὁμολογέω-ἀρνέομαι antithesis is constant, cf. Plato, *Tht.* 165 a; Thucydides 6.603; Epicurus, *Nat.* 29; Aelian, *NA* 2.43; Philo, *Drunkenness* 188, 192; *Spec. Laws* 1.235; *To Gaius* 247; Josephus, *Ant.* 6.151; *P.Phil.* 2, 6; John 1:20; Titus 1:16; 1 John 2:23; etc. Cf. H. F. von Soden, *Untersuchungen zur Homologie in den griechischen Papyri Ägyptens bis Diokletian*, Cologne-Vienna, 1973; W. Kramer, *Christ, Lord, Son of God*, London, 1966, pp. 15ff.

ἀρνέομαι, *arneomai* 203

and submits his life to his Master's will. If this "Christian" later says *no* to this *Amen*, that is, if he officially renounces Jesus, declaring before other people that he is freeing himself from his dependence on the Lord, then the Lord in turn will abandon him and will not exercise his role as advocate and paraclete on his behalf (1 John 2:1). In other words, the baptized person, and especially the apostle, must bear witness publicly to Jesus; their renunciation of Jesus would prompt his official renunciation of them.

Seven times the Gospels use the verb *arneomai* for Peter's "denial" in the courtyard of the high priest.[18] The apostle actually denies knowing Jesus (Luke 22:57) and being one of his disciples (John 18:25), and this renunciation takes place "in front of everyone" (Matt 26:70). This abandonment seems to fulfill perfectly the prediction recorded in Matt 10:32–33, at least in terms of the apparent events; but Peter wept bitterly after his sin, and the Lord, who had predicted it (John 13:38), had also prayed for him that his faith would not fail (Luke 22:32), and afterward he rehabilitated him, giving him the charge to feed his sheep (John 21:15–17). In other words, Peter denied Jesus with his lips, but in his heart he remained constantly faithful to his Lord and Master. The use of the word "denial" for this charade intended to get people to leave him alone is thus problematic. Theodoret commented well: Peter denied Jesus through weakness, but "was held fast by the bonds of love" (*tois tou philtrou desmois katechomenos*, Theodoret, *Car.* 31.10). On the other hand, when the members of the chosen people cry, "We recognize no king but Caesar" (John 19:15), they hand over and "deny Jesus . . . the holy and just one" before Pilate,[19] denying his messianic identity. Through their perjury (their violation of sworn loyalty) they exclude themselves from the covenant and abdicate their privileges along with their obligation to be in submission. This about-face is the same as that of the false teachers and heretics who "in denying the Master who

---

[18] Matt 26:70; Mark 14:68, 70; Luke 22:57; John 13:38; 18:25, 27. Cf. M. Goguel, "Did Peter Deny His Lord?" in *HTR*, 1932, pp. 1–27; C. Masson, "Le Reniement de Pierre: Quelques aspects de la formation d'une tradition," in *RHPR*, 1957, pp. 24–35; B. Schwank, "Petrus verleugnet Jesus (XVIII, 12–27)," in *Sein und Sendung*, 1964, pp. 51–65; P. Benoit, *Passion et résurrection du Seigneur*, Paris, 1966, pp. 61–86; R. Pesch, "Die Verleugnung des Petrus," in *Neues Testament und Kirche, für R. Schnackenburg*, Freiburg, 1974, pp. 42–62. G. Klein and E. Linnemann rejected the historicity of Peter's denial (cf. R. E. Brown, *Peter in the New Testament*, Minneapolis, 1973, p. 63, n. 139; cf. pp. 112, 121, 133), but H. Merkel ("Peter's Curse," in E. Bammel, *The Trial of Jesus*, London, 1970, pp. 66–71) shows that it is unthinkable that the Christian community would have forged this story if Peter had not really denied Jesus.

[19] Acts 3:13–14. Cf. Demosthenes 36.34: ὅταν τὴν διαθήκην ἀρνῆται. M. Wilcox, *The Semitisms of Acts*, Oxford, 1965, pp. 139ff.

redeemed them bring swift perdition upon themselves."[20] They refuse to submit their thought to the only teacher of truth, Christ (John 14:6; 2 Cor 10:5), to whom they have promised unconditional obedience (1 Pet 1:2, 18, 22). They are like slaves whose master has paid the price for their emancipation but who respond with insolence and ingratitude. Their perdition is sure.

Another series of texts gives *arneomai* the meaning "to renounce," referring to self-sacrifice, the giving up of one's own stake: "Anyone who wishes to come after me must deny himself (aorist imperative, *arnēsasthō*), take up his cross each day, and follow me."[21] To say no to oneself firmly and radically is to treat oneself as a negligible quantity that should never enter into consideration, to suppress oneself, in a way; a meaning reinforced by the image of bearing the cross, which leads to death. Conversion to Christianity is a categorical refusal to be in servitude to worldly desires, the goal being to live freely, "with self-control and piety."[22] Faith implies faithfulness, a living adherence to Christ; it requires living in conformity to his teachings. Heretics profess (*homologousin*) to know God, but through their deeds they deny him (*tois de ergois arnountai*).[23] This is repudiation in the most serious sense of the word: "If anyone does not care for his own people, and especially the members of his own household, he has denied the faith (*tēn pistin ērnētai*) and is worse than an infidel" (1 Tim 5:8). This

---

[20] 2 Pet 2:1. Cf. 1 John 2:22—"Who is the liar, if not the one who denies the Jesus is the Christ? He is the Antichrist who denies the Father and the Son," and hence the Incarnation and the Trinity (2 Tim 2:13 says that Christ cannot deny himself; he remains faithful under all circumstances, incapable of any denial whatsoever). 1 John 2:23—"Whoever denies the son does not have the Father either; the one who confesses the Son (*homologōn*) has the Father"; in true faith in the divinity of Jesus Christ there is communion with the Father (John 12:44; 14:6); Jude 4: the impious "deny our only Master and Lord, Jesus Christ."

[21] Luke 9:23 (cf. ἀπαρνησάσθω, Matt 16:24; Mark 8:34); cf. Luke 14:26—μισεῖν τὴν ἑαυτοῦ ψυχήν; Aristodicus: "they renounced life" (*Anth. Pal.* 7.473). R. Völkl, *Die Selbstliebe in der Heiligen Schrift*, 1956, p. 160; C. Spicq, *Théologie morale*, vol. 1, p. 264, n. 3; vol. 2, p. 529; S. Brown, *Apostasy and Perseverance in the Theology of Luke*, Rome, 1969.

[22] Titus 2:12 (A. Fridrichsen, "Zu ἀρνεῖσθαι im N.T. insonderheit in den Pastoralbriefen," in *ConNT*, 1942, pp. 94–96). To live a holy life, i.e., a life that belongs to God, implies not just separation and leaving, but a rejection, a form of violence. Faithfulness is perseverance in this attitude. Christ directs this praise to the church at Pergamum: "You hold fast to my name, and you have not denied my faith" (Rev 2:13), and similarly to the church at Philadelphia: "You have kept my word and not denied my name" (3:8).

[23] Titus 1:16. The impious people of the end times, among their other vices, will maintain the forms of piety but deny its power (2 Tim 3:5). These are impostors. They rob the gospel of its *dynamis*, so that their profession of faith is empty.

ἀρνέομαι, *arneomai*

violation of sworn loyalty means breaking the initial baptismal commitment to live a life of the brotherly love that characterizes the disciple (John 13:35). To fail here is worse than being an unbeliever, who at least is not breaking a promise.[24] Without brotherly *agapē*, the Christian is not only failing to keep his word to the Lord Christ but also stooping beneath common morality. "Melior est canis vivus leone mortuo (Eccl 9:4), id est paganus christiano impio" ("Better a living dog than a dead lion, i.e., better a pagan than an impious Christian," Hugh of St.-Cher).

---

[24] Cf. *b. Šabb.* 116a: "These know and deny, while those deny without knowing"; *b. B. Meṣ.* 71a: Lending for interest is a serious sin, but "to gather a witness, a notary, and ink and sign a document is to deny the God of Israel." Cf. Str-B, vol. 1, p. 585.

ἀρχιποίμην

archipoimēn, **chief shepherd**

"The shepherd's mission is so lofty that it is rightly attributed not only to kings, sages, and souls of perfect purity, but even to the Lord God."[1] In the East, "pastor" is actually used to describe the function and the office of a sovereign;[2] it is also used for Moses, who led Israel in its wanderings;[3] for David;[4] and above all for God.[5] Jesus claimed the designation,[6] and the

---

[1] Philo, *Husbandry* 50. After defining the true shepherd as an overseer, guide, and leader (41ff.), Philo argues that God is the supreme shepherd (49–66). Elsewhere he compares the shepherd and the king, *Moses* 1.60ff.; *Joseph* 2; *Sacr. Abel and Cain* 49ff. Cf. the Mebaqqer at Qumran (CD 13.9).

[2] Cf. M. J. Seux, *Epithètes royales akkadiennes et sumériennes*, Paris, 1967, pp. 244ff. D. Müller, "Der Gute Hirte," in *Zeitschrift für ägyptische Sprache und Altertumskunde*, vol. 86, 1961, pp. 126ff. In the prologue to his code, Hammurabi calls himself pastor (col. 1, 50–51), and he repeats the designation in the epilogue: "I am the pastor, the bearer of salvation. . . . In my bosom I have held the peoples of Sumer and Akkad" (col. 24, 42–43, 49–52). J. Jeremias, ποιμήν, in *TDNT*, vol. 6, pp. 485–502; C. Spicq, *Agapè*, vol. 3, 1959, pp. 235ff. (on John 21:15–17); J. Dauvillier, *Les Temps apostoliques*, Paris, 1970, pp. 147ff.

[3] Cf. H. Kosmala, *Hebräer—Essener—Christen*, Leiden, 1959, pp. 415ff. R. Le Déaut, *Nuit Pascale*, p. 268; Str-B, vol. 2, p. 209.

[4] *Les Paroles des luminaires*, col. IV, 6 (cf. ed. M. Baillet, in *RB* 1961, pp. 205, 222); A. Dupont-Sommer, "Le Psaume CLI et son origine essénienne," in *Sem*, vol. 14, 1964, p. 45.

[5] Isa 40:11; Ezek 34:12ff.; Ps 23. The metaphor suggests watchfulness, care, benevolence, and devotion, cf. C. Spicq, *Agapè: Prolégomènes*, Louvain-Leiden, 1955, p. 110; W. H. Brownlee, *Ezekiel's Poetic Indictment of the Shepherds*, in *HTR*, 1958, pp. 191–204; G. M. Behler, "Le Bon Pasteur: Psaume XXIII," in *VSpir*, 526; 2966, pp. 442–467; J. Dupont, *Le Discours de Milet (Actes, XX, 18, 36)*, Paris, 1962, pp. 143ff.; 149ff.; 167.

[6] John 10:14; cf. Ezek 37:26; Zech 11:14ff.; Matt 25:32; 26:31. L. Sabourin, *Les Noms et les titres de Jésus*, Bruges-Paris, 1963, pp. 71ff. W. Tooley, "The Shepherd and Sheep Image in the Teaching of Jesus," in *NovT*, vol. 7, 1964, pp. 15–25.

---

archipoimēn, S 750; *TDNT* 6.485–499; *EDNT* 1.165; *NIDNTT* 3.564, 568; MM 82; L&N 44.5; BDF §118(2); BAGD 113

faith of the disciple recognized him as the *archēgos* of the new People of God: "the God of peace who brought again from the dead the Shepherd of the sheep, the great one."[7]

If the salvation of all Christians lies in following the "guardian Shepherd" of their souls,[8] the presbyters of the churches of Asia Minor are motivated to behave as models by the thought that "when the Chief Shepherd appears you will receive an unfading crown of glory" (1 Pet 2:4). The term *archipoimēn* is not a Christian coinage, even though it is unknown in the OT (cf. nevertheless its use by Symmachus to translate *noqēd* in 2 Kgs 3:4). It appears for the first time in *T. Jud.* 8.1—"I had many cattle, and my chief herdsman was Hiram and Adullamite" (*ēsan de moi ktēne polla, kai eichon archipoimena Hieram ton Odolomētēn*).[9] It it found again in an inscription of the imperial era on an Egyptian mummy—"Plenis the younger, chief shepherd's, lived . . . years,"[10]—and rather often in rent receipts and transfer orders. Around AD 270: "Aurelius Abous, son of Asemis, of the village of Philadelphia, chief shepherd of Antonius Philoxenos, the most powerful former procurator . . . to Aurelius Kalamos. . . . I have received from you, from those that you hold that belong to the noteworthy (Antonius Philoxenos), twelve goats that I will record among those entered in my accounts";[11] "Aurelius Abous . . . chief shepherd of the livestock of Antonius Philoxenos . . . to Aurelius Neliammon . . . I have received from you from the livestock that you have on location for the account of the noteworthy (Antonius Philoxenos) twenty-eight goats that I will record among the entries of the account of the noteworthy (Antonius Philoxenos)

---

[7] Heb 13:20. In Hebrew, the attributive adjective follows the noun (cf. Sir 39:6—Κύριος ὁ μέγας; Heb 4:14—ἔχοντες οὖν ἀρχιερέα μέγαν; G. D. Kilpatrick, "The Order of Some Noun and Adjective Phrases in the New Testament," in *Donum Gratulatorium Eth. Stauffer*, Leiden, 1962, pp. 111ff.). Here, this modifier, commonly used in antiquity for sovereigns and divinities (cf. C. Spicq, *Epîtres Pastorales*, pp. 249, 269) exalts the King-Priest above Moses and all the *hēgoumenoi* who have died and not yet been resurrected (cf. H. Kosmala, *Hebräer—Essener—Christen*, Leiden, 1959, pp. 415–417). On the participial construction, which is common in the Hellenistic preaching (ὁ ἐγείρας . . .), cf. Isa 64:11 (A. Feuillet, "Le Baptême de Jésus," in *CBQ*, 1959, p. 472); J. Delling, "Partizipiale Gottesprädikationen in den Briefen des Neuen Testaments," in *ST*, vol. 17, 1963, pp. 23ff.

[8] 1 Pet 2:25—ἐπὶ τὸν ποιμένα καὶ ἐπίσκοπον τῶν ψυχῶν ὑμῶν is a hendiadys. Cf. A. Rose, "Jésus-Christ, Pasteur de l'Eglise," in *VSpir*, 1965, pp. 501–515.

[9] Manuscript A has ἦν ὄνομα τοῦ ἀρχιποίμενος μου.

[10] *SB* 3507: Πλῆνις νεώτερος ἀρχιποιμένος ἐβίωσεν ἐτῶν . . . (according to A. Deissmann, *Light*, pp. 100ff.); in the third-fourth century, *PSI* 286, 6; in 338: Καμήτι ἀρχιποιμένι (*P.Lips.* 97, col. XI, 4).

[11] J. Schwartz, "Une Famille de chepteliers au III[e] s. p. C.," in *RechPap*, vol. 3, 1964, p. 56.

as having been handed over by you."[12] On 21 May 270, Dionysius writes to Neilammon, small livestock tenant: "Hand over to Pekysis, the chief shepherd, the small livestock in your keeping that formerly belonged to Kyrilla—fifty sheep, males and females in equal numbers, and five goats—and get an acknowledgement of receipt from him."[13]

The point of these texts is to underline the authority, the competence, and the responsibility of the chief shepherd. He exercises a high level of oversight over the shepherds and the flocks. It is up to him to see to it that the flocks are grazed in the best pastures, that the shepherds are remunerated, that the rent is paid, that the animals entrusted to his care are returned. Thus St. Peter, addressing presbyter-shepherds, suggests that they are only vicars, that they must carry out their duty in union with Christ, the "chief of pastors," in conformity with his instructions and his example.

---

[12] Ibid., p. 57.
[13] Ibid., p. 66 = *SB* 8087, 7–8 (cf. P. Collomp, "Un bail de troupeau," in *Mélanges Maspéro*, Paris, 1955–57, vol. 2, p. 343). Cf. again "Pekynis, the chief shepherd . . . Aurelius Sabinus, the chief shepherd," in an acknowledgement of transfer (J. Schwartz, loc. cit., p. 67, lines 2 and 13).

ἀρχιτέκτων

architektōn, **master builder**

St. Paul, having laid the foundation of the church at Corinth,[1] compares himself to a master architect who is within his rights in requiring his successors to adapt their labors to his own structure.[2] There is nothing to say philologically about the NT hapax *architektōn,* except that its English transliteration is hardly to be defined in terms of our contemporary architects. This is already suggested here by the *architektōn*'s job of laying the foundation; and it is confirmed by Sir 38:27—"Every craftsman and every master worker who works day and night"[3]—and by the papyri and inscriptions.[4]

---

[1] 1 Cor 3:10 (cf. V. P. Furnish, "Fellow Workers in God's Service," in *JBL,* 1961, pp. 364–370; J. Pfammatter, *Die Kirche als Bau,* Rome, 1960, pp. 19–35). The metaphor of founding was common in the *diatribē,* cf. Heb 6:1; Philo, *Dreams* 2.8: "These preliminary considerations will serve as a foundation, but to build the rest, the building itself, let us follow the directives of Allegory, the expert architect, σοφῆς ἀρχιτέκτονος"; (same modifier: σοφὸν ἀρχιτέκτονα, Isa 3:3); *Giants* 30; *Change of Names* 211; Epictetus 2.15.8–9: "Don't you want to establish the principles and the foundation . . . then establish on this foundation the firmness and stability of this decision? But if you put at the base a rotting and crumbling foundation, you must not build"; cf. J. Weiss, *Der erste Korintherbrief,* 10th ed., Göttingen, 1925, p. 79; H. Muszyński, *Fundament, Bild und Metapher in den Handschriften aus Qumran: Studien zur Vorgeschichte des ntl. Begriffs* θεμέλιος, Rome, 1975.

[2] Cf. 2 Macc 2:29—"The architect of a house must concern himself with the whole structure," τῆς ὅλης καταβολῆς = the foundation, in the sense of masonry (cf. F. M. Abel, *Maccabées,* on this text). The architect is distinguished from the painter or the decorator who ornaments the structure after it is built.

[3] Πᾶς τέκτων καὶ ἀρχιτέκτων. The τέκτων is the simple laboror, worker, or artisan working with wood, the joiner or carpenter (*P.Mil.Vogl.* 255, 5; *Prosop.Ptol.,* vol. 5, n. 13234–13294; a papyrus from Strassburg, in *ChrEg,* 1963; p. 135, line 30; A. Orlandos, *Technique architecturale,* pp. 26ff. C. Spicq, *Théologie morale,* vol. 1, p. 378, n. 2; vol. 2, p. 525). The ἀρχιτέκτων could be the foreman, the entrepreneur, whoever directs a work, hence the architect, but here the mechanic or machinist (*P.Lond.* 2074, 2; 2173, 4, 8). Similarly, Strabo associates carpenters and smiths, who have "no conception of beauty or nobility," whereas the poet is a person of quality (Prolegomena, 1.2.5). Cf. A. Bernand, *Pan du désert,* p. 192.

[4] Cf. *Prosop.Ptol.,* n. 182–185, 528–542 (mentions some hyparchitects); 1953, pp. 52–54. On the architect Pathemis (*P.Petr.* III, 43), cf. idem, *Prosopographica* (Studia

---

architektōn, S 753; *EDNT* 1.165; *NIDNTT* 1.279; MM 82; L&N 45.10; BDF §118(2); BAGD 113

At the beginning of the second century AD, Tesenouphos is an engineer or mechanic who complains about the lack of maintenance of the machines (*P.Tebt.* 725, 1, 12, 25). Some hundred years later, Apollonius is a naval engineer;[5] Onasander uses this term for builders of siege engines (42.3). In the second century AD, the declaration of an "architect" who is in charge on the building site is registered (*P.Tebt.* 286, 19). But there are also architects in the literal sense of the word who are summoned when someone wants to build a house (*P.Cair.Zen.* 59233, 2, 7; 59302, 3), who propose changes in the plan that has been proposed to them (59193, 3, 8), and who take care that the dwelling is well outfitted (59200, 3, *kataskeuazētai*). Not only do the Greeks vote them honorific decrees,[6] but they also endlessly praise their concern and devotion.[7]

The architect proper has both speculative and practical capabilities. He works together with the commission set up by the city and he serves as the technical adviser.[8] He establishes the estimates. He goes to the quarries to

---

Hellenistica 9), Louvain, 1953, pp. 52–54: in an adjudication by the *oikonomos* Hermaphilos in the presence of the royal scribe and the architect; the latter comes after the royal scribe but has precedence over the representative of the royal scribe. J. Coupry, *Inscriptions de Délos: Période de l'amphictyonie attico-délienne*, Paris, 1972, n. 104, 4 (notebook of charges, technical conditions imposed, various costs, the assistant architect's remuneration, etc.).

[5] A. Bernand, *Philae*, vol. 1, n. 39 (with the editor's note); B. Boyaval, "Correspondance administrative de l'ingénieur Théodoros," in *Etudes sur l'Egypte et la Soudan anciens*, Lille-Paris, 1973, p. 195, *SB* 8322, 8323 (with the commentary of D. Meredith in *ChrEg*, 1954, pp. 110ff.). M. Guarducci (*Epigrafia Greca*, Rome 1969, vol. 2, pp. 192, 198, 214, 261) translates ἀρχιτέκτων by *ingegnere;* the corresponding Latin term is *faber* (H. J. Mason, *Greek Terms*, p. 26); cf. R. Martin, in *Annuaire de l'Ecole des Hautes Etudes* (4th section), 1973–1974, pp. 221ff.

[6] For Epicratus, at Olbia (Dittenberger, *Syl.* 707, 8, 26), cf. *Syl.* 494, 3; *SB* 8580, 5, 16.

[7] *Epimeleia*, cf. *SEG* vol. 2, 480, 3 = *CIRB*, Moscow-Leningrad, 1965, n. 1112: ἀνεκτίσθη τὸ τεῖχος ἐκ θεμελείων διὰ ἐπιμελείας Εὐτύχους ἀρχιτέκτονος; 1245, 17 (cf. 1249, 11; 1250, 17; 1252, 10; 1258); Dittenberger, *Syl.*, 736, 90, 115. These honors are explained by the architect's having contributed to the embellishment of the city and having built a temple (Dittenberger, *Syl.* 695, 72; 972, 160), but they contrast with the modest honorarium—one drachma per day: "Theodotus, architect, receives an annual salary of 352 drachmas" (C. Michel, *Recueil*, n. 584, 9; with the commentary of the *NCIG*, pp. 131ff.)

[8] *P.Lille* 1, 24. "Harpalos was the most industrious in the science, which requires competency" (E. Bernand, *Inscriptions métriques*, n. 23, 2). For the rebuilding of a temple of Demeter and of Kora, at Tanagra (third century BC), "the commission (elected for three years) will build the sanctuary in the city, consulting on this matter with the polemarchs and the architect" (*RIJG*, vol. 2, n. 36, 14); cf. the treatise on archaeology of Vitruvius; *LSAMSup*, n. 107, 25; idem, *LSCG*, n. 5, 11–12; 41, 29, 42,

select the materials,[9] oversees the manner in which they are rough-hewn and prepared for installation, according to the models or mock-ups (*typoi*) that he has prepared. He is in charge at the work site and manages the execution of all of the jobs, even the lowliest of them. He recruits, gives instructions to, and oversees a multitude of specialized workers: quarriers, masons, inscribers, marble masons, smiths, carpenters, joiners, marqueteurs,[10] etc., whose salaries he pays (cf. *I.Lind.*, 419, 141); and as he is often in charge of the ongoing maintenance of the edifices, he remains on the job for years.

This description allows us to understand better how the apostle can compare himself to an *architektōn*, which should probably be translated "builder";[11] being in charge of *ergōn*, he is within his rights to require of preachers who come to labor on his work site and "add to his construction"[12] that they be strictly faithful to the "canon" that he has determined once for all.[13] "The architect (*ho oikodomos*) . . . the painter . . . the shipbuilder . . . allocate all their materials such that when they are arranged and connected they give the whole work solidity, beauty, and utility" (Plutarch, *Quaest. conv.* 1.2.5).

21; R. Martin, *Architecture grecque*, pp. 172–179; idem, *L'Urbanisme dans la Grèce antique*, Paris, 1956, pp. 69–71.

[9] Cf. J. A. Letronne, *Egypte*, vol. 2, pp. 117–119, 231. A. Bernand, *Koptos*, n. 41, 19 (with the editor's commentary, pp. 89ff.).

[10] Cf. F. Cumont, *L'Egypte des astrologues*, p. 106; L. Robert, *Etudes anatoliennes*, pp. 86ff.

[11] Cf. *MAMA*, vol. 8, 564, 3: σοφιστὴς κτίστης τῶν μεγίστων ἔργων ἐν τῇ πόλει.

[12] 2 Cor 10:12–18; cf. R. Devreesse, "La Deuxième aux Corinthiens," in *Mélanges Tisserant*, vol. 1, pp. 143ff. C. K. Barrett, "Paul's Opponents in II Corinthians," in *NTS*, vol. 17, 1971, pp. 237ff.

[13] In architecture the κανών is "the rule." Cf. H. Oppel, KANΩN, Leipzig, 1937, L. Wenger, *Canon in den römischen Rechtsquellen und in den Papyri*, Vienna, 1941.

ἀσφάλεια, ἀσφαλής, ἀσφαλίζομαι, ἀσφαλῶς

asphaleia, stability, safety, assurance, guarantee; *asphalēs*, safe, sure; *asphalizomai*, to secure, make sure, *asphalōs*, without slipping, securely, safely

These words are formed from the alpha-privative and *sphallō*, which means "stumble, fall," and by extension "fail, be foiled."[1] They are particularly common in the literary (Philo, Josephus) and popular (the papyri) Koine. In the fifteen NT occurrences, St. Luke (eight occurrences) alone uses the substantive, the adjective, the verb, and the adverb; this is probably because these terms belonged to the medical vocabulary,[2] but their use is

---

[1] Cf. Plato, *Resp.* 3.396 d: "faltering (ἐσφαλμένον) because of sickness, love, or even drunkenness"; 404 a: "a habit dangerous (σφαλήν) to the health."

[2] Summarized by W. K. Hobart, *Medical Language*, pp. 199–201 (gives the references to Hippocrates, Galen, Aretaeus) and N. van Brock, *Vocabulaire médical*, p. 184. Cf. Hippocrates, *Aph.* 2.19: "with acute illnesses, predictions either of death or of health are not absolutely certain"; *Epid.* 1.5: "Digestion signals that the turning point is imminent and [return to] health is certain" (ἀσφαλίην = certainty"); 1.11: "the semi-tertian fever, the most dangerous of all"; *Nat. Hom.* 13: "the safest diagnosis" (illnesses whose outcome can be predicted with the most certainty, cf. J. Jouanna, *Hippocrate: La Nature de l'homme*, Berlin, 1975, p. 290); *Acut.* 9: "Medicine can do much to preserve the health of the healthy" (τοῖσιν ὑγιαίνουσιν ἐς ἀσφάλειαν); 58.2: a regular diet is safer for the health and sudden, major changes; 62.1; *Append.* 4.2: "purgation after bleeding requires security and moderation"; 31.4; 54: "foods are not to be prescribed except when completely safe, when the patient is well beyond the spike of the fever"; 57.1; *Liqu.* 6.5: "the greatest sign of recovery" (μέγιστον σεμήϊον ἐς ἀσφάλειαν); *Vict.* 3.76.2: "the safest treatment"; 4.90.1: "a sign of health: a firm step" (ὁδοιπορεῖν τε ἀσφαλῶς); *Oct.* 11.1: "those who are born without risk"; 10.2: "the ones that come head first come out better than the ones that come feet first"; *Dent.* 18: "ulcerations of the tonsils that come without a fever are less troublesome."

---

asphaleia, S 803; *TDNT* 1.506; *EDNT* 1.175–176; *NIDNTT* 1.663–664; MM 88; L&N 21.9, 31.41; BAGD 118 ‖ ***asphalēs***, S 804; *TDNT* 1.506; *EDNT* 1.175–176; *NIDNTT* 1.663; MM 88; L&N 21.10, 31.42; BAGD 119 ‖ ***asphalizomai***, S 805; *TDNT* 1.506; *EDNT* 1.175–176; *NIDNTT* 1.663; MM 88; L&N 18.12, 21.11; BDF §126; BAGD 119 ‖ ***asphalōs***, S 806; *TDNT* 1.506; *EDNT* 1.175–176; *NIDNTT* 1.663; L&N 21.10, 31.42; BAGD 119; ND 3.9

ἀσφάλεια, asphaleia, etc. 213

so widespread that their meanings are considerably nuanced, both in classical Greek and in Hellenistic Greek.

Asphaleia—the condition of not slipping, a firm step[3]—means first of all stability,[4] and then especially security and safety,[5] certainty or assurance: "by far the most surely true answer" (*makrō pros alētheian asphalestaton*, Plato, *Tim.* 50 b). Finally, it is a legal term, meaning security in the sense of a guarantee: "Otherwise he does not affix his seal on an act or sign a guarantee" (*ē asphaleian graphei*, Epictetus 2.13.7; cf. 2 Macc 3:22—keeping deposits safe; Prov 11:15; *BGU* 1149, 24); Polybius 2.11.5: a guarantee against Illyrian violations. The LXX retains especially the meaning security and solidity,[6] as does the *Letter of Aristeas*,[7] which also notes that the translation of the Law had to be done *meta asphaleias*, meaning with care and precision (45; cf. 28; Josephus, *Ant.* 12.56). Philo mentions the security of persons, of property, and of places,[8] notably of the altar and of places of refuge,[9] but also in the intellectual order: stability and

---

[3] Thucydides 3.22.2: "with only the left foot shod for the sake of surefootedness" (ἀσφαλείας ἕνεκα).

[4] Aristotle, *Pol.* 6.5.2: to provide for the stability of constitutions against unsettling elements; Sophocles, *OT* 51: the rescue of a city; Epictetus 2.15.9: "the firmness and stability of this decision."

[5] Plato, *Resp.* 5.467 c: "providing for their safety"; Demosthenes, *1 C. On.* 24; Aeschylus, *Suppl.* 495: an escort of guards "to guarantee our safety"; Thucydides 1.17: the administration of cities by tyrants δι' ἀσφαλείας; 1.120.5: "When a plan is being formed you are safe, but when the time comes for execution fear intervenes"; Xenophon, *Cyr.* 4.5.28: "It is not those who remain seated near their friends who protect them the best" (τὴν ἀσφάλειαν παρέχουσιν); *Hell.* 2.2.2: Lysander gives safe-conducts to the Athenians for their security; Polybius 1.57; 3.97.7: a place of refuge that provides shelter from enemies; Dio Cassius 44.33: "for security reasons, the conspirators retired to . . ."; 45.9.38; 47.11; 55.15; *P.Mich.* XIV, 683, 3: the payment provides a guarantee, εἰς σὴν ἀσφάλειαν.

[6] Lev 26:5; Deut 21:10—"You shall dwell in security" (Hebrew *beṭaḥ*); 1 Macc 14:37; 2 Macc 4:21—Antiochus takes security measures, πραγμάτων τῆς ἀσφαλείας; 9:21; 15:1—Nicanor attacks without risk; 15:11; Ps 104:5—the earth has foundations that are unshakable (Hebrew *mākôn*). In Prov 8:14, ἀσφάλεια (Hebrew *tûšiyâh*) is associated with counsel (βουλή); cf. Philo, *Worse Attacks Better* 36, 37, 42: "safety lies in keeping quiet."

[7] *Ep. Arist.* 115, 118, 172, 230: "gratitude, which is stronger than any argument, assures the greatest safety"; cf. 61: the gems "were fastened with gold pins that crossed them for greater security" (πρὸς τὴν ἀσφάλειαν); 85: "the solidity of the lintel."

[8] Philo, *Joseph* 63 (σωτηρίας καὶ ἀσφαλείας); 251; *Spec. Laws* 4.58; *Moses* 1.178; *Flacc.* 41; *Cherub.* 126: "a house is built for security and protection"; *Creation* 142; *Husbandry* 149, 167; *Plant.* 146: "the security of those most dear"; *Decalogue* 178; *Spec. Laws* 1.75; *Contemp. Life* 22–23; *Conf. Tongues* 103: the solidity of asphalt.

[9] Philo, *Flight* 80; *Spec. Laws* 1.69, 159; 3.130, 132; *Good Man Free* 151; cf. Josephus, *Ant.* 8.13; Dittenberger, *Or.* 81, 16.

balance (*asphaleian kai eukosmian*) in the refutation of sophistry (*Heir* 125; cf. *Spec. Laws* 4.21; *To Gaius* 42); the reasoning faculty with its "sureness and good order" (*asphaleian kai kosmon*, *Change of Names* 111). The meaning personal or military security is predominant in Josephus,[10] who also knows the meanings "holding someone under tight guard,"[11] "assurance, certitude," "victory" (*War* 1.375), "hope" (*Ant.* 15.166), "safety" (17.3). "He reckoned that God would certainly make sure that nothing that he had uttered would prove false" (*Ant.* 2.220; cf. 2.280; 4.31; 6.157). Also present is the legal meaning, a guarantee, security (*Ant.* 17.346): "the principal guarantee of secure peace (*pros asphaleian eirēnēs*) is the legitimate succession of princes" (*War* 4.596).

The adjective *asphalēs*, "not slipping, not falling," means first of all "firm, solid," whether with respect to things (Homer, *Od.* 6.42: Olympus) or persons;[12] then "safe"[13] or "making safe."[14] God has firmly fixed the clouds above (Prov 8:28) and opened a sure path through the sea (Wis 14:3); the ungodly do not lay solid foundations (4:3). But immutable Wisdom never changes in her designs, is of firm, sure, and tranquil mind (*bebaion, asphales, amerimnon,* 7:23). For Philo, "safety lies in staying at home" (*Husbandry* 162); "the safest option is to remain calm."[15] If the adjective

---

[10] *War* 1.567, 623; 2.466, 572, 606, 620; 3.33, 85; *Ant.* 13.263, 266, 307; 14.151, 161; 15.60, 167; *Life* 45, 113, 126, 330; *Ag. Apion* 2.157.

[11] *War* 3.398: "Vespasian commanded that Josephus be guarded most carefully (φρουρεῖν αὐτὸν μετὰ πάσης ἀσφαλείας), intending to send him to Nero as soon as possible"; *Life* 163: "the mission of guarding closely (φυλάξοντας μετ' ἀσφαλείας) anyone who wished to leave."

[12] Sophocles, *OT* 617: "deciding too quickly is not without risk"; Euripides, *Phoen.* 599: "a prudent general is more sure than a fearful general"; Plato, *Soph.* 231 *a;* Euripides, *IT* 1062: "we can count on each other"; Thucydides 1.69.5: "They used to say that you could be counted on!"

[13] Herodotus 1.109: "for the sake of my security this child must die"; Aristophanes, *Av.* 1489: "at this time, it is more secure to be with them"; Sophocles, *Aj.* 1251: "big strapping fellows . . . the most solid"; Xenophon, *Hell.* 5.4.51: "the route of Potniae is the most secure"; Xenophon, *An.* 3.2.19: "it is safer for them to flee than for us"; 8.39.4: "judging themselves to be safe." For Hippocrates: ἀσφαλῆ εἶναι (or ἐν ἀσφαλείᾳ εἶναι) is to be out of danger, on the road to recovery; cf. *Acut.* Suppl. 6: "give barley water when the crisis is past and the patient is out of danger (ἐν ἀσφαλείῃ ἤδη ἦ)"; 11: "next, if the patient seems to be out of danger (ἀσφαλὴς φαίνηται), give him barley water mixed with honey."

[14] Xenophon, *An.* 1.8.22: "That is the safest place for them"; 3.2.19; *Cyr.* 7.1.21: "You will be much safer once you are outside than shut up inside"; *Eq. Mag.* 4.18: "retiring to safety" (εἰς τὸ ἀσφαλές); 5.5: "distance provides the greatest safety and increases the illusion"; Thucydides 1.39.1: "Someone who proceeds in all safety."

[15] *Dreams* 2.92; hence the link with prudence (*Giants* 46; *Flight* 136, 206; *Change of Names* 242); *Drunkenness* 203: "the safest thing is to suspend judgment"; *Moses*

usually modifies a route or a journey,[16] it is also used to define knowledge: "a comprehensive, firm, and solid grasp that reason cannot shake" (*Prelim. Stud.* 141); "to speak more truly (or precisely)" (*to ge asphalesteron eipein, Etern. World* 74); "the sustenance, the support, the strength, the firmness (*bebaiotēs*) of all is the immutable God" (*ho asphalēs theos, Dreams* 1.158). Most of the occurrences in Josephus have to do with security,[17] sometimes in the legal sense;[18] some have to do with prudence,[19] which is very close to the idea of certitude (*Ant.* 1.106; cf. 15.67: uncertain hopes).

The verb *asphalizō*, "to secure, fortify,"[20] is used for the solidity of a building (Neh 3:15; hiphil of Hebrew *ḥāzaq*, "make firm"), for the fastening of an image with iron (Wis 13:15), for putting something in a safe or sheltered place (10:12; cf. 4:17), for supporting with might (Isa 41:10, Hebrew *tāmak*). In Josephus, it means especially to secure the defense of a country or a city, to take measures to ensure its security,[21] especially with a nuance of prudence: the Tiberians "took the precaution (*asphalisthēnai*) of fortifying their walls" (*Life* 317); "being on guard against the appearing of enemies" (*asphalisamenoi periemenon autous, Ant.* 4.160). Josephus also uses the word, however, to describe how he safeguarded himself against those who might criticize his narrative (*Ant.* 10.218), and in a legal sense: "those who read these letters, which are guaranteed by the royal seal—*tas hypo tou basilikou sēmantēros ēsphalismenas epistolas*—shall not oppose what is written herein" (11.271).

The adverb *asphalōs*, "without slipping, solidly, firmly," takes on all of the meanings of the adjective.[22] In the LXX, it always translates the Hebrew

---

1.15: Pharaoh's daughter "judged that it was not safe to take the child to the palace right away."

[16] Abraham 269: "going straight ahead on a safe route (one free of danger) where the ground is not shifting"; *Moses* 2.247; *Spec. Laws* 4.159; *Flacc.* 31, 115; *To Gaius* 247, 361; cf. *Conf. Tongues* 104: "asphalt is solid and sure."

[17] *War* 1.303; 3.174, 457; 4.31, 44, 368, 615; *Ant.* 13.41, 165 (safe-conduct); 20.85; *Life* 108, 118, 269; cf. *War* 3.402: "I ask for a more secure prison (ἀσφαλέστερον) if I have spoken the name of God flippantly."

[18] *Ant.* 17.156: a security deposit; *Life* 347: "to secure themselves against me, they duped me."

[19] *War* 4.143; *Ant.* 3.41; 6.59; 16.327 (examine carefully); *Ag. Apion* 2.224: "It would not be prudent to divulge God's truth to the ignorant mob."

[20] Polybius 1.22.10: "those who came after secured their flanks"; 1.42.7: "a city well defended by its walls"; intransitive: to secure oneself, to be on guard: "Molon secured the support of the neighboring satrapies" (5.43.6); Josephus, *Ag. Apion* 1.77: "Salitis fortified the eastern regions."

[21] *War* 2.609; 4.120; 6.15; *Ant.* 13.22, 175, 183, 202; 14.178.

[22] Homer, *Il.* 13.141: "the stone unfalteringly follows its fixed course"; *Od.* 13.86: "The ship ran on steadily, unwavering." Herodotus 1.86: "In human affairs, nothing is certain"; 2.161: "to reign with greater security over the rest of the population";

beṭaḥ, referring to a safe place (Tob 6:4), a journey made in safety,[23] but we may understand *asphalōs eidotes* to mean knowledge free of any doubt: "knowing with certitude what oaths they trusted in" (Wis 18:6).

All of this would be superfluous except that it helps determine the significance of *asphaleia* at the end of the prologue to the Third Gospel, which is written in purest Greek style, and in which Luke sets out to specify the goal of his work:[24] *heōs an epignōs peri hōn katēchēthēs logōn tēn asphaleian* (Luke 1:4). First of all, we must point out the emphatic position of the last term which is thus spotlighted: *epignōs . . . tēn asphaleian*.[25] Thus we should not hesitate to translate, along with most moderns, "absolute certainty"[26]—the Philonian definition[27]—but at the same time recognizing that it means not just intellectual conviction but also safety, firmness, and stability. Xenophon had already used the word with respect to the certainty of an argument (Xenophon, *Mem.* 4.6.15, *asphaleia logou*); the meaning is identical in the synonym *to asphales*, in *P.Amh.* 131, 3: "until he has certain knowledge of the matter" (*hina to asphales epignō tou pragmatos*, second century); 132, 5; *P.Giss.* 27, 8: "so that I may know with certainty" (*hina to asphales epignō kai stephanēphorian axō*). Finally, we should note the custom of supplying a guarantee or a written assurance.[28]

Plato, *Phd.* 85 d: "the possibility of going on with more security and less risk"; Xenophon, *Eq. Mag.* 6.2: This leader "provides for their safety in retreat"; 7.11; 8.1, 3: "to descend the hillocks in safety" (without the risk of slipping); *I.Priene* 44, 33: an escort seeing to the safety of a judge returning to his country: ἵνα δὲ ἀσφαλῶς παραπεμφθῇ.

[23] Gen 34:25; Bar 5:7; 1 Macc 6:40—the soldiers "advanced steadily and in good order" (ἀσφαλῶς καὶ τεταγμένως); cf. this epitaph from Sosibios: "Depart in all safety."

[24] Cf. Cajetan: "Lucas causam finalem scribendi a se Evangelium, assignat certitudinem rerum Evangelicarum"; C. F. D. Moule, "The Intention of the Evangelists," in A. J. B. Higgins, *New Testament Essays*, pp. 165–179.

[25] E. Delebecque (*Etudes grecques*, p. 8) notes: "It is clear that Luke has detached ἀσφάλειαν from the rest of the prologue by separating it from the verb ('certitude' being the direct object of ἐπιγνῷς) with the relative clause." He translates "afin que tu découvres à propos des instructions que tu as entendues, la certitude," and comments, "The certitude, in short, that will be revealed to Theophilus is the certitude of revelation" (p. 9).

[26] Cf. Acts 2:36; 1 Macc 7:3. J. H. Ropes, "St. Luke's Preface, ἀσφάλεια and παρακολουθεῖν," in *JTS*, 1924, pp. 67–71. W. den Boer ("Some Remarks on the Beginnings of Christian Historiography," in *SP*, vol. 4, Berlin, pp. 348–362) prefers to translate: "precise information."

[27] Cf. above. An intellectual meaning, *Tabula of Cebes* 32.2: the science that confers *paideia* is ἀσφαλὴς δόσις καὶ βεβαία καὶ ἀμετάβλητος; *P.Giss.* 27, 8: ἵνα τὸ ἀσφαλὲς ἐπιγνῶ.

[28] *P.Berl.Zill.* VI, 3: τήνδε τὴν ἔνγραφον ἀσφάλειαν; VIII, 16: δέξασθαι παρ' ἐμοῦ ταύτην τὴν ἔγγραφον παρακλητικὴν ἀσφάλειαν; *P.Mich.* 322 a, 33 (AD 46):

On the other hand, in 1 Thess 5:3 it is a question of stability and safety, which is one of the most common meanings in the papyri:[29] "When they say, 'Peace and safety' (eirēnē kai asphaleia), then sudden destruction will fall upon them."[30] When the officers from the Sanhedrin go to find the imprisoned apostles, they find the prison "locked and secure (en pasē asphaleia) and the guards standing before the gates."[31]

The adjective asphalēs is used three times by St. Luke in the sense of certain, precise, or exact knowledge (Acts 21:34; 22:30; 25:26), for which there is no parallel in the papyri (except for P.Lond. 1916, 26, from the fourth century AD, hina to asphales methōmen kai pisthōmen; SB 11017, 5: tēn asphalēn phasin gnous), which use it only with the meaning "sure,"[32] which

---

κατ' ἔνγραπτον ἀσφαλειας; 607, 13; διὰ τῆς παρούσης ἐγγράφου ἀσφαλείας; P.Flor. 25, 28; 293, 9; P.Wash.Univ. 46, 13: πρὸς σὴν ἀσφάλειαν τούτου; P.Ant. 42, 13; P.Amh. 78, 16: ἀσφάλειαν γραπτήν; P.Princ. 34, 17; P.Soterichos 22, 23, 33; 24, 11, 27; P.Bour. 15, 9; P.Köln 153, 4; C.P.Herm. 32, 26: πρὸς ἀσφάλειαν εἰς πάντα τὰ ἐγγεγραμμένα καὶ εἰς τὴν βεβαίωσιν; P.Erl. 67, 10: διὰ ταύτης ἡμῶν τῆς ἐγγράφου ἀσφαλείας ἐσχηκέναι; 81, 47; P.Oxy. 1891, 5: ὁμολογῶ διὰ ταύτης μου τῆς ἐγγράφου ἀσφαλείας; 1896, 14; 2975, 19; 3365, 11; SB 6704, 7; 10781, 8; etc.

[29] Edict of Tiberius Julius Alexander: "The gods have reserved the safety of the world for this most sacred moment" (BGU 1563, 26; AD 68). An honorific decree of Rhamnus for the stratēgos Theotimus, who "provided for the safety of the countryside, so that the inhabitants might enjoy safety" (J. Pouilloux, Choix, n. 20, 6–7; cf. 22, 44); honorific decree of Phalanna for the judges from Metropolis, granting them "safety in wartime and in peacetime, for them and for their descendants" (NCIG, n. 12, 36; second century BC). With the meaning "guarantee": Thaesis gives full authority to her husband Ptollion to act on her behalf in a lawsuit, "the rights of Thaesis being fully reserved in the recovery of eighty drachmas loaned by her with guarantee (κατὰ ἀσφαλείαν) to Petsiris" (P.Fouad 35, 14; from AD 48); "the guarantee is valid and secure" (ἡ δὲ ἀσφάλεια κυρία καὶ βεβαία, P.Rein. 107, 4; cf. 6, 7). A receipt delivered to an epimelētēs "for more certainty, I have made out this receipt, valid in one copy" (P.Got. 9, 19); C.P.Herm. 18, 17; 19, 8; 29, 5; 40, 4; P.Erl. 79, 9; P.Oxy. 1865, 11–12; 1880, 17; 2411, 34; 2666, col. II, 8; 2780, 23; 2951, 26; PSI 823, 3; P.Ant. 91, 11; 104, 4, 6; P.Mert. 97, 17; P.Mich. 282, 8; 283, 19; P.Amst. 96, 3: so that you may act with all assurance; P.Fam.Tebt. 9, 13: κατὰ ἀσφάλειαν τετελειομένην; 29, 49; P.Aberd. 19, 23; Pap.Lugd.Bat. II, 7, 31; BGU 1659, 7; SB 7201, 22; 10256, 6; 10289, col. I, a 9; 10539, 26; 10810, 5–6; 11215, 7; P.Köln 153, 7. Guarantee in the commercial sense: αἱ ὠναὶ καὶ ἀσφάλειαι = contracts and property titles (P.Tebt. 407, 10; P.Oxy. 3240, 6).

[30] Cf. Philo, Rewards 147: "When they think that they are in safety (ἐν ἀσφαλεῖ) in the cities—an illusion born of false hope—they will perish in their prime, falling into the enemy's snares."

[31] Acts 5:23; cf. Dittenberger, Syl. 547, 30: ὅπως μετὰ πάσης ἀσφαλαίας συντελεσθεῖ; P.Fay. 107, 11: "guard those found guilty in a secure place" (τοὺς φανέντας αἰτίους ἔχιν ἐν ἀσφαλείᾳ); SB 8881, 9. Josephus, War 6.116; Ant. 15.178.

[32] P.Phil. 35, 7: "I sent you a letter through Valerianus . . . a trustworthy man (ἀνθρώπου ἀσφαλοῦς), and I cannot believe that he would not have given you my

corresponds better to Phil 3:1—"It does not hurt me to write the same things to you, and for you it is a guarantee" (*hymin de asphales*, it is safer for you); and especially to Heb 6:19—"We have a soul's anchor that is sure and firm" (*asphalē te kai bebaian*). These metaphors of land or sea routes and anchors were traditional,[33] like the union of the two adjectives.[34]

The four occurrences of the verb *asphalizō* in the NT are all in the middle voice and have to do either with the guard at Jesus' tomb[35] or the Philippian jailer, who "secured the feet (*tous podas ēsphalisato*) of Paul and Silas in stocks" (Acts 16:24; cf. Wis 13:15; *P.Tebt.* 283, 19). This latter meaning is the most common in the papyri where a suspect is captured or secured[36] or where the body of a deceased person is guarded (*P.Princ.*

---

letter"; *P.Oxy.* 2598, *b* 6: "Let me know the price through a trustworthy person (δι' ἀσφαλοῦς ἀνθρώπου) so that I can reimburse you"; 2983, 13; 2984, 12; 3357, 17; *P.Ryl.* 92, 19; *P.Mich.* 657, 11: "you will give the dates to someone who will ship them as safely as possible" (τῷ ἀσφαλέστερον φέροντι; *Pap.Lugd.Bat.* XX, 25, 4; *BGU* 909, 24; *P.Köln* 161, 10; *SB* 6717, 11: ὡς ἀσφαλέστατα = the most reliable; Dittenberger, *Or.* 701, 10: route "across safe and flat terrain along the Red Sea"; *P.Oslo* 128, 12: ἐν ἀσφαλεῖ εἶναι; *P.Oxy.* 2228, 29; 2268, 7; *I.Priene* 114, 10: τὴν δὲ πίστιν καὶ φυλακὴν τῶν παραδοθέντων αὐτῷ γραμμάτων ἐποιήσατο ἀσφαλῆ; 118, 8: ἀσφαλέστατα πρὸς πάντα τὸν χρόνον γενηθῆναι τὰ βραβεῖα; *ZPE*, vol. 10, 1973, p. 105, n. 21, n. 22, 7; *P.Cair.Isid.* 94, 4. Of an arrested suspect, "under close guard" (*P.Oxy.* 1886, 14; *P.Mert.* 29, 6; 66, 9).

[33] Ἀσφαλῶς: the security of a mooring (Strabo 5.4.6; Philo, *Rewards* 58); ἀσφαλεῖς: the security of a route (Strabo 4.6.6). "What security (ἀσφάλεια) can those who navigate have if the sailors do not listen to the pilots?" (Dio Cassius 41.33). For the anchor, cf. Herondas 1.41; Pindar, *Ol.* 6.100; Plato, *Leg.* 12.961 *c*; Philemon, frag. 213, 10: ἐβάλετ' ἄγκυραν καθάψας ἀσφαλείας εἵνεκα (in Stobaeus, *Ecl.* 30.4.10, vol. 3, p. 664); Philo, *Spec. Laws* 2.52: "to cast an anchor of security in an existence free of danger"; Plutarch, *Sol.* 19; *De virt. mor.* 6: "my heart is ready to yield and resists no longer, like the point of an anchor in the sand that is disturbed by the sea"; Heliodorus, *Aeth.* 8.6.9: "cast the anchor of salvation"; 4.19.9. Cf. C. Spicq, " Ἄγκυρα et Πρόδρομος dans Hébr. VI, 19–20," in *ST,* 1949, pp. 185–187; same symbolism in Rabbinic Judaism, cf. R. Mach, *Der Zaddik in Talmud und Midrasch*, Leiden, 1957, pp. 223–241.

[34] To the references given by C. Spicq, *Hébreux*, vol. 2, p. 164, add Philo, *Sacr. Abel and Cain* 141: ἀσφαλὴς καὶ βέβαιος; *Alleg. Interp.* 3.164; *Cherub.* 103; *Conf. Tongues* 106; *Heir* 314; *Prelim. Stud.* 141; Plutarch, *Cat. Mai.* 21.5: "He invested his capital in solid and sure ventures"; Polybius 12.25.2; Heliodorus, *Aeth.* 8.16.1: a troop is sent on ahead to clear the route (τὸ ἀσφαλὲς τῆς ὁδοιπορίας) and through their explorations to secure (βεβαιώσοντες) the march of the bulk of the army.

[35] Matt 27:64, 65, 66. Cf. *Ep. Arist.* 104: "a forward post that guarantees the protection" of the citadel. In the sense of reinforcing a house (*P.Fouad* 30, 24).

[36] *P.Ryl.* 68, 19 (first century BC); *P.Tebt.* 283, 19; 798, 25; 800, 35; 960, 7; *P.Mich.* XIII, 660, 13: "after arresting my husband"; 661, 2; *P.Bour.* 10, 20: if these persons take part in an uprising, "you will do well to secure their persons until we have arrived." —Ἀσφαλίζομαι also means "certify"; *P.Oxy.* 2407, 13, 31, 48, 52; 2956, 22:

ἀσφάλεια, *asphaleia, etc.*

166, 5), but in addition products are seized (*P.Tebt.* 53, 29) and property is secured (407, 4).

The adverb *asphalōs* has the same meaning in Mark 14:44, where Judas asks the soldiers to hold Jesus securely when leading him away, and in Acts 16:23, where the Philippian jailer is ordered to guard Paul and Silas closely (*asphalōs tērein autous*). Similarly *P.Giss.* 19, 14, "so I enjoin you to (guard) yourself closely" (*parakalō se oun asphalōs seauton [tērein]*); and *P.Oxy.* 742, 5: "put them in a secure place" (*thes autas eis topon asphalōs*). But at Pentecost Peter affirms, "Let the whole house of Israel know with certainty (*asphalōs oun ginōsketō hoti*) that God made this Jesus Lord and Christ . . .";[37] a meaning that accords well with Luke 1:4.

"guaranteeing at your own risk"; 3289, 14; *BGU* 1576, 10; *P.Panop.Beatty* 1, 273; *P.Ryl.* 77, 40; *SB* 6002, 18; 6643, 20; 7558, 26; 10253, 3; 10801, 4.

[37] Acts 2:36; cf. γράψον μοι ἀσπαλῶς, "write me without fail" (*P.Oxy.* 3312, 6; *SB* 10529, A 23); ἵνα ἀσφαλῶς ἀναλεύσῃς (*SB* 10557, 9); nuances of security (*P.Hib.* 53, 3: ἀσφαλῶς διεγγυᾶν); *Ep. Arist.* 46: that the books (of the Law), once translated, "return to us with certainty," become our property again; defense of a territory against any attack (*NCIG*, n. VI, 44).

ἀσωτία, ἀσώτως

asōtia, **incurable dissoluteness**; *asōtōs*, **prodigally**

Made up of the alpha-privative and *soō*, *asōtos* normally means "incapable of being saved," and thus "incurable,"[1] and the adverb *asōtōs* "in a hopeless state." With the philosophers and in usage, *asōtia*, literally "lost life," can have two meanings, which are so closely linked that it is not easy to distinguish them:[2] sometimes it means prodigality, sometimes a dissolute life. The transition from the one to the other is explained perfectly by Aristotle: "We label as prodigal those who are incontinent and those who become spendthrifts to satisfy their intemperance. That is why prodigals have such a bad reputation: they have several vices all at once.... Properly speaking, the word *prodigal* refers to the one who has only the sole vicious tendency to destroy his means of subsistence."[3]

Asōtia, dissipation of wealth and debauchery, is very often associated with drinking binges during festivals: "the temple was filled with debaucheries and orgies by dissolute Gentiles and prostitutes" (2 Macc 6:4); "Do not be drunk with wine, which only amounts to licentiousness."[4] Athenaeus

---

[1] Plutarch, *Quaest. nat.* 26; cf. *Alc.* 3.1: The child Alciabiades having fled, Pericles announces "If he is safe (σῶς), the rest of his life will be lost (ἄσωτον)." R. C. Trench, *Synonyms*, p. 54; Foerster, in *TDNT*, vol. 1, p. 506.

[2] According to Plato, false opinions in the soul of the young man introduce "insolence, anarchy, prodigality (ἀσωτίαν) ... and prodigality is called magnificence" (*Resp.* 8.560 e); but in the *Laws*: the totally perverted man who usually lives in debauchery (or prodigality? ὡς ἄσωτος), is altogether impoverished" *Leg.* 5.743 b).

[3] Aristotle, *Eth. Nic.* 4.1.1120^b31ff. Cf. frag. 56 (Rose), cited by Plutarch, *Pel.* 3.2; *De cupid. divit.* 527 a; *Eum.* 13.11: "They transform the camp into a place of debauchery"; *Ant.* 10.4.

[4] Eph 5:18; *T. Jud.* 16.1: φυλάξασθε ... τὸν ὅρον τοῦ οἴνου· ἔστιν γὰρ ἐν αὐτῷ ... ἐπιθυμίας, πυρώσεως, ἀσωτίας καὶ αἰσχροκερδίας. Cf. Philo: "The secret desire

(4.59–67) showed by many examples that the *asōtos* not only wastes his goods, but loses his time, degrades his faculties and abilities, and consumes him. So much did *asōtia* become synonymous with dissoluteness and immorality, and opposed to virtue (*aretē*), that it became a literary topos and is even found in symbolic monuments.[5] It is in this general sense that *asōtia* designates the pagan lifestyle in 1 Pet 4:4—the pagans often find it strange that Christian converts "no longer run with them to the same torrent of licentiousness."

The prodigal spending, these dissolute ways, this flashy existence is often denounced as the vice of the sons of the family, of the younger set, starting with Prov 28:7—"The one whose companions are the debauched (Hebrew *zalal*) brings dishonor to his father." It is in this sense that admission to the presbyterate is allowed only for the father of a family in which the children "are not accused of bad conduct or undisciplined."[6]

We should hesitate to be specific about the conduct of the young man in Luke 15:13—"he wasted all his substance by living *asōtōs*" (*dieskorpisen tēn ousian autou zōn asōtōs*).[7] Because the older brother maligns the younger in verse 30—"this son of yours has consumed your wealth with prostitutes"—we get the idea that the prodigal has lived lasciviously. But our Lord is much more delicate and discreet, and we must translate, with

---

of gluttons . . . devotees of a decadent and dissolute way of life who take pleasure in drinking bouts and wild parties" (*Spec. Laws* 4.91). Drinkers pass their life far from home and hearth; they are enemies of their parents, of their wives, of their children, enemies also of their country, they are also their own enemies. A life spent on drink and licentiousness (ἄσωτος βίος) is a menace for everyone" (*Contemp. Life* 47). "Vitellius left the palace drunk after the most lascivious dinner ever (τῆς ἀσώτου τραπέζης)" (Josephus, *War* 4.651). "Charybdis is a good name for the insatiable, spendthrift debauchery of drinking bouts" (Heraclitus, *All.* 70.10). "Athens offered scarce resources for his intemperance (*asōtia*), so he stocked up in Macedonia" (Plutarch, *De cupid. divit.* 5.525 c). "Everyone berated and reproached him for, among other things, his *asōtia*, since he had a large belly" (Dio Cassius 65.20.3). "Plautianus became the most intemperate of men (ἀσωτότατός), to the point of abandoning himself to good eating and then making himself vomit, since his stomach could no longer digest meats and wine, so much had he loaded it" (ibid. 75.15.7). "He is a good companion, capable of drinking with him and the right one to carouse in the company of a flute girl" (Lucian, *Vit. Auct.* 12).

[5] On the opposition of Ἀρετή and Ἀσωτία, see F. Cumont, *Symbolisme funeraire*, p. 423. In the *Tabula of Cebes* 7, one of the hetaerae, Ἀσωτία, is accompanied by Ἀκρασία, Ἀπληστία, Κολακεία.

[6] Titus 1:6—μὴ ἐν κατηγορίᾳ ἀσωτίας ἢ ἀνυπότακτα; cf. the rebellious (*sārar*) prostitute of Prov 7:11.

[7] Cf. Philo, *Prov.* 2.4: "Parents do not stand aloof from their prodigal sons, τῶν ἀσώτων υἱέων; they take pity on their misfortune, surround them with care, shower attention upon them" (according to Eusebius, *Praep. Evang.* 8.14).

Fr. Lagrange: "He wasted all his substance through a life of foolish spending."[8] The tradition has precisely designated him as "the prodigal son."[9]

---

[8] M. J. Lagrange cites as a good parallel Josephus, Ant. 12.203: ὡς ἀσώτως ζῆν διεγνωκότι = having chosen to live in a foolish manner (a financial contract). This is also the common meaning in the papyri: a cloak guaranteed 2,700 copper drachmas πρὸς ἀσωτείαν (P.Fay. 12, 24; from 103 BC); Pap.Lugd.Bat. XIII, 9, 6 (edict of Praeses of the Thebaïs on maximum interest rates; fourth century AD); likewise the verb ἀσωτεύεσθαι, "dissipate all one's resources"; P.Flor. 99, 7 (first-second century AD): ἐπεὶ ὁ υἱὸς Κάστωρ μεθ' ἑτέρων ἀσωτευόμενος ἐσπάνισε τὰ αὐτοῦ πάντα καὶ ἐπὶ τὰ ἡμῶν μεταβὰς βούλεται ἀπολέσαι κτλ.; PSI 41, 12 (fourth century), a woman complains that her husband is squandering their goods: ἀσαυτεύων [lit. ἀσαυδεύων] καὶ πράττων ἃ μὴ τοῖς εὐγενέσι πρέπι.

[9] Verse 32 corresponds to verse 13: "He was lost, ἀπολωλώς." It remains true that the common title of the parable of the prodigal son does not exactly express its content, because it is the parable of both sons, the one a sinner and the other faithful, and reveals the love of God for the one as for the other, although in two different ways.

> ἀτακτέω, ἄτακτος, ἀτάκτως
>
> *atakteō*, to be disorderly; *ataktos*, undisciplined, disorderly, rebellious; *ataktōs*, in disorder

In 1 Thess 5:14, St. Paul asks the community to take back the brothers who are living in a dissolute manner (*noutheteite tous ataktous*). In his second letter, he more severely prescribes keeping away every brother who is leading a dissolute life (*ataktōs peripatountos*, 2 Thess 3:6, 11), giving himself as an example: "We ourselves did not lead a disorderly life in your midst."[1] It would not be necessary to insist on the meaning of *ataktos*—"not remaining in his/her/its place, out of order, undisciplined"—if a certain number of exegetes did not suggest translating it "idle, lazy."[2] But the usage of the verb, the adjective, and the adverb in the Koine, notably in the first century AD, confirms that the word covers any breach of obligation or convention, disorders of life in general; and the usage is decisive.

On the cosmic level, matter was "disorderly and confused," then God takes it from disorder to order.[3] In military parlance especially, the word is

---

[1] 2 Thess 3:7; cf. W. P. De Boer, *The Imitation of Paul*, Kampen, 1962, p. 126ff. C. Spicq, *Théologie morale*, vol. 2, pp. 720ff. M. F. Wiles, *The Divine Apostle*, Cambridge, 1967, pp. 24ff.

[2] The semantics of this word group has been outlined excellently by B. Rigaux, *Saint Paul: Les Epîtres aux Thessaloniciens*, Paris-Gembloux, 1956, pp. 582ff. Cf. C. Spicq, "Les Thessaloniciens 'inquiets' étaient-ils des paresseux?" in *ST*, vol. 10, 1956, pp. 1–13.

[3] Philo, *Plant.* 3; *Creation* 22: "Matter was on its own without order (ἄτακτος), without quality, without life, without homogeneity, but full of heterogeneity, disharmony, and discord"; *Etern. World* 75: "The nature of the world is order from the disorderly (τὴν τάξιν τῶν ἀτάκτων), accord from the discordant, harmony from the

---

atakteō, S 812; TDNT 8.47–48; EDNT 1.176; MM 89; L&N 88.246; BAGD 119 ‖
ataktos, S 813; TDNT 8.47–48; EDNT 1.176; MM 89; L&N 88.247; BAGD 119 ‖
ataktōs, S 814; TDNT 8.47–78; EDNT 1.177; L&N 88.247; BAGD 119

used with respect to negligent officers (*P.Hib.* 198, 149; from the third century BC), an army in disarray, undisciplined or insubordinate soldiers.⁴ In addition, "disorderly" modifies "multitude, crowd."⁵ In a political context, Josephus compares people who live unencumbered by laws and rules ("those who live in a lawless and disorderly fashion," *tōn anomōs kai ataktōs biountōn*) to those who observe order and common law.⁶ In the social realm, if sons do not meet the financial needs of their parents when necessity arises, they become subject to a penalty of a thousand drachmas, according to testamentary convention.⁷ In apprenticeship agreements, it is provided that if the apprentice is guilty of misconduct or has been absent for one reason or another, he must work additional makeup days.⁸

The moral sense is constant from *T. Naph.* 2.9, which prescribes doing everything "in order and with good intentions, in the fear of God, doing nothing disorderly (*mēden atakton poiēsēte*), out of due season," to Iamblichus, who calls passion "disorderly, culpable, unstable" (*Myst.* 1.10 =

---

unharmonious, union from the disparate . . ."; *Spec. Laws* 1.48. Cf. Ps.-Archytas, in Stobaeus, *Ecl.* 1.41.2 (vol. 1, p. 278); Numenius, in Eusebius, *Praep. Evang.* 15.17.

⁴ In the third century BC, the inhabitants of Soloe in Cilicia complain: "the city is occupied by soldiers who are encamped in disorder, ὑπὸ τῶν στρατιωτῶν ἀτάκτως κατεσκηνωκότων" (C. B. Welles, *Royal Correspondence*, n. 30, 4; reproduced in *C.Ord.Ptol.*, n. 84); Thucydides 3.108.3: "They charged without order and with no discipline"; Aeneas Tacticus, *Polior.* 15.5; 16.2–4; Onasander 10.7; 10.20; 21.7; 27; Josephus, *War* 1.101: "the army of Antiochus in disorder"; 1.382; 2.517; 3.77; *Ant.* 15.150; 17.296; Plutarch, *Phoc.* 12.3; Diodorus Siculus 17.48.4: dispersed, scattered soldiers. In contrast, the ephebes carried out sorties in the coutryside with discipline, εὐτάκτως (*IG* vol. 2, 2, 1011, 15); cf. L. Robert, *Opera Minora Selecta*, vol. 2, p. 1076; idem, *I.Car.*, p. 289, n. 166.

⁵ Herodian 4.14.7: ἄτακτον πλῆθος. Philo, *Rewards* 20: "All that is disorderly (ἄτακτον), unseemly, dissolute, questionable, that is what the crowd is, and keeping company with them is worthless for one who has just passed into virtue"; Josephus, *War* 2.649; *Ant.* 15.152; 3 Macc 1:19. Cf. the confusion of a tumult, θόρυβος ἄτακτος (Philodemus of Gadara, *Hom.*, col. IX, 27).

⁶ Josephus, *Ag. Apion* 2.151; cf. Plutarch, *Cat. Mai.* 16.3: the censors have the right to expel from the senate one whose life is licentious and disorderly; Plutarch, *Cim.* 4.4.

⁷ *P.Eleph.* 2.13 (285–284 BC): ἡ πρᾶξις ἔστω ἐκ τοῦ ἀτακτοῦντος καὶ μὴ ποιοῦντος κατὰ τὰ γεγραμμένα (new edition by *Chrest.Mitt.*, n. 311; commentary in *Jur.Pap.*, pp. 56–60).

⁸ *P.Oxy.* 275, 24 (from AD 66); 725, 39 (AD 183); cf. *P.Oslo* 159, 9; *SB* 10236, 33 (AD 36). The formula ἐάν τις ἀτακτήσῃ is characteristic of corrections or amendments that become effective in case of default on contractual agreements or disobedience, *P.Cair.Zen.* 59596, 18; *BGU* 1125, 8; *P.Wisc.* 4, 22; *SB* 9841, 7; (cf. *P.Oxf.* 10, 23).

1.36.13). Morality lies in not letting reason follow its course with disorderly haste.[9] *Ataktoi andres* (Philodemus of Gadara, *D.* 1.7.6) are *apaideutoi*.[10] Diodorus Siculus goes so far as to equate the life unshackled by moral norms to the life of wild beasts: "settling down into an *ataktos* and beastlike life and go out to various pastures at random" (*en aktatō kai thēriōdei biō kathestōtas sporadēn epi tas nomas exienai* 1.8.1). Finally, the *ataktoi* are rebels, the disobedient, or insurgents,[11] even impious troublemakers; a regulation from Delos covers the possibility that pilgrims may conduct themselves improperly in the sacred places.[12]

In sum, the *ataktos* is the who is defective in action, irregular, against the rule; and since in the Christian life the "order" is established by God or the leaders of the church, disorder can mean sometimes a shortcoming or

---

[9] Philo, *Sacr. Abel and Cain* 85; cf. 45: the νοῦς does not let irrational forces "proceed in disorder or discord, without master or guide." The fool does not know how to act, after the fashion of a coachman who is not in control of his horses; the latter take off on a crazy course (*Husbandry* 74; cf. *Worse Attacks Better* 141; *To Gaius* 344). Philo modifies ἄτακτος with ἄφρων (*Husbandry* 74), the complete opposite of the εὔτακτος, who is σώφρων (*IG*, vol. 9, 750, 18; H. W. Pleket, *Epigraphica*, vol. 2, n. 3, 43; B. 48). This quality is commonly praised in the *neoi* (*MAMA*, vol. 6, 112, 4; 114 A 8; N. Firatli, L. Robert, *Stèles funéraires*, pp. 161–162), and especially in ephebes (*SEG*, vol. 19, 86; 4: πάντες εὐτακτοῦντες καὶ πειθαρχοῦντες; 96, 5; 116, 2; cf. vol. 21, 252, 11; 452, 8; 525, 20; C. Pélékidis, *Ephébie attique*, pp. 38, 181, 235). So the accent is on discipline (cf. J. and L. Robert, "Bulletin épigraphique," in *REG*, 1970, p. 453, n. 553). The inhabitants of Rhamnus vote an honorific decree for Dikaiarchos, who "has correctly and zealously provided for the defense of the citadel and its residents, showing himself to be disciplined (εὔτακτον παρέχων), himself and the soldiers placed under the command of his father" (*I.Rhamn.*, n. 15, p. 130). In sports: "If one of the leaders does not present his runners in good order, the city may fine him ten silver staters" (J. Pouilloux, *Choix*, n. 11, 12). More broadly: "Teachers' stipends should be paid regularly" (ibid. 13, 10); "awarding me a citation for my orderly life, my spirit, and my wisdom" (E. Bernand, *Inscriptions métriques*, n. 114, col. III, 5).

[10] Herodian 7.9.5; cf. Plutarch, *Apoph. lac.* 54. The Stoics used the noun *ataktēma* in the sense of a moral fault, a lapse of discipline, an infraction (cf. *SEG*, vol. 13, 521–59 = Dittenberger, *Or.* 483; complete French translation in R. Martin, *L'Urbanisme dans la Grèce antique*, Paris, 1956, pp. 58ff.).

[11] An edict of the prefect of Egypt, Petronius Quadratus (*P.Haw.* 73, verso; edited by J. G. Milne, in *APF*, vol. 5, 1913, p. 324); Dittenberger, *Syl.* 305, 80. *Ataktéō* = to disturb or shirk one's obligation to the the public order, to free oneself from a regulation, to undertake a revolt (Dittenberger, *Or.* 200, 6).

[12] Ἀτάκτως ἀναστραφεῖ (F. Sokolowski, *Lois sacrées: Supplément*, n. 51, 4). Cf. *SB* 6152, 14: "By their assaults and worse acts of violence *they enter tumultuously* into the temple and commit sacrilegious acts"; *P.Fay.* 337 (second century). Philo, listing the vices of the φιλήδονος, places the ἄτακτος between the seditious and the impious (*Sacr. Abel and Cain* 32).

a discordant note, sometimes law-breaking and moral dissoluteness. The *ataktoi* Thessalonians free themselves from the rule of community life. One thinks of sins against brotherly love, a propensity to favor discord, a refusal to accept the customs or discipline of the church. Certain "troubled" ones seem particularly stormy, befuddled types who disturb the peace (1 Thess 4:11–12). At any rate, "their walk is not in line" (Gal 2:14). They are "culpable" and probably stubborn.

ἀτενίζω

atenizō, **to look attentively, stare**

Among the numerous verbs of seeing in the NT (*blepō, theōreō, eidon, horaō*, etc.), the denominative verb *atenizō* merits special attention.[1] It refers to "attentive and prolonged visual observation of an object,"[2] an insistent fixing of the attention. Thus certain fixed stars "take on a tail . . . in fact, one of the stars, in the constellation of the Dog, had a tail, though a dim one; those who looked at it intently (*atenizousin*) saw only a faint glow" (Aristotle, *Mete.* 343 *b* 9); "Why do we feel ill at ease when we fix our gaze on other objects (*ta all' atenizontes*), but very comfortable when we look at objects that have the green color of grass, cabbage and other plants? It is because we cannot fix our gaze for long (*atenizein*) on white and black."[3] In the medical writers, the verb is used especially with *omma* for a particularly fixed gaze.[4] Moulton-Milligan cite only one papyrus,[5] to which we can

---

[1] Unknown in the LXX (cf. 1 Esdr 6:28; 3 Macc 2:26) and Philo, having only two occurrences, in Josephus, rare in the papyri, ἀτενίζω derives from ἀτενής "all of whose usages can be related to an original meaning 'stretched out,' especially when speaking of eyes or a gaze that are fixed (Aristotle, Lucian, etc.); hence 'straight' (Euripides, frag. 65); intense, excessive (Aeschylus, Callimachus); in speaking of a person's mind 'strained, serious' (Hesiod, Pindar, Plato); 'obstinate' (Arrian, etc.)" (P. Chantraine, *Dictionnaire étymologique*, p. 133).

[2] C. Mugler, *Terminologie optique*, p. 63: "l'observation attentive et prolongée d'un objet par la vue."

[3] Ps.-Aristotle, *Pr.* 959 *a* 24. C. Mugler (*Terminologie optique*) cites also Theon of Alexandria, *In. Alm.*, p. 148, 7: "As for those who attentively peruse books (τῶν ἀτενιζόντων τοῖς βιβλίοις) . . . even they cannot see (ὁρᾶν) all the letters contained in a page"; Olympiodorus, *In Mete.* 223.11: "So if we gaze intently (ἀτενιζόντων), the phenomenon of the halo appears; if we do not gaze intently (μὴ ἀτενιζόντων), it disappears"; "the multicolored halo that appears around lamps . . . if we do not stare right at the lamp" (μὴ ἀκριβῶς ἀτενίσωμεν, ibid. 235.15); John Philoponus, *Comm. de An.* 335.11: "Why do we see neither the sky nor any of the objects of sight, or at least fix our regard toward them?" (ἀτενίζοντες πρὸς αὐτά).

[4] Hippocrates, *Epid.* 7.10: "the gaze of the dying man became fixed"; cf. 7.6: the eyes do not blink; 7.30; Galen, *Remed. Parab.* 1.4: ἀτενίζειν εἰς τὴν χύτραν; Aretaeus, *SA* 5; *SD* 33; W. K. Hobart, *Medical Language*, p. 76.

[5] P.Leid. W, 16, 8: εἰσελθόντος δὲ τοῦ θεοῦ μὴ ἐνατένιζε τῇ ὄψει, ἀλλὰ τῆς (l. τοῖς) ποσί.

---

atenizō, S 816; *EDNT* 1.177; *NIDNTT* 3.520; MM 89; L&N 24.49; BAGD 119 add only *BGU* 1816, 25 (*axiō atenisai eis to megethos tōn proexērithmēmenōn*, a letter from 60/59 BC) and *Pap.Graec.Mag.* 4, 556 ("You will see the gods staring at you and rushing upon you," *opsē de atenizontas soi tous theous kai epi se hormōmemous*) and 711 (with eyes fixed on God, not giving in to any distraction).

This verb is used twelve times by St. Luke (in Luke and in Acts) and twice by St. Paul.[6] In Luke 4:20, it expresses curiosity and extreme attentiveness: in the synagogue at Nazareth, "all eyes were riveted on Jesus." The high priest's servant saw Peter (*idousa*) sitting near the fire, and "after examining him closely (*kai atenisasa autō*) she said, 'This person also was with him' " (Luke 22:56). It was with intensity and a certain amount of anxiety that the apostles, on the day of the ascension, as Jesus disappeared behind a cloud, continued to stare into the sky.[7] When Peter stopped and fixed his gaze on the paralytic who was asking for alms,[8] and when St. Paul looked piercingly at Elymas,[9] this look was both an examination[10] and the point of departure for mental reflection. Several times it connotes an emotional reaction. Thus it is possible to stare in a way that conveys awe, as when the Jews gazed at St. Peter, stupefied that he could perform a miracle (Acts 3:12) and when Cornelius beheld the angel and trembled (10:4). When Herod Agrippa, at the theater of Caesarea, appeared in his luxurious finery, glimmering in the early rays of sunlight, the spectators were seized with holy fright and could not take their eyes off of him (Josephus, *Ant.* 19.344). During the siege of Jerusalem, the Jews, agonizing under the cruelty of the brigands, "breathed their last with their gaze fixed determinedly on the temple" (*War* 5.517). Thecla was not only attentive to Paul's teaching but beside herself with joy (*atenizousa hōs pros euphrasian*, *Acts Paul Thec.* 8).

---

[6] 2 Cor 3:7, 13—the Israelites could not keep their eyes fixed on Moses' face because of the shining brilliance (literally δόξα) of his face.

[7] Acts 1:10; cf. 7:55—St. Stephen keeps his eyes fixed on the heavens; 6:15—the members of the Sanhedrin fixed their gaze on Stephen (ἀτενίσαντες) and saw (εἶδον) his face, which looked like an angel's. Paul was particularly attentive when, before beginning his speech, he kept his eyes fixed on the Sanhedrin (23:1).

[8] Acts 3:4—"Peter fixed his eyes on him (ἀτενίσας) . . . and said, 'Look (βλέψον) at us.' "

[9] Acts 13:9; cf. 14:9—Paul fixed his gaze (ἀτενίσας) on the lame man at Lystra and saw (ἰδών) that he had faith.

[10] Peter fixed his eyes on—stared intently at—the sheet descending from heaven and examined all that it carried (ἀτενίσας κατενόουν, Acts 11:6).

αὐθάδης

authadēs, **presumptuous, arrogant, ill-bred**

The first quality required in a candidate for the *episkopē* is that he be *mē authadē* (Titus 1:7). False teachers, on the other hand, come across as *tolmētai authadeis*.[1] It is quite difficult to specify the meaning of a word that is not illuminated by its context, especially since English happens not to have a term that corresponds exactly to *authadēs*. Etymologically (*autos* + *handanō*) the word would refer to the person who delights in himself (cf. Josephus, *Ant.* 5.39) and is thus self-sufficient and presumptuous. This infatuation and self-centeredness lead to arrogance and even insolence.[2] The *authadēs* is constantly characterized as hard (*sklēros*, Gen 49:3, 7; Polybius 4.21.3; Plutarch, *Lyc.* 11.6) and violent.[3]

Thus it is not simply a matter of self-satisfaction, but of prickly pride, a haughty character who, refusing to hear what is said to him, persists stubbornly in his own opinion;[4] such as Pharaoh and Herod, inflexible and

---

[1] 2 Pet 2:10. These τολμηταί are brassy, insolent, going so far as to insult "the glories," meaning "the glorious ones," i.e., the angels (cf. J. Starcky, "Psaumes apocryphes de la grotte 4 de Qumran, 4 Q Ps^f VIII, 12," in *RB*, 1966, pp. 363–364; the designation Κύριοι ἄγγελοι, in *P.Princ.* 159, 9; *P.Oslo* 1, 44 and 246). Often αὐθάδης (αὐθάδεια) is associated with τόλμη (*P.Mich.* 174, 9; *P.Oslo* 22, 6; *SB* 9458, 11; 9527, 6).

[2] Prov 21:24—one despises and mocks others; Josephus, *War* 6.172: "Jonathan, a braggart by nature, full of disdain for his adversaries"; Plutarch, *Luc.* 7.2. Cf. Bauernfeind, in *TDNT*, vol. 1, p. 508; *BGU* 2240, 7 and 11.

[3] Βίαιος, *PSI* 1323, 6; cf. *P.Fouad* 26, 13: "Through his insolence and violence, he exerts a strong influence on the region"; *P.Mich.* 426, 10: τῇ ἑαυτῶν βίᾳ καὶ αὐθαδίᾳ χρησάμενοι. This latter expression appears constantly in complaints against aggressors (*P.Cair.Isid.* 74, 11; *P.Mert.* 91, 12; *P.Gen.* 31, 9; *P.Mich.* 231, 10; 426, 10; *BGU* 1904, 12); *SB* 4284; 10218, 21: ἁρπαγῇ αὐθάδως ἀναστραφέντες (first-second century); it is glossed (*P.Tebt.* 16, 10) by ἦν ὑβρισμένος οὐ μετρίως (line 7; cf. Josephus, *Ant.* 19.236). Cf. *1 Clem.* 30.8: "Impudence, arrogance, temerity for those cursed by God; benevolence, humility, mildness for those blessed by God"; Plotinus, *Enn.* 2.9.9, line 55: "Great is the αὐθάδεια of humans, even if they were previously humble, modest (μέτριος), simple and profane."

[4] "The general must be neither indecisive (ἄστατος) nor obstinate (αὐθάδης), as if he thought that no one could have a better idea than his own" (Onasander, 3.3); cf. M. Guilmot, "Une lettre de remontrances," in *ChrEg*, 1965, p. 239.

---

authadēs, S 829; *TDNT* 1.508–509; *EDNT* 1.178; MM 91; L&N 88.206; BAGD 120–121 mulish (Philo, *Moses* 1.139; *To Gaius* 301). Not only does this *authadēs* do only what he wants but he is unfriendly, he is brutal[5] and aggressive,[6] at the least a quarreler and quibbler;[7] in sum, ill-bred. In addition, in the catalog of vices in *Sacr. Abel and Cain* 32, Philo places *authadēs* between vainglorious and vulgar. In fact, Josephus attributes this sort of behavior to prisoners (*War* 4.96), the young (*Ant.* 4.263; 16.399), and slaves (*War* 2.356), for example, to Hagar, expecting a child and showing arrogant and insolent pride toward Sarah (*Ant.* 1.189). In Lucian and in the literature, it is a constant trait of the "misanthrope,"[8] who is strictly insufferable.

So it is evident that "presumptuous" and "arrogant"[9] do not convey the depth of meaning of *authadēs*, but it is clear that "God's steward" cannot have this sufficiency, this infatuation, this bad character, these base sentiments, which would confine him to a conspicuous isolation. Someone so unsociable[10] would not be able to carry out the responsibilities of a pastor.

---

[5] Theophrastus, *Char.* 15.1–2: to the simplest question he replies "Leave me alone"; cf. Plutarch, *Cim.* 6.2: Pausanias treated his allies τραχέως καὶ αὐθάδως; Plutarch, *De gen.* 9.

[6] *P.Oxy.* 2563, 43; *Dai papiri della Società Italiana*, Florence, 1965, n. 10, 11; *P.Lond.* 358, 12 (vol. 2, p. 171). P. J. Sijpesteijn, "Einige Papyri aus der Gießener Papyrussammlung," in *Aeg*, 1966, p. 18, 1 21: ὃ τρέφω μέρος προβάτων ἁρπαγῇ αὐθάδως ἀναστραφέντες κτλ. Strabo 11.2.16: "ὑπὸ αὐθαδείας καὶ ἀγριότητος, because of their arrogance and ferocity." Cf. *1 Clem.* 1.1: a revolt "fanned to flame by several rash and self-willed persons."

[7] Philo, *Abraham* 213: The servants of Lot "take liberties, in their *authadeia*, and constantly have disagreements with the most eminent children of the wise Abraham," whose temperament is marked by πραϋπάθεια. In *Heir* 21, Moses' freedom of speech vis-à-vis God is justified, φιλίᾳ μᾶλλον ἢ αὐθαδείᾳ. This nuance must be emphasized in Titus 1:7, given the prescription that follows immediatedly: not quick-tempered or rash (μὴ ὀργίλον).

[8] Cf. J. Bompaire, *Lucien écrivain*, p. 171.

[9] F. Field, (*Notes on the Translation*, p. 219) justifies this translation on etymological grounds—*arrogans, qui sibi aliquid arrogat*—and cites Aristotle: σεμνότης ἐστὶν αὐθαδείας ἀναμέσον τε καὶ ἀρεσκείας (*Mag. Mor.* 1.29). R. C. Trench (*Synonyms*, p. 349) groups this term with φίλαυτος and αὐτάρεσκος, as opposed to εὐπροσήγορος—approachable, affable (Plutarch, *Praec. ger. rei publ.* 31), and cites Aristotle, *Eth. Eud.* 3.7.4: μηδὲν πρὸς ἕτερον ζῶν.

[10] Cf. Strabo 3.4.5: "By *authadeia*, the Greeks refuse to take on mutual obligations. . . . With the Iberians this *authadeia* reaches extreme proportions, being added to a naturally treacherous and deceitful character." Plutarch (*Praec. ger. rei publ.* 13.808 d) cites Plato (*Ep.* 4.321, 321 b): in heads of state, "arrogance mingles with solitude"; *Cat. Min.* 55.6: "the unseasonable pride and arrogance of the son of Pompey"; 58.7: "Scipio presumptuously scorned the opinion of Cato"; *Agis* 5.3: "Epitades, of an arrogant character"; *Cic.* 28.1: "Clodius, of daring and presumptuous character."

αὐτόματος

automatos, **spontaneous, self-moving**

In writing that the iron door of the prison at Jerusalem "opened itself" for the angel and Peter, not only does St. Luke show his Hellenistic culture once again—the expression being a common one—but he also points to the miraculous character of the event.[1]

More delicate is the exegesis of *automatos*—spontaneous, moving of its own accord[2]—in the parable of the grain that comes up without any

---

[1] Acts 12:10—ἥτις αὐτομάτη ἠνοίγη αὐτοῖς. "This aorist passive indicates that the door opened automatically, but at the instance of a supernatural force" (E. Jacquier, *Actes*, p. 364). More precisely, this spontaneous opening of doors is traditionally seen as a prodigy, as much in Greek literature as in Israel; cf. *b. Yoma* 39b: "Our rabbis teach: Forty years before the destruction of the temple . . . the doors of the sanctuary opened themselves, until Yohanan ben Zakkai reproached them, saying, Sanctuary, sanctuary, why are you frightened?"; Xenophon, *Hell.* 6.4.7: "News came to them from their city that the doors of all the temples had opened themselves, πάντες αὐτόματοι ἀνεῴγοντο"; Plutarch, *Tim.* 12.9: "At the moment when battle was joined, the holy door of the temple opened itself, αὐτόματοι διανοιχθεῖεν"; Dio Chrysostom 44.17; Caesar's dream of warning, "the doors of the room where he was sleeping opened themselves, αὐτόμαται ἠνεῴχθησαν"; ibid. 60.35: at the death of Claudius, the doors of the temple of Jupiter the Conqueror opened themselves (αὐτόματος); Josephus, *War* 6.293: "They saw the door of the temple . . . even though it was bronze and so heavy that twenty men could not easily close it at dusk, and it was held in place by bolts fitted with iron chains and with bars . . . open itself (αὐτομάτως ἀνοιγμένη) . . . this portent seemed very favorable to the ignorant"; Artapanus, *De Jud.*, τάς τε θύρας πάσας αὐτομάτως ἀνοιχθῆναι τοῦ δεσμωτηρίου καὶ τῶν φυλάκων (in Eusebius, *Praep. Evang.* 9.27.23), etc.

[2] Cf. Josh 6:15—"The walls of the city fell of their own accord" (cf. Josephus, *War* 5.292); Wis 17:6—the shining pillar, "By itself shined for them an *automatē* (i.e., lighting and fueling itself) and terrifying fire" (cf. Josephus, *Ant.* 3.207); cf. 2 Kgs 19:29; Diodorus Siculus 1.8: "a calamity that was not sent by the gods but came by itself" (Josephus, *War* 1.373: natural disasters); Menander, *Dysk.* 545: "by itself the affair

---

automatos, S 844; *EDNT* 1.179; MM 93; L&N 89.21; BDF §§59(1), 117(2), 243; BAGD 122

tending, without the help of the sower. The earth acts alone:[3] the man sleeps night and day "and the seed sprouts and grows, he knows not how."[4] By itself (*automatē*), the ground produces first the stalk, then the ear, then the full grain in the ear" (Mark 4:27-28). The Lord did not give an explanation of this parable, and the interpretations that have been suggested are widely divergent,[5] but the emphatic position of *automatē* (not translated by the Peshitta) at the beginning of the sentence indicates that it is the most important word and that the interpretation of this teaching depends on understanding it.[6] So what does it mean? That the earth produces, on

---

brought me back to this place"; idem: "He will present himself on his own, αὐτόματος οὗτος παρέσται" (in Plutarch, *Alex.* 17.7; cf. 34.2: πολιτεύειν αὐτονόμους, govern themselves according to their own laws; 35.11; 77.7); Philostratus, *Gym.* 53: "Spontaneous fatigue (of athletes) is the beginning of sickness" (citation of Hippocrates, *Aph.* 2.5; ed. Littré, vol. 4, p. 470); Onasander 10.3: soldiers trained well to place themselves rapidly in formation, "so to speak, automatically, ὡς εἰπεῖν αὐτόματοι." The adverb αὐτομάτως, for spontaneous action (Josephus, *War* 3.386). Αὐτόματος is rare in the papyri; *Stud.Pal.* V, n. 119, I, 16 (third century AD) is too badly damaged to yield any meaning; the other known occurrence is from the sixth century, *P.Stras.* 4, 13: οἰκία μετὰ παντὸς τοῦ ... χρηστηρίου καὶ δικαίου ... αὐτομάτου = naturally, it goes without saying. In an epitaph (*SEG*, vol. 8, 474, 9): δ' αὐτομάτης ... μελίσσης is translated "The Spring sends hither the product of the hard-working bee" by E. Bernand, *Inscriptions métriques*, p. 351.

[3] This is not an allegory, but a parable, peculiar to Mark, the point being "the action of the soil without the help of the sower" (M. J. Lagrange, *Marc*, p. 116).

[4] Mark 4:27—ὡς οὐκ οἶδεν αὐτός, cf. H. Sahlin, "Zum Verständnis von drei Stellen des Markus-Evangeliums," in *Bib*, 1952, pp. 56-57; A. Suhl, *Die Funktion der alttestamentlichen Zitate und Anspielungen im Markusevangelium*, Gütersloh, 1965, pp. 154 and preceding.

[5] For N. A. Dahl ("The Parables of Growth," in *ST*, vol. 5, 1951, pp. 149-150) and J. Jeremias (*Parables*, p. 151), this is the "Parable of the Patient Husbandman," but the passivity of the man is there only to show in relief the immanent activity of nature. According to H. Baltensweiler ("Das Gleichnis von der selbstwachsenden Saats," in *Oikonomia: Festschrift O. Cullmann*, Hamburg, 1967, pp. 69-75), this is "the Parable of the Unbelieving Farmer," the "grotesque" story of a sower who sows without any concern for germination and harvest. K. Weiss ("Mk IV, 26 bis 29—dennoch die Parabel vom zuversichtlichen Sämann," in *BZ*, 1929, pp. 50ff.) does a good job of showing that the farmer's inactivity is only an secondary element of the parable. On ὅταν δὲ παραδοῖ ὁ καρπός, cf. T. W. Manson, "A Note on Mark IV, 28 f.," in *JTS*, 1937, pp. 399-400. For the bibliography, cf. J. Dupont, "La Parabole de la semence qui pousse toute seule," in *RSR*, 1967, pp. 367-392. W. G. Kümmel, "Noch einmal: Das Gleichnis von der selbstwachsenden Saat," in *Festschrift J. Schmid*, Freiburg, 1973, pp. 220-237; J. Dupont, "Encore la parabole de la semence qui pousse toute seule," in *Festschrift W. G. Kümmel*, Göttingen, 1975, pp. 96-108 (defending the unity of the parable).

[6] R. Stuhlmann saw this quite well in "Beobachtungen und Überlegungen zu Markus IV, 26-29," in *NTS*, vol. 19, 1973, pp. 153-162, as did D. Buzy, *Les Paraboles*, Paris, 1932, p. 49: "it is the earth alone that produces in the listing of all the phases

its own, independently of the activity of the farmer, without any human cooperation? Or that it produces without visible cause, in an undiscernible fashion?[7]

We should recall first of all the belief that in the golden age "the soil would produce on its own (*automatē*) an abundant and generous crop,"[8] then the constant use of *automatos* to describe the spontaneous production of uncultivated land, the natural growth of seed, its own energy.[9] Thus this word describes the second crop in Lev 25:5, 11 (*s^{e}pîaḥ*); and Josephus, comparing the sacrifices of Abel and Cain, observes: "God is honored by things that grow spontaneously and according to nature" (*tois automatois kai kata physin*) and not by products fashioned by human ingenuity (*Ant.* 1.54). This word is used when Judas Maccabeus finds the temple at Jerusalem wasted and "plants growing on their own in the sanctuary" (*Ant.* 12.317). Philo similarly contrasts spontaneous growth and the art of agriculture.[10] Given this commonplace, contemporary agricultural usage, it indeed seems that in the Markan parable Jesus is insisting on the wonder of a grain that grows without anyone's tending it; being alive, it accomplishes on its own its germination, growth, and fruit-bearing through mysterious exchanges between itself and the soil that has received it: they

---

of the growth of the grain. . . . The main lesson is that it is the kingdom alone, by its own virtue, by its divine energy, that will develop until the last phase of its perfection." Cf. Plutarch, *An virt. doc.* 1: "excellence that nature produces spontaneously (αὐτομάτως)"; Diodorus Siculus 17.50.6: "the carriers of the god's image proceed randomly, wherever the god directs their steps by a nod of the head."

[7] Cf. Philo, *Flight* 171: "In the spontaneous products of nature that we encounter, we discover neither origins nor ends that could be causes in themselves; thus the origin is the sowing, and the term is the harvest." The secret of growth is imperceptible, like the mystery of life (2 Macc 7:22; Eccl 11:5; Ps 139:13–18) and the nature of the *pneuma* (John 3:8).

[8] Hesiod, *Op.* 118; cf. Heraclitus, *All.* 6.5: "The first humans fed on . . . fruits that grew spontaneously on trees."

[9] Josephus, *Life* 11: Bannus contented himself "for food with that which the land produced spontaneously, τὴν αὐτομάτως φυομένην"; *Ant.* 1.49; 3.281. Philemon, frag. 103: οὐδὲ φύεται αὐτόματον ἀνθρώποισιν . . . μοῦς ὥσπερ ἐν ἀγρῷ θύμος (in Stobaeus, *Ecl.* 2.31.17, vol. 2, p. 204).

[10] Philo, *Creation* 81: "One could hope that God . . . would supply the human race through the spontaneous production of goods all prepared . . . without the art of agriculture, ἄνευ τέχνης γεωργικῆς"; 167: "man deprived of the spontaneous goods that the earth had learned to produce without the art of agriculture"; Philo, *Change of Names* 260: In the seventh sacred season (the sabbatical year), "there will be a growth of spontaneous goods (τῶν αὐτομάτων ἀγαθῶν); they will not be the products of an established art; they will germinate by virtue of a nature capable of begetting itself, sufficient to its ends, and they will bear their natural fruits." Cf. Diphilus, frag. 14: ἥκει φερόμεν' αὐτόματα πάντα τἀγαθά (in Athenaeus 9.370 e).

are linked—"it is the earth alone that produces." Just so the kingdom of God on earth has its own dynamism, an immanent energy, a vital force. Since humans have nothing to do with it, we can conclude that this innate vitality comes from God.[11] In fact this is what is indicated by the fact that the vitality is not easily perceptible; but this invisibility is not mentioned for its own sake; it is a secondary trait.

---

[11] This is what Philo says, *Flight* 170: "Third definition of spontaneous knowledge: it is that which grows by itself, τὸ ἀναβαῖνον αὐτόματον (here he cites Lev 25:11). Natural products require no art, *because it is God who sows them; thanks to his agriculture*, he causes to develop, as if they were growing on their own, products that do not grow on their own, except in the sense that they have no need at all for human attention"; cf. 168: that which one gets from nature is received from God. It is he who causes fecundity (*Rewards* 9, 63, 160; *Abraham* 52–54) and growth (1 Cor 3:6; 2 Cor 9:10; cf. Matt 6:28). Philo loves to exploit metaphorically the "automatism" of knowledge (*Flight* 166ff., *Abraham* 6; *Dreams* 1.68) or of the virtues, which are like seeds innate in the soil of the soul (*Alleg. Interp.* 1.92) and rich in potentiality. At any rate, all that grows spontaneously is supplied or commanded by Providence (Josephus, *Ant.* 1.46), so that "nothing happens by chance" (4.47), and if the walls of Jericho fall by themselves, it is God who makes them fall (5.24). This must indeed be the case, if an event does not fall out "either from natural causes, nor from the activity of others" (*War* 1.378).

αὐτόπτης

autoptēs, eyewitness

→*see also* μάρτυς

Luke the historian calls upon the authority of eyewitnesses of the gospel message preached by Jesus from the beginning of his ministry: *hoi ap' archēs autoptai kai hypēretai genomenoi tou logou*.[1] The noun *autoptēs* (a biblical hapax, unknown in Philo), formed from *opsis* (J. Pollux, *Onom.* 2.57–58), often has the banal meaning of a spectator who sees with his own eyes, as opposed to the "hearer" of a reputation or a bit of news.[2] In the magical papyri, it designates the immediate vision of the divinity.[3] It is often

---

[1] Luke 1:2 (cf. A. Feuillet, " 'Témoins oculaires et serviteurs de la Parole,' Lc. I, 2b," in *NovT*, vol. 15, 1973, pp. 241–259). Αὐτόπται has to do with facts (πραγμάτων), as in Vettius Valens 260.30: πολλὰ δὲ κακῶν καὶ παθῶν αὐτόπτης γενόμενος τῶν πραγμάτων δοκιμάσας συνέγραψα. Cf. Polybius 4.2.2: "We ourselves were present at certain events, and we learned of the others from those who saw them. To extend the account further back in time by setting down hearsay based on hearsay would not, it seems to us, provide a basis either for judgments or even for solid (ἀσφαλεῖς) statements."

[2] Plato, *Leg.* 10.900a: "Whether you know of these spectacles through hearsay (δι' ἀκοῆς) or you have seen the sight yourself with your own eyes (αὐτόπτης)"; Xenophon, *Hell.* 6.2.31: "Since he had not learned from an eyewitness concerning Mnasippos, he feared that it was to deceive him that they made all this fuss . . . but when he received clear reports . . ."; Josephus, *Ant.* 18.342: "Anilaios had heard of the woman's reputation for beauty from the Parthian general (ἀκοῇ τῆς εὐπρεπείας), but when he saw her with his own eyes (αὐτόπτης γενόμενος), he fell in love with her"; 19.125: "Anteios was drawn by the pleasure of seeing Gaius with his own eyes, ὑπὸ ἡδονῆς τοῦ αὐτόπτης γενόμενος Γαΐου"; *War* 6.134: Caesar claimed to be eyewitness and arbiter of all the actions of his soldiers, γένηται δ' αὐτόπτης καὶ μάρτυς ἁπάντων. At the end of the first century AD, Theo writes his sister not to be disturbed during his absence: "αὐτόπτης γάρ εἰμι τῶν τόπων καὶ οὐκ εἰμὶ ξένος τῶν ἐνθάδε, because I am familiar with the places and I am not a stranger here" (*P.Oxy.* 1154, 9).

[3] *P.Lond.* 122, 85 (vol. 1, p. 119 = *Pap.Graec.Mag.* II, p. 49): ἐὰν θέλῃς καὶ αὐτοφαν(πτον) αὐτὸν ἐκάλεσε; cf. αὐτοπτική, αὐτοπτικός (ibid., 121, 319; vol. 1, p. 94; K. Preisendanz, vol. 1, p. 14), line 335: αὐτοπτικὴ ἐὰν βούλῃς σεαυτὸν ἰδεῖν; also line 727 (other references in F. Cumont, *L'Egypte des Astrologues*, Brussels, 1937, p. 165, n. 1; LSJ on this word). For αὐτόπτως, cf. *PSI* 1345, 7: χαίρομαι ὡς ἵνα αὐτοπτῶς προσεκύνουν τὸν δεσπότην μου (sixth-seventh century).

---

autoptēs, S 845; TDNT 5.373; EDNT 1.179; MM 93–94; L&N 24.46; BAGD 122

used by medical writers[4] and can have a juridical meaning[5] after the fashion of *autopsia*, personal inspection.[6]

In Luke 1:2, the *autoptēs*, as opposed to a simple informer who mediates between the sender of a message and its recipient, is a qualified witness who personally affirms both that which he has seen and his conviction, thus making certainty possible. He himself guarantees the truth of the gospel. This term must therefore be understood in its technical sense as a major component in the documentation or factual report that the historian sets out to describe. The eyewitness, who has participated in the events, provides an account that is in accord with reality.[7] From Herodotus on, Greek historians make a distinction in their sources of information between that which they have heard and that which they have seen personally.[8]

---

[4] W. K. Hobart, (*Medical Language*, pp. 89–90) gives a dozen references to Galen (cf. our modern "autopsy"). Xenophon, *Cyr.* 5.4.18: "Cyrus either examined the wounded with his own eyes (αὐτόπτης) or if he could not do so himself he sent people to care for them."

[5] *PSI* 1314, 9 (*episkepsis*, report; first century BC): αὐτόπτην μάχιμον ἐφ᾽ ἡμᾶς ἀποστείλας. Cf. H. Sahlin, *Der Messias und das Gottesvolk: Studien zur protolukanischen Theologie*, Uppsala, 1943, pp. 40–42. The meaning is very close to μάρτυς; cf. John 1:34; 15:27; 19:35; Acts 1:8; 1 John 1:1–2.

[6] *P.Mil.Vogl.* 24, 20: ὡς νῦν οὖν Δημήτριος γενόμενος παρ᾽ ἐμὲ ἐξ αὐτοψίας (second century AD); *P.Tebt.* 286, 20: ἐκ τῆς αὐτοψίας ἣν ἐγὼ ἐπεῖδον (same date); *P.Oxy.* 1272, 19: ἀξιῶ ἐὰν δόξῃ σοι παραγενέσθαι ἐπὶ τὴν αὐτοψίαν (same date); *P.Stras.* 259, 7 (business letter, from the third century. Go to perform an on-site verification); *P.Cair.Isid.* 66, 6 and 10; 67, 8 (third century, I am sending someone to do an inspection); *P.Oxy.* 2233, 9 (fourth century), ὥστε ἐκεῖσαι παραγενέσθαι πρὸς αὐτοψίαν; *P.Amh.* 142, 12; *P.Mil.* 41, 6: ὅθεν ἐπὶ τὴν αὐτοψίαν παραγενόμενοι; the formula is technical.

[7] Cf. ἀκριβῶς (Luke 1:3; Polybius 12.4d). D. Kurz, AKPIBEIA: *Das Ideal der Exaktheit bei den Griechen bis Aristoteles*, dissertation, Tübingen, 1970.

[8] Herodotus 2.99: "To this point what I have said is drawn from what I have seen (ὄψις), from my reflections (γνώμη), from accounts (ἱστορίη) that I have received. From now on, I will recount what the Egyptians say, as I heard it; some things will also be added from what I saw for myself (τῆς ἐμῆς ὄψιος)"; 2.5.106, 122, 131: "Certain people tell (τινες λέγουσι) the following story. . . . This whole account is nothing but rubbish. . . . We have seen for ourselves (ἡμεῖς ὠρῶμεν)"; 3.12; 7.129. With respect to the formation of the earth in Egypt: "In the sphere of human matters, the priests tell me uninimously . . . What they said seemed to me to be correct . . . I readily trust those who told me what I have reported and I am personally convinced that it is so when I see (ἰδών) . . ." (2.4–14); with respect to the origin of the Colchidians: "What I am saying was my personal opinion before I heard it expressed by others (ἀκούσας ἄλλων)" (2.104–105); description of Lake Moeris: "The people of the country told me (ἔλεγον) . . . Since I nowhere saw . . . (οὐκ ὥρων) . . . I asked . . . they told me . . . I had no difficulty believing what they said; for I had heard that something similar had happened at Ninevah" (2.149–150); Thucydides 1.22.1–2: οἷς τε αὐτὸς παρῆν καὶ παρὰ

Only their presence in the theater of action makes their account believable: "As for the history of the war, I wrote it after having been a participant in many of the events (*pollōn autourgos praxeōn*), a witness of a large number of them (*pleistōn d' autoptēs genomenos*); in short, without being unaware of anything that was said or done."[9] The Jewish historian is here plagiarizing Polybius: "On account of the fact that I was not only the witness of the events (*mē monon autoptēs*) but in some a collaborator (*synergos*), in others the architect (*cheiristēs*), I have undertaken to write so to speak a new history from a new point of departure (*archēn allēn*)."[10] According to Dionysius of Halicarnassus, the value of Theopompus of Chios, author of historical works, lay in his having been "eyewitness of most of the events, *pollōn men autoptēs gegenēmenos*."[11] Finally, in the first century, Diodorus Siculus, in describing the Arabian Gulf, distinguishes between the two categories of sources: that which he derived from the Royal Annals kept at Alexandria, and observations that were communicated to him by eyewitnesses, *ta de para tōn autoptōn pepōsmenoi*.[12] Luke 1:2 clearly is in line with this historiographical hermeneutic. Its *autoptai* have all the trustworthiness of persons who have been present at occurrences, of witnesses who merit belief.[13]

τῶν ἄλλων. The two ways of getting information are complementary. Cf. G. Nenci, "Il motive dell' autopsia nella storiografia greca," in *Studi classici e orientali* 3, 1955, pp. 14–46; H. Verdin, "L'Importance des recherches sur le méthode critique des historiens grecs et latins," in *Antidorum W. Peremans sexagenario ab alumnis oblatum* (Studia Hellenistica 16), Louvain, 1968, pp. 298–308; idem, "Notes sur l'attitude des historiens grecs à l'égard de la tradition locale," in *Ancient Society* 1, 1970, pp. 183–200; idem, *De historisch-kritische methode van Herodotus*, Brussels, 1971, pp. 107–154; G. Schepens, "L'Idéal de l'information complète chez les historiens grecs," in *REG*, 1975, pp. 81–93.

[9] Josephus, *Ag. Apion* 1.55; cf. *War* 3.432: "When the news of the catastrophe at Jotapata came to Jerusalem, most people would not at the outset believe it . . . because no eyewitness was available to confirm the report, διὰ τὸ μηδένα τῶν λεγομένων αὐτόπτην παρεῖναι."

[10] Polybius 3.4.13. In 12.25–28, Polybius criticizes the fabrications of Timaeus of Tauromenion, "a historian without culture," and his bookish accounts. Timaeus saw nothing (12.25g4). It isn't enough that he resorted to "the works of his predecessors, spent his time in libraries, and stocked up on scholarship" (12.25e4); "sight is much more of an instrument of observation than hearing" (12.27.1). "Timaeus entirely neglected visual information" (12.27.3). Cf. Marie Laffranque, "L'Ouïe et l'oreille: Polybe et les problèmes de l'information à l'époque hellénistique," in *Revue philosophique*, vol. 93, 1968, pp. 263–272.

[11] Dionysius of Halicarnassus, *Pomp.* 6.3. Cf. Dio Chrysostom 7.1: τόδε μὴν αὐτὸς ἰδών, οὐ παρ' ἑτέρων ἀκούσας, διηγήσομαι.

[12] Diodorus Siculus 3.38.1. These *autoptai* could be travelers, merchants, sailors, soldiers, elephant-hunters, indigenous folk, or explorers; cf. W. Peremans, "Diodore de Sicile et Agatharchide de Cnide," in *Historia*, vol. 16, 1967, pp. 432–455.

[13] E. Delebecque, *Etudes grecques*, pp. 66ff.

ἄφεσις

aphesis, a sending out, point of departure, discharge, settlement, forgiveness, dispensation, acquittal, liberation

This noun, derived from the verb *aphiēmi*, "send out, let go" (Matt 8:22; P.Amh. 37, 10), has multiple shades of meaning, some of them quite everyday, like the sending out of ships (Demosthenes, *Corona* 18.77-78); but there are also technical applications, for example in architecture, and in sports, where it refers to the starting line for the athletes in the *diaulos*;[1] in astrology, it refers to the point of departure, the beginning.[2] In Aristotle, it refers to the emission or expulsion of fish roe,[3] and in Hippocrates it becomes a medical term, the emission of gas being a symptom of illness.[4]

Aphesis is used especially for persons, usually as a legal term for a layoff, for the release of slaves or prisoners (Polybius 1.79.12; Plato, *Plt.* 273 c), the repudiation of a spouse,[5] an exemption from military service (Plutarch, *Ages.* 24.3), a dispensation from an obligation: "A councillor who does not come to the meeting chamber at the appointed time shall pay one drachma for each day's absence unless the council grants him a dispensation" (*ean mē heuriskomenos aphesin tēs boulēs apē*, Aristotle, *Ath. Pol.* 30.6). In Demosthenes, *aphesis* is usually a "discharge" in the technical sense of

---

[1] Diodorus Siculus 4.73; Pausanias 5.15.5; 6.20.9. Cf. J. Delorme, *Gymnasion*, Paris, 1960, pp. 106, 151, 290-291.

[2] Vettius Valens: χρὴ ταῖς λοιπαῖς τῶν ἀστέρων ἀφέσεσι καὶ μαρτυρίαις καὶ ἀκτινοβολίαις προσέχειν (p. 225, 16). Cf. O. Neugebauer, M. B. van Hoesen, *Greek Horoscopes*, Philadelphia, 1959, pp. 87ff., 105ff.

[3] Aristotle, *Gen. An.* 3.5.756a10; *HA* 8.30.68a1; cf. 9.40.626a25: bees release their excrement; 6.22.576a25: a mare remains standing at the moment of delivery; *Part. An.* 4.13.697a24: "the spiracle of cetaceans is for expelling water."

[4] Hippocrates, *Coac.* 3.485 (other references in Hobart, *Medical Language*, pp. 101-102). *Aphesis* can also mean "exhaustion, prostration": "forgetfulness and prostration, loss of voice . . . signs of illness" (*Epid.* 3.6).

[5] Plutarch, *Pomp.* 42.13: "Pompey sent his wife a bill of divorce" (ἔπεμψεν αὐτῇ τὴν ἄφεσιν).

---

aphesis, S 859; *TDNT* 1.509-512; *EDNT* 1.181-183; *NIDNTT* 1.697, 700-703; MM 96; L&N 37.132, 40.8; BAGD 125

freeing someone from an obligation,[6] but also a "settlement" ("My father was able to recover the debt after the settlement," *C. Naus.* 38.14) and a "remission" ("This remission of interest did not wrong the creditors").[7] On rare occasions it refers to the forgiveness of an offense: "What we have said concerning forgiveness of a parricide by a father shall be valid for similar cases" (Plato, *Leg.* 9.869 d). The term does not seem to have been used by the moralists, however.

In the papyri, *aphesis* refers especially to the draining of water from pools (*P.Oxy.* 3167, 10; *P.Petr.* II, 13, 2: *aphesis tou hydatos*; *P.Flor.* 388, 44) and especially to sluice gates ("the sluice gates at Phoboou," *P.Oxy.* 3268, 11; 918, verso 20; *P.Ryl.* 583, 16, 63) or the conduits from which water flows out into the fields.[8] It is difficult to determine the meaning of *gē en aphesei*;[9] scholars disagree.[10] Indeed, it seems that the expression had several meanings, but the very word *aphesis* suggests land "in remission," recalling the *fundi derelecti* of the empire,[11] i.e., either uncultivated land, fallow land (*P.Got.* 20, col. II, 2, 6, 7, 8; *P.Yale* 1674, 57); or land exempted from certain taxes.[12] It seems that *aphesis* also had the meaning "expense" or "disburse-

---

[6] Demosthenes, *C. Apat.* 33.3: "If he had had a release and discharge from all the obligations existing between us"; *P. Phorm.* 26.23: "There was a settling of accounts and a release relative to the bank lease"; *C. Naus.* 28.5: "In every instance where he was given a release and discharge, there was no action. And precisely when there was a discharge, in the presence of numerous witnesses . . ."; 9: "You have been sufficiently informed on that matter by the discharge."

[7] *C. Dionys.* 56.28, 34; remission of a debt, Isocrates, *Phil.* 5.127.

[8] *P.Brem.* 14, 6; *P.Mich.* 92, 5; 103, 6: the sluice gates were open and water flowed out everywhere; 233 (AD 25), the oath of a sluice gate guard (ἀφεσοφύλακες): "the sluice gate of the priests west of the bridge" (line 8), "the sluice gate of the priests to the east" (line 10), "each one guards his sluice" (line 15); 645 (= SB 7174).

[9] *P.Tebt.* 5, 37, 112, 201 (= *C.Ord.Ptol.* 53); 705, 7; *P.Oxy.* 2134, 16; *P.Kroll* col. I, 14 (ed. L. Koenen, *Eine ptolemäische Königsurkunde*, Wiesbaden, 1957, p. 10 = SB 9316); UPZ 110, 177.

[10] Cf. J. Hermann, "Zum Begriff γῆ ἐν ἀφέσει," in *ChrEg*, 1955, pp. 95–106. J. C. Shelton ("Ptolemaic Land ἐν ἀφέσει: An Observation on the Terminology," *ChrEg*, 1971, pp. 113–119) cites *P.Tebt.* 81, 3: "other land ἐν ἀφέσει"; 141, 3 and denounces the restorations of γῆ in many editions of the texts. In the Ptolemaic period, we never find γῆ ἐν ἀφέσει but only ἡ ἐν ἀφέσει γῆ or ἡ ἐν ἀφέσει. As opposed to βασιλικὴ γῆ, land ἐν ἀφέσει is often understood as "ceded, conceded, left" for cultivation by private persons; some see a determination of fiscal status: a land whose produce is freed by the royal administration.

[11] Cf. G. Lumbrose, *Recherches sur l'économie politique de l'Egypte sous les Lagides*, 2d ed., Amsterdam, 1967, p. 90.

[12] Cf. Dittenberger, *Or.* XC, 12: εἰς τέλος ἀφῆκεν; *P.Petr.* II, 2, 1: ὅταν ἡ ἄφεσις δοθῇ; H. A. Rupprecht, *Studien zur Quittung im Recht der graeco-ägyptischen Papyri*, Munich, 1971, p. 60.

ment," for example, in the phrase *logos apheseōs statērōn*, expenses of 130 staters (*P.Tebt.* 404, 1); *apheseōs chōmatos* (*O.Bodl.* 1827: an accounting for the repair of a dike; *P.Tebt.* 706, 11); payment for a route (*P.Tebt.* 815, col. IV, 26); or expenses for the considerable work projects throughout a *nomarchia* (*SB* 8243, 9, *tas apheseis*).

"Dispensations" from *leitourgiai* are well attested. According to a transcript of an audience before a *stratēgos*, a weaver wrongly chosen for a *leitourgia* asks for an exemption (*tēs leitourgias aphesin*, *P.Phil.* 3, 5; second century AD). In the third century, this exemption is a privilege of the artists of Dionysus (*P.Oxy.Hels.* 25, 17). An imperial prescript provides that the prefect of the province shall be able to release a petitioner from a legal obligation (*P.Oxy.* 1020, 6). *Aphesis* is also debt remission: according to a judgment at Cnidos in the second century BC on behalf of Calymna, "a deduction made from the talent that the Calumnians claim was forgiven them by Pausimachus and Cleumedes."[13] Finally, *aphesis* refers to the liberation of a prisoner: *homologia apheseōs* (*SB* 9463, 12–13). A decree at Athens, for the poet Philippides, who used his influence on behalf of his compatriots after the battle of Ipsos, "for all those who were prisoners, after making his case to the king and obtaining their liberation . . . he sent them on their way to their chosen destinations" (Dittenberger, *Syl.* 374, 21). An Iranian act emancipating slaves by consecrating them to the god Sarapis uses the words *tēn aphesin autou*.[14] In a dream in the Serapeum, a vision gives Ptolemy confidence that he will be delivered soon (*aphesis moi ginetai tachy*, *UPZ* 78, 39).

Apart from several occurrences with no original meaning,[15] the LXX gives *aphesis* at least two special meanings. First, the sabbatical "remission": "You shall give the earth release and let it lie fallow" (*aphesin poiēseis*, Hebrew *šāmam*, Exod 23:11; Lev 25:2–7). This sabbatical year is also the occasion of the liberation of Israelite slaves and the return of security held for debts: "At the end of seven years, you shall make a remission . . . a remission of what he has loaned to his neighbor" (*š^emiṭâh*, Deut 15:1, 9; 31:10). Similarly, the jubilee every fiftieth year is the occasion for the freeing (Hebrew *d^erōr*) of all the inhabitants of the land; and the ground lies fallow.[16] Elsewhere, *aphesis* takes on a metaphorical meaning—and for the

---

[13] *RIJG*, vol. 1, n. X, B 7 = C. Michel, *Recueil*, n. 1340; *I.Magn.* 93 *c* 16; Dittenberger, *Syl.* 495, 166: τοῖς μὲν ἀφέσεις ἐποιήσατο τῶν χρημάτων, not requiring interest for the other debtors.

[14] Ed. L. Robert, *Hellenica*, vol. 11, Paris, 1960, p. 85, 8–9.

[15] Exod 18:2—Jethro receives Zipporah back from Moses after her repudiation (Hebrew *šilûḥîm*); Jdt 11:14—"the people with the task of passing on the senate's permission to them"; Lev 16:26—the scapegoat (*aphesis* translates the Hebrew *'^azā'zēl*).

[16] Lev 25:10–13; 25:28, 30: property leaves people hands at the Jubilee (ἐξέρχεσθαι); 27:17–24; Num 36:4; Ezek 46:17 (R. de Vaux, *Ancient Israel*, vol. 1, pp.

first time, a religious, messianic meaning—in Isa 58:6—"to send back free (*en aphesei*, Hebrew *ḥapšîm*) those who have been mistreated."[17] It enters into the vocabulary of instruction in Jer 34:15—"You were converted today . . . and each of you proclaimed freedom to his neighbor" (cf. verse 17).

It is in Jewish literature that *aphesis* receives its full, if not definitive, meaning. For Philo, the term is constantly associated with *eleutheria* and understood to mean complete liberty.[18] Allegorical exegesis takes the sabbatical years and jubilees as referring to "the emancipation and liberation of souls that call upon God" (*Heir* 273) and reject their former errors (*Prelim. Stud.* 108). When Abraham pleads for Sodom, "at first he sets forth the number of the liberation (*tēs apheseōs*) at fifty (righteous), but he stops at ten, the limit of redemption (*tēn apolytrōsin*)" (ibid. 109), i.e., liberation in exchange for ransom (cf. *Spec. Laws* 2.121). Moses offers a goat "as a sacrifice for the remission of our sins" (*thysē peri apheseōs hamartēmatōn, Moses* 2.147; *Spec. Laws* 1.190; cf. 215, 237).

Josephus, who usually uses *aphesis* in its secular literary meaning,[19] also recognizes the meaning "acquittal"[20] and even pardon: Herod "promised to pardon past offenses" (*War* 1.481). *Didous aphesin* could be translated "give absolution."

175ff.). The translation of the Hebrew *yōḇēl* by the substantive σημασία (Lev 25:15) or ἐνιαυτός or ἔτος ἀφέσεως σημασίας (verses 10–13) is elliptical: a sign of the year of liberation, the Jubilee year. Cf. the *hᵃnāḥâh*, the day of rest and relief of debts, in Esth 2:18—"the king gave relief to the provinces"; 1 Macc 10:34—Demetrius writes to the Jews: "All the holy days and Sabbaths . . . shall be days of immunity and release (ἡμέραι ἀτελαίας καὶ ἀφέσεως) for all the Jews who are in the kingdom"; 13:34. —Elsewhere, ἀφέσεις ὑδάτων are "watercourses" (Joel 1:20; Hebrew *'āpîq*; Ezek 47:3) or "rivers of tears" (Lam 3:48; Hebrew *peleg*). A. Deissmann (*Bible Studies*, pp. 98ff.) well noted that this meaning derives from Egyptian usage with respect to irrigation and the pouring out of water and that the translation of the Hebrew *'ᵃpîqê* by ἀφέσεις in 2 Sam 22:16 might have been suggested by the initial *aph-*.

[17] Isa 61:1—"Yahweh has anointed me . . . to proclaim liberation to the captives" (Hebrew *dᵉrôr*); Jer 34:8—Jeremiah's mission is to "proclaim emancipation to the captives" (Hebrew *dᵉrôr*).

[18] Philo, *Sacr. Abel and Cain* 122; *Worse Attacks Better* 63, 144; *Change of Names* 228; *Spec. Laws* 2.67; *Flacc.* 84. "The harvest of fruits that came all alone is called the harvest of liberty" (*Migr. Abr.* 32).

[19] Freeing slaves (*Ant.* 12.40) or prisoners (17.233), letting them go free (*War* 3.533; 7.192), especially the launching of projectiles (2.423, 3.256, 4.580, 5.10, 7.403), and also the discharge of lightning (*Ant.* 5.60).

[20] "Called before the court, he must rejoice at his acquittal" (περὶ τῆς ἀφέσεως εὐχαριστῶν, *War* 1.214; cf. *Ant.* 14.182; 17.185). Compare the formulations of Herodotus (6.30, with respect to the possible pardon by Darius at Histiaeus) and Antiphon (*1 Tetr.* 2, "We have not let the guilty escape," οὐ ἀφέντες).

It is remarkable that the NT writers use *aphesis* thirty-six times, always meaning pardon for sins; there is never a secular meaning, as if this were a technical term reserved for religious use. Its first occurrence is on the lips of Zechariah in his description of the goal of John the Baptist's ministry: namely, to prepare the Messiah's ways "so as to give to his people the knowledge of salvation through the forgiveness of their sins" (*en aphesei hamartiōn autōn*)[21] on account of God's tender mercy (verse 78). The remark that salvation consists of forgiveness of sins shows that the messianic *sōtēria* is spiritual and will not be a political liberation. In effect, Mark 1:4 and Luke 3:3 characterize the ministry of the precursor in the region of the Jordan as a bath of conversion "for the forgiveness of sins" (*eis aphesin hamartiōn*) so as to prepare sinners for the coming of the Messiah. This involves sorrow for offenses committed, penitence, upright intentions; without these things God could not grant pardon. Water baptism is a means of realizing this conversion, and its goal—something altogether new—is a washing, "the remission of sins."[22] In the blood covenant sealed by Jesus with the institution of the Eucharist, the blood is not poured out on the people but drunk by the participants: "This is my blood, the new covenant, shed for the many for the remission of sins."[23] Henceforth it is clear that *aphesis* is the basic element of the redemptive work accomplished on the cross; it is connected with pardon, sanctification, and salvation. Speaking to the disciples at Emmaus, Jesus reminded them of "what was written . . . that in his name repentance for the forgiveness of sins (*eis aphesin hamartiōn*) should be preached to all nations," but he specified that first the Christ had to suffer, die, and be resurrected (Luke 24:47). This point is of the highest importance, because it implies that forgiveness of sins is due to the sufferings of Jesus.

This is what St. Peter keeps teaching to the crowd at Pentecost (Acts 2:38), to the Sanhedrin,[24] and to the centurion Cornelius: concerning

---

[21] Luke 1:77; ἐν ἀφέσει attaches to σωτηρίας or γνῶσιν σωτηρίας, not to δοῦναι.

[22] Ps 51:4, 9, 11, 14; Ezek 36:25-27 (H. Schürmann, *Lukasevangelium*, p. 157). Cf. J. Gnilka, "Die messianischen Tauchbäder und die Johannestaufe," in *RevQ*, vol. 3, 1961, pp. 186—207.

[23] Matt 26:28. Mark 14:24 says simply: "poured out ὑπὲρ πολλῶν"; Luke 22:20—"poured out for you" (τὸ ὑπὲρ ὑμῶν); "εἰς ἄφεσιν ἁμαρτιῶν is probably an addition—correct in its substance—by Matthew" (J. Jeremias, *Eucharistic Words*, p. 114; cf. idem, *Die Abendmahlsworte Jesu*, 3d ed., Göttingen, 1960), apparently inspired by Isa 58:6; 61:1 (cf. Luke 4:18). This means a permanent physical presence of Jesus among his own to communicate the divine life to them, cf. P. Benoit, *Exégèse et théologie*, vol. 1, pp. 163-254.

[24] Acts 5:31—"God raised Jesus to his right hand as leader and Savior so as to grant repentance and forgiveness of sins to Israel."

Christ, "all the prophets bear witness that whoever believes in him receives remission of sins through his Name" (Acts 10:43). This forgiveness depends on faith in the person and the power of Jesus; it is universal, so that everyone can benefit from it. St. Paul said the same thing at Pisidian Antioch,[25] before King Agrippa,[26] and to the Colossians (Col 1:14; *aphesis tōn hamartiōn* is linked with *apolytrōsis*, "redemption").

There remain five texts where *aphesis* is used without a complement or in the variant expression *aphesis tōn paraptōmatōn*, "the remission of trespasses," associated with redemption (*apolytrōsis*, Eph 1:7), the two terms being almost equivalent. In Mark 3:29 the Lord states, "Whoever blasphemes the Holy Spirit will never have forgiveness" (*ouk echei aphesin eis to aiōna*; the last three words are omitted in D and in numerous Latin manuscripts). This unpardonable blasphemy is a willful blindness and hardening.[27] At Nazareth, identifying himself as the Messiah, Jesus cites Isa 58:6, which announces the deliverance (*en aphesei*) of the chosen people (Luke 4:18). The Epistle to the Hebrews uses *aphesis* without a complement for forgiveness, declaring that the absolution of offenses depends on the sacrificial efficacy of the blood: "Without the shedding of blood there is no remission" (*ou ginetai aphesis*).[28] Glossing Jer 31:34 ("I will remember their sins and iniquities no longer"), Hebrews adds, "Now, where there is remission of these (*hopou de aphesis toutōn*), there is no more offering for sin" (Heb 10:18). In fact, since sin has been "remitted" because of the sacrifice

---

[25] Acts 13:38—"It is through him that forgiveness of sins is announced to you (καταγγέλλεται)"; this forgiveness is identified with justification (v. 39) and salvation.

[26] Acts 26:18—The glorified Christ sent Paul to the Jews and the Gentiles "that they might receive (λαβεῖν) by faith in me the forgiveness of sins and the heritage of the saints." Cf. L. Hartman, "Baptism 'into the Name of Jesus' and Early Christology," in *ST*, vol. 28, 1974, pp. 21–48.

[27] Cf. C. Spicq, *Hébreux*, vol. 1; "Excursus IV: Hébr. VI, 4–6: L'Impossible Pénitence," pp. 167–178; O. E. Evans, "The Unforgivable Sin," in *ExpT*, vol. 68, 1957, pp. 240–244; G. Fitzler, "Die Sünde wider den Heiligen Geist," in *TZ*, 1957, pp. 161–182; J. G. Williams, "A Note on the 'Unforgivable Sin' Logion," in *NTS*, vol. 12, 1965, pp. 75–77.

[28] Heb 9:22. Cf. T. C. G. Thornton, "The Meaning of αἱματεκχυσία," in *JTS*, vol. 15, 1964, pp. 63–64; L. Morris, "The Biblical Use of the Term 'Blood,' " *JTS*, 1952, pp. 216–227; 1955, pp. 77–82; J. Dupont, "La Réconciliation dans la théologie de saint Paul," in *EstBib*, 1952, pp. 291ff. L. Sabourin, *Rédemption sacrificielle*, Desclée De Brouwer, 1961, pp. 179, 316; C. Spicq, *Hébreux*, "Excursus VIII: La Théologie et la liturgie du Précieux Sang," pp. 277–285; E. F. Siegman, "The Blood of Christ in St. Paul's Soteriology," in *Precious Blood Study Week*, Carthagena, 1962, pp. 11–35; D. J. McCarthy, "The Symbolism of Blood and Sacrifice," in *JBL*, 1968, pp. 166–176; N. Snaith, "The Sprinkling of Blood," in *ExpT*, vol. 82, 1970, pp. 23–24; S. Lyonnet, L. Sabourin, *Sin, Redemption, and Sacrifice*, Rome, 1970, pp. 167ff.; J. M. Grintz, " 'Do Not Eat of the Blood,' " in *ASTI*, vol. 8, 1970–71, pp. 78–105.

on the cross, we could say that when Jesus died sin died as well, so that a new offering in the future would be nonsensical;[29] "fieret enim injuria hostiae Christi."[30] All these NT usages, which are so perfectly homogeneous, presuppose a catechesis—whose scope and evolution are unknown to us—that added the term *aphesis* to the Christian vocabulary with a precise and exclusive theological meaning.

---

[29] Cf. W. Stott, "The Conception of 'Offering' in the Epistle to the Hebrews," in *NTS*, vol. 9, 1962, p. 66.

[30] For it would be an affront to the sacrifice of Christ," Thomas Aquinas, on this text. Christian theology has correctly understood that Hebrews does not thus exclude the permanent oblation of the earthly church in the sacrifice of the Mass, for just as St. Paul completes that which is lacking in the passion of Christ (Col 1:24), the heavenly High Priest continues to intercede for believers; and the Mass is nothing other than this union of the faithful with the oblation and intercession of the Savior then and now (C. F. D. Moule, *The Sacrifice of Christ*, London, 1956). Cajetan already commented: "Do not think it strange, novice, that the sacrifice of the altar is offered daily in Christ's church; because it is not a new sacrifice, but a commemoration of the very same sacrifice that Christ offered; he himself commanded: Do this in memory of me. So also all the sacraments are nothing other than applications of Christ's passion to those who receive them. Moreover, it is one thing to repeat Christ's passion, but another to repeat the commemoration and application of Christ's passion" ("Nec propterea, novitie, mireris quotidie offerri sacrificium altaris in Christi ecclesia; quoniam non est novum sacrificium, sed illudmet quod Christus obtulit commemoratur; praecipiente ipso: Hoc facite in mei commemorationem. Sacramenta quoque omnia nihil aliud sunt quam applicationes passionis Christi ad suscipientes. Aliud autem est iterare passionem Christi, at aliud iterare commemorationem et applicationem passionis Christi," *Epistolae Pauli et aliorum Apostolorum ad graecam veritatem castigatae*, Venice, 1531, on this text).

ἀφιλάργυρος

aphilargyros, **free of the love of money**

→*see also* αἰσχροκερδής, ἀφιλάργυρος; φιλαργυρία, φιλάργυρος

Since the love of money is one of the signs of belonging to the world, Heb 13:5 addresses to persecuted Christians the charge "that your way of life be *aphilargyros*." This is an echo of Matt 6:24: "You cannot serve God and money." The same virtue is among the qualities required of the candidate for the *episkopē* (1 Tim 3:3). There is not much of significance to add to the citations of this term supplied by T. Nägeli and A. Deissmann[1] unless perhaps from the honorific decrees and in speeches in praise of virtue. The first mention is an honorific decree of Priene, from the second century BC. Unfortunately it is mutilated, but J. Rouffiac finds reason to classify it among "expressions of piety and of the moral ideal" which are common to the vocabulary of the inscriptions and of the NT.[2] More developed is the inscription of the Egyptian delta of 3 May 5 BC, "let *aretē* and *philagathia* and *aphilargyria* be manifest" (*aretē te kai philagathia kai aphilargyria prodēlos geinētai*, SB 8267, 44).

That this absence of avarice was a highly prized virtue is already known from Diodorus Siculus, who emphasizes that Bias never used his oratorical prowess to gain wealth (9.11, *aphilargyria*), but especially from the listing of the qualities of Antoninus Pius: "Hear! In the first place, he had a love of wisdom; in the second place, he did not love money, and in the third place, he loved virtue."[3] But the best parallel to 1 Tim 3:3 is in

---

[1] T. Nägeli, *Wortschatz*, p. 31; A. Deissmann, *Light*, pp. 85–86.

[2] *I.Priene*, 137, 5 (J. Rouffiac, *Caractères du grec*, p. 84). Similarly the adverb ἀφιλαργύρως in the honorific decrees of Istropolis (Dittenberger, *Syl.* 708, 17; first century BC) and of the region around Athens (ibid. 1104, 25, from 37/36 BC).

[3] *P.Oxy.* 33, col. II, 11 (interview with the emperor Marcus Aurelius): ἄκουε, τὸ μὲν πρῶτον ἦν φιλόσοφος, τὸ δεύτερον ἀφιλάργυρος, τὸ τρίτον φιλάγαθος (second century AD).

---

aphilargyros, S 866; *EDNT* 1.183; MM 98; L&N 25.109; BAGD 126

Onasander (1.8), in a list of qualities required in a general: he must be *aphilargyros* because *aphilargyria* guarantees that the leader will be incorruptible in his management of affairs. After all, many who demonstrate courage are blinded by money. The conclusion is that detachment from money will guarantee the probity of the bishop in the administration of material goods and probably also in the handling of spiritual things. One cannot be too strict (*dokimasthēsetai kai prōtē*, Onasander, loc. cit.); hence, similarly, *mē aischrokerdē* (Titus 1:7). It is enough to recall that Judas loved money (John 12:6) as did the Pharisees (Luke 16:14, *philargyroi*) and that Simon Magus expected "to gain the gift of God by paying money" (Acts 8:20).

> ἀφοράω
>
> *aphoraō*, to look from a distance, gaze fixedly
>
> →*see also* ἀποβλέπω

Christians are like athletes who compete together in the arena, where all the believers of the OT cheer them on like "supporters" (Heb 11–12:1). Once the race is begun, the athlete must not allow himself to be distracted by anything. Not only so, but he does not look back (Luke 9:62), nor to left or right, but keeps his attention fixed on the goal, concentrating only on it; and this exclusive attachment is the secret of his endurance and perseverance. Thus Heb 12:2 asks the disciples to "fix their gaze" on Jesus (*aphorōntes eis*).

It does not do justice to this biblical hapax to translate it simply "look at," especially in a letter where the verbs of seeing and considering are so numerous, so varied, and used with careful attention to their particular nuance.[1] The first meaning of *aphoraō* is "look at from a distance,"[2] so it is very close to *apoblepō* (Heb 11:26): just as Moses fixed his eyes on his reward, the believer under the New Covenant thinks only of the heavenly high priest (3:1, *katanoeō*), to whom every step here below in some way brings him closer (12:22–24, *proselēlythate*). But with the particle *eis*, this verb signals the turning of eyes from different points on the same object, in which one faces it[3] and finally fixes one's attention on it.[4] Thus

---

[1] C. Spicq, *Hébreux*, vol. 2, pp. 377ff.

[2] Cf. Josephus, *Ant.* 1.335: the two wives of Jacob are sent to watch from afar the actions of the combatants; 11.329; *War* 5.160: from the high tower of Psephinos at Jerusalem, one could espy Arabia in the distance; 5.445; 15.398.

[3] Josephus, *Ant.* 11.55; 15.401; Lucian, *Philops.* 30: ὁ Ἀρίγνωτος δριμὺ ἀπιδὼν εἰς ἐπέ; *P.Oxy.* 2111, 17: Petronius Mamertinus ἀπιδών εἰς τὴν Ζωσίμην εἶπεν; *PSI* 76, 7; ἀφοράν πρὸς τὴν σὴν λαμπρότητα.

[4] Josephus, *Ant.* 3.36: the people's eyes were fixed on Moses, εἰς αὐτὸν ἀφορῶντα; *War* 5.352: the old wall of Jerusalem is ornamented with spectators so attentive that

---

aphoraō, S 872; *EDNT* 1.183; MM 98; L&N 27.6, 30.31; BDF §74(1); BAGD 127

people look at a model,⁵ a guide or leader,⁶ and above all God himself.⁷ The multitude of citations having to do with looking to God show that a spiritual attitude is intended—whether in a Jewish or a pagan context— the attitude of every human creature face to face with their Creator and Lord.

This attitude entails first and foremost a selectivity, even exclusivity, in attention, as when, for example, the priests refuse to hear the high priests and prominent persons urging them to offer sacrifices for the emperors. They rely on the large numbers and the assistance of the revolutionaries; above all they look to the authority of Eleazar.⁸ When Josephus says that "each of the victims died gazing resolutely toward the temple" (*War* 5.517; cf. 6.123) or that "the army had its eyes on Titus" (7.67, *eis auton apheōra*), or that "when he had to render judgment, he considered only the truth" (*Ant.* 7.110), it is understood that these contemplatives have turned away from other considerations and focused only on one thing. It is precisely in this sense that believers turn and keep their gaze fixed on their *archēgos*, who "in place of the joy that lay before him endured a cross, despising the shame thereof" (Heb 12:2).

In addition, *aphoraō* means "consider, reflect,"⁹ because faith, the evidence of things invisible (Heb 11:1), is a faculty of perception—it "takes in" (verse 3, *noeō*)—but this "observing" is not here purely speculative; *aphoraō* is used for a spectacle that affects the feelings¹⁰ and gives rise to a practical

---

they lean forward to see better. Cf. Plutarch, *Agis* 1.4: those who keep watch from the prow see better than the pilots what is coming up ahead.

⁵ Epictetus 4.1.170: εἰς ταῦτα ἀφόρα τὰ παραδείγματα.

⁶ Josephus, *Ant.* 12.431: the soldiers of Judas Maccabeus, after the death of their leader, think of nothing else . . . ; this στρατηγοῦ τοιούτου στερηθέντες should be compared with the *archēgos* of Christians (Heb 12:2).

⁷ Josephus, *Ag. Apion* 2.166: "Moses urged them all to turn their eyes toward God as the source of all blessings"; *Ant.* 8.290: "Asanos, the king of Jerusalem, was a person of excellent character, keeping his eyes fixed on the divinity (πρὸς τὸν θεῖον ἀφορῶν)," he thought nothing and did nothing that did not orient him to piety and the observance of the laws; 4 Macc 17:10, the epitaph of some Maccabean martyrs: "They avenged our people while looking to God (εἰς τὸν θεὸν ἀφορῶντες) and enduring all torments even unto death"; Epictetus 3.24.16: "looking steadfastly to Zeus, he carried out all his deeds."

⁸ Josephus, *War* 2.410 (μάλιστα δ᾽ ἀφορῶντες εἰς τὸν Ἐλεάζαρον); Epictetus 2.19.29: "It is my intention to free you from every constraint and every fetter . . . directing your gaze toward God in all matters, large and small"; 3.26.11: "Is that also your custom . . . to look to others and hope for nothing from yourself?"

⁹ To behold a spectacle (Josephus, *War* 1.97; 6.233), to consider a situation in its entirety (4.279; cf. *Ant.* 2.42; 2.141; 2.336; 7.350; Plutarch, *Lyc.* 7.4; cf. ἀφίδω, Phil 2:23).

¹⁰ Josephus, *War* 1.142: "the sight of the Romans' perfect order" inspires fear.

response,[11] notably in the papyri where in its rare occurrences it has the sense of "take into account": "but if you take into account that they are slandering you" (*ean de aphidēs hoti diaballousi se*, P.Fouad 54, 29, from the second century; P.Oxy. 1682, 14 from the fourth century); "considering the absolute necessity of this task (= in taking into consideration, *aphorōn to aparaitēton tēs chreias*), bring your zeal to bear . . ." (P.Panop.Beatty 2, 46; third century). Such is the point of the exhortation in Heb 12:2—believers, in meditating on the passion of Jesus, find the model for their own conduct, the source of their *hypomonē* (endurance). They have only to follow the *archēgos*. The best parallel is Plutarch's: "Cato says that in critical circumstances, the senators would turn their eyes toward him (*aphoran . . . pros auton*), as the passengers on a ship turn toward the pilot" (*Cat. Mai.* 19.7).

---

[11] Cf. ἀφίδω; Jonah 4:5—Jonah, sitting outside the city, waited to see what would happen; 4 Macc 17:23—the tyrant Antiochus had observed the courage and patience of the martyrs.

> βαθμός
>
> *bathmos*, **threshold, step, stage, rank**

Formed from *bainō*, "stand or lean on," the NT hapax *bathmos* is an architectural technical term meaning a (raised) threshold of a door or of a temple,[1] a stair step;[2] hence "degree" or "step," whether of the zodiac or a sundial,[3] of a genealogy (*P.Cair.Masp.* 169, 10, from the sixth century; Dio Chrysostom, 41.6), or of time: "Nature has produced stages of life, like steps, as it were, by which people ascend and descend" (Philo, *Etern. World* 58). Hence, in a metaphorical sense, *bathmos* refers to any step of progress toward a goal, levels of vice or of virtue,[4] a stage along the soul's journey.

Thus we may approach 1 Tim 3:13, where deacons "who serve well gain an excellent rank, *bathmon heautois kalon*," a sentence that is something of a *crux interpretum*. It can be understood as saying that deacons, after the fashion of candidates for the *episkopē* (3:1), will not have to be embarrassed at their duties, that they will serve without an inferiority complex;[5] but also that they are in a position to be promoted to a higher level. T. Nägeli,

---

[1] 1 Sam 5:5—"The priests of Dagon and all who enter the temple of Dagon do not step on the threshold of Dagon at Ashdod . . . but they jump over it"; Sir 6:36—"If you know an intelligent man, visit him at dawn. Let your foot be familiar with the threshold of his door." At Laodicea, Apollonia had steps built above the pavements (*IGLS* 1259, 7; cf. 4034: "had the pavement built with steps"; *RB* 1895, p. 76). At Cyzicus, it is the base on which a tower is built (C. Michel, *Recueil*, n. 596, 10); at Didyma, cf. *SEG*, vol. 4, 453, 14. Βαθμοί are bases of stone (*SB* 3919, 8; R. Martin, *Architecture grecque*, p. 207). Cf. the tax on thresholds (*P.Oxy.* 574; second century AD).

[2] Josephus, *War* 1.420: "a stairway of two hundred steps"; 5.195, 5.206: "fifteen steps leading from the women's wall to the great gate"; *Ant.* 8.140 (or ἀναβαθμός); cf. A. Orlandos, *Technique architecturale*, p. 62.

[3] 2 Kgs 20:9–11; Josephus, *Ant.* 10.29; Vettius Valens 31.2; O. Neugebauer, H. B. Hoesen, *Greek Horoscopes*, Philadelphia, 1959, p. 152, n. 12.

[4] Josephus, *War* 4.171: "levels of audacity"; *Corp. Herm.* 13.9: "This stage, my child, is the seat of justice." Cf. Athenaeus 1.1c: "surpassing himself . . . he jumps from level to level."

[5] Cf. P. Dornier, *Les Epîtres Pastorales*, Paris, 1969, p. 65.

---

bathmos, S 898; *EDNT* 1.189–190; MM 101; L&N 87.3; BDF §34(5); BAGD 130

(*Wortschatz*, p. 26) cites an inscription from Mitylene: "kept up to the degrees (*basmoi*) of his rank" (*tois tas axias basmois anelogēse, IG*, vol. 2, 243, 16); P. N. Harrison cites the *Sententiae* of Hadrian, where the emperor asks a soldier who wants to join the praetorian guard first of all to prove himself "in political service, and if you become a good soldier, you will be able to pass on to the praetorium as a third *bathmos*."[6] In any event, the term is used in honorific designations, as seen in the formula used in inscriptions at Sardis and at Side: "*ho lamprotatos komes prōtou bathmou*, vir clarissimus, comes primi ordinis."[7]

The best context is probably Qumran, where the stages of approach to the various offices and the rules determining precedence and hierarchical order (*sereq*) are so detailed: "the priests shall go first, in order according to their spirit, one after the other. The Levites shall go behind them, and all the people third, in order."[8] "In accord with his intelligence and the perfection of his conduct, each one shall keep to his place to carry out the service with which he is charged with respect to a more or less extended group of his brothers. Thus shall be recognized in some *a higher dignity than in others.*"[9]

The diaconal *bathmos kalos* seems to derive from the Lord's teaching on the steward faithful in small things, who carries out a lower duty conscientiously and will also be faithful in higher functions. The Master will place him over his whole household and all his goods, and he will entrust to him the government of ten cities, the managing or dispensation of spiritual riches (Luke 7:44f.; 16:10ff.; 19:17). It is at least with this meaning that our text is understood when it is cited by the first Roman ordination ritual (Hippolytus, *Trad. ap.*) and by the ordination ritual of the patriarchate of Antioch (*Const. App.*).

---

[6] Ἐν τῇ πολιτικῇ στρατείᾳ, καὶ ἐὰν καλὸς στρατιώτης γένῃ, τρίτῳ βαθμῷ δυνήσῃ εἰς πραιτώριον μεταβῆναι. Cf. *SEG*, vol. 21, 505, 7; Eusebius, *Hist. Eccl.* 3.21; P.*Tebt*. 703, 276: "If your conduct is above reproach, you will be taken to be worthy of advancement" (third century BC).

[7] Cf. the texts cited by J. and L. Robert, "Bulletin épigraphique," in *REG*, 1968, p. 518, n. 478.

[8] 1QS 2.20; cf. 2.23: "his allotted place." "They shall be enrolled in order, one after the other, each one in proportion to his intelligence and his works, so that they may obey one another, the lower obeying the higher, . . . that each one may be advanced . . . or demoted" (5.23–24). The progression has to do not only with knowledge (9.18; 1QH 14.13) but also honor (cf. 1 Tim 5:17).

[9] 1QSa 1.17, 18; cf. 2.14–18 (ed. D. Barthélemy, J. T. Milik, *Qumran Cave I*, Oxford, 1955, p. 112). The parallel is pointed out by W. Nauck, "Probleme des frühchristlichen Amtsverständnisses," in *ZNW*, 1957, pp. 216ff.; but H. Braun is skeptical (*Qumran und das N. T.*, Tübingen, 1966, vol. 2, pp. 199, 336).

βαρύς

barys, **important, serious, burdensome, grave, dangerous**

The meaning of this adjective varies according to context and may be either favorable or pejorative.[1] Sometimes it means "worthy, important," like certain commandments of the law, as opposed to those which are "secondary";[2] or the letters of Paul, serious, powerful, impressive;[3] sometimes—most often, in fact—the connotations are negative, as with "heavy burdens," burdensome responsibilities, difficult undertakings,[4] even "grave accusations" (Acts 25:7).

---

[1] The noun βάρος denotes first of all weight (Philo, *Joseph* 140: unequal weights; *Heir* 146; *P.Oxy.* 3008, 12: "the weight is equal"), that which is heavy, like baggage (Judg 18:21; cf. Jdt 7:4; Xenophon, *Oec.* 17.9; *Cyr.* 3.3, 3.42); the adjective means "heavy, weighty"; cf. stone (Prov 27:3), the hands (Homer, *Il.* 1.89; Exod 17:12; Job 23:2; 33:7), an old man (1 Sam 4:18; Job 15:10), a burden carried by camels (Philo, *Post. Cain* 148).

[2] Matt 23:23, τὰ βαρύτερα (ἐντολὴ βαρεῖα-ἐλαφρά); cf. Str-B, vol. 1, pp. 900–905; J. Bonsirven, *Judaïsme palestinien*, pp. 73–80. In the LXX, βαρύς often means "considerable, numerous," describing a people or an army (Num 20:20; 1 Kgs 3:9; 2 Kgs 6:14; 18:17; 2 Chr 9:1; 1 Macc 1:17, 20, 29; 4 Macc 4:5; Ps 35:18; Nah 3:3); cf. Polybius 1.17.3; heavy infantry is distinguished from light infantry (ibid. 1.76.3); Xenophon, *Cyr.* 5.3.37.

[3] 2 Cor 10:10, αἱ ἐπιστολαὶ βαρεῖαι καὶ ἰσχυραί as opposed to his weak physical presence and his speech, which is ineffectual (cf. P. E. Hughes, *Paul's Second Epistle to the Corinthians*, 4th ed., Grand Rapids, 1973, pp. 361ff.); cf. nobility of character (Plutarch, *Cat.* 1.6; 20.2), consideration (*Ages.* 7.1). "Heavy words" can be serious (Job 6:3) or strong-voiced (Aristotle, *Rh.* 3.1.29; cf. 1 Sam 5:11; Philo, *Alleg. Interp.* 1.14; 3.51), or painful: ἐδεξάμην βαρέα ῥήματα (*P.Princ.* 120, 3; *SB* 9616, verso 31); cf. 6263, 26: ἀλλὰ μὴ βαρέως ἔχε μου τὰ γράμματα νουθετοῦντα σε.

[4] Exod 18:12—"The thing is too heavy for you, you cannot do it alone"; Neh 5:18—"the task weighed heavy on this people" (cf. *SB* 6263, 20); Sir 31:2, a grave illness (cf. *P.Tebt.* 52, 11; Philo, *Creation* 125; Diodorus Siculus 17.31.4). In the papyri,

---

barys, S 926; *TDNT* 1.556–558; *EDNT* 1.199; *NIDNTT* 1.260–262; MM 104; L&N 22.4, 65.56, 78.23; BAGD 133

It is in this sense that the scribes and the Pharisees place heavy burdens on people's shoulders (Matt 23:4, *phortia barea*), burdens that are crushing and literally unbearable,[5] after the fashion of sins that weigh on the conscience more than a heavy burden (*hōsei phortion bary ebarynthēsan ep' eme*, Ps 38:4), or of a tax collector who oppresses the taxpayers (*P.Mich.* 529, 28, 35–36; *P.Ant.* 100, 11, *enochlein hymin eti peri toutou moi bary*), or of the "unjust" person who carries very heavy burdens, *pherousa barytata* (Philo, *Husbandry* 20). This constraint is so linked to the person that at times it becomes one with him, as in the case of this man of the second-third century who "wears the yoke of Judaism" (*houtos pherōn Ioudaïkon phortion*, *C.Pap.Jud.* 519, 18; cf. *t. Ber.* 2.7).

Jesus stated that his yoke is easy and his burden light (Matt 11:30), and 1 John 5:3 repeats: "his commands are not *bareiai* (*hai entolai autou bareiai ouk eisin*)."[6] This can be understood as meaning that his precepts are not crushing or oppressive,[7] or that they are not difficult to carry out.[8] The best commentary is Philo's: "God doesn't ask anything burdensome, complicated, or difficult, but something that is simple and easy: to love him as

---

βαρύς describes notably onerous public service (*BGU* 159, 3; *P.Oxy.* 2110, 9, 18, 33, 36; cf. *P.Mich.* 529, 18, λειτουργίας βάρος; *PSI* 1103, 6; 1243, 20; *BGU* 159, 5), urgent necessities (*P.Oxy.* 2131, 12), or the condition of a pregnant woman who miscarries because of blows that she has received, τὴν μὲν Τάησιν βαρέαν οὖσαν ἐκ τῶν πληγῶν αὐτῶν ἐξέτρωσεν τὸ βρέφος (*P.Cair.Goodsp.* 15, 15). Τὸ βάρος, "the burden," commonly describes the child carried in its mother's womb, *P.Brem.* 63, 4 = *C.Pap.Jud.* 442; *SEG*, vol. 8, 802: "she bore the fruit of her womb, and put down her burden in pain"; vol. 15, 876, 1: ἔσχατον ὠδίνων βάρος = the final burden of pains (of childbirth); cf. Philo, *Unchang. God* 15; but also "the burden of the day and of the heat" (Matt 20:12), and all that weighs one down (Gal 6:2; *P.Oxy.* 1062, 14; 2596, 10; *PSI* 27, 7); cf. burden of care (Philo, *Moses* 1.14; *Migr. Abr.* 14).

[5] Cf. Polybius 1.10.6: "They feared that there were troublesome and fearsome neighbors, λίαν βαρεῖς καὶ φορεβοί"; *Anth. Pal.* 11.326: "Do not try to make yourself unbearable, μὴ πάντα βαρὺς θέλε"; Plutarch, *De frat. amor.* 16: older brothers can make themselves unbearable and disagreeable to their juniors, βαρεῖς καὶ ἀηδεῖς.

[6] Cf. G. Lambert, " 'Mon joug est aisé et mon fardeau léger,' " in *NRT*, 1955, pp. 963–969; N. Lazure, *Les Valeurs morales de la théologie johannique*, Paris, 1965, pp. 134ff.; H. D. Betz, "The Logion of the Easy Yoke and of Rest (Mt. XI, 28–30)," in *JBL*, 1967, pp. 10–24.

[7] Sir 40:1—"A heavy yoke was created for the sons of Adam"; cf. 17:21—"a heavy night"; 13:2—βάρος ὑπὲρ σὲ μὴ ἄρῃς; 2 Macc 9:10—"the unbearable weight of his odor"; an epitaph from Doris, from the imperial period: "Death is not equally heavy for all, but the one who is good receives also at the end an easy death" (*SB* 8307, 6): in the sixth century, ὡς βαρυτέρου ὄντος τοῦ ζυγίου (9400, 5).

[8] Dan 2:11—"The thing that the king asks is difficult" (*yaqqîrâh*); Sir 29:28—a hard-to-take insult; Judg 20:34—"the battle was tough"; Philo, *Husbandry* 120, athletes knock to the ground "difficult and heavy adversaries."

benefactor, or at least fear him as master and lord."[9] It seems that this is a traditional description of laws or commands: "the precepts are neither excessive nor too burdensome (*ou hyperonkoi kai baryterai*) for the abilities of those who conform to them" (Philo, *Rewards* 80). More precisely, it is the ideal voiced by Israelite and pagan rulers, but too often contradicted by actual deeds. The assembly of Israel at Shechem stated to Rehoboam: "Your father made our yoke heavy (*ebarynen*); but now you should lighten the harsh servitude of your father and the heavy yoke that he placed on us."[10] The Gadarenes denounced Herod, whose orders were too severe and tyrannical.[11] Pharaoh published ordinances that made demands beyond the abilities of the Jews (Philo, *Moses* 1.37), just as Tarquin had "become hateful and unbearable to the people."[12] But Vespasian forbids burdening the provinces (*IGLS*, 1998, 12, *barynesthai*), and Tiberius Julius Alexander refuses to "weigh down Egypt with new and unjust burdens" (*SB* 8444, 5, *barynomenēn kainais kai adikois eispraxesi*). If the "weight of business" rests on rulers,[13] they acquit themselves honorably when they do not impose overly heavy burdens on their subjects (Acts 15:28; 1 Thess 2:7; Rev 2:24).

When St. Paul preaches to the Ephesian elders, "Grievous wolves (*lykoi bareis*, literally heavy wolves) will enter in among you and will not spare the flock,"[14] he depicts the heretic as a fierce and ravenous animal,[15] a type of the tyrants who exploit the people in Ezek 22:27; Wis 3:3; Prov 28:15 (bear in the Hebrew). Jesus had called them *lykoi harpages* (Matt 7:15; cf. John 10:12) that ravage the flock; the same modifier is used of the wolves

---

[9] Philo, *Spec. Laws* 1.299, οὐδὲν βαρὺ καὶ ποικίλον ἢ δύσεργον, ἀλλὰ ἁπλοῦν καὶ ῥᾴδιον.

[10] 1 Kgs 12:4, 11 (and the whole pericope, 12:1–14, retold in 2 Chr 10:1–14 and Josephus, *Ant.* 8.213); cf. Num 11:14—"I cannot carry this whole people by myself, because they are too heavy a burden for me" (*kabēd*); Josephus, *Ant.* 19.362: a kingdom is a heavy responsibility, εἶναι βαρὺ βάσταγμα βασιλείαν.

[11] Josephus, *Ant.* 15.354, βαρὺν αὐτὸν ἐν τοῖς ἐπιτάγμασι καὶ τυραννικὸν εἶναι.

[12] Plutarch, *Publ.* 1.3: μισῶν καὶ βαρυνόμενος; cf. 2.4. Βαρύς modifies tyranny, "an unbearable burden of excessive constraint" (Philo, *Moses* 1.39; cf. *Conf. Tongues* 92: iron discipline), but also anything that one may suffer (Gen 48:17; Wis 2:15).

[13] Philo, *Plant.* 45: "the heavy burden of the cares of government"; Josephus, *War* 1.461: τὸ βάρος τῶν πραγμάτων; 4.616: τὸ βάρος τῆς ἡγεμονίας; Plutarch, *Per.* 37.1; cf. *UPZ* 110, 176; *P.Ryl.* 659, 4: Let each one stand up under his own burden, ἕκαστον ὑπαντᾶν πρὸς τὰ ἴδια βάρη.

[14] Acts 20:29; cf. G. W. H. Lampe, " 'Grievous Wolves' (Act. XX, 29)," in B. Lindars, S. S. Smalley, *Christ and Spirit in the New Testament* (in honor of C. F. D. Moule), Cambridge, 1973, pp. 253–268; J. Dupont, *Discours de Milet*, p. 209ff.

[15] Cf. Homer, *Il.* 16.352–355: the Achaean chiefs are like wolves that ravage the flocks.

in Gen 49:27, Ezek 22:27, corresponding to the Hebrew *ṭārap*, "tear to pieces": Benjamin is a wolf who tears up his prey, but no parallel is known to the "heavy wolf," which evokes the ideas of violence and of irritation,[16] and which could just as well be translated "dangerous, formidable, voracious, ferocious, rapacious, or cruel."

---

[16] J. Pollux, *Onom.* 5.164, defines ὁ δὲ βίαιος · καλοῖτ' ἂν βαρὺς, ἀλαζών, φορτικός; cf. 3 Macc 5:1, ὀργὴ βαρεῖα; Philo, *Giants* 51, "the violent storm"; Philo, *Moses* 1.119: "pelted by the weight of the hailstones"; Aristophanes, *Ran.* 1394: death, the cruelest of evils, βαρύτατον κακόν; Plutarch, *De cupid. divit.* 5: "an oppressive and cruel mistress of the house"; *De sera* 12: "burdensome old age"; *Demetr.* 10.2: "made unbearable and hateful by the extravagance of the honors that the Athenians voted him"; 28.4: Antigone "hard by nature and scornful"; 19.4: "the heaviness of the body"; *Ant.* 2.5: "heavy debt"; *SEG* 18, 194: "a heavy chain," which is contrasted with freedom; Apollonius Rhodius, *Argon.* 1.272: "a painful life"; 2.1008: "a hard task," etc.

βασιλεία, βασίλειος, βασιλεύς, βασιλεύω, βασιλικός, βασίλισσα

basileia, kingdom, reign; *basileios*, royal; *basileus*, king; *basileuō*, to be king, rule, reign; *basilikos*, royal; *basilissa*, queen

In every language, a "king" is a head of state, a sovereign, a monarch; by extension, a head or representative of a group, one who reigns or presides at an event. A "kingdom" is the land or state governed by a king, and by extension a collective or persons or things ruled by a common principle (cf. the animal kingdom, the plant kingdom). "Reign" is the exercise of royal power, domination, either absolute personal power or dominating influence.

From Homer on, the ideal king fears the gods and lives justly (Homer, *Od.* 19.109); his power and honor come from Zeus,[1] who is kindly disposed toward him (*Il.* 2.196; cf. Hesiod, *Th.* 80–101; 886; Dittenberger, *Syl.* 1014, 110: *Dios basileōs*). In the classical period, Aristotle distinguishes five types of government (*archē*, *Pol.* 3.14.1284^{b}35ff.): (1) Spartan monarchy, law-based (Plato, *Leg.* 3.691 d–692 b) but not entirely sovereign (*ouk esti de kyria pantōn*). (2) Barbarian monarchy, especially in Asia Minor, is law-based and

---

[1] The king is called "offspring of Zeus" (διογενής), *Il.* 1.279; 2.196, 205; 9.98–99. Cf. W. Westrup, "Le Roi de l'Odyssée," in *Mélanges Fournier*, Paris, 1929, pp. 767–786; E. Janssens, "Royauté mycénienne et olympienne," in *Le Pouvoir et le sacré*, Brussels, 1962, pp. 87–102. Cf. E. Peruzzi, "L'Origine minoenne du mot βασιλεύς," in *Onomastica*, 1948, pp. 48–74; *Actes du Colloque international sur l'Idéologie monarchique dans l'Antiquité: Cracovie-Mogilany, du 23 au 26 octobre 1967*, Warsaw-Krakow, 1980.

---

basileia, S 932; *TDNT* 1.564–593; *EDNT* 1.201–205; *NIDNTT* 2.372–382, 386–388; MM 104; L&N 1.82, 11.13, 37.64, 37.65, 37.105; BDF §163; BAGD 134–135 ‖ *basileios*, S 934; *TDNT* 1.564–593; *EDNT* 1.205; *NIDNTT* 2.372–373; MM 104; L&N 37.69; BDF §50; BAGD 136 ‖ *basileus*, S 935; *TDNT* 1.564–593; *EDNT* 1.205–208; *NIDNTT* 1.372–373, 377–378, 389; MM 104–105; L&N 37.67; BDF §§46(2), 146(3), 147(3); BAGD 136 ‖ *basileuō*, S 936; *TDNT* 1.564–593; *EDNT* 1.207–208; *NIDNTT* 2.372–373, 377–378, 380–381; MM 105; L&N 37.22, 37.64; BDF §§177, 234(5), 309(1); BAGD 136 ‖ *basilikos*, S 937; *TDNT* 1.564–593; *EDNT* 1.208; *NIDNTT* 3.372–373; MM 105; L&N 37.69; BAGD 136 ‖ *basilissa*, S 938; *TDNT* 1.564–593; *EDNT* 1.208; *NIDNTT* 2.372–373, 381; MM 105; L&N 37.68; BDF §§34(1), 111(1); BAGD 137

βασιλεία, *basileia*, etc.

hereditary, and thus stable, but despotic and quite close to tyranny, because it favors the sovereign and does not have the consent of the subjects, as with Hieron of Syracuse (Pindar, *Ol.* 1.23; *Pyth.* 3.70, 85); it is a perversion of monarchy (Aristotle, *Eth. Nic.* 8.12.1160^{b}3). (3) Elective tyrrany, as it existed among the ancient Greeks, was called *aisymnēteia*; *aisymnētai* were lawmakers chosen (for a given term or for life) to put an end to civil discord and given extensive powers; such was Pittacus, one of the Seven Sages (Plato, *Hp. Ma.* 281 c; *Prt.* 343 a; *Resp.* 1.335 e; *P.Oxy.* 2506, frag 77). (4) The monarchy of the heroic age, the period of Heracles and Priam, was based on general consent and heredity but regulated by law. The founders of the dynasty were benefactors of the people;[2] their descendants inherited their power, led military operations, judged lawsuits, and presided over sacrifices that were not reserved for the priests. (5) Finally, there was absolute monarchy, under which "one person has authority over everything," as in the domestic government, which is a kind of household monarchy (cf. *Rh.* 1.8.1365^{b}37ff.). But it is more advantageous to be governed by the best laws than by the best person (cf. democracy).

During the Hellenistic period, Xenophon mentions the identification of the good shepherd and the good king (*Cyr.* 8.2.14), which is emphasized by Philo[3] and many others. They are only repeating the image of the shepherd-king from the Code of Hammurabi[4] and the designation of the sovereign as shepherd in Akkadian (*ré'u*) and in Sumerian (*sipa*), a royal and divine title

---

[2] Cf. J. Bielawsky, M. Plezia, *Lettre d'Aristote à Alexandre sur la politique envers les cités*, Wroclaw, 1970, pp. 67–70; R. Monier, G. Cardascia, J. Imbert, *Histoire des institutions et des faits sociaux*, Paris, 1955; J. Gaudemet, *Institutions de l'antiquité*, Paris, 1967.

[3] *Joseph* 2: "The one who has learned the shepherd's art well can be an excellent king, because he has been trained to guide the noblest flock of living beings, namely humans, on a subject matter worthy of less zeal"; *Moses* 1.60–61: "Moses, after he was married, led flocks out to pasture, thus also carrying out an apprenticeship in government, because the care of flocks is a preparatory execise for the monarchy.... So kings are called 'shepherds of flocks' ... a sublime honor"; *Husbandry* 41–48; *Sacr. Abel and Cain* 49–51; *To Gaius* 44: Caligula "like a shepherd has charge of a flock." Cf. A. Dupont-Sommer, "Le Psaume 151," in *Sem*, vol. 14, 1961, pp. 45ff. P. Bogaert, *Apocalypse syr. de Baruch*, Paris, 1969, vol. 2, p. 153; O. Betz, "Die Frage nach dem messianischen Bewußtsein Jesu," in *NovT*, 1963, p. 39, n. 1; W. Tooley, "The Shepherd and Sheep Image in the Teaching of Jesus," ibid., 1964, pp. 15–25; L. Sabourin, *Les Noms et les titres de Jésus*, Bruges-Paris, 1963, pp. 71ff.; A. J. Simonis, *Die Hirtenrede im Johannes-Evangelium*, Rome, 1967; F. Martin, "The Image of Shepherd in the Gospel of Saint Matthew," in *ScEs*, 1975, pp. 261–301; C. Spicq, *Agapè*, vol. 3, pp. 235ff. J. Dauvillier, *Les Temps apostoliques*, Paris, 1970, pp. 147ff. — God is "shepherd and king" (Philo, *Husbandry* 49–54; R. Le Déaut, *Nuit Pascale*, p. 100, n. 84).

[4] Code of Hammurabi, col. 1.50–51; 24.42–43: "I am the shepherd who brings salvation ... I have held the peoples of Sumer and Akkad in my bosom"; 24.49–52.

in Egypt[5] and in the Mediterranean world.[6] Hence the abundant literature on the good king, beginning with the edicts of Asoka in third-century BC India ("king, friend of the gods, with a friendly look"),[7] the Stoics Zeno, Cleanthes, Sphaerus, and Perseus, who wrote treatises *Peri basileias*,[8] and also Diotogenes, Ecphantus, and Sthenidas, whose fragments are preserved in the *Florilegium* of Stobaeus.[9] Two main themes are expounded: monarchy is an institution of divine law, and the king is an image of God's rule over the world. The king conforms to God, and the subjects imitate the king.

The papyri and the inscriptions exalt the title of *basileus* adopted around 334 by Alexander the Great (*I.Priene* I, 1) and preserved in the Antiochian and Egyptian monarchies. Antiochus I of Commagene was called "great king Antiochus the just god" (*basileos megas Antiochos theos dikaios*, IGLS I, 1–2) and even "king of kings" (*basileus basileōn* III, 12–13; cf. A. Deissmann, *Light*, pp. 356, 363ff.). Not only is a king called "great" (*P.Oxy.* 2554, col. I, 13: *ho basileus megas*) but also "very great" (*P.Fouad* 16,

---

[5] M. J. Seux, *Epithètes royales akkadiennes et sumériennes*, Paris, 1967, pp. 244ff., 441ff. D. Müller, "Der Gute Hirte," in *Zeitschrift für ägyptische Sprache und Altertumskunde*, 1961, pp. 126ff.

[6] βασιλεύς (J.-L. Perpillou, *Les Substantifs grecs en* -εύς, Paris, 1973, n. 3.15.49). According to Apollonius Rhodius, *Argon.* 3.1089, "Deucalion was the first to be king over men," but cf. Plutarch, *Dem.* 10.3: "The Athenians were the first of all men to confer on Demetrius and Antigonus the title of king, but they had scruples about accepting, because of all the royal titles that the descendants of Alexander and Philip seemed to possess, this was the only one that remained inaccessible and incapable of being passed on to others"; cf. 18.1–7; A. Aymard, "L'Usage du titre royal dans la Grèce classique et hellénistique," in *RHDFE*, 1949, pp. 579–590; C. Préaux, *Le Monde hellénistique*, Paris, 1978, pp. 181–294; the articles of R. Turcan, J. C. Richard, D. Fishwick, in *ANRW*, vol. 16, 2.

[7] *I.Asok.*

[8] The *Letter of Aristeas* draws inspiration from Stoic ideology (D. Mendels, " 'On Kingship' in the 'Temple Scroll' and the Ideological *Vorlage* of the Seven Banquets in the 'Letter of Aristeas to Philocrates,' " in *Aeg*, 1979, pp. 127–136); cf. Plutarch, *Ad princ. iner.*; Aelius Aristides, *Orat.* 9; Synesius, *De Regno*, an address by the bishop of Ptolemais to Emperor Arcadius (C. Lacombrade, *Le Discours sur la royauté de Synésios de Cyrène*, Paris, 1951). Cf. L. François, "Julien et Dion Chrysostome: Les Περὶ βασιλείας et le second panégyrique de Constance," in *REG*, 1915, pp. 467ff. V. Vademberg, "La Théorie monarchique de Dion Chrysostome," *REG*, 1927, pp. 142ff. E. Goodenough, "The Political Philosophy of Hellenistic Kingship," in *YCS*, vol. 1, 1928, pp. 65ff.

[9] *Flor.*, vol. 4, chapters 6–7, pp. 238–295. Cf. L. Delatte, *Les Traités de la royauté d'Ecphante, Diotogène et Sthénidas*, Paris, 1942. Demetrius of Alexandria (275–194 BC) wrote a work on the kings of Judah (cf. C. Müller, *Fragmenta Historicorum Graecorum*, vol. 3, 214, 224; B. Z. Wacholder, "Biblical Chronology in the Hellenistic World Chronicles," in *HTR*, 1968, pp. 451–481). Musonius states that kings must philosophize (frag. 8), i.e., in the language of the period, must be both virtuous and intelligent.

βασιλεία, basileia, etc.

10: *hyper tou megistou basileōs; BGU* 1816, 23), "eternal" (*PSI* 1314, 17), "most pious" (*P.Oxy.* 2267, 9), the "divinized";[10] oaths are sworn by him (*BGU* 1735-1740); furthermore, Zeus is venerated as *basileus*.[11] So the friendship of kings is a grounds for pride,[12] and those who seek justice resort to them (*P.Yale* 46, col. I, 19; *P.Mert.* 5, 4; *P.Sorb.* 13, 1). It is the king who hears suits (*P.Yale* 42, 30) and gives verdicts (*C.Ord.Ptol.* 21, 14). He commands, and his *prostagmata* are "edicts."[13] If he is enriched by the collection of taxes,[14] he is also a benefactor who gives generously.[15] In return, places of prayer, an altar, a front hall in a temple, etc. are dedicated to him.[16]

Basilissa is a title of the goddess Isis (E. Bernand, *Fayoum*, n. 167, 3; 169, 6), but it is the ordinary term for the wife of a reigning sovereign.[17]

---

[10] *BGU* 1764, 8: the *tychē* of the god and lord king; 1767, 1; 1768, 9; 1789; 1834, 7; 1845, 6; *P.Dura* 18, 1, 12, 13: an act of donation "under the reign of the king of kings Arsaces, the beneficent, the just, a manifest god and friend of the Greeks"; 19, 1; 20, 1; 22, 1–2; *P.Oxy.* 2478, 1: τοῦ θειοτάτου; *SB* 10697, 7: τοῦ θιοτάτου βασιλέως ἡμῶν; H. Engelmann, *I.Ephes.*, IV, 1333, 12. Chronology is a function of the royal reign (*P.Hib.* 198, 199, 201, 202, 205, 209, etc.; *P.Lond.* 1912, 59, 67; 1913, 4; 1914, 30; *P.Mil.* 29, 2, 8, 14). A. Aymard, "Le Protocole royal et son évolution," in *REA*, 1948, pp. 232–263.

[11] At Lebadaia; cf. *NCIG*, n. 22, A 30.

[12] Apollonius is "a benefactor who has been honored by the friendship of kings" (E. Bernand, *Inscriptions métriques*, n. VI, 25); "Diazelmis, honored by kings" (ibid. X, 15). Cf. "Alexander, king of Macedonia, begotten by Ammon" (LXXI, 27); "There is only one Caesar, one great emperor, only one master, only one sovereign (εἷς βασιλεύς)" (LXXI, 27); "Mandoulis, sovereign over all" (CLXVI, 18); "the lion, the king of the animals" (CXXX, 5).

[13] *P.Genova* 54, 6; *C.Ord.Ptol.* 1, 1; 2, 6; 5, 1; 6, 1; 8, 1; 11, 1; etc. *BGU* 1730, 1. King Antigonus entrusts to Epinicus the guard of the citadel of Rhamnus (J. Pouilloux, *Choix*, XIX, 5–6). The councillors of king Eumenes II of Pergamum send him a copy of the decree inscribed on the base of his statue (ibid. XI, 22). Taxes are paid to the king (*P.Mich.* 200, recto 27). Cf. C. B. Welles, *Royal Correspondence*.

[14] According to Diodorus Siculus 17.52, he received more than six thousand talents from Alexandria; cf. Appian, *Praef.* 10.

[15] *NCIG*, VII, col. I, 4, 9, 14. He gives tax exemptions (ibid. col. II, 2); he provides for defense against enemies (ibid. VI, 16, 17, 46); founds many institutions; grants *proxenia* (E. Bernand, *Philae*, n. 128, 17, etc.). An archon-king, assisted by four *epimelēteis*, supervises the celebration of the mysteries (Aristotle, *Ath. Pol.* 57.1). An eponymous official can be called *basileus* (Dittenberger, *Syl.* 57, 22; 1011, 13; 1037, 6; *I.Chalced.* 7, 1; 19, 2; L. Robert, *Hellenica*, vol. 2, Paris, 1946, pp. 51, 53, 63; vol. 8, pp. 76–77). At Miletus, a college of *basileis* worked with the treasurer to sell priesthoods (*NCIG*, VII, col. III, 16); at Chios, it protects the property around the sanctuary (Dittenberger, *Syl.* 986, 8).

[16] E. Bernand, *Fayoum*, n. 1, 2, 3, 4, 83, 84.

[17] *P.Berl.Zill.* I, 38, 57, 64; *BGU* 1730; 1735, 3; 1736, 3; 1738, 4; 1739, 3; *P.Tebt.* 43, 1; 78, 13; 86, 39; 106, 3; 124, 1; *P.Köln* 81, 3, 9, 12; *SB* 6668, 2; 7172, 32; 7783, 1; 7879, 3; *SEG* XXVII, 1206. *Basilissa* describes the sister of King Ptolemy II, hence a nonreigning member of the royal family (Dittenberger, *Or.* 35, 1; third century BC).

She is described as *kyria* (*SB* 7746, 33: *hyper tēs kyrias basilissēs;* 7944, 3), as a priestess (ibid. 8035 *a* 5–6: *hiereias basilissēs Kleopatras theas;* 10763, 3; *hierateuousēs basilissēs*), and as a goddess (*tē thea basilissē*, ibid. 6033, 2; 6156, 3; 6157, 1). Oaths are sworn by her as by the king (ibid. 6261, 13, *P.Sorb.* 32, 6; *P.Eleph.* 23, 10), and Antiochus III orders that worship be offered to "our sister, Queen Laodice."[18]

It is common practice for a document to be dated by the year of the reign of the sovereign or "under the reign of" (*C.Ord.Ptol.* 9, 1), usually with the present participle of the verb *basileuō*, for example: "the twentieth year of Ptolemy's reign."[19] But there is also the figurative statement that Nemesis became queen or began to reign over the world (*basileuousa tou kosmou*).[20]

Basileia is sometimes "kingdom,"[21] sometimes "reign," "government" ("having received from his father the rule over Egypt and Libya," *paralabōn para tou patros tēn basileian Aigyptou kai Libyēs, SB* 8545, A 6; cf. 6003, 14; 8232, 3; 8858, 6; *P.Oxy.* 2899, 3; 2903, 7), sometimes described as "very happy."[22] Βασιλεία (as our word is accented, with an acute on the penult) should not be confused with βασίλεια (accent on the antepenult).[23]

---

[18] L. Robert, *Hellenica*, vol. 7, Paris, 1949, pp. 7–29.

[19] *P.Sorb.* 14 *a* 1; 17 *a* 1; 21, 1, 10; 32, 1; *P.Köln* 50, 17; 51, 1; 81, 1; *P.Corn.* 2, 1; *P.Dura* 18, 1; 19, 1; 20, 1; 22, 1; 24, 1; *P.Mert.* 6, 3; *P.Mich.* 190, 1; *P.Oslo* 16, 1; *PSI* 1016, 16; 1018, 5; 1822, 9; 1824, 1; 1825, 9; *SB* 10859, 1; 11053, 1; 11054; *MAMA* VI, 154, 1; *CII*, n. 683, 1; 690, 2–3; 691, 1. Cf. *Stud.Pal.* V, 125, col. II, 3: ἐπὶ μὲν διατρίβοντός σου ἐπὶ τῆς βασιλευούσης Ῥώμης; *PSI* 965, 4 (cf. Rev 18:7).

[20] *IGUR*, n. 182. In this sense, an *agraphon* of an utterance of Jesus: "surprised, he will reign, and having gotten the royal power, he will rest" (θαμβηθεὶς βασιλεύσει καὶ βασιλεύσας ἀναπαήσεται, *P.Oxy.* 654, 8); this *logion* derives from *Gos. Thom.* 3: "He who seeks must not stop seeking until he finds; and when he finds, he will be bewildered; and if he is bewildered, he will marvel, and will be king over the All"; cf. R. Kasser, *L'Evangile selon Thomas*, Neuchâtel, 1961, pp. 29ff.

[21] "Let none of the subjects of the kingdom be subjected to annoyances contrary to the order" (*C.Ord.Ptol.* 45, 8; cf. 53, 3). Decree of Antiochus III: "Let high priests be appointed for us throughout the whole empire" (κατὰ βασιλείαν, J. Pouilloux, *Choix*, n. XXX, 21).

[22] *P.Panop.Beatty* 1, 132, 396; *P.Oxy.* 1257, 7; *SB* 7634, 31; 8699, 3. Beginning with the fifth century, *basileia* is usually used for chronological notes: βασιλείας τοῦ εὐσεβεστάτου ἡμῶν δεσπότου Φλαουίου Ἡρακλείου (*P.Alex.* 35, 2; 37, 2; *P.Mich.* 607, 1; *P.Warr.* 10, 2; *P.Ant.* 42, 1; *BGU* 1764, 5; *P.Athen.* 40, 3; *P.Berl.Zill.* 7, 1; *P.Erl.* 73, 4; 87, 2; *C.P.Herm.* 65, 2; *P.Princ.* 87, 3; *P.Stras.* 190, 2; 247, 1; 328, 2; 484, 3; *SB* 6271, 2; etc.). In the Rosetta Stone (Dittenberger, *Or.* 90, 43) the *basileiai* are crowns or ornaments: "let the lavatory be crowned with ten headdresses of the king's gold" (τὰς τοὺς βασιλέως χρυσᾶς βασιλείας δέκα, cf. Diodorus Siculus 1.48).

[23] At Lebadaia, εἰς τὰ βασίλεια refers to a Boeotian athletic meet: "the report of the *taxiarchoi* sent to the βασίλεια concerning the sacrifice that they offered"

The adjective basileios, "royal" (Wis 5:16), is rather rare,[24] basilikos on the other hand is extremely common, used especially with reference to the land belonging to the Lagids (basilikē gē),[25] leased out to renters (P.Rev., col. 26, 13; 33, 9–18), cultivated by royal farmers (basilikos geōrgos);[26] hence the "royal grain" (P.Sorb. 17 a 7, b 8) and the royal linens (P.Rein. 120, 3; 121, 3); othonia were a royal monopoly.[27] Everything pertaining to the sovereign was modified by this adjective,[28] notably the royal clerk or scribe (basilikos grammateus), who collaborated with the stratēgos and was an important official in the financial administration;[29] the royal law (nomos basilikos, Jas 2:8), enacted by the sovereign;[30] the oath by the king (basilikos horkos, P.Ryl. 572, 55; 585, 43; P.Lond. 2188, 145; C.Ord.Ptol. 21, 23); the royal treasury (to basilikon, P.Yale 57, 13; P.Lille 14, 6–7; C.Ord. Ptol. 71, 10), made up of the revenues of the royal domains and taxes; or the royal stores, a grain warehouse (P.Cair.Zen. 59015); the royal bank or banker (trapeza, trapezitēs basilikē) that receives all the money due the

---

(NCIG, n. II, 10), a feast in honor of Zeus Basileus in memory of the victory of Leuctra in 371 (cf. M. Holleaux, Etudes d'épigraphie, vol. 1, pp. 131–142); n. XXII a 20: "Xenarchus . . . agōnothetēs of the basileia"; c 47: "the judges of admission to the basileia"; cf. SEG XXVII, 1114. But Isis is "queen of the gods" (E. Bernand, Fayoum, n. 175, col. I, 1; II, 12).

[24] SB 8246, 48; 8299, 45; 10453, 3: βασιλείῳ διοικητῇ; it refers to a type of fig in P.Fouad 77, 17 and a royal residence at Philadelphia (P.Lond. 1974, 9: ἐν τοῖς βασιλείοις; cf. P.Cair.Zen. 59664, 1–2: καινὰ βασιλεῖα), the palace of the satrap Saitaphernes (Dittenberger, Syl. 495, 45), the scepter (P.Lond. 46, 448; vol. 1, p. 79).

[25] CIG III, 4860; P.Athen. 44, 5; P.Berl.Zill. 1, 37; 2, 20; P.Brem. 36, 6; P.Yale 53, 9; P.Köln 137, 33; P.Mich. 555, 6, 8, 13; 557, 7; 564, 9; P.Mert. 5, 22, 25, 27; 11, 7; P.Aberd. 49, 4; 50, 5; P.Got. 2, 5; P.Phil. 1, 38; 15, 9; P.Oxy. 2410, 10; 3205, 13; P.Lond. 2188, 209, 335; P.NYU 20, 9, 10, 16; 21, 19; SB 10880, 7; 10881, 8; 10891, col. I, 13, etc. Cf. C. Préaux, Economie royale, p. 68.

[26] P.Yale 53, 4; P.Tebt. 786, 3–4; 788, 21 (C. Préaux, Economie royale, pp. 438, 553). Cf. γεωργία βασιλική, P.Oxy. 2134, 23; 2722, 32; Pap.Lugd.Bat. XVI, 9, 25; SB 11233, 44.

[27] Cf. βασιλικὸς ἔλαιον, Papyrus 23, 28 (in Notices et extraits des manuscrits de la Bibliothèque impériale, Paris, 1865, XVIII, p. 269); C. Préaux, Economie royale, p. 76. Royal lodgings (C.Ord.Ptol. 1, 4), royal public sales (22, 15), "sacred and royal affairs" (SEG I, 363, 33); arrangements (βασιλικαὶ διατάξεις, SB 10797, 4).

[28] Cf. a royal favor, κατὰ χάριν βασιλικήν (IGUR, n. 240, 14).

[29] P.Laur. 66, 2; 63, 1; P.Köln 86, 2; 94, 15; BGU 1626, 8; P.Oxy. 1219, 15; 2409, 6; P.Mich. 526, 1; P.Bon. 12 g verso 2; P.Brem. 2, 9; 28, 23; 41, 26; P.Phil. 6, 1; 8, 3; P.Sorb. 43, 2; P.Mur. 117, 11; Pap.Lugd.Bat. XVI, 18, 2; 36, 2; P.Oxy. 5 a 12. A. Bernand, Philae, n. 19, 24; cf. P.Vindob.Worp, p. 19.

[30] A. Deissmann (Light, p. 362, n. 5) cites a law from Pergamum on the astynomia: τὸν βασιλικὸν νόμον ἐκ τῶν ἰδίων ἀνέθηκεν.

treasury.[31] Finally, there is the praise implied in the designation of a person as *basilikōtatos*.[32]

The OT uses *melek* for king. The primitive meaning of this root is "to deliberate," then "to decide":[33] the king is the one who governs, who wields supreme power. The first mention of a king is religious: "Yahweh is King." After the crossing of the Red Sea, Moses and the Israelites sing a victory chant: "He is King, Lord forever and ever."[34] This is not a reference to some monarchical government, but rather to the exercise of absolute power[35] to protect and guide the chosen people (Mic 2:13; Ps 74:12); thus Yahweh is King of Israel.[36] Gideon proclaimed "It is the Lord that should be your sovereign" (Judg 8:23), meaning that Israel is the domain or kingdom over which God reigns and in the midst of which he resides (Ps 59:14), Zion being the "city of the great King" (Ps 48:3). As the object of the psalmists' faith, adoration, and supplication, God is called "my King and my God" (Ps 5:2; 44:5; 68:25; 84:4; 145:1), "my Lord, our King" (Add Esth 14:3). The transcendence of this royalty is elaborated over the centuries. Yahweh is

---

[31] *P.Giss.*, col. III, 18; Dittenberger, *Syl.* 577, 17 (C. Préaux, *Economie royale*, pp. 280ff.; R. Bogaert, *Banques et banquiers*, pp. 39, 89–90); cf. the "Royal Street" (ῥύμη βασιλική, *P.Lond.* 2191, 44).

[32] *IGUR*, n. 166, 4. Cf. E. Bernard, *Fayoum*, n. 71, 17: βασιλικὴν τιμήν, "royal dignity."

[33] M. J. Lagrange, "Le Règne de Dieu dans l'Ancien Testament," in *RB*, 1908, pp. 36–51; P. Haupt, "The Hebrew Word *melek*: Counsel," in *JBL*, 1915, pp. 54ff. J. Bonsirven, *Le Règne de Dieu*, Paris, 1957, pp. 11ff. R. Schnackenburg, *God's Rule*; J. Coppens, "Règne de Dieu: Ancien Testament," in *DBSup*, vol. 10, col. 1–58. J. Carmignac, *Le Mirage de l'eschatologie*, Paris, 1979, pp. 13ff. (gives the bibliography). *Malkût* is the reign, *mamlākāh* the kingdom, *mᵉlûkāh* the monarchy but also the kingdom and sometimes the reign. Likewise, the Greek βασιλεία sometimes means royalty (the dignity of the king; cf. Josephus, *War* 1.19, 74), sometimes the exercise of royal power (reign; cf. *War* 1.70, 72), and even the land or people over whom the king's authority is exercised, i.e., the kingdom. See also E. Lipiński, *La Royauté de Yahwé dans la poésie et le culte de l'ancien Israël*, Brussels, 1965.

[34] Exod 15:18; cf. Ps 22:23; 99:1, 4; Mal 1:14—"I am a great king, says Yahweh of Hosts." The bibliography is immense; apart from the works already cited, see especially O. Eissfeldt, *Jahwe als König*, in *ZAW*, 1928, pp. 81–105; H. J. Kraus, *Die Königsherrschaft Gottes im A. T.*, Tübingen, 1951; E. Lipiński, "Yahweh mâlak," in *Bib*, 1963, pp. 405–460; idem, *La Royauté de Yahwé*, Brussels, 1965; G. von Rad, *OT Theology*, pp. 291ff. F. Beisser, *Das Reich Gottes*, Göttingen, 1976; B. D. Chilton, "Regnum Dei Deus Est," in *SJT*, 1978, pp. 261–270; J. Gray, *The Biblical Doctrine of the Reign of God*, Edinburgh, 1979.

[35] Num 23:21; Deut 33:5. Cf. P. Biard, *La Puissance de Dieu*, Paris, 1960; C. H. Powell, *The Biblical Concept of Power*, London, 1963.

[36] Isa 24:23; 33:22; 41:21; 43:15; 44:6; Zech 14:9, 16; Ps 149:2; cf. "your God reigns" (Isa 52:7; Obad 21).

βασιλεία, basileia, etc.

an *eternal* king, "for ever and ever,"[37] whose universal reign will have no end (Ps 66:7; 102:13; Dan 6:27). God is also called King of heaven[38] and of ages (Deut 9:26, LXX; Tob 13:7; 14:15). He is clothed in majesty (Ps 93:1), the King of glory (Ps 24:7, 10; 1 Chr 29:11), sitting enthroned amid a court (Ps 29:10; 93:2; 103:19); so he alone is king (2 Macc 1:24–25), King of kings (Dan 4:34), above all the gods (Ps 95:3–4) and king of the nations, which he rules (Jer 10:7; Ps 22:29; Pss 96—98). He directs the history of the world (Ps 33:13) because "all things are in his power" (Add Esth 13:9, 15; Ps 48:3ff.). As Lord of heaven and earth, he is "King of all things" (Tob 10:13, א). In his special role as King of the chosen people, whom he rewards for their faithfulness, Yahweh has an eschatological kingdom: "The Lord will reign over them forever and ever" (Wis 3:8); "the King of the world will resurrect us to a new life."[39] We can see how the proclamation of this reign would cause the earth to rejoice (Ps 97:1) and how Rabbi Yochanan said "any blessing that is not contained in the kingdom is no real blessing" (*b. Ber.* 12a).

As for human royalty in Israel, certain texts that present it as the product of agitation by the people are unfavorable toward it (1 Sam 8:1–22; 10:18–25; 12:15); but others that attribute the initiative to God are favorable.[40] In any event, this monarchy has a religious character.[41] First of all, the king is enthroned in the sanctuary, where he is anointed (Ps 89:21, 39, 40); this anointing is the essential rite of coronation.[42] Next, at the royal

---

[37] Exod 15:18; Isa 41:21; Ps 10:16; 29:10; 145:12–13; 146:10; 2 Kgs 19:15; 2 Chr 20:6; Add Esth 14:12; Jer 10:10; Wis 3:7; Dan 2:44; 7:14; 2 Macc 3:24; 7:9; 12:15.

[38] Dan 4:34; Tob 1:18 (א); 13:6, 11; Isa 6:5—"my eyes have seen the King, Yahweh of Hosts"; 44:6; 52:7.

[39] 2 Macc 7:9; Prov 9:6 (LXX). Cf. J. Coppens, *La Relève apocalyptique du Messianisme royal: I. La Royauté, le Règne, le Royaume de Dieu cadre de la relève apocalyptique*, Louvain, 1979; J. Gray, *The Biblical Doctrine of the Reign of God*, pp. 182ff., 225ff.

[40] 1 Sam 9:1–10:16; 11:1–11, 15; 13:14. (R. de Vaux, *Ancient Israel*, vol. 1, pp. 94ff. P. Gibert, *La Bible à la naissance de l'histoire: Au temps de Saül, David et Salomon*, Paris, 1979). If Nathan's prophecy gives sacral legitimacy to the throne of David (H. van den Bussche, "Le Texte de la prophétie de Nathan sur la dynastie davadique," in *ETL*, 1948, pp. 354–394), the institution of the monarchy was still in an embryonic stage in Saul's time (*melek*, 1 Sam 11:15); Saul was hardly more than the chief of a clan, having no defined territory, although he had a "king's rights" (1 Sam 8:11–17; his rights were put in writing, 10:25).

[41] J. de Fraine, *L'Aspect religieux de la Royauté israélite*, Rome, 1954; E. Jacob, *Theology of the Old Testament*, trans. A. W. Heathcote and P. J. Allcock, New York, 1958, pp. 234–239; G. von Rad, *OT Theology*, vol. 1, pp. 38ff. Cf. R. Labat, *Le Caractère religieux de la Royauté assyro-babylonienne*, Paris, 1939. N. D. Mettinger, *The Civil and Sacral Legitimation of the Israelite Kings*, Lund, 1976.

[42] Once anointed, the king is called "son of God" (2 Sam 7:14; Ps 2:7), adopted by Yahweh (cf. G. von Rad, *OT Theology*, vol. 1, pp. 320ff., vol. 2, pp. 169ff., 312ff.). This

palace, where he is given the kingly insignia, he is acclaimed and the ranking officials pay him homage. From there the messengers depart, the "evangelists of joy"[43] who carry the news of the investiture into the countryside, where "the earth resounds with their shouts" (1 Kgs 1:40). The Israelite king is essentially a proxy and representative of God, chosen by God to be his people's leader and his own earthly assistant, the mediator of his gifts (2 Sam 16:18; 2 Chr 13:8). Obviously, the king must remain dependent on and obedient to God, not becoming puffed up with pride over his brothers (Deut 17:20). He carries out justice (Jer 22:16). He needs his subjects' prayers (Ps 72:15), but he puts all his trust in Yahweh, who grants him his favor (Ps 21:8).

The NT mentions "the kings of the earth" (*hoi basileis tēs gēs*)[44] and "kings of the nations" (*hoi basileis tōn ethnōn*, Luke 22:25), who hold sway over their peoples and govern them.[45] It is commanded to honor them (1 Pet 2:17), to obey them as sovereigns (2:13), and to pray for them and for all who hold authority,[46] for this authority is from God (John 19:11; Rom

---

unction establishes a special relationship between the king and God, a participation of the king in the holiness of the one whose Spirit he has received (1 Sam 10:10); thus the king becomes inviolable (1 Sam 24:7, 11; 26:9, 11, 16, 23; 2 Sam 1:14–16; 19:22). So it could be said that this unction, which confers a grace, is a sacrament that establishes the king of Israel as God's vassal (R. de Vaux, "Le Roi d'Israël, vassal de Iahvé," in *Mélanges Tisserant*, vol. 1, pp. 119–133). The anointing becomes a characteristic of the messianic King (Jer 23:5; Ezek 37:25; Zech 9:9ff.), "Servant" of God par excellence, or Son of Man (Dan 7:13), causing the rights of Yahweh to triumph on earth, bringing peace through his reign (Isa 7:10–17; 11:1–8; 42:1–4; 49:1–6; 50:4–11; 52:13–53:12; Mic 5:1; Ps 72:12–14). To express the extent to which "Yahweh's anointing" is a source of life, Lam 4:20 calls it "the breath of our nostrils"!

[43] Isa 52:7; 40:9; Zech 9:9; cf. 2 Sam 15:10; 2 Kgs 9:13.

[44] Matt 17:25; Acts 4:26; 9:15; Rev 1:5; 6:15; 17:2; such as Pharaoh, king of Egypt (Acts 7:10) and Aretas (2 Cor 11:32); cf. Rev 16:14—"the kings of the whole world." The *basilissa* of Sheba or of the South (Matt 12:42; Luke 11:31), the Candace (= "queen") of Ethiopia (Acts 8:27). Babylon: "I am seated as queen" (Rev 18:7).

[45] Luke 22:25; Rev 17:12. As administrators (Matt 18:23; cf. R. Sugranyes de Franch, *Etudes sur le droit palestinien à l'époque évangélique*, Fribourg, 1946), kings execute justice (Matt 10:18; Mark 13:9; Luke 21:12), collect taxes (Matt 17:25), wage war (Luke 14:31), and live in luxury (Matt 11:8; 22:2, 7, 11, 13). The holy kings of Israel, like David (Matt 1:6; Acts 13:22), are linked with the prophets in their messianic hope (Luke 10:24).

[46] 1 Tim 2:1–2: "Let supplication be made . . . for kings." These *basileis* are all territorial rulers, whether of lands, towns, large cities, or kingdoms (cf. C. Spicq, *Epîtres Pastorales*, vol. 1, p. 359) and can include the emperor (inscriptions from Argos and Ephesus, cf. J. and L. Robert, "Bulletin épigraphique," in *REG*, 1951, n. 32, 65; 1952, n. 137; *GVI*, n. 514; L. Biehl, *Das liturgische Gebet für Kaiser und Reich*, Paderborn, 1937). Acts 8:27 uses Candace as a proper name for the *basilissē* of the Ethiopians, but it is actually a title of the Ethiopian sovereigns (*ka[n]take* or *ka[n]dakit*), like

βασιλεία, basileia, etc. 265

Rom 13:1). The only true God is acclaimed late as "King of the ages, incorruptible, invisible,"[47] and in a doxology as "the blessed God . . . King of those who reign and Lord of those who have sovereignty."[48] On the other hand, Jesus at his birth is described by the magi as "King of the Jews" (Matt 2:2; cf. 27:11), that is, as Messiah. Nathaniel confesses him as "King of Israel" (John 1:49). After the miracle of the multiplication of the loaves, the crowd wanted "to take him and make him king" (John 6:15), and he was acclaimed as such on the occasion of his messianic entry at Jerusalem: "Your king comes to you" (Matt 21:5; Luke 19:38; John 12:13 = Zech 9:9). In the course of his trial before Pilate, Christ, accused of being King of the Jews, admits "I am a king" (John 18:37), but he adds that his kingdom is not of this world.[49] In fact, he will appear as a glorious king at his Parousia (Matt 25:34), "Lord of lords and King of

---

Pharaoh in Egypt. This queen might be the same as the one who reigned at Meroë under Nero (Pliny, HN 6.186). In a lease from Olymos, there is a βασιλεὺς τοῦ κοινοῦ τῶν Καρῶν, king of the Carian confederation (L. Robert, Etudes anatoliennes, p. 571, n. 2); the city of Istros is under the protection of the basileus Rhemaxus (D. M. Pippidi, Scythica Minora, Budapest-Amsterdam, 1975, pp. 33, 124, 153, 169, 175, 197). Cf. the kings of Thrace (Dittenberger, Syl. 762, 22–25), Amyntas king of Lycaonia and Galatia (Plutarch, Ant. 61.1–2), Mithridates king of Pontus (REG, 1936, pp. 17–37; cf. Plutarch, Ant. 38.3), Pharnaces king of the Bosporus (CIRB, n. 28), Burebistas king of Dacia (Strabo 7.3.11; cf. 7.5.2), Voccio king of Norica (Caesar, BGall. 1.53.4; BCiv. 1.18.5), the Celtic kings Balanos and Catmelus (Livy 44.14.1; cf. 41.1.8; 43.5; cf. P. W. A. Immink, "Gouvernés et gouvernants dans la société germanique," in Gouvernés et gouvernants, Receuils J. Bodin, vol. 23, Brussels, 1968, pp. 365ff.). J. Dobiaš, "King Marobodiius as a Politician," in Klio, 1959, pp. 155–166. In Spain, cf. R. Etienne, Le Culte impérial dans la Péninsule Ibérique d'Auguste à Dioclétien, Paris, 1958, pp. 51ff., 75ff., 88, etc. In the inscriptions, cf. J. Marcillet-Jaubert, A. M. Vérilhac, Index du Bulletin Epigraphique de J. et L. Robert, 1966–1973, Paris, 1979, p. 39.

[47] 1 Tim 1:17 (cf. Tob 13:7; Sir 36:17; C. Spicq, Epîtres Pastorales, vol. 1, p. 346). Jerusalem is "the city of the Great King" (Ps 47:3). Cf. P. Brunner, "Elemente einer dogmatischen Lehre von Gottes Basileia," in Die Zeit Jesu: Festschrift H. Schlier, Freiburg, 1970, pp. 228, 256.

[48] 1 Tim 6:15; Rev 15:3—Almighty God is "King of the nations." On the other hand, the grasshoppers (images of demons) have over them as their king the Angel of the Pit (Rev 9:11).

[49] John 18:36; cf. verses 33, 37; 19:12, 14: "Behold your king"; verse 15: "Shall I crucify your king?" (J. Blank, "Die Verhandlung vor Pilatus Joh. XVIII, 28–XIX, 16 im Lichte johan. Theologie," in BZ, 1959, pp. 60–81; A. George, "La Royauté de Jésus selon l'Evangile de saint Luc," in Sciences Ecclésiastiques, 1962, pp. 57–70; J. Bosc, L'Office royal du Seigneur Jésus-Christ, Geneva, 1957). This proclamation of royalty was official and would be inscribed as the titulus on the cross (Matt 27:37; Mark 15:2, 9, 12, 18, 26; Luke 23:3, 37–38; John 18:39; 19:3, 15, 19, 21); the soldiers make mockery of it (Matt 27:29), and at Calvary the high priests ridicule it: "He is the king of Israel!" (Matt 27:42; Mark 15:32).

kings" (Rev 17:14; 19:16). This is the belief of the primitive church, since at Thessalonica the Jews accuse the Christians of contravening "Caesar's edicts by saying that there is another king, Jesus" (Acts 17:7).

The expression "kingdom of God" (*basileia tou theou*) appears more than 130 times in the NT, and in a new way, especially in Matthew (50 times), whose theology as a whole is summed up by the phrase.[50] It is relatively rare in the Pauline epistles, where it is very close to the concept of justification; this evolution already suggests the variety of meaning of the formula. Jesus begins his preaching with these words: "The time is fulfilled (*pleroō*) and the reign of God has drawn near (*ēngiken*); repent and believe the gospel" (Mark 1:15). As the first phrase of this saying indicates, the proximity is temporal; but inasmuch as this reign comes in the person and the ministry of Jesus, the proximity is also spatial (cf. *P.Oxy.* 1202, 8; *P.Gen.* 74, 17; *P.Thead.* 17, 12) and we may also translate it as "is coming."[51] Since the verb is in the perfect indicative, it means an extreme closeness, immediate imminence (J. Schlosser), even a presence ("It is here"), because the moment of this coming as at the actual beginning of the ministry of

---

[50] This *basileia* basically refers to God's rights as sovereign over his creatures. The formula "kingdom of heaven" does not mean a kingdom that is in heaven but results from Jewish scruples about uttering the divine name (cf. Dan 4:23; 1 Macc 3:18–19; Luke 15:18, 21; Str-B, vol. 1, pp. 172–184). J. Carmignac and R. Schnackenburg give the bibliography; especially worth mention are H. Schlier, "Reich Gottes und Kirche," in *Studia Catholica*, Nijmegen, 1957, pp. 178–189; F. C. Grant, "The Idea of the Kingdom of God in the New Testament," in *The Sacral Kingship* (Supplements to *Numen*, vol. 4), Leiden, 1959, pp. 437–446; W. Dantine, "Regnum Christi—Gubernatio Dei," in *TZ*, 1959, pp. 195–208; S. Aalen, " 'Reign' and 'House' in the Kingdom of God in the Gospels," in *NTS*, vol. 8, 1961, pp. 215–240; G. Lundström, *The Kingdom of God in the Teaching of Jesus*, Richmond, 1963; N. Perrin, *The Kingdom of God in the Teaching of Jesus*, London, 1963; H. Merklein, *Die Gottesherschaft als Handlungsprinzip: Untersuchungen zur Ethik Jesu*; Würzburg, 1978; B. D. Chilton, *God in Strength: Jesus's Announcement of the Kingdom*, Freistadt, 1979; K. Koch, "Offenbaren wird sich das Reich Gottes," in *NTS*, vol. 25, 1979, pp. 158–165; S. Ruager, "Das Reich Gottes und die Person Jesu," in *Arbeiten zum Neuen Testament und Judentum*, vol. 3, Frankfurt, 1979; Margaret Pamment, "The Kingdom of God According to the First Gospel," in *NTS*, 1981, pp. 211–232; especially J. Schlosser, *Le Règne dans les dits de Jésus*, vols. 1–2, Paris, 1980; A. Feuillet, "Règne de Dieu, III: Evangiles synoptiques," in *DBSup*, vol. 10, col. 61–165.

[51] R. F. Berkey, "ἐγγίζειν, φθάνειν and Realized Eschatology," in *JBL*, 1963, pp. 177–187. In the LXX, the verb ἐγγίζω sometimes translates the Hebrew *nāga'* or the Aramaic *meṭā'*, meaning "reach, attain to" (Jer 51:9; Jonah 3:6; Ps 32:6; 88:3; 107:18; Dan 4:11, 22), but usually it translates the Hebrew *qārab* in the sense "arrive" (1 Kgs 8:59; Lam 4:18; Ps 118:169; 1 Macc 9:10); P. Joüon, "Notes philologiques sur les Evangiles," in *RSR*, 1927, pp. 537–540; C. H. Dodd, *The Parables of the Kingdom*, London, 1935, pp. 44ff. J. Gray, *The Biblical Doctrine of the Reign of God*, pp. 317ff.

Jesus. The reign of God has thus indeed come at this point. This is confirmed by Luke 11:20; Matt 12:28, where the Lord concludes, "If I cast out demons by the finger of God, then the reign of God has come" (*ephthasen*). The verb *phthanō*, which means "come before, precede" in classical Greek (cf. again 1 Thess 4:15), in the Koine has the sense "arrive, come upon";[52] here, given the aorist tense and the context, it can mean only the actualization of a past fact whose consequences may be observed; "it expresses not proximity, however great, but effective contact, a presence that has become a reality,"[53] or better, a continued present. This curious link between coming, being close, and being present occurs in John 4:23; 5:25—"The hour is coming and now is."[54] Finally, the *basileia entos hymōn estin* (Luke 17:20-21), which can be taken either as "among you, in your midst," meaning that the reign of God is present in Israel; or "in you," meaning in each person who acts spiritually.[55]

In any event, the reign is progressive and dynamic, like seed sown and growing on its own (Mark 4:26), or a mustard seed that becomes a large tree (Mark 4:30-32; Matt 13:31-32; Luke 13:18-19), or again leavening whose action is mysterious and independent of human action (Matt 13:33). It is given[56] as a demonstration of the Father's love (*eudokēsen*); and Jesus'

---

[52] LXX, Philo, *T. 12 Patr.*, *P.Oxy.* 237, col. VI, 30; VII, 42; 935, 20; 1666, 3; *P.Tebt.* 417, 10; *P.Flor.* 9, 9. In NT usage, φθάνω means to come upon someone, to come at a set time (1 Thess 2:16; Rom 9:31; 2 Cor 10:14; Phil 3:16).

[53] J. Schlosser, *Le Règne dans les dits de Jésus*, p. 138. The actual coming is not visible, cannot be observed: οὐκ ἔρχεται ἡ βασιλεία τοῦ θεοῦ μετὰ παρατηρήσεως (NT hapax, Luke 17:20; cf. R. Le Déaut, *Nuit Pascale*, pp. 272ff.), like an astronomical phenomenon; we cannot be on the lookout for it, because it is spiritual and is not within our reach. Sometimes it is interpreted "the kingdom comes unawares," cf. *Gos. Thom.* 113: "The kingdom does not come when expected."

[54] Ἔρχεται ὥρα καὶ νῦν ἐστιν; John 16:32: ἔρχεται ὥρα καὶ ἐλήλυθεν (cf. Rom 13:11-12; 1 John 2:18). This is not a Semitism, cf. Polybius 4.40.10: ἔσται δὲ καὶ περὶ τὸν Πόντον παραπλήσιον· καὶ γίνεται νῦν.

[55] Cf. A. Rüston, "ἐντὸς ὑμῶν ἐστίν: Zur Deutung von Lukas XVII, 20-21," in *ZNW*, 1960, pp. 197-224; R. Sneed, "The Kingdom of God is Within You (Lc. XVII, 21)," in *CBQ*, 1962, pp. 363-382. J. Schlosser (*Le Règne dans les dits de Jésus*, p. 201ff.) notes that ἐντός followed by the genitive can mean (1) "within, inside" in a temporal sense (a time period not to be exceeded, *P.Oxy.* 724, 11; 728, 18; 1278, 26) or in a local sense (inside a wall, Josephus, *War* 2.531, 632; 4.8, 564), inside a person (Ps 39:3; 109:22), like entrails (Josephus, *Ant.* 2.304; 4.80); within the reach of, in the power of (*P.Oxy.* 1274, 13; 2342, 1, 7, 8; *P.Ross.Georg.* III, 1, 8-9). Finally "in the midst of" (analogous to ἐν μέσῳ), cf. Herodotus 7.100.3; Thucydides 8.5.3; Josephus, *Ant.* 6.315; (2) as an attribute of *basileia*: deep down inside (E. Delebecque, *Evangile de Luc*, on this text); "in you" as a reality that is imminent and already present.

[56] Luke 12:32—δοῦναι ὑμῖν; Matt 21:43. W. Pesch, "Zur Formegeschichte und Exegese von Lk XII," in *Bib*, 1960, pp. 25-40.

disciples are taught to pray that this reign, already inaugurated by him, might "come" to its full, universal blossoming;[57] it then becomes the kingdom of God on earth, a place that one *enters* to take possession of it (*eiserchesthai*, Matt 5:20; 7:21; 18:3; 19:23; 23:13). It is prepared from the creation (25:34), people are called to it (22:10), as to a wedding feast.[58]

It is each person's responsibility to respond to the invitation, to prepare, like the wise virgins (Matt 25:1–13); for "not everyone who says 'Lord, Lord' will enter into the kingdom of heaven" (Matt 7:21; Luke 6:46). A person does not enter the kingdom, does not receive the gospel, without having a little child's qualities of openness and receptivity,[59] without being poor in spirit, that is, aware of one's poverty.[60] These requirements are otherwise expressed as not looking back (Luke 9:62), as renunciation (Mark 9:43–47; Luke 18:29)—just as a person sells everything in order to purchase a pearl or gain possession of a treasure (Matt 13:44–46)—as becoming a eunuch if need be,[61] as doing oneself violence and forcing one's way (Luke 16:16; Matt 11:12–13). In essence, this amounts to being converted and believing (Mark 1:15), possessing a higher righteousness than that of the Pharisees (Matt 5:20; 6:25–33), that is, practicing brotherly love (Matt 18:23–25; cf. Jas 2:5) and being born from above (John 3:3, 5). In a word, it is not enough to wait expectantly for the reign or the kingdom; a total giving of oneself to the divine sovereign is required.

As a wheat field also has tares, so the kingdom of God on earth is composed of good and bad persons (Matt 13:24–30, 36–43, 47–50) and there is a hierarchy in its membership. Because of the excellence of the new

---

[57] Luke 11:2—ἐλθέτω ἡ βασιλεία σου. Manuscript D introduces this petition with ἐφ' ἡμᾶς ("that upon us may come"), which must be a liturgical addition, since it loses the focus on the wishes on God; it breaks the symmetry with "Hallowed be thy name" and "thy will be done" (cf. J. Carmignac, *Recherches sur le 'Notre Père'*, Paris, 1969, pp. 90ff.). This monarchy over souls, triumphing over hostile powers, is a coming of God (Isa 35:4; 40:9; 66:15, 18; Zech 14:5; Mal 3:1–2), the more and more stable and universal establishing of his sovereignty; cf. J. Jeremias, *Abba*, pp. 151–171. — The destruction of Jerusalem, freeing Israel's gospel to bring salvation to the Gentiles, will be a triumphant coming of the reign (Matt 16:28; Mark 9:1; Luke 9:27), one of its "advents" (cf. M. Künzi, *Das Naherwartungslogion Markus IX, 1 par.*, Tübingen, 1977).

[58] Matt 22:2ff.; 25:10ff. Cf. M. J. Lagrange, *Matthieu*, pp. CLff.

[59] Mark 10:14–15; Matt 19:14; Luke 18:17–17. Cf. S. Légasse, *Jésus et l'enfant*, Paris, 1969, pp. 187ff. J. Dupont, "Matthieu XIII, 3: ἐὰν μὴ στραφῆτε καὶ γένησθε ὡς τὰ παιδία," in *Neotestamentica et Semitica: Studies in Honour of M. Black*, Edinburgh, 1969, pp. 50–60; J. I. H. McDonald, "Receiving and Entering the Kingdom: A Study of Mark X, 15," in E. A. Livingstone, *SE*, vol. 6, Berlin, 1973, pp. 328–332.

[60] Matt 5:3; Luke 6:20. The rich have difficulty entering the kingdom because they do not feel their need of God (Mark 10:23–25; Matt 19:23–24; Luke 18:24–25).

[61] Matt 19:12. Cf. "Εἰσὶν εὐνοῦχοι," in *ZNW*, 1957, pp. 254–270.

dispensation, "the one who is least in the kingdom of God is greater than John the Baptist" (Luke 7:28; Matt 11:11). Publicans and prostitutes precede, enter ahead of (*proagousin*) the heirs of the old covenant.[62] There are the small and the great (Matt 5:19–20). The keys of the kingdom are entrusted to Peter (Matt 16:17), the apostles are taught the mysteries of the *basileia*[63] that they must proclaim to all the world (Matt 10:6–8; 24:14), but the scribes and Pharisees shut up the way into these mysteries (Luke 11:52; Matt 23:13).

This reign of God, this kingdom of Christ, a place of blessedness (Luke 14:15), is also eschatological and will have no end (Luke 1:33), is an unshakable kingdom (Heb 12:28), paradise (Luke 23:42), or heavenly glory (Matt 20:21; Mark 10:37). Inaugurated by the resurrection of Jesus, this life in the kingdom is comparable to an eternal banquet where guests beyond number from East and West (Matt 13:11) celebrate at Christ's table.[64]

According to Acts 1:3 (cf. 1:6) Jesus discussed the reign of God with his apostles between the resurrection and the ascension, and this kingdom is also the theme of Philip's preaching (8:12) and of Paul's (19:8; 20:25; 28:23, 31). The latter points out that "it is through many tribulations that we must enter the kingdom of God." His epistles add nothing to the Synoptic theology, but they insist forcefully on the holiness of the members of the *basileia*, which cannot be inherited by the unjust.[65] A person must be worthy of this reward (2 Thess 1:5), even though it is absolutely certain (2 Pet 1:11). The emphasis is on the eschatological royalty of Christ (1 Cor

---

[62] Matt 21:31, 43. Cf. S. Légasse, "Jésus et les prostituées," in *RTL*, 1976, pp. 137–154.

[63] Mark 4:11; Matt 13:11; Luke 8:10. These "secrets" are those of the divine economy, of the making up of a new people, of the forgiveness of sins, of the sharing in the very life of God. These divine intentions can only be known through revelation.

[64] Mark 14:25; Matt 26:29; Luke 22:16, 18, 29, 30. Jesus, in announcing his imminent death, uses this eschatological logion to express the certainty of his triumph over death and his exaltation, perhaps also "the new paschal rite, i.e., the Church" (P. Benoit, *Exégèse et théologie*, p. 198). Cf. M. Rese, "Zur Problematik von Kurz- und Langtext in Luk. XXII, 17ff.," in *NTS*, vol. 22, 1975, pp. 15–31. On the characteristics that permit to a certain extent equating the church and the kingdom of Christ, cf. J. Bonsirven, *Le Règne de Dieu*, pp. 187–200; H. Schlier, "Reich Gottes und Kirche"; R. Schnackenburg, *God's Rule*, pp. 259–270 (urges caution); J. Gray, *The Biblical Doctrine of the Reign of God*, pp. 369ff.; B. Gloege, *Reich Gottes und Kirche im N.T.*, Gütersloh, 1929.

[65] 1 Cor 4:9–10; Gal 5:21; Eph 5:5; cf. Col 1:13. The kingdom is completely spiritual: God reigns in our midst through the virtues and his gifts (Rom 14:17); 1 Cor 15:50, cf. J. Jeremias, "Flesh and Blood Cannot Inherit the Kingdom of God," in *NTS*, vol. 2, 1956, pp. 151–159. Christ's scepter is a scepter of righteousness (Heb 1:8). E. Cothenet, "Règne de Dieu, IV: Epîtres paulienennes," in *DBSup*, vol. 10, col. 165–187.

15:24–25; 1 Tim 4:1) as well as on the power of the reign of God.[66] Hence the acclamations in Revelation. Not only is Christ the "ruler of the kings of the earth" (Rev 1:5), and not only is he thanked for becoming king (11:17), but "he has made of us a kingdom, priests for God his Father" (1:6; 5:10), and his own "will reign as kings forever" (22:5; cf. 1:9). "The reign of our Lord and of his Christ has been established over the world, and he will reign forever and ever."[67]

Basileuō, basileios. — The verb *basileuō*, "be king, reign" (Matt 2:22) has no special meaning in the NT, but it can have the nuance "become king, begin to reign"[68] and is used especially for Christ (Luke 1:33; 14:14, 27) and his victorious domination over his enemies (1 Cor 15:25); for God (Rev 11:15); and for Christians (Rev 5:10; 20:4, 6).

As an adjective in the singular, *basileios* describes the "royal priesthood,"[69] but used as a substantive in the plural, it refers to a royal palace (Luke 7:25), beginning in Herodotus: Croesus lodges Solon *en toisi basilēioisi*.[70] The adjective *basilikos*, much commoner in secular Greek, is applied to an official in the court of Antipas. The description "royal officer" (John 4:46, 49; D and several manuscripts have *basiliskos*) suggests that this is a ranking dignitary (cf. Plutarch, *Sol.* 27.3; Josephus, *Life* 149), as the Old

---

[66] 1 Cor 4:20—οὐ ἐν λόγῳ . . . ἀλλ' ἐν δυνάμει: the virtues of the faithful as well as the community's progress are present realizations of the power of God. 2 Tim 4:18—God saves by bringing his faithful one into his eternal kingdom; cf. R. Deichgräber, *Gotteshymnus und Christushymnus*, Göttingen, 1967, p. 33.

[67] Rev 11:15; cf. 12:10. P. Prigent, "Le Temps et le Royaume dans l'Apocalypse," in J. Lambrecht, *L'Apocalypse johannique et l'Apocalyptique dans le Nouveau Testament*, Gembloux-Louvain, 1980, pp. 231–245.

[68] Rev 11:17; 19:5. It is used metaphorically when it is said that sin and death reign (Rom 5:14, 17, 21; 6:12), i.e., establish their dominion, wielding power and commanding obedience. It is also used for the image of complete fulfillment. St. Paul ironically declares to the Corinthians: "Without us, you have become kings (ἐβασιλεύσατε, ingressive aorist); how I wish that you had really become kings, so that we might be kings with you (συμβασιλεύσωμεν)" (1 Cor 4:8). The verb συμβασιλεύω is used elsewhere only in 2 Tim 2:12—"If we endure, we shall also reign with him."

[69] 1 Pet 2:9 (cf. Exod 19:6, Hebrew *mamlākâh*); 2 Macc 2:17; Philo, *Spec. Laws* 1.142; *Abraham* 56; C. Spicq, *Epîtres de saint Pierre*, pp. 90ff.; P. Sandevoir, "Un Royaume de prêtres," in C. Perrot, *Etudes sur la première Lettre de Pierre*, Paris, 1980, pp. 219–229; cf. J. H. Elliott, *The Elect and the Holy*, Leiden, 1966, pp. 149–154.

[70] Herodotus 1.30; Esth 1:9—Queen Vashti gave a feast in the royal house of King Ahasuerus; Philo, *Flacc.* 92: "the space separating the gates of the arsenal from the royal palace" (ἐν τοῖς βασιλείοις); Josephus, *Ant.* 13.138; cf. Deut 3:10, the royal cities = the cities of the kingdom; Wis 18:15—the royal thrones. — Beginning with Xenophon, the noun in the singular also refers to the king's tent (*Cyr.* 2.4.3; 4 Macc 3:8; Josephus, *Ant.* 6.251), and Philo gives the equation "the palace (βασίλειον) is certainly the house of the king (βασιλέος οἶκος)" (*Sobr.* 66), cf. Prov 18:19 (= citadel).

Latin and the Vulgate interpret it (*regulus*, a king of a small country or person of royal blood). In Acts 12:20—"the land drew its subsistence from the king's land" (*apo tēs basilikēs*). An interesting usage is in Jas 2:8, which describes the precept concerning loving one's neighbor as the "royal law"; Jesus had called this the "great commandment" (*entolē megalē*, Matt 22:36). The expression is already used in Xenophon, *Oec.* 14.7 (*basilikoi nomoi* = laws enacted by the king) and Ps.-Plato, *Min.* 317 (*nomos esti basilikos* = all that is correct is royal law, i.e., is worthy of a statesman),[71] but Philo is the one who gives it its theological elaboration: "the king is a living law" (*ton basilea nomon empsychon*, *Moses* 2.4); "piety is the queen of virtues" (*tē basilidi tōn aretōn*, *Spec. Laws* 4.147); "the sky is the king of the sensible realm . . . astronomy is the queen of the sciences" (*Prelim. Stud.* 50); the "royal road" is the way of perfection, of the word of God (*Post. Cain* 101–102; *Giants* 64; *Unchang. God* 144–145; 159–160; cf. Num 20:17), leading to the truth (*Migr. Abr.* 146). Consequently, if *basilikē* refers to all that comes from the king (Josephus, *Ant.* 9.25), belongs to him, and concerns him (Philo, *Flight* 95, 100, 103; *Dreams* 1.163; *Moses* 2.99), then the "royal law" in Jas 2:8 will mean a precept enunciated by God (Josephus, *Ant.* 11.130) and imposing an absolute obligation. But we might also interpret it as prescribing the highest virtue, *agapē*, the queen of all the others, or even as being addressed to the members, the heirs, of the kingdom of God.[72] Finally, we cannot rule out a connotation of excellence;[73] "royal," a synonym of "august," is an excellent description of the king of commandments!

---

[71] Cf. Ps.-Plato, *Ep.* 8.354 c: "royal power"; 2 Macc 3:13—βασιλικὰς ἐντολὰς = orders received from the king; A. Deissmann (*Light*, p. 362, n. 5) noticed this in an inscription from Pergamum: τὸν βασιλικὸν νόμον ἐκ τῶν ἰδίων ἀνέθηκεν (a law from the royal period on *astynomoi*, published by Dittenberger, *Or.* 483, 2; cf. J. and L. Robert, "Bulletin épigraphique," in *REG*, 1952, p. 171, n. 137; 1955, p. 255, n. 188). The expression is also found in a letter of the imperial musicians to the Dionysiac *technitai*, under Aurelian (*SB* 5225, 15). Cf. M. Gigante, Νόμος βασιλεύς, Naples, 1956; M. Treu, "Νόμος βασιλεύς: alte und neue Probleme," in *RhMus*, 1963, pp. 193–214; O. J. F. Seitz, "James and the Law," in F. L. Cross, *SE*, vol. 2, Berlin, 1964, pp. 472–487.

[72] Cf. J. Marty, *L'Epître de Jacques*, Paris, 1935, pp. 81ff. C. Spicq, *Théologie morale*, vol. 1, p. 36, n. 2; vol. 2, p. 505, n. 2. On the absence of the definite article, cf. J. B. Mayor, *The Epistle of St. James*, 3d ed., London, 1910, pp. 90ff.

[73] Cf. *Jos. Asen.* 5.6; 14.8 (royal scepter); 10.14, 13.2 (royal robe); 13.7 (royal dinner); Josephus, *Ant.* 8.356 (royal authority); 11.277 (royal honors); *Ag. Apion* 1.98; Philo, *Cherub.* 63 and *Plant.* 68; *Virtues* 216; *Good Man Free* 123, 126, 154 (the soul of a king contrasted with a commoner); *Moses* 1.153; *To Gaius* 54; 4 Macc 14:2—reason, royal and free; Polybius 8.24; *SEG* 1.363.3: "sacred and royal business," etc.

> βασκαίνω
>
> *baskainō*, to bewitch, cast a spell, regard enviously
>
> →*see also* φθόνος

Paul's exclamation to the Galatians is not easy to translate: "O foolish Galatians! Who has bewitched you (*tis hymas ebaskanen*), before whose eyes Jesus Christ was portrayed crucified?"[1] An NT hapax, the verb *baskainō*[2] is a denominative formed from *baskanos*, "one who casts a spell";[3] a *baskania* is an evil spell,[4] and the verb, meaning "cast a spell, wish evil, speak ill of," "emphasizes the magical value of the group, which relates properly to an evil spell."[5] Hence the modern translations: "Who has bewitched you, cast a spell on you?"[6] But doesn't this notion of a verbal incantation overplay

---

[1] Gal 3:1. After ἐβάσκανεν, C, D, K, L, and P add τῇ ἀληθείᾳ μὴ πείθεσθαι. The description ἀνόητοι, "unthinking" (cf. verse 3; Luke 24:25; Rom 1:14; 1 Tim 6:9; Titus 3:3) expresses incomprehension in the realm of faith, a lack of discernment, an ignorance of one's own limits. Cf. Ps.-Aristotle, *Mund.* 1.391 *a* 10: the Aloadae, in their folly (οἱ ἀνόητοι), formed the plan to explore the sacred regions of philosophy, when the body is incapable of exploring the heavenly places.

[2] Aorist formed with α, usually with accusative object, cf. F. M. Abel, *Grammaire*, 17 *h*; 43 *e*.

[3] A sorcerer, one with the evil eye; cf. E. Kuhnert, in PW, vol. 6, 2009ff.

[4] Cf. Plato, *Phd.* 95 *b*: "Beware lest some evil eye turn our argument around backward."

[5] C. Bonner, *Magical Amulets*, pp. 97ff. P. Chantraine (*Dictionnaire étymologique*, p. 167) rejects the etymology given by Hesychius, who seems to derive the verb from βάζω, βάσκω (φάσκω), "talk."

[6] Cf. A. Oepke (*Der Brief des Paulus an die Galater*, Leipzig, 1937); H. Schlier (*Der Brief an die Galater*, Göttingen, 1951); F. Mussner (*Der Galaterbrief*, Freiburg, Basel, 1974): "wer hat euch bezaubert." Cf. the bucolic singers of Theocritus 6.39: "In order not to be bewitched (ὡς μὴ βασκανθῶ), I spat three times in my bosom, as old Cotyttaris taught me." There is no room here for the definition of βασκαίνω as "disparage, denigrate"; cf. Demosthenes, *Chers.* 8.19: "do not disparage this army";

---

baskainō, S 940; TDNT 1.594–595; EDNT 1.208; NIDNTT 2.552, 559; MM 106; L&N 53.98, 88.159; BDF §§72, 152(1); BAGD 137

the metaphorical sense of the word? —for surely the sense is metaphorical here. The best approach is to take into account the actual usage of this verb, which is unknown in the papyri.

Baskainō (and related words) is constantly associated with *phthoneō*, "to envy" (cf. Gal 5:26). Callimachus wrote this as his own epitaph: "He sang louder songs than Envy" (*Epigr.* 21), and Stobaeus collected fifty-nine sayings *peri phthonou*, of which the fifty-second goes "They were exceeding *baskanos* and *phthoneros*."[7] In the LXX, in times of famine, "a man will have an evil eye toward (that is, will look askance at, will envy, *sphodra baskanei*, Hebrew *rā'a'*) his brother, the wife of his bosom, his children" (Deut 28:54), and even his wife will jealously spy on her husband and her children (28:56). Moreover, if the miser does not profit from his property, the envious person never has enough and is consumed with the desire to have more, "is grudging to himself" (Sir 14:6). In his insatiability, he commits the grossest injustices to increase his wealth: "The person with the jealous eye is evil" (*ponēros ho baskainōn ophthalmō*, Sir 14:8). This same psychology is evoked by Philo: adversaries, who ought naturally to be jealous of the conqueror, feel no envy toward him" (*baskainein, mē phthoneisthai, Husbandry* 112); "he always looks at happy people with an evil eye (*baskainōn*)."[8] This is also in the vocabulary of Josephus: "Daniel was envied (*ephthonēthē*) because people are jealous (*baskainousi*) of those who are more honored than they themselves by the king" (*Ant.* 10.250; 257); "people made jealous by my fortune invented accusations against me" (*Life* 425); "to remove from those envious of us the last pretext for chicanery" (*Ag. Apion* 1.72). This meaning of *baskainō*, "look at with an evil eye, be envious of," fits with Demosthenes, *C. Lept.* 20.24: "If the possessor of a great fortune did not acquire it at your expense, then there is no room for regarding him with hostility (*baskainein*)."

This envious regard is often considered harmful and injurious; it is described as "the evil eye"[9] and is connected with the magical notion of

---

Corona 189: "He basely disparages"; Josephus, *Ag. Apion* 2.285: "Let them cease disparaging us"; Heraclitus, *All.* 6.3: "envy that always seeks to sully and disparage."

[7] Βάσκανοί τε σφόδρα ἦσαν καὶ φθονεροί. Stobaeus, *Ecl.* 4.38, vol. 3, pp. 708–721. Cf. P. Walcot, *Envy and the Greeks: A Study of Human Behaviour*, Warminster, 1978, pp. 77–84.

[8] *Flacc.* 143; cf. 29: the Alexandrians, "stirred to jealousy (φθόνου)—for Egyptian means spiteful (βάσκανον)"; cf. Plutarch, *De inv. et ot.* 7: "People are even more jealous (βασκαίνουσι μᾶλλον) of those who are considered good because of the thought that they possess the greatest property of all, which is virtue."

[9] Ὀφθαλμὸς πονηρός. This does not mean that there is anything wrong with the eye itself (Matt 6:23; Luke 11:34) but that the eye translates the feelings of the

the casting of an evil spell: "I do not wish to seem to cast an evil spell on (*baskainein en*) the general prosperity" (Lucian, *Nav.* 17; cf. *Philops.* 35). A lead bracelet bears the inscription "Spell-caster begone" (*exō baskanos*);[10] "May Envy and the Evil Eye be far from this happy art."[11] The influence of this *oculus invidiosus*, the symbol of *baskania*, was even attributed to demons, for example, to the she-devil *Baskosyne*.[12] Plutarch, in *Quaestionum convivialum*,[13] tries to explain how "a look can do harm, even though the causal link is difficult to grasp" (680 *f*); he uses the terms "effluence," "emanation," "current," "fascination."[14] Heliodorus draws on this: in the course of a procession, Charicleia "attracted the evil eye (*ophthalmon tina baskanon*). 'You also, like the rabble, believe in the bewitching power of the eyes (*baskanian*).' 'Yes; I say nothing is more real' " (*Aeth.* 3.7.2); "the sickness comes from envy (*ho phthonos*), which is properly called bewitchment (*baskanian*)" (3.7.3; cf. 3.19.2; 4.5.4).

It was difficult to escape the evil eye (Stobaeus 3.38.10), especially when its fascination was worked on the eye of the person to whom harm was

---

heart or soul, in this case envy, cf. Mark 7:22; Matt 20:15; Prov 23:6; 28:22; Sir 14:10. Cf. Plutarch, *De inv. et ot.* 2: envy is like a disease of the eyes.

[10] *SEG* XXV, 1199 = *SB* 10702; cf. 6295: ὀφθαλμὸν ἀπετρύπησα τὸν τοῦ βασκάνου; 6584, 4–5. The decree of association of the athletes of the empire: "Because of all these qualities, malignant Envy (ὁ βάσκανος φθόνος) . . . took from us this common good, of which she was jealous, coming to press on the parts of the body that are most useful to pancratists, namely, the shoulders" (*MAMA* VIII, 417, 19–20; republished, corrected and translated, by L. Robert, *Hellenica*, vol. 13, Paris, 1965, pp. 145ff.). On the linking of βάσκανοι, magicians, evil persons, cf. Strabo 14.2.7; Diodorus Siculus 5.55.3; Callimachus, *Aet.*, in *P.Oxy.* 2079, 17.

[11] Τὸν Φθόνον ἐκ μέσσου καὶ ὄμματα Βασκανίης τῆς ἱλαρῆς τέχνης, *SEG* XXV, 1197 *c* (cf. E. Bernand, *Inscriptions métriques*, n. 122), IX, 818.

[12] In funerary epigrams, Hades is described as βάσκανος (*Anth. Pal.* 7.328, 712; cf. G. Kaibel, *Epigrammata* 345, 379; E. Peterson, ΕΙΣ ΘΕΟΣ, Göttingen, 1926, p. 230; J. Geffcken, "βάσκανος δαίμων," in *Charisteria A. RZACH . . . dargebracht*, Reichenberg, 1930, pp. 36–40). Cf. P. Perdrizet, *Negotium perambulans in tenebris*, Strasbourg, 1922, p. 24: "Envy, jealousy, being the essential nature of evil spirits, and fascination, the evil eye, being their more fearsome weapon of harm." The owl of Athena sometimes sometimes conjured up fascination, sometimes was auxiliary to it. Baskania (Envy) is a chthonic divinity, along with Tartarus, Charon, etc., in *Pap.Graec.Mag.* 4, 1451; cf. I, 1400; VIII, 34 (ed. K. Preisendanz, vol. 1, p. 120). In epitaphs, Ἅδης (or Ἀιδης) is described as βάσκανος (*CIRB*, n. 193, 141; cf. *GVI*, n. 949). On the evil eye, cf. W. Déonna, *Le symbolisme de l'œil*, Berne, 1965, pp. 153–158, who cites an abundant bibliography, especially Elworthy, *The Evil Eye*, London, 1895; Seligmann, *Der Böse Blick und Verwandtes*, 2 vols., 1910.

[13] Plutarch, *Quaest. conv.* 5.7.1.680 *c*: Περὶ τῶν καταβασκαίνειν λεγομένων καὶ βάσκανον ἔχειν ὀφθαλμόν, "On those who are said to cast spells."

[14] Heliodorus, *Aeth.* 2.25.1, writes that the eye captures its object like a net.

wished.¹⁵ Magicians, however, used incantations, talismans, and especially amulets for protection against this sort of influence; "their strange appearance distracts the gaze of the *baskanos* and thus keeps him from fixating on his victim."¹⁶ The epistolary papyri constantly use *abaskantos* with respect to the health of humans, especially children, and even of horses (*O.Florida* 15, 2; 17, 4; *SB* 1022, 6). The writer prays for the health of the recipient and for his preservation from the evil eye.¹⁷

In view of these data, it seems best to translate *tis hymas ebaskanen* "Who put a spell on you?" meaning "Who beclouded your mind?"¹⁸ The Galatians have lost their minds (*anoētoi*); it is not as if they had made some easily explainable mistake in a secular matter, but rather as if their freedom has been put in bondage by the mysterious maneuverings of parties unknown (*tis?*)—*baskania* is often personified (*SEG* XV, 853, 6)—behind whom the working of the devil may be detected; by the jealousy (*phthonō diabolou*) whereby death entered into the world.¹⁹ This would mean Paul's enemies in Galatia, moved by envy, like those Roman preachers who sought to ruin

---

¹⁵ J. B. Lightfoot (*Epistle to the Galatians*, 8th ed., London, 1884) and M. J. Lagrange (*Epître aux Galates*) cite Alexander of Aphrodisias, *Pr.* 2.53: ὥσπερ ἰώδη τινὰ καὶ φθοροποιὸν ἀκτῖνα ἐξιᾶσιν ἀπὸ τῆς κόρης αὐτῶν καὶ αὕτη εἰσιοῦσα διὰ τῶν ὀφθαλμῶν τοῦ φρονουμένου τρέψει τὴν ψυχὴν καὶ τὴν φύσιν; Sir 18:18—δώσις βασκάνου ἐκτήκει ὀφθαλμούς.

¹⁶ Plutarch, *Quaest. conv.* 681 f. In Syria, a drawing to ward off *phthonos* has been found (F. Cumont, *Fouilles de Doura-Europos*, Paris, 1926, p. 138). U. Wilcken has published a Christian amulet from the sixth century: τὸν δαίμονα προβασκανίας (*APF,* 1901, p. 431); cf. Ep Jer 69: "a scarecrow in a field of cucumbers preserves nothing" (βασκάνιον οὐ προβασκάνιον). Definition of amulet by C. Bonner, *Magical Amulets*, p. 2.

¹⁷ *P.Oxy.* 292, 12 (AD 25); 930, 23; 2679, 2; 2981, 24, 30; 3312, 3; 3313, 23; *P.Fay.* 126, 10; *P.Lips.* 108, 9: ἄσπασε τὰ ἀβάσκαντά σου παιδία; *P.Ryl.* 604, 25; *P.Oxy.Hels.* 50, 21; *BGU* 811, 4; *P.Wisc.* 72, 5–6; 74, 16; 76, 26; *P.Stras.* 187, 4; *P.Mil.* 80, 6; *P.Giss.* 23, 10; 24, 7; 25, 3; *P.Mich.* 473, 14. The proper name Abaskantos ("of good omen") is quite widespread in the imperial period: a freedman (*SB* 7515, 390), an archon from Thera (L. Robert, *Hellenica*, in *RevPhil*, 1944, pp. 40–42); T. Drew-Bear, *Phrygie*, Zutphen, 1978, p. 79.

¹⁸ P. Robert's *Dictionnaire . . . de la langue française* cites the expression "Il faut qu'on l'ait ensorcelé" and notes "se dit de quelqu'un dont la conduite paraît inexplicable" and almost diabolical.

¹⁹ Wis 2:24. A. M. Dubarle ("La Tentation diabolique dans le Livre de la Sagesse, II, 24," in *Mélanges Tisserant*, vol. 1, pp. 187–195) compares 1QS 3.23–24, where the angel of darkness misleads the sons of righteousness and "all the spirits of his sort trip up the sons of light"; 1QM 13.11–12; *Enoch* 54.6: the servants of Satan have misled the inhabitants of the earth; *T. Jud.* 23.1, the demons of misleading. The devil's "jealousy" was probably stirred up by God's benevolence toward humankind, whose prerogatives go so far as to include even "dominating the universe" (Wis 10:2, 9ff.).

the apostle's authority and prestige by taking advantage of the powerlessness to which he was reduced by his captivity. They acted *dia phthonon kai erin*, through envious, partisan malice.[20] These jealous folk must have somehow cast an evil eye on Christians, even though they had the wherewithal to conjure against this seduction: "You, before whose eyes Jesus Christ was portrayed crucified."[21] Keeping the eyes fixed on the Crucified One would have been the antidote par excellence.[22]

---

[20] Phil 3:15; cf. 17, ἐξ ἐριθείας. Cf. C. Spicq, *Agapè*, vol. 2, pp. 244–252; J. Gnilka, "Die antipaulinische Mission in Philippi," in *BZ*, 1965, pp. 258–276; A. F. J. Klijn, "Paul's Opponents in Philippians III," in *NovT*, 1965, pp. 278–284; A. E. Harvey, "The Opposition to Paul," in F. L. Cross, *SE*, vol. 4, pp. 319–332.

[21] Προγράφω expresses an official publicness that no one could ignore, a posting, a public notice on a placard; Aristophanes, *Av.* 450: "Let them note what we post on the boards"; Plutarch, *De Pyth. or.* 29: the inscriptions due to the wise; *Dem.* 46.10: "a soldier inscribed before his tent the beginning of the *Oedipus*."

[22] Cf. A. J. Festugière, *Hermétisme et mystique païenne*, Paris, 1967, pp. 188–199, n. 47–48.

βατταλογέω

battalogeō, to babble

Before teaching his disciples the Our Father, our Lord instructed them: "In your prayers, do not babble as the gentiles do,[1] for they think that by using many words they will make themselves heard."[2] This advice seems to recall Eccl 5:1, "Do not be hasty to speak in God's presence . . . let your words be few,"[3] and Sir 7:14—"do not repeat words in your prayer"; but no sure etymology can be given for *battalogeō*.[4] A. Schlatter, pointing out that *legō* can mean "gather, collect" (cf. *poēlogeō*, *blastologeō*, *botanologeō*, *krithologeō*) and that *batos* (Syriac *bata*) means "bramble," relies on Philo (*Alleg. Interp.* 3.253; *Dreams* 2.161; cf. *Moses* 1.65) to arrive at the forced sense of "give oneself over to painful and sterile work."[5] Furthermore, most modern scholars see in this verb a hybrid of the Aramaic *battalta* and the Greek *logos* (in a pejorative sense, cf. *spermologos*, *koprologos*, *sykologeō*) and draw support from the Palestinian Syriac and Sinaitic Syriac versions, "do not be saying (mouthing) *battalata* = vain things."[6] So what is in view is

---

[1] The term *ethnikoi* is pejorative, cf. A. Pelletier, *Josèphe adaptateur*, pp. 79ff.

[2] Matt 6:7, *NJB*; M. J. Lagrange translates, "When you pray, do not stammer on (*bredouillez*) like the Gentiles, because it seems to them that their prayer will be answered thanks to their spate of words" (*Evangile selon saint Matthieu*, 3d ed., Paris, 1927, p. 123); E. Bonnard: "Do not multiply vain words" (*Evangile selon saint Matthieu*, Neuchâtel, 1963, p. 79); the New English Bible: "Do not go babbling on like the heathen"; cf. F. W. Beare, "Speaking with Tongues," *JBL* 1964, pp. 229ff.

[3] Cf. A. Barucq, *Ecclésiaste*, Paris, 1968, pp. 101–102.

[4] Unknown in the Greek language before the *Life of Aesop* (ἐν οἴνῳ μὴ βατταλόγει σοφίαν ἐπιδεικνύμενος, ed. A. Westermann, *Vita Aesopi*, Brunswick, 1845, p. 47) and the commentary on Epictetus by Simplicius in the sixth century (cited by J. J. Wettstein, on this text); cf. G. Delling, in *TDNT*, vol. 1, p. 597.

[5] A. Schlatter, *Der Evangelist Matthäus*, Stuttgart, 1948, p. 206; cf. H. Huber, *Die Bergpredigt*, Göttingen, 1932, pp. 113ff.

[6] Cf. *bata'*, Lev 5:4; Ps 106:33. Cf. BDF §40; BAGD, p. 137; but cf. the summary by G. Zuntz in *Gnomon*, 1958, pp. 20–21.

---

battalogeō, S 945; *TDNT* 1.597; *EDNT* 1.209; MM 107; L&N 33.88, 33.89; BDF §40; BAGD 137 verbiage or constant repetition, as verse 8 specifies—"They think that their prayer will be answered thanks to their torrent of words."[7] Quality matters more than quantity; but above all verbosity and prattling are here denounced.[8] Moulton-Milligan (on this word) cite the nickname given Demosthenes (*battalos*, pouring out torrents of words). *Battalogia* would then be "logorrhea, an endless torrent of prayers and litanies,"[9] which reminds us of the *prophasei makra proseuchomenoi* (making long prayers for show) of the scribes (Mark 12:40). It is not the length of the prayer in terms of time that is denounced, because Jesus spent whole nights in prayer and tarried in prayer (Luke 6:12; 22:14) and his church persevered in prayer (Acts 1:14; 12:5; 1 Tim 5:5; etc.), but abuse and redundancy and canned formulas, in which the cry of the heart becomes mere words.

Liddell-Scott-Jones (*Lexicon*) and M. J. Lagrange (*Evangile selon saint Matthieu*, 3d ed., Paris, 1927) prefer to see this word as onomatopoetic, like *battarizō* (stammer);[10] which should be compared to the "muddling up" of tongues at Babel (Gen 11:7–9), the "babbling" of Isaiah,[11] and the "gurgling" water of Ezek 47:2. By way of an example of the meaningless litanies, cf. the magical incantation of the third century, to which we might compare our *abracadabra:* "Demon, whoever you are, I adjure you by the god Sabarbarbathioth, Sabarbarbathiouth, Sabarbarba-

---

[7] Ἐν τῇ πολυλογίᾳ (Prov 10:19; Job 11:2; cf. 1 Kgs 18:26–29; Isa 1:15; Sir 7:14; Maurer, on this word, in *TDNT*, vol. 6, pp. 545–546).

[8] Cf. περιττολογία, superfluous or excessive exposition, linked with ἄμετρον (in Dionysius of Halicarnassus, *Pomp.* 2), with ἀλαζονεία (in Josephus, *Ant.* 14.111). Cf. πολυλογία, βραχυλογία, μακρολογία, in *Sent. Sextus*, n. 155–157. With good reason, E. J. Bickerman draws a contrast with the simplicity of improvised prayers in Israel ("Bénédiction et prière," in *RB*, 1962, pp. 524ff.). We might think of the custom of shouting acclamations forty or fifty times (cf. Acts 19:34; J. V. Le Clerc, *Des Journaux chez les Romains*, Paris, 1838, p. 420).

[9] D. Buzy, *Evangile selon saint Matthieu*, Paris, 1935, p. 75.

[10] Herodotus 4.155: "The child's speech was confused and stuttering . . . the name Battos was given to him, παῖς ἰσχνόφωνος καὶ τραυλός, τῷ οὔνομα ἐτέθη Βάττος" (cf. F. Chamoux, *Cyrène sous la monarchie des Battiades*, Paris, 1953, pp. 93–98); Plutarch, *De Pyth. or.* 22: "It is not possible to give clear pronunciation to a stutterer or a beautiful voice to one whose organ of speech is weak. It is for this reason, I believe, that Battos, who came here on account of his voice, received from the god the order to go found a colony in Libya, because, if he was a stutterer and had a weak voice, the quality of his spirit was that of a king and a statesman." Cf. the nickname βάτταρος (the stutterer) (*I.Did.*, 425, 4; cf. O. Masson, "En marge du Mime II d'Hérondas: Les surnoms ioniens ΒΑΤΤΑΡΟΣ et ΒΑΤΤΑΡΑΣ," in *REG*, 1970, pp. 356–361; L. Robert, *Noms indigènes dans l'Asie-Mineure gréco-romaine*, Paris, 1963, p. 193, n. 5).

[11] Isa 28:10–11 (W. H. Hallo, "Isaiah XXVIII, 9–13 and the Ugaritic Abecedaries," *JBL* 1958, pp. 324–338).

thioneth, Sabarbarbaphaï . . . ,"[12] or "the secret name Thoathoethathoouthaethousthioaithithethointho."[13] Whether we are talking about unintelligible muttering and stammering or of prattling on unreflectively, the play on words and the results are similar (cf. Herodotus 7.35: "to speak *barbara* and recklessly," *legein barbara te kai atasthala*). "We should see this as a useless spate of words such as that produced by uncultivated people telling their business to lawyers . . . a reference to the eloquence expended by the pagans to persuade the gods" (M. J. Lagrange) and to "tire them out," as the Latins said.[14]

The followers of Jesus Christ have only to say "Our Father" to be heard.[15]

---

[12] G. Milligan, *Selections from the Greek Papyri*, Cambridge, 1927, n. 47; cf. C. Bonner, *Magical Amulets*, pp. 68, 117, passim; cf. the medical-magic prescriptions of *P.Ant.* 66, 45–46 or the Arab amulet (*P.Mur.*, vol. 2, pp. 289–290).

[13] *P.Mert.* 58, 12–14 and the references given by the editors (p. 24). St. Paul preferred to "speak five words intelligently rather than ten thousand 'in tongues' " (1 Cor 14:19).

[14] *Fatigare deos*, cf. Horace, *Carm.* 1.2.26ff.; Livy 1.11.2; Seneca, *Lucil.* 4.2.5; Apuleius, *Met.* 10.26; Martial 7.60.3. Cf. Pherecrates, frag. 137 *a:* τί δ' αὐτὸ λίαν ὧδε λιπαρεῖς θεόν (in J. M. Edmonds, *Attic Comedy*, vol. 1, p. 258).

[15] F. Bussby ("A Note on . . . βαττολογέω in the Light of Qumran," *ExpT*, vol. 76, 1964, p. 26) mentions the meaning of the Aramaic *bâthal* in Ezra 4:24—"the work on the house of God was stopped," and its use in a bill of sale (*P.Mur.*, n. 26, 5; cf. ἐγκόπτω in 1 Pet 3:7) where it means "without legal effect," and comments: "Don't use long prayers—like the pagans—prayers that are *without effect*, so long as you have not called upon God the Father in the right way."

> βέβαιος, βεβαιόω, βεβαίωσις
>
> *bebaios*, solid, durable, sure, valid, guaranteed; *bebaioō*, to make sure, confirm, authenticate, guarantee, carry out; *bebaiōsis*, firmness, juridical definiteness
>
> →*see also* ἀσφάλεια

Bebaios—"that on which one can walk," hence "solid, firm, durable" and finally "sure, certain"—often modifies *logos:* an utterance that is well-founded, authorized, and thus convincing.[1] This firmness-solidity implies immutability when the topic is a promise, an institution, or the word of God.[2] Thus we arrive at the legal meaning, "valid" and even "guaranteed," copiously attested in the papyri and the inscriptions for *bebaios*, the denominative verb *bebaioō*, and *bebaiōsis*.[3] It is in this strong sense that we should

---

[1] Βέβαιος is therefore often associated with πιστός (Plato, *Tim.* 49 b) and ἀληθής (*Phdr.* 90 c). In the third century AD, Sotas writes to Satyros: "Believe it, it is sure, because it can be seen—πίστευε τὸ βεβαία, ἐπεὶ ἰδῖν ἐστίν" (*Pap.Lugd.Bat.* XIII, 19, 7). *SB* 5114, 20: ἐπὶ βεβαίῳ καὶ ἀμεταθέτῳ λόγῳ. Cf. Philo, *Sacr. Abel and Cain* 93: "the simple words of God, in their certitude, differ not at all from oaths . . . it is because of God that an oath itself is sure, ὁ ὅρκος βέβαιος"; Philo, *Dreams* 1.12: "There is nothing about which we can be so sure as the unlimited and infinite nature of wisdom."

[2] The Mosaic constitution is "firm, unshakable, unchanging (βέβαια, ἀσάλευτα, ἀκράδαντα), . . . solidly planted . . . it will endure throughout the future as if immortal" (Philo, *Moses* 2.14). Josephus, *Ag. Apion* 2.156: the law of Moses unshakable for eternity; *War* 4.154: a law solidly established. The formula κυρία καὶ βεβαία is used of an ἐγγύη (*P.Stras.* 50, 8), a διαθήκη (*P.Lond.* 77, 66), an ἀποχή (*P.Flor.* 95, 25; *P.Lips.* 38, 6); cf. *P.Gron.* 10, 20: καὶ ἔστω ἡ χάρις κυρία καὶ βεβαία πανταχοῦ προφερομένη.

[3] This meaning is forcefully supported by A. Deissmann, *Bible Studies*, pp. 104–109. Cf. L. Mitteis, *Grundzüge*, Leipzig-Berlin, 1912, vol. 2, 1, pp. 188ff. R. Taubenschlag, *Law of Greco-Roman Egypt*, New York, 1944, pp. 253–254. Cf. the letter

---

bebaios, S 949; *TDNT* 1.600–603; *EDNT* 1.210–211; *NIDNTT* 1.658–660; MM 107; L&N 28.43, 31.90, 71.15; BDF §59(2); BAGD 138 ‖ **bebaioō**, S 950; *TDNT* 1.600–603; *EDNT* 1.210–211; *NIDNTT* 1.658–659; MM 108; L&N 28.44, 31.91; BAGD 138 ‖ **bebaiōsis**, S 951; *TDNT* 1.600–603; *EDNT* 1.210–211; *NIDNTT* 1.658–659; MM 108; L&N 28.44; BAGD 138

understand Rom 4:16: *bebaian tēn epangelian;* the divine promise is not only firm and immutable, not only assured for all posterity, but it is guaranteed to them. Similarly, in Mark 16:20—*ton logon bebaiountos*—the Lord does more than confirm the word of the apostles by the miracles that accompany him; he also authenticates and guarantees it. Inasmuch as the law of Moses was promulgated by angels, this "word" is valid and authentically divine (*logos bebaios,* Heb 2:2). At the transfiguration, the appearance of Moses and Elijah evokes the messianic prophecies of the OT; these prophecies become more sure, their veracity is guaranteed by the transfiguration of Jesus (*bebaioteron . . . logon,* 2 Pet 1:19).

It is indeed legal language that is used in Heb 9:17, an exceptional scriptural use of the word *diathēkē* in the sense of a will, in order to express our ability to inherit these heavenly goods: it was necessary for Christ, the only Son and heir of God, to die so that we might gain possession of his inheritance; *diathēkē epi nekrois bebaia,* a provision of a will is not valid, has no legal force (*ischuei*) and cannot become operative, until after the demise of the testator.[4]

As for the verb *bebaioō,* it can mean "carry out, realize,"[5] and it is in this sense that we should take Rom 15:8, *eis to bebaiōsai tas epangelias:* Christ "demonstrated God's truthfulness by carrying out the promises made to

---

of Claudius to the Alexandrians: "I guarantee to the ephebes the right to the Alexandrine city" (*P.Lond.* 1912, 54); Wis 6:18—"observing the laws is the guarantee of incorruptibility"; a bill of sale, *P.Rein.* 42, 5 (guarantee that the object sold or bequeathed is clear of tax obligations, first-second century AD), *BGU* 87, 18; 153, 23; *P.Vindob.Worp* 9, 12–13: "I will guarantee to you with all of the guarantees specified below"; a rental contract: "the administrators of the Kytherians guarantee (βεβαιόω) the location to Eucrates" (*RIJG,* vol. 1, n. 13[4] A, 13; 7, 108: "Guarantors and confirmers of the sale of the lands and the house.") A lease, *P.Mich.* 633, 29, 40; 634, 13. In a sale, the guarantee protects the buyer against the danger of eviction (cf. ibid., vol. 2, p. 259); J. Pouilloux, *Choix,* n. 42, 10: "βέβαιον παρεχόντων οἱ βεβιωτῆρες, the guarantors furnishing the guarantee of the sale in the name of the god, conformably to law" (an act emancipating a slave; Delphi, second century BC); *P.Köln* 55, 9. The formula βεβαιώσω πάσῃ βεβαιώσι is normal in contracts, cf. *PSI* 1130, 25 (AD 25); *SB* 9109, 14 (AD 31); *P.Fam.Tebt.* 27, 17–18; *P.Mich.* 188, 23; 189, 30; 259, 32 (AD 33); *P.Princ.* 146, 18 (AD 36); *P.Fay.* 92, 19 (second century); *P.Oslo* 40, 45; etc. up to the sixth century (*P.Michael.* 40, 44; 45, 55; 52, 22, 43, etc.).

[4] We may cite the testament of St. Gregory of Nazianzus: "This is my will, which I want to be firm and valid, τὴν διαθήκην κυρίαν καὶ βεβαίαν" (*PG,* vol. 37, 394). Herod designates Caesar as the guarantor of his will (Josephus, *War* 1.669).

[5] Epictetus 2.11.24: "philosophy consists of examining and establishing these norms." J. Rouffiac (*Caractères du grec,* p. 48) noted this from *I.Priene* 123, 9: a magistrate who had promised to give out beef when he entered into office carried out his promise by making a sacrifice to the gods and giving out the meat to those who were on the list, ἐβεβαίωσεν δὲ τὴν ἐπαγγαλίαν παραστήσας μὲν τοῖς ἐντεμενίοις θεοῖς τὴν θυσίαν.

the fathers"; Heb 2:3—"The salvation that was announced by the Lord . . . was confirmed to us by those who heard him."[6]

When Heb 6:16 appeals to the oath as the juridical proof that nullifies any dispute between adversaries[7]—*eis bebaiōsin ho horkos*—the sense of *eis bebaiōsin* is "definitive, without opposition, with no reconsideration or challenge possible," recalling Lev 25:23, where once Yahweh has affirmed that the Holy Land belongs to him "the land shall not be sold *eis bebaiōsin*" (Hebrew *liṣmitut*); God remains the owner, so the ceding of absolute ownership is forbidden.[8]

Finally, the moral applications of the words of this group are frequent, usually in the sense of firmness, fixity, solidity (1 Cor 1:8; 2 Cor 1:21; Heb 3:14; 13:9; 2 Pet 1:10), notably with respect to faith[9] or hope that is well

---

[6] Εἰς ἡμᾶς ἐβεβαιώθη: having been inaugurated by Christ, salvation is effectively carried out, applied by the apostles to the converted. But given συνεπιμαρτυροῦντος τοῦ θεοῦ (verse 4), the nuance of "guarantee" should be preserved. Through their vigor in certifying the facts for which they bear the guarantees, in communicating grace and performing miracles, the apostles sanction the truth of the message; their proclamation inspires confidence. The twofold sense—"guarantee" and "accomplish"—is also found in 1 Cor 1:6—"the testimony of Christ was established (or accomplished) among you"; Phil 1:7—you associate yourselves with my grace in the defense and the establishing (or realization) of the gospel." *P.Mil.Vogl.* 26, 13: the seller guarantees that the fields purchased by the buyer are free of all taxes; *P.Mich.* 635, 13; cf. H. H. Hobbes, *Preaching Values from the Papyri*, Grand Rapids, 1964, pp. 33–36.

[7] Cf. C. Préaux, "La Preuve à l'époque hellénistique," in *La Preuve* (Recueils de la Société J. Bodin, XVI), Brussels, 1965, pp. 161–222. Cf. Josephus, *Ant.* 17.42: βεβαιώσαντος δι' ὅρκων; Philo, *Abraham* 273: God gives Abraham a guarantee by an oath, τὴν δι' ὅρκου βεβαίωσιν; Philo, *Plant.* 82.

[8] Cf. G. Lumbroso, *Recherches sur l'économie politique de l'Egypte*, 2d ed., Amsterdam, 1967, p. 78. A "solid conversion" (Philo, *Moses* 1.298) is a decisive conversion.

[9] Col 2:7—βεβαιούμενοι τῇ πίστει. This firmness derives from Ps 41:12; 119:28; it is exalted by Philo (*Rewards* 30: "The one who has . . . an unbending and unshakable faith: happy is such a one in truth, and three times blessed"), who demonstrates that βεβαίωσις characterizes the laws of nature, as opposed to positive legislation (*Good Man Free* 37); the soul of the friend of God receives fixity, solidity, and consistency (πῆξιν καὶ βεβαίωσιν καὶ ἵδρυσιν; *Alleg. Interp.* 2.55; cf. *Cherub.* 13). If the divine appearances in the realm of becoming dissipate, those produced by unbegotten being can remain stable, firm, eternal (μόνιμοι καὶ βέβαιοι καὶ ἀΐδιοι, 3.101). There is on earth no stable place, where the security of fortune is assured (τὸ ἀκλινὲς τῆς εὐπραγίας ἐν βεβαίῳ, *Moses* 1.30; cf. *Drunkenness* 170). Βέβαιος is used to describe the true and the good (*Moses* 1.95, 1.220; 2.108; *Spec. Laws* 1.70, 1.77, 1.291; 2.2, etc.), and of friendship (Josephus, *Ant.* 7.203; 14.185; 15.193; 19.317). Plutarch, *Cat. Min.* 1.3: "a character firm in all respects." According to an epigram from Nicomedia, spouses reunited in the same tomb choose to love each other constantly even among the dead, στοργὴν βεβαίαν κἂν αἱρούμενοι (S. Sahin, in *ZPE*, 1975, p. 42, n. 125; 1976, p. 189). Cf. Diodorus Siculus 17.51.2: the god grants firmly (βεβαίως) that which is asked of him.

founded[10] and solidly attached, like an anchor in the heavenly holy of holies: *asphalē te kai bebaian.*[11]

---

[10] 2 Cor 1:7; cf. 4 Macc 17:4. Josephus, *Ant.* 5.176, 8.8, 8.280, 15.153, 16.238; *War* 7.165, 7.413: βεβαίαν ἐλπίδα σωτηρίας.

[11] Ἀσφαλής, "that does not slip," used in medicine for a sick person who is out of danger and on the way to a cure (*P.Oxy.* 939, 5; cf. Thucydides 1.80.1; N. van Brock, *Vocabulaire médical*, pp. 184ff.), for the security of a route (Strabo 4.6.6; Heliodorus, *Aeth.* 8.16.1); ἀσφαλῶς used for the security of a mooring (Strabo 5.4.6) or of a naval escort (Dittenberger, *Syl.* 581, 84); ἀσφάλεια used for the security of sailors who heed their pilots (Dio Cassius 41.33). There is a proverb: "If the vessel does not hold to its anchor, the mooring is not sure" (Herondas, *Pimp* 1.41; cf. Plutarch, *De virt. mor.* 6; *Sol.* 19.2; Philemon, frag. 213—ἐβάλετ' ἄγκυραν καθάψας ἀσφαλείας εἵνεκα—in Stobaeus, *Flor.* 30.4; vol. 3, p. 664, 2); hence "drop the anchor of safety" (Heliodorus, *Aeth.* 8.6.9).—The βέβαιον-ἀσφαλές linkage is constant from Wis 7:23 on; Philo, *Virtues* 216; *Rewards* 30; *Prelim. Stud.* 141; *Conf. Tongues* 106; *Heir* 314; cf. Plutarch, *Cat. Mai.* 21.5: "He invested his capital in solid and sure businesses"; Polybius 12.25ᵃ2: "There will be nothing solid or sure in the sayings of our author"; *P.Rein.* 107, 5: ἡ ἀσφάλεια κυρία καὶ βεβαία; *P.Lips.* 4, 18: ἀνέδωκεν ... πρὸς τὴν κυρίαν ἀπὸ τούτων ἀσφάλειαν καὶ βεβαίωσιν.

βέβηλος, βεβηλόω

bebēlos, **accessible, profane, impure, impious**; *bebēloō*, **to profane, besmirch**

Derived from *bainō*, "go, come," the adjective *bebēlos*, "accessible, profane," unknown in the papyri, is the opposite of *abatos, hieros, hagnos*, "inaccessible, sacred," and is used for places that are not consecrated, where it is permitted to set foot; hence, accessible to everybody (cf. Philo, *Alleg. Interp.* 1.62; Josephus, *Ant.* 3.181; *War* 4.182; Thucydides 4.97.3). The exact equivalent would be "profane" (*pro-fano*): that which is opposite or outside of the sacred. When used of persons it means "uninitiated, profane, impure"[1] and takes on a moral value (Philo, *Sacr. Abel and Cain* 138).

In the language of the Bible, it is highly pejorative (Ezek 21:30—*bebēle anome!*, profane and lawless one); and it is often associated with *anosios* (unholy, 1 Tim 1:9; 3 Macc 2:2), with *pornos* (sexually impure, Heb 12:6), *anieros* (unholy, Philo, *Sacr. Abel and Cain* 138; *Spec. Laws* 4.40); *akathartos* (unclean, *Spec. Laws* 1.150), *amyētos* (uninitiated, Plutarch, *De def. or.* 16). It takes on a technical meaning: the profane is opposed to the sacred as the impure to the pure.[2] The verb *bebēloō*, translating the Hebrew piel *hilel*, in the sense of "profane, besmirch," speaks of a sort of sacrilege.[3] In fact, the

---

[1] Cf. E. Boisacq, *Dictionnaire étymologique*, p. 112; P. Chantraine, *Dictionnaire étymologique*, p. 172. In Josephus, *War* 5.18, 6.271, this word designates lay people, as opposed to priests. In *I.Thas.* 18, 4, μήτε ἱρὴ μήτε βεβήλη can mean an "action sacred or profane" or "private or public."

[2] Lev 10:10; Ezek 22:26 (Philo, *Moses* 2.158). In 1 Sam 21:4—profane loaves as opposed to the sacred loaves. Antiochus Epiphanes "takes with his impure hands (ταῖς μιαραῖς χερσίν) the sacred vessels and gathers up with his profane hands (ταῖς βεβήλοις χερσίν) the offerings" of the temple in Jerusalem (2 Macc 5:16).

[3] One profanes the Sabbath (Isa 56:2, 6; Ezek 20:13, 16, 21; 22:8; 1 Macc 1:43, 45; 2:34; Matt 12:5); the name of God (Lev 18:21; 19:12; 20:3; 21:6; Isa 48:11; Ezek 20:9; 36:20–21; 39:7; Amos 2:7; Mal 1:12); the holiness of Yahweh (Lev 19:8); the sanctuary (Acts 24:6; Lev 21:23; 22:2, 15, 32; Num 18:32; Ezek 23:29; 1 Macc 1:48;

---

bebēlos, S 952; *TDNT* 1.604–605; *EDNT* 1.211; MM 108; L&N 88.115; BAGD 138 ‖
bebēloō, S 953; *TDNT* 1.605; *EDNT* 1.21; L&N 53.33; BAGD 138

profaner is an impious person, after the manner of Esau, who renounced the sacred prerogatives which were his as the firstborn and which made him the fully entitled heir of the messianic promises; thus he was faithless.[4]

In the Pastorals, *bebēlos* is an adjective for heterodox and heretical teaching: "impious fables, old wives' tales."[5] So myth is gratuitous inven-

---

2:12; 2 Macc 8:2; 10:5); that which is holy (Ezek 22:26; Mal 2:11; Zeph 3:4); the altar (1 Macc 4:38, 44, 54); the covenant (Ps 55:20; Mal 2:10; 1 Macc 1:63); the land (Jer 16:18; Ezek 7:21–22); posterity (Sir 47:20). A profane woman is prostituted (Lev 21:7, 14) or besmirched (Sir 42:10; cf. Philo, *Spec. Laws* 1.102; Josephus, *Ant.* 15.90). Cf. a cultic regulation of Cyrene (fourth century BC): ἐς ἱαρὰ καὶ ἐς βάβαλα καὶ ἐς μιαρά (*SEG*, vol. 9, 72, 9; cf. line 21: ὁσία παντὶ καὶ ἁγνῷ καὶ βαβάλῳ).

[4] Heb 12:16—τις πόρνος ἢ βέβηλος (cf. Philo, *Spec. Laws* 1.102). Esau is the type of the φαῦλος, whose concubines are ruinous (*Prelim. Stud.* 54). The Jewish tradition attributed the worst vices to Esau (cf. C. Spicq, *Hébreux*, vol. 2, p. 401); J. D. M. Derrett, *Law in the NT*, p. 120). Codex Neophiti I, on Gen 25:34, glosses: "Esau despised his birthright, he denied the resurrection of the dead, and he denied the life of the world to come." Philo called him senseless (*Prelim. Stud.* 175; cf. 61), "eponym of insanity" (*Sacr. Abel and Cain* 17), "savage and violent, full of fire and passion" (*Rewards* 53). Why was he so criminal? According to *Jubilees*, it was because he broke the oath that his parents made him swear to love Jacob and to do him no harm (*Jub.* 35.24; 36.7–9; 37.1–21; cf. A. Jaubert, *La Notion d'alliance dans le Judaïsme*, Paris, 1963, pp. 109ff.). We know well how legends grow, whether for good as in the case of Rahab (cf. C. Spicq, *Hébreux*, vol. 2, pp. 361ff.) or for evil (M. S. Enslin, "How the Story Grew: Judas in Fact and Fiction," in *Festschrift F. W. Gingrich*, Leiden, 1972, pp. 123–141).

[5] 1 Tim 4:7. St. Thomas Aquinas comments precisely "ineptae et inanes." At root, these are tales or twaddle that grandmothers or nurses tell to small children: monster stories or Aesop's fables (Philo attributes to the mythologers the tradition that ascribes a common language to all animals, *Conf. Tongues* 6); the expression then became a rhetorical characterization and a polemical insult: that which flies in the face of reason and presupposes an incredulity unworthy of an honest person (Heliodorus, *Aeth.* 4.5.3), for example, with respect to the life of separated souls on the moon: "That's a good one to tell women, because it is so fabulous" (Plutarch, *De aud. poet.* 16e; Strabo 1.3; Lucian, *Philops.* 9). "The stories that circulate are for the most part fables dreamed up by women and magicians" (Aristotle, *HA* 8.24.605ᵃ5). According to Strabo, Eratosthenes called the poetry of Homer old wives' tales (Strabo, Prolegomena 1.2.3). "These marvelous phenomena sometimes appear to people. These . . . have been related not only by those who might be suspected of making up fables but also by those who have long shown philosophical rigor" (Numenius, frag. 29; ed. Des Places, p. 80). Listening to such nonsense is appropriate for women (Philo, *Post. Cain* 166). "In his own explanations, he is full of visions, prodigies, and incredible fables, in a word, of low trickery and the sort of fantastic tales appropriate for women" (Polybius 12.24.5). Galen heaps scorn on a certain Pampylos who prescribed certain incantations during the gathering of medicinal herbs, "this person was given to old wives' tales and the practices of Egyptian drivelers" (Galen, *De simpl. medicam. temp.* 6, proem., in C. G. Kühn, *Medic. Graec. opera*, vol. 11, 971; cf. Achilles Tatius, *Leuc. et Clit.* 1.8.4). "This senile foolishness that one readily calls drivel" (Cicero, *Sen.* 36; cf. Horace, *Sat.* 2.6.77: *garrit anilis ex re fabellas*; Quintilian, *Inst.* 1.8); Minucius Felix, *Oct.*

tion (2 Pet 1:16), opposed to true history,[6] against which so many first-century authors protest: Moses urges "putting away the fiction of myths . . . which provoke endless errors" (Philo, *Virtues* 178); "the sophists of Egypt give myths . . . more attention than the evidence for the truth" (*Migr. Abr.* 76); "The ones who spread this idea sacrificed to mythological invention more than to history."[7] When St. Paul calls myth profane, he denounces its incompatibility with the sacred; it is a profanation and an impiety to introduce into gospel teaching these human, fictive elements, which do not mix with religion (cf. Heb 13:9—*didachais xenais*), and which do not encourage true *eusebeia*.[8]

This inanity is again expressed in the prohibition against crude and profane chatter—*tas bebēlous kenophōnias* (1 Tim 6:20; 2 Tim 2:16)—which, under the guise of doctrine, secularize and besmirch the divine truth entrusted to the church. Literally, *kenophōnia* (attested by the best manuscripts instead of *kainophōnia*, empty chatter rather than novel chatter) means: "sounds with no meaning" (cf. 1 Cor 14:7–11), unintelligible words, like those of a baby; hence hazy and vain discourse, inane and empty;[9] called *mataiologia* (1 Tim 1:6; Titus 1:10), they are stigmatized by Plutarch as vain rantings against all that one says (*De tranq. anim.* 468a; *De aud. poet.* 39c). Similarly, Archimedes protests, "I wanted to avoid appearing to some people to have set forth vain words (*kenēn phōnēn*)" (Archimedes, *Eratosth.*, intro.).

This is how the first Christians assessed the "profane" in religious instruction.

11.2: *aniles fabulas adstruunt;* Origen, *Cels.* 6.34: "What old woman, given to wine, spinning out a fable to put a baby to sleep, would not be ashamed to whisper such twaddle?"

[6] Cf. the texts cited in C. Spicq, *Epîtres Pastorales*, pp. 93ff.

[7] Strabo 10.3.20; cf. 22–23; Polybius 3.38.3: "Those who speak or write of it know nothing and are only passing fables along." Plutarch hesitates to retell the myth of Thespesios, because of the thought that his account (*logos*) could pass for a fable (*mythos*) (Plutarch, *De sera* 561b); "this tale is more like a fable . . . than a sensible account" (Plutarch, *De gen.* 21). —The converted pagan Firmicus Maternus wrote a work titled *Against the Error of the Profane Religions.*

[8] 1 Tim 4:7. The piety of the Essenes was thus distinguished: "before sunrise they did not utter a single profane word" (Josephus, *War* 2.128).

[9] Cf. the ἄδολον milk of 1 Pet 2:2 and the οὐ καθαρόν of Hippocrates (*Aff.* 4.55.1). Ἄδολον is nearly synonymous with καθαρόν in *Pap.Lugd.Bat.* XVI, 7, 33.

βιάζομαι

biazomai, to use violence or force

Matt 11:12—*hē basileia tōn ouranōn biazetai, kai biastai harpazousin autēn;* Luke 16:16—*hē basileia tou theou euangelizetai kai pas eis autēn biazetai.* These verses are among the most enigmatic of the NT, and any proposed interpretation can be only a hypothesis. Neither the rabbinic texts[1] nor the papyri[2] provide direction for exegesis. The exegesis depends on whether *biazetai* is passive or middle voice and whether it should be taken in a favorable or an unfavorable sense; but these decisions are determined by the interpretation that one chooses.

We must emphasize that these two texts are not real parallels; each evangelist has not only inserted this logion in a different context but has understood it in a particular way.[3] Matthew seems more primitive and Palestinian; Luke fits with a later stage in the propagation of the gospel. So we cannot use one text to explain the other; each has its own particular significance.[4]

Predominant in Matt 11:12 is the idea of violence against the reign and of effort or aggression on the part of people.[5] All the old versions took *biazetai* as a passive; but is it transitive or intransitive? In the papyri of the

---

[1] D. Daube, *The New Testament and Rabbinic Judaism*, London, 1956, pp. 285–300.

[2] Moulton-Milligan, p. 109.

[3] Cf. M. Black, *Aramaic Approach*, p. 84, n. 2; p. 264, n. 3.

[4] On the exegesis of the first proposition of each verse, cf. W. G. Kümmel, " 'Das Gesetz und die Propheten gehen bis Johannes'—Lukas XVI, 16 im Zusammenhang der heilsgeschichtlichen Theologie der Lukasschriften," in *Verborum Veritas: Festschrift G. Stählin*, Wuppertal, 1980, pp. 89–102.

[5] Βιάζεται, βιασταί, ἁρπάζουσιν. The pair βιάζομαι–ἁρπάζω is also found at least five times in Plutarch (H. Almqvist, *Plutarch und das Neue Testament*, Uppsala, 1946, p. 38). Cf. A. H. M'Neile, *The Gospel According to St. Matthew*, London, 1952, p. 155ff. In Josephus, cf. the precise and thorough study of W. E. Moore, "Βιάζω, Ἁρπάζω and Cognates in Josephus," (in *NTS*, vol. 21, 1975, pp. 519–543) = those who had the first claim on the kingdom of God made themselves unworthy of it by their violence; violence is contrary to the nature of the kingdom, which cannot be established by the force of arms. Cf. Plutarch, *C. Gracch.* 15.4: "It is through violence and steel that proceedings are settled."

---

biazomai, S 971; *TDNT* 1.609–613; *EDNT* 1.216–217; *NIDNTT* 3.712; MM 109–110; L&N 20.9, 20.10; BDF §311(1); BAGD 140; ND 6.98–99

third-fourth century BC, it is used for the violation of a law, as with this woman, who is seeking to have construction banned: "The above-named person coming upon this land in violation of my rights brought in bricks and dug a foundation to build" (*P.Enteux.* 69, 4; *P.Tebt.* 779, 5). It is also used when an orphan complains about the encroachments of a neighbor who despises him (*P.Enteux.* 68, 11). Sometimes what is at issue is the right of the stronger, the compelling of an adversary in spite of himself, without his permission; hence an abuse of power that gives rise to a tort.[6] Sometimes it is a matter of violence as such and a stroke of force; the owner who calls upon a centurion in AD 31 because he has suffered great violence at the hands of his aggressors (*epei de kata polla biazontai me*) explains: *katabiazomenos de kai synarpozomenos* (*P.Oxy.* 2234, 8, 19; cf. *P.Fouad* 26, 33). In several papyri, and constantly in literary texts, the verb is used for forced entry into a house (*P.Tebt.* 804, 9), a route, or a city.[7]

In view of these usages, we may understand Matt 11:12 as follows. From the time of John the Baptist to the present, the reign of God has been the

---

[6] *P.Tebt.* 6, 20 = *C.Ord.Ptol.* n. 47: "Certain ones are seizing land without contracts, not paying the revenues due from them" (a circular of Ptolemy Euergetes II, from 140/139 BC); Dittenberger, *Syl.* 888, 24; *P.Cair.Zen.* 59451, 6: the chief of police Leontiskos forced us to go make bricks; *P.Tebt.* 780, 6; *P.Ryl.* 659, 9: the tax collectors want to compel me; *P.Fay.* 20, 2; *P.Flor.* 296, 24: βιάσασθαί με παρὰ τὸν τοῦ δικαίου λόγον (sixth century AD); *SB* 8033, 15: παρὰ τὸ καθῆκον βιαζόμενος; 7657, 15; 9328, 13: βιάζεται ἡμᾶς παρὰ τὸ ἔθος. Josephus, *Ant.* 4.143: βιάζεται τοὺς νόμους; 14.173: β. τὸ δίκαιον; Menander, *Dysk.* 253: "It is the law that defends him against compulsion, and his character that defends him against persuasion"; Plutarch, *De garr.* 2: "Garrulous people take the floor by force"; *Phoc.* 2.9: "God governs the world without using violence"; 9.7: "you can indeed force me to do what I do not want to do"; *Cat. Min.* 18.4: "those whom one was trying to compel"; *Ti. Gracch.* 19.4; *C. Gracch.* 8.6: "The eminent ones invited Livius Drusus to join them, but without violence, without clashing with the crowd"; 12.7.

[7] 2 Macc 14:41; Philo, *Moses* 1.108, 1.215; Epictetus 4.7.20: "no closed door for me, but for those who want to force it"; Josephus, *War* 2.262: take Jerusalem by force; 4.554: "Vespasian entered Hebron by main force"; 5.59: "Titus forced a way through to his own"; 5.112: force entrance; Josephus, *Ant.* 17.253: he had attempted to take their fortresses by force, etc.; Thucydides 7.83.5; Diodorus Siculus 2.19.7; 17. 68. 2: the Macedonians forced their way, were obliged to withdraw; Polybius 5.4.9: force passage. Often, in the OT and the writers who draw their inspiration from it, βιάζομαι means "do violence to a woman," Deut 22:25 (*ḥāzaq*), 28 (*tapaś*); Esth 7:8 (*kābaš*); Josephus, *Ant.* 2.58, 4.252, 7.152, 7.168, 11.265; *Ag. Apion* 2.201, 2.215; Josephus, *War* 1.439. The verb is frequently used with respect to surgery (cf. W. K. Hobart, *Medical Language*, p. 179). On the meaning of ἀποβιάζομαι, "seize" or "appropriate by force," cf. M.-T. Lenger, "Le Fragment de loi ptolémaïque P. Petrie III, 26," in *Studi in onore U. E. Paoli*, Florence, 1956, pp. 459–467. and M. Jager, M. Reinsma, "Ein mißverstandenes Gesetz aus ptolemäischer Zeit," in *Pap.Lugd.Bat.* XIV, pp. 114–115; but also Prov 22:22; 28:24 (*gazal*) = steal, appropriate unjustly.

object of violence, and violent or fanatical people assault it or attempt to take it by force. The logion would be about violence that is detrimental to the reign on the part of the Pharisees, the Zealots, members of the Sanhedrin, demonic powers, any Jewish or pagan adversary whatsoever, all persecutors (Acts 5:26; 21:35, *bia;* cf. Gal 1:13). Christ is a "sign spoken against" (Luke 2:34); John the Baptist is in prison (Matt 11:2), and it is a characteristic of the kingdom of God on earth to be oppressed by the violent, just as the church is attacked violently by the gates of hell.[8] It would be just as possible to take the passive *biazetai* in a favorable sense as an allusion to the power inherent in the reign of God, which "forces a way for itself" and deploys itself in force,[9] but this interpretation loses sight of the meaning of "violent people," who would then appear to be opponents of this power and would "seize" the reign rather than "receive" it (cf. nevertheless Josephus, *Ant.* 4.121: do violence to the divine will; *War* 6.108: "I strive to save people condemned by God").

The Lucan recension is altogether different. Not only have the *biastai* disappeared, so that it is no longer a question of seizing or ravishing the kingdom in order to plunder it (*harpazō*), but the main clause is controlled by the verb *euangelizetai*,[10] which has its technical biblical sense, "an-

---

[8] Matt 16:18—we might cite Heb 12:3—Jesus suffered a violent assault by sinners against his person. In favor of this exegesis, cf. Schrenk, in *TDNT*, vol. 1, pp. 609–614; A. Schlatter, *Der Evangelist Matthäus*, Stuttgart, 1948, pp. 368ff.; J. Bonsirven, *Le Règne de Dieu*, Paris, 1957, pp. 44ff.; O. Betz, "Jesu Heiliger Krieg," in *NovT*, 1958, pp. 116–137 (comparing our text to the Qumranian eschatological war and identifying the *biastai* with the *'ārûsîm*, hostile demoniac powers and their earthly henchmen: state authorities who presume to preserve the empire of the world and who oppose the blossoming of the reign of God, making it "suffer violence"); M. Brunec, "De legatione Joannis Baptistae, Mt. XI, 2–24," in *VD*, 1957, pp. 321–331; F. W. Danker, "Luke XVI, 16: An Opposition Logion," in *JBL*, 1958, pp. 231–243 (the kingdom suffers violence in a real sense; it is as it were the victim of forced entry by sinners; the Pharisees murmurred against the salvation given to publicans and against soteriological universalism. The rabbis thought that the kingdom of God was vulnerable to violence; they used the verb *kābaš* of a prophet who "does violence" to his message by keeping silent, as Jonah tried to do; of a rabbi who did violence to the halakah by misinterpreting it or rejecting it; of judges who showed favoritism to the powerful; cf. Str-B, vol. 1, pp. 599ff.); L. Ligier, *Péché d'Adam et péché du monde*, Paris, 1961, pp. 87ff.; G. Braumann, " 'Dem Himmelreich wird Gewalt angetan' (Mt. XI, 12 par.)," in *ZNW*, 1961, pp. 104–109; J. Héring, "Remarques sur les bases araméennes et hébraïques des Evangiles synoptiques," in *RHPR*, 1966, p. 28 (proposing the translation "the kingdom of heaven is oppressed and violent people try to plunder it").

[9] M. J. Lagrange, *Matthieu*, p. 221; M. Black, in *ExpT*, vol. 63, 1952, p. 290; C. Spicq, *Agapè*, vol. 1, p. 165; R. Schnackenburg, *God's Rule*, pp. 85f., 129–131.

[10] The formula εὐαγγελίζεσθαι τὴν βασιλείαν τοῦ θεοῦ is peculiar to Luke (4:43; 8:1; Acts 8:12). This evangelization is not aimed at "adversaries," but at the poor (Luke 7:22).

nounce glad tidings, good news"; for example, the granting of a favor, or a victory. The Hebrew *bāśar* (piel *biśśar*) carries the idea of joy; here, it is the joy of deliverance and salvation, which John the Baptist was the first to announce (Luke 3:18). The Acts of the Apostles will then show that when the preaching of the gospel opens the gates of the kingdom, believers receive the good news with joy. So then, how should we take the second part of the verse—*pas eis autēn biazetai?* It is difficult to think of a person entering the kingdom of God as being under compulsion or suffering violence.[11] Commentators just as easily take *biazetai* as a middle, as is often the case in the papyri, either in a positive sense ("everyone strives to get in") or in a negative sense ("everyone uses violence in his own interest"); this last meaning does not yield any sense, because it is too universal.

P. H. Menoud considers the verb to be a passive and suggests translating "each one is expressly invited to enter." He justifies this sense, which harmonizes perfectly with the preceding clause, on the basis of the weakened meaning that *biazomai* has taken on over the centuries.[12] Actually, *biazomai* in the LXX often translates the Hebrew *paṣar*, "urge someone through words or prayers" and has the sense of "insist," with the interlocutor "accepting" the demand made of him of his own free will, having the freedom to refuse (Gen 33:11; Judg 19:7; 2 Sam 13:25, 27; 2 Kgs 5:23); a meaning well attested in the literature[13] and confirmed by a papyrus from

---

[11] I will at least mention the "compel them to come in" of the parable of the impolite guests (Luke 14:23); but on the one hand the purely parabolic expression must not be taken literally; and on the other hand, ἀνάγκασον εἰσελθεῖν can just as well be translated "invite them to enter."

[12] P. H. Menoud, "Le sens du verbe BIAZETAI dans Lc. XVI, 16," in *Mélanges Rigaux*, pp. 207–212 (reprinted in P. Menoud, *Jésus-Christ et la Foi*, Neuchâtel-Paris, 1975, pp. 125–130). He takes up the exegetical position of F. Godet, *Commentaire sur l'Evangile de saint Luc*, 3d ed., Neuchâtel, 1889, vol. 2, p. 259. [ET *A Commentary on the Gospel of Luke*, Edinburgh, 1881–1890, vol. 2, pp. 172–173. It should also be noted that functionaries used violent compulsion (*P.Tebt.* 61b, second century BC), for example, for carrying out an assignation (*UPZ* 110). Cf. W. Dahlmann, Ἡ βία im Recht der Papyri, Cologne, 1968; R. Taubenschlag, *Law of Greco-Roman Egypt*, pp. 446ff.

[13] Josephus, *War* 1.83: "The king insists on knowing"; 3.393: "Certain ones insisted on seeing him at closer range"; psychological or moral pressure, as when Eli compels the prophet by oath (*Ant.* 5.351), Herod "did not cease trying to force Pheroras to separate from his wife" (1.578), certain Romans "strive to have sacrifices offered to God" (6.101); "if one may do this violence to the language" (*Ag. Apion* 2.165; cf. 150). Circumstances can force you to make a certain decision without taking away your freedom: a storm forced them to encamp in the neighboring villages (*War* 1.330; cf. *Ant.* 7.141; 12.429); "I will compel Pharaoh to order the exodus" (*Ant.* 2.271); Titus asks Simon and John not to force the destruction of the city (*War* 5.456); the remedies that the sickness forced him to take (*Ant.* 15.246); the force of fear (13.316); do violence to one's nature or to fate (4 Macc 2:8; 8:24); Xenophon, *Symp.* 2.26; Menander, *Dysk.*

AD 22, in which Serapion confesses that he is the object of friendly persuasion by friends: "I was pressed by my friends to enter the service of Apollonios" (*egō de biazomai hypo philōn genesthai oikakos tou archistatoros Apollōniou*).[14] This weakened sense seems to apply also in a rule relating to the Lycian sanctuary of Men Tyrannos in the second century AD, where *biazomai* has an absolute and reflexive meaning: having detailed the preliminary purification rituals (garlic, pork, sexual abstinence), the founder forbids the offering of any sacrifice out of his presence or without his permission (*aneu tou katheidrysamenou to hieron*), immediately adding: *ean de tis biasētai* (and if anyone violates), his offering will not be pleasing to the god.[15] There is no question of a violator's forcing entrance into the temple, but simply of his transgressing the rule and sacrificing anyway.[16]

If we add that *biazomai* expresses not only obstinate determination (Judg 13:15–16) but the firmness of a decision and zeal in carrying it out,[17] we can understand Luke 16:16 in terms of the *dynamis* inherent in the apostolic preaching: the reign of God is announced with power and absolutely every person—with no categories whatsoever—is in a hurry to follow the way and enter in; "each one forces his entrance."[18]

371: "Why are you so bent on mistreating yourself, τί κακοπαθεῖν σαυτὸν βιάζῃ?" Agathocles, negotiating with the Thracians, convinces them to do no harm to the city, μὴ βιάσασθαι τὴν πόλιν (*NCIG*, n. 6, 19–20; around 200 BC).

[14] *P.Oxy.* 294, 16; cf. *P.Giss.* 19, 13: my father forced me to take food (second century AD). Aseneth compels Joseph to allow her to wash his feet (*Jos. Asen.* 20.3) = a sweet violence! Cf. the insistence of the disciples of Emmaus, παρεβιάσαντο αὐτὸν λέγοντες (Luke 24:29).

[15] Dittenberger, *Syl.*, 1042, 8 (commented on by A. Deissmann, *Bible Studies*, p. 258); cf. *SEG*, vol. 23, 76, 8: ἐὰν δέ τις βιαζόμενος πίνῃ (around 400 BC).

[16] Cf. *P.Wisc.* 14, 14, from AD 131: Pannonios the *epitropos* violated his responsibilities, βιάσηται τὸν ληγᾶτον; 47, 38.

[17] Cf. Exod 19:24—"Let the priests and the people not rush out to ascend to Yahweh" (Hebrew *hāras*, break out); Polybius 1.74.5: "the elephants threw themselves against the encampment, βιασαμένων εἰς τὴν παρεμβολήν." With εἰς, β. is often hostile or pejorative; Josephus, *Ant.* 12.429: "he forced them to flee, εἰς φυγήν"; *War* 3.423: "they strove to get into the open"; Thucydides 1.63.1: "Aristeus decided to force entry into Potidaea, βιάσασθαι ἐς τὴν Ποτείδαιαν"; 7.69.4; *P.Hib.* 265, 3: βιάζονται εἰς τὸν Ἀρσινοίτην.

[18] French "chacun y force son entrée," the translation of E. Delebecque (*Evangile de Luc*, p. 105), who cites Black's translation: "everyone oppresses it," thus harmonizing the verse with Matt 11:12. Delebecque also observes "βία denotes obligation as well as violence": one is legally or morally compelled (*Etudes grecques*, p. 74). Cf. Διὸς βία, or Θεοῦ βία, an expression of extreme compulsion, *P.Laur.*, n. 6.

βλαβερός

blaberos, **harmful**

Derived from *blabē*, "damage, harmfulness" (Wis 11:19), the adjective *blaberos* describes that which does harm, like vinegar to the teeth or smoke to the eyes (Prov 10:26). People who seek to get rich fall prey to "senseless and baneful desires" (*epithymias pollas anoētous kai blaberas*, 1 Tim 6:9). In various contexts, *blaberos* can refer to simple inconveniences,[1] that which is injurious,[2] and even that which is disastrous (Aristotle, *Pol.* 3.15.13; 1286b). Rare in the papyri, it is used for the deterioration of a machine[3] or a person's health.[4]

In 1 Tim 6:9, the strong sense of the word is to be understood, because "terror and violence will lay riches waste" (Sir 21:4): instead of the expected multiplication of profits, covetousness that is never satisfied hastens losses that lead to ruin.[5] Otherwise, the adjective has the judicial and penal sense so often attached to the noun *blabē:* penalty, pecuniary compensation.[6] Eternal perdition (cf. *eis olethron kai apōleian*) would be the compensation, as it were, for the greedy person who prospered here below; that at least is Abraham's verdict (Luke 16:25).

---

[1] *Ep. Arist.* 255: "good counsel in its reflections takes account of the inconveniences associated with the opposed solution."

[2] Aristotle, *Pol.* 3.16.2; 1287a: "it is injurious to the body to give unequal beings equal food or clothing"; *Ep. Arist.* 192: "God shows to those whose prayers he does not answer that which would have been harmful to them"; Plutarch, *An vitiositas* 4: the Parthian poison is injurious and harmful only to those who are sensitized to it; *Phoc.* 12.3: undisciplined soldiers are injurious for the combatants.

[3] *P.Tebt.* 725, 5; a communication from an engineer of the second century BC, μεγάλων βλαβερῶν ἐπιγεγενημένων.

[4] *P.Cair.Goodsp.* II, col. I, 6; medical fragment of the second century AD, ὡς βλαβερωτερόν; Plutarch, *De curios.* 1: "unhealthy and baneful passions."

[5] This annihilation of hope allows the qualification of *epithymiai* by "senseless" (ἀνοήτους), the epithet for the rich person who trusts his fortune to guarantee his future (Luke 12:20, ἄφρων).

[6] *P.Cair.Goodsp.* 13, 13: "in addition to damages and expenses"; *P.Lips.* 3, col. I, 14; 4, 29; 6, col. II, 15; *P.Flor.* 16, 18. Cf. A. Berger, *Die Strafklauseln in den Papyrusurkunden*, 2d ed., Aalen, 1965, pp. 26ff., 133, 186. D. Hennig, "Die Arbeitsverpflichtungen der Pächter," in *ZPE*, 1972, p. 115.

γαστήρ

gastēr, belly, womb

The "belly" is an organ of the body distinct from the stomach (*stomachos*) and the intestines (*koilia*), making up one of its internal parts.[1] "The great blood vessels pass above the belly" (Hippocrates, *Nat. Hom.* 11; 196.4). Its functions, changes, and diseases are described.[2] In the OT, the Hebrew *beṭen*, related to the Akkadian *bântu*, "eminence, prominent part," can refer to a protuberance in a pillar;[3] but usually it refers to the inside

---

[1] Philo, *Creation* 118; *Post. Cain* 8. But man is said to "throw himself on his belly" (*Flight* 31 = position himself at table), and the serpent, "an animal without feet, is slumped on its belly" (*Creation* 157; *Migr. Abr.* 65; *Spec. Laws* 4.113); Josephus, *Ant.* 20.18; *P.Oxy.* 2810, 14.

[2] "The belly has no intelligence, but through it we are aware of thirst or hunger" (*Vict.* 12.2). It is made to feed and strengthen the body, not as an organ for pleasure, like the root of a plant (Musonius, frag. 18 b; ed. C. E. Lutz, p. 118, 9). It has a "prodigious function" (Philo, *Alleg. Interp.* 1.83); tortured by hunger (*Moses* 1.195), it is "filled" with food (*Contemp. Life* 55; cf. *Alleg. Interp.* 3.145; Jer 51:34, Hebrew $k^e r\bar{e}\acute{s}$) and satisfied (Philo, *Spec. Laws* 4.82; *Virtues* 126, 135), but it can be overloaded (Philostratus, *Gym.* 48): "Greeks measure their food by the capacity of their belly" (Xenophon, *Lac.* 2.1). If a person changes habits, "the belly is thrown off" (Hippocrates, *Acut.*, Appendix 42.1); "a walk after dinner dries it out" (*Vict.* 4.49.2; 4.54.2). There can be "pain in the belly" (*Loc. Hom.* 20; 47.4). Agrippa dies after five days of abdominal pain (Josephus, *Ant.* 19.350). The belly is shrunken (Philostratus, *Gym.* 34–35), or swollen (Num 5:22; Hippocrates, *Acut.* 51.1; *Nat. Hom.* 21.214.16; Philo, *Alleg. Interp.* 3.148–150; *Spec. Laws* 3.62) and produces colic (Hippocrates, *Nat. Hom.* 20.212.7); "dropsy can concern the belly alone" (*Aff.* 4.57.2). Philo often identifies or associates the belly with sexual functions (*Alleg. Interp.* 3.157; *Worse Attacks Better* 113; *Post. Cain* 155; *Giants* 15; *Dreams* 1.122; *Moses* 1.160).

[3] 1 Kgs 7:20; cf. P. Dhorme, *Emploi métaphorique*, pp. 107, 133–134. Compare γαστήρ, the rounded part of a shield (Tyrtaeus 11.24); γάστρα, the belly of a vase (Dioscorides 5.103, 144); a swollen pouch of processed meat: a sausage (Aristophanes, *Nub.* 409).

---

gastēr, S 1064; *EDNT* 1.239; MM 121; L&N 8.68, 23.19, 23.50; BAGD 152

of a person, especially in contradistinction to the lips, the organ of externalization.[4] If the seat of wisdom is in the belly (Job 32:18-19; Prov 20:27), it is because certain words, spoken of as if they were delicacies, descend "into the chambers of the belly," to the depths (Prov 18:8; 26:22).

"Belly" is substituted for the mother's womb.[5] The expression "to have in the belly" (*echein en gastri*) as a way of saying that a woman is pregnant is first attested in Herodotus 3.32 with respect to the wife of Cambyses; the LXX uses this expression to translate the Hebrew *hārâh*.[6] It is used almost constantly in the NT,[7] notably for the Virgin Mary (*heurethē en gastri echousa*, Matt 1:18), fulfilling the prophecy of Isa 7:14.

But "to conceive" was also expressed *syllambanein en gastri* (Gen 25:21), especially in the medical writings.[8] It is therefore not surprising that Doctor Luke put the angel's announcement to Mary this way: *kai idou syllēpsē en gastri kai texē huion*.[9]

---

[4] The interior of an object is called "the belly." Jonah (2:3-4) was in "the belly of Sheol . . . in the depths of the sea." Cf. *Flight* 204: "that which is hidden in the belly."

[5] Hebrew *reḥem*. Cf. "the mother's belly" (Judg 16:17), a child described as "son of the belly" or "fruit of the belly" (Gen 30:2; Ps 127:3). Cf. Hippocrates, *Carn.* 6.3: "the child in the belly" (ἐν τῇ γαστρί); *P.Lond.* 1713, 30; *SB* 7288, 2: γαστρὸς ἔχουσα ὄγκον; Philo, *Moses* 1.19. The epitaph for Heroïs, dead at eighteen years: γαστρὸς ἔχουσα ὄγκον (*SB* 5718); cf. Euripides, *Ion* 15. Ps.-Phocylides 184 prescribes: "a woman shall not destroy the fetus in her belly"; likewise *Sib. Or.* 2.281.

[6] With respect to Hagar (Gen 16:4, 5, 11), Samson's mother (Judg 13:3, 5, 7); cf. Gen 38:24-25; Exod 21:22; 2 Kgs 8:12; 15:16; Isa 40:11; Hos 14:1; Job 21:10. It is also a secular usage, Hippocrates, *Nat. Puer.* 15.1; 18.4; 21.3; 30.3-5; *Mul.* 1.1, 3; Artemidorus Daldianus, *Onir.* 2.18; 3.32; *P.Cair.Zen.* 59328, 21; *P.Wisc.* 78, 21; *P.Lond.* 2053, 3; *P.Magd.* 4, 6 (the complaint of a *klērouchos* concerning the theft of eight pigs, not counting the piglets and a pregnant white sow that was killed by the criminals, τὴν ἑτέραν ἀπέκτειναν λευκὴν, ἐν γαστρὶ ἔχουσαν); *P.Tebt.* 800, 29 (142 BC); *P.Ryl.* 68, 13 (89 BC); *PSI* 1440, 1 (second-third century AD); *P.Flor.* 130, 3 (third century).

[7] Matt 24:19—"Woe to the women who are with child" (ταῖς ἐν γαστρὶ ἐχούσαις, Mark 13:17; Luke 21:23). At the Parousia, the woes of humanity are analogous to those of a woman who is going to give birth (ὥσπερ ἡ ὠδὶν τῇ γαστρὶ ἐχούσῃ, 1 Thess 5:3). In Rev 12:2, the Christian community, facing the dragon, "is pregnant (γυνὴ . . . ἐν γαστρὶ ἔχουσα) and cries out in her labor pains." — The NT does not use the expression λαβεῖν ἐν γαστρί, "receive in the womb," i.e., "conceive, carry young" (Hippocrates, *Nat. Puer.* 13.1; *Carn.* 19.1; Aristotle, *HA* 9.50.8; Gen 30:41; 38:18; Exod 2:2, 22; Num 11:12; 2 Sam 11:5; 2 Kgs 4:17; 1 Chr 7:23; Isa 8:3; 26:18; Philo, *Prelim. Stud.* 131, 135, 138), also written λαμβάνειν ἐν γαστρί (Hippocrates, *Nat. Puer.* 15.4; Philo, *Prelim. Stud.* 130, 135).

[8] Hippocrates, Dioscorides, Galen. Numerous references given in Hobart, *Medical Language*, 1882, pp. 91-92.

[9] Luke 1:31. The formula is apparently pleonastic (for Elizabeth, we have only συνέλαβεν, Luke 1:24, 36). R. Laurentin (*Structure et théologie de Luc I–II*, Paris, 1957,

Gastēr is often used with a pejorative nuance, for example in Philo,[10] who denounces its desires (*Creation* 158; *Alleg. Interp.* 3.149; *Spec. Laws* 1.192; 4.96) and its pleasures.[11] It is insatiable (*Dreams* 2.147, 208) and must be mastered (*Prelim. Stud.* 80; *Spec. Laws* 2.195; 4.127). It is with this meaning that Titus 1:12 cites Epimenides of Cnossos, who calls the Cretans "idle bellies" (*gasteres argai*). Already in Homer, Melantheus insults the swineherd by saying that he would rather "fill his belly" than work.[12] The insult became traditional; cf. the disdain of the Muses: "Shepherds . . . who are nothing but bellies" (Hesiod, *Th.* 26). At Rome, L. Veturius was drummed out of the equestrian order because "from neck to groin he was nothing but a belly" (Plutarch, *Cat. Mai.* 9.6); the materialistic turncoats of Alexandria apostasized "for the love of their belly" (3 Macc 7:11; cf. Phil 3:19); "rebels against the divine law, incapable of restraint . . . in the quest for pleasures of the belly and the entrails" (Philo, *Virtues* 182); whereas Socrates considered humans as related to the gods, "we, on the other hand, regard them as bellies, as guts, as sexual organs" (Epictetus 1.9.26). J. M. Edmonds quotes an anonymous writer: "the whole body is a belly."[13]

---

p. 68) thinks that Luke wanted to emphasize the dwelling of Yahweh in the womb (Hebrew *bᵉqerem*) of the Daughter of Zion, in the ark of the covenant (according to Zeph 3:15 *b*, 17 *a*; Isa 12:6). Cf. H. Quecke, "Lukas I, 31 in den alten Übersetzungen," in *Bib*, 1965, pp. 333–348; R. Schürmann, *Das Lukasevangelium*, Freiburg, Basel, Vienna, 1969, p. 46.

[10] *Joseph* 154; *Moses* 2.156; *Spec. Laws* 1.174; *Good Man Free* 156; *To Gaius* 275

[11] *Alleg. Interp.* 1.86; 2.26, 76; 3.62, 114, 138, 141, 144; *Cherub.* 93; *Sacr. Abel and Cain* 33, 49; *Flight* 35; *Joseph* 61; *Moses* 2.23; *Spec. Laws* 1.150; 2.163; 3.43; *Virtues* 208

[12] *Od.* 17.228. P. Chantraine, "Remarques sur la langue et le vocabulaire du Corpus hippocratique," in *La Collection hippocratique* (Colloque de Strasbourg, 1972), Leiden, 1975, pp. 37–39. Cf. Jer 51:34—Nebuchadnezzar "has filled his belly."

[13] Γαστὴρ ὅλον τὸ σῶμα . . . ἕρπον τοῖς ὀδοῦσι θηρίον, J. M. Edmonds, *Attic Comedy*, vol. 3 A, p. 418, n. 392 a. For the Latin writers, cf. C. Spicq, *Epîtres Pastorales*, p. 610; J. Taillardat, *Suétone: Des Terms injurieux*, Paris, 1967, pp. 62, 87.

γνήσιος

gnēsios, **authentic, dear, legitimate**

→*see also* ἀνυπόκριτος, γνήσιος; ὑποκρίνομαι, ὑπόκρισις, ὑποκριτής

As opposed to the adopted son or to the illegitimate child (*nothos*, Heb 12:8; Menander, *Sam.* 236–237; Philo, *Dreams* 2.47), *gnēsios* modifies the child born of a legitimate marriage: "the title of legitimate child belongs to the one who is a son by blood."[1] In practice, this juridical meaning becomes synonymous with "authentic, true, real," and it is with this meaning that Paul addresses Timothy as "*gnēsios* child in (the) faith" (*gnēsiō teknō en pistei*, 1 Tim 1:2) and Titus as "*gnēsios* child according to a common faith" (*gnēsiō teknō kata koinēn pistin*).[2] In the Hellenistic period, this term takes on an emotional density attested notably in the papyri and the inscriptions, where it means "dear" or "much beloved."[3]

I. — It is used for children, with a very affectionate nuance; Isaac is "son . . . *gnēsios*, beloved, and only" (*huios . . . gnēsios, agapētos, kai monos*);[4]

---

[1] Demosthenes, *C. Leoch.* 44.49: τὸ μὲν γὰρ γνήσιόν ἐστιν, ὅταν ἦ γόνῳ γεγονός. The natural father is the πατήρ γόνῳ, the adoptive father ποιητός (Lysias, *C. Agor.* 13.91). *P.Vindob.Bosw.* 5, 11: πρὸς γάμου κοινωνίαν τέκνων γνησίων σπορᾶς ἕνεκεν (with the note of the editor); *P.Oxy.* 1267, 15; cf. F. Schulz, "Roman Registers of Births and Birth Certificates," in *JRS*, 1942, pp. 78–91; 1943, pp. 55–64. M. Scheller, "Griech. γνήσιος, altind. *játya* und Verwandtes," in *Festschrift Debrunner*, Berne, 1954, pp. 399–407.

[2] Titus 1:4. On spiritual begetting and the designation "son" as implying disciple and successor, cf. P. Gutierrez, *Paternité spirituelle*, pp. 225ff. et passim.

[3] This meaning was noted and strongly emphasized by L. Robert, *Hellenica*, vol. 13, Paris, 1966, pp. 218ff.

[4] Philo, *Abraham* 168; cf. *Moses* 1.15: the daughter of Pharaoh takes pity on the infant Moses, "her heart full of maternal affection, as if he were her own child, ὡς ἐπὶ γνησίῳ παιδί"; *Spec. Laws* 4.203: "the sweet hope of begetting legitimate children"; *Good Man Free* 87; *CII* 2, 739; *MAMA* 8, 220: Λούκιος Ἰωάνη ἀναγνώστη φιλτάτῳ καὶ γνησίῳ υἱῷ; cf. 6, 358; 368; 7, 427: τοῦ γνησίου μου τέκνου; 565; H. Gregoire, *Asie Mineure*, n. 74, 310.

---

gnēsios, S 1103; TDNT 1.727; EDNT 1.225; MM 128–129; L&N 73.1; BAGD 162–163

Meltinianos reserves a place in his tomb for "my dear children" (*ta gnēsia mou paidia*, MAMA, VIII, 595; CII 739). It is used for women—mothers or wives—with a clear nuance of love: "in memory of my dear wife Agelais" (*Agelaïdi gynaiki gnēsia mneias heneken*);[5] for parents, "my sweetest and most gnēsios father" (*ton glykytaton kai gnēsion patera*, BCH, 1883, p. 274, n. 15; cf. Philo, *To Gaius* 62, 71; MAMA, I, 361, 365); for brothers and sisters: "do not trade a true brother for gold from Ophir";[6] and finally for friends, compatriots, companions, and "dear colleagues": *gnēsios erastēs*;[7] "let them not forget their true friends."[8] This is the meaning when St. Paul writes, "For your part, Syzygos, true yokefellow, I ask you to come to the aid" of Euodia and Syntyche.[9] In addition to the word-play, the designation is affectionate.[10] To convey this nuance, 1 Tim 1:2 and Titus 1:4 should be translated "dear and true child."

II. — In addition, *gnēsios* is used in a religious sense for the transmitters of revelation. Isis to Horus: "He made me swear not to pass on the revelation, except only to my child and dear friend" (*ei mē monon teknō kai philō*

---

[5] *SEG* 6, 232; cf. *P.Eleph.* 1, 3; MAMA 4, 305: τῇ γλυκυτάτῃ τεκούσῃ Μελτίνῃ καὶ γνησίᾳ γυναικί Ἀμμίᾳ; 1, 358. The superlative *glykytatos*, synonymous with *philtatos*, "dearest," recurs constantly as a feminine epithet (7, 162, 272, 274, 382, 390, 548; 8, 252; *I.Side*, 120; cf. H. Koskenniemi, *Studien zur Idee und Phraseologie des griechischen Briefes*, Helsinki, 1956, pp. 97ff.)

[6] Sir 7:18. Cf. *P.Gron.* 10, 9: ἡ ἐμὴ γνεσιωτάτη ἀδελφὴ Σενεπόνυχος; *P.Osl.* 132, 8; *P.Lond.* 992, 5; 1007, 10; 1244, 5; *P.Michael* 45, 3: Κολλοῦθος γνήσιος αὐτοῦ ἀδελφὸς ἐκ τῶν αὐτῶν γονέων; *P.Oxy.* 48, 12: τοῦ μετηλλαχότος αὐτῆς γνησίου ἀδελφοῦ (AD 86); 2584, 30: πρὸς τὸν ὁμογνήσιόν μου ἀδελφόν; *SB* 9395, 12; 9770, 10; *SEG* 8, 621, 19: "dear Philhermes, who was an affectionate and true brother to me, not according to nature—for by nature he was my cousin—but by his tenderness"; *C.P.Herm.* 49, 3.

[7] "Dear lover," an inscription from the area of Rome (published by L. Robert, *Hellenica*, vol. 4, Paris, 1948, p. 33); *BGU* 86, 19: τὸν γνήσιον αὐτοῦ φίλον. F. Cumont, *Pontica*, n. 20, 26: ἐν πᾶσιν εὔστοργον καὶ γνήσιον φίλον . . . μνημονεύω.

[8] *P.Fouad* 54, 34. M. Naldini, *Il Cristianesimo in Egitto*, n. 58, 5: φίλον γνήσιον; B. Latyschev, *Inscriptiones Antiquae*, vol. 4, n. 425: Callisthenes to Onesimos, τῷ εἰδίῳ γνησίῳ φίλῳ; *P.Apoll.* 24, 1: "I have already written to your remarkable and noble Friendship, τῇ περιβλέπτῳ σου γνηείᾳ φιλίᾳ"; *P.Ness.* 47, 2: ἀσπάζω σε τὸν ἐμοῦ γνησίων φίλων ὄντα, δέσποτα; 68, 2, 7.

[9] Phil 4:3. On this text, cf. C. Spicq, *Théologie morale*, vol. 2, p. 587, n. 5. For the name Syntyche, cf. *P.IFAO* II, n. 7, 1.

[10] Γνήσιος is a common term of affinity; cf. a decree of Tenos: γνησίαν ἔχοντι πρὸς πάντας φιλοστοργίαν (C. Michel, *Recueil*, 394, 49; middle of the first century BC); a decree of Sestos: πρὸ πλείστου θέμενος τὸ πρὸς τὴν πατρίδα γνήσιον καὶ ἐκτενές (ibid., 327, 7); a decree of Chersonese: ἀγάπαν γνασίαν ἐνδείκνυται, (B. Latyschev, *Inscriptiones Antiquae*, vol. 1, 359, 6 = L. Robert, *Opera Minora Selecta*, vol. 1, p. 311, n. 2); letter of Herakleotes to Hadrian: πᾶσαι σπουδαὶ καὶ πάσα φιλοστοργία κεχραμένοι γνασίαι (L. Robert, ibid.); *P.Lond.* 1917, 14: ἀγαπηταὶ γνησιώταται καὶ ἀξιώταται; *I.Delos*, 1512: γνησίως καὶ προθύμως.

gnēsiō).[11] More generally, it modifies the authorized interpreter of a teaching: Aristotle is "the most authentic disciple of Plato";[12] in a more specialized sense, it refers to the legitimate heir to whom a father passes on his authority and command (Philo, *Virtues* 59; *To Gaius* 24; cf. *Spec. Laws* 4.184; Josephus, *Ant.* 17.45). It may stand comparison to the position at court of the "king's friend"; for Eleazer, for example, King Ptolemy is a sincere friend.[13] These latter nuances fit well with the case of the apostle's representatives at Ephesus and Crete. Not only does their spiritual father show tender affection for them that will gain honor for them among Christians,[14] but they are representatives vested with a legitimate authority that cannot rightly be contested; they are, in the final analysis, authentic interpreters of his doctrine, the faithful echo, as it were, of Paul's voice (cf. Philo, *Contemp. Life* 72, and 2 Tim 3:10).

III. — When modifying things, *gnēsios* refers to those which are appropriate, well suited for their purpose;[15] with respect to a service, rendering a service sincerely means rendering it effectively;[16] thus should be understood the exhortation to the Corinthians to be generous toward the saints at Jerusalem (*to tēs hymeteras agapēs gnēsion dokimazōn*, 2 Cor 8:8; cf. *P.Ant.* 188, 16: *to gnēsion endeixesthai*; *P.Lond.* 1041, 2: *gnēsion agapēn*). They must

[11] In M. Berthelot, *Collection des anciens alchimistes grecs*, 2d ed., London, 1963, p. 34, 6; cf. A. J. Festugière, *L'Expérience religieuse du médecin Thessalos*, in *RB*, 1939, p. 51; *Hermès Trismégiste*, vol. 1, p. 259.

[12] Dionysius of Halicarnassus, *Pomp.* 1: ὁ γνησιώτατος αὐτοῦ μαθητής; Claudius to the Alexandrians: "My brother Germanicus, addressing you γνησιωτέραις ὑμᾶς φωναῖς" (*P.Lond.* 1912, 27; with the note of H. I. Bell, *Jews and Christians in Egypt*, p. 31); Philodemus of Gadara, *Adv. Soph.*, frag. y III, 5: γνήσιος ἀναγνώστης; cf. i³, 11–12.

[13] *Ep. Arist.* 41: φίλῳ γνησίῳ (with the commentary of A. Pelletier, *Josèphe adaptateur*, p. 112; idem, *Philon in Flaccum*, Paris, 1967, p. 159); Dittenberger, *Or.* 308, 7–8, 13–15: the Attalid queen Apollonis and her sons.

[14] Cf. this inscription of Palmyra: γνησίως καὶ φιλοτείμως παράσταντα, published by C. Dunant, *Le Sanctuaire de Baalshamin à Palmyre*, Rome, 1971, n. 45 A, 3, and J. T. Milik, *Dédicaces faites par les dieux*, Paris, 1972, p. 74.

[15] *P.Giss.* 47, 4: ἐπὶ τῷ κατὰ τὰς εὐχὰς γνήσια καὶ λείαν ἄξια εὑρῆσθαι; 15: παραζώνιον γὰρ πρὸς τὸ παρὸν γνήσιον οὐκ εὑρέθη; cf. Philo, *Prov.* 2.24: "and who with the thought of the genuine [γνησίων] before them would not disregard the spurious for its sake" (LCL).

[16] Philo, *Unchang. God* 116; *Worse Attacks Better* 21; 3 Macc 3:19—γνήσιον βούλονται φέρειν. This is very often the meaning of the adverb γνησίως; cf. 2 Macc 14:8: "sincere (effective) care for the interests of the king"; Phil. 2:20—"I really have no one like him to take a sincere (effective) interest in your situation"; *P.Tebt.* 326, 11: προστήσεσθαι γνησίως τοῦ παιδίου = he will effectively protect the child; hence the meaning "regularly, conformably to the rule" (*P.Fouad* 6, 10); *SB* 7655, 33; 9935, 15: οἷς ἀπ' ἀρχῆς τήν τε φιλίαν καὶ τὴν συμμαχίαν γνησίως συντετήρηκα; *Pap. Lugd.Bat.* XI, 7, 15.

prove the authenticity of their love, to be sure; but their alms are "normal."[17] The external, material gesture only gives "proper" expression to the internal urgency of love. But there is beauty and honor in showing oneself "true" (cf. Philo, Post. Cain 102), in demonstrating one's intimate feelings: *gnēsiōs kai endoxōs*.[18]

---

[17] Cf. BGU 248, 21: τὰ ἔργα τῶν ἀμπέλων ἰδίων γνησίως γενέσθω; I.Magn. 188, 9: ἐν πάσαις ταῖς τῆς πατρίδος χρείαις γνησίως προνοήσαντα; Dittenberger, Syl. 708, 10: τειχοποιὸς ἀνδρηότατα μὲν καὶ γνησιώτατα τῆς ἐπιμελήας τῶν ἔργων προέστη; SEG, vol. 4, 600, 11.

[18] Dittenberger, Syl. 721, 42; SEG, vol. 15, 849, 3: "Having aided with nobility and generosity (γνησίως καὶ φιλοτείμως) the merchants, the caravans, and the citizens"; cf. Polybius 4.30.4: οἱ γνήσιοι τῶν ἀνδρῶν = well-born men. In the sixth-seventh century, Γνῆσιε = Your Brotherliness, a title of respect (P.Apoll. 37, 12; cf. P.Ant. 188, 1; P.Ness. 75, 1).

δειλία, δειλιάω, δειλός

deilia, **faintheartedness, cowardice, fear;** *deiliaō*, **to be fearful;** *deilos*, **fearful**

Associated with *phobos* (Wis 4:17), *eklysis* (2 Macc 3:24), *anandria* (cf. 4 Macc 6:20), *atolmia* (Philo, *Virtues* 25; Josephus, *Ant.* 4.298; 15.142; Aeneas Tacticus, *Polior.* 16.20), faintheartedness or cowardice can be defined as "a failure of spirit caused by fear."[1] Rarely mentioned in the papyri, it is used for mere reserve or abstention,[2] a lack of courage and of reaction, a sort of torpor,[3] and finally fright (*tarassō*, Ps 55:4; John 14:27; Josephus, *Ant.* 5.216) which can become panic and terror[4] in the face of extreme danger.

I. — Jesus reproaches the apostles for this psychological fear when they are terrified by the storm (Matt 8:26; Mark 4:40), because it involves a

---

[1] Theophrastus, *Char.* 25.1.

[2] A prisoner condemned to die writes to the emperor: "I shall not be afraid to tell you the truth" (*P.Paris* 68 *c* 4); *P.Giss.* 40, 11; Philo, *Good Man Free* 21, 159; Josephus, *Ant.* 10.5: "Out of cowardice, he did not come himself but sent three of his friends."

[3] Lev 26:36—"I will cause them to have weakness of heart, . . . the noise of a falling leaf will put them to flight, they will flee as one flees the sword, and they will fall even when no one is pursuing them"; Prov 19:15; 2 Macc 3:24. Menander, *Sam.* 125: "I am losing heart, now that the matter is at hand" (synonym of weakling, coward, ἀνδρόγυνος; 128). Plutarch, *Fab.* 17.5: "the cowardice and apathy of Fabius (δειλία καὶ ψυχρότης)"; *Cleom.* 33.7: the cravenness of Ptolemy. Cf. Plutarch, *Ant.* 93.4.

[4] 1 Macc 4:32—"Sow panic in their ranks, dissolve their confidence in their might, and let them be distressed by their defeat" (prayer of Judas Maccabeus in the face of the invasion of Lysias); Josephus, *War* 6.212: "Terrified in this circumstance alone" (an account of cannibalism); Quintus of Smyrna, *Posthomerica* 5.187. "Cowardice and faintheartedness" of the soldiers (Polybius 5.85.13).

---

deilia, S 1167; *EDNT* 1.281; MM 138; L&N 25.266; BAGD 173 ‖ *deiliaō*, S 1168; *EDNT* 1.281; MM 138; L&N 25.267; BAGD 173 ‖ *deilos*, S 1169; *EDNT* 1.281; MM 138; L&N 25.268; BAGD 173

δειλία, deilia, etc. 301

moral deficiency:[5] they no longer have faith, or they have but little faith in the presence of the Savior, who has to reassure them. Reference is made to the wisdom literature: when one relies on God, there is nothing to fear.[6]

II. — When Rev 21:8 places the fainthearted and the unbelieving in the lake of fire, it has in view Christians during times of persecution who, out of a fear of suffering, renounce their faith. It is a commonplace that human courage and cowardice are revealed in the face of death;[7] the latter is expressed in flight before danger,[8] but it also lays hold of the lazy farmer (Josephus, *War* 3.42; *P.Tebt.* 58, 27) and the athlete[9] and every human heart that weakens (literally "melts," Isa 13:7, Hebrew *māsas*), even the hearts of apostles facing eschatological trials (John 14:27). Cowardice can then be defined as "a more serious disease than those which afflict the body,

---

[5] For the textual variants, cf. V. Taylor, *The Gospel According to St Mark*, London, 1952, p. 276. The Palestinian and Curetonian Syriac suppress the reproach; Jesus simply says "Fear not" and says nothing about faith (cf. G. Gander, *L'Evangile de l'église*, Geneva, 1970, vol. 1, p. 57). According to Ben Sirach, the heart of the sage, set firmly upon thought-out convictions, will be fearless when the time comes (Sir 22:16); on the other hand, the timid heart, with its foolish convictions, will not stand firm before any fear whatsoever (22:18); cf. J. Hadot, *Penchant mauvais et volonté libre dans la Sagesse de Ben Sira*, Brussels, 1970, p. 117); 2:12—"Unhappy are the faint hearts and the limp hands," which have no strength for combat. Cf. 2 Chr 13:7—"Rehoboam, who was young and weak of heart [literally 'slight,' Hebrew *raq*) could not stand up to them."

[6] Hebrew *pāḥad*; Ps 14:5—"They shall tremble with fear where there is nothing to be afraid of"; 27:1—"Yahweh is the refuge of my life, of whom shall I be afraid?"; 78:53—"Yahweh leads them in safety, they do not tremble"; Sir 34:14—"The one who fears the Lord dreads nothing, he will not be weakhearted, for he is his hope"; *T. Sim.* 2.3; on the fear of the pilot in the storm, cf. Josephus, *War* 3.368.

[7] Ps 55:4—"My heart is troubled within me, the fear of death is upon me"; 2 Macc 15:8—Judas Maccabeus "urged those who were with him not to dread the attack of the Gentiles"; 4 Macc 6:20-21—"It would be a shameful thing for us to prolong our lives for a few days during which our cowardice would make us a general laughing-stock ... if we incur through our faintheartness the scorn of the tyrant"; 14:4—"None of the seven young men trembled, none hesitated in the face of death"; Josephus, *War* 3.365: "it is cowardice to be unwilling to die when necessary"; 7.382; *Ant.* 6.215: Melcha fears for the life of her husband; Plutarch, *De sera* 11; associated with softness (19); with cravenness (*De laude* 13); *Alex.* 50.10-11; 58.4; *Phoc.* 9.2-3 (as a synonym of ἄνανδρος and the opposite of θαρσαλέος); *Cat. Min.* 22.3; 58.8; Diodorus Siculus 17.15.2: "Those who were not willing to die to save the city Phocion reproached for their lack of manliness and their cowardliness."

[8] Menander, *Dysk.* 123: "I beg you, flee! That would be faintheartedness (δειλία)"; Philo, *Worse Attacks Better* 37: "Our enemies treat this evasion (ὄκνον) as cowardliness; for our friends it's prudence."

[9] Philostratus, *Gym.* 25: εἰ θαρσαλέος ἢ δειλός.

because it destroys the faculties of the soul" (Philo, *Virtues* 26) and seen as a major vice, characteristic of base souls.[10]

III. — "God has given us a spirit not of faintheartedness but of strength and love" (2 Tim 1:7). St. Paul encourages his young and timid disciple not to be frightened at the difficulties of his post; more precisely, he stirs up "the good soldier of Jesus Christ" (2 Tim 2:3) to undertake and pursue combat (1 Tim 1:18) according to the traditional military maxim, dating back to Deuteronomy: "Conquer . . . fear not and be not disheartened."[11] The fainthearted are excluded from the army;[12] cravenness was the vice most opposed to courage in combat (Sir 37:11; Philo, *Moses* 1.233; 1.235). It goes without saying that strength and hardiness are required above all in a leader: "faintheartedness and cravenness in private life bring dishonor to those afflicted by them, but in a general charged with responsibilities, they become a public calamity and a great disaster" (Polybius 3.81.7).

---

[10] Wis 9:14; 17:10; Philo, *Husbandry* 17; *Sacr. Abel and Cain* 15; Epictetus 4.1.109. Zeno (in Stobaeus, *Ecl.* 2.7.5*a*; vol. 2, pp. 57–58); an anonymous author of the first century comments: δειλός· τὸν πόνον φεύγων (in J. M. Edmonds, *Attic Comedy*, vol. 3 A, p. 368, n. 115f.). Cf. Lucian, *Nav.* 33: "I am too fainthearted and I would not able to bear being far from home."

[11] The word of Yahweh to Moses before the conquest of the Promised Land (Deut 1:21); Moses to the people: "Be strong and courageous. Fear not, and tremble not before them" (Deut 31:6); to Joshua (Deut 31:8; Josh 1:9; 8:1); Joshua to the people (Josh 10:25).

[12] Deut 20:8; Judg 7:3; 1 Macc 3:56—"He told those who were afraid to return home." Disqualifying cowardice, Philo, *Virtues* 22, 25; *Husbandry* 154; Plutarch, *Fab.* 7.6: "Soldiers weakhearted enough to let themselves be taken by the enemy"; *Aem.* 19.4: "Heracles does not receive fainthearted sacrifices offered by the fainthearted"; cf. Onasander 14.1.

δειπνέω

deipneō, **to dine**

In instituting the Eucharist, the Lord blessed the cup *meta to deipnēsai* (Luke 22:20; 1 Cor 11:25), and he promised the church at Laodicea, "If anyone hears my voice and opens the door, I will come in with him and dine with him (*deipnēsō*) and he with me" (Rev 3:20).

Among the papyri are preserved a certain number of invitations to dinner either in a private home, or in a temple,[1] or above all at the *klinē* of Sarapis,[2] to which have been compared the NT texts cited above and participation "at the Lord's table" (1 Cor 10:21). In effect, the pagan sacrifice was a meal offered to the god;[3] sometimes the god was received at table, sometimes the god invited people to table in the *Hēraion* to rejoice in the divine presence.[4] For example, at the mystery of Panamara, the priest of Zeus writes to the Rhodians: "Although the god invites all men to his feast

---

[1] *P.Oxy.* 111: "Heraïs asks you to dinner on the occasion of the marriage of his children, tomorrow the fifth, at nine o'clock"; *P.Oxy.* 2678 (in the temple of Sabazios).

[2] *P.Oxy.* 110, 523, 1484, 1755, 2592; *P.Oslo* 157; *P.Yale* 85: Ἐρωτᾷ σε Διονύσιος δειπνῆσαι τῇ κα εἰς κλείνην Ἡλίου μεγάλου Σαράπιδος ἀπὸ ὥρας θ΄ ἐν τῇ πατρικῇ ἑαυτοῦ οἰκίᾳ (cf. M. Vandoni, *Feste pubbliche e private nei Documenti greci*, Milan, 1964, n. 138, 140–143, 145); *P.Fouad* 76: "Sarapous invites you to dinner for the sacrifice in honor of Lady Isis, in his house, tomorrow, that is, the twenty-ninth, at the ninth hour"; *P.Köln* 57; *SB* 11049. Cf. J. F. Gilliam, "Invitations to the *Klinē* of Sarapis," in *P.Coll.Youtie* I, pp. 315–324.

[3] A. J. Festugière, *Monde gréco-romain*, vol. 2, pp. 92ff. *P.Oxy.* 3164, 3: ἱερὰ κλίνη.

[4] Cf. *Pap.Colon.* inv. 2555: καλεῖ σε ὁ θεὸς εἰς κλείνην γεινομένην ἐν τῷ Θοηρείῳ αὔριον ἀπὸ ὥρας θ΄ (edited with commentary by I. Koenen, "Eine Einladung zur Kline des Sarapis," in *ZPE*, vol. 1, 1967, pp. 121–126). On the εὐφροσύνη of these communions, cf. A. Laumonier, *Les Cultes indigènes en Carie*, pp. 258, 315ff.; properly speaking, the joy of the dinner parties, cf. L. Robert, *Hellenica*, vol. 10, p. 199, n. 7; vol. 11–12, p. 13, n. 1.

---

deipneō, S 1172; *TDNT* 2.34–35; *EDNT* 1.281–282; *NIDNTT* 2.520–521, 536; *MM* 138; *L&N* 23.20; *BAGD* 173

and to all he offers a common table and equally honorable roles, nevertheless, as he considers your city worthy of special honors . . . and on account of our having shared together in the same holy things, I invite you to come to the god, I urge all citizens of your city to take part in the joy that he offers you."[5] It is the god who offers the meal and presides; one responds to his call; the believer is closely united to his god.

These parallels are interesting from the point of view of linguistics and the history of religions, but the Pauline formulation may be more directly inspired by Mal 1:7, 12; Ezek 39:20; 44:16.

---

[5] *BCH*, 1927, pp. 73–74, n. 11; cited and translated by A. J. Festugière, *Monde gréco-romain*, vol. p. 2, 173; cf. A. Deissmann, *Light*, p. 351. A. Bernand, *El-Kanaïs*, n. 59 bis. On the Theodaisia, the Proixenia, the xenika, the Theoxenia, cf. D. M. Pippidi, *Scythica Minora*, Bucharest-Amsterdam, 1975, pp. 139ff.

δεισιδαίμων, δεισιδαιμονία

deisidaimōn, **superstitious, religious;** *deisidaimonia*, **superstition, religion, reverence**

This adjective and this substantive, unknown in the LXX and the papyri, are among the numerous compounds featuring *daimōn* as the second component.[1] Both have favorable and pejorative usages. Religious fear is always involved;[2] Theophrastus gives the best definition: "Superstition would seem to be a feeling of fear (*deilia*) toward the divine power (*pros to daimonion*)" (*Char.* 16.1).

The favorable meaning—religion and reverence toward the deity—is well attested: "The sovereign will be very zealous toward the gods, because the citizens are less likely to fear that they will suffer from illegal acts when they perceive that the one in authority is religious (*deisidaimona*) and

---

[1] Here, compounded with the verb δείδω-. In Homer, δαίμων refers to "a divine power that one cannot name or does not want to name; hence the meanings of divinity and on the other hand destiny; a δαίμων is not the object of worship" (P. Chantraine, *Dictionnaire étymologique*, on this word; idem, "Le Divin et les dieux chez Homère," in *Entretiens sur l'antiquité classique*, Fondation Hardt, vol. 1, Vandoeuvre-Geneva, 1952, pp. 50ff.); G. François, *Le Polythéisme et l'emploi au singulier des mots ΘΕΟΣ, ΔΑΙΜΩΝ dans la littérature grecque*, Paris, 1957. The documentation is assembled by P. J. Koets, Δεισιδαιμονία, Purmerend, 1929; C. Spicq, "Religion (vertu de)," in *DBSup*, vol. 10, col. 129ff. For the evolution of the meaning of δαίμων, which in part controls that of δεισιδαίμων, E. des Places, " 'Quasi superstitiosiores' (Actes XVII, 22)," in *Studiorum Paulinorum Congressus* (AnBib, vol. 18), Rome, 1963, pp. 183-191; idem, *La Religion grecque*, Paris, 1969, pp. 330-333.

[2] Hesychius explains the word δεισιδαιμονία as φοβοθεία and continues: δεισιδαίμων· ὁ τὰ εἴδωλα σέβων, εἰδωλολάτρης. Ὁ εὐσεβὴς καὶ δειλὸς περὶ θεούς. The Suda: δεισιδαίμων· θεοσεβής· ἢ ἀμφίβολος περὶ τὴν πίστιν, καὶ οἱονεὶ δεδοικώς. According to St. Augustine, Varro (frag. 29 a) "distinguishes the religious person from the superstitious person in that he says that the superstitious person fears the gods, whereas the religious person only reveres them as a father or mother rather than fears them as enemies" (*Civ.* 6.9).

---

deisidaimōn, TDNT 2.20; EDNT 1.282-283; NIDNTT 1.450, 453; MM 139; L&N 53.3; BDF § 244(2); BAGD 173 ‖ *deisidaimonia*, S 1175; EDNT 1.282-283; NIDNTT 1.450, 453; MM 139; L&N 53.2; BAGD 173 solicitous toward the gods" (Aristotle, *Pol.* 5.11.25.1315ᵃ); "Those who fear the gods (*hoi deisidaimones*) are less afraid of men."[3] In the first century, calling punishment down on the guilty inspired "in the king a religious fear and a respect for the deity" (Diodorus Siculus 1.70.8). The repentant Manasseh wanted to show the utmost reverence toward God (*peri auton deisidaimonia*, Josephus, *Ant.* 10.42); when the Jews were not able to tolerate the emperor's ensigns in the temple, Pilate was astonished at such zeal (*to tēs deisidaimonias akraton*).[4] *Deisidaimonia* refers to the Jewish religion. In 49 BC, the consul Lentulus Crus exempted Jewish Roman citizens from military service "on account of their religion."[5]

The pejorative meaning—superstitious and punctilious—is much more commonly attested. It can be seen in Menander's *Deisidaimōn* (The Bigot), in Theophrastus' *Deisidaimōn* (*Char.* 16), and Plutarch's *Peri deisidaimonias* (On superstition). Theophrastus portrays the *deisidaimōn* as very attentive to omens and dreams, careful to avoid defilement, carrying out multiple purifications, reciting prayers suited for the given circumstances, going overboard with the worship of images. Plutarch denounces superstition as an excessive fear of divine signs: "just as unbelief (*apistia*) and disdain of divine signs is a terrible evil, so also is superstition, which, like water, always filters down to the lower levels" (*Alex.* 75.3). "Thanks to Anaxagoras, Pericles raised himself above superstition. Superstition is inspired by celestial phenomena in people who do not know their causes and because of their ignorance are disturbed and frightened regarding religion. Natural science, which banishes this ignorance, replaces timid and feverish superstition with solid piety" (*Per.* 6.1). This terror, which is passed on in traditions[6] and stirred up by accidents (*Marc.* 6.11), bad omens (*Tim.* 26.1),

---

[3] Xenophon, *Cyr.* 3.3.58; "Agesilaus was always a religious man; for him, those who were living well were not yet blessed, but those who had died gloriously had attained to felicity" (*Ages.*11.8).

[4] Josephus, *War* 2.174. When a Roman soldier tore up and burned a copy of the Torah, "the Jews, being drawn together by their religion as by a spring, ran to Cumanus" (2.230); 1.113; *Ant.* 15.277.

[5] Josephus, *Ant.* 14.228: δεισιδαιμονίας ἕνεκεν; cf. 237, 240. The edict of Claudius authorized Jews to observe their customs on the condition that they did not "vilify the religions of other peoples" (19.290); cf. the enclosure of a temple of Aphrodite that is declared to be "of the same right and the same religion" as the temple of Artemis at Ephesus (ἄσυλος ἔστω ταὐτῷ δικαίῳ ταύτῃ τε δεισιδαιμονίᾳ, 39 BC, Dittenberger, *Or.* 455, 11); the epitaph of a mime: πᾶσι φίλος θνητοῖς εἰς τ' ἀθανάτους δεισιδαίμων (G. Kaibel, *Epigrammata*, 607, 3).

[6] Cf. Strabo 5.4.5, the steep slopes of the Avernus used to be covered with forests, which, "according to the superstition, plunged the whole bay in darkness"; Plutarch, *Arat.* 53.2: "an ancient law, fortified further by superstitious fear, forbade burying anyone within the walls."

wonders (*Cleom.* 39.3; *Sol.* 12.5), an eclipse,[7] etc., is a product of human weakness (*Cam.* 6.6); it is a characteristic of barbarians (*Sert.* 11.6), women, and children.[8] So superstition must be driven out from piety[9] and from philosophy, which "Pythagoras (who attached great importance to divination through dreams) and his disciples filled with phantoms, fables, and superstitions" (*De gen.* 9). Upon the death of one of his daughters, Plutarch exhorts his wife to avoid exaggerated mourning and not to have recourse to superstition (*Cons. ux.* 1).

Philo sees "the crushing burden of superstition" (*Giants* 16) as a deviation that mars healthy piety (*Rewards* 40), "the queen of virtues . . . ; adding to it, or on the other hand taking from it, in any way . . . deforms and distorts its appearance . . . because additions breed superstition, and suppression breeds impiety" (*Spec. Laws* 4.147). *Eusebeia* occupies an intermediate position between superstition and impiety (*Unchang. God* 164); *deisidaimonia* is a false respect for God (ibid. 103), an evil parasite that grafts itself onto worship and sacrifice (*Plant.* 107); it spreads in waves and "has

---

[7] Plutarch, *Nic.* 23.1. Thus the general Nicias lost the Athenian army when he was slow to lift the siege of Syracuse because of an eclipse of the moon (Thucydides 7.50; Diodorus Siculus 14.76.4; 14.77.4). Cf. Samaritan Sabbath-observance (Josephus, *Ant.* 12.259), lucky and unlucky days (Plutarch, *Cam.* 19.12), unclean foods (*Ep. Arist.* 129); superstition does not stop at forbidding the killing of animals but extends also to the destruction of plants (Polybius, *Abst.* 1.6.3). In Egypt, there are superstitions related to sacred animals (Diodorus Siculus 1.83.8); the dress and jewelry of kings are "an object of terror and superstitious veneration for the people" (ibid. 1.62.4); 4.51.1 and 3; 17.41.6; 18.61.3; 19.108.2; 20.43.1; etc. Superstition borders on magic (cf. sidereal fatalism). Riess, "Aberglaube," in PW, vol. 1, col. 29–93.

[8] Plutarch, *Dio* 2.4: "Only small children, women, and men whose minds are disturbed by illness . . . have superstition within themselves like an evil genius"; *Caes.* 63.11: "Calpurnia, like so many women, was superstitious"; δεισιδαιμόνια is synonymous with ἄλογον and μυθῶδες (*De gen.* 9.580 C; cf. H. D. Betz, *Plutarch's Theological Writings and Early Christian Literature*, Leiden, 1975, pp. 1–7, 44); Strabo 1.2.8: "A crowd made up of women and all sorts of uneducated people cannot be persuaded by philosophical logic or by this means led to piety, holiness, and faith; but only by the fear of the gods (διὰ δεισιδαιμονίας), which is inseparable from legendary creations and recourse to the miraculous"; Polybius 12.24.5: "He is full of visions, prodigies, and incredible fables, in a word, of base superstition and womanish fantasies." Agatharchides of Cnidos derides Stratonice's superstition, which he cites as an example of weakness (Josephus, *Ag. Apion* 1.208).

[9] Plutarch, *De superst.* 10–15; *De aud. poet.* 12; *Cor.* 24.2; *Fab.* 4.4; Marcus Aurelius 1.16.15: "With respect to the gods, no superstitious fear"; an example is Antoninus, θεοσεβὴς χωρὶς δεισιδαιμονίας (6.30.14); Philo: "It is best not to mingle superstition with piety" (*Worse Attacks Better* 18). Cf. G. Schepens, "Polybius on Timaeus' Account of Phalaris' Bull: A Case of δεισιδαιμονία," in *Ancient Society*, 1978, pp. 117–148.

submerged souls lacking in virility and nobility" (*Change of Names* 138). It is "a sister of impiety" (*asebeia, Sacr. Abel and Cain* 15).

With these two series of texts fresh in our minds, it is easy to see a favorable sense in *desidaimōn* in Acts 17:22, the praise with which St. Paul begins his discourse on the Areopagus: "O Athenians, I see that in all things you are very religious" (*kata panta hōs deisidaimonesterous hymas theōrō*). No judgment for good or for ill is made of this piety; "the fear of the deity can according to its nature be either piety or superstition; this term—a *vox anceps*— . . . is quite fitting for a sentiment that is praiseworthy but directed toward an object that one does not approve."[10] The "very" alludes not only to the altar erected "to an unknown god" (Acts 17:25) but to all the representations of deities that abounded in this city (Acts 17:16), where Plautus's *bon mot* is especially applicable: "It is easier to meet a god there than a mortal" (Plautus, *Satir.* 17). Besides, it was a commonplace to praise the Athenians as surpassing all other nations in the honors they rendered to the gods.[11]

Deisidaimonia has almost the same meaning when Festus uses it in his explanation to King Agrippa of Paul's situation: "His accusers were disputing with him regarding their religion and on the subject of a certain Jesus, who had died but whom Paul affirmed to be alive" (*zētēmata . . . peri tēs idias deisidaimonias eichon*, Acts 25:19). The word could not have meant "superstition," for that would have been an affront to the Jewish king; coming from the Roman prefect, however, it seems to have some pejorative nuance, either like our word "sect" or like the Greek *thrēskeia*, which is used for aberrant cults[12] as well as for worship of the true God (Jas 1:26–27). This ambiguous meaning (suggested by *idias deisidaimonias*) is common.[13]

---

[10] E. Jacquier, *Actes* (following A. Loisy).

[11] Sophocles, *OC* 258: "Athens, most religious of cities" (θεοσεβεστάτας; cf. θεοσεβής, Exod 18:21; Job 1:1, 8; 2:3; Jdt 11:17; Acts 2:5; 8:2); Josephus, *Ag. Apion*: "the Athenians, the most pious of the Greeks"; Philostratus, *VA* 4.19; Pausanias 1.17.1; 1.24.3: Ἀθηναίοις περισσότερόν τι ἢ τοῖς ἄλλοις ἐς τὰ θεῖά ἐστι σπουδῆς. At Athens there was an altar to Piety.

[12] Col 2:18; Wis 11:16; 14:17, 18, 27. Chariton, *Chaer. et Call.* 7.6.6: a sort of religious scruple naturally took hold of the barbarians, θρησκεία τῶν βαρβάρων.

[13] Plutarch, *Lys.* 25.2; Lysander wanted to make an impression on the citizens through the fear of the gods and superstition (φόβῳ θεοῦ τινὶ καὶ δεισιδαιμονίᾳ); *Num.* 8.5: Numa hoped to humble the pride of the Romans through the fear of the gods (*deisidaimonia*), but using apparitions of demons, threatening voices, and the motive of fear; Diodorus Siculus 5.63.3, the wealth of a temple consecrated to Hemithea was protected by "a sort of religious superstition that had been transformed into a custom"; 11.89.6 and 8.

διαλάσσω

dialassō, to reconcile

→*see also* καταλλαγή, καταλλάσσω

"If you are presenting your offering (*to dōron*) at the altar and you remember that your brother has something against you (*echei ti kata sou*), leave your offering there and go first to be reconciled with your brother" (*hypage prōton diallagēthi tō adelphō sou*, Matt 5:23-24). Even though the verb is an imperative (aorist passive, with dative of accompaniment), this is not a cultic rule or a liturgical law but a moral obligation incumbent on a person appearing before God to offer a sacrifice.[1] Apparently, a person who is the object of a brother or sister's animosity must take the initiative in reconciliation; the offended party takes the first step. But J. Jeremias notes that "has something against you" (*echei ti kata sou*) corresponds to the Aramaic adjective *'aketânâ* (= the Greek *mnēsikakos*) and refers to a brother who holds on to the memory of an offense of which he has been the victim.[2] Thus it is not surprising that the true offender should go to him and ask him not to hold a grudge and "gain reconciliation" (*diallagēthi*).

Beginning with Moulton-Milligan, two papyri have been cited that use this verb with the same meaning. In the second century, a prodigal son writes to his mother, "I have written to thee that I am naked (*hoti gymnos eimei* = that I have nothing to wear). I beseech thee, mother, be reconciled

---

[1] Cf. Philo, *Spec. Laws* 1.167: when approaching the altar and offering a victim, one must bring a soul "in a state of absolutely perfect purity, so that when God sees he will not turn away"; *m. Yoma* 8.9: "For offenses between a person and the Place, the Day of Atonement expiates them; but for those between a person and his neighbor, the Day of Atonement does not expiate them as long as the parties are not reconciled to each other."

[2] J. Jeremias, "Laß allda deine Gabe," in *ZNW*, 1937, pp. 150-154; republished in *Abba*, pp. 103-107.

---

dialassō, S 1259; *TDNT* 1.253-254; *EDNT* 1.307; MM 151; L&N 40.2; BDF §193(4); BAGD 186

to me (*dialagēthi moi*). . . . I know that I have sinned."³ A runaway slave begs his owner to be reconciled (*hōste diallagēthi hēmein*).⁴ We may add P.Mich. 502, 8, a letter from Valerius Gemellus, a soldier stationed at Coptus who seeks to end his quarrel with his brother: "I urge you to be reconciled to me, brother (*paraklētheis, adelphe, diallagēthi moi*), so that I may have your confidence while I am in the army." Then there is the case of the concubine of the Levite from Ephraim, who had run away from him and been gone four months. Her husband "went to speak to her and persuade her to be reconciled."⁵

The verb *diallattō* was used often in private law for the reconciliation of persons; *diallaktai* had the job of bringing about *diallagai*.⁶ Augustus urged Herod to be reconciled with his children (Josephus, *Ant.* 16.125; cf. 16.267, 269; 7.192); the reconciliation of Hyrcanus and Aristobulus took place in the temple (*War* 1.122). Conciliation also played a role in ending civil wars but was particularly common in international life between cities⁷ and warring states: the four hundred send heralds to Agis, king of Sparta,

---

³ BGU 846, 10 (cf. A. Deissmann, *Light*, pp. 187–188); cf. 665, col. II, 11: Ἐγὼ τῷ πατρί μου γράψω... περὶ τῆς διαλλαγῆς (first century).

⁴ P.Giss. 17, 13 (republished by *Chrest.Wilck.* n. 481); cf. 1 Esdr 4:31—κολακεύει αὐτὴν ὅπως διαλλαγῇ αὐτῷ.

⁵ Judg 19:3 (Hebrew *šûb*); cf. 1 Sam 29:4—the Philistines fear that David will turn traitor, for otherwise how could he be reconciled to his master? (ἐν τίνι διαλλαγήσεται [Hebrew *rāṣâh*] οὗτος τῷ κυρίῳ αὐτοῦ); 1 Esdr 4:31. *Diallagē* can always be obtained: "If you have spoken up against your friend, do not worry, reconciliation is possible" (Sir 22:22); "for the offense, there is reconciliation" (27:21). The LXX usually gives the verb *diallassō* the meaning "change, give in exchange, modify" (Wis 19:18; 2 Macc 6:27—"If I exchange life for death"; cf. Job 5:12, Hebrew *pārar*); the only meaning in Philo is "be different" (*Sacr. Abel and Cain* 137; *Worse Attacks Better* 164; *Drunkenness* 8; etc.); cf. a testamentary foundation at Thea: "None of the figures that are in the museum . . . shall be pawned or exchanged (μήτε διαλλάξασθαι) or alienated" (C. Michel, *Recueil*, n. 1001, col. II, 14).

⁶ Aristophanes, *Lys.* 1091; Euripides, *Phoen.* 431; Euripides, *Med.* 896; Plato, *Prt.* 346 b. A very common meaning in Josephus: Cassius "reconciled Bassus with Murcus and the separated legions" (*War* 1.219; cf. 454, 510, 530, 591; *Ant.* 16.26, 270, 335, 352, 356; 19.334); Machaeras, "having reflected on his offenses . . . succeeded in reconciling with Herod" (*War* 1.320; *Ant.* 14.438); certain wrongdoers "must think that the penitence of the wrongdoers should be followed immediately by the reconciliation of the victims" (*War* 4.221); even death could not easily reconcile the Jews with Alexander Jannaeus after all the evil that he had done (1.92). Cf. L. Gernet, *Droit et société dans la Grèce ancienne*, Paris, 1955, pp. 103–119, 134; C. Spicq, *Théologie morale*, vol. 1, p. 437, n. 4.

⁷ Aristophanes, *Pax* 540, 1049; Isocrates, *Paneg.* 129, 157, 188; *Phil.* 5.30, 41, 45, 83, 88: Athens and Salamis, regarding cultic matters (F. Sokolowski, *LSCGSup*, n. XIX, 3, 80, 82).

"to say that they wished to come to terms with him" (*legontes diallagēnai boulesthai*).[8] Titus said concerning the Jews, "Let us not wait for agreement to be re-established between our enemies; necessity will reconcile them all too quickly" (Josephus, *War* 3.496). Herod states, "We have learned from messengers of God to reconcile enemies to each other" (*Ant.* 15.136), which entails changing feelings and attitudes (11.54). It is thus that God takes pity on David and is reconciled with him (7.153); so reconciliation is then pardon (6.551).

---

[8] Thucydides 8.70.2; cf. 4.20.2 and 3: "We must be reconciled (Athens and Sparta) by a moderate resolution of our misfortune . . . and bind ourselves with a firm friendship"; 4.59.4; 4.61.2. Y. Garlan ("Etudes d'histoire militaire et diplomatique," in *BCH*, 1978, pp. 97–103) prefers the translation "conciliation" rather than "reconciliation," because diplomatic, not legal, matters are involved, and the adversaries are under no compulsion.

διερμηνεύω, ἑρμηνεία, ἑρμηνεύω

diermēneuō, to translate, interpret, explain; *hermēneia*, interpretation; *hermēneuō*, to translate, interpret

According to Luke 24:27, Christ "explained [to the disciples of Emmaus], in all the Scriptures, that which concerned him."[1] This is the only use of the verb *diermēneuō* in the Gospels. In earlier secular texts, it normally has the sense of "translate" from one language to another,[2] but Luke clearly intends it to mean "interpret," as in 1 Macc 1:36—"Nehemiah called the liquid *nephtar*, which is interpreted as purification (*ho diermēneuetai katharismos*), but most call it naphtha." This usage is clearly attested by Philo, who knows the strict sense "translation,"[3] but more often gives the word a broader meaning: "He will translate your thoughts" (*Migr. Abr.* 81); "that which language expresses" (*Conf. Tongues* 53; cf. *Migr. Abr.* 12). So *diermēneuō* means "express one's thought in words."[4] Thus it is not permitted to express the name of God in literal terms (Philo, *To Gaius* 353; cf. *m. Meg.* 3.41); the precision of thought of a person well-versed in doctrine is expressed in his explications (Philo, *Contemp. Life* 31). To explain the genesis of light is to give its intelligence or to discover the unknown (Philo, *Creation*

---

[1] E. Delebecque translates: "He clarified for them, by means of all the Scriptures, the things that related to him" (*Evangile de Luc*, Paris, 1976).

[2] *Ep. Arist.* 15: "The code that we intend . . . to translate"; 308: "in the presence of the translators, παρόντων τῶν διερμηνευσάντων"; 310: "Now that the translation has been done correctly, with piety, and with a rigorous attitude." A single papyrological attestation: copies of Egyptian reports on the trial of Hermas were translated into Greek, ἀντίγραφα συγγραφῶν Αἰγυπτίων, διηερμηνευμένων δ'ἑλληνιστί (*UPZ* 162, col. V, 4; from 116 BC). The verb does not occur in Josephus.

[3] Philo, *Alleg. Interp.* 3.87: "Isaac is translated: laughter of the soul, joy and happiness" (cf. Philo, *Unchang. God* 144); an "impeccable translation" (*Migr. Abr.* 73, τοῦ διερμηνεύοντες ἀπταίστως); "The high priest was busy choosing translators for the Law" (*Moses* 2.31).

[4] This meaning is unknown in the NT. Cf. Philo, *Change of Names* 56: the word "incapable of expressing the least reality"; 208: the word was instructed to express in a holy manner "holy things in a manner worthy of God."

---

diermēneuō, S 1329; *TDNT* 2.661–666; *EDNT* 2.53–55; *NIDNTT* 1.579–581; MM 160; L&N 33.145, 33.148; BAGD 194 ‖ *hermēneia*, S 2058; *TDNT* 2.661–666; *EDNT* 2.53–55; *NIDNTT* 1.579–582; MM 254; L&N 11.147; BAGD 310 ‖ *hermēneuō*, S 2059; *TDNT* 2.661–666; *EDNT* 2.53–55; *NIDNTT* 1.579–581; MM 254; L&N 33.145; BAGD 310

31). Finally, for Philo, as for St. Luke, this verb means "interpret," and thus it is that Jesus, like Moses, is an interpreter of the holy books.[5]

In Acts 9:36 we have "a disciple named Tabitha, which translated (*hē diermēneuomenē*) means Dorcas." In other NT texts, this idea—which could be put "that is" or "which means"—is expressed by the simple verb *hermēneuō*,[6] which Philo uses extensively for the transcribing into Greek of the meaning of a Hebrew word.[7]

In the papyri, *hermēneuō* usually means the translation of an original text into another language. Thus the will of C. Longinus Castor, written in Latin, was translated into Greek: "I translated the preceding copy" (*hērmēneusa to prokeimenon antigraphon*, BGU 326, col. II, 22 = SB 9298, 26); "copy translated into Greek" (*antigraphon hermēneuthen Ellēnikois grammasi*, P.Oxy. 2231, 26–27); "to translate the letter you sent to me" (*ta hermēneuthēnai to grammation ho diepempsante moi*, P.Stras. 260, 1); "I translated from Latin" (*hermēneusa apo Rhōmaikōn*, P.Ryl. 62, 30); which presupposes a strict correspondence between the two texts. But the correspondence is

---

[5] Philo, *Post. Cain* 1; *Spec. Laws* 4.132. Cf. *Change of Names* 126: "Moses received a considerable gift: the interpretation (ἑρμενείαν) and preaching of the holy laws"; *Moses* 1.1: "Moses, the interpreter of the holy laws"; *Decalogue* 175; *Change of Names* 125; Josephus, *Ant.* 3.87: Moses the hermeneut of God. The διερμενευτής of 1 Cor 14:26 is the translator-interpreter for the charismatic who speaks an unintelligible language.

[6] John 1:42—"You shall be called Cephas, which is translated Peter, ὃ ἑρμηνεύεται Πέτρος"; 9:7—"The pool of Siloam, which is translated Sent"; Heb 7:2—"Melchizedek is translated (ἑρμηνευόμενος) 'king of justice.' " Cf. Ezra 4:7—the text of the letter to King Artaxerxes was written in Aramaic and translated (καὶ ἡρμηνευμένην); Job 42:18 (apocryphal verse): the text claims to be a translation from a Syriac (Aramaic) book—οὗτος ἑρμηνεύεται ἐκ τῆς Συριακῆς βίβλου; *Ep. Arist.* 39: "elders who know their law well and are capable of translating it." C. F. D. Moule (*Birth of the NT*, pp. 276–280) points to Papias: "Matthew joined together the *logia* [of Jesus] in the Hebrew language and each one interpreted them as he was able" (Eusebius, *Hist. Eccl.* 3.39.16). Cf. Heliodorus, *Aeth.* 4.11.4: "having him read the strip, which I translated scrupulously as we went along." Often the verb μεθερμηνεύω is used: Matt 1:23; Mark 5:41; 15:22, 34; John 1:38, 41; Acts 4:36; 8:8 (unknown in Philo).

[7] Nearly 150 times; cf. *Moses* 2.40; *Migr. Abr.* 20: "*Hebrew* is translated emigrant"; *Prelim. Stud.* 51: "*Israel* means 'seeing God' " (= *Dreams* 2.173; *Abraham* 57; *To Gaius* 4). But there are translations that are free (*Migr. Abr.* 169) or broad (*Alleg. Interp.* 1.90), where the interpretation conveys a spiritual exegesis; cf. *Prelim. Stud.* 20. Likewise Josephus, *Ant.* 12.11: Ptolemy Philadelphos translated the Law; 114; *Ag. Apion* 2.46: He asks the Jews to send him men to translate the Law; *War* 7.455: "As to how this was rendered I leave to my readers to assess"; *Ant.* 6.156; but also *Ant.* 6.230: "I express my thought in words"; *War* 5.182: "It is impossible to give an adequate description of the palace"; 5.393: "I would be able to give an adequate account of your extravagances."

broader when an attorney pleads for his client through an interpreter (*di' Anoubiōnos hermēneuontos eipen*, *SB* 8246, 38, 46), and especially in the case of an explanation, as with Isidorus: "Having been given firm information by men who summed up what they knew, and having myself transcribed all these events, I explained to the Greeks the power of the god and of the prince."[8] Finally, to translate feelings is to express them.[9]

So there are translators. Joseph's brother "did not know that Joseph understood, because they were speaking through an interpreter."[10] In a country like Egypt, where many races met,[11] the *hermēneis* (cf. *Ep. Arist.* 310, 318) were not merely multilingual, but seem to have been charged with official duties,[12] such as a certain Apollonius, interpreter for the Ethiopians in Egypt. They could be appointed either by private individuals (*SB* 10743, from the first century) or by the state,[13] because in the first century interpretation was a public function.[14] Furthermore, the papyri often attest to the presence and activity of a *hermēneus tēs kōmēs*.[15] They are employed

---

[8] Ἐγὼ πάντ' ἀναγραψάμενος ἡρμήνηυσ' "Ελλησι θεοῦ δύναμιν τε ἄνακτος (*Hymn to Isis*; *SEG*, vol. 8, 51, 39 = *SB* 8141, 39; V. F. Vanderlip, *Four Greek Hymns*, p. 74, who understands the middle ἡρμήνηυσα as meaning that the author explains himself in his own language). Cf. line 33: "Interpreting his name, the Egyptians call him Porramanres."

[9] *BGU* 140, 20: cf. φιλανθρωπότερον ἑρμηνεύω. Antinous replies with the aid of an interpreter (*P.Vindob.Tandem*, n. VIII, 2–4); cf. *SB* 10288, II, 15.

[10] Gen 42:23 (ἑρμηνευτής; the hiphil of the Hebrew verb *lûṣ*). Ἑρμηνεύς is unknown in the OT. Neither term appears in the NT. Philo never uses the first noun, and Moulton-Milligan cannot supply an example from the Koine, but cf. Josephus, *Ant.* 2.72; Papias: Μάρκος ἑρμηνευτὴς Πέτρου γενόμενος (Eusebius, *Hist. Eccl.* 3.39.15).

[11] Ptolemy Euergetes II decided that there should be different tribunals for hearing cases of Egyptians against Greeks, Greeks against Egyptians, and Egyptians against Egyptians (*P.Tebt.* 5, 207–220); cf. A. Theodorides, "A propos de la loi dans l'Egypte pharaonique," in *RIDA*, 1967, pp. 107–156.

[12] Cf. *CIRB*, Moscow-Leningrad, 1965, n. 698: Παιρίσαλος Σαυρόφου ἑρμηνεύς. There is even a "chief interpreter," δι' ἐπιμελείας Ἡρακᾶ Ποντικοῦ ἀρχερμηνέως (*CIRB* 1053).

[13] Like the ἑρμηνεὺς τῶν Τρυγοδυτῶν, a Berlin papyrus in G. Lumbroso, *Recherches sur l'économie politique de l'Egypte sous les Lagides*, 2d ed., Amsterdam, 1967, p. 256.

[14] Cf. *IGUR*, n. 567: Ἄσπουργος ἑρμηνεὺς Σαρματῶν Βωσπορανός. R. Taubenschlag, "The Interpreters in the Papyri," in *Opera Minora*, Warsaw, 1959, vol. 2, pp. 167–170 (citing Plutarch, *Ant.* 27.2); W. Peremans, "Über die Zweisprachigkeit im ptolemäischen Ägypten," in *Studien zur Papyrologie und antiken Wirtschaftsgeschichte*. Festschrift Oertel, Bonn, 1964, pp. 58ff. On royal interprets paid from the treasury, cf. U. Wilcken, *Actenstücke aus der königlichen Bank zu Theben* (Abhand. der kgl. Preuß. Akad. der Wiss. zu Berlin, 1886, n. 9). On translators in synagogues, cf. *m. Meg.* 2.1; 4.4; *b. Šabb.* 115a; S. Safrai, *The Jewish People in the First Century*, Assen-Amsterdam, 1976, vol. 2, pp. 930ff.

by individuals—not only a general (*SB* 9046, 308) but also private persons.[16] They write (*Stud.Pal.* XXII, 101, 11), are associated with notaries (*P.Oslo* 183, 6, 8), translate from Greek to Latin or from Latin to Greek (*BGU* 140, 326; *P.Stras.* 253, 4; *P.Ryl.* 62, 30; *P.Harr.* 67, col. II, 11), and later from Coptic to Greek (*P.Lond.* 77, 69; vol. 1, p. 235; eighth century). They seem to be entrusted with fairly extensive authority, because they serve as intermediaries: "and we have written also to Apollonius the *hermēneus* concerning these things" (*gegraphamen de kai Apollōniō tō hermēnei peri toutōn*, *SB* 7647, 7; cf. *P.Ryl.* 563, 7; *P.Cair.Zen.* 59065, 2; *PSI* 409, 15). They become parties to lawsuits. For example, to learn if a woman has the right to remain with her husband against the will of her father, the judge prescribes: *ekeleusen di' hermēneōs autēn* (the Egyptian woman) *enechthēnai ti bouletai, eipousēs para tō andri menein* . . . (*P.Oxy.* 237, col. VII, 37). In another case, the judge prescribes that the testimony of Ammonios, Antoninos, and the priest of Sarapis shall be examined *di' hermēneōs*.[17] Thus interpreters are numerous, influential, competent, having certain prerogatives, and indispensable in a cosmopolitan[18] and multilingual[19] society.

---

[15] *P.Tebt.* 450; *P.Ross.Georg.* V, 42, 4; ἑρμενεύς Καρανίδος (*P.Athen.* 21, 11; *P.Mich.* 567, 15; *BGU* 985, 10); ἑρ. Βακχιάδος (*PSI* 879, 12).

[16] *P.Mich.* IV, 1841: Μύσθης ἑρμηνεύς; V, 321, 20: ἐν Ταλὶ ἑρμηνέως; *P.Stras.* 41, 36: δι' ἑρμηνέως Ἀμμώνιον καὶ Ἀντωνίνον κτλ. *P.Oxy.* 1517, 6: Θέων ἑρ.

[17] *P.Stras.* 41, 3 (AD 25); cf. *P.Thead.* 14, 23: ὑδροφύλακες ἀπεκρείναντο δι' ἑρμηνέως; *PSI* 1326, 4; *SB* 8246, 39–40. Cf. F. Cumont, *L'Egypte des Astrologues*, Brussels, 1937, p. 46, n. 3; cf. p. 177, n. 3, on ἑρμηνέα γάμων.

[18] We should keep in mind that ἑρμηνεία in music refers to the execution (what we would call the interpretation) of a sung tune or a melody played on the flute or the cithara, cf. Ps.-Plutarch, *De mus.* 32 and 36. In Philo, ἑρμηνεία is sometimes a verbal expression (τοῦ λόγου τὰς ἑρμηνείας, *Heir* 108; *Prelim. Stud.* 17, 13; *Dreams* 2.262, 2.274; *Virtues* 193; *Worse Attacks Better* 39, 68, 79, etc.), sometimes a translation from one language into another (*Moses* 2.27; *Post. Cain* 74, 120; *Dreams* 2.242), like *Ep. Arist.* 3, 120, 308. This meaning recurs constantly in the papyri, notably for the translation of wills: ἑρμηνία διαθήκης (*Pap.Lugd.Bat.* XIII, 14, 1; *BGU* 326, col. I, 1; 2, 15: ἑρμηνία κωδικίλλων διπτύχων; *P.Oxf.* 7, 12: ἑρμηνείας ἀντίγραφον; *SB* 7640, 8); of receipts (ὑπὲρ ἑρμηνίας, *SB* 9355, col. I, 3; 2, 2; 10288, n. 2, 15), of a document: Διοσκουδίδου χάρτην ἧ ἐνεγράφη τά τε ῥωμαϊκὰ καὶ ἡ τούτων ἑρμηνεία (*P.Oxy.* 2276, 7; cf. 1466, 3: ἑρμηνεία τῶν Ῥωμαϊκῶν; 2472, 3; *PSI* 1364 A and B; *P.Lund* III, 9, 7, published in *SB* 8749, 7); of a letter like that of Diocletian to the inhabitants of the island of Elephantine: τῶν γραμμάτων ἑρμηνεία (*SB* 8393, 20); or of a hearing before a magistrate (*P.Thead.* 13, col. II, 1). In this sense, Sirach Prologue 20: "You are invited to read with care and . . . to show indulgence where we may seem—despite our laborious care in translation—to render certain expressions poorly."

[19] In Palestine, very diverse languages were spoken in the first century. Not only were Hebrew and Aramaic in use (cf. C. Rabin, "Hebrew and Aramaic in the

The special duty of the *hermēneus* is *hermēneia*. If the latter has an almost sacred character in Jewish writings when it designates the Greek version of the Scriptures (the Septuagint, cf. Josephus, *Ant.* 12.39, 87, 104, 106, 107, 108), it also suggests the "explications" supplied by the translator, who thus becomes an interpreter.[20] It is not that he could express his own thoughts:[21] "the soothsayer said nothing personal, he only interpreted someone else's words, when the divine presence seized him" (Philo, *Moses* 1.286); "interpreters of dreams are obligated to tell the truth, because they explain and proclaim divine oracles" (*Joseph* 95). Philo elaborated a theology of the *hermēneus* who carries out a religious function related to prophecy: "The prophets are God's interpreters."[22] In fact, God equips "the perfect interpreter by making the springs of language gush forth for him and by revealing them to him" (*Worse Attacks Better* 44; cf. 68). "The wicked are not permitted to be God's interpreters, so that any evil man is not inspired by God."[23] Only the virtuous "are able to interpret the meaning of the Holy Scriptures" (Josephus, *Ant.* 20.264).

In summary, then, "interpreters" were numerous and important in the secular world of the first century, and they were especially so in Jewish theology. Signal honor was given to the translators of the Hebrew Bible, which had become unintelligible for their contemporaries, and Moses was seen as the outstanding interpreter of the divine revelation. Indeed, prophecy and interpretation were closely associated. With all this in mind,

---

First Century," in S. Safrai, M. Stern, *The Jewish People in the First Century*, Assen-Amsterdam, vol. 2, pp. 1007–1040), but Greek was common: texts of Murabbaʿât, and inscriptions from Nazareth, tombs, ossuaries, and coins, the inscription on the cross; "Hellenists" have Greek names and speak Greek; more than 450 Jewish inscriptions written in Greek have been found in Palestine, etc. Cf. G. Mussie, "Greek in Palestine and the Diaspora," ibid., pp. 1040–1064.

[20] Cf. the interpretation of visions: Mane, thekel, phares—ἐστι δὲ ἡ ἑρμηνεία αὐτῶν (Dan 5:1, LXX [title to Old Greek of Dan 5] = 5:7 NRSV); of Solomon: "For his songs, proverbs, parables, and interpretations the nations admired him" (Sir 47:17); cf. *Ep. Arist.* 32: "a precise interpretation of the text of the Law"; Josephus, *Ant.* 1.29: "I offer this explanation on this point."

[21] Philo, *Moses* 2.34: "What an immense matter, to give a complete translation of the laws dictated by the oracles, without being able to subtract, add, or change anything at all."

[22] Philo, *Spec. Laws* 1.65; 2.189. 3.7; 4.49; *Rewards* 55; *Unchang. God* 138; *Moses* 2.188, 191, 40: the translators of the Law are above all hierophants and prophets; cf. *To Gaius* 99; *Worse Attacks Better* 39–40; *Migr. Abr.* 84.

[23] Philo, *Heir* 259; cf. *Worse Attacks Better* 133. "Evil interpreters" (*Migr. Abr.* 72) are not always truthful (*Spec. Laws* 4.90); "the spirit of the hearers cannot follow explanations spouted forth at high speed and without pauses for breath" (*Contemp. Life* 76).

we can better understand 1 Cor 12:30, where St. Paul makes the interpreter a charismatic, and 14:5, 13, 27, where he requires that speech in incomprehensible tongues be translated for the hearers and clearly explained by an interpreter, who transposes the divine revelation into accessible language.[24] If there is no *diermēneutēs* (verse 28) in the assembly, the one speaking in tongues must be silent or pray for the ability to interpret (verse 13)—which presupposes that the ecstatic discourse has an internal meaning. In any event, it is the Holy Spirit who gives the gift of interpretation of tongues (1 Cor 12:10, *hermēneia glōssōn*), and very likely the *diermēneutēs*, did not stop at giving a pure and simple translation of that which was spoken by the glossalaliac; if necessary, he added explanations and timely clarifications so that the charism might bear all of its fruit for edification (1 Cor 14:26).

---

[24] Cf. J. G. Davies, "Pentecost and Glossalalia," in *JTS*, 1952, pp. 228–231.

> δίκαιος, δικαιοσύνη, δικαιόω, δικαίωμα, δικαίωσις, δικαστής, δίκη
>
> *dikaios*, **conforming to law or custom, right, virtuous;** *dikaiosynē*, **justice, righteousness;** *dikaioō*, **to justify, pronounce just;** *dikaiōma*, **justification, righteousness, righteous decree, just requirement;** *dikaiōsis*, **justification;** *dikastēs*, **judge;** *dikē*, **custom, justice, punishment**
>
> →see also λάθρα

I. *Dikē*. — It is generally agreed that *dikē*, the basic term in this group, is related to *deiknymi*, "show, indicate."[1] Thus its root meaning would be "that which is indicated, is in usage, is customary,"[2] and it is from this starting point that it ends up meaning "justice." The first appearance of this meaning is as a mythical divine being: "There is a virgin, Dike, daughter of Zeus, honored and revered by the gods, inhabitants of Olympia," who denounces the unjust deeds of humans before her father and

---

[1] Cf. E. Boisacq, *Dictionnaire étymologique;* D. Hill, *Greek Words and Hebrew Meanings,* p. 98; P. Chantraine, *Dictionnaire étymologique,* p. 284.

[2] Homer, *Od.* 11.218; 14.59: "my custom is to honor guests." *Dikē* is "that which is established, set, fixed"; δίκη ἐστιν = it is customary (*Od.* 4.691; 19.43); Pindar, *Ol.* 2.18: "what is fitting (just) and what is not" (ἐν δίκα, παρὰ δίκαν); 2 Macc 8:26—"the custom of the eve of the Sabbath" (Aquila); *P.Hamb.* 37, 8 (second century AD): τῇ δίκῃ parallel to τοῦ ἤθους σου; *P.Flor.* 295, 2: "the custom of strangers." The greatest number of secular references are due to G. Quell, G. Schrenk, "δίκη," in *TDNT,* vol. 2, pp. 174–182; cf. V. Ehrenberg, *Die Rechtsidee im frühen Griechentum,* Leipzig, 1921.

---

dikaios, S 1342; *TDNT* 2.174–178, 224–225; *EDNT* 1.324–325; *NIDNTT* 3.352–355, 358, 360–363, 365–370; MM 162; L&N 34.47, 66.5, 88.12; BDF §263(a, b); BAGD 195–196 ‖ *dikaiosynē,* S 1343; *TDNT* 2.174–178, 192–210; *EDNT* 1.325–330; *NIDNTT* 3.352–354, 358, 360–365, 369–372; MM 162; L&N 34.46, 53.4, 57.111, 88.13; BDF §§163, 219(4), 275(3); BAGD 196–197 ‖ *dikaioō,* S 1344; *TDNT* 2.174–178, 211–219; *EDNT* 1.330–334; *NIDNTT* 3.352, 354–355, 358, 360–363, 365, 369–370, 372; MM 162–163; L&N 34.46, 36.22, 37.138, 56.34, 88.16; BDF §§148(4), 195(1e); BAGD 197–198 ‖ *dikaiōma,* S 1345; *TDNT* 2.174–178, 219–223; *EDNT* 1.334–335; *NIDNTT* 3.352, 354, 361–363, 365, 371–372; MM 163; L&N 33.334, 56.34, 88.14; BAGD 198 ‖ *dikaiōsis,* S 1347; *TDNT* 2.174–178, 223–224; *EDNT* 1.335; *NIDNTT* 3.352, 354, 363, 371–372; L&N 34.46, 56.34; BAGD 198 ‖ *dikastēs,* S 1348; *EDNT* 1.336; MM 163; L&N 56.28; BAGD 198 ‖ *dikē,* S 1349; *TDNT* 2.174–182; *EDNT* 1.336; *NIDNTT* 3.92–93, 96; MM 163; L&N 12.27, 38.8; BAGD 198; ND 6.90

δίκαιος, dikaios, etc.

calls for their punishment.[3] But already in Homer, dikē refers to a person's due or share, what he has a right to (Il. 19.180; Od. 24.255) and also to just actions toward someone else (Od. 14.84), giving another person his due (Il. 23.542; Od. 9.215). Aristotle emphasizes mutuality and reciprocity (Eth. Nic. 5.7.1131^b).

Meaning "right" (Homer, Il. 16.388; Hesiod, Op. 219) and "justice" (Josephus, War 5.2), dikē is introduced in legal language, where it refers sometimes to a trial, a legal decision,[4] sometimes to the result of a trial,

---

[3] Hesiod, Op. 256; cf. 279–280: "Zeus has given humans the gift of justice (δίκην), which is by far the best of goods." In Solon, δίκη always has a divine character (frag. 1.8; 3.14ff., ed. Diehl, I, 17 and 23); but Sophocles demythologizes it, representing Dike seated next to the infernal gods, "but the laws were not established for men by these gods. No one knows the day when they appeared; they are unwritten and unshakable" (Ant. 450–467). If the Erinyes are Dike's auxiliaries and bring punishment (Heraclitus, frag. 94 = I, 96, ed. Diels), dikē becomes the universal law, an immanent norm that is obligatory for all people and determines the conduct of each. In Philo, punitive justice is still associated with God: "Justice, seated next to God" (ἡ πάρεδρος θεοῦ δίκη, Change of Names 194; cf. Joseph 48), his follower or companion (Conf. Tongues 118: ἡ ὀπαδὸς τοῦ θεοῦ δίκη), judge or overseer of human affairs (ἔφορος, Joseph 170), unshakable and inflexible (Decalogue 95); "the only father of all things wields his power according to justice and the law over each of his creatures" (Spec. Laws 1.14). Cf. the gnostic amulet of the fourth-fifth century, πλήρος οὐρανὸς καὶ δίκης ἅγιος ὁ δόξης ανιααδα... Μιγαήλ (P.Princ. 107, 17).

[4] Homer, Il. 18.508; Od. 11.570; Hesiod, Op. 225; Philo, Moses 1.46: "He kills without judgment (without trial)." Cf. δικίδιον, "minor case" (Aristophanes, Vesp. 511; Eq. 347). Cf. "the Day of Yahweh" (Joel 4:14; cf. judgment day in a Christian inscription: δίκης μετὰ λοίσθιον ἧμαρ, in G. Kaibel, Epigrammata, n. 173, 17). This meaning, trial-judgment, is constant in the inscriptions (I.Gonn. 77–81, 87, 90, 01; I.Lamps., 3, 4; 6, 5; 7, 41; I.Cumae, 1, 3; 4, 13; 5, 11; 7, 6; 8, 3; I.Ilium: a law against tyranny and oligarchy, 25, 90, 95, 102, 157, 164, 165) and is the most common meaning in the papyri. Cf. this summons in a civil suit in the fourth-third century: ἡ δίκη σοι ἀναγραφήσεται ἐν τῷ ἐν Ἡρακλέους πόλει δικαστηρίῳ, P.Hib. 30, 24; "my mother died before the trial" (P.Achm. 8, 26; cf. P.Oxy. 486, 28; P.Princ. 82, 14); P.Lille 29, 2 (fragment of a law code, third century AD): "If anyone because of a tort has filed suit against another person's slave ..."; line 7: "if he loses his case, let him pay a fine." In an act of emancipation of three Jews at Delphi (second century BC): "They shall fear no trial nor any fine nor any punishment whatsoever" (CII 709); a borrower shall return what he owes "without lawsuit, contest, or chicanery of any sort" (ἄνευ δίκης καὶ κρίσεως καὶ πάσης εὑρεσιλογίας, P.Rein. 15, 21; cf. P.Lond. 298, 16; vol. 2, p. 206). At the time of the Jewish revolt at Alexandria, the insurgents "seek justice (δίκην ἐπαιτοῦντες) violently and unjustly" (C.Pap.Jud., n. 435, col. III, 23; SB 5357, 15; P.Hal. 1, 38: ἡ δίκη ἔστω; 124; P.Rev. 33, 16; 97, 4; P.Mich. 530, 30; 531, 7; R. Taubenschlag, Law of Greco-Roman Egypt, pp. 15, 189ff., 330ff., 416; idem, Opera Minora, vol. 2, pp. 397ff.). A constantly used legal formula is καθάπερ ἐγ δίκης, "as if there had been a judgment (preceding writs of execution), as if there had been a formal court decision," P.Ryl. 582, 20 (42 BC); 585, 38; P.Fam.Tebt. 2, 19; 4, 23; P.Bon.

namely, the execution of sentence, the penalty or punishment:[5] "pursued by your justice" (Wis 11:20); "the slave and the master were stricken with the same punishment" (Wis 18:11). This latter meaning predominates in the LXX: "the avenging sword of vengeance" (Lev 26:25; cf. Exod 21:20); "punishment by fire" (Amos 7:14; cf. 2 Macc 8:11, 13); "the punishment reserved for sinners."[6] The NT knows only this meaning: when St. Paul was bitten by the snake after escaping the shipwreck, the Maltese concluded, "Surely this man is a murderer, since after he has been saved from the sea, Dike (the avenging goddess) does not allow him to live" (Acts 28:4); those who do not obey the gospel "will in punishment suffer eternal loss" (2 Thess 1:9); Sodom and Gomorrah have "suffered the punishment (the consequence of just judgment) of eternal fire" (Jude 7).

II. *Dikaios.* — This adjective modifies persons who conform to custom or law (Homer, *Od.* 6.120) and things that are "normal," i.e., that are as they ought to be (a just judgment, Deut 16:18; John 5:30; Josephus, *Ant.* 9.4; just ways arrive at their goal, Rev 15:3; Josephus, *Ant.* 13.290). Aristotle defines the *dikaios* as "one who conforms to the law (*nomimos*) and is equal (*isos*)."[7] But all of Greek literature includes in the obligations of the just

---

25, 24; *P.Oslo* 37, 15; 39, 20; *P.Mert.* 6, 28; 10, 25; *P.Sakaon* 63–66; 72, 14; 74, 17; 96, 18; cf. H. Meyer-Laurin, "Zur Entstehung und Bedeutung der καθάπερ ἐκ δίκης-Klausel in den griechischen Papyri Ägyptens," in *RIDA*, 1974, pp. 349–350; C. Spicq, *Théologie morale*, vol. 2, p. 743; H. J. Wolff, *Das Justizwesen der Ptolemäer*, Munich, 1962, idem, "Some Observations on Praxis," in *Proceedings* XII, pp. 527–535.

[5] Dike is the goddess who avenges without pity (Hesiod, *Th.* 901; *Op.* 220ff., 256); she pursues the criminal (Dittenberger, *Syl.* 1176); Sophocles, *El.* 528: "justice has condemned him"; *Ant.* 538; Aeschylus (in Stobaeus, *Flor.* 125, 6; vol. 5, p. 1138); *SB* 5103, 13 (third century BC): ὁ θεὸς αὐτῷ τὴν δίκην ἐπιθείη; Josephus, *War* 1.84; 7.34; *Ant.* 6.305; 14.28: punishment for an offense; 4 Macc 4:13—"divine justice, angered at these crimes, drew upon them the hostility of Antiochus"; 9:9; 12:12—"Divine justice holds a more lively fire in reserve for you"; 18:22 (but 8:14, 22, this justice pardons a transgression blamed on compulsion). Cf. E. Gerner, "Zum Begriff δίκη im attischen Recht," in *Festschrift für Leopold Wenger*, Munich, 1945, pp. 242–268.

[6] Wis 14:31; Philo, *Creation* 80: "a punishment was instituted to punish impious conduct"; Josephus, *War* 7.453: God punishes the wicked; *Ant.* 6.288; 18.255: he inflicts punishments. *P.Fay.* 21, 24: a proclamation of the prefect Marcus Petronius Mamertinus, "that creditors might pay the penalties due to their disobedience" (ὅπως τῆς ἀπειθίας ἐκῖνοι τὴν προσήκουσαν δίκην ὑπόσχωσι). In the fourth century, δίκην τὴν ὑπὲρ τῆς ἀμελίας ὑποσχεῖν (*Chrest.Wilck.*, n. 469, 10). Cf. τίμημα τῆς δίκης θάνατος (H. Wankel, *I.Ephes.*, Bonn, 1949, n. II, 11).

[7] Aristotle, *Eth. Nic.* 5.2.1129a33 (cf. this edict of Germanicus: ἐὰν γὰρ δέῃ, αὐτὸς Βαίβιος ἐκ τοῦ ἴσου καὶ δικαίου τὰς ξενίας διαδώσει, *SB* 3924, 17). For Demosthenes (3.21), the δίκαιος πολίτης is the citizen who carries out his obligations toward the

δίκαιος, dikaios, etc. 321

not only their responsibilities toward humans[8] but also toward the gods; the just are so only if they are pious.[9] So if the just person has a political "virtue," it is conceived as the virtue of establishing order and harmony among men (Plato, Resp. 4.443 c–e). To dikaion is an innate idea that belongs to human nature, like the beautiful, the good, and the fitting.[10] Under Stoic influence, Philo makes it a cardinal virtue, but one whose role goes far beyond the legal realm.[11] Depending on the LXX, Josephus has a religious concept of the just person, who is not only faithful to divine commands,[12]

---

state; Philo, Spec. Laws 4.46; Josephus, Ag. Apion 2.293: "What is more just than obeying the laws?"

[8] Cf. Aeschylus, Ag. 1604; Aegisthus declares: "I was marked out (κἀγὼ δίκαιος) to plan this murder."

[9] Δίκαιος is constantly linked with ὅσιος, cf. Plato, Resp. 1.331 a; Grg. 507 b; Euthphr. 12 c–d: "all that is pious is just"; ibid. 12 e: "Here is the part of justice that seems to me to be pious and religious"; Polybius 22.10.8; Philo, Moses 2.108; Flight 63; Josephus, Ant. 8.295; 12.43: "the high priest Onias was surnamed the Just (ὁ δίκαιος) because of his piety toward God and his benevolence toward his compatriots"; 15.138. Aeschylus, Sept. 598: "What presage here links a just person with the impious?"

[10] Epictetus 1.22.1; 2.17.6. Cf. Josephus, Ant. 1.158: Abraham was a δίκαιος ἀνήρ (cf. 6.93), like David (7.110), Uzziah (9.216), and Hezekiah: φύσις δ' ἦν αὐτῷ χρηστὴ καὶ δικαία καὶ εὐσεβής (9.260). Cf. Aeschylus, Sept. 610. Δίκαιος is constantly linked with εὐσεβής (Euripides, Alc. 1147–1148; Philo, Alleg. Interp. 3.10; Josephus, Ant. 6.265; 8.121, 394; 15.182; Ag. Apion 2.170ff. I.Did. 218, 1–2; I.Priene 46, 12, etc.). Cf. ἀληθῶς δικαιοτάτου ἡγεμόνος (H. Wankel, I.Ephes., n. XVIII, 13).

[11] Philo, Alleg. Interp. 2.18: "A person described in terms of the virtues is called, according to the virtues, prudent, temperate, just, courageous"; Sobr. 38; Migr. Abr. 219; cf. ibid. 121: "The just person (ὁ δίκαιος) is the stay of the human race; he brings his personal property to the community and gives unstintingly for the good of those who find a use for it. He then seeks from God, who alone possesses all wealth, that which he does not have"; ibid. 124: "the just among the human race remain in place to push sicknesses away." Worse Attacks Better 121, 123; a man of faith (Alleg. Interp. 3.228); "he discovers that absolutely everything is a gift from God" (ibid. 3.78). God alone is just in the highest degree (Dreams 2.194; Moses 2.279; Flight 82; cf. Josephus, War 7.223; Ant. 2.108; 11.55).

[12] When Samuel anoints David, he exhorts him to be just and to obey the commandments (Josephus, Ant. 6.165; cf. Solomon, Ant. 8.208). One can become just through repentance (6.210) and merit a reward (18.18). More particularly, dikaios means "correct, punctual" (5.197; 15.106; 16.212), notably with respect to things that are well balanced, according to measure, like balances and weights (Lev 19:36; Deut 25:15; Ezek 45:10; Philo, Heir 162), a measuring (P.Hib. 90, 11; 91, 2; P.Oxy. 1126, 7; P.Lille 24, 9; P.Yale 51, 10; O.Amst. 91, 9), prices (SB 5175, 15: τιμὴν δικαίην; P.Tebt. 389, 17), the rising of the Nile as needed (δικαία ἀνάβασις, Dittenberger, Or. 666, 11), well-founded suspicions (ὑποψίας δικαίας, Life 93), "proper" benevolence of spouses (εὔνοια δικαία, Ant. 1.318), things that are appropriate (Ant. 2.272), conformable to the right (δικαία αἰτία, P.Stras. 22, 3; BGU 267, 8; SB 5174, 4).

but a person of honesty, rectitude,[13] keeping to his place and acting according to the divine will. Thus it is the faithful Jew who is just (*Ant.* 9.33), "all the Jews among the Hebrews" (10.38; cf. 14.172). They illustrate the conception of Theognis ("All the virtues are included in justice. If you are just, you are a good person" (1.147–148) or of Isocrates (the best person is the just person, *Nic.* 20; cf. *Hel.* 1). "No sin is the result of justice" (Philo, *Quest. Gen.* 4.64); "Just ways do not know how to do wrong" (*dikaios adikein ouk epistatai trophos*, Menander, in Stobaeus, *Ecl.* 9.8, vol. 3, p. 438; *T. Gad* 5.3).

The LXX affirms and reaffirms that God is "just and upright" (Deut 32:4; Ps 11:7); a "just judge" (Jer 12:1; Ps 7:12; Tob 3:2), acting justly (Gen 18:25; Judg 5:11; Ps 145:17), rewarding or punishing with justice (Ps 62:13); but this justice is linked with goodness: "Yahweh is merciful and just; our God is compassionate" (Ps 116:5). The Messiah is described as just, not only because he carries out God's will, but because he possesses this attribute, which is proper to good sovereigns, and because he establishes justice on earth: "I will raise up from David a just seed. . . . He will practice judgment and justice in the land. . . . He will be called 'Yahweh-our-Justice.'"[14] As for the just person in the OT, he is first of all innocent, in contrast to the impious transgressor (Exod 23:6–8; Ezek 23:45); he is "the one who does the will of the Lord" (Sir 16:3). So he is essentially a religious and perfect person (Gen 6:9), especially impartial (Deut 16:19) and generous (2 Kgs 10:9; 1 Sam 24:18). Not only is he "just before God" (Gen 7:1), he is also a "son of God" (Wis 2:18), and "the souls of the just are in God's hands" (Wis 3:1; 5:1, 15). Even when persecuted (Wis 2:10–18), the just are beloved of God (Ps 146:7) and living (Isa 26:2), and they will be exalted: "Glory to the just!"[15]

---

[13] Δικαίως, as opposed to ἀδόλως (Thucydides 5.18.9; 5.23.2; 5.47.8) means "loyally, without deceit"; cf. ἐπιμελῶς καὶ πιστῶς καὶ δικαίως (B. Latyschev, *Inscriptiones Antiquae*, I, n. 43, 10–11); ἐποιήσαντο ὀρθῶς καὶ δικαίως (*SEG* XIX, 327, 22); δικαιοσύνης καὶ πίστεως = justice and loyalty (Plutarch, *Aem.* 2.6).

[14] Jer 23:5–6; 33:15; cf. Isa 53:11; Zech 9:9; *Pss. Sol.* 17.35—"He is a just king, taught by God, placed over them." Cf. H. Dechent, "Der 'Gerechte': Eine Bezeichnung für den Messias," in *TSK*, vol. 100, 1927–28, pp. 439ff.

[15] Isa 24:16. God rewards this justice (Deut 6:24ff.; 24:13), while the one who turns aside from justice will die (Ezek 3:20; 18:5–26). "The justice of the just will be upon him" (Ezek 18:20) suggests this reward but also hints that this justice is a virtue immanent in the faithful. Cf. Philo, *Sobr.* 38–40; *Sacr. Abel and Cain* 54; *Alleg. Interp.* 2.18; *Prelim. Stud.* 90: "in the soul, that which is just (τὸ δίκαιον) is the perfection and true goal of the acts of Life."

In the NT, several usages of *dikaios* match secular usage,[16] especially the neuter *to dikaion*.[17] The master of the vineyard promises the workers that he will give "whatever is just" (*ho ean ē dikaion*) after the work is done (Matt 20:4). Each one can judge what is right (*krinein to dikaion*, Luke 12:57). Masters must give their slaves what is just and equitable (*to dikaion kai tēn isotēta*, Col 4:1), and St. Peter considers it his responsibility (literally, considers it just, *dikaion hēgeomai*) to keep Christians watchful.[18] But our authors sometimes feel the need to Christianize this obligation, which has its source in God; Peter and John ask their judges "if it is just in God's sight (*ei dikaion estin enōpion tou theou*) to obey you rather than God."[19] Nevertheless, in the great majority of cases, *dikaios* retains its LXX meaning. First of all, in describing God as just in carrying out his promises of salvation, "God shows his justice . . . so that he may be just himself (*eis to einai auton dikaion*) and also make just those who have believed in

---

[16] In the mouth of pagans: Pilate's wife calls Jesus "the just" (Matt 27:19; cf. E. Fascher, *Das Weib des Pilatus*, Halle, 1951), and Pilate repeats the description (27:24), meaning that he is innocent. The centurion at the foot of the cross says "This was a just man" (Luke 23:47)—not guilty, a martyr bringing glory to God. Herod is more influenced by the OT when he respects John the Baptist "knowing that he was a just and holy man" (ἄνδρα δίκαιον καὶ ἅγιον, Mark 6:20); but altogether Greek are Phil 4:8—"whatever is true, honorable, just, pure . . . whatever is good and virtuous . . . think on these things"; and Titus 2:12—"Let us live σωφρόνως καὶ δικαίως καὶ εὐσεβῶς in this present age" (cf. C. Spicq, *Epîtres Pastorales*, vol. 2, p. 638). The adverb δικαίως is used for judging with equity (Deut 1:16; Prov 31:9; Sir 35:18), sinners justly punished (Wis 19:13; *T. Sim.* 4.3); legitimately, according to deserts (Josephus, *Ant.* 2.140), equitably, justly (Epictetus 2.1.3); acting correctly (*P.Tebt.* 702, 21; cf. 19, 14; *P.Oxy.* 653, 23; *P.Fam.Tebt.* 19, 4); legally in possession (*P.Tebt.* 335, 12); money justly due (*P.Fouad* 26, 54). Rather than translate ἐκνήψατε δικαίως (1 Cor 15:34) "return to state of just sobriety," we should understand "sober up rightly" or better "as is fitting, adopting right conduct."

[17] Cf. Aristotle, *Eth. Nic.* 5.2.1129ᵃ34: "the right (τὸ δίκαιον) is that which is conformable to the law and that which is equal"; Polybius 3.21.10; Job 8:3—"Does God pervert what is right?"; Prov 18:5; 21:7; Josephus, *War* 1.507: natural right; *Ant.* 12.121: citizenship rights; 8.296: legal obligation. Xenophon's guests wish for the opportunity for moral conduct: τὰ δίκαια δύνασθαι πρήσσειν (frag. 1.15; ed. J. Defradas, *Les Elégiaques grecs*, Paris, 1962, p. 76).

[18] 2 Pet 1:13; cf. Sir 10:23; 2 Macc 9:12 = it is fitting; Phil 1:7—"It is only just (legitimate, καθώς ἐστιν δίκαιον) for me to feel this way"; Philo, *Husbandry* 80: δίκαιον εἶναι = it is reasonable; *Sacr. Abel and Cain* 74; Menander, *Dysk.* 293, 763; *IG* IX, 1, 582, 22; *C.Pap.Jud.* 4, 3; *P.Tebt.* 50, 25; *P.Oxy.* 1117, 29; cf. 717, 10.

[19] Acts 4:19; cf. 2 Thess 1:6—"It is a just thing with God (δίκαιον παρὰ θεῷ) to return trouble to those who trouble us" (retribution at God's judgment seat, cf. Isa 66:6; Col 3:25; cf. Elisha: "It is just to kill those who have been captured according to the laws of warfare," in Josephus, *Ant.* 9.58); Eph 6:1—"Children, obey your parents in the Lord; this is just," i.e., conformable to the divine will.

Jesus."[20] God is always just in his judgments, punishing the godless and rewarding the faithful.[21] It follows that the law, which comes from God, expresses his will, and binds people to God and their neighbor, "is holy, and the commandment is holy, just, and good" (*hagia kai dikaia kai agathē*, Rom 7:12). This justice clearly goes beyond the realm of the legal or even the equitable; it is almost synonymous with perfection or integrity! Taking up the messianic designation in Isa 53:11; Jer 23:5, St. Peter says to the Sanhedrin, "You disowned the Holy and Just One" (*ton hagion kai dikaion*).[22] Again, the modifier *dikaios* is used for a person of perfect rectitude, one who carries out the will of God;[23] a person set apart, contrasted with the breaker of the law.[24] This person is promised the highest reward: the resurrection of the just (*anastasis tōn dikaiōn*, Luke 14:14; cf. Acts 24:15). *Dikaios* became a term for a Christian, first of all

---

[20] Rom 3:26. Cf. 1 John 1:9—"He is faithful and just to forgive us our sins." In pardoning the guilty who repent, the just God is faithful to his promises of mercy.

[21] The angel of the waters proclaims: "You are just, you who are and who were, the Holy One (ὁ ὅσιος)" (Rev 16:5); "true and just are your judgments" (16:7; 19:2); 1 Pet 2:23—when Christ suffered violence he entrusted himself to "the One who judges with justice" (δικαίως, cf. Jer 11:20; John 8:50; Rom 12:19). Hence Πατὴρ δίκαιε! (John 17:25; 2 Tim 4:8).

[22] Acts 3:14 (cf. 7:52—"the coming of the Just One"; 22:14; 1 Pet 3:18—"Christ died . . . the just for the unjust." 1 John 2:1—"We have an advocate with the Father, Jesus Christ the Just"; *Enoch* 46.3—"the Son of Man who possesses justice and with whom justice dwells"). Christ is a "saint," a "holy one," i.e., one consecrated to God (Ps 16:10; Mark 1:24; Luke 4:34; John 6:69). If he is "just," he is so inasmuch as he fulfills the divine will, and also because he is totally innocent; but this designation also means that he is perfect to an absolute, limitless degree that belongs to the divine realm (cf. τελειόω in Heb 2:10; 5:9; 7:28; τελειωτής, 12:2).

[23] "Just Abel" (Matt 23:35; Heb 11:4); "just Lot" (2 Pet 2:7-8; probably borrowed from a midrashic tradition, *b. Ber.* 54*b*; cf. R. Le Déaut, *Liturgie juive et Nouveau Testament*, Rome, 1965, p. 52, n. 56; cf. S. Rappaport, "Der gerechte Lot," in *ZNW*, 1930, pp. 299–304); "prophets and just ones" (Matt 13:17; cf. 10:41; 23:29; cf. *2 Apoc. Bar.* 85.1, 3, 12; D. Hill, "ΔΙΚΑΙΟΙ as a Quasi-Technical Term," in *NTS*, vol. 11, 1965, pp. 297–302); Zechariah and Elizabeth, "just before God" (Luke 1:6), Simeon, δίκαιος καὶ εὐλαβής (Luke 2:25), Joseph (Matt 1:19—δίκαιος ὤν; cf. C. Spicq, " 'Joseph, son mari, étant juste . . . ,' " in *RB*, 1964, pp. 206–211; A. Tosato, " 'Joseph, Being a Just Man,' " in *CBQ*, 1979, pp. 547–551; cf. the graffito on a Hermes of Roman origin: χαῖρε δίκαιος ὤν, cf. G. Susini, "Le iscrizioni greche di Bologna," in *Atti e memorie*, Bologna, 1963, p. 76), the centurion Cornelius (Acts 10:22). Epitaph of Eleazar, "holy, just, loving his children, loving his brothers, loving the community" (*CII*, n. 321); Plutarch, *Rom.* 23.3. R. Mach, *Der Zaddik in Talmud und Midrasch*, Leiden, 1957.

[24] Δίκαιος as opposed to: ἁμαρτωλός (Matt 9:13; Mark 2:17; Luke 5:32; 15:7; Rom 5:19), ἄδικος (Matt 5:45; Acts 24:15), ἀπειθής (Luke 1:17), ἀσεβής (Rom 5:6–7; 1 Tim 1:9; 1 Pet 4:18), ἄνομος (Matt 13:41; 1 Tim 1:9), πονηρός (Matt 13:49), ὑποκριτής (Matt 23:28; Luke 20:20).

because Christians are purified from sin (Matt 13:43, 49) and acceptable to God (Jas 5:6); they are irreproachable, and their prayers are very powerful (Jas 5:16; 1 Pet 3:12); they are also merciful (Matt 25:37, 46). If they are "saved with difficulty" (1 Pet 4:18; a quotation from Prov 11:31) through many trials, they are sure of receiving "the recompense of the just" (Matt 10:41) and reaching God (Heb 12:23).

St. Paul enriched this OT idea of justice/righteouness. Whereas Ps 14:1 says, "There is no just person, not even one" (quoted Rom 3:10; cf. Eccl 7:20), the apostle adds on the one hand that it is not mere knowledge of the law that makes a person just, but putting it into practice, actualizing it in works.[25] And on the other hand he declares that a new form of justice/righteousness has appeared, no longer a legal or sacrificial justice, nor even moral, but a religious and internal righteousness. Whereas Adam's transgression brought a death sentence for all humans (Rom 5:18), Christ instituted (*kathistēmi*) a dispensation of justifying, life-giving grace: "Through one person's obedience, all will be constituted just" (*dikaioi katastathēsontai hoi polloi*, Rom 5:19); it is no longer Adam's sin that is inherited, but Christ's righteousness. Thus Christ establishes a new humanity of just people, antithetical to sinful humanity.[26] To be clothed with this righteousness, it is enough to believe: "The just will live by faith."[27] It is the gift or the sharing of God's justice/righteousness that makes the believer just, not so much on the moral plane of virtues as in the theological order: the *dikaios* is a new creation (2 Cor 5:17), enters into communion with God, is a new being. So it is indeed faith that is the principle of the religious life (Rom 3:26; Gal 3:7–9) and justification that gives life (*dikaiōsis*

---

[25] Rom 2:13—"It is not those who hear a law read that are just before God (δίκαιοι παρὰ θεῷ), but those who put it into practice are recognized as just (δικαιωθήσονται)"; it is these latter who at judgment will be recognized and declared to be in effect the just, "that which they ought to be," in conformity with what God willed.

[26] This means that this received justice is a gift of God. It is not acquired by individual effort; good "works" are only its manifestation and its fruit. Everything depends on the connection with Christ, like the connection of members to the head or branches to a vine. Cf. J. Coppens, "Le Saddiq-'Juste,' dans le Psautier," in *Mélanges H. Cazelles*, Paris, 1981, pp. 299–306.

[27] Hab 2:4, quoted in Rom 1:17; Gal 3:11; Heb 10:38, in varied terms (cf. the commentaries). A. Feuillet ("La Citation d'Habacuc II, 4 et les huit premiers chapitres de l'Epître aux Romains," in *NTS*, vol. 6, 1959, pp. 52–80) translates, "The one who is just by virtue of faith shall live" ("Celui qui est juste en vertu de la foi vivra") and explains: the text shows "with what justice man must be clothed in order to live." Cf. D. M. Smith, "ὁ δὲ δίκαιος ἐκ πίστεως ζήσεται," in B. L. Daniels, M. J. Suggs, *Studies in the History and Text of the N.T.*, Salt Lake City, 1967, pp. 13–25; G. von Rad, '*Gerechtigkeit*' *und* '*Leben*' *in der Kultsprache der Psalmen*, Göttingen, 1950.

zōēs, Rom 5:18; *to pneuma zōē dia dikaiosynēn*, 8:10). This dynamic and life-giving principle indwells the Christian, who, led by the Holy Spirit (Gal 5:18)—whose role is to lead the children of God (Rom 8:14)—and by faith (Gal 3:11), knows how to discern between good and evil and wants what God wants, just as a child instinctively knows its father's desires and seeks to please him. The law, on the other hand, was established to set rules for sinners and to punish them. Thus "the law was instituted not for the just (those justified by Christ) but for the lawless and rebellious, the godless and sinful."[28]

III. *Dikaiosynē*. — This substantive, unknown in Homer and Hesiod, first appears in Herodotus (1.96), and in the Koine it substituted more and more for *dikē*. Certainly it retains a legal sense,[29] but its meaning is considerably broadened. Not only is it a virtue,[30] notably in sovereigns,

---

[28] 1 Tim 1:9 (cf. C. Spicq, *Epîtres Pastorales*, vol. 1, p. 332). The two other Pauline texts agree with the usage of the LXX and secular usage: "Our bearing among you believers was holy, just, beyond reproach" (ὁσίως καὶ δικαίως καὶ ἀμέμπτως, 1 Thess 2:10; cf. P. E. Langevin, "Le Seigneur Jésus selon un texte prépaulinien, I Th. I, 9–10," in *ScEccl*, 1965, pp. 263–282; the linking of δίκαιος and ἄμεμπτος, as at Job 1:1; 9:10—ὁσίως καί δικαίως; *SEG* XIV, 676, 9; *LSCG*, n. 65, 8). The *episkopos* must be "sober, just, holy, self-controlled" (σώφρονα, δίκαιον, ὅσιον, ἐγκρατῆ, Titus 1:8); "just and holy" as at Deut 32:4; Ps 145:17; 1 Thess 2:10; Eph 4:24; Philo, *Good Man Free* 83. In both cases it is a matter of irreproachable conduct (cf. ὁ βίος δίκαιος, Sallustius, *De Deis et Mundo* 10.2), but "holiness" is recognized in conformity to the will of God. For Antonius Liberalis, the just person is the balanced and proper person or, as we would say, "comme il faut": Hierax, δίκαιος ἀνὴρ καὶ ἐπιφανής (*Met.* 3.1; same link, *P.Dura* XVIII, 1; *IGLS* I, pp. 13–41); Cragaleus, δίκαιος εἶναι καὶ φρόνιμος (IV, 2); Aegypios ἦν μεγαλόφρων καὶ δίκαιος (V, 1); Periphas "was just, rich, and pious" (VI, 1); Mounichos, "a just man" (XIV, 1); his children were all "ἀγαθοὺς καὶ δικαίους, and the gods loved them" (XIV, 2). Δίκαιος is constantly linked with καλός (Philo, *Drunkenness* 197; Josephus, *Ant.* 13.431; Epictetus 1.22.1; 2.17.6; Musonius, frag. 3, ed. C. E. Lutz, p. 40; frag. 7, p. 58; frag. 11, p. 80; *I.Priene* 58, 12; 63, 21; 112, 6; *IGLS* 2740: "Martinus carried out καλῶς καὶ δικαίως the service of lord Cronos and the gods"); with ἀγαθός (ibid. 14, p. 94); Luke 23:50; *SEG* XVII, 711, 15–18; *I.Priene* 58, 12; 63, 21; 112, 6 and 144; *I.Bulg.*, n. 316, 7); with χρηστός (*IG*, II², 12034; Josephus, *Ant.* 2.149; 6.294; 9.166; 11.183; Plutarch, *De frat. amor.* 6; *Publ.* 21.6).

[29] Aristotle, *Rh.* 1.9.1366ᵇ9ff.: "Justice is the virtue thanks to which each person possesses his property in accord with the law" (καὶ ὡς ὁ νόμος); cf. "the legal and just," (τὸ νομικὸν δίκαιον, *Eth. Nic.* 5.12.1136ᵃ12). This is the dominant meaning in the papyri, where plaintiffs appeal to the justice of the *stratēgos* (*BGU* 1138, 4; 1824, 30; *P.Oslo* 128, 10; *P.Oxy.* 1873, 15) and mention their "rights" (*P.Köln* 100, 11, and 23; *P.Petaus* 11, 15; cf. Josephus, *Ant.* 14.403). "In the manner of a brigand and contrary to all justice, he fell upon my sheep and stole eighty-two of them" (*P.Thead.* 23, 9; republished *P.Abinn.* 44). The Christian papyri, which are late, are of no interest here: *SB* 6035, 17; 8763, 15; 8728, 18; 10522, 4: placing Δικαιοσύνη between Ἀγάπη and Εἰρήνη.

[30] Philo, *Change of Names* 197; *Heir* 243; *Abraham* 27, 56, 103, 104; *Creation* 80;

lawmakers, and leaders,[31] that sums up all other virtues;[32] it seems to consist most of all in properly fulfilling one's role in society, at least beginning with Plato (*Phd.* 82 a: *demotikē kai politikē aretē*). Little by little, it becomes a synonym of perfection[33] and an attribute of every honest person,[34] of good comportment (Josephus, *Ant.* 3.67; 4.223; 19.154). Hence its association with *semnos* (Isocrates, *Panath.* 249; Josephus, *War* 4.319), referring to a sort of nobility or at least dignity (Josephus, *Ant.* 11.217; 12.160). *Dikaiosynē*, which implies measure and moderation, goes along with leniency (*praos*, Dio Cassius 49.20) and *epieikeia* (Josephus, *Ant.* 14.13); so it is inclined to forgive (3 Macc 7:6–7; *I.Sard.* 20.1–6). In addition, it is with increasing frequency characterized as being ready to serve[35] and dedicated to serving everyone; doctors who devote them-

---

Alleg. Interp. 1.63; 3.77. Josephus, *Ant.* 9.182; 14.176. An innate virtue (6.36) that is practiced from youth (1.53) and is the beauty of the soul (6.160) and confers prestige (*Life* 7).

[31] Philo, *Spec. Laws* 4.56, 143, *Prelim. Stud.* 179; Josephus, *Ant.* 4.214; *I.Did.* 487, 5. In 111 BC, Queen Cleopatra III is described as "Thea, Philometor, Savior, Justice, Victory-Bringer" (*P.Rein.* 10, 9). Hence its frequent mention in the inscriptions, in honorific decrees. Cf. at Athens, in the fourth century BC, the praise for the commissioners of the Amphiaraion of Oropus "for their justice and their zeal toward god and the people of Athens" (Dittenberger, *Syl.* 298, 31). At Delos in the second century, Aglaos of Cos is praised "for the integrity and justice that he shows in his life on all occasions" (F. Durrbach, *Choix*, n. 92, 18). Cf. R. Hutmacher, *Ehrendekret*, 1965, pp. 43ff. The Romans made justice into one of the four imperial virtues, along with virtue, piety, and clemency (cf. Dionysius of Halicarnassus 2.18.1–2; Diotogenes, *On Kingship*, in Stobaeus, *Flor.* 48; vol. 4, pp. 263ff.; *Mon. Anc.* 34). Cf. B. Lichocka, *Justitia sur les monnaies impériales romaines*, Warsaw, 1974.

[32] Theognis 1.147: "Justice holds in itself all other virtues," cited by Aristotle, *Eth. Nic.* 5.3.1129^b30, who calls it the perfect virtue; it lacks nothing, and nothing surpasses it. Plato, *Euthphr.* 12 e: justice is concerned with relations between humans as well as with the gods; *Prt.* 330 bff. Epictetus 3.26.32; Plutarch, *De fort.* 2; Dittenberger, *Or.* 438, 8. Stobaeus cites Hermes Trismegistus: justice is a harmony in psychic equilibrium (*Ecl.* 1.49.4, vol. 1, p. 322, 10); Philo, *Alleg. Interp.* 1.72, a remedy for all ills (*Worse Attacks Better* 123), justice produces repose (ibid. 122), joy (*Alleg. Interp.* 3.247), and prosperity (Job 8:6; Joel 2:23). The just person is blessed (Ps 69:29; 112:4, 6).

[33] Philo, *Quest. Gen.* 1.97; *Abraham* 33; Josephus, *Ant.* 1.158. It is wisdom put into practice (Philo, *Alleg. Interp.* 1.72).

[34] Cf. Pollux in Lycia, in the second century AD: ἄνδρα καλὸν καὶ ἀγαθὸν καὶ πάσῃ ἀρετῇ καὶ δικαιοσύνῃ διαπρέποντα (*SEG* XVII, 711, 15–18); διὰ τὴν τῶν ἀνδρῶν δικαιοσύνην τε καὶ φιλοτιμίαν (Dittenberger, *Or.* 339, 48); διενένκαντα πίστει καὶ ἀρετῇ καὶ δικαιοσύνῃ καὶ εὐσεβείᾳ καὶ περὶ τοῦ κοινοῦ συνφέροντος (ibid. 438, 8).

[35] It acts in the interest of others (Philo, *Migr. Abr.* 11; Josephus, *Ant.* 11.183; *War* 7.263; Diotogenes, in Stobaeus, *Ecl.* 3.9.46, vol. 3, p. 360; Diogenes Laertius 10.150; *I.Priene* 63, 20). H. Bolkestein, *Wohltätigkeit und Armenpflege im vorchristlichen Altertum*, Utrecht, 1939, pp. 102ff.

selves to the service of all are praised for their *dikaiosynē*.[36] Finally, *dikaiosynē* is linked with beneficence and philanthropy. In the second century BC, Theodorus is praised "for his beneficence and his justice toward all" (*euergesias heneken kai dikaiosynēs tēs pros hapantas*, SB 9974, 7), as is Callicles,[37] and Musonius defines virtue thus: "Virtue (*aretē*) is brotherly love and goodness and *dikaiosynē* and beneficence" (frag. 14, ed. C. E. Lutz, p. 92, 32; frag. 16, p. 104, 33; frag. 17, p. 108, 2; frag. 38, p. 136, 3; cf. frag. 11, p. 82, 33; frag. 13 *b*, p. 90, 13; cf. Philo, *Quest. Gen.* 4.66). *Dikaiosynē* had all of these characteristics when personified, honored, and even divinied,[38] worshiped,[39] given altars.[40]

In the LXX, *dikaiosynē* translates the Hebrew *ṣᵉḏāqâh*, the exact meaning of which is not discoverable but which seems to express fullness and abundance.[41] The justice/righteousness of God, which in itself is indefin-

---

[36] *I.Thas.* 180, 7: δικαίως καὶ φιλαγάθως καὶ ἰατρεύοντα ἐπὶ σωτηρίᾳ τῇ πάντων; *I.Car.* 70 B, 9; *I.Did.* 391B, 1, 13–14: δικαίως καὶ φιλαγάθως; Dittenberger, *Syl.* 193, 19. Aristotle wrote that friendship "is the fullest realization of justice" (*Eth. Nic.* 8.1.1155a22).

[37] SB 10113. Cf. the epitaph of an anonymous person deceased at age eighteen: δίκαιος θεοσεβής, φιλάνθρωπος (E. Bernand, *Inscriptions métriques*, Paris, n. 71, 8); Josephus, *Ag. Apion* 2.146; *Ant.* 11.139; cf. Wis 12:19—"It is fitting that the just should be philanthropic."

[38] At Gerasa: "Diogenes dedicated a statue of Justice" (*SEG* 7.487; L. Vidman, *Sylloge Inscriptionum Religionis Isiacae et Sarapiacae*, Berlin, 1969, n. 6 and 365; *NCIG*, n. 32; L. Robert, *Opera Minora Selecta*, vol. 1, p. 603; vol. 3, p. 1507); at Delos (J. and L. Robert, "Bulletin épigraphique," in *REG*, 1958, p. 289, n. 356); at Athens (*IG*, IV², 407), at Alexandria (Dittenberger, *Or.* 83); cf. *P.Lond.* 46, 403 (vol. 1, p. 78: a magical papyrus, a hymn to Hermes). Justice is sometimes identified with Nemesis (a dedication on Cyprus, cf. J. and L. Robert, "Bulletin épigraphique," in *REG*, 1949, p. 152, n. 203), but more often with Isis: "At Hermopolis the first of the Muses is called both Isis and Justice" (Plutarch, *De Is. et Os.* 3; hymn to Isis in E. Bernand, *Inscriptions métriques* 175, IV, 6; *I.Delos* 2079, 2103).

[39] At Iasos (J. and L. Robert, "Bulletin épigraphique," in *REG*, 1964, p. 222, n. 461); at Termessos: ἱερεὺς Δικαιοσύνης (ibid., 1939, p. 526, n. 501).

[40] In Lycia (J. and L. Robert, "Bulletin épigraphique," in *REG*, 1939, p. 505, n. 384), at Byblos and at Pinara (L. Robert, *Documents*, pp. 25ff.); at Ephesus, on the agora, as was fitting, cf. C. Börker, R. Merkelbach, *I.Ephes.*, Bonn, 1979, n. 503. — H. Lloyd-Jones, *The Justice of Zeus*, Berkeley–Los Angeles, 1971; J. Duchemin, "La Justice de Zeus et le destin d'Io," in *REG*, 1979, pp. 1–54.

[41] Cf. K. H. Fahlgren, *Sedaqa*, Uppsala, 1932; A. Descamps, "La Justice de Dieu dans la Bible grecque," in *Studia Hellenistica*, vol. 5, Paris-Leiden, 1948, pp. 69–92; F. Nötscher, *Die Gerechtigkeit Gottes bei den vorexilischen Propheten*, Münster, 1915, ; F. Rosenthal, *Sedaqa Charity*, in *HUCA*, vol. 33, 1950–51; pp. 411–430; P. Wernberg-Møller, "Tsedeq, Tsadiq, Tsadoq, in the Zadokite Fragments, the Manual of Discipline and the Habakkuk Commentary," in *VT*, 1953, pp. 310–315; J. P. Justesen, "On the Meaning of Sadaq," *AUSS* 2, 1964, pp. 53–61; R. A. Rosenberg, "The Good Sedeq," in *HUCA*, 1965,

able, is always expressed in his relations with the world; it is a relational concept, one that has to do with activities. The believer confesses that on Yahweh's side, all is perfect: "his work is perfect, all his ways are justice" (Deut 32:4); "Justice belongs to the Lord our God" (Bar 1:15; 2:6; Ezra 9:15); "You are just with regard to all that has happened to us."[42] On rare occasions this legislative and retributive divine justice is purely judicial;[43] it is the attribute of an all-powerful sovereign: "You sit enthroned as a just judge" (Ps 9:5; 51:16; 96:13; 111:3; 129:3). He brings to pass exactly what he has announced,[44] but above all, his actions, which are so perfectly just, are always accompanied by goodness and mercy: "Yahweh will do justice to his people and will take pity on his servants" (Deut 32:36; Ps 88:13; 103:17; 116:5; Jer 9:23). He betroths himself to his people in justice, grace, and affection (Hos 2:21); "your great goodness will be remembered and your justice will be proclaimed" (Ps 145:7, 17). The "justices" of Yahweh are his divine favors (Judg 5:11; 1 Sam 12:6ff.; Mic 6:3), a fullness of gifts (Deut 33:21; Amos 5:24), help (Isa 41:10—"I have upheld you by the right hand of my justice"; 42:6),[45] and above all, salvation ("a righteous God and Savior; there is none but me," Isa 45:21; 46:13); "my salvation will soon come, and my justice will appear";[46] "In your justice deliver me, free me, . . .

---

pp. 161–177; A. Descamps, L. Cerfaux, "Justice et justification," in *DBSup*, vol. 4, col. 1417–1510; K. Koch, צדק. *Theolog. Handwörterbuch zum A.T.*, vol. 2, pp. 507–530; J. M. Baumgarten, "The Heavenly Tribunal and the Personification of Ṣedeq in Jewish Apocalyptic," in *ANRW* 2, 19, 1, pp. 219–239; J. W. Olley, *"Righteousness" in the Septuagint of Isaiah*, Missoula, 1979; H. Cazelles, "Amore-Giustizia nella Bibbia," in Giuseppe de Gennaro, *Amore-Giustizia: Analisi semantica dei due termini*, Aquila: Studio Biblico theological aquilano, 1980, pp. 577–590.

[42] Neh 9:33; Dan 9:14; Ps 7:18; cf. Philo, *Moses* 2.237: God shows truth and justice (cf. Rom 3:25ff.); *Unchang. God* 79.

[43] Cf. Isa 43:6—to Israel, God says, "let us come together in trial"; cf. 50:8—"Who will be my opponent at trial?"; 1 Sam 12:7—"Let me go to trial with you before Yahweh"; Isa 20:22—the destruction is "a surge of justice." Josephus, *Ant.* 11.268: God punishes Haman's wickedness.

[44] Neh 9:8—"You have brought your words to pass, for you are just"; Isa 45:19—"I am Yahweh, who says what is just, who announces true things."

[45] Ps 119:40—"In your justice give me life," pardon for sins (Ps 51:16); "Justice and peace will kiss" (85:11–14; cf. 36:6ff.; 145:7); "I am Yahweh, who does mercy, right, and justice on the earth" (Jer 9:23; cf. 23:6; Job 36:2ff.; Zech 8:8); the "sacrifices of justice" (Deut 33:19) assure the success of an undertaking (cf. Ps 4:6; Mal 3:3). P. Benoit describes the δικαιοσύνη θεοῦ in the OT correctly as "compassionate justice" (*Exégèse et théologie*, vol. 2, p. 37 = ET, vol. 2, p. 137); confirmed by H. Cazelles, "A propos de quelques textes relatifs à la justice de Dieu dans l'Ancien Testament," in *RB*, pp. 169–188.

[46] Isa 56:1; cf. 42:6, 21—"Yahweh wanted, for the sake of his justice, to make his law magnificent and glorious"; Ps 65:6—"You will answer us with wonders of justice,

save me" (Ps 71:2). Thus the Messiah, raised up by God's justice and under his protection (Zech 9:9), will execute righteousness and justice (Isa 9:6; 11:4ff.; 32:1). He is the "Just One" who is to come (Jer 23:5) and will be called "Yahweh our Justice" (Jer 32:15).

Human justice/righteousness, which is contrasted with iniquity (*anomia*, Isa 5:7), is defined in relation to God (Zech 8:8, cf. Wis 5:6) and concretely as faithfulness to the law,[47] the proof of total dependence on and submission to the Lord, guaranteeing innocence (Ps 18:21, 25) and perfection (Ps 15:1ff.; 24:3). It is also a cardinal virtue, however (Wis 8:7) and a correct attitude in all human relationships, including, for example, the giving of alms.[48] There are constant appeals to seek (1 Macc 7:12), pursue (Prov 15:9; 21:21; Sir 27:8), practice righteousness and justice (Hos 10:12; Jer 22:3; Ezek 45:9ff.; 2 Sam 8:15). Also quite common are the mentions of the fruits of this justice: pardon for sins (Tob 12:8; 14:9), the way of life (Prov 12:28), and promises of reward: "The one who sows justice will have a guaranteed reward,"[49] for "when one lives with justice, one finds grace with God" (Philo, *Alleg. Interp.* 3.77).

God of our salvation"; 71:15—"My mouth will tell of your justice and your salvation all the day." For a Greek ear, in the first century, salvation is a benevolent manifestation of the deity whose providence preserves and guides the universe (cf. H. Haerens, "Σωτήρ et σωτηρία," in *Studia Hellenistica*, vol. 5, Paris-Leiden, 1948, p. 68). It is always mentioned that the LXX often translates the Hebrew *ḥesed*, "benevolence, grace," as *dikaiosynē* (Gen 19:19; 20:13; 21:23; 24:27; 32:11; Exod 15:13; 34:17; Ps 40:11-12; 88:12; cf. at Qumran the pairing *ḥesed*, *ṣedāqâh*; 1QS 2.24; 5.4; 8.2; 10.28) and that *ṣedāqâh* is translated ἔλεον (Isa 56:1; Ezek 18:19, 21), ἐλεημοσύνη (Deut 6:25; 24:13; Ps 24:5; 33:5; 35:24; 103:6; Sir 3:14; 40:17; Isa 1:27; 28:17; 59:16; Dan 9:6. Cf. Tob 9:6—the just person gives alms). W. Nagel, "Gerechtigkeit oder Almosen?" in *VC*, 1961, pp. 141-145; H. H. Schmid, "Gerechtigkeit und Barmherzigkeit im A. T.," in *Wort und Dienst*, 1973, pp. 31-41; at Qumran, justice is in parallel with goodness (Hebrew *ṭôb*), 1QH 9.11-12; 11.14. In rabbinic Judaism, *ṣedāqâh* means justice, then the leniency of the just, and finally alms; cf. J. Bonsirven, *Judaïsme palestinien*, vol. 1, pp. 198ff.

[47] Deut 6:25; 24:13; Prov 11:5ff.; 21:3; Tob 1:3; 14:7; Wis 14:7; Ps 119:21; Ezek 3:10; 18:5-21; 33:14-19; Zeph 2:3; cf. Josephus, *Ant.* 8.21, 120; 12.291.

[48] Sir 3:30; cf. Matt 25:46. Justice consists in giving each his due (Amos 5:7; Isa 5:7, 23; Jer 22:13); in the city, it is the special responsibility of the judges (Deut 1:16; 16:18-20; Lev 19:15; Ezek 45:9) and of the king (Prov 16:13; 25:5), who must judge disagreements (Deut 25:15); for each person has a "right" (Deut 25:1; Prov 17:15; Isa 5:7, 23).

[49] Prov 11:18; Hos 10:12. Justice/righteousness delivers from death (Prov 11:4) and saves (11:6), gives joy (Tob 14:7), gives a claim on prosperity and honor (Prov 21:21; Ps 112:3, 9). It is in this sense of reward that Abraham, who was acceptable to God because of his complete abandon, was credited with justice/righteousness (Gen 15:6); in a way, Yahweh created it (Hebrew *ḥāšab*) in the soul of the patriarch. As

In the NT, we must immediately distinguish between the *dikaiosynē* taught by St. Paul and that of the evangelists and the non-Pauline epistles.[50] In this last category of writings, all the occurrences are conformable to the LXX,[51] always with a nuance befitting the "ethics" of the new covenant. When John the Baptist objected to baptizing Jesus with a baptism of repentance, the Master replied, "It is appropriate for us to fulfill all righteousness,"[52] that is, to conform to God's plan, what God has decided, what is

---

commentary, cf. at least *Hermes Trismegistus* 13.9: "This level, my child, is the seat of justice. See how, without a trial, it has removed injustice. We have been made just (ἐδικαιώθημεν), child, now that injustice is no longer there."

[50] Cf. A. Descamps, "Le Christianisme comme justice dans le premier Evangile," in *ETL*, 1946, pp. 5–33; idem, *Les Justes et la justice dans les évangiles et le Christianisme primitif hormis la doctrine proprement paulinienne*, Louvain-Gembloux, 1950 (gives the bibliography). F. F. Bruce, "Justification by Faith in the Non-Pauline Writings of the New Testament," in *EvQ*, 1952, pp. 66–77. B. Przybylski, *Righteousness in Matthew and his World of Thought*, Cambridge-London, 1980.

[51] God and Christ judge the world as sovereigns (cf. Heb 7:2—Melchizedek, king of justice/righteousness; 11:33—judges and prophets) who distribute their benefits (2 Pet 1:1), punishment, and rewards (Acts 17:31; 2 Tim 4:8; Heb 1:9; F. Pfister, "Der Wendung ἀπόκειται μοι ὁ τῆς δικαιοσύνης στέφανος," in *ZNW*, 1914, pp. 94–96). It is difficult to specify the content of the λόγος δικαιοσύνης in Heb 5:13—"Whoever drinks milk has no experience of a doctrine of justice/righteousness, for he is a baby." This *logos* is parallel to the "oracles of God" (verse 12); thus *dikaiosynē* would be synonymous with *theos* (cf. 1QM 3.5–6, transforming the enemies of God in Num 10:35 into adversaries of justice), but we could also understand this substantive as the equivalent of *dikaios*: "good, perfect, proper." At Caesarea, Paul "discoursed on justice/righteousness" (Acts 24:25), the rules of natural law and moral prescriptions violated by his hearers (Festus and Agrippa); Noah, the "preacher of justice/righteousness" (2 Pet 2:5), opposed to the godless, by building the ark proclaimed the immunity granted to virtue and could be compared to the Qumran Teacher of Righteousness (cf. G. Vermès, "La Communauté de la nouvelle Alliance," in *ETL*, 1951, pp. 72ff.). On the notion of justice at Qumran, cf. *Words of the Heavenly Lights* 6.2–4 (*RB*, 1961, p. 211), 1QS 11.14–15; S. E. Johnson, "Paul and the Manual of Discipline," in *HTR*, 1955, pp. 160ff.; W. Grundmann, "Der Lehrer der Gerechtigkeit von Qumrân und die Frage der Glaubensgerechtigkeit in der Theologie des Apostels Paulus," in *RevQ*, vol. 6, 1960, pp. 237–259 (reprinted in J. Murphy-O'Connor, *Paul and Qumran*, London, 1968, pp. 85–114). S. Schulz, "Der Rechtfertigung aus Gnaden in Qumrân und bei Paulus," in *ZTK*, 1959, pp. 155–185; O. Betz, "Rechtfertigung in Qumrân," in J. Friedrich, W. Pöhlmann, *Rechtfertigung* (Festschrift E. Käsemann), Tübingen-Göttingen, 1976, pp. 17–36.

[52] Matt 3:15 (cf. A. Fridrichsen, "Accomplir toute justice," in *RHPR*, 1927, pp. 245–252). This refers not to a legal obligation, nor to "fulfilling the ancient legal justice," observing it to perfect it (A. Descamps, in *DBSup*, vol. 4, col. 1464), nor to the Pauline nuance: founding Christian baptism "according to the Spirit" (John 1:33; cf. H. Ljungman, *Das Gesetz erfüllen*, Lund, 1954, p. 97). Still less does it mean "It is appropriate for us to conform to the custom" (R. de Langhe, "Judaïsme ou Hellénisme

pleasing to God. The beatitude of those who hunger after righteousness[53] is the blessedness of moral integrity, the desire for spiritual goods; it is analogous to the beatitude of those "persecuted for the sake of righteousness" (Matt 5:10; 1 Pet 3:14), religious persecution of the disciples, whose moral conduct condemned pagan depravity. But there are different righteousnesses: "If your righteousness does not go beyond that of the scribes and Pharisees you will not enter the kingdom of heaven."[54] For them, righteousness was embodied in spectacular displays; but in the new covenant, it is the heart that counts: right intentions, and especially love. So there is a qualitative change. Justice/righteousness in the new kingdom means fulfilling God's will freely and joyfully, which goes beyond (*perisseuō*) material obedience. This is even clearer in Matt 21:32—"John came to you in the way of righteousness and you did not believe in him,"[55] whereas the

---

en rapport avec le N.T.," in *Recherches Bibliques: L'Attente du Messie*, Bruges, 1954, pp. 173-174). Justice/righteousness is doing what God wants.

[53] Matt 5:6. Cf. J. Dupont, *Béatitudes*, vol. 3, pp. 341ff. A. Descamps, *Les Justes et la justice*, pp. 164-179.

[54] Matt 5:20. Cf. A. Descamps, *Les Justes et la justice*, pp. 180-186; idem, "Le Christianisme comme justice," pp. 15ff.; J. Seynave, " 'La Justice nouvelle,' (Matthieu V, 17-20," in *Message et mission*, Publications de l'Université Lovanium de Kinshasa 23, Louvain-Paris, 1968, pp. 53-75); Matt 6:1—"Take heed not to carry out your righteousness (τὴν δικαιοσύνην ὑμῶν ποιεῖν) before people to be seen by them." This righteousness, which includes all good works and religious obligations (prayer, alms-giving, fasting) is worthless unless it is done to please God and not to require a reputation for holiness; hence very pure intentions and internal rectitude are required: A. George, "La Justice à faire dans le secret (Mt. VI, 1-6 et 16-18)," in *Bib*, 1959, pp. 590-598; B. Gerhardsson, "Geistiger Opferdienst nach Matth. VI, 1-6; 16-21," in *Neues Testament und Geschichte* (Festschrift O. Cullmann), Zurich-Tübingen, 1972, pp. 69-77. "The reign of God and his righteousness" (Matt 6:33) that are to be sought mean both submission to God's sovereignty and also the collection of virtues implied by that submission; so this could be called an "institutional righteousness/justice," since it is coextensive with the kingdom and specific to its members—F. Nötscher, "Das Reich (Gottes) und seine Gerechtigkeit," in *Bib*, 1950, pp. 237-241; reprinted in *Vom Alten zum Neuen Testament*, Bonn, 1962, pp. 226-230; J. M. Fiedler, *Der Begriff der* δικαιοσύνη *im Evangelium des Matthäus, auf seine Grundlagen untersucht*, Halle, 1957.

[55] Ἐν ὁδῷ δικαιοσύνης (cf. 2 Pet 2:21). In the OT, the "way of justice" (Job 24:13; Prov 8:20; 12:28; 16:31; 17:23; 21:16, 21; cf. Rev 15:3; 19:2) was the observance of the law or conduct fixed by God; here it is John's teaching that is willed and guaranteed by God. Thus it was necessary to believe in this prophet, who was preparing and heralding the perfect righteousness given by Christ (cf. G. Strecker, *Die Weg der Gerechtigkeit*, Göttingen, 1962, p. 157: true righteousness leads to receiving God's gift). — The Lucan writings retain the OT meaning even more strictly: the coming of the Messiah will make it possible to serve God "in holiness and righteousness in his presence" (Luke 1:75; cf. Wis 9:3; Eph 4:24), i.e., to fulfill moral and religious perfection. Elymas, the "enemy of all righteousness," was a godless man (Acts 13:10);

publicans and the prostitutes came to be purified. Great sinners were made righteous by believing in the message of the prophet sent by God.

To say that "human wrath does not accomplish the justice/righteousness of God" (Jas 1:20, *dikaiosynē theou;* cf. Rom 10:3) means that it is foreign to the divine will and hence cannot be justice. The quotation of Gen 15:6—"Abraham believed God and this was imputed to him as righteousness"[56]—remains on the Jewish plane: the patriarch is judged by God as being holy in his conduct, so that a nuance of reward is conveyed. Likewise Heb 11:7—Noah "became an heir of righteousness according to faith" (cf. Rom 4:11, 13) and not according to works or through a legal system. Similarly, training through correction (*paideia*), which procures the "peaceable fruit of righteousness,"[57] seems to internalize *dikaiosynē;* the "trainee" acquires this or that virtue as evidence of eternal salvation. This original nuance in the new covenant is found also at 1 Pet 2:24—Christ was crucified "so that we might live for righteousness/justice." Life is transformed by faith and baptism, which make the Christian ready to do God's will, able to serve him, and thus to be genuinely just/righteous, for "whoever fulfills righteousness is born of him" (1 John 2:29). In the new heavens and new earth "the justice/righteousness will dwell for which we wait as the fulfillment of his promise" (2 Pet 3:13). This eschatological righteousness is a perfection in which nothing is lacking; here it is almost synonymous with glory, God's gift if not God himself.

There remain the Johannine usages of *dikaiosynē,* first in the sense of "trial": the Paraclete "will convict the world of guilt with respect to righteousness/justice."[58] Like an advocate in an appeals court, the Holy Spirit will ask each person to make an individual assessment of the original judgment against Jesus: was he guilty or innocent? Everyone must take sides. The Paraclete will convict the original judges of injustice and will exalt the innocence of their convict. As for 1 John 2:29, this verse presupposes the Pauline theology: "Since you know that God is just/righteous, you know

---

the one who fears God and practices justice/righteousness (ἐργαζόμενος δικαιοσύνην), i.e., who is loyal and virtuous, is pleasing to God (Acts 10:35).

[56] Jas 2:23; cf. Ps 106:3—"This was counted to him as righteousness"; 1 Macc 2:52; Philo, *Heir* 90, 94; *Abraham* 262.

[57] Heb 12:1—καρπός δικαιοσύνης, cf. Amos 6:12; Isa 32:17; Prov 11:30; Phil 1:11; Jas 3:18; Philo, *Post. Cain* 118. T. C. de Kruijf, "Justice and Peace in the New Testament," in *Bijdragen,* 1971, pp. 367-383; E. Grässer, "Rechtfertigung im Hebräerbrief," in J. Friedrich, W. Pöhlmann, *Rechtfertigung* (Festschrift E. Käsemann), pp. 79-93.

[58] John 16:8, 10. Cf. M. F. Berrouard, "Le Paraclet défenseur du Christ devant la conscience du croyant (Jo. XVI, 8-11)," in *RSPT,* 1949, pp. 361-389; B. Lindars, "Δικαιοσύνη in Jn. XVI, 8 and 10," in *Mélanges Rigaux,* pp. 275-285; W. Stenger, "Δικαιοσύνη in Jo. XVI, 8, 10," in *NovT,* 1979, pp. 2-12.

also that whoever practices justice/righteousness is born of him." This practice is the whole of Christian ethics (cf. Rev 22:11) and means above all the exercise of brotherly love (1 John 3:10). But the way in which God's righteousness is related to that of his children is remarkable: it is as divinely born ones that Christians resemble their Father. Those who are born of a righteous/just God cannot be other than truly righteous/just (cf. 1 John 3:7).

For St. Paul, *dikaiosynē* is a new and crucial chapter in soteriology.[59] The former Pharisee eliminates the self-proclaimed righteousness obtained through observance of the law (*dikaiosynē ek nomou*),[60] by the "works" that it prescribes (Gal 2:16; Rom 3:20; 4:2; Titus 3:5). This righteousness, after all, would be purely legal, a personal victory and the rightful property of the obedient person;[61] but this *dikaiosynē* cannot give life (Gal 3:21) and is therefore worthless, no longer valid, because in the divine plan the law was intended to be no more than a pedagogue, a transitory institution (Gal 3:15–26). Otherwise "Christ died in vain" (Gal 2:21). But in fact Christ is "the end of the law (*telos nomou*) that righteousness might be given to whoever believes" (Rom 10:4). So a new dispensation is substituted,[62] that of a life-giving justice/righteousness, a participation in God's righteousness (the antithesis of personal human righteousness, Rom 10:3; 2 Cor 5:21). This righteousness is based on faith and is valid for all humanity (Rom

---

[59] M. J. Lagrange, "La Justification selon saint Paul," in *RB*, 1914, pp. 321–343; 481–503; idem, "Note sur la justice de Dieu et la justification," in *Epître aux Romains*, pp. 119–141. E. Tobac, *Le Problème de la justification dans saint Paul*, 2d ed., Gembloux, 1941; K. Kertelge, *Rechtfertigung bei Paulus*, Münster, 1967; idem, "Zur Deutung des Rechtfertigungsbegriffs im Galaterbrief," in *BZ*, 1968, pp. 211–222; P. Stuhlmacher, *Gerechtigkeit Gottes bei Paulus*, Göttingen, 1965; E. Käsemann, "La Justice de Dieu chez Paul," in *Essais exégétiques*, Neuchâtel, 1972, pp. 242–255; J. A. Ziesler, *The Meaning of Righteousness in Paul: A Linguistic and Theological Enquiry*, Cambridge, 1972 (with the critique by N. M. Watson, in *NTS*, vol. 20, 1974, pp. 217–228); L. de Lorenzi, *Battesimo e giustizia in Rom. VI e VIII*, Rome, 1974; A. Lamonnyer, "Justification," in *DTC*, vol. 8, 2, col. 2043–2077; A. Lemonnyer, L. Cerfaux, *Théologie du Nouveau Testament*, Paris, 1963, pp. 95–108; R. Y. K. Fung, "Justification by Faith in I and II Corinthians," in *Pauline Studies: Essays Presented to F. F. Bruce*, Exeter, 1980, pp. 246–261.

[60] Rom 9:31; 10:3—ἡ ἰδία δικαιοσύνη; 10:5; Gal 2:21—διὰ νόμου δικαιοσύνη; 3:11, 20–21; Phil 3:6—δικαιοσύνην τὴν ἐν νόμῳ.

[61] Phil 3:9—"to be found . . . not having my own righteousness, but the righteousness through faith in Christ, the righteousness that comes from God"; cf. Rom 3:21—χωρὶς νόμου.

[62] The Scripture had pointed out a new righteousness in the case of Abraham (Gen 15:6, quoted at Rom 4:3; Gal 3:6—God reckoned Abraham's faith as righteousness). The LXX translated this with an aorist passive, ἐλογίσθη. The verb λογίζομαι, "credit to someone's account," expresses a real equivalency (1 Sam 1:13; Ps 106:31; Isa 29:17; 32:15; 40:17; Hos 8:12; Rom 2:26; 9:8; cf. Acts 19:17).

9:30ff.). In its very essence, therefore, this is no longer a human way of justification but justification through divine intervention. What then is this *dikaiosynē theou*?[63] It is known by its manifestations, because it is essentially active, dynamic,[64] communicating benefits proper to God, making, as it were, a new creation (2 Cor 5:17); and its goal is the justification of humans (Rom 3:25-26). This "righteousness/justice of God" is first of all a divine attribute (Rom 8:33, "it is God who justifies," *theos ho dikaiōn*), notably with respect to his role in retributive justice;[65] but it is seen especially as a merciful will that is gracious and forgiving (Titus 3:5). It is revealed in the cross of Christ, the source of salvation for all who believe:[66] "Christ has become our righteousness" (*Christos egenēthē dikaiosynē*, 1 Cor 1:30; Rom 10:4). Sin is abolished (Gal 2:17; Rom 4:7). This is not a simple acquittal, a verdict of justification (Rom 8:33); this is the merciful justice of God, "who gives life to the dead and calls the nonexistent into existence" (Rom 4:17) and transforms the one who participates in Christ's death and resurrection. He infuses the believer with a *dikaiōsis*

---

[63] Rom 1:17; θεοῦ could be a attributive genitive (righteousness as a divine attribute) or a genitive of author or source (the righteousness that comes from God, which God confers on humans). Better yet: God attributes righteousness to the believer because God himself is righteousness, cf. A. Lemonnyer, in *DTC*, vol. 8, col. 2058ff. J. Drummond, "On the Meaning of 'Righteousness of God' in the Theology of St Paul," in *HibJ*, 1902, pp. 83-95; 272-293; A. Richardson, "δικαιοσύνη θεοῦ," in *JBL*, 1964, pp. 12-16; A. Oepke, "Δικαιοσύνη θεοῦ bei Paulus in neuer Beleuchtung," in *TLZ*, 1953, pp. 257-264; P. Bonnard, *Anamnèsis*, Geneva-Lausanne-Neuchâtel, 1980., pp. 169-176; D. H. van Daalen, "The Revelation of God's Righteousness in Romans 1:17," in E. A. Livingstone, *Studia Biblica 1978* (VI Intern. Congress on Biblical Studies, Oxford, 1978, Sheffield, 1980, pp. 383-389).

[64] It is revealed (ἀποκαλύπτεται, Rom 1:17), manifested (πεφανέρωται, Rom 3:21), demonstrated (ἔνδειξις, Rom 3:25ff.), confirmed (συνίστησις, Rom 3:5), always as *agapē* (5:8). A. Feuillet comments: "In the Pauline perspective, human sin spotlights first of all not the exactitude, but the exactitude of a God of love in the fulfillment of his promises of salvation" ("Le Plan salvifique de Dieu d'après l'Epître aux Romains," in *RB*, p. 349, n. 1).

[65] Rom 3:5; Acts 17:31. Cf. J. Piper, "The Righteousness of God in Romans III, 1-8," in *TZ*, 1980, pp. 3-16; K. Romaniuk, "La Justice de Dieu dans l'Epître de saint Paul aux Romains," in *Collectanea Theologica*, vol. 47, Warsaw, 1977, pp. 139-148.

[66] Rom 3:25; 5:9; cf. "reconciliation" (2 Cor 5:18; Gal 3:13). S. Lyonnet ("De notione 'Justitiae Dei' apud Paulum," in *VD*, 1964, pp. 121-152); the justice/righteousness of God is his salvific action (p. 139). Cf. E. Beaucamp, "Justice divine et pardon," in *A la rencontre de Dieu: Mémorial A. Gelin*, Le Puy-Lyon-Paris, 1961, pp. 129-144; J. Cambier, "Justice de Dieu, salut de tous les hommes et foi," in *RB*, 1964, pp. 537-583; H. Hübner, "Existentiale Interpretation der paulinischen 'Gerechtigkeit Gottes,' " in *NTS*, vol. 21, 1975, pp. 462-488; G. Strecker, *Eschaton und Historie*, Göttingen, 1979, pp. 229-259.

zōēs (Rom 5:18), the infusion of a *pneuma zōē dia dikaiosynēn* (Rom 8:10; Gal 3:2, 5). It is consequently a gift received (*dōrea*, Rom 5:17), a real justice/righteousness (4:4–5) that a person possesses beginning in the present,[67] thanks to Christ. "God made him who knew no sin to be sin for us, so that we might become the righteousness of God in him" (2 Cor 5:21).

Saving faith is precisely this acceptance and this confidence in God acting in the mystery of Christ, in whom the future of salvation is summed up (Rom 3:22). Justice/righteousness and faith are not identical; for it is not faith that justifies, but God who justifies through faith (cf. Lagrange, "La Justification selon saint Paul," p. 140). In faith, a person appropriates Christ's righteousness (Gal 2:17, the efficient cause of our own righteousness, thus becoming the "righteousness of God," 2 Cor 5:21). Righteousness proceeds from faith, which is like a title for obtaining this gift from God. To talk about this relationship between faith and justice/righteousness, St. Paul uses the phrase *ek pisteōs* ("from or of faith," Rom 5:1; Gal 3:24; this is man's part; cf. Gal 3:8); *dia pisteōs* ("through faith," Rom 3:30; with the genitive, *dia* refers to the active role of faith as used by God, Rom 3:22; 9:30; cf. Lagrange, ibid.); finally, the instrumental dative *pistei* (Rom 3:28; 5:2; cf. 5:20; Phil 1:27): a person is justified by means of faith, but the principal agent is God.

Understood thus, justice/righteousness by faith cannot be forensic. The sinner is transformed within, is prepared to life with God, prepared for eternal life (Rom 5:21; 8:10), granted a power (5:17) that allows him to triumph over sin (6:18ff.; 2 Cor 6:4), outfitted with the "weapons of justice/righteousness" (Rom 6:13; 2 Cor 6:7; Eph 6:14). Since the object of this initial justification is a living being, it must continue as an unending process;[68] so in concrete terms it is identified with the Christian life (1 Pet 2:24; 1 John 3:10) and with sanctification.[69]

---

[67] Rom 3:26—"in the present time"; 5:1, 9: "now that we have been justified"; 9:30; 1 Cor 6:11. But this immanent righteousness is a grounds for hope in heavenly glory (Rom 8:30), hence Gal 5:5—"We await the hope of righteousness"; texts that make earth and heaven continuous: those who have been justified will be glorified. W. H. Cadman, "Δικαιοσύνη in Romans III, 21–26," in F. L. Cross, *SE*, vol. 2, Berlin, 1964, pp. 532–534; W. Thüsing, "Rechtfertigungsgedanke und Christologie in den Korintherbriefen," in J. Gnilka, *Neues Testament und Kirche* (Festschrift R. Schnackenburg), Freiburg-Basel, 1974, pp. 301–324.

[68] Rev 22:11. As the fruit of the light (Eph 5:9), righteousness encompasses all the Christian virtues (Phil 1:11). The pastors of the church are "ministers of righteousness" (2 Cor 11:15) and use the inspired Scriptures "for training in righteousness" (2 Tim 3:16). They are themselves models of righteousness and piety (1 Tim 6:11) and "pursue" it tirelessly (2 Tim 2:22).

[69] Cf. the places where δικαιοσύνη is made the equivalent of ἁγιασμός (Rom 6:19; 1 Cor 1:30; 6:11), ὁσιότης (Eph 4:24), peace and joy in the Holy Spirit (Rom 14:17), salvation (Rom 1:16–17), eternal glory (3:23; 8:30).

IV. *Dikaioō*. — The occurrences of this (relatively rare) verb in the secular literature shed no light on the biblical texts. In the literary documents, the predominant meaning is "judge to be good, appreciate, reckon to be just" and hence "pronounce personal judgment."[70] The ten or so occurrences in the papyri have the same meaning,[71] but almost all have a legal sense: "the court's verdict was that we should reimburse the capital."[72]

---

[70] Herodotus 1.89: "I think it just"; Thucydides 2.71: "Pausanias thought it right to leave us to live autonomously"; 4.122.6; Josephus, *Ant.* 9.187; 12.124: "he did not think it right to deprive the Jews of the rights that they possessed"; Philo, *Abraham* 142: the man "did not think it right to go into this place"; 171: Abraham "thought it good that the victim should be laden with objects intended for the sacrifice"; *Moses* 1.44: Moses killed the Egyptian and thought that this was a just action and a pious deed. — The nuance "decide" or "wish" is rather common (Herodotus 2.172; 3.118; Thucydides 5.103.1; Philo, *Drunkenness* 51; *Unchang. God* 9, 159); more common are the nuances "pronounce judgment" in a trial (Dio Cassius 52.24; *P.Oxy.* 653 end) and "condemn, punish," because "to do justice" is to treat in conformity with justice; cf. Herodotus 1.100: "He inflicted on him a punishment proportional to the offense"; 5.92: "A rolling stone . . . will punish Corinth"; Thucydides 3.40.4; Josephus, *Ant.* 17.206; 18.178; Dio Cassius 37.41: "they were handed over for punishment"; 41.28: "punished on the spot"; 49.12: "treated severely"; 54.15.19; 38.11: "Caesar had many to punish"; Plutarch, *Cat. Mai.* 21.4. — This meaning, "to give someone his due" (Aristotle, *Eth. Nic.* 5.10.1136ᵃ18 and 22; Polybius 3.31.9), tends to take on a realistic sense when the subject of the verb is God or the law: "God expects to be called Lord and absolute master" (Philo, *Change of Names* 19); "by natural law it is right (τοῦ φύσει δικαιοῦντος) for each one to be master of his own place" (Josephus, *Ant.* 19.305). Ἐδικαίωσεν ὁ νόμος (Philo, *Spec. Laws* 3.180; cf. 1.67, 109, 140; 2.72; 113; 3.172; Josephus, *Ant.* 4.278) can be translated "the law has judged to be good, has reckoned to be right" but means "the law has established the right, that which should be done." — In the religious sense, *Corp. Herm.* 13.9: "We have been made just (ἐδικαιώθημεν; cf. Rom 3:21–24), child (the initiate), now that the injustice is no longer there" (following the French of A. J. Festugière); but this language about being rid of injustice (or unrighteousness) is probably polemic against Christian justification (cf. G. Schrenk, in *TDNT*, vol. 2, pp. 211–212).

[71] *P.Giss.* 47, 16: "I do not think that it is good to acquire this belt" (second century AD); *P.Ryl.* 654, 8 (minutes of a trial): the masons think that it is always right to consider only their own interests, despite the urgency and magnitude of the needs (cf. the republication by H. C. Youtie, *Scriptiunculae*, vol. 1, pp. 397–401).

[72] *P.Ryl.* 119, 14 (first century); *PSI* 768, 9 (the decision of the tribunal); *SB* 9861 b9 (third century BC); 7033, 30; 10285, 5; *P.Mich.* XIII, 659, 98: it was decided by the public arbiter; *BGU* 1849, 23 (first century BC), a widow writes to the *stratēgos* to obtain τὸ δίκαιον for herself and her child: οἱ ἱερεῖς καὶ Ἀπίων ὁ γυμνασιαρχέσας δεδικαίωκαν, ἐὰν φαίνηται προνοῆσαι ἡμῶν; *P.Tebt.* 444 (first century): "the sums agreed upon by contract" (δεδικαιωμένα, fixed, declared right); *P.Oxy.* 2265, 7, a prefect asks the *stratēgos* to come to the aid of the collector of the *vicesima libertatis*, ἐν οἷς ἐὰν δικαιώσετε.

In the LXX, the passive of *dikaioō*, translating the qal stem of the Hebrew verb *ṣāḏaq*, almost always means "be just," as at Gen 38:26— "Tamar has been more in the right than I."[73] Good judges "pronounce the just just"[74] and do not justify the guilty (Exod 23:7). This justice/righteousness consists in being in order, as by carrying out a vow (Sir 18:22); in being within one's right (niphal of the Hebrew verb *šāpaṭ*, Tob 6:12, 14; cf. Add Esth 10:9); and especially in being "innocent, beyond reproach."[75] It is a gift given by God.[76] Often *dikaioō* means "defend, excuse,"[77] but this declaratory sense (2 Sam 15:4)—which is rather often legal—is purely literary, because it presupposes that no one can effectively justify the sinner[78]—except the Messiah: "My servant, the Just One, will justify the many (hiphil of *ṣāḏaq*); he will take on their iniquities" (Isa 53:11). Here the death of the servant expiates the sins of the people; to justify means to destroy sin, so that sinners recover a real innocence of soul.[79] This heralds Pauline justification.

---

[73] Cf. the demonstration by M. J. Lagrange, "La Justification selon saint Paul," pp. 123ff. and N. M. Watson, "Some Observations of the Use of δικαιόω in the Septuagint," in *JBL*, 1960, pp. 255–266. Ps 19:9—"the judgments of Yahweh are true, they are just"; 51:4 (quoted at Rom 3:4); 143:2—"not one living being is just in your presence"; cf. Isa 42:21; Sir 18:2—"the Lord alone proves to be just" (δικαιωθήσεται).

[74] Deut 25:1 (hiphil of *ṣāḏaq*); 1 Kgs 8:32; 2 Chr 6:23; Ezek 16:51-52: "You have made your sisters appear just by all the abominations that you have committed. . . . They are more just than you." Bad judges justify (acquit) the wicked for a bribe (Isa 5:23).

[75] Δικαιοῦν = Hebrew *zākâh*; Mic 6:11—"Shall I declare innocent deceitful balances and the bag of false scales?"; Ps 73:13—"I have kept my heart pure" (M. J. Lagrange, p. 121, sees this as "the only incontestable OT example of the meaning 'make pure' "). Cf. *nāḵâh*, Sir 9:12—"the godless will not be justified"; *T. Sim.* 6.1—ὅπως δικαιωθῶ ἀπὸ ἁμαρτίας.

[76] Isa 45:26—"In Yahweh the whole race of Israel will obtain justice (ἀπὸ κυρίου δικαιωθήσονται) and be glorified"; 50:8—"The one who justifies me is near at hand."

[77] Gen 44:16—"How shall we speak to justify ourselves?" (hithpael of the Hebrew *ṣāḏaq*); Jer 3:11—"faithless Israel is justified" (in the piel; in the same stem in Job 33:32—"I want you to be justified"); Sir 1:21; 7:5, cf. Isa 1:17—"defend the widow" (δικαιώσατε χήραν, the niphal of *rîḇ*).

[78] Sir 10:29—"Who will justify the one who sins against his soul?"; 12:22; 23:11; 26:29; 31:5; 42:2—"Do not be ashamed (before the pagans) of the law of the Most High and his covenant, the decree that justifies the ungodly"; it would be possible to interpret δικαιῶσαι τὸν ἀσεβῆ as meaning "condemn the ungodly," but this would be the only instance in the OT. The Hebrew text discovered at Masada has the hiphil of *ṣāḏaq*: "When justice (asks) to justify the wicked." Whether the accused is a pagan or a corrupt person, he has the same right to be rendered justice as the unfortunate or the poor (Ps 82:3). This impartiality must not be a cause for embarrassment or scandal.

[79] Exactly as *agapē*—which is in the first place a horror of evil (Rom 12:9)—covers (effaces) a multitude of sins (1 Pet 4:8; cf. Jas 5:20).

δίκαιος, *dikaios, etc.* 339

The Gospels use the aorist passive *edikaiōthē* in the same meaning as the LXX. In the parable about the recalcitrant children—representing people who refused to believe God's message as communicated either by Jesus or John the Baptist—the Master concludes: "Wisdom has been justified by her works" (Matt 11:19) or "by all her children" (Luke 7:35). Far from blaming the precursor for his austerity or Jesus for his open-mindedness, the people and the publicans showed themselves to be teachable and conformed to the dispositions of divine wisdom. Thus they avenged and "justified" this wisdom, proclaiming the excellence and the authenticity of its providential interventions.[80] The "children of wisdom," truly wise people, prove through their adherence that the means used by God to carry out his merciful plan of salvation were effective, well adapted to their goal. The justification in Matt 12:37, which is declaratory (but with cause), is perfectly traditional,[81] as is Matt 16:15, which denounces "those who pass themselves off as just before people" (*hoi dikaiountes heautous*) but whose assessment is at variance with God's.[82]

---

[80] Matt 11:19; Luke 7:29, 35. Same meaning in Philo, *Change of Names* 136: "The disposition of the soul that acknowledges God . . . is justified for the reason that I have not given it to any mortal." Cf. *Pss. Sol.* 2.16—"I acknowledge you to be just, O God, in the uprightness of my heart, because your justice shines forth from your judgments"; 3.5—"the just person has proclaimed the Lord just"; 4.9; 8.7, 23. H. Ljungman ("Un texte de Sifrè éclairant Mt. XI, 18 sv.," in *SEÅ*, vol. 22–23, 1958, pp. 33–35) cites *Sipre Deut.* on Deut 1:12, representing Moses as being exposed to contradictory criticisms. Cf. A. Feuillet, "Jésus et la Sagesse divine d'après les Evangiles synoptiques," in *RB*, 1955, pp. 164–168. — We might compare the hymn or liturgical confession of faith in the risen Christ in 1 Tim 3:16—ἐδικαιώθη ἐν πνεύνατι (G. Richter, "Ist ἐν ein strukturbildendes Element im Logoshymnus Joh. I, 1ff.?" in *Bib*, 1970, p. 543, also compares *Odes Sol.* 19.10–11). The exaltation of Christ in glory manifests his divine nature or power (Rom 1:4; 8:11; Heb 9:14; 1 Pet 3:18) and is also a proof of the justice of Jesus' cause: he is recognized and acclaimed as just. "The return to the Father is God's imprimatur on the justice/righteousness manifested in the life and death of his Son" (E. C. Hoskyns, quoted by R. E. Brown, *John*, vol. 2, p. 713). Cf. C. Spicq, *Epîtres Pastorales*, vol. 1, pp. 468ff. M. J. Fiedler, "Δικαιοσύνη in der diaspora-jüdischen und intertestamentarischen Literatur," in *JSJ*, 1970, pp. 120–143; R. H. Gundry, "The Form, Meaning and Background of the Hymn Quoted in I Timothy III, 16," in W. W. Gasque, R. Martin, *Apostolic History and the Gospel* (presented to F. F. Bruce), Exeter, 1970, pp. 203–222; K. Berger, "Zum traditionsgeschichtlichen Hintergrund christologischer Hoheitstitel," in *NTS*, vol. 17, 1941, p. 405; J. T. Sanders, *The New Testament Christological Hymns*, Cambridge, 1971, pp. 15–94; R. G. Hamerton-Kelly, *Pre-existent Wisdom and the Son of Man*, Cambridge, 1973, pp. 187ff.

[81] "It is from your words that you will be declared just (future passive δικαιωθήσῃ) and from your words that you will be condemned (καταδικασθήσῃ)"; God examines, evaluates, and reveals people's words (and deeds) at the last judgment.

[82] The Sadducees were precisely the "party of justice" and the Pharisees "pretended to be just" (Luke 20:20). As for the teacher of the law, who asked a question

The conclusion of the parable of the Pharisee and the Tax Collector, addressed to certain people who thought of themselves as just (*hoti eisin dikaioi*, Luke 18:9), uses the perfect passive participle *dedikaiōmenos* to express that the tax collector "went down to his house justified rather than the other (the Pharisee)" (verse 14) upon his return from the temple, thanks to his prayer and his humility.[83] Here it is a question of interior justification, which is much more than a verdict of acquittal: God grants that this "sinner" becomes just, he makes him just. This is already the Pauline sense attested in the discourse at Pisidian Antioch: "Through him (Jesus), everyone who believes is justified (*en toutō pas ho pisteuōn dikaioutai*) from everything that you could not be justified from (aorist passive, *dikaiōthēnai*) by the law of Moses."[84]

Several times St. Paul uses *dikaioō* in its forensic OT sense, "declare or acknowledge to be just," especially when he is quoting the OT,[85] but it

---

any child in catechism class could answer and was upset at the answer, he wanted to defend himself, justify himself (δικαιῶσαι ἑαυτόν; Luke 10:29; cf. the hithpael of ṣādaq, Gen 44:16).

[83] Cf. *Prot. Jas.* 10.15—Joachim "went down from the temple of the Lord justified" (δεδικαιωμένος).

[84] Acts 13:38, 39 (cf. Rom 3:20; 10:4; Gal 3:11). The present indicative passive δικαιοῦται, as opposed to δικαιωθῆναι, proves that this justice/righteousness is already acquired by the believer, who is in a new state; not only do believers have a peaceful and loving relationship with God, but their conduct produces new "works," because doing follows being: "let the righteous continue doing right" (Rev 22:11), or we might say "to be sanctified." From an entirely different point of view, Jas 2:21, 24, 25 writes that "man is justified (δικαιοῦται) by works and not by faith alone," and gives Abraham and Rahab as examples. This no longer means the initial justification, but remaining in that original state of righteousness which not only excludes sin but requires practicing the virtues so as to remain just before God (cf. Rom 2:13).

[85] Rom 3:4 (Ps 51:6); 3:20 (Ps 143:2); 4:2 (Gen 15:6). Cf. 1 Cor 4:4—"I am aware of nothing against myself, but that does not mean that I am justified" (δεδικαίωμαι, acquitted, as by a legal verdict; or better, exonerated of any fault in my ministry). — There have been quite a few differing interpretations of Rom 6:7—ὁ γὰρ ἀποθανὼν δεδικαίωται ἀπὸ τῆς ἁμαρτίας, "the one who has died is free (?) from sin." What death does this mean? Can δικαιόω be translated "liberate"? These comments have been offered: (1) The one who is dead (to sin) through baptism is justified, since his sins have been forgiven; (2) A sacrificial death (of a martyr) expiates offenses (K. G. Kuhn, "Röm. VI, 7," in *ZNW*, 1931, pp. 305–310). (3) A general axiom: "Whoever is dead (meaning by natural death) is declared absolved from sin," in the sense that sin can no longer get at him and claim him as its slave (J. Huby, S. Lyonnet, *Saint Paul: L'Epître aux Romains*, 2d ed., Paris, 1957, pp. 211–591, who cite analogous rabbinic pronouncements: "When a man is dead, he is free of the law and its commandments," b. *Nid.* 61b; b. *Šabb.* 30a; Str-B, vol. 3, p. 232). (4) The one who has died is first of all Christ (ὁ ἀποθανών; C. Kearns, "The Interpretation of Romans VI, 7," in *AnBib* 17, Rome, 1968, vol. 1, pp. 301–307; R. Scroggs, "Romans VI, 7," in *NTS*, vol. 10, 1963, pp.

would be wrong to extend this meaning to all the texts. In the first place, this would be to forget that "verbs in *-oō* mean to make whatever the root indicates. Thus *dikaioō* should properly mean 'make just.' This meaning is not found in secular Greek for rather natural reasons."[86] In the second place, it would overlook the fact that St. Paul, as a converted Pharisee, perceived as no one else did the opposition between the new covenant and the old covenant, law and grace, circumcision and baptism, and perhaps especially the inefficacy of the old legal dispensation compared to the efficacy and realism of the dispensation of salvation centered on the cross of Jesus. The consequence is a radical change in ideas concerning righteousness/justification, as is seen in the frequent linking of the verb "justify" with faith in Christ and in the explicit contrast between justification and works of the law; there is a different scheme or process for attributing justice/righteousness in the new covenant than in the old covenant. The apostle gives *dikaioō* a causative sense, as appears from Rom 3:24—"All have sinned and come short of the glory of God (cf. Rom 8:30; 2 Cor 3:18; 5:21); (henceforth) they are justified (present passive participle, *dikaioumenoi*) freely by his grace, through the redemption (*apolytrōsis*) that is in Jesus Christ." God has shown his mercy, but not by pronouncing acquittal pure and simple; through Christ a price was paid, a ransom (*lytron*) with expiatory value (cf. verse 25: *hilastērion*), so that "sinners" have become just, have been made truly righteous.[87] Another clear text is Rom 3:26— "to show his justice/righteousness (his salvific action), so that (it might

---

104–108). (5) It follows that the Christian, united to Christ in baptism, has stripped off his "body of death" (7:24), the body of sin (6:5), and must sin no more (verse 1); cf. 1 Pet 4:1—"The one who has suffered in the flesh has ceased sinning"; 1 John 5:18. M. J. Lagrange understands the perfect passive δεδικαίωται in the sense of "exonerated," as at *T. Sim.* 6.1—ὅπως δικαιωθῶ ἀπὸ τῆς ἁμαρτίας ὑμῶν. A. B. du Toit, "Dikaiosynè in Röm. 6," in *ZTK*, 1979, pp. 261–291.

[86] M. J. Lagrange, "La Justification selon saint Paul," p. 123; cf. A. Lemonnyer, "Justification," in *DTC*, vol. 8, col. 2067ff. We might add that verbs in -όω denote abundance and plenty.

[87] "The sacrifice of Christ has satisfied once and for all the demands for outward justice which God had deposited in the Law, and at the same time it has brought the positive gift of life and inward justice which the latter was unable to give" (P. Benoit, *Exégèse et théologie*, vol. 2, p. 39, n. 2 = ET, vol. 2, p. 39, n. 1); cf. Rom 5:18—"justification gives life." The best commentary is the Trinitarian baptismal text on the "bath of regeneration and renewal" (Titus 3:7), "so that having been justified by the grace of this (Jesus Christ) our Savior (ἵνα δικαιωθέντες τῇ ἐκείνου χάριτι), we might become . . . heirs . . . of eternal life"; the aorist passive participle denotes the present state of this new and internal righteousness that permits entry into heaven, where nothing impure may go in. Cf. H. Rosman, "Iustificare (δικαιοῦν) est verbum causalitatis," in *VD*, 1941, pp. 144–147.

be established that) he himself is just and that he justifies (present active participle, *dikaiounta*) the one who has faith in Jesus": the just God communicates his justice/righteousness and makes just.[88] Again: "We hold that a person is justified (present passive infinitive, *dikaiousthai*) by faith without works of the law";[89] "There is only one God, who will justify (future active indicative, *dikaiōsei* = will make just) the circumcised on the basis of faith and the uncircumcised by means of that same faith" (Rom 3:30).

The realism in this Christian justification is made explicit at Rom 5:1—"Having therefore been justified by faith (aorist passive participle, *dikaiōthentes*), let us maintain peace with God through our Lord Jesus Christ."[90] Whereas sinners were enemies of God, they have now "become righteous/just," i.e., reconciled with God (5:10) in an enduring way (5:2) and have a loving relationship with a holy God in the peace of a purified heart. Such is the standing of the present Christian life. Believers are made so thoroughly just that they are sure of their future glorification: "Those whom God has called he has also justified (aorist active indicative, *edikaiōsen*), those whom he has justified he has also glorified (aorist, anticipating something that is certain, according to Lagrange)" (Rom 8:30). All these verbs are causative; all these acts of God connect to each other and are called by each other's names. Justification is as real and as personal a gift as the gift of faith; the present state is as certain as the future glory.[91]

---

[88] Cf. Rom 4:5—"The one who has no works, but who believes in the One who justifies (δικαιοῦντα) the ungodly, will have his faith counted as righteousness." M. J. Lagrange (on this verse) comments: "δικαιόω in the active cannot mean 'forgive': it has to be 'declare just' or 'make just.' That God should declare the ungodly righteous is a blasphemous proposition. But in addition, when would this declaration be made?" H. W. Heidland (*TDNT*, vol. 4, pp. 288–292) explains λογίζεσθαι: "Justification is not a fiction alongside the reality. If God counts faith as righteousness, man is wholly righteous in God's eyes.... He becomes a new creature through God's λογίζεσθαι."

[89] Rom 3:28; cf. Gal 2:16–17; 3:8, 11, 24; 5:4. W. G. Kümmel, " 'Individualgeschichte' und 'Weltgeschichte' in Gal. 2:15–21," in B. Lindars, S. S. Smalley, *Christ and Spirit in the New Testament* (in honor of C. F. D. Moule), Cambridge, 1973, pp. 157–173.

[90] Cf. Rom 5:9—"How much more, then, having been justified (δικαιωθέντες νῦν) in his blood, shall we be saved by him from wrath." Through the efficacy of the Redeemer's blood, the Christian possesses here and now a real righteousness that assures him of definitive salvation at the Last Judgment. M. Wolter, *Rechtfertigung und zukünftiges Heil: Untersuchungen zu Römer V, 1–11*, Berlin, 1978.

[91] Cf. Rom 8:33—"Who will stand to accuse God's elect? It is God who justifies them" (present active participle, *dikaiōn*). M. J. Lagrange quotes Isa 50:7–8 and interprets thus: "God presents himself as the defender, as the one who comes to make the righteousness of the accused shine out.... God takes up the cause" of the elect person, who is truly just. He can do so because he is the one who made him just.

δίκαιος, dikaios, etc. 343

Finally, 1 Cor 6:11 is decisive: "You have been washed (at baptism), you have been sanctified, you have been justified (aorist passive indicative, *edikaiōthēte*) in the name of the Lord Jesus Christ and in the Spirit of our God." The three aorist verbs show that the events coincide; the two latter verbs in the passive express the reality of the interior change. E. B. Allo notes, "This is a classic passage against imputed righteousness."

V. *Dikaiōma*. — Schrenk (*TDNT*, vol. 2, p. 219) correctly observes that the ending *-ma* indicates the result of an action, in this case the action expressed by *dikaioō*, "to justify." Thus *dikaiōma* will mean "justification" in Rom 5:16, 18, where St. Paul contrasts the death sentence (*katakrima*) that followed Adam's transgression (*di' henos paraptōmatos*) with justification through Christ (*di' henos dikaiōmatos*), justification that gives life (*eis dikaiōsin zōēs*)[92] and is valid for all humankind. Humankind takes on a new religious "status,"[93] not simply on the basis of God's declaration, but because this justice/righteousness has become the property of former sinners who can take advantage of it.[94]

---

[92] On the death-life antithesis, solidarity with Adam and with Christ, the latter being the source of life, cf. A. Feuillet, "Le Règne de la mort et le règne de la vie (Rom V, 12-21)," in *RB*, 1970, pp. 481-521; a causality of grace (J. de Fraine, *Adam et son lignage*, Bruges, 1959, pp. 222ff.).

[93] This is the meaning of *dikaiōma* in Exod 21:9—"the status of the daughters"; 1 Sam 2:13—"the status of the priest"; 8:9—"of the king." Cf. Josephus, *Ant.* 17.108: τὰ τῆς φύσεως δικαιώματα (J. Modrzejewski, "La Règle de droit dans l'Egypte ptolémaïque," in *Essays in Honor of C. B. Welles*, American Studies in Papyrology, vol. 1, New Haven, 1966, p. 142). — In the secular literature and the papyri, δικαίωμα usually means a "right" to something; Josephus, *War* 7.110: the Antiochenes ask Titus to "destroy the bronze tablets on which the rights of the Jews were written"; *Ant.* 19.285: the edict of Claudius confirms the ancient rights of the Alexandrian Jews; *Ag. Apion* 2.37: "the stele that was erected at Alexandria contains the rights granted to the Jews by Caesar the Great" (actually by Augustus); Thucydides 1.41.1: "Such are our *dikaiōmata*, and according to the Greek rule, they are decisive"; Dio Cassius 37.51—"Clodius renounced his patrician title and entered the class of plebeians in order to share in their rights (or statutes)," (πρὸς τὰ τοῦ πλήθους δικαιώματα); 55.2.6—when a man or a woman has not had three children, a law—formerly by the senate, now by the emperor—sometimes grants them the rights of those who have had three children (τὰ τῶν τρὶς γεγεννηκότων δικαιώματα). Cf. 2 Sam 19:29—"What right would I still have to make claims with the king?"; Jer 11:20; *P.Oxy.* 1119, 15: "the exceptional rights (the status) claimed by our native city" (τῶν ἐξαιρέτων τῆς ἡμετέρας πατρίδος δικαιωμάτων); 1890, 9; *P.Grenf.* 60, 23; *Pap.Lugd.Bat.* II, 1, 5 (first century AD), περὶ τούτων δικαιώματι; *CPR* I, 20, 20 (republished as *Stud.Pal.* XX, 54); *P.Mich.* XIII, 659, 49; *SB* 9154, 13; 9228, 11; 9462, 16.

[94] Rev 19:8—"Fine linen is the righteous acts of the saints" (τὰ δικαιώματα τῶν ἁγίων ἐστίν); we are to understand that this garment of innocence is proof of the virtue of the faithful. Quite often δικαίωμα means "supporting document" (J. and L. Robert, "Bulletin épigraphique," in *REG*, 1959, p. 226, n. 323). Litigants have to appear

On the other hand, "God's righteous decree" (*to dikaiōma tou theou*, Rom 1:32), "the requirements of the law" (*ta dikaiōmata tou nomou*, Rom 2:26, cf. 8:4), and "worship regulations" (*dikaiōmata latreias*, Heb 9:1, 10) have the common OT meaning "ordinance, regulation."[95] In accord with the ideal of Jewish piety, Zechariah and Elizabeth, "both just (*dikaioi*) before God, walked in all the commandments and regulations of the Lord" (Luke 1:6). It is more difficult to understand Rev 15:4—"All the people will see and bow down before you, because your justifications are manifest" (*hoti ta dikaiōmata sou ephanerōthēsan*). This could refer to the punishment of the ungodly,[96] but more likely it refers to brilliant manifestations of divine sovereignty (cf. Bar 2:17—in Hades the dead do not return "glory and justice to the Lord"; verse 19).

VI. *Dikaiōsis*. — This rather rare substantive (unknown in Philo, Epictetus, and the papyri) normally means "that which is in accord with the right, the act of establishing justice,"[97] but none of the secular usages shed

---

before the court armed with documents that support their claims (*P.Enteux*. Appendix D 5, p. 248). Archelaus sends Augustus τὰ δικαιώματα, the papers legitimating his royalty, including his father's will (Josephus, *Ant*. 17.228; cf. 17.130: "without other means of justification"). The inhabitants of Priene prove their possession from time immemorial of a certain territory ἐκ τῶν ἄλλων μαρτυριῶν καὶ δικαιωμάτων (Dittenberger, *Or.* XIII, 14; third century BC); *SEG* XVII, 415, 4. A code from the third century AD prescribes that judges should use torture on slaves if the trial documents (δικαιώματα) do not allow them to judge (*P.Lille* 29, 25). Stotoëtis has no property title on a slave who belongs to his mother (*P.Lond*. 360, 8; vol. 2, p. 216); *Stud.Pal*. XXII, 43, 32; *BGU* 113, 265, 847 (= *Chrest.Wilck*., n. 458–460); 1654, 1: notarized copy of a document: ἐκλημφθείσης ἐκ δικαιωμάτων παρατεθέντων; *P.Cair.Zen*. 59368, 6; *P.Oxy*. 3023, col. II, 10; *UPZ* 162, col. III, 21 and 23; col. V, 25; *SB* 3925, 5; 7696, 57: δικαίωμα ἔχουσιν οἱ τρεῖς; 9339, 26; 10254, 14; 10288, 1 a 12; b 17.

[95] Gen 26:5—Abraham "observed by regulation, my orders, my precepts, and my laws"; Deut 4:1, 5, 8; 6:1; 7:11; 30:16; 1 Kgs 2:3; Ps 119:8; Philo, *Worse Attacks Better* 67–68 (quotes Deut 33:10); *Heir* 8 (quotes Gen 26:3–5); *Prelim. Stud*. 163 (quotes Exod 15:23–25). The collection of laws and ordinances of *P.Hal*. 1 was published with the title *P.Hal*. (Berlin, 1913; cf. pp. 25ff.).

[96] Δικαίωμα in the sense of a just decree of condemnation; 1 Kgs 3:28—All the Israelites saw in Solomon "a divine wisdom to pass judgment" (ποιεῖν δικαίωμα); 2 Chr 6:35; Plato, *Leg.* 9.864 e: "he will be exempt from all other punishments." A Jewish epitaph at Rome: "Lord, (grant that) according to your just judgment (ἐν δικαιώματί σου) the repose of Justus, an innocent child, may be peaceful" (*CII* 361). A δικαίωμα is reparation for an unjust act and is the opposite of an ἀδίκημα (Aristotle, *Eth. Nic.* 5.10.1135ª9–14; *Rh*. 1.3.1359ª24ff. Cf. *Cael*. 1.10.279ᵇ9).

[97] This legal meaning is that of the OT hapax at Lev 24:22 (Hebrew *mišpāt*): the same legal statute (literaly, sentence) for the guest as for the native (the *lex talionis*). Cf. Lysias 9.8: "I want to submit legal texts and grounds for rights to you" (νόμους καὶ ἄλλας δικαιώσεις παρασχήσομαι); Thucydides 1.141.1: "every act of claiming a right"; Plutarch, *Demetr*. 18.6. — More common is the meaning "condemnation, punishment"; Josephus, *Ant*. 18.14: the Pharisees believe that there are punishments

δίκαιος, *dikaios*, etc. 345

light on "conferring of justice, act of justification" in Rom 4:25 and 5:18. In the first text: "Jesus our Lord was delivered because of our sins (to do away with them) and raised because of our justification (to obtain it for us, *dia tēn dikaiōsin hēmōn*)";[98] *dia* indicates the goal, the instrumental cause, "with a view to our salvation"; Christ's resurrection is the efficient cause of our justification, for if at baptism the Christian dies with Christ on the cross (Rom 6:4), he enters the new life with Christ emerging from the tomb. Our life is a participation in his, the "life-giving spirit."[99] In Rom 5:18—"As through the trespass of one, condemnation fell on all people, so also the righteousness worked by one man (*di' henos dikaiōmatos*, the state or work of righteousness) procures for all people (in solidarity with him) the justification that gives life (*eis dikaiōsin zōēs*)." This can be understood either as participation in the very life of God or as the existence that concretely carries out justice[100] but necessarily depends on the infusion of grace; justification already means life, as with a fruit seed.

VII. *Dikastēs*. — This substantive is used only by St. Stephen in the NT (Acts 7:27, 35), and it is a quotation from Exod 2:14—"Who set you up as a chief and judge over us?" (*archonta kai dikastēn*, Hebrew *šōp̱ēṭ*). This association suggests that *dikastēs* is not exactly synonymous with *kritēs*: there are different kinds of judges. *Dikastēs* may refer to a magistrate who sits at a tribunal to pass judgment,[101] but also to "elected judges" (Philo,

---

for vices and rewards for virtue; 18.315; Plutarch, *Art.* 14.3: "He took care to punish those who were at fault"; *De sera* 22; Dio Cassius 40.43: Caesar inflicted punishments. Finally, there is "justification" in our sense of the word: "that which serves to justify, to present as just"; cf. Thucydides 3.82.4: "They changed the ordinary relationship of words to acts in the justifications that they gave"; Plutarch, *De virt. mor.* 9: "In their wording they seem to fabricate justifications and evasions"; Dio Cassius 41.54.3: "wrapping themselves in numerous pretexts."

[98] Cf. F. X. Durrwell, *La Résurrection de Jésus mystère de salut*, 2d ed., Le Puy–Paris, 1954; D. M. Stanley, "Ad historiam exegeseos Rom. IV, 25," in *VD*, 1951, pp. 257–274; S. Lyonnet, "La Valeur sotériologique de la Résurrection du Christ selon saint Paul," in *Gregorianum*, 1958, pp. 294–318; J. M. González Ruiz, " 'Muerto por nuestros pecados y resucitado por nuestra justificación" (Rom 4:25), in *Bib*, 1959, pp. 837–858; A. Scrima, "La Résurrection comme centre de l'économie du salut," in E. Dhanis, *Resurrexit*, Vatican City, 1974, pp. 546–553.

[99] 1 Cor 15:45; "He justifies by sending us his Spirit and himself working within us as a spirit" (J. Huby, S. Lyonnet, *Saint Paul: L'Epître aux Romains*, p. 179); "this passage proves that in justification there is an internal element consisting of a life of which the resurrection is the cause" (M. J. Lagrange, on this verse, citing St. Thomas: "dicit esse causam justificationis nostrae, per quam redimus ad novitatem justitiae").

[100] Cf. Rom 6:11, 13, 16, 18, 19, 22, 23; F. J. Leenhardt, *Romans*, pp. 147–148; cf. D. G. Lafont, "Sur l'interpretations de Romains, VI, 15–21," in *RSR*, 1957, pp. 481–513.

[101] Sir 38:33; Philo, *Cherub.* 11: the accused faces the judge; *Alleg. Interp.* 1.87; *Decalogue* 140; *Spec. Laws* 1.121, 277; 3.53, 69; Josephus, *War* 1.452, 618, 622; 2.571;

Unchang. God 112; *Husbandry* 116), delegates,[102] arbiters chosen to settle disputes,[103] such as priests, whose duties include settling contested matters;[104] and finally the conscience, and God, the heavenly judge.[105]

The office of judge is treated with the highest consideration.[106] There are "royal judges," like Dionysius, "king's friend become *politikon stratēgon*" (*SEG* XXIII, 617, 4; cf. *P.Dura* 18, 10, 31; 19, 18; from AD 87/88). There are above all those eminent persons who have a top-level role in the city administration,[107] who are members of a board or of commissions of the assembly charged with preparing for a festival or managing funds.[108] Cities invite foreign judges to "settle disputed contracts"[109] and honor them not

---

Ant. 4.216; 9.3; *Life* 258, *P.Oxy.* 67, 17; 653; 3285, 5, 20, 35; *P.Stras.* 370, 3; *P.Lond.* 971, 19 (vol. 3, p. 129); *P.Hamb.* 168 *a* 13; *b* 2; *C.P.Herm.* 10, 14; *P.Princ.* 118, 8; *PSI* 1310, 15; *SB* 7033, 19; 9225, 3; 10494, 10; Dittenberger, *Or.* 499, 3; 528, 7. In the Ephesian law from 297 BC, the activities of judges are summed up: they go to the site, rectify distributions of property, evaluate, decide in the company of experts, commit their judgment to writing, etc.; cf. Dittenberger, *Syl.* 364; H. Wankel, *I.Ephes.*, Bonn, 1979, n. IV.

[102] *Apokrimata* 51: the praetorian prefect will be delegated as judge; 60; *SB* 7338, 8; 7264, 4: ἔδωκε Ἥρωνα δικαστὴν καὶ μεσείτην τοῦ πράγματος (a private letter from the second century AD).

[103] Philo, *Abraham* 168; *Flacc.* 106; Josephus, *War* 1.458: arbiter of my succession; 2.26; 4.265, 274; Diodorus Siculus 4.33.4: "a dispute in which Phylaeus was named judge."

[104] Josephus, *Ag. Apion* 2.187 (citing Deut 17:8); cf. the parents, who have the authority to judge their son (*Ant.* 4.260; 6.318).

[105] "The conscience is established in the soul as a judge" (Philo, *Creation* 128), "sometimes chief and king, sometimes judge and arbiter in the conflicts of life" (*Worse Attacks Better* 23; *Unchang. God* 50, 128, 183; *Flight* 118; *Decalogue* 87). — God, the supreme judge, cf. 1 Sam 24:16; Philo, *Spec. Laws* 3.205; *Cherub.* 72; *Conf. Tongues* 25; *Heir* 271; *Abraham* 133; *Moses* 2.217, 228; Josephus, *War* 1.630; 5.400; *Ant.* 4.46; 9.169; 18.268; *Acts of Diogenes* 21 (*P.Oxy.* 2664; republished by H. A. Musurillo, *Pagan Martyrs*, p. 27).

[106] *C.P.Herm.* 19, 13: ἐπὶ τὴν σὴν λαμπρότητα, φιλάνθρωπε τῶν δικαστῶν.

[107] Philo, *Creation* 11: "A city without ephors, or arbiters, or judges, upon whom the whole burden of administering and governing rests"; *Joseph* 63: "the magistrates, councillors, or judges who seek to safeguard the common good and security"; *Spec. Laws* 1.55: "councillors, judges, magistrates, members of the assembly." At Sidon, an epigram for a winner in the Nemean games (200 BC): "Diotimius, judge, winner in the chariot race" is the city's first magistrate (*NCIG*, n. XXXV, A 1).

[108] At Athens in the fifth century BC, a regulation concerning the Hephaistia (*LSCG*, n. XIII, 20); at Andonia (92 BC), the judges are part of a commission that manages the revenues of the mysteries (ibid. LXV, 52 and 62 = Dittenberger, *Syl.* 736); *SEG* II, 710, 4. L. Robert (*Documents*, pp. 53–57) studies the δικασταί and the κριταί in decrees from the Hellenistic period in Caria, at Thessalonica, at Temessos, etc.

[109] At Samos, a decree for judges from Myndos, in the third century BC (J. Pouilloux, *Choix*, n. XXI, 3).

only for the fairness of their decisions but also for their behavior.[110] Here we may mention the biblical use of *dikastēs* for a person of high rank, a ruler,[111] a leader of Israel (1 Sam 7:1-2), having official authority and the required powers. Artisans are incapable of these functions (Sir 38:33).

---

[110] A decree of Phalanna for judges from Metropolis (*NCIG*, n. XII, 12 and 25); J. and L. Robert, "Bulletin épigraphique," in *REG*, 1969, p. 463, n. 266; 1971, p. 477, n. 497. The physician Diodorus "spared himself no trouble to care for" the judges invited to Samos who fell ill (J. Pouilloux, *Choix*, n. XIV, 24).

[111] Josh 8:33—"All Israel, with its elders, scribes, and judges, were standing on both sides of the ark, facing the priests and Levites"; 23:2; 24:1; Isa 3:2—the Lord deprives Jerusalem and Judah of "hero and man of war, judge and prophet, diviner and elder"; Bar 2:1—the word of the Lord "against our judges . . . against our kings, against our princes"; Wis 6:1—"Hear, O kings . . . learn, O judges of the ends of the earth"; 9:7. On the judges raised up by God to deliver Israel, cf. R. de Vaux, *Ancient Israel*, vol. 1, pp. 93, 111, 215; vol. 2, pp. 277, 467. The δικασταί instituted at Tyre after the conquest of Nebuchadnezzar are not judges but governors (Menander of Ephesus, in Josephus, *Ag. Apion* 1.156-157), cf. J. Teixidor, "Les Fonctions de rab et de suffète en Phénicie," in *Sem* 1979, pp. 12ff.

δίστομος

distomos, **having two mouths or two edges**

This adjective, which literally means "with two mouths" or "with two openings," is applied to a cave with two entries (*distomos petra*, a rock pierced right through, Sophocles, *Phil.* 16), a road that splits (*distoi hodoi*, the point where two travelers' routes meet, Sophocles, *OC* 900), the post of a door with two entries,[1] a river or canal with a "double mouth" (Polybius 34.10.5); "so that the canal also has two mouths" (*hōste kai distomon einai tēn diōryga*, Strabo 17.4.35). In a letter of September 19, 251, the *dioikētēs* Apollonius asks his steward Zeno to have four hundred birds sent to him to fatten, and one hundred chickens to Ptolemais, "which is on the double mouth."[2]

Euripides speaks of thrusting in a "two-edged sword."[3] The OT uses *distomos* with either the *machaira* or the *rhomphaia*[4] as a way of emphasiz-

---

[1] *P.IFAO* II, n. 31, 8.

[2] Εἰς Πτολεμαίδα τὴν ἐπὶ τοῦ διστόμου, *P.Mich.Zen.* 48, 4; cf. D. Bonneau, "La Terre 'arrosée par le Nil': Neilobrochos," in *BASP*, vol. 16, 1–2; 1979, p. 20. Cf. the double port: δίστομος· οὕτως ἡ Ἐπίδαυρος ἐκαλεῖτο, ἐπεὶ ἀμφιστόμῳ λιμένι ἐκέχρητο . . . συγγραφή (Hesychius). There is also τρίστομον (*P.Tebt.* 112, 3; 121 = p. 502; 208; cf. *BGU* 802, col. II, 8). The Nile delta is called "the mouth of the Nile" in Hebrew (Isa 19:7); today we refer to the "mouths of the Rhone."

[3] Euripides, *Hel.* 983: δίστομον ξίφος; Plutarch, *Cleom.* 26.1: "striking with large staffs in the shape of two-edged swords"; *Pap.Graec.Mag.* 13, 92 (vol. 2, p. 91): ἔχε . . . μαχαῖριν ὁλοσίδηρον δίστομον; in the sixth century, Nonnus of Panopolis applies the same term to an ax (30.141).

[4] There is not too precise a distinction between these two slightly turned back swords or sabers (as opposed to the straight sword, the ξίφος), which were often confused by scribes (cf. the manuscript variants on Luke 21:24). The *machaira* is a soldier's weapon (Polybius 3.114.2–3) but also a sacrificial knife (Gen 22:6, 10; Plutarch, *De def. or.* 41). Cf. the sharp sword of the cherubim (Philo, *Cherub.* 31) or the "sword of fire" (ibid. 20, 21, 25), a shortening of Gen 3:24—"the turning flame of the sword," i.e., double-branched lightning.

---

distomos, S 1366; *EDNT* 1.337; MM 165; L&N 79.94; BAGD 200

ing its penetrating force.⁵ The NT uses the term only metaphorically: the word of God is "sharper than any two-edged sword" (*tomōteros hyper pasan machairan distomon*, Heb 4:12). The comparison is self-evident in Hebrew, first of all because a "word' is "what comes out of the mouth";⁶ and secondly because the word is an offensive weapon,⁷ and God's is irresistible.⁸ The qualification "two-edged," meaning "sharpened on both sides," emphasizes its piercing quality.

Rev 1:16; 2:12; 19:15, in order to symbolize the power of the divine word, have a sword coming out of Christ's mouth and add that this *rhomphaia* is *oxeia*, that is, "sharp, penetrating."⁹ No clearer expression for its force could be devised.

---

⁵ Judg 3:16—"Ehud had a two-edged sword made for himself" (μάχαιραν δίστομον); Ps 149:6—"a two-edged sword in their hands" (ῥομφαῖαι δίστομοι); Prov 5:4—"sharper than a two-edged sword"; Sir 21:3—iniquity is like "a two-edged sword (ὡς ῥομφαία δίστομος); for its wound there is no remedy."

⁶ Deut 8:3; Matt 4:4. "Mouth" in Hebrew is *peh;* "word" or "utterance" is "opening of the mouth" (*pit pî*). "It is because the sword devours the flesh of the enemies (Deut 32:42; cf. 2 Sam 2:26) that it is called a mouth and that a blow is struck 'with the mouth of the sword.' To represent the two edges, the plural *piôt* was used. The vocalization of this form varies in Judg 3:16 and Prov 5:4. Again, the word *pi* is doubled to produce *pîpiyôṭ*, 'two-mouthed, two-edged' (Ps 149:6)" (P. Dhorme, *Emploi métaphorique*, pp. 83–89).

⁷ Isa 49:2—"He made my mouth like a sharp sword"; Hos 6:5; Wis 18:5; Philo, *Cherub.* 28; *Wisdom of Ahikar* 7.100. Cf. Sophocles, *Aj.* 584: "words so cutting do not please me"; Plutarch, *Lyc.* 19.1–15.

⁸ Deut 33:29 compares Yahweh's intervention to a sword that gives the victory to his people; Eph 6:17—"the sword of the Spirit, which is the word of God" (cf. M. Barth, *Ephesians,* pp. 799–800). It is through this weapon that Peter's hearers at Pentecost were "smitten to the heart" and persuaded to be converted (Acts 2:37). Cf. P. Benoit, " 'Et toi-même, un glaive te transpercera l'âme' (Lc. II, 35)," in *CBQ,* 1963, pp. 251–261, reprinted in *Exégèse et théologie,* vol. 3, pp. 216–227.

⁹ Ὀξύς, Isa 49:2; Ezek 5:1; Ps 58:5; cf. Wis 5:20; 18:15.

διχοτομέω

dichotomeō, **to cut in two**

In a collection of "parables of the Parousia," the responsible parties—who have the keys to the kingdom of heaven—are warned that they will be judged with particular rigor. Actually, the steward or servant who mistreats the household staff and carouses with his master's property will be severely punished by the master when he returns: *dichotomēsei auton*.[1] Must we translate literally ("He will cut him in two") or figuratively ("He will remove him" from his service, will show him the door)?

Derived from *temnō*, "to cut, cleave, slice," and hence "smite," the compound *dichotomeō* (unknown in the papyri and in Philo) literally means "cut or divide in two."[2] It is used for the moon (*hē selēnē dichotomousa*), which divides the months into two equal parts.[3] In geometry, it means "to bisect a figure into equal parts by bisecting lines, medians."[4] But the meaning "to separate, to remove from a group or a person" is attested in the fourth century AD in a tomb inscription, probably Christian, at Lycaonia, in which Gordian is separated from his eldest son, Ambrose: "to my

---

[1] Matt 24:51; Luke 12:46. Cf. D. Buzy, "Y a-t-il fusion des paraboles évangéliques?" in *RB*, 1932, pp. 32–35; A. Feuillet, "La Synthèse eschatologique de saint Matthieu (XXIV–XXV)," *RB*, 1950, pp. 78–91.

[2] Plato, *Plt.* 302 e: "Legality and illegality are a principle of dichotomy"; Aristotle, *Part. An.* 1.3.1: "this is how those who practice dichotomy divide" (οἱ διχοτομοῦντες); 1.4.9: "Dichotomy is sometimes impossible, sometimes not useful"; Polybius 6.28.2: "cut a line."

[3] Plutarch, *De fac.* 17.929 f; *Dio* 23.3; cf. Sir 39:12; διχότομος, the first and last quarter of the moon (Philo, *Creation* 101; *Spec. Laws* 1.178); διχότης, the half-moon (*P.Mich.* 149, col. XI, 34–35; second century AD).

[4] C. Mugler, *Terminologie géométrique*, p. 147, cites the paradox of Achilles and the tortoise (the faster runner cannot catch the slower), which Aristotle (*Ph.* 6.9.239b18) compares to dichotomous reasoning.

---

dichotomeō, S 1371; *TDNT* 2.225–226; *EDNT* 1.337; MM 165; L&N 19.19, 37.12; BAGD 200

firstborn son Ambrose, who has cut me off from long life" (*tō hueiō mou tō prōtotokō Ambrosiō tō dichotomēsanti me tou poloetion zēn*, MAMA VIII, 252).

These usages hardly correspond to the usage in the two Synoptics. On the other hand, Josephus, commenting on the judgment of Solomon (1 Kgs 3:25), has the king say *amphotera dichotomēsai ta paidia* ("cut both children in two," *Ant.* 8.31). The only occurrence of the verb in the OT has to do with sacrificial victims: "You shall cut the ram in pieces";[5] and in *3 Apoc. Bar.* 16.3, the Lord commands, "and you shall cut them off with the sword and with death, and their children with demons" (*kai dichotomēsate autous en machaira kai en thanatō, kai ta tekna autōn en daimoniois*). This is the best parallel to the NT texts.

This form of torture is already mentioned by Odysseus to Melantho: "I will tell Telemachus, so that he will carve you (*tamēsin*) limb from limb" (Homer, *Od.* 18.339). According to Herodotus 2.139.2, an Ethiopian received in a vision the advice that he should "cut in two (*diatamein*) across the middle of the body all the priests of Egypt." The prophet Daniel threatens, "The angel of God will cleave you down the middle" (Sus 55, *schisei sou*, LXX). "When the master of the house comes and sees the steward insolently handing out orders, he drags him outside and cuts him" (*helkysas etemen*, Epictetus 3.22.3); Pyrrhus, with his sword, "cleaved the body of the barbarian in two parts that fell simultaneously on each side."[6]

---

[5] Exod 29:17—cf. διχοτόμημα, parts of animals cut in two (Gen 15:11; Philo, *Heir* 215, 311); Herodotus 2.39.5: the Egyptians slit the throat and cut off the head (ἀποτάμνουσι) of animals that they sacrifice.

[6] Διχοτομηθέντος, Plutarch, *Pyrrh.* 24.5. We might mention the "torture with saws" applied by David to the vanquished, according to the LXX (2 Sam 12:31; 1 Chr 20:3). At the time of the uprising of 115, the Jews of Cyrene "sawed [Romans and Greeks] from top to bottom down the middle of the body" (Dio Cassius 58.32). At the time of the Jewish War, a certain Jose Meshita was sawed by the Romans on a sawhorse (*Gen. Rab.* 65.22). Among other torments, the heroes of the faith "were sawn asunder" (ἐπρίσθησαν, Heb 11:37), as Isaiah was by King Manasseh, according to Mart Isa 5:1, 11; *Apoc. Paul* 49 (cf. A. Caquot, "Bref commentaire du 'Martyre d'Isaïe,' " in *Sem*, vol. 23, 1973, pp. 85ff.). The story of the martyrdom of St. Apa Sarapamon specifies that it was "with a saw of olive wood" (H. Hyvernat, *Les Actes des martyrs d'Egypte*, 2d ed., Hildesheim, New York, 1977, p. 309; fol. 175). This belief (cf. St. Justin, *Dial.* 120.5; Origen, *Is.* 1.5) figures in a marginal gloss on Codex Reuchlin on Isa 66:1 (cf. A. Sperber, *The Bible in Aramaic*, Leiden, 1962, vol. 3, pp. 129ff.) and probably originates with the Iranian tradition of the prophet sawn in two (G. Widengren, "Juifs et Iraniens à l'époque des Parthes," in VTSup, vol. 4, 1957, p. 224; A. M. Denis, *Introduction aux Pseudépigraphes grecs de l'Ancien Testament*, Leiden, 1970, p. 171). P. Grelot ("Deux Tosephtas targoumiques inédits sur Isaïe LXVI," in *RB*, 1972, pp. 510ff., 526, 534) found this legend attested in Codex Vatican. Ebr. Urbin. 1, which contains a targum on Chronicles (cf. R. Le Déaut, J. Robert, *Targum des Chroniques*, Rome, 1971), including a midrash on the martyrdom of Isaiah: the prophet took refuge

Such a punishment for the servant in the Gospels is extremely severe, and already St. Jerome explained, "This does not mean that he will cut him in two with the sword, but only that he will cut him off from the society of the saints and will consign him with the hypocrites."[7] So it is possible to treat the text in a more or less softened manner, theologically and morally speaking. But this is not a place for sensitivity. Cut off from the household of God, the unworthy one can only be in Gehenna, as Matt 24:51 notes: "where there is wailing and grinding of teeth" (cf. 8:12; 13:42, 50; 22:13; 25:30). This is the punishment reserved for the "worthless servant" in the parable of the Talents (Matt 25:30; cf. the parable of the Minas: "As for my enemies . . . slaughter them before me," Luke 19:27) and is analogous to the fate of the sterile fig tree (Luke 13:9, *ekkopseis autēn*). The verb *dichotomeō* seems to suggest God's absolute rights and the requirements attached to his gifts.

O. Betz has shown a correspondence to the disciplinary formulations at Qumran,[8] especially 1QS 2.16–17, which formulates a twofold curse: "God will separate him for evil and he will be cut off from the midst of all the sons of light . . . the error that led him astray will win him a place in the midst of those eternally accursed."[9] The dramatic death of Judas ("his body burst open," *elakēsen mesos*, Acts 1:18) could well be a reference to the punishment in Matt 24:51. Finally, the deaths of Ananias and Sapphira, hypocrites who lied to the Holy Spirit (Acts 5:1–11), show that the punishments of unworthy believers are not purely metaphorical.

---

in a carob tree, but "with iron saws the servants of Manasseh cut down the tree, so that Isaiah's blood flowed like water."

[7] *PL*, vol. 26, p. 183. J. Jeremias (*Parables*, p. 57, n. 31) thinks that the Aramaic meaning underlying διχοτομήσει was "he will give him blows and treat him as a profligate." E. Delebecque (*Evangile de Luc*) translates: "Il le réduira de moitié" and takes this to mean that the servant's "ration" will be reduced by half, "cut in two."

[8] O. Betz, "The Dichotomized Servant and the End of Judas Iscariot (Light on the Dark Passages: Matthew 24, 51 and parallel; Acts 1, 18)" in *RevQ*, vol. 17, 1964, pp. 43–58.

[9] Being cut off, separated, is mentioned constantly: "They must separate from all those who are not included in his covenant. . . . He will blot them out of the world; all their works are only defilement before him" (1QS 5.18); 6.24 excludes for one year from the purification of the "congregation" those who lie concerning their property; 7.1, 16 one who has slandered his neighbor; 8.13, 22: "Whoever transgresses one word of the law of Moses deliberately or through negligence shall be excluded from the deliberations of the community"; CD 8.8; 4QpPs 37, col. II, 12; col. III, 11 and 18.

δοκιμάζω, dokimazō, etc.

> δοκιμάζω, δοκιμασία, δοκιμή, δοκίμιον, δόκιμος, ἀδόκιμος
>
> *dokimazō*, to prove, test, verify, examine prior to approval, judge, evaluate, discern; *dokimasia*, verification, testing, authenticity; *dokimē*, proof, trial; *dokimion*, testing, proven worth; *dokimos*, proved, acceptable; *adokimos*, worthless

The exact meaning of these terms is subject to dispute because they are used in so many ways in literary, epigraphic, and papyrological texts. Even their etymology is unsure, although derivation from *dokeō* (*dokaō* is not attested) is the best option and accounts for the intellectual value of the verb *dokimazō*: "put to the proof, test, discern, verify, examine before giving approval."[1]

In the inscriptions and the papyri, beginning with the third century BC, the verb's first meaning is "examine, verify." In a Samian law concerning the distribution of grain: "Let the *chiliasteis* examine mortgage guarantees and the personalities of the guarantors";[2] a *nomarchos* is to examine a petition (*P.Fam.Tebt.* 43, 52; *P.Ryl.* 114, 35; *P.Gen.* 32, 8); an architect "shall visit the site, make an estimate (*dokimasanta*), and set the amount of the rent" (*P.Bour.* 20, 9). Similarly, private individuals estimate prices (*P.Hib.* 207, 8), verify the value of staters (*P.Yale* 79, 10), or evaluate an opportunity

---

[1] P. Chantraine, *Dictionnaire étymologique*, p. 291.
[2] Dittenberger, *Syl.* 976, A 12–13; cf. 958, 14; 807, 9 (first century AD); *SB* 6734, 7 and 9; 6817, 6. In a receipt for military garments, a *chlamys* is δεδοκιμασμένη (*P.Ant.* 40, 6; cf. *P.Tebt.* 703, 86).

---

dokimazō, S 1381; *TDNT* 2.255–260; *EDNT* 1.341–343; *NIDNTT* 3.808–810; MM 167; L&N 27.45, 30.98, 30.114; BDF §§392(3), 405(2), 416(2); BAGD 202 ‖ *dokimasia*, *TDNT* 2.255–260; *EDNT* 1.343; *NIDNTT* 3.808; MM 167; L&N 27.45; BAGD 202 ‖ *dokimē*, S 1382; *TDNT* 2.255–260; *EDNT* 1.341–343; *NIDNTT* 3.808–809; MM 167; L&N 27.45, 65.12, 72.7; BDF §110(2); BAGD 202 ‖ *dokimion*, S 1383; *TDNT* 2.255–260; *EDNT* 1.343; *NIDNTT* 3.808–809; MM 167–168; L&N 27.45, 73.3; BDF §§23, 263(2); BAGD 203 ‖ *dokimos*, S 1384; *TDNT* 2.255–260; *EDNT* 1.341–343; *NIDNTT* 3.808; MM 168; L&N 30.115, 73.4, 87.7; BDF §§23, 263(2); BAGD 203 ‖ *adokimos*, S 96; *TDNT* 2.255–260; *EDNT* 1.33; *NIDNTT* 3.808–810; L&N 65.13, 88.111; BAGD 18

(*P.Oxy.* 2760, 17; Philo, *Moses* 1.263, 306; 2.177). Someone makes an examination in order to be able to judge and decide. This is why the formula "if your majesty approves him" (*ean to megaleion sou dokimasē touton*) comes up so often in petitions to the prefect of Egypt;[3] thus this mother from Theadelphia writes: "I take refuge at your feet, beseeching you on behalf of my minor children to order . . . either the *stratēgos* or whomever your majesty shall decide to force Annous to pay regular rent on the land" (*P.Thead.* 18, 17). When someone submits a case to an authority for examination, it is in order that the authority may evaluate it, decide, and finally approve (*ean dokimazēs*).[4] In a Macedonian law concerning the use of public land, "the councillors approved (*edokimasan*) that those who did the planting . . . should have a share in the harvest."[5] The verb has a religious meaning when a divinity tests, sanctions, and guarantees the virtue of a king and thus qualifies him in his functioning.[6]

In the LXX, the nuance of approbation is attested only once,[7] as is the nuance "discern" (Job 34:3); but "put to the proof, examine" is quite common, especially with respect to metals,[8] and is used for God's examining, sounding, scrutinizing, and testing human hearts, which are purified by "testing"[9]—as silver is purified (Ps 66:10)—and emerge perfect (Sir 31:10). The meaning "verify" (Wis 2:19; 2 Macc 1:34) is also a component of the meaning "test God" (Ps 95:9; Wis 1:3). Philo retains for this verb the

---

[3] *P.Oxy.* 2133, 26; 2407, 5; *P.Ryl.* 659, 13; 701, 14; *P.Col.* VII, 169, 15; *PSI* 767, 50; 769, 4; *P.Cair.Isid.* 74, 18; 76, 18; *P.Mert.* 18, 31; 91, 18; *P.Mich.* 40, 5; *P.Mil.Vogl.* 25, col. V, 5; *SB* 9187, 15; 9188, 21; 11221, 10; cf. 9827 *b* 14; 10800, 19; 11223, 20; *P.Oslo* 148, 9–10.

[4] *BGU* 1787, 11; H. Kling, *P.Giss.Univ.* 20, 38; *P.Mert.* 26, 12; *P.Oxy.* 2726, 22; *SB* 9467, 4: ὅπως δικιμάσας ἀντιγράψῃς μοι; *P.Oxy.* 3253, 8.

[5] *NCIG*, n. 28, 17; cf. *SB* 9016, col. I, 7: ἡ βουλὴ δοκιμάζειν εἴωθεν τοὺς ὑπηρετοῦντας; *P.Fay.* 106, 23: the physicians who made an examination approve an exemption from public service; *P.Eleph.* I, 8 and 10: witnesses approve or confirm; cf. Menander, *Dysk.* 138: approve plans for marriage.

[6] In 196 BC, Ptolemy Epiphanes was approved by Hephaestus, the Greek god of fire: ὃν ὁ Ἥφαιστος ἐδοκίμασεν (Rosetta Stone; Dittenberger, *Or.* 90, 3 = *SB* 8299); likewise Ptolemy IV Philopator (*Chrest.Wilck.*, n. 109, 10 = *SEG* XVIII, 633, 5 = *SB* 10039).

[7] 2 Macc 4:3—"One of those who acted with Simon" (τινος τῶν δεδοκιμασμένων).

[8] Gold and silver, Prov 8:10; 17:3; 27:21; Wis 3:6; Sir 2:5—"It is in fire that gold is proved" (δοκιμάζεται χρυσός); Zech 13:9; the potter's vessels (Sir 27:5); cf. the "reckoned price" (Zech 11:13); Philo, *Alleg. Interp.* 1.77: "gold, a trusty substance, pure, purified in the fire, proved (δεδοκιμασμένη) and precious"; 3.168; *Sacr. Abel and Cain* 80; cf. *Heir* 308.

[9] Judg 7:4; Jer 6:27; 9:6; Ps 17:3; 26:2 (cf. Jer 11:20; 17:10; 20:22); 81:8; 139:1, 23; Jer 12:3; Wis 11:10.

meaning "put to the test,"[10] an examining whose goal is to judge and verify;[11] but he especially emphasizes "evaluate"[12] and "discern values."[13] Josephus was apparently the first to give the word a moral meaning: the character of an Essene novice is put to the test (*to ēthos dokimazetai*) for two years, and only then is he received into the community.[14] God put Abraham's attitude to the test (*Ant.* 1.233) and approved just laws (4.295; cf. 8.380; 14.195); virtue is tested (3.15); the correctness of the lawmaker's conceptions is verified (1.15; 11.94); tribal chiefs are approved by the people as honest and just (3.71; cf. 13.183); Alexander "put to the test the virtue and faithfulness of all the peoples" (*Ag. Apion* 2.42). The meaning "judge, esteem" is also well attested.[15]

The first NT use of *dokimazō* is meteorological. With respect to the impending crisis, Jesus says to his contemporaries, "Hypocrites, you know how to evaluate (*oidate dokimazein*) the appearance of the earth and of the sky; how is it that you do not evaluate this present time?" (Luke 12:56). *Kairos* is the time when a decision is to be made, ought to be made. The Israelites do not "discern" the times and the person of the Messiah; the Master invites them to "verify" his coming and draw out its meaning.[16]

---

[10] Philo, *Worse Attacks Better* 142; *Moses* 1.164: in the desert, God wanted to test his people "to know how they would keep up obedience."

[11] *Post. Cain* 96; *Unchang. God* 128; *Moses* 1.226, 327: after the victory, "the combatants were judged to be without reproach"; 2.34; *Virtues* 32: to choose officers and soldiers, test is made of their state of health and mental balance; 60, 63, 66, 208: the rights of an heir are verified. Likewise Josephus (*War* 5.516; *Ant.* 9.261), a proven friend (*War* 1.516).

[12] *Alleg. Interp.* 2.7: "flavors are evaluated with the aid of the sense of taste"; *Drunkenness* 190; *Migr. Abr.* 48, 51.

[13] *Sacr. Abel and Cain* 77; *Post. Cain* 62; *Drunkenness* 186; *Joseph* 118: "great natures do not take long to be discerned"; *Virtues* 54, 227; *Spec. Laws* 4.153: physicians are discerned through contact with experience; *Good Man Free* 24: it is through practice that a slave is discerned; *To Gaius* 220. A person is judged worthy (*Abraham* 253); athletes are disqualified (μὴ δοκιμασθέντες) and banned from the competition (*Joseph* 138).

[14] *War* 2.138; cf. 161: the Essenes put women who are to be married to the test (δοκιμάζοντες) for three years and marry them only when they have shown their ability to conceive.

[15] *Ant.* 2.176; 5.51: the Gabaonites sent ambassadors to Joshua, choosing those whom they esteemed most capable of acting in their people's interests; 7.321; 11.258: "he deems worthy of honor" (τιμῆς ἄξιον δοκιμάσῃ); 12.18: deem the moment favorable for presenting a petition; 13.51; *Life* 161. Cf. the meanings "prove" (*War* 4.153); "decide" (*Ant.* 1.177; 4.73; 14.209), "verify"; "the priests reconstitute genealogies and scrutinize the remaining women" (*Ag. Apion* 1.35).

[16] The parallel text at Matt 16:3 has διακρίνειν. In the parable of the Great Banquet, one of those invited has bought five yoke of oxen and makes the excuse that

When 1 Pet 1:7 specifies that faith is more precious "than perishable gold, which is nevertheless tried by fire" (*dia pyros de dikomazomenou*), not only does this mean that the fire selects, purifies, refines the material and gives the metal greater value; the text also uses the verb *dokimazō* in the sense that *dokimasia* is constantly given in the papyri (cf. below, *dokimos*), where gold, silver, or pewter is tested by fire to prove its authenticity and to remove impurities.[17] This meaning—"verify, test"—also appears in 1 Cor 3:13, where each apostle's work "will be made manifest by fire" (at the Last Judgment) and "the fire will prove its value (quality)." Fire is the means of verification and control, as with precious metals: that which is worthless is destroyed, but that which is solid and eternal remains.[18] It is through their generosity—and thus by concrete acts, by their behavior—that the Corinthians will verify, test, and prove their love to be genuine, of good alloy (2 Cor 8:8).

Dokimazō means "discern" what it is important to do, the best course to follow, the decision to make,[19] and especially to discern what is pleasing to the Lord (Eph 5:10), which presupposes spiritual renewal and the possession of love, which consequently gives a religious sense, a kind of spiritual instinct that allows a person to recognize true values (Rom 12:2). The Pauline innovation is to apply this verb, with a moral and religious meaning, to Christians themselves: "Examine yourselves."[20] The authenticity of charismatic manifestations must be tested, put to the proof, verified: "Prove all things, hold fast that which is good" (*panta de dokimazete, to kalon katechete*),[21] and thus reject whatever is suspect. St. Paul valued the zeal of the brother (St. Luke?) who accompanied the bearers of the collection; he has had many proofs of his zeal (2 Cor 8:22, *hon edokimasamen*),

---

"I am going to try them out" (Luke 14:19). Cf. Menander, *Dysk.* 816: "You want to make a friend? *Try*—and good luck."

[17] P.Leid. X, 43, 42, 52; R. Helleux, *Les Alchimistes grecs*, Paris, 1981, vol. 1, pp. 52 et passim.

[18] Cf. Rom 1:28—the pagan philosophers did not think it good to retain the knowledge of God; they tested it and rejected it.

[19] Rom 2:18; 14:22; Phil 1:10; C. Spicq, *Agapè*, vol. 2, pp. 233ff.

[20] 2 Cor 13:5—to examine oneself *to find out* if one is in the faith and if Christ dwells within; Gal 6:4—each one must examine, getting behind deceptive appearances, what he has personally accomplished; this clarity will make for a well-founded evaluation; 1 Cor 11:28—before taking communion, people must examine their conscience in order not to partake unworthily (ἀναξίως); they must discern the true nature of this sacred meal, which is entirely different from an ordinary repast. Cf. the only study (and a good one) on this notion, G. Therrien, *Le Discernement dans les écrits pauliniens*, Paris, 1973 (analyzes all the texts and gives the bibliography).

[21] 1 Thess 5:21; 1 John 4:1. Cf. J. Guillet, "Discernement des esprits," in *Dict.spir.*, vol. 3, col. 1222–1267.

δοκιμάζω, *dokimazō*, etc. 357

just as the Corinthians have judged these bearers qualified (*hous ean dokimasēte*, 1 Cor 16:3). God himself had examined the apostle, tested his heart, and pronounced him qualified to preach the gospel (1 Thess 2:4). Finally, candidates for the diaconate are to be examined before being installed in their function: "Let them be tested first (*houtoi dikomazesthōsan prōton*); then, if they are without reproach, let them carry out their office" (1 Tim 3:10). If this *dokimasia* is not explicitly demanded for *episkopoi*, the criteria of discernment are enumerated at length (1 Tim 3:1–7). The "proving" mentioned in these texts is in absolute conformity to Greek custom, whereby before entering upon the duties of public service (a magistrate, a *stratēgos*, a senator), a person was subjected to an examination (inquest, proof, trial period?) to determine if he met the conditions required for the office in question.[22]

Dokimasia. — This word occurs only once in the NT (Heb 3:9), and there it is a quotation from Ps 95:7–11, where the Israelites are so bold as to put Yahweh to the test, and it is also a hapax in the LXX.[23] In Philo, the word means verification, control (*Spec. Laws* 4.106, 157), a testing (*Flight* 155), experience (149; *Flacc.* 130), criterion (Philo, *Virtues* 68: *logia tēs dokimasias*,

---

[22] Aristotle, *Ath. Pol.* 59.4; 55.2–5; 56.1; Dittenberger, *Syl.* 838, 13 (L. Gernet, *Lysias*, 2d ed., Paris, 1955, pp. 3ff., 288; cf. E. Caillemer, "Dokimasia," in *DAGR*, vol. 2, pp. 324–328); the examination is for a life free of reproach (Aeschines, *In Ctes.* 14, 15; Dinarchus, *C. Aristog.* 17; Lysias, *Mantith.* 9), and so also with orators, who are not allowed in court if they have a bad reputation (Aeschines, *In Tim.* 28ff.), the attribution of the rights of citizenship (δοκιμασία δημοποιήτων); ephebes are enrolled on the registers of the deme only after examination by their fellow demesmen, then by the Council of Fifty-Five (Aristotle, *Ath. Pol.* 42, 1; 49, 1; Demosthenes, *C. Eub.* 9–14); the ἰσοτελεῖς at Rhamnus (*SEG* III, 122, 11; C. Pelekidis, *Ephébie attique*, Paris, 1962, pp. 65, 88ff.), the ὀργεῶνες, and the ἐρανισταί: "No one may enter into the most venerable meeting of the ἐρανισταί before being examined for piety, purity, and goodness; this examination must be conducted by the president, the ἀρχερανιστής, the secretary, the treasurers, and the syndics" (P. Foucart, *Les Associations religieuses des Grecs*, Paris, 1873, pp. 10, 146; *LSCG*, n. 59, 32, 34). There are examinations for professional capacity (*P.Fay.* 106, 26; *PSI* 1105, 4, 20; G. Zalateo, "Un nuovo significato della parola δοκιμασία," in *Aeg*, 1957, pp. 32–40). The athlete's constitution is submitted to examination (Philostratus, *Gym.* 26); Moses commanded that priests should be examined for office (τὴν τῶν ἱερέων δοκιμασίαν, Josephus, *Ant.* 4.54; cf. J. Martha, *Les Sacerdoces athéniens*, Paris, 1882, pp. 39ff.). At Qumran, the *mebaqqēr*, the *pāqîd*, and the full assembly examine the postulant several times concerning "his works, his intelligence, his strength, his courage, his possessions" (CD 13.11; cf. 1QS 6.14–21; Josephus, *War* 2.137–138; M. Delcor, "Le Vocabulaire juridique, cultuel et mystique de 'l'initiation' dans la secte de Qumrân," in H. Bardtke, *Qumrân-Probleme*, Berlin, 1963, pp. 117ff.).

[23] Sir 6:21—ὡς λίθος δοκιμασίας. The "stone of testing" is a large stone moved by athletes in contests (Zech 12:3); thus wisdom is a heavy burden for the ignorant and those lacking courage.

ritual formulas for testing); "the test of the soul is that of trouble and bitterness" (*Prelim. Stud.* 164). In the papyri, "six guaranteed gold *solidi*" (*P.Ness.* 18, 14), testing of gold to see if it is pure (*P.Leid.* X, 42–43) testing of bullion for fraud (ibid. X, 62), testing and approval for an office (*P.Mert.* 26, 11; cf. Dittenberger, *Syl.* 972, 29), judged and examined by a common arbiter (*P.Mil.* 659, 55; *PSI* 1105, 20; *SB* 7201, 11).

Dokimos. — This adjective, "proved, acceptable, tried," is abundant in the papyri, but is used almost exclusively for silver, gold, or coins;[24] often there occurs the phrase "three gold *solidi* of imperial coinage, checked for good minting" (*P.Rein.* 105, 1; *SB* 7996, 12, 22, 26; 9193, 18; 11239, 7) or "of imperial minting, authentic and legal."[25] Similarly, in the LXX, it is almost always a question of refined or purified gold or silver (1 Kgs 10:18 = 2 Chr 9:17; 1 Chr 28:18; 29:4; cf. Zech 11:13); but also "four hundred silver shekels of merchants' currency" (Gen 23:16).

Philo was familiar with the use of the word for coinage of good alloy,[26] pure and tested metal (*Sacr. Abel and Cain* 137), but he uses this adjective so frequently that it is often impossible to specify its meaning. Often it is a case of something that after examination has been proven, recognized as authentic, and thus acceptable;[27] sometimes it is objects that are of good quality (*Heir* 180), well-reputed islands (*To Gaius*), a well-bred flock (*Dreams* 1.255), but especially souls that live according to the laws of nature and are accepted into God's circle of friends.[28] With regard to people, *dokimos* means qualified or competent: *en pasi dokimon* (*Joseph* 114), physicians (*Unchang. God* 65; *Spec. Laws* 3.117), scholars (*Creation* 128), artisans (*Heir* 158), priests who are particularly expert at examining animals (*Spec. Laws* 1.166), hence the best (*Plant.* 81) and the noteworthy (*Spec. Laws* 1.78). We

---

[24] Τὸ ἀργύριον δόκιμον (*Stud.Pal.* XX, 63, 17; 85 verso 7 and 10); *P.Dura* 29, 7: ἀργυρίου κάλου δοκίμου δηνάρια; *P.Alex.* 358 (p. 36): χρυσοῦ δοκίμου; *SB* 7816, 20; 8986, 19; 9566, 3 (C. Préaux, "Prêt d'or byzantin du Brooklyn Museum," in *ChrEg*, 1961, p. 354); *P.Tebt.* 815; frag. IV, recto 25: χαλκοῦ δοκίμου; 970, 9.

[25] *P.Fouad* 53, 3: χρυσοῦ νομισμάτια ἁπλᾶ δεσποτικὰ δόκιμα; *Pap.Lugd.Bat.* XIII, 1, 8; *P.Mil.* 56, 9; *P.Michael.* 40, 14; *P.Oxy.* 1891, 7; 1973, 11; 2237, 8; *PSI* 1239, 22; 1263, 20; 1340, 8; *P.Charite* 3, 14; *P.Köln* 102, 7; 151, 10; 155, 2; *P.Rein.* 105, 1. In the metaphorical sense: δεξιὸς ἀνὴρ ἀεὶ δόκιμος παιδείᾳ (*SB* 8542, 5; cf. 8211, 13); a paean at Ptolemais: "Grant that we, joyful and approved (δοκίμους), may see the light of the sun" (E. Bernand, *Inscriptions métriques*, n. 176, 16).

[26] Philo, *Alleg. Interp.* 2.95; 2.104; 3.168; *Conf. Tongues* 159; *Flight* 19; *Change of Names* 208; *Spec. Laws* 1.104; *Contemp. Life* 41. Hence, the "good imprint" of modesty (*Spec. Laws* 3.176) or of constitution (4.47).

[27] *Post. Cain* 96; *Heir* 252; *Spec. Laws* 1.61, 214; 3.119, 120; 4.137; *Dreams* 1.202; *Virtues* 65; *Flacc.* 163: the proven worth of soldiers.

[28] *Husbandry* 66; *Change of Names* 124; *Spec. Laws* 4.196; *Good Man Free* 98; *Plant.* 18; *Sobr.* 20.

δοκιμάζω, *dokimazō*, etc.

could translate "distinguished," with the additional connotation "deserving the respect and esteem of all,"[29] with a nuance of honorableness and celebrity.[30] So Philo considerably enriched the idea of the *dokimos*, and these nuances are found also in Josephus: "the most eminent ones (*hoi dokimōtatoi*) were slaughtered" (*War* 1.35); "the most eminent citizens by birth and intelligence" (2.482; 4.160); the most eminent Jews of Alexandria and of Rome (7.447; *Ant.* 14.21, 43; *Life* 55); Tiberius Alexander, "the most respected of the friends of Titus."[31]

The nuances of honor and celebrity are also found in St. Paul: "Greet Apelles, *ton dokimon en Christō*" (Rom 16:10), which is correctly translated "who has proved himself as a Christian" but must also be understood as praise for an illustrious believer, one of good repute. Likewise 2 Tim 2:15— "Work to present yourself to God as an approved person (*seauton dokimon*), a worker who does not need to be ashamed" (cf. G. Therrien, *Le Discernement dans les écrits pauliniens*, pp. 218–259), tested by his excellent achievements in the gospel ministry but as a result excellent and recognized as such by all. For a Christian who serves Christ in righteousness, peace, and joy in the Holy Spirit is not only pleasing to God but "approved of men," recognized by other people as a true or valuable disciple (Rom 14:18). Obviously these praises presuppose preliminary testing: *hoi dokimoi* are "qualified" Christians,[32] not through their words, but demonstrably,

---

[29] *Flight* 63: a well-thought-of man; *Moses* 2.234: respected; *Joseph* 161, 201: qualified by wisdom; *Abraham* 180: the particularly respected Greeks; *Conf. Tongues* 4: "Homer, the greatest and most respected of the poets"; *Change of Names* 179; *Etern. World* 48: Chrysippus the most esteemed of the Stoics; *Moses* 2.28: the most esteemed of kings; 2.29: the Hebrews of highest repute; 2.187: the most highly respected of the prophets; *Good Man Free* 140: the most distinguished of the ephebes; *Abraham* 189: the child most worthy of respect.

[30] Cf. *Dreams* 2.20: the deeds most worthy of praise; *Moses* 1.221: Moses chooses a leader in each tribe, "those whom he judged the most dependable in order of merit"; 267; *Spec. Laws* 4.174; 2.125: choice of a spouse of real merit, enjoying the respect of all; *Virtues* 201: Noah, one of the truly remarkable people of that period (σφόδρα δοκίμων); *Rewards* 111: "the first grace is to show oneself worthy of respect and honorable"; *To Gaius* 107: "all that was honorable in each city"; 173: "of the most distinguished and most brilliant"; 144: "for leaders the most illustrious of the Romans"; *Alleg. Interp.* 1.66: prudence, the most estimable of the virtues.

[31] *War* 5.45; *Ant.* 12.255: the most worthy of the people and the noblest souls; *Ag. Apion* 1.18: "the most competent (οἱ δοκιμώτατοι) historians contradict each other"; *Life* 228: "the Galileans of highest repute"; 293: "two of the most reputable guards" because of their bravery and trustworthiness.

[32] 1 Cor 11:19—the divisions, oppositions, and schisms in the Corinthian community give "perfect" Christians the opportunity to manifest their love and patience and to overcome evil with good: they are *doikmoi* because they have been purified, strengthened, made better by their trials.

through their deeds (2 Cor 10:18; 2 Cor 13:7). Thus tested, they receive the crown of life.

Dokimē. — "Proof, trial" appears only in the Hellenistic period (Symmachus, Ps 68:11; Dioscorides 4.184 [but LSJ says the word is interpolated here—Tr.]) and is used only by St. Paul in the NT. In an active sense, the testing of the Macedonian churches through multiple afflictions gives them abundant joy (2 Cor 8:2). The Corinthians seek proof that Christ is speaking through St. Paul (13:3); they could verify his apostolic authenticity by the manifestations of power in their community, a proof that the Lord would approve. The other texts have a passive sense: "proven character" (Rom 5:4), a quality of one who has been put to the test (2 Cor 2:9; Phil 2:22), proof (2 Cor 9:13).

Dokimion, dokimios.[33] — In the papyri, the adjective is only used to describe refined gold or silver: "six minas of pure gold according to the Alexandrian standard."[34] Similarly the four occurrences in the LXX: "the words of Yahweh are pure words of refined gold";[35] but in Jas 1:3—"the testing (*to dokimion*) of your faith produces endurance"; faith that has been put to the test is purified, strengthened, verified, and on this account has become precious. In 1 Pet 1:7, the neuter adjective used as a noun also shows the proven character of faith; when it has proved itself, it it worthy of praise; its worth is recognized after examination.

Adokimos. — This word, which means "worthless," seems to have only one occurrence in the papyri, this in the Zeno correspondence: *kai adokimou* in an account of receipts and disbursements seems to mean "not taken into account, not included in the sum total" (*P.Cair.Zen.* 59176, 64). The LXX has only two usages: "dross" (Hebrew *sîg*) to be purged from silver (Prov 25:4); which in Isa 1:22 means "worthless" ("your silver has become dross"). This is the predominant meaning in Philo: the worthless words, desires, and deeds of the fool (*Conf. Tongues* 198); it could even be translated "void, of no account."[36] This nuance is to be retained in many NT texts. In contrast

---

[33] Cf. A. Deissmann, *Bible Studies*, pp. 259ff.; P. Chantraine, *La Formation des noms*, Paris, 1933, p. 53; N. Turner, *Grammatical Insights into the New Testament*, Edinburgh, 1965, pp. 168ff.

[34] *P.Mich.* 262, 13 (in AD 35/36); 343, 3 (in 54/55); 662, 30; 664, 15; *P.Tebt.* 392, 22; *BGU* 1065, 6 (AD 97); *P.Mil.Vogl.* 71, 22 and 28; *Stud.Pal.* XX, 2, 6; *P.Stras.* 237, 15; *SB* 6951, 48; 9264, 7, 22, 28.

[35] Ps 12:6; Prov 27, 21; 1 Chr 29:4; Zech 11:13. The term is unknown in Josephus; it occurs once in Philo: "the divine Word, having tested us . . . , gives us distinction (τὸ δοκίμιον), fame, and brilliance" (*Dreams* 1.226).

[36] *Dreams* 1.227: "acts that cannot be purified, worthlessness (τὸ ἀδόκιμον), nothing but works of darkness"; a false tetradrachma is worthless (*Worse Attacks Better* 162), like certain doctrines (*Conf. Tongues* 34; *Dreams* 2.284). "The word of the

to a fertile field, one that bears "thorns and thistles is worthless (*adokimos*) and in danger of being cursed" (Heb 6:8). Since it is void as far as fertility is concerned, it is not fit for the intended use; it is rejected, abandoned, since one is judged by one's works. After asking "Test yourselves . . . examine yourselves," St. Paul adds "at least unless you should be void" (*ei mēti adokimoi este*, 2 Cor 13:5), meaning that there would be no good to verify. This "incapacity" is that of the mind (*adokimon noun*) of the pagan philosophers, who cannot discern truth and virtue (Rom 1:28) or of latter-day heretics robbed by their corrupt intelligence of the capacity for sound judgment in anything concerning the faith and moral values (2 Tim 3:8). Warped and disordered minds are radically incapable of any good work (Titus 1:16), whereas the apostle is not incapable of proving himself (2 Cor 13:7). In the athletic context of 1 Cor 9:27, the nuance is more precise: St. Paul beats his body and trains it as a slave "for fear lest after preaching to others I myself should be disqualified." He is alluding to the preliminary test at athletic competitions, where the judge, after an examination, "eliminated" certain contestants who were "not acceptable," or in the case of defeat, refused to award them a prize.

---

oracle spoken without judgment is *adokimos* (to be rejected), but tested by judgment is acceptable (*dokimos*)" (*Alleg. Interp.* 3.119). Cf. the hapax in Josephus: "Lysimachuses, Molons . . . worthless sophists (ἀδόκιμοι σοφισταί) who deceive the young" (*Ag. Apion* 2.236).

> δόξα, δοξάζω, συνδοξάζω
>
> *doxa*, expectation, opinion, reputation, honor, glory; *doxazō*, to think, hold an opinion, imagine, praise, glorify; *syndoxazō*, to sanction, agree to, glorify with

The noun *doxa* derives from *dokeō* (future *doxō*, aorist *edoxa*), "think, admit, claim." It means a subjective appraisal, an internal mental judgment, made by an individual or an assembly.[1] But, beginning with its first usages, *doxa* means "expectation, what is thought possible"; "In accord with our expectation, she goes straight to the mark";[2] hence by far the most widespread meaning in secular Greek, "opinion, thought, sentiment,"[3] as

---

[1] Demosthenes, *Fun. Orat.* 60.5: "it seems to me that" (δοκεῖ μοι); Herodotus 7.103: "for myself, I think that"; Plato, *Menex.* 241 b: "The Persians seemed to be invincible by sea"; Sophocles, *Trach.* 718: "Yes, I feel that he will kill him"; Xenophon, *Hell.* 7.5.21: "He gave the enemy the impression that he did not want to join battle that day"; *An.* 2.1.17: "the advice that seems best to you"; Thucydides 2.11.3: "even if we seem (δοκοῦμεν) to be about to attack, having numbers on our side"; A. Bernand, *Philae*, n. 12 bis, 11: "we ask you, if it please you, to order" (δεόμεθά σου, εἰ δοκεῖ). A. Bernand, *Fayoum*, n. 112, 18; 113, 20; 114, 33; etc. Cf. Matt 3:9; 6:7; 17:25; Luke 1:3; Acts 15:22.

[2] Homer, *Od.* 11.344; cf. *Il.* 10.324: "I will not be a vain scout for you, nor will I fall short of your expectation"; Herodotus 1.79: "Croesus found himself in a very awkward position, his affairs having taken an unexpected turn, altogether different from what he had supposed"; 7.203: "whoever came to attack them had to risk being disappointed." Josephus constantly uses παρὰ δόξαν, "contrary to all expectation," for a surprising, unexpected happening: "having escaped alive, by some miracle, from the royal palace at Jerusalem" (*Life* 46; cf. 96; *War* 1.95, 614; 3.289, 518; 4.529; *Ant.* 2.280; 3.210; 5.40; 15.255, 316, 388; 17.330; 18.129, 219; 19.243). Cf. P. Chantraine, *Dictionnaire étymologique*, pp. 290ff. J. Schneider, *Doxa: Eine bedeutungsgeschichtliche Studie*, Gütersloh, 1932.

[3] Plato, *Plt.* 260 b: "Have we made a just division? Yes, in my opinion at least"; Pindar, *Nem.* 11.30; Aeschylus, *Pers.* 29; Philostratus, *Gym.* 17: "following the opinion of certain people (ὡς μὲν δόξα ἐνίων), the Eleans tested during the summer to see if the gymnasts could resist vigorously and burn themselves in the sun"; *P.Mich.*

---

doxa, S 1391; *TDNT* 2.233–253; *EDNT* 1.344–348; *NIDNTT* 2.44–52; *MM* 168–169; *L&N* 1.15, 12.49, 14.49, 25.205, 33.357, 76.13, 79.18, 87.4, 87.23; *BAGD* 203–204 ‖ *doxazō*, S 1392; *TDNT* 2.253–254; *EDNT* 1.348–349; *NIDNTT* 2.44–45, 874; *MM* 169; *L&N* 33.357, 87.8, 87.24; *BDF* §§235(2), 392(3); *BAGD* 204 ‖ *syndoxazō*, S 4888; *TDNT* 2.253–254, 7.766–797; *EDNT* 3.299; *NIDNTT* 2.44; *L&N* 87.10; *BAGD* 785

distinct from *noēsis* (Plato, *Resp.* 7.534.*a*) and *epistēmē*.[4] There are both true and false opinions,[5] especially among the *axiōmata*, the maxims of the philosophers (*Resp.* 3.413 *a*), the *kyriai doxai*,[6] and also illusions produced by the imagination or a miscalculation.[7]

This "opinion" can also be that held by others concerning a person; so *doxa* is renown, reputation. Usually this is favorable: "Philip is in love with fame, he has a passion for it."[8] Hence in the Koine, especially in the inscriptions and the papyri, the meaning "esteem, honor" (expressed by the Latin *gloria* and our word *glory*), is often linked with *timē* (*Pap.Graec.Mag.* 4, 1616), *aretē, epainos*. In an honorific decree of Ptolemy IV for the Cretan auxiliaries (around 150 BC), Aglaos of Cos, through his deeds and his excellent counsel, showed himself "worthy of his country and of the glory (good reputation) that he enjoys."[9] Around the same period, in a decree at

---

XIII, 666, 27: ἐν καιρῷ τοῦ δημοσίου πρὸς τὰ δόξαν = as that seems good; *Stud.Pal.* XXII, 87, 12: ἀξιῶ τὸ δόχαν σοι; *SB* 7558, 11: τὸ δόξαν σοι κελεῦσαι γενέσθαι; 9066, 23: τὸ δόξαν σταθῆναι.

[4] Plato, *Tht.* 187 *b.* Cf. J. Sprute, *Der Begriff der DOXA in der platonischen Philosophie*, Göttingen, 1962, pp. 90ff., 109ff. H. D. Voigtländer, *Der Philosoph und die Vielen*, Wiesbaden, 1980, pp. 177–183; Y. Lafrance, *La Théorie platonicienne de la doxa*, Montreal, 1981.

[5] Plato, *Phlb.* 36 *c*; *Grg.* 458 *a*: δόξα ψευδής; *Resp.* 4.423 *a*; Xenophon, *Cyr.* 1.6.22; *Mem.* 1.7.4.

[6] Of Epicurus (Cicero, *Fin.* 2.7); cf. αἱ κοιναὶ δόξαι (Aristotle, *Metaph.* 2.2.996^{b}28; 3.3.1005^{b}29; K. Held, *Heraklit, Parmenides und der Anfang von Philosophie und Wissenschaft*, Berlin–New York, 1980, pp. 72, 469–471).

[7] Herodotus 8.132; Aeschylus, *Ag.* 275; Thucydides 1.32.4–5: what formerly seemed to be wisdom appeared definitively as folly and weakness. Plato, *Symp.* 218 *e*; G. Kittel, "Δόξα," in *Forschungen und Fortschritte*, vol. 7, 1931, pp. 457–458. On preSocratic δόξα, cf. M. Heidegger, *Einführung in die Metaphysik*, Tübingen, 1953, pp. 79ff. = ET, *An Introduction to Metaphysics*, trans. R. Manheim, New Haven, 1959, pp. 103ff. Parmenides used this word for the world of appearance as grasped by the senses, cf. E. Pax, "Ex Parmenide ad Septuaginta: De notione vocabuli doxa," in *VD*, 1960, pp. 92–102.

[8] Demosthenes, *2 Olynth.* 2.15; cf. *3 Olynth.* 3.24: "The Athenians through their actions have left a renown that defies the envious"; *C. Lept.* 20.10: "the present law deprives our city of this glorious fame"; Euripides, *HF* 157: Heracles has a reputation of bravery for his fights with wild animals; cf. *Hec.* 295: well-known or famous men (τῶν δοκούντων) contrasted to obscure folk (ἀδοκούντων); *Tro.* 613; Diodorus Siculus 15.61.5; Josephus, *Ant.* 4.14: Korah thought that he had a greater right to honor than Moses himself; 19.307; *Life* 274: "They said that the esteem in which I was held was an honor to themselves." Cf. G. Steinkopf, *Untersuchungen zur Geschichte des Ruhmes bei den Griechen*, Halle, 1937, pp. 60ff.

[9] *I.Delos* 1517, 17 = J. Pouilloux, *Choix*, n. 17. The end of an (imperial) decree refers to a dispute concerning the names or rank of cities (πρωτεία). Certain ones are puffed up with a glory that is recent, new (καινῇ δόξῃ, *MAMA* VI, 6, 2) "because

Miletus, "Eirenias has shown the finest zeal for the interests of the city and gives his cooperation to all that pertains to the renown and the glory of our country."[10] According to his epitaph, the officer Apollonius received from the benefactors "the garland, the sacred allotment of the glory that belongs to the king's 'kinsmen.' "[11] A *prytanis* is acclaimed as "glory of the city" (*doxa poleōs*, P.Oxy. 41, 4).

The semantic evolution of *doxa* is probably the most extraordinary in the Bible. Not once in the LXX (except for Eccl 10:1) or the NT does this noun mean "opinion." It translates most often the Hebrew *kābôd*, but also *hôd*, *pe'ēr*, *tip'eret*. *Kābôd*, from the root *kbd*, "be heavy," evokes the idea of weight or that which confers weightiness (cf. 2 Cor 4:17, an eternal weight of glory) and hence esteem or respect, especially power and wealth.[12] In

---

a title has been granted them" (L. Robert, "Les Inscriptions," in J. des Gagniers, *Laodicée*, p. 287).

[10] NCIG, n. 7, col. I, 3. Dittenberger, *Or.* 244, 20: "In the future he shall benefit from all the advantages that confer honor and glory (εἰς τιμὴν καὶ δόξαν); this will be our concern" (= IGLS 992); *Syl.* 700, 35; 724 E 20; 796, 28; *I.Priene* 53, 15: ἀξίως ἐπαίνου καὶ τιμῶν (= C. Michel, *Recueil*, n. 468); 119, 9: μεγίστου τέτευχεν ἐπαίνου καὶ δόξης ἀταράκτου; *I.Olymp.* 472, 12: ἀρετῆς καὶ σωφροσύνης καὶ παιδείας ἕνεκεν καὶ τῆς ὑπὲρ τὴν ἡλικίαν δόξης; *I.Magn.* 53, 48; 131, 3: γένει καὶ δόξῃ καὶ ἀρετῇ καὶ σωφροσύνῃ; 138, 5: ἐπὶ τε τῇ περισσῇ ἀρετῇ τε καὶ δόξῃ καὶ τῇ εὐνοίᾳ.

[11] E. Bernand, *Inscriptions métriques*, n. 5, 5: συγγενικῆς δόξης ἱερὸν γέρας. According to Aphrodisia's epitaph, her husband Ptolemaeus "raised to the heavens the glory of being king's kinsman" (ibid. 35, 10). In the vision of Maximus, the god Mandoulis is "glad for the glory of the Romans," i.e., rejoices in the temple that the imperial government built for him (ibid. 168, 27). "At Elea, the sacred olive tree retains its ancient glory free of profanation" (τὴν ἐκ παλαιοῦ δόξαν, Philostratus, *Gym.* 45). The *gymnastai* dream only of their profits and "do not care for the glory of the athletes" (τῆς μὲν τῶν ἀθλητῶν δόξης, ibid.). The winner in a chariot race notes that he "won a share of glory in life" (τῆς ἐν βίῳ δόξης μετείληφα νεικήσας, P.Oxy. 3116, 5); cf. P.Oslo 85, 13; SB 8542, 2: μεγίστη δόξα διὰ βίου; 8639, 2; 9286, 5; P.Ross.Georg. II, 26, 2: ἐν μείζονι δόξῃ; CIRB 57, 7: μεγάλης δόξης ὁ ἀνὴρ ἔτυχεν; 121, 1; 992, 8; P.Alex. 216 (p. 44); τῆς ὑμετέρας μεγαλοπρεποῦς δόξης; C.P.Herm. 2, 26.

[12] Beginning with the first occurrence, Gen 31:1—Jacob "gained all this fortune from what was our father's"; verse 6; 45:13—Joseph says, "You shall tell my father about all my power in Egypt"; Exod 28:2—"Aaron your brother in glory and in majesty" (same link between δόξα and τιμή, Ps 8:5—"You have crowned man with glory and honor" [cf. the Hebrew text of Sir 49:16—"Above every living thing is the glory of Adam"; T. Abr. A 11; 1QS 4.23; CD 3.20; 1QH 17.15]; Ps 21:6; Job 40:10; 1 Macc 14:21; 2 Macc 5:16); Num 27:20—Moses will confer on Joshua "a little of his majesty"; 1 Kgs 3:13; 1 Chr 29:12, 28; 2 Chr 1:11–12; 17:5; 18:1; 32:27; Esth 6:3; 10:2; Ps 112:3; Prov 3:16; 8:18; 11:16; 22:4; Eccl 6:2; Sir 24:17; 1 Macc 14:4, 9; 15:32, 36, "the wise shall have a share of honor" (Prov 3:35); "the beauty of heaven is the glory of the stars" (Sir 43:9, 12). There is "the glory of the great Raphael" (Tob 3:17), "the glory of athletes" (2 Macc 4:15), and "Yahweh, you are my glory (my pride, my honor)"

this secular meaning, *doxa* can be translated sometimes "majesty" (2 Macc 15:13) or "dignity,"[13] sometimes "renown."[14]

Because Yahweh is the supreme sovereign, he is described as the "king of glory."[15] The whole universe is full of his *doxa*,[16] that is, the splendor of his majesty.[17] We should understand this to mean his mighty deeds, his glorious interventions (Exod 14:18; 16:7) both in overturning his adversaries (Exod 15:7) and in saving his people.[18] In fact, more than once it is said

---

(Ps 3:3, 46:2; 106:20). Glory is like a garment (Job 19:9; 40:10; Sir 6:31; 27:8; 45:7; 50:11; Isa 52:1; Bar 5:1) or an adornment. So there is mention of a crown of glory (Jer 13:18; Bar 5:2) and of a throne of glory (1 Sam 2:8; Isa 22:23; Jer 14:21; 17:12; Bar 5:6; Esth 5:1; Wis 9:10; Sir 7:4; 40:3; 47:11). Glory is preeminently a royal attribute: Solomon is clothed with royal majesty (δόξαν βασιλέως, 1 Chr 29:25; cf. the liturgical acclamation Δόξα σοι ούράνιε βασιλεῦ, *SB* 6584, 10; 7512, 2; 7906, 13; *IGLS* 294, 1; 318, 1; 426, 1; 587; 598); cf. Isa 8:7; 17:4; 21:16; 33:17; Dan 2:37; 4:26–33; 7:14; 11:20; Esth 1:4; Ps 45:13; Prov 14:28; 25:2.

[13] Hos 4:7; Hab 2:16; Isa 16:14; 1 Macc 1:40; 10:58, 64, 86; 11:42; 2 Macc 14:7; Esth 4:17; Job 29:20; Wis 15:9; Sir 1:11, 19; 3:10–11; 8:14; 35:12; 45:2, 20, 23. In the plural, the ἐξουσίαι καὶ δόξαι are high offices (Diodorus Siculus 15.58.1; cf. *PSI* 158, 24 and 41: πάντων ἄλλων δόξας ποιεῖς; 1422, 6), those high dignitaries of the heavenly court that angels are; Philo, *Spec. Laws* 1.45: "Your glory, I mean the Powers that stand guard around you"; *T. Jud.* 25.2—αἱ δυνάμεις τῆς δόξης; Jude 8; 2 Pet 2:10; *P.Princ.* 159, 10: κύριοι ἄγγελοι (= *P.Oslo* 1, 44 and 246), "the cherubim of glory" (Heb 9:5); Ezek 10:4; Sir 49:8), whose spread wings over the place of propitiation symbolize the presence of Yahweh and his powerful interventions on behalf of his people (J. Trinquet, "Gloires," in *Catholicisme*, vol. 5, col. 55). Some have also understood the false teachers of 2 Pet 2:10, who slander the "glorious ones" as those who reject the risen Christ, his extraordinary deeds (2:1—δεσπότην ἀρνούμενοι) or his teachings (κυριότητος καταφρονοῦντας); δόξας would then have its classical meaning "opinion, verdict, axiom, philosophical doctrine," but the plural here would be obscure indeed.

[14] 1 Macc 2:51; 3:3; 9:10; 14:10, 29; 15:9; in all lands (1 Chr 22:5), among the multitudes (Wis 8:10). The forest of cedars is the glory of Lebanon (Isa 35:1ff.; 60:13). Yahwh is the glory of Israel (Ps 3:4; 106:20; Jer 2:2); so also the ark (1 Sam 4:22).

[15] Ps 24:7–10; Isa 24:14; 26:10; 30:30. The glory of Yahweh "is above the heavens" (Ps 113:4); "great is the glory of Yahweh" (Ps 145:5, 11, 12); "Ascribe to Yahweh glory and power" (Ps 29:1–3, 9).

[16] Isa 6:3; 59:19. Not only does God act for his glory (Isa 43:7; 48:11), but his faithful ones "tell of Yahweh's glory to all the nations" (1 Chr 16:24–28; Isa 42:12; 66:19; Ps 96:3, 7–8). Cf. H. Kittel, *Die Herrlichkeit Gottes*, Giessen, 1934; B. Stein, *Der Begriff Kebod Jahwe*, Emsdetten i. W., 1939; A. Plé, "La Gloire de Dieu," in *VSpir*, n. 306, 1946, pp. 479–490; L. Brockington, "The Greek Translator of Isaiah and His Interest in δόξα," in *VT*, 1951, pp. 23ff. P. Deseille, "Gloire de Dieu dans l'Ancien et le Nouveau Testament," in *Dict.spir.*, vol. 6, col. 422–436; J. Duplacy, "Gloire," in *Catholicisme*, vol. 5, col. 47–54.

[17] Isa 2:10, 19, 21; 4:2, 5; 40:1; cf. Bar 4:24—"The splendor of the Eternal."

[18] Isa 12:2; 35:1–4; 44:23; 46:13; Ezek 39:21–29.

that "the glory of Yahweh appeared,"[19] conceived sometimes as a manifestation of the deity (Isa 40:5), sometimes as an image of Yahweh;[20] it is visible.[21] "The spirit of the glory of Yahweh was like a raging fire on the peak of the mountain in the eyes of the children of Israel" (Exod 24:17; Deut 5:24), a sparking of light (Ezek 1) that flames out (Isa 60:1–3). This is how biblical *doxa*, the manifestation of the presence and activity of the invisible and transcendent God answers to sense experience: even though its brilliance cannot be perceived by the eyes of the flesh (Ezek 33:22; Acts 22:11; *Asc. Isa.* 9.37), it is contemplated by the spirit.[22] Biblical *doxa* therefore has a touch of luminescence.[23]

It is worth noting that Hellenistic Jewish writers know nothing of the religious meaning of *doxa*. Nevertheless, the *Letter of Aristeas* has the word in the sense of splendor and brilliance.[24] Philo (in 180 occurrences) has only the meaning "opinion," in accord with the classical tradition, whether true or false opinion (Philo, *Sacr. Abel and Cain* 2–3; *Worse Attacks Better* 32). This latter[25] is described as vicious (*Sacr. Abel and Cain* 5), atheistic (*Alleg. Interp.* 23; *Post. Cain* 42), and especially as vain or empty;[26] it is over

---

[19] Exod 16:10; Lev 9:6, 23; Num 14:10; 16:19; 17:7; 20:6.

[20] Num 12:8 (Hebrew t^emûnâh); Ps 17:15; cf. Ezek 1:28—"the vision of the surrounding brightness was the vision of the image of the glory of Yahweh. I saw and fell on my face." In this epigram from Gofna, on the tomb of an old woman: εἰκόνα δόξης (*GVI*, n. 1185, 3).

[21] Exod 16:7—"You shall see the glory of Yahweh" (who will save you); Exod 33:18–22: Moses asks, "Let me see your glory," and God answers, "I will make all my goodness pass before you"; Deut 5:24—"Yahweh our God made us see his glory and his greatness"; Tob 13:16; Isa 40:5; 60:2; 66:18; Ezek 3:23; Ps 63:2—"I beheld your power and your glory"; 97:6; Sir 17:13; 42:25; 49:8.

[22] Cf. Ezek 1:3; 2:2; 11:24; 2 Cor 3:7; John 1:14—"We have contemplated his glory, glory like that belonging to a Father's only Son"; 2:11—"He manifested his glory, and his disciples believed in him." This *doxa*, which fills the earth (Isa 6:3; Ps 72:19) and the heavens (Ps 8:2; 19:2; 24:7), is manifested especially in the temple (1 Kgs 8:11; Ps 26:8; 2 Chr 5:13–14; 7:1–3; Isa 6:1; Ezek 10:4, 18; 43:4–5).

[23] Cf. *Pap.Graec.Mag.* 13, 189: τὴν δόξαν τοῦ φωτός; 298ff. Cf. C. Mohrmann, "Note sur doxa," in *Sprachgeschichte und Wortbedeutung: Festschrift A. Debrunner*, Bern, 1954, pp. 321–328.

[24] *Ep. Arist.* 96, 98; or dazzling (196); the other occurrences have to do with reputation (3, 37, 226, 234, 242, 269, 283), honor (39, 45), dignity (218, 282, 290). Among all, kings are illustrious and glorious (79, 223, 224).

[25] Ψευδὴς δόξα, *Cherub.* 9, 66, 71; *Post. Cain* 52; *Drunkenness* 70, 76, 162; *Unchang. God* 172; *Conf. Tongues* 106; *Heir* 71; *Dreams* 1.218; *Joseph* 147; *Spec. Laws* 1.59; 4.53, 188.

[26] Κεναὶ δόξαι, *Unchang. God* 172; *Husbandry* 56; *Drunkenness* 36, 38, 144; *Sobr.* 57; *Migr. Abr.* 21; *Prelim. Stud.* 6, 15; *Flight* 47, 128; *Change of Names* 92–94; *Dreams* 1.82; 2.95, 155; *Decalogue* 4; *Spec. Laws* 1.27; *Good Man Free* 66, 158; *Contemp. Life* 17.

against the truth.[27] *Doxa* (often synonymous with *dogma*) refers also to philosophical opinions[28] and especially to wealth, power, honor, and pleasure.[29] These are images and shifting shadows (*Spec. Laws* 1.28), they are uncertain (*Rewards* 29), intoxicating vapors and lies (*Rewards* 21).

For Josephus, *doxa* is opinion, conception, judgment,[30] but especially reputation, renown.[31] In contrast to Philo, he almost always uses *doxa* in a favorable sense ("esteem"), linking it to piety and virtue;[32] but neither of them seem to have been influenced by the LXX.

The NT writers are familiar with almost all of the above-mentioned secular and religious meanings. The Synoptics already attest the meaning "honor, distinction, reputation" for the guest placed by the host in the best place, resulting in "honor before all" (*doxa enōpion pantōn*, Luke 14:10). The devil promises the Messiah royal glory—that attaching to domination, magnificence, splendor (Matt 4:8; Luke 4:6). This was the kind of glory Solomon had (Matt 6:29; Luke 12:27). This glory is luminous,[33] like that of Moses and Elijah at Tabor,[34] signaling a heavenly appearance, a divine manifestation. Peter and his companions, awakened by the dazzling light, "saw his (Christ's) glory" (Luke 9:32). This is a divine state, a condition of honor, of

---

[27] *Alleg. Interp.* 2.56–57; *Cherub.* 83; *Post. Cain* 13; *Joseph* 59; *Spec. Laws* 2.244; 3.164; 4.71; *Rewards* 28; *To Gaius* 279.

[28] Cf. *Post. Cain* 34; *Giants* 39, 62; *Sobr.* 67; *Migr. Abr.* 184; *Heir* 169; *Abraham* 70; *Decalogue* 65; *Spec. Laws* 1.328; *Virtues* 65, 214; *Rewards* 162; *Good Man Free* 3; *Etern. World* 7, 12, 47. The religious meaning is found only in the quotation of Exod 33:18 (*Spec. Laws* 1.45). There is a single instance in Josephus also (*Ant.* 1.155).

[29] Philo, *Creation* 79; *Alleg. Interp.* 1.75; 3.86; *Cherub.* 117; *Worse Attacks Better* 33, 122, 136, 157; *Post. Cain* 112, 117; *Giants* 15; *Drunkenness* 52, 57, 75; *Sobr.* 3, 61; *Conf. Tongues* 112; *Prelim. Stud.* 27; *Flight* 25, 33, 35, 39; *Abraham* 184; *Moses* 2.53; *Decalogue* 153; *Spec. Laws* 1.311; 2.208; 3.1.

[30] *War* 1.375; 2.154, 160; 4.288; 6.264; *Ant.* 2.286; 4.147; etc. (δόξαν παρασκεῖν, cf. *PSI* 1422, 6), the doctrine of the philosophers (*Ag. Apion* 1.165; 2.169) and religious belief (2.179, 221, 224, 239, 254–256, 258).

[31] *War* 1.108, 331; 3.358; 6.260, 267, 442; *Ant.* 1.2, 165, 275, 280; 2.78; 5.290, 351; 7.44, 52 (20.205); *Life* 193, 274); *Ant.* 8.43; 10.59, 272; 11.158; 12.350; 13.63; 17.226; etc. There is the glory of the Olympic games (*War* 1.426), of a victory (4.372; 5.498; *Ant.* 7.304; 8.24), of a success (*Ant.* 5.267; 12.49), of domination (2.175; 7.195), of past glories (1.121).

[32] *Ant.* 2.205; 6.18, 80, 343; 8.196; 9.16; 10.264, 268; 11.121; 12.160; 18.297; 19.211; cf. δόξα καὶ τιμή, 2.268; 6.200; 10.266; 11.217; 12.118.

[33] Cf. Luke 2:32 (relying on Isa 42:6; 49:6): the Messiah is a "light (φῶς) to lighten the nations, and the glory (δόξαν, honor and repute) of your people Israel." Cf. Acts 22:11, Saul on the Damascus road: "I could not see because of the brilliance of that light" (ἀπὸ τῆς δόξης τοῦ φωτὸς ἐκείνου).

[34] Ὀφθέντες ἐν δόξῃ, Luke 9:31. Cf. H. Riesenfeld, *Jésus transfiguré*, Copenhagen, 1947; A. M. Ramsey, *La Gloire de Dieu et la Transfiguration du Christ*, Paris, 1965.

preeminent dignity, of splendor; it belongs especially to Jesus (Mark 10:37), and contrasts with his earthly *morphē* and his passion (Luke 24:26). When the Son of Man appears at the end time as judge and sovereign, his glory will fill the heavens from one end to the other, instantaneously, like lightning.[35] Finally, God's glory (*kābôd*) manifests his presence and his intervention, bathing the shepherds of Bethlehem in light.[36] Also, the angels who praise God (Luke 2:13) acclaim the intervention of God's mercy and might to save humans: "Glory in the highest to God" (*doxa in hypsistois theō*).[37]

St. Paul is the writer who uses the word *glory* most often. As a part of his largely Septuagint-based vocabulary, *doxa* has a depth of meaning that cannot be expressed by a simple translation. Certainly there is the quite basic sense of honor and repute,[38] even beauty and splendor: "If a woman wears her hair long, it is a glory for her";[39] but there is also a religious nuance with those who "seek glory, honor (*doxan kai timēn*) and immortality."[40] To the Israelites "belong the adoption and the glory and the

---

[35] Matt 16:27 (Mark 8:38; Luke 9:26); 19:28; 24:30 (Mark 13:26; Luke 21:27); 25:31.

[36] Luke 2:9 (περιλάμπω = shine about, illumine); like a shining garment. This Semitism appears in Acts 7:2—"the God of glory *appeared* to our father Abraham" (ὁ θεὸς τῆς δόξης ὤφθη). This brilliant light is characteristic of God (Ps 24:7, 9; 29:3; with the article) and shines out from God (M. Black, "The Recovery of the Language of Jesus," in *NTS*, vol. 3, 1957, p. 312); Acts 7:55—Stephen, "his eyes fixed on heaven, saw God's glory" (Exod 16:7; 24:17; Ezek 8:4; 43:2).

[37] Luke 2:14; there is no article and no verb; the style is lapidary (cf. E. Delebecque, *Etudes grecques*, pp. 25–38; cf. C. Westermann, "Alttestamentliche Elemente in Lukas II, 1–20," in *Tradition und Glaube: Festgabe K. G. Kuhn*, Göttingen, 1971, pp. 317–327). On Palm Sunday, the crowd acclaimed the Messiah: "Glory in the highest" (Luke 19:38). After the healing of the ten lepers, "No one was found to return and give glory to (= thank) God except this foreigner" (Luke 17:18). Herod Agrippa, having uttered sacrilegious words and usurped God's glory, is struck dead "because he did not give the glory to God" (Acts 12:23; cf. Rev 19:7).

[38] 1 Thess 2:6—"We have not sought glory from people"; 2:20—"You are our glory and our joy"; Eph 3:13—"The trials that I endure for you are your glory"; the apostle commends himself in his ministry "in the midst of glory and dishonor" (διὰ δόξης καὶ ἀτιμίας, "scorn, shame," 2 Cor 6:8); "Their god is their belly, and their glory is in their shame" (ἡ δόξα ἐν τῇ αἰσχύνῃ αὐτῶν, Phil 3:19); "it is sown in shame, it is raised in glory" (the resurrection, 1 Cor 15:43); "Jesus Christ will transform our body of misery (ταπεινώσεως), conforming it to his glorious body" (Phil 3:21). Cf. M. Carrey, *De la souffrance à la gloire: La Doxa dans la pensée paulinienne*, Neuchâtel, 1964; H. Schlier, "La Notion de doxa dans l'histoire du salut d'après S. Paul," in *Essais sur le Nouveau Testament*, Paris, 1968, pp. 379–412.

[39] 1 Cor 11:15 (for the textual criticism, cf. G. Zuntz, in *RB*, 1952, p. 15); cf. 1 Pet 1:24—"All flesh is like grass, and its glory like a flower of grass" (= Isa 40:6); F. W. Danker, "I Petr. I, 24–II, 7: A Consolatory Pericope," in *ZNW*, 1967, pp. 93–102.

[40] Rom 2:7, 10; 1 Pet 1:7—"Let your faith . . . be found worthy of praise and glory and honor (ἔπαινον καὶ δόξαν καὶ τιμὴν) at the revealing of Jesus Christ."

alliances and the temple worship and the promises" (Rom 9:4). There is the light of this *doxa*, like the shining forth of luminous rays, like the stars, which each have their brilliance and thus a variety of beauty.[41] Thus Moses' face, when he returned from speaking with God, shone brilliantly, even though the light was dissipating (Exod 34:29-35); but the administration of the new covenant according to the Spirit prevails with a preeminent and definitive glory (*tēs hyperballousēs doxēs*),[42] because its light comes from "the knowledge of God's glory (shining) on the face of Christ."[43] The two splendors are not comparable. There is so much variety in luminousness: "man is the image and glory of God, but woman is the glory of man."[44] If Adam and Eve are both the image of God, then the man manifests the royal authority of his Creator and the honor of God (cf. *Num. Rab.* 3.15—"the honor [*kābôd*] of God ascends from men") and the woman "procures honor [i.e., for her husband]" (Prov 11:17). These latter texts can be understood well only as a function of OT *kābôd*. "All have sinned and are deprived of the glory of God" (Rom 3:23) cannot refer to the good opinion that God would have of the righteous (Cajetan), nor to the grace that would be inaugurated glory (a later theological distinction), but to the splendor and beauty that shine out from the divine splendor and

---

[41] 1 Cor 15:40-41: "the brilliance (*doxa*) of heavenly bodies is different from the brilliance of earthly bodies; there is the brilliance of the sun, and the brilliance of the moon, and the brilliance of the stars, for one star differs from another in its brilliance"; cf. Aratus, *Phaen.* 454; Philodemus of Gadara, *Inf.* 9.36; C. Mugler, *Terminologie optique*, pp. 191ff., 352ff.

[42] 2 Cor 3:7-11 (cf. S. Schulz, "Die Decke des Moses," in *ZNW*, 1958, pp. 1-30; R. Le Déaut, "Traditions targumiques dans le Corpus Paulinien," in *Bib*, 1961, pp. 43-47).

[43] 2 Cor 4:6 (cf. C. M. Martini, "Alcuni temi letterari di II Cor. IV, 6 e i racconti della conversione de San Paolo negli Atti," in *AnBib* 17, Rome, 1963, pp. 461-474; G. W. MacRae, "Anti-Dualist Polemic in II Cor. IV, 6?" in F. L. Cross, *SE*, vol. 4, Berlin, 1968, pp. 420-431); cf. 2 Cor 4:4—"the illumination of the gospel of the glory of Christ, who is the image of God" (τὸ φωτισμὸν τοῦ εὐαγγελίου τῆς δόξης τοῦ Χριστοῦ); 1 Tim 1:11—"the gospel of the glory of the blessed God, which was entrusted to me personally," an evocation of the transcendent character of the revealed message, the manifestation of divine power: the epiphany of the Son of God, the Savior. Cf. 2 Cor 7:23—the emissaries of the churches "are the glory of Christ."

[44] 1 Cor 11:7 (Gen 1:26; 2:18-23); cf. the tomb inscription, "[here lies one who was] the glory of Sophronius, blessed Lucilla" (ἡ δόξα Σωφρονίου Λουκίλλα εὐλογημένη, *CII* 135). Cf. C. Spicq, *Théologie morale*, p. 130, n. 7; 690, n. 4; A. Feuillet, "L'Homme 'gloire de Dieu' et la femme 'gloire de l'homme,'" in *RB*, 1974, pp. 161-182; idem, "La Dignité et le rôle de la femme," in *NTS*, vol. 21, 1975, pp. 159ff. S. V. McCasland, "'The Image of God,' according to Paul," in *JBL*, 1950, pp. 85ff. E. E. Ellis, *Paul's Use of the Old Testament*, London, 1957, p. 63; P. Grelot, *Le Couple humain dans l'Ecriture*, Paris, 1962; K. Stendhahl, *The Bible and the Role of Women*, Philadelphia, 1966.

holiness.⁴⁵ The idolatrous pagans "exchanged the glory of the immortal God for images representing a mortal man."⁴⁶

This glory is God in the splendor of his majesty and the omnipotence of his interventions,⁴⁷ "the Father of glory" (*ho patēr tēs doxēs*).⁴⁸ But this predicate *doxa*, which is peculiar to God, is attributed also to Christ, the "Lord of glory."⁴⁹ Heb 1:3 adds the description: "the Son (of God), the effulgence of his (the Father's) glory (*apaugasma tēs doxēs autou*) and the

---

⁴⁵ Cf. Job 19:9—"He has stripped me of my glory"; Bar 5:1—"Put on forever the beauty and glory of God," 4 Ezra 7:122-125; 2 Apoc. Bar. 51.1, 3; 54.15; cf. 2 Thess 1:9—the condemned are "separated from the Lord's presence and from the glory of his might." According to rabbinic theology, the first man, created shining with splendor, shared in the divine *kābôḏ*; he lost this privilege through sin. Glory is one of the six things that were taken from Adam and will be restored to humanity by the Messiah (*Gen. Rab.* 12.5; *Exod. Rab.* 30.2; *Num. Rab.* 13.11, on Num 7:13; cf. *b. Sanh.* 38*b*). Naked, Adam and Eve were clothed with light; sin deprived them of this garment. After eating the forbidden fruit, Eve saw that she had lost the righteousness that had enveloped her and reproached the serpent thus: "Why did you do this? You have robbed me of the glory in which I was clothed" (*Adam and Eve* 20.1-2). Cf. P. Bonnetain, "Grâce," in *DBSup*, vol. 3, col. 775-776; J. B. Frey, "L'Etat originel et la chute de l'homme d'après les conceptions juives au temps de Jésus-Christ," in *RSPT*, 1911, p. 554; W. D. Davies, *Paul and Rabbinic Judaism*, London, 1948, pp. 45ff.; L. Ligier, *Péché d'Adam et péché du monde*, Paris, 1961, pp. 209-210, 245.

⁴⁶ Rom 1:23; cf. N. Hyldahl, "A Reminiscence of the Old Testament at Romans I, 23," in *NTS*, vol. 2, 1956, pp. 285-288; M. D. Hooker, "Adam in Romans I," *NTS*, vol. 6, 1960, pp. 297-306.

⁴⁷ Eph 1:18—ὁ πλοῦτος τῆς δόξης; 3:16; Phil 4:19; Col. 1:27; Rom 9:23; 2 Thess 1:9—τῆς δόξης τῆς ἰσχύος αὐτοῦ; Col. 1:11—τὸ κράτος τῆς δόξης. God has called us ἰδίᾳ δόξῃ καὶ ἀρετῇ (2 Pet 1:3). Cf. L. Cerfaux, *Théologie de l'Eglise suivant saint Paul*, Paris, 1965, p. 35ff., 78, 309ff. Christ, who was raised by the glory of his Father (Rom 6:4), acts to secure the glory of God (15:7), which is manifested through his word, his truth, his faithfulness (3:7). This glory, which appeared on Tabor, is described as "magnificent" or "majestic" (2 Pet 1:17).

⁴⁸ Eph 1:17; P. Benoit in the *Bible de Jérusalem* comments: "that is to say, who possesses in fullness and causes to shine on his elect (verse 18) this brilliant splendor of 'glory' in which all the wealth of the divine essence is expressed." The formula is probably liturgical and of priestly origin (M. Barth, *Ephesians*, vol. 1, p. 148); cf. "God of glory" (Ps 29:3; Acts 7:2), "king of glory" (Ps 24:7), "Lord of glory" (1 Cor 2:8); "Father of mercies" (2 Cor 1:3), "Father of lights" (Jas 1:17).

⁴⁹ 1 Cor 2:8; Jas 2:1. Here *kyrios* is a title of supremacy and even of divinity. Cf. Heb 2:7—"You crowned him with glory and honor" (δόξῃ καὶ τιμῇ, quoting Ps 8:5-7: a lordly crown; cf. F. J. Moloney, "The Re-interpretation of Psalm VIII and the Son of Man Debate," in *NTS*, vol. 27, 1981, pp. 656-672); everything is put under the Messiah's feet (cf. P. Grelot, *Sens chrétien de l'Ancien Testament*, Paris-Tournai, 1962, p. 473; W. H. Schmidt, "Gott und Mensch in Ps. 8," in *TZ*, 1969, pp. 1-15). Christ's glory is superior to that of Moses (πλείονος δόξης), for the builder of a house is more worthy of honor than the house itself (Heb 3:3).

δόξα, *doxa*, etc.   371

image of his substance."⁵⁰ If Christ is the refulgence of God's *doxa*, it is because his origin is divine; he has the same nature as the Father while having his personal independence. The Council of Nicea would give the definition "light from light" (*phōs ek phōtos*). In proclaiming Jesus as his Son at Tabor, God conferred honor and glory upon him (2 Pet 1:17, *timēn kai doxan*); but as a human, Jesus—after the shame of his passion—was glorified by his resurrection,⁵¹ and at the end of time he will appear as an almighty sovereign and in blinding light. His disciples await "the appearing of the glory of our great God and Savior Jesus Christ,"⁵² for they will participate in it (2 Thess 2:14).

Actually, the great innovation of the new covenant is that it calls all believers to share the "eternal glory (of God) in Christ" (1 Pet 5:10). The economy of salvation is order "for our glory" (*eis doxan hēmōn*, 1 Cor 2:7). God calls us "to his kingdom and his glory" (1 Thess 2:12; Rom 5:2; 8:18, 21), and the goal of Jesus' advent on earth was "to lead many sons to glory" (Heb 2:10). Beginning in the present, these contemplate Christ's glory and are metamorphosed in his image "from glory to glory,"⁵³ the objects of

---

⁵⁰ Heb 1:3 is reminiscent of Wis 7:25-26 (cf. Philo, *Plant.* 50; *Dreams* 1.72; *Spec. Laws* 4.123). Ἀπαυγάζω = shine out, emit rays of light and perceive emitted rays; ἀπαυγασμός = shining, rays of light (C. Mugler, *Terminologie optique*, p. 43). In its choice of the word ἀπαύγασμα, Hebrews suggests rays of light emanating from a bright fire, with the idea of splendor, magnificence, beauty: the brilliance of Majesty. Hence, in the passive sense: refulgence, defined by Littré: "the great brilliance formed by the expansion, the reflection of light," perceptible by mortals.

⁵¹ 1 Pet 1:11—the Holy Spirit attested in advance through the prophets "the sufferings in store for the Christ and the glories that would follow" (τὰς μετὰ ταῦτα δόξας); the plural suggests the multiplicity and the greatness of the glorious events following the passion: resurrection, appearances, ascension, session "at the right hand of the Majesty on high" (Heb 1:3; 1 Pet 3:22). The object of Christian faith is God's having raised Christ from the dead and having given him glory (1 Pet 1:21; cf. Acts 3:13). At the ascension, Christ was received up (ἀνελήμφθη ἐν δόξῃ, 1 Tim 3:16). This triumph is not only a transfer to another location, nor the acquisition of almighty *exousia*, but a close communion with God (C. Spicq, *Epîtres Pastorales*, vol. 1, p. 474; J. Coppens, "La Glorification céleste du Christ dans la théologie néotestamentaire," in E. Dhanis, *Resurrexit*, Vatican City, 1974, pp. 31–55).

⁵² Titus 2:13 (C. Spicq, *Epîtres Pastorales*, vol. 1, p. 640; M. J. Harris, "Titus II, 13 and the Deity of Christ," in D. A. Hagner, M. J. Harris, *Pauline Studies: Essays Presented to Professor F. F. Bruce*, Exeter, 1980, pp. 262–277); M. E. Boismard, "Notre glorification dans le Christ d'après saint Paul," in *VSpir*, 1946, pp. 502–517); 1 Pet 4:13.

⁵³ 2 Cor 3:18 (J. Dupont, "Le chrétien miroir de la grâce divine d'après II Cor. III, 18," in *RB*, 1949, pp. 392–411. N. Hugedé, *La Métaphore du miroir dans les épîtres de saint Paul aux Corinthiens*, Neuchâtel-Paris, 1957; C. Mugler, *Terminologie optique*, p. 221; C. Spicq, *Epîtres Pastorales*, vol. 1, pp. 130, 741); Col 1:27—"Christ in you, the hope of glory." This immanent spiritual metamorphosis is progressive and will not

increasing illumination. The life-giving glory of Christ becomes ours and emphasizes our spiritual likeness to the Lord; through this refraction we resemble his image more and more "with unveiled faces." Furthermore, "when Christ, our life, is manifested, then you will be manifested with him en doxē,"[54] that is, in splendor and in the greatest dignity (2 Cor 4:17), symbolized as an incorruptible crown.[55] If doxa became almost synonymous with the heavenly state, the emphasis is on the nobility of this state and the light received from God. This insistence on dignity and eternity— whereas we think especially of "beatitude"—contrasts with the imperfections of earthly, mortal existence but also refers to the glorious condition of the first human being, clothed with God's glory. Finally, it is part of the light mysticism characteristic of inhabitants of the Orient and the Mediterranean.

There is nothing to do but give glory to God, after the fashion of Abraham (Rom 4:20), do everything for God's glory (1 Cor 10:31; 2 Cor 8:19), as an expression of our gratitude and adoration,[56] homage to the almighty and faithful God (2 Cor 1:20; Phil 1:11; 2:11). The fact is that the whole economy of salvation in God's intention has as its goal to draw from the saved a hymn "to the praise of the glory of his grace."[57] Hence more or less developed doxologies acclaim either God's excellence, nature, and activity,[58]

---

be "manifest" until the final eschatological glory, of which it is actually the firstfruits and an anticipation. It is also the work of the "Spirit of glory" (1 Pet 4:14), so designated because he procures the heavenly glory. For the textual criticism of this text, cf. K. Aland, *Die alten Übersetzungen des Neuen Testaments*, Berlin, 1972, p. 100.

[54] Col 3:4. We can translate ἐν δόξῃ "full of glory" (P. Benoit) or "with glory" (C. Masson) or "in glory" (E. Osty). What is certain is that this will be in Christ's glory (cf. Phil 3:21), that which surrounds the Lord at the Parousia (1 Pet 5:1).

[55] 1 Pet 5:4. The crown is the emblem of royalty, or conquerors, or of victors, a symbol of power, success, prosperity, and virtue, cf. J. Köchling, *De Coronarum apud Antiquos Vi atque Usu*, Giessen, 1914; C. Spicq, *Epîtres de saint Pierre*, p. 169.

[56] 2 Cor 4:15 (B. Noak, "A Note on II Cor IV, 15," in *ST*, 1963, pp. 129–132); cf. John 9:24—Δὸς δόξαν τῷ θεῷ (cf. Jos 7:19; 1 Sam 6:5; Jer 13:16).

[57] Eph 1:6, 12, 14. Cf. A. M. Ramsey, *La Gloire de Dieu et la Transfiguration du Christ*, pp. 111–122; F. Dreyfus, "Pour la louange de sa gloire (Eph. I, 13, 14): L'Origine Vétéro-Testamentaire da la formule," in L. de Lorenzi, *Paul de Tarse apôtre de notre temps*, Rome, 1979, pp. 233–248; D. Cohn-Sherbok, "A Jewish Note on τὸ ποτήριον τῆς εὐλογίας," in *NTS*, vol. 27, 1981, pp. 704–709.

[58] Rom 11:36; 16:27—"To God be the glory for ever and ever"; Gal 1:5; Eph 3:21; Phil 4:20; 1 Tim 1:17—"To the King of the ages, incorruptible, invisible, the only God, be honor and glory for ever and ever"; 2 Tim 4:18; Jude 24—"To the one who is able to preserve you from stumbling and establish you spotless before his glory (his majesty and holiness) with joy"; the whole heavenly court acclaims God (Rev 4:9, 11; 7:12; 19:1). Cf. C. Spicq, *Epîtres Pastorales*, pp. 346ff.; A. Solignac, "Honneur de Dieu," in *Dict.spir.*, vol. 7, 704ff.; R. Deichgräber, *Gotteshymnus und Christushymnus*, Göttingen,

or Christ as king, heavenly priest, *archēgos*, shepherd: "Jesus Christ, to whom be the glory for ever and ever."[59]

In the Fourth Gospel, the term *doxa* is almost always placed in the mouth of Jesus, notably in the sense of honor, praise, repute, and to contrast honors given by humans with those that come from God.[60] But St. John worked out a theological concept of glory, Christianized it, attributing it to Jesus Christ, while setting it in relation to the glory of God. It was actually in order to reveal his *doxa* that God sent his Son here below,[61] and because Jesus never failed to glorify God, God in turn glorifies him (8:50, 54; 17:5). In the "Prologue," which sketches a portrait of the person of Christ and the character of his mission, the evangelist first states that "the Word was God" (verse 1); then he was "the true light that illuminates every man, coming into the world" (verse 9); "he sojourned among us."[62] All of this leads up to "We beheld his glory, glory as of the only Son of his Father."[63] Just as in

---

1967. Christian tomb inscriptions usually formulate their doxologies to the glory of the Trinity, *SB* 6035, 21; 7429, 19; 7430, 18; 7432, 21; 8235, 2; 8728, 23; 8765, 21; cf. *O.Bodl.* 415, 7; 2164, 8. Cf. E. C. E. Owen, "Δόξα and Cognate Words," in *JTS*, 1932, pp. 132–150; M. Steinheimer, *Die Δόξα τοῦ θεοῦ in der römischen Liturgie*, Munich, 1951.

[59] Heb 13:21; 1 Pet 4:11; 2 Pet 3:18; Jude 25: "To the only God our Savior, through Jesus Christ our Lord, be glory, majesty, dominion, and power before all ages and now and for all ages"; Rev 1:6; 5:12–13. *IGLS* 2108: "To the glory of Christ our God"; 2157.

[60] John 5:41, 42; 7:18; 8:50; 12:43.

[61] John 4:34; 5:30; 6:38; 7:16; 12:49; 14:24. St. John's Christ is a "divine, incarnate being who is always in the guise of a revealer," seen by his disciples; his Gospel is a revelation discourse, and this revelation is essentially that of the *doxa* that belongs to God (A. J. Festugière, *Observations stylistiques sur l'Evangile de saint Jean*, Paris, 1974, pp. 9ff.; B. Botte, "La Gloire du Christ dans l'Evangile de saint Jean," in *Les Questions liturgiques et paroissiales*, vol. 12, 1927, pp. 65–76; W. Thüsing, *Die Erhöhung und Verherrlichung Jesu im Johannesevangelium*, Münster, 1960; G. B. Caird, "The Glory of God in the Fourth Gospel," in *NTS*, vol. 15, 1969, pp. 265–277).

[62] Glory is often linked to dwelling (Hebrew *šākan*, σκηνή; Num 35:34; Ps 85:10; Sir 24:8; Ezek 43:7). In addition, in Revelation the temple was filled with smoke because of God's glory and power (15:8); thus it was inaccessible; and the heavenly Jerusalem has within it the glory of God (his presence, his dwelling), and its brilliance is splendid like that of a precious stone (21:11). This divine glory illuminates the city (ἐφώτισεν αὐτήν) and its light is the Lamb (21:23); the nations come to it as pilgrims (vv. 24, 26); cf. the earth illuminated by the glory of the angel (18:1).

[63] Ἐθεασάμεθα τὴν δόξαν αὐτοῦ, δόξαν ὡς μονογενοῦς παρὰ πατρός; John 1:14 (cf. A. Feuillet, *Le Prologue du Quatrième Evangile*, Paris, 1968; T. C. de Kruijf, "The Glory of the Only Son," in *Studies in John Presented to Professor Dr J. N. Sevenster*, Leiden, 1970, pp. 111–123). John 12:41—"Isaiah (6:1–5) saw Christ's glory and spoke concerning him." This can mean only Christ's glory before the Incarnation (1 Cor 10:4), hence as God.

the LXX, the apostles saw[64] the *doxa*, the luminous manifestation of the Word incarnate, that is, his divine stature, for this glory is precisely that of the Father.[65] Jesus possesses it by right in his capacity as only Son, that is, by virtue of his eternal filiation (cf. 2 Pet 1:16–17).

This divine glory or power in Jesus was manifested perceptibly in the miracles[66] and first of all in the one at Cana: "He manifested his glory and his disciples believed in him" (*ephanerōsen tēn doxan autou kai episteusan eis auton hoi mathētai autou*, John 2:11). This *doxa* comprises three elements: (a) a manifestation (*phanerōsis*), a light (*phōs*); (b) the seeing (*theōria*) of this manifestation; (c) the faith and praise (*timē*) of the witnesses.[67] *Doxa* is the outcome for Jesus of the faith of the disciples, who recognize him as Messiah or Son of God.[68] Through the miracle, Jesus accomplished a

---

[64] Θεάομαι, see with the eyes of the body (1:32, 38; 4:36; 6:5; 11:45; 1 John 1:1; 4:12, 14); but this verb can also suggest spiritual perception, for divine realities are not the object of physical sight. Nevertheless, the "Word made flesh" is revealed to the senses, at least in part; his divine power and splendor, veiled by the flesh, are perceptible to those who believe; cf. τοῖς πιστεύουσιν, 1:12.

[65] Ὡς is not comparative, but here means "in the capacity of"; παρὰ πατρός is to be connected to δόξαν, not to μονογενοῦς. This *doxa* of the Son belongs to the historical Christ as well as to the Word, since he is the same Person.

[66] Σημεῖα. These signs lead to faith and are revelatory; they must lead to the Son of God and elicit a decision (John 20:30–31); cf. J. P. Charlier, "La Notion de signe (sèméion) dans le IVe Evangile," in *RSPT,* 1959, pp. 434–448; D. Mollat, "Le Semeion johannique," in *Sacra Pagina*, Paris-Gembloux, 1959, vol. 2, pp. 209–218; W. Nicol, *The Semeia in the Fourth Gospel*, Leiden, 1972; L. Erdozáin, *La función del signo en la fe según el quarto Evangelio*, Rome, 1968; S. S. Smalley, "The Sign in John 21," in *NTS* 20, 1974, pp. 275–288; X. Léon-Dufour, "Autour du semeion johannique," in *Die Kirche des Anfangs*, for H. Schürmann, Freiburg-Basel-Vienna, 1978, pp. 363–378; cf. H. C. Youtie, *Scriptiunculae*, "σημεῖον in the Papyri," in *ZPE*, vol. 6, 1970, pp. 105–116, 245ff.

[67] Cf. John 11:4—"This illness is not unto death, but it is for the glory of God (a brilliant manifestation of his power), so that through it the Son of God (the performer of the miracle and sharer in the divine power) might be glorified"; 11:40—"If you believe, you will see God's glory," the brilliant triumph of the divine omnipotence over death and corruption (verse 39); ὁράω is always used for a spiritual vision of heavenly realities (1:51). Martha's faith would enable her to see in the miracle the power of God made manifest in Christ.

[68] Cf. John 11:14; 17:10. The one glorified is glorified through an intermediary (instrument), in (ἐν), through (διά) another: the man is glorified in the woman (1 Cor 11:7), God in his creatures, the Father in the Son (John 14:13; Heb 1:3) and in Christians (John 15:8). The basis of this glorification appears to consist in this: the object that is manifested/seen/praised is taken for what it is, in its essence, but in its essence as an act of visibility, i.e., insofar as it is light (Eph 5:13–14). In the case of an intermediary, when A is glorified in B it is because B participates in A. In so participating, B manifests A to one who sees and praises, because the presence of a cause in its effect, of a principle in that which proceeds from it, manifests this cause or this principle and

self-revelation; in this sign, the disciples discerned his very nature, his "glory," namely, that he was the Messiah (the Word incarnate).

For St. John, it is especially in his passion that Jesus is glorified, because his death is not only that of a martyr showing his patience, faith, and confidence in God, but is also the manifestation of God present and acting in him to save the world (2 Cor 5:19) and ratifying the accomplishment of his mission: "Father, the hour is come; glorify your Son so that your Son may glorify you"[69] through the redemption of humanity, a common labor manifesting the love of the Father and of the Son. In carrying out the Father's *thelēma*, Jesus glorifies him through his obedience and his love (John 17:4). Jesus wants his disciples to behold this heavenly glory openly, to see (*theōrōsin*, present subjunctive) the brilliance and splendor of his divine nature (John 17:24; Heb 12:14). Christ's last will is that his own may see and hence share his *doxa*, which he possesses in common with the Father; for in this order of reality, it is not possible to behold without in some way becoming a participant (2 Cor 3:18). So Jesus asks that his disciples be made capable of receiving this vision face to face with his divinity, "as he is" (1 John 3:2), which they have not seen here below except through the veil of his flesh (1:14). As St. Augustine says concerning spiritual realities, "to see them is to have them" ("videre est ea habere").

Jesus makes believers sharers in precisely this divine *doxa*, which in the OT was incommunicable: "I have given (*dedōka*) to them the glory that you

---

thus glorifies it; "Omne quod est ab alio, manifestat id a quo est" (St. Thomas Aquinas, *In Jo.* 16.14).

[69] John 17:1 (G. Ferraro, "L'ʻhora' della glorificazione del Figlio dell'uomo," in *Aloisiana*, vol. 10, Rome 1974, pp. 178–201); cf. 13:31—when Judas went out, Jesus said, "Now the Son of Man has been glorified, and God has been glorified in him" (the aorist ἐδοξάσθη is a prophetic anticipation of the future; the Savior's victory over sin, death, and Satan would be completed in heavenly triumph; or better, the hour of death is already the hour of glory, that of the elevation on the cross and the exaltation/manifestation of the *exousia* of Jesus); 13:32—"If God has been glorified in him, God will also glorify him in them, and he will glorify him soon," not only in a brilliant manner, in a sovereign and final state, but in accepting him into his intimacy (ἐν αὐτῷ, the glorification fulfilled in God himself, in his presence or pouring out into the Father's bosom); 17:5—"Now, O Father, glorify me with the glory that I had with you before the world was." This is no longer only the heavenly glory that followed the passion, but the specifically divine glory whereby the Son manifests the Father in an original fashion, the glory that Jesus had before the incarnation (1:1); it is the glory of the Son as the second person of the Trinity (παρὰ σοί), God's personal glory. This points to the identity of nature and the equality of the Father and the Son, who are "consubstantial." A. Laurentin (*Doxa*, Paris, 1972, 2 vols.) has collected nearly 400 texts from Greek, Latin, Syriac, and Armenian authors from the second through the thirteenth centuries that comment on John 17:5.

gave me, so that they may be one as we are one" (John 17:22, both verbs in the perfect). This is a reference to divine filiation (1:2), high nobility. This participation in the divine nature (1 Pet 1:23; 2:2; 2 Pet 1:4) and thus in eternal life, this communion in Christ, imparts to all members the same life that belongs to him; obtained through Christ's passion and his Eucharist, it is the principle that unites all Christians with each other and with the three divine persons. Believers are ushered into the presence of the Holy Trinity, receive its splendor, and share in its glory.

So we understand that Jesus continues in heaven the ministry that he carried out on earth; he "finds himself glorified by his disciples" (John 17:10; *dedoxasmai*, perfect passive), as much through their faith as through their fruitful ministry (verse 8; 1 Thess 2:20; Phil 4:1). Similarly, the Father is glorified by their spiritual fruit (John 15:8), after the fashion of a proud vineyard owner who derives honor from the fruitfulness of his vines. Moreover, in the time of the church, the Paraclete, the Spirit of Truth, will glorify Christ (John 16:14) by making his teachings ever better known, by illuminating them. He never stops re-announcing them, re-proclaiming them (*anangellō*). This manifestation will be simultaneously an interior light and a power of visible radiance. Finally, so that the Father may be glorified in the Son, Jesus promises to do whatever his own ask in his name (14:13). Thus the heavenly Christ continues to act as he did on earth, for the glory of his Father.[70]

Doxazō. — In classical Greek this denominative verb expresses both meanings of *doxa*: "think, hold an opinion, imagine,"[71] and "honor, exalt, praise, celebrate."[72] This latter meaning is the only one in the LXX: human

---

[70] In Revelation, "giving glory to God" means being converted to worship him, recognizing him as the only God, 11:13; 14:7; 16:9; 19:7.

[71] Plato, *Grg.* 461 b: "Is that your real opinion?"; *Tim.* 46 d: "most think that . . ."; *Resp.* 1.327 c: "You do not think amiss"; *Tht.* 189 c; 201 c; Thucydides 1.120.5: "The formation of opinions is carried out in safety"; Philo, *Creation* 19: "one must think that . . ."; *Alleg. Interp.* 3.35; *Sacr. Abel and Cain* 95; *Etern. World* 106; *Post. Cain* 25: the fool "has different opinions at different times on the same topics"; *Unchang. God* 21: "professing such opinions"; *Dreams* 1.91, 185. Josephus, *Ant.* 10.281: "If a person wants to judge otherwise. . . ." The nuance "picture to oneself, imagine, suppose" is common; Plato, *Resp.* 2.363 e: "they pass for wicked"; Aeschylus, *Cho.* 844: "Am I to imagine that what I am told is truthful and real?"; *Ag.* 673: "we think his fate will be the same"; *Suppl.* 60: "he will think that he is hearing the voice of Tereus's wife"; Euripides, *Supp.* 1043: "she must be found here, I suppose"; Philo, *Cherub.* 37: "if you imagine such things with regard to us"; 69; Josephus, *Ant.* 4.49: "godless imaginings"; *Ag. Apion* 1.225: "these altogether impudent and foolish men . . . were used to false ideas concerning the gods."

[72] Diodorus Siculus 16.82: Cephalus of Corinth, "celebrated for his knowledge and judgment"; Thucydides 3.45.6: "each one thought too highly of himself";

honors are offered to the king of Israel (2 Sam 6:20; 10:3; 1 Chr 17:18; 19:3) as well as to a slave (Jdt 12:13), to a father, a mother, a priest, a judge, the rich, etc.[73] But in the song of Moses after the crossing of the Red Sea, Yahweh is said to be clothed in glory (Hebrew *gā'âh*) and is exalted (hiphil of *nāwâh*); he wins fame and demonstrates his magnificence by his might (niphal of '*ādar*). "Who is like him, majestic in holiness?" (Exod 15:1, 2, 6, 11; cf. 1 Macc 3:14). Since God manifests his glory in Israel[74] and glorifies his own,[75] it follows that his people will exalt and praise him.[76] This gratitude is the elect people's *raison d'être*.

In the NT, *doxazō* sometimes retains its secular meaning, "praise, acclaim,"[77] while here and there a shade of OT *doxa* is present.[78] But the

---

Josephus, *Ant.* 1.160: "Abram's name is still celebrated in the region of Damascus"; 4.183: "make yourselves more glorious than the foreign races." This author never gives a religious meaning to the verb δοξάζω; nor does Philo, who only uses it with this meaning in quoting Exod 15:1, 21 (*Husbandry* 82; *Dreams* 2.269). On the other hand, although they are late, the magical papyri; Moulton-Milligan cite *P.Lond.* 121, 502 (third century AD): Κυρία Ἴσις . . . δόξασόν μοι (l. με), ὡς ἐδόξασα τὸ ὄνομα τοῦ υἱοῦ σου Ὥρου; Dittenberger, *Or.* 168, 56: ἐν Ἐλεφαντίνῃ δεδοξασμένου ἔτι ἐξ ἀρχαίων (= *SB* 8883, 56; *C.Ord.Ptol.* 58, 10; second century BC). Cf. *P.Oxy.* 924, 13: ἵνα τὸ ὄνομά σου ᾖ διὰ παντὸς δεδοξασμένον; 1874, 14 (Christian letter of condolence, sixth century): "We glorify God, because he has taken back that which he gave."

[73] Sir 3:4, 6, 10; 7:27, 31; 10:24, 30; 44:7; 46:2, 12; 48:4; 49:16; Prov 13:18; Mal 1:6; 1 Macc 2:18, 64; 5:63; 10:65, 68; 11:42, 51; 14:39. Cf. Esth 3:1—King Xerxes honored Haman (elevating him in dignity); 6:6, 7, 9, 11.

[74] Lev 10:3 (niphal of *kābēd*); Isa 44:23; 49:3; 55:5; 60:7, 13: "I will give splendor to the house of my majesty"; 66:5; Ezek 39:13; 1 Macc 14:15; 2 Macc 3:2.

[75] Cf. Moses' face, shining after he has spoken with God (Exod 34:29, 30, 35). God honors those who fear him (Ps 15:4); "You have glorified us after calling us" (Wis 18:8; 19:22; Sir 3:2; 24:12). Cf. Isa 52:13—"My Servant will be raised and lifted up and exalted on high."

[76] Isa 5:16; 24:23; 25:1; 33:10; 42:10; Ps 22:13—"I will praise you in the midst of the congregation" (Sir 35:7; 43:28, 30); 50:15—"I will save you and you will honor me" (v. 23; Isa 43:23); 86:9, 12; Sir 3:20—"The Lord is glorified by the humble"; Dan 4:31 (Theodotion): "I praised and glorified the one who lives eternally"; verse 34. Cf. Judg 9:9—the oil with which gods and men are honored; 13:17; 1 Sam 2:29–30; 15:30.

[77] Matt 6:2—the hypocrites do alms to be praised by people; Luke 4:15—Jesus is acclaimed for his teaching; 1 Cor 12:26—when one member is honored, the other members rejoice; Heb 5:5—Christ did not arrogate to himself the honor of the high priestly office; Rev 18:7—however exalted and vaunted Babylon is, so much torture and grief shall she receive.

[78] 2 Cor 3:10—in comparison with the preeminent glory of the new covenant, the administration of the old was not attended with glory (its illumination was too partial and transitory); Rom 8:30—"those whom God has justified, he has also glorified" (aorist ἐδόξασεν, certain anticipation; cf. M. J. Lagrange); 11:13—"I do honor to my ministry"; 1 Pet 1:8—loving Christ, believers experience an ineffable and glorified (δεδοξασμένη) glory of the same sort as that experienced by the blessed, for

meaning of "glorifying God" is exactly as in the LXX: like lights that shine and give forth light, the good works of the disciples "glorify the Father who is in heaven" (Matt 5:16). God is exalted and praised in view of the manifestations of his sovereignty and power,[79] especially in the miracles whose brilliance draws adoration and thankfulness.[80] If Christians are commanded to "glorify God in your bodies" (1 Cor 6:20; imperative, *doxasate*), it is because the body is the temple of God; not only must it be preserved pure and holy, it is also the locus of sacred acts, of worship that praises and glorifies God (cf. Rom 12:1). All the faithful are joined together in this thanksgiving liturgy.[81] "In everything let God be glorified (acclaimed) through Jesus Christ" (1 Pet 4:11; a doxology follows).

As for St. John, he uses *doxazō* almost exclusively[82] for Christ's glory and his relationship with the Father,[83] exactly as with *doxa*. If "the Spirit was not yet, because Jesus had not yet been glorified" (7:39, passive of *doxazō*, as at 12:16, 23), this must be understood as a reference to the reintegration into eternal glory after the passion and the resurrection, i.e., in the splendor of his majesty and sovereign omnipotence.

Syndoxazō. — This extremely rare verb,[84] a biblical hapax, is only attested three or four times and in each case in a different meaning. Aristotle understands it to mean common approbation: "No profit will be had from

---

it comes from the divine *agapē* and is infused by the Holy Spirit (Rom 5:5; Gal 5:22; cf. 1 John 4:7).

[79] Matt 9:8 (Mark 2:12; Luke 5:25–26); Matt 15:31; Luke 2:20; Rom 1:21—the heathen did not return to God the glory or thanksgiving that was his due; 1 Pet 2:12; Rev 15:4—"Who, O Lord, could fail to glorify your name?"

[80] Luke 7:16; 13:13; 17:15; 18:43. The feeling of the divine presence (23:47); the gift of grace (Acts 11:18), the fruits of the apostolic ministry (3:13; 4:21; 15:48; 21:20; Rom 15:9; Gal 1:24), works of brotherly love (2 Cor 9:13), faithfulness to Christ in persecutions (1 Pet 4:16) are so many signs of God's action and cause him to be glorified.

[81] Rom 15:6—"so that with one heart and one mouth you may glorify the God and Father of our Lord Jesus Christ"; 2 Thess 3:1—"Pray for us, that the word of the Lord may complete its course and be glorified," i.e., may manifest its power to convert and be received with joy, drawing adoration from those converted. According to B. Rigaux (on this text), this is an instance of hendiadys: " 'run gloriously' means 'successfully, triumphing over opposition.' "

[82] With the exception of John 21:29, where it is said that Peter's death would glorify God, providing a witness to the Christian faith.

[83] John 8:54—"It is my Father who glorifies me," by miracles that demonstrate that Jesus shares in the Father's power (11:4), especially in the passion and the resurrection (12:28; 13:31–32; 14:13); cf. Acts 3:13—"the God of our Fathers glorified his servant Jesus" by all the miracles that manifested his messiahship.

[84] Unknown in Philo, the papyri, the lexicons (Hesychius, Phrynichus, Julius Pollux). J. J. Wettstein gives no references at all.

the most beneficent laws, even if they are sanctioned by the unanimity of the citizens (*syndedoxasmenōn hypo pantōn tōn politeuomenōn*), if these latter . . ." (*Pol.* 5.9.12). In Porphyry, it means "agree, consent to."[85] According to Rom 8:17, it is a matter of being "glorified with," together in heaven: "we will suffer with him (Christ) so that we may be glorified with him,"[86] united to him, eternally in his presence, participants in his honor, his joy, and the riches of his kingdom.

---

[85] Διὸ ἐν ταῖς καθάρσεσι τὸ μὲν μὴ συνδοξάζειν τῷ σώματι, ἀλλὰ μόνην ἐνεργεῖς, ὑφίστησι τὸ φρονεῖν (in Stobaeus, *Flor.* 1.123; vol. 3, p. 91, 2–3).

[86] Aorist passive subjunctive συνδοξασθῶμεν. Peace having returned to Antioch, thanks to the prayers of the church, Ignatius asks the Christians of Smyrna "to send one of your people . . . to celebrate with them (ἵνα συνδοξάσῃ) the calm that has been restored to than thanks to God" (Ign. *Smyrn.* 11.3).

δοῦλος, οἰκέτης, οἰκεῖος, μίσθιος, μισθωτός

doulos, **slave**; *oiketēs*, **slave or domestic servant**; *oikeios*, **family member**; *misthios*, **salaried domestic servant**; *misthōtos*, **day laborer**

→*see also* ὑπηρέτης, μισθός, μισθόομαι, μίσθωμα

It is wrong to translate *doulos* as "servant," so obscuring its precise signification in the language of the first century. In the beginning, before it came to be used for slaves, *doulos* was an adjective meaning "unfree," as opposed to *eleutheros*,[1] and this dichotomy remained basic in the first century: *eite douloi, eite eleutheroi*.[2] Gaius defines: "The principal legal

---

[1] F. Gschnitzer, *Studien zur griechischen Terminologie der Sklaverei*, Wiesbaden, 1964, p. 6. The bibliography on slavery is copious. Apart from the articles in the dictionaries and encyclopedias, cf. J. J. Koopmans, *De servitute antiqua et religione christiana capita selecta*, Groningen, 1920; M. Lambertz, "Zur Etymologie von δοῦλος," *Glotta*, vol. 6, 1, pp. 1–18; W. L. Westermann, *The Slave Systems of Greek and Roman Antiquity*, Philadelphia, 1955; S. Lauffer, *Die Bergwerkssklaven von Laureion*, Wiesbaden, vol. 1–2, 1956–1957; M. I. Finley, *Slavery in Classical Antiquity*, Cambridge, 1960; idem, *The Servile Statuses of Ancient Greece*, in *RIDA*, 1960, pp. 165–189; G. Boulvert, *Les Esclaves et les affranchis impériaux sous le haut-empire romain*, 2 vols., Aix-en-Provence, 1964 (cites more than 3,000 inscriptions); L. Halkin, *Les Esclaves publics chez les Romains*, 2d ed., Rome 1965; C. Spicq, "Affranchissement juridique et liberté de grâce," in *Théologie morale*, vol. 2, pp. 828–849; P. Petit, *La Paix romaine*, Paris, 1967, pp. 278, 374ff.; C. Schneider, *Kulturgeschichte des Hellenismus*, Munich, 1967, vol. 2, pp. 167ff.; P. Chantraine, *Freigelassene und Sklaven im Dienst der römischen Kaiser*, Wiesbaden, 1967; F. Kudlien, *Die Sklaven in der griechischen Medizin der klassischen und hellenistischen Zeit*, Wiesbaden, 1968; G. Ramming, *Die Dienerschaft in der Odyssee*, Erlangen, 1973; G. Boulvert, *Domestique et fonctionnaire sous le haut-empire romain*, Paris, 1974; *Actes du Colloque 1972 sur l'Esclavage* (Centre de Recherches d'Histoire ancienne, III), Paris, 1974.

[2] 1 Cor 12:13; Gal 3:28; 4:22–31; Eph 6:8; Col 3:11; Rev 6:15; 13:16; 19:18 (adding the Jewish distinction, small and great; cf. Heb 8:11). *C.P.Herm.* 18, 5: δοῦλος εἶ ἢ ἐλεύθερος; *IGLS* 51, 46; the opposition δουλεία-ἐλευθερία (Rom 6:18–22; 8:21; 1 Cor

---

doulos, S 1401; *TDNT* 2.261–279; *EDNT* 1.349–352; *NIDNTT* 3.592–597; MM 170; L&N 37.3, 87.76; BDF §162(5); BAGD 205 ǁ *oiketēs*, S 3610; *EDNT* 2.495; MM 440; L&N 46.5; BAGD 557 ǁ *oikeios*, S 3609; *TDNT* 5.134–135; *EDNT* 2.494; *NIDNTT* 2.247, 251; MM 440; L&N 10.11; BAGD 556 ǁ *misthios*, S 3407; *TDNT* 4.695–728; *EDNT* 1.432; *NIDNTT* 3.138–139; MM 413; L&N 57.174; BAGD 523 ǁ *misthōtos*, S 3411; *TDNT* 4.695–728; *EDNT* 1.433; *NIDNTT* 3.138–139; MM 414; L&N 57.174;

δοῦλος, *doulos, etc.*

distinction between persons is that of free and slave. Further, among free men, some are *ingenuus*, other are manumitted. The *ingenii* are those who are born free; the manumitted are those who are freed from servitude by a legal proceeding."[3]

The word *slave* refers above all to a legal status, that of an object of property (Latin *res mancipi*). To be a slave is to be attached to a master (Greek *despotēs*; Matt 13:27; Luke 14:21; 1 Tim 6:1; Titus 2:9) by a link of subjection—you are the slave of that which dominates you (2 Pet 2:19; cf. Rom 9:12). A slave is an article of personal property that one buys, sells, leases, gives, or bequeaths, that one can possess jointly;[4] a slave can serve as a pledge or mortgage;[5] is a *res* or a *sōma* (male or female; Rev 18:13), is grouped with the animals[6] as among those *hypo zygon* (under the yoke, 1 Tim 6:1; cf. Gen 27:40; Lev 26:13; Deut 28:48; etc.); and this nuance of abjection is evoked by the *morphē doulou* of the Son of God Incarnate (Phil 2:7; cf. Matt 20:27). Given that Christians are bought and paid for by the Lord,[7] St. Paul, the former rabbi, i.e., theologian-jurist or jurist-theologian,

---

7:21–22; 9:19; Gal 5:1; 2 Pet 2:16, 19; Philo, *Sacr. Abel and Cain* 26; *Abraham* 251; *Good Man Free* 136, 139; Josephus, *War* 7.336). On the analogy of the relationships slave-Lord, disciple-Master, cf. Matt 6:24; 10:24–25; 18:27; 24:45–50; 25:14–30; Luke 12:37–47; John 13:16; 15:20 (slavery in Israel, cf. R. de Vaux, *Ancient Israel*, vol. 1, pp. 80–90).

[3] Gaius, *Inst.* 1.9–11; cf. *BGU* 1730, 14; R. Taubenschlag, *Law of Greco-Roman Egypt*, pp. 50ff., 73ff.; *Opera Minora*, vol. 1, pp. 11ff., 105ff., 332ff., 601ff.

[4] Matt 6:24; Acts 16:16 (τοῖς κυρίοις); cf. *m. Giṭ.* 4.5 (43a); *b. Ḥag.* 4a. Around AD 100, a slave belongs in common to three brothers (F. Durrbach, *Choix d'Inscriptions de Délos*, Paris, 1921, p. 213); a slave is shared between five owners (*Stud.Pal.* XXII, 43); in the third century a slave belongs in common to a brother and a sister, coming from the father's estate, which remains undivided (*P.Oxy.* 1030, 5–6; cf. 716, 722; *BGU* 1581; *PSI* 1115, 1589; cf. I. Biezunska-Malowist, "Les Esclaves en copropriété dans l'Egypte gréco-romaine," in *Aeg*, 1968, pp. 116–129). But, on the psychological level, Euboulos had already formulated the axiom of Matt 6:24—ἀμφίδουλος = οὐδαμόθεν οὐδείς, the slave of two masters is at any given moment no one's slave (cf. J. M. Edmonds, *Attic Comedy*, vol. 2, p. 120).

[5] A debtor agrees not to dispose of or encumber in any way a slave supplied as ὑπάλλαγμα until the debt is paid (*BGU* 1147; cf. *Jur.Pap.* 45, 28).

[6] An inscription of Baetocaece: "Let slaves, cattle (ἀνδράποδα δὲ καὶ τετράποδα), and the other animals be sold on these sites, free of any tax or exaction or complaint" (*IGLS*, 4028, 37–39 = Dittenberger, *Or.* 262). *Doulos* is the term for the defeated bird in a cockfight: "I am a slave bird. — Were you bested by some cock?" (Aristophanes, *Av.* 70–71; cf. *Vesp.* 1490); *P.Oxy.* 3151, 5, with the note of the editor, M. W. Haslam, who cites Plutarch, *Mor.* 762 *f*; *Pel.* 29.11 (ἀλέκτωρ δοῦλος = defeated cock); *Alc.* 4.3, etc.

[7] 1 Cor 6:20; 7:23; Gal 3:13; 4:5; Rev 5:9; 14:3 (E. Pax, "Der Loskauf: Zur Geschichte eines neutestamentlichen Begriffes," in *Anton*, 1962, pp. 239–278; S. Lyonnet, "L'emploi paulinien de ἐξαγοράζειν au sens de 'redimere' est-il attesté dans

transposes this notion of servitude into the supernatural order, accentuating above all the nuance of the Lord's radical seizure of the believer; the latter, being in submission to the discretionary will of his Master, becomes essentially a dependent individual. Furthermore, while only freemen and freedmen enjoy the right to *tria nomina*, the slave bears only a *cognomen* and is specified by the use of the genitive of his owner's name,[8] to which is often joined a title designating the job that he does for his master (*oikonomos, dispensator, medicus, balnearius*, etc.). So when St. Paul officially presents himself as "apostle, slave of Jesus Christ," he proclaims that he belongs exclusively and totally not to any emperor here below but to the Lord of heaven and earth, who owns all rights to him; more precisely, he defines himself, his existence, his mission, all his activities, in terms of Christ, his master. In fact, if the slave is the object of a real right, the *dominica potestas*,[9] then he himself has no legal status as a person,[10] is entitled to no rights: "servile caput nullum jus habet" (Diogenes Laertius 17.32); it is the owner of the slaves who profits from their activity, who has the right to the fruit of their labor; their *opera* are his, just as the fruit of a tree belongs to the owner of the tree. Thus the master will gather the increase on his goods due to the industry of his *douloi* (Matt 25:14; cf. Luke 19:13), the apostle carrying out his ministry expects no salary (1 Cor 9:16–17), and the *douloi archeioi* recognize that they are only

---

la littérature grecque?" in *Biblica*, 1961, pp. 85–89; W. Elert, "Redemptio ab hostibus," in *TLZ*, 1947, pp. 265–270); Rom 7:14—πεπραμένος ὑπὸ τὴν ἁμαρτίαν; cf. *P.Hib*. 203, 10: διὰ τὸ πεπρακέναι μου σώματα δύο; *P.Abinn*. 64, 12; *P.Princ*. 85, 11: τοῦ πεπραμένου δούλου.

[8] In private households, the master of the slaves is designated by his *nomen*; with imperial slaves by Κύριος or Καῖσαρ, *Dominus*; Θάλαμος καὶ Χρηστὴ κυρίων Καισάρων δοῦλοι (*MAMA*, vol. 1, 29; cf. 28; 31 *a*); Λούκιος δοῦλος οὐέρνας τοῦ Κυρίου (*IGRom*. IV, 529; cf. III, 256); Γενεᾶλις Καίσαρος δοῦλος οἰκονόμος (*CIL* 3, 333); οἰκονόμος τοῦ κουρίου . . . Σεουήρου Περτίνακος (*Chrest.Wilck.*, vol. 2, n. 81, 13–14; cf. 79); *P.Oxy*. 735, 6; *P.Tebt*. 296, 11–12; *BGU* 102, 1; cf. G. Boulvert, *Les Esclaves*, pp. 11ff., *Domestique*, p. 30). Likewise δοῦλος τοῦ ἀρχιερέως (Matt 26:51; John 18:26); ἑκατοντάρχου (Luke 7:2); τοῦ θεοῦ Ἰησοῦ Χριστοῦ (2 Pet 1:1; Jude 1). Doulos is a proper name in a papyrus from the third-fourth century (G. Casanova, "Conto de Affitti," in *Aeg*, 1974, p. 100) and *BGU* 802, col. I, 26; 3, 11, etc., from AD 42.

[9] Cf. L. Westermann, *The Slave Systems of Greek and Roman Antiquity*, pp. 22ff.

[10] The slave has no family, having been deprived of the right to marriage (*conubium*); his conjugal union is only a de facto union (*contubernium*; cf. E. Polay, "Die Sklavenehe in antiken Rom," in *Das Altertum*, 1969, p. 86); even his children "born to the household" belong to his owner. The slave has no country—"our *politeuma* is in heaven" (Phil 3:20)—and is considered as a foreigner: no Roman can be a slave at Rome; in Israel, cf. Lev 25:44–45; Exod 12:44; Lev 22:11; at Alexandria (*P.Hal*. 1, 119); among the Germans, cf. Caesar, *BGall*. 4.15.5; Tacitus, *Germ*. 24.

slaves, whose only purpose in life is to carry out that which they are commanded to do;[11] *doulos eis hypokoēn* (Rom 6:16).

If it is true that "slavery is an institution which has as its essential goal to make available to one person the activities of other persons,"[12] a link attaches the *doulos* to his function; the slave is a "worker"[13] or a living tool (*organon*), and his most important role is carrying out his task to the profit of his master. This nuance can be seen in the declaration of the Virgin Mary—"behold the handmaid of the Lord" (*idou hē doulē Kyriou*)[14]; in the expression "his *douloi* the prophets" (Rev 10:7; 11:18; cf. 1:1; Acts 4:29; 16:17); in the texts in the Synoptics that evoke the deeds of slaves (Matt 13:28; 21:34; 22:3-4; 24:46; Luke 15:22; 17:7), "to each his own work" (*hekastō to ergon autou*, Matt 13:34); in the Pauline meaning of the verb *douleuō*—"complete a task, consecrate oneself to a work, devote oneself to a master" (Acts 20:19; Rom 6:6; 7:6, 25; 12:11; 14:18; 16:18; Gal 5:13; Col 3:24; Titus 3:2); and finally, in the ethic of servitude, urging Christian slaves not only to obey their master (Eph 6:5; Col 3:22; Titus 2:9), but to "serve" willingly (Eph 6:7; 1 Tim 6:2).

Slaves are a very diverse lot, from laborers to philosophers, from farmers to physicians.[15] In the imperial administration, the most capable could advance. The job of *praegustator* led to the post of *tricliniarcha* (*CIL*, XI, 3612, n. 10, 68), that of *vestitor* to *procurator*,[16] etc. Even at the heart of the domestic setting there is a hierarchy: the master sets the faithful and

---

[11] Luke 17:10 (Matt 25:30; cf. C. Spicq, *Théologie morale*, vol. 2, pp. 749ff.; A. M. Ward, "Unprofitable Servants," in *ExpT*, 81, 1970, pp. 200-203); *P.Lond.* 1927, 3; cf. Matt 8:9.

[12] G. Boulvert, *Domestique et fonctionnaire*, p. 111; cf. pp. 180ff.

[13] Cf. Gal 4:19; Phil 2:22; E. Boisacq, *Dictionnaire étymologique*, pp. 198, 1107 (from the Dorian δῶλος, activity). In Luke 17:7-8, the function of the *doulos* is to "serve" his owner.

[14] Luke 1:38; the sense is that of consecration to the work of salvation, conformably to the will of God. But in Hebrew, '*ebed* is not only the designation for a social condition, but also a title of honor for those who dedicate themselves to liturgical service (Luke 2:29; Acts 2:18; 2 Tim 2:24; 1 Pet 2:16; Rev 22:3) and the subjects of a king (ministers, officers, cf. Matt 18:23) who are in his service, preeminently the '*ebed Yahweh* (cf. G. Sass, "Zur Bedeutung von δοῦλος bei Paulus," in *ZNW*, 1941, pp. 24-32). In Iran, vassal kings were described as "slaves (*bandak*) of their sovereign," the king of kings. In conformity with Arsacid protocol, Tiridates says to Nero, "Master, I, descendant of Arsaces, brother of the kings Vologeses and Pacorus, am your slave.... My fate will be what you make of it, for you are my destiny and my fortune" (Dio Cassius 63.5.2).

[15] Cf. the slave-steward, δοῦλος πραγματευτής (J. and L. Robert, "Bulletin épigraphique," in *REG*, 1963, p. 167, n. 227).

[16] Cf. G. Boulvert, *Les Esclaves et les affranchis*, vol. 1, pp. 249, 605; W. L. Westermann, *The Slave Systems of Greek and Roman Antiquity*, p. 79; J. Schmidt, *Vie et mort des esclaves dans la Rome antique*, Paris, 1973, pp. 197-232.

prudent *doulos* over all his household (Matt 24:45, 47; Luke 12:41); this slave directs and oversees the subordinate personnel and can come to occupy the highest posts (Matt 28:23ff.). The ideal is liberation, and it is Christ who liberates slaves from sin,[17] making each son of God an *apeleutheros Kyriou* (1 Cor 7:22; cf. Jas 1:25; 2:12).

An *oiketēs* is most often a slave as well,[18] although in many texts it is not possible to say with certainty (Acts 10:7; P.Lund IV, 13, 4), and this term is sometimes substituted for *doulos* as being less dishonorable, as in this epitaph for an Ethiopian slave: "It is to the decurion Pallas, works superintendent of Antinoe, that the god led me as servant (*oiketēs*) from the land of Ethiopia."[19] From its etymology (*oikia*), *oiketēs* would be a "domestic" in the old sense of the word: one who tends to the house and is a part of the family (*famulus*), according to Philo's definition—"the domestics (*hoi oiketai*) . . . are always with us and share our life; they prepare the bread, the drinks, and the dishes for their masters (*tois despotais*), they serve at table" (*Spec. Laws* 1.127). *Oiketai* are "people in service" (1 Pet 2:18; cf. the collective *oiketeia*, Matt 24:45) including all the servants, male and female, free and slaves born in the household, in the service of the master of the house, from cooks and porters to stewards and tutors, but not directly agricultural or industrial workers.[20]

---

[17] John 8:32; 2 Cor 3:17; Gal 5:1, 13; cf. Rom 6:18, 22; 8:2 (H. Francotte, *Mélanges de droit public grec*, 2d ed., Rome, 1964, pp. 207ff.; I. Biezunska-Malowist, "Les Affranchis dans les papyrus de l'époque ptolémaïque et romaine," in *Proceedings* XI, pp. 433–443; P. Petit, *La Paix romaine*, pp. 285ff.; J. Gaudemet, *Institutions de l'antiquité*, Paris, 1967, pp. 555ff.; H. Rädle, *Untersuchungen zum griechischen Freilassungswesen*, Munich, 1969; gives bibliography). Pauline Christians are freed slaves, cf. C. Spicq, *Théologie morale*, vol. 2, pp. 836ff.

[18] Cf. Luke 16:13 and Matt 6:24; Rom 14:4—ἀλλότριον οἰκέτην; Philo, *Post. Cain* 138: "Wisdom gives to the *oiketēs* the name of *Kyrios*"; *Unchang. God* 64: "Undisciplined and scatterbrained *oiketai* deserve to have a master who scares them"; P.Hercul. 18, 4: οἰκέτης ἐστὶν Πατρίκιος = Patricius is a slave; P.Lille 29, 1–2. In the third century, a Roman citizen in his will freed two of the slaves born in his household (P.Oxy. 2474, 29, οἰκέτας). An inscription of Cyrene forbids functionaries to imprison slaves (οἰκέτας) without obtaining a warrant from the circuit judges (SEG 9, 5, 68); P.Vars. 30, 16. Mena is mentioned constantly (διὰ Μηνᾶ οἰκέτου) as acting on the orders of her owner, τῷ ἰδίῳ δεσπότῃ (P.Oxy. 1896, 7; 1898, 11; 1976, 7; 1983, 5; 2420, 6; 2478, 6. Cf. F. Gschnitzer, *Studien zur griechischen Terminologie der Sklaverei*, pp. 16ff.

[19] SB 8071, 3 = GVI, n. 1167 = E. Bernand, *Inscriptions métriques*, n. 26. An analogous designation for the slaves of Priene taking part in the festivities offered for the people (*I.Priene*, Index, pp. 271, 287).

[20] Josephus, *Ag. Apion* 2.181: "Even the women and the servants would tell you"; *Life* 341: "your valet (ὁ σὸς οἰκέτης) found the deceased in this famous affair"; P.Oslo 111, 176: ἡ μήτηρ τοῦ ἀφήλικος καὶ οἱ οἰκέται αὐτοῦ; *Pap.Lugd.Bat.* XIII, 18, 8: ἐκπλεονεξίαν ἐγενάμην διὰ τοῦ ἀγαθοῦ σου οἰκέτου.

δοῦλος, doulos, etc. 385

The adjective *oikeios* used as a noun, however, only designates members of the same family: parents and close relatives.[21] Eph 2:19 opposes this word to foreigners and aliens; 1 Tim 5:8 places *oikeioi* among *hoi idioi*—"those of the household" are a closer group within "his own."[22] Gal 6:10 uses this term for participants in the same faith;[23] the papyri associate it with brother (*BGU* 1871, 4), son (*SB* 8416, 5), with friends;[24] as the object of *philostorgia* (*P.Ant.* 100, 2; cf. *SB* 7558, 35) and of "recommendation" to influential personages.[25]

Among the domestics attached to a household, some are salaried (*misthios*, Sir 37:11); these workers, hired when there is work and discharged when they are no longer needed, are treated without consideration (Luke 15:17, 19); these are workers for hire[26] whose existence is tantamount to servitude (Job 7:1); but they can no more properly be called servants than can day workers who hire themselves out to some concern (Mark 1:20,

---

[21] The *oikeios* is defined by blood relation in Lev 21:2—"the closest flesh to him"; cf. *P.Lille* 7, 5: "I was conversing with Apollonia, my relative"; *P.Magd.* 13, 2: "Theodotus and Agathon are relatives of the mother of Philippos"; J. and L. Robert, "Bulletin épigraphique," in *REG* 1953, p. 174, n. 194; 1965, p. 147, n. 306.

[22] This equivalence of οἱ οἰκεῖοι-οἱ ἴδιοι (already mentioned by A. Deissmann, *Bible Studies*, p. 123, n. 4) is constant. Cf. *Anth. Pal.* 16, 281; *I.Car.* 13, 14; 189, 8: ἡ Κιδραμηνῶν πόλις ἐξ οἰκείων ἀναλωμάτων. Aurelius Heliodorus had a tomb repaired for his wife Aurelia Flavia and for his freed slaves, καὶ τοῖς οἰκείοις αὐτοῦ ἀπελευθέροις (*MAMA* VI, 18; cf. IV, 19c, 5: ἐξ οἰκίων γὰρ πόνων). An act of adoration by members of a thiasos "remembering their own, μνησθέντες τῶν οἰκείων" (E. Bernand, *Philae*, vol. 2, n. 157, 9; cf. 171, 5). Claudius Tiberius Polycharmos built rooms next to the synagogue "from his own resources" or "at his own expense," ἐκ τῶν οἰκείων χρημάτων (B. Lifshitz, *Synagogues juives*, n. X, 13 = *CII* 694); Josephus, *Ant.* 4.88: his own army, troops belonging to him; cf. L. Robert, *Hellenica*, vol. 3, p. 33.

[23] Gal 6:10—μάλιστα δὲ πρὸς τοὺς οἰκείους τῆς πίστεως (cf. *IGLS* 1517: "Diogenes, relative [οἰκῖος] of Eusebius and Antoninus, brothers [ἀδελφῶν] to whom this sepulcre belongs in common"). Compare ἑταῖρος, see Josephus, *Life* 183; *P.Mil.* 129, 3; cf. *PSI* 1414, 22; 1447, 5; *SB* 6799, 7 (cf. *sodalis*, "companion"; *Res gest. divi Aug.* 4.7; H. J. Mason, *Greek Terms*, p. 50). Members of the same religious community are ἑταῖροι (Matt 26:50; cf. F. Rehkopf, in *ZNW*, 1961, pp. 109–115; W. Eltester, " 'Freund, wozu du gekommen bist,' " in *Freundesgabe O. Cullmann*, Leiden, 1962, pp. 70–91); Philo, *Plant.* 65; *Dreams* 1.111; *Contemp. Life* 13; *Flacc.* 2; *C.Pap.Jud.* III, p. 46.

[24] *SB* 9532, 14; cf. Prov 17:9; Plutarch, *Publ.* 3.1; *IGLS* 281, 4; Dittenberger, *Syl.* 591, 59: περὶ τῆς τῶν ἄλλων φίλων καὶ οἰκείων ἀσφαλείας; *I.Magn.*, 33, 15: φιλίαν καὶ οἰκειότητα, friendship and the close relations that exist between the people of Magnesia and those of Gonnoi.

[25] *P.Oslo* 55, 5; *PSI* 383, 2; *P.Princ.* 101, 8; *P.Oxy.* 1869, 20; cf. Jean-Claude Fraisse, *Philia: La Notion d'amitié dans la philosphie antique*, Paris, 1974, pp. 128–149, 338ff.

[26] Lev 19:13 (Hebrew śākîr); 25:50; Job 14:6; Sir 7:20; 24:22; *P.Cair.Isid.* 74, 8; *P.Mert.* 91, 10; *P.Oxy.* 1886, 9; 1894, 12. It is also the soldier who serves for pay (2 Sam 10:6; Jer 46:21), the mercenary (1 Macc 6:29, μισθωτής).

misthōtos), to tend a flock (John 10:12) or to till a field.[27] The emphasis is always on their compensation, and they accordingly have nothing in common with *douloi*. "The *ergatēs* (worker) *has a right* to his food" (Matt 10:10; 1 Tim 5:18; cf. Jas 5:4).

---

[27] *P.Ant.* 89, 12; *P.Oxf.* 13, 37; *P.Mich.* 174, 13; *P.Oslo* 36, 2, 6; 91, 9, 30; but also employed in a public administration (*C.P.Herm.* 19, 6; *P.Harr.* 79, 19; *Pap.Lugd.Bat.* II, 6, 1), a tax collector (*O.Wilb.* 12, 2; *O.Bodl.* II, 461, 966, 967, 1066, 2224; S. J. de Laet, *Portorium*, Bruges, 1949, pp. 329, 361). Μισθωταί are usually farmers for the state (μίσθωσις, farm, *SB* 6800, 28; the hiring out of beasts of burden, *IGLS* 1998, 11) who farm leased tracts (*BGU* 1047, col. 3) and post surety (ibid. 599), cf. N. Hohlwein, *Termes techniques*, pp. 166ff. S. L. Wallace, *Taxation in Egypt*, Princeton, 1938 (index, p. 505); D. Behrend, *Attische Pachturkunden: Ein Beitrag zur Beschreibung der* μίσθωσις *nach den griechischen Inschriften*, Munich, 1970.

> δύσκολος, σκολιός
>
> dyskolos, difficult, causing frustration or unhappiness, disagreeable; skolios, crooked, difficult, perverse

The adjective *dyskolos* and the adverb *dyskolōs* are used in the NT only with respect to the rich, for whom access to the kingdom of God is difficult (Mark 10:24) or who enter it with difficulty (Matt 19:23; Mark 10:23; Luke 18:24). In contemporary literary texts, "the climbing of a wall is difficult" (Josephus, *War* 6.36); "it is difficult (*dyskolos*) and even impossible (*adynaton*) for the defiant mind to receive an education" (Philo, *Rewards* 49); "It is a difficult and hard cure (*dyskolon kai chalepon*) that philosophy undertakes for garrulousness" (Plutarch, *De garr.* 1). Inscriptions evoke difficult or troubled times (Dittenberger, *Syl.* 409, 33; *Or.* 339, 54) and how difficult, almost impossible, it is to express gratitude to match benefits received: "since it is difficult to give thanks to match such good deeds of his" (*epeidē dyskolon men estin tois tosoutois autou euergetēmasin kat' ison eucharistein, Or.* 458.18). In the phrase *ei dynaton ē dyskolon* ("whether possible or difficult," Josephus, *Ant.* 6.203), the difficult has the sense of the impossible (cf. 2.98; 3.72); but God's help is sought in surmounting the difficulty (5.94; 11.134), and a noble soul succeeds in so doing (2.40).

In the papyri, the word is also used for a difficult approach to a city (*dyskolōs anerchometha eis polein, P.Princ.* 102, 9, from the fourth century), for an action that eventually becomes impossible without help from others ("if you cannot open the box yourself, because it opens with difficulty, give it to the locksmith and he will open it for you," *P.Oxy.* 1294, 10); but it is also used with the connotation of "frustrating, disheartening, causing unhappiness": a son writing to this father and giving him the news of the household tells him, "there is nothing *dyskolos* at your house" (*ouden dyskolon eni epi tēs oikias sou*).[1]

---

[1] *P.Oxy.* 1218, 5: "There is nothing frustrating (unpleasant or catastrophic?) at the house"; *BGU* 1881, 8; *PSI* 566, 2 (and again in *SB* 9220 b): ἐπεὶ οὖν δυσκόλως

---

dyskolos, S 1422; EDNT 1.361; MM 173; L&N 22.32; BAGD 209 ‖ **skolios**, S 4646; TDNT 7.403–408; EDNT 3.255; MM 578; L&N 79.90, 88.268; BAGD 756

With reference to persons, *dyskolos* describes a man who cannot be satisfied, who has a bad character or gloomy disposition:[2] the "awkward customer" (Xenophon, *Cyr.* 2.2.2). Philo evokes the "farmhand, struggling under a grumpy and disagreeable boss—*dyskolos* and *dystropos*—who often makes him do things that he does not want to do, which he carries out only painfully and unwillingly."[3] So *dyskolos* can be compared to *skolios*. St. Peter bids household servants: "be submitted to your master with profound reverence, not only to the good and indulgent (*tois agathois kai epieikesin*), but also to the difficult (*kai tois skoliois*)" (1 Pet 2:18). Since *skolios* literally means "twisting, oblique,"[4] we should take this to mean masters who are bizarre, capricious, even wildly eccentric.[5] *Skolia* is the

---

οὕτως ἡμῖν συναντῶσιν. Plutarch, *Praec. ger. rei publ.* 11.806 b; 19.815 c; *Phoc.* 2.2: "δύσκολον τὴν ἀκοήν, the ears are shocked."

[2] Plutarch associates δύσκολος with βάσκανος (*Fab.* 26.3). The type was described by Menander, *Dysk.*, translated by its first editor as *l'Atrabilaire* ("The bilious man," V. Martin, Coligny-Geneva, 1958) and by J. M. Jacques as *Le Bourru* ("The surly man," Paris, 1963, pp. 33ff.). Cf. C. Préaux, "Réflexions sur la misanthropie au théâtre: A propos du Dyscolos de Ménandre," in *ChrEg*, 1959, pp. 327–341. The *dyskolos* is a person of savage disposition, unsociable and solitary, hated by his peers (34); "I flatly told all the neighbors to stay away from me" (508); intractable and ungracious (184, 242), he is hard to put up with (747, 893); "a very inhumane person, hateful to everyone, ... through his whole long life he has never uttered a friendly word"; always ready to punch someone, he frightens those around him (17, 205, 248, 517). This picture can be filled out with the observations of Josephus concerning the unpleasant speech (*Ant.* 8.278) or conduct (8.7, 217, 220; 11.96) of such and such a person toward his followers, and with citations from Plutarch: "One does not show oneself to be a disagreeable person by listening in silence without concocting praises contrary to the evidence" (*De vit. pud.* 6); "Life is hard" (*Cons. ad Apoll.* 6; cf. 28 [generally considered a spurious work—Tr.]); "Cato earned only a reputation for being disagreeable" (*Caes.* 13.6); "if you are unhappy with events" (ibid. 35.7); when anger persists and creates in the soul a negative disposition called irritability, the end result is "rage, bitterness, sullenness (δυσκολίαν)" (*De cohib. ira* 3; cf. 13: φιλαυτία καὶ δυσκολία; 15: τῶν πικρῶν καὶ δυσκόλων; 16: sullenness of judgment); Cicero had a reputation for being cantankerous and sullen (*Cic.* 41.6).

[3] Philo, *Dreams* 1.7; cf. *Spec. Laws* 1.306. The prefix *dys-* is of course pejorative, like un- or mis- in English; cf. δυσγνωστός (*P.Oxy.* 2457, 19), δυσνόητος (2 Pet 3:16), δυσφημία (2 Cor 6:8).

[4] Σκολιός is used for winding paths, full of detours (Prov 2:15; Isa 40:4; cf. Luke 3:5; J. A. Fitzmyer, "The use of Explicit Old Testament Quotations in Qumran Literature and in the New Testament," in *NTS*, vol. 7, 1961, p. 318); uneven terrain (Isa 42:16); Josephus, *War* 3.118: "pioneers with the job of straightening out the curving road"; a piece of twisted wood (Wis 13:13), the twisting serpent (Isa 27:1; Wis 16:5; Aratus, *Phaen.* 70). Cf. Bertram, on this word in *TDNT*, vol. 1, pp. 403–408.

[5] Cf. Josephus, *Ag. Apion* 1.179: "The name of their town is altogether bizarre (πάνυ σκολιόν ἐστιν); they call it Hierusalame"; cf. Job 4:18 (*tāholâh*; the verse is cited by *1 Clem.* 39.4, which A. Jaubert translates "he notes shortcomings in his angels").

opposite of rectitude (*eutheia*) and could be translated: all speech or action that is wrong and perverse (cf. Prov 23:33), contrary to good sense. This might be the term for what we call impossible bosses—never content, always surly, and also, at that period of history, brutal. "Not a single servant stayed; because, already a hard person by nature, he had become even more difficult (*dyskolōteron*) because of his illness" (Isocrates, *Aeginet.* 19.26).

The ethical connotation is often more pejorative. Beginning with Deut 32:5 (commented on by Philo, *Sobr.* 10–11) and Ps 78:8, *skolios* refers to a generation that is wayward, perverse, rebellious (Acts 2:40; Phil 2:15), from whom spotless children of God separate themselves.[6]

The Wisdom writings stigmatize the crooked man (Job 9:20; Prov 16:28; 22:5; 28:18), his thoughts remove him far from God (Wis 1:3), his speech is only deceit and falsehood (Prov 4:24; cf. 8:8); cf. an ambiguous oracle (Diodorus Siculus 16.91).

[6] In *P.Stras.* 578, 10, the hapax δυσκολωτάτῳ (neuter superlative) describes the breach of trust of the baker Serenos, who kept for himself grain that he had solicited for making bread (July 3, 505).

ἔγγυος

engyos, **guarantor**

Derived from *gyē*, "curve, hollow," *engyē* (with the prefix) means "a pledge put in someone's hand," and its first occurrences refer to divinities. When Poseidon declares to Hephaestus, "He (Ares) will pay all the expenses, I give myself as surety before the immortals" (Homer, *Od.* 8.348), Hephaestus answers, "For a poor payer, a poor guarantee" (8.351). At Aeschylus, *Eum.* 898, the Erinyes ask Athena to guarantee their cult in the city of Athens and to guarantee the people her protection: "This surety (*engyēn*) is valid forever." Theognis 286: "take the gods as guarantors of good faith."[1] "From the idea 'palm or hollow of the hand' there developed an original legal group of meanings that were applied to the idea of a security deposit."[2] A person stands surety for another by committing himself to a creditor to supply a guarantee for the execution of an obligation in the event that the debtor defaults.[3] A guarantor is thus one who is responsible for another person's debt; his responsibility becomes operative when the debtor declares himself insolvent with regard to the terms of the contract.[4]

---

[1] Cf. 2 Macc 10:28—the Jews join battle "having as their pledge of success (ἔγγυον ἔχοντες εὐημερίας) and of victory not only their valiance but their reliance on the Lord," a heavenly guarantee.

[2] P. Chantraine, *Dictionnaire étymologique*, p. 240. Cf. two occurrences of ἐγγύη in the OT. "It is a bold man who strikes hands and stands surety for his neighbor" (Prov 17:18); "Do not be one who strikes hands and stands surety for a debt" (Prov 22:26). In Egyptian law, the act of guaranteeing is called "taking the hand" because to guarantee is an act of support or approval on the part of a third party.

[3] Aristotle, *Pol.* 3.8.1280^{b}11: "Law is a mutual guarantee (ἐγγυητὴς ἀλλήλοις) of rights and obligations"; *Eth. Nic.* 5.5.1131^a; 5.8.1133^{b}12.

[4] *P.Rein.* 44. Cf. T. W. Beasley, *Le Cautionnement dans l'ancien droit grec*, Paris, 1902; A. Segrè, "Note sulla ἐγγύη greco-egizia," in *Aeg*, 1929, pp. 3–24. E. Seidl, *Der Eid im römisch-ägyptischen Provinzialrecht*, Munich, 1933–1935; W. Erdmann, *Die Ehe im alten Griechenland*, Munich, 1934, pp. 225, 231, 267ff.; J. Triantaphyllopoulos, "Sponsor," in *RIDA*, 1961, pp. 373–390; cf. 1957, p. 323; F. de Cenival, *Cautionnements démotiques du*

---

engyos, S 1450; *TDNT* 2.329; *EDNT* 1.371; *NIDNTT* 1.372–373; MM 179; L&N 70.8

The guarantor (a relative, a friend; cf. Josephus, *War* 1.460; Plutarch, *Alc.* 5.4: "He is my friend; I stand surety for him") is normally an honorable person who has a fortune at his disposal;[5] being an honest person, he sees to it that the contract is carried out and justice respected.[6] Thus he is above all a person who may be trusted.[7] Ben Sirach, who places standing surety between almsgiving and hospitality, sees it as a brotherly service: "Do not forget the kindness of your surety, for he has given his life for you. It is the deed of a sinner to waste the goods of his surety" (Sir 29:15-16). So there are swindlers and sharpers, or simply unfavorable turns of events, that make the surety's job extremely burdensome: "Surety (*engyē*) has ruined many upright people; it has tossed them like a wave of the sea."[8]

---

début de l'époque ptolémaïque, Paris, 1973 (publishes the Lille Demotic papyri 34–96): a certain person (addressing the *oikonomos* of the *meris*, and the *basilikogrammateus*) stands surety for the payment of a colleague's debt (to the treasury, the payment of a tax). Some guarantee documents include a *paramonē* clause (legal obligation to remain in residence): a worker undertakes to remain in place at a set location, in his store, etc. This is the "guarantee of presence."

[5] Ps.-Aristotle, *Oec.* 2.22.1350ª19: in Macedonia, it was always the rich who bought anchorage rights "because it was necessary to put up a talent of security to guarantee this total of twenty talents"; Isocrates, *Trapez.* 17.37: "As Stratocles asked me who would pay back his money . . . I presented Pasion to him, who obligated himself to return the principal and interest. Now if he had not had any funds belonging to me on deposit, do you suppose that he would have so readily stood surety for me for such a great sum?"; Demosthenes, *C. Apat.* 33.7: "I had no money available; but I was a client of the banker Heraclides. I convinced him to loan the sum, accepting me as guarantor."

[6] Demosthenes, *C. Apat.* 10: "I made arrangements both that I should be freed from my obligation as surety to the bank and that the foreigner should not be defrauded of what he had advanced to Apatourios through my mediation. I placed guards at the ship, and I notified the bank guarantors (ἐγγυηταὶ τῆς τραπέζης) of the seizure."

[7] Philo and Josephus use not the noun ἔγγυος but ἐγγυητής. Philo uses it for one who guarantees the truth: "I shall propose a sure guarantor for my words, Moses, the holiest person of all" (*Cherub.* 45); "For this affirmation we have as guarantor not just any person at all but a prophet who can be trusted, the recorder of the Psalms" (*Husbandry* 50). According to Josephus, Samuel presents himself as guarantor of the promises of God (*Ant.* 6.21); God himself is guarantor of the future (7.72). On the payment of money as guarantee, cf. 14.81; 15.132.

[8] Sir 29:17; cf. verse 19: "the sinner who casts himself (offers himself precipitously) as surety for the purpose of speculation (seeking gain and profit) casts himself into lawsuits (makes himself prey to legal convictions)." Cf. H. M. Weil, "Gage et cautionnement dans la Bible," in *Archives d'histoire du droit oriental*, 1938, pp. 171–241; R. Sugranyes de Franch, *Etudes sur le droit palestinien à l'époque évangélique*, Fribourg, 1946; R. de Vaux, *Ancient Israel*, vol. 1, pp. 171–173; E. Szlechter, "Le Régime des sûretés personnelles à l'époque de la première dynastie de Babylone," in *RIDA*, 1963, pp. 77–90; J. T. Sanders, "Ben Sira's Ethics of Caution," in *HUCA*, 1979, pp. 73–100.

The fact is that those who stood surety risked ruin and imprisonment, and even reduction to slavery, because they were "subject to the same penalties as those for whom they offered themselves as guarantees."[9] According to Philostratus, they could even incur the death penalty: "Among the Egyptians there was a law whereby one who was defeated after being the victor had to be publicly punished by death; actually, he was held in advance for death, or else he had to provide guarantors for his person (*engyētas tou sōmatos*). Since no one was willing to undertake such a guarantee for Attalus, the *gymnastēs* himself fulfilled the legal condition [by standing surety]" (*Gym.* 24; cf. 8). In any event, we can understand the proverb "Surety calls ruin" (*to engyē para d' atē*) and the comment of Theophrastus: "The untimely person goes seeking surety for himself to an unfortunate soul who has just been condemned as surety for someone else (*engyēs*)" (*Char.* 12.4).

The inscriptions confirm these responsibilities of sureties. In a registry of real estate sales at Tenos, "the aforementioned sellers obligate themselves as a body and each for all."[10] On Crete, "if a son stands surety during the lifetime of his father, he will answer with his person and with all the property that he possesses."[11] In an Athenian rental contract: "Exechias of Aphidna stands surety for the execution of the contract within the set time frame; for their part the administrators of the Kytherians guarantee the lease to Eucrates and his descendants; failing which, they undertake to pay him a thousand drachmas."[12] An inscription at Delos (*I.Delos* 502) mentions an *engyos tou pseudous*, a conditional surety that only protects the authorities against the risk of exorbitant bids.[13] At Pergamum, "clients of

---

[9] Andocides, *Myst.* 1.44. In signing the contract, the *engyos* obligated himself (*BGU* 1915, 7; cf. 1961, 10; *P.Amst.* 41, 54 and 78; *P.Cair.Zen.* 59787, 100; *P.Tebt.* 815, frag. 2, verso II, 36; *P.Thead.* 8, 3; *P.Bour.* 19, 31, 42; *P.Laur.* 27, 15). On the clause of execution on the person, cf. A. B. Schwarz, *Die öffentliche und private Urkunde im römischen Ägypten*, Leipzig, 1920, pp. 298–309). On imprisonment for debt (Dittenberger, *Syl.* XLVI, 66; Matt 18:30; R. Sugranyes de Franch, *Etudes sur le droit palestinien*), slavery (*P.Col.* 480, 25; H. Liebesny, "Ein Erlaß des Königs Ptolemaios II Philadelphos," in *Aeg*, 1936, pp. 257–291). In 237 BC, a *prostagma* of Ptolemy Euergetes I specifies the limits of responsibility of those who guaranteed others' appearance in court (ἐγγύη παραμονῆς), cf. *P.Mich.* 70 = *SB* 7447 = *C.Ord.Ptol.* 27. Arrest for debt was banned in 118 by a series of royal edicts (*P.Tebt.* 5) and in AD 68 by the prefect Tiberius Julius Alexander (Dittenberger, *Syl.* 669, 15–17).

[10] §36. *RIJG*, vol. 1, pp. 82 and 100.

[11] *Leg.Gort.* XI, 57; cf. *RIJG*, vol. 1, p. 382.

[12] *Leg.Gort.*, ter, 5; cf. *RIJG*, p. 242; cf. the rental of a field in the fourth century, p. 202; cf. pp. 34ff., 383.

[13] The opposite of ἔγγυος τῆς ἀληθείας; cf. J. and L. Robert, "Bulletin épigraphique," in *REG*, 1942, p. 345, n. 109. Cf. *REG*, 1973, p. 102, n. 236 at Melitaia in

the dormitory shall supply to the god guarantees for the salaries of the physicians to be paid during the year."[14]

In the papyri, the correspondence of Zeno in the third century BC (*P.Cair.Zen.* 59001, 43; 59173, 32; 59340, col. II, 17–18; *SB* 7450, 23; 7532, 19), and especially in the first century AD, the formula *engyoi allēlōn eis ekteisin* recurs constantly; it means that the guarantors are jointly responsible for the payment or settlement of a debt.[15] Most often it is a matter of a monetary loan, but it can also be land leases, contracts for service (*paramonē*, *P.Mich.* 70, 6; *P.Oxy.* 10, 11, 34; 13, 5), even the hiring of a nurse[16] or the payment of a pension (*P.Enteux.* 25, 12). Sometimes it is recalled "that Pythocles has the right of execution on all the property belonging to Spokes and on the property of his surety for debts to the royal treasury" (*P.Sorb.* 17 *a* 17; cf. 10, 3); or that "this man has no right of execution against me . . . let him be barred from bringing any suit against me or molesting either my own person or the above-named sureties, and let him put up security against the possibility of legal damages" (*P.Rein.* 7, 35; second century BC).

Thessaly, where ἔγγυοι τὰς προξενίας are officials who guarantee *proxenia* and the exercise of the attendant privileges. At Delphi, in the endowment of King Attalus II of Pergamum (second century BC): "Let those who wish to borrow . . . present a field as a surety having a value double that of the money received. Let the borrowers establish guarantees acceptable to the commissions; let the same persons be sureties and guarantors of the pledged properties" (J. Pouilloux, *Choix*, n. XIII, 26); cf. Dittenberger, *Syl.* 736, 72; 958, 5; 993, 7.

[14] Ἐγγύους τῶν ἰατρείων τῷ θεῷ, M. Vörrle, *Die Lex Sacra von der Hallenstraße*, line 29, in C. Habicht, *Altertümer von Pergamon*, VIII, 3: *Die Inschriften des Asklepieions*, Berlin, 1969, p. 169. At Epidaurus, in the accounts for the building of the temple of Asclepius, in the fourth century BC, the names are mentioned of those who put up for tender and of the guarantors (C. Michel, *Recueil*, n. 584, 3, 6, 7, 12). At Thyrrheion, in Acarnania, the sums paid out by guarantors are specified (J. and L. Robert, "Bulletin épigraphique," in *REG*, 1969, n. 322). The same citations in *P.Cair.Zen.* 59366, 24; 59504, 8; *P.Oxy.* 2992, 3; *P.Mich.* 190, 25; *P.Hib.* 30 *d* 16.

[15] *P.Corn.* 6, 20 (AD 17); *P.Mich.* 632, 9 (AD 26); 586, 3 and 21; 633, 34 (= *SB* 10535; AD 30); 635, 4 (AD 71); BGU 2044, 12 (AD 46); *P.Oxy.* 2773, 27 (AD 82); *P.Mert.* 6, 29; 78, 3; 108, 7 (in 69–79); 118, 5; *P.Warr.* 8, 7 and 25; *P.Fam.Tebt.* 2, 9; 4, 9; 6, 10; cf. *P.Phil.* 15, 6; *P.Oslo* 131, 17; *P.Amst.* 41, 95; *P.Alex.* 7, 8–10; *P.Athen.* 23, 8; *P.Col.* III, 54, 23; *PSI* 1249, 33; 1311, 10 and 32; *P.Bon.* 25, 9; *P.Gen.* 24, 8; *P.Oxy.* 905, 17; *P.Stras.* 204, 15; 230, 11; 293, 9; *P.NYU* 22, 4, 11, 17, 24; *P.Ryl.* 586, 19; 587, 19; 600, 13; *P.Cair.Isid.* 97, 7; *SB* 10222, 15; 10248, 19; 19779; 10786, 5; 10804, 16; 11059, 9; 11248, 54 and 95; etc. H. W. Van Soest, *De Civielrechtelijke* ΕΓΓΥΗ (*Garantieovereenkomst*) *in de griekse Papyri uit het Ptolemaeische Tijdvak*, Leiden, 1963, pp. 27 and 67.

[16] *P.Rein.* 103, 2 (AD 26): "Taseus, witnessed by her husband Petseiris as trustee and surety for all the clauses of this contract for payment"; cf. *P.Vars.* 10, col. I, 7 and 20; col. II, 15; col. III, 7 and 27; *P.Mil.* 60, 3; *P.Oxy.* 2134, 8.

Sometimes, on the other hand, the surety protests his good faith and obligates himself for the future.[17]

It follows from these texts that in the first century a guarantee was supplied most frequently (1) by a relative or friend of sufficient means; (2) it was always cited by name;[18] (3) it was for the security of the debtor;[19] (4) the surety is often the deity himself or one of his representatives (Moses, the prophets); (5) it expresses his solidarity—his guarantee is an act of benevolence, a *charis* (Sir 19:15); (6) *engyos* in literary texts sometimes has a metaphorical meaning.

Having thus given a certain density and vitality to the term *engyos*, we can understand its usage in Heb 7:22 (NT hapax), where the author, by assessing the quality of a *diathēkē* as a function of the quality of its mediator,[20] proves the superiority of the priesthood of the order of Melchizedek over the Levitical priesthood by the unchangeableness of its founding: "It is established forever." Hence "Jesus has become the surety of a better covenant" (*kreittonos diathēkēs gegonen engyos Iēsous*). God has sworn (Ps 110:4), his decision is immutable (Heb 6:17); the new covenant will be eternal (Heb 13:20) and the new high priest permanent. Consequently, it is characteristic of Jesus to be an indefectible surety for the future, for he remains the same "yesterday and today and forever" (13:8).

The choice of the word *engyos* as much as the connected mention of the name of "Jesus" signals that the author is evoking the legal meaning of this term: if Jesus is given by God as a pledge of his eternal covenant, then he must take on himself all the obligations of a contract of guarantee and is possibly even called upon to give his life.[21] Is he not in solidarity with the parties to the contract—*ex henos pantes* (2:11ff.) and the *archēgos*

---

[17] *P.Lond.* 2045, 6 (correspondence of Zeno): Païs (imprisoned) promises that once he is released he will be faithful to his obligations as surety: ἐγὼ δέ σοι ἐξελθὼν ἐγγύους σοι καταστήσω (according to Greek law, the guarantee is not paid as long as the accused is kept in prison, cf. F. W. Walbank, "Surety in Alexander's Letter to the Chians," in *Phoenix*, 1962, pp. 178–180), cf. 2054, 16: Techestheus makes a similar undertaking: ἐγγύους δέ σοι καταστήσομεν. In a contract of harvesters in the second century AD, these promise, "We will begin the thirtieth of the current month of Pharmouthi and we will not stop . . . being in solidarity with each other" (*P.Sarap.* 51, 17).

[18] Cf. E. Kretschmer, "Beiträge zur Wortgeographie der altgriechischen Dialekte," in *Glotta*, 1930, pp. 89–90.

[19] Cf. in AD 49–50: δι' ἐγγύου ἐμοῦ = for my security, *P.Oxy.* 38, 6; republished in *Aeg*, 1966, p. 237.

[20] As a Greek legal term, ἔγγυος is very close to μεσίτης (Heb 8:6; 9:15; 12:24).

[21] Sir 29:15. J. Héring (*L'Epître aux Hébreux*, p. 71) notes that the covenant is established by means of a sacrifice, and O. Michel (*Der Brief an die Hebräer*, 10th ed., Göttingen, 1957, p. 174) sees here a reference to Christ's passion.

of salvation (verse 10)? Moreover, Christianity is a hope (7:19; 1 Pet 3:15), and salvation will be completed in its fullness only in the future; so it is to be expected that guarantees and sureties will be supplied for the obtaining of the covenant's goods, the realization of the divine promises. The fact that it is Christ who is this living and permanent guarantee, the surety provided by God, who has literally put our salvation "in his hand" (*en-gys*), means that from here on the salvation of each believer is his responsibility (2:10). He has paid our debts. He has freed us from sin. Through his "precious blood" he has bought and paid for our emancipation.[22] Our confidence, the best guarantee there is, must be absolute.

---

[22] Cf. Christ ὁ ῥυόμενος (1 Thess 1:10; Rom 11:26; 2 Tim 3:11; 4:18; cf. Col 1:13). We might mention the analogy of ransom paid for the freeing of prisoners of war or the sum paid in acts of emancipation of slaves by sale to the deity, such that "no one may lay a hand on him throughout his whole life." Cf. *Fouilles de Delphes*, vol. 3, fasc. 6: *Epigraphie*, Paris, 1939; *MAMA* IV, 279; *SEG* XVIII, 225–229; etc. P. Foucart, *Mémoire sur l'affranchissement des esclaves*, Paris, 1867; C. Cromme, "Personen- und Familiengüterrecht in den delphischen Freilassungsurkunden," in *RIDA*, 1962, pp. 177–238.

ἐγκαινίζω

enkainizō, **to renew, inaugurate**

This verb, which literally means "renew," rarely used in secular Greek,[1] is a good instance of a Septuagintism in the NT, where it is only used twice in a religious sense. In Heb 9:18, the first covenant "was not inaugurated without blood";[2] in Heb 10:20, Christ "has inaugurated for us a new and living way through the veil."[3]

In the LXX, it translated either the piel of the Hebrew verb *ḥādaš* or the verb *ḥānak*. The former, "produce something anew, redo," is often used with the moral or psychological connotation of a new beginning;[4] hence, "to install royalty" (1 Sam 11:14), "renew the altar of Yahweh" (2 Chr 15:8); "restore the house of Yahweh" (2 Chr 24:4, 12). It is in this sense, it would seem, that the shedding of blood gives validity to the old covenant (Exod 24) and inaugurates it (Heb 9:18).

As for the verb *ḥānak*, it describes the earliest education of a child; one sets the child on the right path in life (Prov 22:6); hence, "begin to put into use."[5] The word is used for the dedication of the house of God (1 Kgs 8:63; 2 Chr 7:5), and in 1 Macc, *enkainizō* is used for the restoration of the altar (4:54), the repair of the entrances and chambers of the temple (4:57), and

---

[1] Cf. the references given by Behm, on this word in *TDNT*, vol. 3, pp. 453–454. We might add *UPZ* 185, col. II, 6 from the second century AD, but this reading has been restored.

[2] Cf. M. McNamara, *Targum and Testament*, Shannon, 1972, p. 128.

[3] Cf. A. Pelletier, "Le 'Voile' du Temple de Jérusalem," in *Syria*, 1955, pp. 289–307; idem, "La Tradition synoptique du 'voile déchiré,' " in *RSR*, 1958, pp. 161–180.

[4] Ps 51:4—"Renew a firm spirit within me"; 104:30—the earth (in springtime); Lam 5:21—"renew our days as in former times"; Job 10:17—renewed hostilities; cf. Sir 36:5—prodigies and marvels.

[5] Deut 20:5—"Who is the man who has built a new house and has not yet dedicated it?"

---

enkainizō, S 1457; *TDNT* 3.453–454; *EDNT* 1.377; *NIDNTT* 3.670, 673; MM 215; L&N 13.84; BAGD 215

ἐγκαινίζω, enkainizō 397

the restoration of the sanctuary to its former condition (5:1). Hence, the *Enkainia*, the Feast of Dedication (John 10:22) that Judas Maccabeus ordered celebrated from the 25th of the month of Kislev.[6]

So, since Christ the *prodromos* (Heb 6:20) himself opened a new route of access from earth to heaven and was the first to traverse this "new route,"[7] his own can undertake to follow in his steps. So it can be said that he "inaugurated" it, because he opened it for traffic; but since this route leads to the heavenly sanctuary and is a "sacred way" that cannot be traversed except by believing souls purified from sin, *enkainizō* also signifies that Christ "consecrated" this route, which will be that of the liturgical pilgrimage to the heavenly Jerusalem.[8]

---

[6] 1 Macc 4:59; a reproduction of the ceremony instituted by Solomon, then by Ezra at the time of the completion of the sanctuary (2 Macc 2:9; 2 Esdr 6:16–17; Neh 12:27; cf. S. Krauss, "La Fête de Hanoucca," in *REJ*, 1895, pp. 24–43; 204–219; Str-B, vol. 2, pp. 539ff.). Hanukkah is translated by ἐγκαίνισις, ἐγκαίνωσις (Num 7:88), or ἐγκαινισμός (Num 7:10–11, 84; 2 Chr 7:10); the latter term is used for "the dedication of the statue that King Nebuchadnezzar had prepared" (Dan 3:2–3), and for the song for the dedication of the House (the title of Ps 30).

[7] Cf. Heb 9:12. Trajan "had built the new Via Hadriana, from Berenice to Antinoöpolis, across safe and flat terrain . . . at certain distances along the way he built abundant cisterns, stations, and strongholds" (A. Bernand, *El-Kanaïs*, 1912, n. XII, 8, p. 61); M. Bouttier, *La Condition chrétienne selon saint Paul*, Geneva, 1964, p. 21.

[8] Heb 10:20. Philo, *Prelim. Stud.* 114, applies to the soul that is thankful to God an "*enkainia* that is celebrated with the dignity appropriate to the sacred"; on this liturgy of spiritual worship, cf. A. Jaubert, *La Notion d'alliance dans le Judaïsme*, Paris, 1963, pp. 486–489.

> ἐγκακέω
>
> *enkakeō*, to conduct oneself badly, become weary, lose heart

This verb is peculiar to the Koine, where, moreover, it appears only rarely.[1] It can be transitive or intransitive. Its exact meaning ("conduct oneself badly") derives from its etymology,[2] but the nuance varies according to context. The first usage is in Polybius in the sense of doing ill, being at fault, committing culpable negligence: "The Macedonians neglected to send the prescribed help" (*to pempein tas boētheias . . . enekakēsen*).[3] In the second century AD, Didymarion writes to Paniskos that his brother was not the object of any reproach, and he draws the conclusion that he did not conduct himself amiss (*legō mē enekakēsē*, *P.Petaus* 29, 12). But with respect to Gen 27:46, where Rebekah declares, "I am tired of living (*prosochthizō*) because of these Hittite women," Symmachus uses the verb *enkakeō* to mean "lose heart."[4]

The first NT attestation is in St. Luke's introduction of the parable of the Widow and the Judge, which says that the lesson is "that they should always pray *kai mē enkakein*" (present infinitive);[5] that is, that in the most desperate circumstances, they must continue to ask doggedly and intensely and never desist. But how should the verb be translated?[6] The best equiva-

---

[1] It is unknown in the LXX, the *Letter of Aristeas*, Philo, and Josephus. Only three occurrences can be cited from the papyri, but *BGU* 1043, 3 (a letter from the third century AD) is so mutilated that the meaning of the term cannot be made out: μήτηρ παλλαιὰν ἐνκακήσα[ντος? . . .

[2] Thucydides 2.87.3 probably favored the formation of the word: "given courage, inexperience is no excuse for any sort of misconduct" (ἔν τινι κακοὺς γενέσθαι).

[3] Polybius 4.19.10. Cf. *P.Lond.* V, 1708, 92 (arbitration in the sixth century in a family dispute over a will), mistreat: ἐγκακηθέντα καὶ θλιβέντα τὸν ἐμὸν πατέρα.

[4] Idem, on Num 21:5. Cf. be afraid, be frightened, or be in a painful situation; for example a woman giving birth: μὴ, ὡς αἱ ὠδίνουσαι, ἐγκακῶμεν (*2 Clem.* 2.2).

[5] Luke 18:1. Cf. C. Spicq, "La Parabole de la Veuve obstinée et du juge inique aux décisions impromptues," in *RB*, 1961, pp. 68–90.

[6] M. J. Lagrange, P. Joüon, E. Osty, N. Geldenhuys (*Commentary on the Gospel of Luke*, London, 1950), E. Delebecque (*Evangile de Luc*) translate "ne pas se décourager, sans perdre courage" (not become discouraged, without losing heart); the *Bible de*

---

enkakeō, S 1573;*TDNT* 3.486; *EDNT* 1.377; *NIDNTT* 1.561, 563; MM 215; L&N 25.288; BDF §§123(2), 414(2); BAGD 215

lent is "non segnescere" (Bengel), and better yet "not to slacken."[7] It is not so much a matter of omission as of relaxing one's efforts, losing heart in the midst of difficulties, letting go, interrupting one's perseverance before attaining one's goal; giving up rather than continuing the fight. Hence, on the moral level, the exhortation is to overcome lethargy, boredom, duration, even distress in tribulation; one must not give in to the apparent uselessness of appeals to God and succumb to exhaustion, but on the contrary overcome fatigue and continue without yielding or softening.

The five other occurrences are in St. Paul and have the same basic meaning: "Brothers, do not slacken in doing well" (aorist subjunctive, *mē enkakēsēte*, 2 Thess 3:13), do not tire of doing what is good. "Having undertaken a good work, let us not slacken (present subjunctive, *mē enkakōmen*); at the desired time we shall reap, if we do not give up (*mē eklyomenoi*; cf. Matt 15:32; Heb 12:3, 5)" (Gal 6:9). One's perseverance must not weaken in service to one's neighbor, since the harvest will result from our doggedness; a relaxation of effort would be disastrous. "Since we have this ministry, according to the mercy that was shown to us, we do not lose heart" (*ouk enkakoumen*, present indicative, 2 Cor 4:1, 16), or "we do not weaken," "we do not give in"; this is the refusal of all negligence and all laxness. Finally, Eph 3:13—"Do not give in (*mē enkakein*, present infinitive) to the trials (captivity) that I am enduring for you," which might scandalize (in the full sense of the word) believers who see their apostle reduced to inactivity and impotence, apparently abandoned by God. Are there not grounds for discouragement? Hence the exhortation not to lose heart: hold fast, without letting up; always be ardent.

In conclusion, the verb *enkakeō* in the NT is (*a*) found exclusively in the writings of Luke and Paul; (*b*) both made it a Christian technical term to express the unflagging pursuit of the goal of service to neighbor or of apostolic ministry as well as the "tautness" of the determined heart that does not let up, does not lose courage; (*c*) this absence of letting up is a precept of the new morality, a catechetical rule that each Christian must apply in his or her personal life; (*d*) in almost all of these contexts, notably Luke 18:1; Gal 6:9, this moral obligation is expressed as a function of eschatological *peirasmos* and of the Parousia. During the wait for deliverance, judgment, and glory, letting up and weakening are not permitted.

Jérusalem and W. F. Arndt (*The Gospel According to St. Luke*, St. Louis, 1956): "without growing weary" (cf. *NJB*, "never lose heart"); E. Klostermann (*Das Lukas-Evangelium*, Tübingen, 1929): "nicht nachlassen," (without relaxing, slackening); A. R. C. Leaney (*A Commentary on the Gospel According to St. Luke*, London, 1958): "not giving up"; E. E. Ellis (*The Gospel of Luke*, London, 1966): "not lose heart."

[7] H. J. Schonfield, *The Authentic New Testament*, London, n.d.

> ἐγκαταλείπω
>
> *enkataleipō*, to leave, forsake, abandon

Of the ten occurrences of this verb in the NT, half are in quotations from the OT; consequently, its meaning must be understood in terms of the language of the LXX. First of all, Heb 13:5—"He himself has said, I will never leave you nor forsake you." Exegetes rightly attempt to identify the citation,[1] which is very close to Josh 1:5 and Deut 31:6, 8; 1 Chr 28:20; but neither the tenses nor the moods of the verbs are exactly the same. Moreover, our text is exactly identical to that of Philo (*Conf. Tongues* 166), which cites Josh 1:5. The inevitable conclusion is that either Philo or the author of Hebrews had read a recension of the LXX different from that which we possess.

On the literary level, we may note the fivefold pleonastic repetition of the negation, which reinforces the absoluteness of the thought and thus the certainty of divine help: never, never, never, in any circumstance whatsoever, God will not fail. On the theological level, it is impossible to state too emphatically that this OT assertion, in one form or another, is a statement of the unchangeableness of providence,[2] one of the most essen-

---

[1] P. Katz, "Οὐ μή σε ἀνῶ, οὐδέ οὐ μή σε ἐγκαταλίπω, Hebr. XIII, 5: The Biblical Source of the Quotation," in *Bib*, 1952, pp. 523–525.

[2] Yahwah to Jacob (Gen 28:15), to Joshua (Josh 1:5), to Solomon (1 Kgs 6:13); Moses to Israel (Deut 4:31; 31:6), to Joshua (Deut 31:8); David to Solomon (1 Chr 28:20); the professions of faith of the Psalmists: "You will not forsake those who seek you, O Yahweh" (Ps 9:11; cf. 27:9; 37:25, 28, 33; 38:21); "Elohim, you will not forsake me" (Ps 71:18; 114:14; 119:8); the teaching of the sages: "Wisdom did not forsake the just (Joseph) when he was sold" (Wis 10:13); "Who has persevered in the fear of the Lord and been forsaken?" (Sir 2:10; cf. 51:10, 20); the conclusion of history: "He never withdraws his mercy from us; while punishing them with adversity, he does not abandon his people" (2 Macc 6:16; cf. 1:5; Isa 54:7). Unbelievers think that Yahweh has abandoned them (Isa 49:14; Ezek 8:12; 9:9) and they themselves abandon him (Judg 2:12, 13; 10:6, 10, 13; 1 Sam 8:8; 12:10; 1 Kgs 9:9; 19:10, 14; 2 Kgs 17:16; 21:22;

---

enkataleipō, S 1459; *EDNT* 1.377; MM 179; L&N 13.92, 35.54, 68.36; BAGD 215

tial items of Israel's faith. Citing Ps 16:10, St. Peter therefore affirms concerning the Messiah: "You will not abandon my soul in Hades" (Acts 2:27, 31), because being abandoned by God would mean rejection (1 Kgs 8:57; 2 Chr 15:2; Prov 4:6), a sort of desertion (Job 20:13) of which it is unthinkable that the Son of God could become the victim.

Nevertheless, on the cross, citing Ps 22:2, Jesus cried out: "My God, my God, why have you forsaken me?"[3] This cry expresses the completeness of his dereliction at the point where his resistance was lowest (Ps 38:10; 71:9; *Gos. Pet.* 19: "My strength, my strength, you have forsaken me") and death was imminent; but this is not despair:[4] the Messiah was "abandoned to his enemies" (Ps 22:13ff.) and thus he can say that God "remained far off" (verses 12, 20), but his confidence remains complete (verses 21ff.). His trial is analogous to that of Hezekiah, whom "God abandoned to prove him, to learn all that was in his heart" (2 Chr 32:31); and we know that the love and the power of God are sometimes expressed in the *peirasmos* of the just.[5]

Otherwise, *enkataleipō*, which usually translates the Hebrew *'āzab*, often has, like that Hebrew verb, a toned down meaning: to loosen ties, to give out;[6] in the passive: be left defenseless in the hands of an enemy. Expressing the contrast between the power of God and human weakness by four

---

22:17; 1 Chr 14:12; 2 Chr 7:19, 22; 12:1, 5; 24:18, 20, 24; Ezra 9:10; Sir 51:8; Isa 1:4; 65:11; Jer 1:16; 2:13; 5:7; 16:11; 19:4; Bar 3:12; Dan 11:30). But the God of Israel has promised not to forsake his own (Isa 41:9; 17; 54:7) and "Not Forsaken" will be the title of the elect nation (Isa 61:12; cf. 60:15); and believers confess that it is so (Ezra 9:9; Neh 9:17, 19, 31).

[3] Matt 27:46; Mark 15:34; the text is closer to the Aramaic of the Targum than to the official Greek version (cf. the textual variants, in J. Vosté, *De Passione et Morte Jesu Christi*, Rome-Paris, 1937, p. 303; P. Glaue, "Einiger Stellen, die die Bedeutung des Codex D charakterisieren," in *NovT*, 1958, p. 314, and the commentaries of M. J. Lagrange, on this verse; H. Sahlin, "Zum Verständnis von drei Stellen des Markus-Evangeliums," in *Bib*, 1952, pp. 62–66; J. Gnilka, " 'Mein Gott, mein Gott, warum hast du mich verlassen?' " in *BZ*, 1959, pp. 294–297). For the theological explication, cf. G. Jouassard, *L'Abandon du Christ par son Père durant la passion, d'après la tradition patristique et les docteurs du XIIIᵉ siècle*, Lyon, 1923; L. Matthieu, "L'Abandon du Christ en croix," in *Mélanges de science religieuse*, Lille, 1945, pp. 209–242; C. Journet, "La quatrième Parole du Christ en croix," in *Nova et Vetera*, 1952, pp. 47–69; F. W. Danker, "The Demonic Secret in Mark," in *ZNW*, 1970, pp. 48–69.

[4] Cf. the excellent notations of L. Sabourin, *Rédemption sacrificielle*, Desclée De Brouwer, 1961, pp. 438ff. (provides bibliography).

[5] 1 Cor 10:13; Heb 12:5–11. It is when trial bears fruit—in the form of the salvation of sinners—that its benefits are recognized; cf. in Rom 9:29 the citation of Isa 1:9—"If Yahweh of hosts had not left us a remnant," we would be like Sodom and Gomorrah (Ezra 9:15—"We remain as a remnant").

[6] Cf. "leave" (2 Chr 24:25—"leaving him open to serious illnesses"; Ps 37:8), forsake (Sir 7:30), neglect (1 Kgs 12:8, 13; 2 Chr 10:13; Isa 58:2; Prov 4:2; 27:10).

antitheses, St. Paul writes that he is pursued, harassed, pressed, and hunted down, as it were, by his adversaries (*diōkomenoi, all' ouk enkataleipomenoi*, 2 Cor 4:9). If we take this as a metaphor for a race or a manhunt, we will translate "pursued but not overtaken"; but if the reference is to combat, the apostle is not so roughly handled that he gives in (cf. 1 Macc 1:42), that he is put out of commission and abandoned, and in this sense "eliminated."[7]

If you forsake a person, you also leave a place, notably when fleeing;[8] the place is abandoned, and property is often left in disarray;[9] the two go together.[10] It even happens that people forsake worship.[11] This is what happened with certain "Hebrews" who got into the habit of excusing themselves from the meetings of the community,[12] through egotism (refusing to "give themselves" to the common life), through haughtiness (scorning the society of their brothers, cf. 1 Cor 11:18–22; Jude 19, *apodiorizontes*), or perhaps for fear of advertising their faith in a time of persecution, fearing reprisals by the pagan authorities (Heb 10:32), and thus leaving the community to its risks and dangers without giving it the support of their numbers and their courage.[13]

---

[7] Cf. 1 Cor 9:27; C. Spicq, "L'Image sportive de 2 Cor 4:7–9," in *ETL*, 1937, pp. 209–229.

[8] 2 Kgs 7:7—"They abandoned their tents, their horses, their asses, and the camp just as it was, and they fled for their lives"; 2 Chr 11:14—the Levites leave their towns and their possessions; one leaves land, house, or city (Lev 24:43; 2 Kgs 8:6; Isa 6:12; 17:9; 24:12; 32:14; Jer 4:29; 9:18; 12:7; Ezek 36:4; 1 Macc 1:38; 2:28); ἐγκ. τὴν γεωργίαν (*P.Oxy.* 1124, 5; AD 26), τὴν ἰδίαν (*P.Oxy.* 488, 22; *P.Mert.* 92, 12 = *P.Cair.Isid.* 138; cf. *SB* 10196, 7), τὴν ἐπικειμένην ἀσχολίαν (*P.Tebt.* 26, 16; 114 BC), τὴν παραμονήν (*PSI* 1120, 5; service contract from the first century), τὸ κτῆμα (*P.Cair.Zen.* 59367, 37), a payment (τὴν μίσθωσιν, *P.Ross.Georg.* II, 19, 44; *PSI* 32, 18; *P.Mil.Vogl.* 143, 17).

[9] Ἐνκαταλέλοιπαν τὸν παράδεισον ἔρημον καὶ ἀφύλακτον (*SB* 6002, 13; second century BC; 10476, 4). "Soueris changed her mind, left the olive grove, she is gone" (*P.Ryl.* 128, 11; from AD 30); "his departure left me stranded" (*UPZ* 71, 8).

[10] Καὶ μήτε αὐτὸν καὶ τὴν χραίαν ἐγκαταλίπητε (*P.Tebt.* 712, 13; second century BC); ὁ ἀδελφός σου . . . λῃστῶν ἐπικειμένων ἐνκατελελοίπει με ἀποδημήσας (S. Witkowski, *Epistulae Privatae Graecae* 47, 8). In AD 20–50, a woman brings a complaint against her husband: "After mistreating, insulting, and beating me, he abandoned me, leaving me desolate" (*P.Oxy.* 281, 21). Josephus (*Life* 205) draws a connection between leaving the country and forsaking one's friends.

[11] *Stud.Pal.* XX, 33, 11: ἐνκαταλελοιπέναι τὰς θρησκείας; *Chrestomathie*, vol. 1, 72.9: μηδένα δὲ τῶν ἱερέων ἢ ἱερωμένων ἐνκαταλελοιπέναι τὰς θρησκείας.

[12] Heb 10:25—μὴ ἐγκαταλείποντες τὴν ἐπισυναγωγὴν ἑαυτῶν.

[13] A commentary on Heb 10:25 is provided by John Chrysostom, *Discourse 6*, which is addressed to "those who have forsaken the *synaxis*" (A. Wenger, *Jean Chrysostome: Huit catéchèses baptismales*, Paris, 1957, pp. 215ff.).

It is probably this same refusal to compromise themselves that accounts for the abstention of the Roman Christians from St. Paul's first hearing: "At my first defense, no one came to my aid, but all forsook me" (2 Tim 4:16). This must have been a grave sin, since St. Paul immediately adds, "May they not be held accountable for this!" In fact, the five occurrences of *enkataleipō* in Malachi translate the Hebrew *bāgaḏ*, "betray, deceive, break faith" (2:10–16), and the OT always forbade forsaking a dear or honored person.[14]

No doubt it is with this moral flavor that we should understand 2 Tim 4:10—"Demas has forsaken me, having preferred this present age."[15] My coworker walked out on me!

---

[14] Sir 7:30—"With all your strength love the One who made you and do not forsake his ministers"; cf. Deut 12:19—"See that you do not forsake the Levite"; Tob 4:3—"Honor your mother and do not forsake her"; Prov 27:10—"Do not forsake your friend"; Sir 3:16; 9:10; 29:16—"the ingrate forsakes the one who has saved him." —After the Roman conflagration in AD 64, the terrorized Christians had to go underground. Cowardice was common in such circumstances: Heliodorus refused to help Appian by appearing with him before the emperor (*P.Oxy.* 33, 7ff.). Libon, accused of plotting revolution, "went from house to house imploring the support of those close to him, seeking a voice that would be heard in his favor; everyone refused him on various pretexts, but in reality out of fear" (Tacitus, *Ann.* 2.29); "Who among us dreamed of defending Servius Sulla and Publius and M. Leca and C. Cornelius? Who of those here present offered their assistance? No one. Why? Because in other kinds of trials, people of good will think that they are obligated not to abandon even the guilty, when they are their friends; but with an accusation such as this, one would be guilty not only of thoughtlessness, but even in a sense of participation in the crime, if one defended a person that one suspected of being implicated in a coup against the country" (Cicero, *Sull.* 2.6).

[15] Cf. Josh 22:3—"You have not abandoned your brothers." Elisha to Elijah: "I will not leave you" (2 Kgs 2:2); Joseph did not forsake virtue (Josephus, *Ant.* 2.40).

ἐγκομβόομαι

enkomboomai, to attach, fasten

A denominative verb formed from *kombos*, "knot, buckle," this biblical hapax means "attach, fasten."[1] It evokes the large apron that workers or slaves fitted or fastened to their tunics to protect them.[2] 1 Pet prescribes buttoning or fastening to oneself (the verb in the middle voice) humility in mutual relations.[3] There is possibly a reminiscence of the symbolic gesture of Jesus in girding himself with a towel, in the manner of a slave, to wash the feet of his apostles.[4] We might also remember the sash that slaves wore on their shoulder to distinguish them from freemen.[5] In any event any Christian should present himself before his neighbor in an attitude of modesty, reserve, and self-renunciation,[6] thanks to a humility that is solidly fitted and manifest.

---

[1] Epicharmus, frag. 7: εἰ γε μὲν ὅτι ἐγκεκόμβωται καλῶς (G. Kaibel, *Comicorum Graecorum Fragmenta*, p. 92). Apollodorus of Carystus, frag. 4: τὴν ἐπωμίδα πτύξασα διπλῆν ἄνωθεν ἐνεκομβωσάμην (J. M. Edmonds, *Attic Comedy*, vol. 3 A, p. 186).

[2] Longus 2.33.3: "the child cast off his apron (or his coverall, ἐγκόμβωμα) and, light in his tunic, followed his course"; Julius Pollux, *Onom.* 4.18.119, describes one type: τῇ δὲ τῶν δούλων ἐξωμίδι, καὶ ἱματίδιόν τι πρόσκειται λευκὸν, ὃ ἐγκόμβωμα λέγεται. Cf. the aprons (σιμικίνθια) of St. Paul at Ephesus (Acts 19:12). C. Bigg, *Epistles of St. Peter*, Edinburgh, 1901, pp. 190ff.

[3] For the grammatical construction, cf. J. N. D. Kelly, *A Commentary on the Epistles of Peter and of Jude*, London, 1969, p. 205.

[4] John 13:5 (cf. A. Charrue, *Les Epîtres catholiques*, Paris, 1938, p. 471). This would explain the choice of this exceptional verb, when the NT, following the LXX (Ps 109:18-19) uses ἐνδύω for virtues: to put on = to arm oneself with faith and love (1 Thess 5:8; Col 3:12), with strength (Luke 24:49), to put on a panoply of weapons of light (Rom 13:12; Eph 6:11); here, it is a matter of enveloping oneself and keeping oneself tightly wrapped: "wrap yourselves. . . ."

[5] Cf. E. G. Selwyn, *The First Epistle of St. Peter*, London, 1947, pp. 234, 423.

[6] Rom 12:16. The connection humility-modesty-love of neighbor was recognized by the pagans (cf. S. Rehrl, *Das Problem der Demut in der profan-griechischen Literatur*, Münster, 1961, pp. 136ff.) and the Jews (1QS 5.23-25; cf. M. S. Enslin, *The Ethics of Paul*, New York, 1957, pp. 254-276).

ἔθος, εἰθισμένος (ἐθίζω)

ethos, **custom;** *eithismenos (ethizō)*, **accustomed**

The substantive *ethos* has at least four meanings in the NT.

I. — **Personal custom.** — On Thursday of the last week at Jerusalem, Jesus "went according to his custom (*kata to ethos*) to the Mount of Olives" (Luke 22:39; cf. 21:37; John 18:2). This meaning is common in the papyri: "as is your habit (*hōs ethos esti soi*), use your influence" (*P.Fay.* 125, 5); "it is our custom";[1] "even though it is not his custom" (*P.Brem.* 54, 8). Heb 10:25 denounces "the habit of some (*ethos tisin*)" of forsaking church meetings (*tēn episynagōgēn*); many times they excuse themselves individually. Doing so has become a custom,[2] inspired by various motives, all worthy of censure.[3]

---

[1] *P.Laur.* 1, 5 and 12; cf. *PSI* 1333, 12; *SB* 7993, 12; *P.Mert.* 5, 20; *P.Oxy.* 900, 7: "those who habitually fill this job" (cf. 471, 18, a lawyer speaking: "once accustomed to his shame"—ἅπαξ γὰρ ἐν ἔθει τῆς αἰσχύνης γενόμενον); 3057, 27, a disturbed spirit: οὐχ ἔθος ἐχούσης ἠρεμεῖν; *P.Ryl.* 238, 6: "all that they are accustomed to receive"; *P.Oxy.* 2778, 5: "the custom is to give barley to asses"; Josephus, *Ant.* 6.226: it was David's habit to eat with the king; 7.130, to take a walk at that hour; 8.186, to mount his chariot wearing white; 17.183: the habitual manner of Herod to eat an apple; *T. Abr.* A 2.2—"it was his custom to greet and welcome all." *SB* 10989, 52: πονηρὸς ἔθος; 11240, 15: διδόναι τὴν συνήθειαν πρὸς τὸ παλαιὸν ἔθος (AD 6/7); *P.Laur.* 60, 5: "Day before yesterday, after being well closed, according to habit, our enclosure. . . ."

[2] Absolutely contrary to the exigencies of Jewish piety: "Those who love the assemblies of the saints" (οἱ ἀγαπῶντες συναγωγὰς ὁσίων) were diligent at attending synagogue meetings (*Pss. Sol.* 16.20; cf. 18). At Penticapaea in the Crimea, in AD 80, Chreste, the widow of Drusus, frees her slave Heracles, gives him complete liberty, "with the right to go freely wherever he pleases . . . except regarding the *proseuchē*, which he shall owe devotion and diligence" (*CII*, n. 683; cf. 684). Cf. John Chrysostom, *Discourse 6*, which is addressed "to those who have forsaken the synaxis" (A. Wenger, *Jean Chrusostome: Huit catéchèches baptismales*, Paris, 1957, pp. 215ff.).

[3] Through simple negligence, or deliberately; through egoism, refusing to "give oneself" to the common life and thus depriving oneself of the fruits of brotherly love; through pride or scorn for one's brethren (cf. 1 Cor 11:18–22; Jude 19); probably through fear of advertising their faith in times of persecution, not wanting to compromise themselves, they somehow abandon the community with its risks and

---

ethos, S 1485; *TDNT* 2.372–373; *EDNT* 1.384; *NIDNTT* 2.436–438, 455; *MM* 181; *L&N* 41.25; *BAGD* 218–219 ‖ *eithismenos (ethizō)*, *EDNT* 1.381; *MM* 181; *L&N* 41.26; *BAGD* 218

II. — Social, religious, traditional custom. — Propriety requires conforming to the uses and customs sanctioned by the usage of honest folk in certain circles and practiced since a certain time: that which is done in the usual manner.[4] King Alexander sent to Jonathan "a gold buckle such as it is customary to give to the king's relatives."[5] Banking transactions are carried out *kata to ethos* (according to custom);[6] prices are established in advance by usage (*ex ethous*, P.Grenf. I, 48, 15). Rites and liturgical prescriptions set particular behavior of observant folk. It was custom that fixed the drawing of lots to determine which priest would offer the incense.[7] When Joseph of Arimathea and Nicodemus took Jesus' body, wrapped it with bandages and aromatic herbs, and John 19:40 specifies "as is the burial custom of the Jews" (*kathōs ethos estin tois Ioudaiois entaphiazein*), we must

---

dangers, not bringing it the support of numbers and of courage; these are "slackers" (ἐγκαταλείποντες).

[4] P.Wisc. 34, 10; 35, 3; P.Rein. 115, 17: "as is the custom among you, supply the expenses of the soldier"; SB 9328, 5. Epitaph of Hermocrates, a gymnastic trainer: "I did not fail in this custom" (οὐκ ἀπέληγον ἔθους, E. Bernand, *Inscriptions métriques*, n. XXII, col. III, 3); Epitaph of Ammonia: "Say, as is the custom, 'Greetings, excellent Ammonia'" (ibid. XXXIII, 9); epitaph of Makaria (Christian): "it is the custom of pious folk" (ibid. LX, 4). There are demands contrary to custom (P.Fam.Tebt. 15, 86: παρὰ τὸ αἴθος). Each people has its mores or its peculiar customs: the Persians (Philo, *Spec. Laws* 3.13); the Egyptians (Josephus, *Ant.* 1.66; *Ag. Apion* 1.317; 2.139); the Scythians (*Ag. Apion* 2.269); the Greeks (*Ant.* 12.263). These are "foreign customs" (*Ant.* 9.243, 290; 20.47, 81). "Our own Boeotian customs" (Plutarch, *De gen.* 33). Cf. Porphyry, *Abst.* 1.13.5: "This practice exists even among the barbarians"; 1.30.2: "people are impregnated with passions, mores, and usages that do not belong to their race and for which they have been inclined"; Strabo 1.2.8: "the habits of childhood"; Chariton, *Chaer.* 4.1.12: "Mithridates went to bed according to his custom." Before Antiphon, "people were not yet in the habit of writing up their speeches" (Ps.-Plutarch, *X orat.* 832 d).

[5] 1 Macc 10:89; Josephus, *Ant.* 13.102. On *fibulae*, honorific distinctions, cf. L. Robert, *Noms indigènes*, pp. 445ff.

[6] P.Oxy. 370; P.Ryl. 78, 17; P.Grenf. I, 48, 15; P.Lond. 171 b 19 (vol. 2, p. 176); P.Oxy. 2995, 2: "you have given the gold due according to custom" (δέδωκας τὸν ὀφειλόμενον ἐξ ἔθους); Philo, *Unchang. God* 169.

[7] Luke 1:9—κατὰ τὸ ἔθος τῆς ἱερατείας; cf. m. *Tamid* 3.1; 5.2; m. *Yoma* 2.4; Josephus, *War* 6.299: "The priests, according to their custom (ὥσπερ αὐτοῖς ἔθος), entered the temple at night for the ritual worship"; 6.300: "the feast [of tabernacles] for which it is customary that all pitch tents in honor of God"; cf. 1.25, 153; 2.410; 4.182: τῶν ἱερῶν ἐθῶν; 582; *Ant.* 3.129; Bel (Theodotion) 15: "The priests came during the night according to their custom with their wives and their children"; SB 9340, 7: "It is the custom of the priests of the great god Souchou"; P.Fouad 10, 10; BGU 250, 17; P.Oxy. 1848, 5; PSI 208, 6; P.Oxy. 2797, 3: a list of articles for a sacrifice: κατὰ τὸ ἔθος τῆς θυσίας. The custom is to reserve a part of the victim for the priests (inscription of Nimrud Dagh, in *IGLS* I, 152).

translate "regularly," just as circumcision is carried out *kata to ethos* (*SB* 15, 30; 16, 18; 9027, 21; *BGU* 2216, 28).

III. — Common usage and legal rule. — If there is a "force of habit" (Epictetus 3.12.6: *to ethos ischyron proēgētai;* Philo, *Joseph* 83; *Decalogue* 137; *Abraham* 185; *Spec. Laws* 2.109) and if there is a moral obligation to conform to good usages,[8] a custom that is universal and has long been traditional[9] tends to take on more and more of the force of law. Denouncing the divinization of a dead child, Wis 14:16 notes, "This impious custom (*to asebes ethos*) was kept as a law (*hōs nomos ephylachthē*)." *Ethos* is as obligatory as *nomos*. Moreover, "law did not exist in the time of Homer ... peoples continued to follow unwritten customs."[10] The idea has been defended that

---

[8] Cf. Dionysius of Halicarnassus, *Comp.* 6.25.39: "long practice finally gave habit the force of nature."

[9] *P.Lond.* 2041, 10: "This is the custom everywhere" (ἔθος δ'ἐστιν τοῦτο πανταχοῦ); Josephus, *Ant.* 15.288, τῶν κοινῶν ἐθῶν; *P.Köln* 54, 15, πρὸς τὸ παλαιὸν ἔθος; *I.Bulg.* 1581, 28 and 31; *P.Oxy.* 3178, 7: "At my own risk and according to the previous custom (κατὰ τὸ προάγον ἔθος), I choose to serve the above-mentioned *kōmarchia*"; epitaph of the scribe Ammonius: "We invoke you ... with very pure libations and offerings full of regret, according to the ancient custom of our ancestors" (ἀρχαίοις ὡς πάρος ἐστὶν ἔθος, E. Bernand, *Inscriptions métriques,* n. XLIV, 16); κατὰ ἀρχαῖον ἔθισμα Λινδίων (rule relative to the Sminthian Games at Lindus), in *LSCG,* n. 139, 14–15. Josephus, *War* 4.154: ἔθος ἀρχαῖον. The inhabitants of Andromachis deprived the inhabitants of Theadelphia of water, though they had it by long custom (τοῦ ἀρχαίου ἔθους, *P.Ryl.* 653, 9; cf. 676, 12: τὸ ἐξ ἀρχῆς ἔθος; *P.Gen.* 7, 8; *SB* 9016, col. I, 9; II, 14); κατὰ τὸ ἀεὶ ἔθος τοῦ κάστρου (*SB* 5276 a; 5589). We must not forget that for Aristotle habit "is a perfection that our nature is apt to receive" (*Eth. Nic.* 2.1.1103a23–25), the practice of the moral virtues supposes the convergence of nature, intelligence, and habit; hence the three sources of education: φύσις, ἔθος, διδαχή (M. Defourny, *Aristote: Etude sur la "Politics,"* Paris, 1932, pp. 276ff.). Musonius Rufus wonders which is more efficacious for the acquisition of virtue, theory or practice (ἔθος ἢ λόγος)? He answers: theory teaches what good conduct is, while practice is the habit of those who are accustomed to act according to this theory. Practice is more efficacious, as can be seen with physicians, pilots, and musicians who are learned or experienced (frag. 5, ed. C. E. Lutz, p. 48). "One would never go wrong in affirming that character is simply prolonged habit and that the so-called moral virtues are simple virtues acquired by habit" (Ps.-Plutarch, *De lib. ed.* 2 F-3 A); "One must get to the root of the disease of garrulity by creating a habit" (Plutarch, *De garr.* 19.511 E); "the respect of people who are his superiors in merit and in age and will give the garrulous person the habit of holding his peace" (ibid. 23.514 E); habit is a training: God helps us progress in virtue by making us "accustomed" to the virtuous life (*De prof. in virt.* 3.76 D; cf. *Cons. ux.* 9.611 B); "Habit and exercise already permit reason to extirpate a large part of the innate passions" (*De gen.* 15). Cf. E. Schütrumpf, *Die Bedeutung des Wortes ēthos in der Poetik des Aristoteles* (Zemata 49), 1970.

[10] Josephus, *Ag. Apion* 2.155. This author very often links ἔθη καὶ νόμιμα or νόμοι (*Ant.* 11.217; 14.216; 15.254, 328; 16.172; *War* 2.160, 195; 5.237; *Ag. Apion* 2.164; *Life* 198); cf. *Ant.* 9.243: Ahaz, in violation of the laws of his country, immolates his son

in the papyri *ethos* has no normative value and usually expresses only a state of affairs with no constraining force;[11] but in Egypt it has the value of customary law, because judicial sanction raises usages based on practice alone to the rank of positive law.[12] Philo observed that "a custom introduced different legal principles from city to city, not the same principles for all" (*Husbandry* 43; cf. *Migr. Abr.* 90); "customs are unwritten laws, decrees taken by men of former times and inscribed . . . in the souls of those who belong to the same commonwealth" (*Spec. Laws* 4.149; cf. 150; *To Gaius* 115). Thus in AD 68, the prefect of Egypt, Tiberius Julius Alexander, prescribes that "no one shall be compelled to tax farming or to other leasing of inherited property against the general usage of the provinces" (*para to koinon ethos tōn eparchōn*— *BGU* 1563, 30; cf. *P.Princ.* 119, 52; Philo, *To Gaius* 161). In the second century, the edict of the prefect T. Haterius Nepos commands of priests in charge of temples: "They shall avoid infringing customs, in keeping

---

according to Canaanite custom; 11.212; *War* 5.236, 402: "The Romans . . . out of deference for your law, transgress many of their own customs." *I.Bulg.* 317, 7–8: ἀπογράφεσθαι κατὰ τὸν νόμον τῆς πόλεως καὶ τὸ ἔθος. In a lease related to a garden, προστάγματα, διαγράμματα, and customs are mentioned side by side as bases for the ways of paying charges (*BGU* 1118, 22; cf. *C.Ord.Ptol.* 114). These terms are constantly associated in Philo, *Alleg. Interp.* 3.30, 43; *Sacr. Abel and Cain* 15; *Worse Attacks Better* 87; *Post. Cain* 181; *Unchang. God* 17; *Drunkenness* 193, 195, 198; *Prelim. Stud.* 85; *Change of Names* 104; *Dreams* 2.78; *Joseph* 29, 42, 230; *Moses* 1.324; 2.19; *Spec. Laws* 4.16; *Virtues* 65, 219; *Prelim. Stud.* 106; *Flacc.* 52; *To Gaius* 134, 210, 360.

[11] H. D. Schmitz, "Τὸ ἔθος und verwandte Begriffe in den Papyri," diss. Cologne, 1970 (reviewed and criticized by J. Modrzejewski, "Bibliographie de papyrologie juridique," in *APF,* 1978, pp. 184ff.). Cf. the innumerable examples supplied by R. Taubenschlag, "Customary Law and Custom in the Papyri," in *JJP,* 1946, pp. 41–54; republished, idem, *Opera Minora,* vol. 2, pp. 91–106. At Ephesus, the quaestor T. Flavius Vedius Apellas is the object of an honorific decree, λόγων καὶ ἤθους ἔνεκεν (*I.Ephes.,* vol. 3, n. 678, 19).

[12] J. Modrzejewski, *Loi et coutume dans l'Egypte grecque et romaine,* Paris, 1970; idem, "La Règle de droit dans l'Egypte romaine," in *Proceedings* XII, pp. 317–377, cites *P.Oxy.* 583, a constitution of Domitian, forbidding the requisitioning without imperial authorization of lodging and draught animals and denouncing "an ancient and persistent usage that is in danger of gaining the force of law," παλαιὰ καὶ εἴθονος συνήθεια κατ' ὀλίγον χωροῦσα εἰς νόμον (*IGLS,* 1998, 15–16; cf. N. Lewis, "Domitian's Order on Requisitioned Transport and Lodgings," in *RIDA,* 1968, pp. 135–142). Local laws, surviving from provincial customs (*consuetudo provinciae, mores regionis*) were integrated into imperial law after the edict of Caracalla in 212 (Gaius, *Dig.* 21.2.6). Menander of Laodicea, *Epidict.,* notes that the cities are henceforth governed by "the common laws of the Romans who govern us," but that each nevertheless retains "customs that are peculiar to it and worthy of praise."

with [the dignity of the sanctuaries]."¹³ Contracts stipulate obligations in conformity with custom (*P.Brem.* 36, 17; *P.Oxy.* 1887, 11; *P.Ross.Georg.* III, 32, 10).

It is in this sense of Roman *consuetudo* ("repeated usage of a traditional juridical rule") that we must understand Luke 2:42—when Jesus was twelve years old, his parents went up to Jerusalem "as was the custom for the feast (of Passover)"; *kata to ethos tēs heortēs* is, in fact, a legal obligation (Deut 16:16; cf. Exod 23:17; 34:23; *m. Ḥag.* 1.1), imposed only on men but extended by tradition to pious women. With the same meaning: "We must sacrifice today, in the customary fashion (*kata to ethos*) in this feast called Pascha" (Josephus, *Ant.* 2.313; *P.Oxy.* 1464, 4), again with Joseph and Mary taking the child Jesus to the temple "to accomplish the customary requirements of the law regarding him" (Luke 2:27); *kata to eithismenon*, literally, "according to the custom of the law"¹⁴ is the constant way of referring to a legal requirement.¹⁵

IV. — Roman law. — Festus, in explaining to King Agrippa the matter concerning Paul, says, "It is not the custom of the Romans (*ouk estin ethos Rhōmaiois*) to hand over an accused person before he has, in the presence of his accusers, been given the opportunity to respond to the charge."¹⁶ The formula *kata Rhōmaiois ethos* or *kata ta Rhōmaiōn ethē* is copiously used by Josephus¹⁷ and in the papyri,¹⁸ sometimes in the sense of a habitual way

---

¹³ *P.Fouad* 10, 13; cf. *PSI* 1149, 10: ἱερατικὸς νόμος Σεμνουθι = ancient usage; *P.Lund* IV, 1, 6–7.

¹⁴ On the perfect passive participle εἰθισμένος (from ἐθίζω), a NT hapax, cf. 2 Macc 14:30; Philo, *Moses* 2.205; Josephus, *Ag. Apion* 1.225, the Egyptians, who worshiped animals, "had been accustomed from the beginning to false ideas concerning the gods" (εἰθισμένοι δοξάζειν περὶ θεῶν); *Ant.* 11.16; *P.Oxy.* 1454, 16; *BGU* 1073, 12.

¹⁵ Customary right, distinct from written law, is the ensemble of juridical rules made up by customs. These are collective habitual ways of acting, consented to at the outset by those who observe them, and transmitted from generation to generation. Customs are usages, practices, and behaviors rendered normative by their antiquity or frequency.

¹⁶ Acts 25:16. Cf. J. Dupont, "Aequitas Romana: Notes sur Actes 25, 16," in *RSR*, 1961, pp. 354–385.

¹⁷ Josephus, *War* 3.15, Vespasian "arranges the marching order of his army according to the Roman custom"; 124, a centurion watches over him, according to this same custom; 4.13, 17; *SB* 10894, 2; 11233, 2.

¹⁸ Regarding the enrollment of a child "according to Roman law" (*Pap.Lugd.Bat.* II, 2, 4; 6, 2 and 8; *P.Corn.* 12, 10), the registering of an inheritance (*P.Oxf.* 7, 2), of the sale of a slave (*P.Oxy.* 2777, 11), of a grain deposit (3049 A 5; B 6–7), of a woman acting without *kyrios* to sell a part of her house (2236, 8; cf. 2566, col. I, 4; II, 4) or with a *kyrios* κατὰ τὰ Ῥωμαίων ἔθη in an act of emancipation (published by S. Daris, "Note su liberti," in *SPap*, 1979, p. 7) or again pleading from the *jus liberorum* (*P.Mich.* 627, 4; *P.Wisc.* 58, 6; *P.Stras.* 264, 6; *PSI* 1067, 11; 1258, 4; *BGU* 96, 15; 1662, 4, 20;

of acting, constant usage, sometimes—usually—in the technical sense for Roman law. Here we have a clear reference to normative and obligatory usage: that of Roman trial law. The *juris studiosus* that St. Luke was, according to the Muratorian Canon, would admire the equity of the imperial official, because not to take account of the custom would be to scorn *aequitas*.[19] Given respect for legal form, it was absolutely necessary to have witnesses appear and give the accused the chance to defend himself.[20] In this case, *ethos* refers to an inexorable obligation.

V. — The "customs of Moses" and the "customs of our fathers." — In Acts 6:14; 15:1, the *ethē* that Moses passed on to his people are in view. These became the "customs of the Jews" (Acts 26:23; Josephus, *War* 7.50), venerable because they were ancestral[21] and national (Acts 16:21). Not to "walk according to these customs" (*mēde tois ethesin peripatein*) is apostasy against Moses (Acts 21:21; Philo, *Dreams* 2.123). The constantly used plural could allude to religious or liturgical usages like the Sabbath (Josephus, *Ant.* 12.259; 14.245, 246, 258, 263), circumcision (*BGU* 82, 12: *peritmēthēnai kata to ethos*; Josephus, *Ant.* 1.214), ablutions and purifications (Josephus, *Ant.* 6.235), sacrifices (9.262, 263; 16.35), the distinction between clean and

---

2070, col. I, 6; *P.Aberd.* 180, 2; *Stud.Pal.* XX, 29, 14; *SB* 5832; 7838, 5; 7843, 4; 8940, 3; 9573, 5) or a marriage contract (ἔθει Ῥωμαικῷ καὶ χωρεὶς πάσης ἀντιλογίας καὶ ζητήσεως, *P.Ness.* 18, 20; 20, 21) . . . absolutely everyone claims to conform to the requirements of Roman law.

[19] Cf. Cicero, *Verr.* 3.60: "nihil valuisse aequitatem, nihil consuetudinem."

[20] Some cite the trial of Coriolanus (Dionysius of Halicarnassus 7.26 and 52); Plutarch, *C. Gracch.* 3.7: "It is an ancestral custom among us that when a man accused of a capital crime does not appear, a trumpeter is sent to his gate at dawn and calls him with his instrument, and the judges cannot pronounce sentence before. So prudent and circumspect were our fathers in their judgments"; Appian, *BCiv.* 3.54: "The law stipulates that the accused should hear his accusers in person and not be judged before presenting his defense." Claudius, in AD 46 (*BGU* 611 = R. Cavenaile, *Corpus Papyrorum Latinarum*, Wiesbaden, 1956, n. 236) defends the accused against the tyranny of the accusers; likewise Nero (*BGU* 628; R. Cavenaile, *Corpus Papyrorum Latinarum*, n. 237). Hence *Dig.* 48.17.1: "Et hoc jure utimur, ne absentes damnentur neque enim inaudita causa quemquam damnari aequitatis ratio patitur." In truth, this is elementary justice: "Does our law condemn a man without first hearing him and finding out what he has done?" (John 7:51; cf. Josephus, *Ant.* 16.258).

[21] Acts 28:17—τοῖς ἔθεσι τοῖς πατρῴοις; 2 Macc 11:25, Antiochus decides that the temple should be returned to the Jews and that they may live according to their ancestral customs (τὰ ἐπὶ τῶν προγόνων αὐτῶν ἔθη); 4 Macc 18:5; *I.Magn.* 100 *b* 12, κατὰ τὸ πάτριον ἔθος; Josephus, *War* 2.195, 220; 4.102, 136; 7.424; *Ant.* 5.90: ancestral institutions; 5.101, 113; 8.340. Dittenberger, *Syl.* 764, 11: κατὰ τὸ τῶν προγόνων ἔθος (AD 45); 1073, 20: κατὰ τὸ πάτριον τῶν ἀγώνων ἔθος.

unclean animals, fasting (*Ag. Apion* 2.282), etc.[22] In reality, it is a question of the fundamental institutions that the chosen people received from God, namely, the law and the traditional observances necessary for "being saved" (Acts 15:1), that is, for entering the messianic kingdom. These separate Israel from the whole sinful gentile world (Philo, *Moses* 2.193; *Spec. Laws* 3.29; Josephus, *Ant.* 4.137; 16.42). "The customs of the Jews" (*P.Lond.* 1912, 86) can, to be sure, point to a certain way of life, customs proper, and even certain legal provisions, but in actual usage it is a technical term for Israelite religion as practiced by its faithful,[23] opposed as such to the "customs of the Romans."[24]

---

[22] Cf. Josephus, *War* 2.1, 143, 313, 425; 5.236; 6.300. In Israel, "usages that took on the force of law became traditions . . . God's will, received by Moses, transmitted by him and since him in an unbroken chain" (J. Bonsirven, *Judaïsme palestinien*, vol. 1, p. 267).

[23] H. I. Bell, *Jews and Christians in Egypt*, p. 37; cf. Philo, *To Gaius* 115: "The Jews, having been taught from infancy, so to speak . . . by the holy laws (the Torah) and also by the unwritten traditions (τῶν ἱερῶν νόμων καὶ ἔτι τῶν ἀγράφων ἐθῶν) to believe in one God alone"; *Flacc.* 48, 50, 53; *To Gaius* 201, 210; Josephus, *Life* 198: "If they invoked my knowledge of the laws, they would declare: Neither are we ignorant of the customs of our fathers"; *Ant.* 4.198; 9.95: τὰ πάτρια τῶν Ἑβραίων ἔθη καὶ τὴν τοῦ θεοῦ θρησκείαν; 12.126, 261, 271; 13.397; 14.260; 19.283: "Augustus wanted the subject nations to remain faithful to their own customs (ἐμμένοντας τοῖς ἰδίοις ἔθεσιν) and not be compelled to violate the religion of their fathers (τὴν πάτριον θρησκείαν)"; 19.311; 20.75, 139; *Ag. Apion* 2.10, 179. It is known that Josephus never drafted the περὶ ἐθῶν καὶ αἰτιῶν that he said he would write (*Ant.* 1.25; 4.198; 20.268).

[24] Acts 16:21. Cf. W. C. van Unnik (*Sparsa Collecta*, Leiden, 1973, pp. 374–385), who cites Valerius Maximus: the *praetor peregrinus* Gnaeus Cornelius Hispalus required the Jews who had tried to corrupt Roman mores (*Romanos inficere mores*) by the cult of Jupiter Sabazius to return to their country" (in T. Reinach, *Textes d'auteurs grecs et romains relatifs au Judaïsme*, 2d ed., Hildesheim, 1963, p. 259, n. 141); Dio Cassius 50.25.3, Augustus is angry before his soldiers: "Antony today is abandoning the customs of his country (τὰ πάτρια τοῦ βίου ἤθη) to adopt strange and barbarous customs, respecting neither us, nor the laws, nor the gods of our ancestors"; 67.14: Domitian "reproached (the consul Flavius Clemens, his cousin, who had as his wife Domitilla his relative) for impiety, for which also a number of citizens were condemned who were guilty of embracing the Jewish religion" (ἐς τὰ τῶν Ἰουδαίων ἔθη).

εἰκών

eikōn, **image, representation**

The noun "image" is the first word uttered by God in his relations with humans (Gen 1:26–27). It is not said that it was uttered in Hebrew. If its original meaning is difficult to determine, its doctrinal density in the NT is considerable as well, since it is essential to biblical anthropology, to Christology, to soteriology, and to eschatology.[1]

I. — The first meaning of *eikōn* is "image, effigy, representation," whether a painting, a statue, or a figure stamped on a coin (Herodotus 2.130; Philo, *Change of Names* 93; *Virtues* 4; Matt 22:20). "Before a shining mirror, Glauke arranged her hair, smiling at the lifeless image of her person."[2] For Plato, those who observe an eclipse of the sun must look at

---

[1] To the bibliography supplied by C. Spicq, *Théologie morale*, vol. 2, pp. 689ff., add H. Willms, Εἰκών: *Eine begriffsgeschichtliche Untersuchung zum Platonismus*, Münster, 1935; K. L. Schmidt, "Homo imago Dei im Alten und Neuen Testament," in *Eranos*, vol. 15, 1947; F. W. Eltester, *Eikon im Neuen Testament*, Berlin, 1958; J. J. Stamm, *Die Gottebenbildlichkeit des Menschen im Alten Testament*, Zollikon, 1959; J. Jervell, *Imago Dei: Gen I, 26f im Spätjudentum, in der Gnosis und in den paulinischen Briefen*, Göttingen, 1960; J. Caravidopoulos, "Εἰκὼν θεοῦ" καὶ "κατ᾽ εἰκόνα θεοῦ" παρὰ τῷ ἀποστόλῳ Παύλῳ, Thessalonica, 1964; H. Wildberger, "Das Abbild Gottes, Gen I, 26–30," in *TZ*, 1965, pp. 245–259; O. Loretz, *Die Gottebenbildlichkeit des Menschen*, Munich, 1967; G. von Rad, *Genesis*, pp. 55–59; J. Barr, "The Image of God in the Book of Genesis," in *BJRL*, 1968, pp. 11–26; L. Scheffczyk, *Der Mensch als Bild Gottes*, Darmstadt, 1969; J. Jervell, "Imagines und Imago Dei," in *Joseph-Studien* (dedicated to Otto Michel), Göttingen, 1974, pp. 197–204; P. Lamarche, "Image," in *Dict.spir.*, vol. 7, 2, col. 1401–1406 (gives the bibliography).

[2] Euripides, *Med.* 1161, ἄψυχον εἰκών (in contrast to ἔμψυχον εἰκών). Portrait painted (of the king and his ancestors) in the temples: εἰκὼν γράπτη (E. Bernand, *Fayoum*, n. 152, 15, cf. 114, 19; 135, 9. Cf. Plutarch, *De Is. et Os.* 43: "Apis is the living image of Osiris"; Aristaenetus 1.6; Eusebius, *C. Marc.* 1.4); Euripides, *HF* 1002: "then came an image, as Pallas seemed to appear brandishing her spear"; Gorgias, *Hel.* 17: visual perception stamps the images of seen objects on the intellect (cf. C. Mugler, *Terminologie optique*, p. 120). Plato, *Phlb.* 39 b: "a painter, who comes after the writer, draws in the soul images corresponding to the words"; Aristophanes, *Ran.* 537: "to

---

eikōn, S 1504; *TDNT* 2.381–397; *EDNT* 1.388–391; *NIDNTT* 2.286–288, 292–293; MM 183; L&N 6.96, 58.35, 58.61; BAGD 222

εἰκών, eikōn   413

the image of the star in water or some other substance of this type (*Phd.* 99 d). That is to say, the image is very different from the likeness, because it is very close to the shadow: "What I call image is first of all shadows (*tas skias*), then appearances that show themselves in the water and those that form on surfaces that are dense, attractive, and shiny, and every other representation of this sort" (*Resp.* 6.509 e; 510 e: *skiai kai eikones*; Philo, *Alleg. Interp.* 3.96: "God is the image of his shadow, called shadow"—*skia;* cf. Heb 10:1).

In the LXX, *eikōn*'s dominant nuance is "representation, reproduction, figure" (1 Sam 6:11—"the images [Hebrew *ṣelem*] of the tumors" and is sometimes used in an artistic sense: an artisan casts a statue—Isa 40:19, Hebrew *pesel;* Ezek 16:17; Dan 2:31–35; 3:1–18); the images of the Chaldeans (Hebrew *ṣelem*) drawn on the wall in vermilion (Ezek 23:14); the father "makes an image of his child who was too soon snatched away from him" (Wis 14:15). Sometimes it is synonymous with *eidōlon*.[3] In the Hellenistic period, in literary texts,[4] the papyri,[5] and especially the inscriptions, *eikōn* refers to all kinds of art (*P.Oxy.* 3094, 44), painting or statuary, in the sense of "portrait." Apion, a young recruit in the navy of Misenum in the second century BC: "I gave my little portrait to Euctemon to take to you" (*epempsa soi eikonin mou dia Euktēmonos, BGU* 423, 21).

---

be planted there like a painting γεγραμμένην εἰκόν᾽ ἑστάναι." —In rhetoric, εἰκών = comparison; Aristotle, *Rh.* 3.4.1406ᵇ20ff.; Aristophanes, *Nub.* 559: "borrowing my comparison of eels"; Plato, *Resp.* 6.487 e: δι᾽ εἰκόνων, to speak by comparison, similitude, metaphor; Philo, *Rewards* 45; *Abraham* 153: "vision was created as an image of the soul . . . that has no visible nature"; Wis 17:20—"image of darkness."

[3] Deut 4:16 (Hebrew *semel*); 2 Kgs 11:18—the altars and statues (Hebrew *ṣelem*) of the house of Baal are broken; 2 Chr 33:7; Ezek 7:20; 8:5; Dan 3:1–18 (the gold statue prepared by Nebuchadnezzar); Hos 13:2; Wis 13:13, 16; 14:17; 15:5.

[4] Philostratus, *Gym.* 36: "the statues of the fighter Maron" (τὰς εἰκόνας τοῦ παλαιστοῦ Μάρωνος); Philo, *Drunkenness* 110: "man makes himself images of the sun, of the moon"; 132, 134; Herodian 8.6.2. There is a reproduction or correspondence, cf. Philo, *Moses* 2.51: "The laws are the image that most resembles the constitution of the universe."

[5] Sometimes εἰκών is the signature affixed at the end of a document (*P.Cair.Zen.* 59076, 6; *SB* 6782, 20; 6790, 6; 9223, 9), sometimes the description of a person (*P.Oxy.* 2349, 23: λαβόντες αὐτῶν ὑπογραφὰς καὶ εἰκόνας; from AD 70), a description (*BGU* 1059, 7; *P.Tebt.* 32, 21; *P.Oxy.* 1022, 8; *P.Stras.* 79, 10: ἐν ᾧ αἱ εἰκόνες αὐτῆς δηλοῦνται). *P.Fay.* 36, 23: εἰκόνικα means that the scribe "has drawn up" the act (cf. *P.Oxy.* 34, col. I, 12; *P.Mich.* 631, 18). But at the end of the first century εἰκονίζειν, literally "depict," means "establish the identity of" and "sign up for a role" (*UPZ* 126, 12; discussion of the meaning, ibid., pp. 598ff., and C. Préaux, "La Preuve à l'époque héllenistique," in *La Preuve*, Recueils de la Société J. Bodin, vol. 16, Brussels, 1965, p. 187). The εἰκονιστής is an official in charge of establishing descriptions (*P.Oxy.* XXXIV, col. I, 12).

These portraits and statues are ordered out of filial devotion and usually with a religious intention,[6] as is attested by acts of endowment, as in the third century BC Agasicratis established an endowment at Calauria in the Argolid: one adult victim was to be sacrificed to Poseidon and another to Zeus Soter, and "the altar shall be prepared near the statue of Sophanes, the husband of the testatrix."[7] "We have set up this portrait of Neiloussa, wife of Parthenopaios, our mother, in a sanctuary."[8]

Honorific decrees ordering the erection of statues in honor of famous or important people are numerous. Athens ordered "a bronze statue" of the poet Philippides set up at the theater;[9] the priests of Thebes ordered one for the general Callimachus;[10] Miletus ordered one for Eirenias ("let a golden portrait of him be set up at the place designated by the people");[11] the confederation of the Magnesians ordered one in honor of Demetrias, secretary of the federal council ("let his portrait be set up at a place that he shall choose").[12]

Given that the sovereign, such as Ptolemy Epiphanes, is the "living image of Zeus, son of Helios,"[13] numerous statues are raised (tas tōn

---

[6] Plutarch, De Pyth. or. 16.1: "Croesus commissioned a golden statue of his butcher and dedicated it here."

[7] C. Michel, Recueil, n. 1344, 7: Παρὰ τὰν εἰκόνα τὰν ἀνδρὸς αὐτᾶς Σωφάνεος; cf. line 12: "the executors . . . shall clean the statues placed in the most visible place . . . and they shall crown them" (τὰς δὲ εἰκόνας καθαρὰς ποιεῖν); Dittenberger, Syl. 993, 13–14; 1106, 20: endowment of Diomedon, around 300 BC, καθαιρόντω δὲ καὶ τὰς εἰκόνας τὰς τῶν προγόνων τῶν Διομέδοντος.

[8] E. Bernand, Inscriptions métriques, n. 113. A portrait painted of their mother (εἰκὼν γραπτή) was dedicated by the children "in the precincts of Pallas," for whom this mother was a priestess (epitaph from the Cerameicus, in GVI, n. 1741). Some children of a physician dedicate his statue to Asclepius (IGUR, n. 102; cf. 103, 175, 264 B, 6); SB 6154, 10.

[9] Dittenberger, Syl. 374, 63 (en 287 BC); cf. ibid. 493; II, 3; decree of Histiaeus in honor of the banker Athenodorus of Rhodes. At Balboura, an honorific decree mentions that Stephanus raised a gilded bronze image of his master Caesar Antoninus (C. Naour, "Nouvelles inscriptions de Balboura," in Ancient Society 9, 1978, p. 171).

[10] SB 8334, 27; cf. R. Hutmacher, Ehrendekret. The polemarchs of Thasos grant an image (εἰκών), a crown (στέφανος), and honors (τιμαί) to the two brothers Euphrillus and Micas (I.Thas., 192, 16). Some ἱερῶν εἰκόνων, statues or paintings, were given for the cult of the divinities of Samothrace (IG XII [8], 188, 14; cf. P. M. Fraser, Samothrace: The Inscriptions, New York, 1960, p. 112).

[11] NCIG, n. 7, col. II, 13.

[12] SEG XXIII, 447, 28. According to the honorific decree of Cyprus for the Dionysiac artists, the portrait of Isidorus shall be placed in the temple of Aphrodite at Paphos, SB 10097, 4.

[13] Rosetta Stone: εἰκόνος ζώσης τοῦ Διός, υἱοῦ τοῦ ἡλίου (Dittenberger, Or. 90, 3); epithets and titles of protocol, SB 8232, 6, 8, 19; Plutarch, Them. 27.4: ὡς εἰκόνα

basileōn eikonas).[14] They are placed in the temples where they function in the cult.[15] At Athens, during the imperial period, there was a *zakoros*, a religious official, a kind of sacristan, in charge of the "images" of the emperors (*tōn theiōn eikonōn*), that is, their portraits, or more precisely, busts, which were venerated.[16] At Pergamum, *hymnōdoi* are linked to the celebration of the imperial cult (*hymnōdoi eis eikonas tōn Sebastōn, I.Perg.*, 374). In 193 BC, Antiochus III instituted "high priestesses who shall wear gold crowns that shall have her portrait" for the cult of Laodice;[17] that is, they bear the queen's bust. It is easy to understand the indignation of the Jews when the Roman officials presume to set up imperial statues in the synagogues,[18] as well as the denunciation in Rev 13:14–15 of the super-

---

θεοῦ τὰ πάντα σῴζοντος; cf. L. Delatte, *Les Traités de la royauté d'Ecphante, Diotogène et Sthénidas*, Paris, 1942, p. 180.

[14] T. Ihnken, *Die Inschriften von Magnesie am Sipylos*, Bonn, 1978, pp. 27, 106 = Dittenberger, *Or.* 229, 85; cf. 332, 10 (= *I.Perg.*, 246); 383, 27; τὰν εἰκόνα τοῦ βασιλέως Ἀττάλου (Dittenberger, *Syl.* 672, 63). A letter of Marcus Aurelius and Lucius Verus designates these imperial images (in silver: περὶ τῶν ἀργυρῶν εἰκόνων) as τὰς εἰκόνας τῶν αὐτοκρατόρων (Dittenberger, *Or.* 608, 9, 11).

[15] Rosetta Stone: "Let an image (for King Ptolemy, manifested as a god) be set up in each temple in the most conspicuous place" (Dittenberger, *Or.* 90, 38); cf. *Syl.* 1238, 5, τὰς τούτων τῶν ἀγαλμάτων εἰκόνας. At Mytilene, the image of Augustus is designated as τὴν εἰκόνα τοῦ θεοῦ (*IG*, XII, 17). Confirming the privileges granted by Augustus, a letter from Claudius in AD 289 to the Dionysiac artists allows them to raise statues in his honor, thanks to their own devotion, τὰς μὲν ἰκόνας ὃν τρόπον εὐσεβούμετα μετὰ τῆς πρεπούσης τιμῆς ἀνιστάνειν ἐπιτρέπω (*P.Oxy.* 2476, 2). At Adada in Pisidia, a third-century benefactor offers sacrifices "to the imperial images" (προθύσας δὲ καὶ τῶν θείων εἰκόνων καὶ ἀγῶνα ἐπιτελέσας οἴκοθεν, *CIG* 4379, K, 3).

[16] L. Robert, *Opera Minora Selecta*, II, p. 316, cites *Martyrdom of Pionius*, 4, where the images of the imperial cult are associated with divine statues (cf. H. Musurillo, *Christian Martyrs*, p. 143).

[17] L. Robert, *Hellenica*, vol. 7, Paris, 1949, p. 10, line 25. Cf. two [portraits-statues] of King Ptolemy, offered to the god Soknopaïos (*SEG* VIII, 577, 10); "I dedicated this statue of the great Amon" (*SB* 4243; cf. 7216, 15; 8031, 3; 8349 C 4). Honorific decree for Ptolemy IV Philopator, named εἰκόνος ζώσης τοῦ Διός, υἱοῦ Ἡλίου (*SB* 10039, 5; *Chrest.Wilck.*, n. 109, 11).

[18] Philo, *To Gaius* 134, εἰκόνας Γαίου; 138, 334, 346; Philo, *Flacc.* 41. It is reported that Nahum of Tiberias had "never in his life looked upon an image [of the emperor or a divinity] on a coin" (*b. 'Abod. Zar.* 42c). Bar Kochba had scandalous images and inscriptions stamped; did not a denarius of Augustus bear the legend, "Emperor Tiberius, adorable son of the adorable god"? Because of Yahweh's spiritual nature, the OT forbade material representations of him and prohibited images of him (Exod 20:4; Deut 27:15); cf. Kittel, "εἰκών," in *TDNT*, vol. 2, pp. 383–387. J. B. Frey, "Images (chez les Juifs)," in *DBSup*, vol. 4, col. 199ff. J. Gutmann, "The 'Second Commandment' and the Image in Judaism," in *HUCA*, 1961, pp. 161–174; G. von Rad, *OT Theology*, vol. 1, pp. 212ff.

stition regarding talking statues and images of the emperors: "all those who bow down before the image of the Beast shall be killed."[19]

II. — Because an image not only implies the likeness of a copy to a model, but derives from an earler reality, it implies a relation of dependency and of origination; and possessing to some extent the same "form," it resembles its precursor. It is in this sense that God decides, "Let us make man in our image (Hebrew $d^e mût$) and according to our likeness ($ṣelem$)," (Gen 1:26). He has a nature akin to God's (Gen 9:6), like a son begotten by his father.[20] This is clearly a term of honor:[21] man is crowned with glory (Ps 8:5; Sir 17:3ff.). He is sharply distinguished from the animals created before him; he rules the earth,[22] probably because of his faculties

---

[19] Cf. Rev 14:9–11; 15:2; 16:2; 19:20; 20:4. (J. Schwartz, "Tiberius Claudius Balbillus," in *BIFAO*, vol. 49, 1950, pp. 53ff., identifies this prefect of Egypt and councillor to Nero with the "second Beast.") People worshiped images representing divinities, e.g., Isis (*P.Oxy.* 1380, 13 g: αἱ εἰκόνες καὶ τὰ ζῷα πάντων τῶν θεῶν; Dittenberger, *Or.* 56, 61; decree of Canopus) or Artemis, cf. the endowments of C. Vibius Salutaris, in AD 104, for silver and even gold statuettes of the goddess (H. Wankel, *I.Ephes.*, Bonn, 1979, n. XVII, 24, 29, 149, etc.; XXVIII, 17; XXIX, 18; XXX, 17; XXXI, 18; XXXIII, 20; XXXIV, 18; XXXV, 17). Artabanus: "For us, the noblest law is that which orders that people revere the king and bow down before him as before the image of the god who rules the world" (Plutarch, *Them.* 27.4), because "resemblance signifies an exact replica that is presented as a real image" (Philo, *Creation* 72, 134), hence the explanation: "One who respects an old man and an old woman . . . shows that he is thinking of his father and his mother, seeing in them archetypes all of whose reproductions (τὰς εἰκόνας) he reveres" (*Spec. Laws* 2.237).

[20] Gen 5:3—"Adam brought forth a son in his likeness, in his image" (formula which expresses that man has the power to procreate living things); 1 Cor 15:49—"We have borne the likeness of the one who was from the dust." Cf. Plutarch, *De Is. et Os.* 53: "Every generation is an image in the matter of the impregnating substance, and the creature is produced in the likeness of the being that gave it life."

[21] Exploited in 1 Cor 11:7—"man is the image and glory of God." In distinction from woman, man, created directly by God, reflects the supreme authority of his Creator and does not have to veil his face when he addresses him (cf. C. Spicq, *Dieu et l'homme*, p. 186). Cf. Rabbi Aqiba: "Beloved is man because he was made in the image" (*Pirqe 'Abot* 3.14); a saying attributed to R. Meir, *Pirqe 'Abot* 39.8. A. M. Dubarle, "La Conception de l'homme dans l'Ancien Testament," in *Sacra Pagina*, Paris-Gembloux, 1959, vol. 1, pp. 522–536. Theodoret comments on Gen 1:26—Man is the image of God, not according to the body, nor according to the soul, but only according to authority (κατὰ μόνον τὸν ἀρχικόν, *Quaest. XX in Gen.*) in *PG*, vol. 80, 108.

[22] Gen 1:28 (cf. R. McL. Wilson, "The Early History of the Exegesis of Gen. 1:26," in K. Aland, *SP*, Berlin, 1957, pp. 420–437; H. Wildberger, "Das Abbild Gottes, Gen. I, 26–30," in *TZ*, 1965, pp. 245–259; G. Duncker, "L'immagine de Dio nell'uomo [Gen. I, 26–27]: Una semiglianza fisica?" in *Bib*, 1959, pp. 384–392; H. Gross, "Die Gottebenbildlichkeit des Menschen," in *Festschrift H. Junker*, Trèves, 1961, pp. 89–109); 4 Ezra 8:44; *T. Naph.* 2.5.

of intelligence and volition.[23] In any event, "God made man the image of his own eternity" (Wis 2:23), so that we must at least conclude that "to be the image" means "to participate in the being" (Plato, *Prm.* 132 d) and the life; here, that of the "living God."

III. — There are many degrees in representation. There is only one adequate image of God, his Son.[24] Here *eikōn* means not so much resem-

---

[23] Exegetes disagree (R. de Vaux, *La Genèse*, 2d ed., Paris, 1962, p. 42; G. von Rad, *Genesis*, pp. 55–59; C. Spicq, *Dieu et l'homme*, pp. 179ff.), but Sir 15:14–17; 17:3–8 adds to these privileges free will (διαβούλιον). The Wisdom writers, underlining the demands that result from the divine likeness, lay the foundations of an ethic on man "in the image of God." It follows that the soul of the just continues to live after death, not in Sheol, but in true blessedness, in the vision of God (Wis 3:9; cf. M. J. Lagrange, "Le Livre de la Sagesse: La Doctrine des fins dernières," in *RB*, 1907, pp. 85–104; B. Schutz, *Les Idées eschatologiques du Livre de la Sagesse*, Strasbourg, 1935). Philo often commented on Gen 1:26 (*Heir* 23; *Alleg. Interp.* 3.96; *Spec. Laws* 3.83, 207; *Virtues* 205). He distinguishes "two types of people: man born in the image of God and man formed from the earth . . . the image of God is an archetype" (*Alleg. Interp.* 2.4); "the man in the image is not earthly but heavenly" (*Alleg. Interp.* 1.90, 92, 94); "the heavenly man, inasmuch as he is born in the image of God, has no share in a corruptible substance . . . the earthly man is brought forth from a sparse material" (*Alleg. Interp.* 1.31; *Heir* 57); "intelligence, born in the image of God and according to the idea, shared in the breath (πνεῦμα)" (*Alleg. Interp.* 1.42, 53). The resemblance has nothing to do with physical traits; "God does not have a human figure and a human body does not have God's form. The image here applies to the intellect, the guide of the soul" (*Creation* 69). The imprint or mark of the divine power—"Moses calls it by its proper name, 'image,' thereby showing that God is the archetype of rational nature, whereas man is only a copy and a replica" (μίμημα καὶ ἀπεικόνισμα, *Worse Attacks Better* 83, 86–87; *Change of Names* 223); "the one who receives the imprint reproduces perforce the image of the one who gives it out" (*Plant.* 19). God says to Hagar: "I am the God whose image you beheld earlier (the angel) and thought that it was I, and that you raised on a pillar" (*Dreams* 1.241). The most holy Logos is the image of God (*Conf. Tongues* 97, 146–147; *Spec. Laws* 1.81; *Flight* 101), because "an incorporeal being differs in no wise from the divine image" (*Conf. Tongues* 62) and "God has placed on the whole of the universe the seal of his image and idea: his own Word" (*Dreams* 2.45). Cf. J. Giblet, "L'Homme image de Dieu dans les commentaires littéraires de Philon d'Alexandrie," in *Studia Hellenistica*, vol. 5, Louvain-Leiden, 1948, pp. 93–118. According to Wis 7:26: σοφία εἰκὼν τῆς ἀγαθότητος αὐτοῦ (cf. C. Larcher, *Etudes sur le Livre de la Sagesse*, Paris, 1969, pp. 383ff.). Diogenes of Sinope said τοὺς ἀγαθοὺς ἄνδρας θεῶν εἰκόνας εἶναι, according to Diogenes Laertius 6.51. Corinth raised a statue to Regilla, εἰκόνα σωφροσύνης (*I.Cor.* VIII, 1; n. 86, 2; cf. 88, 4); Philo, *To Gaius* 210: "They bear in their soul, as people do with divine statues, the image of the commandments"; *Husbandry* 109. Under a seven-branched candelabrum, a funerary inscription says, εἰκὼν ἐνορῶντος θεοῦ, "image of God who sees" (*CII*, n. 696).

[24] Εἰκὼν τοῦ θεοῦ ἀοράτου, Col 1:15; cf. S. Bartina, " 'Cristo, imagen del Dios invisible,' según los papyros," in *SPap*, 1963, pp. 13–33; A. Feuillet, *Le Christ sagesse de Dieu*, Paris, 1966, pp. 163–273. In a metaphorical sense, the virtues are the image of

blance as derivation and participation; it is not so much the likeness of a copy to its model, but the revelation and, as it were, emanation of the prototype.[25] The image of something is its expression, the thing itself expressed. Here, by the incarnation, Christ manifests the Father (cf. Col 2:9—"in him dwells bodily [by the incarnation] all the fullness of the godhead"). In and by his image, God becomes visible. The emphasis falls simultaneously on the equality, if not identity (*consubstantial* will be the word) of the *eikōn* with the original, and on the authentic representativeness of Jesus, for the one who was *en morphē theou* (in the form of God) and *einai isa theō* (equal with God, Phil 2:6) could say "the one who has seen me has seen the Father."[26]

IV. — In the NT, a new anthropology is superimposed on the old; the elect are predestined to be conformed to the image of the Son of God,[27] associated with his glory (cf. Phil 3:21). On the model of the first creation, the "image" of the baptized is "conformed" to the prototype of the *archēgos*,

---

God (Philo, *Virtues* 205; cf. *Rewards* 114; *Good Man Free* 62); "the beauty of the senses is the image of intelligible beauty" (*Plant.* 50 and 44); the sun is the image and imitation of Wisdom (*Migr. Abr.* 40; *Heir* 112; cf. K. Prümm, "Reflexiones theologicae et historicae ad usum Paulinum termini εἰκών," in *VD*, 1962, pp. 232–257); likewise for Plato, *Resp.* 509 a: Helios, image of the ἰδέα τοῦ ἀγαθοῦ; Hermes: the sun is the image of the heavenly creator god (in Stobaeus, *Ecl.* 1.293.21); "Man was made in the image of the world" (*Corp. Herm.* 8.5; cf. 1.31; 5.2); "Eternity is the image of God, the world is the image of eternity, the sun the image of the world, man the image of the sun" (ibid. 11.15; cf. 12.15). Plutarch, *De E ap. Delph.* 21: "Apollo and the sun are but one"; one contemplates its essence in honoring its image.

[25] Cf. Plato, *Tim.* 92 c: "The world . . . the sensible world formed in the likeness of the intelligible god, very great, very good" (εἰκὼν τοῦ νοητοῦ θεὸς αἰσθητός).

[26] John 14:9; 12:45. The εἰκών is thus not identical to simple resemblance, ὁμοίωσις (cf. R. C. Trench, *Synonyms*, p. 51). Cf. Rabbi Baanah, visiting the tombs of the patriarchs. After seeing Abraham's, he wants to see Adam's; then he hears a voice: "You have seen the resemblance of my image, but my image itself you cannot see" (*b. B. Bat.* 58a). In an analogous sense, the law had "a shadow of good things to come, not the very image (essence) of the realities" (Heb 10:1); men "have exchanged the glory of the immortal God for images representing a mortal man" (ἐν ὁμοιώματι εἰκόνος φθαρτοῦ ἀνθρώπου"—Rom 1:23; cf. Wis 13:13).

[27] Συμμόρφους τῆς εἰκόνος τοῦ υἱοῦ αὐτοῦ, Rom 8:29; Heb 1:3; cf. J. Kürzinger, "Συμμόρφους τῆς εἰκόνος τοῦ υἱοῦ αὐτοῦ, Rom. VIII, 29," in *BZ*, 1958, pp. 294–299; A. R. C. Leaney, " 'Conformed to the Image of His Son' (Rom VIII, 29)," in *NTS*, vol. 10, 1964, pp. 470–479. J. Caravidopoulos, "Εἰκὼν θεοῦ" καὶ "κατ' εἰκόνα θεοῦ"παρὰ τῷ ἀποστόλῳ Παύλῳ; cf. 2 Cor 4:4, 6. St. Thomas Aquinas comments: "Christus perfectissima imago Dei ist; nam ad hoc quod aliquid perfecta sit imago alicujus, tria requiruntur et haec tria perfecta sunt in Christo: similitudo, origo, perfecta aequalitas." Cf. E. Lohse, "Imago Dei bei Paulus," in W. Matthias, *Libertas Christiana: Festschrift Delekat*, Munich, 1057, p. 156; S. V. McCasland, " 'The Image of God' According to Paul," in *JBL*, 1950, p. 87.

because it depends on him and reproduces him, and thus represents or manifests him, because it has the same "form" (cf. Gal 4:19), that is, a new existential condition.[28] The *eikōn* takes on ontological meaning, because the person-image achieves a new spiritual state, we might even say a transformation of his being, which—as a living portrait—will share the glorious condition of the resurrected Son.

This eschatological reproduction will not be consummated until the resurrection; it is realized here below through a progressive assimilation to the one first glorified: "As we have borne the resemblance (*tēn eikona*) of the one who was of the dust, so shall we bear the image of the one who is heavenly" (1 Cor 15:49). The continuous process is evoked in 2 Cor 3:18—"All reflecting on unveiled faces the glory of the Lord, we are metamorphosed into the same resemblance (*tēn autēn eikona metamorphoumetha*) from glory to glory, as by the action of the Lord, [who is] spirit."[29] Glory (*doxa*) is participation in the divine nature (cf. 2 Pet 1:4; Heb 1:3) and puts the emphasis on a luminous manifestation, analogous to that of the transfiguration (cf. Matt 17:2; Mark 9:2). This change or growth in quality is a spiritualization that transfigures Christians to resemble their Lord; they change in form (*morphē*), putting on that of Christ: "The one who cleaves to the Lord is one spirit with him" (*ho kollōmenos tō Kyriō hen pneuma estin*, 1 Cor 6:17).

This conformity to Christ, by grace and by glory, cannot but fulfill the divine plan for the resemblance of man to God (Gen 1:26), according to Col 3:10—"You have put on the new man, that which is directed toward true knowledge in being renewed according to the image of its creator" (*anakainoumenon . . . kat' eikona tou ktisantos auton*). The newness has to do with belonging to the Lord, which implies a vital participation and allows the believer to become an image/reproduction, in the following manner: the Son of God, the firstborn of a multitude of brethren, having assimilated himself to the likeness of our human nature, passes on to us the conformity to his own "exemplary" filiation, by means of which we are authentic sons of God (John 1:12), "of his race" (Acts 17:28), and his heirs. This forms the basis of an entire ethic, that of purification, imitation, and progress.[30]

---

[28] B. Rey, *Créés dans le Christ Jésus*, Paris, 1966, pp. 173ff. E. Bailleux, "A l'image du Fils premier-né," in *RevThom*, 1976, pp. 181–207.

[29] Cf. C. Spicq, *Théologie morale*, vol. 1, p. 131; vol. 2, pp. 741ff. J. Dupont, "Le Chrétien, miroir de la gloire divine d'après II Cor. III, 18," in *RB*, 1949, pp. 392–411; N. Hugedé, *La Métaphore du miroir dans les Epîtres de saint Paul aux Corinthiens*, Neuchâtel-Paris, 1957; R. Koch, "L'Aspect eschatologique de l'Esprit du Seigneur," in AnBib 17, Rome, 1963, pp. 131–141. A. Feuillet, *Le Christ sagesse de Dieu*, pp. 113–161. C. F. D. Moule, "II Cor. III, 18 *b*, καθάπερ ἀπὸ κυρίου πνεύματος," in *Neues Testament und Geschichte* (Festgabe O. Cullmann), Zurich, 1972, pp. 231–237.

[30] Cf. T. Camelot, "La Théologie de l'image de Dieu," in *RSPT*, 1956, pp. 443–472.

εἰλικρίνεια, εἰλικρινής

eilikrineia, **purity, unmixed quality;** *eilikrinēs*, **without mixture, sincere, candid**

The first element of the compound *eilikrinēs* is obscure. It has often been derived from *eilē* (*halea, hēlios*), "distinguished from the sun" (?), suspended in its rays, purified by them; hence, "pure, without spot, immaculate." But P. Chantraine[1] notes that *eilē* literally means "heat of the sun" and prefers to link the adjective to *eilō*, "cause to turn"; the metaphor would be that of grain or wheat, sorted and purified by rolling or bouncing in a screen.

What is certain is that its basic meaning is "without mixture," hence "pure, distinct,"[2] as is attested by its association with *amigēs* ("without mixture"),[3] *amiktos* ("unmixed"),[4] and constantly with *katharos*: "a pure and clear air" (*katharon kai eilikrinea*, Hippocrates, *Vict.* 2.38.5); "If we should bring back the other stars and the whole of heaven to a nature that is pure and without mixture (*eis tina physin katharan kai eilikrinē*), delivered from change. . . . A mixture is an alteration; the primitive substance loses

---

[1] P. Chantraine, *Dictionnaire étymologique*, p. 320.

[2] In the sense in which in current parlance "pure" is used for gold that is unalloyed, wine that is not mixed with water, air that is not fouled with fumes, style that is free of error, being that is in strict conformity to its nature and the law proper to it. Cf. the denominative verb εἰλικρινέω, "purify"; Ps.-Aristotle, *Mund.* 5.397a35: "all is purified (cleaned) below and above the surface."

[3] Plato, *Menex.* 245 d: "We are purely (εἰλικρινῶς) Greek and without barbarian mixture (καὶ ἀμιγεῖς)"; Menander, *Dysk.* 604: "the pure Attic peasant"; Plutarch, *Quaest. Rom.* 26.

[4] Aristotle, *De An.* 3.2.426b: "the sensible qualities cause pleasure when, being first pure and without mixture (εἰλικρινῆ καὶ ἄμικτα), they are brought to a certain proportion"; Plutarch, *De def. or.* 34: "image that is not undefiled and pure" (οὐκ ἄμικτον οὐδ' εἰλικρινές); cf. *De Is. et Os.* 61: "heavenly things are pure and luminous, those below mixed and motley"; 77.

---

eilikrineia, S 1505; *TDNT* 2.397–398; *EDNT* 1.391; MM 183–184; L&N 88.42; BDF §119(4); BAGD 222 ∥ *eilikrinēs*, S 1506; *TDNT* 2.397–398; *EDNT* 1.391; MM 184; L&N 88.41; BDF §119(4); BAGD 222

its purity (*to eilikrines*)" (Plutarch, *De fac.* 16); "that which is one is undefiled and pure (*to hen eilikrines kai katharon*); it is by the mixture of one substance with another that defilement (*ho miasmos*) comes about."[5]

The classical texts are clear: "Steadiness, purity (*to katharon*), truth, and, as we say, integrity (*eilikrines*) in those things that abide always in the same state, in the same manner, free of all mixture (*ameiktotata*)";[6] "by means of thought in itself and by itself and without mixture (*eilikrines*, of the senses and the body), one pursues realities in order to gain the truth";[7] each element of the army "had its distinct place" (*to eilikrinē*, separate).[8]

In the Koine, the meaning has evolved; *eilikrinēs* is used with people and means "sincere, of good faith, candid," especially in the inscriptions and the papyri. Moulton-Milligan cite inscriptions from Didyma in the third century BC (*eilikrinē kai bebaiam poioumenous hymas pros tous philous apodexin*, Dittenberger, *Or.* 227, 12) and from Miletus in the second century BC (*exēgoumenoi sympantos tou plēthous pros hēmas ektenestatēn te kai eilikrinē tēn eunoian*).[9] The adjective appears in the papyri only from Christian pens

---

[5] Plutarch, *De E ap. Delph.* 20; Philo, *Alleg. Interp.* 1.88: immaterial intelligence has "a constitution more pure and less composite" than terrestrial intelligence; *Drunkenness* 101: "the spirit that is mixed with nothing is perfectly pure"; *Prelim. Stud.* 143; *Dreams* 2.20, 74; *Abraham* 129; *Joseph* 145; *Moses* 2.40; *Spec. Laws* 1.99; Josephus, *War* 2.345; *T. Benj.* 6.15—εἰλικρινῆ καὶ καθαρὰν διάθεσιν.

[6] Plato, *Phlb.* 59 c; cf. 53 a: "Among the pure (καθαρά) types, there is the white. In what does pure whiteness consist? In the size or quantity of it, or rather in such integrity (τὸ ἀκρατέστατον) that no part of any other color is mixed with it? —Obviously, the greatest integrity (τὸ μάλιστ' εἰλικρινὲς ὄν)."

[7] Plato, *Phd.* 66 a; cf. 81 c: "Do you think that this soul should, in separating itself from the body, be in itself, by itself, and without mixture (εἰλικρινῆ)?"; *Symp.* 211 e: "a man to whom it would be given to see the good in itself, in the truth of its nature, in its purity, without mixture (τὸ καλὸν ἰδεῖν εἰλικρινές, καθαρόν, ἄμικτον)," without being infected by human flesh, colors, mortal follies; Aristotle, *Eth. Nic.* 10.1176ᵇ20: "to taste a pleasure without mixture"; *Gen. Cor.* 2.3.330ᵇ: "the extreme and purest bodies are fire and earth"; Hippocrates, *Vict.* 1.35.2 and 8; 2.63.2: "pure air (τὸ πνεῦμα τὸ εἰλικρινές) that strikes (the clothed body) does not purify it"; Ps.-Plato, *Ax.* 370 c: "You will enjoy these goods more purely," these pleasures not being mixed with the mortal body.

[8] Xenophon, *Cyr.* 8.5, 14; cf. Stobaeus, *Ecl.* proemium 1.5: μόνον καὶ εἰλικρινές.

[9] Dittenberger, *Or.* 763, 41. This is the meaning of the adverb εἰλικρινῶς; ibid. 441, 5 (first century BC): ἐν παντὶ καιρῷ τὴν πρὸς ἡμᾶς πίστιν εἰλικρινῶς τετηρηκότας; and honorific decree from Tenos in honor of a Roman (same date): εἰλικρινῶς γνησίαν ἔχοντι πρὸς πάντας φιλοστοργίαν εὐχαριστεῖ (C. Michel, *Recueil*, n. 394, 48). Cf. Epictetus 4.2.6: "Formerly, by loving sincerely (εἰλικρινῶς) that which had no value, you pleased your companions." Philo uses the adverb for seeing or knowing distinctly (*Alleg. Interp.* 2.82; 3.111; *Drunkenness* 189; *Prelim. Stud.* 143; *Post. Cain* 134; *Spec. Laws* 1.39, 219).

of the Byzantine era: prayers are addressed to the Lord from a sincere heart (*en ilikrinei dianoia*).[10]

Eilikrinēs is a hapax in the LXX: wisdom is a completely pure, unadulterated exhalation or emanation from the Almighty. Nothing unclean gets into it (Wis 7:25). Philo used this adjective for "the Being purer than the one, more primordial than the monad" (*Contemp. Life* 2), mind,[11] clear light without shadows (*Heir* 308; *Joseph* 145), truths (*Dreams* 2.74), piety (*therapeia*) that is sincere and entirely pure (*Abraham* 129). Josephus has only two occurrences: the most honest and sincere part of the people (*War* 2.345); Agrippa waits for his anger to abate so that he may give a dispassionate judgment (*logismois eilikrinesi*, *Ant.* 19.321).

When the author of 2 Pet 3:1 gives the purpose of his letter as awakening the sincere mind of its recipients (*tēn eilikrinē dianoian*), he seems to be giving the adjective its Philonian meaning; but NT *dianoia* is the religious faculty of perceiving and understanding.[12] Here this faculty has to be healthy, without shadow or stain; it is more than faithfulness—perfect transparency of the spiritual mind, comparable to the candor of doves (Matt 10:16; cf. Luke 11:34). In Phil 1:10, the emphasis is especially on absence of sin: "so that, discerning true values, you may be pure and without reproach on the day of Christ" (*hina ēte eilikrineis kai aproskopoi*).[13] *Eilikrinēs* is here introduced into the vocabulary of salvation and a meaning that is both moral and religious; doing no wrong means not only not sinning but being in conformity to what God expects of the children of light, without participating in the least in the world of darkness. It is an entire spirituality (Rom 12:2).

---

[10] *P.Lond.* 1927, 15 (fourth century); 1711, 35; 1722, 9; 1733, 15. In a letter to some monks, St. Athanasius writes: ἵνα τὴν εὐσεβῆ πίστιν τὴν ἐνεργηθεῖσαν ἐν ὑμῖν θεοῦ χάριτι εἰλικρινῆ καὶ ἄδολον διατηροῦντες (*SB* 8698, 23).

[11] *Creation* 8; *Drunkenness* 190; *Heir* 98; *Moses* 2.40; but "there is nothing pure in the content of sensation" (*Creation* 31); cf. nevertheless the noblest and liveliest sensations (*Spec. Laws* 1.9). Education provides the purest and most useful service (*Contemp. Life* 82).

[12] C. Spicq, *Epîtres de saint Pierre*, on this verse.

[13] It is impossible to give a precise translation for δοκιμάζειν τὰ διαφέροντα; surely the verb means "evaluate, examine, test" and διαφέροντα "differences"; but these have to be understood on the moral level. Often it is taken to mean the essential, the best; sometimes "what matters." It seems that the idea is to evaluate, in the light of faith, each action, thing, or person, giving it its true value. The term is common in Plutarch (*De audiendo* 12; *De adul. et am.* 35) and in the inscriptions: διαφέροντα τῇ πρὸς τὸν δῆμον εὐνοίᾳ (*I.Priene* 247, 4); τὰ διαφέροντα αὐτοῖς (*IGLAM*, vol. 2, 410, 2). Cf. C. Spicq, *Agapè*, vol. 2, pp. 238ff. G. Therrien, *Le Discernement dans les écrits pauliniens*, Paris, 1973, p. 137.

As for the noun *elikrineia*, derived from the preceding adjective and much rarer, its two papyrological meanings, from third-century petitions, give it the sense "probity."[14] In its three Pauline occurrences, it means especially sincerity: the Corinthians are invited to celebrate the Pascha not "with the leaven of vice and perversity, but with the unleavened bread of *elikrineia* and truth."[15] The apostle presents himself thus: "Our pride is in this: the testimony of our conscience, that it is with God's simplicity and purity (*hoti en haplotēti kai eilikrineia tou theou*) that we have conducted ourselves in the world, particularly with regard to you."[16] Frankness and faithfulness are essential to the character of Paul and his apostolic ministry; each term reinforces the other: biblical *haplotēs*, characteristic of the righteous, is always associated with uprightness; here it is reinforced by the transparency and candor of *eilikrineia* and finally confirmed by the superlative "of God"—a sincerity coming from God, derived from his own, given by him! This rectitude is referred to again in 2 Cor 2:17—"We are not like many, who hawk about the word of God, but with God's commission, in God's presence, in Christ do we speak to you." There is no higher way of describing the apostolic faithfulness, which can be referred to Matt 5:37 ("Let your yes be yes, your no, no"); but more precisely, the contrast with falsifications indicates that Paul neither adds to nor subtracts from the message received from the Lord. He transmits it whole, without adding heterogeneous elements, without mixing in his own personal ideas. He only gives voice to what he has heard from the Master and his first apostles. That is why he is trustworthy.

NT *eilikrineia* is "perfect purity" and describes the mind, the heart, one's conduct. Better yet, it describes Christian existence in its relation to God and to people. It is not so much the absence of duplicity or hypocrisy as a fundamental integrity and transparency; it can be compared to innocence, the candor of children, to whom the kingdom of heaven belongs (Mark 10:14).

---

[14] *P.Oxy.* 1252, verso II, 38: προσφεύγω ἐπὶ τὴν σὴν ἰλικρινείαν = I am obliged to have recourse to your probity; *P.Aberd.* 52, 8: Κύριε, τῇ σῇ εἰλικρινείᾳ, κελεύσας τῷ στρατηγῷ κτλ.

[15] 1 Cor 5:8. A targum fragment calls Abraham "the completely unleavened one," perfectly pure and sincere, cf. R. Le Déaut, *Nuit Pascale*, p. 173, n. 110.

[16] 2 Cor 1:12. F. Hahn, "Das Ja des Paulus und das Ja Gottes: Bemerkungen zu II Kor. I, 12–II, 1," in *Neues Testament und Christliche Existenz: Festschrift H. Braun*, Tübingen, 1973, pp. 229–239.

εἰρηνεύω, εἰρήνη, εἰρηνικός, εἰρηνοποιέω, εἰρηνοποιός

eirēneuō, to be at peace, live in peace; *eirēnē*, peace; *eirēnikos*, peaceful; *eirēnopoieō*, to make peace; *eirēnopoios*, making peace; a peacemaker

In secular Greek—classical and Hellenistic—*eirēnē* designates a political and social phenomenon, and first of all the state of a nation that is not at war.[1] It is contrasted with *polemos*.[2] War is enmity (Plato, *Resp.* 5.470 c) and peace is harmonization (Plutarch, *De Alex. fort.* 1.6.329 a-c). Treaties of alliance and of peace almost always link *eirēnē* and *philia*.[3] In other

---

[1] "Peace was nothing other than a contractual interruption of war" (B. Keil, "Εἰρήνη: Eine philologisch-antiquarische Untersuchung," in *Berichte über die Verhandlungen der königl. Sächsischen Gesellschaft der Wissenschaften zu Leipzig*, 1916, p. 18). Cf. von Rad, Foerster, "εἰρήνη," in *TDNT*, vol. 2, pp. 400-420; cf. bibliography in *TWNT*, vol. 10/1, pp. 1069ff. O. Waser, "Eirene," in PW, vol. 5, col. 2128ff. C. Préaux, "La Paix á l'époque hellénistique," in *La Paix* (Recueils de la Société J. Bodin, XIV), Brussels, 1962, pp. 227-231.

[2] Isocrates, *Paneg.* 4.172; Ps.-Plato, *Def.* 413 a: Εἰρήνη· ἡσυχία ἐπ' ἔχθρας πολεμικάς ("the stilling of warlike quarrels"); Philostratus, *Gym.* 19: "The Lacedaemonians used dance—the mildest peacetime occupation—for war." The inscriptions endlessly contrast "in time of war and in time of peace," whether using the genitive πολέμου καὶ εἰρήνης (*I.Gonn.* 5, 8; 12, 5; 17, 4; 42, 24; 70, 7; 72, 2; 92, 2; Dittenberger, *Syl.* 217, 8; *NCIG*, n. XII, 36), or using the prepositional phrase ἐν πολέμῳ καὶ ἐν εἰρήνῃ (*I.Gonn.* 2, 1; 7, 5; 9, 6; 10, 4; 11, 9; 19, 7; 30, 14; 31, 15; 33, 3; 34, 12; 39, 3; 40, 41; 41, 22; 58, 6; 72, 6; 91, 31; *CIRB* III, 4; IV, 2; *SEG* I, 363, 34).

[3] Plato, *Leg.* 1.628 b: "That the death of one party and victory of the other should bring peace after civil war, or that thanks to reconciliation bringing friendship and peace . . ."; Polybius 21.43; Dittenberger, *Syl.* 142, 7: "The inhabitants of Chios, like the Athenians, shall maintain peace, friendship, the oaths, and the conventions in force . . . in no way failing of the texts of the steles relative to the peace." Between the Aetolians and the Acarnanians a treaty establishes "peace and eternal friendship" (*Syl.* 421); "The Magnesians and the Milesians concluded peace on the following conditions. The ambassadors of the following cities came to reconcile them and

---

eirēneuō, S 1514; *TDNT* 2.417-418; *EDNT* 1.394; *NIDNTT* 2.776, 780; MM 185; L&N 88.102; BDF §§227(2), 309(1); BAGD 227 ‖ *eirēnē*, S 1515; *TDNT* 2.400-417; *EDNT* 1.394-397; *NIDNTT* 2.776-783; MM 185-186; L&N 22.42, 25.248; BDF §128(5); BAGD 227-228 ‖ *eirēnikos*, S 1516; *TDNT* 2.418-419; *EDNT* 1.397; *NIDNTT* 3.776, 780, 782; MM 186; L&N 25.249; BAGD 228 ‖ *eirēnopoieō*, S 1517; *TDNT* 2.419-420; *EDNT* 1.397; *NIDNTT* 2.776, 782; L&N 40.4; BAGD 228 ‖ *eirēnopoios*, S 1518; *TDNT* 2.419; *EDNT* 1.397; *NIDNTT* 2.776, 780, 782; L&N 40.5; BAGD 228

words, peace is not only the elimination of war,[4] but an organization of the future, because it guarantees tranquility (*hēsychia*, Plato, *Resp.* 575 b), wealth (Homer, *Od.* 24.486), the cessation of banditry (Epictetus 3.13.9), an opportunity for all sorts of happiness and prosperity,[5] at least if the peace is general: *he koinē eirēnē*.[6] It goes without saying that the king who is "philanthropic" will be interested in restoring order and guaranteeing the peace,[7] because it is recognized that peace is better than war.[8]

If peace is the situation of a nation that is not at war, it also defines the public order, relations between citizens, and social peace, as opposed to discord, trouble, and sedition: "*eirēnē tēs staseōs*, the end of civil war."[9] This

---

restore the former friendship between them. . . . May there be eternal peace and friendship between the Magnesians and the Milesians" (*Syl.* 588).

[4] Cf. the "peace of Phoenix" (Livy 29.12), between Prusias and Byzantium (Polybius 4.52), between Rome and Carthage(Polybius 3.22–25). Reconciliation or agreement is reached ἐν τῇ εἰρήνῃ (*P.Oxy.* 1866, 1; cf. *SB* 7667, 4). There is a nuance of benevolence in letters of commendation: συδέξασθαι αὐτὸν ἐν εἰρήνῃ (*P.Oxy.* 1162, 9; 2785, 6; *P.Alex.* 29, 8).

[5] For Philemon (frag. 71; Stobaeus, *Flor.* 55.5; vol. 4, p. 373: anthology on peace). Eirene is a sort of goddess, loving and kind, who permits marriages, feasts, friends, wealth, health, pleasure. . . . Peace, sealed by oath (Demosthenes, *Treaty Alex.* 18.10; Dittenberger, *Syl.* 260), brings numerous privileges: intervention to help, ἰσοπολιτεία, ἀτέλεια, etc.

[6] Decree establishing the second Athenian confederation (J. Pouilloux, *Choix*, n. 27, 13); *Pap.Lugd.Bat.* XIII, 8, 5: "In the present situation, peace reigns everywhere." Cf. Livy 34.57; E. Bickerman, "Le Droit des gens dans la Grèce classique," in *RIDA*, 1950, pp. 99–127; T. T. Ryder, *Koine Eirene: General Peace and Local Independence in Ancient Greece*, Oxford, 1965. Cf. the *Pax Romana*. At Rome, an altar was dedicated to the goddess Pax in AD 9: *Ara Pacis Augustae;* her symbols were an olive branch, a caduceus, and a horn of plenty; cf. Ovid, *Fast.* 1.711–712; Tibullus 1.10.69f.; Virgil, *Aen.* 6.851–853.

[7] Like Antiochus I at Ilion: "He reestablished peace and the former prosperity" (Dittenberger, *Or.* 219), King Silko (ibid. 201, 7: ἐποίησα εἰρήνην μετ' αὐτῶν; 199, 28); Philip V of Macedon (Polybius 5.100, 102; 18.1–11), Emperor Claudius (*SB* 8899, 2); "O Caesar, in this fulsome peace that you created, what must I suffer!" (Epictetus 3.22.55); "the peace established by our master King Flavius Julianus, the eternal Augustus" (*P.Cair.Goodsp.* 15, 4; cf. *P.Oxy.* 3022, 14). Cf. E. R. Goodenough, "The Political Philosophy of Hellenistic Kingship," in *YCS* I, 1928.

[8] Andocides, *De Pace* 1: "Better a just peace than war; I believe, Athenians, that you all agree"; Ps.-Plato, *Alc.* 109; Aristotle, *Pol.* 1334 *a;* cf. W. E. Caldwell, "Homeric Conceptions of Peace," in *Studies in History, Economics and Public Laws* (Columbia University, Faculty of Political Science, vol. 84, 1919). At the Athenian agora, there was a statue of the goddess Eirene (Pausanias 1.8.2; 9.16.2).

[9] Plato, *Leg.* 1.628 *b;* Isocrates, *Areop.* 51: "the citizens live quietly, at peace with each other (ἡσυχίαν εἶχον) and at peace with the rest of the world"; Epictetus 4.5.35: "These judgments produce friendship in a house, concord in a city, peace among nations"; 3.13.13: "No evil can come to me; no brigand for me, no shaking of the

is the most common usage in the papyri: the *stratēgos* must take measures to guarantee peace and order (*P.Petaus* 53, 17; cf. *P.Stras.* 5, 8).[10] An arrest warrant is addressed "to the *epistatēs* of the peace of the town of Teos" (*epistatē eirēnēs kōmēs Tēeōs, P.Oxy.* 64, 2; cf. *P.Cair.Isid.* 130; *P.Oxy.* 2714, 11; 3035, 2; 3184 *a* 17; *b* 14). So there were guardians of the peace, for example in a list of police officers including *eirēnophylakes* (*SB* 4636), whose responsibility it was to see to it that no one disturbed the course of public services; they may be compared to the municipal functionaries *epi tēs eirēnēs*.[11] *Eirēnē*, finally, refers to the state of a person who is not troubled or disturbed, who is tranquil: "There is nothing to keep you from speaking in peace (without opposition)" (Plato, *Symp.* 189 *b*). But it is quite remarkable that there are no texts evoking the state of soul of a person not troubled by any care, any disquiet, having blessed tranquility[12]—what we call "peace within."

In reading the OT, one has the impression of entering another world, first of all because of the frequency with which peace is mentioned (about 280 times), then because of the new content of this idea,[13] though it is

---

earth; everywhere profound peace, everywhere tranquility (ἀταραξία)"; 4.5.24: "You live at peace with all people, whatever they do, and you mock especially those who think to do you wrong."

[10] Ἐπόπτῃ εἰρήνης Ὀξυρυγχίτου (*P.Oxy.* 1559, 3; cf. 41, 27: εἰρήνη πόλεως), τὴν χώραν ἐν εἰρήνῃ διατετήρηκεν (decree of Canopus, Dittenberger, *Or.* 56, 12); διατηρήσας αὐτὴν (πόλιν) ἐν τῇ πάσῃ εἰρήνῃ (*SB* 8334, 6; 42 BC, cf. R. Hutmacher, *Ehrendekret*, 1965). An *eirēnarchos* of Ptolemais asks the *kōmarchos* of Philadelphia to come to the city of Arsinoë for the feast of peace (*P.Princ.* 99, 5; cf. 20, 18).

[11] *P.Achm.* 7, 8; *P.Oxy.* 2121, 30; 2122, 5; *SB* 9409, VI, 43; 9421, 2; 10075, 34; 10270, XIII, 4–5.

[12] Probably because the Greeks expressed this security, this interior calm, even good humor, using εὐθυμία (cf. Jas 5:13; Plutarch, *Quaest. conv.* 1.1.4; Hipparchus, Περὶ εὐθυμίας, in Stobaeus, *Flor.* 34.81; vol. 4, p. 980; *P.Grenf.* 61; *P.Lips.* 111; *P.Gen.* 53; *P.Giss.* 54; *P.Ross.Georg.* III, 10, 5; V, 6, 26, etc.), or γαλήνη, "serenity" (Plutarch, *De tranq. anim.* 19). We may cite above all in a hymn to Isis: "the sovereign who reigns over Asia and Europe lives in peace, and before him accumulate the fruits that give all sorts of good things" (*SEG* VIII, 550, 14 = *SB* 8140, 14; cf. *UPZ* XX, 4), and the personification of peace by Aristophanes as a woman who has wooers (*Ach.* 32; cf. J. Taillardat, *Images d'Aristophane*, n. 651). We take no account of late Christian papyri (*P.Oxy.* 1865, 11; 2156, 23; *P.Lond.* 1917, 4; 1923, 33; *P.Ross.Georg.* V, 45, 4; *P.Apoll.* 5, 3; 7, 4; *P.Ness.* 68, 6; 70, 9; 74, 10; *O.Bodl.* 2166, 9; *SB* 9748, 1 and 4; 9752, 1; 10514, 1; 10705, 6; 10706, 1). The woman's name is much attested beginning with Hesiod, *Th.* 901: "Equity (Θέμις) was mother of the Horae—Discipline, Justice, and flourishing Peace (Εἰρήνην τεθαλυῖαν)—who watch over mortals." Cf. *P.Tebt.* 818, 8; *BGU* 1102, 18; 1272, 5; *C.Pap.Jud.* 126, 11–12; in Jewish epitaphs, either Εἰρήνη (*CII* 21, 320, 333) or Εἰρήνα (319, 651) or the Latin Irene (72, 240).

[13] Of course, in the LXX we also find the secular contrast between peace and war: Joab "shed the blood of war during peace" (1 Kgs 2:5); "When you draw near to a city to do battle with it, you shall offer peace" (Deut 20:10; cf. 1 Kgs 20:18);

always synonymous with tranquility.[14] *Eirēnē* almost always translates the Hebrew *šālôm;* the sense of the root is "be well, complete, safe and sound," and *šālôm* expresses "the state of a being who lacks nothing and has no fear of being troubled in its quietude; it is euphoria with security. Nothing better can be desired for oneself and for others."[15] There is also a nuance of plenty and prosperity (cf. 1 Macc 14:8); this is how the good health and joyfulness of the woman in Cant 8:10 appears in the eyes of her fiancé (cf. the strong woman who finishes her years in peace, Sir 26:2). Furthermore, the Israelite greeting is a wish for peace, that is, for well-being and happiness.[16] But the great innovation of the OT is to make peace a

---

"Joshua made peace with the Hivites and concluded a treaty allowing them to live" (Josh 9:15); "There was peace between Jabin king of Hazor and Heber the Kenite" (1 Sam 7:14), between Israel and the Amorites (1 Sam 7:14), between Hiram and Solomon (1 Kgs 5:26); Ps 55:18; 120:6; Wis 14:22; Isa 27:5; Mic 2:8; Zech 8:10; 9:10; 1 Macc 5:54; 6:49, 58; 7:13, 28; 9:70; 10:4; 13:37, 40; 2 Macc 12:12; cf. Eccl 3:8—"wartime and peacetime." The διαθήκη εἰρήνης is inspired by secular covenants (Num 25:12; Isa 54:10; Ezek 34:25; 37:26; Mal 2:5; Sir 45:24; 1 Macc 8:20, 22: "treaty of covenant and of peace"), just as the public order and social peace are mentioned at 2 Macc 3:1—"The holy city was administered in complete peace and the laws were observed as closely as possible"; 4:6. Cf. *IGLS* 1320, 6: "Peace and mercy to all our holy community."

[14] 1 Chr 4:40—"the land was calm and tranquil" (εἰρήνη καὶ ἡσυχίᾳ, Hebrew *šāqaṭ);* 22:9—"A son will be born to you who will be a man of peace, and to whom I will grant peace with all his enemies and all around, for his name shall be Solomon, and throughout his years I will give peace and tranquility" (εἰρήνην καὶ ἡσυχίαν δώσω); hence "be at peace" (Judg 6:23; 19:20; Lev 26:6; 2 Sam 17:3), "go in peace" (Judg 18:6; 1 Sam 1:17; 20:13, 42; 25:35; 29:7; 2 Sam 3:21, 24; 15:9, 27; 2 Kgs 5:19; 2 Chr 18:16, 26, 27; 19:1), "return in peace" (Gen 26:29; Judg 8:9; 11:31; 2 Sam 19:25; 1 Kgs 22:17, 27, 28). H. Bietenhard, J. J. Stamm, *Der Weltfriede im Alten und Neuen Testament,* Zurich, 1959.

[15] A. Robert, *Le Cantique des Cantiques,* Paris, 1963, p. 145; cf. G. Gerleman, "*Šālôm,*" in *Theol. Handwörterbuch zum A. T.,* vol. 2, pp. 919, 935; J. Scharbert, "SLM im Alten Testament," in *Lex tua veritas: Festschrift H. Junker,* Trêves, 1961, pp. 209–229; W. Eisenbeis, *Die Wurzel "Slm" im Alten Testament,* Berlin, 1969; H. H. Schmid, *Šālôm "Frieden" im Alten Orient und im Alten Testament,* Stuttgart, 1971 (= *Šalôm: La pace nell' antico Oriente e nell' Antico Testamento,* Brescia, 1977); J. Prignaud, "Un Sceau hébreu de Jérusalem ," in *RB,* 1964, pp. 381ff. The security of εἰρήνη is expressed by the Hebrew *beṭaḥ:* "the poor will sleep in safety" (Isa 14:30; 41:3); they shall be in their land" (Ezek 34:27; 38:8, 11, 14; 39:6, 26; cf. 1 Macc 12:52; 16:10).

[16] Dan 10:19; cf. 1 Sam 20:7; 25:5; 30:21; 2 Sam 8:10; 18:28–29; 2 Kgs 4:23, 26; 1 Chr 18:10; Jdt 15:8; Dan 3:31—"King Nebuchadnezzar to all peoples, nations, and tongues on the whole earth: may your peace be great"; 6:26; 2 Macc 1:1. Those who draw near are asked if they come "for peace" (1 Sam 16:4–5; 1 Kgs 2:13; 2 Kgs 9:17–22; 1 Chr 12:17), but people also wish to "go down in peace to Sheol" (Gen 15:15; 1 Kgs 2:6), to be "received in peace into the tomb" (2 Kgs 22:20; 2 Chr 34:28; Isa 57:2; Sir 44:14), i.e., undefiled, with the requisite decency, with "rest" guaranteed. Hence the

religious idea: it is a gift of God. "Gideon built an altar to Yahweh and called it Yahweh-Peace" (*eirēnē Kyriou*, Judg 6:24); "I am Yahweh—I bring peace" (Isa 45:7); "Great is Yahweh, who wishes peace for his servant" (Ps 35:27). If it is commanded to seek peace (Ps 34:14), much more often it is stated that it is God who secures peace (Isa 26:12; 57:19; 66:12) and that there is no peace for people except for that granted by God when they are in conformity with his will.[17] There can be no peace for the ungodly,[18] but it is granted to those "who walk with God in peace and uprightness."[19] That is to say that Israel will be the people of peace. Not only did God give Moses this formula of blessing: "May Yahweh lift his countenance upon you and give you peace" (Num 6:26); he gives it to the devotees of his temple: "Great will be the glory of this house . . . in this place will I put peace,"[20] and the faithful will implore "Peace upon Israel!" (Ps 125:5; 128:6; cf. Sir 30:23).

It is difficult to specify the content of Israelite *eirēnē*, but it is certain that without excluding the possession of human goods (Ps 4:8), it is in the first instance the fruit of trusting and loving relations[21] with God, who comes to the aid of his own (1 Chr 12:18), hence a characteristic of Israelite religion, a completely original quality of soul of its faithful. With "messengers of peace,"[22] bearers of "good news," peace is synonymous with

---

wish that appears constantly in Jewish epitaphs: "May he rest in peace" (*CII* 7, 13, 18, 35, 44, 85, etc.); sometimes with the addition "with the saints" (n. 45) or variants: "May you lie in peace" (124), "May he sleep in peace" (365, 390), "The Lord [grant that] Justus's rest . . . may be in peace" (358); *SEG* XXVI, n. 1161, 1163, 1168, 1171, 1173, 1185, 1195, 1199, etc. The opposite of εἰρήνη is fear or terror (φόβος, Judg 6:23; Sir 30:5; Tob 12:17) and bitterness (πικρία, Isa 38:17).

[17] Jer 29:7—"by his peace you will have peace"; Bar 3:13—"If you had walked in God's way, you would have dwelt in peace for ever"; 2 Macc 1:4; Lam 3:17—"My soul is deprived of peace, and I have forgotten happiness."

[18] Isa 47:12; cf. 2 Chr 15:5; Jer 6:14; 8:15; 16:5; Ezek 7:25; 13:10, 16; Tob 14:4.

[19] Mal 2:6; Ps 37:11—"the humble will delight in great peace"; 119:165—"Great peace have they who love your law"; 122:6–8; Zech 8:19; Prov 3:2, 17, 23; 4:27; Sir 1:18—"The fear of the Lord makes peace and perfect health flourish"; 38:8; 41:14.

[20] Hag 2:9; 1 Kgs 2:33—"There will be peace forever from Yahweh"; Ps 29:11—"Yahweh will bless his people with peace"; 85:8—"The Lord God speaks of peace to his people and his worshipers"; 85:11—"justice and peace have kissed"; Isa 32:17; 48:18; 54:13—"Great will be the peace of your sons"; 40:17; Bar 5:4—"Your name will be with God: Peace of righteousness"; Tob 13:15—"They will rejoice because of your peace."

[21] Cf. Ps 41:9—the "man of peace" is a close friend. Being or living in peace with others expresses good mutual understanding, goodwill, and harmony, cf. Job 5:23—"the wild beast will be at peace with you"; Sir 47:13, 16: "Solomon reigned in days of peace. God gave him rest all around. . . . You were loved with peace."

[22] Isa 33:7; 52:7; Jer 28:9; Nah 2:1; cf. Rom 10:15.

salvation and victory. A number of these announcements are eschatological, linking justice, peace, and salvation;[23] a certain number are clearly messianic in character: "The government will rest upon his shoulders; his name will be called . . . Prince of Peace. For the growth of his government and peace will be without end."[24] The death of the Messiah/liberator will be expiatory: "The punishment that earned our peace (salvation) has fallen upon him (the Servant of Yahweh)" (Isa 53:5). The NT writers would recognize that this religious peace was accomplished by the Savior Jesus.[25]

The Synoptic Gospels retain the OT meaning of *eirēnē*—"security" (Isa 59:8), but they apply it to Jesus, who guides us "into the way of *eirēnē*" (Luke 1:79), that is, who introduces us to the messianic salvation. Simeon, having beheld the Savior, asks God—as a *doulos* asking his *despotēs*—"Let your servant depart in peace."[26] At Bethlehem, the angels sang, "Glory to God in the highest and peace on earth to people upon whom his favor rests."[27] The Messiah henceforth present brings peace, the gift of God to all people. When Jesus makes his entry into Jerusalem, his disciples sing

---

[23] Isa 26:3; 32:17–18; Ps 29:11; 85:9–14.

[24] Isa 9:5–6; cf. Ezek 34:25—"I Yahweh . . . will establish a covenant of peace with my sheep . . . they will dwell in safety in the wilderness"; Mic 5:4—"By the power of Yahweh he will feed his flock . . . it is he who will be peace"; Zech 9:10—"He will command peace to the nations"; Ps 72:7—"In his days, righteousness and great peace will flourish."

[25] E. Brandenburger, *Frieden im Neuen Testament*, Gütersloh, 1973; E. Dinkler, *Eirene: Der urchristliche Friedensgedanke*, Heidelberg, 1973; K. H. Schelkle, *Theologie des Neuen Testaments*, vol. 3, Düsseldorf, 1970, pp. 141–156; H. Schlier, "Der Friede nach dem Apostel Paulus," in *Geist und Leben*, 1971, pp. 282–296; R. Penna, "L'Evangile de la paix," in L. de Lorenzi, *Paul de Tarse apôtre de notre temps*, Rome, 1979, pp. 175–199.

[26] Luke 2:29—ἀπολύεις τὸν δοῦλόν σου ἐν εἰρήνῃ. The verb ἀπολύω ("loose, unbind, dismiss") is used for the death of Abraham (Gen 15:2), of Aaron (Num 20:29), of Tobias (Tob 3:6), of a martyr (2 Macc 7:9). The present indicative has a semi-modal nuance: Now you can let me die. Simeon had seen "the consolation of Israel." He was happy, like Jacob when he had seen Joseph again: "Now I can die, because I have seen your face and you are still alive" (Gen 46:30).

[27] Luke 2:14. The genitive of quality εὐδοκίας is the opposite of τέκνα ὀργῆς (Eph 2:3). It is not a question of souls well-disposed to benefit from salvation, which would limit salvation to a certain category of people and would limit the divine goodwill (cf. 1 Tim 2:4). The Lucan expression should be compared to the $b^e n\hat{e}$ $r^e\d{s}\hat{o}n\hat{o}$ ("sons of his grace") in the Qumran hymns (1QH 4.32; 11.9), to whom God will give "eternal peace" (1QS 2.4), "full peace" (4.7) at the "time of their peace" (3.15). Cf. E. Vogt, "Pax homnibus bonae voluntatis, Lc. II, 14," in *Bib*, 1953, pp. 427–429; C. H. Hunziger, "Neues Licht auf Lc. II, 14," in *ZNW*, 1952–53, pp. 85–90; idem, "Einer weiterer Beleg zu Lc. II, 14," ibid. 1958, pp. 129ff. J. A. Fitzmyer, "Peace upon Earth among Men of His Good Will," in *TS*, 1958, pp. 225ff. R. Deichgräber, "ἄνθρωποι εὐδοκίας," in *ZNW*, 1960, pp. 132ff.

Ps 118:26 and acclaim the Messiah-king who "comes in the name of the Lord, peace in heaven and glory in the highest places" (Luke 19:38). Jesus, sent by God, carried out the mission that was entrusted to him; salvation is certain, and its author is glorified.[28] Clearly the point is the reconciliation of humans with God, on the spiritual level.

We know that the Israelite greeting was expressed in a wish for peace. Jesus prescribes this greeting to his apostles, but in so doing gives it a religious meaning, namely, benediction: "When you enter into the house, greet it; and if the house is worthy, let your peace come upon it."[29] People also wished each other peace upon parting (1 Sam 1:17; 20:42; 29:7), and there again this commonplace manner of taking one's leave[30] can express not only brotherly love[31] but also the salvation of the soul, the forgiveness of sins; Jesus says to the forgiven sinner, "Go in peace."[32]

---

[28] This is the secular and OT theme of the king who brings, establishes, and guarantees peace. To the contrary, Jesus laments over Jerusalem: "If on that day you had known what was required for peace" (τὰ πρὸς εἰρήνην, Luke 19:42), the conditions of reconciliation with God (contrasted with ruin). Cf. the king who with ten thousand men cannot contend with the one who is attacking with twenty thousand and "sends an embassy to ask for terms of peace" (ἐρωτᾷ τὰ πρὸς εἰρήνην, Luke 14:32). Tyrians and Sidonians asked Herod for peace (ᾐτοῦντο εἰρήνην, Acts 12:20); T. Jud. 9.7—τότε αἰτοῦσιν ἡμῖν τὰ πρὸς εἰρήνην. —In the small, allegorizing parable of Luke 11:21 (inspired by Isa 49:24-26; 53:12), the strong man guards his palace, and his possessions are secure (ἐν εἰρήνῃ ἐστὶν τὰ ὑπάρχοντα). This is Satan and those possessed by him; but Jesus, who is stronger and casts out demons, will despoil him; cf. S. Légasse, "L'Homme fort' de Lc. XI, 21–22," in NovT, 1962, pp. 5–9.

[29] Matt 10:12-13; ἄξιος is the soul open to the apostle's preaching and to the peace that comes from God. Luke 10:5 specifies: "In whatever house you enter, say first of all, 'Peace to this house!' If there is a child of peace (υἱὸς εἰρήνης) there, your peace will rest upon him"; peace is effectively transmitted and possessed by the son of peace as an immanent spiritual good. M. J. Lagrange compares Hillel's saying, which seems already to have a religious value: "The one who loves peace loves creatures, and the one who commands peace leads them to the law of Moses" (Pirqe 'Abot 1.12). Cf. F. W. Danker, "The υἱός Phrase in the New Testament," in NTS, vol. 7, 1960, p. 94; W. Klassen, " 'A Child of Peace' (Luke X, 16) in First Century Context," in NTS, vol. 27, 1981, pp. 488–506.

[30] The Philippian jailer, having received from the praetors the order to release Paul and Silas, frees them and says to them, "Go in peace" (πορεύεσθε ἐν εἰρήνῃ, Acts 16:36). The rich person who refuses to help the poor says to them, "Go in peace (ὑπάγετε ἐν εἰρήνῃ), be warmed and be filled" (Jas 2:16).

[31] Judas and Silas "were sent back with wishes of peace" (ἀπελύθησαν μετ' εἰρήνης) by the community at Antioch (Acts 15:33). The Corinthians are told to treat Timothy with deference and respect, supplying everything he needs to speed him on his way under the best circumstances: προπέμψατε αὐτὸν ἐν εἰρήνῃ (1 Cor 16:11).

[32] Luke 7:50—πορεύου εἰς εἰρήνην. Likewise the woman with the issue of blood, 8:48; Mark 5:34.

In the Fourth Gospel, peace appears only in the "farewell discourse," at precisely at the moment when Jesus is leaving his own, who will be so sorely tested and even terrorized by the passion of their Master. He does not wish them peace; he gives them peace, and not just any peace, but his very own peace,[33] which spreads among them like the sap of the vine to the branches by virtue of their ontological union (*en emoi eirēnē*). It is a legacy that is the fruit of his sacrifice, by which he is victorious over death and Satan; a legacy that will permit his own to know nothing of fright and panic even in the midst of the worst catastrophes.[34] When the resurrected Christ came upon his apostles, his greeting was not the ordinary wish, "Shalom," nor even a benediction, but the confirmation of his gift: "*Eirēnē hymin*" ("Peace to you").[35]

The Acts of the Apostles mentions civil and political peace, like the unity following hostility within a group;[36] but it also mentions the religious, brotherly harmony in the Christian communities;[37] finally, and

---

[33] John 14:27—"I leave you peace, I give you my peace . . . not as the world gives. Let not your heart be troubled, and do not be afraid"; 16:33—"I have told you these things so that in me you may have peace" (ἵνα ἐν ἐμοὶ εἰρήνην ἔχητε). The peace of Christ is a gift of his omnipotence that establishes the disciple in safety, an immanent possession of the "heart" fortified by the "overcomer of the world." The Hebrews did not hesitate to voice a wish of peace at the most critical junctures; cf. the "shalom of war" (2 Sam 11:7), or the Aramaic inscription wishing peace to widows, the most afflicted of all people (C. C. Torrey, *The Excavations at Dura-Europos*, vol. 8, 1, New Haven, 1956, p. 263 *b*, line 14).

[34] This is why the peace of Christ is so different from pagan or Israelite peace; it is entirely spiritual and abides even in renunciation or persecution: "Do not think that I have come to bring peace on the earth; I have come not to bring peace but a sword" (Matt 10:34); members of a family will take sides on account of Christ and will divide and separate themselves according to their choice. Cf. Luke 12:51—"Do you think that I have come to bring peace on the earth? No, I tell you, but dissension" (διαμερισμόν, civil war). Cf. the rider of Rev 6:4, who represents the scourge of war: "It was given to him to take away peace from the earth."

[35] Luke 24:36. Although these words are omitted by D and the Latin manuscripts, it is hard to question their authenticity, which is confirmed by 𝔓75 (*P.Bodm.* XIV) and John 20:19, 21, 26.

[36] Acts 24:2. At Caesarea, Tertullus addresses the procurator Felix: "Enjoying, thanks to you, a profound peace (πολλῆς εἰρήνης τυγχάνοντες) and the reforms that this nation owes to you foresight." This is *tranquillitas ordinis*. Referring to Exod 2:13–14, St. Stephen evokes Moses' intervening between the quarreling Hebrews: "Men, you are brothers; why do you wrong one another?" He unites them for peace (συνήλλασσεν αὐτοὺς εἰς εἰρήνην, Acts 7:26). This is the classic secular sense of peace: the cessation of hostilities. Cf. J. Comblin, "La Paix dans la théologie de saint Luc," in *ETL*, 1956, pp. 439–460.

[37] Acts 9:31—"The church in all of Judea, Galilee, and Samaria enjoyed peace (εἶχεν εἰρήνην), being built up and walking in the fear of the Lord." *Eirēnē* is first of

above all, it defines this peace in terms of Christ. St. Peter says to the centurion Cornelius: "God has sent the word to the sons of Israel, announcing peace by Jesus Christ. He is the Lord of all" (Acts 10:36); *euangelizomenos eirēnēn* evokes the OT messengers of peace, but this has to do with the gospel message, which is the salvation granted by God to all people. This reconciliation translates for them into peace of the soul, thanks to forgiveness of sins. This is already the teaching of St. Paul.[38]

We might almost say that the apostle created a new concept of *eirēnē*, an altogether internal and very spiritual peace, since he locates it at the heart of the Christian life and connects it to each of the persons of the Holy Trinity. The most important text is Rom 5:1–2: "Being therefore justified by faith, let us keep peace with God through our Lord Jesus Christ, to whom we owe our access by faith to this grace in which we stand and our glorying in the hope of the glory of God." The first result of justification was obtaining peace, not only reconciliation with God, the end of a breach and a disorder, but the inauguration of new relations[39] that promise future blessedness: "May the God of hope fill you with all joy and peace, so that you may abound in hope, by the power of the Holy Spirit" (Rom 15:13). This Christian peace, which comes with the call to salvation and endures until the point of entering heaven, is the consequence of all the gifts of a God whom St. Paul describes as "the God of peace,"[40] because he alone creates peace.

---

all tranquility, the absence of persecution (Saul is converted), but also the harmonious union of souls that share the same faith, are united by brotherly love, and live in full submission to the will of God. This is truly the peculiarly Christian peace.

[38] St. Paul, in 43 occurrences of εἰρήνη, has some OT usages: "When they say, 'Peace and safety,' then shall ruin suddenly fall upon them" (1 Thess 5:3; cf. Jer 6:14); Rom 2:10; 3:17—"They have not known the path of peace" (cf. Isa 59:8); cf. Heb 7:2—Melchizedek, priest of the Most High, was "king of Salem, that is, king of peace" (cf. Gen 14:18; Philo, *Alleg. Interp.* 3.79; P. Winter, "Note on Salem-Jerusalem," in *NovT*, 1957, pp. 51–52), hence a type of the Messiah, who establishes peace (Isa 9:5; 32:17; Zech 9:10). Rahab received the spies peaceably (Heb 11:31).

[39] Cf. 1 Cor 7:15—"It is in peace that God has called you" (ἐν δὲ εἰρήνῃ κέκληκεν ὑμᾶς ὁ θεός, cf. Col 3:15; on the Pauline privilege, P. Dulau, "The Pauline Privilege: Is it Promulgated in the First Epistle to the Corinthians?" in *CBQ*, 1951, pp. 146–152; J. Dupont, *Mariage et divorce dans l'évangile*, Bruges, 959, pp. 59, 72, 109, 143; A. Da Ripabottoni, "La dottrina dell'Ambrosiaster sul privilegio paulino," in *Laurentianum*, 1964, pp. 429–447; H. U. Willi, "Das Privilegium Paulinum, I Kor. VII, 15f—Pauli eigene Lebenserinnerung?" in *BZ*, 1978, pp. 100–108); Gal 6:16—"Upon all those who follow this rule (of Christian conduct) be peace and mercy, and upon the Israel of God."

[40] Rom 16:20—"the God of peace will soon crush Satan under your feet"; 1 Thess 5:23—"May the God of peace himself sanctify you wholly"; 2 Thess 3:16—"May the Lord of peace himself give you peace at all times and in every way"; Heb 13:20—"May the God of peace equip you with everything good to do his will"; Rom 15:33—"May

This peace, almost synonymous with salvation, is obtained thanks to Christ, who by his cross reconciled all humans with God. He announces it, and his gospel would be described as the "gospel of peace" (Eph 6:15; cf. Isa 52:7). He effects peace: his own peace (John 14:27; 16:33) is a spiritual reality that rules the minds and hearts of his disciples, making harmony among them, as with the members of a single body: "May the peace of Christ rule in your hearts: this is indeed the goal of the call that has gathered you into one body (the church)" (Col 3:15). What is more, he is himself our peace, because he has not only reconciled us with God but also established peace between Jews and Gentiles, dissolving their indissoluble opposition (there is no longer Jew, nor Greek; they are one in him—Gal 3:28; Col 3:11). He has eliminated the partition (*phragmos*) or the fence (of the Mosaic law and of enmity) or the wall that separated them.[41] This is the teaching of Eph 2:13-17: "You who once were far off have now drawn near, thanks to the blood of Christ. For he himself is our peace, who from the two has made one people . . . breaking down the enmity in his flesh. . . . to create in his person the two in one new man, he who makes peace (*poiōn eirēnēn*), and to reconcile them with God, both in one body, by the cross: in his person he has put the enmity to death. Having thus come he proclaimed peace (*euēngelisato eirēnēn*) to you who were far off and to those who were near."

---

the God of peace be with you all" = 2 Cor 13:11; Phil 4:9; cf. 1 Cor 14:33—"God is not [a God] of turmoil (καταστασίας) but of peace"; *T. Dan* 5.2—ἔσεσθε ἐν εἰρήνῃ ἔχοντες τὸν θεὸν τῆς εἰρήνης. G. Delling ("Die Bezeichnung 'Gott des Friedens' und ähnliche Wendungen in den Paulusbriefen," in E. E. Ellis, E. Grässer, *Jesus und Paulus*, Festschrift W. G. Kümmel, Göttingen, 1975, pp. 76–84) considers "God of peace" a liturgical formula, almost equivalent to "God of all grace," analogous to "God of hope" (Rom 15:13), of patience (Rom 15:5), of compassion (2 Cor 1:3), as at Qumran: "God of justice" (1QM 18.8), of mercy (1QH 10.14; 11.29), of grace (1QM 14.8), of knowledge (1QS 3.15; 1QH 1.26; 12.10), of faithfulness (1QH 1.19). There were angels of peace (*T. Dan* 6.2, 5; *T. Benj.* 6.6; *T. Asher* 6.6; *Enoch* 40.8; 60.24). The Messiah was "Prince of peace" (Isa 9:5; Mic 5:3). In the second century, Rabbi Jose Hagelili refers to the Messiah simply by the name Peace (Str-B, vol. 3, p. 587). Cf. Epictetus 3.13.2: εἰρήνη ὑπὸ τοῦ θεοῦ κεκηρυγμένη διὰ τοῦ λόγου ("this peace proclaimed by God by means of reason [= philosophy])."

[41] Τὸ μεσότοιχον (cf. *Ep. Arist.* 139; cf. Y. Congar, *Le Mystère du temple*, Paris, 1958, pp. 133, 156). G. Ghyssens, "C'est lui qui es notre paix," in *Bible et vie chrétienne*, n. 24, 1958, pp. 28–36; J. Gnilka, "Christus unser Friede—ein Friedens-Erlöserlied in Eph. II, 14–17," in G. Bornkamm, K. Rahner, *Die Zeit Jesu* (Festschrift H. Schlier), Freiburg-Basel-Vienna, 1970, pp. 190–207; A. G. Lamadrid, " 'Ipse est pax nostra," in *EstBib*, 1970, pp. 101–136; 227–266; P. Stuhlmacher, "Er is unser Friede (Eph. II, 4): Zur Exegese und Bedeutung von Eph. II, 14–18," in J. Gnilka, *Neues Testament und Kirche* (for R. Schnackenburg), Freiburg-Basel-Vienna, 1974, pp. 337–358; M. Barth, *Ephesians*, vol. 1, pp. 260–314.

This altogether spiritual peace resides in hearts and thus points to the Holy Spirit, who infuses it in the form of mutual love, harmony, and brotherly unity: "To set the mind on the Spirit is life and peace" (Rom 8:6); "the reign of God is righteousness and peace and joy in the Holy Spirit."[42] So we understand not only that "the peace of God passes all understanding" (Phil 4:7), but that the apostles ceaselessly exhort believers to seek and find peace between themselves, because peace is a distinguishing mark of their religion.[43] This is what gives the *eirēnē* of the apostolic salutations its density of meaning;[44] it includes peace with God, the benefits of salvation, harmony with all people, Christian blessedness, that is, peace of heart or calm in the soul which is purified from its sins; an interior well-being that follows justification by faith and is the work of the Holy Spirit.

In the secular literature, the denominative verb *eirēneuō*, "be or live in peace," is always used in contrast to a state of war,[45] meaning that a kingdom (Josephus, *Ant.* 11.214; 20.49, 133) a city (*War* 6.100), a region[46]

---

[42] Rom 14:17; Gal 5:22—"The fruit of the Spirit is love, joy, peace"; Eph 4:3—"be zealous to maintain the unity of the Spirit by this bond of peace (ἐν τῷ συνδέσμῳ τῆς εἰρήνης). There is but one body and one Spirit."

[43] Rom 12:18—"Be at peace with all people" (εἰρηνεύοντες); 14:19—"We pursue that which contributes to peace and mutual edification"; 2 Tim 2:22—"Pursue righteousness, faith, love, peace with all those who call upon the Lord from a pure heart"; Heb 12:14—"Pursue peace with all" (εἰρήνην διώκετε, Ps 34:15); 1 Pet 3:11; 2 Pet 3:14—"Be zealous to be found by God in peace, without stain or blemish." Sin, being precisely the cause of the separation and hostility with God, is the contradiction of peace (cf. C. Spicq, *Théologie morale*, vol. 1, p. 173; cf. pp. 153ff.; vol. 2, p. 796). The isolated aphorism of Jas 3:18—"A fruit of righteousness in peace is sown for those who spread peace"—means that workers for peace also share in its fruits (Heb 12:11; Hos 10:12; Ps 85:11; Prov 11:21, 30); cf. R. M. Díaz Carbonell, "Nota a Jac. III, 18," in *XXXV Congreso eucaristico internacional*, Barcelona, 1953, vol. 1, pp. 508–509.

[44] The first Pauline salutation is χάρις ὑμῖν καὶ εἰρήνη (1 Thess 1:1); the last salutation of the NT is the Jewish personal wish εἰρήνη σοι (3 John 15). In 2 Thess 1:2 and following, the apostle develops χάρις ὑμῖν καὶ εἰρήνη ἀπὸ θεοῦ πατρὸς καὶ Κυρίου Ἰησοῦ Χριστοῦ (cf. 1 Cor 1:3; 2 Cor 1:2; Gal 1:3; Eph 1:2; cf. 6:23); Phil 1:2; Col 1:2; Phlm 3; Titus 1:4; Rev 1:4. Ἔλεος is inserted between χάρις and εἰρήνη in 1 Tim 1:2; 2 Tim 1:2; 2 John 3; the optative passive of the verb πληθύνω is added at 2 Pet 1:2; Jude 2. The formula of 1 Pet 5:14 is original: "Peace to all of you [who exist] in Christ"; it seems to refer to John 14:27; 16:33.

[45] Plato, *Tht.* 180 b: "Perhaps you have seen men in combat, but in their times of truce (εἰρηνεύουσιν) you have not been with them"; Aristotle, *Rh.* 1.4.1359ᵇ39: "One must know with which peoples one can expect to have war so as to remain at peace (εἰρηνεύηται) with those stronger than oneself."

[46] Polybius 5.8.7: "It is precisely on account of the peace that prevailed (εἰρηνευομένης) so long in this country that the dwellings around the sanctuary and the surrounding places were full of wealth"; Josephus, *Ant.* 20.204; *Life* 78, 211; *War*

is at peace, or that two sovereigns are reconciled (Dio Cassius 77.12; Dittenberger, *Or.* 199, 1; 613, 4). The same meaning occurs sometimes in the LXX,[47] but the verb is most often applied to individuals and means being tranquil,[48] having a human happiness.[49] The NT Christianizes this verb, giving it only a moral and individual meaning, always in parenesis. In its four occurrences, three are in the present imperative and all command keeping harmony and unity. Without a direct object, *eirēneuete* ("live in peace") means "have only one heart and one soul" (2 Cor 13:11); with *en allēlois* (Mark 9:50) or *en heautois* (1 Thess 5:13) it has to do with preserving good brotherly relations; Rom 12:18—"If possible, as much as lies within you, be at peace with all people"[50]—extends the effort to live peaceably to every neighbor. In the context, it is a matter of not returning evil for evil, not getting revenge, suppressing the causes of discord, and especially overcoming evil with good; all requirements of authentic charity.

The adjective *eirēnikos* takes on rather varied nuances:[51] (*a*) an objective meaning: that which has to do with peace ("a man engaged in a peaceful action, not a violent one");[52] (*b*) disposed to peace, opposed to

---

2.367: "forty long ships are sufficient to make peace prevail on the sea"; Dio Cassius 42.15: "although it had been pacified (καίπερ εἰρηνεύσασα) was agitated"; Philo, *To Gaius* 204: "matters of common interest: the means of establishing and maintaining peace everywhere" (ὡς εἰρηνεύεσθαι καὶ ἠρεμεῖσθαι τὰ πανταχοῦ πάντα).

[47] 1 Kgs 22:45—"Jehoshaphat made peace (hiphil of *šālam*) with the king of Israel"; 1 Macc 6:60—"Lysias sent to them to sue for peace" (εἰρηνεῦσαι); 2 Macc 12:4.

[48] 2 Chr 14:5–6; 20:30 (Hebrew *šāqaṭ*); Job 3:26—"I have neither peace (Hebrew *šālāh*) nor calm"; 5:23; 15:21; 16:12; Sir 6:6; 28:9—"the sinful person brings about divisions among those who are at peace" (εἰρηνευόντων); 28:13.

[49] Sir 41:9—death is bitter for "the man who lives in peace (εἰρηνεύοντι) amid his property"; 44:6; Dan 4:1—"I, Nebuchadnezzar, I was tranquil in my house (Aramaic *šᵉlēh*) and satisfied in my palace."

[50] Μετὰ πάντων ἀνθρώπων εἰρηνεύοντες (present participle). Ordinarily Epictetus 4.5.24 is cited: εἰρήνην ἄγεις πάντας ἀνθρώπους. Better to look to a letter from Ammonius (first-second century) in which he exhorts his brother to keep peaceful relations in apparently difficult circumstances, lest we give others opportunity to show their enmity toward us (εἰρηνεύειν καὶ μὴ διδόναι ἀφορμὰς ἑτέροις καθ' ὑμῶν, *P.Oxy.* 3057, 19).

[51] Cf. S. Daniel, *Recherches sur le vocabulaire du culte dans les Septante*, Paris, 1966, pp. 289ff.

[52] Plato, *Resp.* 3.399 *b*; cf. *Leg.* 5.729 *d*: "The Olympic contexts, those of war and of peace"; 7.814 *e*; 815 *a–d*; 816 *d*; 12.949 *d*: "sacrifices in peacetime" (περὶ θυσίας εἰρηνικῆς); 950 *e*: "peace congresses" (εἰρηνικαῖς συνουσίαις); Xenophon, *Oec.* 1.17: "labors of peace" (as opposed to labors of war); 6.1; *Hell.* 3.1.22: the army in peace formation; Josephus, *Ant.* 4.292, laws "for peacetime"; Plutarch, *C. Gracch.* 10.4: "a politics neither wholesome nor peaceable"; *Sert.* 6.9: ἐν ταῖς εἰρηνικαῖς χρείαις; Dio

bellicosity, used of relations between peoples or between parties in a city;[53] (c) that which is calm and peaceable, whether a city or individuals;[54] (d) in Philo, a personal moral quality: serenity, or an inclination to peace, loved for itself—"virtue is of a particularly peaceable nature."[55]

In the LXX, the "man of peace" (Hebrew *šālēm*) is a person who is benevolent and of a friendly disposition,[56] is sincere (Hebrew *kēn*; Gen 42:11, 19, 31, 33, 34) not only in speech[57] but also in conduct; he concludes "peaceful accords" (Zech 6:13; 8:16; 1 Macc 5:25). The peace offering (Hebrew *šelem*) was translated *eirēnikos*, [58] probably because of the idea of salvation, "safe and sound, well-being," with all the semantic richness of the Hebrew *šālôm*: desiring peace and appealing to God to obtain it.[59]

Cassius 41.17: "the garment reserved for peacetime"; 67.7: "artisans skilled in various things useful in peacetime and wartime"; 69.3: Adrian Afer "claimed to know nothing of the arts of peace and of war"; 53.10: "the pacified provinces"; 56.18: "peaceful assemblies."

[53] Isocrates, *De Pace* 136; *Nic.* 24; *Phil.* 5.46; Josephus, *War* 2.302: "the very peaceable sentiments of the people"; 3.30, 458; 4.84; 6.344; 3.448: offers of peace; 5.261, 356; *Ant.* 12.403; *War* 4.120: partisans of peace; 5.30: "Those who dreamed of obtaining peace"; 5.110 (cf. 2.135: εἰρήνης ὑπουργοί, servants of peace); Philo, *Dreams* 2.166; *Joseph* 166; *Moses* 1.243; *Spec. Laws* 4.224.

[54] Plato, *Leg.* 8.829 a: "A good city will live in peace"; Philo, *Abraham* 27: "a calm, tranquil, stable, and peaceable life (εἰρηνικόν βίον) is sought by those who hold virtue in honor"; 61: "a loyal and peaceable life"; *Spec. Laws* 1.224: a peaceable and serene existence; *Virtues* 47: "If you seek justice, holiness, and the other virtues, you will live a life without war in total peace"; *Prelim. Stud.* 25; *Dreams* 1.174: the peaceful repose of the athlete. In the papyri, εἰρηνικός appears only in the fourth century; two νυκτοστράτηγοι are presented as officials responsible for keeping good order: τῶν εἰρηνικῶν τὴν φροντίδα ἀναδεδοιημένοι (*P.Oxy.* 1033, 5); it was incumbent upon the police officer (τῷ τὰ εἰρηνικὰ ἐπιστα[τοῦντι?]) to recover the fugitives from a town (*P.Thead.* 17, 15). In the fifth century a Christian orphan writes to her aunt: "May the Lord keep you in good health through long and peaceful years" (*P.Bour.* 25, 17); in the sixth century, with regard to the repudiation of a fiancée, εἰρηνικόν καὶ ἡσύχιον διάξαι (129, 8; *P.Lond.* 1680, 13; vol. 5, p. 77); *P.Ness.* 29, 1: the peaceable emperor Augustus; *P.Cair.Masp.* 121, 9; *SB* 10522, 11.

[55] Philo, *Abraham* 105; cf. *Conf. Tongues* 49; *Joseph* 167; *Spec. Laws* 3.125; *Rewards* 87: εἰρηνικοὺς τὸ ἦθους, peaceable mores; *Abraham* 225: "the good man is not only peaceable and a friend of righteousness, but also courageous"; *Drunkenness* 76: "how to keep peace in one's soul (εἰρηνικῶς), even in the midst of war?"

[56] Gen 34:21; 37:4; Jer 38:22; Obad 1; Ps 37:37; 2 Macc 5:25.

[57] "Words of peace" (Hebrew *šālôm*), Deut 2:26; 20:11; Jer 9:8; Mic 7:3; Jdt 3:1; 7:24; Ps 35:20; 120:7; 1 Macc 1:30; 5:48; 7:10, 15, 27; 10:3, 47; 11:2; *T. Gad* 6.2.

[58] 1 Sam 10:8; 11:15; 2 Sam 6:17–18; 24:25; 1 Kgs 3:15; 8:63–64; 9:25; 2 Kgs 16:13; Prov 7:14; cf. Josephus, *Ant.* 7.86, 7.333, 7.382.

[59] Cf. S. Daniel, *Recherches sur le vocabulaire du culte dans les Septante*, pp. 291ff.

This nuance is not to be excluded at Heb 12:11, where the rigorous discipline of Israelite education leads finally to the peaceable fruit of righteousness (karpon eirēnikon dikaiosynēs).[60] The adjective eirēnikos refers to the agōn, to the rest of the victorious athlete after the competition (12:1) and to safety after the bloody combat (12:4). It retains the double meaning of biblical šālôm: interior peace with God, and (this-worldly) salvation.[61] Jas 3:17 is in line with LXX usage: Wisdom is first of all pure (hagnē, not stained, because it comes from God), very peaceful (eirēnikē), that is, judging from verse 16, opposed to disorder and intrigues (cf. Prov 3:17; Mal 2:6; Rom 8:6).

Unknown in the papyri, Philo, and Josephus, the verb eirēnopoieō is the equivalent of poieō eirēnēn: "make peace, pacify, conciliate."[62] An OT hapax, "The one who criticizes boldly makes peace" (Prov 10:10), it is also found in the NT. Col 1:20 places this verb in parallel with apokatallassō: God was pleased to reconcile all creatures with himself, "making peace by the blood of his cross." Christ is the instrument and the goal of reconciliation.

The adjective eirēnopoios, which appears for the first time in Xenophon,[63] is a Koine term, synonymous with eirēnikos,[64] but with an emphasis on nobility. Not only did Philo ask that thanks be given to "God who makes peace (tou eirēnopoiou theou) and preserves peace (eirēnophylakos)" (Spec. Laws 2.192); in addition, "peacemaker" was an attribute of the prince. Antony conferred it upon Caesar (ho eirēnopoios, Dio Cassius 44.49), and Commodus applied it to himself (eirēnopoios tēs oikoumenēs).[65]

---

[60] The contrast between the immediate affliction produced by discipline (Hebrew mûsār) and its spiritual fruitfulness is traditional, cf. Wis 3:5; 2 Cor 7:8ff.; Philo, Prelim. Stud. 160, 175; Plutarch, De virt. mor. 12; Aristotle, cited by Diogenes Laertius 5.1.18: τῆς παιδείας ἔφη τὰς μὲν ῥίζας εἶναι πικράς, γλυκεῖς δὲ τοὺς καρπούς.

[61] Deliverance from evil and triumph over one's enemies. Δικαιοσύνης, an appositive genitive, refers to moral rectitude as well as to union with God (cf. ἁγιότης, 12:10) and can even suggest eternal beatitude (11:7; cf. 2 Tim 4:8). The formula καρπὸς δικαιοσύνης is common: Isa 32:17; Amos 6:12; Prov 11:30; Phil 1:11; Jas 3:18; Philo, Post. Cain 118.

[62] Whereas the LXX translates Isa 27:5 ποιήσωμεν εἰρήνην, Aquila, Symmachus, and Theodotion substituted the verb εἰρηνοποιέω: "let them make peace with me." Cf. Hermes Trismegistus: ὅταν δὲ εἰρηνικοί, τότε καὶ αὐτὴ τὸν ἴδιον δρόμον εἰρηνοποιεῖται ("when they [angels and demons] are peaceful, then the soul also makes its course peaceful" [on the earth]), in Stobaeus, Ecl. 1.49.45 (vol. 1, p. 409).

[63] Xenophon, Hell. 6.3.4. Discourse of Callias: "When Athens needs tranquility (ἡσυχίας) it sends us as negotiators of peace (εἰρηνοποιούς)."

[64] Plutarch, Nic. 11.3: "There was opposition between the young, who were in favor of making war (πολεμοποιῶν), and the old, who were in favor of peace (εἰρηνοποιούς)"; Quaest. Rom. 62.

[65] Dio Cassius 72.15; PSI 1036, 28: εἰρηνοποιὸς τοῦ κόσμου (second century AD). Cf. H. Windisch, "Friedensbringer—Gottessöhne," in ZNW, 1925, pp. 240–260. Procuring peace (εἰρήνην παρέχειν) is an imperial duty: "the profound peace that Caesar

Certainly we cannot see this sovereign, political sense in the seventh beatitude of the Sermon on the Mount (*makarioi hoi eirēnopoioi*, Matt 5:9); still less can we see the *pacifici* of the Vulgate.[66] Rather, it is *pacificatori*, that is, persons whose action or influence pacifies or restores peace, favors good understanding, settles quarrels, annuls conflicts, reconciles, and calms minds.[67] The right translation is literal—"peacemakers"—those who pursue it and spread it, establishing it around themselves (the Peshitta translates ab^e day $š^elâmâ$, those who make peace), hence "artisans of peace."[68] At the same time, however, it has to be understood in terms of the function of the messianic messenger who establishes peace (Isa 9:6; Ezek 34:25, 29) and of charity-love, which always tends to come to expression, to act. Peacemakers show themselves to be children of God—of the God of peace (1 Thess 5:23; Phil 4:9; cf. Sir 4:10; *Jub.* 1.24–25).

---

seems to procure for us" (Epictetus 3.13.9–10). Augustus, ὁ εἰρηνοφύλαξ, is the guardian of the peace (Philo, *To Gaius* 144–146) and glories in having pacified the earth and the sea (*Res gest. divi Aug.* 13, 25, 26). Cf. A. Momigliano, "Terra marique," in *Journal of Roman Studies*, 1942, p. 64.

[66] The pacific person is originally "one who cannot be troubled in his possession," hence peaceable; but it is also understood of those who love peace and aspire to peace; cf. meek.

[67] The rabbinic example is Aaron: "Hillel said: Be among the disciples of Aaron, who loved peace; pursue peace, love creatures, and lead them to Torah" (*Pirqe 'Abot* 1.12; cf. *t. Sanh.* 1.2; *Sipre Num.* 42); "restoring peace between a man and his neighbor" profits a person in this world, and the capital goes with him for the world to come (*m. Pe'a* 1.1; *b. Šabb.* 127a; *b. Qidd.* 40a; cf. Str-B, vol. 1, p. 217). P. Fiebig, *Jesu Bergpredigt*, Göttingen, 1924, pp. 11ff.

[68] J. Dupont, *Béatitudes*, vol. 3, Paris, 1973, pp. 635ff. Cf. H. Huber, *Die Bergpredigt*, Göttingen, 1932, pp. 44ff. M. P. Brown, Jr., "Matthew as εἰρηνοποιός," in B. L. Daniels, M. J. Suggs, *Studies . . . in honor of K. W. Clark*, Salt Lake City, 1967, pp. 39–50; E. Dinkler, *Eirene: Der urchristliche Friedensgedanke*, Heidelberg, 1973.

> εἰσακούω, ἐπακούω, ὑπακούω, ὑπακοή
>
> *eisakouō, epakouō,* **to hear, listen to, heed;** *hypakouō,* **to heed, obey;** *hypakoē,* **obedience**
>
> →*see also* παρακοή; πειθαρχέω

The verb *akouō*, "hear, understand," occurs in combination with a number of prefixes (*eis-, ep-, pro-, hyp-,* etc.). *Eisakouō,* used without an object, expresses the idea "listen, heed";[1] with an accusative or genitive of the thing, it emphasizes the attention or the results of the hearing;[2] with the genitive of the person, it means the communication, the passing of information from one person to another (one hears[3] and so understands). Cf. the chorus to Tecmessa: "Listen to this man; he comes to tell us of the fate of Ajax" (Sophocles, *Aj.* 789). With the nuance of a favorable hearing: the ambassadors give a good reception to what Alcibiades has to say (Thucydides 5.45.4). Finally, the verb expresses the idea of taking heed of claims (idem I.126) and submitting to them: Olynthus had obtained the obedience of the closest neighboring cities.[4]

---

[1] Homer, *Il.* 8.97: "divine Ulysses did not listen as he ran on toward the hollow ships."

[2] Sophocles, *El.* 38: "such is the oracle that I heard"; Theocritus 24.34: "Alcmene heard cries and was the first to awaken"; Thucydides 4.34.3: "the cries of the enemy were too loud for them to hear the orders that were given them."

[3] Cf. Euripides, *El.* 416: "He rejoiced . . . when he heard that the child that he had saved was living"; Sophocles, *OC* 1645: "This is what we all heard"; *El.* 884: "From whom did you hear the news, that you believe it so strongly?"

[4] Xenophon, *Hell.* 5.2.13. This meaning is particularly frequent with negation = refuse; Thucydides 3.4.1: the Mytilenians do not obey the generals' message; Herodotus 1.214: Cyrus refuses to hear Tomyris.

---

eisakouō, S 1522; *TDNT* 1.222; *EDNT* 1.400; *NIDNTT* 2.172–173, 175, 177; MM 188; L&N 24.60, 36.15; BDF §173(3); BAGD 232 ‖ *epakouō,* S 1873; *TDNT* 1.222; *EDNT* 2.17; *NIDNTT* 2.172–173, 175, 178; MM 228; L&N 24.60; BDF §173(3); BAGD 282 ‖ *hypakouō,* S 5219; *TDNT* 1.223–224; *EDNT* 3.394–395; *NIDNTT* 2.179; MM 650; L&N 36.15, 46.11; BDF §§163, 173(3), 187(6), 202, 392(3); BAGD 837 ‖ *hypakoē,* S 5218; *TDNT* 1.224–225; *EDNT* 3.394–395; *NIDNTT* 2.179; MM 650; L&N 35.15; BDF §163; BAGD 837

These meanings are also found in the papyri of the third century BC, especially sympathetic hearing and taking heed. In a letter addressed to a *dioikētēs:* "We ask, if it seems good to you, that you summon certain ones of us and hear what they wish to tell you" (*P.Lond.* 1954, 8). Techesteus writes to Zeno, "Summon me and hear what I have to say; I have a proposal concerning how the water should be brought."[5] The usage is elevated in a hymn to Isis: "As for me, I heard from others of an extraordinary wonder";[6] and the goddess herself is the subject in the fourth century AD: "Do not let the gods sleep; Osiris will hear you, because you died prematurely, without child, without wife."[7]

The translators of the LXX obviously knew these secular meanings, but they considered the ear to be the organ of understanding and a channel of teaching;[8] they gave hearing a pedagogical meaning: "The wise listen to advice" (Jer 37:14; Prov 12:15; Hebrew *šōmē'a*). Not only does the LXX call for paying heed to teaching,[9] it attributes blessedness to the one who hears well (Prov 8:34). This hearing well involves having a positive moral disposition, paying heed, and being teachable. *Eisakouō* is thus in effect synonymous with believing, acquiescing, and complying.[10] To hear is to accept a proposition[11] or to pay heed to what has been said, and so to obey.[12]

The great innovation of the OT is to consider revelation as the word of God to humans and to require that people give it a good reception and

---

[5] *P.Lond.* 2054, 21; cf. *PSI* 377, 20: ἔγραψα οὖν σοι ἵνα εἰδῇς, ἐπειδὴ οὐ βούλει μου εἰσακοῦσαι. In the second century AD, Νικάριος εἰσήκουσα, ἐξουσίας οὔσης μεταμισθοῦν (*P.Mil.Vogl.* 130, 9; cf. 131, 14; *SB* 9380, 1; 8210, 14).

[6] E. Bernand, *Inscriptions métriques,* n. 175, col. IV, 35 (= *SB* 8141). Cf. a *proskynēma*: ἐσακοῦσαι θείου φθέγματος ἀπέρχομε (*SB* 8359, 2).

[7] *SB* 11247, 18: εἰσακούσει σε ὁ Οὔσιρις ὅτι; cf. B. Boyaval, "Une malédiction pour viol de sépulture," in *ZPE,* vol. 14, 1974, pp. 71-73 (compares *Pap.Graec.Mag.* 40, 14ff.). *P.Lond.* 1928, 2 is Christian, and εἰσήκουσέν μου is a quotation of Jonah 2:3. Cf. O. Montevecchi, "Quaedam de graecitate psalmorum cum papyris comparata," in *Proceedings* IX, pp. 303ff.

[8] P. Dhorme, *Emploi métaphorique,* p. 89. Cf. Deut 21:18—a rebellious son "does not hear the voice of his father or the voice of his mother; he does not listen to them when they correct him."

[9] Prov 8:6—"Listen, because I am going to tell you important things"; cf. Num 16:8; Isa 32:9; 42:23; Sir 39:13.

[10] Exod 4:8-9; 5:2; Deut 9:23; 13:9. The hardened heart is obstinate, does not listen (Exod 7:13, 22; 11:9), like the uncircumcised ear (Jer 6:10; 7:26) and the hard forehead (Ezek 3:7).

[11] Gen 34:17, 24; 42:21-22; Judg 11:28; 19:25; 20:13; 2 Kgs 10:6; Dan (Theodotion) 1:14.

[12] Hearing or not hearing the voice of Moses (Exod 3:18; 4:1; 6:9, 12, 30; 7:4; 16:20), of Joshua (Deut 34:9; 22:2), of the judges (Judg 2:17), of the angel (Exod 23:21).

submit to it. The verb *eisakouō* (more than 280 occurrences in the LXX) becomes for this reason one of the most important in OT theology when God is its subject. First of all, it is said repeatedly that God hears someone's voice and pays heed,[13] because he is merciful (Exod 22:26). He hears sighs (Exod 2:24; 6:15) as well as murmuring (16:7–9, 12), the cry of the poor (Job 34:28; Ps 34:6; 69:33), of the oppressed (Sir 35:13), of the widow (Jdt 9:4, 12), and the desire of the lowly (Ps 10:17). The faith of Israel is that "my God will hear me" (Mic 7:7), "his ear is not too heavy to hear" (Isa 59:1). It is precisely prayer that has this access to God, and *eisakouein* then means "grant an answer": "God hears the prayer of his servant in the temple";[14] "You will call upon him and he will answer you" (Job 22:27); "Have pity on me—hear my prayer";[15] "You will pray to me and I will answer you" (Jer 29:12). God shows himself propitious (Isa 19:22).

There are nevertheless cases in which God does not hear, refuses to pay heed (Deut 1:45; 3:26), for example when "your hands are bloody";[16] likewise, the great sin of Israel is refusal "to observe (Hebrew *šāmar*) my commandments and my laws" (*eisakouein tas entolas mou*, Exod 16:28), to hear his voice.[17] This religious hearing is obedience to the divine precepts, the carrying out of God's will;[18] better yet, it is loving God, becoming attached to him; "that is life for you" (Deut 30:20).

---

[13] Gen 21:17—"God heard the voice of the boy"; this is a play on the name Ishmael, which could be translated "God hears" or "May God hear" or "In calling upon God" or "Heard by God" (cf. Josephus, *Ant.* 1.190); Exod 22:22—"I will hear his cry"; Num 20:16—"We cried out to Yahweh and he heard our voice"; 21:3; Deut 9:19; 10:10; 26:7; Judg 3:9; 13:9; Neh 9:28; Ps 22:24; 31:22; 34:16, 18; 39:12; 40:1; 106:44; 141:1; Jdt 4:13—"The Lord heard their voice"; 8:17; Sus 35.

[14] 1 Kgs 8:29–30, 32, 34, 36, 39, 43, 45, 52; 2 Chr 6:21, 23, 25, 27, 30, 33; 7:14; cf. Tob 3:16.

[15] Ps 4:1; 5:3—"In the morning you hear my voice"; 6:8—"the voice of my weeping"; 17:2, 6; 27:7; 28:2, 6; 145:19; Jonah 2:3—"From the depths of Sheol I called, and you heard my voice"; Sir 34:24, 26; 51:11—"My prayer was answered; you saved me from ruin"; Bar 2:14, 16; Dan (Theodotion) 9:17, 19; (LXX) 10:12; 2 Macc 1:8—"We prayed to the Lord and we were heard."

[16] Isa 1:15 (cf. Jer 7:16; 11:11, 14; 14:12; Ezek 8:18); that is, the sentiments of the one praying and the object of the request have to be in conformity to God's will (Sir 3:5; 4:6; 2 Macc 8:3).

[17] Num 14:22; Deut 1:43; Jer 11:10; 17:23; 19:15; 25:4, 7; 26:5; 35:15; Bar 2:30; Neh 9:17; Zech 7:11–12.

[18] Deut 11:13, 28; 13:19; 15:5; 19:9; 27:10; 28:1, 2, 9, 15, 45, 58; 30:2, 8, 10, 16, 17; 1 Sam 12:15; Jer 17:27; Ezek 20:8, 39; Dan (Theodotion) 9:10, 11, 14; Zeph 3:2; Zech 1:4; 6:15.

Given the importance of this theology, it is remarkable that Philo's eight occurrences of this verb are all quotations on the OT[19] and the single occurrence in Josephus (*Ant.* 1.190) is likewise a quotation of Gen 16:11— Ishmael was so named "because God heard his supplication."[20]

Of the five NT occurrences of *eisakouō*, four (in the passive) mean to have one's petition granted and, in accord with LXX usage, have to do with prayers addressed to God. The first regards the "Gentiles,"[21] who think "that they will be heard (passive indicative future *eisakousthēsontai*) thanks to their many words,"[22] their verbiage (*polylogia*). This refers particularly to the multiplicity of titles attributed to the many-named divinity in attempts to win favor.[23] In the new religion, it is enough to call upon God as Father; this name alone already constitutes a prayer.[24]

The angel said to Zechariah, "Fear not, Zechariah, for your prayer (the coming of the Messiah) has been heard" (aorist passive indicative *eisēkousthē*, Luke 1:13), as to the centurion Cornelius: "Your prayer has been heard" (*eisēkousthē sou hē proseuchē*, Acts 10:31). According to Heb 5:7, Christ in the garden of agony, having offered prayers and supplications to God with

---

[19] Philo, *Alleg. Interp.* 2.88 (Exod 4:1ff.); *Post. Cain* 12 (Deut 30:20); *Drunkenness* 14 (Deut 21:18–21); *Migr. Abr.* 174 (Exod 23:20–21); *Prelim. Stud.* 70 (Gen 28:7); *Dreams* 1.92 (Exod 22:26–27); 2.175 (Deut 30:9–10).

[20] Διὰ τὸ εἰσακοῦσαι τὸν θεὸν τῆς ἱκεσίας. In the Apocrypha: "The Lord answers the prayer of everyone who fears God" (*Pss. Sol.* 6.8); "that this people might hear my voice and the decrees of my mouth" (Add Jer 7:32); "because they have not heard my voice nor kept my commandments" (*3 Apoc. Bar.* 16.4); "take pity on me and hear me" (*T. Abr.* A 7); "what I asked you, you granted" (ibid. 9); "Lord, Lord, hear my voice" (ibid. 10); "They made this prayer and this supplication for this soul, and God answered them. . . . I have heard your voice and your prayer" (ibid. 14); the archangel to God: "I have obeyed your friend Abraham in all that he said to you" (ibid. 15).

[21] In the pejorative sense of ἐθνικοί, Matt 6:7; cf. A. Pelletier, *Josèphe adaptateur*, pp. 79ff.

[22] Matt 6:7. D. Buzy, *Evangile selon saint Matthieu*, Paris, 1935, pp. 74ff. C. Spicq, *Dieu et l'homme*, p. 64.

[23] Cf. the beginning of Cleanthes' *Hymn to Zeus*: "Most glorious of the immortals, you who are invoked by so many names, eternally all-powerful one, Zeus, author of nature, who govern all things by law, I greet you" (Stobaeus, *Ecl.* 1.1.12; vol. 1, p. 25; cf. A. J. Festugière, *Dieu cosmique*, pp. 310ff.; E. des Places, *La Religion grecque*, Paris, 1969, pp. 263ff.), invocations to Isis (ὑπὸ δὲ τῶν πολλῶν μυριώνυμος κέκληται, Plutarch, *De Is. et Os.* 53; Dittenberger, *Or.* 695, 2; *P.Ross.Georg.* III, 4, 4; *SB* 4101, 2), to Osiris (cf. *The Book of the Dead* 142; ed. P. Barguet, Paris, 1967, pp. 186ff.). A Jewish-Aramaic amulet from Aleppo: "O Holy One . . . sublime, exalted God, my help, Elyeh, Ahmah, etc." (*C.Pap.Jud.* 819, 2ff.).

[24] J. Lewy, "Some Observations Concerning Biblical Prayer," in *HUCA*, vol. 22, 1961, pp. 79ff.

loud cries and tears, was heard because of his piety (*eisakoustheis* [aorist passive participle] *apo tēs eulabeias*).²⁵ *Eulabeia* here is filial devotion, well translated by the Vulgate: "exauditus est pro sua reverentia."²⁶ It is often said that suppliants are saved thanks to their piety (*dia tēn pros theous eusebeian*, Diodorus Siculus 12.57.4; cf. 11.12), that a miracle is obtained because of the piety of the sacrificing priest,²⁷ that an act of adoration is done *eusebias charin*;²⁸ but here (*apo tēs eulabeias*) we have to take *apo* as indicating consequence ("because of"; cf. Exod 3:7; 6:9; Matt 18:7; Luke 19:3; etc.). It was because Christ's piety was outstanding, because he submitted himself wholly to his Father's will, that his prayer was heard with favor and answered.

1 Cor 14:21 is a very free quotation of Isa 28:12—"The Lord will speak to this people through people that babble and in a foreign tongue . . . and they would not hear."²⁹ St. Paul applies this text to glossalalia: "By people of a foreign land and by the lips of foreigners I will speak to this people, and even then they will not listen to me" (*kai oud' houtōs eisakousontai mou*, future middle indicative). Speaking in tongues is not a sign of divine blessing upon a community, not a "sign for believers"; this obscure, even unintelligible mode of expression is above all intended for pagans who will see in it divine revelation! What is clear is that this "hearing" of the glossalalia in the Christian community is to be understood according to its LXX meaning (Hebrew '*ānâh* = respond): accepting the divine message, submitting one's life to it, obeying.

Epakouō. — In classical Greek, this verb is in many cases synonymous with the preceding one and means simply "hear,"³⁰ but its particular

---

²⁵ The text is difficult. On the numerous explications of it, cf. C. Spicq, *Hébreux*, vol. 2, pp. 112ff. Cf. E. Rasco, "La oración sacerdotal de Cristo en la tierra según Hebr. V, 7," in *Gregorianum*, 1962, pp. 723–755; T. Boman, "Der Gebetskampf Jesu," in *NTS*, vol. 10, 1964, pp. 261–273; J. Jeremias, *Abba*, pp. 319–323.

²⁶ Cf. C. Spicq, "Religion (Vertu de)," in *DBSup*, vol. 10, col. 210–232; cf. C. Maurer, " 'Erhört wegen der Gottesfurcht,' Hebr. V, 7," in *Neues Testament und Geschichte* (Festschrift O. Cullmann), Zurich, 1972, pp. 275–284.

²⁷ Πρὸς εὐσέβειαν τοῦ ἱερέως, at Stratonicea in Caria, in L. Robert, *Hellenica*, vol. 12, Paris, 1960, p. 543.

²⁸ *SB* 13, 1167, 8658; *SEG* VIII, 773; *CIRB*, n. 44, 13.

²⁹ Καὶ οὐκ ἠθέλησαν ἀκούειν. This transmission of the word of God by foreigners was as a punishment for the hardening of the elect people, who no longer listened to the voice of the prophets.

³⁰ Herodotus 2.70: "The crocodile hears the cries of the piglet and goes in the direction they are coming from"; Plato, *Grg.* 487 *c:* "One day I heard you deliberating on a point . . ."; cf. Menander, *Dysk.* 821: "I heard your whole conversation from the beginning, while going out the door"; Plutarch, *Flam.* 10.6: the spectators at the Isthmian games "did not all hear, nor hear distinctly, the proclamation" of the herald and ask for a second hearing.

nuance is rather that of paying heed, paying attention. "Men of Ionia, as much as you are able to hear me (*epakountes*), pay heed to what I say" (Herodotus 9.98); "Pay attention to the moment when you hear the voice of the crane call."[31] Hence: "take account, obey an order"; "Histiaeus, obeying the first order" (*epakousas tō prōtō keleusmati,* Herodotus 4.141); "Listen to justice, forget violence" (Hesiod, *Op.* 274). In Homer, however, the verb has a religious meaning and is used for the deity: "Father Zeus, you who see all and hear all" (*pant' epakoueis, Il.* 3.277). When used regarding prayer, it means "hear and answer": "Hear my prayer, accept my offering" (Aristophanes, *Nub.* 274; cf. Aeschylus, *Cho.* 725).

This meaning is well attested in the inscriptions and the papyri. At Iasos, an altar is dedicated to Aphrodite: Aphroditēs epakouousēs kai epēkoou.[32] At Laodicea on the sea, a dedication reads "Karpeina, who was heard (*epakousthisa*) following a vow, has consecrated (this) to the propitious goddesses (*theais epēkoois*)."[33] Invocation to Isis in the second century BC: "Come to me, god of gods, show yourself merciful; hear me; take pity on the Twins."[34] This hearing and answering is also found in secular materials. After King Attalus II of Pergamum made a donation, the city of Delphi acknowledged it thus: "He gave an eager welcome to our requests" (*epakousas prothymōs,* Dittenberger, *Syl.* 672, 6). In a letter to Zeno, the following occurs: "Write me concerning whatever you wish; I will be happy to carry it out" (*hēdeōs epakousomenou, P.Mich.* 103, 15; cf. *P.Cair.Zen.* 59080, 3). The meaning "listen attentively" is common: "Remain and listen for a while to one deceased."[35]

---

[31] Hesiod, *Op.* 448; Plato, *Soph.* 227 c: "Pay attention to me for what follows"; Sophocles, *OT* 708: Jocasta to Oedipus, "Hear me;" Aristophanes, *Eq.* 1080: "Hear this oracle again"; Homer, *Od.* 19.98: "Let the foreigner speak to me and listen to me; I wish to question him." Hence: become informed, "You will learn the trials that await you" (Euripides, *Tro.* 166).

[32] J. and L. Robert, "Bulletin épigraphique," in *REG*, 1973, p. 165, n. 429.

[33] *IGLS* 1262. The word of the prophet is listened to as that of a god, ἐπακούομαι ὡς θεός (Vettius Valens 63, 19; cf. F. Cumont, *L'Egypte des astrologues,* p. 120, n. 5; p. 158, n. 2). Ἐπήκοος is an Egyptian, Greek, and Roman adjective for deities that answer prayers; the classic collection is O. Weinrich, "Θεοὶ ἐπήκοοι," in *Mitteilungen des kaiserlich-deutschen Archaeologischen Instituts,* vol. 37, 1912, pp. 1–68; cf. Y. Grandjean, *Arétalogie d'Isis,* p. 17, line 7: "You have heard, Isis, the prayers that I addressed to you; come for the praises that I intend for you"; p. 30, n. 33; *SB* 4947, 6.

[34] *UPZ* 78, 28: ἐλθέ μοι, θεὰ θεῶν, εἵλεως γινομένη, ἐπάκουσόν μου, ἐλέησον τὰς διδύμας; 81, col. II, 20; *SEG* VIII, 621, 4 (= *SB* 7871); *BGU* 1080, 6; cf. a Christian letter from the fourth century: "May God also hear your prayers" (*P.Oxy.* 1494, 7).

[35] Tomb inscription, in E. Bernand, *Inscriptions métriques,* n. 97, 4 = *SB* 7871, 4. Cf. *P.Oxy.* 2562, 5: "You have heard the decision of my lord the most illustrious prefect of Egypt"; a pilgrim wishes to hear the voice of the Colossus of Memnon (*SEG* XX, 685, 3 - *SB* 101 = A. and E. Bernand, *Memnon,* n. 70, 3); *SB* 11043, 7.

The translators of the LXX (Hebrew *šāmaʻ* and *ʻānâh*) knew this secular meaning,[36] but they almost always used the word for God's hearing with favor[37] and granting an answer: "Isaac prayed to God . . . and God heard him."[38] Beginning with Jacob this granting of an answer is expressed as a response: "I made an altar to God who responded to me in my day of distress" (Gen 35:3); "Samuel cried to God for Israel, and God responded to him."[39] In a corresponding fashion the pious hear the words of the Lord and obey what he commands ("I heard the voice of the Lord" [Deut 26:14; 2 Chr 11:4]) in all that he commands.[40]

Philo knew this religious meaning of the word: "God hears suppliants" (*Worse Attacks Better* 93) and "heeds the prayers of Moses";[41] but most of his occurrences mean simply to hear: "The governor of the land . . . pretended not to hear what he heard."[42] The same commonplace meaning occurs in Josephus: "They were afraid of being heard by the enemy" (*War* 4.331); "Titus heard quietly what was said to him."[43]

The verb is not only a hapax in the NT but a quotation of Isa 49:8 (LXX): "At the favorable time I answered you" (*kairō dektō epēkousa sou*, 2 Cor 6:2). The prophet envisioned the return from exile; St. Paul understands a reference to the messianic age and the apostolic preaching: a fav-

---

[36] Isa 8:9—"Pay heed, all nations of the earth" (hiphil of the Hebrew *ʼāzan*); 10:30 (hiphil of *qāšaḇ*); 55:3; Jdt 14:15—"no one listened"; Cant 5:6—"I called him, but he did not answer"; cf. listen to advice (2 Chr 25:16).

[37] Gen 16:11; 17:20; 21:17; Josh 10:14; Judg 13:9; 2 Chr 6:19; 30:20, 27; Ps 145:19; Jer 18:19; Dan 9:17-19; Prov 15:29—"God hears (answers) the supplications of the righteous"; Sir 4:6. Cf. 2 Sam 21:14—"God showed favor to the land" (ἐπήκουσεν, Hebrew niphal of *ʻātar*); 24:25; 1 Chr 5:20; 21:26; Isa 19:22. J. Barr, "The Meaning of ἐπακούω and cognates in the LXX," in *JTS*, 1980, pp. 67-72.

[38] Gen 25:21—ἐπήκουσε δὲ αὐτοῦ ὁ θεός; 30:6, 17, 22; 2 Sam 22:7; 2 Kgs 13:4; 2 Chr 33:13, 19; Isa 41:17; 49:8; Zech 10:6; Ps 22:24; Sir 48:20; 2 Macc 1:5.

[39] 1 Sam 7:9; 1 Kgs 18:24, 37; Job 33:13; Ps 3:4; 17:6; 20:1, 9; 34:4; 65:5; 69:13, 17; 81:7; 86:1; 91:15; 99:6, 8; 108:6; 118:5, 21; 119:26, 145; 138:3; 143:1; Isa 30:19; 65:24; Hos 2:23; Zech 13:9. C. Cox, "Εἰσακούω and Ἐπακούω in the Greek Psalter," in *Bib*, 1981, pp. 251-258.

[40] Josh 22:2; Isa 45:1; 50:10; cf. Esth 4:17—to effect that which is asked.

[41] *Moses* 1.47; 2.229; *Spec. Laws* 4.32; *Flight* 1 and 5 quoting Gen 16:11. *Joseph* 265: "God sees all and hears all" seems to be a citation of Homer, *Il*. 3.277.

[42] *To Gaius* 132: ὧν ἤκουε μὴ ἐπακούειν; cf. *Post. Cain* 137; *Dreams* 1.129, 191; *Moses* 2.170; *Conf. Tongues* 8.

[43] *War* 7.104; 7.355, 385. In 16 occurrences, only 2 are religious: God hears (answers) prayers (*Ant.* 9.10; 10.41).

orable time for action, since it is God's "accepted" (*dektos*) time for help—hence an opportune time.[44]

Hypakouō. — In classical and Hellenistic Greek, this verb is often synonymous with the preceding forms ("pay heed, listen"), with the emphasis on the attention given. "I awakened Ulysses, I spoke to him, and he paid me heed at once" (Homer, *Od.* 14.485); "Pay heed, hear, O mother, I beg you."[45] The prefix has its force, however, both in Aristophanes, where one seems to bend the head down to listen ("At least listen to the little child," *Lys.* 878) and also in the meaning "listen at a door, answer"; which today is the job of a concierge or porter: "Upon our arrival, the porter (*ho thyrōros*) came out to meet us—he was the one who used to answer (*eiōthei hypakouein*)—and told us to stay there and wait for him" (Plato, *Phd.* 59 e); "Philip, the fool, knocked at the door and told the porter (*tō hypakousanti*) to announce him" (Xenophon, *Symp.* 1.11); "If it is an aged man who answers the door (*tē thyra hypakēko'*) I say at once, 'My father, my dear father.'"[46] Thus when St. Peter knocked on the door, "a young servant-girl named Rhoda went to answer" (Acts 12:13).

The dictionaries give another meaning, "obey," and it is indeed true that this meaning is clearly attested, especially in the political arena;[47] but the shades of meaning—difficult as they are to distinguish—are many. For example, it is obvious that the Samaritans did not "obey" the kings of Syria (Josephus, *Ant.* 13.275) but conformed to their commands (cf. 3.207), because hearing often means "answering an invitation"[48] and "taking into

---

[44] Taking the context into account, L. Cerfaux ("Saint Paul et le 'Serviteur de Dieu' d'Isaïe," in *Miscellanea biblica et orientalia, R. P. A. Miller oblata*, Rome, 1951, p. 359) specifies that the point is the grace offered concretely, at that time, in Paul's mission. The presence and ministry of the apostle, sent and protected by God, offers to the Corinthians "in that moment the irreplaceable opportunity for salvation, their last chance."

[45] Euripides, *Alc.* 400; Ps.-Homer, *H. Aphr.* 1.181: "He eagerly shook off his sleep to listen"; Xenophon, *Cyr.* 8.1.18: "Cyrus did not have the leisure to listen"; 8.1.20; 8.3.21; 8.4.9; 8.7.16; hence, answer and grant the request, Diodorus Siculus 4.34.5

[46] Menander, *Dysk.* 494; Theophrastus, *Char.* 4.12: "If someone knocks on the door, he comes in person to answer"; 28.3—to the question "Who are the women who live in this house?" the slanderous person answers, "They are wantons, women who answer in person when someone knocks at the door"; *P.Oxy.* 2719, 14 (third century).

[47] Herodotus 3.101: "These Indians were never subject to Darius"; the peoples accepted submission to Cyrus (Xenophon, *Cyr.* 1.1.3); the allies were "subjects of the empire" (Thucydides 6.69.3); people submit to the general (ibid. 3.3.11), to the president of a brotherhood (*P.Lond.* 2193 = *SB* 7835, 10), to the laws (Aeschines, *In Tim.* 1.49; Plato, *Leg.* 4.708 d; Dittenberger, *Syl.* 785, 18).

[48] Athenaeus 6.247 d; Plutarch, *Sol.* 31.3: "the accuser did not appear" (οὐχ

εἰσακούω, eisakouō, etc. 447

account" what is asked (Herodotus 3.148). Sometimes it is done willingly, one complies easily (Xenophon, *Cyr.* 2.2.3), and this is the case with the wife who owes obedience to her husband.[49] Sometimes you turn a deaf ear to appeals that are directed to you (Xenophon, *An.* 4.1.9) because to submit to someone else is to compromise your freedom,[50] so one obeys with difficulty;[51] hence the frequent meaning "yield" in Thucydides.[52]

The verb is often used in the papyri, meaning either strict obedience to an order or a law,[53] or an agreement to carry out one's responsibility;[54] or even the spontaneous and loving submission of a wife to her husband (*hypakouousēs moi kai phylattousēs moi pasan eunoian*, P.Lond. 1711, 35; 1727, 12). The commonest meaning, however, is "respond" and "correspond": "I have sworn that I will respond to all questions concerning the vessel" (*P.Oxy.* 87, 19). In the considerations listed in an honorific decree of Athens for the poet Philippides: "He willingly responded to the desires of the people (*hypēkousen tō dēmō ethelontēs*) and celebrated the traditional sacrifices at his own expense" (Dittenberger, *Syl.* 374, 39; third century BC; *Ep. Arist.* 44). In the judicial sphere, it has to do with answering an authoritative summons: "Since Cathytes, summoned before men, has not responded (*ouch' hypēkousen*), I have decided that for his disobedience (*apeithias*) he shall pay 250 denarii."[55] In the third century AD, the verb is used for the

---

ὑπήκουσε). Cf. corresponding to a desire: Eleazar to King Ptolemy—"Every time it is a matter of serving your interests, we will follow your desires" (*Ep. Arist.* 44).

[49] Philemon, frag. 132 K: ἀγαθῆς γυναικός ἐστιν, μὴ κρεῖττον᾽ εἶναι τἀνδρὸς ἀλλ᾽ ὑπήκοον (Stobaeus, *Flor.* 74, 20; vol. IV, 23); Josephus, *Ag. Apion* 2.201: "the wife ought to obey her husband, not to humiliate herself but to be guided, because it is to the man that God has given the power." Cf. Plato, *Lach.* 200 d: "You will know better how to make yourself listen (= obey)."

[50] Thucydides 2.62.3; to submit is to expose oneself in the positive sense to the air (Theophrastus, *Caus. Pl.* 2.12.1), to the cold (ibid. 5.4.2), to the sun's rays (Pindar, *Ol.* 3.44).

[51] Said of certain diseases with regard to the cures, δυσκόλως ὑπακούοντα (Hippocrates, *Epid.* 3.8). Cf. Plutarch, *Thes.* 1.5: "Can we oblige the fables to submit to reason and take on the character of history."

[52] Thucydides 1.141: "You ought to yield before suffering harm"; 5.98; cf. 1.29.1: "The Corinthians did not wish to yield"; 1.26.4; 1.139.2.

[53] *P.Sorb.* 63, 8: "Know well that if you do not obey my orders . . ."; *P.Mich.* 604, 16: submitting to the law of the *stratēgos*; *P.Mil.Vogl.* 237, 12 (oath of obedience to the prefect); *SB* 7835, 10; 9393, 12; 11222, 9; *P.Tebt.* 24, 26 and 28; *P.Oxy.* 900, 9; *P.Cair.Isid.* 102, 10; 113, 10; *P.Mil.* 64, 12. Cf. *P.Hamb.* 169, 5: "Thus far they have not followed up" (241 BC); *P.Cair.Zen.* 59367, 15 = *SB* 6768.

[54] *P.Oxy.* 1889, 21: ὁμολογῶ . . . ὑπακούειν; 1982, 21; *SB* 6266, work contract: ὑπακούειν ὑμῖν ἐν πᾶσι καλοῖς ἔργοις; 6643, 17; 6704, 12; 9503, 12; *P.Aberd.* 19, 11: "If Gaius Julius L., here present, consents to this decision and swears to it . . ."; *P.Oxy.* 2765, 10: present and consenting; *SB* 10205, 14.

identification of a person in court: "This is the person who answered when his name was called."[56]

The LXX gives no special meaning to this verb, treating it as a synonym of *eisakouō* and *epakouō*, in the sense of either hearing[57] or especially of obeying.[58] On the one hand, paying heed already means taking into account (Gen 27:13; Dan [Theodotion] 3:12; cf. Philo, *Flight* 21; *Cherub.* 9) and obeying ("When their ear hears, they obey me," Ps 18:44). On the other hand, most of the usages are religious: hearing God's voice means putting his commandments into practice.[59] Otherwise, *hypakouō* translates the Hebrew *'ānâh* in the sense of "respond": "I called and you did not answer me."[60] Philo gives this verb especially the sense of "obey," but he distinguishes between constrained, forced obedience (*Creation* 142; *Moses* 1.156) and voluntary obedience (*Joseph* 269), the latter being the obedience of children who accept being in submission to their parents' orders (*Spec. Laws* 2.236). He recognizes that "it is very onerous to be compelled to obey a large number of commandments" (*Husbandry* 49) and that the subject (*to hypakouon*) always fears the power of the one who commands even delicately (*Virtues* 114), although people do not obey the commands of the first one to come along (*Good Man Free* 25). But obedience is learned (*hypakouein mathontōn, Conf. Tongues* 55; *Migr. Abr.* 8; cf. Heb 5:8); it is the work of education (*Drunkenness* 198). Obeying someone else does not destroy freedom, as can be seen from the submission of children to parents or that of students to their teacher (*Good Man Free* 36, 156).

In conformity to this evolution, *hypakouō* in the NT always means "obey" (and takes the genitive or the dative) except at Acts 12:13 (cf. above). Unknown in St. John, it is found in the Synoptics only for the winds and

---

[55] *P.Achm.* 8, 28; *BGU* 1826, 25; *P.Mich.* 534, 7, 13; *SB* 7368, 10; 7558, 10; 7696, 36; *P.Fouad* 24, 3: "If they do not respond [to my citation], I will let you distribute"; *PSI* 1100, 10; 1265, 8; *P.Hamb.* 29, 5: κληθέντων τινῶν καὶ μὴ ὑπακουσάντων; *P.Flor.* 6, 24: κληθεὶς μὴ ὑπακούσῃς = if, having been summoned, you do not comply, the consequence will be . . . ; *P.Stras.* 41, 50; *P.Oslo* 80, 24; *P.Oxf.* 5 *a* 6; *P.Oxy.* 3117, 3; P. M. Meyer, *Jur.Pap.*, n. 85.

[56] *P.Oxy.* 2892, col. I, 24; 2894, col. II, 35, 40; col. III, 32; 2895, col. I, 24; 2902, 8, 21, 24; 2922, 13; 2927, 2, 10, etc.; 2930, 7; 2931, 5; 2932, 4; 2936, 29, 31.

[57] Gen 16:2 (Hebrew *šāmāʻ*); 27:13; 39:10; Sir 24:22; cf. 2 Chr 24:19—"they do not heed" (Hebrew *'āzan*).

[58] Gen 41:40—"At Joseph's order, all the people submitted"; 1 Chr 29:23—"all the Israelites obeyed Solomon"; everyone obeyed God (Dan 7:27; Bar 3:33; Sir 42:23) who hears prayers (Prov 15:29; 2 Macc 1:5); obedience to the high priest, 1 Macc 10:38.

[59] Gen 22:18; 26:5; Lev 26:14, 18, 21, 27; Deut 26:14; 30:2; Josh 22:2; Jer 3:13, 25; 11:10; 16:12; Dan 3:30.

[60] Cant 5:6; 2 Sam 22:42: "They cry to Yahweh, and he does not answer them"; Isa 50:2; 65:12, 24; 66:4; Job 5:1; 9:3, 14, 16; 13:22; 14:15; 19:16; Prov 29:19.

εἰσακούω, eisakouō, etc.   449

the sea (Luke 8:25; Matt 8:27; Mark 4:41) and for unclean spirits constrained and forced to submit to Christ's orders; also for the sycamore in Luke 17:6 that would not be able to resist the apostles' faith.

The theological meaning appears in Acts 6:7—at Jerusalem, a great multitude of Jewish priests obey the faith (hypēkouon tē pistei); this imperfect of repetition and duration suggests the continuity of the conversions of those who paid heed to the preaching of the apostles and committed themselves to it, that is, who submitted heart and spirit to what they heard: the doctrine and requirements of the Christian faith (cf. Rom 1:5; 16:26). This would again be called "obedience to the gospel" (2 Thess 1:8; Rom 10:16). The gospel preached and transmitted took form in a "type of teaching" to which people became obedient from the bottom of their hearts,[61] that is to say, with all their being—understanding, will, conduct. In effect, one is the slave of whomever one obeys (douloi este hō hypakouete, Rom 6:16). Whether the master be God or sin, one receives the master's orders and carries them out; serving two masters simultaneously is impossible. If sin is the reigning prince, then one's desires are conformed to it; one consents or yields to it (Rom 6:12). Believers, however, are defined as "those who obey" Christ, the bringer of eternal salvation (Heb 5:9). Thus they correspond to the obedience of the one who submitted to the Father even to the point of death (5:8). In all cases, it is clear that Christian "obedience" is the strictest obedience there is. More than a de facto submission, it is free, complete, and definitive commitment to the one recognized and confessed as a master with full prerogatives. As a subject, the believer is not only dependent upon the Lord's wishes but consecrated to him in life and in death. To have faith is to profess and to make real this "obedience." A fine example of this faith is that of Abraham who "when called, obeyed" God's command right away (Heb 11:12); the juxtaposition

---

[61] Rom 6:17. It is difficult to specify the meaning of τύπος διδαχῆς, given the variety of meanings of the first word. Proposals include form of teaching, norm, rule, model, schema (A. Blumenthal, "Τύπος und Παράδειγμα," in Hermes, 1928, pp. 391–414; G. Roux, "Le Sens de τύπος," in REA, 1961, pp. 5–14). In the papyri, typos is a fixed rule, in contrast to custom (συνήθεια) and a legal term (P.Panop.Beatty 1, 130, 135, 136, 262); in architecture, it is the architect's plan, the mock-up, or the wooden stamp that marks an imprint on the clay (A. Orlandos, Technique architecturale, p. 93). So we could interpret that Christian doctrine puts its authenticating mark on a life in conformity to the will of God and the model of Christ. Cf. J. Kürzinger, "Τύπος διδαχῆς und der Sinn von Röm. VI, 17f," in Bib, 1958, pp. 156–176; F. W. Beare, "On the Interpretation of Romans VI, 17," in NTS, vol. 5, 1959, pp. 206–210; C. H. Dodd, "The Primitive Catechism and the Sayings of Jesus," in New Testament Essays, pp. 109–118; C. Spicq, Théologie morale, vol. 2, pp. 723ff. U. Borse, " 'Abbild der Lehre': Röm. VI, 17," in BZ, 1968, pp. 95–103.

kaloumenos hypēkousen evokes more than consent. According to the usage of the papyri (cf. above) it expresses the exactitude of the human response to the divine will, whatever that will may be.

This religious obedience "in the Lord" is commanded to children with respect to their parents (Eph 6:1; Col 3:1; we can also take *hypakouete* in the sense of "pay heed") and to slaves with respect to their masters . . . as to Christ (Eph 6:5; Col 3:22), desiring to please them. Sarah, a model for Christians, obeyed Abraham, whom she recognized as her lord and master (1 Pet 3:6). Envisioning the public reading of his epistles, St. Paul, after condemning the lazy who will not work, commands, "If anyone will not obey our word (expressed) in this letter . . . no longer have anything to do with him" (2 Thess 3:14). Thanks to God, whether the apostle was present or absent the community at Philippi always obeyed him (Phil 2:12); we could almost translate that they always heard him.

Hypakoē. — This noun, unknown in classical Greek, seems to appear for the first time as a hapax in the LXX,[62] where it translates the Hebrew *"nāwâh* ("humility," cf. Ps 18:36; Prov 15:23). In *Gos. Pet.* 42, it means "response."[63] We could say that it was St. Paul who introduced *hypakoē* into the Greek language and gave it its meaning of strict obedience,[64] first of all with regard to the submission of every person to God,[65] and then of the obedience of Christ as contrasted with Adam,[66] the first disobedient man: "By the obedience of one, all will be constituted righteous" (Rom 5:19). This obedience refers to the mission on which Christ was sent into the

---

[62] 2 Sam 22:36, a song of David: "Your gentleness (ὑπακοή) enlarged me." In *T. Jud.* 17.3 there may be a Christian gloss, ἣν ἔδωκέ μοι Κύριος ἐν ὑπακοῇ πατρός μου.

[63] *Gos. Pet.* 42: a voice from the heavens asks Jesus, " 'Have you preached to those who sleep?' And an answer was heard (ὑπακοὴ ἠκούετο) coming from the cross: 'Yes' "; cf. *Acts John* 94; *Const. App.* 8.13.13. The term is unknown in the papyri until the sixth century, when it appears in a work contract: μεθ' ὑπερτάτης ἀρετῆς καὶ ὑπακοῆς ἐν πᾶσι τοῖς ὀφελίμοις ἔργοις τε καὶ λόγοις (*P.Stras.* 40, 41); *P.Cair. Masp.* 159, 24: μετὰ πάσης ὑποταγῆς καὶ ὑπακοῆς παρ' ἀλλήλων εἰς ἀλλήλους.

[64] Except at Phlm 21, where πεποιθὼς τῇ ὑπακοῇ could be translated "being confident in your teachableness" or "in your mildness." Perhaps the ὑπακοή of the Corinthians with regard to Titus and Paul (2 Cor 7:15) is teachableness or humility rather than obedience in the strict sense (cf. 7:7, 11).

[65] Rom 6:16—When you are in someone's service, it is in order to obey him (εἰς ὑπακοήν), that is, to carry out his orders, as a slave does for his master. Now when a person obeys God, this voluntary submission procures righteousness, ὑπακοῆς εἰς δικαιοσύνην.

[66] Cf. K. Romaniuk, *L'Amour du Père et du Fils dans la sotériologie de saint Paul*, Rome, 1961, pp. 96–150.

world, and especially the crucifixion (*genomenos hypēkoos mechri thanatou*).[67] Heb 5:8 specifies: "Even though he was a Son, he learned obedience by the things that he suffered" (*emathen . . . tēn hypakoēn*).[68] Just as the Savior's whole life was characterized by his submission to God's will, the Christian life is defined by the initial undertaking of baptism, the obedience of the faith (*eis hypakoēn pisteōs*).[69] We recognize and profess that Christ is the only master and Lord of our life; we submit to him our thoughts, will, and conduct better than prisoners of war bound hand and foot and turned over to a new authority: "We take every thought captive to the obedience of Christ (*eis tēn hypakoēn tou Christou*), and we are ready to punish all disobedience, when your obedience shall be complete."[70]

St. Peter's three uses of this term are remarkable. First of all in the primitive definition of baptism: "Having perfectly sanctified your souls by obedience to the truth" (1 Pet 1:22), the heart commitment and public proclamation of this commitment to the divine revelation, which brings definitive belonging to God (perfect participle). The letter is addressed "to

---

[67] Phil 2:8; cf. P. Henry, "Kénose," in *DBSup*, vol. 5, col. 33.

[68] It is a constantly recurring axiom that painful trials teach the wise (Aeschylus, *Ag.* 177; Herodotus 1.207; *Moses* 2.280; cf. J. Coste, "Notion grecque et notion biblique de la souffrance éducatrice: A propos de Hébr. V, 8," in *RSR*, 1955, pp. 481–523; G. Bornkamm, "Sohnschaft und Leiden," in *Judentum, Urchristentum, Kirche: Festschrift J. Jeremias*, Berlin, 1960, pp. 188–198; C. Spicq, *Théologie morale*, vol. 1, p. 46; vol. 2, p. 117). How could the incarnate Son of God, the perfect model of all virtue from his birth on, enroll in the school of suffering to learn a virtue that was innate in him? The answer is that as a human being, Jesus had to experience the constraints, the weaknesses, the temptations of human nature. He had a concrete knowledge of the difficulties of obedience, in the most unhelpful circumstances, especially in the trial of the death that he suffered, a "passion." Thus he acquired a psychologically enriching experience, a practical understanding, a personal appreciation of suffering that was indispensable for his ability to sympathize with his brethren (cf. verse 2). F. Raurell, "La obediencia de Crist, modelo de obediencia del hombre según San Pablo," in *Estudios Franciscanos*, 1963, pp. 249–270.

[69] Rom 1:5; 15:18; 16:19, 26. This can be read as (*a*) submission to the objective faith set forth by the apostle, (*b*) obedience that leads to faith, or more probably (*c*) obedience that is faith: unreserved commitment to God, to what God has said and promised; cf. G. H. Parke-Taylor, "A Note on εἰς ὑπακοὴν πίστεως in Romans I, 5," in *ExpT*, vol. 55, 1943–44, pp. 305ff. W. Wiefel, "Glaubensgehorsam? Erwägungen zu R. I, 5," in *Festschrift E. Schott*, 1967, pp. 137–144.

[70] 2 Cor 10:5–6. The neophyte is like a conqueror's plunder. In the second part of verse 6 (ὅταν πληρωθῇ ὑμῶν ἡ ὑπακοή), J. Héring (*La seconde Epître de saint Paul aux Corinthiens*, Neuchâtel, 1958, p. 58; ET *The Second Epistle of Saint Paul to the Corinthians*, trans. A. W. Heathcote and P. J. Allcock, London, 1967, ad loc) thinks that the aorist is not the equivalent of a preterite or a future perfect but rather has an inchoative sense (cf. Phil 2:7–8; Heb 2:10) that may be translated, "at the moment when your obedience is to be complete." Cf. 2 Cor 2:9—εἰ εἰς πάντα ὑπήκοοί ἐστε.

the elect according to the foreknowledge of God the Father, in the sanctification of the Spirit, for obedience and the sprinkling of the blood of Christ" (*eis hypakoēn kai rhantismon haimatos Iēsou Christou*, 1:2). By the obedience of the faith, the baptized are placed under the lordship of Christ and promise to submit their lives to his precepts. Just as blood seals the *diathēkē* (Matt 26:28; Heb 10:19), the union of obedience and blood refers to the ratification of the old covenant (Exod 24:7–8); the consecration by faith of the person and of all existence is definitive. That is why 1 Pet 1:14 calls Christians "children of disobedience that you were (*hōs tekna hypakoēs*), no longer be conformed to the former covetousnesses."[71]

The frequency and the absoluteness of these NT expressions shows that primitive catechesis was designed to teach believers the idea, the meaning, and the fullness of Christian obedience.[72] Philology alone cannot suffice to fill these out (even with the help of the synonyms *peithō*, *hypatassō*, etc.). In biblical theology, we would have to begin with Matt 11:29–30: the taking of the yoke of Christ and of the baptism in which the disciple recognizes Christ as *Kyrios*. But this submission must be put into context with the love that is the royal law (Jas 2:8), at the same time strictly required and a law of liberty (1:25; cf. 1 Cor 10:23), and which thus governs not slaves but children. Obedience, then, will not consist in material conformity to precepts but in taking heed and being teachable, letting oneself be persuaded, in having a well-disposed heart,[73] and from that point submitting to a rule of life and complying with what is asked. The example of Christ proves that this obedience is the freest and the most spontaneous that there is.

---

[71] Ὑπακοῆς is not a simple genitive of quality describing children of God (cf. verses 3, 17), suggesting the teachableness and submission that every child owes its father (Heb 12:9); it is a Hebraism, like "son of the kingdom" or "son of light," expressing an essential property, a mode of being. We could say that the neophytes are obedient by nature, devoted to obeying God, made to obey.

[72] Cf. O. Kuss, "Der Begriff des Gehorsams im Neuen Testament," in *Theologie und Glaube*, 1935, pp. 695–702; G. Badini, "L'obbedienza nella Bibbia," in *Vita Cristiana*, 1954, pp. 299–312; R. Cai, "L'obbedienza di Gesu Cristo," ibid., pp. 313–329; J. Gnilka, "Zur Theologie des Hörens nach den Aussagen des N.T.," in *Bibel und Leben*, 1961, pp. 71–81. R. Deichgräber, "Gehorsam und Gehorchen in der Verkündigung Jesu," in *ZNW*, 1961, pp. 119–122; R. Schnackenburg, *The Moral Teachings of the New Testament*, trans. J. Holland-Smith and W. J. O'Hara, New York, 1965, pp. 110ff., 207ff.; C. Spicq, *Théologie morale*, vol. 1, pp. 256, 384; vol. 2, pp. 532ff.; 593, n. 3; 623; 659ff. B. Schwank, "Gehorsam (ὑπακοή) im N.T.," in *Erbe und Auftrag*, 1966, pp. 469–476.

[73] One is willing or not willing to be obedient, cf. Acts 7:39—οὐκ ἐθέλησεν ὑπήκοοι γενέσθαι.

ἐκδημέω

ekdēmeō, to leave, be in exile

"Being at home (*endēmountes*) in the body, we are in exile (*ekdēmoumen*) from the Lord. . . . We prefer to be in exile (*ekdēmēsai*) from the body and be at home (*endēmēsai*) with the Lord. That is why whether we are at home in this body or away from it (*eite endēmountes eite ekdēmountes*) it is our desire to be pleasing to him" (2 Cor 5:6, 8, 9). These three occurrences of *ekdēmeō*, the only occurrences in the whole Bible, are rather difficult to translate, because this compound of *dēmos* ("land, territory") is relatively uncommon and has varied meanings.

The first meaning is "leave" (with an accusative of the place or person): "Solon left the country and went to Egypt" (Herodotus 1.30); "Laius had left to consult the oracle."[1] Next, it can mean "go away": "The one who has killed will go away into some other country and to some other place, and he will stay there in exile."[2] It can also mean "travel" and becomes synonymous with *apodēmeō* ("leave on a journey," Matt 25:14; Mark 12:1; Luke 20:9): "These are the conditions imposed on a trip abroad" (Plato, *Leg.* 12.1952 *d*); "The soul completed the journey, because it found a path" (Ps.-Aristotle, *Mund.* 1.391ª11). In *T. Abr.*, the verb is used for death, as in 2 Cor: leaving the body to go to God.[3]

In the papyri, this verb is almost always used for changing one's residence, going from one place to another,[4] leaving one's country or

---

[1] Sophocles, *OT* 114;

[2] Plato, *Leg.* 9.864 *e*; Philo, *Spec. Laws* 4.142: "The inscriptions engraved on the city gates remind those who go away and those who remain alike . . . of what they must say and do"; Josephus, *Life* 388: "An urgent personal matter obliged me to leave the king's domain."

[3] *T. Abr.* A 1: The archangel Michael has the mission of telling Abraham that he is going to die: "You are about to leave this world of vanity and go out of your body (ἐκδημεῖν ἐκ τοῦ σώματος) to your own master among the good"; 7: "At this time you must leave the terrestrial world and go to God" (καὶ πρὸς τὸν θεὸν ἐκδημεῖν); 15: "You are to leave the body (ἐκ τοῦ σώματος ἐκδημεῖν) and appear before the Lord."

[4] *BGU* 1197, 7: ἐκδημήσαντος δὲ σοῦ εἰς τοὺς ἐκτὸς τόπου (4 BC); *P.Lond.* 2019, 1: "Know that I have gone to Crocodilopolis to make a payment" (third century BC).

---

ekdēmeō, S 1553; *TDNT* 2.63–64; *EDNT* 1.408; *NIDNTT* 2.788–790; MM 192; L&N 23.111, 85.21; BAGD 238

moving. In the first century AD, two ephebes state, "If we move or if we leave, we must notify the president."[5] "Ever since we left (*aph' hou exedēmēsamen*) the monarchs have done nothing . . ." (*P.Mich.* 43, 5; third century BC). The meaning "be absent" is well attested: "Be so good as to write Epharmostos to be there and not to be absent (*egdēmountos*) when the matter is judged."[6]

The Pauline use of moving as a metaphor for death, expressed as a play on words, is clear: it is a matter of moving from one country to another, that is, moving out of here in order to move in elsewhere, leaving the body behind to gain heaven and see Christ. Here below, Christians are in exile "apart from the Lord." They live as exiles (*ekdēmeō*) so long as they dwell in this body, which is likened to a tent (*skēnos*—2 Cor 5:1, 4—a symbol of nomadic life) because their citizenship is heavenly (Phil 3:20). The idea could have been comprehensible to pagans: "A little earth envelops and hides his body; his soul, having escaped his members, is possessed by the vast *ouranos*."[7]

An epitaph from the Decapolis in the third century AD mentions that a veteran who has taken part in two wars and traversed the world (τὸν κόσμον ἐκδημήσας; cf. *IG*, XIV, 905: δύσιν καὶ ἀνατολήν) has finally returned to his country (J. and L. Robert, "Bulletin épigraphique," in *REG*, 1952, p. 180, n. 172). Cf. Philo, *Abraham* 65: "Those who have traveled . . . have become expatriates."

[5] *P.Tebt.* 316, 20: ἐὰν δὲ μεταβαίνωμεν ἢ ἐγδημῶμεν μεταδώσωμεν.

[6] *P.Mich.* 80, 4 9 (letter from Eutychides to Zeno); *BGU* 1916, 2; *P.Oxy.* 50, 16: There will be no lost time during the absence (ἐκδημῆσαι) of the delegate; *SB* 6769, 23: καθ' ὃν χρόνον μετὰ τοῦ βασιλέως ἐξεδημοῦμεν; cf. 8940, 4: κατὰ τὴν ἐμὴν ἐκδημίαν. Nothing can be drawn from *P.Yale* 49, 4, which is quite mutilated.

[7] Inscription from Lycabettus, in the Hellenistic period (G. Kaibel, *Epigrammata*, n. 104, 5; cf. 35; 90; 125; 243; 250); "The body has gone to the earth, its parent; the heavenly soul to an imperishable dwelling. The corpse sleeps in the ground; the soul that was given me sojourns in heaven" (ibid. 261, 7–10). A. J. Festugière, *Idéal religieux*, pp. 143–169. For Plutarch, death is like return from an exile (ἐξ ἀποδημίας . . . εἰς πατρίδα). The soul, driven from the body, wanders between the earth and the moon for a variable length of time; "one would speak of banished persons returning to their land after a long absence" (*De fac.* 28.943 *c*); "Socrates said that death was like . . . a great and long journey (ἀποδημία)" (Ps.-Plutarch, *Cons. ad Apoll.* 12; reference to Plato, *Ap.* 40 *c*: "Death is a departure, a passage of the soul from this place to another"; cf. Plato, *Phd.* 67 *d:* "The precise meaning of the word *death* is that a soul is detached and separated from a body"). Epictetus 1.9.16: "The time of the sojourn (τῆς οἰκήσεως) here below is short; we must remain at this post, but wait for God"; Marcus Aurelius 2.17: life is an exile, ξένου ἐπιδημία; Philo, *Heir* 82: "the whole bodily life is an exile (ἀποδημία)"; 267; *Conf. Tongues* 76–82: "The wise person sojourns in the sensible body as in a foreign land" (81); *Dreams* 1.180ff. Cf. F. Cumont, *Symbolisme funéraire*, pp. 177–253; idem, *Lux Perpetua*, pp. 175ff., 275–302; J. Dupont, *Union avec le Christ*, pp. 153–155, 160–165, 168.

ἐκλύομαι

eklyomai, to untie, dissolve, be physically or morally weak

Eklyō, "untie, slacken, dissolve," is used for spilling water (*P.Tebt.* 49, 6; 54, 16; second-first century) and in the context of bathing; in the second century BC, Asclepiades complains about a brawl in which he was victimized by the bath-house employees when, seriously ill, he emerged exhausted from the bath: "and when I emerged *eklelymenos* from the bath" (*kamou anabantos eg balaneiou eglelymenou*, *P.Tebt.* 798, 7). Herod relaxed and finally fainted in a bath full of oil (Josephus, *War* 1.657).

In the passive, the verb is often used of people who are fasting and who faint from hunger. (It was his concern about this eventuality that prompted Jesus to multiply the loaves for the crowd that had followed him on the mountain.)[1] It is also used for men worn out by a long march (1 Sam 30:21, Hebrew *pāgar*, in the piel, too weak) across a wilderness (2 Sam 16:2, Hebrew *yā'ap*) or after battle (2 Sam 21:15, Hebrew *'ûp*; 1 Macc 10:82); they arrive exhausted at their stopping place.[2] This tiredness or physical weakness is expressed in the figure of speech "to have limp, soft, or lifeless hands."[3]

---

[1] Matt 15:32 (aorist passive subjunctive): μή ποτε ἐκλυθῶσιν ἐν τῇ ὁδῷ; Mark 8:3 (future passive indicative): ἐκλυθήσονται ἐν τῇ ὁδῷ. This weakness caused by hunger is mentioned constantly in the OT, cf. Judg 8:15: "so that we might give bread to your exhausted men, τοῖς ἐκλελυμένοις (Hebrew *yā'ēp* = to be tired, faint)"; 1 Sam 14:28—"the people were worn out (Hebrew *'ûp* = to be exausted, to swoon)"; 2 Sam 17:29—"the people were worn out by hunger, fatigue, and thirst in the desert"; unfed, the children collapse (Lam 2:12, 19; Hebrew *'āṭap* = to languish); "how could we fight . . . we are exhausted, for we have eaten nothing today" (1 Macc 3:17).

[2] 2 Sam 16:14—"The king and all the people who were with him arrived exhausted, ἐκλελυμένοι." Diodorus Siculus 13.77: the constant tiredness of the rowers kept the vessels behind. The abuse of pleasures is also tiring, διὰ τὴν τρυφὴν ἐκλελυμένοι (Josephus, *Ant.* 5.134).

[3] Josh 10:6—μὴ ἐκλύσῃς τὰς χεῖράς σου (Hebrew *rāpah* [hithpael], to slacken, weaken); 2 Sam 4:1—his hands slackened; 17:2—Ahithophel says to Absolom, "I will

---

eklyomai, S 1590; EDNT 1.419; NIDNTT 3.177–178; L&N 23.79, 25.288; BAGD 243

But it is also said that the heart weakens,[4] and the present participle *eklyomenos* is used not only for physical weakness but also for moral laxity[5] and thus signifies a lack of spiritual vigor, laxity provoked by weariness, lack of courage, giving up. Hence the expression "he relaxed his eagerness" (*exelyse to prothymon*).[6] This is the meaning in NT exhortations: "Having undertaken to do good, let us not lose courage; at the desired time we shall reap a harvest, if we do not slacken (*mē eklyomenos*)" (Gal 6:9); "Consider [the sufferings of] the one who endured in his own person such contradiction by sinners, so that you may not weaken, your souls may not slacken."[7] Christians who have started out energetically but lack *hypomonē* see their courage fall off bit by bit and are incapable of carrying through. That which is most difficult in the Christian life is not the heroism of a single day, but perseverance in faithfulness to the loftiest ideal: the imitation of the crucified Christ. Hence the present imperative—*mēde eklyou*, quoted from Prov 3:11—in Heb 12:5: "Do not slacken" when you undergo trials at God's hand. Providential training through correction is designed for your good.

---

come upon him when he is tired and his hands are limp"; 2 Chr 15:7—"Be strong, and let your hands not weaken"; Neh 6:9; Isa 13:7; Ezek 7:17.

[4] Deut 20:3—μὴ ἐκλυέσθω (Hebrew *rākak*: to be delicate, troubled, soft); cf. *T. Job* 30.1.

[5] Prov 6:3—ἴσθι μὴ ἐκλυόμενος. Physical tiredness means vulnerability to distress; the one who is weak or worn out is also troubled (Dan 8:27, Hebrew *šāmem*) or disconcerted (1 Macc 9:8). Tiredness causes sagging (Isa 46:1). Cf. Polybius 20.4.7: οὐ μόνον τοῖς σώμασιν ἐξελύθησαν, ἀλλὰ καὶ ταῖς ψυχαῖς; Philostratus, *Gym.* 25: the trainer must not be too talkative, "lest he drain the vigor from the technique by his chattiness."

[6] Josephus, *Ant.* 13.231, 233; 10.119; cf. 17.263: soldiers who spirit was broken (τὰ φρονήματα ἐκλελυμένους); 8.284: God breaks the might (the morale as much as the military strength) of the army. Cf. Philo, *Virtues* 88: if you fail to pay the day laborer promptly "he loses all his vigor at once out of sorrow, τοὺς τόνους ὑπὸ λύπης ἐκλυθείς"; Epictetus 2.19.20: "you will discover that you are . . . quite worn out with the Peripatetics, ἐκλελυμένους." While the "stars do not slacken at their posts" (Sir 43:10), Esau throws off the yoke (Gen 27:40; Hebrew *pāraq*); cf. *Tabula of Cebes* 17; *P.Hib.* 198, 101; soldiers "withdraw" (2 Macc 13:16).

[7] Heb 12:3—ταῖς ψυχαῖς ὑμῶν ἐκλυόμενοι (the perfect passive participle ἐκλελυμένοι is substituted by 𝔓[13, 46], D*, Euthymius). The term is especially well suited to sports contexts (Heb 12:1–4; cf. C. Spicq, *Hébreux*, vol. 2, pp. 382, 390); cf. Aristotle (*Rh.* 3.9.1409ᵇ), which uses it for winded runners who collapse once they have crossed the finished line: ἐπὶ τοῖς καμπτῆρσιν ἐκπνέουσι καὶ ἐκλύονται, προορῶντες γὰρ τὸ πέρας οὐ κάμνουσι πρότερον. Further references in C. Spicq, "Alexandrinismes dans l'Epître aux Hébreux," in *RB*, 1951, p. 487.

ἐκτένεια, ἐκτενής, ἐκτενῶς

ekteneia, fervor, unfailing intensity; *ektenēs, ektenōs*, without ceasing, zealously, urgently

These terms express tautness and, in a moral sense, an effort that can be understood either as perseverance ("without respite, without letting up, assiduously") or as intensity ("with fervor, urgently"). The two meanings are often joined together in a context that makes it difficult to distinguish between them. In the OT, which does not use *ektenēs* (cf. 3 Macc 3:10; 5:29), their usages are religious, notably with respect to the great cries of prayer that Israel voices, forcefully and one might almost say violently, toward God.[1]

Luke also uses *ektenōs* with respect to prayer: in the garden, Jesus prayed with more urgency,[2] and when "Peter was being guarded in prison, the church urgently prayed to God for him."[3] As for 1 Peter, it bids the baptized "Love one another from the bottom of your hearts, intensely"[4]

---

[1] Jdt 4:12 (Hebrew *bᵉḥozqâh*); 4:9; Joel 1:14; Jonah 3:8. Only in 2 Macc 14:38, with respect to Razis, who had risked his body and his life for Judaism, does μετὰ πάσης ἐκτενίας have the meaning of constancy and assiduousness. Cf. Acts 26:7—hoping for the realization of God's promise, the twelve tribes serve God ἐν ἐκτενείᾳ νύκτα καὶ ἡμέραν λατρεῦον.

[2] Luke 22:44—γενόμενος ἐν ἀγωνίᾳ ἐκτενέστερον προσηύχετο; M. J. Lagrange (on this text) notes that ἀγωνία is not agony, but "anxiety or anguish due to a threatening evil that is obscure enough that one cannot know what one is up against."

[3] Acts 12:5—προσευχὴ δὲ ἦν ἐκτενῶς γινομένη ὑπὸ τῆς ἐκκλησίας. The adverb is well attested by 𝔓74, ℵ A* B (Vulg. *sine intermissione*), but A², E, H, L, P, Chrysostom read ἐκτενής, and D says ἐν ἐκτενείᾳ.

[4] 1 Pet 1:22—ἀλλήλους ἀγαπήσατε ἐκτενῶς; cf. C. Spicq, *Agapè*, vol. 2, pp. 312–324 (p. 317 n. 5 points out the imprecision of the articles on this adverb in the lexicons and dictionaries).

---

ekteneia, S 1616; *TDNT* 2.464; *EDNT* 1.422; MM 198; L&N 25.70; BAGD 245 ‖ *ektenēs*, S 1618; *TDNT* 2.463–464; *EDNT* 1.422; MM 198; L&N 25.71, 68.12; BAGD 245 ‖ *ektenōs*, S 1619; *EDNT* 1.422; MM 199; L&N 25.71, 68.12; BAGD 245

and repeats, "Above all, have an intense love between yourselves,"[5] meaning that this love should stretch and be as fervent as possible.[6]

In contemporary usage, especially in the inscriptions, *ektenēs* and *ektenōs* refer to a constant concern to be of service, exacting and untiring zeal, urgent affection, and even lavish gift-giving;[7] things that would be attributed today to "fervent love" (cf. Rom 12:11). As part of the official vocabulary of chancelleries, *ekteneia*, *ektenōs*, and *ektenēs* are in copious supply in honorific decrees,[8] where they enjoy a privileged association with

---

[5] 1 Pet 4:8—πρὸ πάντων τὴν εἰς ἑαυτοὺς ἀγάπην ἐκτενῆ ἔχοντες. The motive given is that love does more than an expiatory sacrifice to "cover a multitude of sins"; cf. C. Spicq, *Agapè*, vol. 2, pp. 332–338; C. Spicq, *Epîtres de saint Pierre*, p. 150; A. Perego, "I peccati sono rimessi e non coperti anche secondo il salmo 31," in *DivThom*, 1960, pp. 205–215.

[6] Cf. ὑπερεκτείνω (unknown before 2 Cor 10:14), which E. B. Allo translates "se distendre" (Eng. slacken, stretch out, relax).

[7] Citizens of the town of Elaia act with consideration toward King Attalus III, given the benefits that they have received from him, ὅπως ἐπὶ τοῖς γεγενημένοις ἀγαθοῖς τῷ βασιλεῖ ἐκτενεῖς οἱ πολῖται φαίνωνται (*I.Perg.*, 246, 4); "who has continually given numerous and great proofs of his devotion toward us and our concerns" (letter of Antiochus III, in *IGLS*, n. 992, 4). King Seleucus, praising his "honored friend" Aristolochus, emphasizes that "he often worked with all possible good will in the service of my father, my brother, and myself, and, in the most critical circumstances, constantly gave tokens of his interest in the affairs of the kingdom" (M. Holleaux, *Etudes d'épigraphie*, vol. 3, pp. 199ff.). *I.Car.*, 166, 7: ἐκτενῶς ἑαυτὸν ἐπιδούς; *I.Ilium*, n. 53, 4: ἐκτενῶς διάκειμαι; cf. 54, 4; *I.Cumae*, n. 13, 84, and 102.

[8] Around 216 BC, an amphictyonic decree from Delphi: ἐκτενῶς πᾶσι τοῖς παραγινομένοις ποτὶ τὸν θεόν (Dittenberger, *Syl*. 538, 17). An honorific decree given by a city to a foreign citizen who has gone to particular trouble on its behalf: τὸ πρὸς τὴν πόλιν ἡμῶν ἐκτενές (*I.Thas*. 166, 6; which the editors, C. Dunant and J. Pouilloux, compare to Dittenberger, *Or.* 339, 7: καὶ πρὸ πλείστου θέμενος τὸ πρὸς τὴν πατρίδα γνήσιον καὶ ἐκτενές). A decree of Samothrace awarding *proxenia* and official standing to Hestiaios "so that the Thasians also may know . . . his zeal on behalf of our people, τὴν πρὸς τὸν δῆμον ἐκτένειαν, and the gratitude of our city" (*I.Thas.*, 169, 26); an honorific decree of Rhodes for Dionysodoros, who constantly took care to supply all the needs of the ambassadors, ἐποιεῖτο τὰν ἐκτενεστάτην πρόνοιαν (ibid. 172, 12). Around AD 283, the prefect Aurelius Mercurious ordered the general of Oxyrhynchus to take inventory of his stock of provisions: πρόνοιαν ποιήσῃ ἐκτενῶς αὐτὰ τρέφεσθαι (*P.Oxy.* 2228, 40; cf. 2861, 4; *P.Panop.Beatty* 1, 376). Ἐπέστειλα τοῖς ἀδελφοῖς μου . . . πρὸς τὸ ἐκτενῶς αὐτοῖς ὑπάρχειν τὰ τῆς εὐθενείας (*P.Michael*. 20, 2). A decree in honor of Eirenias, who "gives proof in all circumstances of the highest zeal for the interests of the city and gives his assistance in everything that pertains to the reputation and glory of our country" (*NCIG*, n. 7, 3). A decree for Isagoras, a Thessalian from Larissa who manifested untiring zeal, φανερὰν ἐνδεικνύμενος τὰν ἰδίαν ἐκτένιαν (*Fouilles de Delphes* 3, 4, n. 49, 7; in 106 BC; cf. 57, 6); συνπροσγεινόμενος ἐκτενῶς πολλὰ τῶν συμφερόντων (*I.Bulg.* 43, 11; cf. 45, A 30); an honorific decree of Iotape: ἀγορανομήσαντος ἐκτενῶς (L. Robert,

prothymia, prothymos, prothymōs, as Hesychius and the *Suda* note. In Thrace: "I have a fervent desire to benefit everyone" (*prothymian gar ektenestatēn echō tou poiein eu pantas, I.Thas.* 186, 10). A decree from Lampsacus sends to the magistrates of Thasos the list of honors conferred upon Dionysodoros, who "shows himself full of ardor and zeal for the interests of the people" (*ektenē kai prothymon heauton eis ta tou dēmou paraskeuazei pragmata,* ibid., 171, 14 = *SEG* XIII, 458 and the commentary of J. Tréheux in *BCH,* 1953, pp. 426–433); "he showed himself full of ardor and zeal for all" (*pasi ektenē kai prothymon auton pareicheto*).⁹ Around 188, the Milesians honor the physician Apollonios, "he showed himself *ektenēs* and *prothymos* likewise according to his art," (*ektenē kai prothymon homoiōs heauton pareicheto kata te tēn technēn,* Dittenberger, *Syl.* 620, 8, 13); the Erythreans fête their praetors, "they proved themselves *ektenēs* and *prothymos* toward the defense of the city" (*ekteneis kai prothymous autous pareschonto pros tēn tēs poleōs phylakēn,* ibid. 442, 9; cf. *SB* 8855, 10). Around 200: "showing himself *ektenēs* and *prothymos* in everything" (*ektenē kai prothymon em pasi paraskeuazomenos, I.Priene* 82, 10–11; cf. *ektenē kai prothymon heauton . . . parechetai, I.Magn.*, 86, 12 and 20); a decree in honor of Boulagoras, "whereas having been chosen several times by the people as their representative during public proceedings, he was unflagging in his activity and zeal—*ektenē kai prothymōs*—and he has secured many advantages and profits for the city."¹⁰ Around 130, an inscription of Pergamum, "so that . . . now in a manner worthy of godlike honors he became most *ektenēs* in his zeal" (*hopōs . . . nyn isotheōn exiōmenos timōn ektenesteros ginētai tē prothymia*).¹¹

The association of zeal and ardor is similar. Cf. a hydrophore of Artemis: *ektenōs kai philoteimōs* (*I.Did.,* 375, 8); "fulfilling the duties of *hydrophoros* in a matter worthy of his race, *philoteimōs*, and performing

---

Documents, p. 75 = G. L. Bean, T. B. Mitford, *Journies in Rough Cilicia,* n. 152, 6; 172ᵃ8); ἐκτενῶς ποτιφερόμενος εἰς τὸν δᾶμον (*SEG* XXII, 266, 7; cf. I, 180; XXIII, 447, 15; XXV, 105, 26; 112, 7, 42). According to a decree of the Athenian cleruchs, Euboulos of Marathon, "who was given responsibility for several diplomatic missions, often succeeded through sustained effort—ἀγωνισάμενος ἐκτενῶς—in securing the interests of the Athenians of Delos" (J. Pouilloux, *Choix,* n. 5, 15). In 164 BC, *P.Paris* 63, 12 prescribes: "καλῶς ποιήσεις τὴν πᾶσαν προσενεγκάμενος ἐκτένειαν καὶ προνοηθείς—You will do well to bring all your zeal to bear and take every precaution"; line 46: ἀλλὰ μετὰ πάσης ἀκριβείας, τὴν ἐκτενεστάτην ποιήσασθαι, in acting in the most correct fashion, you will exercise all diligence" (= *UPZ* 110).

⁹ F. G. Maier, *Griechische Mauerbauinschriften,* Heidelberg, 1959, n. 49, 46; cf. 44, 7; 46, 25; 48, 11.
¹⁰ *SEG* I, 366, 21; J. Pouilloux, *Choix,* n. 3.
¹¹ *IGRom.*, n. 293, col. II, 38.

the mysteries *ektenōs*" (*plērōsasa de kai tēn hydrophorian axiōs tou genous philoteimōs kai ta men mystēria ektenōs telesasa*, ibid. 381, 8). A decree of the Athenian association of soteriasts (worshipers of Artemis Soteira) sets out to reward a certain Diodorus: "the synod having received his *ekteneia* and *philotimia*."[12] The council and people of Sardis honor a priestess Claudia Polla Quintilla, who on the one hand had served the god and the community in an orderly and zealous fashion (*kosmiōs, philoteimōs*) and on the other hand had generously (or constantly) funded public sacrifices out of her own pocket.[13] In 218 BC, a letter-decree from the *kosmoi* (rulers) and city of Gortyn expresses the gratitude of the city to the physician Hermias of Cos, who for five years worked for "citizens and all inhabitants with zeal and constancy—*philotimiōs* and *ekteniōs*—in everything pertaining to his profession and all other cares."[14]

From these usages it emerges that *ekteneia* in the NT is intensity without negligence or failing, whether in prayer or brotherly love. It would not seem that the accent falls on duration or persistence; it is rather fervor, authenticity, magnanimity, a certain lavishness of feeling[15] that characterize Christian *agapē*, eager and generous. To better situate 1 Pet 1:22 and 4:8, we should note that in literary texts *ektenōs*, often in conjunc-

---

[12] Ἡ σύνοδος ἀποδεξαμένη τὴν ἐκτένειαν καὶ φιλοτιμίαν αὐτοῦ, Dittenberger, *Syl*. 1104, 28. Cf. *I.Sinur.*, n. 41, 1.

[13] Δημοτελεῖς θυσίας ἐπιτελέσασαν ἐκ τῶν ἰδίων ἐκτενῶς (*I.Sard.* 52, 11). The *Koinon* of the Cretans conferred proxenia upon the Samian legate, παρεκάλει δὲ ἀμὲ ἐκτενίως καὶ φιλοτίμως καὶ ἀξίως αὐτοσαυτῶ (*I.Cret.* 1, 24, 2; ed. M. Guarducci, vol. 1, p. 282). In AD 43, the Corinthian Junia Theodora is honored by the Lycians for her *philotimia*, her *philostorgia*, and her *ekteneia* (*SEG* 18, 143, 4, 78).

[14] *I.Cret.* 4, 168 (= J. Pouilloux, *Choix*, n. 15); cf. a decree found at Panamara, in L. Robert, *Opera Minora Selecta*, vol. 1, pp. 246, 256, 259 n. 6; vol. 2, p. 746 (a decree for a gymnasiarch of Samos). *I.Bulg.* 43, 11: φιλοτίμως καὶ συνπροσγεινόμενος ἐκτενῶς πολλὰ τῶν συμφερόντων ἡμεῖν συνκατασκευάζεται; Dittenberger, *Or.* 767, 6: ἱερατεύσας τε δὶς Καίσαρος τοῦ θεοῦ ἐκτενῶς καὶ φιλοτείμως; *IG*, X 2, n. 4, 8–9; cf. n. 1, 6. —The intensity of feeling and effort imply eagerness: ἐν πᾶσιν ἐκτενῆ πεφηνότα καὶ σπουδαῖον (*I.Priene* 114, 33); ὁ δῆμος ἀποδεχόμενος αὐτοῦ τὸ φιλόσπουδον καὶ ἐκτενές (Dittenberger, *Or.* 339, 40).

[15] Cf. 3 Macc 6:41—μεγαλοψύχας τὴν ἐκτενίαν ἔχουσαν; Dittenberger, *Syl.* 800, 13: ἐν ταῖς λοιπαῖς δαπάναις πάσαις ἐκτενῶς καὶ μεγαλοψύχως; C. Michel, *Recueil*, n. 544, 4 and 6: ἐκτενῶς καὶ μεγαλομερῶς συνεστράφη (a decree of Themisonion in Phrygia, from 114 BC; cf. the synonyms listed by Julius Pollux, *Onom.* 3.118–119). Agatharchides of Cnidos judges that the Aetolians are more ready than other people to die, because they more than others have the habit of living intensely (in Athenaeus 12.527 *c*; cf. Hierocles, in Stobaeus, 4.25.53; vol. 4, p. 643). Marcus Aurelius would later observe that in order to benefit from the instruction of good teachers in the household, it was necessary to spend generously, δεῖ ἐκτενῶς ἀναλίσκειν (1.4.3).

tion with *philophronōs*[16] and *ektenēs*, often modifies friendship.[17] In fact, *hoi ektenestatoi* is used for the most fervent friends (Polybius 21.22.4). In 182 BC, Eumenes II invites the city of Cos to celebrate games in honor of Athena Nikephora, "with all those who are most *ektenēs* to us among the Greeks."[18] Arcesilas informs his friend Thaumasis that he has drawn up a will in his favor, so greatly has the latter proven his zeal toward him (*ton eis em' ektenōs houtō pephilotimēmenon*, Diogenes Laertius 4.6.44). Attalus II, writing around 160 to Attis, priest of the temple of Cybele at Pessinus, declares "Menodorus, whom you sent to me, gave me your fervent and friendly letter."[19] Arbaces "eagerly forged close relations with the leaders of troops from various nations and succeeded in gaining their friendship" (Diodorus Siculus 2.24.3).

But St. Peter's vision of such generous and constant brotherly love is only possible as a function of the divine rebirth of the children of God. They share in a divine love and give expression to its spontaneity and fervor.

---

[16] The medium of Endor offers Saul generous and friendly sympathy and consolation, the only thing that she possessed in her poverty, ὡς ἐν πενίᾳ τοῦτο παρέσχεν ἐκτενῶς καὶ φιλοφρόνως (Josephus, *Ant.* 6.341). Polybius 8.21.1: Ἀχαιὸς δὲ προσδεξάμενος ἐκτενῶς καὶ φιλοφρόνως τὸν Βῶλιν ἀνέκρινε διὰ πλειόνων ὑπὲρ ἑκάστου τῶν κατὰ μέρος. An honorific decree of Delphi in honor of Euxenos: διότι εὔχρηστον αὐτοσαυτὸν παρασκευάζοι καὶ ἐκτενῆ περὶ τοὺς ἐντυγχάνοντας αὐτῷ τῶν πολιτᾶν καὶ φιλόφρων ὑπάρχει τᾷ πόλει (*SEG* 2, 277, 5), to which should be compared the honorific decree from Busiris in AD 22–23, in favor of its *stratēgos*: ἐκτενῶς καὶ φιλανθρώπως διακείμενος (ibid. 8, 527, 5; cf. C. Michel, *Recueil*, 544, 30: τοὺς οὕτως ἐκενῶς τε καὶ φιλανθρώπως ἀναστρεφομένους).

[17] In friendship, "one party may act generously and the other fall short; ὁ μὲν ἐκτενῶς ποιῇ, ὁ δ' ἐλλείπῃ" (Aristotle, *Mag. Mor.* 2.11.1201ᵃ27). The Stoic Hierocles with respect to mother and father, ἕνεκα τῆς ἐν τοῖς ὀνόμασιν ἐκτενείας (cited by Stobaeus 4.27.23; vol. 4, p. 673). In the third century BC, the comic poet Macon uses the adverb in conjuction with ἀγαπάομαι· ᾔδει δ' ὑπ' αὐτῆς ἀγαπώμενος (in Athenaeus 13.579 *e*).

[18] Σὺν ἅπασι τοῖς ἐκτενεστάτοις ἡμῖν τῶν Ἑλλήνων, C. B. Welles, *Royal Correspondence*, n. 50, 2; cf. ibid. 52, 40: the good will of the people toward Emenes II is profound and sincere, πρὸς ἡμᾶς ἐκτενεστάτην τε καὶ εἰλικρινῆ τὴν εὔνοιαν.

[19] Ἐπιστολὴν ... οὖσαν ἐκτενῆ καὶ φιλικήν (C. B. Welles, *Royal Correspondence*, 58, 4). In an inscription of Cumae, n. xiii, 28, 54, 62, 78, *ekteneia* is associated with *philagathia*; with *philanthropia*, in L. Moretti (*ISE*, vol. 2, n. 55, 2), with *eunoia* (ibid. 33, 7), with *epimeleia* in *ZPE* 25, 1977, p. 270.

ἐκτρέπομαι

ektrepomai, to change direction, deviate, go astray

Very rare in the papyri,[1] the verb *ektrepō* is used only in the middle or passive voice in the NT. It expresses a change of state or direction[2] and seems to have in the first century connotations that vary according to context. Used notably in the moral or religious sphere, it means that one withdraws, deviates, turns aside from one way to go astray, get lost, flee down another. It is in this sense that the word is used four times in the Pastorals, where it seems to have become a technical term of parenesis: the heterodox turn away to wander in empty verbiage, *exetrapēsan eis mataiologian* (1 Tim 1:6; second aorist passive); heretics turn their ears away from the truth, turning instead to fables, *epi de tous mythous ektrapēsontas* (2 Tim 4:4, future passive indicative); Timothy must flee this profane chatter;[3] young widows go astray after Satan (1 Tim 5:15, *exetrapēsan*).

---

[1] I am aware of only three occurrences: a complaint to a priest of Tiberias in AD 33—there is a danger "that the neighboring fields, which are not small, may fall back into an uncultivated state, εἰς ἄσπορον ἐκτραπῆναι" (*P.Ryl.* 133, 22). The same turn of phrase occurs in the second century (*P.Stras.* 259, 12). In the fourth century, the papyrus is mutilated: ἐκτραπῆναι τὰς . . . (*SB* 9136, 8).

[2] In its only OT occurrence, it translates the Hebrew *hāpak*: "turn, change, pass from one state to another"; God changes the shadow of the night to dawn (Amos 5:8). In optics, it designates the deviation of a body in motion from its trajectory (C. Mugler, *Terminologie optique*, p. 133). In a pejorative sense: "Turning aside in that direction (ἐκτραπόμενοι), they sat down and refused to go further" (Xenophon, *An.* 4.5.15); Josephus, *War* 1.614: "All turned aside, no one dared approach him" (Antipater at Caesarea).

[3] 1 Tim 6:20—ἐκτρεπόμενος τὰς βεβήλους κενοφωνίας. Here the present middle participle could be translated "refuse" as in Josephus (*Ant.* 1.194: the Sodomites refusing all relations with others; 1.246: the young girls refused to give them anything to drink) or better, this inscription: ἐνταῦθα δὲ ἐκτρέπεσθαι δεῖ τοὺς σοφιστικοὺς λόγους τούτους (published by H. Usener, "Epikureische Schriften auf Stein," in *RhMus*, 1892, n. 29, 7).

---

ektrepomai, S 1624; *EDNT* 1.423; *NIDNTT* 3.902–903; MM 199; L&N 13.155, 31.65; BAGD 246

ἐκτρέπομαι, ektrepomai 463

The first-century parallels, Jewish and pagan, have this ethical significance: the nouveaux riches do not see the route before them and go astray in areas in which no paths have been cleared, *eis anodias ektrepontai* (Philo, *Spec. Laws* 2.23); "Turn aside from eunuchs (*gallous ektrepesthai*) and flee the company of those who have deprived themselves of their virility" (Josephus, *Ant.* 4.290). The young "turn aside from the ways of their fathers, they take the opposite path" (ibid. 6.34). "Rehoboam went astray in unjust and impious actions, *eis adikous kai asebeis exetrapē praxeis*" (ibid. 8.251); *eis* indicates the direction toward which one turns; cf. 5.98—"If you turn aside to imitate other nations." Hyrcanus, a disciple of the Pharisees, bade them take notice if he committed any fault or turned aside from the way of justice (*tēs hodou tēs dikaias ektrepomenon*) and correct him (ibid. 13.290). In his chapter on training, Musonius says to "do anything to avoid things that are truly evil."[4] T. Nägeli cites an inscription of Oenoanda in Lycia that is very close to the wording of 1 Tim 1:6 and 6:20—*ektrepesthai dei tous sophistikous logous*.[5]

Ektrepomai is also used in medical and surgical contexts—"leave its place, disconnect, dislocate, separate,"[6]—and it is in this sense that we should understand Heb 12:13—"Let the lame person not deviate; let him be healed."[7]

---

[4] In Stobaeus, *Ecl.* 29.78 (vol. 3, p. 650, 18; ed. C. E. Lutz, p. 54, 25). Cf. Epictetus 1.6.42: "letting himself be carried away (ἐκτρεπόμενοι εἰς) to complaints and reproaches against God."

[5] T. Nägeli, *Wortschatz*, p. 19.

[6] Cf. Hippocrates, *Off.* 14, describing the treatment for a dislocated limb; it should be rested on a soft, regular surface, "so that there may be no protruding, no bending, no harmful turning (μήτε ἐκτρέπηται)"; Dioscorides, *Mat. Med.* 2.15. Cf. C. Spicq, "Alexandrinismes dans l'Epître aux Hébreux," in *RB* 1951, p. 488.

[7] The lame person is a sick person (cf. Philo, *Change of Names* 187; *Prelim. Stud.* 164ff.) called by 1QM "a shaker of the knees" (14.6). He represents the hesitant and fearful Christian, in danger of being completely dislocated by trials and incapable of following the narrow path.

ἔκτρωμα

ektrōma, **stillborn child, child born abnormally before term**

After listing the appearances of the risen Christ to the apostles, St. Paul concludes: "And finally, as to a prematurely born child, he appeared even to me; for I am the least of the apostles" (1 Cor 15:8–9). A NT hapax, *ektrōma* is used three times in the LXX, and always in a comparison. Aaron pleads with Moses on behalf of Miriam when she is stricken with leprosy: "Let her not be like a stillborn child (*hōsei ektrōma*, Hebrew *mût*), that emerges from its mother's womb with half its body eaten away" (Num 12:12). "Why was I not like a stillborn child (*hōsper ektrōma*), hidden in its mother's womb, like the little ones who have not seen the light of day?"[1] The rich man, who has fathered a hundred sons and lived a long life, but whose soul is not satisfied and who does not receive a proper burial, is worse off than "the stillborn child, because in vanity it came and in obscurity it went, and in obscurity will its name be hidden; it has not even seen the sun and has not known it" (Eccl 6:3). In all three cases, the *ektrōma* is a stillborn child, a physiological definition that sheds no light on the Pauline metaphor.[2]

There is a single occurrence in the papyri, dating from 142 BC. A pregnant Jewish woman complains that she was attacked by another woman, perhaps in a village of Samaria, and is in danger of having a miscarriage.[3] In the secular literature, the term is not used by gynecologists

---

[1] Job 3:16—ἔκτρωμα translates the Hebrew *nēpel*, which *b. Sota* 22 *a* defines: "a child whose months (in its mother's womb) were not completed." Here it is the fetus that "falls" before term and does not live (cf. Ps 58:9; Eccl 6:3).

[2] More illuminating would be Philo, *Alleg. Interp.* 1.76: "When imprudence is in labor it never gives birth; by nature the soul of the wicked brings nothing viable to light; and that which it produces turns out to be abortions and premature births, ἀμβλωθρίδια . . . καὶ ἐκτρώματα," following a citation of Num 12:12.

[3] *P.Tebt.* 800, 30: κινδυνεύει ὃ ἔχει ἐγ γαστρὶ παιδίον ἔκτρωμα γίνεσθαι μεταλλάξαν τὸν βίον; republished in *C.Pap.Jud.* 133. The corresponding verb is found in AD 362, in a similar context: "Thaesis was pregnant, and by their blows they caused the miscarriage of their child, αὐτῶν ἐξέτρωσεν τὸ βρέφος" (*P.Cair.Goodsp.* 15, 15).

---

ektrōma, S 1626; *TDNT* 2.465–467; *EDNT* 1.423; *NIDNTT* 1.182–183; MM 200; L&N 23.55; BAGD 246

and can be cited only in one text from Aristotle[4] and in the definition of Hesychius: "a child born dead, untimely, something cast out of the woman" (*ektrōma: paidion nekron aōron, ekbolē gynaikos*).

Since the documentation is poor and worthless for shedding light in 1 Cor 15:8, exegetes make the most of a notation by the twelfth-century polygraph J. Tzetzes, who saw the term *ektrōma* as a derogatory label and understood the apostle to be taking up an insult used against him by his adversaries,[5] like "ordure" (*peripsēma*) in 1 Cor 4:13. But J. Schneider (*TDNT*, vol. 2, pp. 465–467) has demonstrated that this polemical interpretation does not square with the kerygmatic material that precedes. Thus it seems preferable to see in this word an expression of humility, as it was understood by Ignatius of Antioch,[6] the Greek Fathers, and a number of moderns.[7]

Cf. *Apoc. Pet.* 26: "Some women were seated, with pus up to their necks. Across from them, there were babies that had been brought into the world before term; seated, they were crying. . . . These were women who did not want to conceive and had abortions"; Diodorus Siculus 3.64.4 (the birth of Bacchus): "Semele fell dead and miscarried. Jupiter took up her premature son and hid him in his thigh. The body of the child there grew perfectly"; 4.2.3. Eusebius, *Hist. Eccl.* 5.1.45: "It was a great joy for the virgin mother [the church] to receive alive those whom she had ejected dead from her womb, οὓς ὡς νεκροὺς ἐξέτρωσε" (a text used by E. Schwartz in *Nachrichten der Gesellsch. der Wissenschaften zu Göttingen*, 1907, p. 276). A cultic rule from Ptolemaïs in Egypt in the first century considers a miscarriage (ἐκτρωσμός) as a defilement for the mother (*LSCGSup*, n. 119, 5 and 10).

[4] Aristotle, *Gen. An.* 4.5.773^{b}18: "The fetuses detach as in the case called miscarriage, τοῖς καλουμένοις ἐκτρώμασιν"; cf. *HA* 7.3.583^{b}12: "Outflow (ἐκρύσεις) is the term for the abortion of the fetus during the first seven days, and miscarriage (ἐκτρωσμοί) for expulsion within forty days"; cf. Hippocrates, *Septim.* 9 (ed. Littré, vol. 7, p. 448).

[5] A. von Harnack, "Die Verklärungsgeschichte Jesu," in *Sitzungsberichte der preußischen Akademie der Wissenschaften zu Berlin*, 1922, p. 72, n. 3; A. Fridrichsen, "Paulus Abortivus," in *Symbolae Philologicae O. A. Danielsson*, Uppsala, 1932, pp. 78–85 (traces the history of the exegesis, noting that ἔκτρωμα refers to the result, not the action); G. Björk, "Nochmals Paulus Abortivus," in *ConNT*, vol. 3, 1938, pp. 3–8 (on the basis of modern Greek usage, translates "monster, object of horror" making the word a synonym of τέρας and ἄμβλωμα); J. Munck, "Paulus Tanquam Abortivus," in A. J. B. Higgins, *New Testament Essays*, pp. 180–193 (criticizes his latest predecessor). C. K. Barrett, *A Commentary on the First Epistle to the Corinthians*, London, 1968, p. 344, emphasizes that this expression of scorn on the part of adversaries could be based as much on Paul's physique ("a man of three cubits," according to Chrysostom; "small in height" in *Acts Paul Thec.* 3; cf. σαῦλος = a person who waddles when he walks) as on the externals of his presentation (cf. Acts 14:12; 2 Cor 10:1, 10).

[6] Ign. *Rom.* 9.2: "I blush at being reckoned among them (Syrian Christians) because I am not worthy, being the last of them and an abortive child (ἔκτρωμα)."

[7] F. Field, *Notes on the Translation*, p. 179; F. Godet, *Commentaire sur la première Epître aux Corinthiens*, Paris-Neuchâtel, 1886, vol. 1, pp. 339ff. [ET *A Commentary on*

T. Boman points out the triply depreciative expression: the last of the series—like a stillborn child—the lowliest or most minuscule of the apostles (*elachistos*, imperceptible); and he cites the Latin *abortivus* (dwarfish, infantile, falling short in maturity) which was not unknown to Paul.[8] In effect, St. Irenaeus knew an analogous meaning: "shapeless and formless, like an *ektrōma*."[9] So *ektrōma*, derived from *ektitrōskō* (pierce, tear), literally means a fetus born before its time and violently; metaphorically, the Pauline image would be that of a body ripped by force from a woman's womb (the synagogue). The reference would be to the abnormal and sudden character of Paul's birth to the Christian faith and the apostolic ministry. His case is indeed different from that of the Twelve. He, Saul, was in a way a "premature birth," in an immature stage of his gestation in grace, "only a spiritual embryo" (T. Boman, p. 49). He immediately explains: "since I had persecuted the church of God" (verse 9). Moreover, in the occurrences of *ektrōma*, the emphasis is always placed in the abnormal birth, before term, whether the baby is dead or living (Schneider). It required an omnipotent intervention by Christ to give this persecutor, in one stroke, both faith and the apostolic calling.[10]

St. Paul's First Epistle to the Corinthians, Edinburgh, 1886, ad loc]; A. Plummer, *First Epistle of St. Paul to the Corinthians*, Edinburgh, 1911, p. 339. J. Weiss, *Der erste Korintherbrief*, 10th ed., Göttingen, 1925, pp. 351ff.

[8] T. Boman, "Paulus Abortivus," in *ST*, 1964, pp. 46–50, and again in *Die Jesus-Überlieferung im Lichte der neueren Volkskunde*, Göttingen, 1967, pp. 236ff. Str-B (vol. 1, pp. 496ff.; vol. 3, p. 471) points out several occurrences of ἔκτρωμα to designate disciples of the rabbis.

[9] Ἄμορφος καὶ ἀνείδεος, ὥσπερ ἔκτρωμα, Irenaeus, *Haer.* 1.4.7 (cf. *Extracts of Theodotus* 68—the Valentinians called matter ἔκτρωμα, transposing the Egyptian myth of the birth of Harpocrates, "born before term and weak with inferior limbs"; cf. A. Torhoudt, *Een onbekend gnostisch systeem in Plutarchus' de Iside et Osiride*, Louvain, 1942, pp. 50–52, 96). Cf., in the first half of the first century, Ps.-Longinus, *Subl.* 14.3: "If an author was afraid of not being heard beyond his own life and his own times, the conceptions of his thought would necessarily turn out no better than incomplete and blind productions, like abortions (ὥσπερ ἀμβλοῦσθαι), completely unable to come to term and gain renown among posterity." In French, *avorton* designates "a fetus that has emerged from the mother's womb before term," then "that which is arrested in its evolution or had not achieved the development normal for its species," and finally "that which is puny, feeble, malformed, scrawny" (P. Robert, *Dictionnaire . . . de la langue française*, Paris, 1965, vol. 1, p. 376).

[10] Cf. L. de Grandmaison, *Jésus-Christ*, 13th ed., Paris, 1931, vol. 2, pp. 378–379; J. Blank, *Paulus und Jesus*, Munich, 1968, pp. 187–190. Ἐκτιτρώσκω = cause an abortion, in *P.Tebt.Tait* 40, 2.

ἐκψύχω

ekpsychō, to be short of breath, expire

Instead of the classical *apopsychō*,[1] the Koine uses—though rarely—the verb *ekpsychō*, which has quite variable meanings. It appears for the first time in Epicharmus in the sense "dry out,"[2] but in Ps.-Aristotle it means "be short of breath" (Ps.-Aristotle, *Pr.* 882^{a}36; 886^{b}14). In Plutarch: "Cooling off (*to ekpsychesthai*) not only hardens bodies but also causes them to melt" (*Quaest. conv.* 6.8.6; 695 D).

In Judg 4:21, Alexandrinus translates the Hebrew *'ûp* as *exepsyxen* (Sisera "fell motionless and died"),[3] whereas the piel of *kāhâh* in Ezek 21:12 has to be translated *ekpsyxei pasa sarx kai pan pneuma* ("all flesh and every spirit will weaken").[4] The only three occurrences of the verb (in the aorist indicative) in the NT are in St. Luke, and they all mean "give up the ghost." Ananias "fell down and expired" (Acts 5:5); so also Sapphira (5:10) and Herod Agrippa I ("he was eaten by worms and expired," 12:23). Perhaps this was the medical meaning in the first century,[5] but its usages in Hippocrates (quoted by Hesychius) refer to "a patient who blacks out" (*Aff.* 1.5, 1.18).

---

[1] Ἀποψύχω (a biblical hapax) means "exhale," then "lose strength, faint," and finally "expire"; Luke 21:26—"men fainting with fright and in apprehension at the things that are happening," hence, "frozen with fear"; 4 Macc 15:18—"the eldest expired."

[2] *P.Oxy.* 2427, frag. 27, 6 = C. Austin, *Comicorum Graecorum Fragmenta*, n. 85, 245.

[3] Moulton-Milligan provides no papyrological occurrence but cites Herondas, *Mimes* 4.29: ἐν τάχα ψύξειν.

[4] Or "collapse"; *kāhâh* is also used for a light that dims, an eye that becomes dull, darkens.

[5] Cf. Hobart, *Medical Language*, p. 37, who cites texts from Hippocrates, Galen, and Aretaeus.

---

ekpsychō, S 1634; *EDNT* 1.424; MM 200; L&N 23.99; BAGD 247

> ἔλαττον (ἐλάσσων), ἐλαττονέω, ἐλαττόω
>
> *elatton (elassōn)*, **smaller, lesser;** *elattoneō*, **to have less, have too little;** *elattoō*, **to diminish**

If it is true that in the Hellenistic era the double consonant *ss* replaced the Attic *tt*,[1] this is not a general rule. It applies most of the time in the LXX,[2] but *elatton* is much more common than *elassōn* in the papyri.[3] The NT confirms this variety of usage, with *elassōn* twice (John 2:10; Rom 9:12) and *elatton* twice (1 Tim 5:9; Heb 7:7).

Elassōn, very common in comparisons of size,[4] functions as the comparative of *mikros*, "smaller, lesser," and the opposite of *meizōn* (to designate a younger sibling),[5] of *kreittōn* ("the lesser is blessed by the greater"),[6]

---

[1] Cf. F. M. Abel, *Grammaire*, n. 4r.

[2] Cf. ἔλαττον, Exod 16:17–18; Lev 25:16; Num 26:54; 33:54; 35:8; Dan 2:39; 2 Macc 5:5; 8:9.

[3] Ἐλάσσων is hardly found at all outside of *SB* 9225, 1 (fragment of a law from the third century BC). P.Paris 63, 28 (= P.Petr. III, p. 20, from the second century BC) and in the second-third century AD, P.Fouad (Crawford) 18, 5; P.Mich. 501, 16; *BGU* 1564, 12–13; 1663, 7; 1734, 12; P.Giss. 1, 61, 18; *PSI* 187, 10 (fourth century); cf. E. Mayser, *Grammatik*, p. 223.

[4] Cf. C. Mugler, *Terminologie géométrique*, p. 169. Gen 1:16; Exod 16:17–18; Prov 13:11; 30:24; Dan 2:39.

[5] Rom 9:12 (citation of Gen 25:23; Hebrew *ṣā'îr*); cf. Josh 6:25; P.Ryl. 77, 39: ἀναδεξάμενος τὴν μείζονα ἀρχὴν οὐκ ὀφείλει τὴν ἐλάττον' ἀποφεύγειν. The term takes on a pejorative flavor: "the least, miniscule," cf. 2 Kgs 18:24; Job 30:1; Wis 9:5: "I am too small to understand judgment and the laws"; Isa 60:22; P.Cair.Isid. 73, 3: "we who are small farmers." Cf. *C.Ord.Ptol.* 53, 70: "those who bear responsibilities in the least of the temples, ἐν τοῖς ἐλάσσοσιν ἱεροῖς"; 53, 96: "they will be taxed at a reduced rate." Menander, *Dysk.* 679: "I cared less than nothing for the wounded one." P.Tebt. 88, 61; 1117, 1 = the lesser priests.

[6] Heb 7:7; cf. 1 Sam 9:21; Prov 22:16. Philo, *Alleg. Interp.* 2.3; Plutarch, *Praec. ger. rei publ.* 8.804 *a*: ἠλαττοῦτο πολλῶν. In the first century BC, Geminus wrote indifferently ἔλασσον or ἔλαττον with respect to measures of space and time: "certain circles are sometimes greater, sometimes smaller" (*Intro. to Astronomy* 5.30.35; 6.27; 14.3), "the smallest displacement" (14.4–5; 17.17; 18.2); "the distance is sometimes

---

elatton (elassōn), S 1640; *TDNT* 4.648–659; *EDNT* 1.426; *NIDNTT* 2.427–428; MM 201; L&N 59.3, 67.116, 87.67; BDF §§34(1), 47(2), 61(1), 185(4), 263(3); BAGD 248 ‖ *elattoneō*, S 1641; *EDNT* 1.426; MM 201; L&N 57.41; BAGD 248 ‖ *elattoō*, S 1642; *EDNT* 1.426; MM 201; L&N 87.68; BAGD 248

ἔλαττον (ἐλάσσων), elatton (elassōn), etc. 469

of *kalon* (the wine that is less good is served at the end of the meal),[7] or of *pleiōn* (Exod 16:17; Num 26:54; 33:54; P.Mich. 636, 8); thus the neuter *mē elatton* is used in 1 Tim 5:9—a woman is not to be enrolled with the widows until she is "at least sixty years old."[8]

The denominative verb *elattoneō*, "have less or too little, lack," a NT hapax (2 Cor 8:15) is a citation of Exod 16:18—"the one who had less manna did not go wanting."[9] It is rare in the papyri, but attested in 217 BC: a defrauder in a wine delivery will be required "to restore to us the difference, fourteen missing jugs" (*to diaphoron tōn elattonountōn* ιδ′ *keramiōn*, P.Magd. 26, 12). In 11 BC, the word is used for the lack of the price of 230 *kotylai* of oil (BGU 1195, 19); and in the third century AD: "it is my joy and my glory to produce more and lose nothing" (*pleon exeurein kai mē elattonin*, P.Oxy. 2407, 54).

Elattoō also has the meaning "lack, be deprived of,"[10] as well as "decrease," like the present passive infinitive in John 3:30—"he must become

---

smaller, sometimes greater" (5.47); "the signs of the zodiac take less time to rise, ἐν ἐλάττονι χρόνῳ"; (7.11; 14.2); "the smallest beginning of an eclipse."

[7] John 2:10. On this verse, cf. P. W. Meyer, "John II, 10," in *JBL*, 1967, pp. 191–197; J. D. M. Derrett, *Law in the NT*, pp. 228–246; B. Lindars, "Two Parables in John," in *NTS*, vol. 16, 1970, pp. 318–324.

[8] The formula is common: οὐκ ἐλάττους = not less than a thousand people, than five thousand, than twenty thousand (2 Macc 5:5; 8:9, 35; 10:18; 12:4, 10; Diodorus Siculus 17.19.15; 17.21.26; 17.31.2; 17.36.6; 17.64.4; etc.) and in the papyri often designates a price less than the total or the agreed-upon sum: "not less than 800 drachmas" (*Pap.Lugd.Bat.* XIII, 14, 28; a will from the second century AD); P.Achm. 8, 17; P.Oxy. 237; col. VIII, 11: when threatened, those from who one is demanding repayment of a debt are tempted to agree to a "reduction" (AD 138); P.Lille 29, col. I, 31; 2, 34: "not less than two witnesses." J. Pouilloux, *Recherches sur l'histoire et les cultes de Thasos*, Paris, 1954, vol. 1, n. 141: the polemarchs will give the boys greaves and breastplates . . . "the value of which shall be not less than three minas, μὴ ἐλάσσονος ἄξια τριῶν μνῶν." The expression πλέον ἔλαττον means "more or less, approximately" (P.Oxy. 1895, 5, 8; 1907, 10; 2347, 6; P.Vindob.Tandem, n. 28, 8; H. J. July, *Die Klauseln hinter den Maßangaben der Papyrusurkunden*, Cologne, 1966, pp. 96ff.). The brother of Phoibammon must buy at Alexandria a robe of Antioch "worth ten keratia, more or less" (P.Fouad 74, 7); cf. BGU 1663, 7; C.P.Herm. 34, 11: "two *arourai*, more or less, of arable land"; P.Cair.Isid. 103, 9; P.Mert. 17, 14, 20; P.Ross.Georg. II, 14, 2 (first century AD); 5, 25, 2; 42, 7; SB 9253, 9; 9293, 11; etc.

[9] The verb is well attested in the LXX, where is is used for the subsiding waters of the flood (Gen 8:3, 5; cf. Philo, *Etern. World* 120); for the fifty righteous people, of whom five may be lacking (Gen 18:28); for the poor man who shall not pay less then a half-shekel (Exod 30:15; cf. Lev 25:16; Prov 11:24). A decrease in numbers is contrasted with an increase (Jer 30:19); "For the one who hates idle chatter will have less evil" (Sir 19:6–7). The verb is also used for military defeat (2 Macc 12:11; 13:19).

[10] 1 Sam 2:5; 21:16; 2 Sam 3:29; Jer 51:18; Ezek 24:10; Ps 34:11—"Those who seek Yahweh lack no good thing"; Sir 32:24. One is deprived or stripped of wisdom

greater, but I must decrease."[11] The decreasing can be monetary[12] or solar (Dio Cassius 45.17: "the light of the sun seems to diminish and go out") or physical (Philo, *Virtues* 46; *Etern. World* 65); but also psychological or social. In 180 BC, Orthagoras of Araxa is the object of an honorific decree because "sent on a mission to the confederation, he so conducted the debates with words and with deeds that he gained advantages for our people and we avoided suffering the least diminution, *kai en mēdeni elattōthēnai*."[13] It can refer to a decrease in quality (Sir 16:23; Philo, *Giants* 27); "the science of gymnastics is not inferior to any other art" (Philostratus, *Gym.* 1). It is in this sense that God made man slightly, hardly (*ēlattōsas brachy*) lower than the angels (Heb 2:7, citing Ps 8:5).

(Sir 29:23), of intelligence (19:24; 25:2; 47:23); one is freed of something (Sir 22:10; 28:8; 38:24).

[11] Cf. Sir 18:6—"There is nothing to take away, nothing to add"; 42:21—"jealousy and wrath shorten life"; 31:30—"drunkenness diminishes strength"; 39:18. In the papyri, the perfect passive participle with negation—μὴ ἠλαττουνένου (-νης)—is a clause that occurs constantly in contracts. It means that the lender or lessor will not be subject to any loss, damage, or prejudice in the recovery of that which is due him, cf. "associated with you in the business related to the city's account, I recognize that you will be subject to no loss with respect to what my brother and I owe you, ὁμολογῶ κατὰ μηδέν σε ἐλαττοῦσθαι περὶ ὧν ὀφείλομέν σοι ἐγώ τε καὶ ὁ ἀδελφός μου" (*P.Oxy.* 2134, 5, 15); μὴ ἐλαττουμένου σου τοῦ Ἀπίωνος τοῦ καὶ Πετοσοράπιος ἐν τῇ πράξει ὧν ἄλλων ὀφείλω σοι (*P.Oslo* 40, 63; cr. 123, 33); μὴ ἐλαττουμένου σου ἐν οἷς ὠφείλησα τῷ ἀδελφῷ σου τῷ μετηλλαχότι Παυσανίς ἐν τῇ πράξει (*P.Mert.* 14, 15); *P.Alex.* 7, 16; *BGU* 1573, 29; *P.Ross.Georg.* II, 18, 59; *Pap.Lugd.Bat.* VI, 9, 19; 20, 43 (= *SB* 6611; cf. 10787, 14; 10989, 35); 36, 7 (= *P.Hamb.* 67); 36, 18; *P.Fouad* 35, 13 (from AD 48; the rights of Thaesis are fully reserved in the recovery of eighty drachmas loaned by her, with guarantee, to Petsiris); *P.Ryl.* 677, 11; *P.Sarap.* 2, 19; 39, 7; *P.Mich.* 562, 15; 615, 31, 34; *P.Tebt.* 382, 13 (between 30 BC and AD 1); *P.Vars.* 10 (cf. *Berichtigungsliste* IV, p. 102, n. 10 I 25). Cf. G. Häge, "Die ΜΗ ΕΛΑΤΤΟΥΜΕΝΟΥ-Klausel in den griechischen Papyri Aegyptens," in *Proceedings* XII, pp. 195–205; H. A. Rupprecht, *Studien zur Quittung im Recht der graeco-ägyptischen Papyri*, Munich, 1971, pp. 18ff.

[12] Num 26:54; 33:54. Cf. the request of the priests of the inner sanctum of Philae: "in view of the fact that these abuses are impoverishing the sanctuary (ἐλαττοῦσθαι τὸ ἱερὸν) and we run the risk ..." (*C.Ord.Ptol.* 52 - *SB* 8396, 28 = A. Bernand, *Philae*, vol. 1, n. 19 and p. 190). Ἐλασσώματος is a real-estate reduction, the nonproductive area deducted from the acreage on which one pays land tax (*P.Bour.* 42, 32; *BGU* 20, 8; *APF*, 1976, p. 106).

[13] J. Pouilloux, *Choix*, n. 4, 53; cf. *I.Magn.* 90, 15. Plutarch, *Dem.* 11, 1: "to correct his physical defects (τοῖς σωματικοῖς ἐλαττώμασι) he resorted to exercises."

ἐλεέω, ἔλεος

eleeō, to have compassion, show favor or mercy; *eleos*, compassion, mercy

Eleos is an irregular noun. Normally masculine, it is most commonly neuter in the Hellenistic period.[1] It refers to a "feeling,"[2] namely, the feeling of one who is moved by the sight of another's suffering and in a way shares in it: compassion.[3] Such a sensitivity to misery is unacceptable without controls or objective motives.[4] Furthermore, Aristotle specifies that "pity

---

[1] Τὸ ἔλεος; cf. F. M. Abel, *Grammaire*, n. 9 *t*. The verb ἐλεέω ("take pity") is regular, but some of its forms presuppose a primitive parallel ἐλεάω—in the second person plural imperative ἐλεᾶτε (Jude 23) and in the genitive participle ἐλεῶντος (Rom 9:16). Cf. the adjectives ἐλεήμων (Homer, *Od.* 5.191: "My heart is all pity"; Aristophanes, *Pax* 425; Ps 112:4—ἐλεήμων καὶ οἰκτίρμων; Matt 5:7; Heb 2:17), ἐλεεινός, "pitiable" (Menander, *Dysk.* 297; *Thras.* 387, 390; 1 Cor 15:19; Rev 3:17), the substantive ἐλεημοσύνη (Callimachus, *Hymn.* 4.152: "for the pity that you show me"; *P.Gen.* 51, 26; Matt 6:4; Luke 11:41; Acts 9:36).

[2] Aristotle, *Eth. Nic.* 3.1.1109b32: "The domain of virtue is feelings and actions. . . . When these are involuntary, they may elicit forgiveness or even pity"; 3.2.1111a30.

[3] Plato, *Euthd.* 288 d: "let them take pity on me (ἐλεήσαντέ με) and be compassionate (οἰκτίραντε)"; Sophocles, *Phil.* 308–309: "Those people took pity on me (ἐλεοῦσι) and even sometimes gave me food out of compassion (οἰκτίραντες)"; Euripides, *IT* 227–228; *Hel.* 944. The historian Phylarchus describes terrible scenes in order to "provoke the pity of his readers (εἰς ἔλεος ἐκκαλεῖσθαι τοὺς ἀναγινώσκοντας) and make them have feelings for his account (καὶ συμπαθεῖς ποιεῖν τοῖς λεγομένοις)" (Polybius 2.56.7). The linking of ἐλεήμων and οἰκτίρμων is common in the LXX, Exod 34:6; Neh 9:17; Ps 86:15; 103:4; 111:4; Sir 2:11; etc.

[4] Polybius 2.56.3: οὔτ᾽ ἐλεεῖν εὐλόγως οὔτ᾽ ὀργίζεσθαι καθηκόντως. Seneca, *Clem.* 2.4.4: "Compassion is the morbid condition of souls that feel an excess of misery. Making it a responsibility of the wise person almost requires of him lamentations and obsequious groanings that would be foreign to him"; Philo, *Joseph* 144: "No one pities envious poverty"; *Spec. Laws* 4.76–77.

---

eleeō, S 1653; TDNT 2.477–485; EDNT 1.429–431; NIDNTT 2.594; MM 202; L&N 88.76; BDF §§90, 148(2), 176(1); BAGD 249 ‖ *eleos*, S 1656; TDNT 2.477–485; EDNT 1.429–431; NIDNTT 2.593–597, 600; MM 203; L&N 88.76; BDF §51(2); BAGD 250

has as its object a being that does not deserve its misfortune" (Aristotle, *Poet.* 13.1453ᵃ4) and defines *eleos* as "a pain following upon the sight of a destructive or painful evil that strikes a person who does not deserve it and that one might expect to suffer oneself or see one's own dear ones suffer. . . . To feel pity, one must obviously be able to think that one is exposed" (*Rh.* 2.8.1385ᵇ13–14). One must be moved only at the sight or the thought of someone suffering wrongly. This idea was taken up by the whole Greek tradition,[5] notably by Polybius,[6] and became even more categorical with the Cynics: "The Cynic must feel neither envy nor pity."[7] Of course, even philosophers sometimes show themselves more favorable to altruistic feelings,[8] but even so, pity remains suspect, even a weakness.[9]

---

[5] Ps.-Andronicus, *Pass.* 2: ἔλεος μὲν οὖν ἐστι λύπη ἐπ' ἀλλοτρίοις κακοῖς ἀναξίως πάσχοντος ἐκείνου (*SVF,* vol. 3, 414); Diogenes Laertius 7.1.111: "pity is a sorrow felt for one who suffers evils undeservedly"; Cicero, *Tusc.* 4.8.1: "Misericordia est aegritudo ex miseria alterius injuria laborantis." Cf. Sir 12:13—"Who will pity the charmer bit by a snake?"

[6] "Their past attempts at rebellion (the cities of Hippocritae and Utica) leave no place for pity or pardon" (τόπον ἐλέους μηδὲ συγγνώμης, Polybius 1.88.2); "Those who owe their reversals to fortune find pity accompanied by indulgence and aid; but those who owe them to their own stupidity get only blame and reprobation from sensible people" (ibid. 2.7.3; cf. 2.58.11; 6.58.10; 9.10.7; 23.10.11; 25.4.4; 30.8.3; 33.11.3; 38.3.2; 38.16.7; 38.17.7). Cf. A. Ničev, "Questions éthiques et esthétiques chez Polybe: Ἔλεος chez Polybe et Aristote," in *REG,* 1978, pp. 149–157.

[7] Epictetus 3.22.13. Cf. 2.17.26: "The one who feels pity has received no philosophical education"; 4.1.4; 4.6.1ff. Plutarch alludes to this school: "Some philosophers criticize even pity inspired by misfortunes, thinking that it is good to help, not to feel compassion" (*De tranq. anim.* 7).

[8] Epictetus 1.18.9: "If, contrary to the arrangements of nature, you absolutely need to have feelings regarding the evils suffered by another, pity him (ἐλέει) rather than hate him"; 1.28.9; 2.21.3 and 5; Marcus Aurelius 7.26.

[9] Nero's declaration is significant in his discourse of AD 67 granting freedom to the Greeks: "On this day it is not pity but only goodwill (οὐ δι' ἔλεον ὑμᾶς, ἀλλὰ δι' εὔνοιαν) that makes me generous toward you" (Dittenberger, *Syl.* 814, 21). That is also why ἔλεος is so rarely mentioned in the papyri and the inscriptions and hardly appears at all except from the pens of Christians, who know God's mercy. For example, there is this graffito by Christian deserters in the Theban mountains in the fourth-fifth century: ἕως ἂν ἐλέησεν ὁ θεὸς καὶ ἐξάγαγεν ἡμᾶς ἐν σωτήριον χωρὶς ἁμαρτιῶν καὶ σώσωμεν πάντας (*SB* 9802, 1); *P.Ant.* 198, 5: τὸ ἔλεος τοῦ θεοῦ; *P.Erl.* 120, 12; *SEG* 24, 1224; *SB* 7872, 11: δωῇ ἔλεος ὁ κύριος τῷ 'Ονησιφόρου οἴκῳ (= 2 Tim 1:16). God's mercy is invoked (*IGLS* 317, 412, 500, 601, 633, 747; at Ephesus, cf. J. and L. Robert, "Bulletin épigraphique," in *REG,* 1953, p. 168, n. 177), or Christ's (ibid. 2358, 1), "Peace and mercy to all our holy community" (ibid. 1320, 6; cf. Ps 84:8–9; Rom 9:6; Gal 6:16). People call themselves bishop, archpriest, archdeacon, and priest "by the mercy of God" (*P.Ness.* 50, 10; 51, 1; 57, 1–2, 24, 26, 27; 107, 3; *P.Oxy.* 1951, 4; 1989, 27; *SB* 9146, 22; 9590, 26–27). In a Jewish epitaph at Rachelis: "I have good hope of mercy" (ἐλέους ἐλπίδα ἀγαθὴν ἐγὼ προσδέχομαι, *C.Pap.Jud.* 1513, 7 = *SEG*

R. Bultmann ("ἔλεος," in *TDNT*, vol. 2, p. 478) mentions the large role played by pity in the administration of justice. The litigant or the accused always seeks to gain the judge's *eleos;* they bring before the court "pity, excuses, humanity, but no human law, no divine law, allows the accrual of profit from this unclean wretch."[10] "He begged and supplicated the judges with many tears . . . to stir their compassion."[11] In the third century BC, an old man, victim of the theft of grain, asks for the king's help and concludes, "Thus, thanks to you, O king, I will enjoy the effects of justice and mercy for the rest of my days."[12]

With the LXX, we enter an entirely new world, in the first place because pity is exalted with considerable frequency, and secondly because it becomes a religious virtue[13] and especially a divine attribute,[14] so much

---

I, 573, 6; cf. *P.Oxy.* 2828, 7; 1 Thess 4:13; 2 Thess 2:16; Titus 2:13). E. Peterson (ΕΙΣ ΘΕΟΣ, Göttingen, 1926, pp. 164–167) compared the Christian Κύριε ἐλέησον to a Roman amulet (Πουβλικιανέ/Εἷς Ζεὺς/Σέραπις/ἐλέησον, *IGIS* 2413, 3; cf. *UPZ* 78, 24), to a medal (Κύρια Νέμεθι ἐλήσον, *CIG* 7036, *e*); Epictetus 2.7.12 on divination: "We hold the diviner's hand and call upon him as upon a god; we pray, 'Lord, have mercy on me' "; Josephus, *Ant.* 9.64: δέσποτα ἐλέησον; Achilles Tatius 3.5.4.

[10] Demosthenes, *C. Aristog.* 1; 25.81; cf. *C. Mid.* 21.100; Antiphon 1.21; 1.25: the guilty parties were "pitiless and merciless" in committing their crime and ought to be stricken by justice.

[11] Plato, *Ap.* 34 *c*, ἵνα ὅ τι μάλιστα ἐλεηθείη; 35 *b*. *Leg.* 5.731 *d:* "The criminal deserves pity (ἐλεεινός) in the same way as any person afflicted with an evil"; Philo, *Unchang. God* 115: "Your suffering and groaning will help you find pity"; Josephus, *War* 1.637; 5.318; *Ant.* 14.172; *Jos. Asen.* 28.2–3.

[12] *P.Magd.* 18, 6. A *colonus* addresses a petition to his patron: παρακαλῶ τοῦ ὑμετέρου ἐλέους τυχεῖν (*P.Oxy.* 2479, 23; cf. 3126, col. II, 11). A request for the deferment of a debt (*PSI* 767, 37); *P.Lund* II, 5, 15; *P.Fay.* 106, 16; *P.Flor.* 378, 3; *I.Bulg.* 2236, 95: ἵνα ἐλεηθέντες διὰ τὴν θείαν σου πρόνοιαν (under Gordian).

[13] Hos 6:6—"I want mercy, not sacrifice"; Mic 6:8—"What God requires of you is to love mercy . . ." or faithfulness (cf. B. Renaud, *La Formation du livre de Michée*, Paris, 1977, pp. 298ff.); Prov 14:21—"Happy is the one who takes pity on the miserable"; Wis 6:6—"The lowly person deserves pardon and pity"; 1 Macc 2:57— "David, for his mercy, inherited a royal throne." "Men of mercy" (Sir 44:10; 46:7) have compassion on their sisters and on orphans (Hos 2:3; 14:5), on the poor and on adolescents (Prov 14:31; Deut 28:50), on old and weak people (Lam 4:16; Prov 19:17; 28:8; 4 Macc 6:12; 8:20), and on themselves (4 Macc 12:6). This is a benevolence that gives others a good welcome (Gen 19:19; 24:49; 40:14; Num 11:15; Josh 2:12, 14; Judg 1:24; 6:17; 21:22; 1 Sam 15:6; Sir 18:13; etc.), in contrast to cruelty (Jer 50:42; Isa 13:18; 49:15; 2 Macc 7:27) and insults (Tob 3:15); it is full of understanding (Job 19:21), is compassionate and sheds tears (2 Macc 4:37; cf. 4 Macc 9:4), prompts one to help (Sir 29:1).

[14] One of the forms of God's benevolence (2 Sam 7:15; 15:20; 1 Kgs 3:6; 8:23; 1 Chr 17:13; 2 Chr 1:8; 6:14; Ps 26:6; Wis 15:1; Sir 18:5), that shows grace to the thousandth generation (Exod 20:6; Num 14:19; Deut 5:10; 7:9). The pious give thanks

so that Israel's religion appears to be the cult of a God of mercy,[15] which is an innovation—despite the altar raised by the Athenians to *Eleos* (Pausanias 1.17.1; Diodorus Siculus 13.22.7) and the Epidaurian belief (*Eleos epieikēs theos*, IG IV, 1282). After all, *eleeō* and *eleos* are translation Greek; all, *eleeō* and *eleos* are translation Greek; they reflect the content of the Hebrew original. Most commonly the verb *eleeō* translates the Hebrew *ḥānan*, "show favor or grace," with the nuance of a freely given favor, a generous gift.[16] Thus the usages of the verb connote preferential love for

---

to Yahweh "because he is good, for his mercy endures forever" (1 Chr 16:34; 2 Cor 5:13; 7:3–6; Neh 1:5; 9:32; Jdt 13:14; Ps 31:21; 88:1–2; 92:1–2; 100:5; 103:17; 106:1; 107:1; 118:1–4; 136:1ff.; Sir 51:8, 29; Jer 33:11; 1 Macc 4:24). "I am Yahweh who shows mercy" (Jer 9:24); "I am merciful" (Jer 3:12); "God is compassionate" (Ps 116:5). "With an everlasting mercy will I have mercy on you" (Isa 54:8, 10; 60:10; 63:7); "Yahweh's steadfast love does not cease; his mercies never come to an end" (Lam 3:22, 32).

[15] Israel prays that the Lord will have pity (Tob 8:4, 17; Jdt 7:30; Ps 25:67; 26:11; 27:7; 30:11; 51:1, 3; 67:2; 86:3, 16; 119:58, 132; Isa 33:2), as do Joseph (Gen 43:29) and Habakkuk ("Yahweh, even in your wrath remember to have pity"—Hab 3:2) and the faithful in the temple (Ps 48:9; cf. 1 Macc 3:44; 13:46; 2 Macc 8:3). Believers hope and have confidence in God's grace and mercy (Ps 13:5; 33:18, 22; 52:8; 147:11; Sir 2:9). They know that "all the paths of Yahweh are mercy and truth" (Ps 25:10; 26:3), that "the earth is full of Yahweh's grace" (Ps 33:5; 119:64). In the past he has shown mercy and satisfied his servants with all good things (Gen 33:5, 11; 2 Kgs 13:23; Tob 8:17; 11:16); his mercy is constant (Isa 49:10), and it is certain that he will always show himself to be merciful (Tob 6:18): "God will have pity on you" (Deut 30:3; Isa 14:1; 54:7; 55:7; Jer 12:15; 30:18; 31:20; 42:12; Ezek 39:25). Of course this mercy is completely free ("I will have mercy on whom I will have mercy," Exod 33:19), and one cannot always be sure of its manifestation ("Perhaps Yahweh will have mercy on what remains of Joseph," Amos 5:15; Mal 1:9; 2 Sam 12:22). And so the reasons for intervention are specified: "Have pity on me, Yahweh, for I languish" (Ps 6:2; 9:13), "because I am alone and unhappy" (Ps 25:6; cf. Jdt 6:19); "because I am in distress" (Ps 31:9; 51:2; 123:3), "because I have sinned against you" (Ps 51:5). This merciful benevolence is the basis of the covenant ("I will betroth you to myself . . . in pity and in mercy," Hos 2:19), the motive for providence ("The one who takes pity on them will lead them," Isa 49:10), the source of salvation ("Save me, Yahweh, by virtue of your grace," Ps 6:4; 17:7; 31:16; 85:7; 86:13; 109:26; 119:41), of liberation from enemies (Ps 143:12), of pardon for sins (Wis 11:23; 15:1; Bar 3:2; Sir 16:9; 18:14; 36:1; 2 Macc 2:18; 11:10), of comfort (Isa 12:1; 49:13; 52:9; Zech 1:17) and of joy (Ps 31:8). Certainly it is the same God who chastises and who shows mercy (Tob 13:2, 5); but if he punishes, it is with mercy (Wis 11:9; 12:22; 2 Macc 6:16), and his grace is always beneficent (Ps 69:16; 90:14; 94:18) and "better than life" (Ps 63:3). Since God dispenses his grace and truth so generously (Ps 57:3, 10; 59:10, 16, 17; 61:7; 62:12; 69:13; 84:11; 85:10; 88:14; 108:5; 138:2), we can understand the deep significance of the formula of benediction: "You shall bless the children of Israel in this way . . . The Lord be gracious to you" (Num 6:25).

[16] The substantive *ḥēn* has the aesthetic meaning of χάρις, "grace, charm, attractiveness," and it often suggests an accommodating attitude, the source of favors

a certain person that is shown in the generosity with which favors are granted.[17] Fairly often *eleeō* translates the piel of the Hebrew *rāḥam*, "have pity, show mercy," but also "love tenderly."[18] On the other hand, there are 172 instances in which the LXX uses *eleos* to translate *ḥesed̠*, a word whose significance is varied and disputed[19] but whose basic meaning is "goodness, benevolence, favorable disposition," covering the spectrum from plain sympathy and goodness to mercy and clemency. It is fundamentally a species of love (and is often linked with love— "love *ḥesed̠*" [Amos 5:5] means to love tenderly); and most of its occurrences have to do with God's mercy or lovingkindness. The description of God as *rāḇ-ḥesed̠*, literally "great in favor," is to be understood as meaning "abundant in mercy" (*polyeleos*, Num 14:18; Joel 2:13; Ps 86:5, 15). Translators of the NT must keep these

---

and gifts. With God, it is mercy or lovingkindness. Cf. C. Spicq, *Agapè: Prolégomènes*, Appendix II, pp. 125–129; P. Bonnetain, "Grâce," in *DBSup*, vol. 3, col. 727–737; W. F. Lofthouse, "*Hen* and *Hesed* in the Old Testament," in *ZAW*, 1933, pp. 29–35; W. L. Reed, "Some Implications of *Hen* for Old Testament Religion," in *JBL*, 1954, pp. 36–41; K. W. Neubauer, *Der Stamm* Chnn *im Sprachgebrauch des Alten Testaments*, Berlin, 1964.

[17] A fourth-century inscription, translating the priestly benediction (Num 6:25), substitutes ἀγαπήσει (line 9) for ἐλεήσει in the original; an equivalence justified by the editors B. Lifshitz and J. Schiby, "Une Synagogue samaritaine à Thessalonique," in *RB*, 1968, pp. 370ff.

[18] In six passages, the LXX translates *rāḥam* with ἀγαπάω. The singular noun *reḥem* refers to the mother's womb, the uterus (Jer 1:5), the locus of the mother's pity for her children (1 Kgs 3:26), the plural *raḥᵃmîm* refers to the intestines, which are moved with compassion and love (Cant 5:4; Gen 43:30). Hence the anthropomorphic descriptions of God's mercy: "Have the yearning of your entrails and your compassion toward me been withheld?" (Isa 63:15); "My entrails are still moved on [Ephraim's] account; I truly pity him" (Jer 31:20).

[19] *Ḥesed̠* is linked with righteousness but put in relation with the covenant; it expresses the idea of faithfulness. Cf. C. Spicq, *Agapè: Prolégomènes*, Appendix I, pp. 120–124; I. Elbogen, "חסד, Verpflichtung, Verheißung, Bekräftigung," in *P. Haupt Festschrift*, Leipzig, 1922, pp. 43–46; N. Glueck, *Das Wort* hesed *im alttestamentlichen Sprachgebrauch als menschliche und göttliche gemeinschaftgemäße*, Giessen, 1927; H. J. Stoebe, "Die Bedeutung des Wortes Häsäd im Alten Testament," in *VT*, 1952, pp. 244–254; U. Masing, "Der Begriff Hésed im alttestamentlichen Sprachgebrauch," in *Charisteria I. Kõpp . . . oblata*, Holmiae, 1954, pp. 27–63; C. Ryder Smith, *The Bible Doctrine of Grace*, London, 1956, pp. 8–55; A. R. Johnson, "Hesed and Hasid," in N. A. Dahl, A. S. Kapelrud, *Interpretationes ad Vetus Testamentum pertinentes S. Mowinckel . . . missae*, Oslo, 1965, pp. 100–112; A. Caquot, " 'Les Grâces de David': A propos d'Isaïe LV, 3 b," in *Sem*, 1965, pp. 45–59; W. Zimmerli, "חסד im Schriftum von Qumran," in *Hommages à A. Dupont-Sommer*, Paris, 1971, pp. 439–449; and above all Katherine Doob Sakenfeld, *The Meaning of Hesed in the Hebrew Bible*, Missoula, 1978. This bibliography may be filled out from that in *TWNT*, vol. 10, p. 1072.

nuances in mind wherever they must render the rich meaning of formally biblical *eleos*.[20]

The NT takes up Israel's faith in God's mercy in exactly the same form and continues it. It gives much greater emphasis, however, to the precept of brotherly mercy,[21] which it makes into an active, internal virtue, an indispensable condition of eternal blessedness[22] and an imitation of the heavenly Father. In the parable of the Unmerciful Servant,[23] Jesus first contrasts two debts—one enormous (ten thousand talents), the other miniscule (a hundred denarii)—then the two creditors. The king is moved by a visceral compassion (*splanchnistheis*, Matt 18:27) when he hears his debtor's supplications and forgives the whole debt; but the latter shuts out all feelings of pity and not only refuses to forgive the debt owed him but throws the debtor into prison. So this is the motivation for the king's (God's) judgment: "Contemptible servant,[24] ought you not also to have had pity

---

[20] The Jewish writings add nothing to the OT meaning. Pity is a "generous feeling" (χρηστὸς πάθος, Josephus, *War* 4.384), "the most essential feeling, the closest to reflective thought" (Philo, *Virtues* 144), "the altar of mercy" (*Rewards* 154), which has as its object the indigent (*Change of Names* 40; *Dreams* 1.95–96) and the orphans (Philo, *Worse Attacks Better* 145; *Spec. Laws* 4.180; Josephus, *War* 1.556; *Ant.* 16.15, 17). It is above all a divine attribute (Philo, *Flight* 162; *Spec. Laws* 1.308; Josephus, *Ant.* 4.239, 269; *Pss. Sol.* passim), a saving mercy (τὸν σωτήριον ἔλεον, *Unchang. God* 74; *Dreams* 2.149) bestowed by God even upon the unworthy (*Unchang. God* 76). "In God's mercy all things repose together" (*Sacr. Abel and Cain* 42). Cf. *Ep. Arist.* 208: "You shall be led to have pity (πρὸς τὸν ἔλεον), for God is merciful (ἐλεήμων)"; *T. Zeb.* 5.3—Ἔχετε οὖν ἔλεος ἐν σπλάγχνοις ὑμῶν, ὅτι εἴ τι ἂν ποιήσῃ τῷ πλησίον αὐτοῦ, οὕτω Κύριος ποιήσει; *T. Abr.* B 10.

[21] Matt 9:13; 12:7 take up Hos 6:6—"I desire mercy and not sacrifice" (cf. D. Hill, "On the Use and Meaning of Hosea VI, 6 in Matthew's Gospel," in *NTS*, vol. 24, 1977, pp. 107–119). In Matt 23:23, Jesus accuses the Pharisees of neglecting the most important points of the law, the fundamental, most serious, obligations that it imposes (τὰ βαρύτερα τοῦ νόμου): righteousness or justice, compassion (τὸ ἔλεος), and good faith; cf. Zech 7:9; Prov 14:21–22.

[22] Jas 2:13—"Judgment (condemnation) will be without mercy (ἀνέλεος) for the one who has not shown mercy; mercy triumphs over judgment." It is the condition for the forgiveness of sins (Sir 28:2; *T. Zeb.* 8.1–3). The adjective ἀνέλεος, a biblical hapax, is found elsewhere only in the papyri, in the fourth century (*P.Lips.* 39, 12); cf. ἀνελεήμων (Rom 1:32).

[23] C. Spicq, *Dieu et l'homme*, pp. 54–61; J. D. M. Derrett, *Law in the NT*, pp. 32–47; W. J. Thompson, *Matthew's Advice to a Divided Community*, Rome, 1970, pp. 203ff.; J. Dupont, *Béatitudes*, vol. 3, pp. 620ff.

[24] Δοῦλε πονηρέ is usually translated "wicked servant" (18:32), but πονηροί is the adjective used for sycophants (Demosthenes, *C. Eub.* 57.32), that is, the dishonest, and means "rascals, rogues" (cf. J. Taillardat, *Images d'Aristophane*, p. 241, n. 430), miserable types (Plutarch, *De cupid. divit.* 5), the villainous (*De vit. pud.* 11; *De sera* 11), vile (Josephus, *Ant.* 2.55; 16.296), foul individual (Josephus, *Life* 134).

on your fellow-servant, since I took pity on you?" (*ouk edei kai se eleēsai ton syndoulon sou, hōs kagō se eleēsa*, 18:33). And he hands him over to the torturers. Jesus explains the teaching of the parable: "So also will my heavenly Father do to you, if each of you does not forgive (*mē aphēte*) his brother from the heart" (18:35). On the one hand, "from the heart" contrasts with forgiveness merely spoken with the lips;[25] it is a matter of not only overlooking the offenses of which one has been victim, but of loving one's neighbor, that is, of wishing and doing him well in every circumstance (Matt 5:44). On the other hand, God will treat us according to the way we treat our brethren. The motivation for brotherly compassion is imitation of God; which puts the emphasis on the interiority and sincerity of the forgiveness. The one who shows compassion has a good heart.

The good Samaritan is a model, because he was moved by compassion at the sight of the wounded stranger (*idōn esplanchnisthē*, Luke 10:33) and helped him, showing himself to be the "neighbor" of the man who fell into the hands of the brigands.[26] Just the opposite of the priest and the Levite, who passed by the wounded man, remaining indifferent strangers and even turning aside for fear of contracting a legal defilement, the Samaritan was completely spontaneous, quick to act, disinterested, and efficient in his generosity simply because he was good-hearted and was moved (*ho poiēsas to eleos met' autou*, 10:37), because he knew himself and showed himself to be the brother of the stranger.

The apostles praise this virtue: "The wisdom from on high is . . . full of mercy and good fruit" (*mestē eleous kai karpōn agathōn*, Jas 3:17); a love that originates with God reflects the very wisdom of God and is made manifest in "good works." It is beneficent, especially toward the unfortunate. The one who carries out such a ministry in the church will radiate goodness: "Let the one who practices mercy (do so) with joy" (*ho eleōn en hilarotēti*, Rom 12:8; cf. Prov 22:8 a, LXX), not only because God loves a cheerful giver (2 Cor 9:7) or to build up the unfortunate with a smile but

---

[25] The insensitivity and cruelty of the unmerciful debtor contrasts with the so generous compassion of the king, who was moved by his servant's distress. God's heart (1 John 3:20) and even "entrails" are stirred; cf. the father of the prodigal (Luke 15:20–21).

[26] Cf. B. Gerhardsson, "The Good Samaritan," in *ConNT*, vol. 16, 1958; C. Spicq, *Agapè*, vol. 1, pp. 137–148; H. Binder, "Das Gleichnis vom barmherzigen Samariter," in *TZ*, 1959, pp. 176–194; W. Monselewski, *Der barmherzige Samariter*, Tübingen, 1966; C. Daniel, "Les Esséniens et l'arrière-fond historique de la parabole du Bon Samaritain," in *NovT*, 1969, pp. 71–104; H. Zimmermann, "Das Gleichnis vom barmherzigen Samariter," in G. Bornkamm, *Die Zeit Jesu* (Festschrift H. Schlier), Freiburg-Basel-Vienna, 1970, pp. 58–69; Bo Reicke, "Der barmherzige Samariter," in *Verborum Veritas* (Festschrift F. Stählin), Wuppertal, 1970, pp. 103–109.

because "there is greater happiness in giving than in receiving" (Acts 20:35). Jude (21–22) addresses all Christians: "Keep yourselves in the love of God, awaiting the mercy of our Lord Jesus Christ for life everlasting (*prosdechomenoi to eleos tou kyriou hēmōn*). Have pity on those who are deciding" (or "disputing," *kai hous men eleate diakrinomenous*—the textual variants are numerous). This whole catechesis was already contained in the promise of divine mercy to those who pardon their neighbor: "Blessed are the merciful, for they themselves shall be shown mercy."[27]

As for God, his mercy is revealed in the coming of the messianic salvation and is sung by the Virgin Mary and the priest Zechariah in terms borrowed from the OT.[28] It is a gratuitous favor, a grace that presupposes God's love and the intervention of his omnipotence. In addition, it is manifested in Elizabeth's motherhood (Luke 1:58), as it is shown to the Gerasene demoniac (Mark 5:19), to St. Paul (1 Cor 7:25; 2 Cor 4:1; 1 Tim 1:13, 16), to Epaphroditus (Phil 2:27), to the house of Onesiphorus (2 Tim 1:16; cf. *SB* 1872). It extends to all believers (Gal 6:16) and together with Christ's mercy becomes the content of the apostle's wish for a whole church: "Grace, mercy, and peace from God the Father and Christ our Savior" (1 Tim 1:2; 2 Tim 1:2; Jude 2; 2 John 3). Thus it is God's mercy that accounts for the conversion of a persecutor and his sending as an apostle, for the healing of a sick person, for the casting out of a demon, for purification from sin and a life united to God. Blind, epileptic, and leprous folk all appeal to Jesus' compassion, always with success,[29] and it is thanks to his intercession that believers can "approach the throne of grace to receive mercy and find grace to help in time of need" (Heb 4:16).

Certainly God is free to grant or deny his favors and his forgiveness (Rom 9:15–18; cf. Exod 33:19); but those who yesterday were "Not pitied" are today "Pitied" (1 Pet 2:10; cf. Hos 1:6–9). St. Paul's innovation in the biblical theology of *eleos* is to locate God's mercy at the beginning and at the end of the plan of salvation: "Formerly you were disobedient to God; now you have obtained mercy. . . . God has consigned all people to dis-

---

[27] Μακάριοι οἱ ἐλεήμονες ὅτι αὐτοὶ ἐλεηθήσονται, Matt 5:7. Ἐλεήμων, in 25 of its 30 occurrences in the LXX, refers to an attribute of God (cf. of Christ, Heb 2:17) and usually translates the Hebrew *ḥannûn* (cf. J. Dupont, *Béatitudes*, vol. 3, pp. 604–633). God punishes sin but also has mercy on the sinner (Jonah 4:2; Joel 2:13; Isa 55:7; Jer 3:12), especially on the person who is compassionate (Luke 6:36–38; Eph 4:32; Col 3:12) and forgiving (Matt 6:12; Luke 11:5–6); cf. the parable of the Last Judgment (Matt 25:31–46).

[28] Luke 1:50 (= Ps 102:17); 1:54 (Ps 97:3); 1:72 (= Mic 7:20); 1:78, διὰ σπλάγχνα ἐλέους θεοῦ ἡμῶν.

[29] Mark 10:47; Matt 9:27; 17:15; Luke 17:13; cf. Luke 16:24—the wicked rich man—"Father Abraham, have mercy on me."

obedience so as to show mercy to all" (Rom 11:30–32). Universal mercy extends to Gentiles as well as Jews (Rom 15:9) and consists in the forgiveness of sins. It is made effective for each one in baptism ("He has saved us according to his mercy through a bath of regeneration and renewal in the Holy Spirit" (Titus 3:5), and it has an eschatological bearing ("God wished to make known the wealth of his glory in vessels of mercy that he has prepared for glory").[30] The whole Christian life here below consists in "waiting for the mercy of our Lord Jesus Christ for life everlasting" (Jude 21).

---

[30] Rom 9:23; 1 Pet 1:3—"The God and Father of our Lord Jesus Christ, through whose great mercy we have been born again to a living hope"; 2 Tim 1:18—"May the Lord grant to Onesiphorus to find mercy with the Lord on that Day" (to Onesiphorus, who was so devoted to the church at Ephesus and so charitable toward St. Paul when he was imprisoned at Rome). Thus the prayers of the apostle and of Christians provoke God to compassion.

ἐλπίζω, ἐλπίς
elpizō, to hope; *elpis*, hope

We note that the noun *elpis* is absent from the four Gospels and thus that the Lord did not use the word *hope*.[1] The verb *elpizō* is used only twice in its secular sense ("If you lend to those from whom you hope to receive . . ." [Luke 6:34; cf. *elpizōn . . . apodōsei*, L. Robert, *Gladiateurs*, n. 55]; "Herod hoped to see Jesus perform some miracle" [Luke 23:8]) and three times in its religious sense,[2] all in accord with the OT meaning.[3] The more the

---

[1] That is to say that in working out a NT theology of hope we have to take other terms into account: ἀναμένω, ἀπεκδέχομαι, γρηγορέω, ἐκδέχομαι, ἐπέχω, προσδέχομαι, προσδοκάω, ὑπομονή, etc.; cf. ἀπελπίζω (Luke 6:35), προελπίζω (Eph 1:12). Cf. C. Spicq, *Théologie morale*, vol. 1, pp. 292–380; J. de Guibert, "Sur l'emploi d'ἐλπίς et ses synonymes dans le N.T.," in *RSR*, 1913, pp. 565–569; A. Gelin, *Les Idées maîtresses de l'Ancien Testament*, Paris, 1949, pp. 27ff.; T. C. Vriezen, "Die Hoffnung im Alten Testament," in *TLZ*, 1953, col. 577–586; J. van der Ploeg, "L'Espérance dans l'A.T.," in *RB*, 1954, pp. 481–507; W. Grossouw, "L'Espérance dans le N.T.," ibid., pp. 508–532; J. Guillet, *Thèmes bibliques*, Paris, 1954, pp. 160ff.; D. L. Fidele, *La speranza cristiana nelle lettere de S. Paulo*, Naples, 1960; C. F. D. Moule, *The Meaning of Hope* (Facet Books, 5), Philadelphia, 1963; H. Schlier, *Essais sur le Nouveau Testament*, Paris, 1968, pp. 159–170, 356ff.; K. Hanhart, "Paul's Hope in the Face of Death," in *JBL*, 1969, pp. 445–457; F. Raurell, *La esperanze en la Biblia* (XXX Semana Biblica Española), in *Analecta sacra Tarraconensia*, 1970, pp. 325–359; J. R. Flecha Andrés, *Esperanza y moral en el Nuevo Testamento*, Léon, 1975; H. Zimmermann, *Das Bekenntnis der Hoffnung: Tradition und Redaktion im Hebräerbrief*, Cologne, 1977; P. Grelot, *L'Espérance juive à l'heure de Jésus*, Paris, 1978.

[2] Matt 12:21 (Rom 15:12), a quotation of Isa 42:4—"My servant . . . in his name the nations shall place their hope"; Luke 24:21—the disciples from Emmaus hoped that Jesus would deliver Israel; John 5:45—the Jews place their hope in Moses (the perfect form ἠλπίκατε has a parallel in *P.Oslo* 159, 18, ἤλπικα, in the third century).

[3] Ἐλπίζω is construed with the accusative, the dative (Thucydides 3.97.2: "Demosthenes hoped in his fortune," τῇ τύχῃ ἐλπίσας), or the infinitive; or with ὅτι and many prepositions: εἰς τινα, ἐν τινι, ἐπί τινα, ἐπί τι, ἐπί τινι. In the LXX, it translates

---

elpizō, S 1679; *TDNT* 2.517–533; *EDNT* 1.437–441; *NIDNTT* 2.238–246; MM 204; L&N 25.59, 30.54; BDF §§14, 74(1), 187(6), 233(2), 235(2), 337(2), 338(3), 341, 350, 397(2); BAGD 252 ‖ *elpis*, S 1680; *TDNT* 2.517–533; *EDNT* 1.437–441; *NIDNTT* 2.238–246; MM 204–205; L&N 25.59, 25.61, 25.62; BDF §§14, 235(2), 400(1); BAGD 252–253; ND 2.77

proclamation of the gospel of salvation advanced in Asia Minor and in Europe, the more the apostles, especially St. Paul, came in contact with pagans, whom they defined as "those who have no hope."[4] These pagans are amazed by the unique *elpis* (Eph 4:4; Heb 3:6; cf. *P.Brem.* 1, 1: *mia ēn elpis kai loipē prosdokia*; *UPZ* 42, 39; *C.P.Herm.* 116; Josephus, *War* 5.64; 6.160) that animates all the members of the new religion.[5] They cry for help (Acts 16:9—*boēthēson hēmin*), so that the preaching of the faith is oriented more and more toward a preaching of hope (cf. Heb 11:1), and the confession of faith becomes a *homologia tēs elpidos aklinē* ("unwavering confession of hope," Heb 10:23).

---

the Hebrew words *qāwâh*, "await, hope" (cf. P. A. H. de Boer, "Etude sur le sense de la racine QWH," in *Oudtestamentlische Studiën*, vol. 10, 1954, pp. 225–246); *bāṭaḥ*, "have confidence in, feel secure"; *yāḥal*, "wait for someone"; *ḥākâh*, "wait with confidence or certitude"; *ḥāsâh*, "entrust oneself to someone, find shelter (*maḥᵃseh*, refuge, shelter), have recourse to someone." While in secular Greek ἐλπίς and ἐλπίζω especially mean wait for, count on, expect, suppose (notably in Josephus), hope for, in the LXX, the preponderant nuance is trust, have recourse to, place one's hope in someone.

[4] 1 Thess 4:13; Eph 2:12. Certainly the Romans had a cult of Hope, for whom they had many temples (PW, vol. 3, A, 2, col. 1634ff.; K. Thylander, *Inscriptions du port d'Ostie*, Lund, 1952, n. B, 335, 32); they thought that the cult of Hope restored courage (Cicero, *Nat. D.* 2.23; Dio Cassius 2.23). At Rome, A. Atilius Calatinus had built a temple to Spes (Hope) on the Forum Holitorium during the First Punic War; later a temple to Spes Vetus was erected on the Esquiline (Cicero, *Leg.* 2.11.28); but Elpis does not have a place in the index of Stoic technical terms or in that of E. des Places' *La Religion grecque* (Paris, 1969), since it is a passion and as such as little desirable as any other passion. According to the myth of Pandora, the jar from which escaped all the evils that spread among humankind was closed before Hope, which was still down inside it, could get out (Hesiod, *Op.* 42–105). Certainly some religious souls hoped in the gods' help (Philemon: οἱ γὰρ θεὸν σέβοντες, ἐλπίδας καλὰς ἔχουσιν εἰς σωτηρίαν, in J. M. Edmonds, *Attic Comedy*, vol. 3 A, p. 82), but in the first century, sadness and discouragement are constant: "We can no longer bear either our vices or their cures" (Livy, preface). Archias of Mitylene thought that it was good to bewail the birth of sons, who would advance relentlessly among evils of all sorts, and that the dead were blessed in that they had left life and found in death the cure for all ills (*Anth. Pal.* 9.11; cf. *P.Oxy.* 115). It has been observed that in the sculpture of the first century, the eyes often express sadness, "a sort of desperate numbness" (J. P. Milliet, "Les Yeux hagards," in *Mélanges Nicole*, Geneva, 1905, pp. 357–366). A common epitaph: "I was not, I came to be, I am no longer; it amounts to nothing" (*MAMA*, vol. 8, 353; cf. R. Lattimore, *Epitaphs*). Cf. A. J. Festugière, *Idéal religieux*, pp. 163–164; idem, *Vie spirituelle*, pp. 159ff. C. Spicq, *Vie morale*, pp. 10ff. = ET, *Trinity*, pp. 3ff.; J. M. Aubert, "La Voix de l'espérance dans l'âme grecque antique," in *BAGB*, 1961, pp. 205–216.

[5] 1 Pet 3:15. Cf. E. Cothenet, "Le Réalisme de l'espérance chrétienne selon I Pierre," in *NTS* 27, 1981, pp. 564–572.

I. — Secular objects of hope. — If hope is defined as "expectation of something good,"[6] then there are many good things (Sir 2:9): returning to one's country (Jer 44:14; Philo, *Spec. Laws* 4.17; Polybius 3.63.7), freedom (Isa 25:9; cf. Jdt 6:9; Ps 112:7), receiving a teaching (Isa 42:4; cf. Philo, *Change of Names* 8), help (2 Macc 3:29), a wage (Wis 2:22, *misthon*), money,[7] a harvest (Philo, *Virtues* 159; *Rewards* 129; 1 Cor 9:10); escaping an illness (2 Macc 3:29; Philo, *Sacr. Abel and Cain* 123; Josephus, *War* 1.657; *Ant.* 17.172), a shipwreck (Acts 27:20), a disaster (Job 2:9); what in Greek is called salvation (Philo, *Flacc.* 11; *To Gaius* 151, 329; 4 Macc 11:7). Philo specifies that people hope for useful goods, like wealth, health, reputation (*Alleg. Interp.* 3.86; *Decalogue* 91; *To Gaius* 11), pleasures (*Dreams* 2.209), favors and compliments (*Abraham* 128; *To Gaius* 137), a calm and tranquil life (*Moses* 1.214), a contemplative life (*Migr. Abr.* 70), wellbeing (*Joseph* 162), freedom (*Alleg. Interp.* 3.194; *Moses* 1.171, 193; *Virtues* 123), fatherhood (*Alleg. Interp.* 3.85; *Spec. Laws* 1.138; 4.203; *Decalogue* 126; *Virtues* 207), motherhood (*Spec. Laws* 3.62), marriage (*Husbandry* 158; *Prelim. Stud.* 5; Aristaenetus 1.21.14: *elpizomenos estin ho gamos hēdys*), victory (*Spec. Laws* 4.28; *Good Man Free* 111; *To Gaius* 356; *Husbandry* 162; *Joseph* 138), booty (*Cherub.* 75), happiness (*Flight* 145; *Abraham* 7; *To Gaius* 82), perfection (*Heir* 311; *Decalogue* 113). St. Paul and St. John express several times their desire to visit a community, to prolong a visit, to be free to meet a disciple.[8] This meaning is in conformity with common usage as expressed in the papyri: "Tell Longinus that I hope to meet him again."[9] The desire is expressed that a certain order will be carried out (*P.Ant.* 188, 10), that a guilty person will be imprisoned (*SB* 9616, 28), that a certain person will make an effort

---

[6] Ps.-Plato, *Def.* 416: ἐλπίς· προσδοκία ἀγαθοῦ; cf. Xenophon, *Cyr.* 1.6.19.

[7] Acts 24:26—ἐλπίζων ὅτι χρήματα δοθήσεται αὐτῷ; Luke 6:34—ἐλπίζετε λαβεῖν; a profit (ἐργασία, Acts 16:19; cf. κέρδος, Josephus, *War* 2.587; 6.383; *Ant.* 18.7; *Life* 325). The poor person who has hope (Hebrew *tiqwâh*; Job 4:16; *Pss. Sol.* 5.13; 15.2; 18.3; Philo, *Abraham* 47: "The one who hopes is poor") directs his desire to what is due him (Deut 24:15). The hope for a tree is that it will renew itself (Job 14:7; 19:10); the merchant's hope is profit (Philo, *Rewards* 11).

[8] Rom 15:24—ἐλπίζω θεάσασθαι ὑμᾶς; 1 Cor 16:7—ἐλπίζω ἐπιμεῖναι; Phil 2:19, 23; Phlm 22; 1 Tim 3:14; 2 John 12; 3 John 14; cf. Tob 10:8—Tobias's parents have no more hope of seeing him again. In the sense "expect, count on," St. Paul uses the verb ἐλπίζω to express his confidence in the good feelings of his correspondents ("I hope that you will understand . . ." [2 Cor 1:13; 5:11; 8:5; 10:15; 13:6]) or in their faithfulness (2 Cor 1:7). Cf. the letter of Sempronius in the second century: "I expect (ἐλπίζω) that our brother Valerius realizes how deep the sorrow is that we feel" (*P.Wisc.* 84, 12).

[9] *P.Mich.* 476, 25 (third century); 481, 14; *P.Gron.* 18, 7; *P.Oxy.* 1829, 7, 17; 1940, 3; 2190, 9. A son's hope is that upon his return he will find his mother in good health (letter of Ammon, edited by W. H. Willis, in *Proceedings* XV, p. 108, l. 17).

(*P.Brem.* 5, 8: *dōsein ergasian;* a Latinism, cf. Luke 12:58), that someone will carry out our business (*P.Oxy.* 3147, 8, *hoti poiei to pragma hēmōn*), that a field will be sown (*P.Ryl.* 243, 8), that certain things will be pleasing (*PSI* 1242, 3: *auta hēdista;* first century; cf. *SB* 9528). Someone counts on receiving money (*P.Mich.* 480, 15; *Pap.Lugd.Bat.* XI, 28, 10; *P.Oslo* 50, 7; *P.Laur.* 39, 8) or help.[10] Soldiers hope for promotion.[11] In the midst of trials, the danger is that one will lose all hope.[12] Is a happy life not sustained by hope?[13] In contracts for divorce by mutual consent, the spouses recognize that they were united in a legal marriage and in a common life "for the procreation of children, according to the human custom, with good hopes" (*epi chrēstais elpisin, C.P.Herm.* 29, 10 = *SB* 9278; *C.Pap.Jud.* 513). In all these texts, we can conclude on the one hand that human hope is the expectation—uncertain, confident, or anguished—of a desired good; it glimpses as possible or probable the realization of that which it counts on. On the other hand, the birthright of every human being, man or woman, but above all of the poor and unfortunate, is to retain hope. "Thales, when asked what the commonest thing was, answered, 'Hope—for even those who have nothing else still have this.' "[14]

---

[10] *P.Mich.* 529, 15: Aurelius ἐλπίζων τῆς τοῦ κυρίου μου βοηθείας, hoping for my lord's assistance (the lord in question being the prefect of Egypt, Maevius Honoratianus); *P.Tebt.* 787, 15: ἐλπίδα ἔχοντες τῆς σῆς ἀντιλήψεως.

[11] In 107, the soldier Apollinarus writes to his brother Sabinus that the consular Claudius Severus has told him: "I will make you a secretary of the legion, with hope of advancement" (ἐφ' ἐλπίδων, *P.Mich.* 466, 30); "I hope to be promoted soon" (*BGU* 423, 27). Cf. *SB* 6717, 7: ἐλπίζω σε στεφανωθήσεσθαι; *P.Lond.* 1941, 8.

[12] Ἄλλην ἐλπίδα οὐκ ἔχομεν, *P.Giss.* (ed. H. Kling) 31, 14; *P.Oxy.* 1678, 7; *P.Mich.* 502, 12: μάλιστα δέ τις ἄλλη ἐλπὶς οὐκ ἔστιν ὡς ἡ παρησία τῶν ἀδελφῶν (second century); Josephus, *Ant.* 10.11: τῷ μηδεμίαν ἄλλην ἐλπίδα ἔχοντι σωτηρίας. An insolvent debtor saw his children seized by creditors; he himself was arrested; it could be said that he had been almost forced to lose blessed hope: ὥστε ὡς ἔπος εἰπεῖν ἀναγκασθῆναι τῆς μακαρίας ἐλπίδος (cf. Titus 2:13; Antiochus I of Commagene, in *IGLS* 1, 108); ἡμῶν ἀποστερηθῆναι (*P.Lond.* 1915, 9). The legal ἀνάπαυσις was not respected in the assigning of a *leitourgia* to a complainant who thus lost "the time to have good hopes" (ἔχειν περὶ ἐμαυτῷ χρηστὰς τὰς ἐλπίδας, *SB* 10199). En route to Hades: εἰς φλόγα καὶ σποδιὴν ἐλπίδας ἐξέχεεν (*CIRB* 141, 5). The author of a letter, in a difficult situation, has no hope other than the help of his correspondent: νῦν ἐν σοὶ μοί εἰσιν αἱ ἐλπίδες τοῦ σωίζεσθαι (sic), *P.Cair.Zen.* 59844, 6. It is hoped that some evil will not happen: ὅπερ ἐλπίζω μηδὲν τούτων γενήσεσθαι (*P.Mil.Vogl.* 76, 8).

[13] Βίον ἀγαθὸν εἰς ἐλπίδα (Antiochus I of Commagene, in *IGLS* 47, col. VI, 14); ἐλπίδα τοῦ βιώσεσθαι (Josephus, *Ant.* 15.204; cf. 17.1). New fruits give the best hopes (*BGU* 486, 6; cf. education, Philo, *Post. Cain* 97; *Heir* 310). *SB* 9528, 11; *PSI* 1312, 9 (letters of Chomenis to his brother): ἀγαθὰς οὖν ἐλπίδας ἔχε; *UPZ* 13, 28.

[14] Θάλης ἐρωτηθεὶς τί κοινότατον, ἀπεκρίνατο· ἐλπίς· καὶ γὰρ οἷς ἄλλο μηδέν, αὕτη πάρεστιν, Stobaeus, *Flor.* 110.46, n. 24 (vol. 5, p. 1001); Plato, *Phlb.* 39 e:

Otherwise, in biblical as in secular Greek, *elpizō (en)* means to hope in someone, to place one's confidence in people or in earthly realities: the people of Shechem put their hope in Gaal (Judg 9:26; cf. 20:36), Hezekiah put his in Egypt and his horsemen (2 Kgs 18:24), the Assyrians put theirs in their shields and spears;[15] Israel in Bethel (Jer 48:13) and Egypt (Ezek 29:16); but Jer 17:5 curses the person who trusts in a human (Philo, *Flacc.* 22). This same meaning, "placing one's confidence," is found in the papyri: "For we would not have expected him to perish (future infinitive of *diapiptō*) in so short a time" (*ou gar an ēlpisamen en houtō brachei chronō diapesein auton*, *SB* 6787, 39; third century BC); "but I hope that I shall be saved through your prayers" (*elpizō de diasōthēsesthai me dia tōn euchōn sou*, ibid. 7872, col. II, 10; *C.P.Herm.* 5, 11). It is attested especially in Jewish and Christian tomb inscriptions: "I expect a good hope of mercy";[16] but then the verb has a religious meaning.

II. — Religious objects of hope. — Pagans placed their confidence in God to obtain earthly goods.[17] In the first century AD, according to Orphic and mystery traditions,[18] souls aspire to immortality, to a blessed survival after death, and it was thought that Dionysus would protect his faithful ones after death. But this hope was never named as such, and it is only

---

"Throughout our lives, we do not cease to be full of hope"; Theocritus 4.42: "There is hope as long as one is living; it is when one is dead that there is no more hope"; Xenophon, *An.* 7.6.11: "When one is human one must expect everything" (cited by Bultmann, "ἐλπίς," in *TDNT*, vol. 2, pp. 517–518). Philo, *Worse Attacks Better* 138–139: "Is there is anything more properly human than the hope or expectation of possessing goods that God will give? . . . Those who do not hope in God do not share in a rational nature . . . only humans have hope . . . whoever despairs is not human"; *Rewards* 14: "No one could be taken for a human being who does not hope in God"; 72; *Abraham* 8, 10.

[15] Jdt 9:7; Ps 44:6; Hos 10:13—"You hoped in the multitude of your valiant men." A person may have confidence in dreams (Sir 34:7; cf. hope through magic, Rhetorius, ἐλπίσι χρησμῶν ἀναλαμβανομένους, in *CCAG*, VIII, IV, p. 165, 8), in a lie (Isa 28:15; Jer 13:25), wickedness (Isa 47:10: ἐλπίς τῆς πονηρίας σου) or extortion (Isa 30:12). Fools put their hope in dead things: ἐν νεκροῖς = in idols (Wis 13:10; cf. 15:6, 10).

[16] Ἐλέους ἐλπίδα ἀγαθὴν ἐγὼ προσδέχομαι, epitaph of a Jew of Rachelis, dead at age 30, *CII* 1513, 7 = *SB* 6650, 4. In classical Greek, ἔχειν τὴν ἐλπίδα ἐπί = place one's hope in someone; cf. Euripides, *Or.* 1059; Diodorus Siculus 14.101.

[17] Ἐλπίζω σὺν θεῷ, παρὰ θεοῦ, μετὰ θεόν, εἰς θεόν. In the papyri, most of these attestations are Christian and late, *P.Iand.* 11, 2; *P.Ant.* 198, 6–7; *PSI* 301, 9; *SB* 7655, 15; 9139, 15; 10269, 5; *IGLS* 2546.

[18] Cf. M. J. Lagrange, *Les Mystères: L'Orphisme*, Paris, 1937; A. Boulanger, "L'Orphisme," in *REA*, 1937, pp. 45–48; especially F. Cumont, *Lux Perpetua*, pp. 240ff., 401ff. A. J. Festugière, *Etudes de religion*, pp. 13–63. For Cicero (*Leg.* 2.14.36), Eleusis brought men nothing better than a reason to live with joy and to die "with good hope."

Plutarch who states that the initiates into the mysteries undergo "a sudden thrill mixed with hope" (*met' elpidos idias echousi*, *De fac.* 28; 943 c), when they are in the act of clinging to the moon.

A veritable semantic revolution is effected by the LXX, which gives *elpis* and *elpizō* a strictly religious meaning. Hope, which is always directed toward God, is no longer any expectation whatsoever, but a sure and certain confidence in Yahweh. It is not only the virtue of certain individuals[19] but also the faith, piety, and spirituality of Israel, as these are expressed by the psalmists and the sages: "The hope of the righteous is full of immortality" (Wis 3:4). "The hope of those who fear God is placed in the one who saves them."[20] No object is given to *elpis*. It is only a matter of finding one's refuge in Yahweh[21] and having full and complete confidence in him.[22] The twelve prophets have throughout history strengthened the chosen people "by certitude and constancy of hope" (*en pistei elpidos*, Sir 49:10). Just as pagans denounce the vain and deceptive hope that animates humans without God—for destiny laughs at hopes (Josephus, *War* 1.233)—so does Israel affirm the blessedness of *elpis* based on the true God: "Happy is the one whose hope is in Yahweh, his God" (Ps 146:5; cf. Sir 14:2); "Yahweh of Hosts, blessed is the person who hopes in you" (Ps 84:12). "Blessed is the person who trusts in Yahweh; the Lord is his hope" (Jer 17:7); "The hope of the righteous is joy, but the hope of the wicked will perish."[23]

---

[19] 2 Kgs 18:5 (Hezekiah); Ps 21:7; 26:1; 28:7; 32:10; 34:8, 22; 56:2, 4, 11; 91:2; 147:11; Sus 60: "God saves those who hope in him"; 1 Macc 2:61; Judas Maccabeus "holding an unshakeable confidence had full hope of obtaining help from the Lord" (2 Macc 15:7); 4 Macc 17:4.

[20] Sir 34:13; Dan 3:28—"His servants trusted in him"; Ps 22:4, 5; 25:20.

[21] Ps 7:1; 13:5; 14:6; 16:1; 17:7; 18:2, 30; 31:1; 61:3; 62:7; 71:1; 73:28; 91:1–3, 9; 94:22; Prov 14:26.

[22] Ps 4:5—Have confidence in Yahweh; 9:10; 40:4; 52:5, 11; 43:5; 71:5; 115:9–11; Isa 26:4; Bar 4:22; Sir 2:6. God is "the hope of all the ends of the earth" (Ps 65:5); even "the islands will hope" in him and will count on his arms (Isa 51:5). With Noah, "the hope of the world found refuge on a raft" (Wis 14:6). This confidence, which will not be disappointed (Prov 23:18) contrasts with the vain hope of fools (κενὴ ἡ ἐλπίς αὐτῶν, Wis 3:11, 18; 5:14), which is empty and deceitful (Sir 34:1), which is never fulfilled (Job 8:13; 27:8; Prov 11:7, 23; 26:12; 29:20). "The hope of the wicked is to breathe their last" (Job 11:20); that of the ingrate melts "like the wintry frost" (Wis 16:29).

[23] Prov 10:28. This hope-confidence is found in all the writers who share in the faith of Israel: *Pss. Sol.* 5.13; 6.8; 8.37; 9.19; 17.3, 38, 44. The Qumran psalmist hopes in the love, the goodness, the grace of God (1QH 9.10, 14; 10.16; 11.31; cf. 3.20; 6.6); Philo: "Only the one who has placed his hope in God is worthy of approval" (*Rewards* 13); "Holy and praiseworthy is the one who hopes" (*Abraham* 14–16); "Those who are truly well-born are full of hope" (*To Gaius* 195); "The greatest hope is hope in God"

St. Paul—who would be imprisoned "because of the hope of Israel" (Acts 28:20)—is the faithful heir of this language, this lexicon, and this faith: "God, in whom we have placed our hope (*eis hon ēlpikamen*) . . . will deliver us, with you helping us through prayer."[24] "It is for this reason that we toil and strive, that we have placed our hope in the living God (*ēlpikamen epi theō zōnti*), who is the Savior of all people, especially of believers" (1 Tim 4:10). The verb in the perfect emphasizes that the hope is immutable and is the source of all the efforts, like that of the widow who "has placed her hope in God" (*ēlpiken epi theon*, 1 Tim 5:5) and whose prayer is almost constant, because God is her only help.[25] This is the example given by the holy women of Israel who "placed their hope in God" (*gynaikes hai elpizousai eis theon*, 1 Pet 3:5). This is still the traditional contrast: expecting the pleasures that this world can offer or expecting from God alone the regard and recompense of virtuous conduct.

The object of this hope is rarely specified and never defined. 2 Thess 2:16 is content to say that Christ and God our Father have given us "a good hope graciously" (*elpida agathēn en chariti*),[26] but Heb 7:19 states that the

---

(*Spec. Laws* 1.310; cf. *Virtues* 67, 75; *Flacc.* 176). The faithful place their hope in God's merciful nature (*Spec. Laws* 2.196; cf. *Abraham* 9; *Flight* 99). Josephus: to place one's hope in God (τὰς ἐλπίδας ἔχειν ἐν τῷ θεῷ, *Ant.* 8.282) is to have confidence in his help (βοηθὸν ἐλπίζειν τὸν θεόν, 2.331; cf. *War* 2.391; 6.99–100) and to find salvation (*Ant.* 12.344). Moses had confidence that God would save his people (*Ant.* 2.276) and Darius hoped that the deity would save Daniel (10.258); cf. *T. Job* 37.1, 5.

[24] 2 Cor 1:10–11. Prayer obtains God's granting of the thing hoped for (Job 6:8); hence the association of ἐλπίς and εὐχή, *P.Berl.Zill.* 14, 16: ἐλπίδας ἔχω εἰς τὸν θεὸν καὶ τὰς εὐχὰς ὑμῶν (sixth century); *P.Oxy.* 939, 9–10; *P.Lond.* 1928, 15: διὰ τῶν ὑμῶν εὐχῶν προσδοκομένη ἐλπίς; Dittenberger, *Syl.* 364, 5; Phlm 22. In 1 Cor 15:19, the Christ-mediator or God-man is substituted for God as the basis of hope: "If we have hoped in Christ (ἐν Χριστῷ ἠλπικότες) in this life only, then we are of all people most to be pitied," since we would be deprived of the very point: future blessedness (cf. *IGLS* 2546: "O Christ, help Helenis, your servant, for the one who hopes in you [will not perish?]").

[25] Cf. 1 Tim 6:17—"Command the rich in this age . . . not to place their hope in (μηδὲ ἠλπικέναι ἐπί) the uncertainty of wealth but in God who procures all things richly for our enjoyment." Earthly goods are unstable and deceptive. A Christian must count only on God, who is the rich one par excellence (2 Cor 8:9; Eph 2:4) and loves to give.

[26] The adjective ἀγαθή is constantly used to describe hopes of happiness; cf. Socrates (in Stobaeus, vol. 5, p. 1002, n. 26); Xenophon, *Cyr.* 1.6.19; Josephus, *Ant.* 1.325; 5.222; 8.214; 13.201; 14.96. (Cf. the numerous uses collected by F. Cumont, *Lux Perpetua*, especially in relation to the mysteries of Eleusis.) It alternates with καλή (*Ep. Arist.* 261; Plutarch, *Brut.* 40.1), γλυκεῖα (Bion, in Stobaeus, vol. 5, p. 1000, 17), ἱλαρά (Critias, frag. 6, ed. Diels; Josephus, *War* 1.616; 2.106); cf. εὔελπις (Plato, *Ap.* 41 d; *Phd.* 64 a).

ἐλπίζω, elpizō, etc. 487

new covenant introduced "a better hope (*kreittonos elpidos*) whereby we draw near to God"; not only is the certitude complete, but the things hoped for are far superior.[27] We may distinguish hope in the realization of the promises of the Messiah and his kingdom,[28] the fervent expectation of salvation,[29] eternal life,[30] glory, (Rom 5:2; 8:21; Eph 1:18; Col 1:27), resurrection,[31] the appearing-epiphany of Christ[32] and of all the good

---

[27] Κρεῖττον (Josephus, *Ant.* 2.110; 3.83) alternates with μεγάλη (*War* 7.76; *Ep. Arist.* 18), βέλτιον (Dittenberger, *Syl.* 731, 35), χρηστή (*Ant.* 6.275; 7.234; 8.419; 13.421; 15.302; 18.284; *P.Oxy.* 1070, 10), and βεβαία (2 Cor 1:7; 4 Macc 17:4; Josephus, *War* 7.165, 413; *Ant.* 8.8), sometimes in the superlative βεβαιοτάτη (Philo, *Plant.* 88; Josephus, *Ant.* 8.280). 1 Pet 1:3—"God has regenerated us εἰς ἐλπίδα ζῶσαν"; 1:13—τελείως; Heb 10:23—ἀκλινής; Titus 2:13; *P.Lond.* 1915, 9: μακαρία. To express firm hope, one can say πολλὴ ἐλπίς (2 Macc 9:22).

[28] Acts 26:6–7. Cf. Col 1:23—"the hope promised by the gospel"; Heb 6:17–18. Thus Abraham, trusting in God's promise, hoped against all hope (παρ' ἐλπίδα ἐπ' ἐλπίδι, Rom 4:18). The expression "saved against all hope" (σωθεὶς . . . παρ' ἐλπίδα), used with respect to Mithridates (Josephus, *War* 1.192; cf. *Ant.* 17.331), is common in this author (*War* 1.331, 580; 4.657, etc.).

[29] 1 Thess 5:8—ἐλπὶς σωτηρίας (objective genitive; cf. Job 2:9; *T. Job* 24.1; Aeneas Tacticus, prol. l. 14; Philo, *To Gaius* 329). The expression recurs constantly in Josephus, especially with regard to military victories (*War* 1.390; 3.194, 204; 4.312, 338; 5.64, 306, 512, 535; 6.160, 181; 7.165, 331, 413; *Ant.* 1.327; 2.140; 7.158; 13.399; 15.153; 16.238, 389); cf. 2 Thess 2:13; Rom 5:9–10; 1 Tim 4:10. In Rom 8:24 (τῇ γὰρ ἐλπίδι ἐσώθημεν), "hope" can be understood in the objective sense of a salvation fully realized, consummated (cf. Gal 5:5—"We await the hope of righteousness"); already saved now (the aorist ἐσώθημεν; cf. 1 Cor 1:18), Christians are on the way to to definitive salvation, to complete possession, what Heb 6:11 calls the πληροφορία τῆς ἐλπίδος. They live, then, under a dispensation of hope. Some understand "hope" in the subjective and instrumental sense: salvation is realized through hope-patience. For the discussion cf. M. F. Lacan, " 'Nous sommes sauvés par l'espérance' (Rom. VIII, 24)," in *A la rencontre de Dieu: Mémorial A. Gelin*, Le Puy-Lyon-Paris, 1961, pp. 331–339; J. Cambier, "L'Espérance et le salut dans Rom. 8, 24," in *Message et mission: Recueil commémorative du Xe anniversaire de la Faculté de Théologie* (of Kinshasa), Louvain-Paris, 1968, pp. 77–107.

[30] Titus 1:2—"Paul, an apostle . . . for the hope of eternal life (ἐπ' ἐλπίδι ζωῆς αἰωνίου), which God, who cannot lie, has promised"; 3:7; cf. Rom 6:22; 1 Cor 15:22; Gal 6:8.

[31] Acts 23:6—"It is on account of the hope of the resurrection of the dead that I am on trial"; 24:15—"Having this hope in God . . . that there will be a resurrection of the just and the unjust"; 2:26 (= Ps 16:9)—"My very flesh will rest in hope (of the resurrection)"; Phil 3:20–21; Rom 8:23. Even the creation, subjected to vanity, retains a hope of renewal (8:20). Cf. *1 Enoch* 46.6—unbelievers "will have no hope of rising from their slumber."

[32] Titus 2:13 (cf. *marana-tha*, 1 Cor 16:22; C. Spicq, *Agapè*, vol. 3, pp. 83ff.; C. F. D. Moule, "A Reconsideration of the Context of Maranatha," in *NTS*, vol. 6, 1960, pp. 307–310; S. Schulz, "Maranatha und Kyrios Jesus," in *ZNW*, 1962, pp. 125–144). The

things implied in the concept of the heavenly inheritance (Rom 8:17; 1 Cor 15:50; Eph 1:18; Titus 3:7) or kingdom (2 Thess 1:5; 2 Tim 4:18), notably the vision of God (1 Cor 13:12; 1 John 3:2), which is presently impossible (2 Cor 4:18). The specific character of the Christian *elpis* is to expect not only a future good but "what we do not see" (*ou blepomen elpizomen*, Rom 8:25; cf. 2 Cor 4:18).

Whatever the diversity of these objects of hope, they are all summed up in Christ "our hope" (*elpis hēmōn*, 1 Tim 1:1), not only because his disciples await the coming (1 Thess 1:10; Phil 3:8–13, 20; 1 Tim 6:14; 2 Tim 4:8) of the victorious one (Rev 2:21; 5:5; 6:2; 17:14), who will lead to glory the multitude of the children of God (Heb 2:10; 10:22; 12:22–24; "to be with him," Phil 1:22–23), but especially because it is through him alone—and no longer through Moses (John 5:45)—that they may obtain the future glory (Col 1:27). They are "those who have placed their hope in Christ" (1 Cor 15:19; cf. Rom 5:1) or in the grace that he has brought (1 Pet 1:13). He is the "pioneer of salvation" (*archēgos tēs sōtērias*, Heb 2:10). Their religious life is summed up in the person of the one who is the "living hope" (Heb 10:23).[33]

Christian hopes for the coming of Christ (1 Cor 1:7; 1 Pet 1:13) as the servant hopes for that of his master (Luke 12:36); it is his reason for living. His whole watchful and patient life is determined by this waiting (1 Thess 1:10; Phil 3:12, 20; cf. C. Spicq, *Théologie morale*, vol. 1, pp. 311ff.).

[33] Jer 17:7 had stated: ἔσται κύριος ἐλπὶς αὐτοῦ (cf. *P.Oxy.* 1059, 1, a Christian prayer from the fifth century, κύριε θεέ καὶ ἐλπίς μου); Ps 71:5—κύριος ἡ ἐλπίς μου; Sir 34:14—"The one who fears the Lord will not be timid, for his hope is in him"; Thucydides 3.57.4: "You Lacedaemonians, our only hope." According to 1 *Enoch* 48.4, the Son of Man "will be the hope of those who suffer in their heart." Hesiod personifies Ἐλπίς (*Op.* 96), like the allegorists who "call Moses' sister *Elpis* because she observes from afar" (Philo, *Dreams* 2.142), and many women named Elpis are known (*BGU* 632, 20; *GVI*, n. 1103, 1; L. Robert, "Les Inscriptions," in J. des Gagniers, *Laodicée*, p. 352) or Elpidis (L. Robert, "Bulletin épigraphique," in *REG*, 1953, p. 188, n. 218). A physician of Corinth is named Gaius Vibius Euelpistus (*I.Cor.* VIII, 3, n.206); the same name in upper Pannonia, cf. V. Hoffiler, B. Soria, *Antike Inschriften aus Jugoslawien*, Amsterdam, 1970, I, n. 517, 4. In the fourth century, a Christian servant asks for prayers for his sick mistress, ἐν γὰρ αὐτῇ πάντες τὰς ἐλπίδας ἔχομεν (*P.Oxy.* 939, 9; cf. 1 Thess 2:19). For Theognis 1135 ("Elpis is the only deity who is beneficent toward humans") people must count on her; for this *parthenē* appears to them, like Artemis or Athena (Artemidorus Daldianus, *Onir.* 2.44). In 1 Tim 1:1; Col 1:27, the personification of Hope = Christ seems to intend an anti-imperial apologetic, because the Romans applauded their sovereign as the hope of the universe: "Caesar Augustus at his appearing realized the hopes of our ancestors. . . . He leaves future benefactors of humanity no hope of surpassing him" (*I.Priene* 105; Dittenberger, *Or.* 458, 37–40). ". . . So that with greater confidence you may hope for everything (πάντα ἐλπίζητε), the salvation as well as the material happiness of the benefactor Augustus, Emperor

So NT hope is not only a personal feeling (*peri tēs en hymin elpidos*, 1 Pet 3:15), nor even the thing awaited (1 Thess 2:19; Eph 2:12), but the whole economy of the new covenant, the dispensation under which all believers live, the goal and the meaning of their calling (Eph 4:4), whose full actualization they await (Gal 5:5). They are exhorted to "hold fast to the hope set forth" (Heb 6:18), to "keep their confession of hope unshakable" (*tēn homologian tēs elpidos*, Heb 10:23), that is, their profession of faith.[34]

III. — Hope as a virtue. — A feeling of confidence, hope resides in the heart (Jdt 6:9; Ps 28:7); it is a virtue[35] infused by "the God of hope" (Rom 15:13) or the Holy Spirit (Rom 15:13; cf. 5:5)—the pledge of the world to come (2 Cor 1:22; 5:5)—and by means of the Scriptures (Rom 15:4). It is associated with faith and charity.[36] Being confident of the future (*chrēstas peri tōn mellontōn echein elpidas*, Josephus, *Ant.* 6.275), it is a source of optimism: "charity hopes all things" (1 Cor 13:7), sure of the triumph of the good. This hope is always joyful,[37] since it already pos-

---

Galba" (edict of Tiberius Julius Alexander; ibid. 669 = *BGU* 1563, 15). In 54, Nero is referred to as ὁ τῆς οἰκουμένης καὶ προσδοκηθεὶς καὶ ἐλπισθείς (*P.Oxy.* 1021, 6). In 37: ἐπεὶ ἡ κατ' εὐχὴν πᾶσιν ἀνθρώποις ἐλπισθεῖσα Γαΐου Καίσαρος Γερμανικοῦ Σεβαστοῦ ἡγεμονία κατήγγελται, οὐδὲν δὲ μέτρον χαρᾶς εὕρηκεν ὁ κόσμος (Dittenberger, *Syl.* 797, 5).

[34] 1 Pet 3:15 (cf. the two lamps of Antinoöpolis bearing this inscription: Πίστις ἐλπίς [τοῦ ἁγίου Σεργίου?], in *SB* 6023). Hope is part of the description of faith: πίστις ἐλπιζομένων ὑπόστασις (Heb 11:1), cf. C. Spicq, *Hébreux*, vol. 2, pp. 336ff. To believe is to hope, Rom 4:18; 2 Cor 1:9; 2 Tim 1:12.

[35] Rom 5:4—"Virtue when tested produces hope."

[36] In 1 Thess 1:3; 5:8; 1 Cor 13:13—"Now there abide (or remain valid; μένω, Rom 9:11; Isa 14:24; cf. W. Grossouw, "L'Espérance dans le N.T.," *RB*, 1954, p. 517) faith, hope, and charity." On this triad, cf. C. Spicq, *Agapè*, vol. 2, pp. 104ff., 365–378; trinitarian sequences are common in the *Orac. Chald.* (5.26; E. des Places, *Jamblique: Les Mystères d'Egypte*, Paris, 1966, p. 182, n. 2), in language, and in music (Philo, *Husbandry* 136–137; *Alleg. Interp.* 1.3; *Abraham* 122ff.; *Quest. Gen.* 4.8); cf. H. Usener, *Dreiheit: Ein Versuch mythologischer Zahlenlehre*, 2d ed., Hildesheim, 1966; E. von Dobschütz, "Zwei- und dreigliedrige Formeln: Ein Beitrag zur Vorgeschichte der Trinitätsformel," in *JBL*, 1931, pp. 117–147. —On 1 Cor 13:13, the Pauline triad taking precedence over justice, peace, truth, etc. (Christian inscription from Tafeh, in *SB* 8705); cf. F. M. Lacan, "Les Trois qui demeurent," in *RSR*, 1958, pp. 321–348 (with the critique by A. Feuillet, in *NTS*, vol. 6, p. 513, n. 2); J. Moss, "I Cor. XIII," in *ExpT*, vol. 73, 1962, p. 253; F. Dreyfus, " 'Maintenant, la foi, l'espérance et la charité demeurent toutes les trois,' " in *Studiorum Paulinorum Congressus*, Rome, 1963, pp. 403–412; W. Marxsen, "Das 'Bleiben' in I Kor. XIII, 13," in *Neues Testament und Geschichte* (Festgabe O. Cullmann), Zurich, 1972, pp. 223–229; E. Miguens, "I Cor. XIII, 8–13 Reconsidered," in *CBQ*, 1975, pp. 76–97.

[37] 1 Thess 2:19; Rom 12:12—τῇ ἐλπίδι χαίροντες; 15:13. Philo brings it up over and over again: *Alleg. Interp.* 3.87; *Change of Names* 161, 163; *Worse Attacks Better* 138; *Rewards* 161.

sessed the pledge of the promised blessedness (Rom 14:17; Gal 5:22). It eliminates timidity and hesitation and gives the hopeful person "great boldness,"[38] made up of assurance and pride, letting one keep the "head high" (cf. Lev 26:13) and remain unshakable before criticisms and even fearless before God's judgment (1 John 2:28; 3:21; 4:17). This certitude and confidence which belong to "sharers in a heavenly calling" (Heb 3:1) are for them a *kauchēma*, a subject of pride and honor, a claim to glory, attributed again by Heb 3:6 to hope.[39] But this essentially dynamic virtue demands the sanctification and purification of the Christian, because the end demands the use of means to attain it: "Whoever has such a hope in God purifies himself, as he himself is pure" (1 John 3:3). Only the pure, after all, will see God (Matt 5:8; Heb 12:14), and nothing impure will ever enter into the heavenly city (Rev 21:27; 22:11). So those whose entire hope is to draw near to God, and to see God, purify themselves from every evil (Acts 24:15–16; 2 Cor 5:9).

IV. — The certitude of the Christian hope. — Unlike human hope, whose props are often weak, whose goals are often bad,[40] whose expectations are often disappointed,[41] NT *elpis* is sure and certain first of all by virtue of its semantic origin in the LXX (Hebrew *bāṭaḥ*), where it means essentially having confidence, being assured. Then, by virtue of its object

---

[38] 2 Cor 3:12; Phil 1:20; Heb 3:6; P. Joüon, "Divers sens de παρρησία dans le N.T.," in *RSR*, 1940, pp. 239–241. A. M. Denis, "L'Apôtre Paul, Prophète 'messianique' des Gentils," in *ETL*, 1957, pp. 249–259; D. Smolders, "L'Audace de l'apôtre selon saint Paul: Le Thème de la parrèsia," in *Collectanea Mechlinensia*, 1958, pp. 16–30, 117–133; W. C. van Unnik, " 'With Unveiled Faces': An Exegesis of 2 Corinthians III, 12–18," in *NovT*, vol. 6, 1963, pp. 159ff. (= idem, *Sparsa Collecta*, Leiden, 1973, pp. 200ff.). Cf. G. J. M. Bartelink, "Quelques observations sur Παρρησία dans la littérature paléo-chrétienne," in *Graecitas et latinitas Christianorum primaeva*, *Supplementa*, vol. 2, Nijmegen, 1970, pp. 7–57. L. Engels, "Fiducia dans la Vulgate: Le Problème de traduction παρρησία-fiducia," ibid., *Supplementa*, vol. 1, 1964, pp. 99–141.

[39] Heb 3:6. J. S. Bosch, *'Gloriarse' según San Pablo y teologia de* καυχάομαι (AnBib 40), Rome, 1970. E. Fuchs, "Gloire de Dieu et gloire de l'homme: Essai sur les termes kaukastai . . . dans la Septante," in *RTP*, 1977, pp. 321–332.

[40] Cf. Josephus, *Ant.* 15.79: τὴν ἐλπίδα τῆς πλεονεξίας.

[41] Sir 13:6—the wicked rich person gives (deceptive) hope to the poor. The pejorative adjectives for this hope are many: κακή (Euripides, in Stobaeus, vol. 5, p. 999, 13; Menander, ibid., p. 998, 8), ἄδηλος (uncertain, 2 Macc 7:34), ματαία (Isa 31:2; Lucian, *Alex.* 47), ἀπάτη (Philo, *Rewards* 147), πονηρά (Isa 28:19; 47:10; Socrates, in Stobaeus, 5, p. 1001, n. 21; Josephus, *Ant.* 11.247), κενή (Job 7:6; Wis 3:11; Sir 31:1; Philo, *Moses* 1.195), ἀτελής (Philo, *Spec. Laws* 4.158; *Virtues* 29; *Rewards* 149; *CIRB* 130, 16), ψευδής (Euripides, in Stobaeus, vol. 5, p. 1004, n. 5), ἀβέβαια (Philo, *Flacc.* 109), ἀλόγιστος (ill-considered, Josephus, *War* 2.346), ἀναιδής (ibid. 6.337), σφαλερά (1.357), μικρά (7.77; *Ant.* 15.232). A distant hope is abandoned (Plutarch, *Arat.* 4.3).

and its own nature, it is solid (*bebaia*, 2 Cor 1:7; Heb 6:19), indefectible (*aklinēs*, Heb 10:23); since it places its confidence in God it cannot be disappointed. What is more, it is sure because it is based on many statements in inspired Scripture.[42] Finally, it is sure because St. Paul expressly states it and justifies it: "Hope does not disappoint, because the love of God is shed abroad in our hearts by the Holy Spirit that has been given to us."[43] Hope's certitude is the certitude of God's unchanging and efficacious love and of his infinite mercy, in which he has willed that none should perish and set in motion the whole economy of forgiveness and salvation.[44] Now this divine *agapē* comes to indwell the souls of the faithful—justification is already present, actual—because the Holy Spirit has poured it out in them, so that it becomes their possession. They abide in God (1 John 2:5–6). So there is no break between earth and heaven (cf. the metaphor of the anchor, Heb 6:19). Divine love is like a spring that wells up to eternal life (John 4:14; 7:38).

Thus it is certain that hope placed in God will not be disappointed. The verb *kataischynō*, used almost eighty times in the LXX,[45] expresses the idea of disappointment in a context of confidence (Luke 13:17). The wicked person who plots evil but cannot actualize his plans is embarrassed by his failure, but the faithful person who waits on God for salvation will not be confounded—a litotes—will not regret having entrusted his whole life to God. A "dis-grace" means being rejected by one's Lord—this would be opprobrium, shame (cf. *aischynomai*; Phil 1:20); it would mean becoming the object of mocking by unbelievers who would laugh at the unfortunate, disappointed righteous person. It is as with the man who wanted to build a tower and had laid the foundation, but was unable to complete the project: "everyone ridiculed him" (Luke 14:29, *empaizō*). For a member of the new and eternal covenant in Jesus Christ,

---

[42] "Your expectation (Hebrew *tiqwâh*) will not be disappointed" (Prov 23:18; 24:14). God does not look upon us with scorn (Jdt 8:20; cf. 2 Macc 2:18). Those who hope in him have not been confounded (Ps 22:6; 25:3, 20; 31:1, 6, 14, 19, 24; 71:1; 119:116; Sir 2:6). He saves them (Sus 60; Bar 4:22; Isa 25:9).

[43] Rom 5:5 (a verse that was cited 201 times by St. Augustine; cf. A. M. Bonnardière, "Le Verset paulinien Rom. V, 5 dans l'œuvre de Saint Augustine," in *Augustinus Magister*, Paris, 1954, vol. 2, pp. 657–665); Phil 1:20.

[44] Eph 2:4–5; Titus 3:4–5; 1 Pet 1:3; John 3:6; 1 John 4:9–10.

[45] In the sense "dishonor, taint" (2 Sam 16:21; 19:6; Prov 19:26; Sir 22:4–5; 42:11; 1 Cor 11:5, 22), humiliate and molest (Ruth 2:15), expresses simultaneously the ideas of punishment and derision: Mic 3:7 (linked with καταγελάω); Ps 44:8; 1 Cor 1:27; 1 Pet 3:16; cf. C. Spicq, *Agapè*, vol. 2, pp. 173ff.; J. M. Lochmann, *Trägt oder trügt die christliche Hoffnung?*, Zurich, 1974.

such an emptying out of hope is unthinkable (cf. Rom 8:32), since it is God himself who has given us this "good hope."[46]

---

[46] 2 Thess 2:15 (cf. P. Otzen, " 'Gute Hoffnung' bei Paulus," in *ZNW*, 1958, pp. 283-285). St. Thomas Aquinas glosses this text: " We look for a good hope, that is, the certainty of eternal goods" ("Expectamus spem bonam, id est bonorum aeternorum infallibilitatem"). On 2 Cor 5:5—"He has given us the Spirit as a pledge," St. Thomas comments: "That is, the Holy Spirit giving us certainty of this good thing with which we wish to be filled. . . . A pledge is kept and held as a surety that something will be had. That is how it is with the Holy Spirit, because the Holy Spirit is worth as much as heavenly glory, but the mode of possession is different in each case: because we have the Spirit now as a surety that that glory will follow; in heaven, however, we will have that glory as something that is already ours and possessed by us." ("Id est Spiritum Sanctum causantem in nobis certitudinem hujus rei qua desideramus impleri. . . . Pignus servatur et tenetur quasi pro certitudine rei habendae. Ita est de Spiritu Sancto, quia Spiritus Sanctus tantum valet quantum gloria coelestis, sed differt modo habendi, quia nunc habemus eum quasi ad certitudinem consequendi illam gloriam; in patria vero habebimus ut rem jam nostram et a nobis possessam.")